Algebra 1

Timothy D. Kanold

Edward B Burger

Juli K Dixon

Matthew R. Larson

Steven J. Leinwand

Printed in the U.S.A.

ISBN 978-1-328-90002-9

3 4 5 6 7 8 9 10 0868 26 25 24 23 22 21 20 19 18

4500712737   A B C D E F G H

Authors

Timothy D. Kanold, Ph.D., is an award-winning international educator, author, and consultant. He is a former superintendent and director of mathematics and science at Adlai E. Stevenson High School District 125 in Lincolnshire, Illinois. He is a past president of the National Council of Supervisors of Mathematics (NCSM) and the Council for the Presidential Awardees of Mathematics (CPAM). He

has served on several writing and leadership commissions for NCTM during the past decade. He presents motivational professional development seminars with a focus on developing professional learning communities (PLC's) to improve the teaching, assessing, and learning of students. He has recently authored nationally recognized articles, books, and textbooks for mathematics education and school leadership, including *What Every Principal Needs to Know about the Teaching and Learning of Mathematics*.

Edward B. Burger, Ph.D., is the President of Southwestern University, a former Francis Christopher Oakley Third Century Professor of Mathematics at Williams College, and a former vice provost at Baylor University. He has authored or coauthored more than sixty-five articles, books, and video series; delivered over five hundred addresses and workshops throughout the world; and made more than fifty radio and

television appearances. He is a Fellow of the American Mathematical Society as well as having earned many national honors, including the Robert Foster Cherry Award for Great Teaching in 2010. In 2012, Microsoft Education named him a "Global Hero in Education."

Juli K. Dixon, Ph.D., is a Professor of Mathematics Education at the University of Central Florida. She has taught mathematics in urban schools at the elementary, middle, secondary, and post-secondary levels. She is an active researcher and speaker with numerous publications and conference presentations. Key areas of focus are deepening teachers' content knowledge and communicating and justifying

mathematical ideas. She is a past chair of the NCTM Student Explorations in Mathematics Editorial Panel and member of the Board of Directors for the Association of Mathematics Teacher Educators.

Matthew R. Larson, Ph.D., is the K-12 mathematics curriculum specialist for the Lincoln Public Schools and served on the Board of Directors for the National Council of Teachers of Mathematics from 2010 to 2013. He is a past chair of NCTM's Research Committee and was a member of NCTM's Task Force on Linking Research and Practice. He is the author of several books on

implementing the Common Core Standards for Mathematics. He has taught mathematics at the secondary and college levels and held an appointment as an honorary visiting associate professor at Teachers College, Columbia University.

Steven J. Leinwand is a Principal Research Analyst at the American Institutes for Research (AIR) in Washington, D.C., and has over 30 years in leadership positions in mathematics education. He is past president of the National Council of Supervisors of Mathematics and served on the NCTM Board of Directors. He is the author of

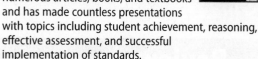

numerous articles, books, and textbooks and has made countless presentations with topics including student achievement, reasoning, effective assessment, and successful implementation of standards.

Performance Task Consultant

Robert Kaplinsky
Teacher Specialist, Mathematics
Downey Unified School District
Downey, California

STEM Consultants
Science, Technology, Engineering, and Mathematics

Michael A. DiSpezio
Global Educator
North Falmouth, Massachusetts

Michael R. Heithaus
Executive Director, School of Environment, Arts, and Society
Professor, Department of Biological Sciences
Florida International University
North Miami, Florida

Reviewers

Mindy Eden
Richwoods High School
Peoria School District
Peoria, IL

Dustin Johnson
Badger High School Math Teacher
Department Chair
Lake Geneva-Genoa City Union
High School District
Lake Geneva, WI

Ashley D. McSwain
Murray High School
Murray City School District
Salt Lake City, UT

Rebecca Quinn
Doherty Memorial High School
Worcester Public Schools District
Worcester, MA

Ted Ryan
Madison LaFollette High School
Madison Metropolitan School District
Madison, WI

Tony Scoles
Fort Zumwalt School District
O'Fallon, MO

Cynthia L. Smith
Higley Unified School District
Gilbert, AZ

Phillip E. Spellane
Doherty Memorial High School
Worcester Public Schools District
Worcester, MA

Mona Toncheff
Math Content Specialist
Phoenix Union High School District
Phoenix, AZ

Quantities and Modeling

MODULE 1

Quantitative Reasoning

MODULE 2

Algebraic Models

Understanding Functions

Functions and Models

Patterns and Sequences

Linear Functions, Equations, and Inequalities

MODULE 5

Linear Functions

MODULE 6

Forms of Linear Equations

UNIT 3

MODULE 7

Linear Equations and Inequalities

Statistical Models

© Houghton Mifflin Harcourt Publishing Company • Image Credits: (t) ©Daniel Padavona/Shutterstock; (b) ©Duane Osborn/Somos Images/Corbis

MODULE 8

Multi-Variable Categorical Data

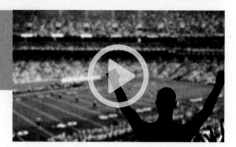

MODULE 9

One-Variable Data Distributions

MODULE 10

Linear Modeling and Regression

© Houghton Mifflin Harcourt Publishing Company · Image Credits: ©John Elk III/Alamy

Linear Systems and Piecewise-Defined Functions

Solving Systems of Linear Equations

Modeling with Linear Systems

Piecewise-Defined Functions

Exponential Relationships

UNIT 6

MODULE 14

Rational Exponents and Radicals

MODULE 15

Geometric Sequences and Exponential Functions

MODULE **16** Exponential Equations and Models

© Houghton Mifflin Harcourt Publishing Company • Image Credits: ©Everett Collection Inc/Alamy Images

Polynomial Operations

MODULE 17

Adding and Subtracting Polynomials

Multiplying Polynomials

Quadratic Functions

MODULE 19

Graphing Quadratic Functions

MODULE 20

Connecting Intercepts, Zeros, and Factors

MODULE 21
Using Factors to Solve Quadratic Equations

MODULE 22
Using Square Roots to Solve Quadratic Equations

MODULE 23

Linear, Exponential, and Quadratic Models

Real-World Video 857
Are You Ready? 858

Inverse Relationships

MODULE 24

Functions and Inverses

Contents of Student Edition Resources

Quantities and Modeling

MODULE 1
Quantitative Reasoning

MODULE 2
Algebraic Models

MATH IN CAREERS

Personal Trainer A personal trainer works with clients to help them achieve their personal fitness goals. A personal trainer needs math to calculate a client's heart rate, body fat percentage, lean muscle mass, and calorie requirements. Personal trainers are often self-employed, so they need to understand the mathematics of managing a business.

If you are interested in a career as a personal trainer, you should study these mathematical subjects:
- Algebra
- Business Math

Research other careers that require knowledge of the mathematics of business management. Check out the career activity at the end of the unit to find out how **personal trainers** use math.

© Houghton Mifflin Harcourt Publishing Company • Image Credits: ©OJO Images Ltd/Alamy

Reading Start-Up

Visualize Vocabulary

Copy the chart and use the ✔ words to complete it. Put one term in each section of the square.

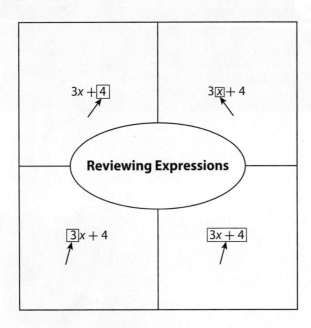

Understand Vocabulary

To become familiar with some of the vocabulary terms in this unit, consider the following. You may refer to the module, the glossary, or a dictionary.

1. The level of detail of a measurement, determined by the unit of measure,

   is ___?___ .

2. A statement that two ratios are equal is called a ___?___ .

3. A ___?___ is a comparison of two quantities by division.

Active Reading

Two-Panel Flip Book Before beginning the lessons, create a two-panel flip chart to help you compare concepts in this unit. Label the flaps "Creating and Solving Equations" and "Creating and Solving Inequalities." As you study each lesson, write important ideas under the appropriate flap. Include any examples that will help you remember the concepts later when you look back at your notes.

Quantitative Reasoning

Essential Question: How do you use quantitative reasoning to solve real-world problems?

REAL WORLD VIDEO
In order to function properly and safely, electronics must be manufactured to a high degree of precision. Material tolerances and component alignment must be precisely matched in order to not interfere with each other.

© Houghton Mifflin Harcourt Publishing Company • Image Credits: Photodisc/Getty Images

MODULE PERFORMANCE TASK PREVIEW

What an Impossible Score!

Darts is a game of skill in which small pointed darts are thrown at a circular target mounted on a wall. The target is divided into regions with different point values, and scoring depends on which segment the dart hits. Is there some score that is impossible to achieve no matter how many darts are thrown in a simple game of darts? Keep your eye on the target and let's figure it out!

Are YOU Ready?

Complete these exercises to review skills you will need for this module.

One-Step Equations

Example 1 Solve.

$$y - 11 = 7$$

$$y - 11 + 11 = 7 + 11 \quad \text{Isolate the variable by adding 11}$$
$$y = 18 \qquad \qquad \text{to both sides of the equation.}$$

Solve each equation.

1. $4x = 32$

2. $9 + a = 23$

3. $\dfrac{n}{3} = 16$

Scale Factor and Scale Drawings

Example 2 Length of car: 132 in. Length of model of car: 11 in.

$$\frac{\text{model length}}{\text{actual length}} = \frac{11}{132} \qquad \text{Write a ratio using the given dimensions comparing the model length to the actual length.}$$

$$= \frac{1}{12} \qquad \text{Simplify.}$$

The scale factor is $\dfrac{1}{12}$.

Identify the scale factor.

4. Length of room: 144 in.
Length of room on scale drawing: 18 in.

5. Wingspan of airplane: 90 ft
Wingspan of model of airplane: 6 ft

Significant Digits

Example 3 Determine the number of significant digits in 37.05.

The significant digits in 37.05 are 3, 7, 0, and 5.

37.05 has 4 significant digits.

Significant digits are nonzero digits, zeros at the end of a number and to the right of a decimal point, and zeros between significant digits.

Determine the number of significant digits.

6. 0.0028

7. 970.0

8. 50,000

9. 4000.01

1.1 Solving Equations

Resource Locker

Essential Question: How do you solve an equation in one variable?

 Explore **Solving Equations by Guess-and-Check or by Working Backward**

An **equation** is a mathematical sentence that uses the equal sign $=$ to show two expressions are equivalent. The expressions can be numbers, variables, constants, or combinations thereof.

There are many ways to solve an equation. One way is by using a method called *guess-and-check*. A guess-and-check method involves guessing a value for the variable in an equation and checking to see if it is the solution by substituting the value in the equation. If the resulting equation is a true statement, then the value you guessed is the solution of the equation. If the equation is not a true statement, then you adjust the value of your guess and try again, continuing until you find the solution.

Another way to solve an equation is by *working backward*. In this method, you begin at the end and work backward toward the beginning.

Solve the equation $x - 6 = 4$ using both methods.

Use the *guess-and-check* method to find the solution of the equation $x - 6 = 4$.

(A) Guess 11 for x.

$$x - 6 = 4$$

$$\boxed{?} - 6 \overset{?}{=} 4$$

$$\boxed{?} \overset{?}{=} 4$$

Is 11 the solution

of $x - 6 = 4$? $\boxed{?}$

(B) The value 11 is too high.

Guess 10 for x.

$$x - 6 = 4$$

$$\boxed{?} - 6 \overset{?}{=} 4$$

$$\boxed{?} \overset{?}{=} 4$$

Is 10 the solution

of $x - 6 = 4$? $\boxed{?}$

(C) Use the *working backward* method to find the solution of the equation $x - 6 = 4$.

$4 + 6 = \boxed{?}$ Is this the value of x before taking away 6?

$\boxed{?} - 6 \overset{?}{=} 4$ $\boxed{?}$

Reflect

1. Discussion Which method of solving do you think is more efficient? Explain your answer.

A **solution of an equation** is a value for the variable that makes the equation true. To determine the solution of an equation, you will use the Properties of Equality.

Properties of Equality		
Words	**Numbers**	**Algebra**
Addition Property of Equality You can add the same number to both sides of an equation, and the statement will still be true.	$3 = 3$ $3 + 2 = 3 + 2$ $5 = 5$	$a = b$ $a + c = b + c$
Subtraction Property of Equality You can subtract the same number from both sides of an equation, and the statement will still be true.	$7 = 7$ $7 - 5 = 7 - 5$ $2 = 2$	$a = b$ $a - c = b - c$
Multiplication Property of Equality You can multiply both sides of an equation by the same number, and the statement will still be true.	$3 = 3$ $3 \cdot 4 = 3 \cdot 4$ $12 = 12$	$a = b$ $a \cdot c = b \cdot c$
Division Property of Equality You can divide both sides of an equation by the same nonzero number, and the statement will still be true.	$15 = 15$ $\frac{15}{3} = \frac{15}{3}$ $5 = 5$	$a = b$ $\frac{a}{c} = \frac{b}{c}$, where $c \neq 0$

Example 1   Solve the equation by using Properties of Equality.

(A) $3x - 2 = 6$

Use the Addition Property of Equality. $3x - 2 + 2 = 6 + 2$

Combine like terms. $3x = 8$

Now use the Division Property of Equality. $\frac{3x}{3} = \frac{8}{3}$

Simplify. $x = \frac{8}{3}$

(B) $\frac{1}{2}z + 4 = 10$

Use the Subtraction Property of Equality. $\frac{1}{2}z + 4 - \boxed{4} = 10 - \boxed{4}$

Combine like terms. $\frac{1}{2}z = \boxed{6}$

Now use the Multiplication Property of Equality to multiply each side by 2. $2 \cdot \frac{1}{2}z = 2 \cdot \boxed{6}$

Simplify. $z = \boxed{12}$

Reflect

2. **Discussion** What is the goal when solving a one-variable equation?

Your Turn

Solve the equation by using Properties of Equality.

3. $5x - 10 = 20$

4. $\frac{1}{3}x + 9 = 21$

🔧 Explain 2 Solving Equations to Define a Unit

One useful application of algebra is to use an equation to determine what a unit of measure represents. For instance, if a person uses the unit of time "score" in a speech and there is enough information given, you can solve an equation to find the quantity that a "score" represents.

Example 2 Solve an equation to determine the unknown quantity.

Ⓐ In 1963, Dr. Martin Luther King, Jr., began his famous "I have a dream" speech with the words "Five score years ago, a great American, in whose symbolic shadow we stand, signed the Emancipation Proclamation." The proclamation was signed by President Abraham Lincoln in 1863. But how long is a score? We can use algebra to find the answer.

Let s represent the quantity (in years) represented by a score.

s = number of years in a score

Calculate the quantity in years after President Lincoln signed the Emancipation Proclamation.

$$1963 - 1863 = 100$$

Dr. Martin Luther King, Jr. used "five score" to describe this length of time. Write the equation that shows this relationship.

$$5s = 100$$

Use the Division Property of Equality to solve the equation.

$$\frac{5s}{5} = \frac{100}{5}$$

$$s = 20$$

A score equals 20 years.

Ⓑ An airplane descends in altitude from 20,000 feet to 10,000 feet. A gauge at Radar Traffic Control reads that the airplane's altitude drops 1.8939 miles. How many feet are in a mile?

Let m represent the quantity (in feet) represented by a mile.

m = number of feet in a mile

Calculate the quantity in feet of the descent.

$20,000 - \boxed{10,000} = \boxed{10,000}$

A gauge described this quantity as 1.8939 miles. Write the equation that shows this relationship.

$1.8939m = \boxed{10,000}$

Use the Division Property of Equality to solve the equation.

$$\frac{1.8939m}{1.8939} = \frac{10{,}000}{1.8939}$$

Round to the nearest foot.

$$m \approx \boxed{5280}$$

There are 5280 feet in a mile.

Your Turn

Solve an equation to determine the unknown quantity.

5. 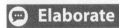 An ostrich that is 108 inches tall is 20 inches taller than 4 times the height of a kiwi. What is the height of a kiwi in inches?

6. An emu that measures 60 inches in height is 70 inches less than 5 times the height of a kakapo. What is the height of a kakapo in inches?

💬 Elaborate

7. How do you know which operation to perform first when solving an equation?

8. How can you create an equivalent equation by using the Properties of Equality?

9. When a problem involves more than one unit for a characteristic (such as length), how can you tell which unit is more appropriate to report the answer in?

10. **Essential Question Check-In** Describe each step in a solution process for solving an equation in one variable.

☆ Evaluate: Homework and Practice

- Online Homework
- Hints and Help
- Extra Practice

Use the *guess-and-check* method to find the solution of the equation. Show your work.

1. $2x + 5 = 19$

Use the *working backward* method to find the solution of the equation. Show your work.

2. $4y - 1 = 7$

Solve each equation using the Properties of Equality. Check your solutions.

3. $4a + 3 = 11$

4. $8 = 3r - 1$

5. $42 = -2d + 6$

6. $3x + 0.3 = 3.3$

7. $15y + 31 = 61$

8. $9 - c = -13$

9. $\frac{x}{6} + 4 = 15$

10. $\frac{1}{3}y + \frac{1}{4} = \frac{5}{12}$

11. $\frac{2}{7}m - \frac{1}{7} = \frac{3}{14}$

12. $15 = \frac{a}{3} - 2$

13. $4 - \frac{m}{2} = 10$

14. $\frac{x}{8} - \frac{1}{2} = 6$

Justify each step.

15. $2x - 5 = -20$

$2x = -15$

$x = -\frac{15}{2}$

16. $\frac{x}{3} - 7 = 11$

$\frac{x}{3} = 18$

$x = 54$

17. $\frac{9x}{4} = -9$

$9x = -36$

$x = -4$

18. In 2003, the population of Zimbabwe was about 12.6 million people, which is 1 million more than 4 times the population in 1950. Write and solve an equation to find the approximate population p of Zimbabwe in 1950.

19. Julio is paid 1.4 times his normal hourly rate for each hour he works over 30 hours in a week. Last week he worked 35 hours and earned \$436.60. Write and solve an equation to find Julio's normal hourly rate, r. Explain how you know that your answer is reasonable.

20. The average weight of the top 5 fish at a fishing tournament was 12.3 pounds. Some of the weights of the fish are shown in the table.

Top 5 Fish	
Caught by	**Weight (lb)**
Wayne S.	
Carla P	12.8
Deb N.	12.6
Vincente R.	11.8
Armin G.	9.7

What was the weight of the heaviest fish?

21. Paul bought a student discount card for the bus. The card allows him to buy daily bus passes for \$1.50. After one month, Paul bought 15 passes and spent a total of \$29.50. How much did he spend on the student discount card?

22. Jennifer is saving money to buy a bike. The bike costs \$245. She has \$125 saved, and each week she adds \$15 to her savings. How long will it take her to save enough money to buy the bike?

© Houghton Mifflin Harcourt Publishing Company

23. Astronomy The radius of Earth is 6378.1 km, which is 2981.1 km greater than the radius of Mars. Find the radius of Mars.

24. Maggie's brother is 3 years younger than twice her age. The sum of their ages is 24. How old is Maggie?

25. Analyze Relationships One angle of a triangle measures 120°. The other two angles are congruent. Write and solve an equation to find the measure of the congruent angles.

26. Explain the Error Find the error in the solution, and then solve correctly.

$$9x + 18 + 3x = 1$$
$$9x + 18 = -2$$
$$9x = -20$$
$$x = -\frac{20}{9}$$

27. Check for Reasonableness Marietta was given a raise of $0.75 per hour, which gave her a new wage of $12.25 per hour. Write and solve an equation to determine Marietta's hourly wage before her raise. Show that your answer is reasonable.

Lesson Performance Task

The formula $p = 8n - 30$ gives the profit p when a number of items n are each sold at $8 and expenses totaling $30 are subtracted.

a. If the profit is $170.00, how many items were bought?

b. If the same number of items were bought but the expenses changed to $40, would the profit increase or decrease, and by how much? Explain.

1.2 Modeling Quantities

Essential Question: How can you use rates, ratios, and proportions to solve real-world problems?

Resource Locker

🧭 Explore   Using Ratios and Proportions to Solve Problems

Ratios and *proportions* are very useful when solving real-world problems. A **ratio** is a comparison of two numbers by division. An equation that states that two ratios are equal is called a **proportion**.

A totem pole that is 90 feet tall casts a shadow that is 45 feet long. At the same time, a 6-foot-tall man casts a shadow that is x feet long.

The man and the totem pole are both perpendicular to the ground, so they form right angles with the ground. The sun shines at the same angle on both, so similar triangles are formed.

90 ft

6 ft

45 ft x ft

Ⓐ Write a ratio of the man's height to the totem pole's height. $\dfrac{?}{?}$

Ⓑ Write a ratio of the man's shadow to the totem pole's shadow. $\dfrac{?}{?}$

Ⓒ Write a proportion.

$$\frac{\text{man's height}}{\text{pole's height}} = \frac{\text{man's shadow}}{\text{pole's shadow}} \qquad \frac{?}{?} = \frac{?}{?}$$

Ⓓ Solve the proportion by $\boxed{?}$ both sides by 45.

Ⓔ Solve the proportion to find the length of the man's shadow in feet. $x = \boxed{?}$

Reflect

1. **Discussion** What is another ratio that could be written for this problem? Use it to write and solve a different proportion to find the length of the man's shadow in feet.

2. **Discussion** Explain why your new proportion and solution are valid.

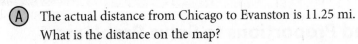

🎸 Explain 1 Using Scale Drawings and Models to Solve Problems

A **scale** is the ratio of any length in a *scale drawing* or *scale model* to the corresponding actual length. A drawing that uses a scale to represent an object as smaller or larger than the original object is a **scale drawing**. A three-dimensional model that uses a scale to represent an object as smaller or larger than the actual object is called a **scale model**.

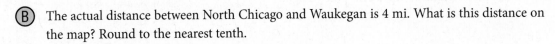

Example 1 Use the map to answer the following questions.

Ⓐ The actual distance from Chicago to Evanston is 11.25 mi. What is the distance on the map?

Write the scale as a fraction.

$$\frac{\text{map}}{\text{actual}} \rightarrow \frac{1 \text{ in.}}{18 \text{ mi}}$$

Let d be the distance on the map.

$$\frac{1}{18} = \frac{d}{11.25}$$

Multiply both sides by 11.25.

$$\frac{11.25}{18} = d$$

$$0.625 = d$$

The distance on the map is about 0.625 in.

Ⓑ The actual distance between North Chicago and Waukegan is 4 mi. What is this distance on the map? Round to the nearest tenth.

Write the scale as a fraction.   Let d be the distance on the map.   Multiply both sides by 4.

$$\frac{\text{map}}{\text{actual}} \rightarrow \frac{1 \text{ in.}}{18 \text{ mi}}$$ $$\frac{1}{18} = \frac{d}{4}$$ $$\frac{4}{18} = d$$

$$\boxed{0.2} \approx d$$

The distance on the map is about 0.2 in.

Your Turn

3. A scale model of a human heart is 196 inches long. The scale is 32 to 1. How many inches long is the actual heart? Round your answer to the nearest whole number.

Explain 2 · Using Dimensional Analysis to Convert Measurements

Dimensional analysis is a method of manipulating unit measures algebraically to determine the proper units for a quantity computed algebraically. The comparison of two quantities with different units is called a **rate**. The ratio of two equal quantities, each measured in different units, is called a **conversion factor**.

Example 2 Use dimensional analysis to convert the measurements.

(A) A large adult male human has about 12 pints of blood. Use dimensional analysis to convert this quantity to gallons.

Step 1 Convert pints to quarts.

Multiply by a conversion factor whose first quantity is quarts and whose second quantity is pints.

$$12 \text{ pt} \cdot \frac{1 \text{ qt}}{2 \text{ pt}} = 6 \text{ qt}$$

12 pints is 6 quarts.

Step 2 Convert quarts to gallons.

Multiply by a conversion factor whose first quantity is gallons and whose second quantity is quarts.

$$6 \text{ qt} \cdot \frac{1 \text{ gal}}{4 \text{ qt}} = \frac{6}{4} \text{ gal} = 1\frac{1}{2} \text{ gal}$$

A large adult male human has about $1\frac{1}{2}$ gallons of blood.

(B) The length of a building is 720 in. Use dimensional analysis to convert this quantity to yards.

Step 1 Convert inches to feet.

Multiply by a conversion factor whose first quantity is feet and whose second quantity is inches.

$$720 \text{ in.} \cdot \frac{\boxed{1} \text{ ft}}{\boxed{12} \text{ in.}} = \boxed{60} \text{ ft}$$

720 inches is $\boxed{60}$ feet.

Step 2 Convert feet to yards.

Multiply by a conversion factor whose first quantity is yards and whose second quantity is feet.

$$\boxed{60} \text{ ft} \cdot \frac{\boxed{1} \text{ yd}}{\boxed{3} \text{ ft}} = \boxed{20} \text{ yd}$$

$\boxed{60}$ feet is $\boxed{20}$ yards.

Therefore, 720 inches is 20 yards.

Your Turn

Use dimensional analysis to convert the measurements. Round answers to the nearest tenth.

4. 7500 seconds ≈ __?__ hours

5. 3 feet ≈ __?__ meters

6. 4 inches ≈ __?__ yards

Explain 3 **Using Dimensional Analysis to Convert and Compare Rates**

Use dimensional analysis to determine which rate is greater.

Example 3 During a cycling event for charity, Amanda traveled 105 kilometers in 4.2 hours and Brenda traveled at a rate of 0.2 mile per minute. Which girl traveled at a greater rate? Use 1 mi = 1.61 km.

(A) Convert Amanda's rate to the same units as Brenda's rate.
Set up conversion factors so that both kilometers and hours cancel.

$$\frac{x \text{ miles}}{\text{minute}} \approx \frac{105 \text{ km}}{4.2 \text{ h}} \cdot \frac{1 \text{ mi}}{1.61 \text{ km}} \cdot \frac{1 \text{ h}}{60 \text{ min}}$$

$$\approx \frac{105 \text{ mi}}{4.2 \cdot 1.61 \cdot 60 \text{ min}}$$

$$\approx 0.2588 \text{ mi/min}$$

Amanda traveled approximately 0.26 mi/min.

Amanda traveled faster than Brenda.

(B) A box of books has a mass of 4.10 kilograms for every meter of its height. A box of magazines has a mass of 3 pounds for every foot of its height. Which box has a greater mass per unit of height? Use 1 lb = 0.45 kg and 1 m = 3.28 ft. Round your answer to the nearest tenth.

Convert the mass of the box of books to the same units as the mass of the box of magazines. Set up conversion factors so that both kilograms and meters cancel.

$$\frac{x \text{ lb}}{\text{ft}} \approx \frac{4.10 \text{ kg}}{1 \text{ m}} \cdot \frac{\boxed{1} \text{ lb}}{\boxed{0.45} \text{ kg}} \cdot \frac{\boxed{1} \text{ m}}{\boxed{3.28} \text{ ft}} \approx \frac{\boxed{4.10} \text{ lb}}{\boxed{0.45 \cdot 3.28} \text{ ft}} \approx \boxed{2.8} \text{ lb/ft}$$

The box of magazines has a greater mass per unit of height.

Reflect

7. Why is it important to convert rates to the same units before comparing them?

Your Turn

Use dimensional analysis to determine which rate is greater.

8. Alan's go-kart travels 1750 feet per minute, and Barry's go-kart travels 21 miles per hour. Whose go-kart travels faster? Round your answer to the nearest tenth.

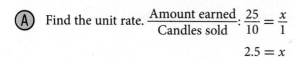 Graphing a Proportional Relationship

To graph a proportional relationship, first find the unit rate, then create scales on the *x*- and *y*-axes and graph points.

Example 4 Simon sold candles to raise money for the school dance. He raised a total of $25.00 for selling 10 candles. Find the unit rate (amount earned per candle). Then graph the relationship.

Ⓐ Find the unit rate. $\dfrac{\text{Amount earned}}{\text{Candles sold}} : \dfrac{25}{10} = \dfrac{x}{1}$

$$2.5 = x$$

The unit rate is $2.50 per candle.

Using this information, create scales on the *x*- and *y*-axes.

The *x*-axis will represent the candles sold, since this is the independent variable.

The *y*-axis will represent the amount earned, since this is the dependent variable.

The origin represents what happens when Simon sells 0 candles. The school gets $0.

Simon sold a total of 10 candles, so the *x*-axis will need to go from 0 to 10.

Since the school gets a total of $25 from Simon, the *y*-axis will need to go from 0 to 25.

Plot points on the graph to represent the amount of money the school earns for the different numbers of candles sold.

A local store sells 8 corn muffins for a total of $6.00. Find the unit rate. Then graph the points.

Ⓑ Find the unit rate. $\dfrac{\text{Amount earned}}{\text{Muffins sold}} : \dfrac{\boxed{6}}{\boxed{8}} = \dfrac{x}{1}$

$$\boxed{0.75} = x$$

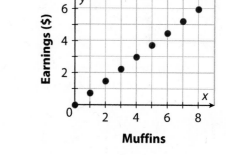

The unit rate is $0.75 per muffin.

Using this information, create scales on the *x*- and *y*-axes.

The *x*-axis will represent the muffins being sold, since this is the independent variable.

The *y*-axis will represent the earnings (in dollars), since this is the dependent variable.

The origin in this graph represents what happens when zero muffins are sold, earning $0.

The *x*-axis will need to go from 0 to 8. The *y*-axis will need to go from 0 to 6.

Plot points on the graph to represent the earnings from the different numbers of muffins sold.

9. In Example 4A, Simon raised a total of $25.00 for selling 10 candles. If Simon raised $30.00 for selling 10 candles, would the unit rate be higher or lower? Explain.

Find the unit rate. On a grid, create scales on the x- and y-axes, and then graph the function.

10. Alex drove 135 miles in 3 hours at a constant speed.

11. Max wrote 10 pages of his lab report in 4 hours.

Elaborate

12. Give three examples of proportions. How do you know they are proportions? Then give three nonexamples of proportions. How do you know they are not proportions?

13. If a scale is represented by a ratio less than 1, what do we know about the actual object? If a scale is represented by a ratio greater than 1, what do we know about the actual object?

14. How is dimensional analysis useful in calculations that involve measurements?

15. **Essential Question Check In** How is finding the unit rate helpful before graphing a proportional relationship?

☆ Evaluate: Homework and Practice

1. **Represent Real-World Problems** A building casts a shadow 48 feet long. At the same time, a 40-foot-tall flagpole casts a shadow 9.6 feet long. What is the height of the building?

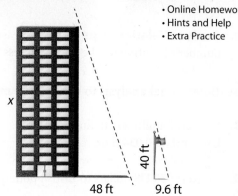

Use the table to answer questions 2–4. Select the best answer. Assume the shadow lengths were measured at the same time of day.

2. The flagpole casts an 8-foot shadow, as shown in the table. At the same time, the oak tree casts a 12-foot shadow. How tall is the oak tree?

3. How tall is the goal post?

4. What is the length of the fence's shadow?

Object	Length of Shadow (ft)	Height (ft)
Flagpole	8	20
Oak tree	12	?
Goal post	18	?
Fence	?	6.5

5. **Decorating** A particular shade of paint is made by mixing 5 parts red paint with 7 parts blue paint. To make this shade, Shannon mixed 12 quarts of blue paint with 8 quarts of red paint. Did Shannon mix the correct shade? Explain.

6. **Geography** The scale on a map of Virginia shows that 1 inch represents 30 miles. The actual distance from Richmond, VA, to Washington, D.C., is 110 miles. On the map, how many inches are between the two cities?

7. Sam is building a model of an antique car. The scale of his model to the actual car is 1:10. His model is $18\frac{1}{2}$ inches long. How long is the actual car?

8. **Archaeology** Stonehenge II in Hunt, Texas, is a scale model of the ancient construction in Wiltshire, England. The scale of the model to the original is 3 to 5. The Altar Stone of the original construction is 4.9 meters tall. Write and solve a proportion to find the height of the model of the Altar Stone.

For 9–11, tell whether each scale *reduces*, *enlarges*, or *preserves* the size of an actual object.

9. 1 m to 25 cm

10. 8 in. to 1 ft

11. 12 in. to 1 ft

12. Analyze Relationships When a measurement in inches is converted to centimeters, will the number of centimeters be greater or less than the number of inches? Explain.

Use dimensional analysis to convert the measurements.

13. Convert 8 milliliters to fluid ounces. Use 1 mL ≈ 0.034 fl oz.

14. Convert 12 kilograms to pounds. Use 1 kg ≈ 2.2 lb.

15. Convert 950 US dollars to British pound sterling. Use 1 US dollar = 0.62 British pound sterling.

16. The dwarf sea horse *Hippocampus zosterae* swims at a rate of 52.68 feet per hour. Convert this speed to inches per minute.

Use dimensional analysis to determine which rate is greater.

17. Tortoise A walks 52.0 feet per hour and tortoise B walks 12 inches per minute. Which tortoise travels faster? Explain.

18. The pitcher for the Robins throws a baseball at 90.0 miles per hour. The pitcher on the Bluebirds throws a baseball 121 feet per second. Which pitcher throws a baseball faster? Explain.

19. For a science experiment, Marcia dissolved 1.0 kilogram of salt in 3.0 liters of water. For a different experiment, Bobby dissolved 2.0 pounds of salt in 7.0 pints of water. Which person made a more concentrated salt solution? Explain. Use 1 L = 2.11 pints. Round your answer to the nearest hundredth.

20. Will a stand that can hold up to 40 pounds support a 21-kilogram television? Explain. Use 2.2 lb = 1 kg.

Find the unit rate. On a grid, create scales on the *x*- and *y*-axes, and then graph the function.

21. Brianna bought a total of 8 notebooks and got 16 free pens.

22. Mason sold 10 wristbands and made a total of 5 dollars.

23. Match each graph to the data it goes with. Explain your reasoning.

A.
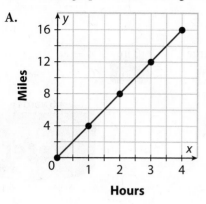

B.
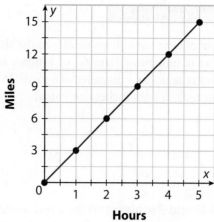

C.
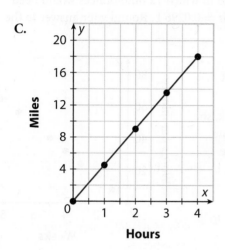

D.
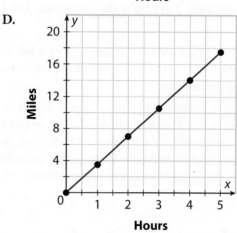

a. __?__ Mike walks 3 miles per hour for 5 hours.

b. __?__ Brad walks 3.5 miles per hour for 5 hours.

c. __?__ Jesse walks 4 miles per hour for 4 hours.

d. __?__ Josh walks 4.5 miles per hour for 4 hours.

24. Multi-Step A can of tuna has a shape similar to the shape of a large water tank. The can of tuna has a diameter of 3 inches and a height of 2 inches. The water tank has a diameter of 6 yards. What is the height of the water tank in both inches and yards?

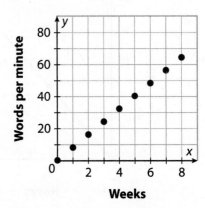

25. Represent Real-World Problems Write a real-world scenario in which 12 fluid ounces would need to be converted into liters. Then make the conversion. Use 1 fl oz = 0.0296 L. Round your answer to the nearest tenth.

26. Find the Error The graph shown was given to represent this problem. Find the error(s) in the graph and then create a correct graph to represent the problem.

Jamie took an 8-week keyboarding class. At the end of each week, she took a test to find the number of words she could type per minute and found out she improved the same amount each week. Before Jamie started the class, she could type 25 words per minute, and by the end of week 8, she could type 65 words per minute.

Lesson Performance Task

The Wright Flyer was the first successful powered aircraft. A model was made to display in a museum with the length of 35 cm and a wingspan of about 66.9 cm. The length of the actual plane was 21 ft 1 in., and the height was 2.74 m. Compare the length, height, and wingspan of the model to the actual plane and explain why any errors may occur. (Round any calculations to the nearest whole number.)

1.3 Reporting with Precision and Accuracy

Resource Locker

Essential Question: How do you use significant digits when reporting the results of calculations involving measurement?

⊘ Explore   Comparing Precision of Measurements

Numbers are values without units. They can be used to compute or to describe measurements. Quantities are real-word values that represent specific amounts. For instance, 15 is a number, but 15 grams is a quantity.

Precision is the level of detail of a measurement, determined by the smallest unit or fraction of a unit that can be reasonably measured.

Accuracy is the closeness of a given measurement or value to the actual measurement or value. Suppose you know the actual measure of a quantity, and someone else measures it. You can find the accuracy of the measurement by finding the absolute value of the difference of the two.

Ⓐ Copy and complete the table to choose the more precise measurement.

Measurement 1	Measurement 2	Smaller Unit	More Precise Measurement
4 g	4.3 g	?	?
5.71 oz	5.7 oz	?	?
4.2 m	422 cm	?	?
7 ft 2 in.	7.2 in.	?	?

Ⓑ Eric is a lab technician. Every week, he needs to test the scales in the lab to make sure that they are accurate. He uses a standard mass that is exactly 8.000 grams and gets the following results.

Scale	Mass
Scale 1	8.02 g
Scale 2	7.9 g
Scale 3	8.029 g

Scale 1   Scale 2   Scale 3

Copy and complete the statement:

The measurement for Scale ? is the most precise because it measures to the

nearest ? , which is smaller than the smallest unit measured on the other two scales.

Ⓒ Find the accuracy of each of the measurements in Step B.

Scale 1: Accuracy $= \left| 8.000 - \boxed{?} \right| = \boxed{?}$

Scale 2: Accuracy $= \left| 8.000 - \boxed{?} \right| = \boxed{?}$

Scale 3: Accuracy $= \left| 8.000 - \boxed{?} \right| = \boxed{?}$

Copy and complete the statement: The measurement for Scale $\boxed{?}$, which is $\boxed{?}$ grams,

is the most accurate because $\boxed{?}$.

Reflect

1. **Discussion** Given two measurements of the same quantity, is it possible that the more precise measurement is not the more accurate? Why do you think that is so?

🔊 Explain 1   Determining Precision of Calculated Measurements

As you have seen, measurements are reported to a certain precision. The reported value does not necessarily represent the actual value of the measurement. When you measure to the nearest unit, the actual length can be 0.5 unit less than the measured length or less than 0.5 unit greater than the measured length. So, a length reported as 4.5 centimeters could actually be anywhere between 4.45 centimeters and 4.55 centimeters, but not including 4.55 centimeters. It cannot include 4.55 centimeters because 4.55 centimeters reported to the nearest tenth would round *up* to 4.6 centimeters.

Example 1   **Calculate the minimum and maximum possible areas. Round your answers to the nearest square centimeter.**

Ⓐ The length and width of a book cover are 28.3 centimeters and 21 centimeters, respectively.

Find the range of values for the actual length and width of the book cover.

Minimum length $= (28.3 - 0.05)$ cm and maximum length $= (28.3 + 0.05)$ cm, so 28.25 cm $\leq$ length $<$ 28.35 cm.

Minimum width $= (21 - 0.5)$ cm and maximum width $= (21 + 0.5)$ cm, so 20.5 cm $\leq$ width $<$ 21.5 cm.

Find the minimum and maximum areas.

Minimum area $=$ minimum length $\cdot$ minimum width

$\qquad\qquad = 28.25$ cm $\cdot$ 20.5 cm ≈ 579 cm^2

Maximum area $=$ maximum length $\cdot$ maximum width

$\qquad\qquad = 28.35$ cm $\cdot$ 21.5 cm ≈ 610 cm^2

So 579 cm$^2 \leq$ area $<$ 610 cm^2.

B The length and width of a rectangle are 15.5 centimeters and 10 centimeters, respectively.

Find the range of values for the actual length and width of the rectangle.

Minimum length $= (15.5 - 0.05)$ cm and maximum length $= (15.5 + 0.05)$ cm, so $15.45 \leq$ length < 15.55.

Minimum width $= (10 - 0.5)$ cm and maximum width $= (10 + 0.5)$ cm, so $9.5 \leq$ width < 10.5.

Find the minimum and maximum areas.

Minimum area $=$ minimum length $\cdot$ minimum width

$$= 15.45 \text{ cm} \cdot 9.5 \text{ cm} \approx 147 \text{ cm}^2$$

Maximum area $=$ maximum length $\cdot$ maximum width

$$= 15.55 \text{ cm} \cdot 10.5 \text{ cm} \approx 163 \text{ cm}^2$$

So $147 \text{ cm}^2 \leq$ area $< 163 \text{ cm}^2$.

Reflect

2. How do the ranges of the lengths and widths of the books compare to the range of the areas? What does that mean in terms of the uncertainty of the dimensions?

Your Turn

Calculate the minimum and maximum possible areas. Round your answers to the nearest whole square unit.

3. Sara wants to paint a wall. The length and width of the wall are 2 meters and 1.4 meters, respectively.

4. A rectangular garden plot measures 15 feet by 22.7 feet.

Explain 2   Identifying Significant Digits

Significant digits are the digits in measurements that carry meaning about the precision of the measurement.

Identifying Significant Digits	
Rule	**Examples**
All nonzero digits are significant.	55.98 has 4 significant digits.
	115 has 3 significant digits.
Zeros between two other significant digits are significant.	102 has 3 significant digits.
	0.4000008 has 7 significant digits.
Zeros at the end of a number to the right of a decimal point are significant.	3.900 has 4 significant digits.
	0.1230 has 4 significant digits.
Zeros to the left of the first nonzero digit in a decimal are *not* significant.	0.00035 has 2 significant digits.
	0.0806 has 3 significant digits.
Zeros at the end of a number without a decimal point are assumed to be *not* significant.	60,600 has 3 significant digits.
	77,000,000 has 2 significant digits.

Example 2 Determine the number of significant digits in a given measurement.

Ⓐ 6040.0050 m

Significant Digits Rule	Digits	Count
Nonzero digits:	⑥ 0 ④ 0 . 0 0 ⑤ 0	3
Zeros between two significant digits:	6 ⓪ 4 ⓪ . ⓪⓪ 5 0	4
End zeros to the right of a decimal:	6 0 4 0 . 0 0 5 ⓪	1
	Total	8

So, 6040.0050 m has 8 significant digits.

Ⓑ 710.080 cm

Significant Digits Rule	Digits	Count
Nonzero digits:	⑦ ① 0 . 0 ⑧ 0	3
Zeros between two significant digits:	7 1 ⓪ . ⓪ 8 0	2
End zeros to the right of a decimal:	7 1 0 . 0 8 ⓪	1
	Total	6

710.080 cm has 6 significant digits.

Reflect

5. **Critique Reasoning** A student claimed that 0.045 m and 0.0045 m have the same number of significant digits. Do you agree or disagree?

Your Turn

Determine the number of significant digits in each measurement.

6. 0.052 kg

7. 10,000 ft

8. 10.000 ft

⊘ Explain 3 Using Significant Digits in Calculated Measurements

When performing calculations with measurements of different precision, the number of significant digits in the solution may differ from the number of significant digits in the original measurements. Use the rules from the following table to determine how many significant digits to include in the result of a calculation.

Rules for Significant Digits in Calculated Measurements	
Operation	**Rule**
Addition or Subtraction	The sum or difference must be rounded to the same place value as last significant digit of the least precise measurement.
Multiplication or Division	The product or quotient must have no more significant digits than the least precise measurement.

Example 3 **Find the perimeter and area of the given object. Make sure your answers have the correct number of significant digits.**

Ⓐ A rectangular swimming pool measures 22.3 feet by 75 feet.

Find the perimeter of the swimming pool using the correct number of significant digits.

Perimeter = sum of side lengths
= 22.3 ft + 75 ft + 22.3 ft + 75 ft
= 194.6 ft

The least precise measurement is 75 feet. Its last significant digit is in the ones place. So round the sum to the ones place. The perimeter is 195 ft.

Find the area of the swimming pool using the correct number of significant digits.

Area = length · width
= 22.3 ft · 75 ft = 1672.5 ft²

The least precise measurement, 75 feet, has two significant digits, so round the product to a number with two significant digits. The area is 1700 ft².

Ⓑ A rectangular garden plot measures 21 feet by 25.2 feet.

Find the perimeter of the garden using the correct number of significant digits.

Perimeter = sum of side lengths
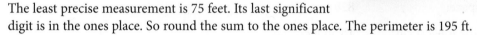
= [21 ft] + [25.2 ft] + [21 ft] + [25.2 ft] = [92.4 ft]

The least precise measurement is 21 ft. Its last significant digit is in the ones place. So round the sum to the ones place. The perimeter is 92 ft.

Find the area of the garden using the correct number of significant digits.

Area = length · width
= [21 ft] · [25.2 ft] = [529.2 ft²]

The least precise measurement, 21 ft, has 2 significant digits, so round to a number with 2 significant digits. The area is 530 ft².

9. In the example, why did the area of the garden and the swimming pool each have two significant digits?

10. Is it possible for the perimeter of a rectangular garden to have more significant digits than its length or width does?

Your Turn

Find the perimeter and area of the given object. Make sure your answers have the correct number of significant digits.

11. A children's sandbox measures 7.6 feet by 8.25 feet.

12. A rectangular door measures 91 centimeters by 203.2 centimeters.

🔑 Explain 4   Using Significant Digits in Estimation

Real-world situations often involve estimation. Significant digits play an important role in making reasonable estimates.

> A city is planning a classic car show. A section of road 820 feet long will be closed to provide a space to display the cars in a row. In past shows, the longest car was 18.36 feet long and the shortest car was 15.1 feet long. Based on that information, about how many cars can be displayed in this year's show?

🧩 Analyze Information

- Available space: 820 feet
- Length of the longest car: 18.36 feet
- Length of the shortest car: 15.1 feet

🧩 Formulate a Plan

The word *about* indicates that your answer will be an estimate.

$$\text{Available Space} = \text{Number of Cars} \cdot \text{Length of Car}$$

Find the number of longest cars and the number of shortest cars, and then use the average.

🧩 Solve

Longest:

$$820 = L \cdot \boxed{18.36}$$

$$L = \frac{820}{\boxed{18.36}} \approx \boxed{45}$$

Shortest:

$$820 = S \cdot \boxed{15.1}$$

$$S = \frac{820}{\boxed{15.1}} \approx \boxed{54}$$

To find a numerical estimate for the number of cars, average the two estimates.

$$\text{Number of cars} = \frac{L + S}{2} = \frac{\boxed{45} + \boxed{54}}{2} \approx \boxed{50}$$

So, on average, 50 cars can be displayed.

Justify and Evaluate

Because the cars will probably have many different lengths, a reasonable estimate is a whole number between the estimates of S and L.

Reflect

13. In the example, why wouldn't it be wise to use the length of a shorter car?

14. Critical Thinking How else might the number of cars be estimated? Would you expect the estimate to be the same? Explain.

Your Turn

Estimate the quantity needed in the following situations. Use the correct number of significant digits.

15. Claire and Juan are decorating a rectangular wall of 433 square feet with two types of rectangular pieces of fabric. One type has an area of 9.4 square feet and the other has an area of 17.2 square feet. About how many decorative pieces can Claire and Juan fit in the given area?

16. An artist is making a mosaic and has pieces of smooth glass ranging in area from 0.25 square inch to 3.75 square inches. Suppose the mosaic is 34.1 inches wide and 50.0 inches long. About how many pieces of glass will the artist need?

Elaborate

17. Given two measurements, is it possible that the more accurate measurement is not the more precise? Justify your answer.

18. What is the relationship between the range of possible error in the measurements used in a calculation and the range of possible error in the calculated measurement?

19. Essential Question Check-In How do you use significant digits to determine how to report a sum or product of two measurements?

1. Choose the more precise measurement from the pair 54.1 cm and 54.16 cm. Justify your answer.

Choose the more precise measurement in each pair.

2. 1 ft; 12 in.   3. 5 kg; 5212 g   4. 7 m; 7.7 m   5. 123 cm; 1291 mm

6. True or False? A scale that measures the mass of an object in grams to two decimal places is more precise than a scale that measures the mass of an object in milligrams to two decimal places. Justify your answer.

7. Every week, a technician in a lab needs to test the scales in the lab to make sure that they are accurate. She uses a standard mass that is exactly 4 g and gets the following results.

   Scale 1   Scale 2   Scale 3

   a. Which scale gives the most precise measurement?

   b. Which scale gives the most accurate measurement?

8. A manufacturing company uses three measuring tools to measure lengths. The tools are tested using a standard unit exactly 7 cm long. The results are as follows.

   a. Which tool gives the most precise measurement?

   b. Which tool gives the most accurate measurement?

Measuring Tool	Length
Tool 1	7.033 cm
Tool 2	6.91 cm
Tool 3	7.1 cm

Given the following measurements, calculate the minimum and maximum possible areas of each object. Round your answer to the nearest square whole square unit.

9. The length and width of a book cover are 22.2 centimeters and 12 centimeters, respectively.

10. The length and width of a rectangle are 19.5 centimeters and 14 centimeters, respectively.

11. Chris is painting a wall with a length of 3 meters and a width of 1.6 meters.

12. A rectangular garden measures 15 feet by 24.1 feet.

Show the steps to determine the number of significant digits in the measurement.

13. 123.040 m

14. 0.00609 cm

Determine the number of significant digits in each measurement.

15. 0.0070 ft   16. 3333.33 g   17. 20,300.011 lb

Find the perimeter and area of each garden. Report your answers with the correct number of significant digits.

18. A rectangular garden plot measures 13 feet by 26.6 feet.

19. A rectangular garden plot measures 24 feet by 25.3 feet.

20. Samantha is putting a layer of topsoil on a garden plot. She measures the plot and finds that the dimensions of the plot are 5 meters by 21 meters. Samantha has a bag of topsoil that covers an area of 106 square meters. Should she buy another bag of topsoil to ensure that she can cover her entire plot? Explain.

21. Tom wants to tile the floor in his kitchen, which has an area of 320 square feet. In the store, the smallest tile he likes has an area of 1.1 square feet and the largest tile he likes has an area of 1.815 square feet. About how many tiles can be fitted in the given area? Explain your answer.

H.O.T. Focus on Higher Order Thinking

22. Communicate Mathematical Ideas Consider the calculation 5.6 mi ÷ 9s = 0.62222 mi/s. Why is it important to use significant digits to round the answer?

23. Find the Error A student found that the dimensions of a rectangle were 1.20 centimeters and 1.40 centimeters. He was asked to report the area using the correct number of significant digits. He reported the area as 1.7 cm^2. Explain the error the student made.

24. Make a Conjecture Given two values with the same number of decimal places and significant digits, is it possible for the sum or product of the two values to have a different number of decimal places or significant digits than the original values?

Lesson Performance Task

The sun is an excellent source of electrical energy.
A field of solar panels yields 16.22 Watts per square feet.
Determine the amount of electricity produced by a field of
solar panels that is 305 feet by 620 feet.

Quantitative Reasoning

Essential Question: How do you use quantitative reasoning to solve real-world problems?

Key Vocabulary

accuracy *(exactitud)*

conversion factor
(factor de conversión)

dimensional analysis
(análisis dimensional)

equation *(ecuación)*

precision *(precisión)*

proportion *(proporción)*

rate *(tasa)*

ratio *(razón)*

scale *(escala)*

significant digits
(dígitos significativos)

solution of an equation
(solución de una ecuación)

KEY EXAMPLE   *(Lesson 1.1)*

Two fortnights have passed from January 3rd to January 31st. How many days long is a fortnight?

$31 - 3 = 28$	*Calculate the number of days that have passed.*
$2f = 28$	*Write an equation.*
$\dfrac{2f}{2} = \dfrac{28}{2}$	*Use the division property of equality.*
$f = 14$	

A fortnight equals 14 days.

KEY EXAMPLE   *(Lesson 1.2)*

The scale on a map is 1 in: 8 mi. The distance from Cedar Park, TX to Austin, TX on the map is 2.5 in. How long is the actual distance?

$\dfrac{\text{actual}}{\text{map}} \rightarrow \dfrac{8 \text{ mi}}{1 \text{ in.}}$	*Write the scale as a fraction.*
$\dfrac{8}{1} = \dfrac{d}{2.5}$	*Let d be the actual distance.*
$2.5 \times 8 = 2.5 \times \dfrac{d}{2.5}$	*Multiply both sides by 2.5.*
$20 = d$	

The actual distance is 20 mi.

KEY EXAMPLE   *(Lesson 1.3)*

Find the sum and product of the following measurements using the correct number of significant digits: 15 ft and 9.25 ft.

$15 \text{ ft} + 9.25 \text{ ft} = 24.25 \text{ ft}$	*Round to the place value of the last significant digit of the least precise measurement.*
24 ft	*The last significant digit of 15 is in the ones place.*
$15 \text{ ft} \times 9.25 \text{ ft} = 138.75 \text{ ft}^2$	*Round so it has the number of significant digits of the least precise measurement.*
140 ft^2	*15 has 2 significant digits.*

EXERCISES

Solve. Check your solutions. *(Lesson 1.1)*

1. $z - 12 = 30$

2. $-\dfrac{y}{7} = 8$

3. $5x + 13 = 48$

4. $25 - 3p = -11$

5. The height of a scale model building is 15 in. The scale is 5 in. to 32 in. Find the height of the actual building in inches and in feet. *(Lesson 1.2)*

6. Which of the following measurements is least precise, and how many significant digits does it have? *(Lesson 1.3)*

$$50.25 \text{ cm, } 12.5 \text{ cm, } 101 \text{ cm}$$

7. A square countertop has a side length of 28 inches. Find the perimeter and area of the countertop using the correct number of significant digits. *(Lesson 1.3)*

MODULE PERFORMANCE TASK

What an Impossible Score!

The simple dartboard shown has two sections, a 5-point outer ring and a 7-point inner circle. What is the largest integer score that is impossible to achieve for this simple dartboard, even if you are allowed to throw as many darts as you want?

Start by listing how you plan to tackle the problem. Then complete the task. Be sure to write down all your data and assumptions. Then use graphs, numbers, words, or algebra to explain how you reached your conclusion.

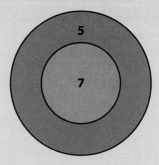

Ready to Go On?

1.1–1.3 Quantitative Reasoning

- Online Homework
- Hints and Help
- Extra Practice

Solve. *(Lesson 1.1)*

1. $7 = 4s + 19$

2. $\dfrac{x}{4} + 8 = 16$

3. A student's pay of $23 an hour at a new job is $6 more than twice the amount the student earned per hour at an internship. Write and solve an equation to find the hourly pay of the internship. *(Lesson 1.1)*

4. Susan enlarged to scale a rectangle with a height of 4 cm and length of 11 cm on her computer. The length of the new rectangle is 16.5 cm. Find the height of the new rectangle. *(Lesson 1.2)*

5. An instructional video is 5.4 minutes long. How long is the video in seconds? How long is it in hours? *(Lesson 1.2)*

Solve using the correct number of significant digits. *(Lesson 1.3)*

6. 70.8 m × 11 m

7. 16.5 ft + 2.25 ft + 12.5 ft

ESSENTIAL QUESTION

8. How do you calculate correctly with real-world measurements?

Assessment Readiness

1. Look at each equation and possible solution. Tell whether each solution is correct.

   A. $-3x = -30; x = -10$

   B. $25 - 2y = 13; y = 6$

   C. $\frac{z}{3} + 2 = 6; z = 16$

2. During a 5-kilometer run to raise money for the school band, Tabitha ran 0.08 kilometer per minute. Use 1 mi $\approx$ 1.61 km. Determine if each statement is True or False.

   A. Tabitha ran 4.8 miles per hour.

   B. Tabitha ran about 0.05 mile per minute.

   C. Tabitha ran faster than 4 kilometers per hour.

3. A carpenter took the following measurements: 3.4 m, 10.25 m, 20.2 m, and 19 m. Determine if each statement is True or False.

   A. The most precise measurement has 4 significant digits.

   B. The least precise measurement has 2 significant digits.

   C. Written using the correct number of significant digits, the sum of the measurements should be rounded to the tenths place.

4. Stanley is putting wallpaper strips on his bathroom walls that have a total area of 450 square feet. Each strip of wall paper covers between 20 and 24 square feet. Estimate how many strips of wallpaper Stanley will need. Explain how you solved this problem.

Algebraic Models

Essential Question: How can you use algebraic models to solve real-world problems?

REAL WORLD VIDEO
In a grocery store receipt, some items are taxed and some items are not taxed. You can write an expression that shows a simplified method for calculating the total grocery bill.

MODULE PERFORMANCE TASK PREVIEW
Menu Math

What if you opened a menu in a restaurant and saw this: "Special Today!!! All G's just $2.95 a piece! M's reduced 20%!" You might decide to try another restaurant. On the other hand, you might decide that you wanted to decipher the code. Deciphering codes is one way of describing what you do when you solve equations. In this module, you'll decipher a lot of codes and then use what you've learned to discover the mathematics of menus!

Are YOU Ready?

Complete these exercises to review skills you will need for this module.

• Online Homework
• Hints and Help
• Extra Practice

One-Step Inequalities

| Example 1 | Solve. |

$$x + 8 < 15$$

$$x + 8 - 8 < 15 - 8 \qquad \text{Isolate the variable by subtracting 8}$$
$$\text{from both sides of the inequality.}$$

$$x < 7$$

Solve each inequality.

1. $n - 23 \geq 17$ **2.** $p + 14 \leq 9$ **3.** $\dfrac{n}{5} > -13$

Two-Step Equations

| Example 2 | Solve. |

$$6k - 12 = 18$$

$$6k - 12 + 12 = 18 + 12 \quad \text{Add 12 to both sides of the equation.}$$

$$6k = 30$$

$$\dfrac{6k}{6} = \dfrac{30}{6} \qquad \text{Divide both sides of the equation by 6.}$$

$$k = 5$$

Solve each equation.

4. $3n + 19 = 28$ **5.** $34 - 4b = 18$ **6.** $\dfrac{2}{3}y + 7 = 15$

Two-Step Inequalities

| Example 3 | Solve. |

$$15 - 3f > 75$$

$$15 - 15 - 3f > 75 - 15 \quad \text{Subtract 15 from both sides of the inequality.}$$

$$-3f > 60$$

$$\dfrac{-3f}{-3} < \dfrac{60}{-3} \qquad \text{Divide both sides of the inequality by } -3.$$
$$\text{Reverse the inequality symbol.}$$

$$f < -20$$

Solve each inequality.

7. $8c - 21 < 35$ **8.** $-6h + 17 > 41$ **9.** $\dfrac{r}{5} - 2 \leq 9$

2.1 Modeling with Expressions

Essential Question: How do you interpret algebraic expressions in terms of their context?

Explore Interpreting Parts of an Expression

An **expression** is a mathematical phrase that contains operations, numbers, and/or variables. The **terms** of an expression are the parts that are being added. A **coefficient** is the numerical factor of a variable term. There are both *numerical expressions* and *algebraic expressions*. A **numerical expression** contains only numbers while an **algebraic expression** contains at least one variable.

(A) Identify the terms and the coefficients of the expression $8p + 2q + 7r$.

terms: ⬚ ? ; coefficients: ⬚ ?

(B) Identify the terms and coefficients of the expression $18 - 2x - 4y$. Since the expression involves ⬚ ? rather than addition, rewrite the expression as the ⬚ ? of the terms:

$18 - 2x - 4y = $ ⬚ ? . So, the terms of the expression are ⬚ ? and the coefficients

are ⬚ ? .

(C) Identify the terms and coefficients in the expression $2x + 3y - 4z + 10$. Since the expression involves both ⬚ ? and addition, rewrite the expression as the ⬚ ?

of the terms: $2x + 3y - 4z + 10 = $ ⬚ ? . So, the terms of the expression are ⬚ ?

and the coefficients are ⬚ ? .

Tickets to an amusement park are $60 for adults and $30 for children. If a is the number of adults and c is the number of children, then the cost for a adults and c children is $60a + 30c$.

(D) What are the terms of the expression? ⬚ ?

(E) What are the factors of $60a$? ⬚ ?

(F) What are the factors of $30c$? ⬚ ?

(G) What are the coefficients of the expression? ⬚ ?

(H) Interpret the meaning of the two terms of the expression. ⬚ ?

The price of a case of juice is $15.00. Fred has a coupon for 20 cents off each bottle in the case. The expression to find the final cost of the case of juice is $15 - 0.2b$, wherein b is the number of bottles.

(I) What are the terms of the expression? ⬚ ?

Ⓙ What are the factors of each term? [?] is the only factor of the [?]

term and [?] and [?] are the factors of the [?] term.

Ⓚ Do both terms have coefficients? Explain. [?]

What are the coefficients? [?]

Ⓛ What does the expression $15 - 0.2b$ mean in the given situation? [?]

Reflect

1. Sally identified the terms of the expression $9a + 4b - 18$ as $9a$, $4b$, and 18. Explain her error.

2. What is the coefficient of b in the expression $b + 10$? Explain.

⊘ Explain 1   Interpreting Algebraic Expressions in Context

In many cases, real-world situations and algebraic expressions can be related. The coefficients, variables, and operations represent the given real-world context.

Interpret the algebraic expression corresponding to the given context.

Example 1

Ⓐ Curtis is buying supplies for his school. He buys p packages of crayons at \$1.49 per package and q packages of markers at \$3.49 per package. What does the expression $1.49p + 3.49q$ represent?

Interpret the meaning of the term $1.49p$. What does the coefficient 1.49 represent?

The term $1.49p$ represents the cost of p packages of crayons. The coefficient represents the cost of one package of crayons, \$1.49.

Interpret the meaning of the term $3.49q$. What does the coefficient 3.49 represent?

The term $3.49q$ represents the cost of q packages of markers. The coefficient represents the cost of one package of markers, \$3.49.

Interpret the meaning of the entire expression.

The expression $1.49p + 3.49q$ represents the total cost of p packages of crayons and q packages of markers.

Ⓑ Jill is buying ink jet paper and laser jet paper for her business. She buys 8 more packages of ink jet paper than p packages of laser jet paper. Ink jet paper costs \$6.95 per package and laser jet paper costs \$8 per package. What does the expression $8p + 6.95(p + 8)$ represent?

Interpret the meaning of the first term, $8p$. What does the coefficient 8 represent?

The term $8p$ represents the cost of p packages of laser jet paper. The coefficient represents the cost of one package of laser jet paper, \$8.

Interpret the meaning of the second expression, $6.95(p + 8)$. What do the factors 6.95 and $(p + 8)$ represent?

© Houghton Mifflin Harcourt Publishing Company

The term $6.95(p + 8)$ represents the cost of the ink jet paper. 6.95 represents the cost of one package of ink jet paper. $(p + 8)$ represents the total cost of packages of ink jet and laser jet paper that Jill bought.

Interpret the expression $8p + 6.95(p + 8)$.

The expression represents the total cost of packages of ink jet and laser jet paper that Jill bought.

Your Turn

Interpret the algebraic expression corresponding to the given context.

3. George is buying watermelons and pineapples to make fruit salad. He buys w watermelons at $4.49 each and p pineapples at $5 each. What does the expression $4.49w + 5p$ represent?

4. Sandi buys 5 fewer packages of pencils than p packages of pens. Pencils costs $2.25 per package and pens costs $3 per package. What does the expression $3p + 2.25(p - 5)$ represent?

⚙ Explain 2 Comparing Algebraic Expressions

Given two algebraic expressions involving two variables, we can compare whether one is greater or less than the other. We can denote the inequality between the expressions by using $<$ or $>$ symbols. If the expressions are the same, or **equivalent expressions**, we denote this equality by using $=$.

Suppose x and y give the populations of two different cities where $x > y$. Compare the expressions and tell which of the given pair is greater.

Example 2

(A) $x + y$ and $2x$

The expression $2x$ is greater.

- Putting the lesser population, y, together with the greater population, x, gives a population that is less than double the greater population.

(B) $\frac{x}{y}$ and $\frac{y}{x}$

Since $x > y$, $\frac{x}{y}$ will be greater than 1 and $\frac{y}{x}$ will be less than 1.

So $\frac{x}{y} > \frac{y}{x}$.

Your Turn

Suppose x and y give the populations of two different cities where $x > y$ and $y > 0$. Compare the expressions and tell which of the given pair is greater.

5. $\frac{x}{x + y}$ and $\frac{x + y}{x}$

6. $2(x + y)$ and $(x + y)^2$

🔑 Explain 3   Modeling Expressions in Context

The table shows some words and phrases associated with the four basic arithmetic operations. These words and phrases can help you translate a real-world situation into an algebraic expression.

Operation	Words	Examples
Addition	the sum of, added to, plus, more than, increased by, total, altogether, and	1. A number increased by 2 2. The sum of n and 2 3. $n + 2$
Subtraction	less than, minus, subtracted from, the difference of, take away, taken from, reduced by	1. The difference of a number and 2 2. 2 less than a number 3. $n - 2$
Multiplication	times, multiplied by, the product of, percent of	1. The product of 0.6 and a number 2. 60% of a number 3. $0.6n$
Division	divided by, division of, quotient of, divided into, ratio of	1. The quotient of a number and 5 2. A number divided by 5 3. $n \div 5$ or $\frac{n}{5}$

Example 3   Write an algebraic expression to model the given context.
Give your answer in simplest form.

(A)   the price of an item plus 6% sales tax

Price of an item $+$ 6% sales tax

p $+$ $0.06p$

The algebraic expression is $p + 0.06p$, or $1.06p$.

(B)   the price of a car plus 8.5% sales tax

The price of a car $+$ 8.5% sales tax

p $+$ $0.085p$

The algebraic expression is $p + 0.085p$, or $p + 0.085p = 1.085p$.

Reflect

7.   Use the Distributive Property to show why $p + 0.06p = 1.06p$.

8.   What could the expression $3(p + 0.06p)$ represent? Explain.

Your Turn

Write an algebraic expression to model the given context. Give your answer in simplest form.

9.   the number of gallons of water in a tank, that already has 300 gallons in it, after being filled at 35 gallons per minute for m minutes

10.   the original price p of an item less a discount of 15%

11. When given an algebraic expression involving subtraction, why is it best to rewrite the expression using addition before identifying the terms?

12. How do you interpret algebraic expressions in terms of their context?

13. How do you simplify algebraic expressions?

14. Essential Question Check In How do you write algebraic expressions to model quantities?

⊛ Evaluate: Homework and Practice

Identify the terms and the coefficients of the expression.

- Online Homework
- Hints and Help
- Extra Practice

1. $-20 + 5p - 7z$

2. $8x - 20y - 10$

Identify the factors of the terms of the expression.

3. $5 + 6a + 11b$

4. $13m - 2n$

5. Erin is buying produce at a store. She buys c cucumbers at $0.99 each and a apples at $0.79 each. What does the expression $0.99c + 0.79a$ represent?

6. The number of bees that visit a plant is 500 times the number of years the plant is alive, where t represents the number of years the plant is alive. What does the expression $500t$ represent?

7. Lorenzo buys 3 shirts at s dollars apiece and 2 pairs of pants at p dollars a pair. What does the expression $3s + 2p$ represent?

8. If a car travels at a speed of 25 mi/h for t hours, then travels 45 mi/h for m hours, what does the expression $25t + 45m$ represent?

9. The price of a sandwich is $1.50 more than the price of a smoothie, which is d dollars. What does the expression $d + 1.5$ represent?

10. A bicyclist travels 1 mile in 5 minutes. If m represents minutes, what does the expression $\frac{m}{5}$ represent?

11. What are the factors of the expression $(y - 2)(x + 3)$?

12. Explain the Error A student wrote that there are two terms in the expression $3p - (7 - 4q)$. Explain the student's error.

13. Yolanda is buying supplies for school. She buys n packages of pencils at $1.40 per package and m pads of paper at $1.20 each. What does each term in the expression $1.4n + 1.2m$ represent? What does the entire expression represent?

14. Chris buys p pairs of pants and 4 more shirts than pairs of pants. Shirts cost $18 each and pair of pants cost $25 each. What does each term in the expression $25p + 18(p + 4)$ represent? What does the entire expression represent?

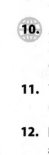

Suppose a and b give the populations of two states where $a > b$. Compare the expressions and tell which of the given pair is greater or if the expressions are equal. Justify your answer.

15. $\dfrac{b}{a+b}$ and 0.5

16. $a + 13c$ and $b + 13c$, where c is the population of a third state

17. $\dfrac{a-b}{2}$ and $a - \dfrac{b}{2}$

18. $a + b$ and $2b$

19. $5(a + b)$ and $(a + b)5$

Write an algebraic expression to model the given context. Give your answer in simplest form.

20. the price s of a pair of shoes plus 5% sales tax.

21. the original price p of an item less a discount of 20%

22. the price h of a recently bought house plus 10% property tax

23. the principal amount P originally deposited in a bank account plus 0.3% interest

24. Match each statement with the algebraic expression that models it.

A. the price of a winter coat and a 20% discount

B. the base salary of an employee and a 2% salary increase

C. the cost of groceries and a 2% discount with coupons

D. the number of students attending school last year and a 20% increase from last year

a. ___?___ $x + 0.02x = 1.02x$

b. ___?___ $x - 0.20x = 0.80x$

c. ___?___ $x + 0.20x = 1.20x$

d. ___?___ $x - 0.02x = 0.98x$

H.O.T. Focus on Higher Order Thinking

25. **Critique Reasoning** A student is given the rectangle and the square shown. The student states that the two figures have the same perimeter. Is the student correct? Explain your reasoning.

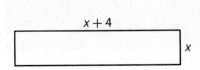

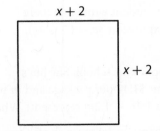

26. Multi-Step Yon buys tickets to a concert for himself and a friend. There is a tax of 6% on the price of the tickets and an additional booking fee of $20 for the transaction. Write an algebraic expression to represent the price per person. Simplify the expression if possible.

27. Persevere in Problem Solving Jerry is planting white daisies and red tulips in his garden and he wants to choose a pattern in which the tulips surround the daisies. He uses tiles to generate patterns starting with two rows of three daisies. He surrounds these daisies with a border of tulips. The design continues as shown.

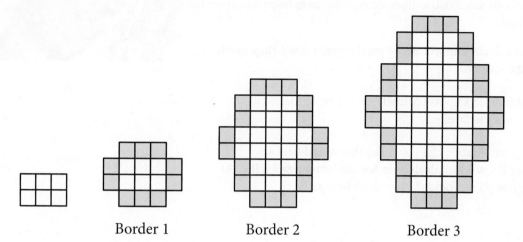

Border 1   Border 2   Border 3

a. Jerry writes the expression $8(b - 1) + 10$ for the number of tulips in each border, wherein b is the border number and $b \geq 1$. Explain why Jerry's expression is correct.

b. Elaine wants to start with two rows of four daisies. Her reasoning is that Jerry started with two rows of three daisies and his expression was $8(b - 1) + 10$, so if she starts with two rows of four daisies, her expression will be $10(b - 1) + 10$. Is Elaine's statement correct? Explain.

Lesson Performance Task

Becky and Michele are both shopping for a new car at two different dealerships. Dealership A is offering $500 cash back on any purchase, while Dealership B is offering $1000 cash back. The tax rate is 5% at Dealership A but 8% at Dealership B. Becky wants to buy a car that is $15,000, and Michele is planning to buy a car that costs $20,000. Use algebraic expressions to help you answer the following questions.

    a. At which dealership will Becky get the better deal? How much does she save?

    b. At which dealership will Michele get the better deal? How much does she save?

    c. What generalization can you make that would help any shopper know which dealership has the better deal? [Hint: At what price point would the two deals be equal?]

© Houghton Mifflin Harcourt Publishing Company · Image Credits: ©Tom Grill/ Corbis

2.2 Creating and Solving Equations

Essential Question: How do you use an equation to model and solve a real-world problem?

🧭 Explore — Creating Equations from Verbal Descriptions

You can use what you know about writing algebraic expressions to write an equation that represents a real-world situation.

Suppose Cory and his friend Walter go to a movie. Each of their tickets costs the same amount, and they share a frozen yogurt that costs $5.50. The total amount they spend is $19.90. How can you write an equation that describes the situation?

(A) Identify the important information.

The word [?] tells you that the relationship describes an equation.

The word *total* tells you that the operation involved in the relationship is [?].

What numerical information do you have? [?]

What is the unknown quantity? [?]

(B) Write a verbal description.

Choose a name for the variable. In this case, use *c* for [?].

The verbal description is: Twice the cost of [?] plus the cost of [?] equals [?].

(C) To write an equation, write a numerical or [?] expression for each quantity and insert

an equal sign in the appropriate place. An equation is: [?].

Reflect

1. How can you use a verbal model to write an equation for the situation described?

2. Could you write a different equation to describe the situation? Explain your reasoning.

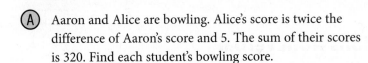

When you create an equation to model a real-world problem, your equation may involve the Distributive Property. When you solve a real-world problem, you should always check that your answer makes sense.

Example 1 Write and solve an equation to solve each problem.

(A) Aaron and Alice are bowling. Alice's score is twice the difference of Aaron's score and 5. The sum of their scores is 320. Find each student's bowling score.

Write a verbal description of the basic situation.

The sum of Aaron's score and Alice's score is 320.

Choose a variable for the unknown quantity and write an equation to model the detailed situation.

Let a represent Aaron's score. Then $2(a - 5)$ represents Alice's score.

$$a + 2(a - 5) = 320$$

Solve the equation for a.

$$a + 2(a - 5) = 320$$

$$a + 2a - 10 = 320 \qquad \text{Distributive Property}$$

$$3a - 10 = 320$$

$$3a - 10 + 10 = 320 + 10 \qquad \text{Addition Property of Equality}$$

$$3a = 330$$

$$\frac{3a}{3} = \frac{330}{3} \qquad \text{Division Property of Equality}$$

$$a = 110$$

So, Aaron's score is 110 and Alice's score is $2(a - 5) = 2(110 - 5) = 2(105) = 210$.

Check that the answer makes sense.

$110 + 210 = 320$, so the answer makes sense.

(B) Mari, Carlos, and Amanda collect stamps. Carlos has five more stamps than Mari, and Amanda has three times as many stamps as Carlos. Altogether, they have 100 stamps. Find the number of stamps each person has.

Write a verbal description of the basic situation.

The total of the numbers of stamps Mari, Carlos, and Amanda have is 100.

Choose a variable for the unknown quantity and write an equation to model the detailed situation.

Let s represent the number of stamps Mari has. Then Carlos has $s + 5$ stamps, and Amanda has $3(s + 5)$ stamps.

$$s + \boxed{s + 5} + 3\left(\boxed{s + 5}\right) = \boxed{100}$$

Solve the equation for s.

$$s + \boxed{s + 5} + 3\left(\boxed{s + 5}\right) = \boxed{100}$$

$s + s + 5 + 3s + \boxed{15} = \boxed{100}$	Distributive Property
$\boxed{5s} + \boxed{20} = \boxed{100}$	Combine like terms
$\boxed{5}\,s = \boxed{80}$	Subtraction Property of Equality
$s = \boxed{16}$	Division Property of Equality

So, Mari has 16 stamps, Carlos has 21 stamps, and Amanda has 63 stamps.

Check that the answer makes sense.

$$\boxed{16} + \boxed{21} + \boxed{63} = \boxed{100}$$
$$\boxed{100} = \boxed{100}$$
; the answer makes sense.

Reflect

3. Would a fractional answer make sense in this situation?

4. **Discussion** What might it mean if a check revealed that the answer to a real-world problem did not make sense?

Your Turn

Write and solve an equation to solve the problem.

5. A rectangular garden is fenced on all sides with 256 feet of fencing. The garden is 8 feet longer than it is wide. Find the length and width of the garden.

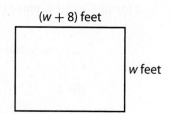
$(w + 8)$ feet

w feet

Creating and Solving Equations with Variables on Both Sides

In some equations, variables appear on both sides. You can use the properties of equality to collect the variable terms so that they all appear on one side of the equation.

Example 2   Write and solve an equation to solve each problem.

Ⓐ Janine has job offers at two companies. One company offers a starting salary of $28,000 with a raise of $3000 each year. The other company offers a starting salary of $36,000 with a raise of $2000 each year. In how many years would Janine's salary be the same with both companies? What will the salary be?

Write a verbal description of the basic situation.

Let n represent the number of years it takes for the salaries to be equal.

Base Salary A plus $3000 per year raise = Base Salary B + $2000 per year raise

$$28{,}000 + 3000n = 36{,}000 + 2{,}000n$$

$$28{,}000 + 3000n - 2000n = 36{,}000 + 2{,}000n - 2000n \qquad \text{Subtraction Property of Equality}$$

$$28{,}000 + 1000n = 36{,}000 \qquad \text{Combine like terms.}$$

$$28{,}000 + 1000n - 28{,}000 = 36{,}000 - 28{,}000 \qquad \text{Subtraction Property of Equality}$$

$$1000n = 8000$$

$$\frac{1000n}{1000} = \frac{8000}{1000} \qquad \text{Division Property of Equality}$$

$$n = 8$$

$$28{,}000 + 3{,}000(8) = 36{,}000 + 2{,}000(8)$$

$$52{,}000 = 52{,}000$$

In 8 years, the salaries offered by both companies will be $52,000.

Ⓑ One moving company charges $800 plus $16 per hour. Another moving company charges $720 plus $21 per hour. At what number of hours will the charge by both companies be the same? What is the charge?

Write a verbal description of the basic situation. Let t represent the number of hours that the move takes.

Moving Charge A plus $16 per hour = Moving Charge B plus $21 per hour

$$800 + \boxed{16}\, t = 720 + \boxed{21}\, t$$

$$800 + \boxed{16}\, t - \boxed{16}\, t = 720 + \boxed{21}\, t - \boxed{16}\, t \qquad \text{Subtraction Property of Equality}$$

$$800 = 720 + \boxed{5}\, t$$

$$800 - 720 = 720 + \boxed{5}\; t - 720 \qquad \text{Subtraction Property of Equality}$$

$$\boxed{80} = \boxed{5}\; t$$

$$\frac{\boxed{80}}{\boxed{5}} = \frac{\boxed{5}}{\boxed{5}}\, t \qquad \text{Division Property of Equality}$$

$$t = \boxed{16}$$

The charges are the same for a job that takes 16 hours.

Substitute the value 16 in the original equation.

$$800 + 16t = 720 + 21t$$

$$800 + 16\left(\boxed{16}\right) = 720 + 21\left(\boxed{16}\right)$$

$$800 + \boxed{256} = 720 + \boxed{336}$$

$$\boxed{1056} = \boxed{1056}$$

After 16 hours, the moving charge for both companies will be $1056.

Reflect

6. Suppose you collected the variable terms on the other side of the equal sign to solve the equation. Would that affect the solution?

Your Turn

Write and solve an equation to solve each problem.

7. Claire bought just enough fencing to enclose either a rectangular garden or a triangular garden, as shown. The two gardens have the same perimeter. How many feet of fencing did she buy?

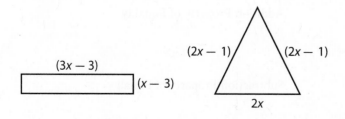

8. A veterinarian is changing the diets of two animals, Simba and Cuddles. Simba currently consumes 1200 Calories per day. That number will increase by 100 Calories each day. Cuddles currently consumes 3230 Calories a day. That number will decrease by 190 Calories each day. The patterns will continue until both animals are consuming the same number of Calories each day. In how many days will that be? How many Calories will each animal be consuming each day then?

Explain 3 Constructing Equations from an Organized Table

You can use a table to organize information and see relationships.

Example 3 Construct and solve an equation to solve the problem.

Kim works 4 hours more each day than Jill does, and Jack works 2 hours less each day than Jill does. Over 2 days, the number of hours Kim works is equal to the difference of 4 times the number of hours Jack works and the number of hours Jill works. How many hours does each person work each day?

Analyze Information

Identify the important information.

- Kim works [4] hours more per day than Jill does.

- Jack works [2] hours less per day than Jill does.

Formulate a Plan

Make a table using the information given. Let x be the number of hours Jill works in one day.

	Hours Worked Per Day	Hours Worked Over 2 Days
Kim	$x + 4$	$2(x + 4)$
Jill	x	$2x$
Jack	$x - 2$	$2(x - 2)$

Over 2 days, the number of hours Kim works is equal to the difference of 4 times the number of hours Jack works and the number of hours Jill works.

$$2(x + 4) = 4 \cdot 2(x - 2) - 2x$$

Solve

$$2(x + 4) = 4 \cdot 2(x - 2) - 2x$$

$2(x + 4) = \boxed{8}\ (x - 2) - 2x$ 　　　Simplify.

$2x + \boxed{8} = 8x - \boxed{16} - 2x$ 　　　Distributive Property

$2x + 8 = \boxed{6}\ x - 16$

$2x + 8 + \boxed{16} = 6x - 16 + \boxed{16}$ 　　　Addition Property of Equality

$2x + \boxed{24} = 6x$

$2x + 24 - \boxed{2}\ x = 6x - \boxed{2}\ x$ 　　　Subtraction Property of Equality

$24 = \boxed{4}\ x$

$\dfrac{24}{\boxed{4}} = \dfrac{\boxed{4}\ x}{\boxed{4}}$ 　　　Division Property of Equality

$\boxed{6} = x$

Jill works ☐6☐ hours per day, Kim works ☐10☐ hours per day, and

Jack works ☐4☐ hours per day.

 **Justify and Evaluate**

Substitute $x = 6$ into the original equation.

$$2(6 + 4) = 4 \cdot 2(6 - 2) - 2x$$

$$2\boxed{10} = 8\boxed{4} - 2\boxed{6}$$

$$\boxed{20} = \boxed{20}$$

Your Turn

Write and solve an equation to solve the problem.

9. Lisa is 10 centimeters taller than her friend Ian. Ian is 14 centimeters taller than Jim. Every month, their heights increase by 2 centimeters. In 7 months, the sum of Ian's and Jim's heights will be 170 centimeters more than Lisa's height. How tall is Ian now?

💬 **Elaborate**

10. How can you use properties to solve equations with variables on both sides?

11. How is a table helpful when constructing equations?

12. When solving a real-world problem to find a person's age, would a negative solution make sense? Explain.

13. **Essential Question Check-In** How do you write an equation to represent a real-world situation?

⭐ **Evaluate: Homework and Practice**

• Online Homework
• Hints and Help
• Extra Practice

Write an equation for each description.

1. The sum of 14 and a number is equal to 17.

2. A number increased by 10 is 114.

3. The difference between a number and 12 is 20.

4. Ten times the sum of half a number and 6 is 8.

5. Two-thirds a number plus 4 is 7.

6. Tanmayi wants to raise $175 for a school fundraiser. She has raised $120 so far. How much more does she need to reach her goal?

7. Hector is visiting a cousin who lives 350 miles away. He has driven 90 miles. How many more miles does he need to drive to reach his cousin's home?

8. The length of a rectangle is twice its width. The perimeter of the rectangle is 126 feet.

Write and solve an equation for each situation.

9. In one baseball season, Peter hit twice the difference of the number of home runs Alice hit and 6. Altogether, they hit 18 home runs. How many home runs did each player hit that season?

10. The perimeter of a parallelogram is 72 meters. The width of the parallelogram is 4 meters less than its length. Find the length and the width of the parallelogram.

ℓ meters

$(\ell - 4)$ meters

11. One month, Ruby worked 6 hours more than Isaac, and Svetlana worked 4 times as many hours as Ruby. Together they worked 126 hours. Find the number of hours each person worked.

12. In one day, Annie traveled 5 times the sum of the number of hours Brian traveled and 2. Together they traveled 20 hours. Find the number of hours each person traveled.

13. Xian and his cousin Kai both collect stamps. Xian has 56 stamps, and Kai has 80 stamps. The boys recently joined different stamp-collecting clubs. Xian's club will send him 12 new stamps per month. Kai's club will send him 8 new stamps per month. After how many months will Xian and Kai have the same number of stamps? How many stamps will each have?

14. Kenya plans to make a down payment plus monthly payments in order to buy a motorcycle. At one dealer she would pay $2,500 down and $150 each month. At another dealer, she would pay $3,000 down and $125 each month. After how many months would the total amount paid be the same for both dealers? What would that amount be?

15. Community Gym charges a $50 membership fee and a $55 monthly fee. Workout Gym charges a $200 membership fee and a $45 monthly fee. After how many months will the total amount of money paid to both gyms be the same? What will the amount be?

16. Tina is saving to buy a notebook computer. She has two options. The first option is to put $200 away initially and save $10 every month. The second option is to put $100 away initially and save $30 every month. After how many months would Tina save the same amount using either option? How much would she save with either option?

Use the table to answer each question.

	Starting Salary	Yearly Salary Increase
Company A	$24,000	$3000
Company B	$30,000	$2400
Company C	$36,000	$2000

17. After how many years are the salaries offered by Company A and Company B the same?

18. After how many years are the salaries offered by Company B and Company C the same?

19. Paul started work at Company B ten years ago at the salary shown in the table. At the same time, Sharla started at Company C at the salary shown in the table. Who earned more during the last year? How much more?

20. George's page contains twice as many typed words as Bill's page and Bill's page contains 50 fewer words than Charlie's page. If each person can type 60 words per minute, after one minute, the difference between twice the number of words on Bill's page and the number of words on Charlie's page is 210. How many words did Bill's page contain initially? Use a table to organize the information.

21. Geometry Sammie bought just enough fencing to border either a rectangular plot or a square plot, as shown. The perimeters of the plots are the same. How many meters of fencing did she buy?

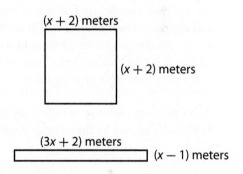

(x + 2) meters

(x + 2) meters

(3x + 2) meters

(x − 1) meters

22. Justify Reasoning Suppose you want to solve the equation $2a + b = 2a$, where a and b are nonzero real numbers. Describe the solution to this equation. Justify your description.

23. Multi-Step A patio in the shape of a rectangle, is fenced on all sides with 134 feet of fencing. The patio is 5 feet less wide than it is long.

ℓ feet

$(\ell - 5)$ feet

   a. What information can be used to solve the problem? How can you find the information?

   b. Describe how to find the area of the patio. What is the area of the patio?

24. **Explain the Error** Kevin and Brittany write an equation to represent the following relationship, and both students solve their equation. Who found the correct equation and solution? Why is the other person incorrect?

5 times the difference of a number and 20 is the same as half the sum of 4 more than 4 times a number.

Kevin: Brittany:

$$5(x - 20) = \frac{1}{2}(4x + 4)$$ $$5(20 - x) = \frac{1}{2}(4x + 4)$$

$$5x - 100 = 2x + 2$$ $$100 - 5x = 2x + 2$$

$$3x - 100 = 2$$ $$100 - 7x = 2$$

$$3x = 102$$ $$-7x = -98$$

$$x = 34$$ $$x = 14$$

25. **What If?** Alexa and Zack are solving the following problem.

The number of miles on Car A is 50 miles more than the number of miles on Car B, and the number of miles on Car B is 30 miles more than the number of miles on Car C. All the cars travel 50 miles in 1 hour. After 1 hour, twice the number of miles on Car A is 70 miles less than 3 times the number of miles on Car C. How many miles were there on Car B initially?

Alexa assumes there are m miles on Car B. Zack assumes there are m miles on Car C. Will Zack's answer be the same as Alexa's answer? Explain.

Lesson Performance Task

Stacy, Oliver, and Jivesh each plan to put a certain amount of money into their savings accounts that earn simple interest of 6% per year. Stacy puts $550 more than Jivesh, and Oliver puts in 2 times as much as Jivesh. After a year, the amount in Stacy's account is 2 times the sum of $212 and the amount in Oliver's account. How much does each person initially put into his or her account? Who had the most money in his or her account after a year? Who had the least? Explain.

2.3 Solving for a Variable

Essential Question: How do you rewrite formulas and literal equations?

Resource Locker

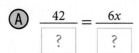 **Explore** **Rearranging Mathematical Formulas**

Literal Equations are equations that contain two or more variables. There are many literal equations in the form of math, science, and engineering formulas. These formulas may seem like they can only be solved for the variable that is isolated on one side of the formula. By using inverse operations and the properties of equality, a formula can be rearranged so any variable in the formula can be isolated. It is no different than how equations are solved by using inverse operations and the properties of equality.

How can you solve the equation $42 = 6x$?

(A) $\dfrac{42}{\boxed{?}} = \dfrac{6x}{\boxed{?}}$ What is the reason for dividing? $\boxed{?}$

Why divide by this quantity? $\boxed{?}$

$\boxed{?} = x$ By rearranging the equation, x was isolated and the solution was found.

The mathematical formula for the volume of a rectangular prism, $B = Vh$ or $V = \ell wh$, is a literal equation. V represents volume, ℓ represents length, w represents width, and h represents height. Using inverse operations, the formula can be rearranged to solve for any one of the variables that might be unknown. Like solving for x, a formula can be rearranged to isolate a variable.

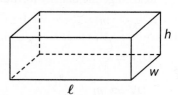

(B) In the formula $V = \ell wh$, the variable h needs to be isolated.

The operation of $\boxed{?}$ is used in the formula.

The inverse operation, $\boxed{?}$, should be used to isolate $\boxed{?}$.

(C) $\dfrac{V}{\boxed{?}} = \dfrac{\ell wh}{\boxed{?}}$

$\dfrac{V}{\boxed{?}} = \boxed{?}$

The formula rearranged in this way can easily produce the height of the rectangular prism, when the volume, length, and width are known.

Reflect

1. Using the formula for a rectangular prism, rewrite the formula to solve for ℓ.

© Houghton Mifflin Harcourt Publishing Company

⚙ Explain 1 Rearranging Scientific Formulas

Use inverse operations to isolate the unknown variable in a scientific formula.

The formula for density is $D = \frac{m}{V}$. Lead has a very high density of 11,340 kg/m³. Plastic foam has a very low density of 75 kg/m³. The formula for density can be rearranged to solve for V, volume or m, mass.

Example 1

(A) A sinker on a fishing line is made of lead and has a volume of 0.000015 m³. What is the mass of the sinker?

The density formula can be rearranged to isolate m, the mass. The values for volume and density can then be substituted into the formula to find the mass.

$$D = \frac{m}{V}$$
$$DV = \left(\frac{m}{V}\right)V$$
$$DV = m$$
$$\left(11{,}340 \text{ kg/m}^3\right)\left(0.000015 \text{ m}^3\right) = m$$
$$0.17 \text{ kg} \approx m$$

(B) The design for a life preserver requires 0.3 kilogram of plastic foam to provide proper buoyancy. What is the volume of the plastic foam required?

Rearrange the density formula to isolate V.

$$D = \frac{m}{V}$$
$$(D)V = \frac{m}{V}\boxed{V}$$
$$DV = \boxed{m}$$
$$\frac{DV}{\boxed{D}} = \frac{m}{\boxed{D}}$$
$$V = \boxed{\frac{m}{D}}$$

Now substitute the given values.

$$V = \frac{\boxed{0.3 \text{ kg}}}{\boxed{75 \text{ kg/m}^3}}$$

$$V = \boxed{0.004} \text{ m}^3$$

Your Turn

2. For altitudes up to 36,000 feet, the relationship between ground temperature and atmospheric temperature can be described by the formula $t = -0.0035a + g$, in which t is the atmospheric temperature in degrees Fahrenheit, a is the altitude, in feet, at which the atmospheric temperature is measured, and g is the ground temperature in degrees Fahrenheit. Determine the altitude in feet when t is -27.5 °F and g is 60 °F.

Explain 2 **Rearranging Literal Equations**

Using inverse operations to rearrange literal equations can be applied to any formula. The interest formula, $I = prt$, is another example of a literal equation. In the formula, I represents interest, p the principal or the initial amount to which interest will be applied, r the rate at which interest will be paid, and t is the time in years.

Example 2

(A) Find the number of years used in the calculation of a $1000 loan at an interest rate of 5% with interest totaling $600.

Solve the formula for t.

$$I = prt$$

$$\frac{I}{pr} = \frac{prt}{pr}$$

$$\frac{I}{pr} = t$$

Substitute the given values. Since the interest rate is 5%, $r = 0.05$.

$$\frac{\$600}{\$1000 \cdot 0.05} = t$$

$$12 = t$$

So the length of time for the loan is 12 years.

(B) Determine the interest rate for a $2000 loan that will be paid off in 4 years with interest totaling $640. In order to find the interest rate, solve the formula for **r**.

$$I = prt$$

$$\frac{I}{\boxed{pt}} = \frac{prt}{\boxed{pt}}$$

$$\frac{I}{\boxed{pt}} = r$$

Now substitute the values and simplify.

$$\frac{\boxed{\$640}}{\left(\boxed{\$2000}\right)\left(\boxed{4}\right)} = r$$

$$0.08 = r$$

So the interest rate is 8% per year.

Your Turn

3. The formula $y = mx + b$ is the slope-intercept form of the equation of a line. Solve the equation for m.

4. **Discussion** What could be a reason for isolating a variable in a literal equation?

5. Describe a situation in which a formula could be used more easily if it were rearranged. Include the formula in your description.

6. **Essential Question Check-In** How do you isolate a variable?

⭐ Evaluate: Homework and Practice

- Online Homework
- Hints and Help
- Extra Practice

Solve for the indicated variable in each mathematical formula.

1. $C = 2\pi r$ for r

2. $A = \frac{1}{2}bh$ for b

3. $y = mx + b$ for x

4. $A = \frac{1}{2}(a + b)h$ for h

5. $V = \pi r^2 h$ for h

6. $SA = 2\pi r^2 + 2\pi rh$ for h

Solve for the indicated variable in each scientific formula.

7. $d = rt$ for t

8. $PV = nRT$ for T

9. $A = \frac{FV - OV}{T}$ for OV

10. $C = \frac{Wtc}{1000}$ for W

Solve for the indicated variable in each literal equation.

11. $2p + 5r = q$ for p

12. $-10 = xy + z$ for x

13. $\frac{a}{b} = c$ for b

14. $\frac{h - 4}{j} = k$ for j

15. $\frac{x}{5} - g = a$ for x

16. $5p + 9c = p$ for c

17. $\frac{2}{5}(z + 1) = y$ for z

18. $g\left(h + \frac{2}{3}\right) = 1$ for h

19. $a(n - 3) + 8 = bn$ for n

20. Which is a possible way to rewrite the equation $y = 3x + 3b$ to solve for b?

   A. $b = \frac{y - 3x}{3}$

   C. $b = \frac{y - 3}{3x}$

   B. $b = 3(y - 3x)$

   D. $b = x(y - 3)$

21. **Sports** To find a baseball pitcher's earned run average (ERA), you can use the formula $Ei = 9r$, in which E represents ERA, i represents the number of innings pitched, and r represents the number of earned runs allowed. Solve the equation for E. What is a pitcher's ERA if he allows 5 earned runs in 18 innings pitched?

22. Meteorology For altitudes up to 36,000 feet, the relationship between ground temperature and atmospheric temperature can be described by the formula $t = -0.0035a + g$, in which t is the atmospheric temperature in degrees Fahrenheit, a is the altitude, in feet, at which the atmospheric temperature is measured, and g is the ground temperature in degrees Fahrenheit. Solve the equation for a. If the atmospheric temperature is $-65.5\ °F$ and the ground temperature is $57\ °F$, what is the altitude?

H.O.T.   Focus on Higher Order Thinking

23. Explain the Error A student was asked to use the formula for the perimeter of a rectangle, $P = 2\ell + 2w$, to solve for ℓ. The student came up with an answer, $P - 2w = 2\ell$. What error did the student make? Explain. Then solve for ℓ.

24. Multi-Step The formula $c = 5p + 215$ relates c, the total cost in dollars of hosting a birthday party at a skating rink, to p, the number of people attending. If Allie's parents are willing to spend $300 for a party, how many people can attend?

25. Multi-Step The formula for the area of a triangle is $A = \frac{1}{2}bh$, in which b represents the length of the base and h represents the height. If a triangle has an area of 192 mm^2 and the height is 12 mm, what is the measure of the base?

Lesson Performance Task

The following table shows the average low temperatures in Fahrenheit for the city of Boston for several months during the year. The formula $F = \frac{9}{5}C + 32$ allows you to determine the temperature in Fahrenheit when given the temperature in Celsius.

Month	Temperature in Fahrenheit	Temperature in Celsius
January	22°	?
April	41°	?
July	65°	?
October	47°	?
December	28°	?

a. Use the information given to determine the average low temperatures in Celsius.

b. Would it ever be possible for the temperature in Celsius to have a greater value than the temperature in Fahrenheit? Explain why or why not.

© Houghton Mifflin Harcourt Publishing Company

2.4 Creating and Solving Inequalities

Essential Question: How do you write and solve an inequality that represents a real-world situation?

Explore   Creating Inequalities from Verbal Descriptions

An **inequality** is a statement that compares two expressions that are not strictly equal by using one of the following inequality signs.

Symbol	Meaning
<	is less than
≤	is less than or equal to
>	is greater than
≥	is greater than or equal to
≠	is not equal to

You have probably seen a sign at an amusement park saying something like, "You must be at least 48 inches tall to ride this ride." This statement could be written as $h \geq 48$ in., where h represents the height of a person allowed to ride.

Nora is planning a birthday party for her little sister, Colleen. Nora's budget will allow her to spend no more than $50 for party supplies. Eight children, including Colleen, will attend the party, and Nora wants to determine how much she could spend on party favors for each child. She will also purchase a cake for $10. Write an inequality that represents the situation, and find possible solutions.

(A) First, let c represent the cost of a party favor for each child. Write an expression for the total cost of the party as a function of c.

$$\boxed{?} \; c + \boxed{?}$$

(B) Which inequality symbol should be used to represent the phrase "no more than"? $\boxed{?}$

(C) Write the inequality that represents Nora's budget goal.

$$8c + 10 \leq \boxed{?}$$

(D) Suppose Nora finds party favors that cost $4 each. Use a value of 4 for c and check to see if this inequality is true.

$$8 \cdot 4 + 10 \overset{?}{\leq} 50$$

$$\boxed{?} \overset{?}{\leq} 50$$

Is the inequality true?

 Could Nora buy $6 party favors for all of her guests without going over budget? [?]

Reflect

1. Why does an inequality represent Nora's budget calculation better than an equation?

2. The solution set of an inequality consists of all values that make the statement true. Describe the whole dollar amounts that are in the solution set for this situation.

✏️ Explain 1   Creating and Solving Inequalities Involving the Distributive Property

You may need to use the Distributive Property before you can solve an inequality.

Distributive Property	If a, b, and c are real numbers, then $a(b + c) = ab + ac$.

The inequality sign must be reversed when multiplying or dividing both sides of an inequality by a negative number.

Example 1

(A) Trina is buying 12 shirts for the drama club. She will choose a style for the blank shirts and then pay an additional charge of $2.75 for each shirt to have the club logo. If Trina cannot spend more than $99, how much can she spend on each blank shirt? Write and solve an inequality to find the possible cost of each blank shirt.

Let s represent the cost of each blank shirt.

Write an inequality to represent the situation.	$12(s + 2.75) \le 99$
Use the Distributive Property.	$12s + 33 \le 99$
Subtraction Property of Inequality	$12s + 33 - 33 \le 99 - 33$
Simplify.	$12s \le 66$
Division Property of Inequality	$\frac{12s}{12} \le \frac{66}{12}$
Simplify.	$s \le 5.5$

Check your answer.

Since $s \le 5.5$, check a smaller number. $12(5 + 2.75) \le 99$

Trina can order blank shirts that cost $5.50 or less. $93 \overset{?}{\le} 99$ true

(B) Sergio needs to buy gifts for 8 friends. He wants to give the same gift to all his friends and he plans to have the gifts wrapped for an additional charge of $1.50 each. If Sergio spends at least $70, he will receive free shipping on his order. Write and solve an inequality to determine how much Sergio needs to spend on each gift in order to receive free shipping.

Let g be the cost of one gift.

Write an inequality to represent the situation.

$$8\left(g + \boxed{1.50}\right) \geq 70$$

Use the Distributive Property.

$$\boxed{8}\,g + \boxed{12} \geq 70$$

Subtraction Property of Inequality

$$\boxed{8}\,g + 12 - \boxed{12} \geq 70 - \boxed{12}$$

Simplify.

$$8g \geq \boxed{58}$$

Division Property of Inequality

$$\frac{8g}{\boxed{8}} \geq \frac{58}{\boxed{8}}$$

Simplify.

$$g \geq \boxed{7.25}$$

Check your answer.

Since $g \geq 7.25$, check a larger number.

$$8(8 + 1.50) \overset{?}{\geq} 70$$

Sergio must spend at least $\boxed{\$7.25}$ on each gift.

$$\boxed{76} \overset{?}{\geq} 70 \text{ true}$$

Reflect

3. Discussion Why is the first step in solving the inequality to use the Distributive Property instead of working inside the parentheses?

Your Turn

4. Zachary is planning to send a video game to each of his two brothers. If he buys the same game for both brothers and pays $4.75 to ship each game, how much can he spend on each game without spending more than $100? Write and solve an inequality for this situation.

Solve each inequality.

5. $\frac{4}{3}(6x + 9) < 4$

6. $-2\left(\frac{1}{4}x + 2\right) \geq 5$

⚙ Explain 2 **Creating and Solving Inequalities with Variables on Both Sides**

Some inequalities have variable terms on both sides of the inequality symbol. You can solve these inequalities the same way you solved equations with variables on both sides. Use the properties of inequality to collect all the variable terms on one side and all the constant terms on the other side.

Example 2

Ⓐ The *Daily Info* charges a fee of $650 plus $80 per week to run an ad. The *People's Paper* charges $145 per week. For how many weeks must an ad run for the total cost at the *Daily Info* to be less expensive than the cost at the *People's Paper*? Let w be the number of weeks the ad runs in the paper.

Write an inequality to represent the situation.

$$650 + 80w < 145w$$

Subtraction Property of Inequality

$$650 + 80w - 80w < 145w - 80w$$

Simplify.

$$650 < 65w$$

© Houghton Mifflin Harcourt Publishing Company

Division Property of Inequality

$$\frac{650}{65} < \frac{65w}{65}$$

Simplify.

$$10 < w$$

The total cost at the *Daily Info* is less than the cost at the *People's Paper* if the ad runs for more than 10 weeks.

B The Home Cleaning Company charges $312 to power-wash the siding of a house plus $12 for each window. Power Clean charges $36 per window, and the price includes power-washing the siding. How many windows must a house have to make the total cost from The Home Cleaning Company less expensive than Power Clean? Let w be the number of windows.

Write an inequality to represent the situation.

$$\boxed{312} + 12w < 36w$$

Subtraction Property of Inequality

$$312 + 12w - \boxed{12w} < 36w - \boxed{12w}$$

Simplify.

$$312 < \boxed{24w}$$

Division Property of Inequality

$$\frac{312}{\boxed{24}} < \frac{24w}{\boxed{24}}$$

Simplify.

$$\boxed{13} < w$$

A house must have more than 13 windows for The Home Cleaning Company to be less expensive than Power Clean.

Reflect

7. How would the final inequality change if you divided by -24 in the next to last step?

Your Turn

8. The school band will sell pizzas to raise money for new uniforms. The supplier charges $100 plus $4 per pizza. The band members sell the pizzas for $7 each. Write and solve an inequality to find how many pizzas the band members will have to sell to make a profit.

💬 Elaborate

9. Which inequality symbol would you use to represent the following words or phrases? Can you come up with more examples?

   a. at most   **b.** farther than   **c.** younger than   **d.** up to

10. Discussion How are the steps to solving an inequality similar to those for solving an equation? How are they different?

11. Essential Question Check-In How can you write an inequality that represents a real-world situation?

Write an inequality that represents the description, and then solve.

1. Max has more than 5 carrots (number of carrots Max has = c).

2. Brigitte is shorter than 5 feet (Brigitte's height = h).

3. Twice a number (x) is less than 10.

4. Six more than five times a number (x) is at least twenty-one.

5. Dave has \$15 to spend on an \$8 book and two birthday cards (c) for his friends. How much can he spend on each card if he buys the same card for each friend?

6. Toni can carry up to 18 lb in her backpack. Her lunch weighs 1 lb, her gym clothes weigh 2 lb, and her books (b) weigh 3 lb each. How many books can she carry in her backpack?

Solve each inequality.

7. $3(x - 2) > -3$

8. $5 + 5(x + 4) \leq 20$

9. $3 + \frac{1}{2}(3 - x) < -7$

10. $3(x + 6) - 2(x + 2) \geq 10$

11. $5(3 - x) - 4(2 - 3x) > 2$

12. $\frac{1}{2}(4x - 2) - \frac{2}{3}(6x + 9) \leq 4$

13. $x + 1 > -5(7 - 2x)$

14. $\frac{5}{3}(6x + 3) \leq 2x - 7$

15. $2x \leq -\frac{2}{3}(4x + 4)$

16. $\frac{1}{2}(-2x - 10) > 3(4 - 6x)$

17. $-5 - 3x \geq 2(10 + 2x) + 3$

18. $-3(9x + 20) \geq 15x - 20$

19. $8\left(\frac{1}{4}x - 3\right) + 24 < 4(x + 5)$

20. $6x - 2(x + 2) > 2 - 3(x + 3)$

21. **Physics** A crane cable can support a maximum load of 15,000 kg. If a bucket has a mass of 2,000 kg and gravel has a mass of 1,500 kg for every cubic meter, how many cubic meters of gravel (g) can be safely lifted by the crane?

22. Find the solution set of each inequality below, and then determine which inequalities have the same solution set as $\frac{1}{3}(-5x - 3) < 14$.

a. $\frac{1}{3}(5x + 3) > -14$

b. $\frac{2}{5}(10x + 20) > 44$

c. $-\frac{2}{5}(10x + 20) < -44$

d. $-\frac{1}{3}(5x + 3) < 14$

e. $\frac{2}{5}(10x - 20) > -44$

f. $\frac{1}{3}(5x + 3) < -14$

H.O.T. Focus on Higher Order Thinking

23. **Explain the Error** Sven is trying to find the maximum amount of time he can spend practicing the five scales of piano music he is supposed to be working on. He has 60 minutes to practice piano and would like to spend at least 35 minutes playing songs instead of practicing scales. So, Sven sets up the following inequality, where t is the number of minutes he spends on each scale, and solves it.

$$60 - 5t \leq 35$$
$$-5t \leq -25$$
$$t \geq 5$$

Sven has concluded that he should spend 5 minutes or more on each scale. Is this correct? If not, what mistake did he make? Find the correct answer.

24. Critical Thinking Anika wants to determine the maximum number of tulip bulbs (*t*) she can purchase if each bulb costs $1.50. She will also need to purchase separate pots for each bulb at $1.25 each and a bag of potting soil for $10.00. Set up an inequality to determine how many tulip bulbs Anika can purchase without spending more than $20.00, and solve it. Can Anika buy exactly enough bulbs and pots to spend the full $20.00? Explain. Can you think of a better inequality to describe the answer?

25. Geometry The area of the triangle shown is no more than 10 square inches.

   a. Write an inequality that can be used to find *x*.

   b. Solve the inequality from part **a**.

   c. What is the maximum height of the triangle?

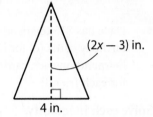

$(2x - 3)$ in.

4 in.

Lesson Performance Task

When planning an airplane route, the trip planner must be careful to consider the range the aircraft can travel and the availability of airports to stop and refuel.

A large commercial jet airplane burns approximately 5 gallons of fuel per mile flown, plus about 8500 gallons of fuel per trip to reach cruising altitude. With a useable fuel capacity of 50,000 gallons (there is additional fuel reserved for emergencies), describe the acceptable distance for which an airline could establish a non-stop flight.

For flights originating from Chicago, determine which cities in the table could be safely reached by a non-stop flight.

City	Distance from Chicago (miles)
Bangalore, India	8530
Jakarta, Indonesia	9810
Johannesburg, South Africa	8680
Moscow, Russia	4970
Paris, France	4130
Perth, Australia	10,970
Tokyo, Japan	6300

2.5 Creating and Solving Compound Inequalities

Essential Question: How can you solve a compound inequality and graph the solution set?

⊘ Explore Truth Tables and Compound Statements

A **compound statement** is formed by combining two or more simple statements. A compound statement can be true or false. A compound statement involving **AND** is true when *both* simple statements are true. A compound statement involving **OR** is true when *either* one simple statement *or both* are true.

Ⓐ Copy and complete the truth table.

P	Q	P True or False?	Q True or False?	P AND Q True or False?
A dog is a mammal.	Red is a color.	?	?	?
A dog is a mammal.	Red is not a color.	?	?	?
A dog is a fish.	Red is a color.	?	?	?
A dog is a fish.	Red is not a color.	?	?	?

Ⓑ *P* **AND** *Q* is true when [?] .

Ⓒ Copy and complete the truth table.

P	Q	P True or False?	Q True or False?	P OR Q True or False?
1 is an odd number.	2 is an even number.	?	?	?
1 is an odd number.	2 is an odd number.	?	?	?
1 is an even number.	2 is an even number	?	?	?
1 is an even number.	2 is an odd number.	?	?	?

Ⓓ *P* **OR** *Q* is true when [?] .

Reflect

1. Give two simple statements *P* and *Q* for which *P* **AND** *Q* is false and *P* **OR** *Q* is true.

 **Explain 1** **Solving Compound Inequalities Involving AND**

Combining two or more simple inequalities forms a **compound inequality**. The graph of a compound inequality involving **AND** is the **intersection**, or the overlapping region, of the simple inequality graphs.

Compound Inequalities: AND		
Words	**Algebra**	**Graph**
All real numbers greater than 2 **AND** less than 6	$x > 2$ **AND** $x < 6$ $2 < x < 6$	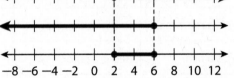
All real numbers greater than or equal to 2 **AND** less than or equal to 6	$x \geq 2$ **AND** $x \leq 6$ $2 \leq x \leq 6$	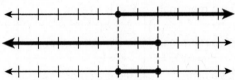

Example 1 Solve each compound inequality and graph the solutions.

Ⓐ $4 \leq x + 2 \leq 8$

$4 \leq x + 2$	**AND**	$x + 2 \leq 8$	Write the compound inequality using AND.
$4 - 2 \leq x + 2 - 2$		$x + 2 - 2 \leq 8 - 2$	Subtract 2 from both sides of each simple inequality.
$2 \leq x$		$x \leq 6$	Simplify.

Graph $2 \leq x$.

Graph $x \leq 6$.

Graph the intersection by finding where the two graphs overlap.

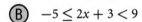

Ⓑ $-5 \leq 2x + 3 < 9$

$-5 - \boxed{3} \leq 2x + 3 - \boxed{3} < 9 - \boxed{3}$ Subtract $\boxed{3}$ from each part of the inequality.

$\boxed{-8} \leq 2x < \boxed{6}$ Simplify.

$\dfrac{-8}{\boxed{2}} \leq \dfrac{2x}{\boxed{2}} < \dfrac{6}{\boxed{2}}$ Divide each part of the inequality by $\boxed{2}$.

$\boxed{-4} \leq x < \boxed{3}$ Simplify.

Graph $-4 \leq x$.

Graph $x < 3$.

Graph the intersection by finding where the two graphs overlap.

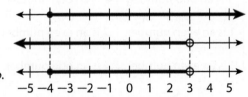

Reflect

2. **Discussion** Explain why $2 \leq x \leq 6$ can be considered the *short method* for writing the **AND** compound inequality $x \geq 2$ **AND** $x \leq 6$.

© Houghton Mifflin Harcourt Publishing Company

Solve each compound inequality and graph the solutions.

3. $-2 < x - 3 < 5$

4. $-10 < 3x + 2 \leq 8$

🎸 Explain 2   Solving Compound Inequalities Involving OR

The graph of a compound inequality involving **OR** is the **union**, or the combined region, of the simple inequality graphs.

Compound Inequalities: OR		
Words	**Algebra**	**Graph**
All real numbers less than 2 **OR** greater than 6	$x < 2$ **OR** $x > 6$	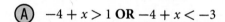
All real numbers less than or equal to 2 **OR** greater than or equal to 6	$x \leq 2$ **OR** $x \geq 6$	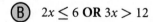

Example 2   Solve each compound inequality and graph the solutions.

(A) $-4 + x > 1$ **OR** $-4 + x < -3$

$-4 + x > 1$ **OR** $-4 + x < -3$	Write the compound inequality using OR.
$-4 + 4 + x > 1 + 4$ $-4 + 4 + x < -3 + 4$	Add 4 to both sides of each simple inequality.
$x > 5$ $x < 1$	Simplify.

Graph $x > 5$.

Graph $x < 1$.

Graph the union by combining the graphs.

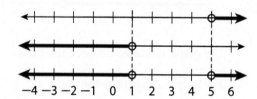

(B) $2x \leq 6$ **OR** $3x > 12$

$2x \leq 6$ **OR** $3x > 12$	Write the compound inequality using OR.
$\dfrac{2x}{\boxed{2}} \leq \dfrac{6}{\boxed{2}}$ **OR** $\dfrac{3x}{\boxed{3}} > \dfrac{12}{\boxed{3}}$	Divide the first simple inequality by $\boxed{2}$.
	Divide the second simple inequality by $\boxed{3}$.
$x \leq \boxed{3}$ **OR** $x > \boxed{4}$.	Simplify.

Graph $x \leq 3$.

Graph $x > 4$.

Graph the union by combining the graphs.

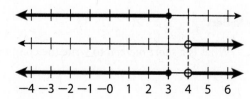

Reflect

5. Critical Thinking What kind of compound inequality has no solution?

Your Turn

Solve each compound inequality and graph the solutions.

6. $x - 5 \geq -2$ **OR** $x - 5 \leq -6$

7. $4x - 1 < 15$ **OR** $8x \geq 48$

🧭 Explain 3 Creating Compound Inequalities From Graphs

Given a number line graph with a solution set graphed, you can create a compound inequality to fit the graph.

Example 3 Write the compound inequality shown by each graph.

(A)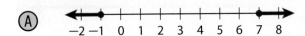

The shaded portion of the graph is not between two values, so the compound inequality involves OR.

On the left, the graph shows an arrow pointing left from -1 and a solid circle, so use $\leq$.

The inequality is $x \leq -1$.

On the right, the graph shows an arrow pointing right from 7 and a solid circle, so use $\geq$.

The inequality is $x \geq 7$.

The compound inequality is $x \leq -1$ **OR** $x \geq 7$.

(B)

The graph is shaded between the values 0 and 6 , so the compound inequality involves **AND**.

The graph is shaded to the right of 0 and the circle is solid, so use the inequality symbol $\geq$.

The inequality is $x \geq 0$.

The graph is shaded to the left of 6 and the circle is open, so use the inequality symbol $<$.

The inequality is $x < 6$.

The compound inequality is $x \geq 0$ AND $x < 6$.

Reflect

8. What is a *short method* to write the compound inequality $x \geq 0$ AND $x < 6$?

Write the compound inequality shown by each graph.

9.

$$\xleftarrow{\quad}\underset{-10\,-9\,-8\,-7\,-6\,-5\,-4\,-3\,-2\,-1\quad 0}{\overset{\circ\!\!\rule[0.5ex]{4em}{0.4pt}\!\!\circ}{\,}}\xrightarrow{\quad}$$

10.

$$\xleftarrow{\quad}\underset{-5\,-4\,-3\,-2\,-1\ \ 0\ \ 1\ \ 2\ \ 3\ \ 4\ \ 5}{\overset{\circ\!\!\rule[0.5ex]{4em}{0.4pt}\!\!\bullet}{\,}}\xrightarrow{\quad}$$

⚙ Explain 4 Expressing Acceptable Levels with Compound Inequalities

You can express quality-controls levels in real-world problems using compound inequalities.

Example 4 Write a compound inequality to represent the indicated quality-control level, and graph the solutions.

Ⓐ The recommended pH level for swimming pool water is between 7.2 and 7.6, inclusive.

Let p be the pH level of swimming pool water.

7.2	is less than or equal to	pH level	is less than or equal to	7.6
7.2	$\leq$	p	$\leq$	7.6

The compound inequality is $7.2 \leq p \leq 7.6$.

Graph the solutions.

$$\xleftarrow{\quad}\underset{7.0\ 7.1\ 7.2\ 7.3\ 7.4\ 7.5\ 7.6\ 7.7\ 7.8\ 7.9\ 8.0}{\overset{\bullet\!\!\rule[0.5ex]{4em}{0.4pt}\!\!\bullet}{\,}}\xrightarrow{\quad}$$

Ⓑ The recommended free chlorine level for swimming pool water is between 1.0 and 3.0 parts per million, inclusive.

Let c be the free chlorine level in the pool.

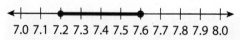

1.0	is less than or equal to	free chlorine level	is less than or equal to	3.0
1.0	$\leq$	c	$\leq$	3.0

The compound inequality is $1.0 \leq c \leq 3.0$.

Graph the solutions.

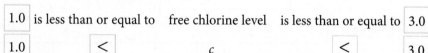

Reflect

11. Discussion What does the phrase "between 7.2 and 7.6, inclusive" mean?

Your Turn

Write a compound inequality to represent the indicated quality-control level, and graph the solutions.

12. The recommended alkalinity level for swimming pool water is between 80 and 120 parts per million, inclusive.

13. Explain the difference between graphing a compound inequality involving **AND** and graphing a compound inequality involving **OR**.

14. How can you tell whether a compound inequality involves **AND** or **OR** from looking at its graph?

15. **Essential Question Check-In** Explain how to find the solutions of a compound inequality.

☆ Evaluate: Homework and Practice

- Online Homework
- Hints and Help
- Extra Practice

Copy and complete the truth tables.

1.

P	Q	P True or False?	Q True or False?	P AND Q True or False?
An apple is a fruit.	A carrot is a vegetable.	?	?	?
An apple is a fruit.	A carrot is a fruit.	?	?	?
An apple is a vegetable.	A carrot is a vegetable.	?	?	?
An apple is a vegetable.	A carrot is a fruit.	?	?	?

2.

P	Q	P True or False?	Q True or False?	P OR Q True or False?
Blue is a color.	Five is a number.	?	?	?
Blue is a color.	Five is a color.	?	?	?
Blue is a number.	Five is a number.	?	?	?
Blue is a number.	Five is a color.	?	?	?

Solve each compound inequality and graph the solutions.

3. $-3 < 3x \le 9$

4. $0 \le 2x - 10 \le 20$

5. $x - 5 < 3$ **OR** $x - 5 \ge 8$

6. $1 \le x + 7 < 7$

7. $4x + 3 < -5$ **OR** $4x + 3 > 23$

8. $\frac{x}{5} - 2 \le -6$ **OR** $8x + 1 \ge 41$

9. $-6 < \frac{x - 12}{4} < -2$

10. $x + 7 \le 7$ **OR** $5 + 2x > 7$

Write the compound inequality shown by each graph.

11.
$$\xleftarrow{\hspace{1cm}} \begin{array}{ccccccccccc} -2 & -1 & 0 & 1 & 2 & 3 & 4 & 5 & 6 & 7 & 8 \end{array} \xrightarrow{\hspace{1cm}}$$

12.
$$\begin{array}{ccccccccccc} -10 & -9 & -8 & -7 & -6 & -5 & -4 & -3 & -2 & -1 & 0 \end{array}$$

13.
$$\begin{array}{ccccccccccc} 5 & 6 & 7 & 8 & 9 & 10 & 11 & 12 & 13 & 14 & 15 \end{array}$$

14.
$$\begin{array}{ccccccccccc} -4 & -3 & -2 & -1 & 0 & 1 & 2 & 3 & 4 & 5 & 6 \end{array}$$

15.
$$\begin{array}{ccccccccccc} 0 & 1 & 2 & 3 & 4 & 5 & 6 & 7 & 8 & 9 & 10 \end{array}$$

16.
$$\begin{array}{ccccccccccc} -5 & -4 & -3 & -2 & -1 & 0 & 1 & 2 & 3 & 4 & 5 \end{array}$$

Write a compound inequality to show the levels that are within each range. Then graph the solutions.

17. Biology An iguana needs to live in a warm environment. The temperature in a pet iguana's cage should be between 70 °F and 95 °F, inclusive.

18. Meteorology One layer of Earth's atmosphere is called the stratosphere. At one point above Earth's surface, the stratosphere extends from an altitude of 16 kilometers to an altitude of 50 kilometers.

19. Music A typical acoustic guitar has a range of three octaves. When the guitar is tuned to "concert pitch," the range of frequencies for those three octaves is between 82.4 Hertz and 659.2 Hertz, inclusive.

20. Transportation The cruise-control function on Georgina's car should keep the speed of the car within 3 miles per hour of the set speed. The set speed is 55 miles per hour.

21. Chemistry Water is not a liquid if its temperature is above 100 °C or below 0 °C.

22. Sports The ball used in a soccer game may not weigh more than 16 ounces or less than 14 ounces at the start of the match. After 1.5 ounces of air were added to a ball, the ball was approved for use in a game.

23. Match the compound inequalities with the graphs of their solutions.

A. $-26 < 6x - 8 < 16$

a. _____?_____
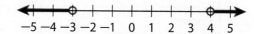
$$\begin{array}{ccccccccccc} -5 & -4 & -3 & -2 & -1 & 0 & 1 & 2 & 3 & 4 & 5 \end{array}$$

B. $-\dfrac{1}{3} \le \dfrac{x+2}{3} \le 2$

b. _____?_____
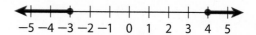
$$\begin{array}{ccccccccccc} -5 & -4 & -3 & -2 & -1 & 0 & 1 & 2 & 3 & 4 & 5 \end{array}$$

C. $4x + 1 < -11$ **OR** $\dfrac{x}{2} - 5 > -3$

c. _____?_____
$$\begin{array}{ccccccccccc} -5 & -4 & -3 & -2 & -1 & 0 & 1 & 2 & 3 & 4 & 5 \end{array}$$

D. $\dfrac{x-6}{3} \le -3$ **OR** $2x + 8 \ge 16$

d. _____?_____
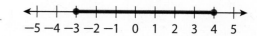
$$\begin{array}{ccccccccccc} -5 & -4 & -3 & -2 & -1 & 0 & 1 & 2 & 3 & 4 & 5 \end{array}$$

24. **Multi-Step** Jenna's band is going to record a CD at a recording studio. They will pay $225 to use the studio for one day and $80 per hour for sound technicians. Jenna has $200 and can reasonably expect to raise up to an additional $350 by taking pre-orders for the CDs.

    a. Explain how the inequality $200 \leq 225 + 80n \leq 550$ can be used to find the number of hours Jenna and her band can afford to use the studio and sound technicians.

    b. Solve the inequality. Are there any numbers in the solution set that are not reasonable in this situation?

    c. Suppose Jenna raises $350 in pre-orders. How much more money would she need to raise if she wanted to use the studio and sound technicians for 6 hours?

25. **Explain the Error** A student solves the compound inequality $15 \leq 2x + 5 \leq 17$ and finds the solutions of the compound inequality to be all real numbers. Explain and correct the student's mistake. Graph the actual solutions to back up your answer.

26. **Communicate Mathematical Thinking** Describe the solutions of the compound inequalities.

    $x > 9 \text{ AND } x < 9$

    $x < 9 \text{ OR } x > 9$

    $x \geq 9 \text{ AND } x \leq 9$

    $x \leq 9 \text{ OR } x \geq 9$

Lesson Performance Task

The table gives the melting point and boiling point of various elements. Write a compound inequality for each element to show the temperature range of the element in its liquid state. Graph the solutions of each.

Suppose you were to set the temperature of each element to its melting point and increase the temperature of each element at the same rate. Which element will remain liquid for the longest amount of time? Which element will reach its boiling point first? Explain.

Element	Melting Point (°C)	Boiling Point (°C)
Gold	1064	2856
Copper	1085	2562
Iron	1538	2861
Lead	327	1749
Aluminum	660	2519

Algebraic Models

Essential Question: How can you use algebraic models to solve real-world problems?

KEY EXAMPLE   (Lesson 2.1)

Write an expression for each situation.

The total cost of two notebooks that cost x dollars each and a pen that costs $3.50

$2x + 3.5$

The price of three identical items that are each 25% off

$3(p - 0.25p) = 2.25p$

KEY EXAMPLE   (Lesson 2.2)

Solve the equation $3(2y - 5) = 9$ for y.

$3(2y - 5) = 9$

$6y - 15 = 9$ *Distributive Property*

$6y = 24$ *Addition Property of Equality*

$y = 4$ *Division Property of Equality*

KEY EXAMPLE   (Lesson 2.3)

The formula for the area of a triangle is $A = \frac{1}{2}bh$. The base b of a triangle is 8 cm, and the area A is 40. Solve the formula for h, and then find the height of the triangle.

$A = \frac{1}{2}bh$

$\dfrac{2A}{b} = h$ *Solve for h.*

$\dfrac{2(40)}{8} = h$ *Substitute 40 for A and 8 for b.*

$10 = h$ *Simplify.*

KEY EXAMPLE   (Lesson 2.4)

Solve the inequality for a.

$-2a - 13 \leq 9a + 20$

$-11a - 13 \leq 20$ *Subtract 9a from both sides.*

$-11a \leq 33$ *Add 13 to both sides.*

$a \geq -3$ *Divide by −11. Reverse the inequality sign.*

Key Vocabulary

algebraic expression
(expresión algebraica)

coefficient *(coeficiente)*

expression *(expresión)*

inequality *(desigualdad)*

literal equation
(ecuación literal)

numerical expression
(expresión numérica)

term *(término)*

EXERCISES

Write an expression for each situation. *(Lesson 2.1)*

1. The original price of an item plus a sales tax of 8.5%

2. The total cost of 6 pens and 3 folders. A folder costs $1.15 more than a pen.

3. The sum of Andre and Brandon's scores on a math quiz is 180. Andre's score is 2 times as much as 30 less than Brandon's score. Find each student's quiz score. *(Lesson 2.2)*

4. The formula for finding the area of a trapezoid is $A = \frac{1}{2}(b_1 + b_2)h$ where A represents the area of the trapezoid, b_1 and b_2 are bases, and h represents the height. Solve the formula for h. *(Lesson 2.3)*

5. Solve $7(3 - x) \leq 5x - 15$ for x. *(Lesson 2.4)*

MODULE PERFORMANCE TASK

Menu Math

You and some friends have ordered from this restaurant menu. When the checks come, you find that your server has written all the orders as equations such as "$c + f + 2s = 6.70$," using the first letter of each menu item as the variable. Use the menu to write an equation to challenge a classmate, letting x represent the price of an unknown item. ($x + t = 3.45$. What's x?) You can use coefficients, fractions, decimals, percents, the distributive property, verbal descriptions, and all of the elements of writing and solving equations that you've learned.

Start by listing some of your ideas. Then complete the task.

Menu	
Hamburger	$1.95
Cheeseburger	$2.45
Veggie burger	$2.15
Fries	$1.25
Green salad	$1.65
Tomato soup	$1.80
Juice	
Small	$1.50
Large	$2.25

(Ready) to Go On?

2.1–2.5 Algebraic Models

Personal Math Trainer

• Online Homework
• Hints and Help
• Extra Practice

Write an expression in simplest form for each verbal description. *(Lesson 2.1)*

1. The sum of the cost of dinner d and a $12 tip divided equally between 3 people

2. The total pay for 12 hours of work at a base rate of p per hour plus a temporary raise of $2.50 per hour

3. Given $x < y$, compare the following expressions and determine which is greater: $2x - y$; $2y - x$. Explain your answer. *(Lesson 2.1)*

4. The formula $y - y_1 = m(x - x_1)$ is the point-slope form of the equation of a line where m is the slope of the line and (x, y) and (x_1, y_1) are points of the line. Solve the equation for m, and find the slope of a line that includes the points $(4, -2)$ and $(5, 0)$. *(Lesson 2.3)*

Solve. *(Lessons 2.2, 2.4, 2.5)*

5. $-17 - 5(x + 3) = 3x$

6. $100x - 200 > 50x - 75$

7. $12 < 2x + 2 \leq 22$

8. $-13 < -x + 5 < 8$

ESSENTIAL QUESTION

9. What is the general process for solving an equation with one variable?

Assessment Readiness

1. Consider the new expression that is obtained by simplifying $8(x - 1) + 15$. Determine if each statement is True or False.

   A. The new expression has 3 terms.

   B. The coefficient of x in the new expression is 8.

   C. The constant in the new expression is 14.

2. Look at each equation and possible solution. Tell whether each solution is correct.

   A. $3 - m = -2(m + 6); m = -15$

   B. $5(p + 3) = -35; p = -4$

   C. $8q = 3(10 + q); q = 6$

3. The formula for finding the volume of a triangular prism $V = \frac{1}{2}(bh)\ell$ where b represents the base length, h represents the base height, and ℓ represents the length of the prism. Determine if each statement is True or False.

   A. The formula solved for h is $h = \dfrac{2V\ell}{b}$.

   B. The formula solved for ℓ is $\ell = \dfrac{2V}{bh}$.

   C. The formula solved for b is $b = \dfrac{2V}{bh}$.

4. Sherman hopes to get at least a 90 average on his science tests. He has one more test before the end of the school year. His past test scores are 79, 94, 91, and 92. Write and solve an inequality that represents this situation. What is the lowest score Sherman can get on his final test and reach his goal? Show your work.

• Online Homework
• Hints and Help
• Extra Practice

1. Consider each equation and solution. Tell whether each solution is correct.

    A. $6 = -\dfrac{r}{3}; r = -2$

    B. $1 - 2s = 3; s = 5$

    C. $4 + 6t = -20; t = -4$

2. The distance from Town A to Town B on a map is 6 inches. The actual distance from Town B to Town C is 12 miles. The scale on the map is 1 in: 4 mi. Determine if each statement is True or False.

    A. The actual distance from A to B is 24 mi.

    B. The distance from B to C on the map is 36 in.

    C. The actual distance from A to C is 4.5 mi.

3. The dimensions of a storage container in the shape of a rectangular prism are 54 in. × 32.25 in. × 24.5 in. Determine if each statement is True or False.

    A. The most precise dimension has 4 significant digits.

    B. Written using the correct number of significant digits, the volume of the container has 3 significant digits.

    C. Written using the correct number of significant digits, the surface area of the container is rounded to the ones place.

4. Hank bought 3 more boxes of cereal than gallons of milk. He bought x boxes of cereal at $2.79 each. Each gallon of milk costs $4.49. Consider the expression $2.79x + 4.49(x - 3)$. Determine if each statement is True or False.

    A. The term $x - 3$ represents the number of gallons of milk.

    B. The coefficient 2.79 represents the cost of one box of cereal.

    C. The expression represents the total number of boxes of cereal and gallons of milk.

5. The formula $y = mx + b$ is the slope-intercept form of the equation of a line where m is the slope of the line, b is the y-intercept, and (x, y) is a solution of the equation. Determine whether each statement is True or False.

   A. The equation solved for b is $b = y - mx$.

   B. The equation solved for x is $x = \dfrac{y - b}{m}$.

   C. The equation solved for m is $m = x(y - b)$.

6. Carla and Ross competed in the long-jump at a track meet. Carla jumped 3.5 meters. Ross jumped 99 inches. Who jumped farther and by approximately how many feet? Use 1 m $\approx$ 3.27 ft. Explain how you solved this problem.

7. Solve the following equation for x: $\dfrac{1}{2}(5x + 12) = 2x - 3$. Show your work.

8. A factory produces 5-packs of pencils. To be within the weight specifications, a pack of 5 pencils should weigh between 60 grams and 95 grams. The cardboard for each package has a mass of 15 grams. Write a compound inequality to represent the mass of a single pencil in a pack. Can each pencil have a mass of 10.5 grams? Explain.

Performance Tasks

★ 9. Fernando is starting a new sales job and needs to decide which of two salary plans to choose from. For plan A, he will earn $100/week plus 15% commission on all sales. For plan B, he will earn $150/week plus 10% commission on all sales.

   A. Write an expression for each salary plan if Fernando's total weekly sales are s.

   B. For what amount of weekly sales is plan B better than plan A?

★★**10.** An electronics company has developed a new hand-held device. The company predicts that the start-up cost to manufacture the new product will be $125,000, and the cost to make one device will be $6.50.

   A. If the company plans on selling the device at a wholesale price of $9, write and solve an inequality to determine how many must be sold for the company to make a profit. Show your work.

   B. The cost of making one device is 10% more than the company predicted. What is the new cost of making one device? How many devices must it now sell at the same wholesale price to make a profit?

   C. Suppose the company wants to start making a profit after selling the same number of devices you found in part **A**. What should the new wholesale price be? Explain how you found this price.

★★★**11.** A company that sells computers and other electronic equipment wants to hire some new sales staff. The company offers salary packages that combine a base salary and commissions from sales. It is willing to pay a base salary of between $20,000 and $30,000 per year and a commission rate between 2.5% and 6.5% of total sales per year. The company has a rule that if someone makes the maximum base salary, he or she cannot earn the highest commission rate, and vice versa.

   A. Javier is very confident in his ability to generate large sales. What salary package would appeal to him? Explain your reasoning, and write an algebraic expression for Javier's salary package.

   B. Catherine prefers to have a more stable income that is less affected by sales. What salary package would appeal to her? Explain your reasoning, and write an algebraic expression for her salary package.

   C. For what amounts of sales will Catherine make more than Javier? Use your expressions from parts **A** and **B** to write and solve an inequality to find the answer.

Personal Trainer Kayla is a personal trainer and is working with Jed to devise a plan to help him lose weight. Kayla explained to Jed that each pound of body fat is equal to 3500 Calories. So, if Jed eliminates 500 Calories per day through diet and exercise, he will lose one pound per week. The table shows how many Calories are burned per hour of exercise for people of different weights who are walking or running at various speeds.

Calories Burned per Hour of Exercise by Body Weight				
	Body Weight			
Exercise (1 Hour)	**130 lb**	**155 lb**	**180 lb**	**205 lb**
Walking 2.0 mph	148	176	204	233
Walking 3.0 mph	195	232	270	307
Walking 4.0 mph	295	352	409	465
Running 5.0 mph	472	563	654	745
Running 6.0 mph	590	704	817	931
Running 7.0 mph	649	774	899	1024

Jed currently weighs 205 pounds. He walks on a treadmill at a speed of 3 miles per hour and runs at a speed of 5 miles per hour, and he exercises for 30 minutes each day.

a. Use the information in the table to find an expression for the number of Calories Jed burns while walking for t minutes.

b. If Jed exercises for 30 minutes, then $30 - t$ is the number of minutes Jed runs at 5.0 miles per hour. Write an expression for the number of Calories Jed burns while running for t minutes.

c. Write an equation relating the total number of Calories Jed burns to the number of minutes he walks each day.

d. What is the domain of the equation you found in part c?

e. Is it possible for Jed to burn 500 Calories per day from exercising for 30 minutes? Explain how you determined your answer.

Understanding Functions

MATH IN CAREERS

Interior Designer Interior designers create and improve interior spaces in homes and buildings, making them safe, functional, and visually pleasing. Interior designers must understand the geometry of spaces and how to interpret measurements on blueprints. They also need to be able to calculate the amount and cost of materials needed for a project.

If you are interested in a career as an interior designer, you should study these mathematical subjects:
- Algebra
- Geometry
- Trigonometry
- Business Math

Research other careers that require determining costs and amounts of materials for a project. Check out the career activity at the end of the unit to find out how **interior designers** use math.

Visualize Vocabulary

Use the ✔ words to identify a–e in the graphic. Select one term for each letter.

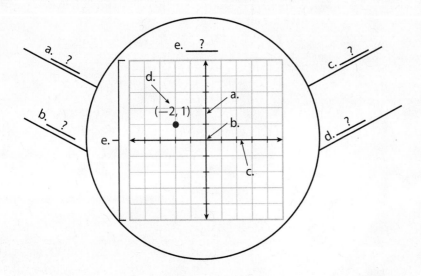

Vocabulary

Review Words
✔ coordinate plane
   (plano cartesiano)
✔ input *(entrada)*
✔ ordered pair
   (par ordenado)
✔ origin *(origen)*
✔ output *(salida)*
✔ *x*-axis *(eje x)*
✔ *y*-axis *(eje y)*

Preview Words
continuous graph
   (gráfica continua)
discrete graph
   (gráfica discreta)
domain *(dominio)*
function *(función)*
function rule *(regla de función)*
range *(rango)*
relation *(relación)*
sequence *(sucesión)*

Understand Vocabulary

Match the term on the left to the correct expression on the right.

1. ___?___ discrete graph   **A.** a graph made up of connected lines or curves

2. ___?___ function rule   **B.** a graph made up of unconnected points

3. ___?___ continuous graph   **C.** a set of ordered pairs

4. ___?___ relation   **D.** an algebraic expression that describes how the output comes from the input

Active Reading

Booklet Before beginning the unit, create a booklet for taking notes as you learn the concepts in this unit. Write the main idea of each module on the appropriate pages to create an outline of the unit. As you study each lesson, write the important details that support the main idea, such as vocabulary and formulas. Refer to your finished booklet as you work on assignments and study for tests.

Functions and Models

Essential Question: How can you use functions to solve real-world problems?

REAL WORLD VIDEO
A function can be thought of as an industrial machine, only accepting certain predefined inputs, performing a series of operations on what it's been fed, and delivering an output dependent on the initial input.

MODULE PERFORMANCE TASK PREVIEW

Season Passes

Decisions, decisions! Wild Planet Theme Park has just opened, and you've decided to buy a season pass but aren't sure which payment option is the least expensive. How can you decide? Looks like the theme of this theme park is mathematics!

Complete these exercises to review skills you will need for this module.

Graphing Linear Relationships

• Online Homework
• Hints and Help
• Extra Practice

Example 1 Tell whether the graph represents a linear nonproportional or proportional relationship.

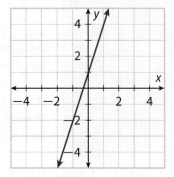

The graph of a linear nonproportional relationship is a straight line that does not pass through the origin.

The graph of a linear proportional relationship is a straight line that passes through the origin.

The graph represents a linear nonproportional relationship because it is a straight line that does not pass through the origin.

Tell whether the graph represents a linear nonproportional or proportional relationship.

1.
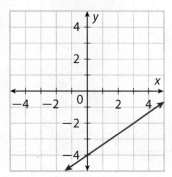

2.
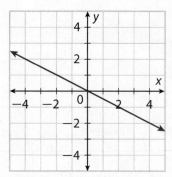

Linear Functions

Example 2 Tell whether $y = x^2 + 5$ represents a linear function.

$y = x^2 + 5$ does not represent a linear function because x has an exponent of 2.

When a linear equation is written in standard form, the following are true.

• x and y both have exponents of 1.

• x and y are not multiplied together.

• x and y do not appear in denominators, exponents, or radicands.

Tell whether the equation represents a linear function.

3. $0.3x + y = 7$

4. $xy - 2 = 9$

5. $y = 2^x + 5$

3.1 Graphing Relationships

Essential Question: How can you describe a relationship given a graph and sketch a graph given a description?

⊘ Explore   Interpreting Graphs

The distance a delivery van is from the warehouse varies throughout the day. The graph shows the distance from the warehouse for a day from 8:00 am to 5:00 pm.

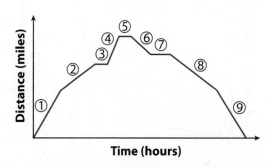

(A) Segment 1 shows that the delivery van moved away from the warehouse. What does segment 2 show?

(B) Based on the time frame, what change in the distance from the warehouse is represented by segment 6?

(C) Which line segments show intervals where the distance did not change?

(D) What is a possible explanation for these segments?

Reflect

1. **Discussion** Explain how the slope of each segment of the graph is related to whether the delivery truck is not moving, is moving away from, or is moving toward the warehouse.

⚙ Explain 1 Relating Graphs to Situations

Graphs can often be drawn to represent real life situations. These graphs are not always easily derived from equations, but rather represent certain situations. For example, these graphs may include the amount of rain over a certain period of time, or the height of a bouncing ball over a certain period of time.

Example 1 Three hoses fill three different water barrels. A green hose fills a water barrel at a constant rate. A black hose is slowly opened when filling the barrel. A blue hose is completely open at the beginning and then slowly closed. The three graphs of the situations are shown.

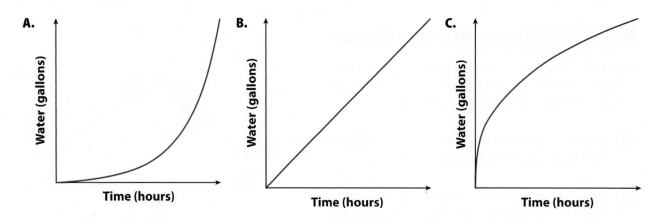

Ⓐ Which graph best represents the amount of water in the barrel filled by the green hose?

Since the flow of the water is constant, the amount of water in the barrel should be a steady increase. Thus, graph B best represents the situation.

Ⓑ Describe the water level represented by each graph. Then determine which graph represents each situation.

The water level for graph A begins slowly and then increases rapidly over time.

The water level for graph C increases rapidly and then slows down over time.

Graph A represents the black hose and graph C represents the blue hose.

Reflect

2. Could a graph of the amount of water in a water barrel slant downward from left to right? Explain.

You and a friend are playing catch. You throw three different balls to your friend. You throw the first ball in an arc and your friend catches it. You throw the second ball in an arc, but this time the ball gets stuck in a tree. You throw the third ball directly at your friend, but it lands in front of your friend, and rolls the rest of the way on the ground. The three graphs of these situations are shown.

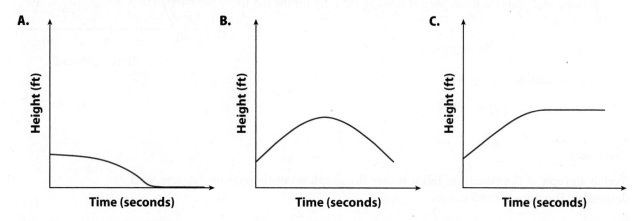

A. Height (ft) / Time (seconds)

B. Height (ft) / Time (seconds)

C. Height (ft) / Time (seconds)

3. Which graph represents the situation where the ball gets stuck in the tree?

4. Describe the height of the ball represented by the other two graphs.

🔑 Explain 2 Sketching Graphs for Situations

Some graphs that represent real-world situations are drawn without any interruptions. In other words, they are *continuous graphs*. A **continuous graph** is a graph that is made up of connected lines or curves. Other types of graphs are not continuous. They are made up of distinct, unconnected points. These graphs are called **discrete graphs**.

Example 2 Sketch a graph of the situation, tell whether the graph is continuous or discrete, and determine the domain and range.

(A) A student is taking a test. There are 10 problems on the test. For each problem the student answers correctly, the student received 10 points.

The graph is made up of multiple unconnected points, so the graph is discrete.

The student can get anywhere from 0 to 10 questions right, so the domain is the whole numbers from 0 to 10.

If the student gets 0 problems correct, the student gets 0 points. If the student gets 10 problems correct, the student gets 100 points. So the range is whole number multiples of 10 from 0 to 100.

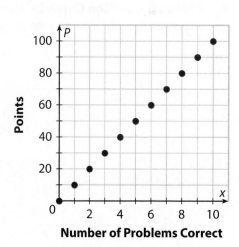

Points / Number of Problems Correct

Ⓑ A bathtub is being filled with water. After 10 minutes, there are 75 quarts of water in the tub. Then someone accidentally pulls the drain plug while the water is still running, and the tub begins to empty. The tub loses 15 quarts in 5 minutes, and then someone plugs the drain and the tub fills for 6 more minutes, gaining another 45 quarts of water. After a 15-minute bath, the person gets out and pulls the drain plug. It takes 11 minutes for the tub to drain.

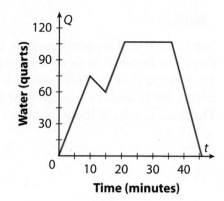

The graph is a continuous graph.

The domain is $0 \leq t \leq 47$.

The range is $0 \leq Q \leq 105$.

Your Turn

Sketch a graph of the situation, tell whether the graph is continuous or discrete, and determine the domain and range.

5. At the start of a snowstorm, it snowed two inches an hour for two hours, then slowed to one inch an hour for an additional hour before stopping. Three hours after the snow stopped, it began to melt at one-half an inch an hour for two hours.

6. A local salesman is going door to door trying to sell vacuums. For every vacuum he sells, he makes $20. He can sell a maximum of 10 vacuums a day.

💬 Elaborate

7. When interpreting graphs of real world situations, what can the slope of each part tell you about the situation?

8. **Discussion** What is the best way to sketch the graph of a situation?

9. **Essential Question Check-In** How can you tell when to use a discrete graph as opposed to using a continuous graph? Give an example of each.

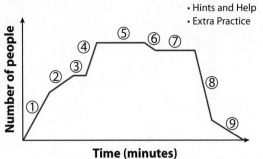
The graph shows the attendance at a hockey game, and the rate at which the fans enter and exit the arena.

1. Compare segments 1 and 2. What do they represent?

2. What does segment 8 represent in terms of the game?

3. What is the significance of segments 5 and 7?

4. What does segment 6 mean?

Use Graphs A–D for Exercises 5–8. Janelle alternates between running and walking. She begins by walking for a short period, and then runs for the same amount of time. She takes a break before beginning to walk again. Consider the graphs shown.

A.

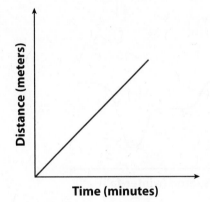

B.

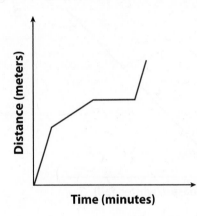

C.

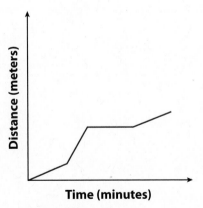

D.

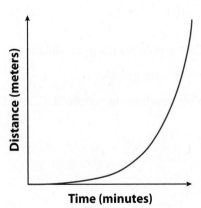

5. Which graph best represents the given situation?

6. Describe the other three graphs.

7. What if Janelle began by running, then slowed to a walk, stopped, and then began running again. Which graph would represent this situation?

8. What are possible situations for graphs A and D?

Use Graphs A–D for Exercises 9–11. During the winter, the amount of water that flows down a river remains at a low constant. In the spring, when the snow melts, the flow of water increases drastically, until it decreases to a steady rate in the summer. The flow then slowly decreases through the fall into the winter. Consider the graphs shown.

A.

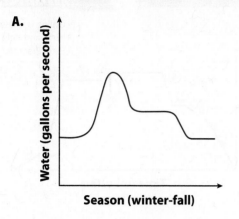

B.

C.

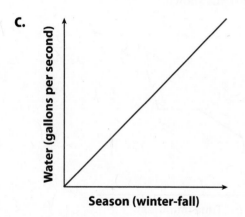

D.

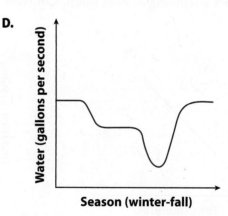

9. Which graph best represents the given situation?

10. Describe the other three graphs.

11. What are possible situations for graphs B, C, and D?

Two children are selling lemonade. They are charging \$1 for a cup. They only sell 10 cups. Consider the graphs shown.

A.

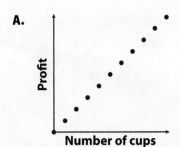

B.

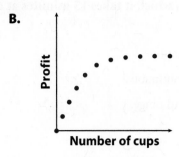

C.

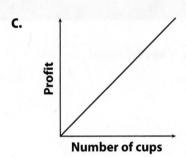

D.

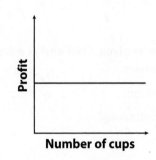

12. Which graph best represents the given situation?

13. What situations could the other graphs represent?

14. Is the graph that represents the given situation discrete or continuous?

A plane takes off and climbs steadily for 15 minutes until it reaches 30,000 feet. It travels at that altitude for 2 hours until it begins to descend to land, which it takes 15 minutes at a constant rate.

15. Sketch a graph of the situation.

16. Is the graph discrete or continuous?

17. Determine the domain and range.

A contestant on a game show is given $100 and is asked five questions. The contestant loses $20 for every wrong answer.

18. Sketch a graph of the situation.

19. Is the graph discrete or continuous?

20. Determine the domain and range.

You decide to hike up a mountain. You climb steadily for 2 hours, then take a 30 minute break for lunch. Then you continue to climb, faster than before. When you make it to the summit, you enjoy the view for an hour. Finally, you decide to climb down the mountain, but stop halfway down for a short break. Then you continue down at a slower pace than before.

21. Sketch a graph of the situation.

22. Is the graph discrete or continuous?

| H.O.T. | Focus on Higher Order Thinking |

23. **Analyze Relationships** Write a possible situation for the graph shown.

24. Represent Real-World Problems Scientists are conducting an experiment on a bacteria colony that causes its population to fluctuate. The population of a bacteria colony is shown in the graph.

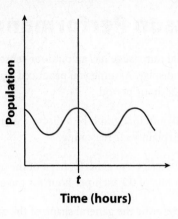

a. What happened to the bacteria colony before time *t*?

b. Suppose at time *t*, a second colony of bacteria is added to the first. Draw a new graph to show how this action might affect the population after time *t*.

c. Suppose at some point after time *t*, scientists add a substance to the colony that destroys some of the bacteria. Describe how your graph from part b might change.

25. Explain the Error A student is told to draw a graph of the situation which represents the height of a skydiver with respect to time. He drew the following graph. Explain the student's error and draw the correct graph.

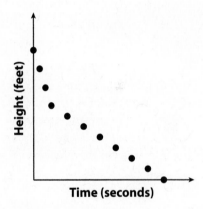

Lesson Performance Task

A digital rain gauge has an outdoor sensor that collects rainfall and transmits data to an indoor display. Assume you produced a graph of all the data collected by the rain gauge over a 24-hour period.

a. Would that graph be a discrete graph or a continuous graph? Explain your reasoning.

b. Describe the general shape of the graph assuming it rained at a rate of 0.1 inch per hour for the entire 24-hour period.

c. Describe the general shape of the graph assuming it rained 0.1 inch per hour for 6 hours, stopped raining for 6 hours, and then rained 0.2 inch for 12 hours.

3.2 Understanding Relations and Functions

Essential Question: How do you represent relations and functions?

⊘ Explore   Understanding Relations

A **relation** is a set of ordered pairs (x, y) where x is the input value and y is the output value. The **domain** is all possible inputs of a relation, and the **range** is all possible outputs of a relation. For example, the given relation represents the number of whole-wheat cracker boxes sold and the money earned.

$\{(1, 4), (2, 8), (3, 12), (4, 16)\}$.

Domain: $\{1, 2, 3, 4\}$ Range: $\{2, 8, 12, 16\}$

(A) For the following relation, the input, x, is the ages of boys and the output, y, is their corresponding height, in inches.

$\{(7, 41), (8, 45), (9, 49), (10, 52), (10, 53), (11, 55), (12, 59)\}$

(B) Create a table of x- and y-values.

(C) Plot the points on a graph.

(D) Copy and complete the mapping diagram.

(E) State the domain of the relation.

(F) State the range of the relation.

Age (yr)	Height (in.)
7	41
8	45
9	49
10	52
11	53
12	55
	59

1. **Discussion** The number 10 appears twice in the x column of the table. How many times is it written in the domain? Explain.

🔑 Explain 1 Recognizing Functions

A **function** is a type of relation in which there is only one output value for each input value.

For every input value, there is a unique output value.

Example: $y = x^2$. When $x = 3$, y will always be equal to 9.

Example 1 **Give the domain and range of each relation. State the corresponding outputs for the given inputs in context and explain whether the relation is a function.**

Ⓐ The given relation represents the number of students and the number of classrooms the school has to have for the corresponding number of students.

Students x	Classrooms y
40	2
45	3
50	4

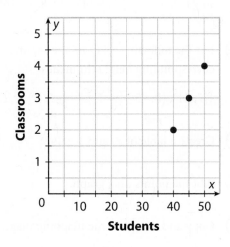

Domain: {40, 45 50}

The domain represents the number of students.

Range: {2, 3, 4}

The range represents the number of classrooms.

For an input of 40 students, there is an output of 2 classrooms.

For an input of 45 students, there is an output of 3 classrooms.

For an input of 50 students, there is an output of 4 classrooms.

This relation is a function. Each domain value is paired with exactly one range value.B

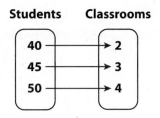

B The given relation represents the amount of gas in gallons and the distance traveled in miles from that amount of gas.

Gas (gal)	Distance (mi)
10	150
16	240
17	240
20	300

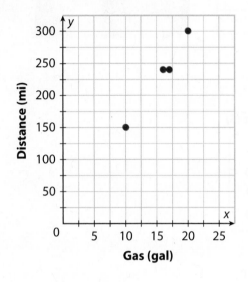

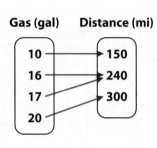

Domain: {10, 16, 17, 20}

The domain represents the different amounts of gas.

Range: {150, 240, 300}

The range represents the distance traveled.

For an input of 10 gallons of gas, there is an output of 150 miles.

For an input of 16 gallons of gas, there is an output of 240 miles.

For an input of 17 gallons of gas, there is an output of 240 miles.

For an input of 20 gallons of gas, there is an output of 300 miles.

This relation is a function. Each domain value is paired with exactly one range value.

Reflect

2. If each month in a year was paired with all the possible numbers of days in the month, will the result be a function? Explain.

Give the domain and range of each relation and interpret them in context. State the corresponding outputs for the given inputs in context and explain whether the relation is a function.

3. The relation represents the number of books sold and the price for the corresponding number of books.

Number of books sold	Price ($)
2	4
3	6
4	7
5	9

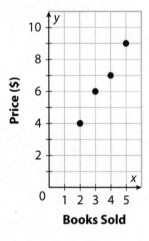

Books Sold

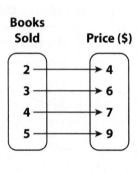

4. The relation represents the time spent exercising and the number of calories burned during that time.

Time (min)	Calories burned
20	50
30	85
35	85
60	100

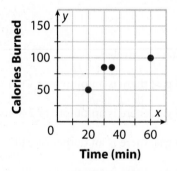

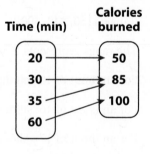

⚙ Explain 2 — Understanding the Vertical Line Test

A test, called the *vertical line test*, can be used to determine if a relation is a function. The **vertical line test** states that a relation is a function if and only if a vertical line does not pass through more than one point on the graph of the relation.

Example 2   Use the vertical line test to determine if each relation is a function. Explain.

Ⓐ   Draw a vertical line through each point of the graph.

Does any vertical line touch more than one point? Yes

Since a vertical line does pass through more than one point, the graph fails the vertical line test. So, the relation is not a function.

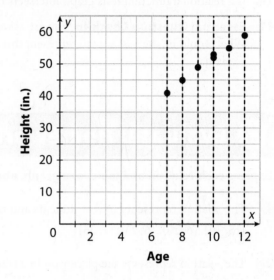

Ⓑ   Draw a vertical line through each point of the graph.

Does any vertical line touch more than one point? No.

Since a vertical line does not pass through more than one point, the graph passes the vertical line test. So, the relation is a function.

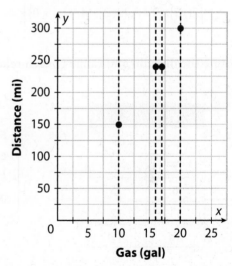

Reflect

5.   Why does the vertical line test work?

Your Turn

Use the vertical line test to determine if each relation is a function.

6.

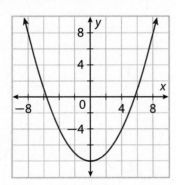

7.

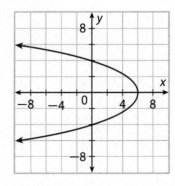

8. How can you use a mapping diagram to determine the domain and the range of a relation?

9. Discussion For a discrete function, can the number of elements in the range be greater than the number of elements in the domain? Explain.

10. Is a relation a function if its graph intersects the *y*-axis twice?

11. Essential Question Check-In You are asked to determine if the relation $y = x^2 - 8x + 4$ is a function. What would be the best way to represent this relation in order to determine if it is a function or not? Explain.

☆ Evaluate: Homework and Practice

• Online Homework
• Hints and Help
• Extra Practice

Express each relation as a table, as a graph, and as a mapping diagram.

1. The relation represents ages of students and the number of words they can write per minute.
$$\{(5, 10), (6, 20), (6, 23), (7, 35)\}$$

2. The relation represents the place won in a track meet and the number of points that place finish is worth.
$$\{(1, 5), (2, 3), (3, 2), (4, 1), (5, 0)\}$$

State the domain and range of each relation.

3.

x	y
2	5
7	8
8	15
11	12
15	19

4.

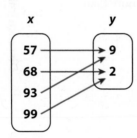

5.

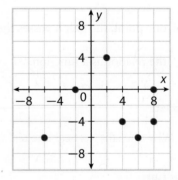

State the domain and range of each relation, interpret in context, and explain if it is a function or not.

6. The relation represents the age of each student and the number of pets the student has.

Age	Number of Pets
6	3
8	2
9	0
11	1
11	2

7. The relation represents time driven in hours and the number of miles traveled at the end of each hour.

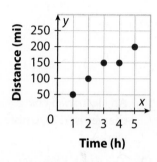

State the domain and range of each relation, interpret in context, and explain if it is a function or not.

8. The relation represents the number of hours a person is able to rent a canoe and the cost of renting the canoe for that many hours.

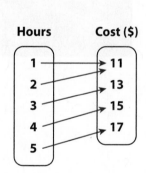

9. A person can burn about 6 calories per minute bicycling. Let x represent the number of minutes bicycled, and let y represent the number of calories burned. Create a mapping diagram to show the number of calories burned by bicycling for 60, 120, 180, or 240 minutes.

10. The table represents a sample of ages of people and their shoe size.

Age	Shoe Size
x	y
11	7
12	8
13	10
15	10
15	10.5
16	11

11. An electrician charges a base fee of $75 plus $50 for each hour of work. The minimum the electrician charges is $175. Create a table that shows the amount the electrician charges for 1, 2, 3, and 4 hours of work.

12. The graph represents the average soccer goals scored for players of different ages. Determine the domain and range of the relation in context and explain whether or not this represents a function.

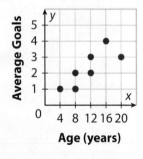

Express each relation as a mapping diagram and explain whether or not the relation represents a function.

13. $\{(13, 33), (17, 25), (22, 22), (25, 17), (33, 17)\}$

14. $\{(1, 2), (5, 2), (5, 4), (7, 6), (11, 6) (11, 8)\}$

Use the vertical line test to determine if each relation is a function.

15.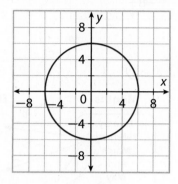

16.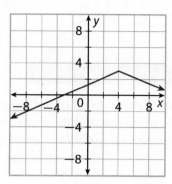

Use the vertical line test to determine if each relation is a function.

17.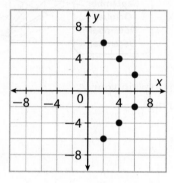

18.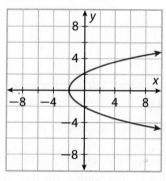

19.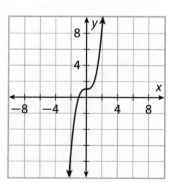

20.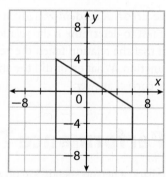

21.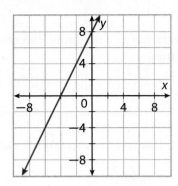

22.

23. **Draw Conclusions** Examine the mapping diagram. The first set is the months of the year, and the second set is the possible number of days per month. Is the relation a function? Explain.

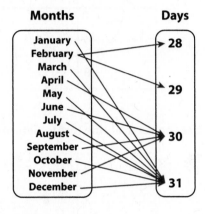

24. **Justify Reasoning** Tell whether each situation represents a function. Explain your reasoning. If the situation represents a function, give the domain and range.

   a. Each U.S. coin is mapped to its monetary value.

   b. A $1, $5, $10, $20, $50, or $100 bill is mapped to all the sets of coins that are the same as the total value of the bill.

25. **Explain the Error** A student was given a graph and asked to use the vertical line test to determine if the relation was a function or not. The student said that the relation failed the vertical line test and the graph was not a function. What error did the student make? Explain the error and give the correct answer.

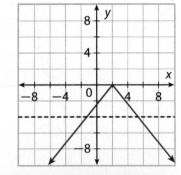

Lesson Performance Task

At an amusement park, a person spends $30 on admission and food, and then goes on *r* number of rides that cost $2 each.

   a. Write an equation to represent the total amount *A* spent at the amusement park if a person goes on anywhere from 0 to 5 rides.

   b. Represent the relation as a table, as a graph, and as a mapping diagram.

   c. Find the domain and range, and then determine whether the relation is a function or not.

3.3 Modeling with Functions

Essential Question: What is function notation and how can you use functions to model real-world situations?

Resource Locker

⊘ Explore 1 Identifying Independent and Dependent Variables

The input of a function is the **independent variable**. The output of the function is the **dependent variable**. The value of the dependent variable depends on, or is a function of, the value of the independent variable.

Identify dependent and independent variables in each situation.

In the winter, more electricity is used when the outside temperature goes down, and less is used when the outside temperature rises.

(A) The [?] depends on the [?] .

(B) Dependent: [?]

Independent: [?]

(C) The cost of shipping a package is based on its weight.

The [?] depends on the [?] .

(D) Dependent: [?] Independent: [?]

(E) The faster Tom walks, the quicker he gets home.

The [?] depends on the [?] .

(F) Dependent: [?] Independent: [?]

Reflect

1. **Discussion** Give a situation where "time" is the dependent variable and "distance" is the independent variable.

2. In Explore 1, explain how you know that the amount of electricity used is not the independent variable.

⊘ Explore 2 Applying Function Notation

If x is the independent variable and y is the dependent variable, then you can use **function notation** to write $y = f(x)$, which is read "y equals f of x," where f names the function. When an equation in two variables describes a function, you always can use function notation to write it.

The dependent variable	is	a function of	the independent variable.
y	is	a function of	x.
y	$=$	f	(x)

Write an equation in function notation.

Amanda babysits and charges $5 per hour.

Time Worked in Hours (x)	1	2	3	4
Amount Earned in Dollars (y)	5	10	15	20

Ⓐ The ⬚? is $5 times the ⬚? .

Ⓑ An algebraic expression that defines a function is a **function rule**. Write an equation using two variables to show this relationship.

Amount earned   is $5   times   the number of hours worked.
   ↓   ↓   ↓   ↓   ↓
  ⬚?   =   5   •   ⬚?

Ⓒ The dependent variable is a function of the independent variable. Write the equation in function notation.

Amount earned   is $5   times   the number of hours worked.
   ↓   ↓   ↓   ↓   ↓
   y =   5   • x
  ⬚?   =   5   • x

Reflect

3. **Discussion** Can y be used instead of $f(x)$ in function notation? If so, tell why. If not, give an example of a function not written in function notation and the same function written in function notation.

⊘ Explain 1 Modeling Using Function Notation

The value of the dependent variable depends on, or is a function of, the value of the independent variable. If x is the independent variable and y is the dependent variable, then the function notation for y will read "f of x," where f names the function. When an equation in two variables describes a function, you can use function notation to write it.

Example 1 For each example identify the independent and dependent variables. Write an equation in function notation for each situation, and then use the equation to solve the problem.

(A) A lawyer's fee is $180 per hour for his services. How much does the lawyer charge for 5 hours?

The fee for the lawyer depends on how many hours he works.

Dependent: fee; Independent: hours

Let h represent the number of hours the lawyer works.

The function for the lawyer's fee is $f(h) = 180h$.

$f(h) = 180h$
$f(5) = 180(5)$　　　Substitute 5 for h.
　　$= 900$　　　　　Simplify.

The lawyer charges $900 for 5 hours of work.

(B) The admission fee at a carnival is $9. Each ride costs $1.75. How much does it cost to go to the carnival and then go on 12 rides?

The total cost depends on the the number of rides, plus $9.

Dependent: total cost; Independent: the number of rides

Let r represent the number of rides. The function for the total cost of the carnival is

$f(r) = 1.75r + 9$.

Substitute 12 for r into the function for the total cost of the carnival, and find the total cost.

$$f\left(\boxed{12}\right) = \boxed{1.75(12) + 9}$$
$$f\left(\boxed{12}\right) = \boxed{30}$$

It costs $30 to go to the carnival and go on 12 rides.

Your Turn

Identify the independent and dependent variables. Write an equation in function notation. Then use the equation to solve the problem.

4. Kate earns $7.50 per hour. How much money will she earn after working 8 hours?

🔑 Explain 2　Choosing a Reasonable Domain and Range

When a function describes a real-world situation, every real number is not always a reasonable choice for the domain and range. For example, a number representing the length of an object cannot be negative, and only whole numbers can represent a number of people.

Example 2 Write a function in function notation for each situation. Find a reasonable domain and range for each function.

(A) Manuel has already sold $20 worth of tickets to the school play. He has 4 tickets left to sell at $2.50 per ticket. Write a function for the total amount collected from ticket sales.

Let t represent the number of tickets to sell.

Total amount collected from ticket sales	is	$2.50	per	ticket	plus	tickets already sold
$f(t)$	=	$2.50	•	t	+	20

Manuel has only 4 tickets left to sell, so a reasonable domain is {0, 1, 2, 3, 4}.

Substitute these values into the function rule $2.50t + 20$ to find the range values.

The range is {$20, $22.50, $25, $27.50, $30}.

(B) A telephone company charges $0.25 per minute for the first 5 minutes of a call plus a $0.45 connection fee per call. Write a function for the total cost in dollars of making a call.

Let m represent the number of minutes used.

Total cost for one call	is	$0.25	per	minute	plus	$0.45 fee.
$f(m)$	=	$0.25	•	m	+	$0.45

The charges only occur if a call is made, so a reasonable domain is {1, 2, 3, 4, 5}.

Substitute these values into the function rule $0.25m + 0.45$ to find the range values.

The range is {$0.70, $0.95, $1.20, $1.45, $1.70}.

Your Turn

Write a function in function notation for each situation. Find a reasonable domain and range for each function.

5. The temperature early in the morning is 17 °C. The temperature increases by 2 °C for every hour for the next 5 hours. Write a function for the temperature in degrees Celsius.

6. Takumi earns $8.50 per hour proofreading advertisements at a local newspaper. He works no more than 5 hours a day. Write a function for his earnings.

💬 Elaborate

7. How can you identify the independent variable and the dependent variable given a situation?

8. Describe how to write $3x + 2y = 12$ in function notation. Assume that y represents the dependent variable.

9. **Discussion** What is the advantage of using function notation instead of using y?

10. **Essential Question Check-In** Explain how to find reasonable domain values for a function.

⭐ Evaluate: Homework and Practice

1. Identify the dependent and independent variables in each situation.

A. The total cost of running a business is based on its expenses.

B. The price of a house depends on its area.

C. The time it takes you to run a certain distance depends on the distance.

D. The number of items in a carton depends on the size of the carton.

2. Charles will babysit for up to 4 hours and charges $7 per hour.

Write a function in function notation for this situation.

For each situation, identify the independent and dependent variables. Write a function in function notation. Then use the function to solve the problem.

3. Almira earns $50 an hour. How much does she earn in 6 hours?

4. Stan, a local delivery driver, is paid $3.50 per mile driven plus a daily amount of $75. On Monday, he is assigned a route that is 30 miles long. How much is he being paid for that day?

5. Bruce owns a small grocery store and charges $4.75 per pound of produce. If a customer orders 5 pounds of produce, how much does Bruce charge the customer?

6. Georgia, a florist, charges $10.95 per flower bundle plus a $15 delivery charge per order. If Charlie orders 8 bundles of flowers and has them delivered, how much does Georgia charge Charlie?

7. Allison owns a music store and sells DVDs at $17.75 per DVD. If Craig orders 5 DVDs, how much does it cost?

8. Anne buys used cars at auction for $2000 per car. There is a $150 fee to take part in the auction. If Anne buys 13 used cars, how much does she pay in total?

9. Harold, a real estate developer, sells houses at $250,000 per house. If he sells 9 houses, how much does he earn?

10. Gordon buys 3 HD TVs for $1200 each. There is a shipping charge of $90 to have the TVs delivered to his house. How much does Gordon pay in total?

11. Cindy is buying jackets for her local community charity's auction. Each jacket costs $50. If Cindy bought 23 jackets, what is the total cost?

12. Autumn sells laptop computers for $600 each. If she sells 68 computers, how much money does she earn?

Write a function using function notation to describe each situation. Find a reasonable domain and range for each function.

13. Elijah has already sold $40 worth of tickets for a local raffle. He has 5 tickets left to sell at $5 per ticket.

14. Mary has already sold $55 worth of tickets to the benefit concert. She has 3 tickets left to sell at $7 per ticket.

15. A law firm charges $100 per hour for the first 3 hours plus a $300 origination fee for its services.

16. A pay-for-service Internet company charges $5 per hour for the first 3 hours of service plus a $10 connection fee.

17. A high definition radio station charges $200 per year in addition to $50 per month for the first 3 months to receive its broadcast.

18. A newspaper charges $3 per line for the first 4 lines plus a $20 fee to advertise.

19. Matt has already sold $72 worth of tickets to the benefit concert. He has 6 tickets left to sell at $9 per ticket.

20. Sarah has sold $33 worth of tickets to the comedy show. She has 4 tickets left to sell at $11 per ticket.

H.O.T. Focus on Higher Order Thinking

21. Justify Reasoning The function $f(x) = -6x + 11$ has a range given by {−37, −25, −13, −1}. Select the domain values of the function from the list 1, 2, 3, 4, 5, 6, 7, 8. Explain how you arrived at your answer.

22. Represent Real-World Problems Victor needs to find the volume of 6 cube-shaped boxes with sides lengths of between 2 feet and 7 feet. The side lengths of the boxes can only be whole numbers. The volume of a cube-shaped box with a side length of s is given by the function $V(s) = s^3$.

  a. What is a reasonable domain for this situation? Explain.

  b. What is a reasonable range for this situation? Explain.

23. Represent Real-World Problems Tanya is printing a report. There are 100 sheets of paper in the printer, and the number of sheets of paper p left after t minutes of printing is given by the function $p(t) = -8t + 100$.

  a. How many minutes would it take the printer to use all 100 sheets of paper? Show your work.

  b. What is a reasonable domain for this situation? Explain.

  c. What is a reasonable range for this situation? Explain.

Lesson Performance Task

Jenna's parents have given her an interest-free loan of $100 to buy a new pair of running shoes. She plans to pay back the loan with monthly payments of $20 each.

  a. Write a function rule for the balance function $B(p)$, where p represents the number of payments that Jenna has made.

  b. After how many payments will Jenna have paid back more than half the loan? Explain your reasoning.

  c. Suppose the loan amount were $120 and the monthly payments were $15. Write a rule for the new balance function and use it to determine how long it would take Jenna to pay off the loan.

3.4 Graphing Functions

Essential Question: How do you graph functions?

Resource Locker

⊘ Explore   Graphing Functions Using a Given Domain

Recall that the domain of a function is the set of input values, or x-values, of the function and that the range is the set of corresponding output values, or y-values, of the function. One way to understand a function and its features is to graph it. You can graph a function by finding ordered pairs that satisfy the function.

Graph the function for the given domain.

$x + 3y = 15$ D: $\{0, 3, 6, 9\}$

Ⓐ You have been given the input values, x, of the domain. You need to solve the function for y.

$x + 3y = 15$

$\underline{-x \qquad -x}$ Subtract x from both sides.

$3y = \boxed{?}$

$\dfrac{3y}{3} = \dfrac{\boxed{?}}{\cdot \ 3}$ Since y is multiplied by 3, divide both sides by 3.

$y = \boxed{?} + \boxed{?}$ Rewrite the right side as two separate fractions.

$y = \boxed{?} + \boxed{?}$ Simplify.

Ⓑ Substitute the given values of the domain for x to find the values of y.

x	$y = -\frac{1}{3}x + 5$	(x, y)
0	$y = -\frac{1}{3}(0) + 5 = \boxed{?}$	$\left(0, \boxed{?}\right)$
3	$y = -\frac{1}{3}\left(\boxed{?}\right) + 5 = 4$	$\left(\boxed{?}, 4\right)$
6	$y = -\frac{1}{3}(6) + 5 = \boxed{?}$	$\left(6, \boxed{?}\right)$
9	$y = -\frac{1}{3}\left(\boxed{?}\right) + 5 = 2$	$\left(\boxed{?}, \boxed{?}\right)$

Ⓒ Graph the ordered pairs.

1. **Discussion** Why do you not connect the points of the graph?

2. **Discussion** How would the graph be different if the domain was $0 \leq x \leq 9$?

🔧 Explain 1 Graphing Functions Using a Domain of All Real Numbers

If the domain of a function is all real numbers, any number can be used as an input value producing an infinite number of ordered pairs that satisfy the function. Arrowheads are drawn at both ends of a smooth line or curve to represent the infinite number of ordered pairs. If a domain is not provided, it should be assumed that the domain is all real numbers.

Graphing Functions Using a Domain of All Real Numbers	
Step 1	Use the function to generate ordered pairs by choosing several values of x.
Step 2	Plot enough points to see a pattern for the graph.
Step 3	Connect the points with a line or smooth curve.

Example 1 Graph each function.

(A) $y = x^2$

Use several values of x to generate ordered pairs. Plot the points from the table, and draw a smooth curve through the points. Include an arrowhead at each end.

x	$y = x^2$	(x, y)
-3	$y = (-3)^2 = 9$	$(-3, 9)$
-2	$y = (-2)^2 = 4$	$(-2, 4)$
-1	$y = (-1)^2 = 1$	$(-1, 1)$
0	$y = (0)^2 = 0$	$(0, 0)$
1	$y = (1)^2 = 1$	$(1, 1)$
2	$y = (2)^2 = 4$	$(2, 4)$
3	$y = (3)^2 = 9$	$(3, 9)$

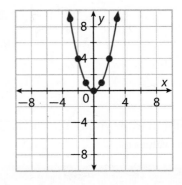

(B) $f(x) = 3x - 5$

Use several values of x to generate ordered pairs.

x	$f(x) = 3x - 5$	$(x, f(x))$
-1	$f(-1) = 3(-1) - 5 = \boxed{-8}$	$(-1, \boxed{-8})$
0	$f\boxed{0} = 3\boxed{0} - 5 = -5$	$(\boxed{0}, -5)$
1	$f(1) = 3(1) - 5 = (\boxed{-2})$	$(1, \boxed{-2})$
2	$f\boxed{2} = 3(\boxed{2}) - 5 = 1$	$(\boxed{2}, 1)$
3	$f(3) = 3(3) - 5 = (\boxed{4})$	$(3, \boxed{4})$
4	$f\boxed{4} = 3(\boxed{4}) - 5 = 7$	$(\boxed{4}, \boxed{7})$

Plot the points from the table to see a pattern.

The points appear to form a line. Draw a line through all the points to show the ordered pairs that satisfy the function.

Draw arrowheads on both ends of the graph.

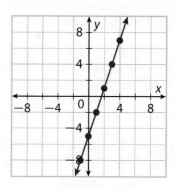

Reflect

3. When graphing a function, does it matter if the function is written in function notation? Explain.

Your Turn

Graph each function.

4. $y = -x^2$

5. $y = -4x + 2$

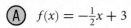 Explain 2   Using a Graph to Find Values

To find the value of a function for a given value of x using a graph, locate the value of x on the x-axis, move up or down to the graph of the function, and then move left or right to the y-axis to find the corresponding value of y.

Example 2   Use a graph to find the value of $f(x)$ when $x = -2$ for each function.

(A) $f(x) = -\frac{1}{2}x + 3$

Use a graphing calculator to graph $y = -\frac{1}{2}x + 3$, and use TRACE to find the function value when $x = -2$.

Therefore, the value of y is 4 when x is -2.

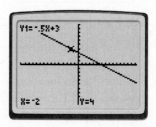

(B) $f(x) = \frac{3}{2}x - 4$

First graph the line. Locate −2 on the x-axis. Draw a vertical line segment from −2 on the x-axis to the graph of the function and a horizontal line segment from the graph of the function to the y-axis.

The value of y on the y-axis is the value of the function. Therefore, the value of $f(x)$ is −7 when x is −2.

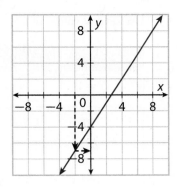

Your Turn

6. Use a graph to find the value of $f(x)$ when $x = 3$ for the function $f(x) = -x + 7$.

 Explain 3 **Modeling Using a Function Graph**

The domain of a real-world situation may have to be limited in order to have reasonable answers. Only nonnegative numbers can be used to represent quantities such as time, distance, and the number of people. When both the domain and the range of a function are limited to nonnegative values, the function is graphed only in Quadrant I.

The Mid-Atlantic Ridge separates the North and South American Plates from the Eurasian and African Plates. The function $y = 2.5x$ relates the number of centimeters y the Mid-Atlantic Ridge spreads after x years. Graph the function and use the graph to estimate how many centimeters the Mid-Atlantic Ridge spreads in 4.5 years.

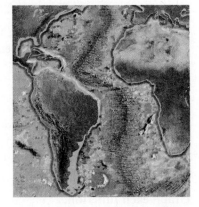

Analyze Information

Identify the important information:

- The function $y = 2.5x$ describes how many centimeters the Mid-Atlantic Ridge spreads after x years.

Formulate a Plan

Only use nonnegative values of x and y. Use a graph to find the value of y when x is 4.5.

 Solve

Choose several values of x that are in the domain of the function to find values of y.

x	$y = 2.5x$	(x, y)
0	$y = 2.5(\boxed{0}) = 0$	$(\boxed{0}, 0)$
2	$y = 2.5(2) = \boxed{5}$	$(2, \boxed{5})$
4	$y = 2.5(\boxed{4}) = 10$	$(\boxed{4}, 10)$
5	$y = 2.5(5) = \boxed{12.5}$	$(5, \boxed{12.5})$

Plot the points that represent the ordered pairs on the graph. Draw a line through all of the points because the points appear to form a line.

Use the graph to estimate the *y*-value when *x* is 4.5.

The Mid-Atlantic Ridge spreads about 11.25 centimeters after 4.5 years.

Mid-Atlantic Ridge Spreading

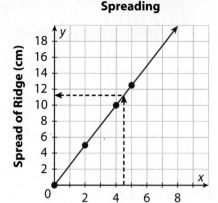

Justify and Evaluate

The distance of the Mid-Atlantic Ridge spread increases as the number of years increases, so the graph is reasonable. When *x* is between 4 and 5, *y* is between 10 and 12.5. Since 4.5 is between 4 and 5, it is reasonable to estimate *y* to be 11.25 when *x* is 4.5.

Your Turn

7. A cruise ship is currently 5 kilometers away from its port and is traveling away from the port at 15 kilometers per hour. The function $y = 15x + 5$ relates the number of kilometers *y* the ship will be from its port *x* hours from now. Graph the function and use the graph to determine how far the cruise ship will be from its port 2.5 hours from now.

Elaborate

8. Is it enough to plot two points to see a pattern for a graph? Explain.

9. **Discussion** When you use a graph to find the value of a function for a specific value of *x*, do you always get an exact answer? Explain.

10. **Essential Question Check-In** How do you graph a function that has a domain of all real numbers?

• Online Homework
• Hints and Help
• Extra Practice

Graph each function for the given domain.

1. $y = 2x$ D:$\{-2, 0, 2, 4\}$

2. $y = \frac{1}{4}x + 5$ D:$\{-8, -4, 0, 4\}$

3. $-3x - 5y = 20$ D:$\{-10, -5, 0, 5\}$

4. $y = x^2 - 3$ D:$\{-2, -1, 0, 1, 2\}$

Graph each function.

5. $y = -x^2 + 5$

6. $y = \frac{2}{3}x - 1$

7. $x + y = 0$.

8. $y = \frac{1}{4}x^2 - 8$

Use a graphing calculator to find the value of $f(x)$ when $x = 3$ for each function.

9. $f(x) = \frac{1}{3}x - 2$

10. $f(x) = -x^2 - 4$

Use a graphing calculator to find the value of $f(x)$ when $x = -4$ for each function.

11. $f(x) = x^2 - 3$

12. $f(x) = -4x - \frac{3}{2}$

13. $f(x) = -\frac{9}{2}x^2 - 5$

14. Graph $f(x) = 8 + 2x$. Then find the value of $f(x)$ when $x = \frac{1}{2}$.

15. Graph $f(x) = 0.5 - 2x^2$. Then find the value of $f(x)$ when $x = 0$.

16. Graph $f(x) = \frac{1}{4}x^2$. Then find the value of $f(x)$ when $x = -6$.

17. The fastest recorded Hawaiian lava flow moved at an average speed of 6 miles per hour. The function $y = 6x$ describes the distance y the lava moved on average in x hours. Graph the function. Use the graph to estimate how many miles the lava moved after 4.5 hours.

18. The total cost of a cab ride can be represented by the function $f(x) = 3x + 2.5$, where x is the number of miles driven. Graph the function. Use the graph to estimate how much the cab will cost if the cab ride is 8 miles.

19. Joshua is driving to the store. The average distance d in miles he travels over t minutes is given by the function $d(t) = 0.5t$. Graph the function. Use the graph to estimate how many miles he drove after 5 minutes.

20. The production cost for g graphing calculators is $C(g) = 15g$. Graph the function and then evaluate it when $g = 15$. What does the value of the function at $g = 15$ represent?

21. The temperature, in degrees Fahrenheit, of a liquid that is increasing can be represented by the equation $f(t) = 64 + 4t$, where t is the time in hours. Graph the function to show the temperatures over the first 10 hours. Use the graph to find the temperature after 7 hours.

22. A snowboarder's elevation, in feet, can be represented by the function $E(t) = 3000 - 70t$, where t is in seconds. Graph the function and find the elevation of the snowboarder after 30 seconds.

23. **Explain the Error** Student A and student B were given the following graph and asked to find the value of $f(x)$ when $x = 1$. Student A gave an answer of 0 while student B gave an answer of -2. Who is incorrect? Explain the error.

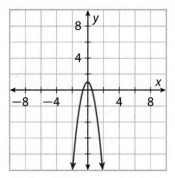

24. **Justify Reasoning** Without graphing, tell which statement(s) are true for the graph of the function $y = x^2 + 1$. Explain your choices.

   I. All points on the graph are above the origin.

   II. All points on the graph have positive x-values.

   III. All points on the graph have positive y-values.

Lesson Performance Task

The Japanese Shinkansen, or bullet train, can accelerate rapidly to reach its maximum traveling speed of about 170 miles per hour. The table gives the speed of the train in feet per second at several different times.

Time (seconds)	Speed (feet per second)
0	0
1	2.5
4	10
6	15
10	25

a. Convert the data from the table to a set of ordered pairs and graph them on a coordinate grid. Connect the points with a line. What does the line represent?

b. What is the slope of the line? What does the slope represent?

c. If the acceleration remains constant, how long will it take the train to reach its maximum speed of 170 miles per hour (mph)? [1 mph equals about 1.5 feet per second]

Functions and Models

Essential Question: How can you use functions to solve real-world problems?

KEY EXAMPLE   *(Lesson 3.1)*

The graph below represents Robert's total distance traveled during his walk to school. Write a possible situation for the graph.

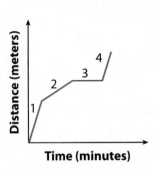

Sections 1 and 4 are steeper than section 2, so Robert was walking faster during these times.

Section 3 is horizontal, so Robert was not moving during this time.

Possible Situation: Robert walked quickly at the beginning of his walk, then he walked at a slower pace. He stopped for a while to talk to some friends. Then, he walked quickly the rest of the way to school.

Key Vocabulary

continuous graph
   (gráfica continua)
dependent variable
   (variable dependiente)
discrete graph
   (gráfica discreta)
domain *(dominio)*
function *(función)*
function notation
   (notación de función)
independent variable
   (variable independiente)
range *(rango)*
relation *(relación)*

KEY EXAMPLE   *(Lesson 3.2)*

Give the domain and range of the relation. Explain whether the relation is a function.

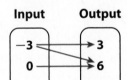

The domain is all inputs, or $\{-3, 0, 2\}$.

The range is all outputs, or $\{3, 6, 9\}$.

A function has at most one output value for each input. The relation is not a function, because the input value -3 has more than one output.

KEY EXAMPLE   *(Lessons 3.3, 3.4)*

Write an equation in function notation for the following example, and graph the function.

A study skills tutor charges $8 an hour for sessions lasting 1, 2, 3, or 4 hours.

The independent variable x is the number of hours.

The dependent variable $f(x)$ is the total cost.

The function for the total cost is $f(x) = 8x$.

The ordered pairs for the function $f(x) = 8x$ for the domain $\{1, 2, 3, 4\}$ are $(1, 8)$, $(2, 16)$, $(3, 24)$, and $(4, 32)$.

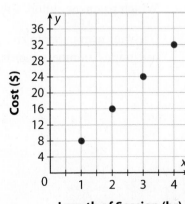

Length of Session (hr)

EXERCISES

1. Sketch a graph that represents the following situation. A person gets on a ride at an amusement park. The ride rises slowly and then quickly to its highest point. Then, to build anticipation, the ride stops for a period of time before quickly falling. Then, the ride descends more slowly before coming to a stop. *(Lesson 3.1)*

2. Identify the independent and dependent variables of the following relation. Give the domain and range, and explain whether the relation is a function.

   A farmer has up to 3 pigs at a time on his farm. The given relation represents the average number of pounds of feed needed for *x* pigs daily. *(Lesson 3.2)*

Number of Pigs, x	Pounds of Feed, y
1	55
2	110
3	165

3. A store sells roasted peanuts in 1, 2, 2.5, and 4 pound bags. The peanuts cost $4 per pound. Write an equation in function notation that represents the cost of the peanuts in terms of the number of pounds, and graph the function. *(Lessons 3.3, 3.4)*

MODULE PERFORMANCE TASK

Season Passes

Wild Planet Theme Park offers three season-pass purchase options.

Plan A	Plan B	Plan C
One payment of $500	$80 down payment 6 payments of $75 every other month	$60 down payment 11 monthly payments of $45

Which payment option is the least expensive?

Use your own paper to complete the task. Be sure to write down all your data. Then use graphs, numbers, words, or algebra to explain how you reached your conclusion.

(Ready) to Go On?

3.1–3.4 Functions and Models

1. The graph shown represents the altitude of a hiker during a period of time. Write a possible situation represented by the graph. *(Lesson 3.1)*

2. Use the vertical line test to determine if the relation represented on the graph from **Exercise 1** is a function. Explain. *(Lesson 3.2)*

3. A math test is made up of 7 problems, each worth 10 points. There is no partial credit. Every test taker receives 30 points for taking the test. Write a function to describe the test score determined by the number of correct answers. Graph the function using a reasonable domain and range. *(Lessons 3.3, 3.4)*

ESSENTIAL QUESTION

4. What is a function?

Assessment Readiness

1. Kyle is installing new baseboards and carpet in his rectangular living room. He measured the length as 24.25 feet and the width as 16.4 feet. Tell whether each statement is correct.

   A. The length is a more precise measurement.

   B. The area of the room should be given with 3 significant digits.

   C. The perimeter of the room should be given with 4 significant digits

2. The graph represents the function $f(x) = -x^2 + 2$. Determine if each statement is True or False.

   A. When $x = 1$, $f(x) = 1$.

   B. When $f(x) = 2$, $x = -2$.

   C. When $x = -1$, $f(x) = 1$.

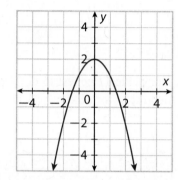

3. The mapping diagram represents the age, in years, and height, rounded to the nearest inch, of a group of friends. Does the diagram represent a function? Explain your answer.

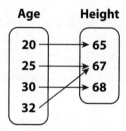

4. An amusement park charges an entrance fee of $25 plus $3.50 per ride. Write a function to represent this situation. How much would it cost to go to the park and ride 8 rides?

Patterns and Sequences

Essential Question: How are patterns and sequences used to solve real-world problems?

REAL WORLD VIDEO
Today's calculators, apps, and computer software can perform even the most complex calculations almost instantly. Programming based on patterns and sequences makes these modern marvels possible.

MODULE PERFORMANCE TASK PREVIEW
There Has to Be an Easier Way

Carl Friedrich Gauss, one of the greatest mathematicians of all time, showed his genius at a very early age. When he was just ten, his teacher presented a math problem that the teacher thought would keep the class occupied for a long time. Surprise! Gauss solved the problem almost before the teacher had finished stating it. In this module, you'll get a chance to tackle the same problem Gauss solved. Use a creative method to find the answer and you'll be famous too!

Are **YOU** Ready?

Complete these exercises to review skills you will need for this module.

Number Patterns

Example 1   Find the next three numbers in the pattern 2, 5, 8, 11, …

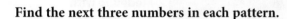

2   5   8   11

$+3$ $+3$ $+3$

Study the pattern in the sequence.

Each number is 3 more than the number before it.

$11 + 3 = 14$

$14 + 3 = 17$

$17 + 3 = 20$

The next 3 numbers will be 14, 17, and 20.

Find the next three numbers in each pattern.

1. 2, 4, 8, 16, …

2. 5, 11, 17, 23, …

3. 50, 43, 36, 29, …

4. 1, 4, 9, 16, …

Algebraic Expressions

Example 2   Evaluate $2x + 3y$ for $x = 4$ and $y = -5$.

$2x + 3y$

$2(4) + 3(-5)$ Substitute 4 for *x* and -5 for *y*.

$8 + (-15)$ Multiply.

-7 Add.

Evaluate each expression for the given values of the variables.

5. $4p - 7p$ for $p = 8$ and $q = 5$

6. $(n - 1)^2$ for $n = -4$

7. $8d + 5e - 11$ for $d = 6$ and $e = -9$

8. $a^2 - b$ for $a = 7$ and $b = 12$

4.1 Identifying and Graphing Sequences

Essential Question: What is a sequence and how are sequences and functions related?

Resource Locker

⊘ Explore   Understanding Sequences

A go-kart racing track charges $5 for a go-kart license and $2 for each lap. If you list the charges for 1 lap, 2 laps, 3 laps, and so on, in order, the list forms a sequence of numbers:

$$7, 9, 11, 13, \ldots$$

A **sequence** is a list of numbers in a specific order. Each element in a sequence is called a **term**. In a sequence, each term has a position number. In the sequence 7, 9, 11, 13, . . ., the second term is 9, so its position number is 2.

Ⓐ The total cost (term) of riding a go-kart for different numbers of laps (position) is shown below. Complete the table.

Position number, n	1	2	3	?	5	?	Domain
Term of the sequence, $f(n)$	7	9	?	13	?	17	Range

Ⓑ You can use the term and position number of a sequence to write a function. Using function notation, $f(2) = 9$ indicates that the second term is 9. Use the table to complete the following statements.

$f(1) = \boxed{?}$ $f(3) = \boxed{?}$ $f(6) = \boxed{?}$ $f\left(\boxed{?}\right) = 13$ $f\left(\boxed{?}\right) = 15$

Ⓒ Identify the domain of the function $f(n)$. $\boxed{?}$

Ⓓ Identify the range of the function $f(n)$. $\boxed{?}$

Reflect

1. **Discussion** What does $f(4) = 13$ mean in the context of the go-kart problem?

2. **Discussion** Explain how to find the missing values in the table.

3. **Communicate Mathematical Ideas** Explain why the relationship between the position numbers and the corresponding terms of a sequence can be considered a function.

⚙ Explain 1 · Solving One-Variable Two-Step Equations

An **explicit rule** for a sequence defines the nth term as a function of n for any whole number n greater than 0. Explicit rules can be used to find any specific term in a sequence without finding any of the previous terms.

Example 1   Write the first 4 terms of the sequence defined by the explicit rule.

Ⓐ $f(n) = n^2 + 2$

Make a table and substitute values for $n = 1, 2, 3, 4$ to find the first 4 terms.

The first 4 terms of the sequence defined by the explicit rule $f(n) = n^2 + 2$ are 3, 6, 11, and 18.

n	$f(n) = n^2 + 2$	$f(n)$
1	$f(1) = 1^2 + 2 = 3$	3
2	$f(2) = 2^2 + 2 = 6$	6
3	$f(3) = 3^2 + 2 = 11$	11
4	$f(4) = 4^2 + 2 = 18$	18

Ⓑ $f(n) = 3n^2 + 1$

Make a table and substitute values for $n = 1, 2, 3, 4$.

The first 4 terms are 4, 13, 28, and 49.

n	$f(n) = 3n^2 + 1$	$f(n)$
1	$f\left(\boxed{1}\right) = 3\left(\boxed{1}\right)^2 + 1 = \boxed{4}$	$\boxed{4}$
2	$f\left(\boxed{2}\right) = 3\left(\boxed{2}\right)^2 + 1 = \boxed{13}$	$\boxed{13}$
3	$f\left(\boxed{3}\right) = 3\left(\boxed{3}\right)^2 + 1 = \boxed{28}$	$\boxed{28}$
4	$f\left(\boxed{4}\right) = 3\left(\boxed{4}\right)^2 + 1 = \boxed{49}$	$\boxed{49}$

Reflect

4. **Communicate Mathematical Ideas**   Explain how to find the 20th term of the sequence defined by the explicit rule $f(n) = n^2 + 2$.

5. **Justify Reasoning**   The number 125 is a term of the sequence defined by the explicit rule $f(n) = 3n + 2$. Which term in the sequence is 125? Justify your answer.

Your Turn

6. Write the first 4 terms of the sequence defined by the explicit rule $f(n) = n^2 - 5$.

7. Find the 15th term of the sequence defined by the explicit rule $f(n) = 4n - 3$.

⚙ Explain 2 Generating Sequences Using a Recursive Rule

A **recursive rule** for a sequence defines the nth term by relating it to one or more previous terms.

The following is an example of a recursive rule:

$$f(1) = 4, f(n) = f(n-1) + 10 \text{ for each whole number } n \text{ greater than } 1$$

This rule means that after the first term of the sequence, every term $f(n)$ is the sum of the pervious term $f(n-1)$ and 10.

Example 2 Write the first 4 terms of the sequence defined by the recursive rule.

Ⓐ $f(1) = 2, f(n) = f(n-1) + 3$ for each whole number n greater than 1

For the first 4 terms, the domain of the function is 1, 2, 3, and 4.

The first term of the sequence is 2.

n	$f(n) = f(n-1) + 3$	$f(n)$
1	$f(1) = 2$	2
2	$f(2) = f(1) + 3 = 2 + 3 = 5$	5
3	$f(3) = f(2) + 3 = 5 + 3 = 8$	8
4	$f(4) = f(3) + 3 = 8 + 3 = 11$	11

The first 4 terms are 2, 5, 8, and 11.

Ⓑ $f(1) = 4, f(n) = f(n-1) + 5$ for each whole number n greater than 1

For the first 4 terms, the domain of the function is 1, 2, 3, and 4

The first term of the sequence is 4 .

n	$f(n) = f(n-1) + 5$	$f(n)$
1	$f(1) =$ 4	4
2	$f(2) = f\left(1 \right) + 5 =$ 4 $+ 5 =$ 9	9
3	$f(3) = f\left(2 \right) + 5 =$ 9 $+ 5 =$ 14	14
4	$f(4) = f\left(3 \right) + 5 =$ 14 $+ 5 =$ 19	19

The first 4 terms are 4, 9, 14, and 19.

Reflect

8. Describe how to find the 12th term of the sequence in Example 2A.

9. Suppose you want to find the 40th term of a sequence. Would you rather use a recursive rule or an explicit rule? Explain your reasoning.

Write the first 5 terms of the sequence.

10. $f(1) = 35$ and $f(n) = f(n-1) - 2$ for each whole number n greater than 1.

11. $f(1) = 45$ and $f(n) = f(n-1) - 4$ for each whole number n greater than 1.

🔧 Explain 3   Constructing and Graphing Sequences

You can graph a sequence on a coordinate plane by plotting the points $(n, f(n))$ indicated in a table that you use to generate the terms.

Example 3   Construct and graph the sequence described.

Ⓐ The go-kart racing charges are $5 for a go-kart license and $2 for each lap. Use the explicit rule $f(n) = 2n + 5$.

Complete the table to represent the cost for the first 4 laps.

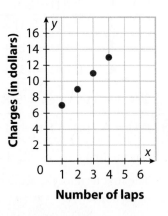

n	$f(n) = 2n + 5$	$f(n)$
1	$f(1) = 2(1) + 5 = 2 + 5 = 7$	7
2	$f(2) = 2(2) + 5 = 4 + 5 = 9$	9
3	$f(3) = 2(3) + 5 = 6 + 5 = 11$	11
4	$f(4) = 2(4) + 5 = 8 + 5 = 13$	13

The ordered pairs are $(1, 7)$, $(2, 9)$, $(3, 11)$, $(4, 13)$.

Graph the sequence using the ordered pairs.

Notice that the graph is a set of points that are not connected.

Ⓑ A movie rental club charges $20 a month plus a $5 membership fee. Use the explicit rule $f(n) = 20n + 5$.

Complete the table to represent the charges paid for 6 months.

n	$f(n) =$ ⟦20⟧ $n +$ ⟦5⟧						$f(n)$
1	$f($ 1 $) =$ 20 $($ 1 $) +$ 5 $=$ 25						25
2	$f($ 2 $) =$ 20 $($ 2 $) +$ 5 $=$ 45						45
3	$f($ 3 $) =$ 20 $($ 3 $) +$ 5 $=$ 65						65
4	$f($ 4 $) =$ 20 $($ 4 $) +$ 5 $=$ 85						85
5	$f($ 5 $) =$ 20 $($ 5 $) +$ 5 $=$ 105						105
6	$f($ 6 $) =$ 20 $($ 6 $) +$ 5 $=$ 125						125

The ordered pairs are (1, 25), (2, 45), (3, 65), (4, 85), (5, 105), and (6, 125).

Graph the sequence using the ordered pairs.

Notice that the graph is a set of points that are not connected.

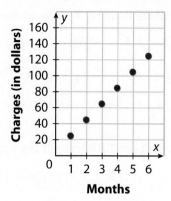

Reflect

12. Explain why the points in the graphs in Example 3 are not connected.

Your Turn

Construct and graph the sequence described.

13. A pizza place is having a special. If you order a large pizza for a regular price $17, you can order any number of additional pizzas for $8.50 each. Use the recursive rule $f(1) = 17$ and $f(n) = f(n - 1) + 8.5$ for each whole number n greater than 1.

14. A gym charges $100 as the membership fee and $20 monthly fee. Use the explicit rule $f(n) = 20n + 100$ to construct and graph the sequence.

Elaborate

15. What is the difference between an explicit rule and a recursive rule?

16. Describe how to use an explicit rule to find the position number of a given term in a sequence.

17. Explain why the graph of a sequence is a set of points that are not connected.

18. **Essential Question Check-In** Why can the rule for a sequence be considered a function?

⭐ Evaluate: Homework and Practice

• Online Homework
• Hints and Help
• Extra Practice

Copy and complete the table, and state the domain and range for the sequence it represents. Assume that the sequence continues without end.

1.

n	1	2	3	?	5	?
f(n)	15	30	?	60	?	90

2.

n	1	?	3	4	?	6
f(n)	6	8	10	?	14	?

Write the first 4 terms of the sequence defined by the given rule.

3. $f(1) = 65{,}536,\ f(n) = \sqrt{f(n-1)}$

4. $f(n) = n^3 - 1$

5. $f(1) = 7,\ f(n) = -4 \cdot f(n-1) + 15$

6. $f(n) = 2n^2 + 4$

7. $f(1) = 3,\ f(n) = [f(n-1)]^2$

8. $f(n) = (2n - 1)^2$

Find the 10th term of the sequence defined by the given rule.

9. $f(1) = 2,\ f(n) = f(n-1) + 7$

10. $f(n) = \sqrt{n+2}$

11. $f(1) = 30,\ f(n) = 2 \cdot f(n-1) - 50$

12. $f(n) = \frac{1}{2}(n-1) + 3$

The explicit rule for a sequence and one of the specific terms is given. Find the position of the given term.

13. $f(n) = 1.25n + 6.25;\ 25$

14. $f(n) = -3(n-1);\ -51$

15. $f(n) = (2n - 2) + 2;\ 52$

The recursive rule for a sequence and one of the specific terms is given. Find the position of the given term.

16. $f(1) = 8\frac{1}{2};\ f(n) = f(n-1) - \frac{1}{2};\ 5\frac{1}{2}$

17. $f(1) = 99,\ f(n) = f(n-1) + 4;\ 119$

18. $f(1) = 33.3,\ f(n) = f(n-1) + 0.2;\ 34.9$

Graph the sequence that represents the situation on a coordinate plane.

19. Jessica had $150 in her savings account after her first week of work. She then started adding $35 each week to her account for the next 5 weeks. The savings account balance can be represented by a sequence.

20. Carrie borrowed $840 from a friend to pay for a car repair. Carrie promises to repay her friend in 8 equal monthly payments. The remaining amount Carrie has to repay can be represented by a sequence.

21. A park charges $12 for one round of miniature golf and a reduced fee for each additional round played. If Tom paid $47 for 6 rounds of miniature golf, what is the reduced fee for each additional round played?

22. Analyze Relationships Construct a recursive rule to describe the sequence: 2, 4, 6, 8,…

23. Explain the Error To find the 5th term of a sequence where $f(1) = 4$ and $f(n) = 2 \cdot f(n-1) + 1$ for each whole number greater than 1, Shane calculates $(4 \cdot 2 \cdot 2 \cdot 2 \cdot 2) + 1 = 65$. Is this correct? Justify your answer.

24. Critical Thinking Write a recursive rule for a sequence where every term is the same.

Lesson Performance Task

A museum charges $10 per person for admission and $2 for each of 8 special exhibits.

a. Use function notation to write an equation to represent the cost for attending *n* events.

b. Make a table to represent the total cost of admission plus 1, 2, and 3 special exhibits.

c. What would $f(0) = 10$ represent?

d. What would the total cost be for going to all 8 special exhibits?

e. Determine an explicit rule for the total cost if the first special exhibit were free.

4.2 Constructing Arithmetic Sequences

Essential Question: What is an arithmetic sequence?

🧭 Explore Exploring Arithmetic Sequences

You can order tickets for the local theater online. There is a fee of $2 per order. Matinee tickets cost $10 each. The total cost, in dollars, of ordering n matinee tickets online can be found by using $C(n) = 10n + 2$. The table shows the cost of 1, 2, 3, and 4 tickets.

Ⓐ Copy and complete the table of values for
$C(n) = 10n + 2$.

Tickets	1	2	3	4
Total Cost ($)	?	?	?	?

What is the domain of the sequence? 🔲 ?

Ⓑ What is the range of the sequence? 🔲 ?

Ⓒ What is the first term of the sequence? 🔲 ?

Ⓓ Find the difference between each two consecutive terms in the sequence:

$22 - 12 =$ 🔲 ? $32 - 22 =$ 🔲 ? $42 - 32 =$ 🔲 ?

Reflect

1. **Discussion** Suppose you extended the table for up to 15 tickets. Would you expect the difference between consecutive terms to be the same? Explain your reasoning.

2. **Communicate Mathematical Ideas** Explain how the domain is limited in this situation.

✏️ Explain 1 Constructing Rules for Arithmetic Sequences

In an **arithmetic sequence,** the difference between consecutive terms is always equal. This difference, written as d, is called the **common difference.**

An arithmetic sequence can be described in two ways, explicitly and recursively. As you saw earlier, in an **explicit** rule for a sequence, the nth term of the arithmetic sequence is defined as a function of n. In a **recursive** rule for a sequence, the first term of the sequence is given and the nth term is defined by relating it to the previous term. An arithmetic sequence can be defined using either a recursive rule or an explicit rule.

Example 1 Write a recursive rule and an explicit rule for the sequence described by each table.

(A) The table shows the monthly balance in a savings account with regular monthly deposits. The savings account begins with $2000, and $500 is deposited each month.

Time (months)	n	1	2	3	4	5
Balance	$f(n)$	2000	2500	3000	3500	4000

Write a recursive rule.

$f(1) = 2000$, and the common difference d is 500.

The recursive rule is $f(1) = 2000$, $f(n) = f(n-1) + 500$ for $n \geq 2$.

Write an explicit rule.

n	$f(n)$	$f(1) + d \cdot x = f(n)$
1	2000	$2000 + 500(0) = 2000$
2	2500	$2000 + 500(1) = 2500$
3	3000	$2000 + 500(2) = 3000$

Since d is always multiplied by a number equal to $(n-1)$, you can generalize the result from the table. The explicit rule is $f(n) = 2000 + 500(n-1)$.

(B) The table shows the monthly balance in a savings account with regular monthly deposits.

Time (months)	n	1	2	3	4	5
Balance	$f(n)$	5000	6000	7000	8000	9000

Write a recursive rule.

$f(1) = 5000$ and the common difference d is 1000.

The recursive rule is $f(1) = 5000$, $f(n) = f(n-1) + 1000$ for $n \geq 2$.

Write an explicit rule.

n	$f(n)$	$f(1) + d \cdot x = f(n)$
1	5000	$5000 + 1000(0) = 5000$
2	6000	$5000 + 1000(1) = 6000$
3	7000	$5000 + 1000(2) = 7000$

Since d is always multiplied by a number equal to $(n-1)$, you can generalize the result from the table. $f(n) = 5000 + 1000(n-1)$.

Reflect

3. **Critique Reasoning** Jerome says that the sequence 1, 8, 27, 64, 125,... is not an arithmetic sequence. Is that correct? Explain.

4. An arithmetic sequence has a common difference of 3. If you know that the third term of the sequence is 15, how can you find the fourth term?

5. The table shows the number of plates left at a buffet after n hours. Write a recursive rule and an explicit rule for the arithmetic sequence represented by the table.

Time (hours)	n	1	2	3	4	5
Number of plates	$f(n)$	155	141	127	113	99

⚙ Explain 2 Using a General Form to Construct Rules for Arithmetic Sequences

Arithmetic sequences can be described by a set of general rules. Values can be substituted into these rules to find a recursive and explicit rule for a given sequence.

General Recursive Rule	General Explicit Rule
Given $f(1)$, $f(n) = f(n-1) + d$ for $n \geq 2$	$f(n) = f(1) + d(n-1)$

Example 2 Write a general recursive and general explicit rule for each arithmetic sequence.

(A) 100, 88, 76, 64, . . .

$f(1) = 100$, common difference $= 88 - 100 = -12$

The recursive rule is $f(1) = 100$, $f(n) = f(n-1) - 12$ for $n \geq 2$.

The explicit rule is $f(n) = 100 - 12(n-1)$.

(B) 0, 8, 16, 24, 32, . . .

$f(1) = 0$, common difference $= 8 - 0 = 8$.

The recursive rule is $f(1) = 0$, $f(n) = f(n-1) + 8$ for $n \geq 2$.

The explicit rule is $f(n) = 0 + 8\,(n-1)$.

Reflect

6. What is the recursive rule for the sequence $f(n) = 2 + (-3)(n-1)$? How do you know?

7. Write a recursive rule and an explicit rule for the arithmetic sequence 6, 16, 26, 36, . . .

⚙ Explain 3 Relating Arithmetic Sequences and Functions

The explicit rule for an arithmetic sequence can be expressed as a function. You can use the graph of the function to write an explicit rule.

Example 3 Write an explicit rule in function notation for each arithmetic sequence.

(A) The cost of a whitewater rafting trip depends on the number of passengers. The base fee is $50, and the cost per passenger is $25. The graph shows the sequence.

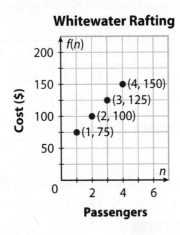

Whitewater Rafting

Step 1 Represent the sequence in a table.

Number of passengers n	1	2	3	4
Cost ($) $f(n)$	75	100	125	150

Step 2 Find the common difference.

$f(2) - f(1) = 100 - 75 = 25$

$f(3) - f(2) = 125 - 100 = 25$

$f(4) - f(3) = 150 - 125 = 25$

The common difference d is 25.

Step 3 Write an explicit rule for the sequence.

Substitute 75 for $f(1)$ and 25 for d.

$f(n) = f(1) + d(n - 1)$

$f(n) = 75 + 25(n - 1)$

(B) The number of seats per row in an auditorium depends on which row it is. The first row has 6 seats, the second row has 9 seats, the third row has 12 seats, and so on. The graph shows the sequence.

Step 1 Represent the sequence in a table.

Row number n	1	2	3	4
Number of seats $f(n)$	6	9	12	15

Step 2 Find the common difference.

$f(2) - f(1) = \boxed{9} - \boxed{6} = \boxed{3}$

$f(3) - f(2) = \boxed{12} - \boxed{9} = \boxed{3}$

$f(4) - f(3) = \boxed{15} - \boxed{12} = \boxed{3}$

Auditorium Seats

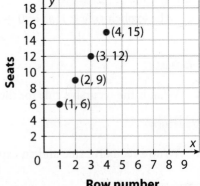

The common difference is $d = 3$.

Step 3 Write an explicit rule for the sequence.

$$f(n) = f(1) + d(n-1)$$

Substitute 6 for $f(1)$ and 3 for d.

$$f(n) = \boxed{6} + \boxed{3}(n-1)$$

Reflect

8. **Analyze Relationships** Compare the graph of the function $f(x) = 3 + 5(x-1)$ and the graph of the sequence $f(n) = 3 + 5(n-1)$.

YourTurn

9. Jerry collects hats. The total number of hats in Jerry's collection depends on how many years he has been collecting hats. After the first year, Jerry had 10 hats. Each year he has added the same number of hats to his collection. The graph shows the sequence. Write an explicit rule in function notation for the arithmetic sequence.

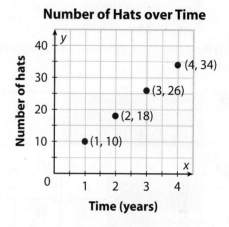

Number of Hats over Time

Elaborate

10. What information do you need to write a recursive rule for an arithmetic sequence that you do not need to write an explicit rule?

11. Suppose you want to be able to determine the ninetieth term in an arithmetic sequence and you have both an explicit and a recursive rule. Which rule would you use? Explain.

12. **Essential Question Check-In** The explicit equation for an arithmetic sequence and a linear equation have a similar form. How is the value of m in the linear equation $y = mx + b$ similar to the value of d in the explicit equation $f(n) = f(1) + d(n-1)$?

⭐ Evaluate: Homework and Practice

- Online Homework
- Hints and Help
- Extra Practice

1. Farah pays a $25 signup fee to join a car sharing service and a $7 monthly charge. The total cost of using the car sharing service for n months can be found using $C(n) = 25 + 7n$. The table shows the cost of the service for 1, 2, 3, and 4 months.

   a. Copy and complete the table for $C(n) = 25 + 7n$

Months	n	1	2	3	4
Cost ($)	$f(n)$	?	?	?	?

   b. What are the domain and range of the sequence?

   c. What is the common difference d?

Tell whether each sequence is an arithmetic sequence.

2.
a. 6, 7, 8, 9, 10,…

b. 5, 10, 20, 35, 55,…

c. 0, −1, 1, −2, 2,…

d. 1, 16, 81, 625, 1296

e. −2, −4, −6, −8, −10, …

3. **Chemistry** A chemist heats up several unknown substances to determine their boiling point. Use the table to determine whether the sequence is arithmetic. If it is arithmetic, write an explicit rule and a recursive rule for the sequence. If not, explain why it is not arithmetic.

Substance	1	2	3	4	5
Boiling Point (°F)	100	135	149	165	188

Write a recursive rule and an explicit rule for the arithmetic sequence described by each table.

4.

Month	n	1	2	3	4	5
Account balance ($)	$f(n)$	35	32	29	26	23

5.

Tickets	n	1	2	3	4	5
Total cost (S)	$f(n)$	58	65	72	79	86

6.

Month	n	1	2	3	4	5
Total deposits ($)	$f(n)$	84	100	116	132	148

7.

Delivery number	n	1	2	3	4	5
Weight of truck (lb)	$f(n)$	4567	3456	2345	1234	123

8.

Week	n	1	2	3	4	5
Account owed ($)	$f(n)$	125	100	75	50	25

9.

Skaters	n	1	2	3	4	5
Charge for lesson ($)	$f(n)$	60	80	100	120	140

Write a recursive rule and an explicit rule for each arithmetic sequence.

10. 95, 90, 85, 80, 75,…

11. 63, 70, 77, 84, 91,…

12. 86, 101, 116, 131, 146,…

13. 112, 110, 108, 106, 104,…

14. 5, 9, 13, 17, 21,…

15. 67, 37, 7, −23, −53,…

Write an explicit rule in function notation for each arithmetic sequence.

16. A student loan needs to be paid off beginning the first year after graduation. Beginning at Year 1, there is $52,000 remaining to be paid. The graduate makes regular payments of $8,000 each year. The graph shows the sequence.

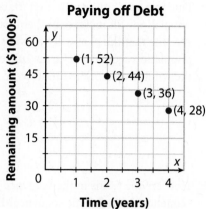

Paying off Debt

17. A grocery cart is 38 inches long. When the grocery carts are put away in a nested row, the length of the row depends on how many carts are nested together. Each cart added to the row adds 12 inches to the row length. The graph shows the sequence.

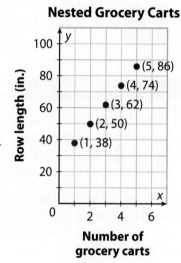

Nested Grocery Carts

18. A dog food for overweight dogs claims that a dog weighing 85 pounds will lose about 2 pounds per week for the first 4 weeks when following the recommended feeding guidelines. The graph shows the sequence.

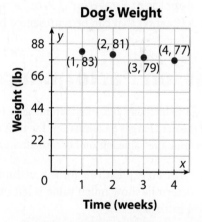

Dog's Weight

19. A savings account is opened with $6300. Monthly deposits of $1100 are made. The graph shows the sequence.

Savings Account Balance

20. Biology The wolf population in a local wildlife area is currently 12. Due to a new conservation effort, conservationists hope the wolf population will increase by 2 animals each year for the next 50 years. Assume that the plan will be successful. Write an explicit rule for the population sequence. Use the rule to predict the number of animals in the wildlife area in the fiftieth year.

21. How are the terms in the sequence in the table related? Is the sequence an arithmetic sequence? Explain.

n	1	2	3	4	5
f(n)	3	9	27	81	243

H.O.T. Focus on Higher Order Thinking

22. Explain the Error The cost of a hamburger is $2.50. Each additional hamburger costs $2.00. Sully wrote this explicit rule to explain the sequence of costs: $f(n) = 2 + 2.5(n - 1)$. Using this rule, he found the cost of 12 hamburgers to be $29.50. Is this number correct? If not, identify Sully's error.

23. Critical Thinking Lucia knows the fourth term in a sequence is 55 and the ninth term in the same sequence is 90. Explain how she can find the common difference for the sequence. Then use the common difference to find the second term of the sequence.

24. Represent Real-World Problems Write and solve a real-world problem involving a situation that can be represented by the sequence $f(n) = 15 + 2(n - 1)$.

Lesson Performance Task

For Carl's birthday, his grandparents gave him a $50 gift card to a local movie theater. The theater charges $6 admission for each movie. How can Carl use an arithmetic sequence to determine the value left on his card after each movie he sees?

a. Write an explicit rule for the arithmetic sequence and use it to determine how much value is left on the card after Carl has seen 4 movies.

b. How much is left on the card after Carl has seen the maximum number of movies?

4.3 Modeling with Arithmetic Sequences

Essential Question: How can you solve real-world problems using arithmetic sequences?

⊙ Explore Interpreting Models of Arithmetic Sequences

You can model real-world situations and solve problems using models of arithmetic sequences. For example, suppose watermelons cost $6.50 each at the local market. The total cost, in dollars, of n watermelons can be found using $c(n) = 6.5n$.

(A) Copy and complete the table of values for 1, 2, 3, and 4 watermelons.

Watermelons n	1	2	3	4
Total cost ($) $c(n)$	?	?	?	?

(B) What is the common difference?

(C) What does n represent in this context?

(D) What are the dependent and independent variables in this context?

(E) Find $c(7)$. What does this value represent?

Reflect

1. **Discussion** What domain values make sense for $c(n) = 6.5n$ in this situation?

🔧 Explain 1 Modeling Arithmetic Sequences From a Table

Given a table of data values from a real-world situation involving an arithmetic sequence, you can construct a function model and use it to solve problems.

Example 1 Construct an explicit rule in function notation for the arithmetic sequence represented in the table. Then interpret the meaning of a specific term of the sequence in the given context.

Ⓐ Suppose the table shows the cost, in dollars, of postage per ounce of a letter.

Number of ounces	n	1	2	3	4
Cost ($) of postage	$f(n)$	0.35	0.55	0.75	0.95

Determine the value of $f(9)$, and tell what it represents in this situation.

Find the common difference, d. $d = 0.55 - 0.35 = 0.20$

Substitute 0.35 for $f(1)$ and 0.20 for d.

$f(n) = f(1) + d(n - 1)$

$f(n) = 0.35 + 0.20(n - 1)$

$f(9) = 0.35 + 0.20(8) = 1.95$

So, the cost of postage for a 9-ounce letter is $1.95.

Ⓑ The table shows the cumulative total interest paid, in dollars, on a loan after each month.

Number of months	n	1	2	3	4
Cumulative total ($)	$f(n)$	160	230	300	370

Determine the value of $f(20)$ and tell what it represents in this situation.

Find the common difference, d. $d = \boxed{230} - 160 = \boxed{70}$

Substitute $\boxed{160}$ for $f(1)$ and $\boxed{70}$ for d.

$f(n) = f(1) + d(n - 1)$

$f(n) = \boxed{160} + \boxed{70}\,(n - 1)$

Find $f(20)$ and interpret the value in context.

$f(n) = f(1) + d(n - 1)$

$f\left(\boxed{20}\right) = \boxed{160} + \boxed{70}\left(\boxed{19}\right) = \boxed{1490}$

So, the cumulative total interest paid after 20 months is $1490.

Your Turn

Construct an explicit rule in function notation for the arithmetic sequence represented in the table. Then interpret the meaning of a specific term of the sequence in the given context.

2. The table shows $f(n)$, the distance, in miles, from the store after Mila has traveled for n hours.

Time (h)	n	1	2	3	4
Distance (mi)	$f(n)$	20	32	44	56

Determine the value of $f(10)$ and tell what it represents in this situation.

3. The table below shows the total cost, in dollars, of purchasing n battery packs.

Number of battery packs	n	1	2	3	4
Total cost ($)	$f(n)$	4.90	8.90	12.90	16.90

Determine the value of $f(18)$ and tell what it represents in this situation.

Explain 2 **Modeling Arithmetic Sequences From a Graph**

Given a graph of a real-world situation involving an arithmetic sequence, you can construct a function model and use it to solve problems.

Example 2   Construct an explicit rule in function notation for the arithmetic sequence represented in the graph, and use it to solve the problem.

(A) D'Andre collects feather pens. The graph shows the number of feather pens D'Andre has collected over time, in weeks. According to this pattern, how many feather pens will D'Andre have collected in 12 weeks?

Represent the sequence in a table.

n	1	2	3	4
$f(n)$	18	37	56	75

Find the common difference.

$d = 37 - 18 = 19$

Use the general explicit rule for an arithmetic sequence to write the rule in function notation. Substitute 18 for $f(1)$ and 19 for d.

$f(n) = f(1) + d(n - 1)$

$f(n) = 18 + 19(n - 1)$

To determine the number of feather pens D'Andre will have collected after 12 weeks,

find $f(12)$.

$f(n) = 18 + 19(n - 1)$

$f(12) = 18 + 19(11)$

$f(12) = 18 + 209$

$f(12) = 227$

So, if this pattern continues, D'Andre will have collected 227 feather pens in 12 weeks.

(B) Eric collects stamps. The graph shows the number of stamps that Eric has collected over time, in months. According to this pattern, how many stamps will Eric have collected in 10 months?

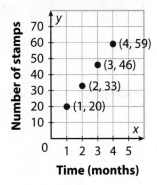

Represent the sequence in a table.

n	1	2	3	4
$f(n)$	20	33	46	59

Find the common difference.

$$d = \boxed{33} - 20 = \boxed{13}$$

Use the general explicit rule for an arithmetic sequence to write the rule in function notation.

Substitute $\boxed{20}$ for $f(1)$ and $\boxed{13}$ for d.

$$f(n) = f(1) + d(n - 1)$$

$$f(n) = \boxed{20} + \boxed{13}\,(n - 1)$$

To determine the number of stamps Eric will have collected in 10 months, find $f\left(\boxed{10}\right)$.

$$f(n) = f(1) + d(n - 1)$$
$$f\left(\boxed{10}\right) = \boxed{20} + \boxed{13}\left(\boxed{9}\right) = \boxed{137}$$

So, if this pattern continues, Eric will have collected 137 stamps in 10 months.

Reflect

4. How do you know which variable is the independent variable and which variable is the dependent variable in a real-world situation involving an arithmetic sequence?

Your Turn

Construct an explicit rule in function notation for the arithmetic sequence represented in the graph, and use it to solve the problem.

5. The graph shows the height, in inches, of a stack of boxes on a table as the number of boxes in the stack increases. Find the height of the stack with 7 boxes.

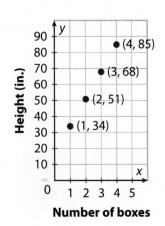

6. Quynh begins to save the same amount each month to save for a future shopping trip. The graph shows total amount she has saved after each month, *n*. What will be the total amount Quynh has saved after 12 months?

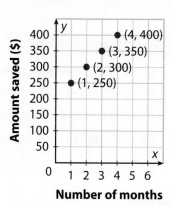

Explain 3 Modeling Arithmetic Sequences From a Description

Given a description of a real-world situation involving an arithmetic sequence, you can construct a function model and use it to solve problems.

Example 3 Construct an explicit rule in function notation for the arithmetic sequence represented, and use it to solve the problem. Justify and evaluate your answer.

The odometer on a car reads 34,240 on Day 1. Every day the car is driven 57 miles. If this pattern continues, what will the odometer read on Day 15?

Analyze Information

- The odometer on the car reads 34,240 miles on Day 1.
- Every day the car is driven 57 miles.

$f(1) = 34{,}240$ and
$d = 57$

Formulate a Plan

Write an explicit rule in function notation for the arithmetic sequence, and use it to find $f(15)$, the odometer reading on Day 15.

Solve

$$f(n) = f(1) + d(n - 1)$$

$$f(n) = \boxed{34{,}240} + \boxed{57}\ (n - 1)$$

$$f\left(\boxed{15}\right) = \boxed{34{,}240} + \boxed{57}\left(\boxed{14}\right)$$

$$f\left(\boxed{15}\right) = \boxed{35{,}038}$$

On the Day 15, the odometer will show 35,038 miles.

Using an arithmetic sequence model is reasonable because the number of miles on the odometer increases by the same amount each day.

By rounding and estimation:

$34{,}200 + 60(14) = \boxed{34{,}200} + \boxed{840} = \boxed{35{,}040}$ miles

So 35,038 miles is a reasonable answer.

Your Turn

Construct an explicit rule in function notation for the arithmetic sequence represented, and use it to solve the problem. Justify and evaluate your answer.

7. Ruby signed up for a frequent-flier program. She receives 3400 frequent-flier miles for the first round-trip she takes and 1200 frequent-flier miles for all additional round-trips. How many frequent-flier miles will Ruby have after 5 round-trips?

8. A gym charges each member $100 for the first month, which includes a membership fee, and $50 per month for each month after that. How much money will a person spend on their gym membership for 6 months?

💬 Elaborate

9. What domain values usually make sense for an arithmetic sequence model that represents a real-world situation?

10. When given a graph of an arithmetic sequence that represents a real-world situation, how can you determine the first term and the common difference in order to write a model for the sequence?

11. What are some ways to justify your answer when creating an arithmetic sequence model for a real-world situation and using it to solve a problem?

12. Essential Question Check-In How can you construct a model for a real-world situation that involves an arithmetic sequence?

⭐ Evaluate: Homework and Practice

- Online Homework
- Hints and Help
- Extra Practice

1. A T-shirt at a department store costs $7.50. The total cost, in dollars, of a T-shirts is given by the function $C(a) = 7.5a$.

a. Copy and complete the table of values for 4 T-shirts.

T-shirts	1	2	3	4
Cost ($)	?	?	?	?

b. Determine the common difference.

c. What does the variable a represent? What are the reasonable domain values for a?

2. A car dealership sells 5 cars per day. The total number of cars C sold over time in days is given by the function $C(t) = 5t$.

   a. Copy and complete the table of values for the first 4 days of sales.

Time (days)	1	2	3	4
Number of Cars	?	?	?	?

   b. Determine the common difference.

   c. What do the variables represent? What are the reasonable domain and range values for this situation?

3. A telemarketer makes 82 calls per day. The total number of calls made over time, in days, is given by the function $C(t) = 82t$.

   a. Copy and complete the table of values for 4 days of calls.

Time (days)	1	2	3	4
Number of Calls	?	?	?	?

   b. Determine the common difference.

   c. What do the variables represent? What are the reasonable domain and range values for this situation?

Construct an explicit rule in function notation for the arithmetic sequence represented in the table. Then determine the value of the given term, and explain what it means.

4. Darnell starts saving the same amount from each week's paycheck. The table shows the total balance $f(n)$ of his savings account over time in weeks.

Time (weeks) n	1	2	3	4
Savings Account Balance($) $f(n)$	$250	$380	$510	$640

Determine the value of $f(9)$, and explain what it represents in this situation.

5. Juan is traveling to visit universities. He notices mile markers along the road. He records the mile markers every 10 minutes. His father is driving at a constant speed. Copy and complete the table.

   a.

Time Interval	Mile Marker
1	520
2	509
3	498
4	?
5	?
6	?

   b. Find $f(10)$, and tell what it represents in this situation.

Construct an explicit rule in function notation for the arithmetic sequence represented in the graph. Then determine the value of the given term, and explain what it means.

6. The graph shows total cost of a whitewater rafting trip and the corresponding number of passengers on the trip. Find $f(8)$, and explain what it represents.

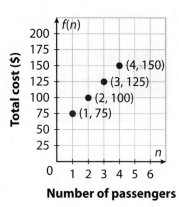

7. Ed collects autographs. The graph shows the total number of autographs that Ed has collected over time, in weeks. Find $f(12)$, and explain what it represents.

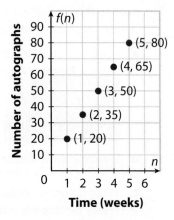

8. Finance Bob purchased a bus pass card with 320 points. Each week costs 20 points for unlimited bus rides. The graph shows the points remaining on the card over time in weeks. Determine the value of $f(10)$, and explain what it represents.

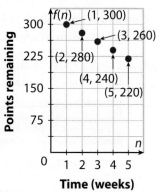

9. Biology The local wolf population is declining. The graph shows the local wolf population over time, in weeks. Find $f(9)$, and explain what it represents.

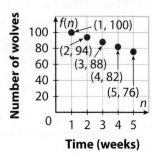

Construct an explicit rule in function notation for the arithmetic sequence. Then determine the value of the given term, and explain what it means.

10. **Economics** To package and ship an item, it costs $5.75 for the first pound and $0.75 for each additional pound. Find the 12th term, and explain what it represents.

11. A new bag of cat food weighs 18 pounds. At the end of each day, 0.5 pound of food is removed to feed the cats. Find the 30th term, and explain what it represents.

12. Carrie borrows $960 interest-free to pay for a car repair. She will repay $120 monthly until the loan is paid off. How many months will it take Carrie to pay off the loan? Explain.

13. The rates for a go-kart course are shown.

Number of Laps n	1	2	3	4
Total cost ($) $f(n)$	7	9	11	13

   a. What is the total cost for 15 laps?

   b. Suppose that after paying for 9 laps, the 10th lap is free. Will the sequence still be arithmetic? Explain.

14. **Multi-Part** Seats in a concert hall are arranged in the pattern shown.

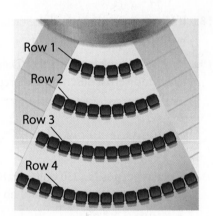

   a. The numbers of seats in the rows form an arithmetic sequence. Write a rule for the arithmetic sequence.

   b. How many seats are in Row 15?

   c. Each ticket costs $40. If every seat in the first 10 rows is filled, what is the total revenue from those seats?

   d. An extra chair is added to each row. Write the new rule for the arithmetic sequence and find the new total revenue from the first 10 rows.

H.O.T. **Focus on Higher Order Thinking**

15. **Explain the Error** The table shows the number of people who attend an amusement park over time, in days.

Time (days) n	1	2	3	4
Number of people $f(n)$	75	100	125	150

Sam writes an explicit rule for this arithmetic sequence:
$$f(n) = 25 + 75(n - 1)$$

He then claims that according to this pattern, 325 people will attend the amusement park on Day 5. Explain the error that Sam made.

16. **Communicate Mathematical Ideas** Explain why it may be harder to find the nth value of an arithmetic sequence from a graph if the points are not labeled.

17. **Make a prediction** Verona is training for a marathon. The first part of her training schedule is given in the table.

Session *n*	1	2	3	4	5	6
Distance (mi) *f*(*n*)	3.5	5	6.5	8	9.5	11

a. Is this training schedule an arithmetic sequence? Explain. If it is, write an explicit rule for the sequence.

b. If Verona continues this pattern, during which training session will she run 26 miles?

18. If Verona's training schedule starts on a Monday and she runs every third day, on which day will she run 26 miles?

19. **Multiple Representations** Determine whether the following graph, table, and verbal description all represent the same arithmetic sequence.

Time (months) *n*	1	2	3	4
Amount of money ($) *f*(*n*)	250	300	350	400

A person deposits $250 dollars into a bank account. Each month, he adds $25 dollars to the account, and no other transactions occur in the account.

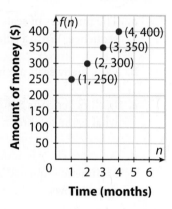

Lesson Performance Task

The graph shows the population of Ivor's ant colony over the first four weeks. Assume the ant population will continue to grow at the same rate.

a. Write an explicit rule in function notation.

b. If Ivor's ants have a mass of 1.5 grams each, what will be the total mass of all of his ants in 13 weeks?

c. When the colony reaches 1385 ants, Ivor's ant farm will not be big enough for all of them. In how many weeks will the ant ipopulation be too large?

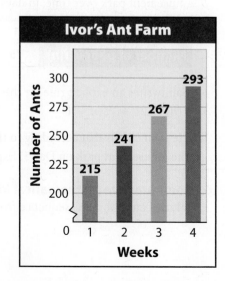

Patterns and Sequences

Essential Question: How are patterns and sequences used to solve real-world problems?

© Houghton Mifflin Harcourt Publishing Company

Key Vocabulary

arithmetic sequence
(sucesión aritmética)

common difference
(diferencia común)

explicit rule *(fórmula explícita)*

recursive rule
(fórmula recurrente)

sequence *(sucesión)*

term *(término)*

KEY EXAMPLE   *(Lesson 4.1)*

A software subscription is \$4 a month plus a start-up fee of \$8. Use the explicit rule $f(n) = 4n + 8$. Construct and graph the first 4 terms of the sequence described.

n	1	2	3	4
f(n)	12	16	20	24

Represent the sequence in a table.

(1, 12), (2, 16), (3, 20), (4, 24)   *Generate ordered pairs.*

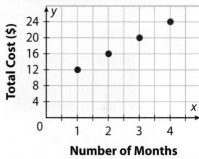

KEY EXAMPLE   *(Lesson 4.2)*

Write a recursive rule and an explicit rule for the sequence 20, 14, 8, 2 ….

$f(1) = 20, d = 14 - 20 = -6$ *Find the first term and common difference.*

Given $f(1), f(n) = f(n - 1) + d$ for $n \geq 2$.   *Use the general form of the recursive rule.*

Recursive Rule: $f(1) = 20, f(n) = f(n - 1) - 6$

$f(n) = f(1) + d(n - 1)$ *Use the general form of the explicit rule.*

Explicit Rule: $f(n) = 20 - 6(n - 1)$

KEY EXAMPLE   *(Lesson 4.3)*

Construct an explicit rule in function notation for the arithmetic sequence represented in the graph, and use it to solve the problem.

The graph shows the total predicted sales $f(n)$ for the next n days at a clothing store. What are the total predicted sales on day 10?

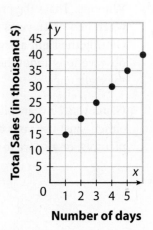

15, 20, 25, 30…   *Write a sequence to represent the information.*

$d = 20 - 15 = 5$ *Find the common difference.*

$f(n) = f(1) + d(n - 1)$ *Use the general explicit rule.*

$f(n) = 15 + 5(n - 1)$

$f(10) = 15 + 5(10 - 1)$ *Find $f(10)$.*

$f(10) = 60$

The total predicted sales on day 10 are \$60,000.

EXERCISES

Write the first 4 terms of each sequence following the given rule. *(Lesson 4.1)*

1. $f(n) = n^2 - 4$

2. $f(1) = -12, f(n) = 2f(n-1)$

Determine if each of the following sequences is arithmetic. If so, write a recursive rule and an explicit rule for the sequence. If not, explain why. *(Lesson 4.2)*

3. $-8, -1, 6, 13\ldots$

4. $1, 8, 27, 81\ldots$

5. The table below shows the balance of a savings account each month after being opened. The balance can be represented with an arithmetic sequence. Write an explicit rule and a recursive rule for the sequence. What will the account balance be after 10 months? *(Lesson 4.3)*

Time (months)	1	2	3	4
Balance ($)	750	715	680	645

MODULE PERFORMANCE TASK

There Has to Be an Easier Way

Quick, now, what's the sum: $1 + 2$?

Okay, you got that one. How about this: $1 + 2 + 3$?

You're really sailing along! Okay, how about this one: $1 + 2 + 3 + \ldots + 98 + 99 + 100$?

Whoops. That's the problem that mathematician Carl Friedrich Gauss solved quickly when he was 10 years old. And that's the problem you're being asked to solve now. Getting the right answer isn't as important as coming up with some interesting observations about the problem or some ideas that might lead you in the direction of the right answer.

Gauss was 10 years old in 1787, so he didn't have a calculator! No calculator for you either—just use your own paper to work on the task. Then use numbers, words, pictures, or algebra to explain how you reached your conclusion.

(Ready) to Go On?

4.1–4.3 Patterns and Sequences

- Online Homework
- Hints and Help
- Extra Practice

Write the first 4 terms of each sequence defined by the rule given. *(Lesson 4.1)*

1. $f(1) = 8, f(n) = f(n-1) - 4$

2. $f(n) = \dfrac{n^2}{2}$

Write a recursive rule and an explicit rule for each arithmetic sequence. Then, find the 20th term of each sequence. *(Lessons 4.2, 4.3)*

3. $2, 0, -2, -4 \ldots$

4. $45, 55, 65, 75 \ldots$

5. Each Saturday, Tina mows lawns to earn extra money which she puts into a savings account. The graph shows the balance of Tina's savings account over the first six weeks of mowing lawns. Write an explicit function to describe this sequence. According to this pattern, how much will Tina have in her account after 15 weeks of mowing lawns? *(Lesson 4.3)*

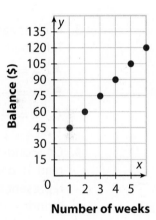

Number of weeks

ESSENTIAL QUESTION

6. What are two ways of representing an arithmetic sequence?

Assessment Readiness

1. Consider a sequence defined by the recursive rule $f(1) = 15$; $f(n) = f(n - 1) - 6$ for $n \geq 2$. Determine if each statement is True or False.

   A. The second term of the sequence is 8.

   B. The third term of the sequence is 3.

   C. The fourth term of the sequence is -3.

2. The cost of renting a moped for 1, 2, 3, or 4 hours and can be represented by an arithmetic sequence. The base fee is $30, and the cost per hour is $15. The graph shows the sequence. Determine if each statement is True or False.

   A. The domain of the sequence is $\{1, 2, 3, 4\}$.

   B. The range of the sequence is the set of all real numbers.

   C. An explicit rule for the sequence is $f(n) = 15 + 30n$.

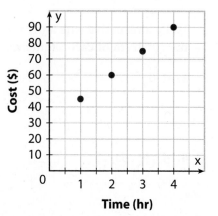

3. Look at each possible solution of the inequality $-12 < 2x + 8 < -6$ below. Tell whether each solution is correct.

   A. $x = -10$

   B. $x = -8$

   C. $x = -14$

4. On Monday, Mr. Sanchez started reading a 225-page biography. He plans to read 15 pages each day until he finishes the book. Write an explicit function to represent the number of pages he has left to read depending on the day number; Monday is day number 1, Tuesday is day number 2, and so on. Find f(5) and interpret its meaning in this situation.

• Online Homework
• Hints and Help
• Extra Practice

1. Write $18z - 7(-3 + 2z)$ in simplest form. Determine if each statement is True or False.

   A. The expression has 2 terms.

   B. The coefficient of z is 13.

   C. The constant is 21.

2. The relation shown in the table represents the number of various books sold and their total cost.

Number of books sold, x	Cost ($), y
1	5
2	6
2	8
4	12

   Determine if each statement is True or False.

   A. The domain is all real numbers.

   B. The range is $\{5, 6, 8, 12\}$.

   C. The relation is a function.

3. A dog walker charges a flat rate of $6 per walk plus an hourly rate of $30. How much does the dog walker charge for a 45 minute walk? Write an equation in function notation for the situation, and then use it to solve the problem. Determine if the given statement is True or False.

   A. The dependent variable is the number of hours.

   B. The function for the walker's fee is $f(h) = 30h + 6$.

   C. The dog walker charges $22.50 for a 45 minute walk.

4. Consider a sequence defined by the explicit rule $f(n) = -8 + 3(n - 1)$. Determine if each statement is True or False.

   A. $f(1) = -8$

   B. The common difference is 3.

   C. The fifth term of the sequence is 7.

5. Graph $f(x) = -2x + 4$. What is x when $f(x) = -8$? Explain how you found x.

6. Find the first 4 terms of the sequence defined by the explicit rule $f(n) = 7(n - 1) - 10$. Is it an arithmetic sequence? Explain your answer.

Performance Tasks

★ **7.** A construction company's cost to build a new home is $35,000 plus $95 for each square foot of floor space.

    A. Find a function for the cost c to build a house with f square feet of floor space.

    B. Use your function to determine how much it will cost to build a house that contains 1600 square feet.

★★ **8.** The weight in pounds that can be supported by a diving board is given by the function $w(x) = \dfrac{5000}{x}$, where x is the distance in feet from the base to a point along the length of the diving board.

    A. What is the domain of the function? Can the domain include zero? Explain.

    B. Make a table of values and generate five ordered pairs to represent the function.

    C. Plot the ordered pairs (x, w), and draw a smooth curve connecting the points.

★★★ **9.** The results of a test of an alloy are shown in the table. Stress is the tension force per unit area, and strain is deformation of the alloy.

Strain (m/m)	0.01	0.02	0.03	0.04	0.05	0.06	0.07	0.08	0.09
Stress (MPa)	100	200	300	400	500	540	560	550	525

A. Make a graph of the data using strain on the horizontal axis.

B. Hooke's law states that stress is directly proportional to strain. For what domain does the material obey Hooke's law? How did you determine your answer?

C. Write a function to represent Hooke's law for this material.

D. The ultimate tensile strength is the maximum stress value on the stress-strain curve. What are the stress and strain values for this material's ultimate tensile strength?

Interior Designer Ben is an interior designer and plans to have part of a floor tiled with 36 square tiles. The tiles come in whole-number side lengths from 2 to 6 inches.

a. Write a function for the area, $A(s)$, where s is the side length of the tile.

b. Identify the domain of this function.

c. Make a table of values for this domain. Write the results as ordered pairs in the form (independent variable, dependent variable).

d. Graph the function by plotting the ordered pairs.

e. What does the function evaluated at $s = 3$ mean in this context?

UNIT 3

Linear Functions, Equations, and Inequalities

MATH IN CAREERS

Wildlife Field Researcher Wildlife field researchers observe wildlife and their habitats. Wildlife field researchers utilize geometry and trigonometry when surveying habitats. They use statistics, exponential functions, and differential equations to study population changes.

If you are interested in a career as a wildlife field researcher, you should study these mathematical subjects:
- Algebra
- Geometry
- Trigonometry
- Calculus
- Differential Equations

Research other careers that require using exponential equations to understand populations. Check out the career activity at the end of the unit to find out how **wildlife field researchers** use math.

Visualize Vocabulary

Copy the diagram and use the ✔ words to complete it. You will put one word in each oval.

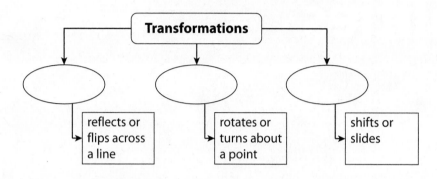

Vocabulary

Review Words
✔ function (*función*)
✔ reflection (*reflexión*)
✔ rotation (*rotación*)
✔ transformation (*transformación*)

Preview Words
boundary line *(línea de límite)*
constant of variation *(constante de variación)*
parent function *(función madre)*
rate of change *(tasa de cambio)*
slope *(pendiente)*
x-intercept *(intersección con el eje x)*
y-intercept *(intersección con el eje x)*

Understand Vocabulary

Complete the sentences using the preview words.

1. The __?__ of a graph is the *y*-coordinate of the point where the graph intersects the *y*-axis.

2. The __?__ of a graph is the *x*-coordinate of the point where the graph intersects the *x*-axis.

3. A __?__ is a line that divides a coordinate plane into two halves.

Active Reading

Layered Book Before beginning the unit, create a layered book to help you learn the concepts in this unit. Label the flaps "Linear Functions," "Forms of Linear Equations," and "Linear Equations and Inequalities." As you study the lessons in each module, write important ideas, such as vocabulary, and sample problems under the appropriate flap.

Linear Functions

Essential Question: How can you use a linear function to solve real-world problems?

REAL WORLD VIDEO
Cyclists adjust their gears to climb up a steep grade or through rocky terrain. Check out how gear ratios, rates of speed, and slope ratios can be used to solve problems involving speed, distance, and time when mountain biking.

MODULE PERFORMANCE TASK PREVIEW

How Many Cups Do You Need?

Paper or foam cups are convenient for drinking out of, but they can also be used to explore mathematical concepts. They can be used to build a structure by stacking individual cups. Just how many cups would you need to build a structure the same height as your math teacher? Get ready to discover the mathematics of cup-stacking!

Are YOU Ready?

Complete these exercises to review skills you will need for this module.

Slope

Example 1   Describe the slope of the line that joins the points.

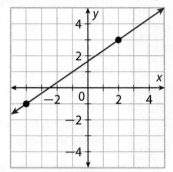

The slope is positive if the line slants up.

The slope is negative if the line slants down.

The slope is 0 if the line is horizontal.

The slope is undefined if the line is vertical.

The line slants up, so the slope is positive.

Describe the slope of the line that joins the points.

1.

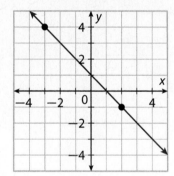

2.

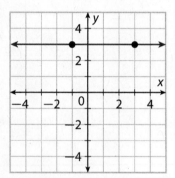

Multi-Step Equations

Example 2   Solve.

$$3x + 5 + 4x - 9 = 24$$

$$7x - 4 = 24 \qquad \text{Combine like terms.}$$

$$7x - 4 + 4 = 24 + 4 \qquad \text{Add 4 to both sides of the equation.}$$

$$7x = 28$$

$$\frac{7x}{7} = \frac{28}{7} \qquad \text{Divide both sides of the equation by 7.}$$

$$x = 4$$

Solve each equation.

3. $3(2n - 7) + 12 = 39$

4. $4a + 23 - 9a - 17 = 21$

5.1 Understanding Linear Functions

Essential Question: What is a linear function?

⊘ Explore 1 Recognizing Linear Functions

A race car can travel up to 210 mph. If the car could travel continuously at this speed, $y = 210x$ gives the number of miles y that the car would travel in x hours. Solutions are shown in the graph below.

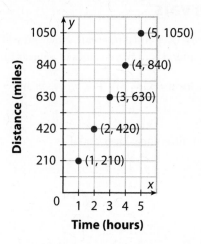

The graph of the car's speed is a function because every x-value is paired with exactly one y-value. Because the graph is a non-vertical straight line, it is also a **linear function.**

(A) Create a table of x- and y-values using the data points from the graph above.

(B) Using the table, check that x has a constant change between consecutive terms.

(C) Now check that y has a constant change between consecutive terms.

(D) Using the answers from before, what change in x corresponds to what change in y?

(E) All linear functions behave similarly to the one in this example. Based on this information,

a generalization can be made that a [?] change in x will correspond to a [?] change in y.

1. **Discussion** Will a non-linear function have a constant change in x that corresponds to a constant change in y?

2. $y = x^2$ represents a typical non-linear function. Using the table of values, check whether a constant change in x corresponds to a constant change in y.

x	$y = x^2$
1	1
2	4
3	9
4	16
5	25

⊘ Explore 2   Proving Linear Functions Grow by Equal Differences Over Equal Intervals

Linear functions change by a constant amount (change by equal differences) over equal intervals. Now you will explore the proofs of these statements. $x_2 - x_1$ and $x_4 - x_3$ represent two intervals in the x-values of a linear function.

It is also important to know that any linear function can be written in the form $f(x) = mx + b$, where m and b are constants.

Copy and complete the proof that linear functions grow by equal differences over equal intervals.

Given: $x_2 - x_1 = x_4 - x_3$

f is a linear function of the form $f(x) = mx + b$.

Prove: $f(x_2) - f(x_1) = f(x_4) - f(x_3)$

Proof: 1. $x_2 - x_1 = x_4 - x_3$ Given.

      2. $m(x_2 - x_1) = \boxed{?}\ (x_4 - x_3)$ Mult. Property of Equality

      3. $mx_2 - \boxed{?} = mx_4 - \boxed{?}$ $\boxed{?}$

      4. $mx_2 + b - mx_1 - b = mx_4 + \boxed{?} - mx_3 - \boxed{?}$ $\boxed{?}$

      5. $mx_2 + b - (mx_1 + b) = mx_4 + b - \boxed{?}$ $\boxed{?}$

      6. $f(x_2) - f(x_1) = \boxed{?}$ Definition of $f(x)$

3. **Discussion** Consider the function $y = x^3$. Use two equal intervals to determine if the function is linear. The table for $y = x^3$ is shown.

x	$y = x^3$
1	1
2	8
3	27
4	64
5	125

4. In the given of the proof it states that: f is a linear function of the form $f(x) = mx + b$. What is the name of the form for this linear function?

🔗 Explain 1   Graphing Linear Functions Given in Standard Form

Any linear function can be represented by a linear equation. A **linear equation** is any equation that can be written in the **standard form** expressed below.

Standard Form of a Linear Equation

$Ax + By = C$ where A, B, and C are real numbers and A and B are not both 0.

Any ordered pair that makes the linear equation true is a **solution of a linear equation in two variables**. The graph of a linear equation represents all the solutions of the equation.

Example 1   Determine whether the equation is linear. If so, graph the function.

Ⓐ $5x + y = 10$

The equation is linear because it is in the standard form of a linear equation:
$A = 5$, $B = 1$, and $C = 10$.

To graph the function, first solve the equation for y.

Make a table and plot the points. Then connect the points.

x	−1	0	1	2	3
y	15	10	5	0	−5

Note that because the domain and range of functions of a non-horizontal line are all real numbers, the graph is continuous.

$$5x + y = 10$$
$$y = 10 - 5x$$

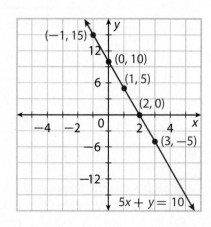

(B) $-4x + y = 11$

The equation is linear because it is in the standard form of a linear equation:

$A = -4$, $B = 1$, and $C = 11$.

$$-4x + y = 11$$

To graph the function, first solve the equation for y.
Make a table and plot the points. Then connect the points.

$$y = 11 + 4x$$

x	−4	−2	0	2	4
y	−5	3	11	19	27

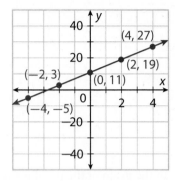

Reflect

5. Write an equation that is linear but is not in standard form.

6. If $A = 0$ in an equation written in standard form, how does the graph look?

Your Turn

7. Determine whether $6x + y = 12$ is linear. If so, graph the function.

🔑 Explain 2   Modeling with Linear Functions

A **discrete function** is a function whose graph has unconnected points, while a **continuous function** is a function whose graph is an unbroken line or curve with no gaps or breaks. For example, a function representing the sale of individual apples is a discrete function because no fractional part of an apple will be represented in a table or a graph. A function representing the sale of apples by the pound is a continuous function because any fractional part of a pound of apples will be represented in a table or graph.

Example 2   Graph each function and give its domain and range.

(A) Sal opens a new video store and pays the film studios $2.00 for each DVD he buys from them. The amount Sal pays is given by $f(x) = 2x$, where x is the number of DVDs purchased.

x	$f(x) = 2x$
0	$f(0) = 2(0) = 0$
1	$f(1) = 2(1) = 2$
2	$f(2) = 2(2) = 4$
3	$f(3) = 2(3) = 6$
4	$f(4) = 2(4) = 8$

DVD Purchases

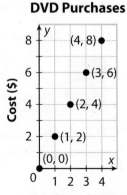

Number of DVDs

This is a discrete function. Since the number of DVDs must be a whole number, the domain is $\{0, 1, 2, 3, \ldots\}$ and the range is $\{0, 2, 4, 6, 8 \ldots\}$.

(B) Elsa rents a booth in her grandfather's mall to open an ice cream stand. She pays $1 to her grandfather for each hour of operation. The amount Elsa pays each hour is given by $f(x) = x$, where x is the number of hours her booth is open.

x	$f(x) = x$	
0	$f(0) =$	0
1	$f(1) =$	1
2	$f(2) =$	2
3	$f(3) =$	3
4	$f(4) =$	4

Ice Cream Booth Rental

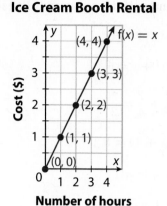

This is a continuous function. The domain is all real numbers greater than 0 and the range is all real numbers greater than 0.

Reflect

8. Why are the points on the graph in Example 2B connected?

9. **Discussion** How is the graph of the function in Example 2A related to the graph of an arithmetic sequence?

Your Turn

10. Kristoff rents a kiosk in the mall to open an umbrella stand. He pays $6 to the mall owner for each umbrella he sells. The amount Kristoff pays is given by $f(x) = 6x$, where x is the number of umbrellas sold. Graph the function and give its domain and range.

💬 **Elaborate**

11. What is a solution of a linear equation in two variables?

12. What type of function has a graph with a series of unconnected points?

13. **Essential Question Check-In** What is the standard form for a linear equation?

Determine if the equation is linear. If so, graph the function.

1. $2x + y = 4$

2. $2x^2 + y = 6$

3. $\frac{2}{x} + \frac{y}{4} = \frac{3}{2}$

4. $3x + 4y = 8$

5. $x + y^2 = 1$

6. $x + y = 1$

State whether each function is discrete or continuous.

7. The number of basketballs manufactured per day

8. $x = \frac{y}{4}$, where x is the number of hours and y is the miles walked

9. The number of bulls eyes scored for each hour of practice

10. $y = 4^4x$, where x is the time and y is gallons of water

11. $y = 35x^1$, where x is distance and y is height

12. The amount of boxes shipped per shift

Graph each function and give its domain and range.

13. Hans opens a new video game store and pays the gaming companies $5.00 for each video game he buys from them. The amount Hans pays is given by $f(x) = 5x$, where x is the number of video games purchased.

14. Peter opens a new bookstore and pays the book publisher $3.00 for each book he buys from them. The amount Peter pays is given by $f(x) = 3x$, where x is the number of books purchased.

15. Steve opens a jewelry shop and makes $15.00 profit for each piece of jewelry sold. The amount Steve makes is given by $f(x) = 15x$, where x is the number of pieces of jewelry sold.

16. Anna owns an airline and pays the airport $35.00 for each ticket sold. The amount Anna pays is given by $f(x) = 35x$, where x is the number of tickets sold.

17. A hot air balloon can travel up to 85 mph. If the balloon travels continuously at this speed, $y = 85x$ gives the number of miles y that the hot air balloon would travel in x hours.

Create a table of x- and y-values using the data points from the graph. Determine whether x and y have constant change between consecutive terms and whether they are in a linear function.

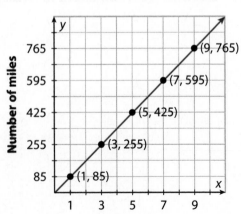

18. State whether each equation is in standard form.

    a. $3x + y = 8$ **b.** $x - y = 15z$ **c.** $x^2 + y = 11$

    d. $3xy + y^2 = 4$ **e.** $x + 4y = 12$ **f.** $5x + 24y = 544$

19. Physics A physicist working in a large laboratory has found that light particles traveling in a particle accelerator increase velocity in a manner that can be described by the linear function $-4x + 3y = 15$, where x is time and y is velocity in kilometers per hour. Use this function to determine when a certain particle will reach 30 km/hr.

20. Travel The graph shows the costs of a hotel for one night for a group traveling. The total cost depends on the number of hotel rooms the group needs. Does the plot follow a linear function? Is the graph discrete or continuous?

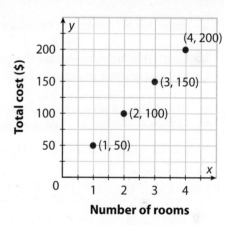

21. Biology The migration pattern of a species of tree frog to different swamp areas over the course of a year can be described using the graph below. Create a table of x- and y-values and express whether this pattern follows a linear function. If the migration pattern is a linear function, express what constant change in y corresponds to a constant change in x.

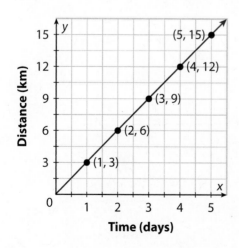

22. Representing Real-World Problems Write a real-world problem that is a discrete non-linear function.

23. Explain the Error A student used the following table of values and stated that the function described by the table was a linear function. Explain the student's error.

x	−1	0	2	3	4
y	−5	0	5	10	15

24. Communicate Mathematical Ideas Explain how graphs of the same function can look different.

Lesson Performance Task

Jordan has started a new dog-walking service. His total profits over the first 4 weeks are expressed in this table.

a. Show that his profits can be described by a linear function.

b. Graph this function and use the graph to predict his business profit 9 weeks after he opens.

c. Explain why it is or is not a good idea to project his profits so far into the future. Give examples to support your answer.

Time (weeks)	Profits($)
1	150
2	300
3	450
4	600

5.2 Using Intercepts

Essential Question: How can you identify and use intercepts in linear relationships?

⊙ Explore   Identifying Intercepts

Miners are exploring 90 feet underground. The miners ascend in an elevator at a constant rate over a period of 3 minutes until they reach the surface. In the coordinate grid, the horizontal axis represents the time in minutes from when the miners start ascending, and the vertical axis represents the miners' elevation relative to the surface in feet. Copy the grid and complete the graph.

Ⓐ What point represents the miners' elevation at the beginning of the ascent?

   Plot this point.

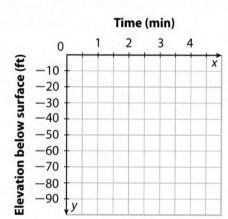

Ⓑ What point represents the miners' elevation at the end of the ascent?

   Plot this point.

Ⓒ Connect the points with a line segment.

Ⓓ What is the point where the graph crosses the y-axis? [?] the x-axis? [?]

Reflect

1. **Discussion** The point where the graph intersects the y-axis represents the beginning of the miners' ascent. Will the point where a graph intersects the y-axis always be the lowest point on a linear graph? Explain.

⊙ Explain 1   Determining Intercepts of Linear Equations

The graph in the Explore intersected the axes at (0, −90) and (3, 0).

The **y-intercept** of a graph is the y-coordinate of the point where the graph intersects the y-axis. The x-coordinate of this point is always 0. The y-intercept of the graph in the Explore is −90.

The **x-intercept** of a graph is the x-coordinate of the point where the graph intersects the x-axis. The y-coordinate of this point is always 0. The x-intercept of the graph in the Explore is 3.

Example 1
Find the *x*- and *y*-intercepts.

(A) $3x - 2y = 6$

To find the *x*-intercept, replace *y* with 0 and solve for *x*.

$3x - 2(0) = 6$

$3x = 6$

$x = 2$

The *x*-intercept is 2.

To find the *y*-intercept, replace *x* with 0 and solve for *y*.

$3(0) - 2y = 6$

$-2y = 6$

$y = -3$

The *y*-intercept is −3.

(B) $-5x + 6y = 60$

To find the *x*-intercept, replace *y* with 0 and solve for *x*.

$-5x + 6\left(\boxed{0}\right) = 60$

$-5x = 60$

$x = \boxed{-12}$

The *x*-intercept is −12.

To find the *y*-intercept, replace *x* with 0 and solve for *y*.

$-5\left(\boxed{0}\right) + 6y = 60$

$6y = 60$

$y = \boxed{10}$

The *y*-intercept is 10.

Reflect

2. If the point (5, 0) is on a graph, is (5, 0) the *y*-intercept of the graph? Explain.

Your Turn

Find the *x*- and *y*-intercepts.

3. $8x + 7y = 28$

4. $-6x - 8y = 24$

🎯 Explain 2 Interpreting Intercepts of Linear Equations

You can use intercepts to interpret a situation that is modeled by a linear function.

Example 2 Find and interpret the *x*- and *y*-intercepts for each situation.

Ⓐ The Sandia Peak Tramway in Albuquerque, New Mexico, travels a distance of about 4500 meters to the top of Sandia Peak. Its speed is 300 meters per minute. The function $f(x) = 4500 - 300x$ gives the tram's distance in meters from the top of the peak after *x* minutes.

To find the *x*-intercept, replace $f(x)$ with 0 and solve for *x*.

$$f(x) = 4500 - 300x$$
$$0 = 4500 - 300x$$
$$x = 15$$

It takes 15 minutes to reach the peak.

To find the *y*-intercept, replace *x* with 0 and find $f(0)$.

$$f(x) = 4500 - 300x$$
$$f(0) = 4500 - 300(0) = 4500$$

The distance from the peak when it starts is 4500 m.

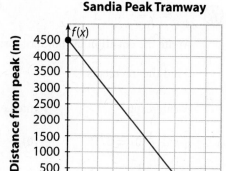

Sandia Peak Tramway

Ⓑ A hot air balloon is 750 meters above the ground and begins to descend at a constant rate of 25 meters per minute. The function $f(x) = 750 - 25x$ represents the height of the hot air balloon after *x* minutes.

To find the *x*-intercept, replace $f(x)$ with 0 and solve *x*.

$$f(x) = 750 - 25x$$
$$\boxed{0} = 750 - 25x$$
$$x = \boxed{30}$$

It takes 30 minutes to reach the ground.

To find the *y*-intercept, replace *x* with 0 and find $f(0)$.

$$f(x) = 750 - 25x$$
$$f(0) = 750 - 25\left(\boxed{0}\right) = 750$$

The height above ground when it starts is 750 meters.

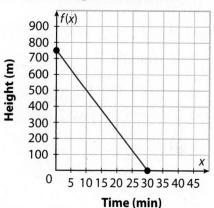

Height of Hot Air Balloon

Reflect

5. **Critique Reasoning** A classmate says that the graph shows the path of the tram. Do you agree?

Your Turn

6. The temperature in an experiment is increased at a constant rate over a period of time until the temperature reaches 0 °C. The equation $y = \frac{5}{2}x - 70$ gives the temperature *y* in degrees Celsius *x* hours after the experiment begins. Find and interpret the *x*- and *y*-intercepts.

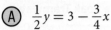

You can use the *x*- and *y*-intercepts to graph a linear equation.

Example 3 **Use intercepts to graph the line described by each equation.**

(A) $\frac{1}{2}y = 3 - \frac{3}{4}x$

Write the equation in standard form. $\frac{3}{4}x + \frac{1}{2}y = 3$

Find the intercepts.

x-intercept:

$\frac{3}{4}x + \frac{1}{2}(0) = 3$

$\frac{3}{4}x = 3$

$x = 4$

y-intercept:

$\frac{3}{4}(0) + \frac{1}{2}y = 3$

$\frac{1}{2}y = 3$

$y = 6$

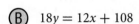

Graph the line by plotting the points (4, 0) and (0, 6) and drawing a line through them.

(B) $18y = 12x + 108$

Write the equation in standard form. $\boxed{-12x + 18y} = 108$

Find the intercepts.

x-intercept:

$-12x + 18\left(\boxed{0}\right) = 108$

$-12x = 108$

$x = \boxed{-9}$

y-intercept:

$-12\boxed{0} + 18y = 108$

$18y = 108$

$y = \boxed{6}$

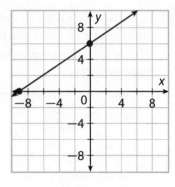

Graph the line by plotting the points $(-9, 0)$ and $(0, 6)$ and drawing a line through them.

Your Turn

7. Use intercepts to graph $3y = -5x - 30$.

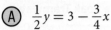 Elaborate

8. A line intersects the *y*-axis at the point (a, b). Is $a = 0$? Is $b = 0$? Explain.

9. What does a negative *y*-intercept mean for a real-world application?

10. Essential Question Check-in How can you find the *x*-intercept of the graph of a linear equation using the equation? How is using the graph of a linear equation to find the intercepts like using the equation?

Evaluate: Homework and Practice

• Online Homework
• Hints and Help
• Extra Practice

Identify and interpret the intercepts for each situation, plot the points on a graph, and connect the points with a line segment.

1. An electronics manufacturer has 140 capacitors, and the same number of capacitors is needed for each circuit board made. The manufacturer uses the capacitors to make 35 circuit boards.

2. A dolphin is 42 feet underwater and ascends at a constant rate for 14 seconds until it reaches the surface.

Find the x- and y-intercepts.

3. $2x - 3y = -6$

4. $-4x - 5y = 40$

5. $8x + 4y = -56$

6. $-9x + 6y = 72$

7. $\frac{3}{5}x + \frac{1}{2}y = 30$

8. $-\frac{3}{4}x + \frac{5}{6}y = 15$

Interpret the intercepts for each situation. Use the intercepts to graph the function.

9. **Biology** A lake was stocked with 350 trout. Each year, the population decreases by 14. The population of trout in the lake after x years is represented by the function $f(x) = 350 - 14x$.

10. The air temperature is $-6\,°C$ at sunrise and rises $3\,°C$ every hour for several hours. The air temperature after x hours is represented by the function $f(x) = 3x - 6$.

11. The number of brake pads needed for a car is 4, and a manufacturing plant has 480 brake pads. The number of brake pads remaining after brake pads have been installed on x cars is $f(x) = 480 - 4x$.

12. Connor is running a 10-kilometer cross country race. He runs 1 kilometer every 4 minutes. Connor's distance from the finish line after x minutes is represented by the function $f(x) = 10 - \frac{1}{4}x$.

Use intercepts to graph the line described by each equation.

13. $-6y = -4x + 24$

14. $9y = 3x + 18$

15. $y = \frac{1}{5}x + 2$

16. $-3y = 7x - 21$

17. $\frac{3}{2}x = -4y - 12$

18. $\frac{2}{3}y = 2 - \frac{1}{2}x$

19. Kim owes her friend $245 and plans to pay $35 per week. Write an equation of the function that shows the amount Kim owes after x weeks. Then find and interpret the intercepts of the function.

20. Explain the Error Arlo incorrectly found the x-intercept of $9x + 12y = 144$. His work is shown.

$$9x + 12y = 144$$

$$9(0) + 12y = 144$$

$$12y = 144$$

$$y = 12 \quad \text{The } x\text{-intercept is 12.}$$

Explain Arlo's error.

21. Determine whether each point could represent an x-intercept, y-intercept, both, or neither.

A. $(0, 5)$ **B.** $(0, 0)$ **C.** $(-7, 0)$

D. $(3, -4)$ **E.** $(19, 0)$

22. A bank employee notices an abandoned checking account with a balance of $360. The bank charges an $8 monthly fee for the account.

a. Write and graph the equation that gives the balance $f(x)$ in dollars as a function of the number of months, x.

b. Find and interpret the x- and y-intercepts.

23. Kathryn is walking on a treadmill at a constant pace for 30 minutes. She has programmed the treadmill for a 2-mile walk. The display counts backward to show the distance remaining.

a. Write and graph the equation that gives the distance $f(x)$ left in miles as a function of the number x of minutes she has been walking.

b. Find and interpret the x- and y-intercepts.

H.O.T. Focus on Higher Order Thinking

24. Represent Real-World Problems Write a real-world problem that could be modeled by a linear function whose x-intercept is 6 and whose y-intercept is 60.

25. Draw Conclusions For any linear equation $Ax + By = C$, what are the intercepts in terms of A, B, and C?

26. Multiple Representations Find the intercepts of $3x + 40y = 1200$. Explain how to use the intercepts to determine appropriate scales for the graph and then create a graph.

Lesson Performance Task

A sail on a boat is in the shape of a right triangle. If the sail is superimposed on a coordinate plane, the point where the horizontal and vertical sides meet is $(0, 0)$ and the sail is above and to the right of $(0, 0)$. The equation of the line that represents the sail's hypotenuse in feet is $10x + 4y = 240$.

a. Find and interpret the intercepts of the line and use them to graph the line. Then use the triangle formed by the x-axis, y-axis, and the line described by the above equation to find the area of the sail.

b. Now find the area of a sail whose hypotenuse is described by the equation $Ax + By = C$, where A, B, and C are all positive.

5.3 Interpreting Rate of Change and Slope

Essential question: How can you relate rate of change and slope in linear relationships?

⊘ Explore Determining Rates of Change

For a function defined in terms of x and y, the **rate of change** over a part of the domain of the function is a ratio that compares the change in y to the change in x in that part of the domain.

$$\text{rate of change} = \frac{\text{change in } y}{\text{change in } x}$$

The table shows the year and the cost of sending 1-ounce letter in cents.

Years after 2000 (x)	3	4	6	8	13
Cost (cents)	37	37	39	42	46

Find the rate of change, $\dfrac{\text{change in postage}}{\text{change in year}}$, for each time period using the table.

Ⓐ From 2003 to 2004: $\dfrac{\boxed{?} - \boxed{?}}{4 - 3} = \boxed{?}$ cent(s) per year

Ⓑ From 2004 to 2006: $\dfrac{\boxed{?} - \boxed{?}}{6 - 4} = \boxed{?} = \boxed{?}$ cent(s) per year

Ⓒ From 2006 to 2008: $\dfrac{\boxed{?} - \boxed{?}}{8 - 6} = \boxed{?} = \boxed{?}$ cent(s) per year

Ⓓ From 2008 to 2013: $\dfrac{\boxed{?} - \boxed{?}}{13 - 8} = \boxed{?} = \boxed{?}$ cent(s) per year

E Plot the points represented in the table. Connect the points with line segments to make a statistical line graph.

Find the rate of change for each time period using the graph.

F Label the vertical increase (*rise*) and the horizontal increase (*run*) between points (4, 37) and (6, 39). Then find the rate of change, $\frac{rise}{run}$.

$$\frac{rise}{run} = \frac{\boxed{?}}{\boxed{?}} = \boxed{?} \text{ cent(s) per year}$$

G Label the vertical increase (*rise*) and the horizontal increase (*run*) between points (6, 39) and (8, 42). Then find the rate of change, $\frac{rise}{run}$.

$$\frac{rise}{run} = \frac{\boxed{?}}{\boxed{?}} = \boxed{?} \text{ cent(s) per year}$$

H Label the vertical increase (*rise*) and the horizontal increase (*run*) between points (8, 42) and (13, 46). Then find the rate of change, $\frac{rise}{run}$.

$$\frac{rise}{run} = \frac{\boxed{?}}{\boxed{?}} = \boxed{?} \text{ cent(s) per year}$$

Reflect

1. **Discussion** Between which two years is the rate of change $\frac{\text{change in postage}}{\text{change in years}}$ the greatest?

2. **Discussion** Compare the line segment between 2006 and 2008 with the line segment between 2008 and 2013. Which is steeper? Which represents a greater rate of change?

3. **Discuss** How do you think the steepness of the line segment between two points is related to the rate of change it represents?

🔧 **Explain 1** **Determining the Slope of a Line**

The rate of change for a linear function can be calculated using the rise and run of the graph of the function. The **rise** is the difference in the *y*-values of two points on a line. The **run** is the difference in the *x*-values of two points on a line.

The **slope** of a line is the ratio of rise to run for any two points on the line.

$$\text{Slope} = \frac{rise}{run} = \frac{\text{difference in } y\text{-values}}{\text{difference in } x\text{-values}}$$

Example 1 **Determine the slope of each line.**

A Use (3, 4) as the first point. Subtract *y*-values to find the change in *y*, or rise. Then subtract *x*-values to find the change in *x*, or run.

$$\text{slope} = \frac{4-1}{3-2} = \frac{3}{1} = 3.$$

Slope of the line is 3.

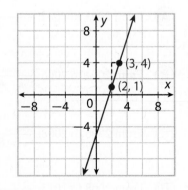

B Use $\left(-2, \boxed{3}\right)$ as the first point. Subtract y-values to find the change in y, or rise. Then subtract x-values to find the change in x, or run.

$$\text{slope} = \frac{\boxed{3} - \boxed{0}}{\boxed{-2} - \boxed{1}} = \frac{3}{-3} = \boxed{-1}.$$

The slope of the line is $\boxed{-1}$.

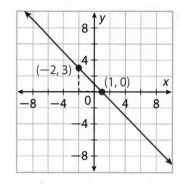

Reflect

4. Find the rise of a horizontal line. What is the slope of a horizontal line?

5. Find the run of a vertical line. What is the slope of a vertical line?

6. **Discussion** If you have a graph of a line, how can you determine whether the slope is positive, negative, zero, or undefined without using points on the line?

Your Turn

Find the slope of each line.

7.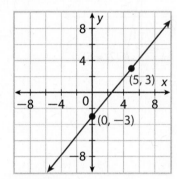

8.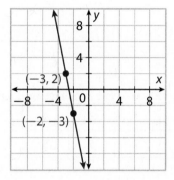

🖊 Explain 2 Determining Slope Using the Slope Formula

The **slope formula** for the slope of a line is the ratio of the difference in y-values to the difference in x-values between any two points on the line.

Slope Formula

If (x_1, y_1) and (x_2, y_2) are any two points on a line, the slope of the line is $m = \dfrac{y_2 - y_1}{x_2 - x_1}$.

Example 2 Find the slope of each line passing through the given points using the slope formula. Describe the slope as positive, negative, zero, or undefined.

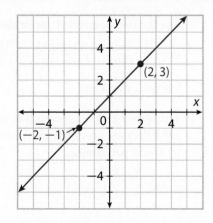

A The graph shows the linear relationship.

$$y_2 - y_1 = 3 - (-1) = 3 + 1 = 4$$

$$x_2 - x_1 = 2 - (-2) = 2 + 2 = 4$$

$$m = \frac{y_2 - y_1}{x_2 - x_1} = \frac{4}{4} = 1$$

The slope is positive. The line rises from left to right.

x	3	3	3	3
y	2	4	6	8

Let $\boxed{3}, 4$ be (x_1, y_1) and $\boxed{3}, 8$ be (x_2, y_2).

$y_2 - y_1 = 8 - \boxed{4} = \boxed{4}$

$x_2 - x_1 = \boxed{3} - \boxed{3} = \boxed{0}$

$m = \dfrac{y_2 - y_1}{x_2 - x_1} = \dfrac{\boxed{4}}{\boxed{0}}$

The slope is undefined and the line is vertical.

Your Turn

Find the slope of each line passing through the given points using the slope formula. Describe the slope as positive, negative, zero, or undefined.

9. The graph shows the linear relationship.

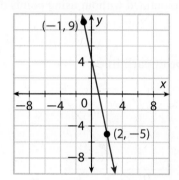

10.

x	1	2	3	4
y	5	5	5	5

⚙ Explain 3 Interpreting Slope

Given a real-world situation, you can find the slope and then interpret the slope in terms of the context of the situation.

Example 3 **Find and interpret the slope for each real-world situation.**

Ⓐ The graph shows the relationship between a person's age and his or her estimated maximum heart rate.

Use the two points that are labeled on the graph.

$$\text{slope} = \frac{\text{rise}}{\text{run}} = \frac{180 - 150}{20 - 50} = \frac{30}{-30} = -1$$

Interpret the slope.

The slope being -1 means that for every year a person's age increases, his or her maximum heart rate decreases by 1 beat per minute.

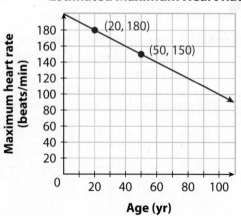

Estimated Maximum Heart Rate

© Houghton Mifflin Harcourt Publishing Company

Ⓑ The height of a plant *y* in centimeters after *x* days is a linear relationship. The points (30, 15) and (40, 25) are on the line.

Use the two points that are given.

$$\text{slope} = \frac{\text{rise}}{\text{run}} = \frac{\boxed{25} - \boxed{15}}{\boxed{40} - \boxed{30}} = \frac{\boxed{10}}{\boxed{10}} = \boxed{1}$$

Interpret the slope.

The slope being 1 means the plant's height increases by 1 cm each day.

Your Turn

Find and interpret the slope.

11. The graph shows the relationship between the temperature expressed in °F and the temperature expressed in °C.

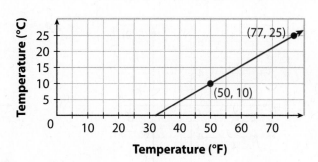

12. The number of cubic feet of water *y* in a reservoir *x* hours after the water starts flowing into the reservoir is a linear function. The points (40, 3000) and (60, 4000) are on the line of the function.

💬 **Elaborate**

13. How can you relate the rate of change and slope in the linear relationships?

14. How is the slope formula related to the definition of slope?

15. How can you interpret slope in a real-world situation?

Determine the slope of each line.

1.

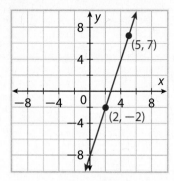

2.

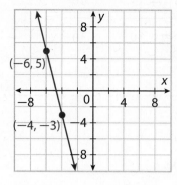

3.

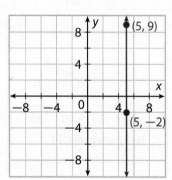

4.

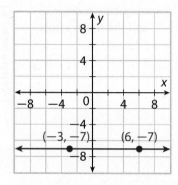

5.

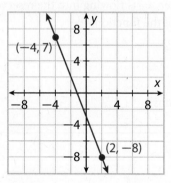

6.

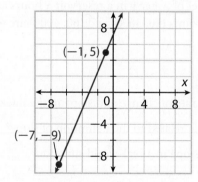

Find the slope of each line passing through the given points using the slope formula. Describe the slope as positive, negative, zero, or undefined.

7. $(5, 3)$ and $(10, 8)$

8. $(-5, 14)$ and $(-1, 2)$

9. $(-5, 6)$ and $(8, 6)$

10. $(-4, -17)$ and $(-4, -3)$

11. $(12, -7)$ and $(2, -2)$

12. $(-3, -10)$ and $(-1, -1)$

Find and interpret the slope for each real-world situation.

13.

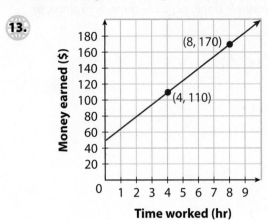

14.

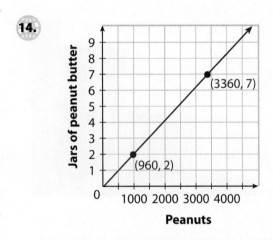

15.

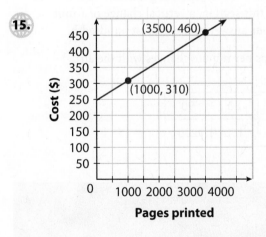

16.

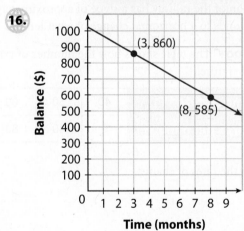

17. **a.** The table shows the distance that a group of hikers has traveled from the start of the trail.

Time (hr)	0.5	1	2	3
Distance (km)	3	5	7	13

Use the table to plot the 4 points on a graph and join the points using line segments.

b. Find the slope for each of the three line segments.

c. Which line segment has the greatest slope? Does this line segment appear to be the steepest on the graph?

18. Determine whether each set of points is on a line that has a positive slope, negative slope, zero slope, or undefined slope.

    a. $(5, 0)$ and $(8, 4)$

    b. $(-6, 1)$ and $(-6, 9)$

    c. $(2, 6)$ and $(11, -3)$

    d. $(3, 4)$ and $(-2, 12)$

    e. $(-3, 5)$ and $(7, 5)$

19. What is the slope of the segment shown for a staircase with 10-inch treads and 7.75-inch risers? As you walk up (or down) the stairs, your vertical distance from the floor is a linear function of your horizontal distance from the point on the floor where you started. Is the function discrete or continuous? Explain.

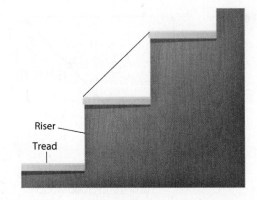

Riser

Tread

20. The Mount Washington Cog Railway in New Hampshire is one of the steepest cog railways in the world. A section of the railway has a slope of approximately 0.37. In this section, a vertical change of 1 unit corresponds to a horizontal change of what length? Round your answer to the nearest hundredth.

21. a. Biology The table shows how the number of cricket chirps per minute changes with the air temperature.

Temperature (°F)	40	50	60	70	80	90
Chirps per minute	0	40	80	120	160	200

Find the rates of change.

b. Is the graph of the data a line? If so, what is the slope? If not, explain why not.

22. **Explain the Error** A student is asked to find the slope of a line containing the points (4, 3) and (−2, 15) and finds the slope as shown. Explain the error.

$$\text{slope} = \frac{\text{rise}}{\text{run}} = \frac{4 - (-2)}{3 - 15} = \frac{6}{-12} = -\frac{1}{2}$$

23. **Critical Thinking** In this lesson, you learned that the slope of a line is constant. Does this mean that all lines with the same slope are the same line? Explain.

24. **a. Represent Real-World Problems** A ladder is leaned against a building. The bottom of the ladder is 11 feet from the building. The top of the ladder is 19 feet above the ground. What is the slope of the ladder?

    b. What does the slope of the ladder mean in the real world?

    c. If the ladder were set closer to the building, would it be harder or easier to climb? Explain in terms of the slope of the ladder.

25. **a.** The table shows the cost, in dollars, charged by an electric company for various amounts of energy in kilowatt-hours. Graph the data and show the rates of change.

Energy (kWh)	0	200	400	600	1000	2000
Cost ($)	8	8	34	60	112	157

    b. Compares the rates of change for each interval. Are they all the same? Explain.

    c. What do the rates of change represent?

    d. Describe in words the electric company's billing plan.

Lesson Performance Task

A city has three Internet service providers (ISP), each of which charges a usage fee when a subscriber goes over 100 megabytes (MB) per billing cycle. The table below relates the amount of data a subscriber uses with the cost for each ISP.

ISP	100 MB	200 MB	400 MB
A	$54	$74	$94
B	$42	$57	$87
C	$60	$72	$96

Use the table to find the rate of change for each interval of each ISP, and use the rates of change to determine whether the usage fee is constant for each ISP. Interpret the meaning of the rates of change for each ISP. Then determine and explain which ISP would be the least expensive and which ISP would be the most expensive for a subscriber that uses a high amount of data.

Linear Functions

Essential Question: How can you use a linear function to solve real-world problems?

Key Vocabulary

continuous function
(función continua)

discrete function *(función discreta)*

linear function *(función lineal)*

slope *(pendiente)*

KEY EXAMPLE   *(Lesson 5.1)*

Determine whether $4x + y = 7$ is linear. If so, graph the function.

The equation is linear because it is in the standard form of a linear equation: $A = 4$, $B = 1$, and $C = 7$.

To graph the function, first solve the equation for y.

$$4x + y = 7$$

$$\underline{-4x \qquad\qquad -4x}$$

$$y = 7 - 4x$$

Make a table and plot the points. Then connect the points.

x	−1	0	1	2
y	11	7	3	−1

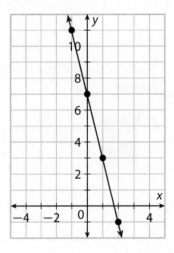

KEY EXAMPLE   *(Lesson 5.3)*

Find the slope of the line passing through the given points using the slope formula. Describe the slope as positive, negative, zero, or undefined.

x	1	2	3	4
y	7	7	7	7

Let $(1, 7)$ be (x_1, y_1) and $(3, 7)$ be (x_2, y_2).

$$y_2 - y_1 = 7 - 7 = 0$$

$$x_2 - x_1 = 3 - 1 = 2$$

$$m = \frac{y_2 - y_1}{x_2 - x_1} = \frac{0}{2} = 0$$

The slope is zero.

EXERCISES

Determine whether each equation is linear. *(Lesson 5.1)*

1. $4x^2 + y = 8$

2. $7x + y = 3$

Find the *x*- and *y*-intercepts. *(Lesson 5.2)*

3. $2x - 3y = 12$

4. $-6x + 8y = 24$

5. $3x + y = 5$

6. $5x - 2y = 0$

Find the slope of the line passing through the given points using the slope formula. *(Lesson 5.3)*

7.

x	0	1	2	3
y	2	5	8	11

8.

x	0	2	4	6
y	6	5	4	3

MODULE PERFORMANCE TASK

How Many Stacked Cups Do You Need?

You want to stack paper, plastic, or foam cups one inside the next so that the height of the stack is equal to your math teacher's height. How can you determine the number of cups you would need?

Start by listing the questions you will need to answer in order to tackle the problem. Then complete the task. Be sure to write down all your data and assumptions. Then use graphs, numbers, words, or algebra to explain how you reached your conclusion.

(Ready) to Go On?

5.1–5.3 Linear Functions

- Online Homework
- Hints and Help
- Extra Practice

Determine whether each equation is linear. If it is linear, graph the equation, determine the slope, and find the *x*- and *y*-intercepts. *(Lessons 5.1, 5.2, 5.3)*

1. $x^3 + y = 8$

2. $4x + 2y = 6$

3. $-5x + 4y = 0$

4. $5xy + y = 9$

ESSENTIAL QUESTION

5. What do the slope and *y*-intercept of a real-world linear function represent?

Assessment Readiness

1. Tell whether each equation is linear.

   A. $\frac{1}{3}x - 2y = 7$

   B. $y = x^2 - 8$

   C. $3x + \frac{7}{y} = -5$

2. Consider the equation $8x - 2y = 24$. Determine if each statement is True or False.

   A. The x-intercept is 3.

   B. The y-intercept is 12.

   C. It is equivalent to $y = 4x - 12$.

3. Consider the sequence –8, –4, 0, 4, 8, 12, …. Determine if each statement is True or False.

   A. A recursive rule for the sequence is $f(1) = -8$; $f(n) = -4(n - 1)$ for all $n \geq 2$.

   B. An explicit rule for the sequence is $f(n) = -8 + 4(n - 1)$.

   C. The tenth term is 28.

Use the graph to answer questions 4 and 5.

4. Is the relation represented on the graph a function? Explain.

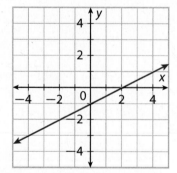

5. What is the slope of the line shown on the graph? Explain how you got your answer.

Forms of Linear Equations

Essential Question: How can you use different forms of linear equations to solve real-world problems?

REAL WORLD VIDEO
Periodic comets have orbital periods of less than 200 years. Halley's comet is the only short-period comet that is visible to the naked eye. It returns every 76 years. You can build functions to represent and model predictable occurrences, such as the return of Halley's comet.

© Houghton Mifflin Harcourt Publishing Company • Image Credit: ©Cessna152/Shutterstock

MODULE PERFORMANCE TASK PREVIEW

Who Wins the Race

A marathon is a long-distance run that is 26.2 miles long. Marathon events are hosted all over the world, and participants are a mix of athletes with different skill levels. Most runners train for many months to prepare for a marathon. How can linear equations be used to compare the running speeds of two different runners? Stay on track and find out!

Are (YOU) Ready?

Complete these exercises to review skills you will need for this module.

Constant Rate of Change

Example 1   Tell if the rate of change is constant.

x	1	2	3	4
y	16	22	28	34

$$+6 \quad +6 \quad +6$$

The rate of change, $\frac{6}{1}$, is constant.

For a function defined in terms of x and y, the rate of change of the function is a ratio that compares the change in y to the change in x.

$$\text{rate of change} = \frac{\text{change in } y}{\text{change in } x} = \frac{6}{1}$$

Tell if the rate of change is constant.

1.

x	2	5	8	11
y	6	15	24	33

2.

x	3	6	9	12
y	2	6	11	17

Two-Step Equations

Example 2   Solve.

$$10 = 3x - 11$$
$$10 + 11 = 3x - 11 + 11 \qquad \text{Add 11 to both sides of the equation.}$$
$$21 = 3x$$
$$\frac{21}{3} = \frac{3x}{3} \qquad \text{Divide both sides of the equation by 3.}$$
$$7 = x$$

Solve each equation.

3. $7n + 17 = 59$

4. $24 - 4y = 20$

5. $34 = 49 - 3b$

Linear Functions

Example 3   Tell whether $y = \frac{4}{x} - 8$ represents a linear function.

$y = \frac{4}{x} - 8$ does not represent a linear function because x appears in the denominator.

When a linear equation is written in standard form, the following are true.

- x and y both have exponents of 1.
- x and y are not multiplied together.
- x and y do not appear in denominators, exponents, or radicands.

Tell whether the equation represents a linear function.

6. $8x^2 + y = 16$

7. $6x + y = 12$

8. $3y = 2x + 5$

6.1 Slope-Intercept Form

Essential Question: How can you represent a linear function in a way that reveals its slope and y-intercept?

Resource Locker

🧭 Explore Graphing Lines Given Slope and y-intercept

Graphs of linear equations can be used to model many real-life situations. Given the slope and y-intercept, you can graph the line, and use the graph to answer questions.

Andrew wants to buy a smart phone that costs $500. His parents will pay for the phone, and Andrew will pay them $50 each month until the entire amount is repaid. The loan repayment represents a linear situation in which the amount y that Andrew owes his parents is dependent on the number x of payments he has made.

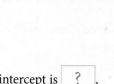

(A) When $x = 0$, $y = \boxed{?}$.

The y-intercept of the graph of the equation that represents

the situation is $\boxed{?}$.

(B) The rate of change in the amount Andrew owes over time is $\boxed{?}$

per month.

The slope is $\boxed{?}$.

(C) Use the y-intercept to plot a point on a graph of the equation. The y-intercept is $\boxed{?}$,

so plot the point $\boxed{?}$.

(D) Using the definition of slope, plot a second point.

$$\text{Slope} = \frac{\text{Change in } y}{\text{Change in } x} = \frac{\boxed{?}}{1} = \boxed{?}.$$

Start at the point you plotted. Count $\boxed{?}$ units down and $\boxed{?}$ unit right and plot another point.

(E) Draw a line through the points you plotted.

Reflect

1. **Discussion** How can you use the same method to find two more points on that same line?

2. How many months will it take Andrew to pay off his loan? Explain your answer.

🔑 Explain 1   Creating Linear Equations in Slope-Intercept Form

You can use the slope formula to derive the slope-intercept form of a linear equation.

Consider a line with slope m and y-intercept b.

The slope formula is $m = \dfrac{y_2 - y_1}{x_2 - x_1}$.

Substitute $(0, b)$ for (x_1, y_1) and (x, y) for (x_2, y_2).

$$m = \frac{y - b}{x - 0}$$

$$m = \frac{y - b}{x}$$

$$mx = y - b \qquad \text{Multiply both sides by } x \ (x \neq 0).$$

$$mx + b = y \qquad \text{Add } b \text{ to both sides.}$$

$$y = mx + b$$

Slope-Intercept Form of an Equation

If a line has slope m and y-intercept $(0, b)$, then the line is described by the equation $y = mx + b$.

Example 1   **Write the equation of each line in slope-intercept form.**

Ⓐ   Slope is 3, and $(2, 5)$ is on the line.

    Step 1: Find the y-intercept.

$y = mx + b$	Write the slope–intercept form.
$5 = 3(2) + b$	Substitute 3 for m, 2 for x, and 5 for y.
$5 = 6 + b$	Multiply.
$5 - 6 = 6 + b - 6$	Subtract 6 from both sides.
$-1 = b$	Simplify.

    Step 2: Write the equation.

$y = mx + b$	Write the slope–intercept form.
$y = 3x + (-1)$	Substitute 3 for m and -1 for b.
$y = 3x - 1$	

Ⓑ   The line passes through $(0, 5)$ and $(2, 13)$.

    Step 1: Use the points to find the slope. $m = \dfrac{y_2 - y_1}{x_2 - x_1}$

Substitute $(0, 5)$ for (x_1, y_1) and $\boxed{2}, \boxed{13}$ for (x_2, y_2). $m = \dfrac{\boxed{13 - 5}}{\boxed{2 - 0}} = \dfrac{\boxed{8}}{2} = \boxed{4}$

Step 2: Substitute the slope and x- and y-coordinates
of either of the points in the equation $y = mx + b$.

$$y = mx + b$$

$$\boxed{13} = \boxed{4} \left(\boxed{2} \right) + b$$

Step 3: Substitute 4 for m and 5 for
b in the equation $y = mx + b$.

$$\boxed{13} = \boxed{8} + b$$

The equation of the line is $\boxed{y = 4x + 5}$.

$$\boxed{13} - \boxed{8} = \boxed{8} + b - \boxed{8}$$

$$\boxed{5} = b$$

Your Turn

Write the equation of each line in slope-intercept form.

3. Slope is -1, and $(3, 2)$ is on the line.

4. The line passes through $(1, 4)$ and $(3, 18)$.

🎼 Explain 2   Graphing from Slope-Intercept Form

Writing an equation in slope-intercept form can make it easier to graph the equation.

Example 2   **Write each equation in slope-intercept form. Then graph the line.**

(A) $y = 5x - 4$

The equation $y = 5x - 4$ is already in slope-intercept form.

Slope: $m = 5 = \dfrac{5}{1}$

y-intercept: $b = -4$

Step 1: Plot $(0, -4)$

Step 2: Count 5 units up and 1 unit to the right and plot another point.

Step 3: Draw a line through the points.

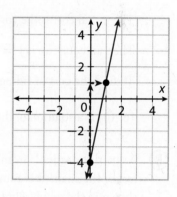

(B) $2x + 6y = 6$

Step 1: Write the equation in slope-intercept form by solving for y.

$$2x + 6y - 2x = 6 - \boxed{2x} \qquad \text{Slope: } \boxed{-\dfrac{1}{3}}$$

$$6y = \boxed{-2x} + 6 \qquad \text{y-intercept: } \boxed{1}$$

$$y = \boxed{-\dfrac{1}{3}} x + \boxed{1}$$

Step 2: Graph the line.

Plot $\left(\boxed{0} , \boxed{1} \right)$. Move 1 unit down and 3 units to the right
to plot a second point. Draw a line through the points.

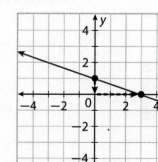

Write each equation in slope-intercept form. Then graph the line.

5. $2x + y = 4$

6. $2x + 3y = 6$

🧭 Explain 3 Determining Solutions of Equations in Two Variables

Given a real-world linear situation described by a table, a graph, or a verbal description, you can write an equation in slope-intercept form. You can use that equation to solve problems.

Example 3 Identify the slope and y-intercept of the graph that represents each linear situation and interpret what they mean. Then write an equation in slope-intercept form and use it to solve the problem.

(A) For one taxi company, the cost y in dollars of a taxi ride is a linear function of the distance x in miles traveled. The initial charge is \$2.50, and the charge per mile is \$0.35. Find the cost of riding a distance of 10 miles.

The rate of change is \$0.35 per mile, so the slope, m, is 0.35.

The initial cost is the cost to travel 0 miles, \$2.50, so the y-intercept, b, is 2.50.

Then an equation is $y = 0.35x + 2.50$.

$$y = 0.35x + 2.50$$

To find the cost of riding 10 miles, substitute 10 for x.

$$= 0.35(10) + 2.50$$
$$= 6$$

$(6, 10)$ is a solution of the equation, and the cost of riding a distance of 10 miles is \$6.

(B) A chairlift descends from a mountain top to pick up skiers at the bottom. The height in feet of the chairlift is a linear function of the time in minutes since it begins descending as shown in the graph. Find the height of the chairlift 2 minutes after it begins descending.

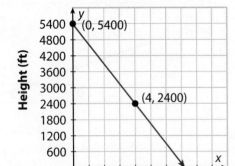

Height of a Chairlift

The graph contains the points (0, 5400) and (4, 2400).

The slope is $\dfrac{\boxed{2400} - 5400}{\boxed{4} - 0} = \boxed{-750}$.

It represents the rate at which the chairlift descends.

The graph passes through the point (0, 5400), so the y-intercept is 5400. It represents the height of the chairlift 0 minutes after it begins descending.

Let x be the time in minutes after the chairlift begins to descend.

Let y be the height of the chairlift in feet.

The equation is $y = -750x + 5400$.

To find the height after 2 minutes, substitute 2 for x and simplify.

$$\boxed{y} = \boxed{-750}\left(\boxed{2}\right) + 5400$$

$$= \boxed{-1500} + 5400$$

$$= \boxed{3900}$$

$(2, 3900)$ is a solution of the equation, and the height of the chairlift 2 minutes after it begins descending is 3900 feet.

Reflect

7. In the example involving the taxi, how would the equation change if the cost per mile increased or decreased? How would this affect the graph?

Your Turn

Identify the slope and y-intercept of the graph that represents the linear situation and interpret what they mean. Then write an equation in slope-intercept form and use it to solve the problem.

8. A local club charges an initial membership fee as well as a monthly cost. The cost C in dollars is a linear function of the number of months of membership. Find the cost of the membership after 4 months.

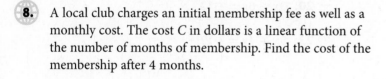

Membership Cost	
Time (months)	Cost ($)
0	100
3	277
6	454

Elaborate

9. What are some advantages to using slope-intercept form?

10. What are some disadvantages of slope-intercept form?

11. Essential Question Check-In When given a real-world situation that can be described by a linear equation, how can you identify the slope and y-intercept of the graph of the equation?

☆ Evaluate: Homework and Practice

For each situation, determine the slope and *y*-intercept of the graph of the equation that describes the situation.

1. John gets a new job and receives a $500 signing bonus. After that, he makes $200 a day.

2. Jennifer is 20 miles north of her house, and she is driving north on the highway at a rate of 55 miles per hour.

Sketch a graph that represents the situation.

3. Morwenna rents a truck. She pays $20 plus $0.25 per mile.

4. An investor invests $500 in a certain stock. After the first six months, the value of the stock has increased at a rate of $20 per month

Write the equation of each line in slope-intercept form.

5. Slope is 3, and $(1, 5)$ is on the line.

6. Slope is -2, and $(5, 3)$ is on the line.

7. Slope is $\frac{1}{4}$, and $(4, 2)$ is on the line.

8. Slope is 5, and $(2, 6)$ is on the line.

9. Slope is $-\frac{2}{3}$, and $(-6, -5)$ is on the line.

10. Slope is $-\frac{1}{2}$, and $(-3, 2)$ is on the line.

11. Passes through $(5, 7)$ and $(3, 1)$

12. Passes through $(-6, 10)$ and $(-3, -2)$

13. Passes through $(6, 6)$ and $(-2, 2)$

14. Passes through $(-1, -5)$ and $(2, 6)$

Write each equation in slope-intercept form. Identify the slope and *y*-intercept. Then graph the line described by the equation.

15. $y = 2x + 3$

16. $y = -x + 2$

17. $y = \frac{2}{3}x - 4$

18. $y = -\frac{1}{2}x - 1$

19. $-4x + 2y = 10$

20. $3x - 6y = -12$

21. $-5x - 2y = 8$

22. $3x + 4y = -12$

23. Sports A figure skating school offers introductory lessons at $25 per session. There is also a registration fee of $30. Write a linear equation in slope-intercept form that represents the situation. You want to take at least 6 lessons. Can you pay for those lessons using a $200 gift certificate? If so, how much money, if any, will be left on the gift certificate? If not, explain why not.

24. Represent Real World Problems Lorena and Benita are saving money. They began on the same day. Lorena started with $40. Each week she adds $8. The graph describes Benita's savings plan. Which girl will have more money in 6 weeks? How much more will she have? Explain your reasoning.

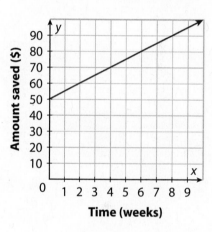

H.O.T. Focus on Higher Order Thinking

25. Analyze Relationships Julio and Jake start their reading assignments the same day. Jake is reading a 168-page book at a rate of 24 pages per day. Julio's book is 180 pages long and his reading rate is $1\frac{1}{4}$ times Jake's rate. After 5 days, who will have more pages left to read? How many more? Explain your reasoning.

26. Explain the Error John has $2 in his bank account when he gets a job. He begins making $107 dollars a day. A student found that the equation that represents this situation is $y = 2x + 107$. What is wrong with the student's equation? Describe and correct the student's error.

27. Justify Reasoning Is it possible to write the equation of every line in slope-intercept form? Explain your reasoning.

Lesson Performance Task

The graph shows the cost of a gym membership in each of two years. What are the values that represent the sign-up fee and the membership monthly fee? How did the values change between the years?

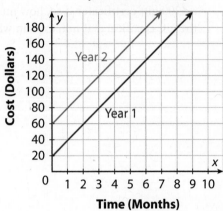

Gym Memberships

a. Write an equation in slope-intercept form for each of the two lines in the graph.

b. What are the values that represent the sign-up fee and the membership cost? How did the values change between the years?

6.2 Point-Slope Form

Essential Question: How can you represent a linear function in a way that reveals its slope and a point on its graph?

🧭 Explore   Deriving Point-Slope Form

Suppose you know the slope of a line and the coordinates of one point on the line. How can you write an equation of the line?

Ⓐ A line has a slope m of 4, and the point $(2, 1)$ is on the line. Let (x, y) be any other point on the line. Substitute the information you have in the slope formula.

$$m = \frac{y_2 - y_1}{x_2 - x_1}$$

$$\boxed{?} = \frac{y - \boxed{?}}{x - \boxed{?}}$$

Ⓑ Use the Multiplication Property of Equality to get rid of the fraction.

$$\boxed{?}\left(x - \boxed{?}\right) = \left(\frac{y - \boxed{?}}{x - \boxed{?}}\right)\left(x - \boxed{?}\right)$$

Ⓒ Simplify.

$$\boxed{?}\left(x - \boxed{?}\right) = \left(y - \boxed{?}\right)$$

Reflect

1. **Discussion** The equation that you derived is written in a form called *point-slope form*. The equation $y = 2x + 1$ is in slope-intercept form. How can you rewrite it in point-slope form?

🔑 Explain 1   Creating Linear Equations Given Slope and a Point

Point-Slope Form

The line with slope m that contains the point (x_1, y_1) can be described by the equation $y - y_1 = m(x - x_1)$.

Example 1   Write an equation in point-slope form for each line.

Ⓐ Slope is 3.5, and $(-3, 2)$ is on the line.

$y - y_1 = m(x - x_1)$	Point-slope form
$y - 2 = 3.5\big(x - (-3)\big)$	Substitute.
$y - 2 = 3.5(x + 3)$	Simplify.

Ⓑ Slope is 0, and $(-2, -1)$ is on the line.

$y - y_1 = m(x - x_1)$	Point-slope form
$y - \boxed{(-1)} = \boxed{0}\left(x - \boxed{(-2)}\right)$	Substitute.
$y + \boxed{1} = \boxed{0}$	Simplify.

2. **Communicate Mathematical Ideas** Suppose that you are given that the slope of a line is 0. What is the only additional information you need to write an equation of the line? Explain.

Your Turn

Write an equation in point-slope form for each line.

3. Slope is 6, and (1, 2) is on the line.

4. Slope is $\frac{1}{3}$, and $(-3, 1)$ is on the line.

🛠 Explain 2 Creating Linear Models Given Slope and a Point

You can write an equation in point-slope form to describe a real-world linear situation. Then you can use that equation to solve a problem.

Example 2 **Solve the problem using an equation in point-slope form.**

(A) Paul wants to place an ad in a newspaper. The newspaper charges $10 for the first 2 lines of text and $3 for each additional line of text. Paul's ad is 8 lines long. How much will the ad cost?

Let x represent the number of lines of text. Let y represent the cost in dollars of the ad. Because 2 lines of text cost $10, the point $(2, 10)$ is on the line. The rate of change in the cost is $3 per line, so the slope is 3.

Write an equation in point-slope form.

$y - y_1 = m(x - x_1)$ Point-slope form

$y - 10 = 3(x - 2)$ Substitute 3 for m, 2 for x_1, and 10 for y_1.

To find the cost of 8 lines, substitute 8 for x and solve for y.

$y - 10 = 3(8 - 2)$ Substitute

$y - 10 = 18$ Simplify.

$y = 28$

The cost of 8 lines is $28.

(B) Paul would like to shop for the best price to place the ad. A different newspaper has a base cost of $15 for 3 lines and $2 for every extra line. How much will an 8-line ad cost in this paper?

$y - y_1 = m(x - x_1)$ Point-slope form

$y - \boxed{15} = 2\left(x - \boxed{3}\right)$ Substitute.

$y - \boxed{15} = 2\left(\boxed{8} - \boxed{3}\right)$ Substitute for x.

$y - \boxed{15} = \boxed{10}$ Simplify the right side.

$y = \boxed{25}$ Solve for y.

The cost of 8 lines is $ \boxed{25} .

5. **Analyze Relationships** Suppose that you find that the cost of an ad with 8 lines in another publication is $18. How is the ordered pair (8, 18) related to the equation that represents the situation? How is it related to the graph of the equation?

Your Turn

6. Daisy purchases a gym membership. She pays a signup fee and a monthly fee of $11. After 4 months, she has paid a total of $59. Use a linear equation in point-slope form to find the signup fee.

🔑 Explain 3   Creating Linear Equations Given Two Points

You can use two points on a line to create an equation of the line in point-slope form. There is more than one such equation.

Example 3   Write an equation in point-slope form for each line.

(A) (2, 1) and (3, 4) are on the line.

Let $(2, 1) = (x_1, y_1)$ and let $(3, 4) = (x_2, y_2)$.

Find the slope of the line by substituting the given values in the slope formula.

$$m = \frac{y_2 - y_1}{x_2 - x_1}$$
$$= \frac{4 - 1}{3 - 2}$$
$$= 3$$

You can choose either point and substitute the coordinates in the point-slope form.

$y - y_1 = m(x - x_1)$	Point-slope form
$y - 1 = 3(x - 2)$	Substitute 3 for m, 2 for x_1, and 1 for y_1.

Or:

$y - y_1 = m(x - x_1)$	Point-slope form
$y - 4 = 3(x - 3)$	Substitute 3 for m, 3 for x_1, and 4 for y_1.

(B) (1, 3) and (2, 3) are on the line.

Let $(1, 3) = (x_1, y_1)$ and let $(2, 3) = (x_2, y_2)$.

Find the slope of the line by substituting the given values in the slope formula.

$$m = \frac{y_2 - y_1}{x_2 - x_1}$$
$$= \frac{\boxed{3} - \boxed{3}}{\boxed{2} - \boxed{1}}$$
$$= \boxed{0}$$

Choose either point and substitute the coordinates in the point-slope form.

$y - y_1 = m(x - x_1)$	Point-slope form
$y - \boxed{3} = \boxed{0}\left(x - \boxed{1}\right)$	Substitute 0 for m, 1 for x_1, and 3 for y_1.

Or:

$y - y_2 = m(x - x_2)$	Point-slope form
$y - \boxed{3} = \boxed{0}\left(x - \boxed{2}\right)$	Substitute 0 for m, 2 for x_2, and 3 for y_2.

7. Given two points on a line, Martin and Minh each found the slope of the line. Then Martin used (x_1, y_1) and Minh used (x_2, y_2) to write the equation in point-slope form. Each student's equation was correct. Explain how they can show both equations are correct.

Your Turn

Write an equation in point-slope form for each line.

8. $(2, 4)$ and $(3, 1)$ are on the line.

9. $(0, 1)$ and $(1, 1)$ are on the line.

 Explain 4 **Creating a Linear Model Given Two Points**

In a real-world linear situation, you may have information that represents two points on the line. You can write an equation in point-slope form that represents the situation and use that equation to solve a problem.

Example 4 **Solve the problem using an equation in point-slope form.**

An animal shelter asks all volunteers to take a training session and then to volunteer for one shift each week. Each shift is the same number of hours. The table shows the numbers of hours Joan and her friend Miguel worked over several weeks. Another friend, Lili, plans to volunteer for 24 weeks over the next year. How many hours will Lili volunteer?

Volunteer	Weeks worked	Hours worked
Joan	6	15
Miguel	10	23

Analyze Information

Identify the important information.
- Joan worked for 6 weeks for a total of 15 hours.
- Miguel worked for 10 weeks for a total of 23 hours.
- Lili will work for 24 weeks.

Formulate a Plan

To create the equation, identify the two ordered pairs represented by the situation. Find the slope of the line that contains the two points. Write the equation in point-slope form. Substitute the number of weeks that Lili works for x to find y, the number of hours that Lili works. Let x represent the number of weeks worked and y represent the number of hours worked. The points (6, 15) and (10, 23) are on the line. Substitute the coordinates in the slope formula to find the slope.

$$m = \frac{y_2 - y_1}{x_2 - x_1}$$

$$m = \frac{\boxed{23} - \boxed{15}}{\boxed{10} - \boxed{6}}$$

$$m = \boxed{2}$$

Next choose one of the points and find an equation of the line in point-slope form.

$y - y_1 = m(x - x_1)$ Point-slope form

$y - \boxed{15} = \boxed{2}\left(x - \boxed{6}\right)$ Substitute $\boxed{2}$ for m, $\boxed{6}$ for x_1, and $\boxed{15}$ for y_1.

Or:

$y - y_2 = m(x - x_2)$ Point-slope form

$y - \boxed{23} = \boxed{2}\left(x - \boxed{10}\right)$ Substitute $\boxed{2}$ for m, $\boxed{10}$ for x_2, and $\boxed{23}$ for y_2.

Finally, substitute 24 in the equation to find y.

$y - \boxed{15} = \boxed{2}\left(x - \boxed{6}\right)$ Substitute $\boxed{2}$ for m, $\boxed{6}$ for x_1, and $\boxed{15}$ for y_1.

$y - \boxed{15} = \boxed{2}\left(\boxed{24} - \boxed{6}\right)$ Substitute $\boxed{24}$ for x.

$y - \boxed{15} = \boxed{2}\left(\boxed{18}\right)$ Simplify.

$y = \boxed{51}$ Simplify.

Or:

$y - \boxed{23} = \boxed{2}\left(x - \boxed{10}\right)$ Substitute $\boxed{2}$ for m, $\boxed{10}$ for x_2, and $\boxed{23}$ for y_2.

$y - \boxed{23} = \boxed{2}\left(\boxed{24} - \boxed{10}\right)$ Substitute $\boxed{24}$ for x.

$y - \boxed{23} = \boxed{2}\left(\boxed{14}\right)$ Simplify.

$y = \boxed{51}$ Simplify.

Lili will work a total of 51 hours.

The ordered pair ($\boxed{24}$, $\boxed{51}$) is a solution of both equations obtained using the given information.

$y - \boxed{15} = \boxed{2} \left(x - \boxed{6} \right)$ Substitute 2 for m, 6 for x_1, and 15 for y_1.

$\boxed{51} - \boxed{15} = \boxed{2} \left(\boxed{24} - \boxed{6} \right)$ Substitute $\boxed{24}$ for x and $\boxed{51}$ for y.

$\boxed{36} = \boxed{36}$ Simplify.

Or:

$y - \boxed{23} = \boxed{2} \left(x - \boxed{10} \right)$ Substitute 2 for m, 10 for x_2, and 23 for y_2.

$\boxed{51} - \boxed{23} = \boxed{2} \left(\boxed{24} - \boxed{10} \right)$ Substitute $\boxed{24}$ for x and $\boxed{51}$ for y.

$\boxed{28} = \boxed{28}$ Simplify.

The answer makes sense because the rate of change in the number of hours is the slope, 2. Because Lili will work 14 more weeks than Miguel, she will work $23 + 2(14)$ hours, or 51 hours.

Your Turn

Solve the problem using an equation in point-slope form.

10. A gas station has a customer loyalty program. The graph shows the amount y dollars that two members paid for x gallons of gas. Use an equation in point-slope to find the amount a member would pay for 22 gallons of gas.

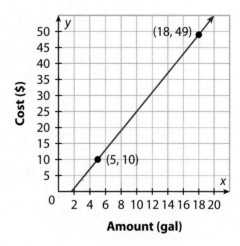

11. A roller skating rink offers a special rate for birthday parties. On the same day, a party for 10 skaters cost $107 and a party for 15 skaters cost $137. How much would a party for 12 skaters cost?

12. Can you write an equation in point-slope form that passes through any two given points in a coordinate plane?

13. Compare and contrast the slope-intercept form of a linear equation and the point-slope form.

14. **Essential Question Check-In** Given a linear graph, how can you write an equation in point-slope form of the line?

⭐ Evaluate: Homework and Practice

- Online Homework
- Hints and Help
- Extra Practice

1. Is the equation $y + 1 = 7(x + 2)$ in point-slope form? Justify your answer.

Write an equation in point-slope form for each line.

2. Slope is 1 and $(-2, -1)$ is on the line.

3. Slope is -2, and $(1, 1)$ is on the line.

4. Slope is 0, and $(1, 2)$ is on the line.

5. Slope is $\frac{1}{4}$, and $(1, 2)$ is on the line.

6. $(1, 6)$ and $(2, 3)$ are on the line.

7. $(-1, 1)$ and $(1, -1)$ are on the line.

8. $(7, 7)$ and $(-3, 7)$ are on the line.

9. $(0, 3)$ and $(2, 4)$ are on the line.

Solve the problem using an equation in point-slope form.

10. An oil tank is being filled at a constant rate. The depth of the oil is a function of the number of minutes the tank has been filling, as shown in the table. Find the depth of the oil one-half hour after filling begins.

Time (min)	Depth (ft)
0	3
10	5
15	6

11. James is participating in a 5-mile walk to raise money for a charity. He has received $200 in fixed pledges and raises $20 extra for every mile he walks. Use a point-slope equation to find the amount he will raise if he completes the walk.

12. Keisha is reading a 325-page book at a rate of 25 pages per day. Use a point-slope equation to determine whether she will finish reading the book in 10 days.

13. Lizzy is tiling a kitchen floor for the first time. She had a tough time at first and placed only 5 tiles the first day. She started to go faster, and by the end of day 4, she had placed 35 tiles. She worked at a steady rate after the first day. Use an equation in point-slope form to determine how many days Lizzy took to place all of the 100 tiles needed to finish the floor.

14. The amount of fresh water left in the tanks of a nineteenth-century clipper ship is a linear function of the time since the ship left port, as shown in the table. Write an equation in point-slope form that represents the function. Then find the amount of water that will be left in the ship's tanks 50 days after leaving port.

Time (days)	Amount (gal)
1	3555
8	3240
15	2925

15. At higher altitudes, water boils at lower temperatures. This relationship between altitude and boiling point is linear. At an altitude of 1000 feet, water boils at 210 °F. At an altitude of 3000 feet, water boils at 206 °F. Use an equation in point-slope form to find the boiling point of water at an altitude of 6000 feet.

16. In art class, Tico is copying a detail from a painting. He paints slowly for the first few days, but manages to increase his rate after that. The graph shows his progress after he increased his rate. How many square centimeters of his painting will he finish in 5 days after the increase in rate?

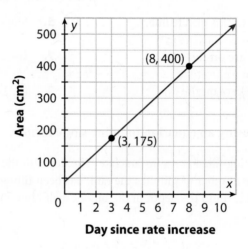

17. A hot air balloon in flight begins to ascend at a steady rate of 120 feet per minute. After 1.5 minutes, the balloon is at an altitude of 2150 feet. After 3 minutes, it is at an altitude of 2330 feet. Use an equation in point-slope form to determine whether the balloon will reach an altitude of 2500 feet in 4 minutes.

18. A candle burned at a steady rate. After 32 minutes, the candle was 11.2 inches tall. Eighteen minutes later, it was 10.75 inches tall. Use an equation in point-slope form to determine the height of the candle after 2 hours.

19. **Volume** A rectangular swimming pool has a volume capacity of 2160 cubic feet. Water is being added to the pool at a rate of about 20 cubic feet per minute. Determine about how long it will take to fill the pool completely if there were already about 1200 gallons of water in the pool. Use the fact that 1 cubic foot of space holds about 7.5 gallons of water.

20. **Multi-Step** Marisa is walking from her home to her friend Sanjay's home. When she is 12 blocks away from Sanjay's home, she looks at her watch. She looks again when she is 8 blocks away from Sanjay's home and finds that 6 minutes have passed.

a. What do you need to assume in order to treat this as a linear situation?

b. Identify the variables for the linear situation and identify two points on the line. Explain the meaning of the points in the context of the problem.

c. Find the slope of the line and describe what it means in the context of the problem.

d. Write an equation in point-slope form for the situation and use it to find the number of minutes Marisa takes to reach Sanjay's home. Show your work.

21. Match each equation with the pair of points used to create the equation.

A. $y - 10 = 1(x + 2)$ **a.** __?__ $(0, 0), (-1, 1)$

B. $y - 0 = 1(x - 0)$ **b.** __?__ $(1, 1), (-1, -1)$

C. $y - 3 = -1(x + 3)$ **c.** __?__ $(-2, 10), (0, 12)$

D. $y - 3 = 0(x - 2)$ **d.** __?__ $(1, 3), (-3.5, 3)$

22. **Explain the Error** Carlota wrote the equation $y + 1 = 2(x - 3)$ for the line passing through the points $(-1, 3)$ and $(2, 9)$. Explain and correct her error.

23. **Communicate Mathematical Ideas** Explain why it is possible for a line to have no equation in point-slope form or to have infinitely many, but it is not possible that there is only one.

24. **Persevere in Problem Solving** If you know that $A \neq 0$ and $B \neq 0$, how can you write an equation in point-slope form of the equation $Ax + By = C$?

Lesson Performance Task

Alberto is snow boarding down a mountain with a constant slope. The slope he is on has an overall length of 1560 feet. The top of the slope has a height of 4600 feet, and the slope has a vertical drop of 600 feet. It takes him 24 seconds to reach the bottom of the slope.

a. If we assume that Alberto's speed down the slope is constant, what is his height above the bottom of the slope at 10 seconds into the run?

b. Alberto says that he must have been going 50 miles per hour down the slope. Do you agree? Why or why not?

6.3 Standard Form

Essential Question: How can you write a linear equation in standard form given properties of the line including its slope and points on the line?

⊘ Explore Comparing Forms of Linear Equations

You have seen that the standard form of a linear equation is $Ax + By = C$ where A and B are not both zero. For instance, the equation $2x + 3y = -12$ is in standard form. You can write equivalent equations in slope-intercept form and point-slope form. For instance, the equation in slope-intercept form and an equation in point-slope are shown.

$$\text{Standard form: } 2x + 3y = -12$$

$$\text{Slope-intercept form: } y = -\tfrac{2}{3}x - 4$$

$$\text{Point-slope from: } y + 8 = -\tfrac{2}{3}(x - 6)$$

Use the three forms of the equation shown to complete each step.

Ⓐ Determine whether you can read the slope from the equation.

Standard form ⸤ ? ⸥

Slope-intercept form ⸤ ? ⸥

Point-slope form ⸤ ? ⸥

Ⓑ The slope is ⸤ ? ⸥.

Ⓒ Determine whether you can read the y-intercept from the equation.

Standard form ⸤ ? ⸥

Slope-intercept form ⸤ ? ⸥

Point-slope form ⸤ ? ⸥

Ⓓ Identify the y-intercept ⸤ ? ⸥

Reflect

1. Explain how you can find both intercepts using the standard form.

2. How can you find a point on the line using the slope-intercept form?

Explain 1 **Creating Linear Equations in Standard Form Given Slope and a Point**

Given the slope of a line and a point on the line, you can write an equation of the line in standard form.

Example 1 Write an equation in standard form for each line.

(A) Slope is 2 and $(-2, 2)$ is on the line.

Method 1: Use the point-slope form. Substitute the given slope and the coordinates of the given point.

$y - 2 = 2(x - (-2))$ Point-slope form | Rewrite in standard form.

$y - 2 = 2x + 4$ Simplify. | $y - 2 = 2x + 4$

 | $-2x + y = 6$

Method 2: Use the slope-intercept form. Substitute the given slope and the coordinates of the given point. Solve for b.

$y = mx + b$ Slope-intercept form | The slope-intercept form is $y = 2x + 6$.

$2 = 2(-2) + b$ Substitute for x. | Rewrite in standard form as in Method 1: $-2x + y = 6$

$6 = b$ Simplify.

(B) Slope is 5, and $(-2, 4)$ is on the line.

Method 1: Use the point-slope form. Substitute the given slope and the coordinates of the given point.

$y - \boxed{4} = \boxed{5}\left(x - \left(\boxed{-2}\right)\right)$ Point-slope form

$y - \boxed{4} = \boxed{5}\,x + \boxed{10}$ Simplify.

Rewrite in standard form.

$y - \boxed{4} = \boxed{5}\,x + \boxed{10}$

$\boxed{-5}\,x + y = \boxed{14}$

Method 2: Use the slope-intercept form and substitute the slope and point into the equation to solve for b.

$\boxed{4} = \boxed{5} \cdot \boxed{-2} + b$ | This gives the equation $y = \boxed{5}\,x + \boxed{14}$.

$\boxed{4} = \boxed{-10} + b$ | Rewrite in standard form as in Method 1:

$\boxed{14} = b$ | $\boxed{-5}\,x + y = \boxed{14}$

3. **Discussion** Which method do you prefer? Why?

Write an equation in standard form for each line.

4. Slope is -2, and $(-7, -10)$ is on the line

5. Slope is 4, and $(-3, 0)$ is on the line.

🔑 **Explain 2** **Creating Linear Equations in Standard Form Given Two Points**

You can use two points on a line to create an equation of the line in standard form.

Example 2 **Write an equation in standard form for each line.**

Ⓐ $(-2, -1)$ and $(0, 4)$ are on the line.

Find the slope using the given points.

$$m = \frac{y_2 - y_1}{x_2 - x_1} = \frac{4 - (-1)}{0 - (-2)} = \frac{5}{2}$$

Substitute the slope and the coordinates of either of the given points in the point-slope form.

$$y - y_1 = m(x - x_1)$$

$$y - 4 = \frac{5}{2}(x - 0)$$

$$y - 4 = \frac{5}{2}x$$

Rewrite in standard form.

$$2y - 8 = 5x$$

$$5x - 2y = -8$$

Ⓑ $(5, 2)$ and $(3, -6)$ are on the line.

Find the slope.

$$m = \frac{y_2 - y_1}{x_2 - x_1} = \frac{\boxed{-6} - \boxed{2}}{\boxed{3} - \boxed{5}} = \frac{\boxed{-8}}{\boxed{-2}} = \boxed{4}$$

Substitute the slope and the coordinates of either of the given points in the point-slope form.

$$y - y_1 = m(x - x_1)$$

$$y - \boxed{2} = \boxed{4}\left(x - \boxed{5}\right)$$

$$y - \boxed{2} = \boxed{4}\ x - \boxed{20}$$

Or:

$$y - \boxed{(-6)} = \boxed{4}\left(x - \boxed{3}\right)$$

$$y + \boxed{6} = \boxed{4}\ x - \boxed{12}$$

Rewrite in standard form.

6. Why does it not matter which of the two given points you use in the point-slope form?

Write an equation in standard form for each line.

7. $(4, -7)$ and $(2, -3)$ are on the line.

8. $(1, 5)$ and $(-10, -6)$ are on the line.

🔀 Explain 3 Creating Linear Models in Standard Form

Equations in standard form can be used to model real-world linear situations.

Example 3 **Write an equation in standard form to model the linear situation.**

Ⓐ A tank is filling up with water at a rate of 3 gallons per minute. The tank already had 3 gallons in it before it started being filled.

Let x represent the time in minutes since the filling began and y represent the amount of water in gallons. Since 3 gallons were in the tank before filling started, the point $(0, 3)$ is on the line.

The rate is 3 gallons per minute, so $m = 3$.

Substitute the slope and the coordinates of the point in the point-slope form and rewrite in standard form.

$y - 3 = 3(x - 0)$

$y - 3 = 3x$

$3x - y = -3$

Ⓑ A hot tub filled with 440 gallons of water is being drained. After 1.5 hours, the amount of water had decreased to 320 gallons.

The initial amount of water in the hot tub was 440 gallons, so $(0, 440)$ is on the line.

After 1.5 hours, the amount of water had decreased to 320 gallons, so $(1.5, 320)$ is on the line.

Use the given information to find the slope.

$$m = \frac{\boxed{320} - \boxed{440}}{\boxed{1.5} - \boxed{0}} = \frac{\boxed{-120}}{\boxed{1.5}} = \boxed{-80}$$

Substitute the slope and the coordinates of one of the points in the point-slope form, and rewrite in standard form.

$y - \boxed{440} = \boxed{-80}\left(x - \boxed{0}\right)$

$y - \boxed{440} = \boxed{-80}\,x$

$\boxed{80x + y = 440}$

9. Your school sells adult and student tickets to a school play. Adult tickets cost $15 and student tickets cost $4. The total value of all the tickets sold is $7000. How could you write an equation in standard form to describe the linear situation?

Your Turn

Write an equation in standard form to model the linear situation.

10. A tank is being filled with gasoline at a rate of 4.5 gallons per minute. The gas tank contained 1.5 gallons of gasoline before filling started.

11. A pool that is being drained contained 18,000 gallons of water. After 2 hours, 12,500 gallons of water remain.

⊡ Elaborate

12. Describe a method other than the one given in the example for writing an equation in standard form given two points on a line.

13. Why might you choose the standard form of an equation over another form?

14. **Essential Question Check-In** When writing a linear equation in standard form, what other forms might you need to use?

☆ Evaluate: Homework and Practice

• Online Homework
• Hints and Help
• Extra Practice

Identify the form of each equation.

1.   **a.** $5x + 4y = 8$ **b.** $y - 3 = 8(x - 2)$

      c. $y = 3x + 6$ **d.** $2x - 3y = -7$

Rewrite each equation in standard form.

2. $y = 6x - 4$

3. $y - 2 = -(x + 7)$

4. $y = \frac{4}{3}x - \frac{2}{3}$

5. $y - 4 = \frac{7}{3}(x - 3)$

Use the information given to write an equation in standard form.

6. Slope is 3, and (1, 4) is on the line.

7. Slope is −2, and (4, 3) is on the line.

8. Slope is −3, and (0, −4) is on the line.

9. Slope is 0, and (0, 5) is on the line.

10. Slope is $\frac{4}{7}$, and (1, 3) is on the line.

11. Slope $= -\frac{3}{2}$, and (2, 3) is on the line.

12. (−1, 1) and (0, 4) are on the line.

13. (6, 11) and (5, 9) are on the line.

14. (2, −5) and (−1, 1) are on the line.

15. (25, 34) and (35, 50) are on the line.

16. Use the information on the graph to write an equation in standard form.

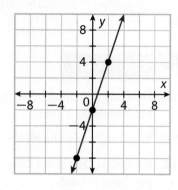

Write an equation in standard form to model the linear situation.

17. A bathtub that holds 32 gallons of water contains 12 gallons of water. You begin filling it, and after 5 minutes, the tub is full.

18. A barrel of oil was filled at a constant rate of 7.5 gal/min. The barrel had 10 gallons before filling began.

19. **Represent Real-World Situations**
A restaurant needs to plan seating for a party of 150 people. Large tables seat 10 people and small tables seat 6. Let x represent the number of large tables and y represent the number of small tables. An expression like the total number of people you can seat using A large tables and B small tables is called a *linear combination*. For instance, 150 people could be seated using 12 large tables and 5 small tables. Use that expression to write an equation in standard form that models all the different combinations of tables the restaurant could use. Then identify at least one possible combination of tables other than $(12, 5)$.

20. Match each equation with an equivalent equation in standard form.

A. $y = \frac{2}{3}x + 3$ a. __?__ $7x + 6y = 6$

B. $6 - y = -5x + 8$ b. __?__ $5x - y = 2$

C. $y - 3 = 4(x - 3)$ c. __?__ $2x - 3y = -9$

D. $-\frac{7}{6}x + 1 = y$ d. __?__ $4x - y = 9$

---

21. **Explain the Error** Cody was given two points $\left(\frac{1}{2}, 4\right)$ and $\left(\frac{2}{3}, 1\right)$, on a line and asked to create a linear equation in standard form. Cody's work is shown. Identify any errors and correct them.

$$m = \frac{1 - 4}{\frac{2}{3} - \frac{1}{2}} = -\frac{3}{\frac{1}{6}} = -\frac{1}{2}$$

$$y - 1 = -\frac{1}{2}\left(x - \frac{2}{3}\right)$$

$$y - 1 = -\frac{1}{2}x + \frac{1}{3}$$

$$2y - 2 = -x + \frac{2}{3}$$

$$x + 2y = \frac{8}{3}$$

22. **Communicate Mathematical Ideas** In the equation $Ax + By = C$, A and B cannot both be zero. What if only A is zero? What if only B is zero? Explain.

Lesson Performance Task

An airplane takes off with a full tank of 40,000 gallons of fuel and flies at an average speed of 550 miles per hour. After 8 hours in flight, there are 14,000 gallons of fuel left. It will take another 3.5 hours for the plane to reach its destination. How much fuel will be left in the tank when the plane lands? What is the total distance of the flight?

6.4 Transforming Linear Functions

Essential Question: What are the ways in which you can transform the graph of a linear function?

⊘ Explore 1 Building New Linear Functions by Translating

Investigate what happens to the graph of $f(x) = x + b$ when you change the value of b.

Ⓐ Use a graphing calculator. Start with the standard viewing window, which you can obtain by pressing Zoom and selecting ZStandard. Because the distances between consecutive tick marks on the x-axis and on the y-axis are not equal, you can make them equal by pressing Zoom again and selecting ZSquare.

What interval on each axis does the viewing window now show? (Press Window to find out.)

Ⓑ Graph the function $f(x) = x$ by pressing Y= and entering the function's rule next to $Y_1 =$. As shown, the graph of the function is a line that makes a 45° angle with each axis.

What are the slope and y-intercept of the graph of $f(x) = x$?

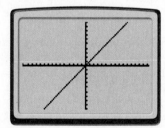

Ⓒ Graph other functions of the form $f(x) = x + b$ by entering their rules next to $Y_2 =$, $Y_3 =$, and so on. Be sure to choose both positive and negative values of b. For instance, graph $f(x) = x + 2$ and $f(x) = x - 3$.

What do the graphs have in common? How are they different?

Reflect

1. **Discussion** A *vertical translation* moves all points on a figure the same distance either up or down. Use the idea of a vertical translation to describe what happens to the graph of $f(x) = x + b$ when you increase the value of b and decrease the value of b.

2. In this Explore, we replaced the linear function $f(x)$ by $f(x) + k$. Show how replacing $f(x)$ by $f(x + k)$ has exactly the same effect.

Explore 2 Building New Linear Functions by Stretching, Shrinking, or Reflecting

Investigate what happens to the graph of $f(x) = mx$ when you change the value of m.

Ⓐ Use a graphing calculator. Press Y= and clear out all but the function $f(x) = x$ from the previous Explore Activity. Then graph other functions of the form $f(x) = mx$ by entering their rules next to $Y_2 =$, $Y_3 =$, and so on. Use only values of m that are greater than 1. For example, graph $f(x) = 2x$ and $f(x) = 6x$.

What do the graphs have in common? How are they different?

As the value of m increases from 1, does the graph become steeper or less steep?

Ⓑ Again, press Y= and clear out all but the function $f(x) = x$. Then graph other functions of the form $f(x) = mx$ by entering their rules next to $Y_2 =$, $Y_3 =$, and so on. This time use only values of m that are less than 1 but greater than 0. For instance, graph $f(x) = 0.5x$ and $f(x) = 0.2x$.

As the value of m decreases from 1 to 0, does the graph become steeper or less steep?

Ⓒ Again, press Y= and clear out all but the function $f(x) = x$. Then graph the function $f(x) = -x$ by entering its rule next to $Y_2 =$.

What are the slope and y-intercept of the graph of $f(x) = -x$?

How are the graphs of $f(x) = x$ and $f(x) = -x$ geometrically related?

Ⓓ Again, press Y= and clear out all the functions. Graph $f(x)= -x$ by entering its rule next to $Y_1 =$. Then graph other functions of the form $f(x) = mx$ where $m < 0$ by entering their rules next to $Y_2 =$, $Y_3 =$, and so on. Be sure to choose values of m that are less than -1 as well as values of m between -1 and 0.

Describe what happens to the graph of $f(x) = mx$ as the value of m decreases from -1, and as it increases from -1 to 0.

Reflect

3. **Discussion** When $m > 1$, will the graph of $f(x) = mx$ be a *vertical stretch* or a *vertical shrink* of the graph of $f(x) = x$? When $0 < m < 1$, will the graph of $f(x) = mx$ be a *vertical stretch* or a *vertical shrink* of the graph of $f(x) = x$? Explain your answers.

⊘ Explore 3 Understanding Function Families

Investigate what happens to the graph of $f(x) = mx$ when you change the value of m.

(A) A **family of functions** is a set of functions whose graphs have basic characteristics in common. What do all these variations on the original function $f(x) = x$ have in common?

(B) The most basic function of a family of functions is called the **parent function**. What is the parent function of the family of functions explored in the first two Explore Activities?

(C) A **parameter** is one of the constants in a function or equation that determines which variation of the parent function one is considering. For functions of the form $f(x) = mx + b$, what are the two parameters?

Reflect

4. **Discussion** For the family of all linear functions, the parent function is $f(x) = x$, where the parameters are $m = 1$ and $b = 0$. Other examples of families of linear functions are shown below. The example on the left shows a family with the same parameter m and differing parameters b. The example on the right shows a family with the same parameter b and differing parameters m.

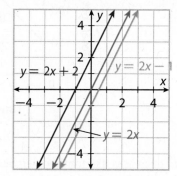

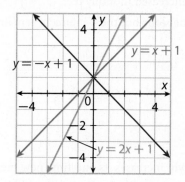

Describe the parameter that is left unchanged in the equations of the lines in the first graph.

🔑 Explain 1 Interpreting Parameter Changes in Linear Models

Many real-world scenarios can be modeled by linear functions. Changes in a particular scenario can be analyzed by making changes in the corresponding parameter of the linear function.

Example 1 A gym charges a one-time new member fee of $50 and then a monthly membership fee of $25. The total cost C of being a member of the gym is given by the function $C(t) = 25t + 50$, where t is the time (in months) since joining the gym. For each situation described, sketch a graph using the given graph of $C(t) = 25t + 50$ as a reference.

(A) The gym decreases its one-time fee for new members.

What change did you make to the graph of $C(t) = 25t + 50$ to represent a lower one-time fee?

I decreased the y-intercept but the slope remained the same.

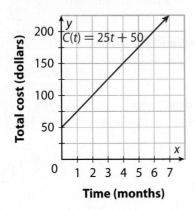

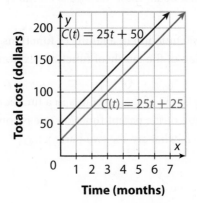

(B) The gym increases its monthly membership fee.

What change did you make to the graph of $C(t) = 25t + 50$ to represent an increased monthly fee?

I increased the slope but the y-intercept remained the same.

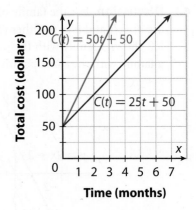

Reflect

5. Suppose the gym increases its one-time new member fee *and* decreases its monthly membership fee. Describe how you would alter the graph of $C(t) = 25t + 50$ to illustrate the new cost function.

Your Turn

Determine what will happen to the graph of the original function when the described changes occur.

6. Once a year the gym offers a special in which the one-time fee for joining is waived for new members. What impact does this special offer have on the graph of the original function $C(t) = 25t + 50$?

7. Suppose the gym increases its one-time joining fee *and* decreases its monthly membership fee. Does this have any impact on the domain of the function? Does this have any impact on the range of the function? Explain your reasoning.

💬 Elaborate

8. How do changes to m in the equation $f(x) = mx$ affect the graph of the equation?

9. How do changes to b in the equation $f(x) = x + b$ affect the graph of the equation?

10. Which parameter causes the steepness of the graph of the line to change for the family of linear functions of the form $f(x) = mx + b$?

11. **Essential Question Check-In** What are the different types of transformations?

• Online Homework
• Hints and Help
• Extra Practice

In Exercises 1–4, refer to the graph of $f(x) = x + 2$.

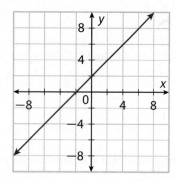

1. Graph two more functions in the same family for which the parameter being changed is the y-intercept, b.

2. Graph two more functions in the same family for which the parameter being changed is the slope, m, and is greater than 1.

3. Graph two more functions in the same family for which the parameter being changed is the slope, m, and is between 0 and 1.

4. Graph two more functions in the same family for which the parameter being changed is the slope, m, and is less than 0.

5. The graph of the parent linear function $f(x) = x$ is shown in black on the coordinate grid. Write the function that represents this function with the indicated parameter changes.

   a. m increased, b unchanged

   b. m decreased, b unchanged

   c. m unchanged, b increased

   d. m unchanged, b decreased,

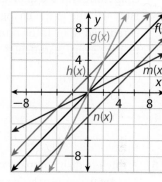

6. For each linear function graphed on the coordinate grid, state the value of m and the value of b.

   a. $f(x)$

   b. $g(x)$

   c. $h(x)$

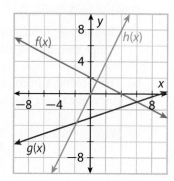

Describe the transformation(s) on the graph of the parent function $f(x) = x$ that results in the graph of $g(x)$.

7. $g(x) = -x + 9$

8. $g(x) = 3x$

9. $g(x) = \frac{1}{4}x$

10. $g(x) = 7x - 8$

11. $g(x) = -\frac{3}{4}x + 5$

Use the parent function and the description of the transformation to write the new function.

12. Transform the graph of $f(x) = -x + 2$ in such a way that it has the same steepness in the opposite direction.

13. Reflect the graph of $f(x) = x - 1$ across the y-axis, and then translate it 4 units down.

Determine how changes in parameters will affect a graph. Write the new function.

14. For large parties, a restaurant charges a reservation fee of $25, plus $15 per person. The total charge for a party of x people is $f(x) = 15x + 25$. How will the graph of this function change if the reservation fee is raised to $50 and if the per-person charge is lowered to $12?

15. The number of chaperones on a field trip must include 1 teacher for every 4 students, plus a total of 2 parents. The function describing the number of chaperones for a trip of x students is $f(x) = \frac{1}{4}x + 2$. How will the graph change if the number of parents is reduced to 0? If the number of teachers is raised to 1 for every 3 students?

16. A satellite dish company charges a one-time installation fee of $75 and then a monthly usage charge of $40. The total cost C of using that satellite service is given by the function $C(t) = 40t + 75$, where t is the time (in months) since starting the service. For the situation given below, describe the new function using the graph of $C(t) = 40t + 75$ as a reference.

   a. The satellite dish company reduces its one-time installation fee to $60. What change would you make to the graph of $C(t) = 40t + 75$ to obtain the new graph?

   b. The satellite dish company decreases its monthly fee to $30. What change would you make to the graph of $C(t) = 40t + 75$ to obtain the new graph?

   c. What is the new function with both changes?

17. A salesperson earns a base monthly salary of $2000 plus a 10% commission on sales. The salesperson's monthly income I (in dollars) is given by the function $I(s) = 0.1s + 2000$, where s is the sales (in dollars) that the salesperson makes. Sketch a graph to illustrate each situation using the graph of $I(s) = 0.1s + 2000$ as a reference.

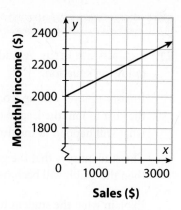

a. The salesperson's base salary is increased.

b. The salesperson's commission rate is decreased.

18. Mr. Resnick is driving at a speed of 40 miles per hour to visit relatives who live 100 miles away from his home. His distance d (in miles) from his destination is given by the function $d(t) = 100 - 40t$, where t is the time (in hours) since his trip began. Sketch a graph to illustrate each situation. The graph shown already represents the function $d(t)$.

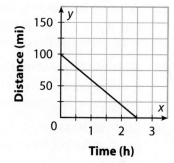

a. He increases his speed to get to the destination sooner. (Hint: His distance from the destination decreases faster.)

b. His starting distance from the destination is increased because a detour forces him to take a longer route.

c. Give an example of another linear function within the same family of functions as $d(t) = 100 - 40t$. Explain the meaning of each parameter in your example.

19. A book club charges a membership fee of $20 and then $12 for each book purchased.

a. Write a function to represent the cost y of membership in the club based on the number of books purchased x.

b. Write a second function to represent the cost of membership if the club raises its membership fee to $30.

c. Describe the relationship between the functions from parts A and B.

20. Match each effect on a graph with the appropriate change in m. The *steepness* of a line refers to the absolute value of its slope. The greater the absolute value of the slope, the steeper the line.

How the Value of m Changes	Effect on the Graph of $f(x) = mx$
A. Increase m when $m > 1$.	**a.** _?_ Graph becomes steeper.
B. Decrease m when $0 < m < 1$.	**b.** _?_ Graph becomes less steep.
C. Decrease m when $m < -1$.	**c.** _?_ Graph becomes steeper.
D. Increase m when $0 > m > -1$.	**d.** _?_ Graph becomes less steep.

21. Explain the Error A student is asked to explain what happens with each of the parameters for the following situation.

It costs a player $20 up front to join a basketball league and then $5 a week to play. If the cost to join the league is reduced to $19 and the weekly fee increases to $6 a week, what will happen to the function of the graph?

The student says that the graph will shift up because the value of b has increased and then the graph will become less steep because the value of m has decreased.

Explain what the student has done incorrectly.

22. Critique Reasoning Geoff says that changing the value of m while leaving b unchanged in $f(x) = mx + b$ has no impact on the intercepts of the graph. Marcus disagrees with this statement. Who is correct? Explain your reasoning.

23. Multiple Representations The graph of $y = x + 3$ is a vertical translation of the graph of $y = x + 1$, 2 units upward. Examine the intercepts of both lines and state another way that the geometric relationship between the two graphs can be described.

24. Critique Reasoning Stephanie says that the graphs of $y = 3x + 2$ and $y = 3x - 2$ are parallel. Isabella says that the graphs are perpendicular. Who is correct? Explain your reasoning.

25. Critical Thinking It has been shown that the graph of $g(x) = x + 3$ is the result of translating the graph of $f(x) = x$ three units up. However, this can also be thought of as a horizontal translation—that is, a translation left or right. Describe the horizontal translation of $f(x) = x$ to get the graph of $g(x) = x + 3$.

Lesson Performance Task

High-demand cars that are also in low supply tend to retain their value better than other cars. The data in the table is for a car that won a resale value award.

Year	1	3	5
Value (%)	84	64	44

a. Write a function to represent the change in the percentage of the car's value over time. Assume that the function is linear for the first 5 years.

b. According to the model, by what percent did the car's value drop the day it was purchased and driven off the lot?

c. Would the linear model be useful after 10 years? Explain why or why not.

d. Suppose months were used instead of years to write the function. How would the model change? What is the relationship of the new function to the original function?

6.5 Comparing Properties of Linear Functions

Essential Question: How can you compare linear functions that are represented in different ways?

🧭 Explore Comparing Properties of Linear Functions Given Algebra and a Description

Comparing linear relationships can involve comparing relationships that are expressed in different ways.

Dan's Plumbing and Kim's Plumbing have different ways of charging their customers. The function $D(t) = 35t$ represents the total amount in dollars that Dan's Plumbing charges for t hours of work. Kim's Plumbing charges \$35 per hour plus a \$40 flat-rate fee.

(A) Define a function $K(t)$ that represents the total amount Kim's Plumbing charges for t hours of work. Then copy and complete the tables.

Cost for Dan's Plumbing		
t	$D(t) = 35t$	$(t, D(t))$
0	?	?
1	?	?
2	?	?
3	?	?

Cost for Kim's Plumbing		
t	$K(t) = $?	$(t, K(t))$
0	?	?
1	?	?
2	?	?
3	?	?

(B) What domain and range values for the functions $D(t)$ and for $K(t)$ are reasonable in this context? Explain.

(C) Graph the two cost functions for the appropriate domain values.

(D) Compare the graphs. How are they alike? How are they different?

Reflect

1. Discussion What information could be found about the two functions without changing their representation?

⊘ Explain 1 Comparing Properties of Linear Functions Given Algebra and a Table

A table and a rule are two ways that a linear relationship may be expressed. Sometimes it may be helpful to convert one representation to the other when comparing two relationships. There are other times when comparisons are possible without converting either representation.

Example 1 Compare the initial value and the range for each of the linear functions $f(x)$ and $g(x)$.

(A) The domain of each function is the set of all real numbers x such that $5 \leq x \leq 8$. The table shows some ordered pairs for $f(x)$. The function $g(x)$ is defined by the rule $g(x) = 3x + 7$.

x	f(x)
5	20
6	24
7	28
8	32

The initial value is the output that is paired with the least input. The least input for $f(x)$ and $g(x)$ is 5.

The initial value of $f(x)$ is $f(5) = 20$.

The initial value of $g(x)$ is $g(5) = 3(5) + 7 = 22$.

Since $f(x)$ is a linear function and its domain is the set of all real numbers from 5 to 8, its range will be the set of all real numbers from $f(5)$ to $f(8)$. Since $f(5) = 20$ and $f(8) = 32$, the range of $f(x)$ is the set of all real numbers such that $20 \leq f(x) \leq 32$.

Since $g(x)$ is a linear function and its domain is the set of all real numbers from 5 to 8, its range will be the set of all real numbers from $g(5)$ to $g(8)$. Since $g(5) = 22$ and $g(8) = 3(8) + 7 = 31$, the range of $g(x)$ is the set of all real numbers such that $22 \leq g(x) \leq 31$.

(B) The domain of each function is the set of all real numbers x such that $6 \leq x \leq 10$. The table shows some ordered pairs for $f(x)$. The function $g(x)$ is defined by the rule $g(x) = 5x + 11$.

x	f(x)
6	36
7	42
8	48
9	54
10	60

The initial value is the output that is paired with the least input. The least input for $f(x)$ and $g(x)$ is 6.

The initial value of $f(x)$ is $f(6) = 36$.

The initial value of $g(x)$ is $g(6) = 5(6) + 11 = 41$.

Since $f(x)$ is a linear function, and its domain is the set of all real numbers from 6 to 10, its range

will be the set of all real numbers from $f\left(\boxed{6} \right)$ to $f(10)$. Since $f\left(\boxed{6} \right) = \boxed{36}$ and $f(10) = \boxed{60}$, the

range of $f(x)$ is the set of all real numbers such that $\boxed{36} \leq f(x) \leq \boxed{60}$.

Since $g(x)$ is a linear function and its domain is the set of all real numbers from 6 to 10, its

range will be the set of all real numbers from $g\left(\boxed{6} \right)$ to $g(10)$. Since $g\left(\boxed{6} \right) = \boxed{41}$ and

$g(10) = 5\left(\boxed{10} \right) + 11 = \boxed{61}$, the range of $g(x)$ is the set of all real numbers such

that $\boxed{41} \leq g(x) \leq \boxed{61}$.

2. **Discussion** How can you use a table of values to find the rate of change for a linear function?

Your Turn

3. Find the rate of change for the linear function $f(x)$ that is shown in the table.

x	f(x)
3	22
4	29
5	36
6	43
7	50

4. The rule for $f(x)$ in Example 1B is $f(x) = 6x$. If the domains were extended to all real numbers, how would the slopes and y-intercepts of $f(x)$ and $g(x) = 5x + 11$ in Example 1B compare?

⭐ Explain 2 Comparing Properties of Linear Functions Given a Graph and a Description

Information about a linear relationship may have to be inferred from the context given in the problem.

Example 2 Write a rule for each function, and then compare their domain, range, slope, and y-intercept.

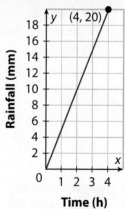

(A) A rainstorm in Austin lasted for 3.5 hours, during which time it rained a steady rate of 4.5 mm per hour. The function $A(t)$ represents the amount of rain that fell in t hours.

The graph shows the amount of rain that fell during the same rainstorm in Dallas, $D(t)$ (in millimeters), as a function of time t (in hours).

Write a rule for each function. $A(t) = 4.5t$ for $0 \leq t \leq 3.5$

The line representing $D(t)$ has endpoints at $(0, 0)$ and $(4, 20)$. The slope of $D(t)$ is $\frac{20 - 0}{4 - 0} = 5$. The y-intercept is 0, so substituting 5 for m and 0 for b in $y = mx + b$ produces the equation $y = 5x$. This can be represented by the function $D(t) = 5t$, for $0 \leq t \leq 4$.

The domains of each function both begin at 0 but end for different values of t, because the lengths of time that it rained in Austin and Dallas were not the same.

The range for $A(t)$ is $0 \leq A(t) \leq 15.75$. The range for $D(t)$ is $0 \leq A(t) \leq 20$.

The slope for $D(t)$ is 5, which is greater than the slope for $A(t)$, which is 4.5.

The y-intercepts of both functions are 0.

Rainfall (mm) / Time (h)

B One group of hikers hiked at a steady rate of 6.5 kilometers per hour for 4 hours. The function $f(t)$ represents the distance this group of hikers hiked in t hours.

The graph shows the distance a second group of hikers hiked, $g(t)$ (in kilometers), as a function of t (in hours).

Write a rule for each function.

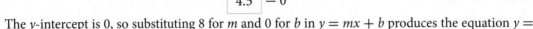

$f(t) = \boxed{6.5t}$ for $\boxed{0} \leq t \leq \boxed{4}$

The line representing $g(t)$ has endpoints at $(0, 0)$

and $\left(\boxed{4.5} , \boxed{36} \right)$. The slope of $g(t)$ is $\dfrac{36 - 0}{\boxed{4.5} - 0} = \boxed{8}$.

The y-intercept is 0, so substituting 8 for m and 0 for b in $y = mx + b$ produces the equation $y = \boxed{8x}$.

This can be represented by the function $g(t) = \boxed{8t}$ for $\boxed{0} \leq t \leq \boxed{4.5}$.

The domains of each function both begin at 0 and end at different values of t.

The range for $f(t)$ is $\boxed{0} \leq f(t) \leq \boxed{26}$ and the range for $g(t)$ is $\boxed{0} \leq g(t) \leq \boxed{36}$.

The slope for $g(t)$ is greater than the slope for $f(t)$.

The y-intercepts are both 0.

Reflect

5. What is the meaning of the y-intercepts for the functions $A(t)$ and $D(t)$ in Example 2A?

Your Turn

6. An experiment compares the heights of two plants over time. A plant was 5 cm tall at the beginning of the experiment and grew 0.3 centimeters each day. The function $f(t)$ represents the height of the plant (in centimeters) after t days. The graph shows the height of the second plant, $g(t)$ (in centimeters), as a function of time t (in days).

Find the rate of change $g(t)$ and compare it to the rate of change for $f(t)$.

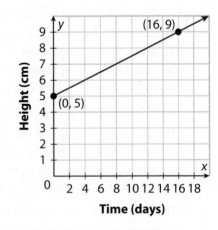

💬 Elaborate

7. When would representing a linear function by a graph be more helpful than by a table?

8. When would representing a linear function by a table be more helpful than by a graph?

9. **Essential Question-Check-In** How can you compare a linear function represented in a table to one represented as a graph?

Evaluate: Homework and Practice

• Online Homework
• Hints and Help
• Extra Practice

Compare the initial value and the range for each of the linear
functions $f(x)$ and $g(x)$.

1. The domain of each function is the set of all real numbers x such that $2 \le x \le 5$.
The table shows some ordered pairs for $f(x)$. The function $g(x)$ is defined by the
rule $g(x) = x + 6$.

x	f(x)
2	5
3	7
4	9
5	11

2. The domain of each function is the set of all real numbers x such that $8 \le x \le 12$.
The table shows some ordered pairs for $f(x)$. The function $g(x)$ is defined by the
rule $g(x) = 7x - 3$.

x	f(x)
8	34
9	38
10	42
11	46
12	50

3. The domain of each function is the set of all real numbers x such that
$-4 \le x \le -1$. The function $f(x)$ is defined by the rule $f(x) = 2x + 9$.
The table shows some ordered pairs for $g(x)$.

x	g(x)
−4	10
−3	9
−2	8
−1	7

4. The domain of each function is the set of all real numbers x such that $0 \le x \le 4$.
The function $f(x)$ is defined by the rule $f(x) = -3x + 15$. The table shows some
ordered pairs for $g(x)$.

x	g(x)
0	23
1	19
2	15
3	11
4	7

5. The domain of each function is the set of all real numbers x such that
$10 \le x \le 13$. The table shows some ordered pairs for $f(x)$. The function
$g(x)$ is defined by the rule $g(x) = \frac{1}{2}x + 12$.

x	f(x)
10	22
11	$\frac{47}{2}$
12	25
13	$\frac{53}{2}$

© Houghton Mifflin Harcourt Publishing Company

6. The domain of each function is the set of all real numbers x such that $2 \leq x \leq 6$. The function $f(x)$ is defined by the rule $f(x) = -\frac{3}{4}x + 10$. The table shows some ordered pairs for $g(x)$.

x	g(x)
2	14
3	$\frac{51}{4}$
4	$\frac{23}{2}$
5	$\frac{41}{4}$
6	9

Write a rule for each function f and g, and then compare their domains, ranges, slopes, and y-intercepts.

7. The function $f(x)$ has a slope of 6 and has a y-intercept of 20. The graph shows the function $g(x)$.

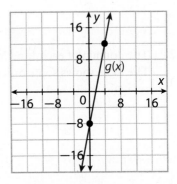

8. The function $f(x)$ has a slope of -3 and has a y-intercept of 5. The graph shows the function $g(x)$.

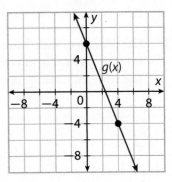

Write a rule for each function, and then compare their domains, ranges, slopes, and y-intercepts.

9. Jeff, an electrician, had a job that lasted 5.5 hours, during which time he earned \$32 per hour and charged a \$25 service fee. The function $J(t)$ represents the amount Jeff earns in t hours.

Brendan also works as an electrician. The graph of $B(t)$ shows the amount in dollars that Brendan earns as a function of time t in hours.

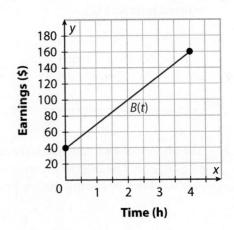

10. Apples can be bought at a farmer's market up to 10 pounds at a time, where each pound costs $1.10. The function $a(w)$ represents the cost of buying w pounds of apples.

The graph of $p(w)$ shows the cost in dollars of buying w pounds of pears.

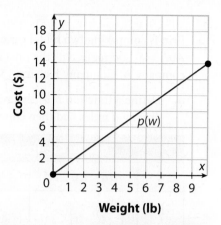

11. **Biology** A gecko travels for 6 minutes at a constant rate of 19 meters per minute. The function $g(t)$ represents the distance the gecko travels after t minutes.

The graph of $m(t)$ shows the distance in meters that a mouse travels after t minutes.

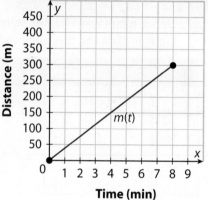

12. Cindy is buying a water pump. The box for Pump A claims that it can move 48 gallons per minute. The function $A(t)$ represents the amount of water (in gallons) Pump A can move after t minutes.

The graph of $B(t)$ shows the amount of water in gallons that Pump B can move after t minutes.

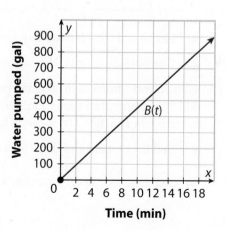

13. Erin is comparing two rental car companies for an upcoming trip. The function $A(d) = 0.20d$ represents the total amount in dollars of driving a car d miles from company A. Company B charges $0.10 per mile and a $10 fee.

a. Define a function $B(d)$ that represents the total amount company B charges for driving d miles and then copy and complete the tables.

Cost for Company A		
d	$A(d) = 0.20d$	$(d, A(d))$
0	?	?
20	?	?
40	?	?

Cost for Company B		
d	$B(d) =$	$(d, B(d))$
0	?	?
20	?	?
40	?	?

b. Graph and label the two cost functions for all appropriate domain values.

c. Compare the graphs. How are they alike? How are they different?

14. Snow is falling in two cities. The function $C(t) = 2t + 8$ represents the amount of snow on the ground, in centimeters, in Carlisle t hours after the snowstorm begins. There was 8 cm of snow on the ground in York when the storm began and the snow accumulates at 1.5 cm per hour.

a. Define a function $Y(t)$ that represents the amount of snow on the ground after t hours in York and then copy and complete the tables.

Carlisle		
t	$C(t) = 2t + 8$	$(t, C(t))$
0	?	?
1	?	?
2	?	?

York		
t	$Y(t) =$	$(t, Y(t))$
0	?	?
1	?	?
2	?	?

b. Graph and label the two cost functions for all appropriate domain values.

c. Compare the graphs. How are they alike? How are they different?

15. Gillian works from 20 to 30 hours per week during the summer. She earns $12.50 per hour. Her friend Emily also has a job. Her pay for t hours each week is given by the function $e(t) = 13t$, where $15 \leq t \leq 25$.

a. Find the domain and range of each function.

b. Compare their hourly wages and the amount they earn per week.

16. The function $A(p)$ defined by the rule $A(p) = 0.13p + 15$ represents the cost in dollars of producing a custom textbook that has p pages for college A, where $0 < p \le 500$. The table shows some ordered pairs for $B(p)$, where $B(p)$ represents the cost in dollars of producing a custom textbook that has p pages for college B, where $0 < p \le 500$. For both colleges, only full pages may be printed.

Compare the domain, range, slope, and y-intercept of the functions. Interpret the comparisons in context.

p	B(p)
0	24
50	30
100	36
150	42

17. Copy and complete the table so that $f(x)$ is a linear function with a slope of 4 and a y-intercept of 7. Assume the domain includes all real numbers between the least and greatest values shown in the table. Compare $f(x)$ to $g(x) = 4x + 7$ if the range of $g(x)$ is $-1 \le g(x) \le 11$.

x	f(x)
−2	?
−1	?
0	?
1	?

18. Which of the following functions have a rate of change that is greater than the one shown in the graph?

a. $f(x) = \dfrac{1}{2}x - 5$

b. $g(x) = x + 6$

c. $h(x) = \dfrac{3}{4}x - 9$

d. $j(x) = \dfrac{1}{4}x + 8$

e. $k(x) = x$

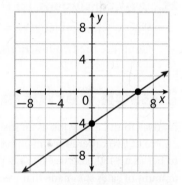

19. Does the function $f(x) = 5x + 5$ with the domain $6 \le x \le 8$ have the same domain as function $g(x)$, whose only function values are shown in the table? Explain.

x	g(x)
6	35
7	40
8	45

20. The linear function $f(x)$ is defined by the table, and the linear function $g(x)$ is shown in the graph. Assume that the domain of $f(x)$ includes all real numbers between the least and greatest values shown in the table.

a. Find the domain and range of each function, and compare them.

b. What is the slope of the line represented by each function? What is the y-intercept of each function?

x	f(x)
−1	−7
0	−4
1	−1
2	2
3	5

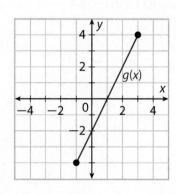

21. The linear function $f(x)$ is defined by $f(x) = -\frac{1}{4}x + 6$ for all real numbers, and the linear function $g(x)$ is shown in the graph.

    a. Find the domain and range of each function, and compare them.

    b. What is the slope of the line represented by each function? What is the y-intercept of each function?

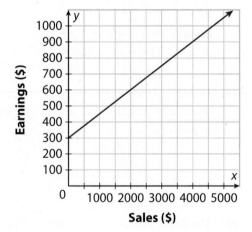

22. **Communicate Mathematical Ideas** Describe a linear function for which the least value in the range does not occur at the least value of the domain (a function for which the least value in the range is not the initial value.)

23. **Draw Conclusions** Two linear functions have the same slope, same x-intercept, and same y-intercept. Must these functions be identical? Explain your reasoning.

24. **Draw Conclusions** Let $f(x)$ be a line with slope -3 and y-intercept 0 with domain $\{0, 1, 2, 3\}$, and let $g(x) = \{(0, 0), (1, -1), (2, -4), (3, -9)\}$. Compare the two functions.

25. **Draw Conclusions** Let $f(x)$ be a line with slope 7 and y-intercept -17 with domain $0 \le x \le 5$, and let $g(x) = \left\{(0, -17), (1, -10), (2, -3), (3, 4), (4, 11), (5, 18)\right\}$. Compare the two functions.

Lesson Performance Task

Lindsay found a new job as an insurance salesperson. She has her choice of two different compensation plans. Plan F was described to her as a $450 base weekly salary plus a 10% commission on the amount of sales she made that week. The function $f(x)$ represents the amount Lindsay earns in a week when making sales of x dollars with compensation plan F. Plan G was described to her with the graph shown. The function $g(x)$ represents the amount Lindsay earns in a week when making sales of x dollars with compensation plan G.

Write a rule for the functions $f(x)$ and $g(x)$; then identify and compare their domain, range, slope, and y-intercept. Compare the benefits and drawbacks of each compensation plan. Which compensation plan should Lindsay take? Justify your answer.

Essential Question: How can you use different forms of linear equations to solve real-world problems?

Key Vocabulary

family of functions *(familia de funciones)*

parameter *(parámetro)*

parent function *(función madre)*

KEY EXAMPLE   *(Lesson 6.1)*

For one taxi company, the cost y in dollars of a ride is a linear function of the miles traveled x. The initial charge is $2.00, and the charge per mile is $0.40. Identify the slope and y-intercept of the graph that represents this situation and interpret what they mean. Then write an equation in slope-intercept form and use it to find the cost of riding 15 miles.

The rate of change is $0.40 per mile, so the slope m is 0.4.

The initial cost is the cost to travel 0 miles, $2.00, so the y-intercept b is 2.

So, the equation in slope-intercept form is $y = 0.4x + 2$.

To find the cost of riding 15 miles, substitute 15 for x and simplify.

$$y = 0.4x + 2$$
$$= 0.4(15) + 2$$
$$= 6 + 2$$
$$= 8$$

(15, 8) is a solution of the equation, and the cost of riding 15 miles is $8.

KEY EXAMPLE   *(Lesson 6.3)*

Write an equation in standard form for the line that contains $(-3, 4)$ and $(5, 0)$.

Find the slope using the given points.

$$m = \frac{y_2 - y_1}{x_2 - x_1} = \frac{0 - 4}{5 - (-3)} = \frac{-4}{8} = -\frac{1}{2}$$

Substitute the slope and the coordinates of either of the points in point-slope form.

$$y - y_1 = m(x - x_1)$$
$$y - 0 = -\frac{1}{2}(x - 5)$$
$$y = -\frac{1}{2}x + \frac{5}{2}$$

Rewrite in standard form. $x + 2y = 5$

EXERCISES

Write the equation of each line in slope-intercept form. *(Lesson 6.1)*

1. slope is 4 and contains (3, 6)

2. contains (5, 0) and (9, 4)

Write the equation of each line in point-slope form. *(Lesson 6.2)*

3. slope is −1 and contains (2, 7)

4. contains (−2, 8) and (4, −4)

Write the equation of each line in standard form. *(Lesson 6.3)*

5. slope is 3 and contains (1, 6)

6. contains (0, −2) and (10, 2)

7. Describe a series of transformations of the graph of $f(x) = x$ that results in the graph of $g(x) = −x + 6$. *(Lesson 6.4)*

8. Compare the domain and range of $f(x) = −3x + 5$ and $g(x) = 4x − 6$. *(Lesson 6.5)*

MODULE PERFORMANCE TASK

Who Wins the Race?

Jamal and Kendra are running in a 26.2-mile marathon. Jamal's friend is recording his times in the table as shown, while Kendra's friend uses a scatter plot to show her progress. If both runners continue at the same average pace, who will arrive at the finish line first? How much longer will it take for the other person to finish?

Jamal's Race	
Distance (mi)	Time (min)
4	26
8	56
12	90
16	128
20	170

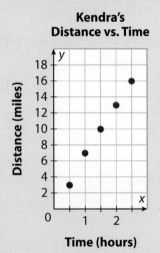

Kendra's Distance vs. Time

Distance (miles) — Time (hours)

Be sure to write down all your data and assumptions. Then use graphs, numbers, words, or algebra to explain how you reached your conclusion.

(Ready) to Go On?

6.1–6.5 Forms of Linear Equations

Write an equation for each line in the given form. *(Lessons 6.1, 6.2, 6.3)*

1. slope is -2 and $(1, 7)$ is on the line; standard form

2. contains the points $(3, 4)$ and $(6, 10)$; slope-intercept form

3. slope is 4 and $(-3, 8)$ is on the line; point-slope form

4. Describe a transformation of the graph of $f(x) = x$ that results in the graph of $g(x) = 4x$. *(Lesson 6.4)*

5. Jan works from 30 to 40 hours per week during the summer. She earns $12.00 per hour. Her friend Rachel also has a job. Rachel's pay for t hours is given by the function $r(t) = 11t$, where $20 \le t \le 30$. Find the domain and range of each function. Compare their hourly wages and the amount they earn per week. *(Lesson 6.5)*

ESSENTIAL QUESTION

6. What type or types of transformations can affect the slope of a linear function? What type or types cannot?

Assessment Readiness

1. Look at each equation. Tell whether each equation represents a line with slope $m = 5$, containing the point $(3, 8)$.

   A. $5x - y = 7$

   B. $3x + 8y = 5$

   C. $10x - 2y = 14$

2. Consider the function $f(x) = 3x - 2$. Determine if each statement is True or False.

   A. The y-intercept is 2.

   B. The x-intercept is $\frac{2}{3}$.

   C. The slope is 3.

3. Look at each statement. Tell whether each statement describes a transformation of the graph of $f(x) = x$ that would result in the graph of $g(x) = x + 2$.

   A. The graph of the parent function is reflected across the y-axis.

   B. The graph of the parent function is translated 2 units up.

   C. The graph of the parent function is translated 2 units down.

4. What is the x-intercept of $y + 12 = 3(x - 9)$? Explain how you solved this problem.

5. Write $5x - 3y = -12$ in slope-intercept form. What is the slope? Show your work.

Linear Equations and Inequalities

Essential Question: How can you use linear equations and inequalities to solve real-world problems?

REAL WORLD VIDEO
In some sports, such as boxing and wrestling, the athletes and their competitions are categorized by weight. The weight divisions are defined by specific upper and lower weight limits, which can be efficiently described using inequalities.

MODULE PERFORMANCE TASK PREVIEW

Making Weight

Wrestling is a physically demanding contact sport in which two athletes grapple on a mat with the goal of out-maneuvering and gaining control over the opponent. Opponents are matched up based on weight, and there are several weight classes. How can athletes use models to help them meet their weight class goals? Let's hit the mat and find out!

Are YOU Ready?

Complete these exercises to review skills you will need for this module.

Algebraic Expressions

- Online Homework
- Hints and Help
- Extra Practice

Example 1 Evaluate $5x + 6y$ for $x = -9$ and $y = 7$.

$5x + 6y$

$5(-9) + 6(7)$ Substitute -9 for x and 7 for y.

$-45 + 42$ Multiply.

-3 Add.

Evaluate each expression for the given values of the variables.

1. $7p + 3q$ for $p = 2$ and $q = -6$

2. $(n + 1)^2$ for $n = -9$

3. $4d - 2e - 13$ for $d = 5$ and $e = -7$

4. $a^2 - b$ for $a = 4$ and $b = 5$

Graphing Linear Proportional Relationships

Example 2 Tell whether the graph represents a linear proportional relationship.

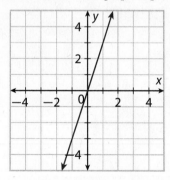

The graph of a proportional relationship is a straight line that passes through the origin.

The graph is a straight line that passes through $(0, 0)$, so it represents a linear proportional relationship.

Tell whether the graph represents a linear proportional relationship.

5.

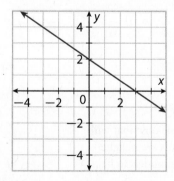

6.

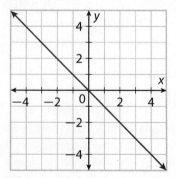

© Houghton Mifflin Harcourt Publishing Company

7.1 Modeling Linear Relationships

Essential Question: How can you model linear relationships given limited information?

⊘ Explore Modeling Linear Relationships with Slope-Intercept Form

A department store offers a frequent-buyers card to earn rewards for purchases customers make at the store. Each transaction is worth 12 points, and customers automatically earn 25 points when they sign up.

Write an equation for the function that gives the card value based on the number of transactions that have occurred.

(A) What units would be associated with the variables in this function? $\boxed{?}$

(B) Complete the verbal model for the frequent-buyers card function. Include units.

Card Value (points) = Initial Value (points) + $\boxed{?}$

(C) Write the function rule for the card-value function C.

$C(t) = \boxed{?} + \boxed{?}\ t$, where t is the number of transactions.

(D) For each 100 points, the customer receives a gift certificate. How many transactions will it take for the customer to earn the first gift certificate? $\boxed{?}$

(E) What is the y-intercept for this linear function, and what does it represent? $\boxed{?}$

(F) What is the slope for this linear function, and what does it represent? $\boxed{?}$

Reflect

1. **Discussion** Use the function rule to show that the units for $C(t)$ are points.

2. **Critical Thinking** What types of number are appropriate for the domain of $C(t)$?

3. Using inequalities, express the restrictions on the range of $C(t)$.

Explain # Creating and Interpreting Linear Models

You can create linear equations and inequalities to model some real-world situations.

Example **Given the real-world situation, solve the problem.**

Fundraising The Band Booster Club is selling T-shirts and blanket wraps to raise money for a trip. The band director has asked the club to raise at least $1000.

The booster club president wants to know how many T-shirts and how many blanket wraps the club needs to sell to meet their goal of $1000. The T-shirts cost $10 each, and the blanket wraps cost $25 each. Write a linear equation that describes the problem, and then graph the linear equation. How can the booster club president use the sales price of each item to meet the goal?

Analyze Information

Identify the important information.

- T-shirts cost $10 each.

- Blanket wraps cost $25 each.

- The booster club needs to raise a total of $1000 .

Formulate a Plan

The total amount of revenue earned by selling T-shirts is $10t$. The total amount of revenue earned from selling blanket wraps is $25b$. These two results can be added and set equal to the sales goal to find the number of T-shirts and blanket wraps that need to be sold to reach $1000. Graph this function to find all of the possible combinations of T-rts and blanket wraps sold to reach $1000.

 ### Solve

Write a linear equation for the sales goal.

$$\boxed{25}\, b + \boxed{10}\, t = \boxed{1000}$$

Calculate three pairs of values for t and b, and graph a line through those points to find possible solutions. Be sure to label the graph.

t	b
0	40
50	20
100	0

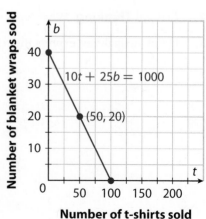

Number of blanket wraps sold

Number of t-shirts sold

$10t + 25b = 1000$

(50, 20)

© Houghton Mifflin Harcourt Publishing Company • Image Credits: ©B Christopher/Alamy

Justify and Evaluate

The *x*-intercept represents the number of T-shirts that need to be sold if no blanket wraps are sold. The *y*-intercept represents the number of blanket wraps to be sold if no T-shirts are sold. The booster club president can use the line to find the possible combinations of T-shirts and blankets to reach $1000.

Reflect

4. **Critical Thinking** Technically, the graph of possible combinations of T-shirts and blanket wraps that reach the goal of $1000 should be discrete, but for convenience the graph is shown as a connected line. Explain why the solutions to this problem would be only the points on the line that have whole-number coordinates.

Your Turn

5. **Business** A sandwich shop sell sandwiches for $5 each and bottles of water for $1 each. The owner of this shop needs to earn a total of $100 by the end of the day. Write a linear equation that describes the problem; then graph the linear equation. Make sure to label both axes with appropriate titles. Then use the graph to determine how many sandwiches the shop must sell if no waters are sold.

 Elaborate

6. How can the graph of a linear function be used to find answers to a real-world problem?

7. **Essential Question Check-In** What is the first step when modeling linear relationships given limited information?

• Online Homework
• Hints and Help
• Extra Practice

Food A baker sells bread for $3 a loaf and rolls for $1 each. The baker needs to sell $24 worth of baked goods by the end of the day.

1. Write a linear equation that describes the problem.

2. Graph the linear equation. Make sure to label both axes with appropriate titles.

3. Use the graph to approximate how many loaves of bread the baker must sell if 12 rolls are sold.

Charity A local charity is selling seats to a baseball game. Seats cost $20 each, and snacks cost an additional $5 each. The charity needs to raise $400 to consider this event a success.

4. Write a linear equation that describes the problem.

5. Graph the linear equation. Make sure to label both axes with appropriate titles.

6. Use the graph to approximate how many snacks the charity must sell if 10 seats are sold.

Movies A movie theater sells tickets to a new show for $10 each. The theater also sells small containers of popcorn for $6 each. The theater needs to make $3000 in order to break even on the show.

7. Write a linear equation that describes the problem.

8. Graph the linear equation. Make sure to label both axes with appropriate titles.

9. Use the graph to approximate how many buckets of popcorn must the movie theater must sell if it sells 210 movie tickets.

Sports A golf course charges $18 for a package including the full 18-hole course. The course also sells buckets of golf balls for $20 each. The golf course would like to earn $400 by the end of the day.

10. Write a linear equation that describes the problem.

11. Graph the linear equation. Make sure to label both axes with appropriate titles.

12. Use the graph to approximate how many buckets of balls the golf course must sell if it sells 10 course packages.

Reading A bookstore sells textbooks for $80 each and notebooks for $4 each. The bookstore would like to sell $800 in merchandise by the end of the week.

13. Write a linear equation that describes the problem.

14. Graph the linear equation. Make sure to label both axes with appropriate titles.

15. Use the graph to approximate how many textbooks the bookstore must sell if it sells 40 notebooks.

Fitness A gym is selling monthly memberships for $30 each and reusable water bottles for $7 each. The gym needs to make $1050 by the end of the month.

16. Write a linear equation that describes the problem.

17. Graph the linear equation. Make sure to label both axes with appropriate titles.

18. Use the graph to approximate the number of water bottles that the gym must sell if it sells 28 gym memberships.

A shoe store offers a frequent-buyers card. Each transaction is worth 8 points, and customers automatically earn 20 points when they sign up.

19. The value of the card is a function of the number of transactions. What are the units for a card?

20. Copy and complete the verbal model for the transaction function. Include units.

$$\begin{array}{c} \text{Card Value} \\ \text{(points)} \end{array} = \begin{array}{c} \text{Initial Value} \\ \text{(points)} \end{array} + \boxed{?} \cdot \boxed{?}$$

21. Write the function rule for the transaction function.

$$N(p) = \boxed{?} + \boxed{?}\ p$$

In graphing the function, $\boxed{?}$ would be the slope and $\boxed{?}$ would be the y-intercept.

22. In each equation of the form $ax + by = c$, state a, b, and c.

$y = 2$

$3x = 0$

$3x + 2y = 6$

$5x - y = 1$

$4y + 2x = 3$

H.O.T. Focus on Higher Order Thinking

23. **Critical Thinking** Suppose that you were given the graph of a monthly revenue function that is a linear relationship and are asked to interpret a point. What would it mean if the point were located on the graph, two units to the right of the origin and slightly above the y-intercept?

24. **Represent Real-World Problems** Describe a situation not used in the lesson that is best described by a linear relationship

25. **Explain the Error** Consider the following situation. Lacie pays a babysitter an initial fee of $35 in addition to $6 per hour.

When trying to model this situation, Juan created the function $y = 35x + 6$. Explain his error.

Lesson Performance Task

A computer store sells both tablets and laptops. One brand of tablet costs $200. That same brand of laptop costs $400. The store manager wants to sell enough of this brand of tablets and laptops to reach the sales goal of $20,000.

    a. Write an equation that models the situation. Then graph the equation.

    b. Interpret the x- and y-intercepts.

    c. Will the store manager meet her goal if the sales team sells 45 tablets and 25 laptops? If so, explain. If not, find how many more tablets need to be sold to meet the goal.

    d. Will the store manager meet her goal if the sales team sells 80 tablets and 10 laptops? If so, explain. If not, find how many more tablets need to be sold to meet the goal.

7.2 Using Functions to Solve One-Variable Equations

Resource Locker

Essential Question: How can you use functions to solve one-variable equations?

⊘ Explore   Creating Functions to Solve One-Variable Equations

Finance Susan wants to hire a babysitter for this weekend for her 3 children. She has two choices. Babysitter A charges $10 per child and $5 per hour. Babysitter B charges $15 per child and $2 per hour. When will they charge the same amount of money?

Ⓐ   Write and solve a one-variable equation to find the number of hours for which the two babysitters will charge the same amount of money. Let x represent the number of hours.

Ⓑ   Write a function for each babysitting service. Enter the two functions in a graphing calculator. Use the graphing calculator to compare their tables and find the intersection point of their graphs. Copy and complete the table.

x	$f(x) = y_1$	$g(x) = y_2$
0	?	?
1	?	?
2	?	?
3	?	?
4	?	?
5	?	?
6	?	?

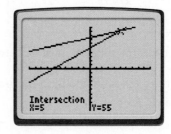

Reflect

1. **Discussion** Why are the x-coordinates of the points where the graphs of the equations $f(x) = y_1$ and $g(x) = y_2$ intersect the solutions of the equation $f(x) = g(x)$?

2. **Discussion** How should the graph provided by the graphing calculator be changed to make the graph an accurate representation of this situation?

⚙ Explain 1 Using Intersections to Determine Approximate Solutions of One-Variable Equations

You can use tables and graphs of the functions $y_1 = f(x)$ and $y_2 = g(x)$ to solve an equation of the form $f(x) = g(x)$.

Example 1 Use a table and a graphing calculator to estimate the solution.

(A) John needs to hire a painter. Painter A is offering his services for an initial $175 in addition to $14.25 per hour. Painter B is offering her services for an initial $200 in addition to $11 per hour. For what number of hours will the two painters charge the same amount of money?

$f(x) = 175 + 14.25x$
$g(x) = 200 + 11x$

x	f(x)	g(x)
0	175	200
1	189.25	211
2	203.5	222
3	217.75	233
4	232	244
5	246.25	255
6	260.5	266
7	274.75	277
8	289	288

From the table, the solution must be between 7 and 8 hours.

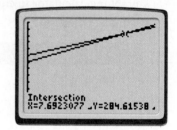

Based on the intersection point in the graph, the solution is approximately 7.7 hours.

(B) Georgia is in need of an electrician. Electrician A is offering his services for an initial fee of $125 in addition to $45 per hour. Electrician B is offering her services for an initial fee of $150 in addition to $38 per hour. For what number of hours will the two electricians charge the same amount of money?

$$f(x) = 125 + 45x \qquad g(x) = 150 + 38x$$

x	f(x)	g(x)
0	125	150
1	170	188
2	215	226
3	260	264
4	305	302
5	350	340
6	395	378

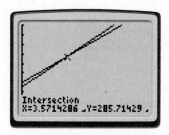

From the table, the solution must be between 3 and 4 hours. From the graph, the solution is about 3.6 hours.

Reflect

3. What limitations, if any, exist on the range of the functions?

4. Why is using a graph better than using a table when finding the solution to a one-variable equation?

Your Turn

5. Sarah would like to hire a clown for her daughter's birthday party. Clown A is offering his services for an initial fee of $100 in addition to $11 per hour. Clown B is offering her services for an initial $150 fee in addition to $8 per hour. When will the two clowns charge the same amount of money? Use a table and a graphing calculator to estimate the solution.

Explain 2 | Using Intercepts to Determine Approximate Solutions for One-Variable Equations

When the amount in a bank account is less than the amount of the payment due, an automatic payment would overdraw the account. That is, the value of the account would be less than zero. In discrete situations like the ones described in the examples, there is no actual point at which the value of the account would be zero, unless the amount in the account is a multiple of the monthly payment. However, you can use the related continuous functions to make an estimation of when the account would theoretically reach zero.

Example 2 Use a table to estimate the solution to the given situation. Then use a graphing calculator to approximate the x-intercept.

(A) Tara has $800 in a bank account. that she uses to make automatic payments of her $101.51 monthly cable bill. If Tara stops making deposits to that account, when would automatic payments make the value of the account zero?

The function that describes the amount in the account after x automatic payments is $f(x) = 800 - 101.51x$.

The other function that describes the situation is $g(x) = 0$.

x	f(x)	g(x)
0	800	0
1	698.49	0
2	596.98	0
3	495.47	0
4	393.96	0
5	292.45	0
6	190.94	0
7	89.43	0
8	−12.08	0

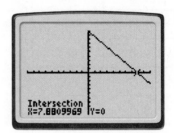

From the table, the value of the account would be 0 between 7 and 8 months. From the graph, the x-intercept is about 7.9.

(B) Craig has $1850 dollars in a bank account. that he uses to make automatic payments of $400.73 on his car loan. If Craig stops making deposits to that account, when would automatic payments make the value of the account zero?

The function that describes the amount in the account after x automatic payments is $f(x) = 1850 - 400.73 x$.

The other function that describes the situation is $g(x) = 0$.

x	f(x)	g(x)
0	1850	0
1	1449.27	0
2	1048.54	0
3	647.81	0
4	247.08	0
5	−153.65	0

From the table, the value of the account would be 0 between 4 and 5 months. From the graph, the x-intercept is about 4.6.

Reflect

6. How are the examples in this section similar to the examples in the previous section?

7. **Discussion** Name one way to better approximate the solution without the use of technology.

8. Cassandra has $2000 dollars in a bank account that she uses to make automatic $900.01 mortgage payments each month. If Cassandra stops making deposits to that account, when would automatic payments make the value of the account zero? Use a table to estimate the solution. Then use a graphing calculator to approximate the x-intercept.

💬 Elaborate

9. Throe would like to hire a guitarist for his charity concert. Guitarists A and B are offering their services to Throe but each guitarist charges different initial fees and hourly rates. How can Throe check to see when they will charge the same amount of money? Name three ways to perform this task.

10. **Essential Question Check-In** What is the first step in using functions to solve one-variable equations?

⭐ Evaluate: Homework and Practice

Use a table to find the solution for each situation.

- Online Homework
- Hints and Help
- Extra Practice

1. Bridget needs an actor. Actor A is offering her services for an initial $250 in addition to $50 per day. Actor B is offering her services for an initial $200 in addition to $60 per day. When will the two actors charge the same amount of money?

2. Yuma needs a singer. Singer A is offering her services for an initial $50 in addition to $20 per hour. Singer B is offering his services for an initial $100 in addition to $10 per hour. When will the two singers charge the same amount of money?

3. Sam needs a web designer. Designer A is offering her services for an initial $500 in addition to $100 per hour. Designer B is offering her services for an initial $600 in addition to $50 per hour. When will the two designers charge the same amount of money?

4. Lindsey needs a jeweler to repair her earrings. Jeweler A is offering her services for an initial $125 in addition to $15 per hour. Jeweler B is offering his services for an initial $140 in addition to $12 per hour. When will the two jewelers charge the same amount of money?

5. Stan needs a mime. Mime A is offering his services for an initial $75 in addition to $25 per hour. Mime B is offering her services for an initial $30 in addition to $40 per hour. When will the two mimes charge the same amount of money?

6. Lottie needs a driver. Driver A is offering his services for an initial $200 in addition to $80 per hour. Driver B is offering his services for an initial $230 in addition to $70 per hour. When will the two drivers charge the same amount of money?

7. Garrett needs a baseball coach. Coach A is offering her services for an initial $5000 in addition to $450 per hour. Coach B is offering her services for an initial $4000 in addition to $700 per hour. When will the two coaches charge the same amount of money?

8. Zena needs a salesperson. Salesperson A is offering his services for an initial $50 in addition to $5 per hour. Salesperson B is offering her services for $15 per hour. When will the two salespeople charge the same amount of money?

In Exercises 9–14, each person uses the given bank account to make automatic monthly payments and stops making deposits to the account. Use a table to find when automatic payments would make the value of the account zero.

9. Charles has $1600 dollars in his account and makes automatic $400 monthly payments on a utility bill.

10. Lena has $2800 dollars in her account and makes automatic $700 monthly payments on a cell phone bill.

11. Malcolm has $3600 dollars in his account and makes automatic $600 monthly mortgage payments.

12. Isabelle has $4900 dollars in her account and makes automatic $700 monthly payments on a home loan.

13. Larry's small business has $60,000 dollars in its account and makes automatic monthly payments that total $12,000.

14. Sharon has $12,000 dollars in her account and makes automatic monthly payments that total $6000.

Use a graphing calculator to find the solution for each situation.

15. Aaron needs to hire a waiter. Waiter A is offering his services for an initial $25 in addition to $5.25 per hour. Waitress B is offering her services for an initial $30 in addition to $4.25 per hour. When will the two waiters charge the same amount of money?

16. Finance Lucy needs to hire a host. Host A is offering his services for an initial $60 in addition to $13.25 per hour. Hostess B is offering her services for an initial $75 in addition to $11.50 per hour. When will the two hosts charge the same amount of money?

17. Ida needs to hire a singer for her wedding. Singer A is offering his services for an initial $90 in addition to $13.15 per hour. Singer B is offering her services for an initial $100 in addition to $11.85 per hour. When will the two singers charge the same amount of money?

18. Emily needs to hire a pilot. Pilot A is offering his services for an initial $32 in addition to $22.18 per hour. Pilot B is offering her services for an initial $46.75 in addition to $18.24 per hour. When will the two pilots charge the same amount of money?

In Exercises 19–22, each person uses the given bank account to make automatic monthly payments and stops making deposits to the account. Use a graphing calculator to approximate the x-intercept of the point where the value of the account would be zero.

19. Rafael has $1875 in his account and makes automatic monthly payments of $225.18 for a smartphone service plan.

20. Zach has $43,408 dollars in his account and makes automatic monthly rent payments of $4500.

21. Rebecca has $326.74 dollars in her account and makes automatic monthly payments of $113.51 for bike rental.

22. Greg has $1464.54 in his account and makes automatic monthly payments of $321.46 for a car loan.

23. Given that $f(x)$ and $g(x)$ are equal, write a one-variable equation. No solutions need to be found for this problem.

   a. $f(x) = 45x + 12, g(x) = 244x + 234$

   b. $f(x) = 13x + 48, g(x) = 24x + 47$

   c. $f(x) = 71x + 145, g(x) = 43x + 17$

   d. $f(x) = 8x + 11, g(x) = 55x + 123$

24. Critical Thinking Given a table of values for a one-variable linear equation, how can $f(x)$ be found?

25. Communicate Mathematical Ideas In a real-world problem one variable is solved with a graphing calculator. What quadrants of the graph are never used for the problem?

26. Explain the Error A student was trying to solve a problem and came up with this table as a result:

Time (Weeks)	Profit($)
1	200
2	500
3	800
4	1100
5	1400
6	1700
7	2000
8	2300
9	2600

The student stated that the range of this function is all real numbers. What is wrong with the student's answer?

Lesson Performance Task

Laura wants to hire a lawyer to file deeds for some properties she owns. The graph illustrates costs for her two choices of lawyers. Using the points on the graph, construct a table of results and two equations. Which lawyer is a better choice for her if she has 8 deeds? Which lawyer is a better choice if she has 2 deeds? Why? Over the long run, which lawyer is more cost-effective?

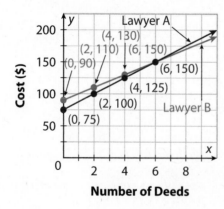

7.3 Linear Inequalities in Two Variables

Essential Question: How do you write and graph linear inequalities in two variables?

⊘ Explore   Graphing Linear Inequalities Involving ≤ or ≥

A **linear inequality in two variables** can be written in one of the following forms: $Ax + By < C$, $Ax + By \leq C$, $Ax + By \geq C$, or $Ax + By > C$, where A, B, and C are constants and A and B are not both 0. The **solution of an inequality in two variables** is one or more ordered pairs that make the inequality true.

Some students at a music recital perform 3-minute pieces and some perform 5-minute pieces. The total time of this part of the recital needs to be at least 30 minutes long. An inequality that represents this is $3x + 5y \geq 30$.

(A) Solve the inequality for y.

(C) Graph the boundary line. The inequality $y \geq -\frac{3}{5}x + 6$ uses the symbol $\geq$, so the line will be solid, to show that the points on the boundary line are part of the solution set.

(B) Replace the inequality symbol in the inequality with an equal sign. The inequality is now an equation that will be used to graph a line. The line is called the **boundary line** of the solution set of the inequality. Write the equation of the line.

(D) The part of the coordinate plane containing the solution set to the inequality, which may include the line, is called a **half-plane**. Since the inequality symbol is $\geq$, two conditions must be met. (1) The boundary line is solid, and (2) the half-plane above the boundary line is shaded. Shade the appropriate part of the graph.

(E) Check the solution by filling in the table.

Point	Above or Below Line	Inequality	True or False?
(0, 0)	?	$3\left(\boxed{?}\right) + 5\left(\boxed{?}\right) \geq 30$	?
(8, 8)	?	$3\left(\boxed{?}\right) + 5\left(\boxed{?}\right) \geq 30$	?

Reflect

1. **Discussion** How would the graph change if the inequality were $>$ instead of $\geq$?

⊘ Explain 1   Graphing Linear Inequalities Involving < or >

Example 1   Graph the solution set for the given inequality using the method given.

Ⓐ   Graph $21 - 3y < 9x$ using a graphing calculator.

Solve the inequality for y.

$$21 - 3y < 9x$$
$$-3y < 9x - 21$$
$$y > -3x + 7$$

Enter the equation into Y_1 in the graphing calculator.

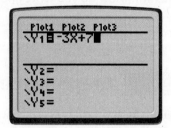

Go to the far left and hit enter two times until it looks like this.

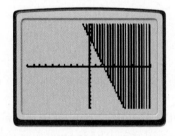

Now view the graph. Note that the calculator will draw a solid line. Determine whether the line should be solid or not.

Since the inequality is strictly greater than, the line should be dashed.

Ⓑ   Graph $-14 + 2y < -x$ by hand.

Solve the inequality for y.

$$-14 + 2y < -x$$
$$+ 2y < -x + \boxed{14}$$
$$y < \frac{-x + \boxed{14}}{\boxed{2}}$$
$$y < -\boxed{\frac{1}{2}}x + \boxed{7}$$

Graph the boundary line. The inequality uses the symbol $<$, so use a dashed line to show that points on the line are not part of the solution.

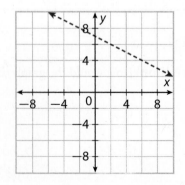

Shade the appropriate part of the graph. The inequality uses the symbol $<$, so shade below the boundary line.

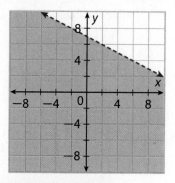

Check the solution by filling in the table.

Point	Above or Below Line	Inequality	True or False?
$(0, 0)$	Below	$-14 + 2\left(\boxed{0}\right) < -\left(\boxed{0}\right)$	True
$(8, 8)$	Above	$-14 + 2\left(\boxed{8}\right) < -\left(\boxed{8}\right)$	False

Reflect

2. Is $(6, 4)$ part of the solution?

Your Turn

Graph the inequality.

3. $3 - y < -5x$

4. $10x + 8y < 64$

🔑 Explain 2 Creating Models with Linear Inequalities

Example 2 Write a linear inequality to represent the information or graph given.

(A) Elijah can spend at most $8.25 on snacks for a party. Carrots cost $2.00 per package and grapes cost $0.75 per bag.

Write a linear inequality to describe the situation.

Let x represent the number of packages of carrots and let y represent the number of bags of grapes.

Use $\leq$ for "at most".

Total cost of carrots	Plus	Total cost of grapes	is at most	$8.25
$2x$	$+$	$0.75y$	$\leq$	8.25

Solve the inequality for y.

$$2x + 0.75y \le 8.25$$

$$0.75y \le -2x + 8.25$$

$$y \le -\frac{8}{3}x + 11$$

 B

The slope of the line is $\frac{4}{3}$.

The y-intercept of the line is 3.

The boundary line is $y = \boxed{\frac{4}{3}x + 3}$.

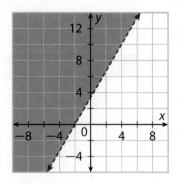

The boundary line on the graph is dashed and the shaded region is above the graph so the symbol will be $>$.

So the inequality is $\boxed{y > \frac{4}{3}x + 3}$.

Your Turn

5. Complete the linear inequality that represents the relationship shown in the table: $y \boxed{?} 2x$

x	y
−3	−8
−2	−10
−1	−2.5
0	0
1	1
2	4
3	0

6. Ramona has $18 that she can spend on food for her dog. Dry dog food costs $5.50 per small bag and wet dog food costs $2.00 per can. Write a linear inequality that describes how many bags and cans of dog food Ramona can buy.

💬 Elaborate

7. Describe a real-world problem situation that can be represented by a linear inequality in two variables. Write an inequality and explain what each part means. Are there any solutions of the solution set that are not solutions to the problem?

8. How can you tell which side of the boundary line should be shaded?

9. **Essential Question Check-In** How do you graph a linear inequality in two variables?

★ Evaluate: Homework and Practice

In order to graph the inequality using a graphing calculator, tell what function to enter for the boundary line, whether the graph should be shaded above or below the line, and if the boundary line is included in the solution.

1. $30 + 5y \geq 4x$

2. $-\frac{1}{2} + y \leq 6x$

3. $-\frac{1}{2}y \leq -\frac{3}{4}x + \frac{5}{4}$

4. $-\frac{8}{3}x \geq y + 9$

Graph the inequality.

5. $4x - 4y \geq 28$

6. $3x + 2y \leq 12$

7. $y \leq 3$

8. $5x - y \geq 4$

In order to graph the inequality using a graphing calculator, tell what function to enter for the boundary line, whether the graph should be shaded above or below the line, and if the boundary line is included in the solution.

9. $x + 5y > 25$

10. $-x - 7y \geq 0$

11. $-\frac{9}{2}x - y \geq -10y + 3$

12. $15x + 20y < 140$

Graph the inequality.

13. $4y + 3x - y > -6x + 12$

14. $-15y > 30x - 45$

15. $10x - 6y > -36$

16. $7x + 2y < 2$

Write a linear inequality to represent the information or graph given.

17. Shanley would like to give $5 gift cards and $4 teddy bears as party favors. Shanley has $120 to spend on party favors. Write an inequality to find the number of gift cards x and teddy bears y Shanley could purchase. Give one solution to the inequality.

18. The total fees for the high school play are $250. Tickets to the play cost $5 for students and $8 for nonstudents. Write a linear inequality that describes the number of student and nonstudent tickets that need to be sold for the drama class to be able to pay the fees.

19.

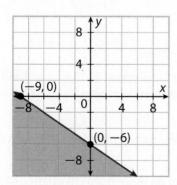

20.

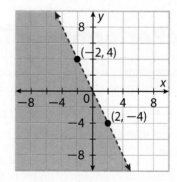

21. Complete the linear inequality that represents the relationship shown in the table:

$$y \boxed{?} x + 1$$

x	y
−3	0
−2	−1
−1	5
0	1
1	3
2	4
3	4

22. Complete the linear inequality that represents the relationship shown in the table:

$$y \boxed{?} 3x - \frac{1}{2}$$

x	y
−3	−10.5
−2	−7
−1	−4
0	−1
1	1
2	5
3	7.5

23. Critique Reasoning Austin thinks that the inequality $6x - 4y \geq 10$ should be shaded above the boundary line because it uses the $\geq$ inequality symbol. Is he correct? Explain.

24. Analyze Relationships For the graph of $x > 10$, the boundary line is the vertical line $x = 10$. Would you shade to the left or right of the boundary? Explain.

25. Multi-step The fare for a taxi cab is $2.50 per passenger and $0.75 for each mile. A group of friends has $22.00 for cab fare.

a. Write a linear inequality to represent how many miles, y, the group can travel if there are x people in the group.

b. If there are 3 people in the group, how far can they travel by taxi? Show all work.

c. If the group wants to travel 10 miles, what is the greatest number of passengers that can travel by taxi? Explain.

26. Communicate Mathematical Ideas How is graphing a linear inequality on a coordinate plane similar to graphing an inequality on a number line?

Lesson Performance Task

Students are raising money for a field trip by selling candles and soap. The candles cost $0.75 each and will be sold for $2.75, and the soap costs $1.50 per bar and will be sold for $4. The students need to raise at least $300 to cover their trip costs.

a. Write an inequality that relates the number of candles c and the number of bars of soap s to the needed income.

b. The wholesaler can supply no more than 100 bars of soap and no more than 130 candles. Graph the inequality from part a and the inequalities that represent the constraints. Graph the number of candles on the vertical axis.

c. What does the shaded area of your graph represent?

Linear Equations and Inequalities

Essential Question: How can you use linear equations and inequalities to solve real-world problems?

KEY EXAMPLE   *(Lesson 7.1)*

A clothing store offers a rewards program in which customers earn points by making purchases at the store. Every item bought is worth 8 points, and customers earn 20 points when they sign up. Write an equation for the function that gives the number of points based on the number of items bought. How many points will a customer have after making 16 purchases?

Write a verbal model for the situation.

Total points = Initial points + Points Per Item · Number of Items.

Define the variables that you will use for the function.

$n =$ number of items; $P(n) =$ total points

Using the verbal model, variables, and information from the problem, write a function rule.

$P(n) = 20 + 8n$

Substitute $n = 16$ into the function, and solve to find the total points.

$P(16) = 20 + 8(16)$

$P(16) = 148$

The customer will have 148 points after making 16 purchases.

KEY EXAMPLE   *(Lesson 7.2)*

Sandi is in need of an electrician. Electrician A is offering his services for an initial fee of $50 and $12 per hour. Electrician B is offering her services for an initial fee of $32 and $15 per hour. When will the two electricians charge the same amount of money? Use a table to find the solution.

$f(x) = 12x + 50$

$g(x) = 15x + 32$

x	f(x)	g(x)
0	50	32
1	62	47
2	74	62
3	86	77
4	98	92
5	110	107
6	122	122

The solution is 6 hours.

Key Vocabulary

linear inequality in two variables *(desigualdad lineal en dos variables)*
solution of an inequality in two variables *(solución de una desigualdad en dos variables)*

EXERCISES

Write a linear equation that models the situation. *(Lesson 7.1)*

1. A kiosk sells magazines for $4 each and paperback books for $6 each. The owner would like to make $180 by the end of the day.

2. A theater is selling children's tickets at $8 and adult tickets at $18. The theater would like to sell tickets worth a total of $720 for a performance.

3. Maxine needs a stunt driver. Driver A is offering his services for an initial $150 and $90 per hour. Driver B is offering his services for an initial $210 and $70 per hour. When will the two drivers charge the same amount of money? Create a table to find the solution. *(Lesson 7.2)*

4. Solve $-9x + 3y \leq 6$ for y and show your work. Graph the solution. *(Lesson 7.3)*

MODULE PERFORMANCE TASK
Making Weight

The National Federation of State High School Associations designates 14 weight classes for wrestlers. Coach Silva has two wrestlers who would like to compete in the 182-pound weight class, Jake and Tawa. Jake weighs 194.6 pounds, Tawa weighs 176 pounds. Coach Silva wants to put each on a diet regimen so that they can meet their weight goal in 6 weeks. For health reasons, neither athlete should lose or gain more than 1.5% of his body weight per week.

If Coach Silva would like for each boy to gain or lose weight at a steady rate over the 6-week time frame, how much does each boy's weight need to change per week? Is this a reasonable goal for each athlete, given the 1.5% per week body weight restriction? Work out your answer on a separate piece of paper.

(Ready) to Go On?

7.1–7.3 Linear Equations and Inequalities

- Online Homework
- Hints and Help
- Extra Practice

Write a linear equation that models the situation. *(Lesson 7.1)*

1. A drugstore sells pens for $1.50 each and notebooks for $4 each. The owner would like to sell $35 of these items each day.

2. A movie theater sells tickets to a film for $12 each. The theater also sells beverages for $3. The theater needs to make $1700 in all in order to break even on the film.

3. Sylvia has $14,000 in a bank account that she uses to make automatic payments that total $7000 each month. If Sylvia stops making deposits to that account, when would automatic payments make the value of the account zero? *(Lesson 7.2)*

4. Solve $10x + 5y \geq 20$ for y and show your work. Graph the solution. *(Lesson 7.3)*

ESSENTIAL QUESTION

5. How can you use the graph of a linear equation to graph an inequality in two variables?

Assessment Readiness

1. Look at each equation. Tell whether the graph of each equation includes the point $(-6, 3)$.

   A. $y = -2x - 6$

   B. $y + 3 = 2(x + 9)$

   C. $y - 4 = \frac{1}{2}(x + 4)$

2. Consider the inequality represented by the graph. Determine if each statement is True or False.

   A. $(1, 4)$ is a solution of the inequality.

   B. $(-3, -2)$ is a solution of the inequality.

   C. The inequality represented is $y < 6x - 2$.

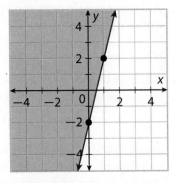

3. Look at each equation. Tell whether each given equation is linear.

   A. $-3x + y = 8$

   B. $3 = xy + 9$

   C. $y = x^3 - 3$

4. Andre is a small business owner who wants to hire an accountant. Accountant A is offering his services for $50 an hour. Accountant B is offering her services for $35 an hour plus an initial fee of $375. Write a function to represent the cost charged by Accountant A. Write a function to represent the cost charged by Accountant B. For how many hours of work do the two accountants charge the same amount of money? Show your work.

1. Tell whether each equation is linear.

   A. $-\dfrac{3}{4}x - \dfrac{1}{2}y = 2$

   B. $y = x^2 - 5$

   C. $-\dfrac{2}{x} = y + 12$

2. Consider the equation $2x - \dfrac{3}{5}y = -6$.
   Determine if each statement is True or False.

   A. The y-intercept is 10.

   B. It is equivalent to $x = \dfrac{3}{10}y - 3$.

   C. It is equivalent to $y = \dfrac{10}{3}x + 10$.

3. A line is represented by the equation $y - 5 = 6\left(x + \dfrac{1}{2}\right)$.
   Does the given statement describe the line?

   A. The slope of the line is -6.

   B. $\left(-\dfrac{1}{2}, 5\right)$ is a point on the line.

   C. The y-intercept of the line is 3.

4. Does the given statement describe a step in the transformation of the graph of $f(x) = x$ that would result in the graph of $g(x) = -\dfrac{1}{3}x - 4$?

   A. The parent function is reflected across the y-axis.

   B. The parent function is translated 4 units down.

   C. The parent function becomes more steep.

5. Consider the graph of the inequality $2y - 10 \leq -\dfrac{2}{4}x$. Tell whether each statement is correct.

   A. The boundary line is dashed.

   B. The boundary line is $y = -\dfrac{1}{2}x + 5$.

   C. The half-plane below the boundary line is shaded.

6. Leia and Thaddeus are reading the same 225 page book. Leia starts reading the book and plans to read 25 pages a day. Thaddeus has already read 45 pages and is reading 20 pages a day. Determine if each statement is True or False.

   A. Leia will finish the book in 9 days.

   B. $f(x) = 20x$ represents the number of pages Thaddeus has read after x days.

   C. They will both finish the book in 9 days.

© Houghton Mifflin Harcourt Publishing Company

7. Write $5x = -2y + 6$ in slope-intercept form, and graph the line. Explain how you graphed the line.

8. Donnie and Tania are math tutors. The amount Donnie charges for a session h hours long is represented by the function $D(h) = 40h + 10$. Tania charges a flat fee of $30 plus $15 an hour. Write a function, $T(h)$, that represents the amount in dollars that Tania charges for h hours of tutoring. Graph both functions on the same coordinate grid, and label each line. Compare the slopes and y-intercepts of the graphs.

Performance Tasks

★ **9.** A bicycle computer or cyclometer uses a magnetic counter that records each wheel rotation to calculate the bike's total distance traveled. To set up the computer, you select a calibration constant for the bike's wheel size. The computer multiplies this constant times the number of tire rotations to find the total distance in miles. Write a function for the distance d in miles if the calibration number is 0.00125. If the function is incorrect and your tire is actually slightly smaller, how should the function change?

★★10. A marina rents party boats for large social gatherings. They charge the following amounts for a 2-hour rental.

Number of People	10	20	35	50
Cost	$165	$192.50	$233.75	$275

  A. Write an equation that represents the data. Include a definition of your variables.

  B. What are the intercepts of the graph of your equation? What is the slope? What do they mean in this context?

  C. Use your equation to predict the cost of providing a party boat for 75 people.

  D. The marina actually charges $460 for 75 people. What might be a reason for the difference?

★★★11. High demand cars that are also in low supply tend to retain their value better than other cars. The data in the table are for a car that won a resale value award.

Year	1	3	5
Value (%)	84	64	44

  A. Write a function to represent the car's value over time, assuming that the car's value is linear for the first 5 years.

  B. According to your model, how much did the car's value drop the day it was purchased and driven off the lot?

  C. Do you think the linear model would still be useful after 10 years? Explain.

  D. Suppose you used months instead of years to write a function. How would your model change?

Wildlife Field Researcher Alexa is a wildlife field researcher who is studying the American black bear. American black bears are the most common bears in the United States. They can be found in 11 of the 21 counties in New Jersey. Most wild male black bears weigh between 125 and 600 pounds, while females generally weigh between 90 and 300 pounds. Their weight depends upon their age, the season of the year, and how much food is available.

a. Write inequalities to show the range of weights for male and female black bears.

b. Black bears hibernate for about 5 months in the winter. They must store 50 to 60 pounds of fat to survive hibernation. During the month before hibernation, a black bear may consume up to 20,000 Calories per day. If a bear consumes an average of 18,500 Calories per day in the month of August, about how many total calories will he consume that month?

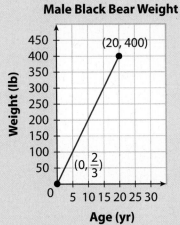

Male Black Bear Weight

c. Use the graph to estimate how much a male bear, weighing $\frac{2}{3}$ pound at birth and 400 pounds at the age of his death, 20 years, weighed when he was 7 years old.

d. A white-tailed deer is running from a black bear at 20 miles per hour. It is $\frac{1}{3}$ mile in front of the bear. The bear is running at 30 miles per hour. How many minutes will it take the bear to catch the deer? Assume both continue running at a constant pace.

e. During the hibernation months, the bear's heart rate slows to about 10 beats per minute. If the bear hibernates for 155 days, how many times will its heart beat?

Statistical Models

MATH IN CAREERS

Geologist A geologist is a scientist who studies Earth—its processes, materials, and history. Geologists investigate earthquakes, floods, landslides, and volcanic eruptions to gain a deeper understanding of these phenomena. They explore ways to extract materials from the earth, such as metals, oil, and groundwater. Geologists devise and use mathematical models and use statistical methods to help them understand Earth's geological processes and history.

If you are interested in a career as a geologist, you should study these mathematical subjects:

- Algebra
- Geometry
- Trigonometry
- Statistics
- Calculus

Research other careers that require using statistical methods to understand natural phenomena. Check out the career activity at the end of the unit to find out how **geologists** use math.

© Houghton Mifflin Harcourt Publishing Company • Image Credits: ©Ulrich Doering/Alamy

Visualize Vocabulary

Copy the graphic, then use the ✔ words to complete it. Put one word in each oval.

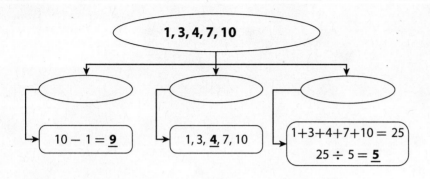

Review Words

✔ data *(datos)*
✔ mean *(media)*
✔ median *(mediana)*
✔ range *(rango)*

Preview Words

box plot *(gráfica de caja)*
categorical data *(datos categoricos)*
dot plot *(diagrama de puntos)*
frequency table *(table de frecuencia)*
histogram *(histograma)*
normal distribution *(distribución normal)*
outlier *(valor extremo)*
quartile *(cuartil)*
scatter plot *(diagram de dispersión)*
trend line *(línea de tendencia)*

Understand Vocabulary

To become familiar with some of the vocabulary terms in the module, consider the following. You may refer to the module, the glossary, or a dictionary.

1. A __?__ is the median of the upper or lower half of a data set.

2. A graph with points plotted to show a possible relationship between two sets of data is a __?__.

3. A __?__ is a bar graph used to display data grouped in intervals.

4. A data value that is far removed from the rest of the data is an __?__.

Active Reading

Booklet Before beginning each module in this unit, create a booklet to help you learn the vocabulary and concepts in the module. Each page of the booklet should contain a main topic from each lesson. As you study each lesson, write details of the main topic, with definitions, diagrams, graphs, and examples, to create an outline that summarizes the main content of the lesson.

Multi-Variable Categorical Data

Essential Question: How can you use multi-variable categorical data to solve real-world problems?

REAL WORLD VIDEO
With emotions riding high, it can be difficult to evaluate popular opinion concerning personal preferences, such as favorite sports teams. Polls and surveys use a methodical, mathematical approach to reduce or eliminate bias.

MODULE PERFORMANCE TASK PREVIEW

Survey Says?

You won't be surprised to learn that the activities people enjoy change with age. Most six-year-olds like climbing on jungle-gyms. Most twenty-year-olds don't, but they do like to attend pop music concerts. In this module, you'll learn ways to analyze surveys of public opinions and preferences. Then you'll look at data relating to the vacation preferences of two different age groups and decide what you can learn from the data.

Are (YOU) Ready?

Complete these exercises to review skills you will need for this module.

Percents

Example 1	What percent of 14 is 21?

$$\frac{x}{100} \cdot 14 = 21 \qquad \text{Write an equation.}$$

$$\frac{x}{100} \cdot 14 \cdot \frac{100}{14} = 21 \cdot \frac{100}{14} \qquad \text{Multiply both sides by } \frac{100}{14}.$$

$$x = 150 \qquad \text{Simplify.}$$

21 is 150% of 14.

Solve each equation.

1. What percent of 24 is 18?

2. What percent of 400 is 2?

3. What percent of 880 is 924?

Two-Way Frequency Tables

Example 2	The table shows the number of adults, teens, and children under 13 who visited the local petting zoo one week. How many people visited it on Friday?

	Su	M	Tu	W	Th	F	Sa
Adult	112	40	33	52	29	8	90
Teen	29	0	6	22	4	2	10
Child	61	32	56	65	38	16	48

Friday is the second to last column. It shows that 8 adults, 2 teens, and 16 children visited that day. The sum is $8 + 2 + 16 = 26$.

The number of people who visited the petting zoo on Friday is 26.

Use the table shown to answer the questions.

4. How many children under 13 visited the petting zoo that week?

5. How many adults visited the petting zoo on the weekend?

6. To the nearest whole percent, what percent of the visitors were teens?

8.1 Two-Way Frequency Tables

Essential Question: How can categorical data for two categories be summarized?

Resource Locker

⊘ Explore Categorical Data and Frequencies

Data that can be expressed with numerical measurements are **quantitative data**. In this lesson you will examine qualitative data, or **categorical data**, which cannot be expressed using numbers. Data describing animal type, model of car, or favorite song are examples of categorical data.

Ⓐ Which of the following is a categorical data variable? Justify your choice. ☐?

      temperature   weight   height   color

Ⓑ Identify whether the given data is categorical or quantitative.

    large, medium, small ☐?

    120 ft^2, 130 ft^2, 140 ft^2 ☐?

Ⓒ A **frequency** table shows how often each item occurs in a set of categorical data. Use the categorical data listed on the left to complete the frequency table.

Ways Students Get to School
bus car walk car car car bus
walk walk walk bus bus car
bus bus walk bus car bus car

Way	Frequency
bus	8
car	?
?	?

Reflect

1. How did you determine the numbers for each category in the frequency column?

2. What must be true about the sum of the frequencies in a frequency table?

✎ Explain 1 Constructing Two-Way Frequency Tables

If a data set has two categorical variables, you can list the frequencies of the paired values in a **two-way frequency table**.

Example 1 Complete the two-way frequency table.

Ⓐ A high school's administration asked 100 randomly selected students in the 9th and 10th grades about what fruit they like best. Complete the table.

Preferred Fruit				
Grade	Apple	Orange	Banana	Total
9th	19	12	23	?
10th	22	9	15	?
Total	?	?	?	?

Row totals:

9th: 19 + 12 + 23 = 54

10th: 22 + 9 + 15 = 46

Column totals:

Apple: 19 + 22 = 41

Orange: 12 + 9 = 21

Banana: 23 + 15 = 38

Grand total:

Sum of row totals: 54 + 46 = 100

Sum of column totals: 41 + 21 + 38 = 100

Both sums should equal the grand total.

Preferred Fruit				
Grade	Apple	Orange	Banana	Total
9th	19	12	23	54
10th	22	9	15	46
Total	41	21	38	100

(B) Jenna asked some randomly selected students whether they preferred dogs, cats, or other pets. She also recorded the gender of each student. The results are shown in the two-way frequency table below. Each entry is the frequency of students who prefer a certain pet and are a certain gender. For instance, 8 girls prefer dogs as pets. Complete the table.

Preferred Pet				
Gender	Dog	Cat	Other	Total
Girl	8	7	1	16
Boy	10	5	9	24
Total	18	12	10	40

Row totals:

Girl: 8 + 7 + 1 = 16

Boy: 10 + 5 + 9 = 24

Column totals:

Dog: 8 + 10 = 18

Cat: 7 + 5 = 12

Other: 1 + 9 = 10

Grand total:

Sum of row totals: 16 + 24 = 40

Sum of column totals:

18 + 12 + 10 = 40

Both sums should equal the grand total.

Reflect

3. Look at the totals for each row. Was Jenna's survey evenly distributed among boys and girls? Explain.

4. Look at the totals for each column. Which pet is preferred by the most students? Justify your answer.

Your Turn

Complete the two-way frequency table.

5. Antonio surveyed 60 of his classmates about their participation in school activities and whether they have a part-time job. The results are shown in the two-way frequency table below. Copy and complete the table.

	Activities				
Job	**Clubs Only**	**Sports Only**	**Both**	**Neither**	**Total**
Yes	12	13	16	4	?
No	3	5	5	2	?
Total	?	?	?	?	?

6. Jen surveyed 100 students about whether they like baseball or basketball. Copy and complete the table.

	Like Basketball		
Like Baseball	**Yes**	**No**	**Total**
Yes	61	13	?
No	16	10	?
Total	?	?	?

🕹 Explain 2   Reading Two-Way Frequency Tables

You can extract information about paired categorical variables by reading a two-way frequency table.

Example 2   Read and complete the two-way frequency table.

Ⓐ Suppose you are given the circled information in the table and instructed to complete the table.

	Eat Cereal for Breakfast		
Gender	**Yes**	**No**	**Total**
Girl	(42)	(12)	(54)
Boy	36	(10)	46
Total	78	22	(100)

Find the total number of boys by subtracting: $100 - 54 = 46$

Find the number of boys who do eat cereal by subtracting: $46 - 10 = 36$

Add to find the total number of students who eat cereal and the total number of students who do not eat cereal.

B One hundred students were surveyed about which beverage they chose at lunch. Some of the results are shown in the two-way frequency table below. Complete the table.

Gender	Lunch Beverage			
	Juice	Milk	Water	Total
Girl	10	13	17	40
Boy	15	24	21	60
Total	25	37	38	100

Find the total number of girls by subtracting: $100 - 60 = \boxed{40}$

So, the total number of girls is $\boxed{40}$. The number of girls who do not choose milk is

$\boxed{17} + \boxed{10} = \boxed{27}$.

Find the number of girls who chose milk by subtracting: $\boxed{40} - \boxed{27} = \boxed{13}$

Reflect

7. Which lunch beverage is the least preferred? How do you know?

Your Turn

Read and complete the two-way frequency table.

8. 100 students were asked what fruit they chose at lunch. The two-way frequency table shows some of the results of the survey. Copy and complete the table.

Gender	Lunch Fruit			
	Apple	Pear	Banana	Total
Girl	?	17	11	49
Boy	?	10	16	?
Total	?	?	?	?

9. 200 high school teachers were asked whether they prefer to use the chalkboard or projector in class. The two-way frequency table shows some of the results of the survey. Copy and complete the table.

Gender	Preferred Teaching Aid		
	Chalkboard	Projector	Total
Female	?	56	99
Male	44	?	?
Total	87	113	200

10. You are making a two-way frequency table of 5 fruit preferences among a survey sample of girls and boys. What are the dimensions of the table you would make? How many entries would you need to fill the table with frequencies and totals?

11. A 3 categories-by-3 categories two-way frequency table has a row with 2 numbers, and no row or column totals. Can you fill the row?

12. **Essential Question Check-In** How can you summarize categorical data for 2 categories?

⭐ Evaluate: Homework and Practice

• Online Homework
• Hints and Help
• Extra Practice

1. Identify whether the given data is categorical or quantitative.
gold medal, silver medal, bronze medal
100 m, 200 m, 400 m

2. A theater company asked its members to bring in canned food for a food drive. Use the categorical data to complete the frequency table.

Cans Donated to Food Drive
peas corn peas soup corn
corn soup soup corn peas
peas corn soup peas corn
peas corn peas corn soup
corn peas soup corn corn

Cans	Frequency
soup	?
peas	?
?	?

Complete the two-way frequency table.

3. James surveyed some of his classmates about what vegetable they like best. Copy and complete the table.

	Preferred Vegetable			
Grade	**Carrots**	**Green Beans**	**Celery**	**Total**
9th	30	15	24	?
10th	32	9	20	?
Total	?	?	?	?

4. A high school's extracurricular committee surveyed a randomly selected group of students about whether they like tennis and soccer. Copy and complete the table.

	Like Tennis		
Like Soccer	**Yes**	**No**	**Total**
Yes	37	20	?
No	16	15	?
Total	?	?	?

5. After a school field trip, Ben surveyed some students about which animals they liked from the zoo. Copy and complete the table.

Grade	Preferred Animal at a Zoo			
	Lion	Zebra	Monkey	Total
11th	9	15	14	?
12th	4	17	15	?
Total	?	?	?	?

6. Jill asked some randomly selected students whether they preferred blue, green, or other colors. She also recorded the gender of each student. The results are shown in the two-way frequency table below. Copy and complete the table.

Gender	Preferred Color			
	Green	Blue	Other	Total
Girl	15	3	10	?
Boy	3	16	6	?
Total	?	?	?	?

7. Kevin surveyed some students about whether they preferred soccer, baseball, or another sport. He also recorded their gender. Copy and complete the table.

Gender	Preferred Sport			
	Soccer	Baseball	Other	Total
Girl	33	7	10	?
Boy	15	27	7	?
Total	?	?	?	?

8. A school surveyed a group of students about whether they like backgammon and chess. They will use this data to determine whether there is enough interest for the school to compete in these games. Copy and complete the table.

Like Chess	Like Backgammon		
	Yes	No	Total
Yes	10	61	?
No	5	3	?
Total	?	?	?

9. Hugo surveyed some 9th and 10th graders in regard to whether they preferred math, English, or another subject. The results of the survey are in the following table. Copy and complete the table.

Grade	Preferred Subject			
	Math	English	Other	Total
9th	40	35	20	?
10th	41	32	17	?
Total	?	?	?	?

10. Luis surveyed some middle school and high school students about the type of music they prefer. Copy and complete the table.

School Level	Preferred Music			
	Country	Pop	Other	Total
Middle School	18	13	23	?
High School	7	32	15	?
Total	?	?	?	?

11. Natalie surveyed some teenagers and adults on whether they prefer standard cars, vans, or convertibles. Her results are in the following table. Copy and complete the table.

Age	Preferred Car Type			
	Standard	Van	Convertible	Total
Adults	10	25	9	?
Teenagers	11	7	24	?
Total	?	?	?	?

12. Eli surveyed some teenagers and adults on whether they prefer apples, oranges, or bananas. His results are in the following table. Copy and complete the table.

Age	Preferred Fruit			
	Apple	Orange	Banana	Total
Adults	22	12	10	?
Teenagers	24	9	9	?
Total	?	?	?	?

200 students were asked to name their favorite science class. The results are shown in the two-way frequency table. Use the table for the following questions.

Gender	Favorite Science Class			
	Biology	Chemistry	Physics	Total
Girl	42	39	23	104
Boy	?	45	32	?
Total	?	?	?	?

13. How many boys were surveyed? Explain how you found your answer.

14. Copy and complete the table. How many more girls than boys chose biology as their favorite science class? Explain how you found your answer.

The results of a survey of 150 students about whether they own an electronic tablet or a laptop are shown in the two-way frequency table.

Gender	Device				
	Electronic tablet	Laptop	Both	Neither	Total
Girl	15	54	?	9	88
Boy	?	35	8	5	?
Total	?	?	?	?	?

15. Copy and complete the table. Do the surveyed students own more laptops or more electronic tablets?

16. Which group had more people answer the survey, boys or students who own an electronic tablet only? Explain.

17. The table shows the results of a survey about students' preferred frozen yogurt flavor. Copy and complete the table, and state the flavors that students preferred the most and the least.

Gender	Preferred Flavor			
	Vanilla	Mint	Strawberry	Total
Girl	?	15	18	45
Boy	17	25	?	?
Total	?	?	?	100

18. Teresa surveyed 100 students about whether they like pop music or country music. Out of the 100 students surveyed, 42 like only pop, 34 like only country, 15 like both pop and country, and 9 do not like either pop or country. Copy and complete the two-way frequency table.

Like Country	Like Pop		
	Yes	No	Total
Yes	?	?	?
No	?	?	?
Total	?	?	?

19. Forty students in a class at an international high school were surveyed about which non-English language they can speak. Copy and complete the table.

Gender	Foreign Language			
	Chinese	Spanish	French	Total
Girl	7	8	?	?
Boy	?	6	7	18
Total	?	?	?	?

Luis surveyed 100 students about whether they like soccer. The number of girls and the number of boys completing the survey are equal.

20. Copy and complete the table.

Gender	Likes Soccer		
	Yes	No	Total
Girl	?	20	?
Boy	?	35	?
Total	?	?	100

21. Twice as many girls like soccer as the number that like tennis. The same number of students like soccer as like tennis. Construct a table containing the tennis data.

22. A group of 200 high school students were asked about their use of email and text messages. The results are shown in the two-way frequency table. Copy and complete the table.

Email	Text Messages		
	Yes	**No**	**Total**
Yes	72	?	90
No	?	45	?
Total	?	?	?

23. Determine whether each data set is categorical.

A. 75°, 79°, 77°, 85°

B. apples, oranges, pears

C. male, female

D. blue, green, red

E. 2 feet, 5 feet, 12 feet

F. classical music, country music

G. 1 centimeter, 3 centimeters, 9 centimeters

24. **Explain the Error** Find the mistake in completing the two-way frequency table for a survey involving 50 students. Then copy and complete the table correctly.

Gender	Favorite Foreign Language Class			
	Russian	**German**	**Italian**	**Total**
Girl	8	8	8	24
Boy	42	9	7	58
Total	50	?	?	?

H.O.T. **Focus on Higher Order Thinking**

25. **Justify Reasoning** Charles surveyed 100 boys about their favorite color. Of the 100 boys surveyed, 44 preferred blue, 25 preferred green, and 31 preferred red.

a. Explain why it is not possible to make a two-way frequency table from the given data.

b. Suppose Charles also surveyed some girls. Of the girls surveyed, 30 preferred blue and 43 preferred green. Can Charles make a two-way frequency table now? Can he complete it?

26. **Persevere in Problem Solving** Shown are two different tables about a survey involving students. Each survey had a few questions about musical preferences. All students answered all questions. Copy and complete the tables. What type of music do the students prefer?

Gender	Likes Classical Music		
	Yes	No	Total
Girl	21	?	?
Boy	?	22	?
Total	?	?	100

Gender	Likes Blues Music		
	Yes	No	Total
Girl	?	15	49
Boy	?	15	?
Total	?	?	?

Lesson Performance Task

Two hundred students were asked about their favorite sport. Of the 200 students surveyed, 98 were female. Some of the results are shown in the following two-way frequency table.

Gender	Favorite Sport				
	Football	Baseball	Basketball	Soccer	Total
Female	?	?	36	12	?
Male	38	19	?	?	?
Total	64	?	?	36	?

a. Copy and complete the table.

b. Which sport is the most popular among the students? Which is the least popular? Explain.

c. Which sport is most popular among the females? Which sport is most popular among the males? Explain.

8.2 Relative Frequency

Essential Question: How can you recognize possible associations and trends between two categories of categorical data?

Explore Relative Frequencies

To show what portion of a data set each category in a frequency table makes up, you can convert the data to *relative frequencies*. The **relative frequency** of a category is the frequency of the category divided by the total of all frequencies.

The frequency table below shows the results of a survey Kenesha conducted at school. She asked 80 randomly selected students whether they preferred basketball, football, or soccer.

Favorite Sport	Basketball	Football	Soccer	Total
Frequency	20	32	28	80

(A) Use the frequencies to make a relative frequency table expressed with decimals.

Favorite Sport	Basketball	Football	Soccer	Total
Relative Frequency	$\frac{20}{80} = 0.25$	?	?	$\frac{80}{80} =$?

(B) Rewrite the relative frequency table using percents instead of decimals.

Favorite Sport	Basketball	Football	Soccer	Total
Relative Frequency	25%	?	?	?

Reflect

1. Explain what the numerator and denominator of the ratio $\frac{20}{80}$ refer to in part A.

2. What types of numbers can you use to write relative frequencies?

Explain 1 Two-Way Relative Frequency Tables

Two types of relative frequencies are found in a relative frequency table:

1. A **joint relative frequency** is found by dividing a frequency that is not in the Total row or the Total column by the grand total. It tells what portion of the total has both of the two specified characteristics.

2. A **marginal relative frequency** is found by dividing a row total or a column total by the grand total. It tells what portion of the total has a specified characteristic.

Example 1 Complete a two-way relative frequency table from the data in a two-way frequency table. Identify the joint relative frequencies and the marginal relative frequencies.

Ⓐ For her survey about sports preferences, Kenesha also recorded the gender of each student. The results are shown in the two-way frequency table for Kenesha's data.

Gender	Preferred Sport			
	Basketball	Football	Soccer	Total
Girl	6	12	18	36
Boy	14	20	10	44
Total	20	32	28	80

To find the relative frequencies, divide each frequency by the grand total.

Gender	Preferred Sport			
	Basketball	Football	Soccer	Total
Girl	$\frac{6}{80} = 0.075$	$\frac{12}{80} = 0.15$	$\frac{18}{80} = 0.225$	$\frac{36}{80} = 0.45$
Boy	$\frac{14}{80} = 0.175$	$\frac{20}{80} = 0.25$	$\frac{10}{80} = 0.125$	$\frac{44}{80} = 0.55$
Total	$\frac{20}{80} = 0.25$	$\frac{32}{80} = 0.4$	$\frac{28}{80} = 0.35$	$\frac{80}{80} = 1$

The joint relative frequencies tell what percent of all those surveyed are in each category:

- 7.5% are girls who prefer basketball.
- 15% are girls who prefer football.
- 22.5% are girls who prefer soccer.

- 17.5% are boys who prefer basketball.
- 25% are boys who prefer football.
- 12.5% are boys who prefer soccer.

The marginal relative frequencies tell what percent of totals has a given single characteristic:

- 25% prefer basketball.
- 40% prefer football.
- 35% prefer soccer.

- 45% are girls.
- 55% are boys.

Ⓑ Millie performed a survey of students in the lunch line and recorded which type of fruit each student selected along with the gender of each student. The two-variable frequency data she collected is shown in the table.

	Fruit			
	Apple	Banana	Orange	Total
Girl	16	10	14	40
Boy	25	13	14	52
Total	41	23	28	92

Fruit				
	Apple	**Banana**	**Orange**	**Total**
Girl	17.4%	10.9%	15.2%	43.5%
Boy	27.2%	14.1%	15.2%	56.5%
Total	44.6%	25.0%	30.4%	100.0%

The joint relative frequencies:

- 17.4% are girls who selected an apple.
- 27.2% are boys who selected an apple.

- 10.9% are girls who selected a banana.
- 14.1% are boys who selected a banana.

- 15.2% are girls who selected an orange.
- 15.2% are boys who selected an orange.

The marginal relative frequencies:

- 44.6% selected an apple.
- 43.5% are girls.

- 25% selected a banana.
- 56.5% are boys.

- 30.4% selected an orange.

Reflect

3. **Discussion** Explain how you can use joint and marginal relative frequencies to check your relative frequency table.

Your Turn

Use the two-way table of data from another student survey to answer the following questions.

	Like Aerobic Exercise		
Like Weight Lifting	**Yes**	**No**	**Total**
Yes	7	14	21
No	12	7	19
Total	19	21	40

4. Find the joint relative frequency of students surveyed who like aerobics exercise but dislike weight lifting.

5. What is the marginal relative frequency of students surveyed who like weight lifting?

© Houghton Mifflin Harcourt Publishing Company

⚙ Explain 2 Conditional Relative Frequencies

A **conditional relative frequency** describes what portion of a group with a given characteristic also has another characteristic. A conditional relative frequency is found by dividing a frequency that is not in the Total row or the Total column by the total for that row or column.

Example 2 Use the joint relative frequencies to calculate the associated conditional relative frequencies and describe what each one means.

(A) Use the data from Example 1A. Find the conditional relative frequency that a a person in Kenesha's survey prefers soccer, given that the person is a girl.

Divide the number of girls who prefer soccer by the total number of girls.

$$\frac{\text{Number of girls who prefer soccer}}{\text{Total number of girls}} = \frac{18}{36} = 0.5 = 50\%$$

Half of the girls in the sample prefer soccer.

(B) Use the data from Example 1B. Find the conditional relative frequency that a student in Millie's survey chose an orange, given that the student is a boy.

$$\frac{\text{Number of } \boxed{\text{boys}} \text{ who chose an orange}}{\text{Total number of } \boxed{\text{boys}}} = \frac{\boxed{14}}{\boxed{52}} \approx 0.269 = \boxed{26.9}\%$$

Your Turn

Use the data from Your Turn Exercises 4 and 5 after Example 1.

6. What is the conditional relative frequency that a student likes to lift weights, given that the student does not like aerobics?

7. Find the conditional relative frequency that a student likes to lift weights, given that the student likes aerobics.

⚙ Explain 3 Finding Possible Associations

You can analyze two-way frequency tables to locate possible associations or patterns in the data.

Example 3 Analyze the results of the surveys to determine preferences by gender.

Kenesha is interested in the question, "Does gender influence what type of sport students prefer?" If there is no influence, then the distribution of gender within each sport preference will roughly equal the distribution of gender within the whole group. Analyze the results of Kenesha's survey from Example 1. Determine which sport each gender is more likely to prefer.

(A) Analyze the data about girls that were surveyed.

Step 1: Identify the percent of all students surveyed who are girls.

$$\frac{36}{80} = 0.45 = 45\%$$

Step 2: Determine each conditional relative frequency.

Basketball	Football	Soccer
Of the 20 students who prefer basketball, 6 are girls. $$\frac{6}{20} = 0.3 = 30\%$$	Of the 32 students who prefer football, 12 are girls. $$\frac{12}{32} = 0.375 = 37.5\%$$	Of the 28 students who prefer soccer, 18 are girls. $$\frac{18}{28} \approx 0.643 = 64.3\%$$

Step 3: Interpret the results by comparing each conditional relative frequency to the percent of all students surveyed who are girls, 45%.

Basketball	Football	Soccer
30% < 45%	37.5% < 45%	64.3% > 45%
Girls are less likely to prefer basketball.	Girls are less likely to prefer football.	Girls are more likely to prefer soccer.

(B) Analyze the data about boys that were surveyed.

Step 1: Identify the percent of all students surveyed who are boys.

$$\frac{44}{80} = \boxed{0.55} = \boxed{55}\%$$

Step 2: Determine each conditional relative frequency.

Basketball	Football	Soccer
Of the 20 students who prefer basketball, $\boxed{14}$ are boys. $$\frac{14}{20} = \boxed{0.7} = \boxed{70}\%$$	Of the $\boxed{32}$ students who prefer football, $\boxed{20}$ are boys. $$\frac{20}{32} = \boxed{0.625} = \boxed{62.5}\%$$	Of the $\boxed{28}$ students who prefer soccer, $\boxed{10}$ are boys. $$\frac{10}{28} = \boxed{0.357} = \boxed{35.7}\%$$

Step 3: Interpret the results by comparing each conditional relative frequency to the percent of all students surveyed who are boys, $\boxed{55}$ %.

Basketball	Football	Soccer
70% > 55%	62.5% > 55%	35.7% < 55%
Boys are more likely to prefer basketball.	Boys are more likely to prefer football.	Boys are less likely to prefer soccer.

Reflect

8. **Making Connections** How can the statement "6 out of the 20 students who prefer basketball are girls" be stated as a conditional relative frequency?

9. Analyze the data given in the Your Turn after Example 1 to determine if liking aerobic exercise influences whether a person also likes weight lifting. Explain.

💬 Elaborate

10. What does it mean to say there is an association between characteristics in a two-way frequency table?

11. **Essential Question Check-In** How can you use two-way frequency data to recognize possible associations between the two categories of categorical data?

⭐ Evaluate: Homework and Practice

• Online Homework
• Hints and Help
• Extra Practice

Use the table of frequency data for Exercises 1–4.

Class Survey of Favorite Colors

Favorite Color	Red	Orange	Yellow	Green	Blue	Purple	Total
Frequency	2	5	1	6	8	2	24

1. Copy and complete the relative frequency table for this data using decimals rounded to the nearest thousandth.

Class Survey of Favorite Colors

Favorite Color	Red	Orange	Yellow	Green	Blue	Purple	Total
Relative Frequency	?	?	?	?	?	?	?

2. Copy and complete the relative frequency table for this data using percents rounded to the nearest tenth.

Class Survey of Favorite Colors

Favorite Color	Red	Orange	Yellow	Green	Blue	Purple	Total
Relative Frequency	?	?	?	?	?	?	?

3. What is the relative frequency of having blue as a favorite color, expressed as a decimal?

4. Which color is a favorite color with a relative frequency of 25%?

The following frequency data shows the number of states, including the District of Columbia, that favored each party in the presidential popular vote in 1976 and in 2012.

1976 Election	2012 Election		
	Democrat	Republican	Total
Democrat	12 = [?]	12 = [?]	24 = [?]
Republican	15 = [?]	12 = [?]	27 = [?]
Total	27 = [?]	24 = [?]	51 = [?]

5. Complete the table above with relative frequencies using percents.

6. What percent switched from Democrat in 1976 to Republican in 2012? What type of frequency is this?

7. What percent voted Republican in 1976? What type of frequency is this?

The results of a survey of 45 students and the foreign language they are studying are shown in the two-way frequency table.

Gender	Language			
	Chinese	French	Spanish	Total
Girl	2	8	15	25
Boy	4	4	12	20
Total	6	12	27	45

8. Create a table of two-way relative frequencies using decimals, rounded to the nearest thousandth.

9. What fraction of the surveyed students are boys taking Spanish?

10. What fraction of the surveyed students are taking Chinese?

In some states, a driver of a vehicle may not use a handheld cell phone while driving. In one state with this law, 250 randomly selected drivers were surveyed to determine the association between drivers who know the law and drivers who obey the law. The results are shown in the table below.

11. Copy and complete the table of two-way relative frequencies using percents.

Obeys the Law	Knows the Law		
	Yes	No	Total
Yes	160 = ?	45 = ?	?
No	25 = ?	20 = ?	?
Total	?	?	?

12. What is the relative frequency of drivers who know and obey the law?

13. What is the relative frequency of drivers who know the law?

Refer to the election data from Exercises 5–7. Answer using percents rounded to the nearest tenth.

14. What is the conditional relative frequency of a state's popular vote being won by the Democrat in 2012, given that it was won by the Democrat in 1976?

15. What is the conditional relative frequency of a state's popular vote being won by the Democrat in 1976, given that it was won by the Democrat in 2012?

Refer to the language data from Exercises 8–10. Answer using decimals rounded to the nearest thousandth.

16. What fraction of girls are studying French?

17. What fraction of Spanish students are boys?

Refer to the cell phone law data from Exercises 11–13. Answer using percents rounded to the nearest tenth.

18. What percent of drivers obey the law despite not knowing the law?

19. What is the conditional relative frequency of drivers who obey the law, given that they know the law?

Use the previously described data to determine whether there are associations between the categories surveyed.

20. Refer to the election data from Exercises 5–7. Is there an association between the party that won the popular vote in a state in 1976 and in 2012?

21. Refer to the language data from Exercises 8–10. Can you use gender to predict a preference for taking Spanish?

22. Refer to the language data from Exercises 8–10. Is there an association between gender and a preference for French?

23. Refer to the cell phone law data from Exercises 11–13. Most drivers who don't know that it is illegal to operate a cell phone while driving obey the law anyway, presumably out of a general concern for safe driving. Does this mean there is no association between knowledge of the cell phone law and obeying the cell phone law?

24. **Multipart Classification** Classify each statement as describing a *joint*, *marginal*, or *conditional* relative frequency.

    a. In a study on age and driving safety, 33% of drivers were considered younger and a high accident risk.

    b. In a study on age and driving safety, 45% of older drivers were considered a high accident risk.

    c. In a study on age and driving safety, 67% of drivers were classified as younger.

    d. In a pre-election poll, 67% of the respondents who preferred the incumbent were men.

    e. In a pre-election poll, 33% of women preferred the challenger.

    f. In a pre-election poll, 16% of respondents were men who preferred the challenger.

H.O.T. Focus on Higher Order Thinking

25. **Explain the Error** In the survey on gender and fruit selection (Example 1B), Millicent notices that given a preference for oranges, the conditional relative frequencies of a student being a boy or a girl are the same. She concludes that there is no association between gender and orange preference. Explain her error.

26. **Communicate Mathematical Ideas** Can a joint relative frequency be greater than either of the conditional relative frequencies associated with it? Explain your reasoning.

27. **Explain the Error** Refer to the cell phone data from Exercises 11–13. Cole found the conditional relative frequency that a driver surveyed does not know the law, given that the driver obeys the law, by dividing 45 by 250. Explain Cole's error.

Lesson Performance Task

Eighty students were surveyed about playing an instrument. The results are shown in the two-way frequency table.

Gender	Play an Instrument		
	Yes	No	Total
Female	28	17	45
Male	20	15	35
Total	48	32	80

a. Create a two-way relative frequency table for the data.

b. What percent of the students surveyed play an instrument? What percent of the males surveyed do not play an instrument? Identify what type of frequency each percent is.

c. Is there an association between the sex of a student and whether the student plays an instrument? Explain.

Multi-Variable Categorical Data

Essential Question: How can you use multi-variable categorical data to solve real-world problems?

© Houghton Mifflin Harcourt Publishing Company

Key Vocabulary
categorical data
   (datos categóricos)
conditional relative frequency
   (frecuencia relativa condicional)
frequency table *(tabla de frecuencia)*
joint relative frequency
   (frecuencia relativa conjunta)
marginal relative frequency
   (frecuencia relativa marginal)
quantitative data *(datos cuantitativos)*
relative frequency *(frecuencia relativa)*

KEY EXAMPLE   *(Lesson 8.1)*

The principal of a high school surveyed 9th and 10th graders as to whether they want to go on a field trip to the museum, zoo, or botanical garden. The results of the survey are in the following table. Complete the table.

Grade	Preferred Field Trip			
	Museum	Zoo	Botanical Garden	Total
9th	42	28	31	
10th		52	62	142
Total	70	80	93	

$42 + 28 + 31 = 101$ Find the 9th grade row total.

$70 - 42 = 28$ Total who prefer the museum − 9th graders who prefer the museum

$70 + 80 + 93 = 243$ and $101 + 142 = 243$ Find the grand total.

Grade	Preferred Field Trip			
	Museum	Zoo	Botanical Garden	Total
9th	42	28	31	101
10th	28	52	62	142
Total	70	80	93	243

KEY EXAMPLE   *(Lesson 8.2)*

The principal wants to know if the percent of 10th graders who prefer the zoo is greater than the percent of total students who prefer the zoo. Find the conditional relative frequency of 10th graders who prefer the zoo and the marginal relative frequency of students who prefer the zoo. Compare the results.

The percent of 10th graders who prefer the zoo is given by the conditional relative frequency:

$$\frac{\text{Number of 10th graders who prefer the zoo}}{\text{Total number of 10th graders}} = \frac{52}{142} \approx 0.37.$$

The percent of total students who prefer the zoo is given by the marginal relative frequency:

$$\frac{\text{Number of students who prefer the zoo}}{\text{Total number of students}} = \frac{80}{243} \approx 0.33.$$

Since 37% > 33%, the percent of 10th graders who prefer the zoo is greater than the percent of total students that prefer the zoo.

EXERCISES

1. Copy and complete the two-way frequency table. Interpret the meaning of the number in the starred cell of the table. *(Lesson 8.1)*

	Preferred Mode of Transportation			
Age	Bike	Car	Bus	Total
Adults	25	3	12	?
Teenagers	5	28	12	?
Total	?	? *	?	?

2. A middle school student surveyed middle school and high school teachers on whether they preferred to have their students write in pen. *(Lesson 8.2)*

	Prefer Students Use Pen		
Grade Level	Yes	No	Total
Middle School	3	18	21
High School	7	12	19
Total	10	30	40

Are middle school teachers or high school teachers more likely to prefer that their students use pen? Explain.

MODULE PERFORMANCE TASK

Survey Says?

Students in grades 7–12 were surveyed about which of the following they would most like to do during 2 weeks of a summer vacation: visit a foreign country, attend camp, or visit a national park. The students were divided into two groups, Grades 7–9 and Grades 10–12. Here are the results:

	Visit a Foreign Country	Attend Camp	Visit a National Park
Grades 7–9	25	40	15
Grades 10–12	70	20	30

- Make a table showing the relative frequency of each of the six categories in the table.
- Make a circle graph, histogram, or bar graph showing the frequencies or relative frequencies of each of the six categories in the table.
- Write and answer at least five questions involving conditional relative probability that can be answered by referring to the table.
- Describe any trends you see in the data.

Use numbers, words, or algebra to explain how you reached your conclusion.

(Ready) to Go On?

8.1–8.2 Multi-Variable Categorical Data

- Online Homework
- Hints and Help
- Extra Practice

1. A researcher surveyed 135 people, 85 females and 50 males. The researcher asked each person which of the following types of movies they preferred: action, comedy, or drama. Copy and complete the table. *(Lesson 8.1)*

Gender	Favorite Type of Movie			
	Action	**Comedy**	**Drama**	**Total**
Female	35	?	18	?
Male	12	28	?	?
Total	?	?	28	?

2. Based on the data given in the frequency table below, does a greater percent of 11th or 12th graders surveyed like tennis? Use conditional relative frequencies to support your answer. *(Lesson 8.2)*

Grade	Like Tennis		
	Yes	**No**	**Total**
11th	55	55	110
12th	64	32	96
Total	119	87	206

ESSENTIAL QUESTION

3. How can you compare values in tables of two-variable categorical data?

Assessment Readiness

1. Look at each variable. Tell whether each variable is best represented by categorical data.

   A. Favorite song

   B. Car color

   C. Weight

2. Mazin asked his classmates whether they like soccer and whether they like running. The table shows the results of his survey.

Like Soccer	Like Running		
	Yes	**No**	**Total**
Yes	12	?	?
No	?	6	18
Total	24	31	?

Copy and complete the table. Determine if each statement is True or False.

   A. 12 students like soccer but not running.

   B. Mazin surveyed 55 students in all.

   C. 25 students like soccer.

Use the following information for questions 3 and 4.

Samantha is preparing to do a survey of the language classes taken by ninth and tenth graders at her high school. Each student in ninth and tenth grade takes one language class. From school records, she knows there are 158 students in the ninth grade, as shown in the table.

Grade	Language			
	French	**Mandarin**	**Spanish**	**Total**
9	r	s	t	158
10	x	y	z	?
Total	?	?	?	?

3. Write an expression to represent the conditional relative frequency that a student takes Mandarin, given that the student is a tenth grader. Explain how you created the expression.

4. Based on school records, Samantha finds out that there are 65 students in ninth grade who take Spanish and 35 students in ninth grade that take French. Find the conditional probability that a student takes Mandarin, given that the student is a ninth grader. Show your work.

One-Variable Data Distributions

Essential Question: How can you use one-variable data distributions to solve real-world problems?

REAL WORLD VIDEO
In baseball, there are many options for how a team executes a given play. The use of statistics for in-game decision making sometimes reveals surprising strategies that run counter to the common wisdom.

MODULE PERFORMANCE TASK PREVIEW

Baseball Stats

Most baseball fans keep track of a few statistics relating to their favorite team—the number of home runs their favorite player has hit, for example. An entire field of statistics called sabermetrics goes much farther, keeping track of incredibly detailed data about teams and their players. One website lists 111 such statistics. In this module, you'll study ways to analyze these numbers and then apply what you've learned to some actual baseball stats.

Are YOU Ready?

Complete these exercises to review skills you will need for this module.

Measures of Center

Example 1   Find the mode, median, and mean of these data.

8, 4, 16, 8, 12, 19, 35, 8, 4, 11

4, 4, 8, 8, 8, 11, 12, 16, 19, 35   Order the data.

The mode is 8.

The middle two entries are 8 and 11.

Their mean is $\frac{8 + 11}{2} = 9.5$.

The median is 9.5.

The sum of all the data is 125.

There are 10 entries.

The mean is $\frac{125}{10}$, or 12.5.

Mode: The number with the greatest frequency is the mode.

Median: Find the middle entry or the mean of the two middle entries of the ordered data.

Mean: Find the sum of all the entries and divide it by the number of entries.

Use these data to find the measures of center.
26, 19, 14, 30, 12, 21, 30, 4

1. What is the mean?

2. What is the mode?

3. What is the median?

Box Plots

Example 2   The box plot shown represents the ages people of a certain community were when they purchased their first automobile. What is the range of ages?

The box plot extends from 22 to 31, so the range of ages is 31 − 22, or 9 years.

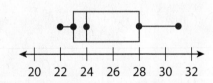

Use the box plot shown to answer the questions.

4. What is the median?

5. What is the first quartile?

6. What is the third quartile?

9.1 Measures of Center and Spread

Resource Locker

Essential Question: How can you describe and compare data sets?

⊘ Explore   Exploring Data

Caleb and Kim have bowled three games. Their scores are shown in the chart below.

Name	Game 1	Game 2	Game 3	Average Score
Caleb	151	153	146	?
Kim	122	139	189	?

Copy and complete the table.

(A) Find Caleb's average score over the three games and enter it in the table.

$$\frac{151 + 153 + 146}{3} = \frac{\boxed{?}}{3} = \boxed{?}$$

(B) Find Kim's average score over the three games and enter it in the table.

$$\frac{122 + 139 + 189}{3} = \frac{\boxed{?}}{3} = \boxed{?}$$

(C) How do their average scores compare? ?

(D) Whose scores are more consistent? ?

(E) Are Caleb's scores farther from or closer to the average than Kim's. ?

They bowl a fourth game, where Caleb scores 150 and Kim scores a 175. How does this affect their averages?

(F) Caleb's average ? .   (G) Kim's average ? .

(H) Does the Game 4 score affect the consistency of their scores? Explain. ?

Reflect

1. **Discussion** Is the average an accurate representation of Caleb's bowling?

2. **Discussion** Is the average an accurate representation of Kim's bowling?

⚙ Explain 1 Measures of Center: Mean and Median

Two commonly used measures of center for a set of numerical data are the mean and median. Measures of center represent a central or typical value of a data set. The **mean** is the sum of the values in the set divided by the number of values in the set. The **median** is the middle value in a set when the values are arranged in numerical order.

Example 1   Find the mean and median of each data set.

(A) The number of text messages that Isaac received each day for a week is shown.

47, 49, 54, 50, 48, 47, 55

Find the mean. Divide the sum by the numbers of data values.

$\frac{350}{7} = 50$. The mean is 50 text messages a day.

Find the median. Rewrite the values in increasing order.

47, 47, 48, ⟨49⟩ 50, 54, 55. The median is 49 text messages a day.

(B) The amount of money Elise earned in tips per day for 6 days is listed below.

$75, $97, $360, $84, $119, $100

Find the mean to the nearest $0.01. Divide the sum by the number of data values.

$\frac{835}{6} = \boxed{\$139.17}$ The mean is $139.17.

Find the median. Rewrite the values in increasing order.

75, $\boxed{84}$, ⟨$\boxed{97}$, $\boxed{100}$⟩, $\boxed{119}$, 360

Find the mean of the middle two values. $\dfrac{\boxed{97} + \boxed{100}}{2} = \boxed{98.5}$

The median is $98.50.

Reflect

3. **Discussion** For the data on tips, which measure of center is more accurate in describing the typical value? Explain.

Your Turn

Find the mean and median of each data set.

4. Niles scored 70, 74, 72, 71, 73, and 96 on his 6 geography tests.

5. Raul recorded the following golf scores in his last 7 games.

84, 94, 93, 89, 94, 81, 90

🎸 Explain 2 Measures of Spread: Range and IQR

Measures of spread are used to describe the consistency of data values. They show the distance between data values and their distance from the center of the data. Two commonly used measures of spread for a set of numerical data are the *range* and *interquartile range (IQR)*. The **range** is the difference between the greatest and the least data values. **Quartiles** are values that divide a data set into four equal parts. The **first quartile (Q_1)** is the median of the lower half of the set, the **second quartile (Q_2)** is the median of the whole set, and the **third quartile (Q_3)** is the median of the upper half of the set. The **interquartile range (IQR)** of a data set is the difference between the third and first quartiles. It represents the range of the middle half of the data.

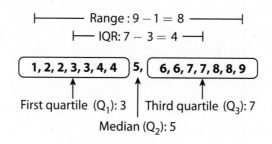

Example 2 Find the median, range, and interquartile range for the given data set.

(A) The April high temperatures for 5 years in Boston are 77 °F, 86 °F, 84 °F, 93 °F, and 90 °F

Order the data values.

Median: 77, 84, 86, 90, 93   Range: $93 - 77 = 16$
                 median
Interquartile range:

lower half   upper half
77, 84, 86, 90, 93 $Q_1 = \dfrac{77 + 84}{2} = 80.5$ and $Q_3 = \dfrac{90 + 93}{2} = 91.5$
         median

$IQR = Q_3 - Q_1 = 91.5 - 80.5 = 11$

Ⓑ The numbers of runs scored by a softball team in 20 games are given.

3, 4, 8, 12, 7, 5, 4, 12, 3, 9, 11, 4, 14, 8, 2, 10, 3, 10, 9, 7

Order the data values.

2, 3, 3, 3, 4, 4, 4, 5 , 7 , 7 , 8 , 8 , 9 , 9, 10, 10, 11, 12, 12, 14

<u>median</u>

$$\text{Median} = \frac{\boxed{7} + \boxed{8}}{2} = \boxed{7.5}$$

$$\text{Range} = 14 - 2 = \boxed{12}$$

Interquartile range.

$$Q_1 = \frac{\boxed{4} + \boxed{4}}{2} = 4 \text{ and } Q_3 = \frac{\boxed{10} + \boxed{10}}{2} = \boxed{10}$$

$$IQR = Q_3 - Q_1$$

$$= \boxed{10} - \boxed{4}$$

$$= \boxed{6}$$

The median is 7.5.

The range is 12.

The IQR is 6.

Reflect

6. **Discussion** Why is the IQR less than the range?

Your Turn

Find the median, range, and interquartile range for the given data set.

7. 21, 31, 26, 24, 28, 26

8. The high temperatures in degrees Fahrenheit on 11 days were 68, 71, 75, 74, 75, 71, 73, 71, 72, 74, and 79.

Measures of Spread: Standard Deviation

Another measure of spread is the **standard deviation**, which represents the square root of the average of the squared differences between individual data values and the mean.

The formula for finding the standard deviation of the data set $\{x_1, x_2, x_2, x_2 \cdots, x_n\}$, with n elements and mean x, is shown below.

$$\text{standard deviation} = \sqrt{\frac{(x_1 - \bar{x})^2 + (x_2 - \bar{x})^2 + \cdots + (x_n - \bar{x})^2}{n}}$$

Example 3

Ⓐ Find the standard deviation of 77, 86, 84, 93, 90.

Find the mean.

$$\text{mean} = \frac{77 + 86 + 84 + 93 + 90}{5}$$
$$= \frac{430}{5}$$
$$= 86$$

Complete the table.

Data Value, x	Deviation from Mean, x x	Squared Deviation, $(x - \bar{x})^2$
77	$77 - 86 = -9$	$(-9)^2 = 81$
86	$86 - 86 = 0$	$0^2 = 0$
84	$84 - 86 = -2$	$(-2)^2 = 4$
93	$93 - 86 = 7$	$7^2 = 49$
90	$90 - 86 = 4$	$4^2 = 16$

Find the mean of the squared deviations.

$$\text{mean squared deviation} = \frac{81 + 0 + 4 + 49 + 16}{5}$$
$$= \frac{150}{5}$$
$$= 30$$

Find the square root of the mean of the squared deviations, rounding to the nearest tenth. $\sqrt{30} = 5.5$

The standard deviation is approximately 5.5.

Ⓑ Find the standard deviation of 3, 4, 8, 12, 7, 5, 4, 12, 3, 9, 11, 4, 14, 8, 2, 10, 3, 10, 9, 7.

Find the mean.

$$\text{mean} = \frac{2 + 3 + 3 + 3 + 4 + 4 + 4 + 5 + 7 + 7 + 8 + 8 + 9 + 9 + 10 + 10 + 11 + 12 + 12 + 14}{20}$$
$$= \frac{\boxed{145}}{20}$$
$$= \boxed{7.25}$$

Complete the table.

Data Value, x	Deviation from Mean, $x - \bar{x}$	Squared Deviation, $(x - \bar{x})^2$
2	$2 - \boxed{7.25} = \boxed{-5.25}$	$\left(\boxed{-5.25}\right)^2 = \boxed{27.5625}$
3	$3 - \boxed{7.25} = \boxed{-4.25}$	$\left(\boxed{-4.25}\right)^2 = \boxed{18.0625}$
3	-4.25	18.0625
3	-4.25	18.0625
4	$4 - \boxed{7.25} = \boxed{-3.25}$	$\left(\boxed{-3.25}\right)^2 = \boxed{10.5625}$
4	-3.25	10.5625
4	-3.25	10.5625
5	$5 - \boxed{7.25} = \boxed{-2.25}$	$\left(\boxed{-2.25}\right)^2 = \boxed{5.0625}$
7	$7 - \boxed{7.25} = \boxed{-0.25}$	$\left(\boxed{-0.25}\right)^2 = \boxed{0.0625}$
7	-0.25	0.0625
8	$8 - \boxed{7.25} = \boxed{0.75}$	$\left(\boxed{0.75}\right)^2 = \boxed{0.5625}$
8	0.75	0.5625
9	$9 - \boxed{7.25} = \boxed{1.75}$	$\left(\boxed{1.75}\right)^2 = \boxed{3.0625}$
9	1.75	3.0625
10	$10 - \boxed{7.25} = \boxed{2.75}$	$\left(\boxed{2.75}\right)^2 = \boxed{7.5625}$
10	2.75	7.5625
11	$11 - \boxed{7.25} = \boxed{3.75}$	$\left(\boxed{3.75}\right)^2 = \boxed{14.0625}$
12	$12 - \boxed{7.25} = \boxed{4.75}$	$\left(\boxed{4.75}\right)^2 = \boxed{22.5625}$
12	4.75	22.5625
14	$14 - \boxed{7.25} = \boxed{6.75}$	$\left(\boxed{-6.25}\right)^2 = \boxed{45.5625}$

Find the mean of the squared deviations.

$$\text{mean squared deviation} = \frac{\boxed{\begin{array}{c} 27.5625 + 3(18.0625) + 3(10.5625) + 5.0625 + 2(0.0625) + 2(0.5625) \\ + 2(3.0625) + 2(7.5625) + 14.0625 + 2(22.5625) + 45.5625 \end{array}}}{20}$$

$$= \frac{\boxed{245.75}}{20}$$

$$= \boxed{12.2875}$$

Find the square root of the mean of the squared deviations, rounding to the nearest tenth.

$$\sqrt{\boxed{12.2875}} = \boxed{3.5}$$

The standard deviation is approximately 3.5.

Reflect

9. In terms of data values used, what makes calculating the standard deviation different from calculating the range?

Your Turn

10. Find the standard deviation of 21, 31, 26, 24, 28, 26.

11. Find the standard deviation of 68, 71, 75, 74, 75, 71, 73, 71, 72, 74, and 79.

💬 Elaborate

12. In Your Turn 11, what is the mean of the deviations before squaring? Use your answer to explain why squaring the deviations is helpful.

13. How can you determine the first and third quartiles of a data set?

14. How can you determine the standard deviation of a data set?

15. **Essential Question Check-In** What does the measure of center of a data set indicate?

☆ Evaluate: Homework and Practice

1. The data set {13, 24, 14, 15, 14} gives the times of Tara's one-way ride to school (in minutes) for one week. Is the average (mean) of the times a good description of Tara's ride time? Explain.

Find the mean and median of each data set.

2. The numbers of hours Cheri works each day are 3, 7, 4, 6, and 5.

3. The weights in pounds of 6 members of a basketball team are 125, 136, 150, 119, 150, and 143.

4. 36, 18, 12, 10, 9

5. The average yearly gold price for the period from 2000–2009:

$279.11, $271.04, $309.73, $363.38, $409.72, $444.74, $603.46, $695.39, $871.96, $972.35

6. There are 28, 30, 29, 26, 31, and 30 students in a school's six Algebra 1 classes.

7. 13, 14, 18, 13, 12, 17, 15, 12

8. The numbers of members in five karate classes are 13, 12, 10, 16, and 19.

9. Find the range and interquartile range for 3, 7, 4, 6, and 5.

10. Find the range and interquartile range for 125, 136, 150, 119, 150, and 143.

11. Find the range and interquartile range for 36, 18, 12, 10, and 9.

12. Find the range and interquartile range for $279.11, $271.04, $309.73, $363.38, $409.72, $444.74, $603.46, $695.39, $871.96, and $972.35.

13. Find the range and interquartile range for 28, 30, 29, 26, 31, and 30.

14. Find the range and interquartile range for 13, 14, 18, 13, 12, 17, 15, and 12.

15. Find the range and interquartile range for 13, 12, 15, 17, and 9.

16. Find the standard deviation of 3, 7, 4, 6, and 5.

17. Find the standard deviation of 125, 136, 150, 119, 150, and 143.

18. Find the standard deviation of 36, 18, 12, 10, and 9.

19. Find the standard deviation of $279.11, $271.04, $309.73, $363.38, $409.72, $444.74, $603.46, $695.39, $871.96, and $972.35. Round the mean to the nearest $0.01 and the squared deviations to the nearest whole number.

20. Find the standard deviation of 28, 30, 29, 26, 31, and 30.

21. Find the standard deviation of 13, 14, 18, 13, 12, 17, 15, and 12.

22. Determine whether or not the third quartile has the same value as a member of the data set.

    A. {79, 91, 90, 99, 91, 80, 80, 90}

    B. {98, 96, 96, 95, 91, 81, 87}

    C. {88, 95, 89, 93, 88, 93, 84, 93, 85, 92}

    D. {97, 84, 96, 82, 93, 88, 82, 91, 94}

    E. {94, 85, 95, 80, 97}

    F. {85, 89, 81, 89, 85, 84}

Use this data for Exercises 23 and 24. The numbers of members in 6 yoga clubs are 80, 74, 77, 71, 75, and 91.

23. Find the standard deviation of the numbers of members to the nearest tenth.

H.O.T. **Focus on Higher Order Thinking**

24. **Explain the Error** Suppose a person in the club with 91 members transfers to the club with 71 members. A student claims that the measures of center and the measures of spread will all change. Correct the student's error.

25. **What If?** If all the values in a set are increased by 10, does the range also increase by 10? Explain.

26. **Communicate Mathematical Ideas** Jorge has a data set with the following values: 92, 80, 88, 95, and x. If the median value for this set is 88, what must be true about x? Explain.

27. **Critical Thinking** If the value for the median of a set is not found in the data set, what must be true about the data set? Explain.

Lesson Performance Task

The table lists the ages of the soprano and bass singers in a town choir. Find the mean, median, range, interquartile range, and standard deviation for each type of singer in the data set. Interpret each result. What can you conclude about the ages of the different types of singers?

Age of Soprano Singers	63	42	28	45	36	48	32	40	57	49
Age of Bass Singers	32	34	53	35	43	41	29	35	24	34

© Houghton Mifflin Harcourt Publishing Company

9.2 Data Distributions and Outliers

Resource Locker

Essential Question: What statistics are most affected by outliers, and what shapes can data distributions have?

⊘ Explore   Using Dot Plots to Display Data

A **dot plot** is a data representation that uses a number line and Xs, dots, or other symbols to show frequency. Dot plots are sometimes called *line plots*.

Finance Twelve employees at a small company make the following annual salaries (in thousands of dollars): 25, 30, 35, 35, 35, 40, 40, 40, 45, 45, 50, and 60.

(A) Which number line has the most appropriate scale for this problem? Explain your reasoning.

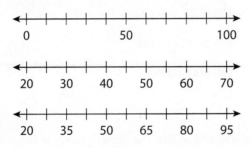

(B) Create and label a dot plot of the data. Put an X above the number line for each time that value appears in the data set.

Reflect

1. **Discussion** Recall that quantitative data can be expressed as a numerical measurement. Categorical, qualitative data is expressed in categories, such as attributes or preferences. Is it appropriate to use a dot plot for displaying quantitative data, qualitative data, or both? Explain.

🖉 Explain 1   The Effects of an Outlier in a Data Set

An **outlier** is a value in a data set that is much greater or much less than most of the other values in the data set. Outliers are determined by using the first or third quartiles and the IQR.

How to Identify an Outlier
A data value x is an outlier if $x < Q_1 - 1.5(\text{IQR})$ or if $x > Q_3 + 1.5(\text{IQR})$.

Example 1 Create a dot plot for the data set using an appropriate scale for the number line. Determine whether the extreme value is an outlier.

(A) Suppose that the list of salaries from the Explore is expanded to include the owner's salary of $150,000. Now the list of salaries is 25, 30, 35, 35, 35, 40, 40, 40, 45, 45, 50, 60, and 150.

To choose an appropriate scale, consider the minimum and maximum values, 25 and 150.

A number line from 20 to 160 will contain all the values. A scale of 5 will be convenient for the data. Label tick marks by 20s.

Plot each data value to see the distribution.

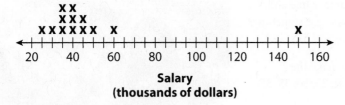

Salary
(thousands of dollars)

Find the quartiles and the IQR to determine whether 150 is an outlier.

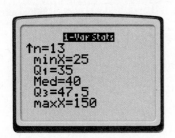

$150 \overset{?}{>} Q_3 + 1.5(IQR)$

$150 \overset{?}{>} 47.5 + 1.5(47.5 - 35)$

$150 > 66.25$ True

150 is an outlier.

(B) Suppose that the salaries from Part A were adjusted so that the owner's salary is $65,000.

Now the list of salaries is 25, 30, 35, 35, 35, 40, 40, 40, 45, 45, 50, 60, and 65.

To choose an appropriate scale, consider the minimum and maximum data values, 25 and 65.

A number line from 20 to 70 will contain all the data values.

A scale of 5 will be convenient for the data.

Label tick marks by 10s.

Plot each data value to see the distribution.

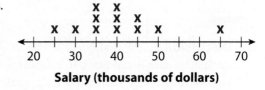

Salary (thousands of dollars)

Find the quartiles and the IQR to determine whether 65 is an outlier.

$65 \overset{?}{>} Q_3 + 1.5(IQR)$

$65 \overset{?}{>} \boxed{47.5} + 1.5\left(\boxed{47.5} - \boxed{35} \right)$

$65 > \boxed{66.25}$ False

Therefore, 65 is not an outlier.

Reflect

2. Explain why the median was NOT affected by changing the max data value from 150 to 65.

Your Turn

3. **Sports** Baseball pitchers on a major league team throw at the following speeds (in miles per hour): 72, 84, 89, 81, 93, 100, 90, 88, 80, 84, and 87.

Create a dot plot using an appropriate scale for the number line. Determine whether the extreme value is an outlier.

🔧 Explain 2   Comparing Data Sets

Numbers that characterize a data set, such as measures of center and spread, are called **statistics**. They are useful when comparing large sets of data.

Example 2   Calculate the mean, median, interquartile range (IQR), and standard deviation for each data set, and then compare the data.

Ⓐ **Sports** The tables list the average ages of players on 15 teams randomly selected from the 2010 teams in the National Football League (NFL) and Major League Baseball (MLB). Describe how the average ages of NFL players compare to those of MLB players.

NFL Players' Average Ages, by Team
25.8, 26.0, 26.3, 25.7, 25.1, 25.2, 26.1, 26.4, 25.9, 26.6, 26.3, 26.2, 26.8, 25.6, 25.7

MLB Players' Average Ages, by Team
28.5, 29.0, 28.0, 27.8, 29.5, 29.1, 26.9, 28.9, 28.6, 28.7, 26.9, 30.5, 28.7, 28.9, 29.3

On a graphing calculator, enter the two sets of data into L_1 and L_2.

Use the "1-Var Stats" feature to find statistics for the data in lists L_1 and L_2. Your calculator may use the following notations: mean $\bar{x}$, standard deviation σ_x.

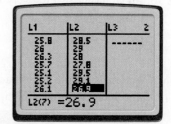

Scroll down to see the median (Med), Q_1, and Q_3. Complete the table.

	Mean	Median	IQR ($Q_3 - Q_1$)	Standard deviation
NFL	25.98	26.00	0.60	0.46
MLB	28.62	28.70	1.10	0.91

Compare the corresponding statistics.

The mean age and median age are lower for the NFL than for the MLB, which means that NFL players tend to be younger than MLB players. In addition, the IQR and standard deviation are smaller for the NFL than for the MLB, which means that the ages of NFL players are closer together than those of MLB players.

B The tables list the ages of 10 contestants on 2 game shows.

Game Show 1
18, 20, 25, 48, 35, 39, 46, 41, 30, 27

Game Show 2
24, 29, 36, 32, 34, 41, 21, 38, 39, 26

On a graphing calculator, enter the two sets of data into L_1 and L_2.

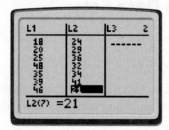

Complete the table. Then circle the correct items to compare the statistics.

	Mean	Median	IQR ($Q_3 - Q_1$)	Standard deviation
Show 1	32.9	32.5	16	10.00
Show 2	32	33	12	6.45

The mean is lower for the 2nd game show, which means that contestants in the 2nd game show are on average younger than contestants in the 1st game show. However, the median is lower for the 1st game show, which means that although contestants are on average younger on the 2nd game show, there are more young contestants on the 1st game show. Finally, the IQR and standard deviation are higher for the 1st game show, which means that the ages of contestants on the 1st game show are further apart than the age of contestants on the 2nd game show.

Your Turn

 4. The tables list the age of each member of Congress in two randomly selected states. Copy and complete the table and compare the data.

Illinois
26, 24, 28, 46, 39, 59, 31, 26, 64, 40, 69, 62, 31, 28, 26, 76, 57, 71, 58, 35, 32, 49, 51, 22, 33, 56

Arizona
42, 37, 58, 32, 46, 42, 26, 56, 27

	Mean	Median	IQR ($Q_3 - Q_1$)	Standard deviation
Illinois	?	?	?	?
Arizona	?	?	?	?

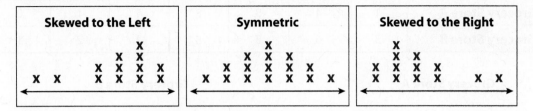

♪ Explain 3   Comparing Data Distributions

A data distribution can be described as **symmetric**, **skewed to the left**, or **skewed to the right**, depending on the general shape of the distribution in a dot plot or other data display.

Example 3   For each data set, make a dot plot and determine the type of distribution. Then explain what the distribution means for each data set.

Ⓐ   **Sports** The data table shows the number of miles run by members of two track teams during one day.

Miles	3	3.5	4	4.5	5	5.5	6
Members of Team A	2	3	4	4	3	2	0
Members of Team B	1	2	2	3	3	4	3

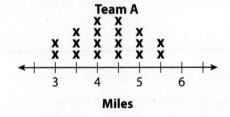

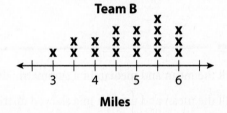

The data for team A show a symmetric distribution. This means that the distances run are evenly distributed about the mean.

The data for team B show a distribution skewed to the left. This means that more than half the team members ran a distance greater than the mean.

B The table shows the number of days, over the course of a month, that specific numbers of apples were sold by competing grocers.

Number of Apples Sold	0	50	100	150	200	250	300
Grocery Store A	1	4	8	8	4	1	0
Grocery Store B	3	6	8	8	2	2	1

Grocery Store A

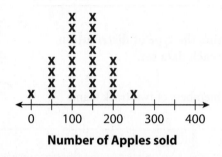

Number of Apples sold

Grocery Store B

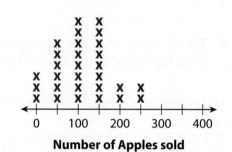

Number of Apples sold

The distribution for grocery store A is symmetric. This means that the number of apples sold each day is evenly distributed about the mean.

The distribution for grocery store B is right-skewed. This means that the number of apples sold each day is unevenly distributed about the mean.

Reflect

7. Will the mean and median in a symmetric distribution always be approximately equal? Explain.

8. Will the mean and median in a skewed distribution always be approximately equal? Explain.

Your Turn

9. **Sports** The table shows the number of free throws attempted during a basketball game. Make a dot plot and determine the type of distribution. Then explain what the distribution means for the data set.

Free Throws Shot	0	2	4	6	8
Members of Team A	2	2	4	2	2
Members of Team B	3	4	2	2	1

💬 Elaborate

10. If the mean increases after a single data point is added to a set of data, what can you tell about this data point?

11. How can you use a calculation to decide whether a data point is an outlier in a data set?

12. **Essential Question Check-In** What three shapes can data distributions have?

⭐ Evaluate: Homework and Practice

Fitness The numbers of members in 8 workout clubs are 100, 95, 90, 85, 85, 95, 100, and 90. Use this information for Exercises 1–2.

1. Create a dot plot for the data set using an appropriate scale for the number line.

2. Suppose that a new workout club opens and immediately has 150 members. Is the number of members at this new club an outlier?

Sports The number of feet to the left outfield wall for 10 randomly chosen baseball stadiums is 315, 325, 335, 330, 330, 330, 320, 310, 325, and 335. Use this information for Exercises 3–4.

3. Create a dot plot for the data set using an appropriate scale for the number line.

4. The longest distance to the left outfield wall in a baseball stadium is 355 feet. Is this stadium an outlier if it is added to the data set?

Education The numbers of students in 10 randomly chosen classes in a high school are 18, 22, 26, 31, 25, 20, 23, 26, 29, and 30. Use this information for Exercises 5–6.

5. Create a dot plot for the data set using an appropriate scale for the number line.

6. Suppose that a new class is opened for enrollment and currently has 7 students. Is this class an outlier if it is added to the data set?

Sports The average bowling scores for a group of bowlers are 200, 210, 230, 220, 230, 225, and 240. Use this information for Exercises 7–8.

7. Create a dot plot for the data set using an appropriate scale for the number line.

8. Suppose that a new bowler joins this group and has an average score of 275. Is this bowler an outlier in the data set?

The tables describe the average ages of employees from two randomly chosen companies. Use this information for Exercises 9–10.

Company A	Company B
23, 29, 35, 46, 51, 50, 42, 37, 30	24, 23, 45, 45, 42, 52, 55, 47, 55

9. Calculate the mean, median, interquartile range (IQR), and standard deviation for each data set.

10. Compare the data sets.

The tables describe the size of microwaves, in cubic feet, chosen randomly from two competing companies. Use this information for Exercises 11–12.

Company A
1.8, 2.1, 3.1, 2.0, 3.3, 2.9, 3.3, 2.1, 3.2

Company B
1.9, 2.6, 1.8, 3.0, 2.5, 2.8, 2.0, 3.6, 3.1

11. Calculate the mean, median, interquartile range (IQR), and standard deviation for each data set.

12. Compare the data sets.

For each data set, make a dot plot and determine the type of distribution. Then explain what the distribution means for each data set.

13. Sports The data table shows the number of miles run by members of two teams running a marathon.

Miles	5	10	15	20	25
Members of Team A	3	5	10	5	3
Members of Team B	6	10	4	1	5

14. Sales The data table shows the number of days that specific numbers of turkeys were sold. These days were in the two weeks before Thanksgiving.

Number of Turkeys	10	20	30	40
Grocery Store A	2	5	5	2
Grocery Store B	5	5	1	3

15. State whether each set of data is left-skewed, right-skewed, or symmetrically distributed.

A. 3, 5, 5, 3

B. 1, 1, 3, 1

C. 7, 9, 9, 11

D. 5, 5, 3, 3

E. 19, 21, 21, 19

16. What If? Given the data set 8, 15, 12, 10, and 5, what happens to the mean if you add a data value of 40? Is 40 an outlier of the new data set?

17. Critical Thinking Can an outlier be a data value between Q_1 and Q_3? Justify your answer.

18. Justify Reasoning If the distribution has outliers, why will they always have an effect on the range?

19. Education The data table describes the average testing scores in 20 randomly selected classes in two randomly selected high schools, rounded to the nearest ten. For each data set, make a dot plot, determine the type of distribution, and explain what the distribution means in context.

Average Scores	0	10	20	30	40	50	60	70	80	90	100
School A	0	1	2	2	3	4	3	2	2	1	0
School B	0	1	1	1	2	4	5	4	2	0	0

Lesson Performance Task

The tables list the daily car sales of two competing dealerships.

Dealer A			
14	13	15	12
15	16	15	17
17	12	16	14
15	16	14	16
13	14	18	15

Dealer B			
16	17	15	20
18	19	18	17
19	10	19	18
15	17	20	19
18	18	16	17

A. Calculate the mean, median, interquartile range (IQR), and standard deviation for each data set. Compare the measures of center for the two dealers.

B. Create a dot plot for each data set. Compare the distributions of the data sets.

C. Determine if there are any outliers in the data sets. If there are, remove the outlier and find the statistics for that data set(s). What was affected by the outlier?

9.3 Histograms and Box Plots

Essential Question: How can you interpret and compare data sets using data displays?

Resource Locker

⊘ **Explore** **Understanding Histograms**

A **histogram** is a bar graph that is used to display the frequency of data divided into equal intervals. The bars must be of equal width and should touch but not overlap. The heights of the bars indicate the frequency of data values within each interval.

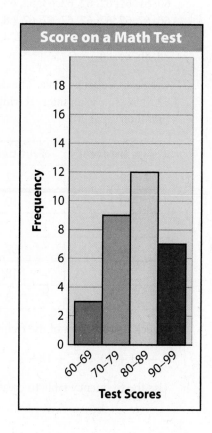

Ⓐ Look at the histogram of "Scores on a Math Test." Which axis indicates the frequency?

The ⬚? axis shows the frequency for each interval.

Ⓑ What does the horizontal axis indicate?

The horizontal axis shows the ⬚? .

Ⓒ How is the horizontal axis organized?

It is organized in groups of ⬚? .

Ⓓ How many had scores in the interval 60–69? ⬚?

Ⓔ How many had scores in the interval 70–79? ⬚?

Ⓕ How many had scores in the interval 80–89? ⬚?

Ⓖ How many had scores in the interval 90–99? ⬚?

Reflect

1. What statistical information can you tell about a data set by looking at a histogram? What statistical information cannot be determined by looking at a histogram?

2. How many test scores were collected? How do you know?

⏀ Explain 1 Creating Histograms

When creating a histogram, make sure that the bars are of equal width and that they touch without overlapping. Create a frequency table to help organize the data before constructing the histogram. Consider the range of the data values when creating intervals.

Example 1 Create a frequency table from the data. Then use the frequency table to create a histogram.

Ⓐ Listed are the ages of the 100 U.S. senators at the start of the 112th Congress on January 3, 2011.

39, 39, 42, 44, 46, 47, 47, 47, 48, 49, 49, 49, 50, 50, 51, 51, 52, 52, 53, 53, 54, 54, 55, 55, 55, 55, 55, 55, 56, 56, 57, 57, 57, 58, 58, 58, 58, 58, 59, 59, 59, 59, 60, 60, 60, 60, 60, 60, 60, 61, 61, 62, 62, 62, 63, 63, 63, 63, 64, 64, 64, 64, 66, 66, 66, 67, 67, 67, 67, 67, 67, 67, 68, 68, 68, 68, 69, 69, 69, 70, 70, 70, 71, 71, 73, 73, 74, 74, 74, 75, 76, 76, 76, 76, 77, 77, 78, 86, 86, 86

Create a frequency table. The data values range from 39 to 86, so use an interval width of 10 and start the first interval at 30.

Age Interval	Frequency
30–39	2
40–49	10
50–59	30
60–69	37
70–79	18
80–89	3

Check that the sum of the frequencies is 100.

$2 + 10 + 30 + 37 + 18 + 3 = 100$

Use the frequency table to create a histogram.

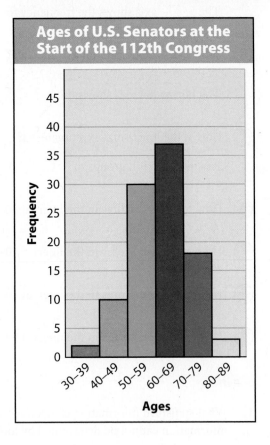

Ages of U.S. Senators at the Start of the 112th Congress

(B) Listed are the scores from a golf tournament.

68, 78, 76, 71, 69, 73, 72, 74, 76, 70, 77, 74, 75, 76, 71, 74

Create a frequency table. The data values range from ☐68☐ to ☐78☐,

so use an interval width of 3, and start the first interval at ☐68☐.

Score Interval	Frequency
68– 70	3
71– 73	4
74– 76	7
77– 79	2

Check that the sum of the frequencies is ☐16☐.

$3 + 4 + 7 + 2 =$ ☐16☐

Use the frequency table to create a histogram.

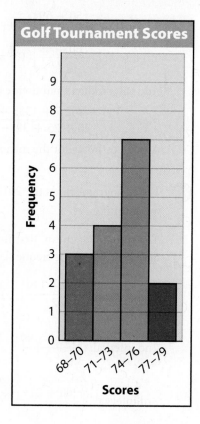

Golf Tournament Scores

Reflect

3. Describe the shape of the distribution of senators' ages. Interpret the meaning.

Your Turn

4. Listed are the heights of players, in inches, on a basketball team. Create a frequency table from the data. Then use the frequency table to create a histogram.

79, 75, 74, 68, 63, 76, 74, 73, 69, 65, 71, 68, 74, 73, 70

🔑 Explain 2 **Estimating from Histograms**

You can estimate statistics by studying a histogram.

Example 2 **Estimate the mean of the data set displayed in each histogram.**

(A) The histogram shows the ages of teachers in a high school.

To estimate the mean, first find the midpoint of each interval, and multiply by the frequency.

1st interval: $\left(\dfrac{20 + 29}{2}\right)(20) = (24.5)(20) = 490$

2nd interval: $\left(\dfrac{30 + 39}{2}\right)(25) = (34.5)(25) = 862.5$

3rd interval: $\left(\dfrac{40 + 49}{2}\right)(30) = (44.5)(30) = 1335$

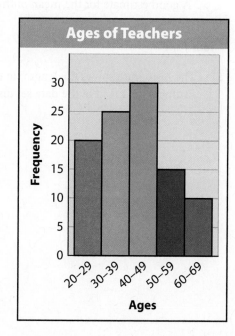

Ages of Teachers

4th interval: $\left(\dfrac{50 + 59}{2}\right)(15) = (54.5)(15) = 817.5$

5th interval: $\left(\dfrac{60 + 69}{2}\right)(10) = (64.5)(10) = 645$

Add the products and divide by the sum of the frequencies.

Mean: $\dfrac{490 + 862.5 + 1335 + 817.5 + 645}{20 + 25 + 30 + 15 + 10} = \dfrac{4150}{100} = 41.5$

A good estimate for the mean of this data set is an age of 41.5.

(B) The histogram shows the 2012 Olympic results for women's weightlifting.

To estimate the mean, first find the midpoint of each interval, and multiply by the frequency.

1st interval: $\left(\dfrac{160 + 179}{2}\right)\boxed{1} = \boxed{169.5} \cdot \boxed{1} = \boxed{169.5}$

2nd interval: $\left(\dfrac{180 + 199}{2}\right)\boxed{2} = \boxed{189.5} \cdot \boxed{2} = \boxed{379}$

3rd interval: $\left(\dfrac{200 + 219}{2}\right)\boxed{4} = \boxed{209.5} \cdot \boxed{4} = \boxed{838}$

4th interval: $\left(\dfrac{220 + 239}{2}\right)\boxed{9} = \boxed{229.5} \cdot \boxed{9} = \boxed{2065.5}$

5th interval: $\left(\dfrac{240 + 259}{2}\right)\boxed{1} = \boxed{249.5} \cdot \boxed{1} = \boxed{249.5}$

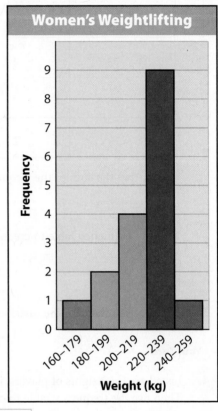

Add the results and divide by the total number of values in the data set.

Mean: $\dfrac{169.5 + 379 + 838 + 2065.5 + 249.5}{1 + 2 + 4 + 9 + 1} = \dfrac{\boxed{3701.5}}{17} \approx \boxed{217.7}$

A good estimate for the mean of this data set is $\boxed{217.7}$ kg.

Your Turn

5. The histogram shows the length, in days, of Maria's last vacations. Estimate the mean of the data set displayed in the histogram.

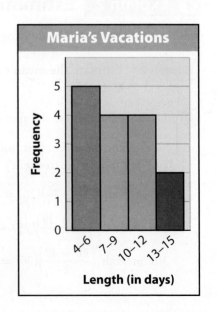

🎸 Explain 3 Constructing Box Plots

A box plot can be used to show how the values in a data set are distributed. You need 5 values to make a box plot: the minimum (or least value), first quartile, median, third quartile, and maximum (or greatest value).

Example 3 Use the data to make a box plot.

Ⓐ The numbers of runs scored by a softball team in 20 games are given.

3, 4, 8, 12, 7, 5, 4, 12, 3, 9, 11, 4, 14, 8, 2, 10, 3, 10, 9, 7

Order the data from least to greatest.

2, 3, 3, 3, 4, 4, 4, 5, 7, 7, 8, 8, 9, 9, 10, 10, 11, 12, 12, 14

Identify the 5 needed values. Those values are the minimum, first quartile, median, third quartile, and maximum.

2, 3, 3, 3, | 4, 4, | 4, 5, 7, | 7, 8, | 8, 9, 9, | 10, 10, | 11, 12, 12, | 14

↑	↑	↑	↑	↑
Minimum	Q₁	Median	Q₃	Maximum
2	4	7.5	10	14

Draw a number line and plot a point above each of the 5 needed values. Draw a box whose ends go through the first and third quartiles, and draw a vertical line segment through the median. Draw horizontal line segments from the box to the minimum and maximum.

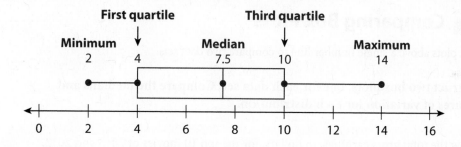

Ⓑ 13, 14, 18, 13, 12, 17, 15, 12, 13, 19, 11, 14, 14, 18, 22, 23

Order the data from least to greatest.

11 , 12, 12, 13 , 13 , 13, 14, 14 , 14 , 15, 17, 18 , 18 , 19, 22 23

Identify the 5 needed values. Those values are the minimum, first quartile, median, third quartile, and maximum.

11 , 12, 12, | 13, 13, | 13, 14, | 14, 14, | 15, 17, | 18, 18, | 19, 22, | 23

↑	↑	↑	↑	↑
Minimum	Q₁	Median	Q₃	Maximum
11	13	14	18	23

Draw a number line and plot a point above each of the 5 needed values. Draw a box whose ends go through the first and third quartiles, and draw a vertical line through the median. Draw horizontal lines from the box to the minimum and maximum.

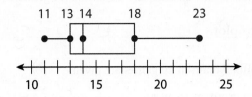

Reflect

6. The lines that extend from the box in a box plot are sometimes called "whiskers." What part (lower, middle, or upper) and about what percent of the data does the box represent? What part and about what percent does each "whisker" represent?

7. Which measures of spread can be determined from the box plot, and how are they found? Calculate each measure.

Your Turn

Use the data to make a box plot.

8. 25, 28, 26, 16, 18, 15, 25, 28, 26, 16

9. The numbers of goals scored by Lisa's soccer team in 13 games are listed below.

2, 3, 4, 1, 1, 3, 4, 2, 6, 2, 2, 3, 2

Explain 4 Comparing Box Plots

You can plot two box plots above a single number line to compare two data sets.

Example 4 Construct two box plots, one for each data set. Compare the medians and measures of variation for each distribution.

(A) The tables show the total gross earnings, in dollars, for the top 10 movies of 2013 and 2012.

Total Gross Earnings by the Top 25 Movies of 2013 & 2012			
Rank	Total Gross in 2013	Rank	Total Gross in 2012
1	$420,468,544	1	$623,357,910
2	$409,013,994	2	$448,139,099
3	$368,061,265	3	$408,010,692
4	$352,946,000	4	$304,360,277
5	$291,045,518	5	$303,003,568
6	$268,492,764	6	$292,324,737
7	$262,547,000	7	$262,030,663
8	$253,029,814	8	$237,283,207
9	$238,679,850	9	$218,815,487
10	$234,911,825	10	$216,391,482

Analyze Information

For each set of data, identify the five values you need to make a box plot: the minimum, first quartile, median, third quartile, and maximum. In this case, the data is from least to greatest reading from the bottom to the top.

 Formulate a Plan

With the 5 needed values for each data set, construct 2 box plots on the same number line. The number line for both plots can go from $200 million to $650 or 700 million. Interpret the box plots to compare the gross earnings for the top 10 movies in 2012 and 2013.

 Solve

Using the statistics feature of a graphing calculator, find the five needed values for both 2013 and 2012, rounded to the nearest hundred million. Use them to make the box plots.

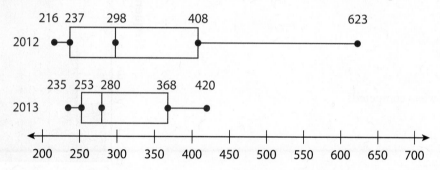

The medians for both years are very close together, but gross earnings for 2013 did not vary as much as in 2012. The range and interquartile range were greater for the 2012 data than for the 2013 data. The maximum value in the 2012 data appears to be an outlier, but because 623 is not greater than 665, it is not an outlier.

 Justify and Evaluate

Considering the little difference between minimum values but the great difference between maximum values the data sets, it makes sense that their measures of variation would not be alike.

Your Turn

Construct two box plots, one for each data set. Compare the medians and measures of variation for each distribution.

10. The net worth of the 10 richest people in the world for 2012 and 2013 (in billions) are:

2012: 69, 61, 44, 41, 37.5, 36, 30, 26, 25.5, 25.4 **2013:** 73, 67, 57, 53.5, 43, 34, 34, 31, 30, 29

11. The ages of the 10 richest people in the world for 2012 and 2013 (in years) are:

2012: 72, 56, 81, 63, 75, 67, 55, 64, 83, 92 **2013:** 72, 57, 76, 82, 68, 77, 72, 84, 90, 63

💬 **Elaborate**

12. How can you create a histogram from a data set?

13. How can you create a box plot from a data set?

14. Essential Question Check-In How can you use histograms and box plots to interpret and compare data sets?

☆ Evaluate: Homework and Practice

Use the histogram to answer the following questions.

1. What does each axis indicate?

2. How is the horizontal axis organized?

3. How many bowlers competed?

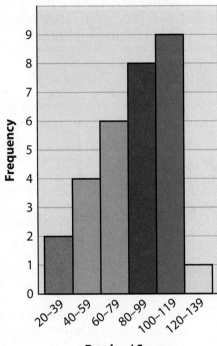

Bowlers' Scores

4. Describe the general shape of the distribution.

Create a histogram for the given data.

5. Listed are the ages of the first 44 U.S. presidents on the date of their first inauguration.

57, 61, 57, 57, 58, 57, 61, 54, 68, 51, 49, 64, 50, 48, 65, 52, 56, 46, 54, 49, 51, 47, 55, 55, 54, 42, 51, 56, 55, 51, 54, 51, 60, 62, 43, 55, 56, 61, 52, 69, 64, 46, 54, 47

6. Listed are the breathing intervals, in minutes, of gray whales.

8, 5, 13, 7 ,16, 9, 15, 11, 8, 6, 10, 9, 9, 11, 14, 12, 13, 15, 16, 11, 14, 9, 15, 6, 14

7. Listed are the heights, in inches, of the students in Marci's karate class.

42, 44, 47, 50, 51, 53, 53, 55, 56, 57, 57, 58, 59, 60, 66

8. Listed are the starting salaries, in thousands of dollars, for college graduates.

34, 20, 32, 45, 32, 48, 34, 32, 20, 35, 34, 32, 40, 47, 21, 37, 21, 47, 30, 31, 40, 31, 21, 22, 30, 22, 34, 48, 35, 37, 22, 46, 38, 39, 45, 37, 52, 25, 26, 26, 27, 43, 34, 28, 55, 29, 31, 42, 24, 21, 42, 42, 31, 30, 20, 39, 23, 41, 24, 33, 49, 24, 36, 36, 23, 38, 33, 33, 54

Estimate the mean of the data set displayed in each histogram.

9. The histogram shows the GPAs of the students in George's class.

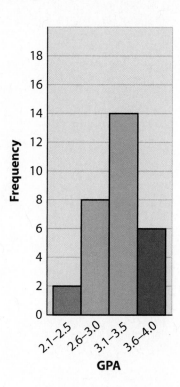

10. The histogram shows long jump distances, in feet, for a track and field team.

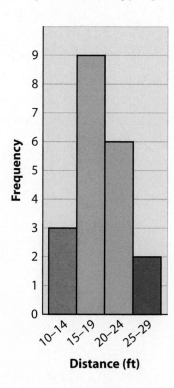

11. The histogram shows the speeds of downhill skiers, in miles per hour, during a competition.

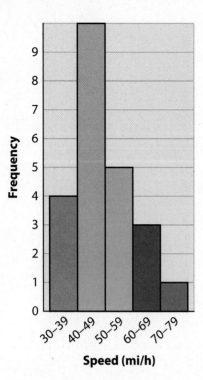

12. The histogram shows the depths a diver has been to, in meters.

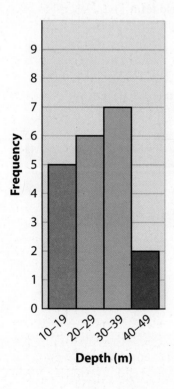

Use the data to make a box plot.

13. The numbers of points Julia's basketball team scored in 11 games are listed below.

50, 62, 37, 36, 34, 44, 44, 36, 37, 42, 36

14. The numbers of baskets Kelly's team scored in 9 games are listed below.

14, 24, 29, 15, 16, 20, 24, 15, 15

15. The numbers of runs Jane's baseball team scored in 9 games are listed below.

0, 2, 3, 2, 4, 11, 3, 4, 3

16. The numbers of field goals James' football team scored in 12 games are listed below.

3, 2, 5, 3, 5, 2, 1, 0, 5, 4, 4, 2

17. The numbers of points scored by Jane in 8 basketball games are listed below.

0, 13, 12, 2, 0, 16, 3, 14

18. The numbers of goals Claudia's soccer team scored in 21 games are shown below.

0, 5, 4, 3, 3, 2, 1, 1, 6, 2, 2, 1, 1, 1, 2, 2, 0, 1, 0, 1, 4

19. Mario and Carlos, two brothers, play for the same basketball team. Here are the points they scored in 10 games:

Game	1	2	3	4	5	6	7	8	9	10
Mario	15	X	X	12	7	11	12	11	10	11
Carlos	10	X	9	12	15	X	19	11	12	12

(Xs mark games each one missed.) Which brother had the highest-scoring game? How many more points did he score in that game than the other brother did in his highest-scoring game?

20. Communicate Mathematical Ideas Describe how you could estimate the IQR of a data set from a histogram.

21. Critical Thinking Suppose the minimum in a data set is the same as the first quartile. How would this affect a box plot of the data? Explain.

22. Draw Conclusions Dolly and Willie's scores are shown. Dolly claims that she is the better student, but Willie claims that he is the better student. What statistics make either Dolly or Willie seem like the better student? Explain.

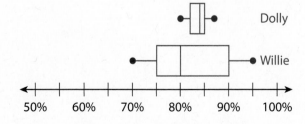

Lesson Performance Task

The batting averages for the starting lineup of two competing baseball teams are given in the table.

Batting Averages for Team A	0.270	0.260	0.300	0.290	0.260	0.280	0.280	0.240	0.270	0.280
Batting Averages for Team B	0.290	0.270	0.240	0.280	0.230	0.280	0.230	0.270	0.250	0.270

a. Create a box plot for each data set on the same number line.

b. Compare the distributions of the batting averages for each team.

c. Which team has a better starting lineup? Explain.

9.4   Normal Distributions

Essential Question: How can you use characteristics of a normal distribution to make estimates and probability predictions about the population that the data represents?

⊘ Explore   Investigating Symmetric Distributions

A bell-shaped, symmetric distribution with a tail on each end is called a **normal distribution**.

Use a graphing calculator and the infant birth mass data in the table below to determine if the set represents a normal distribution.

Birth Mass (kg)				
3.3	3.6	3.5	3.4	3.7
3.6	3.5	3.4	3.7	3.5
3.4	3.5	3.2	3.6	3.4
3.8	3.5	3.6	3.3	3.5

(A) Enter the data into a graphing calculator as a list. Calculate the "1-Variable Statistics" for the distribution of data.

Mean, $x \approx$ [?]   Standard deviation, $\sigma_x \approx$ [?]

Median = [?] $IQR = Q_3 - Q_1 =$ [?]

(B) Use the intervals shown to sketch a histogram. Always include labels for the axes and the bar intervals.

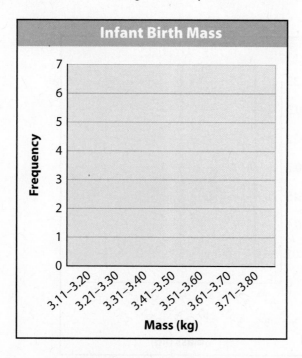

(C) Could this data be described by a normal distribution? Explain.

1. Which intervals on the histogram had the fewest values? Which interval had the greatest number of values?

2. **Make a Conjecture** For the normal distribution, the mean and the median are the same. Is this true for every normal distribution? Explain.

3. **Counterexamples** Allison thinks that every symmetric distribution must be bell-shaped. Provide a counterexample to show that she is incorrect.

⊘ Explore 2 Investigating Symmetric Relative Frequency Histograms

The table gives the frequency of each mass from the data set used in the first Explore.

Mass (kg)	3.2	3.3	3.4	3.5	3.6	3.7	3.8
Frequency	1	2	4	6	4	2	1

(A) Use the frequency table to make a relative frequency table.
Notice that there are 20 data values.

Mass (kg)	3.2	3.3	3.4	3.5	3.6	3.7	3.8
Relative Frequency	$\frac{1}{20} = 0.05$	?	?	?	?	?	?

What is the sum of the relative frequencies? ?

(B) On a grid with axes labeled as shown, sketch a relative frequency histogram. The heights of the bars now indicate relative frequencies.

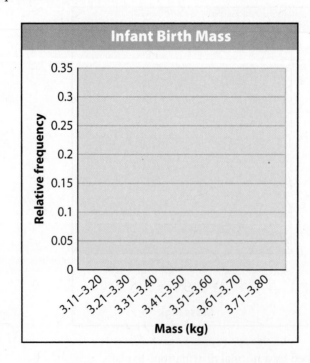

Infant Birth Mass

Ⓒ Recall from the first Explore that the mean of this data set is 3.5 and the standard deviation is 0.14. By how many standard deviations does a birth mass of 3.2 kg differ from the mean? Round to one decimal place. Justify your answer.

$3.5 - 3.2 = \boxed{\ ?\ }$ and $\boxed{\ ?\ } \div 0.14 = \boxed{\ ?\ }$, so a birth mass of 3.2 kg is $\boxed{\ ?\ }$

standard deviations below the mean.

Reflect

4. Identify the interval of values that are within one standard deviation of the mean. Use the frequency table to determine what percent of the values in the set are in this interval.

5. Identify the interval of values that are within two standard deviations of the mean. Use the frequency table to determine what percent of values in the set are in this interval.

⚙ Explain 1 Using Properties of Normal Distributions

The smaller the intervals are in a symmetric, bell-shaped relative frequency histogram, the closer the shape of the histogram is to a curve called a *normal curve*. Let σ represent the standard deviation.

A **normal curve** has the following properties:

- about 68% of the data fall within 1 standard deviation of the mean.

- about 95% of the data fall within 2 standard deviations of the mean.

- about 99.7% of the data fall within 3 standard deviations of the mean.

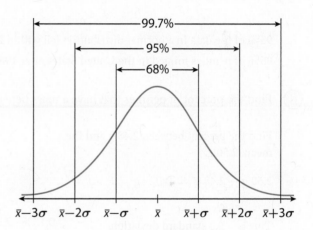

The symmetry of a normal curve allows you to separate the area under the curve into eight parts and know what percent of the data is contained in each part.

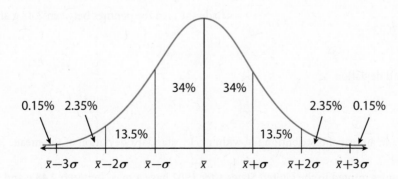

Example 1 The masses (in grams) of pennies minted in the United States after 1982 are normally distributed with a mean of 2.50 g and a standard deviation of 0.02 g.

(A) Find the percent of these pennies that have a mass between 2.46 g and 2.54 g.

Find the percent between 2.46 g and the mean, 2.50 g.

2.50 g − 2.46 g = 0.04 g

This is 2 standard deviations below the mean.

Find the percent between 2.54 g and the mean, 2.50 g.

2.54 g − 2.50 g = 0.04 g

This is 2 standard deviations above the mean.

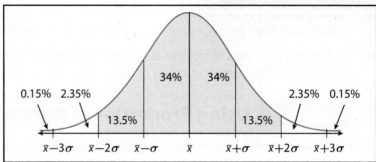

The shaded area represents pennies between 2.46 g and 2.54 g.

95% of the data in a normal distribution fall within 2 standard deviations of the mean.

95% of pennies minted in the United States after 1982 have a mass between 2.46 g and 2.54 g.

(B) Find the percent of pennies that have a mass between 2.48 g and 2.52 g.

Find the percent between 2.48 g and the mean, 2.50 g.

2.50 g − 2.48 g = $\boxed{0.02}$ g

This is $\boxed{1}$ standard deviation below the mean.

Find the distance between 2.52 g and the mean, 2.50 g.

2.52 g − 2.50 g = $\boxed{0.02}$ g

This is $\boxed{1}$ standard deviation above the mean.

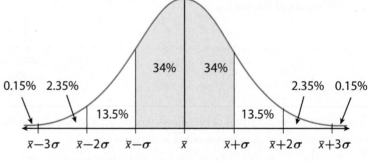

Shade the area for pennies between 2.48 g and 2.52 g.

$\boxed{68}$ % of the data in a normal distribution fall within $\boxed{1}$ standard deviation of the mean.

So, $\boxed{68}$ % of pennies minted in the United States after 1982 have a mass between 2.48 g and 2.52 g.

6. Find the percent of these pennies that have a mass between 2.44 g and 2.56 g.

7. Find the percent of these pennies that have a mass between 2.46 g and 2.50 g.

⚙ Explain 2   Estimating Probabilities in Approximately Normal Distributions

You can use the properties of a normal distribution to make estimations about the larger population that the distribution represents.

Example 2   **The masses (in grams) of pennies minted in the United States after 1982 are normally distributed with a mean of 2.50 g and a standard deviation of 0.02 g.**

Ⓐ Estimate the probability that a randomly chosen penny has a mass greater than 2.52 g.

Find the percent greater than 2.52 g.
2.52 g − 2.50 g = 0.02 g
2.52 g is 1 standard deviation above the mean.

Shade in the percent of data greater than 1 standard deviation above the mean.

$13.5\% + 2.35\% + 0.15\% = 16\%$

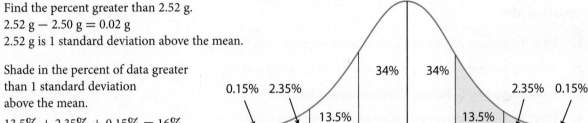

The probability that a randomly chosen penny has a mass greater than 2.52 g is about 16%.

Ⓑ Estimate the probability that a randomly chosen penny has a mass greater than 2.56 g.

Find the percent greater than 2.56 g.

$\boxed{2.56}$ g − $\boxed{2.50}$ g = $\boxed{0.06}$ g

$\boxed{2.56}$ g is $\boxed{3}$ standard deviations above the mean.

Shade in the percent of data greater than $\boxed{3}$ standard deviations above the mean.

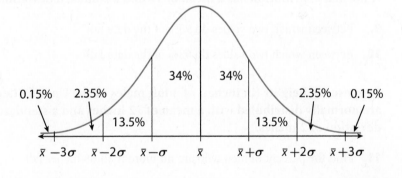

$\boxed{0.15}$ % is shaded.

The probability that a randomly chosen penny has a mass greater than 2.56 g is about $\boxed{0.15}$ %.

8. Find the probability that a randomly chosen penny has a mass less than 2.54 g.

9. Find the probability that a randomly chosen penny has a mass greater than 2.44 g.

10. For data described by a normal distribution, how do the mean and median compare?

11. What does the symmetry of the normal distribution tell you about the areas above and below the mean?

12. How can you tell if data follow a normal distribution by looking at a histogram of the data?

13. **Essential Question** How do you find percents of data and probabilities of events associated with normal distributions?

⭐ Evaluate: Homework and Practice

- Online Homework
- Hints and Help
- Extra Practice

The scores on a test given to all juniors in a school district are normally distributed with a mean of 74 and a standard deviation of 8.

1. Find the percent of juniors whose score is no more than 90.

2. Find the percent of juniors whose score is between 58 and 74.

3. Find the percent of juniors whose score is at least 74.

4. Find the percent of juniors whose score is below 66.

5. Find the probability that a randomly chosen junior has a score above 82.

6. Find the probability that a randomly chosen junior has a score between 66 and 90.

7. Find the probability that a randomly chosen junior has a score below 74.

8. Find the probability that a randomly chosen junior has a score above 98.

A normal distribution has a mean of 10 and a standard deviation of 1.5.

9. Between which two values do 95% of the data fall?

10. Between which two values do 68% of the data fall?

Suppose the heights (in inches) of adult males in the United States are normally distributed with a mean of 72 inches and a standard deviation of 2 inches.

11. Find the percent of men who are no more than 68 inches tall.

12. Find the percent of men who are between 70 and 72 inches tall.

13. Find the percent of men who are at least 76 inches tall.

14. Find the probability that a randomly chosen man is more than 72 inches tall.

15. Find the probability that a randomly chosen man is between 68 and 76 inches tall.

16. Find the probability that a randomly chosen man is less than 76 inches tall.

17. **Multi-Step** Ten customers at Fielden Grocery were surveyed about how long they waited in line to check out. Their wait times, in minutes, are shown.

16	15	10	7	5
5	4	3	3	2

   a. What is the mean of the data set?

   b. How many data points are below the mean, and how many are above the mean?

   c. Does the data appear to be normally distributed? Explain.

18. Kori is analyzing a normal data distribution, but the data provided is incomplete. Kori knows that the mean of the data is 120 and that 84% of the data values are less than 130. Find the standard deviation for this data set.

19. Suppose compact fluorescent light bulbs last, on average, 10,000 hours. The standard deviation is 500 hours. What percent of light bulbs burn out within 11,000 hours?

20. The numbers of raisins per box in a certain brand of cereal are normally distributed with a mean of 339 raisins and a standard deviation of 9 raisins. Find the percent of boxes of this brand of cereal that have fewer than 330 raisins. Explain how you solved this problem.

Suppose the heights of professional basketball players in the United States are distributed normally, with a mean of 79 inches and a standard deviation of 4 inches.

21. How far below the mean is 71 inches and how many standard deviations is this?

22. How far below the mean is 75 inches and how many standard deviations is this?

Suppose the upper-arm length (in centimeters) of adult males in the United States is normally distributed with a mean of 39.4 cm and a standard deviation of 2.3 cm.

23. **Justify Reasoning** What percent of adult males have an upper-arm length between 34.8 cm and 41.7 cm? Explain how you got your answer.

24. **Communicate Mathematical Ideas** Explain how you can determine whether a set of data is approximately normally distributed.

25. Critical Thinking The distribution titled "Heads Up" shows results of many trials of tossing 6 coins and counting the number of "heads" that land facing up. The distribution titled "Number 1s Up" shows results of many trials of tossing 6 number cubes and counting the number of 1s that land facing up. For which distribution is it reasonable to use a normal distribution as an approximation? Justify your answer.

Heads Up

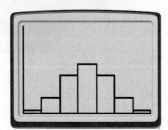

Number 1s Up

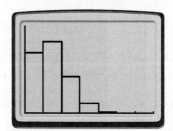

Lesson Performance Task

During a series of 100-meter races, the times of the runners are normally distributed with a mean of 12.5 seconds and a standard deviation of 0.3 seconds.

a. Find the percent of runners that have a time between 11.6 seconds and 12.8 seconds. Explain how you got your answer.

b. Find the probability that a randomly selected runner has a time greater than 12.8 seconds and less than 13.4 seconds.

One-Variable Data Distributions

Essential Question: How can you use one-variable data distributions to solve real-world problems?

KEY EXAMPLE   *(Lesson 9.2)*

The dot plot given shows the high score of 12 members of a bowling club. A new member joins whose high score is 294. Determine if the new score is an outlier.

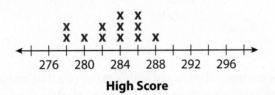

High Score

The scores are 278, 278, 280, 282, 282, 284, 284, 284, 286, 286, 286, 288, and 294.

Median = 284 $Q_1 = \dfrac{280 + 282}{2} = 281$ $Q_3 = \dfrac{286 + 286}{2} = 286$ IQR = 286 − 281 = 5

A data value is an outlier if $x < Q_1 - 1.5(IQR)$ or if $x > Q_3 + 1.5(IQR)$.

Since 294 > 286 + 1.5(5), the new score is an outlier.

KEY EXAMPLE   *(Lesson 9.4)*

A machine produces plastic skateboard wheels with diameters that are normally distributed with a mean diameter of 52 mm and a standard deviation of 0.15 mm. Find the percent of wheels made by the machine that have a diameter of less than 51.7 mm.

$52 - 51.7 = 0.3$ $\dfrac{0.3}{0.15} = 2$

51.7 is 2 standard deviations below the mean.

The percent of data that is 2 standard deviations below the mean is 0.15% + 2.35% = 2.5%.

2.5% of the wheels have a diameter less than 51.7 mm.

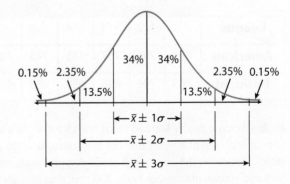

EXERCISES

Find the mean, median, range, and interquartile range of each data set. *(Lesson 9.1)*

1. {12, 12, 13, 14, 16, 20, 32,}

2. {4, 8, 9, 9, 11, 12, 15, 15}

3. Make a box plot to represent the data set {28, 30, 32, 32, 34, 35, 36, 38}. *(Lesson 9.3)*

4. The weights of a small box of Healthy Oats are normally distributed with a mean of 8.9 oz and a standard deviation of 0.1 oz. Find the probability that a randomly chosen box of Healthy Oats weighs more than 8.8 oz. Express the probability as a decimal. *(Lesson 9.4)*

MODULE PERFORMANCE TASK
Baseball Stats

The table below gives the total number of runs scored by each of the 15 teams in each of baseball's two major leagues, the American League and the National League, during the 2013 season.

League	Team														
	1	2	3	4	5	6	7	8	9	10	11	12	13	14	15
American	853	796	767	745	745	733	730	712	700	650	648	624	614	610	598
National	783	706	698	688	685	656	649	640	634	629	619	618	610	602	513

In this module you've learned many ways to analyze a set of data, both numerically and graphically. Which ways might be useful in helping someone to make sense of the statistics in the runs-scored table? Decide on the ones you'll use and apply them, either through numerical calculations or pictorial representations or both. You may also explain why you decided not to calculate certain data measures.

Use numbers, words, or algebra to explain how you reached your conclusion.

(Ready) to Go On?

9.1–9.4 One-Variable Data Distributions

- Online Homework
- Hints and Help
- Extra Practice

1. The dot plot given represents the scores of 10 students on a standardized test. An eleventh student was sick on the test date, took a make-up test, and made a score of 212. Copy and complete the table. If necessary, round to the nearest tenth. *(Lesson 9.1)*

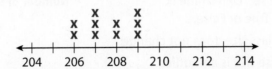

	Mean	Median	Range	IQR	Standard Deviation
Without Make-up Test	?	?	?	?	?
With Make-up Test	?	?	?	?	?

2. The ages of students in a tango class are represented by the data set {24, 41, 33, 36, 28, 30, 32, 22, 26, 44}. Copy and complete the frequency table and make a histogram to represent the data. *(Lesson 9.3)*

Age Interval	Frequency
20–24	?
25–29	?
30–34	?
35–39	?
40–44	?

ESSENTIAL QUESTION

3. When is it better to use a histogram than a dot plot?

© Houghton Mifflin Harcourt Publishing Company

Assessment Readiness

1. The dot plot shown represents the number of students enrolled in each of the 16 courses at a community college. A new course has started and has 65 enrolled students. Consider the effect of the addition of the new course to the data set. Determine if each statement is True or False.

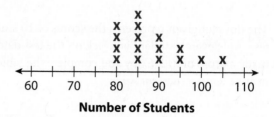

Number of Students

   A. The median class size does not change.

   B. The new course size is an outlier.

   C. The range increases by 40.

2. The histogram shows the number of tomato plants Susan has in each height range. Determine if each statement is True or False.

   A. Susan has 11 plants.

   B. Susan has the same number of plants that are 7 to 9 inches high as plants that are 10 to 12 inches high.

   C. The median height of the plants could be about 11 inches.

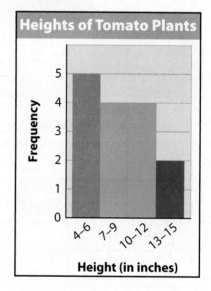

3. The high temperature, in °F, for the past 4 days was 45, 38, 46, and 35. Carlos knows that the mean high temperature for the past 5 days was 42°F. Write and solve an equation to find the high temperature on the first day. Show your work.

4. Write an equation in slope-intercept form to represent a line that includes the points (3, −4) and (5, 2). Explain how you wrote the equation.

Linear Modeling and Regression

Essential Question: How can you use linear modeling and regression to solve real-world problems?

REAL WORLD VIDEO
A fossil is a remnant or trace of an organism from a past geologic age that has been preserved in the earth's crust. Fossils are often dated by using interpolation, a type of calculation that uses an observed pattern to estimate a value between two known values.

MODULE PERFORMANCE TASK PREVIEW

How Does Wingspan Compare with Weight in Birds?

The wingspan of a bird is the distance from one wingtip to the other wingtip. Birds that fly have to support their body weight when in flight. What, if any, relationship exists between the wingspan and body weight for different species of birds? Let's use math to find out!

Are (YOU) Ready?

Complete these exercises to review skills you will need for this module.

Scatter Plots

Personal Math Trainer

• Online Homework
• Hints and Help
• Extra Practice

Example 1   Tell whether the correlation is positive or negative, or if there is no correlation.

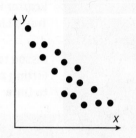

Scatter plots can help you see relationships between two variables.

- In a positive correlation, as the value of one variable increases, the value of the other variable increases.

- In a negative correlation, as the value of one variable decreases, the value of the other variable increases.

- Sometimes there is no correlation, meaning there is no relationship between the variables.

The scatter plot has a negative correlation.

Tell whether the correlation is positive or negative, or if there is no correlation.

1.
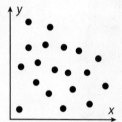

2.
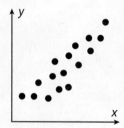

Linear Associations

Example 2   Estimate the correlation coefficient.

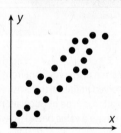

One measure of the strength and direction of a correlation is the correlation coefficient, denoted by r. The stronger the correlation, the closer the correlation coefficient will be to -1 or 1. The weaker the correlation, the closer r will be to zero.

The points lie close to a line with positive slope. r is close to 1.

Estimate the correlation coefficient.

3.
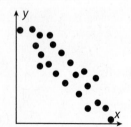

4.
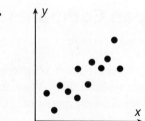

10.1 Scatter Plots and Trend Lines

Essential Question: How can you describe the relationship between two variables and use it to make predictions?

Resource Locker

⊘ Explore   Describing How Variables Are Related in Scatter Plots

Two-variable data is a collection of paired variable values, such as a series of measurements of air temperature at different times of day. One method of visualizing two-variable data is called a **scatter plot**: a graph of points with one variable plotted along each axis. A recognizable pattern in the arrangement of points suggests a mathematical relationship between the variables.

Correlation is a measure of the strength and direction of the relationship between two variables. The correlation is positive if both variables tend to increase together, negative if one decreases while the other increases, and we say there is "no correlation" if the change in the two variables appears to be unrelated.

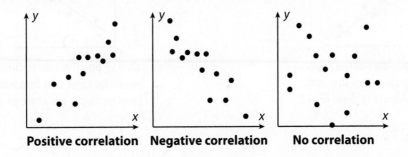

Positive correlation   **Negative correlation**   **No correlation**

(A) The table below presents two-variable data for seven different cities in the Northern hemisphere.

City	Latitude (°N)	Average Annual Temperature (°F)
Bangkok	13.7	82.6
Cairo	30.1	71.4
London	51.5	51.8
Moscow	55.8	39.4
New Delhi	28.6	77.0
Tokyo	35.7	58.1
Vancouver	49.2	49.6

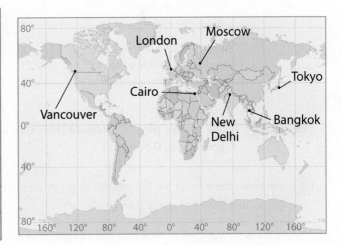

The two variables are ⬚ ? and ⬚ ? .

Ⓑ Plot the data on a grid, with latitude on the *x*-axis, and temperature on the *y*-axis.

Ⓒ The variables are ⬚? correlated.

Reflect

1. **Discussion** Why are the points in a scatter plot not connected in the same way plots of linear equations are?

⚙ Explain 1 Estimating the Correlation Coefficient of a Linear Fit

One way to quantify the correlation of a data set is with the **correlation coefficient**, denoted by *r*. The correlation coefficient varies from −1 to 1, with the sign of *r* corresponding to the type of correlation (positive or negative). Strongly correlated data points look more like points that lie in a straight line, and have values of *r* closer to 1 or −1. Weakly correlated data will have values closer to 0.

There is a precise mathematical formula that can be used to calculate the correlation coefficient, but it is beyond the scope of this course. It is still useful to learn the qualitative relationship between the appearance of the data and the value of *r*. The chart below shows examples of strong correlations, with *r* close to −1 and 1, and weak correlations with *r* close to 0.5. If there is no visible correlation, it means *r* is closer to 0.

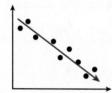

Strong negative correlation; points lie close to a line with negative slope. *r* is close to −1.

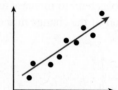

Strong positive correlation; points lie close to a line with positive slope. *r* is close to 1.

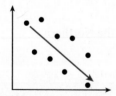

Weak negative correlation; points loosely follow a line with negative slope. *r* is between 0 and −1.

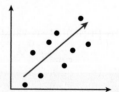

Weak positive correlation; points loosely follow a line with positive slope. *r* is between 0 and 1.

Example 1 Use a scatter plot to estimate the value of *r*. Indicate whether *r* is closer to −1, −0.5, 0, 0.5, or 1.

Ⓐ Estimate the *r*-value for the relationship between city latitude and average temperature using the scatter plot you made previously.

This is strongly correlated and has a negative slope, so *r* is close to −1.

Ⓑ

Winning vs Losing Scores

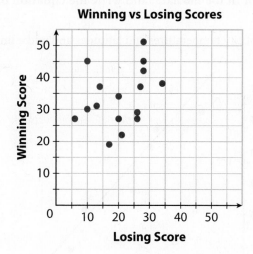

This data represents the football scores from one week with winning score plotted versus losing score.

r is close to [0].

Your Turn

Use a scatter plot to estimate the value of *r*. Indicate whether *r* is closer to −1, −0.5, 0, 0.5, or 1.

2.

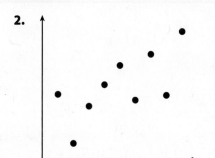

3.

✏️ Explain 2   Fitting Linear Functions to Data

A **line of fit** is a line through a set of two-variable data that illustrates the correlation. When there is a strong correlation between the two variables in a set of two-variable data, you can use a line of fit as the basis to construct a linear model for the data.

There are many ways to come up with a line of fit. This lesson addresses a visual method: Using a straight edge, draw the line that the data points appear to be clustered around. It is not important that any of the data points actually touch the line; instead the line should be drawn as straight as possible and should go through the middle of the scattered points.

Once a line of fit has been drawn onto the scatter plot, you can choose two points on the line to write an equation for the line.

© Houghton Mifflin Harcourt Publishing Company

Example 2   Determine a line of fit for the data, and write the equation of the line.

(A)   Go back to the scatter plot of city temperatures and latitudes and add a line of fit.

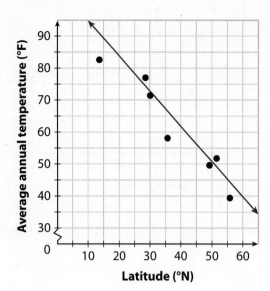

A line of fit has been added to the graph. The points (10, 95) and (60, 40) appear to be on the line.

$$m = \frac{40 - 95}{60 - 10} = -1.1$$

$$y = mx + b$$

$$95 = -1.1(10) + b$$

$$106 = b$$

The model is given by the equation

$$y = -1.1x + 106$$

(B)   The boiling point of water is lower at higher elevations because of the lower atmospheric pressure. The boiling point of water in some different cities is given in the table.

City	Altitude (feet)	Boiling Point (°F)
Chicago	597	210
Denver	5300	201
Kathmandu	4600	205
Madrid	2188	207
Miami	6	210

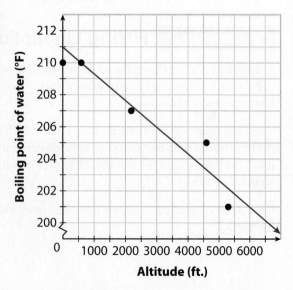

A line of fit may go through points $\left(\boxed{0}, \boxed{211}\right)$ and $\left(\boxed{6000}, \boxed{201}\right)$.

$$m = \dfrac{\boxed{-10}}{\boxed{6000}} \quad b = \boxed{211}$$

The equation is of this line of fit is $y = \dfrac{\boxed{-10}}{6000}\, x + \boxed{211}$.

Reflect

4. In the model from Example 2A, what do the slope and y-intercept of the model represent?

Your Turn

5. Aoiffe plants a tree sapling in her yard and measures its height every year. Her measurements so far are shown. Make a scatter plot and find a line of fit if the variables have a correlation. What is the equation of your line of fit?

Years after Planting	Height (ft)
0	2.1
1	4.3
2	5
3	7.3
4	8.1
5	10.2

Explain 3   Using Linear Functions Fitted to Data to Solve Problems

Interpolation and **extrapolation** are methods of predicting data values for one variable from another based on a line of fit. The domain of the model is determined by the minimum and maximum values of the data set. When the prediction is made for a value within the extremes (minimum and maximum) of the original data set, it is called interpolation. When the prediction is made for a value outside the extremes, it is called extrapolation. Extrapolation is not as reliable as interpolation because the model has not been demonstrated, and it may fail to describe the relationship between the variables outside the domain of the data. Extrapolated predictions will also vary more with different lines of fit.

Example 3   Use the linear fit of the data set to make the required predictions.

(A) Use the model constructed in Example 2A to predict the average annual temperatures for Austin (30.3°N) and Helsinki (60.2°N).

$$y = -1.1x + 106$$

Austin: $y = -1.1 \cdot 30.3 + 106 = 72.67\ °F$

Helsinki: $y = -1.1 \cdot 60.2 + 106 = 39.78\ °F$

(B) Use the model of city altitudes and water boiling points to predict the boiling point of water in Mexico City (altitude = 7943 feet) and in Fargo, North Dakota (altitude = 3000 feet)

$$y = -0.00167x + 211$$

Mexico City: $y = \boxed{-0.00167} \cdot 7943 + \boxed{211} = 197.74$

Fargo: $y = \boxed{-0.00167} \cdot 3000 + \boxed{211} = 205.99$

Reflect

6. **Discussion** Which prediction made in Example 3B would you expect to be more reliable? Why?

Your Turn

7. Use the model constructed in YourTurn 5 to predict how tall Aoiffe's tree will be 10 years after she planted it.

⚙ Explain 4 Distinguishing Between Correlation and Causation

A common error when interpreting paired data is to observe a correlation and conclude that causation has been demonstrated. Causation means that a change in the one variable results directly from changing the other variable. In that case, it is reasonable to expect the data to show correlation. However, the reverse is not true: observing a correlation between variables does not necessarily mean that the change to one variable caused the change in the other. They may both have a common cause related to a variable not included in the data set or even observed (sometimes called lurking variables), or the causation may be the reverse of the conclusion.

Example 4 Read the description of the experiments, identify the two variables and describe whether changing either variable is likely, doubtful, or unclear to cause a change in the other variable.

(A) The manager of an ice cream shop studies its monthly sales figures and notices a positive correlation between the average air temperature and how much ice cream they sell on any given day.

The two variables are ice cream sales and average air temperatures.

It is likely that warmer air temperatures cause an increase in ice cream sales.

It is doubtful that increased ice cream sales cause an increase in air temperatures.

(B) A traffic official in a major metropolitan area notices that the more profitable toll bridges into the city are those with the slowest average crossing speeds.

The variables are profit and crossing speed.

It is doubtful that increased profit causes slower crossing speed.

It is doubtful that slower crossing speeds cause an increase in profits.

8. Explain your reasoning for your answers in Example 4B and suggest a more likely explanation for the observed correlation.

Your Turn

9. HDL cholesterol is considered the "good" cholesterol as it removes harmful bad cholesterol from where it doesn't belong. A group of researchers are studying the connection between the number of minutes of exercise a person performs weekly and the person's HDL cholesterol count. The researchers surveyed the amount of physical activity each person did each week for 10 weeks and collected a blood sample from 67 adults. After analyzing the data, the researchers found that people who exercised more per week had higher HDL cholesterol counts. Identify the variables in this situation and determine whether it describes a positive or negative correlation. Explain whether the correlation is a result of causation.

💬 Elaborate

10. Why is extrapolating from measured data likely to result in a less accurate prediction than interpolating?

11. What will the effect be on the correlation coefficient if additional data is collected that is farther from the line of fit? What will the effect be if the newer data lies along the line of fit? Explain your reasoning.

12. **Essential Question Check-In** How does a scatter plot help you make predictions from two-variable data?

☆ Evaluate: Homework and Practice

Use a scatter plot to estimate the value of r. Indicate whether r is closest to -1, -0.5, 0, 0.5 or 1 for the following data sets.

• Online Homework
• Hints and Help
• Extra Practice

1.

x	y
1	8
2	4.037522
3	7.200593
4	4.180245
5	4.763788
6	1
7	1.047031
8	2.436249
9	1.844607

2. The table below presents exam scores earned by six students and how long they each studied.

Hours of Study	Exam Score
2	63
2	71
2.5	75
3	67
4.5	82
5	95

3. Raymond opens a car wash and keeps track of his weekly earnings, as shown in the table.

Weeks after Opening	Earnings ($)
0	1050
1	1700
2	2400
3	2000
4	3500
5	3600

4. Rafael is training for a race by running a mile each day. He tracks his progress by timing each trial run.

Trial	Run Time (min)
1	8.2
2	8.1
3	7.5
4	7.8
5	7.4
6	7.5
7	7.1
8	7.1

Make a scatter plot, determine a line of fit for the data, and write the equation of your line.

5.

x	y
1	7.15
2	8.00
3	4.81
4	7.14
5	3.56
6	2.12
7	1.00
8	3.76
9	1.42

6.

Studying Time (Hours)	Test Score (%)
2	63
2	71
2.5	75
3	67
4.5	82
5	95

7.

Weeks After Opening	Weekly Revenue (dollars)
0	1050
1	1700
2	2400
3	2000
4	3500
5	3600

8.

Training Run	Run Time (min)
1	8.2
2	8.1
3	7.5
4	7.8
5	7.4
6	7.5
7	7.1
8	7.1

Use the linear models found in problems 5–8 for 9–12, respectively, to make predictions, and classify each prediction as an interpolation or an extrapolation.

9. Find y when $x = 4.5$.

10. What grade might you expect after studying for 4 hours?

11. How much money might Raymond hope to earn 8 weeks after opening if the trend continues?

12. What mile time does Rafael expect for his next run?

Read each description. Identify the variables in each situation and determine whether it describes a positive or negative correlation. Explain whether the correlation is a result of causation.

13. A group of biologists is studying the population of wolves and the population of deer in a particular region. The biologists compared the populations each month for 2 years. After analyzing the data, the biologists found that as the population of wolves increases, the population of deer decreases.

14. Researchers at an auto insurance company are studying the ages of its policyholders and the number of accidents per 100 policyholders. The researchers compared each year of age from 16 to 65. After analyzing the data, the researchers found that as age increases, the number of accidents per 100 policyholders decreases.

15. Educational researchers are investigating the relationship between the number of musical instruments a student plays and a student's grade in math. The researchers conducted a survey asking 110 students the number of musical instruments they play and went to the registrar's office to find the same 110 students' grades in math. The researchers found that students who play a greater number of musical instruments tend to have a greater average grade in math.

16. Researchers are studying the relationship between the median salary of a police officer in a city and the number of violent crimes per 1000 people. The researchers collected the police officers' median salary and the number of violent crimes per 1000 people in 84 cities. After analyzing the data, researchers found that a city with a greater police officers' median salary tends to have a greater number of violent crimes per 1000 people.

17. The owner of a ski resort is studying the relationship between the amount of snowfall in centimeters during the season and the number of visitors per season. The owner collected information about the amount of snowfall and the number of visitors for the past 30 seasons. After analyzing the data, the owner determined that seasons that have more snowfall tend to have more visitors.

18. Government researchers are studying the relationship between the price of gasoline and the number of miles driven in a month. The researchers documented the monthly average price of gasoline and the number of miles driven for the last 36 months. The researchers found that the months with a higher average price of gasoline tend to have more miles driven.

19. **Interpret the Answer** Each time Lorelai fills up her gas tank, she writes down the amount of gas it took to refill her tank, and the number of miles she drove between fill-ups. She makes a scatter plot of the data with miles driven on the y-axis and gallons of gas on the x-axis, and observes a very strong correlation. The slope is 35 and the y-intercept is 0.83. Do these numbers make sense, and what do they mean (besides being the slope and intercept of the line)?

20. **Multi-Step** The owner of a maple syrup farm is studying the average winter temperature in Fahrenheit and the number of gallons of maple syrup produced. The relationship between the temperature and the number of gallons of maple syrup produced for the past 8 years is shown in the table.

a. Make a scatter plot of the data and draw a line of fit that passes as close as possible to the plotted points.

Temperature (°F)	Number of gallons of maple syrup
24	154
26	128
25	141
22	168
28	104
21	170
24	144
22	160

b. Find the equation of this line of fit.

c. Identify the slope and y-intercept for the line of fit and interpret it in the context of the problem.

21. The table below shows the number of boats in a marina during the years 2007 to 2014.

Years Since 2000	7	8	9	10	11	12	13	14
Number of Boats	26	25	27	27	39	38	40	39

a. Make a scatterplot by using the data in the table as the coordinates of points on the graph. Use the calendar year as the x-value and the number of boats as the y-value.

b. Use the pattern of the points to determine whether there is a positive correlation, negative correlation, or no correlation between the number of boats in the marina and the year. What is the trend?

22. **Multiple Response** Which of the following usually have a positive correlation? List all that apply.

a. the number of cars on an expressway and the cars' average speed

b. the number of dogs in a house and the amount of dog food needed

c. the outside temperature and the amount of heating oil used

d. the weight of a car and the number of miles per gallon

e. the amount of time studying and the grade on a science exam

H.O.T. Focus on Higher Order Thinking

23. **Justify Reasoning** Does causation always imply linear correlation? Explain.

24. **Explain the Error** Olivia notices that if she picks a very large scale for her y-axis, her data appear to lie more along a straight line than if she zooms the scale all the way in. She concludes that she can use this to increase her correlation coefficient and make a more convincing case that there is a correlation between the variables she is studying. Is she correct?

25. **What if?** If you combined two data sets, each with r values close to 1, into a single data set, would you expect the new data set to have an r value between the original two values?

Lesson Performance Task

A 10-team high school hockey league completed its 20-game season. A team in this league earns 2 points for a win, 1 point for a tie, and 0 points for a loss. One of the team's coaches compares the number of goals each team scored with the number of points each team earned during the season as shown in the table.

a. Plot the points on the scatter plot, and use the scatterplot to describe the correlation and estimate the correlation coefficient. If the correlation coefficient is estimated as −1 or 1, draw a line of fit by hand and then find an equation for the line by choosing two points that are close to the line. Identify and interpret the slope and y-intercept of the line in context of the situation.

Goals Scored	Points
46	15
48	11
49	17
51	20
57	18
58	21
59	25
60	23
62	27
64	24

b. Use the line of fit to predict how many points a team would have if it scored 35 goals, 54 goals, and 70 goals during the season.

c. Use the results to justify whether the coach should only be concerned with the number of goals his or her team scores.

10.2 Fitting a Linear Model to Data

Essential Question: How can you use the linear regression function on a graphing calculator to find the line of best fit for a two-variable data set?

⊘ Explore 1   Plotting and Analyzing Residuals

For any set of data, different lines of fit can be created. Some of these lines will fit the data better than others. One way to determine how well the line fits the data is by using residuals. A **residual** is the signed vertical distance between a data point and a line of fit.

After calculating residuals, a residual plot can be drawn. A **residual plot** is a graph of points whose x-coordinates are the variables of the independent variable and whose y-coordinates are the corresponding residuals.

Looking at the distribution of residuals can help you determine how well a line of fit describes the data. The plots below illustrate how the residuals may be distributed for three different data sets and lines of fit.

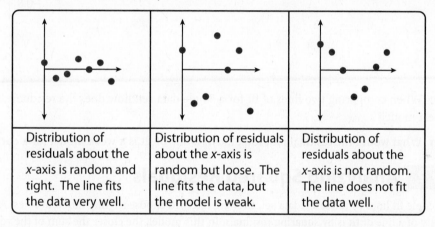

Distribution of residuals about the x-axis is random and tight. The line fits the data very well.	Distribution of residuals about the x-axis is random but loose. The line fits the data, but the model is weak.	Distribution of residuals about the x-axis is not random. The line does not fit the data well.

The table lists the median age of females living in the United States, based on the results of the United States Census over the past few decades. Follow the steps listed to complete the task.

Ⓐ   Use the table to create a table of paired values for x and y. Let x represent the time in years after 1970 and y represent the median age of females.

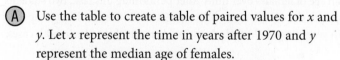

Year	Median Age of Females
1970	29.2
1980	31.3
1990	34.0
2000	36.5
2010	38.2

(B) Use residuals to calculate the quality of fit for the line $y = 0.25x + 29$, where y is median age and x is years since 1970.

x	Actual y	Predicted y based on $y = 0.25x + 29$	Residual Subtract Predicted from Actual to Find the Residual.
0	29.2	?	?
10	31.3	?	?
20	34.0	?	?
30	36.5	?	?
40	38.2	?	?

(C) Plot the residuals on a grid like the one shown.

(D) Evaluate the quality of fit to the data for the line $y = 0.25x + 29$.

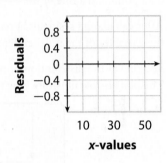

Reflect

1. **Discussion** When comparing two lines of fit for a single data set, how does the residual size show which line is the best model?

2. **Discussion** What would the residual plot look like if a line of fit is a weak model for a data set?

⊘ Explore 2 Analyzing Squared Residuals

When different people fit lines to the same data set, they are likely to choose slightly different lines. Another way to compare the quality of a line of fit is by squaring residuals. In this model, the closer the sum of the squared residuals is to 0, the better the line fits the data.

In the previous section, a line of data was fit for the median age of females over time. After performing this task, two students came up with slightly different results. Student A came up with the equation $y = 0.25x + 29.0$ while Student B came up with the equation $y = 0.25x + 28.8$, where x is the time in years since 1970 and y is the median age of females in both cases.

(A) Copy and complete each table below.

$y = 0.25x + 29.0$			
x	y (Actual)	y (Predicted)	Residual	Square of Residual
0	29.2	?	?	?
10	31.3	?	?	?
20	34.0	?	?	?
30	36.5	?	?	?
40	38.2	?	?	?

$y = 0.25x + 28.8$				
x	y (Actual)	y (Predicted)	Residual	Square of Residual
0	29.2	?	?	?
10	31.3	?	?	?
20	34.0	?	?	?
30	36.5	?	?	?
40	38.2	?	?	?

Ⓑ Find the sum of squared residuals for each line of fit.

$y = 0.25x + 29.0 :$ [?]

$y = 0.25x + 28.8 :$ [?]

Ⓒ Which line has the smaller sum of squared residuals? [?]

Reflect

3. How does squaring a residual affect the residual's value?

4. Are the sums of residuals or the sum of the squares of residuals a better measure of quality of fit?

🔑 Explain 1 Assessing the Fit of Linear Functions from Residuals

The quality of a line of fit can be evaluated by finding the sum of the squared residuals. The closer the sum of the squared residuals is to 0, the better the line fits the data.

Example 1 The data in the tables are given along with two possible lines of fit. Calculate the residuals for both lines of fit and then find the sum of the squared residuals. Identify the lesser sum and the line with better fit.

Ⓐ

x	2	4	6	8
y	7	8	4	8

$y = x + 2.2$

$y = x + 2.4$

a. Find the residuals of each line.

x	y (Actual)	y Predicted by $y = x + 2.4$	Residual for $y = x + 2.4$	y Predicted by $y = x + 2.2$	Residual for $y = x + 2.2$
2	7	4.4	2.6	4.2	2.8
4	8	6.4	1.6	6.2	1.8
6	4	8.4	−4.4	8.2	−4.2
8	8	10.4	−2.4	10.2	−2.2

b. Square the residuals and find their sum.

$y = x + 2.4: (2.6)^2 + (1.6)^2 + (-4.4)^2 + (-2.4)^2 = 6.76 + 2.56 + 19.36 + 5.76 = 34.44$

$y = x + 2.2: (2.8)^2 + (1.8)^2 + (-4.2)^2 + (-2.2)^2 = 7.84 + 3.24 + 17.64 + 4.84 = 33.56$

The sum of the squared residuals for $y = x + 2.2$ is smaller, so it provides a better fit for the data.

(B)

x	1	2	3	4
y	5	4	6	10

$y = 2x + 3$

$y = 2x + 2.5$

a. Find the residuals of each line.

x	y (Actual)	y Predicted by $y = 2x + 3$	Residual for $y = 2x + 3$	y Predicted by $y = 2x + 2.5$	Residual for $y = 2x + 2.5$
1	5	5	0	4.5	0.5
2	4	7	−3	6.5	−2.5
3	6	9	−3	8.5	−2.5
4	10	11	−1	10.5	−0.5

b. Square the residuals and find their sum.

$y = 2x + 3: \left(\boxed{0}\right)^2 + \left(\boxed{-3}\right)^2 + \left(\boxed{-3}\right)^2 + \left(\boxed{-1}\right)^2 = \boxed{0} + \boxed{9} + \boxed{9} + \boxed{1} = \boxed{19}$

$y = 2x + 2.5: \left(\boxed{0.5}\right)^2 + \left(\boxed{-2.5}\right)^2 + \left(\boxed{-2.5}\right)^2 + \left(\boxed{-0.5}\right)^2 = \boxed{0.25} + \boxed{6.25} + \boxed{6.25} + \boxed{0.25} = \boxed{13}$

The sum of the squared residuals for $y = \boxed{2}\, x + \boxed{2.5}$ is smaller, so it provides a better fit for the data.

Reflect

5. How do negative signs on residuals affect the sum of squared residuals?

6. Why do small values for residuals mean that a line of best fit has a tight fit to the data?

Your Turn

7. The data in the table are given along with two possible lines of fit. Calculate the residuals for both lines of fit and then find the sum of the squared residuals. Identify the lesser sum and the line with better fit.

x	1	2	3	4
y	4	7	8	6

$y = x + 4$

$y = x + 4.2$

⊘ Explain 2 Performing Linear Regression

The least-squares line for a data set is the line of fit for which the sum of the squared residuals is as small as possible. Therefore the least-squares line is a line of best fit. A **line of best fit** is the line that comes closest to all of the points in the data set, using a given process. **Linear regression** is a method for finding the least-squares line.

Example 2 Given latitudes and average temperatures in degrees Celsius for several cities, use your calculator to find an equation for the line of best fit. Then interpret the correlation coefficient and use the line of best fit to estimate the average temperature of another city using the given latitude.

City	Latitude	Average Temperature (°C)
Barrow, Alaska	71.2°N	−12.7
Yakutsk, Russia	62.1°N	−10.1
London, England	51.3°N	10.4
Chicago, Illinois	41.9°N	10.3
San Francisco, California	37.5°N	13.8
Yuma, Arizona	32.7°N	22.8
Tindouf, Algeria	27.7°N	22.8
Dakar, Senegal	14.0°N	24.5
Mangalore, India	12.5°N	27.1

Estimate the average temperature in Vancouver, Canada at 49.1°N.

Enter the data into data lists on your calculator. Enter the latitudes in column **L1** and the average temperatures in column **L2**.

Create a scatter plot of the data.

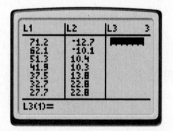

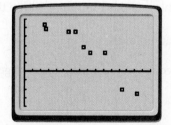

Use the Linear Regression feature to find the equation for the line of best fit using the lists of data you entered. Be sure to have the calculator also display values for the correlation coefficient r and r^2.

The correlation coefficient is about −0.95, which is very strong. This indicates a strong correlation, so we can rely on the line of fit for estimating average temperatures for other locations within the same range of latitudes.

The equation for the line of best fit is $y \approx -0.693x + 39.11$.

Graph the line of best fit with the data points in the scatter plot.

Use the TRACE function to find the approximate average temperature in degrees Celsius for a latitude of 49.1°N.

The average temperature in Vancouver should be around 5°C.

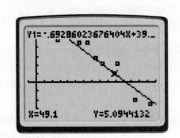

Ⓑ

City	Latitude	Average Temperature (°F)
Fairbanks, Alaska	64.5°N	30
Moscow, Russia	55.5°N	39
Ghent, Belgium	51.0°N	46
Kiev, Ukraine	50.3°N	49
Prague, Czech Republic	50.0°N	50
Winnipeg, Manitobia	49.5°N	52
Luxembourg	49.4°N	53
Vienna, Austria	48.1°N	56
Bern, Switzerland	46.6°N	59

Estimate the average temperature in degrees Fahrenheit in Bath, England, at 51.4°N.

Enter the data into data lists on your calculator.

Use the Linear Regression feature to find the equation for the line of best fit using the lists of data you entered. Be sure to have the calculator also display values for the correlation coefficient r and r^2.

The correlation coefficient is about -0.95, which indicates a very strong correlation. The correlation coefficient indicates that the line of best fit is reliable for estimating temperatures of other locations within the same range of latitudes.

The equation for the line of best fit is $y \approx -$ [1.60] $x +$ [131.05].

Use the equation to estimate the average temperature in Bath, England at 51.4°N.

$y \approx -$ [1.60] $x +$ [131.05]

The average temperature in degrees Fahrenheit in Bath, England, should be around [49] °F.

Graph the line of best fit with the data points in the scatter plot. Then use the TRACE function to find the approximate average temperature in degrees Fahrenheit for a latitude of 51.4°N.

Reflect

8. Interpret the slope of the line of best fit in terms of the context for Example 2A.

9. Interpret the y-intercept of the line of best fit in terms of the context for Example 2A.

10. Use the given data and your calculator to find an equation for the line of best fit. Then interpret the correlation coefficient and use the line of best fit to estimate the average temperature of another city using the given latitude.

City	Latitude	Average Temperature (°F)
Anchorage, United States	61.1°N	18
Dublin, Ireland	53.2°N	29
Zurich, Switzerland	47.2°N	34
Florence, Italy	43.5°N	37
Trenton, New Jersey	40.1°N	?
Algiers, Algeria	36.5°N	46
El Paso, Texas	31.5°N	49
Dubai, UAE	25.2°N	56
Manila, Philippines	14.4°N	61

💬 Elaborate

11. What type of line does linear regression analysis make?

12. Why are squared residuals better than residuals?

13. **Essential Question Check-In** What four keys are needed on a graphing calculator to perform a linear regression?

⭐ Evaluate: Homework and Practice

- Online Homework
- Hints and Help
- Extra Practice

The data in the tables below are shown along with two possible lines of fit. Calculate the residuals for both lines of fit and then find the sum of the squared residuals. Identify the lesser sum and the line with better fit.

1.

x	2	4	6	8
y	1	3	5	7

$y = x + 5$

$y = x + 4.9$

2.

x	1	2	3	4
y	1	7	3	5

$y = 2x + 1$

$y = 2x + 1.1$

3.

x	2	4	6	8
y	2	8	4	6

$y = 3x + 4$

$y = 3x + 4.1$

4.

x	1	2	3	4
y	2	1	4	3

$y = x + 1$

$y = x + 0.9$

5.

x	2	4	6	8
y	1	5	4	3

$y = 3x + 1.2$

$y = 3x + 1$

6.

x	1	2	3	4
y	4	1	3	2

$y = x + 5$

$y = x + 5.3$

7.

x	2	4	6	8
y	3	6	4	5

$y = 2x + 1$

$y = 2x + 1.4$

8.

x	1	2	3	4
y	5	3	6	4

$y = x + 2$

$y = x + 2.2$

9.

x	2	4	6	8
y	1	5	7	3

$y = x + 3$

$y = x + 2.6$

10.

x	1	2	3	4
y	2	5	4	3

$y = x + 1.5$

$y = x + 1.7$

11.

x	1	2	3	4
y	2	9	7	12

$y = 2x + 3.1$

$y = 2x + 3.5$

12.

x	1	3	5	7
y	2	6	8	13

$y = 1.6x + 4$

$y = 1.8x + 4$

13.

x	1	2	3	4
y	7	5	11	8

$y = x + 5$

$y = 1.3x + 5$

14.

x	1	2	3	4
y	4	11	5	15

$y = 2x + 3$

$y = 2.4x + 3$

Use the given data and your calculator to find an equation for the line of best fit. Then interpret the correlation coefficient and use the line of best fit to estimate the average temperature of another city using the given latitude.

15.

City	Latitude	Average Temperature (°F)
Calgary, Alberta	51.0°N	24
Munich, Germany	48.1°N	26
Marseille, France	43.2°N	29
St. Louis, Missouri	38.4°N	34
Seoul, South Korea	37.3°N	36
Tokyo, Japan	35.4°N	38
New Delhi, India	28.4°N	43
Honolulu, Hawaii	21.2°N	52
Bangkok, Thailand	14.2°N	58
Panama City, Panama	8.6°N	?

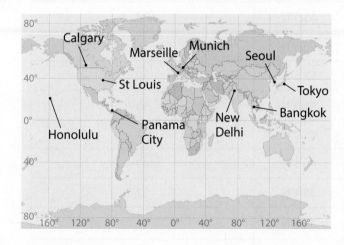

16.

City	Latitude	Average Temperature (°F)
Oslo, Norway	59.6°N	21
Warsaw, Poland	52.1°N	28
Milan, Italy	45.2°N	34
Vatican City, Vatican City	41.5°N	41
Beijing, China	39.5°N	42
Tel Aviv, Israel	32.0°N	48
Kuwait City, Kuwait	29.2°N	?
Key West, Florida	24.3°N	55
Bogota, Columbia	4.4°N	64
Mogadishu, Somalia	2.0°N	66

17.

City	Latitude	Average Temperature (°F)
Tornio, Finland	65.5°N	28
Riga, Latvia	56.6°N	36
Minsk, Belarus	53.5°N	39
Quebec City, Quebec	46.5°N	45
Turin, Italy	45.0°N	47
Pittsburgh, Pennsylvania	40.3°N	49
Lisbon, Portugal	38.4°N	52
Jerusalem, Israel	31.5°N	?
New Orleans, Louisiana	29.6°N	60
Port-au-Prince, Haiti	18.3°N	69

18.

City	Latitude (°N)	Average Temperature (°F)
Juneau, Alaska	58.2	15
Amsterdam, Netherlands	52.2	24
Salzburg, Austria	47.5	36
Belgrade, Serbia	44.5	38
Philadelphia, Pennsylvania	39.6	41
Tehran, Iran	35.4	44
Nassau, Bahamas	25.0	52
Mecca, Saudi Arabia	21.3	56
Dakar, Senegal	14.4	?
Georgetown, Guyana	6.5	65

Demographics Each table lists the median age of people living in the United States, based on the results of the United States Census over the past few decades. Use residuals to calculate the quality of fit for the line $y = 0.5x + 20$, where y is median age and x is years since 1970.

19.

Year	Median age of men
1970	25.3
1980	26.8
1990	29.1
2000	31.4
2010	35.6

20.

Year	Median Age of Texans
1970	27.1
1980	29.3
1990	31.1
2000	33.8
2010	37.6

21. State the residuals based on the actual y and predicted y-values.

    a. Actual: 23, Predicted: 21

    b. Actual: 25.6, Predicted: 23.3

    c. Actual: 24.8, Predicted: 27.4

    d. Actual: 34.9, Predicted: 31.3

H.O.T. Focus on Higher Order Thinking

22. Critical Thinking The residual plot of an equation has x-values that are close to the x-axis from $x = 0$ to $x = 10$, but has values that are far from the axis from $x = 10$ to $x = 30$. Is this a strong or weak relationship?

23. Communicate Mathematical Ideas In a squared residual plot, the residuals form a horizontal line at $y = 6$. What does this mean?

24. Interpret the Answer Explain one situation other than those in this section where squared residuals are useful.

Lesson Performance Task

The table shows the latitudes and average temperatures for the 10 largest cities in the Southern Hemisphere.

City	Latitude (°S)	Average Temperature (°F)
Sao Paulo, Brazil	23.9	69
Buenos Aires, Argentina	34.8	64
Rio de Janeiro, Brazil	22.8	76
Jakarta, Indonesia	6.3	81
Lodja, DRC	3.5	73
Lima, Peru	12.0	68
Santiago de Chile, Chile	33.2	58
Sydney, Australia	33.4	64
Melbourne, Australia	37.7	58
Johannesburg, South Africa	26.1	61

    a. Use a graphing calculator to find a line of best fit for this data set. What is the equation for the best-fit line? Interpret the meaning of the slope of this line.

    b. The city of Piggs Peak, Swaziland, is at latitude 26.0°S. Use the equation of your best-fit line to predict the average temperature in Piggs Peak. The actual average temperature for Piggs Peak is 65.3 °F. How might you account for the difference in predicted and actual values?

    c. Assume that you graphed the latitude and average temperature for 10 cities in the Northern Hemisphere. Predict how the line of best fit for that data set might compare with the best-fit line for the Southern Hemisphere cities.

Linear Modeling and Regression

Essential Question: How can you use linear modeling and regression to solve real-world problems?

Key Vocabulary

correlation *(correlación)*

line of best fit *(línea de mejor ajuste)*

linear regression *(regresión lineal)*

scatter plot *(diagrama de dispersión)*

KEY EXAMPLE   *(Lesson 10.1)*

The boiling point of water is lower at higher elevations because of the lower atmospheric pressure. The boiling point of water at some different elevations is given in the table.

Altitude (feet)	Boiling Point (°F)
500	211
1500	209
5250	202
3650	205.5
2000	207.5

Determine a line of fit for the data, and write the equation of the line. Then use your model to predict the boiling point of water at an altitude of 6400 feet.

Plot the points and sketch a line of fit. One possible line of fit goes through points (0, 212) and (5250, 202).

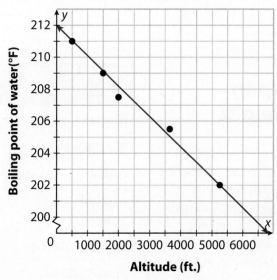

$m = -\dfrac{10}{5250}, b = 212$

The equation of this line of fit is $y = -0.0019x + 212$.

Substituting 6400 feet for x gives you $y = 199.84$. So the boiling point of water at 6400 feet is approximately 199.84°F.

EXERCISES

Estimate the correlation coefficient for each data set, indicating whether it is closest to –1, –0.5, 0, 0.5, or 1. *(Lesson 10.1)*

1.

x	y
1	2.569
2	4.236
3	3.49
4	5.62
5	4.3
6	6.1

2.

x	y
1	9.6
2	6.3
3	2.8
4	8.73
5	5.9
6	1.2

3. Calculate the residuals and give the sum of the squared residuals for the data in the table and the given line of fit. *(Lesson 10.2)*

x	1	3	5	7
y	4	6	9	10

$y = 2x - 1$

How Does Wingspan Compare with Weight in Birds?

How can we use a mathematical model to describe the relationship between wingspan and weight for birds? The table shows the weights and wingspans of several small birds. Use the data to explore a possible mathematical model, and explain how you can use your model to predict weight or wingspan of different birds.

Be sure to write down all your data and assumptions. Then use graphs, numbers, words, or algebra to explain how you reached your conclusion.

Bird	Weight (ounces)	Wingspan (inches)
Blue Jay	3	16
Black-Billed Magpie	6	25
Red-Winged Blackbird	1.8	13
Brown-Headed Cowbird	1.5	12
European Starling	2.9	16
Rusty Blackbird	2.1	14
Brewer's Blackbird	2.2	15.5
Yellow-Headed Blackbird	2.3	15

(Ready) to Go On?

10.1–10.2 Linear Modeling and Regression

- Online Homework
- Hints and Help
- Extra Practice

1. The table shows test averages of eight students.

U.S. History Test Average	88	68	73	98	88	83	78	88
Science Test Average	78	73	70	93	90	80	78	90

If $x =$ the U.S. History Test Average, and $y =$ the Science Test Average, the equation of the least-squares line for the data is $y \approx 0.77x + 17.65$ and $r \approx 0.87$. Discuss correlation and causation for the data set. *(Lesson 10.1)*

2. The table shows numbers of books read by students in an English class over a summer and the students' grades for the following semester.

Books	0	0	0	0	1	1	1	2	2	3	5	8	10	14	20
Grade	64	68	69	72	71	74	76	75	79	85	86	91	94	99	98

Find an equation for the line of best fit. Calculate and interpret the correlation coefficient. Then use your equation to predict the grade of a student who read 7 books. *(Lessons 10.1, 10.2)*

ESSENTIAL QUESTION

3. How can you use statistical methods to find relationships between sets of data?

Assessment Readiness

1. Some students were surveyed about how much time they spent playing video games last week and their overall test averages. The equation of the least-squares line for the data is $y \approx -2.82x + 87.50$ and $r \approx -0.89$. Determine if each statement is True or False.

   A. The variables are time spent playing games and test averages.

   B. The variables have a negative correlation.

   C. The variables have a weak correlation.

2. Consider $f(x) = -3x - 12$. Determine if each statement is True or False.

   A. The slope is -3.

   B. The y-intercept is -12.

   C. The x-intercept is 4.

3. Look at each equation. Tell whether each equation has a solution of $x = 3$.

   A. $2x - 8 = 19 - 7x$

   B. $-2(3x - 4) = 10$

   C. $\dfrac{-6x}{2} = -9$

4. Use your calculator to write an equation for the line of best fit for the following data.

x	12	15	19	31	43	57
y	36	41	44	61	72	94

   Calculate and interpret the correlation coefficient. Use your equation to predict the value of y when $x = 25$.

The data plot shown represents the age of the members of a jogging club.

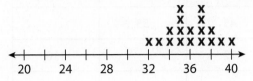

```
            X X
            X X
          X X X X
        X X X X X X X X X
    +--+--+--+--+--+--+--+--+--+--+-->
    20    24    28    32    36    40
```

1. Find the median, range, and interquartile range of the data.
   Tell whether each statement is correct.

   A. The median age is 36.

   B. The range of ages is 8.

   C. The interquartile range is 4.

2. A new member who is 30 joins the jogging club. Determine if each statement is True or False.

   A. The range increases by 2.

   B. The median decreases by 1.

   C. The age of the new member is an outlier.

3. Tell whether the equation represents a linear function.

   A. $y = -\frac{4}{5}x$

   B. $y = 5x^2 - 2$

   C. $y = -7$

4. Several hundred people were surveyed about their salary and the length of their commute to work. The equation of the line of best fit for the data is $y \approx 1.14x + 1.45$ and $r \approx 0.45$. Tell whether each phrase accurately describes the data set.

   A. The variables have a strong correlation.

   B. The variables have a positive correlation.

   C. This study shows that there is no correlation between the length of a person's commute and their salary.

5. A student notices that as the town population has gone up steadily over several years, the price of a quart of milk has also gone up steadily. Describe the correlation, if any. Then explain whether you think the situation implies causation.

6. Vivian surveyed 10th and 11th graders about whether they like reading comics. Some of the results are shown in the frequency table shown. Copy and complete the table. Find the conditional relative frequency that a student enjoys reading comics given that the student is an 11th grader. Explain how you solved this problem.

Grade	Enjoy Reading Comics		
	Yes	No	Total
10th	45	53	
11th	72		110
Total		91	208

7. Thomas drew a line of best fit for the scatter plot as shown.

Write an equation for the line of best fit in slope-intercept form. Show your work.

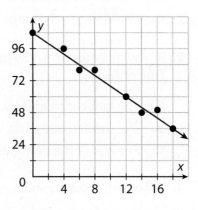

Performance Tasks

★ **8.** Gail counted the number of cars passing a certain store on Tuesday from 4 P.M. to 4:05 P.M. and on Saturday from 4 P.M. to 4:05 P.M. for 6 weeks. Her data sets are shown below.

Week	1	2	3	4	5	6
Cars on Tuesday	10	8	12	3	9	15
Cars on Saturday	24	8	31	36	29	32

A. Use the most appropriate measure of central tendency to compare the centers of these two data sets. Explain your choice.

B. Draw two box plots on the same number line to represent the data.

★★ **9.** A total of 150 students in two grades at Lowell High School were asked whether they usually ate lunch in the cafeteria. If they did not, they were asked if they would or would not eat lunch in the cafeteria if it had a salad bar.

	Now eat in cafeteria	Would eat if salad bar	Would not eat if salad bar
9th graders	36	14	32
10th graders	25	10	28

A. Use the given frequency table to make a new table showing the joint and marginal relative frequencies. Round to the nearest tenth of a percent.

B. The school board has decided that a salad bar should be added to the cafeteria if at least 30% of the students who currently do not eat in the cafeteria would start doing so. Should the salad bar be added?

★★★**10.** A scientist theorizes that you can estimate the temperature by counting how often crickets chirp. The scientist gathers the data in the table shown.

Number of chirps in a 14-second interval	37	32	42	37	46	35	34
Temperature (°F)	78	72	81	77	88	75	76

A. How many cricket chirps would you expect to indicate a temperature of 85 degrees? Include a graph and an equation as part of the justification of your answer.

B. What might be the lowest temperature your model could be applied to? Explain your reasoning.

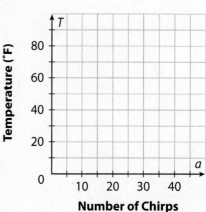

Geologist A geologist is studying the sediment discharged from several U.S. rivers, as shown in the table.

River	Amount of Sediment Discharged (millions of tons)
Mississippi River	230
Copper River	80
Yukon River	65
Columbia River	40
Susitna River	25
Eel River	15
Brazos River	11

For Parts **a–c**, round your answers to the nearest whole number, if necessary.

a. Find the mean and the median of the data for all seven rivers. Which measure represents the data better? Explain.

b. Find the mean of the data for the six rivers, excluding the Mississippi River. Does this mean represent the data better than the mean you found in part a? Explain.

c. Find the range and standard deviation of the data of all seven rivers. Describe what the measures tell you about the dispersion of the data.

Linear Systems and Piecewise-Defined Functions

MATH IN CAREERS

Personal Shopper Personal shoppers assist clients in their needs for a variety of merchandise, which can include furniture, clothing, groceries, or gifts. Personal shoppers must have a good understanding of financial math, including percentages. They must be able to stay within the budgetary constraints of their clients. They must also be able to calculate expenses such as transportation costs and reasonable rates for their services.

If you are interested in a career as a personal shopper, you should study these mathematical subjects:
- Algebra
- Business Math

Research other careers that require staying within the constraints of a budget. Check out the career activity at the end of the unit to find out how **personal shoppers** use math.

Reading Start-Up

Visualize Vocabulary

Use the ✔ words to complete the chart.

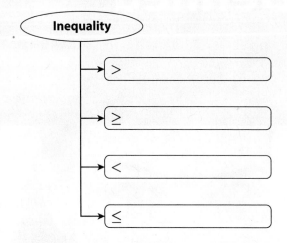

Inequality

> [ ]

≥ [ ]

< [ ]

≤ [ ]

Vocabulary

Review Words

✔ greater than *(mayor que)*

✔ greater than or equal to *(mayor que o igual a)*

✔ less than *(menor que)*

✔ less than or equal to *(menor que o igual a)*

✔ *x*-intercept *(intersección con el eje x)*

✔ *y*-intercept *(intersección con el eje y)*

Preview Words

absolute-value function *(función de valor absolute)*

consistent system *(sistema consistente)*

dependent system *(sistema dependiente)*

independent system *(sistema independiente)*

piecewise function *(función a trozos)*

system of linear equations *(sistema de ecuaciones lineales)*

system of linear inequalities *(sistema de desigualdades lineales)*

Understand Vocabulary

Complete the sentences using the preview words. Match the term on the left to the example on the right.

1. __?__ independent system

A. a system of equations that has an infinite number of solutions

2. __?__ consistent system

B. a system of equations or inequalities that has at least one solution

3. __?__ dependent system

C. a system of equations that has exactly one solution

Active Reading

Three-Panel Flip Chart Create a three-panel flip chart to help you understand the concepts in this unit. Label one flap "Solving Systems of Linear Equations," another "Modeling with Linear Systems," and the last flap "Piecewise-Defined Functions." As you study each module, write important ideas under the appropriate flap. Include any sample equations, inequalities, and functions that will help you remember the concepts later when you look back at your notes.

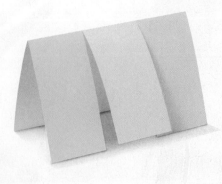

Solving Systems of Linear Equations

Essential Question: How can you use a system of linear equations to solve real-world problems?

REAL WORLD VIDEO
A Mars rover is sent into space to land on Mars. This feat requires planning the trajectory of the rover to intersect with the orbit of Mars. Systems of equations are used to find the intersection of graphs.

© Houghton Mifflin Harcourt Publishing Company • Image Credit: ©Handout/ Reuters/Corbis

MODULE PERFORMANCE TASK PREVIEW
Do Hybrid Cars Pay for Themselves?

Hybrid cars often get better gas mileage than traditional cars, which can lead to savings on gas money. The longer you drive a hybrid car, the more you are likely to save on gas. In this module, you will explore the question of how many years it would take to save enough money on gas to pay for the extra cost of a hybrid car. Buckle up and let's find out!

Are YOU Ready?

Complete these exercises to review skills you will need for this module.

Graphing Linear Relationships

Example 1 Tell whether the graph represents a linear nonproportional or proportional relationship.

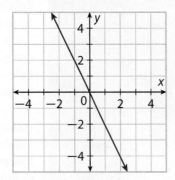

The graph of a linear nonproportional relationship is a straight line that does not pass through the origin.

The graph of a linear proportional relationship is a straight line that passes through the origin.

The graph is a straight line that passes through the origin, so it represents a linear proportional relationship.

Tell whether the graph represents a linear nonproportional or proportional relationship.

1.
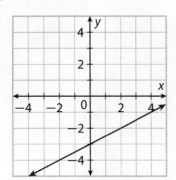

2.
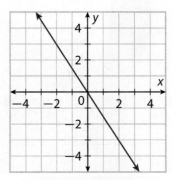

Algebraic Expressions

Example 2 Evaluate $3x + 4y$ for $x = -2$ and $y = 4$.

$3x + 4y$

$3(-2) + 4(4)$ Substitute −2 for x and 4 for y.

$-6 + 16$ Multiply.

10 Add.

Evaluate each expression for the given values of the variables.

3. $6p - 2q$ for $p = 3$ and $q = -7$

4. $5a - 2b$ for $a = -2$ and $b = 5$

5. $8m + 5n$ for $m = 3$ and $n = -5$

6. $7x + 9y$ for $x = -3$ and $y = 2$

11.1 Solving Linear Systems by Graphing

Essential Question: How can you find the solution of a system of linear equations by graphing?

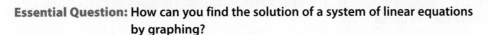

⊘ Explore Types of Systems of Linear Equations

A **system of linear equations,** also called a *linear system,* consists of two or more linear equations that have the same variables. A **solution of a system of linear equations** with two variables is any ordered pair that satisfies all of the equations in the system.

Graph A

(A) Describe the relationship between the two lines in Graph A.

(B) What do you know about every point on the graph on a linear equation?

(C) How many solutions does a system of two equations have if the graphs of the two equations intersect at exactly one point?

Graph B

(D) Describe the relationship between the two lines that coincide in Graph B.

(E) How many solutions does a system of two equations have if the graphs of the two equations intersect at infinitely many points?

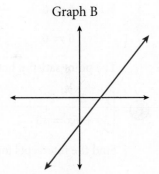

Graph C

(F) Describe the relationship between the two lines in Graph C .

(G) How many solutions does a system of two equations have if the graphs of the two equations do not intersect?

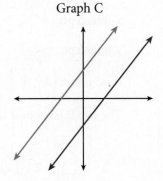

Reflect

1. Discussion Explain why the solution of a system of two equations is represented by any point where the two graphs intersect.

Explain 1 # Solving Consistent, Independent Linear Systems by Graphing

A **consistent system** is a system with at least one solution. Consistent systems can be either independent or dependent.

An **independent system** has exactly one solution. The graph of an independent system consists of two lines that intersect at exactly one point. A **dependent system** has infinitely many solutions. The graph of a dependent system consists of two coincident lines, or the same line.

A system that has no solution is an **inconsistent system**.

Example 1 Solve the system of linear equations by graphing. Check your answer.

 (A) $\begin{cases} 2x + y = 6 \\ -x + y = 3 \end{cases}$

Find the intercepts for each equation, plus a third point for a check. Then graph.

$2x + y = 6$	$-x + y = 3$
x-intercept: 3	x-intercept: -3
y-intercept: 6	y-intercept: 3
third point: $(-1, 8)$	third point: $(3, 6)$

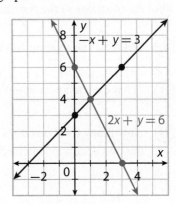

The two lines appear to intersect at $(1, 4)$. Check.

$2x + y = 6 \qquad\qquad -x + y = 3$

$2(1) + 4 \stackrel{?}{=} 6 \qquad -(1) + 4 \stackrel{?}{=} 3$

$6 = 6 \qquad\qquad\quad 3 = 3$

The point satisfies both equations, so the solution is $(1, 4)$.

(B) $\begin{cases} y = 2x - 2 \\ 3y + 6x = 18 \end{cases}$

Find the intercepts for each equation, plus a third point for a check. Then graph.

$y = 2x - 2$	$3y + 6x = 18$
x-intercept: $\boxed{1}$	x-intercept: $\boxed{3}$
y-intercept: $\boxed{-2}$	y-intercept: $\boxed{6}$
third point: $\left(3, \boxed{4}\right)$	third point: $\left(1, \boxed{4}\right)$

The two lines appear to intersect at $\boxed{(2, 2)}$. Check.

$y = 2x - 2 \qquad\qquad\qquad y + 2x = 6$

$\boxed{2} \stackrel{?}{=} 2\left(\boxed{2}\right) - 2 \qquad \boxed{2} + 2\left(\boxed{2}\right) \stackrel{?}{=} 6$

$\boxed{2} = \boxed{2} \qquad\qquad\qquad \boxed{6} = 6$

The point satisfies both equations, so the solution is $\boxed{(2, 2)}$.

Reflect

2. How do you know that the systems of equations are consistent? How do you know that they are independent?

Your Turn

Solve the system of linear equations by graphing. Check your answer.

3. $\begin{cases} y = -2x - 2 \\ x + 2y = 2 \end{cases}$

4. $\begin{cases} y = -2x - 2 \\ -x + y = 6 \end{cases}$

⚙ Explain 2　Solving Special Linear Systems by Graphing

Example 2　Solve the special system of equations by graphing and identify the system.

Ⓐ　$\begin{cases} y = 2x - 2 \\ -2x + y = 4 \end{cases}$

Find the intercepts for each equation, plus a third point for a check.

$y = 2x - 2$	$-2x + y = 4$
x-intercept: 1	x-intercept: -2
y-intercept: -2	y-intercept: 4
third point: (2, 2)	third point: (2, 8)

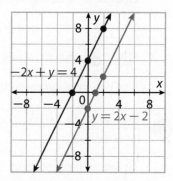

The two lines don't intersect, so there is no solution.
The two lines have the same slope and different y-intercepts
so they will never intersect.
This is an inconsistent system.

Ⓑ　$\begin{cases} y = 3x - 3 \\ -3x + y = -3 \end{cases}$

Find the intercepts for each equation, plus a third point for a check.

$y = 3x - 3$	$-3x + y = -3$
x-intercept: 　1	x-intercept: 　1
y-intercept: 　-3	y-intercept: 　-3
third point: $\left(2, \boxed{3}\right)$	third point: $\left(2, \boxed{3}\right)$

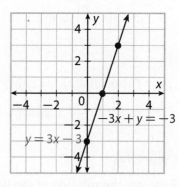

The two lines coincide, so there are infinitely many solutions.

They have the same slope and y-intercept; therefore, they are the same line.

This is a consistent and dependent system.

Solve the special system of linear equations by graphing. Check your answer.

5. $\begin{cases} y = -x - 2 \\ x + y + 2 = 0 \end{cases}$

6. $\begin{cases} y = \dfrac{2}{3}x - 1 \\ -\dfrac{2}{3}x + y = 1 \end{cases}$

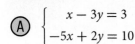 **Explain 3** **Estimating Solutions of Linear Systems by Graphing**

You can estimate the solution of a linear system of equations by graphing the system and finding the approximate coordinates of the intersection point.

Example 3 **Estimate the solution of the linear system by graphing.**

(A) $\begin{cases} x - 3y = 3 \\ -5x + 2y = 10 \end{cases}$

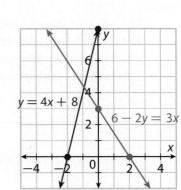

Graph the equations using a graphing calculator.

$Y1 = (3 - X)/(-3)$ and $Y2 = (10 + 5X)/2$

Find the point of intersection.

The two lines appear to intersect at about $(-2.8, -1.9)$.

(B) $\begin{cases} 6 - 2y = 3x \\ y = 4x + 8 \end{cases}$

Graph each equation by finding intercepts.

The two lines appear to intersect at about $\boxed{(-1, 4.5)}$.

Check to see if $\boxed{(-1, 4.5)}$ makes both equations true.

$$6 - 2y = 3x \qquad\qquad y = 4x + 8$$
$$6 - 2\left(\boxed{4.5}\right) \overset{?}{=} 3\left(\boxed{-1}\right) \qquad \boxed{4.5} \overset{?}{=} 4\left(\boxed{-1}\right) + 8$$
$$\boxed{-3} \approx \boxed{-3} \qquad\qquad \boxed{4.5} \approx \boxed{4}$$

The point does not satisfy both equations, but the results are close.

So, $\boxed{(-1, 4.5)}$ is an approximate solution.

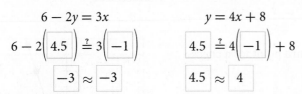

Your Turn

Estimate the solution of the linear system of equations by graphing.

7. $\begin{cases} 2y = -5x + 10 \\ -15 = -3x + 5y \end{cases}$

8. $\begin{cases} 3x + 3y = -9 \\ y = \dfrac{1}{2}x - 1 \end{cases}$

🎸 Explain 4 Interpreting Graphs of Linear Systems to Solve Problems

You can solve problems with real-world context by graphing the equations that model the problem and finding a common point.

Example 4 Rock and Bowl charges $2.75 per game plus $3 for shoe rental. Super Bowling charges $2.25 per game and $3.50 for shoe rental. For how many games will the cost to bowl be approximately the same at both places? What is that cost?

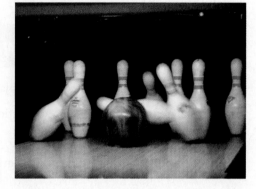

🧩 Analyze Information

Identify the important information.

- Rock and Bowl charges $ ⬚2.75 per game plus $ ⬚3 for shoe rental.

- Super Bowling charges $ ⬚2.25 per game and $ ⬚3.50 for shoe rental.

- The answer is the number of games played for which the total cost is approximately the same at both bowling alleys.

🧩 Formulate a Plan

Write a system of linear equations, where each equation represents the price at each bowling alley.

$$\begin{cases} y = 2.75x + 3 \\ y = 2.24x + 3.50 \end{cases}$$

🧩 Solve

Graph $y = 2.75x + 3$ and $y = 2.25x + 3.50$.

The lines appear to intersect at $(1, 5.75)$. So, the cost at both places will be the same for 1 game bowled and that cost will be $5.75.

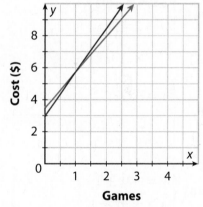

🧩 Justify and Evaluate

Check $(1, 5.75)$ using both equations.

$$2.75\left(\boxed{1} \right) + 3 = \boxed{5.75} \qquad 2.25\left(\boxed{1} \right) + 3.5 = \boxed{5.75}$$

Reflect

9. Which bowling alley costs more if you bowl more than 1 game? Explain how you can tell by looking at the graph.

Your Turn

10. Video club A charges $10 for membership and $4 per movie rental. Video club B charges $15 for membership and $3 per movie rental. For how many movie rentals will the cost be the same at both video clubs? What is that cost? Write a system and solve by graphing.

11. When a system of linear equations is graphed, how is the graph of each equation related to the solutions of that system?

12. Essential Question Check-In How does graphing help you solve a system of linear equations?

✪ Evaluate: Homework and Practice

- Online Homework
- Hints and Help
- Extra Practice

1. Is the following statement correct? Explain.

A system of two equations has no solution if the graphs of the two equations are coincident lines.

Solve the system of linear equations by graphing. Check your answer.

2. $\begin{cases} y = 2x - 4 \\ x + 2y = 12 \end{cases}$

3. $\begin{cases} y = -\dfrac{1}{3}x + 2 \\ y + 4 = -\dfrac{4}{3}x \end{cases}$

4. $\begin{cases} y = -x - 6 \\ y = x \end{cases}$

5. $\begin{cases} y = \dfrac{4}{3}x - 4 \\ y = 4 \end{cases}$

6. $\begin{cases} y = -2x + 2 \\ y + 2 = 2x \end{cases}$

7. $\begin{cases} y = \dfrac{1}{2}x + 5 \\ \dfrac{2}{3}x + y = -2 \end{cases}$

8. $\begin{cases} y = \dfrac{1}{2}x - 2 \\ -\dfrac{1}{2}x + y - 3 = 0 \end{cases}$

9. $\begin{cases} y = 2x + 4 \\ -4x + 2y = 8 \end{cases}$

10. $\begin{cases} y = -3x + 1 \\ 12x + 4y = 4 \end{cases}$

11. $\begin{cases} y = 4x + 4 \\ -4x + y + 4 = 0 \end{cases}$

12. $\begin{cases} y = -\dfrac{3}{4}x + \dfrac{1}{4} \\ \dfrac{3}{4}x + y - 2 = 0 \end{cases}$

13. $\begin{cases} y = 5x - 1 \\ -5x + y + 4 = 3 \end{cases}$

Estimate the solution of the linear system of equations by graphing.

14. $\begin{cases} 3y = -5x + 15 \\ -14 = -2x + 7y \end{cases}$

15. $\begin{cases} 2y + 5x = 14 \\ -35 = -5x + 7y \end{cases}$

16. $\begin{cases} \dfrac{4}{7}y = x + 4 \\ 2x - 5y = 10 \end{cases}$

17. $\begin{cases} 6y = 5x + 30 \\ 2 = -\dfrac{2}{7}x + y \end{cases}$

Solve by graphing. Give an approximate solution if necessary.

18. Wren and Jenni are reading the same book. Wren is on page 12 and reads 3 pages every night. Jenni is on page 7 and reads 4 pages every night. After how many nights will they have read the same number of pages? How many pages will that be?

19. Rusty burns 6 calories per minute swimming and 10 calories per minute jogging. In the morning, Rusty burns 175 calories walking and swims for x minutes. In the afternoon, Rusty will jog for x minutes. How many minutes must he jog to burn at least as many calories y in the afternoon as he did in the morning? Round your answer up to the next whole number of minutes.

20. A gym membership at one gym costs $10 every month plus a one-time membership fee of $15, and a gym membership at another gym costs $4 every month plus a one-time $40 membership fee. After about how many months will the gym memberships cost the same amount?

21. Malory is putting money in two savings accounts. Account A started with $150 and Account B started with $300. Malory deposits $16 in Account A and $12 in Account B each month. In how many months will Account A have a balance at least as great as Account B? What will that balance be?

22. Critical Thinking Write *sometimes*, *always*, or *never* to complete the following statements.

a. If the equations in a system of linear equations have the same slope, there are _____?_____ infinitely many solutions for the system.

b. If the equations in a system of linear equations have different slopes, there is _____?_____ one solution for the system.

c. If the equations in a system of linear equations have the same slope and a different y-intercept, there is _____?_____ any solution for the system.

H.O.T. Focus on Higher Order Thinking

23. Critique Reasoning Brad classifies the system below as inconsistent because the equations have the same y-intercept. What is his error?

$\begin{cases} y = 2x - 4 \\ y = x - 4 \end{cases}$

24. Explain the Error Alexa solved the system

$$\begin{cases} 5x + 2y = 6 \\ x - 3y = -4 \end{cases}$$

by graphing and estimated the solution to be about $(1.5, 0.6)$.
What is her error? What is the correct answer?

25. Represent Real-World Problems Cora ran 3 miles last week and will run 7 miles per week from now on. Hana ran 9 miles last week and will run 4 miles per week from now on. The system of linear equations $\begin{cases} y = 7x + 3 \\ y = 4x + 9 \end{cases}$ can be used to represent this situation. Explain what x and y represent in the equations. After how many weeks will Cora and Hana have run the same number of miles? How many miles? Solve by graphing.

Lesson Performance Task

A boat takes 7.5 hours to make a 60-mile trip upstream and 6 hours on the 60-mile return trip. Let v be the speed of the boat in still water and c be the speed of the current. The upstream speed of the boat is $v - c$ and the downstream boat speed is $v + c$.

a. Use the distance formula to write a system of equations relating boat speed and time to distance, one equation for the upstream part of the trip and one for the downstream part.

b. Graph the system to find the speed of the boat in still water and the speed of the current.

c. How long would it take the boat to travel the 60 miles if there were no current?

11.2 Solving Linear Systems by Substitution

Essential Question: How can you solve a system of linear equations by using substitution?

⊘ Explore   Exploring the Substitution Method of Solving Linear Systems

Another method to solve a linear system is by using the substitution method.

In the system of linear equations shown, the value of y is given. Use this value of y to find the value of x and the solution of the system.

$$\begin{cases} y = 2 \\ x + y = 6 \end{cases}$$

(A) Substitute the value of y in the second equation and solve for x.

$$x + y = 6$$

$$x + \boxed{?} = 6$$

$$x = \boxed{?}$$

(B) The values of x and y are known. What is the solution of the system?

Solution: $\left(\boxed{?}, \boxed{?} \right)$

(C) Graph the system of linear equations. How do your solutions compare? $\boxed{?}$

(D) Use substitution to find the values of x and y in this system of linear equations. Substitute $4x$ for y in the second equation and solve for x. Once you find the value for x, substitute it into either original equation to find the value for y.

$$\begin{cases} y = 4x \\ 5x + 2y = 39 \end{cases}$$

Solution: $\left(\boxed{?}, \boxed{?} \right)$

Reflect

1. **Discussion** For the system in Step D, what equation did you get after substituting $4x$ for y in $5x + 2y = 39$ and simplifying?

2. **Discussion** How could you check your solution in part D?

The **substitution method** is used to solve a system of equations by solving an equation for one variable and substituting the resulting expression into the other equation. The steps for the substitution method are as shown.

1. Solve one of the equations for one of its variables.
2. Substitute the expression from Step 1 into the other equation and solve for the other variable.
3. Substitute the value from Step 2 into either original equation and solve to find the value of the other variable.

Example 1 Solve each system of linear equations by substitution.

Ⓐ $\begin{cases} 3x + y = -3 \\ -2x + y = 7 \end{cases}$

Solve an equation for one variable.

$3x + y = -3$	Select one of the equations.
$y = -3x - 3$	Solve for y. Isolate y on one side.

Substitute the expression for y in the other equation and solve.

$-2x + (-3x - 3) = 7$	Substitute the expression for y.
$-5x - 3 = 7$	Combine like terms.
$-5x = 10$	Add 3 to both sides.
$x = -2$	Divide each side by -5.

Substitute the value for x into one of the equations and solve for y.

$3(-2) + y = -3$	Substitute the value of x into the first equation.
$-6 + y = -3$	Simplify.
$y = 3$	Add 6 to both sides.

So, $(-2, 3)$ is the solution of the system.

Check the solution by graphing.

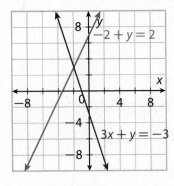

$3x + y = -3$ $-2x + y = 7$

x-intercept: -1 x-intercept: $-\dfrac{7}{2}$

y-intercept: -3 y-intercept: 7

The point of intersection is $(-2, 3)$.

(B) $\begin{cases} x - 3y = 9 \\ x + 4y = 2 \end{cases}$

Solve an equation for one variable.

$x - 3y = 9$ Select one of the equations.

$x = \boxed{3y + 9}$ Solve for x. Isolate x on one side.

Substitute the expression for x in the other equation and solve.

$\left(\boxed{3y + 9}\right) + 4y = 2$ Substitute the expression for x.

$\boxed{7y + 9} = 2$ Combine like terms.

$\boxed{7y} = \boxed{-7}$ Subtract $\boxed{9}$ from both sides.

$y = \boxed{-1}$ Divide each side by $\boxed{7}$.

Substitute the value for y into one of the equations and solve for x.

$x - 3\left(\boxed{-1}\right) = 9$ Substitute the value of y into the first equation.

$\boxed{x + 3} = 9$ Simplify.

$x = \boxed{6}$ Subtract $\boxed{3}$ from both sides.

So, $\left(\boxed{6}, \boxed{-1}\right)$ is the solution by graphing.

Check the solution by graphing.

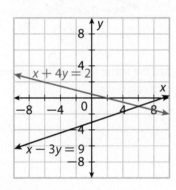

$x - 3y = 9$ $x + 4y = 2$

x-intercept: $\boxed{9}$ x-intercept: $\boxed{2}$

y-intercept: $\boxed{-3}$ y-intercept: $\boxed{\frac{1}{2}}$

The point of intersection is $\left(\boxed{6}, \boxed{-1}\right)$.

Reflect

3. Explain how a system in which one of the equations is of the form $y = c$, where c is a constant, is a special case of the substitution method.

4. Is it more efficient to solve $-2x + y = 7$ for x than for y? Explain.

Your Turn

5. Solve the system of linear equations by substitution.

$\begin{cases} 3x + y = 14 \\ 2x - 6y = -24 \end{cases}$

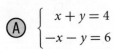

You can use the substitution method for systems of linear equations that have infinitely many solutions and for systems that have no solutions.

Example 2 Solve each system of linear equations by substitution.

(A) $\begin{cases} x + y = 4 \\ -x - y = 6 \end{cases}$

Solve $x + y = 4$ for x.

$$x = -y + 4$$

Substitute the resulting expression into the other equation and solve.

$$-(-y + 4) - y = 6 \qquad \text{Substitute.}$$
$$-4 = 6 \qquad \text{Simplify.}$$

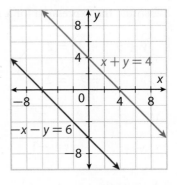

The resulting equation is false, so the system has no solutions.

The graph shows that the lines are parallel and do not intersect.

(B) $\begin{cases} x - 3y = 6 \\ 4x - 12y = 24 \end{cases}$

Solve $x - 3y = 6$ for x.

$$x = \boxed{3y + 6}$$

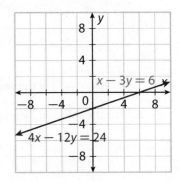

Substitute the resulting expression into the other equation and solve.

$$4\left(\boxed{3y + 6}\right) - 12y = 24 \qquad \text{Substitute.}$$
$$\boxed{24} = 24 \qquad \text{Simplify.}$$

The graphs are the same line. so the system has infinitely many solutions.

The resulting equation is true, so the system has infinitely many solutions.

Reflect

6. Provide two possible solutions of the system in Example 2B. How are all the solutions of this system related to one another?

Your Turn

Solve each system of linear equations by substitution.

7. $\begin{cases} -2x + 14y = -28 \\ x - 7y = 14 \end{cases}$

8. $\begin{cases} -3x + y = 12 \\ 6x - 2y = 18 \end{cases}$

🎸 Explain 3   Solving Linear System Models by Substitution

You can use a system of linear equations to model real-world situations.

Example 3   Solve each real-world situation by using the substitution method.

(A)   Fitness center A has a \$60 enrollment fee and costs \$35 per month. Fitness center B has no enrollment fee and costs \$45 per month. Let t represent the total cost in dollars and m represent the number of months. The system of equations $\begin{cases} t = 60 + 35m \\ t = 45m \end{cases}$ can be used to represent this situation. In how many months will both fitness centers cost the same? What will the cost be?

$60 + 35m = 45m$	Substitute $60 + 35m$ for t in the second equation.
$60 = 10m$	Subtract $35m$ from each side.
$6 = m$	Divide each side by 10.
$t = 45m$	Use one of the original equations.
$= 45(6) = 270$	Substitute 6 for m.
$(6, 270)$	Write the solution as an ordered pair.

Both fitness centers will cost \$270 after 6 months.

(B)   High-speed Internet provider A has a \$100 setup fee and costs \$65 per month. High-speed internet provider B has a setup fee of \$30 and costs \$70 per month. Let t represent the total amount paid in dollars and m represent the number of months. The system of equations $\begin{cases} t = 100 + 65m \\ t = 30 + 70m \end{cases}$ can be used to represent this situation. In how many months will both providers cost the same? What will that cost be?

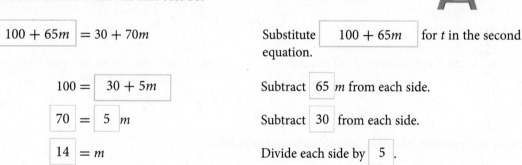

$\boxed{100 + 65m} = 30 + 70m$	Substitute $\boxed{100 + 65m}$ for t in the second equation.
$100 = \boxed{30 + 5m}$	Subtract $\boxed{65}\,m$ from each side.
$\boxed{70} = \boxed{5}\,m$	Subtract $\boxed{30}$ from each side.
$\boxed{14} = m$	Divide each side by $\boxed{5}$.

$t = 30 + 70m$	Use one of the original equations.
$t = 30 + 70\left(\boxed{14}\right)$	Substitute $\boxed{14}$ for m.
$t = \boxed{1010}$	
$\left(\boxed{14}\,,\,\boxed{1010}\right)$	Write the sulotion as an ordered pair.

Both Internet providers will cost \$1010 after 14 months.

9. If the variables in a real-world situation represent the number of months and cost, why must the values of the variables be greater than or equal to zero?

10. A boat travels at a rate of 18 kilometers per hour from its port. A second boat is 34 kilometers behind the first boat when it starts traveling in the same direction at a rate of 22 kilometers per hour to the same port. Let d represent the distance the boats are from the port in kilometers and t represent the amount of time in hours. The system of equations $\begin{cases} d = 18t + 34 \\ d = 22t \end{cases}$ can be used to represent this situation. How many hours will it take for the second boat to catch up to the first boat? How far will the boats be from their port? Use the substitution method to solve this real-world application.

💬 Elaborate

11. When given a system of linear equations, how do you decide which variable to solve for first?

12. How can you check a solution for a system of equations without graphing?

13. **Essential Question-Check-In** Explain how you can solve a system of linear equations by substitution.

⭐ Evaluate: Homework and Practice

• Online Homework
• Hints and Help
• Extra Practice

1. In the system of linear equations shown, the value of y is given. Use this value of y to find the value of x and the solution of the system.
$\begin{cases} y = 12 \\ 2x - y = 4 \end{cases}$

    a. What is the solution of the system?

    b. Graph the system of linear equations. How do the solutions compare?

Solve each system of linear equations by substitution.

2. $\begin{cases} 5x + y = 8 \\ 2x + y = 5 \end{cases}$

3. $\begin{cases} x - 3y = 10 \\ x + 5y = -22 \end{cases}$

4. $\begin{cases} 5x - 3y = 22 \\ -4x + y = -19 \end{cases}$

5. $\begin{cases} x + 7y = -11 \\ -2x - 5y = 4 \end{cases}$

6. $\begin{cases} 2x + 6y = 16 \\ 3x - 5y = -18 \end{cases}$

7. $\begin{cases} 7x + 2y = 24 \\ -6x + 3y = 3 \end{cases}$

Solve each system of linear equations by substitution.

8. $\begin{cases} x + y = 3 \\ -4x - 4y = 12 \end{cases}$

9. $\begin{cases} 3x - 3y = -15 \\ -x + y = 5 \end{cases}$

10. $\begin{cases} x - 8y = 17 \\ -3x + 24y = -51 \end{cases}$

11. $\begin{cases} 5x - y = 18 \\ 10x - 2y = 32 \end{cases}$

12. $\begin{cases} -2x - 3y = 12 \\ -4x - 6y = 24 \end{cases}$

13. $\begin{cases} 3x + 4y = 36 \\ 6x + 8y = 48 \end{cases}$

Solve each real-world situation by using the substitution method.

14. The number of DVDs sold at a store in a month was 920 and the number of DVDs sold decreased by 12 per month. The number of Blu-ray discs sold in the same store in the same month was 502 and the number of Blu-ray discs sold increased by 26 per month. Let d represent the number of discs sold and t represent the time in months.

The system of equations $\begin{cases} d = 920 - 12t \\ d = 502 + 26t \end{cases}$ can be

used to represent this situation. If this trend continues, in how many months will the number of DVDs sold equal the number of Blu-ray discs sold? How many of each is sold in that month?

15. One smartphone plan costs $30 per month for talk and messaging and $8 per gigabyte of data used each month. A second smartphone plan costs $60 per month for talk and messaging and $3 per gigabyte of data used each month. Let c represent the total cost in dollars and d represent the amount of data used in gigabytes. The system of equations $\begin{cases} c = 30 + 8d \\ c = 60 + 3d \end{cases}$ can be used to represent this situation. How many gigabytes would have to be used for the plans to cost the same? What would that cost be?

16. A movie theater sells popcorn and fountain drinks. Brett buys 1 popcorn bucket and 3 fountain drinks for his family, and pays a total of $9.50. Sarah buys 3 popcorn buckets and 4 fountain drinks for her family, and pays a total of $19.75. If p represents the number of popcorn buckets and d represents the number of drinks, then the system of equations $\begin{cases} 9.50 = p + 3d \\ 19.75 = 3p + 4d \end{cases}$ can be used to represent this situation. Find the cost of a popcorn bucket and the cost of a fountain drink.

17. Jen is riding her bicycle on a trail at the rate of 0.3 kilometer per minute. Michelle is 11.2 kilometers behind Jen when she starts traveling on the same trail at a rate of 0.44 kilometer per minute. Let d represent the distance in kilometers the bicyclists are from the start of the trail and t represent the time in minutes.

The system of equations $\begin{cases} d = 0.3t + 11.2 \\ d = 0.44t \end{cases}$ can be used to represent this situation. How many minutes will it take Michelle to catch up to Jen? How far will they be from the start of the trail? Use the substitution method to solve this real-world application.

18. Geometry The length of a rectangular room is 5 feet more than its width. The perimeter of the room is 66 feet. Let L represent the length of the room and W represent the width in feet. The system of equations $\begin{cases} L = W + 5 \\ 66 = 2L + 2W \end{cases}$ can be used to represent this situation. What are the room's dimensions?

19. A cable television provider has a \$55 setup fee and charges \$82 per month, while a satellite television provider has a \$160 setup fee and charges \$67 per month. Let c represent the total cost in dollars and t represent the amount of time in months. The system of equations $\begin{cases} c = 55 + 82t \\ c = 160 + 67t \end{cases}$ can be used to represent this situation.

a. In how many months will both providers cost the same? What will that cost be?

b. If you plan to move in 12 months, which provider would be less expensive? Explain.

20. Determine whether each of the following systems of equations have one solution, infinitely many solutions, or no solution.

a. $\begin{cases} x + y = 5 \\ -6y - 6y = 30 \end{cases}$

b. $\begin{cases} x + y = 7 \\ 5x + 2y = 23 \end{cases}$

c. $\begin{cases} 3x + y = 5 \\ 6x + 2y = 12 \end{cases}$

d. $\begin{cases} 2x + 5y = -12 \\ x + 7y = -15 \end{cases}$

e. $\begin{cases} 3x + 5y = 17 \\ -6x - 10y = -34 \end{cases}$

21. Finance Adrienne invested a total of \$1900 in two simple-interest money market accounts. Account A paid 3% annual interest and account B paid 5% annual interest. The total amount of interest she earned after one year was \$83. If a represents the amount invested in dollars in account A and b represents the amount invested in dollars in account B, the system of equations $\begin{cases} a + b = 1900 \\ 0.03a + 0.05b = 83 \end{cases}$ can represent this situation. How much did Adrienne invest in each account?

22. **Real-World Application** The Sullivans are deciding between two landscaping companies. Evergreen charges a $79 startup fee and $39 per month. Eco Solutions charges a $25 startup fee and $45 per month. Let c represent the total cost in dollars and t represent the time in months. The system of equations $\begin{cases} c = 39t + 79 \\ c = 45t + 25 \end{cases}$ can be used to represent this situation.

   a. In how many months will both landscaping services cost the same? What will that cost be?

   b. Which landscaping service will be less expensive in the long term? Explain.

23. **Multiple Representations** For the first equation in the system of linear equations below, write an equivalent equation without denominators. Then solve the system.

$$\begin{cases} \dfrac{x}{5} + \dfrac{y}{3} = 6 \\ x - 2y = 8 \end{cases}$$

24. **Conjecture** Is it possible for a system of three linear equations to have one solution? If so, give an example.

25. **Conjecture** Is it possible to use substitution to solve a system of linear equations if one equation represents a horizontal line and the other equation represents a vertical line? Explain.

Lesson Performance Task

A company breaks even from the production and sale of a product if the total revenue equals the total cost. Suppose an electronics company is considering producing two types of smartphones. To produce smartphone A, the initial cost is $20,000 and each phone costs $150 to produce. The company will sell smartphone A at $200. Let $C(a)$ represent the total cost in dollars of producing a units of smartphone A. Let $R(a)$ represent the total revenue, or money the company takes in due to selling a units of smartphone A. The system of

equations $\begin{cases} C(a) = 20{,}000 + 150a \\ R(a) = 200a \end{cases}$ can be used to represent the situation for phone A.

To produce smartphone B, the initial cost is $44,000 and each phone costs $200 to produce. The company will sell smartphone B at $280. Let $C(b)$ represent the total cost in dollars of producing b units of smartphone B and $R(b)$ represent the total revenue from

selling b units of smartphone B. The system of equations $\begin{cases} C(b) = 44{,}000 + 200b \\ R(b) = 280b \end{cases}$ can be

used to represent the situation for phone B.

Solve each system of equations and interpret the solutions. Then determine whether the company should invest in producing smartphone A or smartphone B. Justify your answer.

11.3 Solving Linear Systems by Adding or Subtracting

Resource Locker

Essential Question: How can you solve a system of linear equations by adding and subtracting?

Explore Exploring the Effects of Adding Equations

Systems of equations can be solved by graphing, substitution, or by a third method, called **elimination.**

(A) Look at the system of linear equations.

$$\begin{cases} 2x - 4y = -10 \\ 3x + 4y = 5 \end{cases}$$

What do you notice about the coefficients of the y-terms? [?]

(B) What is the sum of $-4y$ and $4y$? How do you know? [?]

(C) Find the sum of the two equations by combining like terms.

$$\begin{array}{ccc} 2x & -4y & = & -10 \\ +3x & +4y & = & +5 \\ \hline \end{array}$$

[?] + [?] = [?]

(D) Use the equation from Step C to find the value of x.

$x =$ [?]

(E) Use the value of x to find the value of y. What is the solution of the system?

$y =$ [?]

Solution: [?]

Reflect

1. **Discussion** How do you know that when both sides of the two equations were added, the resulting sums were equal?

2. **Discussion** How could you check your solution?

🛠 Explain 1   Solving Linear Systems by Adding or Subtracting

The **elimination method** is a method used to solve systems of equations in which one variable is eliminated by adding or subtracting two equations in the system.

Steps in the Elimination Method
1. Add or subtract the equations to eliminate one variable, and then solve for the other variable.
2. Substitute the value into either original equation to find the value of the eliminated variable.
3. Write the solution as an ordered pair.

Example 1   Solve each system of linear equations using the indicated method. Check your answer by graphing.

Ⓐ Solve the system of linear equations by adding.

$$\begin{cases} 4x - 2y = 12 \\ x + 2y = 8 \end{cases}$$

Add the equations.

$$4x - 2y = 12$$

$$\underline{x + 2y = 8}$$
$$5x + 0 = 20$$

$$5x = 20$$

$$x = 4$$

Substitute the value of x into one of the equations and solve for y.

$$x + 2y = 8$$
$$4 + 2y = 8$$
$$2y = 4$$
$$y = 2$$

Write the solution as an ordered pair.

$$(4, 2)$$

Check the solution by graphing.

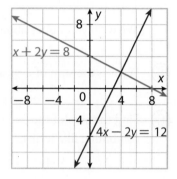

Ⓑ Solve the system of linear equations by subtracting.

$$\begin{cases} 2x + 6y = 6 \\ 2x - y = -8 \end{cases}$$

Subtract the equations.

$$2x + 6y = 6$$
$$\underline{-(2x - y = -8)}$$
$$\boxed{0} \boxed{+ 7y} = \boxed{14}$$
$$y = 2$$

Substitute the value of y into one of the equations and solve for x.

$$2x - y = -8$$
$$2x - 2 = -8$$
$$2x = -6$$
$$x = -3$$

Write the solution as an ordered pair. $(-3, 2)$

Check the solution by graphing.

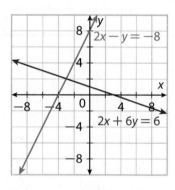

3. Can the system in part A be solved by subtracting one of the original equations from the other? Why or why not?

4. In part B, what would happen if you added the original equations instead of subtracting?

Solve each system of linear equations by adding or subtracting.

5. $\begin{cases} 2x + 5y = -24 \\ 3x - 5y = 14 \end{cases}$

6. $\begin{cases} 3x + 2y = 5 \\ x + 2y = -1 \end{cases}$

✪ Explain 2 Solving Special Linear Systems by Adding or Subtracting

Example 2 Solve each system of linear equations by adding or subtracting.

Ⓐ $\begin{cases} -4x - 2y = 4 \\ 4x + 2y = -4 \end{cases}$

Add the equations.

$$\begin{array}{r} -4x - 2y = 4 \\ +4x + 2y = -4 \\ \hline 0 + 0 = 0 \\ 0 = 0 \end{array}$$

The resulting equation is true, so the system has infinitely many solutions.

Graph the equations to provide more information.

The graphs are the same line, so the system has infinitely many solutions.

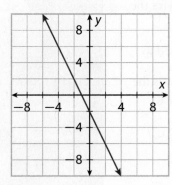

Ⓑ $\begin{cases} x + y = -2 \\ x + y = 4 \end{cases}$

Subtract the equations.

$$x + y = -2$$
$$-(x + y = 4)$$
$$\overline{}$$
$$0 + 0 = -6$$
$$0 = -6$$

The resulting equation is false, so the system has no solutions.

Graph the equations to provide more information.

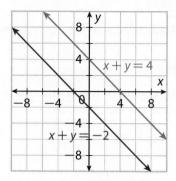

The graph shows that the lines are parallel and do not intersect.

Your Turn

Solve each system of linear equations by adding or subtracting.

7. $\begin{cases} 4x - y = 3 \\ 4x - y = -2 \end{cases}$

8. $\begin{cases} x - 6y = 7 \\ -x + 6y = -7 \end{cases}$

⚙ Explain 3 Solving Linear System Models by Adding or Subtracting

Example 3 Solve by adding or subtracting.

Ⓐ Perfect Patios is building a rectangular deck for a customer. According to the customer's specifications, the perimeter should be 40 meters and the difference between twice the length and twice the width should be 4 meters.

The system of equations $\begin{cases} 2\ell + 2w = 40 \\ 2\ell - 2w = 4 \end{cases}$ can be used to

represent this situation, where ℓ is the length and w is the width. What will be the length and width of the deck?

Add the equations.

$$2\ell + 2w = 40$$
$$\underline{2\ell - 2w = 4}$$
$$4\ell + 0 = 44$$
$$4\ell = 44$$
$$\ell = 11$$

Substitute the value of ℓ into one of the equations and solve for w.

$$2\ell + 2w = 40$$
$$2(11) + 2w = 40$$
$$22 + 2w = 40$$
$$2w = 18$$
$$w = 9$$

Write the solution as an ordered pair.

$$(\ell, w) = (11, 9)$$

The length of the deck will be 11 meters and the width will be 9 meters.

(B) A video game and movie rental kiosk charges \$2 for each video game rented, and \$1 for each movie rented. One day last week, a total of 114 video games and movies were rented for a total of \$177. The system of equations $\begin{cases} x + y = 114 \\ 2x + y = 177 \end{cases}$ represents this situation, where x represents the number of video games rented and y represents the number of movies rented. Find the numbers of video games and movies that were rented.

Subtract the equations.

$$x + y = 114$$
$$\underline{-(2x + y = 177)}$$
$$-x + 0 = -63$$
$$-x = -63$$
$$x = 63$$

Substitute the value of x into one of the equations and solve for y.

$$x + y = 114$$
$$63 + y = 114$$
$$y = 51$$

Write the solution as an ordered pair.

$$(63, 51)$$

63 video games and 51 movies were rented.

Your Turn

9. The perimeter of a rectangular picture frame is 62 inches. The difference of the length of the frame and twice its width is 1. The system of equations $\begin{cases} 2\ell + 2w = 62 \\ \ell - 2w = 1 \end{cases}$ represents this situation, where ℓ represents the length in inches and w represents the width in inches. What are the length and the width of the frame?

💬 Elaborate

10. How can you decide whether to add or subtract to eliminate a variable in a linear system? Explain your reasoning.

11. **Discussion** When a linear system has no solution, what happens when you try to solve the system by adding or subtracting?

12. **Essential Question Check-In** When you solve a system of linear equations by adding or subtracting, what needs to be true about the variable terms in the equations?

© Houghton Mifflin Harcourt Publishing Company

⭐ **Evaluate: Homework and Practice**

• Online Homework
• Hints and Help
• Extra Practice

1. Which method of elimination would be best to solve the system of linear equations? Explain.

$$\begin{cases} \dfrac{1}{2}x + \dfrac{3}{4}y = -10 \\ -x - \dfrac{3}{4}y = 1 \end{cases}$$

Solve each system of linear equations by adding or subtracting.

2. $\begin{cases} 3x + 2y = 10 \\ 3x - y = 22 \end{cases}$

3. $\begin{cases} -2x + y = 3 \\ 3x - y = -2 \end{cases}$

4. $\begin{cases} x + y = 5 \\ x - 3y = 3 \end{cases}$

5. $\begin{cases} 7x + y = -4 \\ 2x - y = 1 \end{cases}$

6. $\begin{cases} -5x + y = -3 \\ 5x - 3y = -1 \end{cases}$

7. $\begin{cases} 2x + y = -6 \\ -5x + y = 8 \end{cases}$

8. $\begin{cases} 6x - 3y = 15 \\ 4x - 3y = -5 \end{cases}$

9. $\begin{cases} 8x - 6y = 36 \\ -2x + 6y = 0 \end{cases}$

10. $\begin{cases} \dfrac{1}{2}x - \dfrac{7}{9}y = -\dfrac{20}{3} \\ -\dfrac{1}{2}x + \dfrac{7}{9}y = 6\dfrac{2}{3} \end{cases}$

11. $\begin{cases} -10x + 2y = -7 \\ -10x + 2y = -2 \end{cases}$

12. $\begin{cases} -2x + 5y = 7 \\ 2x - 5y = -7 \end{cases}$

13. $\begin{cases} x + y = 0 \\ -x - y = 0 \end{cases}$

14. $\begin{cases} -5x - y = -3 \\ -5x - y = -2 \end{cases}$

15. $\begin{cases} ax - by = c \\ ax - by = c \end{cases}$

16. The sum of two numbers is 65, and the difference of the numbers is 27. The system of linear equations $\begin{cases} x + y = 65 \\ x - y = 27 \end{cases}$ represents this situation, where x is the larger number and y is the smaller number. Solve the system to find the two numbers.

17. A rectangular garden has a perimeter of 120 feet. The length of the garden is 24 feet greater than twice the width. The system of linear equations $\begin{cases} 2\ell + 2w = 120 \\ \ell - 2w = 24 \end{cases}$ represents this situation, where ℓ is the length of the garden and w is its width. Find the length and width of the garden.

18. The sum of two angles is 90°. The difference of twice the larger angle and the smaller angle is 105°. The system of linear equations $\begin{cases} x + y = 90 \\ 2x - y = 105 \end{cases}$ represents this situation where x is the larger angle and y is the smaller angle. Find the measures of the two angles.

19. Max and Sasha exercise a total of 20 hours each week. Max exercises 15 hours less than 4 times the number of hours Sasha exercises. The system of equations $\begin{cases} x + y = 20 \\ x - 4y = -15 \end{cases}$ represents this situation, where x represents the number of hours Max exercises and y represents the number of hours Sasha exercises. How many hours do Max and Sasha exercise per week?

20. The sum of the digits in a two-digit number is 12. The digit in the tens place is 2 more than the digit in the ones place. The system of linear equations $\begin{cases} x + y = 12 \\ x - y = 2 \end{cases}$ represents this situation, where x is the digit in the tens place and y is the digit in the ones place. Solve the system to find the two-digit number.

21. A pool company is installing a rectangular pool for a new house. The perimeter of the pool must be 94 feet, and the length must be 2 feet more than twice the width.

The system of linear equations $\begin{cases} 2\ell + 2w = 94 \\ \ell = 2w + 2 \end{cases}$ represents this situation, where ℓ is the length and w is the width. What are the dimensions of the pool?

22. Use one solution, no solutions, or infinitely many solutions to complete each statement.

    a. When the solution of a system of linear equations yields the equation $4 = 4$, the system has ____?____.

    b. When the solution of a system of linear equations yields the equation $x = 4$, the system has ____?____.

    c. When the solution of a system of linear equations yields the equation $0 = 4$, the system has ____?____.

H.O.T. Focus on Higher Order Thinking

23. Multiple Representations You can use subtraction to solve the system of linear equations shown.

$$\begin{cases} 2x + 4y = -4 \\ 2x - 2y = -10 \end{cases}$$

Instead of subtracting $2x - 2y = -10$ from $2x + 4y = -4$, what equation can you add to get the same result? Explain.

24. Explain the Error Liang's solution of a system of linear equations is shown. Explain Liang's error and give the correct solution.

$$\begin{cases} 3x - 2y = 12 \\ -x - 2y = -20 \end{cases}$$

$$3x - 2y = 12$$
$$\underline{-x - 2y = -20}$$
$$2x = -8$$
$$x = -4$$

$$3x - 2y = 12$$
$$3(-4) - 2y = 12$$
$$-12 - 2y = 12$$
$$-2y = 24$$
$$y = -12$$

Solution: $(-4, -12)$

25. Represent Real-World Problems For a school play, Rico bought 3 adult tickets and 5 child tickets for a total of $40. Sasha bought 1 adult ticket and 5 child tickets for a total of $25.

The system of linear equations $\begin{cases} 3x + 5y = 40 \\ x + 5y = 25 \end{cases}$ represents this

situation, where x is the cost of an adult ticket and y is the cost of a child ticket. How much will Julia pay for 5 adult tickets and 3 child tickets?

Lesson Performance Task

A local charity run has a Youth Race for runners under the age of 12. The entry fee is $5 for an individual or $4 each for two runners from the same family. Carter is collecting the registration forms and fees. After everyone has registered, he picks up the cash box and finds a dollar on the ground. He checks the cash box and finds that it contains $200 and the registration slips for 47 runners. Does the dollar belong in the cash box or not? Explain your reasoning. (Hint: You can use the system of equations $i + f = 47$ and $5i + 4f = 200$, where i equals the number of individual tickets and f equals the number of family tickets.)

11.4 Solving Linear Systems by Multiplying First

Essential Question: How can you solve a system of linear equations by using multiplication and elimination?

⊘ Explore 1 Understanding Linear Systems and Multiplication

A system of linear equations in which one of the like terms in each equation has either the same or opposite coefficients can that be readily solved by elimination.

How do you solve the system if neither of the pairs of like terms in the equations have the same or opposite coefficients?

(A) Graph and label the following system of equations.
$$\begin{cases} 2x - y = 1 \\ 4x + 4y = 8 \end{cases}$$

(B) The solution to the system is $\boxed{?}$.

(C) When both sides of an equation are multiplied by the same value, is the equation still true?
$\boxed{?}$

(D) Multiply both sides of the first equation by 2.

(E) Write the resulting system of equations.
$\boxed{?}$

$$4x + 4y = 8$$

(F) Graph and label the new system of equations.
Solution: $\boxed{?}$

(G) Can the new system of equations be solved using elimination now that $4x$ appears in each equation? $\boxed{?}$

Reflect

1. **Discussion** How are the graphs of $2x - y = 1$ and $4x - 2y = 2$ related?

2. **Discussion** How are the equations $2x - y = 1$ and $4x - 2y = 2$ related?

⊘ Explore 2 Proving the Elimination Method with Multiplication

The previous example illustrated that rewriting a system of equations by multiplying a constant term by one of the equations does not change the solutions for the system. What happens if a new system of equations is written by adding this new equation to the untouched equation from the original system?

(A) Original System → New System

$$\begin{cases} 2x - y = 1 \\ 4x + 4y = 8 \end{cases} \rightarrow \begin{cases} 4x - 2y = 2 \\ 4x + 4y = 8 \end{cases}$$

Add the equations in the new system.

$4x - 2y = 2$
$\underline{4x + 4y = 8}$

$\boxed{?}$

(B) Write a new system of equations using this new equation.

$$\begin{cases} 2x - y = 1 \\ \boxed{?} \end{cases}$$

(C) Graph and label the equations from this new system of equations.

(D) Is the solution to this new system of equations the same as the solution to the original system of equations? Explain $\boxed{?}$.

(E) If the original system is $Ax + By = C$ and $Dx + Ey = F$, where A, B, C, D, E, and F are constants, then multiply the second equation by a nonzero constant k to get $kDx + kEy = kF$. Add this new equation to $Ax + By = C$.

$$\begin{array}{c}
\quad Ax + \qquad\quad By = \quad C \\
+ \quad\quad \underline{kDx + \qquad\quad kEy = \quad kF} \\
\boxed{?} + \quad \boxed{?} = \boxed{?}
\end{array}$$

(F) So, the original system is $\begin{cases} Ax + By = C \\ Dx + Ey = F \end{cases}$, and the new system is

$$\begin{cases} Ax + By = C \\ \boxed{?} \end{cases}$$

(G) Let (x_1, y_1) be the solution to the original system. Fill in the missing parts of the following proof to show that (x_1, y_1) is also the solution to the new system.

(H) $Ax_1 + By_1 = \boxed{?}$ \qquad Given.

(I) $Dx_1 + Ey_1 = \boxed{?}$ \qquad Given.

© Houghton Mifflin Harcourt Publishing Company

Ⓙ $\boxed{?}(Dx_1 + Ey_1) = kF$ $\boxed{?}$ Property of Equality

Ⓚ $kDx_1 + kEy_1 = kF$ $\boxed{?}$

Ⓛ $\boxed{?} + kDx_1 + kEy_1 = C + kF$ $\boxed{?}$ Property of Equality

Ⓜ $Ax_1 + \boxed{?} + kDx_1 + kEy_1 = C + kF$ Substitute $Ax_1 + \boxed{?}$ for $\boxed{?}$ on the left.

Ⓝ $Ax_1 + \boxed{?} + By_1 + kEy_1 = C + kF$ $\boxed{?}$ Property of Addition

Ⓞ $(Ax_1 + kDx_1) + (By_1 + kEy_1) = C + kF$ $\boxed{?}$ Property of Addition

Ⓟ $(A + kD)x_1 + \left(\boxed{?}\right)y_1 = C + kF$ $\boxed{?}$

Ⓠ   Therefore, (x_1, y_1) is the solution to the new system.

Reflect

3. **Discussion** Is a proof required using subtraction? What about division?

🎷 Explain 1   Solving Linear Systems by Multiplying First

In some systems of linear equations, neither variable can be eliminated by adding or subtracting the equations directly. In these systems, you need to multiply one or both equations by a constant so that adding or subtracting the equations will eliminate one or more of the variables.

Steps for Solving a System of Equations by Multiplying First
1.   Decide which variable to eliminate.
2.   Multiply one or both equations by a constant so that adding or subtracting the equations will eliminate the variable.
3.   Solve the system using the elimination method.

Example 1 Solve each system of equations by multiplying. Check the answers by graphing the systems of equations.

Ⓐ $\begin{cases} 3x + 8y = 7 \\ 2x - 2y = -10 \end{cases}$

Multiply the second equation by 4.

$4(2x - 2y = -10) \Rightarrow 8x - 8y = -40$

Add the result to the first equation.

$$\begin{array}{r} 3x + 8y = 7 \\ + \ 8x - 8y = -40 \\ \hline 11x = -33 \end{array}$$

Solve for x.

$11x = -33$

$x = -3$

Substitute -3 for x in one of the original equations, and solve for y.

$3x + 8y = 7$

$3(-3) + 8y = 7$

$-9 + 8y = 7$

$8y = 16$

$y = 2$

The solution to the system is $(-3, 2)$.

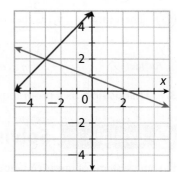

Ⓑ $\begin{cases} -3x + 2y = 4 \\ 4x - 13y = 5 \end{cases}$

Multiply the first equation by 4 and multiply the second equation by 3 so the x terms in the system have coefficients of -12 and 12 respectively.

$\boxed{4} \ (-3x + 2y = 4)$ $-12x + \boxed{8} \ y = \boxed{16}$

$\qquad\qquad\qquad\qquad\quad \Rightarrow$

$\boxed{3} \ (4x - 13y = 5)$ $12x - \boxed{39} \ y = \boxed{15}$

Add the resulting equations.

$-12x + \boxed{8} \ y = \boxed{16}$

$+12x - \boxed{39} \ y = \boxed{15}$

$\rule{4cm}{0.4pt}$

$\boxed{-31} \ y = \boxed{31}$

Solve for y.

$\boxed{-31} \ y = \boxed{31}$

$y = \boxed{-1}$

Solve the first equation for x when $y = \boxed{-1}$.

$$-3x + 2y = 4$$

$$-3x + 2\left(\boxed{-1}\right) = 4$$

$$-3x + \boxed{-2} = 4$$

$$-3x = \boxed{6}$$

$$x = \boxed{-2}$$

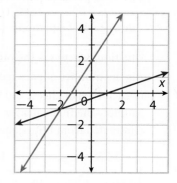

The solution to the system is $\boxed{(-2, -1)}$.

Your Turn

Solve each system of equations by multiplying. Check the answers by graphing the systems of equations.

4. $\begin{cases} -3x + 4y = 12 \\ 2x + y = -8 \end{cases}$

5. $\begin{cases} 2x + 3y = -1 \\ 5x - 2y = -12 \end{cases}$

🔧 Explain 2   Solving Linear System Models by Multiplying First

You can solve a linear system of equations that models a real-world example by multiplying first.

Example 2   Solve each problem by multiplying first.

(A) Jessica spent $16.30 to buy 16 flowers. The bouquet contained daisies, which cost $1.75 each, and tulips, which cost $0.85 each. The system of equations $\begin{cases} d + t = 16 \\ 1.75d + 0.85t = 16.30 \end{cases}$ models this situation, where d is the number of daisies and t is the number of tulips. How many of each type of flower did Jessica buy? Multiply the first equation by -0.85 to eliminate t from each equation. Then, add the equations.

$$\begin{cases} -0.85(d + t) = -0.85(16) \\ 1.75d + 0.85t = 16.30 \end{cases} \Rightarrow$$

$$\begin{array}{rcl} -0.85d - 0.85t &=& -13.60 \\ +1.75d + 0.85t &=& 16.30 \\ \hline 0.9d &=& 2.70 \\ d &=& 3 \end{array}$$

Find t. $d + t = 16$

$$3 + t = 16$$

$$t = 13 \qquad \text{The solution is } (3, 13).$$

Jessica bought 3 daisies and 13 tulips.

(B) The Tran family is bringing 15 packages of cheese to a group picnic. Cheese slices cost $2.50 per package. Cheese cubes cost $1.75 per package. The Tran family spent a total of $30 on cheese.

The system of equations $\begin{cases} s + c = 15 \\ 2.50s + 1.75c = 30 \end{cases}$ represents this

situation, where s is the number of packages of cheese slices and c is the number of packages of cheese cubes. How many packages of each type of cheese did the Tran family buy?

Multiply the first equation by a constant so that c can be eliminated from both equations, and then subtract the equations.

$$\begin{cases} \boxed{1.75}\ (s + c) = \boxed{1.75}\ (15) \\ 2.50s + 1.75c = 30 \end{cases} \Rightarrow \begin{array}{l} \boxed{1.75}\ s + \boxed{1.75}\ c = \boxed{26.25} \\ \underline{-(2.50s + 1.75c\ )\qquad\quad = -30} \\ \boxed{-0.75}\ s \qquad\qquad\quad = \boxed{-3.75} \\ \qquad\qquad\qquad\qquad s = \boxed{5} \end{array}$$

Find c.
$$\begin{array}{l} s + c = 15 \\ \boxed{5} + c = 15 \\ c = \boxed{10} \end{array}$$

The solution is $\boxed{(5,\ 10)}$.

The Tran family bought 5 packages of sliced cheese and 10 packages of cheese cubes.

Your Turn

6. Jacob's family bought 4 adult tickets and 2 student tickets to the school play for $64. Tatianna's family bought 3 adult tickets and 3 students tickets for $60. The system of equations $\begin{cases} 4a + 2s = 64 \\ 3a + 3s = 60 \end{cases}$ models this situation, where a is the cost of an adult ticket and s is the cost of a student ticket. How much does each type of ticket cost?

💬 Elaborate

7. When would you solve a system of linear equations by multiplying?

8. How can you use multiplication to solve a system of linear equations if none of the coefficients are multiples or factors of any of the other coefficients?

9. **Essential Question Check-In** How do you solve a system of equations by multiplying?

For each linear equation,

   a. find the product of 3 and the linear equation;

   b. solve both equations for y.

1. $2y - 4x = 8$ **2.** $-5y + 7x = 12$

3. $4x + 7y = 18$ **4.** $x - 2y = 13$

For each linear system, multiply the first equation by 2 and add the new equation to the second equation. Then, graph this new equation along with both of the original equations.

5. $\begin{cases} 2x + 4y = 24 \\ -12x + 8y = -16 \end{cases}$ **6.** $\begin{cases} 2x + 2y = 16 \\ -15x + 3y = -12 \end{cases}$

Solve each system of linear equations by multiplying. Verify each answer by graphing the system of equations.

7. $\begin{cases} 5x - 2y = 11 \\ 3x + 5y = 19 \end{cases}$ **8.** $\begin{cases} -2x + 2y = 2 \\ -4x + 7y = 16 \end{cases}$

9. $\begin{cases} 3x + 4y = 13 \\ 2x - 2y = -10 \end{cases}$ **10.** $\begin{cases} x - 4y = -1 \\ 5x + 2y = 17 \end{cases}$

Solve each system of linear equations using multiplication.

11. $\begin{cases} -3x + 2y = 4 \\ 5x - 3y = 1 \end{cases}$ **12.** $\begin{cases} 3x + 3y = 12 \\ 6x + 11y = 14 \end{cases}$

Solve each problem by multiplying first.

13. The sum of two angles is 180°. The difference between twice the larger angle and three times the smaller angle is 150°. The system of equations $\begin{cases} x + y = 180 \\ 2x - 3y = 150 \end{cases}$ models this situation, where x is the measure of the larger angle and y is the measure of the smaller angle. What is the measure of each angle?

14. The perimeter of a rectangular swimming pool is 126 feet. The difference between the length and the width is 39 feet. The system of equations $\begin{cases} 2x + 2y = 126 \\ x - y = 39 \end{cases}$ models this situation, where x is the length of the pool and y is the width of the pool. Find the dimensions of the swimming pool.

15. Jamian bought a total of 40 bagels and donuts for a morning meeting. He paid a total of $33.50. Each donut cost $0.65 and each bagel cost $1.15. The system of equations $\begin{cases} b + d = 40 \\ 1.15b + 0.65d = 33.50 \end{cases}$ models this situation, where b is the number of bagels and d is the number of donuts. How many of each did Jamian buy?

16. A clothing store is having a sale on shirts and jeans. 4 shirts and 2 pairs of jeans cost $64. 3 shirts and 3 pairs of jeans cost $72. The system of equations $\begin{cases} 4s + 2j = 64 \\ 3s + 3j = 72 \end{cases}$ models this situation, where s is the cost of a shirt and j is the cost of a pair of jeans. How much does one shirt and one pair of jeans cost?

17. Jayce bought 5 bath towels and returned 2 hand towels. His sister Jayna bought 3 bath towels and returned 4 hand towels. Jayce paid a total of $124 and Jayna paid a total of $24. The system of equations $\begin{cases} 5b - 2h = 124 \\ 3b - 4h = 24 \end{cases}$ models this situation, where b is the price of a bath towel and h is the price of a hand towel. How much does each kind of towel cost?

18. Apples cost $0.95 per pound and bananas cost $1.10 per pound. Leah bought a total of 8 pounds of apples and bananas for $8.05.

The system of equations $\begin{cases} a + b = 8 \\ 0.95a + 1.10b = 8.05 \end{cases}$ models this situation, where a is the number of pounds of apples and b is the number of pounds of bananas. How many pounds of each did Leah buy?

19. Which of the following are possible ways to eliminate a variable by multiplying first?

$\begin{cases} -x + 2y = 3 \\ 4x - 5y = -3 \end{cases}$

    a. Multiply the first equation by 4.

    b. Multiply the first equation by 5 and the second equation by 2.

    c. Multiply the first equation by 4 and the second equation by 2.

    d. Multiply the first equation by 5 and the second equation by 4.

    e. Multiply the first equation by 2 and the second equation by 5.

    f. Multiply the second equation by 4.

20. Explain the Error A linear system has two equations $Ax + By = C$ and $Dx + Ey = F$. A student begins to solve the equation as shown. What is the error?

$$Ax + By = C$$

$$\underline{+ \, k(Dx + Ey) = F}$$

$$(A + kD)x + (B + kE)y = C + F$$

21. Critical Thinking Suppose you want to eliminate y in this system: $\begin{cases} 2x + 11y = -3 \\ 3x + 4y = 8 \end{cases}$

By what numbers would you need to multiply the two equations in order to eliminate y? Why might you choose to eliminate x instead?

H.O.T. Focus on Higher Order Thinking

22. Justify Reasoning Solve the following system of equations by multiplying.

$\begin{cases} x + 3y = -14 \\ 2x + y = -3 \end{cases}$ Would it be easier to solve the system by using substitution? Explain your reasoning.

23. Multi-Step The school store is running a promotion on school supplies. Different supplies are placed on two shelves. You can purchase 3 items from shelf A and 2 from shelf B for $16. Or you can purchase 2 items from shelf A and 3 from shelf B for $14. This can be represented by the following system of equations.

a. Solve the system of equations $\begin{cases} 3A + 2B = 16 \\ 2A + 3B = 14 \end{cases}$ by multiplying first.

b. If the supplies on shelf A are normally $6 each and the supplies on shelf B are normally $3 each, how much will you save on each package plan from part A?

Lesson Performance Task

A chemist has a bottle of 1% acid solution and a bottle of 5% acid solution. She wants to mix the two solutions to get 100 mL of a 4% acid solution.

a. Copy and complete the table to write the system of equations.

	1% Solution	+	5% Solution	=	4% Solution
Amount of Solution (mL)	x	+	y	=	?
Amount of Acid (mL)	$0.01x$	+	?	=	$0.04(100)$

b. Solve the system of equations to find how much she will use from each bottle to get 100 mL of a 4% acid solution.

Solving Systems of Linear Equations

Essential Question: How can you use a system of linear equations to solve real-world problems?

Key Vocabulary

elimination method
  (*eliminación*)
substitution method
  (*sustitución*)
system of linear equations
  (*sistema de ecuaciones lineales*)

KEY EXAMPLE   (*Lesson 11.2*)

Solve $\begin{cases} 4x + y = 7 \\ -6x + y = -3 \end{cases}$ **by substitution.**

Solve an equation for one variable.

$-6x + y = -3$ Select one of the equations.

$y = 6x - 3$ Solve for y. Isolate y on one side.

Substitute the expression for y in the other equation and solve.

$4x + (6x - 3) = 7$ Substitute the expression for y.

$10x - 3 = 7$ Combine like terms.

$10x = 10$ Add 3 to both sides.

$x = 1$ Divide each side by 10.

Substitute the value for x into one of the equations and solve for y.

$4(1) + y = 7$ Substitute the value of x into the first equation.

$4 + y = 7$ Simplify.

$y = 3$ Subtract 4 from both sides.

So, $(1, 3)$ is the solution of the system.

KEY EXAMPLE   (*Lesson 11.3*)

Solve $\begin{cases} -6x + 8y = 19 \\ 6x - 8y = -19 \end{cases}$ **by adding.**

Add the equations.

$-6x + 8y = 19$

$+6x - 8y = -19$

$\overline{ 0 + 0 = 0}$

$0 = 0$

The resulting equation is always true, so the system has infinitely many solutions.

EXERCISES

Solve each system of equations. *(Lessons 11.1, 11.2, 11.3, 11.4)*

1. $\begin{cases} 3x + 7y = -5 \\ 8x + 9y = 6 \end{cases}$

2. $\begin{cases} -5x + 2y = 13 \\ 3x - 2y = -11 \end{cases}$

3. $\begin{cases} 9x - 2y = -5 \\ -6x + y = -1 \end{cases}$

4. $\begin{cases} 7x - 9y = -11 \\ 7x - y = -9 \end{cases}$

5. $\begin{cases} -3x + 5y = 8 \\ 3x - 5y = -8 \end{cases}$

6. $\begin{cases} -2x + 6y = 6 \\ -4x - 8y = 12 \end{cases}$

MODULE PERFORMANCE TASK

Do Hybrid Cars Pay for Themselves?

Your family wants to buy a specific model of new car and is considering buying the hybrid version. Use the information shown for the two cars to determine how long it will take to save enough money on gas to pay for the extra cost of the hybrid. Then make a recommendation on which car to buy.

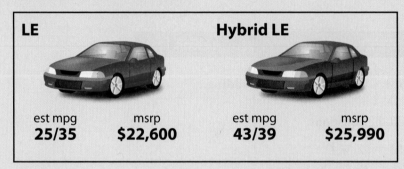

LE		Hybrid LE	
est mpg	msrp	est mpg	msrp
25/35	**$22,600**	**43/39**	**$25,990**

Start by listing the information you will need to solve the problem. Be sure to write down all your data and assumptions. Then use graphs, numbers, words, or algebra to explain how you reached your conclusion.

(Ready) to Go On?

11.1–11.4 Solving Systems of Linear Equations

- Online Homework
- Hints and Help
- Extra Practice

Solve each system of equations using the given method. *(Lessons 11.1, 11.2, 11.3, 11.4)*

1. $\begin{cases} -3x + y = 6 \\ 5x + 2y = 23 \end{cases}$; substitution

2. $\begin{cases} -4x + 9y = 14 \\ 12x - 10y = -8 \end{cases}$; multiplication

3. $\begin{cases} 7x + 2y = 8 \\ -5x - 2y = -12 \end{cases}$; addition

4. $\begin{cases} 6x - 12y = 15 \\ 2x - 4y = 6 \end{cases}$; multiplication

5. $\begin{cases} 5x - 3y = 3 \\ 3x - y = 9 \end{cases}$; graphing

6. $\begin{cases} 9x - 2y = 8 \\ -2x + 2y = 6 \end{cases}$; addition

ESSENTIAL QUESTION

7. When must a system of linear equations be solved algebraically, not graphically?

Assessment Readiness

1. A system of equations is represented on the graph. Tell whether each equation is part of the system.

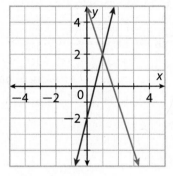

   A. $3x + y = 5$

   B. $2x + 3y = 8$

   C. $-8x + 2y = -4$

2. Consider the lines and solution set of the system of equations $\begin{cases} -8x - 6y = 8 \\ 4x + 3y = 2 \end{cases}$.

   Determine if each of the following statements is True or False.

   A. The lines have the same y-intercept.

   B. The lines have the same slope.

   C. The system has no solutions.

3. Solve the system of equations $\begin{cases} 5x + y = 10 \\ 2x + 3y = -9 \end{cases}$. Explain how you solved this system.

4. The perimeter of a picture frame is 68 inches. The difference between the length of the frame and three times its width is 2. The system of equations $\begin{cases} 2\ell + 2W = 68 \\ 2\ell - 6W = 4 \end{cases}$ represents this situation, where ℓ represents the length in inches and W represents the width in inches. What is the width of the frame? What is the length of the frame?

Modeling with Linear Systems

Essential Question: How can you model with linear systems to solve real-world problems?

REAL WORLD VIDEO
When you're playing an arcade game, chances are that you don't have math on your mind. But you might be surprised to find that mathematical reasoning can sometimes help you figure out the best strategy for the winning the game.

MODULE PERFORMANCE TASK PREVIEW
How to Win at an Arcade Game

Many arcades have a game that is somewhat like bowling. Players roll a hand-sized ball up an inclined lane so that the ball lands in one of several different holes, each with varying point values. The goal is to collect as many points as possible. How can you use mathematics to help you win at this game? Let's find out!

Are (YOU) Ready?

Complete these exercises to review skills you will need for this module.

One-Step Inequalities

Example 1   Solve.

$$x + 13 \leq 9$$
$$x + 13 - 13 \leq 9 - 13$$
$$x \leq -4$$

Isolate the variable by subtracting 13 from both sides of the inequality.

Solve each inequality.

1. $k - 12 \geq 5$

2. $y + 2 < -9$

3. $\dfrac{n}{4} > -7$

Two-Step Equations and Inequalities

Example 2   Solve.

$$4b - 19 = 17$$
$$4b - 19 + 19 = 17 + 19$$ Add 19 to both sides of the equation.
$$4b = 36$$
$$\dfrac{4b}{4} = \dfrac{36}{4}$$ Divide both sides of the equation by 4.
$$b = 9$$

Solve each equation.

4. $3a + 17 = 38$

5. $27 - 5c = 12$

6. $\dfrac{3}{4}m - 8 = 10$

Example 3   Solve.

$$11 - 7t < 67$$
$$11 - 11 - 7t < 67 - 11$$ Subtract 11 from both sides of the inequality.
$$-7t < 56$$
$$\dfrac{-7t}{-7} > \dfrac{56}{-7}$$ Divide both sides of the inequality by –7.
$$t > -8$$ Reverse the inequality symbol.

Solve each inequality.

7. $9p + 23 < 41$

8. $-6w - 16 \geq 44$

9. $\dfrac{v}{3} + 12 > 7$

12.1 Creating Systems of Linear Equations

Essential Question: How do you use systems of linear equations to model and solve real-world problems?

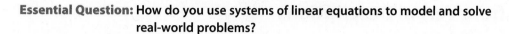

Explore   Creating Linear System Models by Changing Parameters

Investigate how a system of equations can help you compare and interpret situations where rates of change affect the outcome.

After leaving her hotel, a student is walking to a café to have breakfast and do some sightseeing. On the way, she passes two stores that rent bicycles. The first shop charges an initial fee of $7.00 and $2.75 for each hour. The second shop charges a flat fee of $3.00 per hour. Over breakfast, the student needs to decide which rental agency to use. How should she start?

(A) Begin by finding functions that represent the cost of each rental. Let $f(t)$ represent the cost of renting a bicycle for t hours from the first shop, and let $g(t)$ represent the cost of renting a bicycle from the second shop.

(B) What is the initial cost of renting a bicycle from the first shop? ❓

(C) This represents the ❓ of the model for the first business.

(D) The slope of this linear model represents the ❓ of the cost, as a function of time.

(E) The slope of the first model is ❓ .

(F) This makes $f(t) =$ ❓ .

(G) Similarly, the function modeling the cost for renting a bicycle from the second shop is $g(t) =$ ❓ .

(H) Once the student decides the length of time she plans to spend on her bike ride, she can solve the linear system of the two functions, ❓ ❓ , to determine from which company she wants to rent a bicycle.

Reflect

1. **Discussion** Under what conditions would this type of real-world situation have no solution?

2. **Discussion** Under what conditions would this type of real-world situation have infinitely many solutions?

 Explain 1 **Creating Linear System Models from Verbal Descriptions**

Often, a company will charge a start-up fee for its services, followed by a monthly or per unit cost. This can be written as a linear function in slope-intercept form.

When the costs of the same services from two different companies must be compared, the variable amount for each must represent the same thing, and both models should produce values with the same type of unit. For example, if one function models yearly income in terms of thousands of dollars and the other function models monthly income in terms of hundreds of dollars, the comparison will not be accurate.

Example 1 **Determine when the cost of the two services will be the same amount, and what the price will be.**

Video streaming service Atomic Stream charges $10 for membership and $1.00 for each movie download. Blitz Video charges $15 for a membership and $0.50 per movie download. How many movies would you need to download for the services to have identical costs? What is that cost?

 Analyze Information

Identify the important information.

Atomic Stream has a $10 membership fee.

Atomic Stream has a $1 per download fee.

Blitz Video has a $15 membership fee.

Blitz Video has a $0.50 per download fee.

 Formulate a Plan

Create two functions to model the cost of each service, $A(x)$ and $B(x)$, where x represents the number of videos downloaded.

The solution can be found by setting up an equation so that the function $A(x)$ is equal to the function $B(x)$ and then solving for x.

Solve

The model for Atomic Stream is $A(x) = \boxed{10 + x}$.

The model for Blitz Video is $B(x) = \boxed{15 + 0.5x}$.

The two functions are $\begin{cases} A(x) = 10 + x \\ B(x) = 15 + 0.5x \end{cases}$.

Solve using substitution. You can use substitution because you are solving for the value where $A(x) \boxed{=} B(x)$.

$$\boxed{10+x} \boxed{=} \boxed{15+0.5x} \qquad\qquad A(x) = \boxed{10+x}$$

$$0.5x = 5 \qquad\qquad\qquad\qquad A\left(\boxed{10}\right) = \boxed{10+10}$$

$$x = \boxed{10} \qquad\qquad\qquad\qquad\qquad = \boxed{20}$$

The cost of each service is $20 when 10 movies are screened.

Justify and Evaluate

It is reasonable to expect the cost of the services to be the same after a number of uses. The businesses are in the same market but can appeal to different customers.

Atomic Stream is more affordable for customers who stream less than 10 movies a month, while Blitz Video is a better deal for people who stream more than 10 movies a month.

Your Turn

Determine when the cost of the two services will be the same amount, and what the price will be.

3. One cable television provider has a $60 setup fee and charges $80 per month, and another cable provider has a $160 equipment fee and charges $70 per month.

4. The Strauss family is deciding between two lawn-care services. Green Lawn charges a $49 startup fee plus $29 per month. Yard Guard charges a $25 startup fee plus $37 per month.

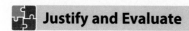 Explain 2 — Creating Linear System Models from Tables

Sometimes, there is not enough information to model an equation. Businesses may have a table of rates posted to explain their pricing. To compare the cost of items or services from two or more businesses, table entries can be used to create and solve a linear system.

Example 2 **Use the cost tables for two services to create a linear system of equations. Then solve the system to determine when the cost of the two services will be equal.**

(A) Two garden supply companies deliver mulch according to the following table.

Mulch (Cubic Yards)	Yard Depot	Lawn & Garden
1	$60	$80
2	$90	$105
3	$120	$130
4	$150	$155

© Houghton Mifflin Harcourt Publishing Company

Yard Depot	Lawn & Garden
Use points $(1, 60)$ and $(2, 90)$.	Use points $(1, 80)$ and $(2, 105)$.
$m = \dfrac{90 - 60}{2 - 1} = 30$	$m = \dfrac{105 - 80}{2 - 1} = 25$
Write the equation.	Write the equation.
$y - 60 = 30(x - 1)$	$y - 80 = 25(x - 1)$
$y = 30x + 30$	$y = 25x + 55$

The system of equations is: $\begin{cases} f(x) = 30s + 30 \\ g(x) = 25x + 55 \end{cases}$

Solve for x when $f(x) = g(x)$ to find the amount of cubic yards, x, for which both companies charge the same amount.

$$30s + 30 = 25x + 55$$

$$x = 5 \Rightarrow f(5) = 30(5) + 30 = 180$$

Both companies charge $180 for 5 cubic yards of mulch.

(B) The table shows canoe rental prices for two companies.

Time t (in hours)	Canoe Depot	Paddle and Oar
1	$14	$20
2	$19	$23
3	$24	$26

Canoe Depot	Paddle & Oar
Use points $\left(1, \boxed{14}\right)$ and $\left(2, \boxed{19}\right)$.	Use points $\left(1, \boxed{20}\right)$ and $\left(2, \boxed{23}\right)$.
$m = \dfrac{\boxed{19} - \boxed{14}}{2 - 1} = \boxed{5}$	$m = \dfrac{\boxed{23} - \boxed{20}}{2 - 1} = \boxed{3}$
Write the equation.	Write the equation.
$y - \boxed{14} = \boxed{5}(x - 1)$	$y - \boxed{20} = \boxed{3}(x - 1)$
$y = \boxed{5}x + \boxed{9}$	$y = \boxed{3}x + \boxed{17}$

The system of equations is $\begin{cases} C(x) = \boxed{5}x + \boxed{9} \\ P(x) = \boxed{3}x + \boxed{17} \end{cases}$

Solve for x when $C(x) = P(x)$ to find the number of hours, x, for which both canoe rental places charge the same amount.

$$\boxed{5}x + \boxed{9} = \boxed{3}x + \boxed{17}$$

$$x = \boxed{4} \Rightarrow C\left(\boxed{4}\right) = \boxed{29}$$

Both companies charge $ \boxed{29} for \boxed{4} hours of canoe rental.

Use the cost tables for two services to create a linear system of equations. Then solve the system to determine when the cost of the two services will be equal.

5. Two garden supply companies deliver pea stone according to the following table.

Pea Stone x (in cubic yards)	Yard Depot	Lawn & Garden
1	$75	$45
2	$110	$85
3	$145	$125

6. Two beachfront stores rent surfboards according to the following table.

Time t (in hours)	Hang Ten	Waverider
1	$28	$46
2	$48	$63
3	$68	$80
4	$88	$97

🔑 Explain 3 Creating Linear System Models from Graphs

In newspapers and magazines, information is often displayed in the form of a graph. You can use the graph of a linear system to write the function models that are represented.

Example 3 Use the graph to make a linear model of each function. Describe the meaning of the terms in the models. Then create the linear system, and state what the solution represents.

Ⓐ

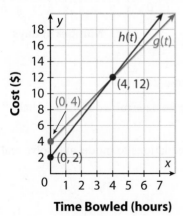

$g(x)$	$h(x)$
The y-intercept b is 4. Initial cost is $4. Use $(0, 4)$ and $(4, 12)$: $$m = \frac{12 - 4}{4 - 0} = 2$$ Charge per hour: $2.00/h $y = 2x + 4$	The y-intercept b is 2. Initial cost is $2. Use $(0, 2)$ and $(4, 12)$: $$m = \frac{12 - 2}{4 - 0} = 2.5$$ Charge per hour: $2.50/h $y = 2.5x + 2$

The system of equations is: $\begin{cases} g(x) = 2x + 4 \\ h(x) = 2.5x + 2 \end{cases}$

The solution $(4, 12)$ represents the same charge of $12 for 4 hours that both bowling alleys charge.

Ⓑ

Cost ($) (y-axis) vs **Trail Mix (pounds)** (x-axis)

Graph showing g(x) and f(x) with points (0, 8), (0, 1), and (7, 15).

$f(x)$	$g(x)$
The *y*-intercept *b* is 8 .	The *y*-intercept *b* is 1 .
Initial cost is $ 8 .	Initial cost is $ 1 .
Use $\left(0, \boxed{8}\right)$ and $(7, 15)$:	Use $\left(0, \boxed{1}\right)$ and $(7, 15)$:
$m = \dfrac{15 - \boxed{8}}{\boxed{7} - 0} = \boxed{1}$	$m = \dfrac{15 - \boxed{1}}{7 - 0} = \boxed{2}$
Rate of change: $ 1 /lb	Rate of change: $ 2 /lb
$y = \boxed{1}\,x + \boxed{8}$	$y = \boxed{2}\,x + \boxed{1}$

The system of equations is $\begin{cases} f(x) = \boxed{1}\,x + \boxed{8} \\ g(x) = \boxed{2}\,x + \boxed{1} \end{cases}$

The solution (7, 15) represents the same charge of $ 15 for 7 pounds of trail mix.

Your Turn

7. Use the graph to make a linear model of each function. Describe the meaning of terms in the models. Then create the linear system and state what the solution represents.

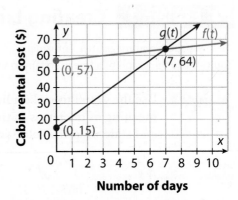

Cabin rental cost ($) (y-axis) vs **Number of days** (x-axis). Graph showing g(t) and f(t) with points (0, 57), (0, 15), and (7, 64).

💬 **Elaborate**

8. When writing a linear model of a situation, what does the slope represent?

9. **Discussion** Compare and contrast the system of equations that can be determined from a verbal description of a relationship, a table of values, and a graph.

10. **Essential Question Check-In** How do you use systems of linear equations to model and solve real-world problems?

• Online Homework
• Hints and Help
• Extra Practice

1. In the graph shown, what do the parameters of each line represent?

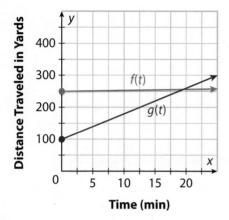

Set up and solve a system of equations to solve the problem.

2. Casey wants to buy a gym membership. One gym has a $150 joining fee and costs $35 per month. Another gym has no joining fee and costs $60 per month. When would Casey pay the same amount to be a member of either gym? How much would he pay?

3. A jar contains n nickels and d dimes. There are 20 coins in the jar, and the total value of the coins is $1.40. How many nickels and how many dimes are in the jar?

4. Helene invested a total of $1000 in two simple-interest bank accounts. One account paid 5% annual interest; the other paid 6% annual interest. The total amount of interest she earned after 1 year was $58. Find the amount invested in each account.

5. A local boys club sold 176 bags of mulch and made a total of $520. It sold two types of mulch: hardwood for $3.50 a bag and pine bark for $2.75 a bag. How many bags of each kind of mulch did it sell?

6. The school band sells carnations on Valentine's Day for $2 each. It buys the carnations from a florist for $0.50 each, plus a $16 delivery charge. When will the cost of the carnations be equal to the revenue from selling them? How many carnations does it need to sell to reach this point?

Use the given cost tables for the same product from two different companies to create a linear system. Then solve the system to determine when the cost of the product will be the same and what the price will be.

7. Two online spice retailers sell paprika by the pound using the following pricing chart.

Paprika (lb)	iSpice	Spice Magic
1	$15.75	$26.25
2	$27.50	$36.50
3	$39.25	$46.75
4	$51	$57

8. Two online retailers sell organic vanilla extract by the ounce using the following pricing chart.

Vanilla Extract (oz)	Chef Mate	Grocery Gourmet
2	$12.50	$17
3	$17.25	$21
4	$22	$25
5	$26.75	$29

9. Two dry cleaning companies offer a home pick-up and delivery service. The monthly cost depends on the number of garments laundered, and is shown in the following table.

Number of Garments	Company 1	Company 2
5	$55.25	$31.25
10	$75.50	$57.50
15	$95.75	$83.75

10. A small town in the mountains needs to buy road salt for the coming winter. It has found two companies that use the following pricing table.

Road Salt (tons)	Company 1	Company 2
5	$1775	$2750
10	$3350	$4000
15	$4925	$5250

11. A restaurant needs to stock paper towels in its kitchen and bathrooms. It has found two vendors using the following case price chart.

Paper Towels (cases)	Restaurant Warehouse	Supply Side
5	$300.20	$220.20
10	$480.15	$420.15
15	$660.10	$620.10

Use the graph to make a linear model of each function. Describe the meaning of the terms in the models. Then create the linear system, and state what the solution represents.

12.

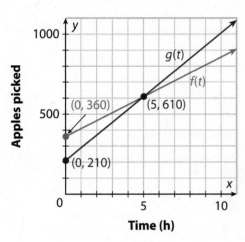

13.

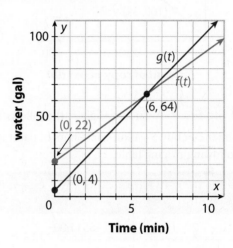

14.

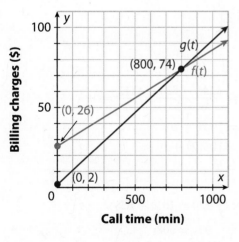

15.

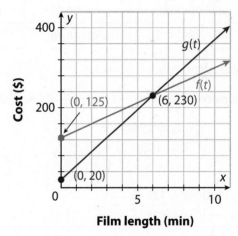

16. Two office supply stores sell their brand of copy paper by the pound. One company offers a flat rate shipping charge and the other offers free shipping. Use the graph provided to construct a linear system to model this situation. Solve the system to determine the amount of copy paper for which the cost is the same at both stores. Use the graph to verify that your answer is reasonable.

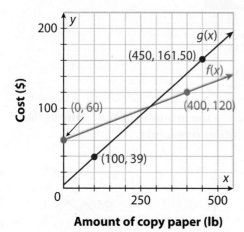

17. Find the Error A student is given the following problem:

A painter can buy 5-gallon containers of paint from two different stores based on the following pricing table.

Containers of Paint	Company A	Company B
2	$512.00	$422.00
4	$904.00	$834.00
6	$1296.00	$1246.00
8	$1688.00	$1658.00

The student's work is shown.

Company A: $m = \dfrac{904 - 512}{4 - 2} = \dfrac{392}{2} = 196$ Company B: $m = \dfrac{1246 - 834}{6 - 2} = \dfrac{412}{4} = 103$

$$A(x) = 196x + b$$
$$512 = 196(2) + b$$
$$120 = b$$

$$B(x) = 103x + b$$
$$834 = 103(2) + b$$
$$628 = b$$

$$\begin{cases} A(x) = 196x + 120 \\ B(x) = 103x + 628 \end{cases}$$

$$196x + 120 = 103x + 628$$
$$93x = 508$$
$$x = 5.5$$

The student knows that the function values for Company A would be less than those of Company B for x-values greater than that of the intersection. This is not true if the x-coordinate of the intersection is 5.5, so he concludes that his results must contain an error. Find the error and the correct solution.

18. Two friends, Jorge and Mark, are taking a trip to the mountains for a camping trip, but they are not leaving together. Both friends separately record the distance they each have traveled from home every hour on the second day. The distance each friend is from his home can be modeled by a linear function of the hours spent traveling. Determine if the linear system created by the models for each situation has a unique solution with a positive value for time.

    a. Jorge and Mark traveled the same distance on the first day and they are traveling at the same speed on the second day.

    b. Jorge travels 25 miles on the first day and drives 65 miles per hour on the second day. Mark travels 100 miles on the first day and also drives 65 miles per hour on the second day.

    c. Jorge travels 25 miles on the first day and drives 65 miles per hour on the second day. Mark travels 100 miles on the first day and drives 45 miles per hour on the second day.

    d. Jorge traveled 45 miles on the first day and drives 55 miles per hour on the second day. Mark arrived at the campsite on the first day after traveling 300 miles. Assume Jorge lives at least 300 miles from the campsite and that he keeps driving on the second day until he gets there.

    e. Jorge gets sick before the trip and doesn't get in touch with Mark. Mark travels 40 miles on the first day and drives 67 miles per hour on the second day.

19. **Communicate Mathematical Ideas** Given a set of data measuring the distance two planes have traveled after takeoff as a function of when they both passed over the same point, how would you find when they have both traveled the same distance since takeoff?

20. **Analyze Relationships** How can you use the slope and the *y*-intercept of each model in a linear system to determine whether or not there will be a solution?

Lesson Performance Task

A family is going on vacation and they need to bring their dog to a kennel. Alpha Kennel charges an initial fee of $75 and a daily rate of $30. Beta Kennel charges a flat fee of $34.95 a day. Find linear functions modeling the cost of boarding a dog for n days in each kennel. Set up and solve a system of linear equations. Then interpret the solution.

What if the family has two dogs? Alpha Kennel runs a special where you receive a 10% discount if you board more than one pet. Modify the linear models to give the price of boarding two dogs. Set up, solve, and interpret the linear system covering this case.

12.2 Graphing Systems of Linear Inequalities

Resource Locker

Essential Question: How do you solve a system of linear inequalities?

⊘ Explore   Determining Solutions of Systems of Linear Inequalities

A **system of linear inequalities** consists of two or more linear inequalities that have the same variables. The **solutions of a system of linear inequalities** are all the ordered pairs that make all the inequalities in the system true.

Solve the system of equations by graphing.

$$\begin{cases} x + 3y > 3 \\ -x + y \leq 6 \end{cases}$$

(A) First look at $x + 3y > 3$. The equation of the boundary line is   ? .

(B) What are the x-and y-intercepts?   ?

(C) The inequality symbol is $>$ so use a   ?   line.

(D) Shade   ?   the boundary line for solutions that are greater than the inequality.

(E) Graph $x + 3y > 3$.

(F) Look at $-x + y \leq 6$. The equation of the boundary line is   ? .

(G) What are the x-and y-intercepts?   ?

(H) The inequality symbol is $\leq$ so use a   ?   line.

(I) Shade   ?   the boundary line for solutions that are less than the inequality.

(J) Graph $-x + y \leq 6$ on the same graph as $x + 3y > 3$.

Ⓚ Identify the solutions. They are represented by the ⬚? shaded regions.

Ⓛ Check your answer by using a point in each region. Copy and complete the table.

Ordered Pair	Satisfies $x + 3y > 3$?	Satisfies $-x + y \leq 6$?	In the overlapping shaded regions?
(0, 0)	?	?	?
(2, 3)	?	?	?
(−8, 2)	?	?	?
(−4, 6)	?	?	?

Reflect

1. **Discussion** Why is (0, 0) a good point to use for checking the answer to this system of linear inequalities?

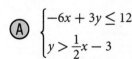

Solving Systems of Linear Inequalities by Graphing

You can use a graph of a system of linear inequalities to determine and identify solutions to the system of linear inequalities.

Example 1 Graph the system of linear inequalities. Give two ordered pairs that are solutions and two that are not solutions.

Ⓐ $\begin{cases} -6x + 3y \leq 12 \\ y > \frac{1}{2}x - 3 \end{cases}$

Solve the first inequality for y.   Graph the system.

$-6x + 3y \leq 12$ $\begin{cases} y \leq 2x + 4 \\ y > \frac{1}{2}x - 3 \end{cases}$
$\quad 3y \leq 6x + 12$
$\quad\quad y \leq 2x + 4$

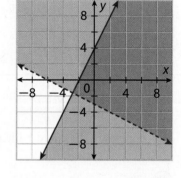

(0, 0) and (2, 8) are solutions. (−6, −4) and (−4, 4) are not solutions.

Ⓑ $\begin{cases} 3x + y \leq 1 \\ y > \frac{2}{3}x - 2 \end{cases}$

Solve the first inequality for y.   Graph the system.

$3x + y \leq 1$ $\begin{cases} y \leq \boxed{-3x + 1} \\ y > \frac{2}{3}x - 2 \end{cases}$
$\quad\quad y \leq \boxed{-3x + 1}$

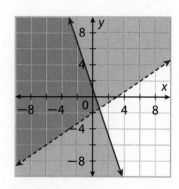

(0, 0) and (−8, 0) are solutions. (0, −8) and (4, 4) are not solutions.

Reflect

2. Is $(-6, -6)$ a solution of the system?

Your Turn

Graph the system of linear inequalities. Give two ordered pairs that are solutions and two that are not solutions.

3. $\begin{cases} y \le x + 3 \\ y < -3 \end{cases}$

4. $\begin{cases} y > x - 8 \\ 2x + 4y < 16 \end{cases}$

⚙ Explain 2 Graphing Systems of Inequalities with Parallel Boundary Lines

If the lines in a system of linear equations are parallel, there are no solutions. However, if the boundary lines in a system of linear inequalities are parallel, the system may or may not have solutions.

Example 2 Graph each system of linear inequalities. Describe the solutions.

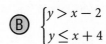

Ⓐ $\begin{cases} y < 4x - 3 \\ y > 4x + 2 \end{cases}$

Ⓑ $\begin{cases} y > x - 2 \\ y \le x + 4 \end{cases}$

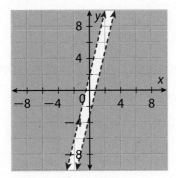

This system has no solution.

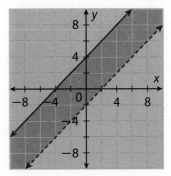

The solutions are all points between the parallel lines and on the solid line.

Your Turn

Graph each system of linear inequalities. Describe the solutions.

5. $\begin{cases} y \le -2x - 3 \\ y \le -2x + 1 \end{cases}$

6. $\begin{cases} y < \frac{1}{3}x - 6 \\ y \ge \frac{1}{3}x + 5 \end{cases}$

7. Is it possible for a system of two linear inequalities to have every point in the plane as solutions? Why or why not?

8. **Discussion** How would you write a system of linear inequalities from a graph?

9. **Essential Question Check-In** How does testing specific ordered pairs tell you that the solution you graphed is correct?

☆ Evaluate: Homework and Practice

1. Match the inequality with the correct boundary line. Answers may be used more than once.

- Online Homework
- Hints and Help
- Extra Practice

A. $y = 3x$

a. ___?___ $-x + 3y \leq 0$

B. $y = \frac{1}{3}x$

b. ___?___ $y > -x + \frac{1}{2}$

C. $y = x - 0.5$

c. ___?___ $y \leq \frac{1}{3}x$

D. $y = -x + \frac{1}{2}$

d. ___?___ $\frac{2}{3} + \frac{1}{3}y \geq x$

E. $y = 3x - 2$

e. ___?___ $-y > x - 0.5$

F. $y = x$

f. ___?___ $\frac{1}{3}y \geq x$

Determine if the given point satisfies either inequality and is a solution of the system of inequalities.

2. $\begin{cases} 4y - 20x < 6 \\ \frac{5}{2}y \geq 5x - 10 \end{cases}$; $(0, 0)$

3. $\begin{cases} x + 5y > -10 \\ x - y \leq 4 \end{cases}$; $(2.5, -1.5)$

Determine if the given point is a solution of the system of inequalities. If not, find a point that is.

4. $(-9, 4)$

5. $(6, -2)$

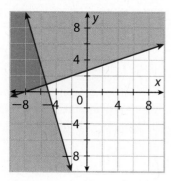

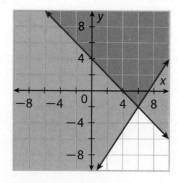

6. $(0, -4)$

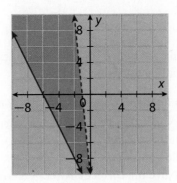

Graph the system of linear inequalities. Give two ordered pairs that are solutions and two that are not solutions.

7. $\begin{cases} x > 2 \\ y \le -\frac{1}{2}x - 2 \end{cases}$

8. $\begin{cases} y > -x \\ y \ge x \end{cases}$

9. $\begin{cases} y < -x + 10 \\ y < \frac{1}{10}x + 7 \end{cases}$

10. $\begin{cases} y \le \frac{1}{2}x - 5 \\ y \ge -2x + 12 \end{cases}$

11. $\begin{cases} y \le -\frac{3}{5}x \\ y > -x - 4 \end{cases}$

12. $\begin{cases} y \ge 2x + 6 \\ y < -\frac{1}{2}x - 1 \end{cases}$

13. $\begin{cases} y \le \frac{4}{5}x - 4 \\ y < 2x - 8 \end{cases}$

14. $\begin{cases} x \ge -6 \\ y < 3 \end{cases}$

Graph each system of linear inequalities. Describe the solutions.

15. $\begin{cases} y \le 3x + 6 \\ y < 3x - 8 \end{cases}$

16. $\begin{cases} y \ge \frac{2}{5}x + 4 \\ y \le \frac{2}{5}x - 6 \end{cases}$

17. $\begin{cases} y \ge \frac{5}{4}x - 6 \\ y \ge \frac{5}{4}x \end{cases}$

18. $\begin{cases} y \ge -\frac{3}{2}x - 3 \\ y \le -\frac{3}{2}x + 10 \end{cases}$

19. $\begin{cases} x < 6 \\ x \ge -3 \end{cases}$

20. $\begin{cases} y \ge \frac{9}{4}x - 1 \\ y < \frac{9}{4}x - 9 \end{cases}$

21. $\begin{cases} y < -\frac{3}{5}x + 3 \\ y \ge -\frac{3}{5}x - 4 \end{cases}$

22. $\begin{cases} y > -\frac{1}{2}x + 5 \\ y > -\frac{1}{2}x - 1 \end{cases}$

23. **Persevere in Problem Solving** Write and graph a system of linear inequalities for which the solutions are all the points in the second quadrant, not including points on the axes.

24. **Critical Thinking** Can the solutions of a system of linear inequalities be the points on a line? Explain.

25. **Explain the Error** A student was asked to graph the system $\begin{cases} y < \frac{3}{2}x - 8 \\ y \le \frac{3}{2}x + 2 \end{cases}$ and describe the solution set. The student gave the following answer. Explain what the student did wrong, then give the correct answer.

The solutions are the same as the solutions of $y \le \frac{3}{2}x + 2$.

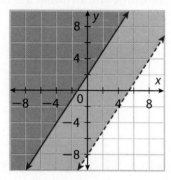

Lesson Performance Task

Successful stock market investors know a lot about inequalities. They know up to what point they are willing to accept losses, and at what point they are willing to "lock in" their profits and not subject their investments to additional risk. They often have these inequalities all mapped out at the time they purchase a stock, so they can tell instantly if they are sticking to their investment strategy. Graph the system of linear inequalities. Then describe the solution set and give two ordered pairs that are solutions and two that are not. Is there anything particular to note about the shape of this system?

$$\begin{cases} y < -\frac{3}{5}x + 4 \\ y \le \frac{3}{2}x + 8 \\ y > -\frac{3}{5}x - 8 \\ y > \frac{3}{2}x - 6 \end{cases}$$

12.3 Modeling with Linear Systems

Resource Locker

Essential Question: How can you use systems of linear equations or inequalities to model and solve contextual problems?

⊘ Explore   Modeling Real-World Constraints with Systems

Real-world situations can often be modeled by systems of equations. Usually, information about prices and the total number of items purchased is given, and the system is solved to find the number of each item purchased.

Joe goes to the store to buy jeans and some T-shirts. The jeans cost $40 each and the T-shirts cost $20 each. If Joe spends $160 on 5 items, how many pairs of jeans and how many T-shirts did he buy?

(A) Write an expression to represent the amount that Joe spent on x pairs of jeans. [?]

(B) Write an expression to represent the amount that Joe spent on y T-shirts. [?]

(C) Now write an equation that represents the total amount spent on jeans and T-shirts.

Amount spent on jeans	+	Amount spent on T-shirts	=	Total amount spent
[?]	+	[?]	=	[?]

(D) What variable represents the number of jeans purchased? [?]

(E) What variable represents the number of T-shirts purchased? [?]

(F) Write an equation to represent the total number of items purchased. [?]

(G) Write the system that represents the situation.

[?] = 160

[?] = 5

Reflect

1. What units are associated with the two expressions that you wrote in steps A and B?

2. When you add the units for the expressions representing the amounts spent on jeans and T-shirts, what units do you get for the total amount spent?

⚙ Explain 1 Modeling Real-World Constraints with Systems of Linear Equations

You can model real-world constraints, such as the number of items needed and the amount of money one has to spend, with systems of linear equations.

Example 1 Write a system of equations to represent the situation, and then solve the system.

(A) Bobby will buy coffee and hot chocolate for his co-workers. Each cup of coffee costs $2.25 and each cup of hot chocolate costs $1.50. If he pays a total of $15.75 for 8 cups, how many of each did he buy?

Create a table to organize the information.

	Coffee	Hot Chocolate	Total
Number of Cups	c	h	8
Cost	$\$2.25c$	$\$1.50h$	$\$15.75$

Use the information to write a system of equations.

$2.25c + 1.50h = 15.75$ Total amount spent on c cups of coffee and h cups of hot chocolate

$c + h = 8$ Total number of cups bought

Multiply the second equation by -2.25 to get opposite coefficients for c.

$-2.25(c + h = 8)$

$-2.25c - 2.25h = -18$

Add the new equation to the first equation.

$2.25c + 1.50h = 15.75$

$+(-2.25c - 2.25h = -18)$
_____

$-0.75h = -2.25$

Solve for h.

$-0.75h = -2.25$

$h = 3$

Substitute the value found for h back into one of the original equations and solve for c.

$c + h = 8$

$c + 3 = 8$

$c = 5$

So Bobby bought 5 cups of coffee and 3 cups of hot chocolate.

B A student is buying pens and markers for school. Packs of pens cost $2.75 each and packs of markers cost $3.25 each. If she bought a total of 6 packs and spent $17.50, how many of each did she buy?

Create a table to organize the information.

	Pens	Markers	Total
Number of packs	p	m	6
Cost	$2.75p$	$3.25m$	$17.50

Use the information to write a system of equations.

$$\boxed{2.75p} + \boxed{3.25m} = 17.50 \qquad \text{Total amount spent on } p \text{ packs of pens and } m \text{ packs of markers}$$

$$p + m = \boxed{6} \qquad \text{Total number of packs bought}$$

Multiply the second equation by -2.75 to get opposite coefficients for p.

$$\boxed{-2.75}\left(p + m = \boxed{6}\right)$$

$$\boxed{-2.75}\, p + \boxed{-2.75}\, m = \boxed{-16.50}$$

Add the new equation to the first equation.

$$\boxed{2.75}\, p + \boxed{3.25}\, m = 17.50$$

$$+ \boxed{-2.75}\, p + \boxed{-2.75}\, m = \boxed{-16.50}$$

$$\rule{3cm}{0.4pt}$$

$$\boxed{0.5}\, m = \boxed{1}$$

Solve for m, the number of markers.

$$m = \boxed{2}$$

Substitute the value found for m back into one of the original equations and solve for p.

$$p + m = \boxed{6}$$

$$p + \boxed{2} = \boxed{6}$$

$$p = \boxed{4}$$

So the student bought 4 packs of pens and 2 packs of markers.

Reflect

3. What's another possible way to solve the problem?

Your Turn

Write a system of equations to represent the situation, and then solve the system.

4. A company has to buy computers and printers. Each computer costs $550 and each printer costs $390. If the company spends $8160 and buys a total of 16 machines, how many of each did it buy?

⚙ Explain 2 Modeling Real-World Constraints with Systems of Linear Inequalities

You can use a system of linear inequalities and its graph to model many real-world situations.

Example 2 Set up and solve the system of linear equalities.

Ⓐ Sue is buying T-shirts and shorts. T-shirts cost $14 and shorts cost $21. She plans on spending no more than $147 and buy at least 5 items. Show and describe all combinations of the number of T-shirts and shorts she could buy.

First write the system. Let x represent the number of T-shirts, and let y represent the number of shorts.

$x + y \geq 5$ She wants to buy at least 5 items.

$14x + 21y \leq 147$ She wants to spend no more than $147.

Graph the system of inequalities: $\begin{cases} x + y \geq 5 \\ 14x + 21y \leq 147 \end{cases}$

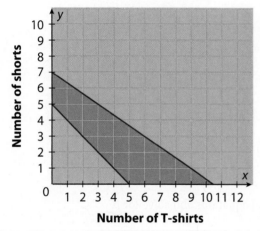

T-shirts and Shorts

Number of shorts (y-axis, 0–10)
Number of T-shirts (x-axis, 0–12)

The possible solutions are where the shaded regions overlap. So, a possible solution is 5 T-shirts and 2 shorts. Substitute this value into the inequalities to make sure it is a reasonable solution.

$$\begin{cases} x + y \geq 5 \\ 14x + 21y \leq 147 \end{cases} \rightarrow \begin{cases} 5 + 2 \overset{?}{\geq} 5 \\ 14(5) + 21(2) \overset{?}{\leq} 147 \end{cases} \rightarrow \begin{cases} 7 \geq 5 \\ 112 \leq 147 \end{cases}$$

The result is two inequalities that are true, so this is a reasonable answer.

Ⓑ John has to buy two different kinds of rope. Rope A costs $0.60 per foot and Rope B costs $0.90 per foot. John needs to buy at least 15 feet of rope, but he wants to spend no more than $18. Show and describe all combinations of the number of feet of each type of rope John can buy.

First write the system. Let x represent the amount of Rope A, and let y represent the amount of Rope B.

$\boxed{x} + \boxed{y} \geq 15$

$\boxed{0.6x} + 0.9y \boxed{\leq} \boxed{18}$

Graph the system.

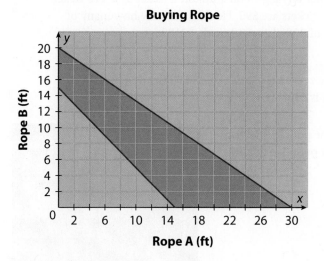

Buying Rope

Describe the solutions to the system.

The possible solutions are all of the ordered pairs that lie in the region shared by the two inequalities and on the solid boundary lines.

Your Turn

Write a system of inequalities for the given situation and graph the system. Then determine if the point (8, 4) is a solution to the system.

5. A student has to buy graph paper and printer paper. The printer paper costs $2 a pack, while the graphing paper costs $3 a pack. She wants to buy at least 6 packs of paper but wants to spend at most $27.

6. Now assume that she wants to buy at least 7 packs and will spend at most $30.

Elaborate

7. Is it possible for a system of two linear inequalities to only have one solution?

8. Why can't a system of inequalities be solved using the same methods as solving systems of equations?

9. **Essential Question Check-In** When writing a system of equations or inequalities from a situation, how do you know that you have possibly written the system correctly?

☆ Evaluate: Homework and Practice

- Online Homework
- Hints and Help
- Extra Practice

Write a system of equations that corresponds to the situation. Do not solve.

1. Lisa spends part of her year as a member of a gym. She then finds a better deal at another gym, so she cancels her membership with the first gym and spends the rest of the year with the second gym. The membership to the first gym costs $75 per month, while the membership for the second gym costs $50 per month. She ends up spending a total of $775 over the course of the year.

2. Jack is selling tickets to an event. Attendees can either buy a general admission ticket or a VIP ticket. The general adimission tickets are $60 and the VIP tickets are $90. He doesn't know how many of each type he has sold, but he knows he sold a total of 29 tickets and made $2100.

3. There are 200 adults and 300 children at a zoo. The zoo makes a total of $7000 from the entrance fees, and the cost for an adult and a child to attend is $30.

4. A local fish market is selling fish and lobsters by the pound. The fish costs $4.50 a pound, while the lobster costs $9.50 a pound. The fish market sells 25.5 pounds and makes $189.75.

5. Jennifer has 12 nickels and dimes. The value of her coins is $1.

6. The sum of 5 times one number and 2 times a second number is 57. The sum of the two numbers is 18.

7. Gary goes to the grocery store to buy hot dogs and hamburgers for a cookout. He buys a total of 8 packages for a total of $28.52. A package of hot dogs costs $2.29 and a package of hamburgers costs $5.69.

8. The sum of two numbers is 28, and the sum of 6 times the first number and 3 times the second number is 105.

Find a system of equations that corresponds to the situation and then solve the resulting system.

9. Jan spends part of her year as a member of a gym. She then finds a better deal at another gym, so she cancels her membership with the first gym and spends the rest of the year with the second gym. The membership to the first gym costs $80 per month, while the membership for the second gym costs $45 per month. If she ends up spending a total of $645 over the course of the year, how much time did she spend at each gym?

10. John is selling tickets to an event. Attendees can either buy a general admission ticket or a VIP ticket. The general adimission tickets are $70 and the VIP tickets are $105. If he knows he sold a total of 33 tickets and made $2730, how many of each type did he sell?

11. There are 150 adults and 225 children at a zoo. If the zoo makes a total of $5100 from the entrance fees, and the cost of an adult and a child to attend is $31, how much does it cost each for a parent and a child?

12. A local fish market is selling fish and lobsters by the pound. The fish costs $5.25 a pound, while the lobster costs $10.50 a pound. The fish market sells 28.5 pounds and makes $215.25.

13. Nicole has 15 nickels and dimes. If the value of her coins is $1.20, how many of each coin does she have?

14. The sum of 4 times one number and 3 times a second number is 64. If the sum of the two numbers is 19, find the two numbers.

15. Meaghan goes to the grocery store to buy hot dogs and hamburgers for a cookout. She buys a total of 6 packages for a total of $30.46. If a package of hot dogs costs $2.65 and a package of hamburgers costs $6.29, determine how many packs of each she bought.

16. The sum of two numbers is 33, and the sum of 7 times the first number and 5 times the second number is 197.

Write the system of inequalities that represents the situation. Then graph the system and describe the solutions. Give one possible solution.

17. Angelique is buying towels for her apartment. She finds some green towels that cost $8 each and blue towels that cost $10 each. She wants to buy at least 4 towels but doesn't want to spend more than $70. How many of each towel can she purchase?

18. The sum of two numbers is at least 8, and the sum of one of the numbers and 3 times the second number is no more than 15.

19. The sum of two numbers is at most 12, and the sum of 3 times the first number and 8 times the second number is at least 48.

20. Katie is purchasing plates and mugs for her house. She would like to buy at least 8 items. Determine the possibilities if the plates cost $8 each and the mugs cost $7 each, and she plans to spend no more than $112.

21. Christine is selling tickets at a museum. She knows that she has sold at least 40 tickets. The adult tickets cost 14 dollars and the children's tickets cost 12 dollars. If she knows she has sold no more than $720 worth of tickets, what are the possible combinations?

22. Mike is bringing cans and bottles to a recycling center. For a type A can or bottle he gets 5 cents, and for a type B can or bottle he gets 10 cents. He knows that he has redeemed at least 11 cans but has no more than 95 cents. What are the possible combinations?

H.O.T. Focus on Higher Order Thinking

23. Explain the Error A student is given the following system. He graphs the system as shown and determines that a solution is $(7, 0)$. Where did the student go wrong? What should the correct answer be?

$x + y = 6$
$x + 2y = 8$

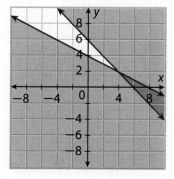

24. Justify Reasoning Molly went shopping to buy jewelry. All of the earrings cost $15.25 and the necklaces cost $40.75. If she spends $127.25 and buys 5 items, how many necklaces and pairs of earrings did she buy? Justify your answer.

25. Check for Reasonableness Chris is at the florist and has to buy flowers. Arrangements of daisies are $4.25 and arrangements of roses are $6.50. He wants to spend less than $39 and wants to buy more than 4 arrangements. What are possible combinations that Chris can buy? Check to make sure your answer is reasonable.

Lesson Performance Task

Amy is at the store to buy shirts and pants. The shirts cost $40 each and the pants cost $50 each. She plans to spend no more than $400 and buy at least 5 items. Find a possible combination of shirts and pants she can buy. How do you know this is a solution? What are two possible ways to show that this is a solution?

Modeling with Linear Systems

Essential Question: How can you model with linear systems to solve real-world problems?

KEY EXAMPLE   *(Lesson 12.1)*

One cable television provider has a $50 setup fee and charges $90 per month, and another cable provider has a $150 equipment fee and charges $80 per month. Determine when the cost of the two services will be the same amount, and what the price will be.

Let $f(t)$ represent the cost for the first cable company and let $g(t)$ represent the cost of the second cable company, where t is the number of months.

The system of equations is $\begin{cases} f(t) = 50 + 90t \\ g(t) = 150 + 80t \end{cases}$.

Solve the system when $f(t) = g(t)$.

$50 + 90t = 150 + 80t$

$90t - 80t = 150 - 50$

$10t = 100$

$t = 10$

$f(t) = 50 + 90t$

$f(10) = 50 + 90(10)$

$f(10) = 950$

A subscriber would have paid either company $950 for 10 months of service.

KEY EXAMPLE   *(Lesson 12.2)*

Graph the system of linear inequalities $\begin{cases} y \leq 2x - 2 \\ y > 0.5x + 1 \end{cases}$.

Graph the line $y = 2x - 2$. Use a solid line because the inequality symbol is $\leq$. Lightly shade below the line.

Graph the line $y = 0.5x + 1$. Use a dashed line because the inequality symbol is $>$. Lightly shade above the line.

The intersection of the two shaded areas contains the solution set to the system of linear inequalities. For example, (4, 4) is within the intersection and satisfies both inequalities.

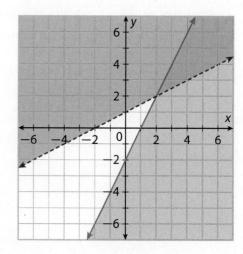

EXERCISES

1. **Jacob wants to buy a gym membership. The table below shows the total cost of two gyms after several months, including any startup fees.**

Month	2	4	6	8
Tony's Gym	$220	$300	$380	$460
Mickey's Gym	$120	$240	$360	$480

Use the data to write a system of equations. Then solve to find out in how many months both memberships will cost the same. What will that cost be? *(Lesson 12.1)*

2. Graph $\begin{cases} y \leq -2x + 3 \\ 3y \geq 9x - 6 \end{cases}$. Give two ordered pairs that are solutions and two that are not

   solutions. *(Lesson 12.2)*

3. A local fish market is selling fish and lobster by the pound. The fish costs $5.00 a pound, while the lobster costs $10.50 a pound. The fish market sells 30 total pounds and makes $194. Represent this situation with a system of equations and solve it to find how many pounds of fish and lobster were sold. *(Lesson 12.3)*

MODULE PERFORMANCE TASK

How to Win at an Arcade Game

You are playing an arcade game that involves rolling a ball up a ramp. If you earn at least 450 points, you win the grand prize. You want to figure out a winning strategy. Here is some background information that will help you to formulate your plan.

- One round of the game uses 9 balls.
- Earning 100, 50, 40, 30, and 20 points is fairly obvious as the ball has to go down the corresponding hole. However, if you miss all of those holes, a big curve catches the balls and empties into the 10-points hole. So, you will almost always earn at least 10 points.

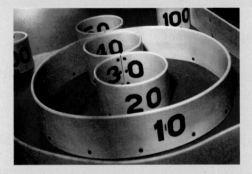

Be sure to write down all your data and assumptions. Then use graphs, numbers, words, or algebra to explain how you reached your conclusion.

12.1–12.3 Modeling with Linear Systems

- Online Homework
- Hints and Help
- Extra Practice

1. A jar contains n nickels and d dimes. There are 30 coins in the jar, and the total value of the coins is \$2.10. Set up and solve a system of equations to find how many nickels and how many dimes are in the jar. *(Lesson 12.1)*

Tell whether each ordered pair is a solution of $\begin{cases} y < 2x + 5 \\ 4y > -4x - 8 \end{cases}$. *(Lesson 12.2)*

2. $(1, 2)$

3. $(0, 6)$

4. $(-1, -2)$

5. $(-1, 2)$

6. Nathan buys coffee and hot chocolate for his co-workers. Each cup of coffee costs \$1.75 and each cup of hot chocolate costs \$1.20. If he pays a total of \$11.15 for 7 cups, how many of each does he buy? *(Lesson 12.3)*

ESSENTIAL QUESTION

7. How can the graph of a system of linear equations help you find the solution to a real-world problem?

Assessment Readiness

1. Consider each ordered pair. Is the ordered pair a solution of $\begin{cases} y \leq 3x + 5 \\ y \geq -\frac{2}{3}x + 5 \end{cases}$?

   A. $(-1, 4)$

   B. $(0, 5)$

   C. $(2, 9)$

2. Consider the graph of $y - 5 = \frac{1}{5}(x + 2)$.
   Determine whether each statement is True or False.

   A. The slope of the graph is $\frac{1}{5}$.

   B. The graph includes the point $(0, 2)$.

   C. The graph includes the point $(2, -5)$.

3. The sum of 4 times one number and 3 times a second number is 65. The sum of the two numbers is 18. Write and solve a system of equations to find the two numbers. Show your work.

4. Steven wants to buy a couch that costs $475. He has already saved $120. He plans to save $25 a week. Write a function to represent the amount Steven will have saved in x weeks. Will he have enough to buy the couch in 10 weeks? Explain your answer.

Piecewise-Defined Functions

Essential Question: How can you use piecewise-defined functions to solve real-world problems?

REAL WORLD VIDEO
Optimizing sales prices is key to running a successful retail business. Cost and pricing structures are rarely linear, instead taking "jumps" at certain price points.

MODULE PERFORMANCE TASK PREVIEW

A Taxing Situation

United States citizens pay sales taxes on items they buy, gasoline taxes when they fill up their cars at the pump, and property taxes if they own a home. Everyone who earns more than a certain minimum amount also pays the federal government a tax on their income. The amount paid is defined not as a percent of income but by a "piecewise" function. You'll learn about these functions in this module and then use them to analyze the income tax system.

Are (YOU) Ready?

Complete these exercises to review skills you will need for this module.

- Online Homework
- Hints and Help
- Extra Practice

Multi-Step Equations

Example 1   Solve. $\frac{3}{4}b + 2 = 38$

$$\frac{3}{4}b = 36 \qquad \text{Subtract 2 from both sides.}$$

$$b = 48 \qquad \text{Multiply both sides by } \frac{4}{3}.$$

Solve each equation.

1. $10x - 15 = -4$

2. $5x - 7 = 2(3x + 1)$

3. $5(8v - 4) = -2$

Two-Step Inequalities

Example 2   Solve. $-2w + 3 \leq 4$

$$-2w \leq 1 \qquad \text{Subtract 3 from both sides.}$$

$$w \geq -0.5 \qquad \text{Divide both sides by } -2 \text{ and flip the sign.}$$

Solve.

4. $n - 7 \geq -4$

5. $\frac{3x}{2} < -6$

6. $5 - 9a \leq 32$

Absolute Value

Example 3   Use the definition of absolute value to write two equations that represent the equation $|3x - 11| = 1$.

If $3x - 11 > 0$, then $3x - 11 = 1$.

If $3x - 11 < 0$, then $3x - 11 = -1$.

The two equations are $3x - 11 = 1$ and $3x - 11 = -1$.

Write two equations that represent the given function.

7. $\left|\dfrac{k}{9} + \dfrac{1}{3}\right| = 12$

8. $\left|6(r - 4)\right| = 4.8$

9. $\left|\dfrac{n}{22}\right| = 16$

13.1 Understanding Piecewise-Defined Functions

Resource Locker

Essential Question: How are piecewise-defined functions different from other functions?

🧭 Explore Exploring Piecewise-Defined Function Models

A **piecewise function** has different rules for different parts of its domain. The following situation can be modeled by a piecewise function.

Armando drives from his home to the grocery store at a speed of 0.9 mile per minute for 4 minutes, stops for 2 minutes to buy snacks, and then drives to the soccer field at a speed of 0.7 mile per minute for 3 minutes. The graph shows Armando's distance from home.

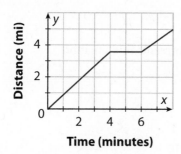

Time (minutes)

The three different sections in the graph show that there are three different parts to the function. The function for this graph will have three function rules, each for a different range of values for x.

The following steps can be used to build the piecewise function to model this situation.

(A) Determine the function rule for the first 4 minutes for the domain, $0 \leq x \leq 4$.
The rate of change is Armando's speed in miles per minute.

$$m = \frac{\boxed{?} \text{ mi}}{\boxed{?} \text{ min}} = \boxed{?}$$

The y-intercept is $\boxed{?}$.

The function for the first 4 minutes is $y = \boxed{?}$.

(B) Determine the function rule for the next 2 minutes for the domain, $4 < x \leq 6$.

Because the distance is not changing, the rate of change is $m = \dfrac{\boxed{?} \text{ mi}}{\boxed{?} \text{ min}} = \boxed{?}$.

The function for the next 2 minutes is a constant function. The constant y-value is Armando's distance from home at the end of the first 4 minutes.

$$y = 0.9x$$

$$y = 0.9(4) = \boxed{?}$$

(C) Determine the function rule for the last 3 minutes.
The rate of change is Armando's speed in miles per minute.

$$m = \frac{\boxed{?} \text{ mi}}{\boxed{?} \text{ min}} = \boxed{?}$$

The point at which the function begins is $\left(\boxed{?}, \boxed{?} \right)$.

Use the point and slope to construct the function rule for the last 3 minutes.

$$y - \boxed{?} = \boxed{?} \left(x - \boxed{?} \right)$$

$$y - \boxed{?} = \boxed{?} \, x - \boxed{?}$$

$$y = \boxed{?} \, x - \boxed{?}$$

(D) Use all three parts to build the piecewise function that represents this situation.

$$f(x) = \begin{cases} \boxed{?} & \text{if } 0 \leq x \leq 4 \\ \boxed{?} & \text{if } 4 < x \leq 6 \\ \boxed{?} & \text{if } 6 < x \leq 9 \end{cases}$$

Reflect

1. **Discussion** Describe how the domain is constructed so that the piecewise function is a function with no more than one value of the dependent variable for any value of the independent variable.

🔑 Explain 1 Evaluating Piecewise-Defined Functions

The **greatest integer function** is a piecewise function whose rule is denoted by $\lfloor x \rfloor$, which represents the greatest integer less than or equal to x. The greatest integer function is an example of a **step function**, a piecewise function in which each function rule is a constant function. To evaluate a piecewise function for a given value of x, substitute the value of x into the rule for the part of the domain that includes x.

Example 1   **Evaluate each piecewise function for the given values.**

(A) Find $f(-3)$, $f(-2.9)$, $f(0.7)$, and $f(1.06)$ for $f(x) = \lfloor x \rfloor$.

The greatest integer function $f(x) = \lfloor x \rfloor$ can also be written in the form below.

$$f(x) = \begin{cases} \vdots \\ -3 & \text{if } -3 \le x < -2 \\ -2 & \text{if } -2 \le x < -1 \\ -1 & \text{if } -1 \le x < 0 \\ 0 & \text{if } 0 \le x < 1 \\ 1 & \text{if } 1 \le x < 2 \\ 2 & \text{if } 2 \le x < 3 \\ \vdots \end{cases}$$

-3 is in the interval $-3 \le x < -2$, so $f(-3) = -3$.

-2.9 is in the interval $-3 \le x < -2$, so $f(-2.9) = -3$.

0.7 is in the interval $0 \le x < 1$, so $f(0.7) = 0$.

1.06 is in the interval $1 \le x < 2$, so $f(1.06) = 1$.

(B) Find $f(-3)$, $f(-0.2)$, $f(0)$, and $f(2)$ for $f(x) = \begin{cases} -x & \text{if } x < 0 \\ x + 1 & \text{if } x \ge 0 \end{cases}$

$-3 < 0$, so $f(-3) = -(-3) = \boxed{3}$ $0 \ge 0$, so $f(0) = \boxed{0} + 1 = \boxed{1}$

$-0.2 < 0$, so $f(-0.2) = \boxed{-(-0.2)} = 0.2$ $2 \ge 0$, so $f(2) = \boxed{2} + \boxed{1} = \boxed{3}$

Reflect

2.   For positive numbers, how is applying the greatest integer function different from the method of rounding to the nearest whole number?

Your Turn

3.   Find $f(-2)$, $f(-0.4)$, $f(3.7)$, and $f(5)$ for $f(x) = \begin{cases} -x & \text{if } x < 2 \\ 2x + 3 & \text{if } 2 \le x < 4. \\ x^2 & \text{if } x \ge 4 \end{cases}$

 Explain 2   **Graphing Piecewise-Defined Functions**

You can graph piecewise-defined functions to illustrate their behavior.

Example 2   **Graph each function.**

(A) $f(x) = \begin{cases} -x & \text{if } x < 0 \\ x + 1 & \text{if } x \ge 0 \end{cases}$

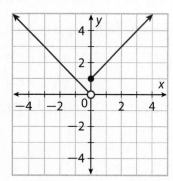

Make a table of values.

x	−3	−2	−1	0	1	2
f(x)	3	2	1	1	2	3

(B) $f(x) = \lfloor x \rfloor$

Make a table of values.

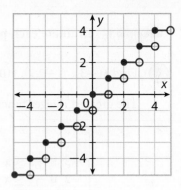

x	-3	-2.9	-2.1	-2	-1.5	-1	0	1	1.5	2
$f(x)$	-3	-3	-3	-2	-2	-1	0	1	1	2

Reflect

4. Why does the graph in Example 2A use rays and not lines?

5. Use the graph of the greatest integer function from Example 2B to explain why this function is called a step function.

Your Turn

6. $f(x) = \begin{cases} x & \text{if} & x < 2 \\ 2x + 3 & \text{if} & 2 \le x < 4 \\ x^2 & \text{if} & x \ge 4 \end{cases}$

⚙ Explain 3 Modeling with Piecewise-Defined Functions

Some real-world situations can be described by piecewise functions.

Example 3 Write a piecewise function for each situation. Then graph the function.

(A) **Travel** On her way to a concert, Maisee walks at a speed of 0.03 mile per minute from her car for 5 minutes, waits in line for a ticket for 3 minutes, and then walks to her seat for 4 minutes at a speed of 0.01 mile per minute.

Express the Maisee's distance traveled d (in miles) as a function of time t (in minutes).

For $0 \le t \le 5$, $m = 0.03$ and $b = 0$, so $d(t) = 0.03t$.

For $5 < t \le 8$, $m = 0$ and $b = 0.15$, so $d(t) = 0.15$.

For $8 < t \le 12$, $m = 0.01$ beginning at $(8, 0.15)$, so $d(t) = 0.01t + 0.07$.

$d(t) = \begin{cases} 0.03t & \text{if } 0 \le t \le 5 \\ 0.15 & \text{if } 5 < t \le 8 \\ 0.01t + 0.07 & \text{if } 8 < t \le 12 \end{cases}$

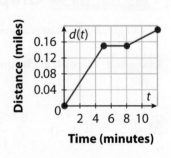

© Houghton Mifflin Harcourt Publishing Company

Ⓑ **Travel** On his way to class from his dorm room, a college student walks at a speed of 0.05 mile per minute for 3 minutes, stops and talks to a friend for 1 minute, and then to avoid being late for class, runs at a speed of 0.10 mile per minute for 2 minutes.

Express the student's distance traveled d (in miles) as a function of time t (in minutes).

For $0 \leq t \leq 3$, $m =$ 0.05 and $b = 0$, so $d(t) =$ 0.05 t.

For $3 < t \leq$ 4 , $m = 0$ and $b = 0.15$, so $d(t) = 0.15$.

For $4 < t \leq 6$, $m =$ 0.1 beginning at (4, 0.15), so $y =$ 0.1 $x -$ 0.25 .

$$d(t) = \begin{cases} 0.05\ t & \text{if } 0 \leq t \leq 3 \\ 0.15 & \text{if } 3 < t \leq 4 \\ 0.1\ t - 0.25 & \text{if } 4 < t \leq 6 \end{cases}$$

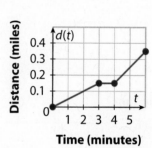

Your Turn

7. **Finance** A savings account earns 1.4% simple interest annually for balances of $100 or less, 2.4% simple interest for balances greater than $100 and up to $500, and 3.4% simple interest for balances greater than $500. Write a function rule for the interest paid by the account and graph the function.

🔑 Explain 4 Building Piecewise-Defined Functions from Graphs

You can find the function rules for a piecewise function when you are given the graph of the function.

Example 4 Write an equation for each graph.

Ⓐ

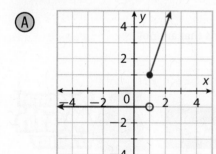

Find the equation of the ray on the right.

$m = \dfrac{1 - 4}{1 - 2} = \dfrac{-3}{-1} = 3$

Because the point $(1, 1)$ is on the ray, $y - 1 = 3(x - 1)$, so $y = 3x - 2$

The equation of the line that contains the horizontal ray is $y = -1$.

The equation for the function is $y = \begin{cases} -1 & \text{if } x < 1. \\ 3x - 2 & \text{if } x \geq 1 \end{cases}$

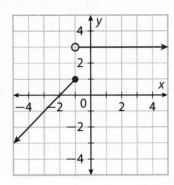

Ⓑ Find the equation for the ray on the left.

$$m = \frac{1 - \boxed{-2}}{-1 - \boxed{-4}} = \frac{\boxed{3}}{\boxed{3}} = \boxed{1}$$

Because the point $(-1, 1)$ is on the ray, $y \boxed{-1} = \boxed{1} \left(x \boxed{+1}\right)$,

so $y = \boxed{x + 2}$

The equation of the horizontal ray is $y = \boxed{3}$.

The equation for the function is $y = \begin{cases} \boxed{1} \, x + \boxed{2} & \text{if } x \le -1 \\ \boxed{3} & \text{if } x > -1 \end{cases}$

Your Turn

8.

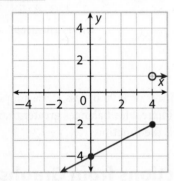

💬 Elaborate

9. How are the greatest integer function and $f(x) = 2\lfloor x \rfloor$ related?

10. **Essential Question Check-In** How many function rules do functions that are not piecewise-defined have?

⭐ Evaluate: Homework and Practice

- Online Homework
- Hints and Help
- Extra Practice

Evaluate each piecewise function for the given values.

1. Find $f(-4)$, $f(-3.1)$, $f(1.2)$, and $f(2.8)$ for $f(x) = \lfloor x \rfloor$.

2. Find $f(-3)$, $f(-2.1)$, $f(0.6)$, and $f(3.3)$ for $f(x) = \begin{cases} -1 & \text{if } x \le 0 \\ 3x & \text{if } 0 < x < 1 \\ x + 3 & \text{if } x \ge 1 \end{cases}$.

3. Find $f(-4)$, $f(-2.9)$, and $f(1.9)$ for $f(x) = \begin{cases} -5 & \text{if } x \le -3 \\ x + 2 & \text{if } -3 < x \le 0 \\ x^2 + 7 & \text{if } x \ge 0 \end{cases}$.

© Houghton Mifflin Harcourt Publishing Company

4. Find $f(-6)$, $f(-2.2)$, $f(1.4)$ and $f(3.6)$ for $f(x) = -2\lfloor x \rfloor$.

5. Find $f(-3)$, $f(-1)$, and $f(1)$ for $f(x) = \begin{cases} \dfrac{2}{x} & \text{if } x \le -2 \\ x & \text{if } -2 < x \le 0. \\ 1 & \text{if } x \ge 0 \end{cases}$

6. Find $f(-2)$, $f(-1)$, $f(0)$, $f(4)$, and $f(9)$ for $f(x) = \begin{cases} -x^2 & \text{if } x \le -2 \\ 2x & \text{if } -2 < x < 2 \\ x + 6 & \text{if } 2 \le x \le 4 \\ \sqrt{x} + 8 & \text{if } x > 4 \end{cases}$.

7. Find $f(-2.8)$, $f(-1.2)$, $f(0.4)$, and $f(1.6)$ for $f(x) = \lfloor x \rfloor^2$.

8. Find $f(0)$, $f(2)$, and $f(4)$ for $f(x) = \begin{cases} 8 & \text{if } x \le 0 \\ 0 & \text{if } x > 0 \end{cases}$.

Graph each piecewise function.

9. $f(x) = \begin{cases} -x + 1 & \text{if } x < 0 \\ x & \text{if } x \ge 0 \end{cases}$

10. $f(x) = \begin{cases} -1 & \text{if } x < 1 \\ 2x - 2 & \text{if } x \ge 1 \end{cases}$

11. $f(x) = \lfloor x \rfloor + 1$

12. $f(x) = 2\lfloor x \rfloor - 2$

Write an equation for each graph.

13.

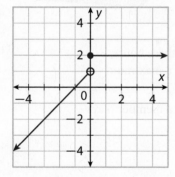

14.

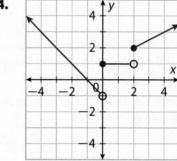

15.

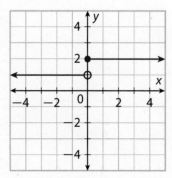

16.

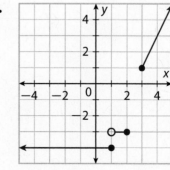

Write a piecewise function for each situation. Then complete the table and graph the function.

17. Finance A garage charges the following rates for parking (with an 8 hour limit):

$4 per hour for the first 2 hours

$2 per hour for the next 4 hours

No additional charge for the next 2 hours

Express the cost C (in dollars) as a function of the time t (in hours) that a car is parked in the garage.

t	0	1	2	3	4	5	6	7	8
$C(t)$	?	?	?	?	?	?	?	?	?

18. Cost Analysis The cost to send a package between two cities is $8.00 for any weight less than 1 pound. The cost increases by $4.00 when the weight reaches 1 pound and again each time the weight reaches a whole number of pounds after that.

Express the shipping cost C (in dollars) as a function of the weight (in pounds). Express your answer in terms of the greatest integer function $\lfloor w \rfloor$.

w	0.5	1	1.5	2	2.5
$C(w)$	?	?	?	?	?

19. Golfing A local golf course charges members $30 an hour for the first three hours, $35 an hour for the next five hours, and nothing for the last 2 hours, for a maximum of 10 hours.

Express the cost C (in dollars) as a function of the time t (in hours) that a member plays golf at this golf course.

t	2	4	6	8	10
$C(t)$	?	?	?	?	?

20. Construction A construction company is building a new parking garage and is charging the following rates: $5000 a month for the first 2 months; $8000 a month for the next 4 months; $6000 in total for the last 4 months, when the garage will be completed. This amount will be paid in a lump sum at the end of the 6th month.

Express the cost C (in thousands of dollars) as a function of the time t (in months) that the construction company works on the parking garage.

t	2	4	6	8	10
$C(t)$	?	?	?	?	?

21. State the domain and range of each piecewise function.

A. $y = \begin{cases} 5 & \text{if } 0 < x \le 1 \\ 0 & \text{if } x > 1 \end{cases}$
B. $y = \begin{cases} -x & \text{if } x \le 0 \\ x & \text{if } x > 0 \end{cases}$
C. $y = \begin{cases} x^2 & \text{if } x \le 4 \\ x^3 & \text{if } x > 4 \end{cases}$

D. $y = \begin{cases} x^2 + 1 & \text{if } x \le -2 \\ x^3 & \text{if } -2 < x < 4 \\ x^x & \text{if } x \ge 4 \end{cases}$
E. $y = \begin{cases} 1 & \text{if } x \le -3 \\ 1 & \text{if } -3 < x < 8 \\ 1 & \text{if } x \ge 8 \end{cases}$

H.O.T. Focus on Higher Order Thinking

22. Critical Thinking Rewrite the piecewise function into a function of the greatest integer function.

$$f(x) = \begin{cases} -6 & \text{if } -2 \le x < -1 \\ -3 & \text{if } -1 \le x < 0 \\ 0 & \text{if } 0 \le x < 1 \\ 3 & \text{if } 1 \le x < 2 \\ 6 & \text{if } 2 \le x < 3 \end{cases}$$

23. Explain the Error Clara was given the following situation and told to write a piecewise function to describe it.

While exercising, a person loses weight in the following manner:
0.5 pound per hour for the first hour
0.7 pound per hour for the next three hours
0.1 pound per hour until the workout is finished

Clara produced the following result. What did she do wrong and what is the correct answer?

$$W(t) = \begin{cases} 0.5t & \text{if } 0 \le t \le 1 \\ 0.7t & \text{if } 1 \le t < 4 \\ 0.1t & \text{if } t \ge 4 \end{cases}$$

24. Critical Thinking Write an equation for the shown graph. Express the answer in terms of $\lfloor x \rfloor$.

25. Communicate Mathematical Ideas Is a piecewise function still a function if it contains a vertical line? Explain why or why not.

Lesson Performance Task

Suppose someone is traveling from New York City to Miami, Florida. The following table describes the average speeds at various intervals on this 1200-mile trip.

Distance Traveled (hundreds of miles)	Average Speed (mi/h)
$0 < d \leq 2$	37.7
$2 < d \leq 4$	46.6
$4 < d \leq 6$	63.3
$6 < d \leq 8$	45.5
$8 < d \leq 10$	64.4
$10 < d \leq 12$	49.9

A. Graph the distance function. Make sure to use appropriate labels.

B. Write the piecewise function that is given by the table.

C. Suppose the destination was changed from Miami, Florida to Minneapolis, Minnesota instead. Explain why it is not okay to use the piecewise function created for the trip from New York to Miami when traveling to Minneapolis, even though the distance is comparable.

13.2 Absolute Value Functions and Transformations

Essential Question: What are the effects of parameter changes on the graph of $y = a|x - h| + k$?

Explore   Understanding the Parent Absolute Value Function

The most basic **absolute value function** is a piecewise function given by the following rule.

$$f(x) = |x| = \begin{cases} x & \text{if } x \geq 0 \\ -x & \text{if } x < 0 \end{cases}$$

This function is sometimes called the parent absolute value function. Complete each step to graph this function.

(A) Copy and complete the table of values.

x	$f(x) = |x|$
−3	3
−2	?
−1	?
0	?
1	?
2	?
3	3

(B) Plot these points on a graph and using two rays, connect them to display the absolute value function.

(C) The vertex of an absolute value function is the single point that both rays have in common. Identify the vertex of the parent absolute value function.

Reflect

1. What is the domain of $f(x) = |x|$? What is the range?

2. For what values of x is the function $f(x) = |x|$ increasing? decreasing?

© Houghton Mifflin Harcourt Publishing Company

⚙ Explain 1 Graphing Translations of Absolute Value Functions

You can compare the graphs of absolute value functions in the form $g(x) = |x - h| + k$, where h and k are real numbers, with the graph of the parent function $f(x) = |x|$ to see how h and k affect the parent function.

Example 1 Graph each absolute value function with respect to the parent function $f(x) = |x|$.

(A) $g(x) = |x + 3| - 5$

First, create a table of values for x and $g(x)$.

x	$g(x) = |x + 3| - 5$
−6	−2
−3	−5
−1	−3
0	−2
1	−1
3	1
6	4

Now graph the function along with the parent function.

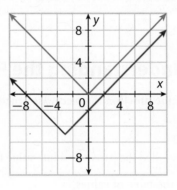

(B) $g(x) = |x - 4| + 2$

First, create a table of values for x and $g(x)$.

x	$g(x) = |x - 4| + 2$
−5	11
−3	9
−1	7
0	6
1	5
3	3
5	3

Now graph the function along with the parent function.

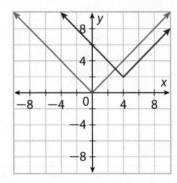

Reflect

3. How is the graph of $g(x) = |x - 4| + 2$ related to the graph of the parent function $f(x) = |x|$?

4. In general, how is the graph of $g(x) = |x - h| + k$ related to the graph of $f(x) = |x|$?

YourTurn

5. Graph the absolute value function $g(x) = |x + 1| + 2$ along with the parent function $f(x) = |x|$.

Explain 2 **Constructing Functions for Given Graphs of Absolute Value Functions**

You can write an absolute value function from a graph of the function.

Example 2 Write an equation for each absolute value function whose graph is shown.

(A)

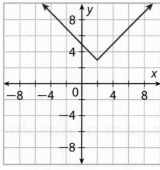

- h is the number of units that the parent function is translated horizontally. For a translation to the right, h is positive; for a translation to the left, h is negative. In this situation, $h = 2$.

- k is the number of units that the parent function is translated vertically. For a translation up, k is positive; for a translation down, k is negative. In this situation, $k = 3$.

The function is $g(x) = |x - 2| + 3$.

(B)

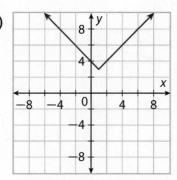

- h is the number of units that the parent function is translated horizontally. For a translation to the right, h is positive; for a translation to the left, h is negative. In this situation, $h = \boxed{1}$.

- k is the number of units that the parent function is translated vertically. For a translation up, k is positive; for a translation down, k is negative. In this situation, $k = \boxed{3}$.

The function is $g(x) = \left| x - \boxed{1} \right| + \boxed{3}$.

Reflect

6. If the graph of an absolute value function is a translation of the graph of the parent function, explain how you can use the vertex of the translated graph to help you determine the equation for the function.

Write an equation for the absolute value function whose graph is shown.

7.

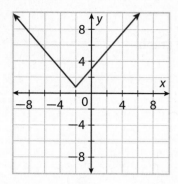

⊘ **Explain 3** **Graphing Stretches and Compressions of Absolute Value Functions**

You can compare the graphs of absolute value functions in the form $g(x) = a|x|$, where a is a real number, with the graph of the parent function $f(x) = |x|$ to see how a affects the absolute value function.

Example 3 **Graph each absolute value function.**

Ⓐ $g(x) = -2|x|$

Ⓑ $g(x) = \frac{1}{4}|x|$

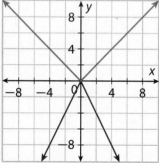

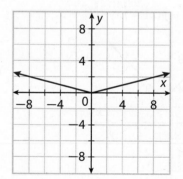

The graph of the parent function is shown in red for comparison.

Reflect

8. Describe how the graphs of $g(x) = \frac{1}{4}|x|$ and $h(x) = -2|x|$ compare with the graph of $f(x) = |x|$. Use either the word *stretch* or *shrink*, and include the directions of movement.

9. What other transformation occurs when the value of a in $g(x) = a|x|$ is negative?

Your Turn

Graph each absolute value function.

10. $g(x) = -\frac{1}{2}|x|$

11. $g(x) = 4|x|$

12. Why is it important to note both the direction and the distance that a point has been translated either vertically or horizontally?

13. How does knowing a point in the graph other than the vertex help you find the value of a?

14. When graphing an absolute value function, how are $g(x) = a|x|$ and $h(x) = -a|x|$ related?

15. **Essential Question Check-In** How would the graph of the parent function $f(x) = |x|$ be affected if $h > 0$, $k < 0$ and $a > 1$?

⭐ Evaluate: Homework and Practice

- Online Homework
- Hints and Help
- Extra Practice

Graph each absolute value function.

1. $g(x) = |x + 1| + 1$

2. $g(x) = |x - 4| + 2$

3. $g(x) = |x - 3| - 5$

4. $g(x) = |x + 7| - 1$

5. $g(x) = |x + 3| - 1$

6. $g(x) = |x + 5| - 3$

Write an equation for each absolute value function whose graph is shown.

7.

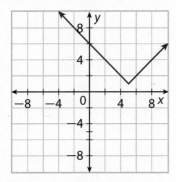

8.

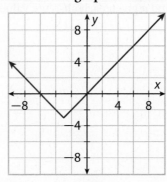

9.

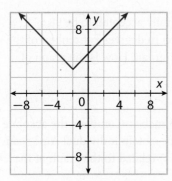

10.

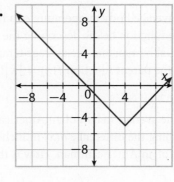

11.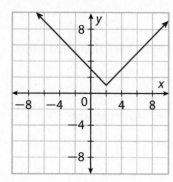

12.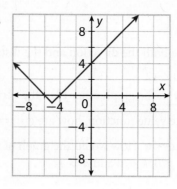

Determine the domain and range of each function.

13. $g(x) = |x + 3| - 1$

14. $g(x) = |x + 2| + 2$

15. $g(x) = |x| + 1$

16. $g(x) = |x - 9| + 6$

Graph each absolute value function.

17. $g(x) = 3|x|$

18. $g(x) = -2.5|x|$

19. $g(x) = \frac{1}{2}|x|$

20. $g(x) = -\frac{2}{3}|x|$

21. Identify the values of h, k, and a given each absolute value function.

A. $f(x) = 3|x - 2| + 2$

B. $f(x) = -0.2|x - 3| + 4$

C. $f(x) = -5|x + 6| - 1$

D. $f(x) = 0.5|x + 2| - 7$

E. $f(x) = 0.8|x| + 3$

22. **Body Temperature** The average body temperature of a human is generally accepted to be 98.6 °F. Complete the absolute value function below describing the difference $d(x)$ in degrees Fahrenheit of the temperature x of an individual human and the average temperature of a human. How is the graph of $d(x)$ related to the graph of the parent function $f(x) = |x|$?

$d(x) = \left| x - \boxed{} \right|$

23. **Population Statistics** The average height of an American man is 69.3 inches. Complete the absolute value function below describing the difference $d(x)$ in inches of the height x of an individual American man and the average height of an American man. How is the graph of $d(x)$ related to the graph of the parent function $f(x) = |x|$?

$d(x) = \left| x - \boxed{} \right|$

24. **Make a Prediction** Copy and complete the table and graph all the functions on the same coordinate plane. How do the graphs of $f(x) = a|x|$ and $g(x) = |ax|$ compare?

x	−6	−3	0	3	6
$g(x) = \frac{1}{3}|x|$	?	?	?	?	?
$g(x) = \left|\frac{1}{3}x\right|$	?	?	?	?	?
$g(x) = -\frac{1}{3}|x|$	?	?	?	?	?
$g(x) = \left|-\frac{1}{3}x\right|$	?	?	?	?	?

Multiple Representations Write an equation for each absolute value function whose graph is shown.

25.

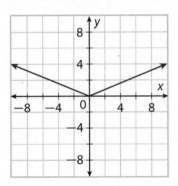

Note: One point on this graph is $(10, 4)$

26.

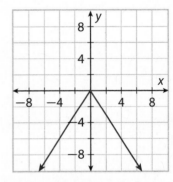

Note: One point on this graph is $(6, -9)$.

27. **Represent Real-World Problems** From his driveway at point $(4, 6)$, Kerry is adjusting his rearview mirror before backing out onto the street. The farthest object behind him to the left he can see is a neighbor's mailbox at $(-4, 12)$. The farthest object behind him to the right he can see is a telephone pole at $(20, 18)$. Create an absolute value function in the form $f(x) = a|x - h| + k$, with Kerry at the vertex, to represent the boundaries of Kerry's visual field in the rearview mirror. Graph the function, and label Kerry, the mailbox, and the telephone pole.

Lesson Performance Task

Geese are initially flying south in a V-shaped pattern that can be modeled by the absolute value function $f(x) = a|x - h| + k$, where a represents the growth or shrinkage of the distance between geese, k represents the height change of the flock, and h represents a left or right shift in the flock.

A. Graph the original flock function, $g(x) = |x|$. State the function's domain and range in words.

B. While flying south, the flock encounters a jet stream and is forced to drop 2 feet. Write the new equation and graph this function along with the original. State the new function's domain and range in words.

C. A short while after passing through the jet stream, the flock of geese encounters a rain storm and is forced to double the distance between each of its members in order to avoid colliding with one another. Write the new equation and graph all three functions. State the new function's domain and range in words.

13.3 Solving Absolute Value Equations

Essential Question: How can you solve an absolute value equation?

⊘ Explore Solving Absolute Value Equations Graphically

Absolute value equations differ from linear equations in that they may have two solutions. This is indicated with a **disjunction**, a mathematical statement created by a connecting two other statements with the word "or." To see why there can be two solutions, you can solve an absolute value equation using graphs.

(A) Solve the equation $2|x - 5| - 4 = 2$.

Plot the function $f(x) = 2|x - 5| - 4$ on a grid. Then plot the function $g(x) = 2$ as a horizontal line on the same grid, and mark the points where the graphs intersect.

The points are $\boxed{?}$ and $\boxed{?}$.

(B) Write the solution to this equation as a disjunction:

$x = \boxed{?}$ or $x = \boxed{?}$

Reflect

1. Why might you expect most absolute value equations to have two solutions? Why not three or four?

2. Is it possible for an absolute value equation to have no solutions? one solution? If so, what would each look like graphically?

✎ Explain 1 Solving Absolute Value Equations Algebraically

To solve absolute value equations algebraically, first isolate the absolute value expression on one side of the equation the same way you would isolate a variable. Then use the rule:

If $|x| = a$ (where a is a positive number), then $x = a$ OR $x = -a$.

Notice the use of a **disjunction** here in the rule for values of x. You cannot know from the original equation whether the expression inside the absolute value bars is positive or negative, so you must work through both possibilities to finish isolating x.

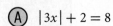

Example 1 Solve each absolute value equation algebraically. Graph the solutions on a number line.

(A) $|3x| + 2 = 8$

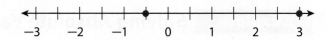

Subtract 2 from both sides. $|3x| = 6$

Rewrite as two equations. $3x = 6$ or $3x = -6$

Solve for x. $x = 2$ or $x = -2$

(B) $3|4x - 5| - 2 = 19$

Add 2 to both sides. $3|4x - 5| = \boxed{21}$

Divide both sides by 3. $|4x - 5| = \boxed{7}$

Rewrite as two equations. $4x - 5 = \boxed{7}$ or $4x - 5 = \boxed{-7}$

Add 5 to all four sides. $4x = \boxed{12}$ or $4x = \boxed{-2}$

Solve for x. $x = \boxed{3}$ or $x = -\dfrac{\boxed{1}}{\boxed{2}}$

Your Turn

Solve each absolute value equation algebraically. Graph the solutions on a number line.

3. $\frac{1}{2}|x + 2| = 10$

4. $-2|3x - 6| + 5 = 1$

⚙ Explain 2 Absolute Value Equations with Fewer than Two Solutions

You have seen that absolute value equations have two solutions when the isolated absolute value expression is equal to a positive number. When the absolute value is equal to zero, there is a single solution because zero is its own opposite. When the absolute value expression is equal to a negative number, there is no solution because absolute value is never negative.

Example 2 Isolate the absolute value expression in each equation to determine if the equation can be solved. If so, finish the solution. If not, write "no solution."

(A) $-5|x + 1| + 2 = 12$

Subtract 2 from both sides. $-5|x + 1| = 10$

Divide both sides by -5. $|x + 1| = -2$

Absolute values are never negative. No Solution

(B) $\frac{3}{5}|2x-4|-3=-3$

Add 3 to both sides.	$\frac{3}{5}|2x-4|=$	0
Multiply both sides by $\frac{5}{3}$.	$|2x-4|=$	0
Rewrite as one equation.	$2x-4=$	0
Add 4 to both sides.	$2x=$	4
Divide both sides by 2.	$x=$	2

Your Turn

Isolate the absolute value expression in each equation to determine if the equation can be solved. If so, finish the solution. If not, write "no solution."

5. $3\left|\frac{1}{2}x+5\right|+7=5$

6. $9\left|\frac{4}{3}x-2\right|+7=7$

💬 Elaborate

7. Why is important to solve both equations in the disjunction arising from an absolute value equation? Why not just pick one and solve it, knowing the solution for the variable will work when plugged back into the equation?

8. **Discussion** Discuss how the range of the absolute value function differs from the range of a linear function. Graphically, how does this explain why a linear equation always has exactly one solution while an absolute value equation can have one, two, or no solutions?

9. **Essential Question Check-In** Describe, in your own words, the basic steps to solving absolute value equations and how many solutions to expect.

⭐ Evaluate: Homework and Practice

- Online Homework
- Hints and Help
- Extra Practice

Solve the following absolute value equations by graphing.

1. $|x-3|+2=5$

2. $2|x+1|+5=9$

3. $-2|x+5|+4=2$

4. $\left|\frac{3}{2}(x-2)\right|+3=2$

Solve each absolute value equation algebraically. Graph the solutions on a number line.

5. $|2x|=3$

6. $\left|\frac{1}{3}x+4\right|=3$

7. $3|2x-3|+2=3$

8. $-8|-x-6|+10=2$

Isolate the absolute value expressions in the following equations to determine if they can be solved. If so, find and graph the solution(s). If not, write "no solution".

9. $\frac{1}{4}|x+2|+7=5$

10. $-3|x-3|+3=6$

11. $2(|x+4|+3)=6$

12. $5|2x+4|-3=-3$

Solve the absolute value equations.

13. $|3x-4|+2=1$

14. $7\left|\frac{1}{2}x+3\frac{1}{2}\right|-2=5$

15. $|2(x+5)-3|+2=6$

16. $-5|-3x+2|-2=-2$

17. The bottom of a river makes a V-shape that can be modeled with the absolute value function, $d(h)=\frac{1}{5}|h-240|-48$, where d is the depth of the river bottom (in feet) and h is the horizontal distance to the left-hand shore (in feet).

A ship risks running aground if the bottom of its keel (its lowest point under the water) reaches down to the river bottom. Suppose you are the harbormaster and you want to place buoys where the river bottom is 30 feet below the surface. How far from the left-hand shore should you place the buoys?

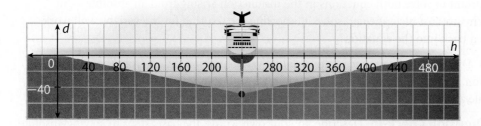

18. A flock of geese is flying past a photographer in a V-formation that can be described using the absolute value function $b(d)=\frac{3}{2}|d-50|$, where $b(d)$ is the distance (in feet) of a goose behind the leader, and d is the distance from the photographer. If the flock reaches 27 feet behind the leader on both sides, find the distance of the nearest goose to the photographer.

19. Geometry Find the points where a circle centered at (3, 0) with a radius of 5 crosses the x-axis. Use an absolute value equation and the fact that all points on a circle are the same distance (the radius) from the center.

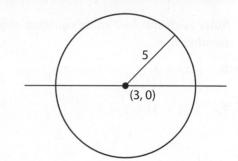

20. Select the value or values of x that satisfy the equation $-\frac{1}{2}|3x - 3| + 2 = 1$.

A. $x = \frac{5}{3}$ B. $x = -\frac{5}{3}$

C. $x = \frac{1}{3}$ D. $x = -\frac{1}{3}$

E. $x = 3$ F. $x = -3$

G. $x = 1$ H. $x = -1$

21. Terry is trying to place a satellite dish on the roof of his house at the recommended height of 30 feet. His house is 32 feet wide, and the height of the roof can be described by the function $h(x) = -\frac{3}{2}|x - 16| + 24$, where x is the distance along the width of the house. Where should Terry place the dish?

22. Explain the Error While attempting to solve the equation $-3|x - 4| - 4 = 3$, a student came up with the following results. Explain the error and find the correct solution:

$-3|x - 4| - 4 = 3$

$\qquad -3|x - 4| = 7$

$\qquad\qquad |x - 4| = -\frac{7}{3}$

$\qquad\qquad x - 4 = -\frac{7}{3}$ or $x - 4 = \frac{7}{3}$

$\qquad\qquad\qquad x = \frac{5}{3}$ or $\qquad x = \frac{19}{3}$

23. Communicate Mathematical Ideas Solve this absolute value equation and explain what algebraic properties make it possible to do so.

$3|x - 2| = 5|x - 2| - 7$

24. Justify Your Reasoning This absolute value equation has nested absolute values. Use your knowledge of solving absolute value equations to solve this equation. Justify the number of possible solutions.

$\left| |2x + 5| - 3 \right| = 10$

25. Check for Reasonableness For what type of real-world quantities would the negative answer for an absolute value equation not make sense?

Lesson Performance Task

A snowball comes apart as a child throws it north, resulting in two halves traveling away from the child. The child is standing 12 feet south and 6 feet east of the school door, along an east-west wall. One fragment flies off to the northeast, moving 2 feet east for every 5 feet north of travel, and the other moves 2 feet west for every 5 feet north of travel. Write an absolute value function that describes the northward position, $n(e)$, of both fragments as a function of how far east of the school door they are. How far apart are the fragments when they strike the wall?

13.4 Solving Absolute Value Inequalities

Resource Locker

Essential Question: What are two ways to solve an absolute value inequality?

Explore Visualizing the Solution Set of an Absolute Value Inequality

You know that when solving an absolute value equation, it's possible to get two solutions. Here, you will explore what happens when you solve absolute value inequalities.

(A) Determine whether each of the integers from -5 to 5 is a solution of the inequality $|x| + 2 < 5$. Write *yes* or *no* for each number. If a number is a solution, plot it on a number line.

(B) Determine whether each of the integers from -5 to 5 is a solution of the inequality $|x| + 2 > 5$. Write *yes* or *no* for each number. If a number is a solution, plot it on a number line.

(C) State the solutions of the equation $|x| + 2 = 5$ and relate them to the solutions you found for the inequalities in Steps A and B.

(D) If x is any real number and not just an integer, graph the solutions of $|x| + 2 < 5$ and $|x| + 2 > 5$.

Reflect

1. It's possible to describe the solutions of $|x| + 2 < 5$ and $|x| + 2 > 5$ using inequalities that don't involve absolute value. For instance, you can write the solutions of $|x| + 2 < 5$ as $x > -3$ and $x < 3$. Notice that the word *and* is used because x must be both greater than -3 and less than 3. How would you write the solutions of $|x| + 2 > 5$? Explain.

2. Describe the solutions of $|x| + 2 \leq 5$ and $|x| + 2 \geq 5$ using inequalities that don't involve absolute value.

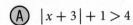

⚙ Explain 1 Solving Absolute Value Inequalities Graphically

You can use a graph to solve an absolute value inequality of the form $f(x) > g(x)$ or $f(x) < g(x)$, where $f(x)$ is an absolute value function and $g(x)$ is a constant function. Graph each function separately on the same coordinate plane and determine the intervals on the x-axis where one graph lies above or below the other. For $f(x) > g(x)$, you want to find the x-values for which the graph $f(x)$ is above the graph of $g(x)$. For $f(x) < g(x)$, you want to find the x-values for which the graph of $f(x)$ is below the graph of $g(x)$.

Example 1 Solve the inequality graphically.

Ⓐ $|x + 3| + 1 > 4$

The inequality is of the form $f(x) > g(x)$, so determine the intervals on the x-axis where the graph of $f(x) = |x + 3| + 1$ lies above the graph of $g(x) = 4$.

The graph of $f(x) = |x + 3| + 1$ lies above the graph of $g(x) = 4$ to the left of $x = -6$ and to the right of $x = 0$, so the solution of $|x + 3| + 1 > 4$ is $x < -6$ or $x > 0$.

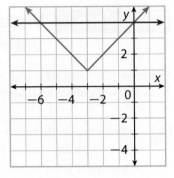

Ⓑ $|x - 2| - 3 < 1$

The inequality is of the form $f(x) < g(x)$, so determine the intervals on the x-axis where the graph of $f(x) = |x - 2| - 3$ lies below the graph of $g(x) = 1$.

The graph of $f(x) = |x - 2| - 3$ lies below the graph of

$g(x) = 1$ between $x = \boxed{-2}$ and $x = \boxed{6}$, so the solution of

$|x - 2| - 3 < 1$ is $x > \boxed{-2}$ and $x < \boxed{6}$.

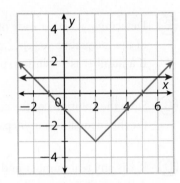

Reflect

3. Suppose the inequality in Part A is $|x + 3| + 1 \geq 4$ instead of $|x + 3| + 1 > 4$. How does the solution change?

4. In Part B, what is another way to write the solution $x > -2$ and $x < 6$?

5. **Discussion** Suppose the graph of an absolute value function $f(x)$ lies entirely above the graph of the constant function $g(x)$. What is the solution of the inequality $f(x) > g(x)$? What is the solution of the inequality $f(x) < g(x)$?

Your Turn

6. Solve $|x + 1| - 4 \leq -2$ graphically.

⚙ Explain 2 Solving Absolute Value Inequalities Algebraically

To solve an absolute value inequality algebraically, start by isolating the absolute value expression. When the absolute value expression is by itself on one side of the inequality, apply one of the following rules to finish solving the inequality for the variable.

Solving Absolute Value Inequalities Algebraically
1. If $|x| > a$ where a is a positive number, then $x < -a$ or $x > a$.
2. If $|x| < a$ where a is a positive number, then $-a < x < a$.

Example 2 Solve the inequality algebraically. Graph the solution on a number line.

Ⓐ $|4 - x| + 15 > 21$

$$|4 - x| > 6$$

$4 - x < -6$ or $4 - x > 6$

$-x < -10$ or $-x > 2$

$x > 10$ or $x < -2$

The solution is $x > 10$ or $x < -2$.

Ⓑ $|x + 4| - 10 \le -2$

$$|x + 4| \le \boxed{8}$$

$x + 4 \ge \boxed{-8}$ and $x + 4 \le \boxed{8}$

$x \ge \boxed{-12}$ and $x \le \boxed{4}$

The solution is $x \ge \boxed{-12}$ and $x \le \boxed{4}$,

or $\boxed{-12} \le x \le \boxed{4}$.

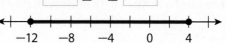

Reflect

7. In Part A, suppose the inequality were $|4 - x| + 15 > 14$ instead of $|4 - x| + 15 > 21$. How would the solution change? Explain.

8. In Part B, suppose the inequality were $|x + 4| - 10 \le -11$ instead of $|x + 4| - 10 \le -2$. How would the solution change? Explain.

Your Turn

Solve the inequality algebraically. Graph the solution on a number line.

9. $3|x - 7| \ge 9$

10. $|2x + 3| < 5$

 **Explain 3** **Solving a Real-World Problem with Absolute Value Inequalities**

Absolute value inequalities are often used to model real-world situations involving a margin of error or *tolerance*. Tolerance is the allowable amount of variation in a quantity.

Example 3

A machine at a lumber mill cuts boards that are 3.25 meters long. It is acceptable for the length to differ from this value by at most 0.02 meters. Write and solve an absolute value inequality to find the range of acceptable lengths.

 Analyze Information

Identify the important information.

- The boards being cut are $\boxed{3.25}$ meters long.
- The length can differ by at most 0.02 meters.

 Formulate a Plan

Let the length of a board be ℓ. Since the sign of the difference between ℓ and 3.25 doesn't matter, take the absolute value of the difference. Since the absolute value of the difference can be at most 0.02, the inequality that models the situation is

$$\left|\ell - \boxed{3.25}\right| \leq \boxed{0.02}.$$

 Solve

$$|\ell - 3.25| \leq 0.02$$

$$\ell - 3.25 \geq -0.02 \text{ and } \ell - 3.25 \leq 0.02$$

$$\ell \geq \boxed{3.23} \text{ and } \qquad \ell \leq \boxed{3.27}$$

So, the range of acceptable lengths is $\boxed{3.23} \leq \ell \leq \boxed{3.27}$.

Justify and Evaluate

The bounds of the range are positive and close to $\boxed{3.25}$, so this is a reasonable answer.

The answer is correct since $\boxed{3.23} + 0.02 = 3.25$ and $\boxed{3.27} - 0.02 = 3.25$.

Your Turn

11. A box of cereal is supposed to weigh 13.8 oz, but it's acceptable for the weight to vary as much as 0.1 oz. Write and solve an absolute value inequality to find the range of acceptable weights.

Elaborate

12. Describe the values of x that satisfy the inequalities $|x| < a$ and $|x| > a$ where a is a positive constant.

13. How do you algebraically solve an absolute value inequality?

14. Explain why the solution of $|x| > a$ is all real numbers if a is a negative number.

15. Essential Question Check-In How do you solve an absolute value inequality graphically?

ⓐ Evaluate: Homework and Practice

• Online Homework
• Hints and Help
• Extra Practice

1. Determine whether each of the integers from -5 to 5 is a solution of the inequality $|x - 1| + 3 \geq 5$. If a number is a solution, plot it on a number line.

2. Determine whether each of the integers from -5 to 5 is a solution of the inequality $|x + 1| - 2 \leq 1$. If a number is a solution, plot it on a number line.

Solve each inequality graphically.

3. $2|x| \leq 6$

4. $|x - 3| - 2 > -1$

5. $\dfrac{1}{2}|x| + 2 < 3$

6. $|x + 2| - 4 \geq -2$

Match each graph with the corresponding absolute value inequality. Then give the solution of the inequality.

A. $2|x| + 1 > 3$ **B.** $2|x + 1| < 3$ **C.** $2|x| - 1 > 3$ **D.** $2|x - 1| < 3$

7.

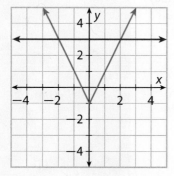

8.

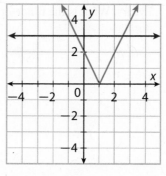

9.

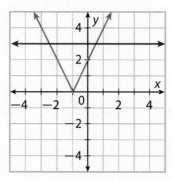

10.

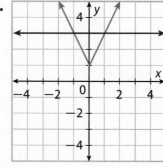

Solve each absolute value inequality algebraically. Graph the solution on a number line.

11. $2\left|x - \dfrac{7}{2}\right| + 3 > 4$

12. $|2x + 1| - 4 < 5$

13. $3|x + 4| + 2 \geq 5$

14. $|x + 11| - 8 \leq -3$

15. $-5|x - 3| - 5 < 15$

16. $8|x + 4| + 10 < 2$

Solve each problem using an absolute value inequality.

17. The thermostat for a house is set to 68 °F, but the actual temperature may vary by as much as 2 °F. What is the range of possible temperatures?

18. The balance of Jason's checking account is $320. The balance varies by as much as $80 each week. What are the possible balances of Jason's account?

19. On average, a squirrel lives to be 6.5 years old. The lifespan of a squirrel may vary by as much as 1.5 years. What is the range of ages that a squirrel lives?

20. You are playing a history quiz game where you must give the years of historical events. In order to score any points at all for a question about the year in which a man first stepped on the moon, your answer must be no more than 3 years away from the correct answer, 1969. What is the range of answers that allow you to score points?

21. The speed limit on a road is 30 miles per hour. Drivers on this road typically vary their speed around the limit by as much as 5 miles per hour. What is the range of typical speeds on this road?

H.O.T. **Focus on Higher Order Thinking**

22. **Represent Real-World Problems** A poll of likely voters shows that the incumbent will get 51% of the vote in an upcoming election. Based on the number of voters polled, the results of the poll could be off by as much as 3 percentage points. What does this mean for the incumbent?

23. **Explain the Error** A student solved the inequality $|x - 1| - 3 > 1$ graphically. Identify and correct the student's error.

I graphed the functions $f(x) = |x - 1| - 3$ and $g(x) = 1$. Because the graph of $g(x)$ lies above the graph of $f(x)$ between $x = -3$ and $x = 5$, the solution of the inequality is $-3 < x < 5$.

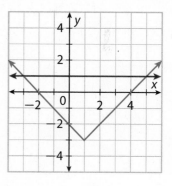

24. **Multi-Step** Recall that a literal equation or inequality is one in which the constants have been replaced by letters.

a. Solve $|ax + b| > c$ for x. Write the solution in terms of a, b, and c. Assume that $a > 0$ and $c \geq 0$.

b. Use the solution of the literal inequality to find the solution of $|10x + 21| > 14$.

c. Explain why you must assume that $a > 0$ and $c \geq 0$ before you begin solving the literal inequality.

Lesson Performance Task

The distance between the Sun and each planet in our solar system varies because the planets travel in elliptical orbits around the Sun. Here is a table of the average distance and the variation in the distance for the five innermost planets in our solar system.

	Average Distance	Variation
Mercury	36 million miles	7.5 million miles
Venus	67.2 million miles	0.5 million miles
Earth	92.75 million miles	1.75 million miles
Mars	141 million miles	13 million miles
Jupiter	484 million miles	24 million miles

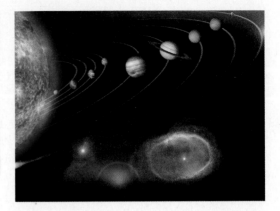

a. Write and solve an inequality to represent the range of distances that can occur between the Sun and each planet.

b. Calculate the percentage variation (variation divided by average distance) in the orbit of each of the planets. Based on these percentages, which planet has the most elliptical orbit?

Piecewise-Defined Functions

Essential Question: How can you use piecewise-defined functions to solve real-world problems?

Key Vocabulary

absolute-value equation
  (ecuación de valor absoluto)

absolute-value function
  (función de valor absolute)

mean *(media)*

greatest integer function
  (función de entero mayor)

piecewise function *(función a trozos)*

step function *(función escalón)*

KEY EXAMPLE   (Lesson 13.1)

Graph the piecewise function $f(x) = \begin{cases} -2x & \text{if } x \le 2 \\ \frac{1}{2}x + 1 & \text{if } x > 2 \end{cases}$.

x	−4	−2	0	2	4	6
f(x)	$-2(-4) = 8$	$-2(-2) = 4$	$-2(0) = 0$	$-2(2) = -4$	$\frac{1}{2}(4) + 1 = 3$	$\frac{1}{2}(6) + 1 = 4$

The transition from one rule to the other occurs at $x = 2$. Show a closed dot at $(2, -4)$, since this point is part of the graph. Show an open dot at $(2, 2)$, since this is not part of the graph.

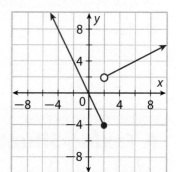

KEY EXAMPLE   (Lesson 13.3)

Solve $-4\,|x + 5| = -2$.

$|x + 5| = \frac{1}{2}$ Divide both sides by −4.

$x + 5 = \frac{1}{2}$ or $x + 5 = -\frac{1}{2}$ Write as two equations.

$x = -4\frac{1}{2}$ or $x = -5\frac{1}{2}$ Subtract 5 from both sides.

KEY EXAMPLE   (Lesson 13.4)

Solve $\frac{1}{2}|x| - 3 \le 1$ graphically.

Let $f(x) = \frac{1}{2}|x| - 3$ and $g(x) = 1$.

Graph $f(x)$ and $g(x)$.

Determine when $f(x) \le g(x)$.

The solution is $x \ge -8$ and $x \le 8$.

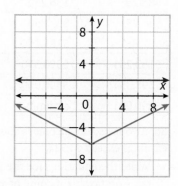

---

1. Copy and complete the table of values for $f(x) = \begin{cases} x - 3 & \text{if } x < -1 \\ -2x + 4 & \text{if } x \geq -1 \end{cases}$. Graph the function. *(Lesson 13.1)*

x	f(x)
−3	?
−2	?
−1	?
0	?
1	?
2	?
3	?

−4

Solve each equation and inequality. *(Lesson 13.3)*

2. $6|x| + 4 = -2$

3. $2|4x - 1| = 6$

4. $|2x + 3| + 7 = 7$

5. $|x + 4| - 12 \leq 20$

MODULE PERFORMANCE TASK

A Taxing Situation

The table below defines the amount of income tax a single U.S. taxpayer must pay to the federal government for income earned in 2013.

If taxable income is over	but not over	the tax is
$0	$8,925	10% of the amount over $0
$8,926	$36,250	$892.50 plus 15% of the amount over $8,925
$36,251	$87,850	$4,991.25 plus 25% of the amount over $36,250
$87,851	$183,250	$17,891.25 plus 28% of the amount over $87,850
$183,251	$398,350	$44,603.25 plus 33% of the amount over $183,250
$398,351	$400,000	$115,586.25 plus 35% of the amount over $398,350
$400,001	no limit	$116,163.75 plus 39.6% of the amount over $400,000

So, if your taxable income is $30,000, you owe $892.50 plus 15% of the amount by which your earnings exceed $8,925.

- Write the equations for the piecewise-defined function that gives the income tax y on taxable income of x (where $x \leq \$100,000$).
- Graph the function.
- Find the percent of total taxable income that a person making $50,000 and a person making $100,000 pay in income tax.

Use numbers, words, or algebra to explain how you reached your conclusion.

13.1–13.4 Piecewise-Defined Functions

- Online Homework
- Hints and Help
- Extra Practice

Write a function to represent each graph shown. *(Lesson 13.1)*

1.

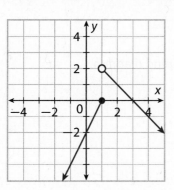

2.

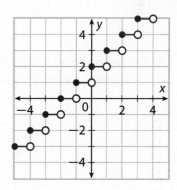

3. The graph of $g(x)$ is a transformation of the graph of $f(x) = |x|$ left 2 units and reflected across the x-axis. Write a function for $g(x)$, and graph $g(x)$. *(Lesson 13.2)*

Solve each equation and inequality. *(Lessons 13.3, 13.4)*

4. $|5x| + 4 = 19$

5. $|2x| + 3 \geq 11$

6. $|4x + 2| - 2 = -18$

7. $|x + 8| - 5 < 2$

ESSENTIAL QUESTION

8. Write a real-world situation that could be modeled by $|x - 14| \leq 3$.

Assessment Readiness

1. Consider the function $f(x) = \begin{cases} 3 & \text{if } x < 2 \\ -x + 1 & \text{if } 2 \leq x < 6 \\ x & \text{if } x \geq 6 \end{cases}$. Tell whether each of the following is a solution of $f(x)$.

   A. $(-5, 3)$

   B. $(2, -1)$

   C. $(8, -7)$

2. Consider the relation represented by the mapping diagram.
   Determine if each statement is True or False.

   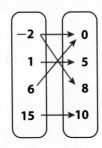

   A. The domain is $\{-2, 1, 6, 15\}$.

   B. The range is $\{0, 5, 8, 10\}$.

   C. The relation is a function.

3. Find the intercepts and slope of $8x - \frac{1}{2}y = 12$. Determine if each statement is True or False.

   A. The x-intercept is 4.

   B. The y-intercept is -24.

   C. The slope is 8.

4. How many solutions does the equation $|x + 6| - 4 = c$ have if $c = 5$?
   If $c = -10$? Justify your answers.

• Online Homework
• Hints and Help
• Extra Practice

1. One equation of a system of two equations is $y = \frac{2}{5}x - 3$. If the second equation is one of the following, is the given number of solutions correct?

   A. $y = \frac{2}{5}x + 1$; no solutions

   B. $y = -2x - 3$; 1 solution

   C. $y = -\frac{2}{5}x - 3$; infinite number of solutions

2. Solve the system of equations $\begin{cases} 2x + 3y = 18 \\ x + y = 6 \end{cases}$.

   Determine if each statement is True or False.

   A. $x = 0$.

   B. $y = 6$.

   C. The only solution is $(0, 6)$.

3. Determine whether each of the following is a solution of the system $\begin{cases} y < 2x + 5 \\ y \geq -\frac{1}{2}x - 2 \end{cases}$.

   A. $(-1, 3)$

   B. $(5, 2)$

   C. $(0, 8)$

4. Asif spent $745.10 on 13 new file cabinets for his office. Small file cabinets cost $43.50 and large file cabinets cost $65.95. Write and solve a system of equations to find the number of small cabinets and large cabinets he purchased.

   Determine if each statement is True or False.

   A. He purchased 5 small cabinets.

   B. He purchased 7 large cabinets.

   C. He spent $527.60 on large cabinets.

5. Solve $\frac{2}{3}|x - 6| \leq 8$. Is each of the following a solution of the inequality?

   A. $x = -6$

   B. $x = 0$

   C. $x = 20$

6. Graph $y = \frac{1}{2}|x - 2| - 6$. Is the relation a function? Explain why or why not.

7. Write the system represented on the graph below. Find and explain the meaning of the point of intersection of the lines.

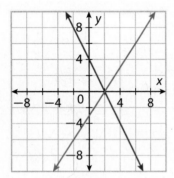

Performance Tasks

★ **8.** A coffee shop purchased 60 pounds of Guatemalan coffee beans and 90 pounds of Nicaraguan coffee beans. The total purchase price was $180. The next week it purchased 80 pounds of Guatemalan coffee and 20 pounds of Nicaraguan coffee, and the cost was $100. Write and solve a system of equations to find the cost per pound for both the Guatemalan and Nicaraguan coffee beans.

★★ **9.** A boat takes 6.5 hours to make a 70-mile trip upstream and 5 hours on the 70-mile return trip. Let *v* be the speed of the boat in still water and *c* be the speed of the current. Therefore, the upstream speed of the boat is $v - c$, and the downstream boat speed is $v + c$.

    A. Write two equations, one for the upstream part of the trip and one for the downstream part, relating boat speed, distance, and time.

    B. Solve the equations in part **A** for the speed of the current.

    C. How long would it take the boat to travel the 70 miles if there were no current? How did you determine your answer?

★★★**10.** Students are raising money for a field trip by selling scented candles and specialty soap. The candles cost $0.75 each and will be sold for $1.75. The soap costs $1.25 per bar and will be sold for $3.25. The students need to raise at least $200 to cover their trip costs.

    A. What is the profit per item for the candles and soap?

    B. Write an inequality that relates the number of candles *c* and the number of bars of soap *s* to the needed income.

    C. The wholesaler can supply no more than 80 bars of soap and no more than 140 candles. Graph the inequality from part **B** and these constraints, using number of candles for the vertical axis.

    D. What does the shaded area of your graph represent?

Personal Shopper Delia is a personal shopper and is tasked with purchasing jeans and T-shirts for her client. Jeans cost $35 and T-shirts cost $15.

a. Write an equation to represent the total amount Delia will pay for x pairs of jeans and y T-shirts if her client wants to spend $115.

b. Delia's client wants a total of 5 items. Write an equation in x and y representing the total number of items Delia will purchase.

c. Solve the system of equations found in parts **a** and **b** algebraically. Show your work.

d. Graph the system, and state the point of intersection.

e. Was it easier to solve the system algebraically or by graphing? Explain your reasoning.

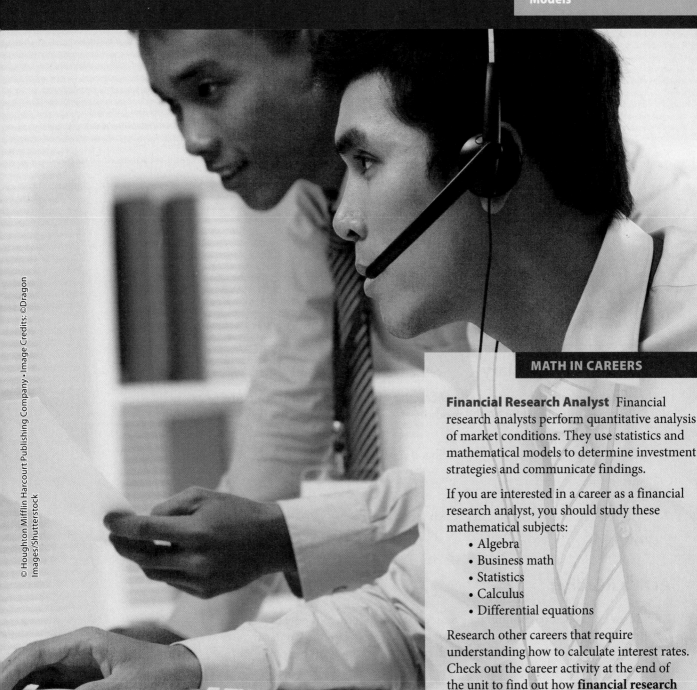

Exponential Relationships

MATH IN CAREERS

Financial Research Analyst Financial research analysts perform quantitative analysis of market conditions. They use statistics and mathematical models to determine investment strategies and communicate findings.

If you are interested in a career as a financial research analyst, you should study these mathematical subjects:
- Algebra
- Business math
- Statistics
- Calculus
- Differential equations

Research other careers that require understanding how to calculate interest rates. Check out the career activity at the end of the unit to find out how **financial research analysts** use math.

Visualize Vocabulary

Copy the Summary Triangle, then use the ✔ words to complete it.

Write one word in each box.

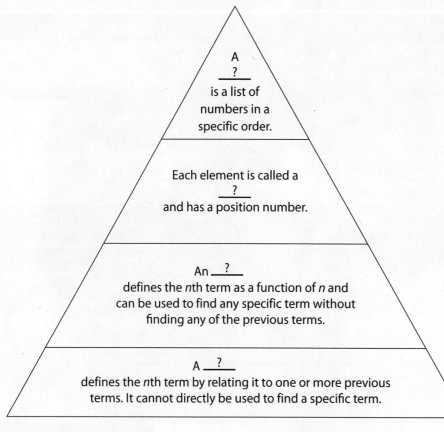

A
___?___
is a list of
numbers in a
specific order.

Each element is called a
___?___
and has a position number.

An ___?___
defines the *n*th term as a function of *n* and
can be used to find any specific term without
finding any of the previous terms.

A ___?___
defines the *n*th term by relating it to one or more previous
terms. It cannot directly be used to find a specific term.

Vocabulary

Review Words

✔ explicit rule (*fórmula explícita*)
exponent (*exponente*)
irrational number (*número irracional*)

✔ linear function (*función lineal*)
rational number (*número racional*)

✔ recursive rule (*fórmula recurrente*)

✔ sequence (*sucesión*)

✔ term (*término*)

Preview Words

exponential function (*función exponencial*)
index (*índice*)
radical expression (*expresión radical*)
radicand (*radicando*)
rational exponent (*exponente racional*)

Understand Vocabulary

To become familiar with some of the vocabulary terms in this unit, consider the following. You may refer to the module, the glossary, or a dictionary.

1. A ___?___ can be expressed as $\frac{m}{n}$ such that if *m* and *n* are integers and $n > 1$, then $a^{\frac{m}{n}} = \sqrt[n]{a^m} = \left(\sqrt[n]{a}\right)^m$.

2. The ___?___ in the ___?___ indicates which root to take of the ___?___.

Active Reading

Key-Term Fold Before beginning the unit, create a key-term fold note to help you organize what you learn. Write a vocabulary term on each tab of the key-term fold. Under each tab, write the definition of the term and an example of the term.

Rational Exponents and Radicals

Essential Question: How can you use rational exponents and radicals to solve real-world problems?

REAL WORLD VIDEO
Zoo managers must determine the amount of food needed for a healthy diet for the animals.

MODULE PERFORMANCE TASK PREVIEW
How Much Should We Feed the Animals?

You have been selected to be the next reptile chef at the local zoo. This means you are in charge of feeding the reptiles. Reptiles get much of their moisture from the foods they eat, so they need food to stay hydrated as well as to keep from starving. Of course, if they don't get enough food, they starve. If they get too much food, however, they can develop serious health issues that may cause death. So, how much food is enough? How much is too much? Let's find out!

Are YOU Ready?

Complete these exercises to review skills you will need for this module.

Exponents

Example 1　Write $(-4)^3$ as a multiplication of factors. Then find its value.

$(-4)^3 = (-4)(-4)(-4)$　Write the base -4 multiplied by itself 3 times.

$(-4)(-4)(-4) = -64$　Multiply.

Write each expression as a multiplication of factors. Then find its value.

1. 13^2

2. $(-5)^4$

3. 9^3

4. 2^5

Algebraic Expressions

Example 2　Evaluate $x^2 + 4$ for $x = -2$.

$x^2 + 4$

$(-2)^2 + 4$　Substitute -2 for x.

$4 + 4$　Evaluate the exponent.

8　Add.

Evaluate each expression for the given value of the variables.

5. $p^3 - 2$ for $p = 3$

6. $5a + b^2$ for $a = -3$ and $b = 4$

7. $6m - n^2$ for $m = 5$ and $n = -7$

8. $x^2 - y^3$ for $x = 6$ and $y = -2$

Real Numbers

Example 3　Tell if 13 is a rational number or an irrational number.

13 can be written as $\frac{13}{1}$,

so 13 is a rational number.

A rational number can be expressed in the form $\frac{p}{q}$, where p and q are integers and $q \neq 0$.

An irrational number cannot be written as the quotient of two integers.

Tell if the number is a rational number or irrational number.

9. -23

10. $\sqrt{8}$

11. $\frac{3}{8}$

14.1 Understanding Rational Exponents and Radicals

Essential Question: How are radicals and rational exponents related?

⊘ Explore 1   Understanding Integer Exponents

Recall that powers like 3^2 are evaluated by repeating the base (3) as a factor a number of times equal to the exponent (2). So $3^2 = 3 \cdot 3 = 9$. What about a negative exponent, or an exponent of 0? You cannot write a product with a negative number of factors, but a pattern emerges if you start from a positive exponent and divide repeatedly by the base.

(A)   Starting with powers of 3:

$$3^3 = \boxed{?}$$

$$3^2 = \boxed{?}$$

$$3^1 = \boxed{?}$$

(B)   Dividing a power of 3 by 3 is equivalent to $\boxed{?}$ the exponent by $\boxed{?}$.

(C)   Complete the pattern:

$$3^3 \xrightarrow{\div 3} 3^2 \xrightarrow{\div 3} 3^1 \xrightarrow{\div 3} 3^0 \xrightarrow{\div 3} 3^{-1} \xrightarrow{\div 3} 3^{-2}$$

$$27 \xrightarrow{\div 3} 9 \xrightarrow{\div 3} 3 \xrightarrow{\div 3} \boxed{?} \xrightarrow{\div 3} \boxed{?} \xrightarrow{\div 3} \boxed{?}$$

(D) $3^{-1} = \dfrac{1}{3}, \ 3^{-2} = \dfrac{1}{9} = \dfrac{1}{3}$

Integer exponents less than 1 can be summarized as follows:

Words	Numbers	Variables
Any non-zero number raised to the power of 0 is 1; 0^0 is undefined	$3^0 = 1$ $(2.4)^0 = 1$	$x^0 = 1$ for $x \neq 0$
Any non-zero number raised to a negative power is equal to 1 divided by the same number raised to the opposite, positive power.	$3^{-2} = \dfrac{1}{3^2} = \dfrac{1}{9}$	$x^{-n} = \dfrac{1}{x^n}$ for $x \neq 0$, and integer n.

Reflect

1.   **Discussion** Why does there need to be an exception in the second rule for the case of $x = 0$?

Explore 2 Exploring Rational Exponents

A **radical expression** is an expression that contains the radical symbol, $\sqrt{\ }$.

For $\sqrt[n]{a}$, n is called the **index** and a is called the **radicand**. n must be an integer greater than 1. a can be any real number when n is odd, but must be non-negative when n is even. When $n = 2$, the radical is a square root and the index 2 is usually not shown.

You can write a radical expression as a power. First, note what happens when you raise a power to a power.

$$\left(2^3\right)^2 = (2\cdot2\cdot2)^2 = (2\cdot2\cdot2)(2\cdot2\cdot2) = 2^6, \text{ so } \left(2^3\right)^2 = 2^{3\cdot2}.$$

In fact, for all real numbers a and all rational numbers m and n, $\left(a^m\right)^n = a^{m\cdot n}$. This is called the **Power of a Power Property.**

A radical expression can be written as an exponential expression: $\sqrt[n]{a} = a^k$. Find the value for k when $n = 2$.

(A) Start with the equation. $\sqrt{a} = a^k$

    Square both sides. $\left(\sqrt{a}\right)^{\boxed{?}} = \left(a^k\right)^{\boxed{?}}$

(B) Definition of square root $\boxed{?} = \left(a^k\right)^2$ (D) Equate exponents. $1 = \boxed{?}$

(C) Power of a power property $a^1 = a^{\boxed{?}}$ (E) Solve for k. $k = \boxed{?}$

Reflect

2. What do you think will be the rule for other values of the radical index n?

Explain 1 Simplifying Numerical Expressions with *n*th Roots

For any integer $n > 1$, the nth root of a is a number that, when multiplied by itself n times, is equal to a.
$$x = \sqrt[n]{a} \Rightarrow x^n = a$$
The nth root can be written as a radical with an index of n, or as a power with an exponent of $\frac{1}{n}$.
An exponent in the form of a fraction is a **rational exponent**.
$$\sqrt[n]{a} = a^{\frac{1}{n}}$$
The expressions are interchangeable, and to evaluate the nth root, it is necessary to find the number, x, that satisfies the equation $x^n = a$.

Example 1 Find the root and simplify the expression.

(A) $64^{\frac{1}{3}}$

    Convert to radical. $64^{\frac{1}{3}} = \sqrt[3]{64}$

    Rewrite radicand as a power. $= \sqrt[3]{4^3}$

    Definition of nth root $= 4$

(B) $81^{\frac{1}{4}} + 9^{\frac{1}{2}}$

    Convert to radicals. $81^{\frac{1}{4}} + 9^{\frac{1}{2}} = \sqrt[4]{\boxed{81}} + \sqrt{\boxed{9}}$

    Rewrite radicands as powers. $= \sqrt[4]{\boxed{3}^{\,4}} + \sqrt{\boxed{3}^{\,2}}$

    Apply definition of nth root. $= \boxed{3} + \boxed{3}$

    Simplify. $= \boxed{6}$

Find the root and simplify the expression.

3. $8^{\frac{1}{3}}$

4. $16^{\frac{1}{2}} + 27^{\frac{1}{3}}$

 Explain 2 **Simplifying Numerical Expressions with Rational Exponents**

Given that for an integer n greater than 1, $\sqrt[n]{a} = a^{\frac{1}{n}}$, you can use the Power of a Power Property to define $a^{\frac{m}{n}}$ for any positive integer m.

$$a^{\frac{m}{n}} = a^{\frac{1}{n} \cdot m}$$

$$a^{\frac{m}{n}} = a^{m \cdot \frac{1}{n}}$$

$$= \left(a^{\frac{1}{n}}\right)^{m} \qquad \text{Power of a Power Property} \qquad = \left(a^{m}\right)^{\frac{1}{n}}$$

$$= \left(\sqrt[n]{a}\right)^{m} \qquad \text{Definition of } a^{\frac{1}{n}} \qquad = \sqrt[n]{a^{m}}$$

The definition of a number raised to the power of $\frac{m}{n}$ is the nth root of the number raised to the mth power. The power of m and the nth root can be evaluated in either order to obtain the same answer, although it is generally easier to find the nth root first when working without a calculator.

Example 2 Simplify expressions with rational exponents.

(A) $27^{\frac{2}{3}}$

Definition of $a^{\frac{m}{n}}$ $\qquad 27^{\frac{2}{3}} = \left(\sqrt[3]{27}\right)^{2}$

Rewrite radicand as a power. $\qquad = \left(\sqrt[3]{3^{3}}\right)^{2}$

Definition of cube root $\qquad = 3^{2}$

$\qquad = 9$

(B) $25^{\frac{3}{2}}$

Definition of $a^{\frac{m}{n}}$ $\qquad 25^{\frac{3}{2}} = \left(\sqrt{25}\right)^{3}$

Rewrite radicand as a power. $\qquad = \left(\sqrt{5^{2}}\right)^{3}$

Definition of $\boxed{\text{square}}$ root $\qquad = 5^{3}$

$\qquad = \boxed{125}$

Simplify the expressions with rational exponents.

5. $32^{\frac{3}{5}}$

6. $4^{\frac{5}{2}} - 4^{\frac{3}{2}}$

7. Why can you evaluate an odd root for any radicand, but even roots require non-negative radicands?

8. In evaluating powers with rational exponents with values like $\frac{2}{3}$, why is it usually better to find the root before the power? Would it change the answer to switch the order?

9. **Essential Question Check-In** How can radicals and rational exponents be used to simplify expressions involving one or the other?

⭐ Evaluate: Homework and Practice

- Online Homework
- Hints and Help
- Extra Practice

Evaluate the expressions.

1. 10^{-2}

2. 56^{-1}

3. 2^{-4}

4. $\left(\frac{1}{3}\right)^{-2}$

5. $(-2)^0$

6. $3 \cdot 6^{-2}$

Find the root(s) and simplify the expression.

7. $81^{\frac{1}{2}}$

8. $125^{\frac{1}{3}}$

9. $49^{\frac{1}{2}} - 4^{\frac{1}{2}}$

10. $16^{\frac{1}{4}} + 32^{\frac{1}{5}}$

Simplify the expressions with rational exponents.

11. $49^{\frac{3}{2}}$

12. $8^{\frac{5}{3}}$

13. $27^{\frac{4}{3}} + 4^{\frac{3}{2}}$

14. $25^{\frac{3}{2}} + 16^{\frac{3}{2}}$

Simplify the expressions.

15. $25^{-\frac{1}{2}}$

16. $8^{-\frac{1}{3}}$

17. $1^{-\frac{2}{3}}$

18. $8^{\frac{2}{3}} + 8^{-\frac{2}{3}}$

19. $\dfrac{25^{\frac{1}{2}}}{27^{\frac{1}{3}}}$

20. $7 \cdot 10^{-3}$

21. $\left(\frac{1}{4}\right)^{-\frac{3}{2}}$

22. $2 \cdot 36^{-\frac{1}{2}} + 6^{-1}$

23. Geometry The volume of a cube is related to the area of a face by the formula $V = A^{\frac{3}{2}}$.

What is the volume of a cube whose face has an area of 100 cm²?

24. Biology The approximate number of Calories, C, that an animal needs each day is given by $C = 72m^{\frac{3}{4}}$, where m is the animal's mass in kilograms. Find the number of Calories that a 16 kilogram dog needs each day.

25. Rocket Science Escape velocity is a measure of how fast an object must be moving to escape the gravitational pull of a planet or moon with no further thrust. The escape velocity for the moon is

given approximately by the equation $V = 5600 \cdot \left(\dfrac{d}{1000}\right)^{-\frac{1}{2}}$, where v is the escape velocity in miles

per hour and d is the distance from the center of the moon (in miles). If a lunar lander thrusts upwards until it reaches a distance of 16,000 miles from the center of the moon, about how fast must it be going to escape the moon's gravity?

26. Multiple Response Which of the following expressions cannot be evaluated?

a. $4^{\frac{1}{2}}$

b. $(-4)^{-\frac{1}{2}}$

c. 4^{-2}

d. $(-4)^{-2}$

e. $0^{-\frac{1}{2}}$

f. 0^{-2}

27. Explain the Error Yuan is asked to evaluate the expression $(-8)^{\frac{2}{3}}$ on his exam, and writes that it is unsolvable because you cannot evaluate a negative number to an even fractional power. Is he correct, and if so, why? If he is not correct, what is the correct answer?

28. Communicate Mathematical Ideas Show that the nth root of a number, a, can be expressed with an exponent of $\dfrac{1}{n}$ for any positive integer, n.

29. Explain the Error Xia, Yen, and Zane are working on homework together, and come to the problem "Find $\left(-\dfrac{1}{64}\right)^{-\frac{2}{3}}$." Xia says "It's undefined because you can't find a square root of a negative number." Yen says "No, it's $1365\dfrac{1}{3}$ because I entered $\left(-\dfrac{1}{64}\right)^{-\frac{2}{3}}$ on a scientific calculator and got 1365.333333." Zane says "No, it's −512, look…" and shows this work:

$$\left(-\frac{1}{64}\right)^{-\frac{2}{3}} = \frac{1}{-\left(\dfrac{1}{64}\right)^{\frac{3}{2}}} = \frac{1}{-\left(\sqrt{\dfrac{1}{64}}\right)^{3}} = \frac{1}{-\left(\dfrac{1}{8}\right)^{3}} = \frac{1}{-\dfrac{1}{512}} = -512$$

Who's right, if anyone? Explain.

Lesson Performance Task

Carbon-14 dating is used to determine the age of archeological artifacts of biological (plant or animal) origin. Items that are dated using carbon-14 include objects made from bone, wood, or plant fibers. This method works by measuring the fraction of carbon-14 remaining in an object. The fraction of the original carbon-14 remaining can be expressed by the function,

$$f = 2^{\left(-\frac{t}{5700}\right)},$$

where t is the length of time since the organism died.

a. Copy and complete the following table to see what fraction of the original carbon-14 still remains after the passage of time.

t	$\dfrac{t}{5700}$	Fraction of Carbon-14 Remaining
0	?	?
5700	?	?
11,400	?	?
17,100	?	?

b. The duration of 5700 years is referred to as the "half-life" of carbon-14 because the amount of carbon-14 drops in half 5700 years after any starting point (not just $t = 0$ years). Verify this property by comparing the amount of remaining carbon-14 after 11,400 years and 17,100 years.

c. Write the corresponding expression for the remaining fraction of uranium-234, which has a half-life of about 80,000 years.

14.2 Simplifying Expressions with Rational Exponents and Radicals

Resource Locker

Essential Question: How can you write a radical expression as an expression with a rational exponent?

⊙ Explore   Exploring Operations with Rational and Irrational Numbers

What happens when you add two rational numbers? Is the result always another rational number or can it be irrational? Will the sum of two irrational numbers always be rational, always be irrational, or can it be either? What about the product of two irrational numbers?

These questions are all used to determine whether a set of numbers is closed under an operation. If the sum of two rational numbers is always rational, the set of rational numbers would be said to be closed under addition. The following tables will combine rational and irrational numbers in various ways. The various sums and products should provide a general idea of which sets are closed under the different operations.

(A) Define rational and irrational numbers.

(B) Copy and complete the following addition table. Note that there are both rational and irrational addends.

+	$-\pi$	7	$\frac{1}{4}$	0	$\sqrt{3}$	$-\sqrt{3}$
$-\pi$	-2π	?	?	?	?	$-\sqrt{3}-\pi$
7	?	?	?	?	?	?
$\frac{1}{4}$	?	?	?	?	?	?
0	?	?	?	?	?	?
$\sqrt{3}$	?	?	?	?	?	?
$-\sqrt{3}$	?	?	?	?	?	?

(C) Based on the results in the table, will the sum of two rational numbers sometimes, always, or never be a rational number?

(D) What about the sum of two irrational numbers?

(E) And finally, the sum of a rational number and an irrational number?

(F) Now copy and complete the following multiplication table. Similarly, it has both rational and irrational factors.

×	$-\pi$	7	$\frac{1}{4}$	0	$\sqrt{3}$	$\frac{1}{\sqrt{3}}$
$-\pi$	π^2	?	?	?	?	?
7	?	?	?	?	?	?
$\frac{1}{4}$	?	?	?	?	?	?
0	?	?	?	?	?	?
$\sqrt{3}$	$-\pi\sqrt{3}$	?	?	?	?	?
$\frac{1}{\sqrt{3}}$	?	?	?	?	?	?

(G) Based on the results in the table, will the product of two rational numbers sometimes, always, or never be a rational number?

(H) What about the product of two irrational numbers?

(I) And finally, the product of a rational number and an irrational number?

Reflect

1. Prove that the product of two rational numbers is a rational number by confirming the general case.

2. **Discussion** Consider the following statement: The product of two rational numbers is an irrational number. Is it a true statement? Justify your answer.

© Houghton Mifflin Harcourt Publishing Company

Explain 1   Simplifying Multivariable Expressions Containing Radicals

As you have seen, to simplify expressions containing radicals, you can rewrite the expressions as powers with rational exponents. You can use properties of exponents. You have already seen the Power of a Power Property of exponents. There are additional properties of exponents that are suggested by the following examples.

$$2^2 \cdot 2^3 = (2 \cdot 2)(2 \cdot 2 \cdot 2) = 2^5 = 2^{2+3}$$

$$\frac{2^3}{2^2} = \frac{2 \cdot 2 \cdot 2}{2 \cdot 2} = 2^1 = 2^{3-2}$$

$$(2 \cdot 3)^2 = (2 \cdot 3)(2 \cdot 3) = (2 \cdot 2)(3 \cdot 3) = 2^2 \cdot 3^2$$

$$\left(\frac{2}{3}\right)^2 = \frac{2}{3} \cdot \frac{2}{3} = \frac{2 \cdot 2}{3 \cdot 3} = \frac{2^2}{3^2}$$

$$\left(2^3\right)^2 = (2 \cdot 2 \cdot 2)^2 = (2 \cdot 2 \cdot 2)(2 \cdot 2 \cdot 2) = 2^6 = 2^{2 \cdot 3}$$

These relationships are formalized in the table.

In the previous lesson, $a^{\frac{1}{n}}$ was defined as $a^{\frac{1}{n}} = \sqrt[n]{a}$ for an integer $n > 1$ and a real number a ($a \geq 0$ for even n) in order to demonstrate that $a^{\frac{m}{n}} = (\sqrt[n]{a})^m$ where m is an integer:

$$a^{\frac{m}{n}} = a^{\frac{1}{n} \cdot m} = \left(a^{\frac{1}{n}}\right)^m = (\sqrt[n]{a})^m$$

The properties of integer exponents now extend to rational exponents.

Properties of Exponents	
Let a and b be real numbers and m and n be rational numbers.	
Product of Powers Property	$a^m \cdot a^n = a^{m+n}$
Quotient of Powers Property	$\dfrac{a^m}{a^n} = a^{m-n},\ a \neq 0$
Power of a Product Property	$\left(a \cdot b\right)^n = a^n \cdot b^n$
Power of a Quotient Property	$\left(\dfrac{a}{b}\right)^n = \dfrac{a^n}{b^n},\ b \neq 0$
Power of a Power Property	$\left(a^m\right)^n = a^{mn}$

Example 1   **Simplify each expression. Assume all variables are positive.**

Ⓐ $\sqrt[3]{(xy)^9}$

$\sqrt[3]{(xy)^9} = (xy)^{\frac{9}{3}}$ Rewrite using rational exponent.

$\quad\quad\quad = (xy)^3$ Simplify the fraction in the exponent.

$\quad\quad\quad = x^3 y^3$ Power of a Product Property

B $\sqrt[5]{x}\,\sqrt{x}$

$$\sqrt[5]{x}\,\sqrt{x} = x^{\boxed{\frac{1}{5}}}\,x^{\frac{1}{2}}$$ Rewrite using rational exponents.

$$= x^{\boxed{\frac{1}{5}} + \boxed{\frac{1}{2}}}$$ Product of Powers Property

$$= x^{\boxed{\frac{7}{10}}}$$ Simplify the exponent.

$$= \sqrt[\boxed{10}]{x^{\boxed{7}}}$$ Rewrite the expression in radical form.

Reflect

3. **Discussion** Why is $\sqrt[n]{a}$ not defined when n is even and $a < 0$?

4. Kris says that $\frac{1}{\sqrt[n]{a}} = \frac{1}{a^{\frac{1}{n}}} = a^{-\frac{1}{n}} = a^{\frac{1}{-n}} = \sqrt[-n]{a}$. Is this true? If not, explain the mistake in reasoning.

Your Turn

Simplify each expression. Assume all variables are positive.

5. $\left(x^2 y\right)^2 \sqrt[4]{y^4}$

6. $\dfrac{\sqrt[4]{x^8}}{\sqrt[4]{x^6}}$

Explain 2 Simplifying Multivariable Expressions Containing Rational Exponents

Use properties of rational exponents to simplify expressions.

Example 2 Simplify each expression. Assume all variables are positive.

A $\left(8x^9\right)^{\frac{2}{3}}$

$$\left(8x^9\right)^{\frac{2}{3}} = \left(2^3\right)^{\frac{2}{3}}\left(x^9\right)^{\frac{2}{3}}$$ Power of a Product Property

$$= 2^{\left(3 \cdot \frac{2}{3}\right)}x^{\left(9 \cdot \frac{2}{3}\right)}$$ Power of a Power Property

$$= 2^2\,x^6$$ Simplify within the parentheses.

$$= 4x^6$$ Simplify.

B $\left(64x^{12}\right)^{\frac{1}{6}}$

$$\left(64x^{12}\right)^{\frac{1}{6}} = \left(2^{\boxed{6}}\right)^{\boxed{\frac{1}{6}}}\left(x^{12}\right)^{\boxed{\frac{1}{6}}}$$ Power of a Product Property

$$= \left(2^{\boxed{6 \cdot \frac{1}{6}}}\right)\left(x^{\boxed{12 \cdot \frac{1}{6}}}\right)$$ Power of a Power Property

$$= 2^{\boxed{1}}\,x^{\boxed{2}}$$ Simplify within the parentheses.

$$= \boxed{2}\,x^{\boxed{2}}$$ Simplify.

7. Simplify $(8x^9)^{-\frac{2}{3}}$. How is it related to the simplified form of $(8x^9)^{\frac{2}{3}}$ found in example 2A? Verify the relationship if one exists.

Your Turn

Simplify each expression. Assume all variables are positive.

8. $\left(\dfrac{1}{4x^4} \cdot x^{12}\right)^{-\frac{1}{2}}$

9. $\left(\dfrac{1}{9x^{12}} \cdot x^4\right)^{\frac{1}{2}}$

⏱ Explain 3 Simplifying Real-World Expressions with Rational Exponents

The relationship between some real-world quantities can be more complicated than a linear or quadratic model can accurately represent. Sometimes, in the most accurate model, the dependent variable is a function of the independent variable raised to a rational exponent. Use the properties of rational exponents to solve the following real-world scenarios.

Example 3 **Biology Application** The approximate number of Calories C that an animal needs each day is given by $C = 72m^{\frac{3}{4}}$, where m is the animal's mass in kilograms.

(A) Find the number of Calories that a 625 kg bear needs each day.
To solve this, evaluate the equation when $m = 625$.

$$C = 72m^{\frac{3}{4}}$$

$$= 72(625)^{\frac{3}{4}} \qquad \text{Substitute 625 for } m.$$

$$= 72\left(\sqrt[4]{625}\right)^3 \qquad \text{Definition of } a^{\frac{m}{n}}$$

$$= 72\left(\sqrt[4]{5^4}\right)^3$$

$$= 72(5)^3$$

$$= 72(125) = 9000$$

A 625 kilogram bear needs 9000 Calories each day.

(B) A particular panda consumes 1944 Calories each day. How much does this panda weigh?

Substitute $\boxed{1944}$ for C in the original equation and solve for m.

$C = 72m^{\frac{3}{4}}$	Original equation
$\boxed{1944} = 72m^{\frac{3}{4}}$	Substitute for C.
$\dfrac{\boxed{1944}}{72} = m^{\frac{3}{4}}$	Divide each side by 72.
$\boxed{27} = m^{\frac{3}{4}}$	Simplify.
$3^3 = m^{\frac{3}{4}}$	Rewrite the left side as a power.
$\left(3^3\right)^{\boxed{\frac{4}{3}}} = \left(m^{\frac{3}{4}}\right)^{\boxed{\frac{4}{3}}}$	Raise both sides to the $\boxed{\frac{4}{3}}$ power.
$3^{\left(3 \cdot \boxed{\frac{4}{3}}\right)} = m^{\left(\frac{3}{4} \cdot \boxed{\frac{4}{3}}\right)}$	Power of a Power Property
$3^4 = m$	Simplify inside the parentheses.
$m = \boxed{81}$	Simplify.

The panda weighs $\boxed{81}$ kilograms.

Your Turn

Solve each real-world scenario.

10. The speed of light is the product of its frequency f and its wavelength w. In air, the speed of light is 3×10^8 m/s.

   a. Write an equation for the relationship described above, and then solve this equation for frequency.

   b. Rewrite this equation with w raised to a negative exponent.

   c. What is the frequency of violet light when its wavelength is approximately 400 nanometers $\left(1 \text{ nm} = 10^{-9} \text{ m}\right)$?

11. Geometry The formula for the surface area S of a sphere in terms of its volume V is $S = (4\pi)^{\frac{1}{3}} (3V)^{\frac{2}{3}}$. What is the surface area of a sphere that has a volume of 36π cm cubed? Leave the answer in terms of π. What do you notice?

12. A set of elements is said to be closed under some operation if performance of that operation on elements of the set always produces an element of the set. Examine the set of integers and the set of rational numbers. Is each set closed under each of the following operations: addition, multiplication, division, and subtraction? Provide a counterexample if the set is not closed under an operation.

13. Why are integers closed under multiplication?

14. Is the set of all numbers of the form a^x, where a is a positive constant and x is a rational number, closed under multiplication? Justify your answer.

15. **Essential Question Check-In** How can you write a radical expression as a power with a rational exponent?

☆ Evaluate: Homework and Practice

- Online Homework
- Hints and Help
- Extra Practice

1. Why are the addition and multiplication tables in the Explore activity symmetric about the diagonal from the upper-left corner to the lower-right? For example, why is the entry in the third row of the second column equal to the entry in the second row of the third column? Would a subtraction table be symmetric about the same diagonal?

2. Prove that the rational numbers are closed under addition.

Simplify the given expression.

3. $\sqrt[3]{\left(27x^3\right)^4}$

4. $\sqrt[3]{\left(8x^3\right)^2}$

5. $\sqrt[3]{\left(8y^3\right)^4}\sqrt[6]{\left(8y^3\right)^4}$

6. $\sqrt[10]{0x}$

7. $\sqrt{(2x)^2\sqrt{2y}}$

8. $\dfrac{\sqrt{8x}}{\sqrt[3]{16x}}$

9. $(0x)^{\frac{1}{3}}$

10. $10,000^{\frac{1}{4}} \cdot z + 10,000^{\frac{1}{2}} \cdot z$

11. $\left(\dfrac{1}{25x} \cdot x^9\right)^{-\frac{1}{2}}$

12. $\left(\dfrac{1}{125x^3}\right)^{-\frac{1}{3}}$

13. $\left[(2x)^x(2x)^{2x}\right]^{\frac{1}{x}}$

14. $\left[\left(1,000,000x^6\right)^{-\frac{1}{3}}\right]^{-\frac{1}{2}}$

15. $\left(x^2y\right)^3\sqrt[2]{y^4}$

16. $\dfrac{\left[\left(x^2y\right)^4\right]^{\frac{1}{2}}}{\left[\left(x^2y\right)^{\frac{1}{2}}\right]^4}$

17. $\left(x^{\frac{1}{8}}y^{\frac{1}{4}}z^{\frac{1}{2}}\right)^8$

18. $\left(\sqrt{z\sqrt{y\sqrt{x}}}\right)^8$

19. $\dfrac{\left(x^{10}\right)^{\frac{1}{5}}}{\sqrt[2]{x^8}}$

20. $\dfrac{\left[\left(x^{-8}\right)^{\frac{1}{4}}\right]^{-1}\sqrt[3]{x^2}}{\sqrt[6]{x^4}}$

21. $\left(x^2y\right)^4\left(\sqrt{y^{\frac{1}{2}}}\right)$

22. $\left(\sqrt{y^{\frac{1}{4}}}\right)^8$

23. **Biology** Biologists use a formula to estimate the mass of a mammal's brain. For a mammal with a mass of m grams, the approximate mass B of the brain, also in grams, is given by $B = \frac{1}{8}m^{\frac{2}{3}}$. Find the approximate mass of the brain of a mouse that has a mass of 64 grams.

24. **Multi-Step** Scientists have found that the life span of a mammal living in captivity is related to the mammal's mass. The life span in years L can be approximated by the formula $L = 12m^{\frac{1}{5}}$, where m is the mammal's mass in kilograms. How much longer is the life span of a lion compared with that of a wolf?

Typical Mass of Mammals	
Mammal	Mass (kg)
Koala	8
Wolf	32
Lion	243
Giraffe	1024

Tim and Tom are painters. Use the given information to provide the desired estimate.

25. Tim and Tom use a liters of paint on a building. If the next building they need to paint is similar but has twice the volume, how much paint should they plan on buying?

26. Tim and Tom are painting a building. Tom paints 10 square feet per minute. They painted a particular building in 1 day. Tim uses a sprayer and is 4.7 times as fast as Tom. How long would it take them to paint a building with twice the volume and of similar shape?

27. Determine whether each of the following is rational or irrational.

a. The product of $\sqrt{2}$ and $\sqrt{50}$

b. The product of $\sqrt{2}$ and $\sqrt{25}$

c. $C = 2\pi r$ evaluated for $r = \pi^{-1}$

d. $C = 2\pi r$ evaluated for $r = 1$

e. $A = 2\pi r^2$ evaluated for $r = \pi^{\frac{1}{2}}$

f. The product of $\sqrt{\dfrac{2}{\pi}}$ and $\sqrt{50\pi}$

g. The product of $\sqrt{2}$ and $\sqrt{\dfrac{9}{2}}$

28. **Explain the Error** Jim tried to show how to write a radical expression as a power with a rational exponent.

Suppose that $(\sqrt[n]{a}) = a^k$.

$(\sqrt[n]{a})^n = (a^k)^n$	Raise each side to the nth power.
$a = (a^k)^n$	Definition of nth root
$a = a^{\frac{n}{k}}$	Power of a Power Property
$a^1 = a^{\frac{n}{k}}$	
$1 = \dfrac{n}{k}$	Equate exponents.
$k = n$	Solve for k.

Jim claimed to have shown that $\sqrt[n]{a} = a^n$. Explain and correct his error.

29. **Communicate Mathematical Ideas** Given that the set of rational numbers is closed under multiplication, prove by contradiction that the product of a nonzero rational number and an irrational number is an irrational number. To do this, assume the negation of what you are trying to prove and show how it will logically lead to something contradicting a given statement. Let $a \neq 0$ be rational, let b be irrational, and let $a \cdot b = c$. Assume that a nonzero rational number times an irrational number is rational, so c is rational.

$a \cdot b = c$	Given
$\left(\frac{1}{a}\right) \cdot a \cdot b = \left(\frac{1}{a}\right) \cdot c$	Multiply both sides by $\frac{1}{a}$.
$b = \left(\frac{1}{a}\right) \cdot c$	Simplify.

Provide the contradiction statement to finish the proof.

30. **Communicate Mathematical Ideas** Prove by contradiction that a rational number plus an irrational number is irrational. To do this assume the negation of what you are trying to prove and show how it will logically lead to something contradicting the given. Assume that a rational number plus an irrational number is rational.

$r_1 + i_1 = r_2$	Given
$r_1 + i_1 - r_1 = r_2 - r_1$	Subtract r_1 from both sides.
$i_1 = r_2 - r_1$	Simplify left side.

Provide the contradiction statement to finish the proof.

31. **Critical Thinking** Show that a number raised to the $\frac{1}{3}$ power is the same as the cube root of that number.

Lesson Performance Task

The balls used in soccer, baseball, basketball, and golf are spheres. How much material is needed to make each of the balls in the table?

The formula for the surface area of a sphere is $S_A = 4\pi r^2$, and the formula for the volume of a sphere is $V = \frac{4}{3}\pi r^3$. Use algebra to find the formula for the surface area of a sphere given its volume.

Copy and complete the table with the surface area of each ball.

Ball	Volume (in cubic inches)	Surface Area (in square inches)
soccer ball	356.8	?
baseball	12.8	?
basketball	455.9	?
golf ball	2.48	?

Rational Exponents and Radicals

Essential Question: How can you use rational exponents and radicals to solve real-world problems?

Key Vocabulary

index *(índice)*
radical expression
  (expresión radical)
radicand *(radicando)*
rational exponent
  (exponente racional)

KEY EXAMPLE *(Lesson 14.1)*

Evaluate the expression 3^{-4}.

$3^{-4} = \frac{1}{3^4}$ Definition of negative exponent

$= \frac{1}{81}$ Evaluate.

KEY EXAMPLE *(Lesson 14.1)*

Simplify $64^{\frac{2}{3}}$.

$64^{\frac{2}{3}} = \left(\sqrt[3]{64}\right)^2$ Definition of $b^{\frac{m}{n}}$

$= \left(\sqrt[3]{4^3}\right)^2$ Rewrite radicand as a power.

$= 4^2$ Definition of cube root

$= 16$

Simplify $128^{-\frac{8}{7}}$.

$128^{-\frac{8}{7}} = \frac{1}{\left(\sqrt[7]{128}\right)^8}$ Definition of negative exponent and $b^{\frac{m}{n}}$

$= \frac{1}{\left(\sqrt[7]{2^7}\right)^8}$ Rewrite radicand as a power.

$= \frac{1}{2^8}$ Definition of nth root

$= \frac{1}{256}$

KEY EXAMPLE *(Lesson 14.2)*

Simplify $\frac{\sqrt[3]{x^8}}{\sqrt[3]{x^6}}$. Assume x is positive.

$\frac{\sqrt[3]{x^8}}{\sqrt[3]{x^6}} = \frac{x^{\frac{8}{3}}}{x^{\frac{6}{3}}}$

$= x^{\frac{8}{3} - \frac{6}{3}}$

$= x^{\frac{2}{3}}$

$= \sqrt[3]{x^2}$

EXERCISES

Simplify each expression. *(Lesson 14.1)*

1. $25^{\frac{3}{2}}$

2. $81^{\frac{1}{2}} - 16^{\frac{1}{2}}$

3. $27^{\frac{4}{3}}$

4. $8^{\frac{5}{3}} + 4^{\frac{5}{2}}$

Simplify each expression. *(Lesson 14.2)*

5. $1{,}000{,}000^{\frac{1}{3}} \cdot d + 1{,}000{,}000^{\frac{1}{2}} \cdot d$

6. $\sqrt[3]{\left(64x^3\right)^4}$

7. $\sqrt[3]{\left(27x^3\right)^2}$

8. $\left(\dfrac{1}{216x^3}\right)^{-\frac{1}{3}}$

MODULE PERFORMANCE TASK

How Much Should We Feed the Reptiles?

The zoo is expecting a new alligator to arrive in a few days. The previous Reptile Chef fed other species of reptiles currently at the zoo according to the information in the table. You speak with the Mammal Chef, who uses the formula $y = 72m^{\frac{3}{4}}$ to determine the daily Calorie intake for mammals, where y is the number of Calories eaten and m is the mammal's mass in kilograms. You wonder if a similar formula might help determine the number of Calories for the new alligator. Substitute data pairs from the table into the formula to find a number a so that the expression $y = am^{\frac{3}{4}}$ gives the daily number of Calories required by a reptile with a mass of m kilograms.

Reptile Type	Mass	Daily Calories
Bearded Dragon	0.4 kg	5.0
Spur-thighed Tortoise	4.2 kg	29.3
Spectacled Caiman	34 kg	142
Rhinoceros Iguana	7.4 kg	44.9
Giant Tortoise	250 kg	629

If the alligator has a mass of 400 kilograms, how many Calories will it require per day?

Use graphs, numbers, words, or algebra to support your conclusion.

(Ready) to Go On?

14.1–14.2 Rational Exponents and Radicals

- Online Homework
- Hints and Help
- Extra Practice

Simplify each expression. *(Lesson 14.1)*

1. $216^{\frac{1}{3}} - 125^{\frac{1}{3}}$

2. $3 \cdot 49^{-\frac{1}{2}} + 7^{-1}$

Simplify each expression. *(Lesson 14.2)*

3. $\left(\dfrac{1}{16x} \cdot x^7 \right)^{-\frac{1}{2}}$

4. $\left(xy^2 \right)^2 \sqrt[2]{y^8}$

5. The volume of a cube is related to the area of a face by the formula $V = A^{\frac{3}{2}}$. What is the volume of a cube whose face has an area of 25 mm²? *(Lesson 14.1)*

6. Biologists use a formula to estimate the mass of a mammal's brain. For a mammal with a mass of m grams, the approximate mass B of the brain, also in grams, is given by $B = \frac{1}{8}m^{\frac{2}{3}}$. Find the approximate mass of the brain of a shrew that has a mass of 27 grams. *(Lesson 14.2)*

ESSENTIAL QUESTION

7. How are rational exponents and radicals related?

Assessment Readiness

1. Consider each expression. Is the expression equivalent to $\frac{512^{\frac{1}{3}}}{64^{\frac{2}{3}}}$?

   A. $\left(\dfrac{64^{\frac{2}{3}}}{512^{\frac{1}{3}}} \right)^{-1}$

   B. $\left(64^{\frac{2}{3}} \times 512^{-\frac{1}{3}} \right)^{-1}$

   C. $\dfrac{64^{-\frac{2}{3}}}{512^{-\frac{1}{3}}}$

2. Consider each set. Does the set represent a function?

   A. $\left\{ (5, -2), (5, 0), (5, 2), (5, 4) \right\}$

   B. $\left\{ (3, 4), (4, 4), (5, 2), (6, 4) \right\}$

   C. $\left\{ (-4, 1), (-2, 3), (0, 4), (2, 3) \right\}$

3. Consider the graph of $y = \left(\sqrt[3]{8x^3} \right) + 8$. Determine if each of the following statements is True or False.

   A. The slope is 8.

   B. The y-intercept is 8.

   C. The x-intercept is -4.

4. Simplify $216^{\frac{2}{3}}$.

5. Jasmine believes that the sum of two positive irrational numbers can be a rational number. She gives the following example: $\sqrt{2} + \sqrt{2}$. Do you agree with Jasmine? Explain why or why not.

Geometric Sequences and Exponential Functions

Essential Question: How can you use geometric sequences and exponential functions to solve real-world problems?

REAL WORLD VIDEO
Pythons originally kept as pets but later released into the Florida ecosystem find themselves in an environment with no natural predators and prey ill-equipped to evade or defend itself. As a result, the python population can grow exponentially, causing havoc among local wildlife and pets.

MODULE PERFORMANCE TASK PREVIEW
What Does It Take to Go Viral?

You have just created a great video, and you share it with some of your friends. Then each of them shares it with the same number of their own friends. If this pattern continues, to how many friends should you show your video to make it go viral within a few days? Let's find out!

Are (YOU) Ready?

Complete these exercises to review skills you will need for this module.

Exponents

Example 1   Evaluate $(-6)^3$.

$(-6)^3 = (-6)(-6)(-6)$ Write the base -6 multiplied by itself 3 times.

$(-6)(-6)(-6) = -216$ Multiply.

Evaluate each power.

1. 2^4

2. $(-3)^5$

3. 5^0

Example 2   Simplify $x^3 \cdot x^5$.

$x^3 \cdot x^5 = x^{3+5} = x^8$ When multiplying powers with the same base, add the exponents.

Simplify.

4. $x \cdot x^6$

5. $x^3 y^2 \cdot y^4$

6. $3a^2 b \cdot 5a^2 b^4$

7. $4mno \cdot 7n^2 o^2 \cdot mn$

Algebraic Expressions

Example 3   Evaluate $\frac{2}{3}x^2$ for $x = 6$.

$\frac{2}{3}(6)^2$ Substitute 6 for *x*.

$\frac{2}{3}(36)$ Evaluate the power.

24 Multiply.

Evaluate each expression for the given value of the variables.

8. $\frac{1}{2}x^3$ for $x = 4$

9. $\frac{3}{4}x^4$ for $x = -2$

10. $8x^2$ for $x = \frac{1}{2}$

11. $18x^3$ for $x = -\frac{1}{3}$

15.1 Understanding Geometric Sequences

Essential Question: How are the terms of a geometric sequence related?

⊘ Explore 1 Exploring Growth Patterns of Geometric Sequences

The sequence 3, 6, 12, 24, 48, … is a *geometric sequence*. In a **geometric sequence**, the ratio of successive terms is constant. The constant ratio is called the **common ratio**, often represented by *r*.

(A) Complete each division.

$\dfrac{6}{3} = \boxed{?}$ $\dfrac{12}{6} = \boxed{?}$ $\dfrac{24}{12} = \boxed{?}$ $\dfrac{48}{24} = \boxed{?}$

(B) The common ratio *r* for the sequence is $\boxed{?}$.

(C) Use the common ratio you found to identify the next term in the geometric sequence.

The next term is $48 \cdot \boxed{?} = \boxed{?}$.

Reflect

1. Suppose you know the twelfth term in a geometric sequence. What do you need to know to find the thirteenth term? How would you use that information to find the thirteenth term?

2. **Discussion** Suppose you know only that 8 and 128 are terms of a geometric sequence. Can you find the term that follows 128? If so, what is it?

⊘ Explore 2 Comparing Growth Patterns of Arithmetic and Geometric Sequences

Recall that in arithmetic sequences, successive (or consecutive) terms differ by the same nonzero number *d*, called the common difference. In geometric sequences, the ratio *r* of successive terms is constant. In this Explore, you will examine how the growth patterns in arithmetic and geometric sequences compare. In particular, you will look at the arithmetic sequence 3, 5, 7, … and the geometric sequence 3, 6, 12, … .

The tables show the two sequences.

3, 5, 7, …	
Term Number	**Term**
1	3
2	5
3	7
4	9
5	11

3, 6, 12, …	
Term Number	**Term**
1	3
2	6
3	12
4	24
5	48

(A) The common difference d of the arithmetic sequence is $5 - 3 = 2$. The common ratio r of the geometric sequence is $\dfrac{6}{\boxed{?}} = \boxed{?}$.

(B) Copy and complete the table. Find the differences of successive terms.

Arithmetic: 3, 5, 7, ...		
Term Number	Term	Difference
1	3	—
2	5	$5 - 3 = \boxed{?}$
3	7	$7 - 5 = \boxed{?}$
4	9	$9 - 7 = \boxed{?}$
5	11	$11 - 9 = \boxed{?}$

Geometric: 3, 6, 12, ...		
Term Number	Term	Difference
1	3	—
2	6	$6 - 3 = \boxed{?}$
3	12	$12 - 6 = \boxed{?}$
4	24	$24 - 12 = \boxed{?}$
5	48	$48 - 24 = \boxed{?}$

(C) Compare the growth patterns of the sequences based on the tables. $\boxed{?}$

(D) Graph both sequences in the same coordinate plane. Compare the growth patterns based on the graphs. $\boxed{?}$

Reflect

3. Which grows more quickly, the arithmetic sequence or the geometric sequence?

🔑 Explain 1 Extending Geometric Sequences

In Explore 1, you saw that each term of a geometric sequence is the product of the preceding term and the common ratio. Given terms of a geometric sequence, you can use this relationship to write additional terms of the sequence.

Finding a Term of a Geometric Sequence
For $n \geq 2$, the nth term, $f(n)$, of a geometric sequence with common ratio r is $$f(n) = f(n - 1)r.$$

© Houghton Mifflin Harcourt Publishing Company

Example 1 Find the common ratio r for each geometric sequence and use r to find the next three terms.

(A) 6, 12, 24, 48, …

$\dfrac{12}{6} = 2$, so the common ratio r is 2.

For this sequence, $f(1) = 6$, $f(2) = 12$, $f(3) = 24$, and $f(4) = 48$.

$f(4) = 48$, so $f(5) = 48(2) = 96$.

$f(5) = 96$, so $f(6) = 96(2) = 192$.

$f(6) = 192$, so $f(7) = 192(2) = 384$.

The next three terms of the sequence are 96, 192, and 384.

(B) 100, 50, 25, 12.5, …

$\dfrac{50}{100} = \boxed{0.5}$, so the common ratio r is $\boxed{0.5}$.

For this sequence, $f(1) = 100$, $f(2) = 50$, $f(3) = 25$, and $f(4) = 12.5$.

$f(4) = 12.5$, so $f(5) = \boxed{12.5}\,(0.5) = \boxed{6.25}$.

$f(5) = \boxed{6.25}$, so $f(6) = \boxed{6.25}\,(0.5) = \boxed{3.125}$.

$f(6) = \boxed{3.125}$, so $f(7) = \boxed{3.125}\,(0.5) = \boxed{1.5625}$.

The next three terms of the sequence are $\boxed{6.25}$, $\boxed{3.125}$, and $\boxed{1.5625}$.

Reflect

4. **Communicate Mathematical Ideas** A geometric sequence has a common ratio of 3. The 4th term is 54. What is the 5th term? What is the 3rd term?

Your Turn

Find the common ratio r for each geometric sequence and use r to find the next three terms.

5. 5, 20, 80, 320, …

6. $9, -3, 1 -\dfrac{1}{3}, …$

Recognizing Growth Patterns of Geometric Sequences in Context

You can find a term of a sequence by repeatedly multiplying the first term by the common ratio.

Example 2

(A) A bungee jumper jumps from a bridge. The table shows the bungee jumper's height above the ground at the top of each bounce. The heights form a geometric sequence. What is the bungee jumper's height at the top of the 5th bounce?

Bounce	Height (feet)
1	200
2	80
3	32

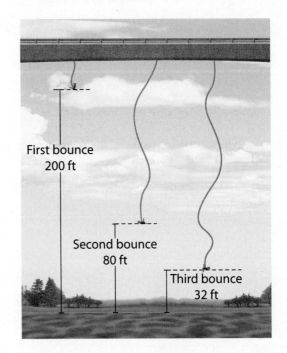

First bounce
200 ft

Second bounce
80 ft

Third bounce
32 ft

Find r.

$$\frac{80}{200} = 0.4 = r$$

$f(1) = 200$

$f(2) = 80$

$\quad = 200(0.4)$ or $200(0.4)^1$

$f(3) = 32$

$\quad = 80(0.4)$

$\quad = 200(0.4)(0.4)$

$\quad = 200(0.4)^2$

In each case, to get $f(n)$, you multiply 200 by the common ratio, 0.4, $n-1$ times. That is, you multiply 200 by $(0.4)^{n-1}$.

The jumper's height on the 5th bounce is $f(5)$.

Multiply 200 by $(0.4)^{5-1} = (0.4)^4$.

$200(0.4)^4 = 200(0.0256)$

$\quad\quad = 5.12$

The height of the jumper at the top of the 5th bounce is 5.12 feet.

Example 2

(B) A ball is dropped from a height of 144 inches. Its height on the 1st bounce is 72 inches. On the 2nd and 3rd bounces, the height of the ball is 36 inches and 18 inches, respectively. The heights form a geometric sequence. What is the height of the ball on the 6th bounce to the nearest tenth of an inch?

Find r.

$$\frac{36}{72} = \frac{1}{2} = r$$

$$f(1) = \boxed{72}$$

$$f(2) = \boxed{36}$$

$$= 72\left(\boxed{\frac{1}{2}}\right) \text{ or } 72\left(\boxed{\frac{1}{2}}\right)^1$$

$$f(3) = \boxed{18}$$

$$= 36\left(\boxed{\frac{1}{2}}\right)$$

$$= 72\left(\boxed{\frac{1}{2}}\right)\left(\boxed{\frac{1}{2}}\right)$$

$$= 72\left(\boxed{\frac{1}{2}}\right)^2$$

In each case, to get $f(n)$, you multiply 72 by the common ratio, $\frac{1}{2}$, $n - 1$ times. That is, you multiply 72 by $\left(\frac{1}{2}\right)^{n-1}$.

The height of the ball on the 6th bounce is $f\left(\boxed{6}\right)$.

Multiply 72 by $\left(\frac{1}{2}\right)^{6-1} = \left(\frac{1}{2}\right)^5$.

$$72\left(\frac{1}{2}\right)^5 = 72\left(\frac{1}{32}\right)$$

$$= 72(0.3125)$$

$$= 2.25$$

The height of the ball at the top of the 6th bounce is about 2.3 inches.

Reflect

7. Is it possible for a sequence that describes the bounce height of a ball to have a common ratio greater than 1?

8. **Physical Science** A ball is dropped from a height of 8 meters. The table shows the height of each bounce. The heights form a geometric sequence. How high does the ball bounce on the 4th bounce? Round your answer to the nearest tenth of a meter.

Bounce	Height (m)
1	6
2	4.5
3	3.375

💬 Elaborate

9. Suppose all the terms of a geometric sequence are positive, and the common ratio r is between 0 and 1. Is the sequence increasing or decreasing? Explain.

10. **Essential Question Check-In** If the common ratio of a geometric sequence is less than 0, what do you know about the signs of the terms of the sequence? Explain.

⭐ Evaluate: Homework and Practice

- Online Homework
- Hints and Help
- Extra Practice

Find the common ratio r for each geometric sequence and use r to find the next three terms.

1. 5, 15, 45, 135 …

2. −2, 6, −18, 54 …

3. 4, 20, 100, 500, …

4. 8, 4, 2, 1, …

5. 72, −36, 18, −9, …

6. 200, −80, 32, −12.8, …

7. 10, 30, 90, 270, …

8. 5, 3, 1.8, 1.08, …

9. 18, 36, 72, 144

10. 243, 162, 108, 72, …

Find the indicated term of each sequence by repeatedly multiplying the first term by the common ratio. Use a calculator.

11. 1, 8, 64, …; 5th term

12. 16, −3.2, 0.64, …; 7th term

13. −50, 15, −4.5, …; 5th term

14. 3, −12, 48, …; 6th term

Solve. You may use a calculator and round your answer to the nearest tenth of a unit if necessary.

15. **Physical Science** A ball is dropped from a height of 900 centimeters. The table shows the height of each bounce. The heights form a geometric sequence. How high does the ball bounce on the 5th bounce?

Bounce	Height (cm)
1	800
2	560
3	392

16. Leo's bank balances at the end of months 1, 2, and 3 are $1500, $1530, and $1560.60, respectively. The balances form a geometric sequence. What will Leo's balance be after 9 months?

17. **Biology** A biologist studying ants started on day 1 with a population of 1500 ants. On day 2, there were 3000 ants, and on day 3, there were 6000 ants. The increase in an ant population can be represented using a geometric sequence. What is the ant population on day 5?

18. **Physical Science** A ball is dropped from a height of 625 centimeters. The table shows the height of each bounce. The heights form a geometric sequence. How high does the ball bounce on the 8th bounce?

Bounce	Height (cm)
1	500
2	400
3	320

19. **Finance** The table shows the balance in an investment account after each month. The balances form a geometric sequence. What is the amount in the account after month 6?

Month	Amount ($)
1	1700
2	2040
3	2448

20. **Biology** A turtle population grows in a manner that can be represented by a geometric sequence. Given the table of values, determine the turtle population after 6 years.

Year	Number of Turtles
1	5
2	15
3	45

21. Consider the geometric sequence −8, 16, −32, ... Determine whether each statement is correct.

   a. The common ratio is 2.

   b. The 5th term of the sequence is −128.

   c. The 7th term is 4 times the 5th term.

   d. The 8th term is 1024.

   e. The 10th term is greater than the 9th term.

22. **Justify Reasoning** Suppose you are given a sequence with $r < 0$. What do you know about the signs of the terms of the sequence? Explain.

23. **Critique Reasoning** Miguel writes the following: 8, x, 8, x, ... He tells Alicia that he has written a geometric sequence and asks her to identify the value of x. Alicia says the value of x must be 8. Miguel says that Alicia is incorrect. Who is right? Explain.

Lesson Performance Task

Multi-Step Gifford earns money by shoveling snow for the winter. He offers two payment plans: either pay $400 per week for the entire winter or pay $5 for the first week, $10 for the second week, $20 for the third week, and so on. Explain why each plan does or does not form a geometric sequence. Then determine the number of weeks after which the total cost of the second plan will exceed the total cost of the first plan.

15.2 Constructing Geometric Sequences

Essential Question: How do you write a geometric sequence?

🧭 Explore   Understanding Recursive and Explicit Rules for Sequences

You learned previously that an explicit rule for a sequence defines the nth term as a function of n. A recursive rule defines the nth term of a sequence in terms of one or more previous terms.

You can use what you know to identify recursive and explicit rules for sequences, and identify whether the sequences are arithmetic, geometric, or neither.

A rule for the sequence 6, 9, 13.5,... is $f(n) = 6\left(\dfrac{3}{2}\right)^{n-1}$.

(A) The given rule is a(n) [?] rule because you do not need to know the

value of [?].

(B) The only unknown in the expression is [?], which

represents [?].

(C) The sequence is a(n) [?] sequence because each term is

the [?] of the previous term and $\dfrac{3}{2}$.

Reflect

1. **Discussion** How can you differentiate between a geometric sequence and an arithmetic sequence?

2. How can you tell by looking at a function rule for a sequence whether it is a recursive rule?

Constructing Recursive and Explicit Rules for Given Geometric Sequences

To write a recursive rule for a sequence, you need to know the first term, and a rule for successive terms.

Example 1   **Write a recursive rule and an explicit rule for each geometric sequence.**

Ⓐ Makers of Japanese swords in the 1400s repeatedly folded and hammered the metal to form layers. The folding process increased the strength of the sword.

The table shows how the number of layers depends on the number of folds.

Number of Folds	n	1	2	3	4	5
Number of Layers	$f(n)$	2	4	8	16	32

To write a recursive rule, find the common ratio by calculating the ratio of consecutive terms.

$\frac{4}{2} = 2$

The common ratio r is 2.

The first term is 2, so $f(1) = 2$.

All terms after the first term are the product of the previous term and the common ratio:

$f(2) = f(1) \cdot 2, f(3) = f(2) \cdot 2, f(4) = f(3) \cdot 2, \ldots$

State the recursive rule by providing the first term and the rule for successive terms.

$f(1) = 2$

$f(n) = f(n - 1) \cdot 2$ for $n \geq 2$

Write an explicit rule for the sequence by writing each term as the product of the first term and a power of the common ratio.

n	$f(n)$
1	$2(2)^0 = 2$
2	$2(2)^1 = 4$
3	$2(2)^2 = 8$
4	$2(2)^3 = 16$
5	$2(2)^4 = 32$

Generalize the results from the table: $f(n) = 2 \cdot 2^{n-1}$.

n	1	2	3	4	5
f(n)	5	15	45	135	405

To write a recursive rule, find the common ratio by calculating the ratio of consecutive terms.

$$\frac{\boxed{15}}{5} = \boxed{3}$$

The common ratio r is 3.

The first term is 5. So, the recursive rule is:

$$f(n) = f(n-1) \cdot 3 \text{ for } n \geq 2$$

Write an explicit rule for the sequence by writing each term as the product of the first term and a power of the common ratio.

n	f(n)
1	$5(3)^0 = \boxed{5}$
2	$5(3)^1 = \boxed{15}$
3	$5(3)^2 = \boxed{45}$
4	$5(3)^3 = \boxed{35}$
5	$5(3)^4 = \boxed{405}$

Generalize the results from the table: $f(n) = \boxed{5 \cdot 3}^{\,n-1}$.

Reflect

3. Explain why the sequence 5, 10, 20, 40, 80, … appears to be a geometric sequence.

4. **Draw Conclusions** How can you use properties of exponents to simplify the explicit rule $f(n) = 2 \cdot 2^{n-1}$?

Your Turn

Write a recursive rule and an explicit rule for each geometric sequence.

5.

n	1	2	3	4	5
f(n)	7	14	28	56	112

6. Write a recursive rule and an explicit rule for the geometric sequence 128, 32, 8, 2, 0.5, … .

Deriving the General Forms of Geometric Sequence Rules

Example 2 Use each geometric sequence to help write a recursive rule and an explicit rule for any geometric sequence. For the general rules, the values of n are consecutive integers starting with 1.

(A) 6, 24, 96, 384, 1536, …

Find the common ratio.

Numbers

6, 24, 96, 384, 1536,…

Common ratio = 4

Algebra

$f(1), f(2), f(3), f(4), f(5),…$

Common ratio = r

Write a recursive rule.

Numbers

$f(1) = 6$ and

$f(n) = f(n-1) \cdot 4$ for $n \geq 2$

Algebra

Given $f(1)$,

$f(n) = f(n-1) \cdot r$ for $n \geq 2$

Write an explicit rule.

Numbers

$f(n) = 6 \cdot 4^{n-1}$

Algebra

$f(n) = f(1) \cdot r^{n-1}$

(B) 4, 12, 36, 108, 324,…

Find the common ratio.

Numbers

4, 12, 36, 108, 324,…

Common ratio = $\boxed{3}$

Algebra

$f(1), f(2), f(3), f(4), f(5),…$

Common ratio = $\boxed{r}$

Write a recursive rule.

Numbers

$f(1) = \boxed{4}$ and

$f(n) = f(n-1) \cdot \boxed{3}$ for $n \geq \boxed{2}$

Algebra

Given $f(1)$,

$f(n) = f(n-1) \cdot \boxed{r}$ for $n \geq \boxed{2}$

Write an explicit rule.

Numbers

$f(n) = \boxed{4} \cdot \boxed{3}^{\,n-1}$

Algebra

$f(n) = f\left(\boxed{1}\right) \cdot \boxed{r}^{\,n-1}$

7. **Discussion** The first term of a geometric sequence is 81 and the common ratio is $\frac{1}{3}$. Explain how the 4th term of the sequence can be determined.

8. What is the recursive rule for the sequence $f(n) = 5(4)^{n-1}$?

Your Turn

Use the geometric sequence to help write a recursive rule and an explicit rule for any geometric sequence.

9. 6, 12, 24, 48, 96,...

⚿ Explain 3   Constructing a Geometric Sequence Given Two Terms

The explicit and recursive rules for a geometric sequence can also be written in subscript notation. In subscript notation, the subscript indicates the position of the term in the sequence. a_1, a_2, and a_3 are the first, second, and third terms of a sequence respectively. In general, a_n is the nth term of a sequence.

Example 3   **Write an explicit rule for each sequence using subscript notation.**

Ⓐ **Photography** The shutter speed settings on a camera form a geometric sequence where a_n is the shutter speed in seconds and n is the setting number. The fifth setting on the camera is $\frac{1}{60}$ second and the seventh setting on the camera is $\frac{1}{15}$ second.

Identify the given terms in the sequence.

The fifth setting is $\frac{1}{60}$ second, so the 5th term of the sequence is $\frac{1}{60}$.

$$a_5 = \frac{1}{60}$$

The seventh setting is $\frac{1}{15}$ second, so the 7th term of the sequence is $\frac{1}{15}$.

$$a_7 = \frac{1}{15}$$

Find the common ratio.

$a_7 = a_6 \cdot r$	Write the recursive rule for a_7.
$a_6 = a_5 \cdot r$	Write the recursive rule for a_6.
$a_7 = a_5 \cdot r \cdot r$	Substitute the expression for a_6 into the rule for a_7.
$\frac{1}{15} = \frac{1}{60} \cdot r^2$	Substitute $\frac{1}{15}$ for a_7 and $\frac{1}{60}$ for a_5.
$4 = r^2$	Multiply both sides by 60.
$2 = r$	Definition of positive square root

Find the first term of the sequence.

$$a_n = a_1 \cdot r^{n-1}$$ Write the explicit rule.

$$\frac{1}{60} = a_1 \cdot 2^{5-1}$$ Substitute $\frac{1}{60}$ for a_n, 2 for r, and 5 for n.

$$\frac{1}{60} = a_1 \cdot 16$$ Simplify.

$$\frac{1}{960} = a_1$$ Divide both sides by 16.

Write the explicit rule.

$$a_n = a_1 \cdot r^{n-1}$$ Write the general rule.

$$a_n = \frac{1}{960} \cdot (2)^{n-1}$$ Substitute $\frac{1}{960}$ for a_1 and 2 for r.

 Viral Video You tell a number of friends about an interesting video you saw online. Each of those friends tells the same number of friends about it. This pattern continues, and there are no repeats in the people told. The numbers of people who hear about this video through you form a geometric sequence. There are 256 people at the fourth round and 4096 people at the sixth round.

Identify the given terms in the sequence.

The 4th term of the sequence is $\boxed{256}$.

$$a_4 = \boxed{256}$$

The 6th term of the sequence is $\boxed{4096}$.

$$a_6 = \boxed{4096}$$

Find the common ratio.

$$a_6 = \boxed{a_5} \cdot r$$ Write the recursive rule for a_6.

$$a_6 = \boxed{a_4} \cdot r$$ Write the recursive rule for a_5.

$$a_6 = \boxed{a_4} \cdot \boxed{r} \cdot r$$ Substitute the expression for a_5 into the rule for a_6.

$$\boxed{4096} = \boxed{256} \cdot r^2$$ Substitute $\boxed{4096}$ for a_6 and $\boxed{256}$ for a_4.

$$\boxed{16} = r^2$$ Divide both sides by 256.

$$\boxed{4} = r$$ Definition of positive square root.

Find the first term of the sequence.

$$a_n = a_1 \cdot r^{n-1}$$ Write the explicit rule.

$$\boxed{256} = a_1 \cdot \boxed{4}^{\,4-1}$$ Substitute $\boxed{256}$ for a_n, $\boxed{4}$ for r, and $\boxed{4}$ for n.

$$\boxed{256} = a_1 \cdot \boxed{64}$$ Simplify.

$$\boxed{4} = a_1$$ Divide both sides by $\boxed{64}$.

Write the explicit rule.

$$a_n = a_1 \cdot r^{n-1}$$ Write the general rule.

$$a_n = \boxed{4} \cdot \left(\boxed{4}\right)^{n-1}$$ Substitute $\boxed{4}$ for a_1 and $\boxed{4}$ for r.

10. Finding the common ratio in the shutter speed example involved finding a square root. Why was the negative square root not considered?

Your Turn

Write an explicit rule for the sequence using subscript notation.

11. The third term of a geometric sequence is $\frac{1}{27}$ and the fifth term is $\frac{1}{243}$. All the terms of the sequence are positive.

💬 Elaborate

12. What If Suppose you are given the terms a_3 and a_6 of a geometric sequence. How can you find the common ratio r?

13. If you know the second term and the common ratio of a geometric sequence, can you write an explicit rule for the sequence? If so, explain how.

14. Essential Question Check-In How can you write the explicit rule for a geometric sequence if you know the recursive rule for the sequence?

☆ Evaluate: Homework and Practice

- Online Homework
- Hints and Help
- Extra Practice

For each geometric sequence, write a recursive rule by finding the common ratio by calculating the ratio of consecutive terms. Write an explicit rule for the sequence by writing each term as the product of the first term and a power of the common ratio.

1.

n	1	2	3	4	5
a_n	2	6	18	54	162

2.

n	1	2	3	4	5
a_n	10	3	0.9	0.27	0.081

3.

n	1	2	3	4	5
a_n	5	20	80	320	1280

4.

n	1	2	3	4	5
a_n	6	−3	1.5	−0.75	0.375

5.

n	1	2	3	4	5
a_n	9	6	4	$2\frac{2}{3}$	$1\frac{7}{9}$

6.

n	1	2	3	4	5
a_n	−12	6	−3	1.5	−0.75

7.

n	1	2	3	4	5
a_n	4	24	144	864	5184

8.

n	1	2	3	4	5
a_n	10	5	2.5	1.25	0.625

9.

n	1	2	3	4	5
a_n	3	21	147	1029	7203

10.

n	1	2	3	4	5
a_n	8	72	648	5832	52,488

11.

n	1	2	3	4	5
a_n	6	30	150	750	3750

Use the geometric sequence to help write a recursive rule and an explicit rule for any geometric sequence. For the general rules, the values of n are consecutive integers starting with 1.

12. 5, 15, 45, 135, 405,…

13. 10, 40, 160, 640, 2,560,…

14. 5, 10, 20, 40, 80,…

15. 18, 90, 450, 2250, 11,250,…

Write an explicit rule for each geometric sequence using subscript notation. Use a calculator and round your answer to the nearest tenth if necessary.

16. The fifth term of the sequence is 5. The sixth term is 2.5.

17. The third term of the sequence is 120. The fifth term is 76.8.

18. The fourth term of the sequence is 216. The sixth term is 96.

19. **Sports** The numbers of teams remaining in each round of a single-elimination tennis tournament represent a geometric sequence where a_n is the number of teams competing and n is the round. There are 32 teams remaining in round 4 and 8 teams in round 6.

20. **Video Games** The numbers of points that a player must accumulate to reach each next level of a video game form a geometric sequence where a_n is the number of points needed to complete level n. You need 20,000 points to complete level 3 and 8,000,000 points to complete level 5.

21. **Conservation** A state began an effort to increase the deer population. In year 2 of the effort, the deer population in a state forest was 1200. In year 4, the population was 1728.

22. **Biology** The growth of a local raccoon population approximates a geometric sequence where a_n is the number of raccoons in a given year and n is the year. After 6 years there are 45 raccoons and after 8 years there are 71 raccoons.

23. **Chemistry** A chemist measures the temperature in degrees Fahrenheit of a chemical compound every hour. The temperatures approximate a geometric sequence where a_n is the temperature at a given hour, and n is the hour. At hour 4, the temperature is 70 °F and at hour 6 the temperature is 80 °F.

24. Yusuf was asked to write a recursive rule for a sequence. Which of the following is an appropriate answer? Select all that apply.

    a. $f(n) = 11(5)^{n-1}$ **b.** $f(n) = 11f(n-1), f(1) = 555$ **c.** $f(n) = f(n-1) + 15, f(1) = 36$

    d. $f(n) = 12 + 19 \cdot f(n-1)$ **e.** $f(n) = -4\left(\dfrac{2}{3}\right)^{n-1}$

H.O.T. Focus on Higher Order Thinking

25. **Multi-Step** An economist predicts that the cost of food will increase by 4% per year for the next several years.

    a. Write an explicit rule for the sequence that gives the cost $f(n)$ in dollars of a box of cereal in year n that costs $3.20 in year 1. Justify your answer.

    b. What is the fourth term of the sequence? What does it represent in this situation? Justify your answer.

26. **Analyze Relationships** Suppose you know the 8th term of a geometric sequence and the common ratio r. How can you find the 3rd term of the sequence without writing a rule for the sequence? Explain.

27. **Explain the Error** Given that the second term of a sequence is 64 and the fourth term is 16, Francis wrote the explicit rule $a_n = 128 \cdot \left(\dfrac{1}{4}\right)^{n-1}$ for the sequence. Explain his error.

28. **Communicate Mathematical Ideas** Suppose you are given two terms of a geometric sequence like the ones in Example 3, except that both terms are negative. Explain how writing the explicit rule for the sequence would differ from the examples in this lesson.

Lesson Performance Task

The table shows how a population of rabbits has changed over time. Write an explicit rule for the geometric sequence described in the table. In what year will there be more than 5000 rabbits?

Time (years), n	Population, a_n
1	800
2	1200
3	1800
4	2700

15.3 Constructing Exponential Functions

Essential Question: What are discrete exponential functions and how do you represent them?

⊘ Explore   Understanding Discrete Exponential Functions

Recall that a discrete function has a graph consisting of isolated points.

(A) The table represents the cost of tickets to an annual event as a function of the number *t* of tickets purchased. Copy and complete the table by *adding* 10 to each successive cost. Plot each ordered pair from the table on a coordinate grid.

Tickets *t*	Cost ($)	$(t, f(t))$
1	10	(1, 10)
2	20	(2, 20)
3	?	(3, ?)
4	?	(4, ?)
5	?	(5, ?)

(B) The number of people attending an event doubles each year. The table represents the total attendance at each annual event as a function of the event number *n*. Copy and complete the table by *multiplying* each successive attendance by 2. Plot each ordered pair from the table on a coordinate grid.

Event Number *n*	Attendance	$(n, g(n))$
1	20	(1, 20)
2	40	(2, 40)
3	?	(3, ?)
4	?	(4, ?)
5	?	(5, ?)

(C) Copy and complete the table.

Function	Linear?	Discrete?
$f(t)$	Yes	?
$g(n)$	?	?

Reflect

1. Communicate Mathematical Ideas What are the limitations on the domains of these functions? Why?

Explain 1   Representing Discrete Exponential Functions

An **exponential function** is a function whose successive output values are related by a constant ratio. An exponential function can be represented by an equation of the form $f(x) = ab^x$, where a, b, and x are real numbers, $a \neq 0$, $b > 0$, and $b \neq 1$. The constant ratio is the base b.

When evaluating exponential functions, you will need to use the properties of exponents, including zero and negative exponents.

Recall that, for any nonzero number c:

$$c^0 = 1, c \neq 0$$

$$c^{-n} = \frac{1}{c^n}, c \neq 0.$$

Example 1   Complete the table for each function using the given domain. Then graph the function using the ordered pairs from the table.

(A) $f(x) = 3 \cdot \left(\frac{1}{2}\right)^x$ with a domain of $\left\{-1, 0, 1, 2, 3, 4\right\}$

$f(-1) = 3 \cdot \left(\frac{1}{2}\right)^{-1} = 3 \cdot \dfrac{1}{\left(\frac{1}{2}\right)} = 3 \cdot 2 = 6$

x	$f(x)$	$(x, f(x))$
-1	6	$(-1, 6)$
0	3	$(0, 3)$
1	$1\frac{1}{2}$	$\left(1, 1\frac{1}{2}\right)$
2	$\frac{3}{4}$	$\left(2, \frac{3}{4}\right)$
3	$\frac{3}{8}$	$\left(3, \frac{3}{8}\right)$
4	$\frac{3}{16}$	$\left(4, \frac{3}{16}\right)$

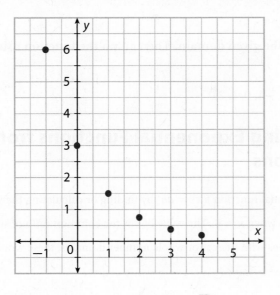

(B) $f(x) = 3\left(\dfrac{4}{3}\right)^x$; domain = $\left\{-2, -1, 0, 1, 2, 3\right\}$

$$f(-3) = 3\left(\dfrac{4}{3}\right)^{-2} = 3 \cdot \dfrac{1}{\left(\dfrac{4}{3}\right)^{-2}} = 3 \cdot \dfrac{\boxed{3}^{-2}}{\boxed{4}^{-2}} = 3 \cdot \dfrac{\boxed{9}}{\boxed{16}} = \dfrac{27}{16} = 1\dfrac{11}{16}$$

x	f(x)	(x, f(x))
−2	$1\dfrac{11}{16}$	$\left(-2, 1\dfrac{11}{16}\right)$
−1	$2\dfrac{1}{4}$	$\left(-1, 2\dfrac{1}{4}\right)$
0	3	$(0, 3)$
1	4	$(1, 4)$
2	$5\dfrac{1}{3}$	$\left(2, 5\dfrac{1}{3}\right)$
3	$7\dfrac{1}{9}$	$\left(3, 7\dfrac{1}{9}\right)$

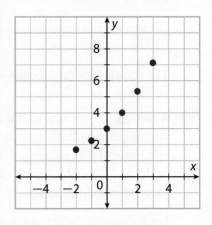

Reflect

2. **What If** What would happen to the function $f(x) = ab^x$ if a were 0? What if b were 1?

3. **Discussion** Why is a geometric sequence a discrete exponential function?

Make a table for the function using the given domain. Then graph the function using the ordered pairs from the table.

4. $f(x) = 4\left(\dfrac{3}{2}\right)^x$; domain $= \left\{-3, -2, -1, 0, 1, 2\right\}$

🔧 Explain 2 Constructing Exponential Functions from Verbal Descriptions

You can write an equation for an exponential function $f(x) = ab^x$ by finding or calculating the values of a and b. The value of a is the value of the function when $x = 0$. The value of b is the common ratio of successive function values, $b = \dfrac{f(x+1)}{f(x)}$. For discrete functions with integer or whole number domains, these will be successive values of the function.

Example 2 Write an equation for the function.

(A) When a piece of paper is folded in half, the total thickness doubles. Suppose an unfolded piece of paper is 0.1 millimeter thick. The total thickness $t(n)$ of the paper is an exponential function of the number of folds n.

The value of a is the original thickness of the paper before any folds are made, or 0.1 millimeter.

Because the thickness doubles with each fold, the value of b (the constant ratio) is 2.

The equation for the function is $t(n) = 0.1(2)^n$.

(B) A savings account with an initial balance of $1000 earns 1% interest per month. That means that the account balance grows by a factor of 1.01 each month if no deposits or withdrawals are made. The account balance in dollars $B(t)$ is an exponential function of the time t in months after the initial deposit.

Let B represent the balance in dollars as a function of time t in months.

The value of a is the original balance, 1000.

The value of b is the factor by which the balance changes every month, 1.01.

The equation for the function is $B(t) = 1000(1.01)^t$.

Reflect

5. Why is the exponential function in the paper-folding example discrete?

Your Turn

6. A piece of paper that is 0.2 millimeters thick is folded. Write an equation for the thickness t of the paper in millimeters as a function of the number n of folds.

Explain 3 **Constructing Exponential Functions from Input-Output Pairs**

You can use two given successive values of a discrete exponential function to write an equation for the function.

Example 3 Write an equation for the function that includes the points.

Ⓐ $(3, 12)$ and $(4, 24)$

Find b by dividing the function value of the second pair by the function value of the first: $b = \frac{24}{12} = 2$.

Evaluate the function for $x = 3$ and solve for a.

Write the general form.	$f(x) = ab^x$
Substitute the value for b.	$f(x) = a \cdot 2^x$
Substitute a pair of input-output values.	$12 = a \cdot 2^3$
Simplify.	$12 = a \cdot 8$
Solve for a.	$a = \dfrac{3}{2}$
Use a and b to write an equation for the function.	$f(x) = \dfrac{3}{2} \cdot 2^x$

Ⓑ $(1, 3)$ and $\left(2, \dfrac{9}{4}\right)$

Find b by dividing the function value of the second pair by the first: $b = \dfrac{9}{4} \div 3 = \boxed{\dfrac{3}{4}}$.

Write the general form.	$f(x) = \boxed{ab^x}$
Substitute the value for b.	$f(x) = a \cdot \boxed{\left(\dfrac{3}{4}\right)}$
Substitute a pair of input-output values.	$\boxed{3} = a \cdot \left(\dfrac{3}{4}\right)^{\boxed{1}}$
Simplify.	$3 = a \cdot \boxed{\dfrac{3}{4}}$
Solve for a.	$a = \boxed{4}$
Use a and b to write an equation for the function.	$f(x) = \boxed{4\left(\dfrac{3}{4}\right)^x}$

Your Turn

Write an equation for the function that includes the points.

7. $\left(-2, \dfrac{2}{5}\right)$ and $(-1, 2)$

8. Explain why the following statement is true: For $0 < b < 1$ and $a > 0$, the function $f(x) = ab^x$ decreases as x increases.

9. Explain why the following statement is true: For $b > 1$ and $a > 0$, the function $f(x) = ab^x$ increases as x increases.

10. **Essential Question Check-In** What property do all pairs of adjacent points of a discrete exponential function share?

☆ Evaluate: Homework and Practice

- Online Homework
- Hints and Help
- Extra Practice

Make a table for each function using the given domain. Then graph the function using the ordered pairs from the table.

1. $f(x) = \frac{1}{2} \cdot 4^x$; domain $= \left\{-2, -1, 0, 1, 2\right\}$.

2. $f(x) = 9\left(\frac{1}{3}\right)^x$; domain $= \left\{0, 1, 2, 3, 4, 5\right\}$.

3. $f(x) = 6\left(\frac{2}{3}\right)^x$; domain $= \left\{-1, 0, 1, 2, 3, 4\right\}$.

4. $f(x) = 6\left(\frac{4}{3}\right)^x$; domain $= \left\{-3, -2, -1, 0, 1\right\}$.

Write an equation for each function.

5. **Business** A recent trend in advertising is viral marketing. The goal is to convince viewers to share an amusing advertisement by e-mail or social networking. Imagine that the video is sent to 100 people on day 1. Each person agrees to send the video to 5 people the next day, and to request that each of those people send it to 5 people the day after they receive it. The number of viewers $v(n)$ is an exponential function of the number n of days since the video was first shown.

6. A pharmaceutical company is testing a new antibiotic. The number of bacteria present in a sample when the antibiotic is applied is 100,000. Each hour, the number of bacteria present decreases by half. The number of bacteria remaining $r(n)$ is an exponential function of the number n of hours since the antibiotic was applied.

7. **Optics** A laser beam with an output of 5 milliwatts is directed into a series of mirrors. The laser beam loses 1% of its power every time it reflects off of a mirror. The power $p(n)$ is a function of the number n of reflections.

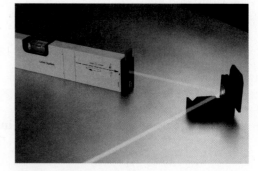

8. The NCAA basketball tournament begins with 64 teams, and after each round, half the teams are eliminated. The number of remaining teams $t(n)$ is an exponential function of the number n of rounds already played.

Write an equation for the function that includes the points.

9. $(2, 100)$ and $(3, 1000)$

10. $(-2, 4)$ and $(-1, 8)$

11. $\left(1, \frac{4}{5}\right)$ and $\left(2, \frac{2}{3}\right)$

12. $\left(-3, \frac{1}{16}\right)$ and $\left(-2, \frac{3}{8}\right)$

Use two points to write an equation for the function.

13.

x	f(x)
1	2
2	$\frac{2}{7}$
3	$\frac{2}{49}$
4	$\frac{2}{343}$

14.

x	f(x)
−4	0.53
−3	5.3
−2	53
−1	530

15.

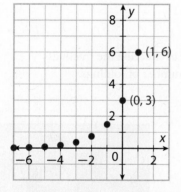

16.

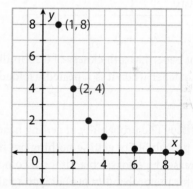

17. The height $h(n)$ of a bouncing ball is an exponential function of the number n of bounces. One ball is dropped and on the first bounce reaches a height of 6 feet. On the second bounce it reaches a height of 4 feet.

18. A child starts a playground swing from standing and doesn't use her legs to keep swinging. On the first swing she swings forward by 18 degrees, and on the second swing she only comes 13.5 degrees forward. The measure in degrees of the angle $m(n)$ is an exponential function of the number n of swings.

19. Make a Prediction A town's population has been declining in recent years. The table shows the population since 1980. Is this data consistent with an exponential function? Explain. If so, predict the population for 2010 assuming the trend holds.

Year	Population
1980	5000
1990	4000
2000	3200
2010	

20. A piece of paper has a thickness of 0.15 millimeters. Write an equation to describe the thickness $t(n)$ of the paper when it is repeatedly folded in thirds, where n is the number of foldings.

21. Probability The probability of getting heads on a single coin flip is $\frac{1}{2}$. The probability of getting nothing but heads on a series of coin flips decreases by $\frac{1}{2}$ for each additional coin flip. Write an exponential function for the probability $p(n)$ of getting all heads in a series of n coin flips.

22. **Multipart Classification** Determine whether each of the functions is exponential or not.

   a. $f(x) = x^2$

   b. $f(x) = 3 \cdot 2^x$

   c. $f(x) = 3 \cdot \frac{1}{2} x$

   d. $f(x) = 1.001^x$

   e. $f(x) = 2 \cdot x^3$

   f. $f(x) = \frac{1}{10} \cdot 5^x$

23. **Explain the Error** Biff observes that in every math test he has taken this year, he has scored 2 points higher than the previous test. His score on the first test was 56. He models his test scores with the exponential function $s(n) = 28 \cdot 2^n$ where $s(n)$ is the score on his nth test. Is this a reasonable model? Explain.

24. **Find the Error** Kaylee needed to write the equation of an exponential function from points on the graph of the function. To determine the value of b, Kaylee chose the ordered pairs (1, 6) and (3, 54) and divided 54 by 6. She determined that the value of b was 9. What error did Kaylee make?

Lesson Performance Task

In ecology, an invasive species is a plant or animal species newly introduced to an ecosystem, often by human activity. Because invasive species often lack predators in their new habitat, their populations typically experience exponential growth. A small initial population grows to a large population that drastically alters an ecosystem. Feral rabbits that populate Australia and zebra mussels in the Great Lakes are two examples of problematic invasive species that grew exponentially from a small initial population.

An ecologist monitoring a local stream has been collecting samples of an unfamiliar fish species over the past four years and has summarized the data in the table.

Here are the results so far:

Year	Average Population Per Mile
2009	32
2010	48
2011	72
2012	108
2013	
2014	

a. Look at the data in the table and confirm that the growth pattern is exponential.

b. Write the equation that represents the average population per square meter as a function of years since 2009.

c. Predict the average populations expected for 2013 and 2014.

d. Graph the population versus time since 2009 and include the predicted values.

15.4 Graphing Exponential Functions

Essential Question: How do you graph an exponential function of the form $f(x) = ab^x$?

Resource
Locker

⊘ Explore   Exploring Graphs of Exponential Functions

Exponential functions follow the general shape $y = ab^x$.

(A) Graph the exponential functions on a graphing calculator, and match the graph to the correct function rule.

1. $y = 3(2)^x$

2. $y = 0.5(2)^x$

3. $y = 3(0.5)^x$

4. $y = -3(2)^x$

a.
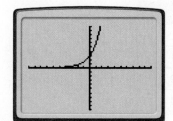

b.
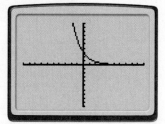

c.
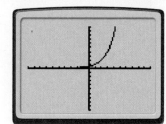

d.
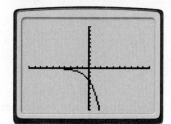

(B) In all the functions 1–4 above, the base $b > 0$.

Use the graphs to make a conjecture: State the domain and range of $y = ab^x$ if $a > 0$.

(C) In all the functions 1–4 above, the base $b > 0$.

Use the graphs to make a conjecture: State the domain and range of $y = ab^x$ if $a < 0$.

(D) What is the y-intercept of $f(x) = 0.5(2)^x$?

(E) Note the similarities between the y-intercept and a. What is their relationship?

Reflect

1. **Discussion** What is the domain for any exponential function $y = ab^x$?

2. **Discussion** Describe the values of b for all functions $y = ab^x$.

🔑 Explain 1 Graphing Increasing Positive Exponential Functions

The symbol ∞ represents *infinity*. We can describe the *end behavior* of a function by describing what happens to the function values as x approaches positive infinity $(x \rightarrow \infty)$ and as x approaches negative infinity $(x \rightarrow -\infty)$.

Example 1 Graph each exponential function. After graphing, identify a and b, the y-intercept, and the end behavior of the graph.

(A) $f(x) = 2^x$

Choose several values of x and generate ordered pairs.

x	$f(x) = 2^x$
−1	0.5
0	1
1	2
2	4

Graph the ordered pairs and connect them with a smooth curve.

$a = 1$

$b = 2$

y-intercept: $(0, 1)$

End Behavior: As x-values approach positive infinity $(x \rightarrow \infty)$, y-values approach positive infinity $(y \rightarrow \infty)$.
As x-values approach negative infinity $(x \rightarrow -\infty)$, y-values approach zero $(y \rightarrow 0)$.

Using symbols only, we say: As $x \rightarrow \infty, y \rightarrow \infty$, and as $x \rightarrow -\infty, y \rightarrow 0$.

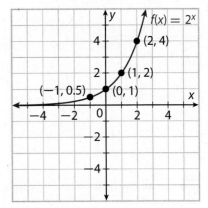

(B) $f(x) = 3(4)^x$

Choose several values of x and generate ordered pairs.

x	$f(x) = 3(4)^x$
−1	0.75
0	3
1	12
2	48

Graph the ordered pairs and connect them with a smooth curve.

$a = \boxed{3}$

$b = \boxed{4}$

y-intercept: $\left(\boxed{0}, \boxed{3}\right)$

End Behavior: As $x \to \infty$, $y \to \boxed{\infty}$ and as $x \to -\infty$, $y \to \boxed{0}$.

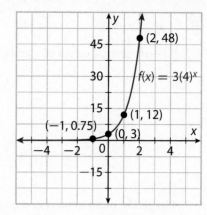

Reflect

3. If $a > 0$ and $b > 1$, what is the end behavior of the graph?

4. Describe the y-intercept of the exponential function $f(x) = ab^x$ in terms of a and b.

Your Turn

5. Graph the exponential function $f(x) = 2(2)^x$
After graphing, identify a and b, the y-intercept, and the end behavior of the graph.

🔧 Explain 2   Graphing Decreasing Negative Exponential Functions

You can use end behavior to discuss the behavior of a graph.

Example 2   Graph each exponential function. After graphing, identify a and b, the y-intercept, and the end behavior of the graph. Use end behavior to discuss the behavior of the graph.

(A) $f(x) = -2(3)^x$

Choose several values of x and generate ordered pairs.

x	$f(x) = -2(3)^x$
-1	-0.7
0	-2
1	-6
2	-18

Graph the ordered pairs and connect them with a smooth curve.

$a = -2$

$b = 3$

y-intercept: $(0, -2)$

End Behavior: As $x \to \infty$, $y \to -\infty$ and as $x \to -\infty$, $y \to 0$.

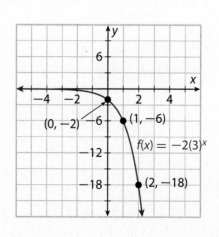

(B) $f(x) = -3(4)^x$

Choose several values of x and generate ordered pairs.

x	$f(x) = -3(4)^x$
−1	−0.75
0	−3
1	−12
2	−48

Graph the ordered pairs and connect them with a smooth curve.

$a = \boxed{-3}$

$b = \boxed{4}$

y-intercept: $\left(\boxed{0}, \boxed{-3}\right)$

End Behavior: As $x \to \infty$, $y \to \boxed{-\infty}$ and as $x \to -\infty$, $y \to \boxed{0}$.

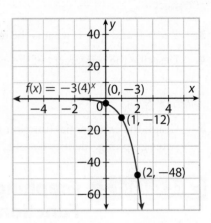

Reflect

6. If $a < 0$ and $b > 1$, what is the end behavior of the graph?

Your Turn

7. Graph the exponential function. $f(x) = -3(3)^x$
   After graphing, identify a and b, the y-intercept, and the end behavior of the graph.

⊙ Explain 3   Graphing Decreasing Positive Exponential Functions

Example 3   Graph each exponential function. After graphing, identify a and b, the y-intercept, and the end behavior of the graph.

(A) $f(x) = (0.5)^x$

Choose several values of x and generate ordered pairs.

x	$f(x) = (0.5)^x$
−1	2
0	1
1	0.5
2	0.25

Graph the ordered pairs and connect them with a smooth curve.

$a = 1$

$b = 0.5$

y-intercept: $(0, 1)$

End Behavior: As $x \to \infty$, $y \to 0$ and as $x \to -\infty$, $y \to \infty$.

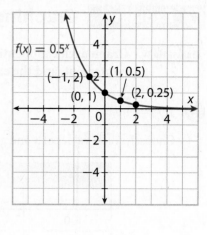

(B) $f(x) = 2(0.4)^x$

Choose several values of x and generate ordered pairs.

x	$f(x) = 2(0.4)^x$
−1	5
0	2
1	0.8
2	0.32

Graph the ordered pairs and connect them with a smooth curve.

$a = \boxed{2}$

$b = \boxed{.4}$

y-intercept: $\left(\boxed{0} , \boxed{2} \right)$

End Behavior: As $x \to \infty$, $y \to \boxed{0}$ and as $x \to -\infty$, $y \to \boxed{\infty}$.

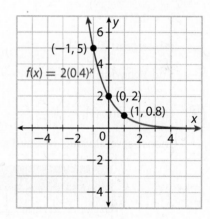

Reflect

8. If $a > 0$ and $0 < b < 1$, what is the end behavior of the graph?

Your Turn

9. Graph the exponential function. After graphing, identify a and b, the y-intercept, and the end behavior of the graph.

$f(x) = 3(0.5)^x$

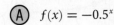 **Explain 4** **Graphing Increasing Negative Exponential Functions**

Example 4 Graph each exponential function. After graphing, identify a and b, the y-intercept, and the end behavior of the graph.

(A) $f(x) = -0.5^x$

Choose several values of x and generate ordered pairs.

x	$f(x) = -0.5^x$
-1	-2
0	-1
1	-0.5
2	-0.25

Graph the ordered pairs and connect them with a smooth curve.

$a = -1$

$b = 0.5$

y-intercept: $(0, -1)$

End Behavior: As $x \to \infty$, $y \to 0$ and as $x \to -\infty$, $y \to -\infty$.

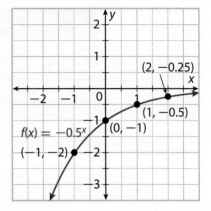

(B) $f(x) = -3(0.4)^x$

Choose several values of x and generate ordered pairs.

x	$f(x) = -3(0.4)^x$
-1	-7.5
0	-3
1	-1.2
2	-0.48

Graph the ordered pairs and connect them with a smooth curve.

$a = \boxed{-3}$

$b = \boxed{0.4}$

y-intercept: $\left(\boxed{0}, \boxed{-3} \right)$

End Behavior: As $x \to \infty$, $y \to \boxed{0}$ and as $x \to -\infty$, $y \to \boxed{-\infty}$.

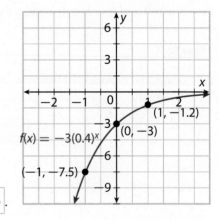

Reflect

10. If $a < 0$ and $0 < b < 1$, what is the end behavior of the graph?

Your Turn

11. Graph the exponential function. After graphing, identify a and b, the y-intercept, and the end behavior of the graph.

$f(x) = -2(0.5)^x$

Elaborate

12. Why is $f(x) = 3(-0.5)^x$ not an exponential function?

13. Essential Question Check-In When an exponential function of the form $f(x) = ab^x$ is graphed, what does a represent?

⊛ Evaluate: Homework and Practice

- Online Homework
- Hints and Help
- Extra Practice

State a, b, and the y-intercept then graph the function on a graphing calculator.

1. $f(x) = 2(3)^x$

2. $f(x) = -6(2)^x$

3. $f(x) = -5(0.5)^x$

4. $f(x) = 3(0.8)^x$

5. $f(x) = 6(3)^x$

6. $f(x) = -4(0.2)^x$

7. $f(x) = 7(0.9)^x$

8. $f(x) = -3(2)^x$

State a, b, and the y-intercept then graph the function and describe the end behavior of the graphs.

9. $f(x) = 3(3)^x$

10. $f(x) = 5(0.6)^x$

11. $f(x) = -6(0.7)^x$

12. $f(x) = -4(3)^x$

13. $f(x) = 5(2)^x$

14. $f(x) = -2(0.8)^x$

15. $f(x) = 9(3)^x$

16. $f(x) = -5(2)^x$

17. $f(x) = 7(0.4)^x$

18. $f(x) = 6(2)^x$

19. Identify the domain and range of each function. Make sure to provide these answers using inequalities.

   a. $f(x) = 3(2)^x$

   b. $f(x) = 7(0.4)^x$

   c. $f(x) = -2(0.6)^x$

   d. $f(x) = -3(4)^x$

   e. $f(x) = 2(22)^x$

20. Statistics In 2000, the population of Massachusetts was 6.3 million people and was growing at a rate of about 0.32% per year. At this growth rate, the function $f(x) = 6.3(1.0032)^x$ gives the population, in millions x years after 2000. Using this model, find the year when the population reaches 7 million people.

21. Physics A ball is rolling down a slope and continuously picks up speed. Suppose the function $f(x) = 1.2(1.11)^x$ describes the speed of the ball in inches per minute. How fast will the ball be rolling in 20 minutes? Round the answer to the nearest whole number.

H.O.T. Focus on Higher Order Thinking

22. Draw Conclusions Assume that the domain of the function $f(x) = 3(2)^x$ is the set of all real numbers. What is the range of the function?

23. What If? If $b = 1$ in an exponential function, what will the graph of the function look like?

24. Critical Thinking Using the graph of an exponential function, how can b be found?

25. Critical Thinking Use the table to write the equation for the exponential function.

x	f(x)
−1	$\frac{4}{5}$
0	4
1	20
2	100

Lesson Performance Task

A pumpkin is being grown for a contest at the state fair. Its growth can be modeled by the equation $P = 25(1.56)^n$, where P is the weight of the pumpkin in pounds and n is the number of weeks the pumpkin has been growing. By what percentage does the pumpkin grow every week? After how many weeks will the pumpkin be 80 pounds?

After the pumpkin grows to 80 pounds, it grows more slowly. From then on, its growth can be modeled by $P = 25(1.23)^n$, where n is the number of weeks since the pumpkin reached 80 pounds. Estimate when the pumpkin will reach 150 pounds.

15.5 Transforming Exponential Functions

Essential Question: How does the graph of $f(x) = ab^x$ change when a and b are changed?

◎ Explore   Changing the Value of b in $f(x) = b^x$

Investigate the effect of b on the function $f(x) = b^x$.

(A) Copy and complete the table of values for the functions $f_1(x) = 1.2^x$ and $f_2(x) = 1.5^x$. Use a calculator to find the values and round to the nearest thousandth if necessary.

x	$f_1(x) = 1.2^x$	$f_2(x) = 1.5^x$
−2	0.694	?
−1	?	0.667
0	?	?
1	1.2	1.5
2	?	?

(B) Which function increases more quickly as x increases? ?

Which function approaches 0 more quickly as x decreases? ?

(C) The y-intercept of $f_1(x)$ is ? . The y-intercept of $f_2(x)$ is ? .

(D) Copy and complete the table of values for the functions $f_3(x) = 0.6^x$ and $f_4(x) = 0.9^x$. Round to the nearest thousandth again.

x	$f_3(x) = 0.6^x$	$f_4(x) = 0.9^x$
−2	2.778	?
−1	?	1.111
0	?	?
1	0.6	0.9
2	?	?

(E) Which function increases more quickly as x decreases? ?

Which function approaches 0 more quickly as x increases? ?

(F) The y-intercept of $f_3(x)$ is ? . The y-intercept of $f_4(x)$ is ? .

Reflect

1. Consider the function, $y = 1.3^x$. How will its graph compare with the graphs of $f_1(x)$ and $f_2(x)$? Discuss end behavior and the y-intercept.

✪ Explain 1   Changing the Value of *a* in $f(x) = ab^x$ with $b > 1$

Multiplying a growing exponential function $(b > 1)$ by a constant a does not change the growth rate, but it does stretch or compress the graph vertically, and reflects the graph across the x-axis if $a < 0$.

A **vertical stretch** of a graph is a transformation that pulls the graph away from the x-axis. By multiplying the y-value of each (x, y) pair by a, where $|a| > 1$, the graph is stretched by a factor of $|a|$.

A **vertical compression** of a graph is a transformation that pushes the graph toward the x-axis. By multiplying the y-value of each (x, y) pair by a, where $|a| < 1$, the graph is compressed by a factor of $|a|$.

Example 1   Make a table of values for the function given. Then graph it on the same coordinate plane with the graph of $y = 1.5^x$. Describe the end behavior and find the y-intercept of each graph.

(A) $f(x) = 0.3(1.5)^x$

x	$f(x) = 0.3(1.5)^x$
−2	0.133
−1	0.2
0	0.3
1	0.45
2	0.675
3	1.013
4	1.519

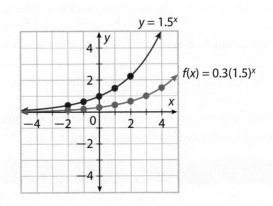

End Behavior:

$f(x) \to \infty$ as $x \to \infty$

$f(x) \to 0$ as $x \to -\infty$

y-intercept: 0.3

Ⓑ $f(x) = -2(1.5)^x$

x	$f(x) = -2(1.5)^x$
−4	−0.395
−3	−0.593
−2	−0.889
−1	−1.333
0	−2
1	−3
2	−4.5

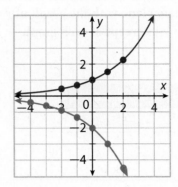

End Behavior:

$f(x) \rightarrow \boxed{-\infty}$ as $x \rightarrow \infty$

$f(x) \rightarrow \boxed{0}$ as $x \rightarrow -\infty$

y-intercept: $\boxed{-2}$

Reflect

2. **Discussion** What can you say about the common behavior of graphs of the form $f(x) = ab^x$ with $b > 1$? What is different when a changes sign?

Your Turn

Graph each function, and describe the end behavior and find the y-intercept of each graph.

3. $f(x) = -0.5(1.5)^x$

4. $f(x) = 4(1.5)^x$

🖉 Explain 2 Changing the Value of a in $f(x) = ab^x$ with $0 < b < 1$

Multiplying a decaying exponential function $(b < 1)$ by a constant a does not change the growth rate, but it does stretch or compress the graph vertically.

Example 2 Make a table of values for the function given. Then graph it on the same coordinate plane with the graph of $y = 0.6^x$. Describe the end behavior and find the y-intercept of each graph.

Ⓐ $f(x) = -3(0.6)^x$

x	$f(x) = -3(0.6)^x$
−1	−5
0	−3
1	−1.8
2	−1.08
3	−0.648

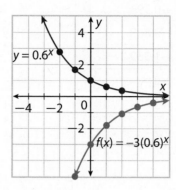

End behavior:

$f(x) \rightarrow 0$ as $x \rightarrow \infty$

$f(x) \rightarrow -\infty$ as $x \rightarrow -\infty$

y-intercept: −3

Ⓑ $f(x) = 0.5\,(0.6)^x$

x	$f(x) = 0.5(0.6)^x$
−4	3.858
−3	2.315
−2	1.389
−1	0.833
0	0.5
1	0.3
2	0.18

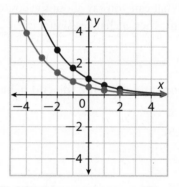

End Behavior:

$f(x) \rightarrow \boxed{0}$ as $x \rightarrow \infty$

$f(x) \rightarrow \boxed{\infty}$ as $x \rightarrow -\infty$

y-intercept: $\boxed{0.5}$

Reflect

5. **Discussion** What can you say about the common behavior of graphs of the form $f(x) = ab^x$ with $0 < b < 1$? What is different when a changes sign?

Graph each function, and describe its end behavior and *y*-intercept.

6. $f(x) = 2(0.6)^x$

7. $f(x) = -0.25(0.6)^x$

🔑 Explain 3 Adding a Constant to an Exponential Function

Adding a constant to an exponential function causes the graph of the function to translate up or down, depending on the sign of the constant.

Example 3 Make a table of values for each function and graph them together on the same coordinate plane. Find the *y*-intercepts, and explain how they relate to the translation of the graph.

Ⓐ $f(x) = 2^x$ and $g(x) = 2^x + 2$

x	$f(x) = 2^x$	$g(x) = 2^x + 2$
−2	0.25	2.25
−1	0.5	2.5
0	1	3
1	2	4
2	4	6

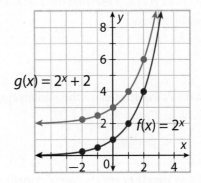

The *y*-intercept of $f(x)$ is 1.

The *y*-intercept of $g(x)$ is 3.

The *y*-intercept of $g(x)$ is 2 more than that of $f(x)$ because $g(x)$ is a vertical translation of $f(x)$ up by 2 units.

Ⓑ $f(x) = 0.7^x$ and $g(x) = 0.7^x - 3$

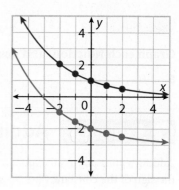

x	$f(x) = 0.7^x$	$g(x) = 0.7^x - 3$
−2	2.041	−0.959
−1	1.429	−1.571
0	1.0	−2
1	0.7	−2.3
2	0.49	−2.51

The y-intercept of $f(x)$ is [1] .

The y-intercept of $g(x)$ is [−2] .

The y-intercept of $g(x)$ is 3 less than that of $f(x)$ because $g(x)$ is a vertical translation of $f(x)$ down by 3 units.

Reflect

8. What do you think will happen to the y-intercept of an exponential function with both a stretch and a translation, such as $f(x) = 3(0.7)^x + 2$?

YourTurn

Graph the functions together on the same coordinate plane. Find the y-intercepts, and explain how they relate to the translation of the graph.

9. $f(x) = 0.4^x$ and $g(x) = 0.4^x + 4$

10. $f(x) = 2(1.5)^x$ and $g(x) = 2(1.5)^x - 3$

💬 Elaborate

11. How do you determine the y-intercept of an exponential function $f(x) = ab^x + k$ that has been both stretched and translated?

12. Describe the end behavior of a translated exponential function $f(x) = b^x + k$ with $b > 1$ as x approaches $-\infty$.

13. **Essential Question Check-in** If a and b are positive real numbers and $b \neq 1$, how does the graph of $f(x) = ab\ x$ change when b is changed?

☆ Evaluate: Homework and Practice

Exercises 1 and 2 refer to the functions $f_1(x) = 2.5^x$ and $f_2(x) = 3^x$.

1. Which function grows faster as x increases toward ∞?

2. Which function approaches 0 faster as x decreases toward $-\infty$?

Exercises 3 and 4 refer to the functions $f_1(x) = 0.5^x$ and $f_2(x) = 0.7^x$.

3. Which function grows faster as x decreases toward $-\infty$?

4. Which function approaches 0 faster as x increases toward ∞?

Describe each of the following functions, $g(x)$, as a vertical stretch or a vertical compression of the parent function, $f(x)$, and tell whether it is reflected about the x-axis.

5. $g(x) = 0.7(0.5)^x$, $f(x) = 0.5^x$

6. $g(x) = -1.2(5)^x$, $f(x) = 5^x$

7.

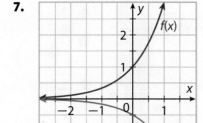

8.

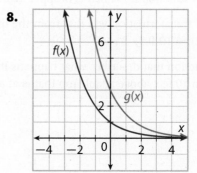

Find the y-intercept for each of the functions, $g(x)$, from Exercises 5–8.

9. $g(x) = 0.7(0.5)^x$

10. $g(x) = -1.2(5)^x$

11. Use $g(x)$ from Exercise 7.

12. Use $g(x)$ from Exercise 8.

Describe the translation of each of the functions, $g(x)$, compared to the parent function, $f(x)$.

13. $f(x) = 0.4^x$, $g(x) = 0.4^x + 5$

14. $f(x) = -2(1.5)^x$, $g(x) = -2(1.5)^x - 2$

15.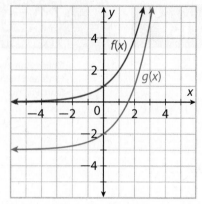

16.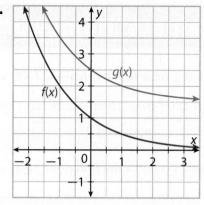

The height *h* above the floor of the *n*th bounce of a bouncy ball dropped from a height of 10 feet above the floor can be characterized by a decaying exponential function, $h(n) = 10(0.8)^n$, where each bounce reaches 80% of the height of the previous bounce.

17. Write the new function if the ball is dropped from 5 feet.

18. What kind of transformation was that from the original function, $h(n) = 10(0.8)^n$?

19. Write the function that describes what happens if the ball is dropped from 10 feet above a table top that is at a height of 3 feet.

20. Biology Unrestrained growth of cells in a petri dish can be extremely rapid, with a single cell growing into a number of cells, *N*, given by the formula, $N(t) = 8^t$, after *t* hours.

   a. Write the formula for the number of cells in the petri dish when a culture is started with 50 isolated cells.

   b. How many cells do you expect after 3 hours?

A bank account with an initial deposit of $1000 and an interest rate of 5% increases by 5% each year. The balance (B) as a function of time in years (t) can be described by an exponential function: $B(t) = 1000(1.05)^t$

21. What parameter of the exponential form $f(x) = ab^x + k$ represents the initial balance of $1000?

22. What is the y-intercept of $B(t)$?

23. What parameter would change if the interest rate were changed to 7%?

24. Which bank account balance grows faster, the one with 5% interest or the one with 7% interest?

25. What kind of transformation is represented by changing the initial balance to $500?

26. Match the graph to the characteristics of the function $f(x) = ab^x$.

A. $a < 0, b > 1$ **B.** $a > 0, 0 < b < 1$ **C.** $a > 0, b > 1$ **D.** $a < 0, 0 < b < 1$

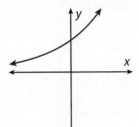

a.

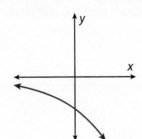

b.

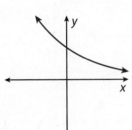

c.

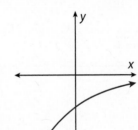

d.

H.O.T. Focus on Higher Order Thinking

27. Critical Thinking Describe how the graph of $f(x) = ab^x$ changes for a given positive value of a as you increase the value of b when $b > 1$. Discuss the rise and fall of the graph and the y-intercept.

28. Communicate Mathematical Ideas Consider the functions $f_1(x) = (1.02)^x$ and $f_2(x) = (1.03)^x$. Which function increases more quickly as x increases to the right of 0? How do the growth factors support your answer?

29. Communicate Mathematical Ideas Consider the function $f_1(x) = (0.94)^x$ and $f_2(x) = (0.98)^x$. Which function decreases more quickly as x increases to the right of 0? How do the growth factors support your answer?

Lesson Performance Task

A coffee shop serves two patrons cups of coffee. The initial temperature of the coffee is 170 °F. As the coffee sits in the 70 °F room, the temperature follows the pattern of a transformed exponential function. One patron leaves her coffee untouched, resulting in a slow cooling toward room temperature. The other patron is in a hurry and stirs her coffee, resulting in a faster cooling rate.

Both cups of coffee can be modeled with transformed exponential functions of the form $T(t) = ab^t + k$.

Each minute, the unstirred coffee gets 10% closer to room temperature, and the stirred coffee gets 20% closer. Find the functions $T_s(t)$ and $T_u(t)$ for the stirred and unstirred cups of coffee, copy and complete the table of values, and graph the functions. Determine how long it takes each cup to drop below 130 °F (don't try to solve the equations exactly, just use the table to answer to the nearest minute).

Time (minutes)	Temperature (°F, unstirred)	Temperature (°F, stirred)
0	?	?
1	?	?
2	?	?
3	?	?
4	?	?
5	?	?

Geometric Sequences and Exponential Functions

Essential Question: How can you use geometric sequences and exponential functions to solve real-world problems?

KEY EXAMPLE   *(Lesson 15.1)*

Find the common ratio r for the geometric sequence 2, 6, 18, 54, ... and use r to find the next three terms.

$\frac{6}{2} = 3$, so the common ratio r is 3.

For this sequence, $f(1) = 2$, $f(2) = 6$, $f(3) = 18$, and $f(4) = 54$.

$f(4) = 54$, so $f(5) = 54(3) = 162$.

$f(5) = 162$, so $f(6) = 162(3) = 486$.

$f(6) = 486$, so $f(7) = 486(3) = 1458$.

The next three terms of the sequence are 162, 486, and 1458.

KEY EXAMPLE   *(Lesson 15.3)*

Write an equation for the exponential function that includes the points $(2, 8)$ and $(3, 16)$.

Find b by dividing the function value of the second pair by the function value of the first: $b = \frac{16}{8} = 2$.

Evaluate the function for $x = 2$ and solve for a.

$f(x) = ab^x$	Write the general form.
$f(x) = a \cdot 2^x$	Substitute the value for **b**.
$8 = a \cdot 2^2$	Substitute a pair of input-output values.
$8 = a \cdot 4$	Simplify.
$a = 2$	Solve for **a**.
$f(x) = 2 \cdot 2^x$	Use **a** and **b** to write an equation for the function.

KEY EXAMPLE   *(Lesson 15.5)*

Describe the transformations of the function $g(x) = 2(3)^x + 5$ as compared to the parent function $f(x) = 3^x$.

a has changed from 1 to 2.

This corresponds to a vertical stretch by a factor of 2.

The constant has changed from 0 to 5.

This corresponds to a translation of 5 units up.

$g(x)$ has been stretched by a factor of 2 and translated 5 units up.

EXERCISES

Find the common ratio *r* for each geometric sequence and use *r* to find the next three terms. *(Lesson 15.1)*

1. 1701, 567, 189,…

2. 5, 20, 80,…

Write a recursive rule and an explicit rule for each geometric sequence. *(Lesson 15.2)*

3. 4, 12, 36, 108, 324,…

4. 6, 30, 150, 750, 3750,…

Write an equation for the exponential function that includes the pair of given points. *(Lesson 15.3)*

5. $(2, 16)$ and $(3, 32)$

6. $(2, 4)$ and $(3, 2)$

7. Find *a*, *b*, and the *y*-intercept for $f(x) = 5(2)^x$, and then describe its end behavior. *(Lesson 15.4)*

MODULE PERFORMANCE TASK

What Does It Take to Go Viral?

You want your newest video to be so popular that it gets more than 750,000 daily views within a week after you post it. You share it with friends and assume that each friend will share the video with the same number of people that you do, and so on. How can you determine the smallest number of friends you need to show your video to? What answer do you think would be too big? Too small?

Start by listing how you plan to tackle the problem. Then complete the task. Be sure to write down all your data and assumptions. Then use numbers, tables, or algebra to explain how you reached your conclusion.

15.1–15.5 Geometric Sequences and Exponential Functions

- Online Homework
- Hints and Help
- Extra Practice

Write a recursive rule and an explicit rule for each geometric sequence, and then find the next three terms. *(Lessons 15.1, 15.2)*

1. 2, 8, 32,…

2. 1024, 512, 256,…

Write an equation for the exponential function that includes the pair of given points. Find *a*, *b*, and the *y*-intercept, and then graph the function and describe its end behavior. *(Lessons 15.3, 15.4)*

3. $(1, 12)$ and $(-1, 0.75)$

4. $(-1, -8)$ and $(1, -2)$

5. Describe the transformations of the function $g(x) = 0.25(5)^x - 2$ as compared to the parent function $f(x) = 5^x$. *(Lesson 15.5)*

ESSENTIAL QUESTION

6. How does the rate of change of an exponential function behave as the value of *x* increases?

Assessment Readiness

1. Consider the geometric sequence 6, 24, 96, 384, …. Determine if each statement is True or False.

   A. The sixth term is 1536.

   B. The explicit rule is $f(n) = 6(4)^{n-1}$.

   C. The recursive rule is $f(1) = 4; f(n) = f(n-1) \cdot 6$.

2. Tell whether the given system of equations has exactly one solution.

   A. $\begin{cases} 3x - 2y = 6 \\ 2x + 2y = 14 \end{cases}$

   B. $\begin{cases} y = -4x - 5 \\ y = -4x + 2 \end{cases}$

   C. $\begin{cases} 5x - 3y = 15 \\ 5x + 3y = 15 \end{cases}$

3. Tell whether the given number is a term in both the sequence $f(n) = f(n-1) + 5$ and the sequence $f(n) = 3(2)^{n-1}$, if $f(1) = 3$.

   A. 8

   B. 18

   C. 24

   D. 48

4. A laser beam with an output of 6 milliwatts is focused at a series of mirrors. The laser beam loses 2% of its power every time it reflects off of a mirror. The power $p(n)$ is an exponential function of the number of reflections in the form of $p(n) = ab^n$. Write the equation $p(n)$ for this laser beam. Explain how you determined the values of a and b.

Exponential Equations and Models

Essential Question: How can you use exponential equations to represent real-world situations?

REAL WORLD VIDEO
Scientists have found many ways to use radioactive elements that decay exponentially over time. Uranium-235 is used to power nuclear reactors, and scientists use Carbon-14 dating to calculate how long ago an organism lived.

MODULE PERFORMANCE TASK PREVIEW

Half-Life

Accidents at nuclear reactors like the one in Fukushima, Japan, in 2011 commonly release the radioactive isotopes iodine-131 and cesium-137. Iodine-131 often causes thyroid problems, whereas cesium-137 permeates the entire body and can cause death. Each isotope decays over time but at very different rates. How can you figure out the concentration of isotopes at a nuclear accident? Let's find out!

Are YOU Ready?

Complete these exercises to review skills you will need for this module.

Constant Rate of Change

Example 1   Tell if the rate of change is constant.

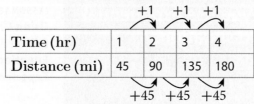

Time (hr)	1	2	3	4
Distance (mi)	45	90	135	180

The rate of change is constant.

rate of change = $\dfrac{\text{change in miles}}{\text{change in hours}}$

$= \dfrac{45}{1}$

Tell if the rate of change is constant.

1.

Age (mo)	3	6	9	12
Weight (lb)	12	16	18	20

2.

Hours	2	4	6	8
Pay ($)	16	32	48	64

Percent

Example 2   Write 7% as a decimal.

$7\% = \dfrac{7}{100} = 0.07$

Write the percent in the form $\dfrac{r}{100}$ and then write the decimal.

Write the percent as a decimal.

3. 21%

4. 3.5%

5. 108%

6. 0.25%

Exponents

Example 3   Find the value of $2(3)^4$.

$2(3)^4 = 2(3 \cdot 3 \cdot 3 \cdot 3)$

$\quad\quad\quad = 162$

Write the power as a multiplication expression. Multiply.

Find the value.

7. $3(4)^2$

8. $24(0.5)^3$

9. $5(2)^5$

10. $350(0.1)^3$

16.1 Using Graphs and Properties to Solve Equations with Exponents

Resource Locker

Essential Question: How can you solve equations involving variable exponents?

⊘ Explore 1 Solving Exponential Equations Graphically

In previous lessons, variables have been raised to rational exponents and you have seen how to simplify and solve equations containing these expressions. How do you solve an equation with a rational number raised to a variable? In certain cases, this is not a difficult task. If $2^x = 4$ it is easy to see that $x = 2$ since $2^2 = 4$. In other cases, like $3(2)^x = 96$, where would you begin? Let's find out.

(A) Solve for $3(2)^x = 96$ for x.

(B) Let $f(x) = 3(2)^x$. Copy and complete the table for $f(x)$.

(C) Using the table of values, graph $f(x)$.

x	f(x)
1	6
2	?
3	?
4	?
5	?
6	?
7	?

(D) Let $g(x) = 96$. Copy and complete the table for $g(x)$.

(E) Using the table, graph $g(x)$ on the same axes as $f(x)$.

x	g(x)
1	96
2	?
3	?
4	?
5	?
6	?
7	96

© Houghton Mifflin Harcourt Publishing Company

(F) The graphs intersect at point(s): $\boxed{?}$

This means that $f(x) = \boxed{?}$

when $x = \boxed{?}$.

Reflect

1. **Discussion** Consider the function $h(x) = -96$. Where do $f(x)$ and $h(x)$ intersect?

2. Divide the equation $3(2)^x = 96$ by 3 on both sides (an Algebraic Step) and utilize the same method as in Explore 1 to graph each side of the equation as a function. What would the point of intersection be?

   Is this the same point of intersection? Is this the same answer? Can this be done? Elaborate as to why or why not.

⊘ Explore 2 Solving Exponential Equations Algebraically

Recall the example $2^x = 4$, with the solution $x = 2$. What about a slightly more complicated equation? Can an equation like $5(2)^x = 160$ be solved using algebra?

(A) Solve $5(2)^x = 160$ for x. The first step in isolating the term containing the variable

on one side of the equation is to $\boxed{?}$.

$$\frac{5(2)^x}{\boxed{?}} = \frac{160}{\boxed{?}}$$

(B) Simplify.

$(2)^x = \boxed{?}$

(C) Rewrite the right hand side as a power of 2.

$(2)^x = (2)^{\boxed{?}}$

(D) Solve.

$x = \boxed{?}$

Reflect

3. **Discussion** The last step of the solution process seems to imply that if $b^x = b^y$ then $x = y$. Is this true for all values of b? Justify your answer.

4. In Reflect 2, we started to solve $3(2)^x = 96$ algebraically. Finish solving for x.

Solving Equations by Equating Exponents

Solving the previous exponential equation for x used the idea that if $2^x = 2^5$, then $x = 5$. This will be a powerful tool for solving exponential equations if it can be generalized to if $b^x = b^y$ then $x = y$. However, there are values for which this is clearly not true. For example, $0^7 = 0^3$ but $7 \neq 3$. If the values of b are restricted, we get the following property.

Equality of Bases Property

Two powers with the same positive base other than 1 are equal if and only if the exponents are equal.

Algebraically, if $b > 0$ and, $b \neq 1$, then $b^x = b^y$ if and only if $x = y$.

Example 1 **Solve by equating exponents and using the Equality of Bases Property.**

Ⓐ
$$\frac{2}{5}(5)^x = 250$$

$$\frac{5}{2} \cdot \frac{2}{5}(5)^x = 250 \cdot \frac{5}{2} \qquad \text{Multiply both sides by } \frac{5}{2}.$$

$$5^x = 625 \qquad \text{Simplify.}$$

$$5^x = 5^4 \qquad \text{Rewrite the right side as a power of 5.}$$

$$x = 4 \qquad \text{Equality of Bases Property.}$$

Ⓑ
$$2\left(\frac{5}{3}\right)^x = \frac{250}{27}$$

$$\frac{2\left(\frac{5}{3}\right)^x}{\boxed{2}} = \frac{\frac{250}{27}}{\boxed{2}} \qquad \text{Divide both sides by } \boxed{2}.$$

$$\left(\frac{5}{3}\right)^x = \frac{\boxed{125}}{27} \qquad \text{Simplify.}$$

$$\left(\frac{5}{3}\right)^x = \left(\boxed{\frac{5}{3}}\right)^3 \qquad \text{Rewrite the right side as a power of } \boxed{\frac{5}{3}}.$$

$$x = \boxed{3} \qquad \text{Equality of Bases Property.}$$

Reflect

5. Suppose while solving an equation algebraically you are confronted with:

$5^x = 15$

$5^x = 5$

Can you find x using the method in the examples above?

Solve by equating exponents and using the Equality of Bases Property.

6. $\frac{2}{3}(3)^x = 18$

7. $\frac{3}{2}\left(\frac{4}{3}\right)^x = \frac{8}{3}$

 Explain 2   **Solving a Real-World Exponential Equation by Graphing**

Some equations cannot be solved using the method in the previous example because it isn't possible to write both sides of the equation as a whole number power of the same base. Instead, you can consider the expressions on either side of the equation as the rules for two different functions. You can then solve the original equation in one variable by graphing the two functions. The solution is the input value for the point where the two graphs intersect.

Example 2   **Solve by graphing two functions.**

An animal reserve has 20,000 elk. The population is increasing at a rate of 8% per year. There is concern that food will be scarce when the population has doubled. How long will it take for the population to reach 40,000?

 Analyze Information

Identify the important information.

- The starting population is   20,000.

- The ending population is   40,000.

- The growth rate is   8% or 0.08.

Formulate a Plan

With the given situation and data there is enough information to write and solve an exponential model of the population as a function of time. Write the exponential equation and then solve it using a graphing calculator.

Set $f(x) = $ the target population and $g(x) = $ the exponential model.

Input $Y_1 = f(x)$ and $Y_2 = g(x)$ into a graphing calculator, graph the functions, and find their intersection.

Solve

Write a function $P(t) = ab^t$, where $P(t)$ is the population and t is the number of years since the population was initially measured.

a represents the initial population of elk

$a = \boxed{20{,}000}$

b represents the yearly growth rate of the elk population

$b = \boxed{1.08}$

The function is $P(t) = \boxed{20{,}000}\left(\boxed{1.08}\right)^t$.

To find the time when the population is 40,000, set the function or $P(t)$ equal to 40,000 and solve for t.

$40{,}000 = \boxed{20{,}000}\left(\boxed{1.08}\right)^t$.

Write functions for the expressions on either side of the equation.

$f(x) = 40{,}000$

$g(x) = 20{,}000\,(1.08)^x$

Using a graphing calculator, set $Y_1 = f(x)$ and $Y_2 = g(x)$. View the graph.
Use the intersect feature on the CALC menu to find the intersection of the two graphs.

The approximate x-value where the graphs intersect is $\boxed{9.006468}$.

Therefore, the population will double in just a little over $\boxed{9}$ years.

Justify and Evaluate

Check the solution by evaluating the function at $t = \boxed{9}$.

$P\left(\boxed{9}\right) = 20{,}000 \cdot \boxed{(1.08)^9}$

$= 20{,}000 \cdot \left(\boxed{1.9990}\right)$

$= \boxed{39{,}980}$

Since $\boxed{39{,}980} \approx 40{,}000$, it is accurate to say the population will double in 9 years.

This prediction is reasonable because $1.08^{\boxed{9}} \approx \boxed{2}$.

Your Turn

Solve using a graphing calculator.

8. There are 225 wolves in a state park. The population is increasing at the rate of 15% per year. You want to make a prediction for how long it will take the population to reach 500.

9. There are 175 deer in a state park. The population is increasing at the rate of 12% per year. You want to make a prediction for how long it will take the population to reach 300.

Elaborate

10. Explain how you would solve $0.25 = 0.5^x$. Which method can always be used to solve an exponential equation?

11. What would you do first to solve the equation $\frac{1}{4}(6)^x = 54$?

12. How does isolating the power in an exponential equation like $\frac{1}{4}(6)^x = 54$ compare to isolating the variable in a linear equation?

13. Given a population decreasing by 1% per year, when will the population double? What will this type of situation look like when graphed on a calculator?

14. Solve $0.5 = 1.01^x$ graphically. Suppose this equation models the point where a population increasing at a rate of 1% per year is halved. When will the population be halved?

15. **Essential Question Check-In** How can you solve equations involving variable exponents?

✪ Evaluate: Homework and Practice

- Online Homework
- Hints and Help
- Extra Practice

1. Would it have been easier to find the solution to the equation in Explore 1, $3(2)^x = 96$, algebraically? Justify your answer. In general, if you can solve an exponential equation graphing by hand, why can you solve it algebraically?

2. The equation $2 = (1.01)^x$ models a population that has doubled. What is the rate of increase? What does x represent?

3. Can you solve exponential equations using both algebraic and graphical methods? Explain.

Solve the given equation.

4. $4(2)^x = 64$

5. $7(3)^x = 63$

6. $\dfrac{6^x}{4} = 54$

7. $\left(\dfrac{1}{4}\right)\left(\dfrac{5}{6}\right)^x = \dfrac{75}{432}$

8. $2\left(\dfrac{7}{2}\right)^x = \dfrac{49}{2}$

9. $3(11)^x = 3993$

10. $2(9)^x = 162$

11. $2\left(\dfrac{1}{9}\right)^x = \dfrac{2}{81}$

12. $2\left(\dfrac{4}{13}\right)^x = \dfrac{32}{169}$

13. $\left(\dfrac{1}{2}\right)\left(\dfrac{2}{3}\right)^x = \left(\dfrac{1}{4}\right)\left(\dfrac{16}{27}\right)$

14. $(8)\left(\dfrac{2}{3}\right)^x = (4)\left(\dfrac{16}{27}\right)$

15. $\left(\dfrac{2}{5}\right)\left(\dfrac{2}{5}\right)^x = \dfrac{8}{125}$

16. $\left(\dfrac{2}{5}\right)^x\left(\dfrac{2}{5}\right)^x = \left(\dfrac{8}{125}\right)\left(\dfrac{8}{125}\right)$

17. There is a drought and the oak tree population is decreasing at the rate of 7% per year. If the population continues to decrease at the same rate, how long will it take for the population to be half of what it is?

18. An animal reserve has 40,000 elk. The population is increasing at a rate of 11% per year. How long will it take for the population to reach 80,000?

19. A lake has a small population of a rare endangered fish. The lake currently has a population of 10 fish. The number of fish is increasing at a rate of 4% per year. When will the population double? How long will it take the population to be 80 fish?

20. Tim has a savings account with the bank. The bank pays him 1% per year. He has $5000 and wonders when it will reach $5200. When will his savings reach $5200?

21. Tim is considering a different savings account that pays 1%, but this time it is compounded monthly.

(When interest is compounded monthly, the bank pays interest every month instead of every year. The function representing compounded interest is $S(t) = P\left(1 + \dfrac{r}{n}\right)^{nt}$, where P is the principal, or initial deposit in the account, r is the interest rate, n is the number of times the interest is compounded per year, t is the year, and $S(t)$ is the savings after t years.)

How many years will it take Tim to earn $200 at this bank? Should he switch?

22. Lisa has a credit card that charges 3% interest on a monthly balance. She buys a $200 bike and plans to pay for it by making monthly payments of $100. How many months will it take her to pay it off? Assume the first payment she makes is charged no interest because she paid it before the first bill.

23. **Analyze Relationships** A city has 175,000 residents. The population is increasing at the rate of 10% per year.

a. You want to make a prediction for how long it will take for the population to reach 300,000. Round your answer to the nearest tenth of a year.

b. Suppose there are 350,000 residents of another city. The population of this city is decreasing at a rate of 3% per year. Which city's population will reach 300,000 sooner? Explain.

24. **Explain the Error** Jean and Marco each solved the equation $9(3)^x = 729$. Whose solution is incorrect? Explain your reasoning. How could the person who is incorrect fix the work?

Jean

$$9(3)^x = 729$$

$$\left(\frac{1}{9}\right) \cdot 9(3)^x = \left(\frac{1}{9}\right) \cdot 729$$

$$3^x = 81 = 3^4$$

$$x = 4$$

Marco

$$9(3)^x = 729$$

$$3^2 \cdot (3)^x = 729$$

$$3^{2+x} = 729 = 3^6$$

$$x = 6$$

25. **Critical Thinking** Without solving, identify the equation with the greater solution. Explain your reasoning.

$$\left(\frac{1}{3}\right)(3)^x = 243 \qquad\qquad \left(\frac{1}{3}\right)(9)^x = 243$$

Lesson Performance Task

A town has a population of 78,918 residents. The town council is offering a prize for the best prediction of how long it will take the population to reach 100,000. The population rate is increasing 6% per year. Find the best prediction in order to win the prize. Write an exponential equation in the form $y = ab^x$ and explain what a and b represent.

16.2 Modeling Exponential Growth and Decay

Essential Question: How can you use exponential functions to model the increase or decrease of a quantity over time?

Explore 1 Describing End Behavior of a Growth Function

When you graph a function $f(x)$ in a coordinate plane, the x-axis represents the independent variable and the y-axis represents the dependent variable. Therefore, the graph of $f(x)$ is the same as the graph of the equation $y = f(x)$. You will use this form when you use a calculator to graph functions.

(A) Use a graphing calculator to graph the exponential growth function $f(x) = 200(1.10)^x$, using Y_1 for $f(x)$. Use a viewing window from -20 to 20 for x, with a scale of 2, and from -100 to 1000 for y, with a scale of 50. Sketch the curve.

(B) To describe the end behavior of the function, you describe the function values as x increases or decreases without bound. Using the TRACE feature, move the cursor to the right along the curve. Describe the end behavior as x increases without bound.

(C) Using the TRACE feature, move the cursor to the left along the curve. Describe the end behavior as x decreases without bound.

Reflect

1. Describe the domain and range of the function using inequalities.

2. Identify the y-intercept of the graph of the function.

3. An asymptote of a graph is a line the graph approaches more and more closely. Identify an asymptote of this graph.

4. **Discussion** Why is the value of the function always greater than 0?

Explore 2 Describing End Behavior of a Decay Function

Use the form from the first Explore exercise to graph another function on your calculator.

(A) Use a graphing calculator to graph the exponential decay function $f(x) = 500(0.8)^x$, using Y_1 for $f(x)$. Use a viewing window from -10 to 10 for x, with a scale of 1, and from -500 to 5000 for y, with a scale of 500. Sketch the curve.

(B) Using the TRACE feature, move the cursor to the right along the curve. Describe the end behavior as x increases without bound.

(C) Using the TRACE feature, move the cursor to the left along the curve. Describe the end behavior as x decreases without bound.

Reflect

5. **Discussion** Describe the domain and range of the function using inequalities.

6. Identify the y-intercept of the graph of the function.

7. Identify an asymptote of this graph. Why is this line an asymptote?

🔧 Explain 1 Modeling Exponential Growth

Recall that a function of the form $y = ab^x$ represents exponential growth when $a > 0$ and $b > 1$. If b is replaced by $1 + r$ and x is replaced by t, then the function is the **exponential growth model** $y = a(1 + r)^t$, where a is the initial amount, the base $(1 + r)$ is the growth factor, r is the growth rate, and t is the time interval. The value of the model increases with time.

Example 1 Write an exponential growth function for each situation. Graph each function and state its domain, range and an asymptote. What does the y-intercept represent in the context of the problem?

(A) A painting is sold for $1800, and its value increases by 11% each year after it is sold. Find the value of the painting in 30 years.

Write the exponential growth function for this situation.

$$y = a(1 + r)^t$$
$$= 1800(1 + 0.11)^t$$
$$= 1800(1.11)^t$$

Find the value in 30 years.

$$y = 1800(1.11)^t$$
$$= 1800(1.11)^{30}$$
$$\approx 41{,}206.13$$

After 30 years, the painting will be worth approximately $41,206.

Create a table of values to graph the function.

t	y	(t, y)
0	1800	(0, 1800)
8	4148	(8, 4148)
16	9560	(16, 9560)
24	22,030	(24, 22,030)
32	50,770	(32, 50,770)

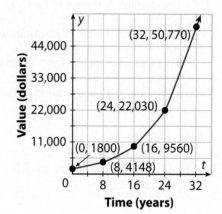

Determine the domain, range and an asymptote of the function.

The domain is the set of real numbers t such that $t \geq 0$.

The range is the set of real numbers y such that $y \geq 1800$.

An asymptote for the function is $y = 0$.

The y-intercept is the value of y when $t = 0$, which is the value of the painting when it was sold.

(B) A baseball trading card sold for $2, and its value increases by 8% each year after it is sold. Find the value of the baseball trading card in 10 years.

Write the exponential growth function for this situation.

$y = a(1 + r)^t$

$= \boxed{2}\left(1 + \boxed{0.08}\right)^t$

$= \boxed{2}\left(\boxed{1.08}\right)^t$

Find the value in 10 years.

$y = a(1 + r)^t$

$= \boxed{2}\left(\boxed{1.08}\right)^t$

$= \boxed{2}\left(\boxed{1.08}\right)^{\boxed{10}}$

$\approx \boxed{4.32}$

After 10 years, the baseball trading card will be worth approximately $4.32.

Create a table of values to graph the function.

t	y	(t, y)
0	2	(0, 2)
3	2.52	(3, 2.52)
6	3.17	(6, 3.17)
9	4.00	(9, 4.00)
12	5.04	(12, 5.04)

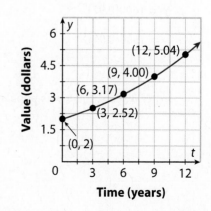

Determine the domain, range, and an asymptote of the function.

The domain is the set of real numbers t such that $t \geq \boxed{0}$.

The range is the set of real numbers y such that $y \geq \boxed{2}$.

An asymptote for the function is $y = 0$.

The y-intercept is the value of y when $t = 0$, which is the value of the card when it was sold.

Reflect

8. Find a recursive rule that models the exponential growth of $y = 1800(1.11)^t$.

9. Find a recursive rule that models the exponential growth of $y = 2(1.08)^t$.

Your Turn

10. Write and graph an exponential growth function, and state the domain and range. Tell what the y-intercept represents. Sara sold a coin for $3, and its value increases by 2% each year after it is sold. Find the value of the coin in 8 years.

⚙ Explain 2 Modeling Exponential Decay

Recall that a function of the form $y = ab^x$ represents exponential decay when $a > 0$ and $0 < b < 1$. If b is replaced by $1 - r$ and x is replaced by t, then the function is the **exponential decay model** $y = a(1 - r)^t$, where a is the initial amount, the base $(1 - r)$ is the decay factor, r is the decay rate, and t is the time interval.

Example 2 Write an exponential decay function for each situation. Graph each function and state its domain and range. What does the y-intercept represent in the context of the problem?

Ⓐ The population of a town is decreasing at a rate of 3% per year. In 2005, there were 1600 people. Find the population in 2013.

Write the exponential decay function for this situation.

$y = a(1 - r)^t$

$\quad = 1600(1 - 0.03)^t$

$\quad = 1600(0.97)^t$

Find the value in 8 years.

$y = 1600(0.97)^t$

$\quad = 1600(0.97)^8$

$\quad \approx 1254$

After 8 years, the town's population will be about 1254 people.

Create a table of values to graph the function.

t	y	(t, y)
0	1600	(0, 1600)
8	1254	(8, 1254)
16	983	(16, 983)
24	770	(24, 770)
32	604	(32, 604)

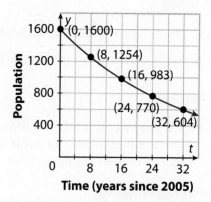

Determine the domain and range of the function.

The domain is the set of real numbers t such that $t \geq 0$. The range is the set of real numbers y such that $0 < y \leq 1600$.

The y-intercept is the value of y when $t = 0$, the number of people before it started to lose population.

(B) The value of a car is depreciating at a rate of 5% per year. In 2010, the car was worth $32,000. Find the value of the car in 2013.

Write the exponential decay function for this situation.

$y = a(1 - r)^t$

$= \boxed{32{,}000}\left(1 - \boxed{0.05}\right)^t$

$= \boxed{32{,}000}\left(\boxed{0.95}\right)^t$

Find the value in 3 years.

$y = a(1 - r)^t$

$= \boxed{32{,}000}\left(\boxed{0.95}\right)^t = \boxed{32{,}000}\left(\boxed{0.95}\right)^3 \approx \boxed{27{,}436}$

After 3 years, the car's value will be $\boxed{27{,}436}$.

Create a table of values to graph the function.

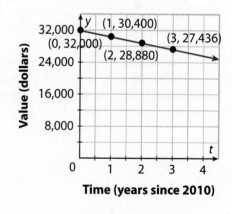

t	y	(t, y)
0	32,000	(0, 32,000)
1	30,400	(1, 30,400)
2	28,880	(2, 28,880)
3	27,436	(3, 27,436)

Determine the domain and range of the function.

The domain is the set of real numbers t such that $t \geq \boxed{0}$. The range is the set of real numbers y such that $\boxed{0} < y \leq \boxed{32{,}000}$.

The y-intercept, 32,000, is the value of y when $t = 0$, the original value of the car.

© Houghton Mifflin Harcourt Publishing Company

11. Find a recursive rule that models the exponential decay of $y = 1600(0.97)^t$.

12. Find a recursive rule that models the exponential decay of $y = 32,000(0.95)^t$.

13. The value of a boat is depreciating at a rate of 9% per year. In 2006, the boat was worth $17,800. Find the worth of the boat in 2013. Write an exponential decay function for this situation. Graph the function and state its domain and range. What does the y-intercept represent in the context of the problem?

⚙ Explain 3   Comparing Exponential Growth and Decay

Graphs can be used to describe and compare exponential growth and exponential decay models over time.

Example 3   **Use the graphs provided to write the equations of the functions. Then describe and compare the behaviors of both functions.**

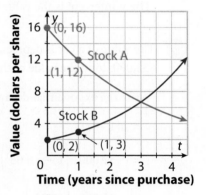

(A)   The graph shows the value of two different shares of stock over the period of 4 years since they were purchased. The values have been changing exponentially.

The graph for Stock A shows that the value of the stock is decreasing as time increases.

The initial value, when $t = 0$, is 16. The value when $t = 1$ is 12. Since $12 \div 16 = 0.75$, the function that represents the value of Stock A after t years is $A(t) = 16(0.75)^t$. $A(t)$ is an exponential decay function.

The graph for Stock B shows that the value of the stock is increasing as time increases.

The initial value, when $t = 0$, is 2. The value when $t = 1$ is 3. Since $3 \div 2 = 1.5$, the function that represents the value of Stock B after t years is $B(t) = 2(1.5)^t$. $B(t)$ is an exponential growth function.

The value of Stock A is going down over time. The value of Stock B is going up over time. The initial value of Stock A is greater than the initial value of Stock B. However, after about 3 years, the value of Stock B becomes greater than the value of Stock A.

B The graph shows the value of two different shares of stocks over the period of 4 years since they were purchased. The values have been changing exponentially.

The graph for Stock A shows that the value of the stock is decreasing as time increases.

The initial value, when $t = 0$, is $\boxed{100}$. The value when $t = 1$

is $\boxed{50}$. Since $\boxed{50} \div \boxed{100} = \boxed{0.5}$, the function that

represents the value of Stock A after t years is $A(t) = \boxed{100} \left(\boxed{0.5}\right)^t$.

$A(t)$ is an exponential decay function.

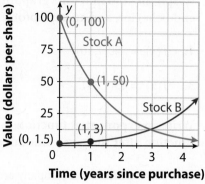

The graph for Stock B shows that the value of the stock is increasing as time increases.

The initial value, when $t = 0$, is $\boxed{1.5}$. The value when $t = 1$ is $\boxed{3}$. Since $\boxed{3} \div \boxed{1.5} = \boxed{2}$, the

function that represents the value of Stock B after t years is $B(t) = \boxed{1.5}\left(\boxed{2}\right)^t$. $B(t)$ is an exponential growth function.

The value of Stock A is going down over time. The value of Stock B is going up over time.

The initial value of Stock A is greater than the initial value of Stock B. However, after about $\boxed{3}$ years, the value of Stock B becomes greater than the value of Stock A.

Reflect

14. Discussion In the function $B(t) = 1.5(2)^t$, is it likely that the value of B can be accurately predicted in 50 years?

Your Turn

15. The graph shows the value of two different shares of stocks over the period of 4 years since they were purchased. The values have been changing exponentially. Use the graphs provided to write the equations of the functions. Then describe and compare the behaviors of both functions.

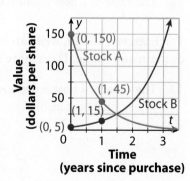

💬 Elaborate

16. If $b > 1$ in a function of the form $y = ab^x$, is the function an example of exponential growth or an example of exponential decay?

17. What is an asymptote of the function $y = 35(1.1)^x$?

18. Essential Question Check-In What equation should be used when modeling an exponential function that models a decrease in a quantity over time?

Graph the function on a graphing calculator, and state its domain, range, end behavior, and an asymptote.

1. $f(x) = 300(1.16)^x$

2. $f(x) = 800(0.85)^x$

3. $f(x) = 65(1.64)^x$

4. $f(x) = 57(0.77)^x$

Write an exponential function to model each situation. Then find the value of the function after the given amount of time.

5. Annual sales for a company are $155,000 and increases at a rate of 8% per year for 9 years.

6. The value of a textbook is $69 and decreases at a rate of 15% per year for 11 years.

7. A new savings account is opened with $300 and gains 3.1% yearly for 5 years.

8. The value of a car is $7800 and decreases at a rate of 8% yearly for 6 years.

9. The starting salary at a construction company is fixed at $55,000 and increases at a rate of 1.8% yearly for 4 years.

10. The value of a piece of fine jewelry is $280 and decreases at a rate of 3% yearly for 7 years.

11. The population of a town is 24,000 and is increasing at a rate of 6% per year for 3 years.

12. The value of a new stadium is $3.4 million and decreases at a rate of 2.39% yearly for 10 years.

For Exercises 13–20, write an exponential function for each situation. Graph each function and state its domain and range. Determine what the y-intercept represents in the context of the problem.

13. The value of a boat is depreciating at a rate of 7% per year. In 2004, the boat was worth $192,000. Find the value of the boat in 2013.

14. The value of a collectible baseball card is increasing at a rate of 0.5% per year. In 2000, the card was worth $1350. Find the value of the card in 2013.

15. The value of an airplane is depreciating at a rate of 7% per year. In 2004, the airplane was worth $51.5 million. Find the value of the airplane in 2013.

16. The value of a movie poster is increasing at a rate of 3.5% per year. In 1990, the poster was worth $20.25. Find the value of the poster in 2013.

17. The value of a couch is decreasing at a rate of 6.2% per year. In 2007, the couch was worth $1232. Find the value of the couch in 2014.

18. The population of a town is increasing at a rate of 2.2% per year. In 2001, the town had a population of 34,567. Find the population of the town in 2018.

19. A house is losing value at a rate of 5.4% per year. In 2009, the house was worth $131,000. Find the worth of the house in 2019.

20. An account is gaining value at a rate of 4.94% per year. The account held $113 in 2005. What will the bank account hold in 2017?

Use a calculator to graph the functions. Describe and compare each pair of functions.

21. $A(t) = 13(0.6)^t$ and $B(t) = 4(3.2)^t$

22. $A(t) = 9(0.4)^t$ and $B(t) = 0.6(1.4)^t$

23. $A(t) = 547(0.32)^t$ and $B(t) = 324(3)^t$

24. $A(t) = 2(0.6)^t$ and $B(t) = 0.2(1.4)^t$

25. Identify the y-intercept of each of the exponential functions.

    a. $3123(432,543)^x$

    b. $76(89,047,832)^x$

    c. $45(54)^x$

H.O.T. Focus on Higher Order Thinking

26. Explain the Error A student was asked to find the value of a $2500 item after 4 years. The item was depreciating at a rate of 20% per year. What is wrong with the student's work?

$2500(0.2)^4$

$4

27. Make a Conjecture The value of a certain car can be modeled by the function $y = 18000(0.76)^t$, where t is time in years. Will the value of the function ever be 0?

28. Communicate Mathematical Ideas Explain how a graph of an exponential function may resemble the graph of a linear function.

Lesson Performance Task

Archeologists have several methods of determining the age of recovered artifacts. One method is radioactive dating.

All matter is made of atoms. Atoms, in turn, are made of protons, neutrons, and electrons. An "element" is defined as an atom with a given number of protons. Carbon, for example, has exactly 6 protons. Carbon atoms can, however, have different numbers of neutrons. These are known as "isotopes" of carbon. Carbon-12 has 6 neutrons, carbon-13 has 7 neutrons, and carbon-14 has 8 neutrons. All carbon-based life forms contain these different isotopes of carbon.

Carbon-12 and carbon-13 account for over 99% of all the carbon in living things. Carbon-14, however, accounts for approximately 1 part per trillion or 0.0000000001% of the total carbon in living things. More importantly, carbon-14 is unstable and has a half-life of approximately 5700 years. This means that, within the span of 5700 years, one-half of any amount of carbon will "decay" into another atom. In other words, if you had 10 g of carbon-14 today, only 5 g would remain after 5700 years.

But, as long as an organism is living, it keeps taking in and releasing carbon-14, so the level of it in the organism, as small as it is, remains constant. Once an organism dies, however, it no longer ingests carbon-14, so the level of carbon-14 in it drops due to radioactive decay. Because we know how much carbon-14 an organism had when it was alive, as well as how long it takes for that amount to become half of what it was, you can determine the age of the organism by comparing these two values.

Use the information presented to create a function that will model the amount of carbon-14 in a sample as a function of its age. Create the model $C(n)$ where C is the amount of carbon-14 in parts per quadrillion (1 part per trillion is 1000 parts per quadrillion) and n is the age of the sample in half-lives. Graph the model.

16.3 Using Exponential Regression Models

Essential Question: How can you use exponential regression to model data?

Explore 1 Fitting an Exponential Function to Data

One of the reasons data is valuable is that it allows us to make predictions for values that fall outside of the data set. In order to do this, the data needs to be synthesized into a function. An **exponential regression** is a graphing calculator tool used to generate an exponential equation that fits data exhibiting exponential growth or decay. The statistical tools on a graphing calculator offer several possible methods for finding a regression model for a set of data. Use a graphing calculator to find the exponential regression equation that models the data provided.

Number of Internet Hosts							
Years since 2001	0	1	2	3	4	5	6
Number (millions)	110	147	172	233	318	395	433

(A) Enter the data from the table on a graphing calculator, with years since 2001 in L1. Input the number of Internet hosts in L2. Create a scatter plot of the data on the calculator. Plot the data points on a coordinate grid.

(B) Use the statistical calculation features of a graphing calculator to calculate the exponential regression equation for the data you entered into L1 and L2.

The exponential regression function is [?].
(Round to three significant digits.)

(C) Graph the exponential regression equation with the data points on the calculator. Sketch a graph of the exponential regression equation on the grid with the data points that you plotted.

Reflect

1. **Discussion** Which parameter, *a* or *b*, represents the initial value of the function? Explain how you know.

2. What is the growth rate of this exponential model?

Plotting and Analyzing Residuals of Exponential Models

Recall that a residual is the difference between the actual y-value in the data set and the predicted y-value. Residuals can be used to assess how well a model fits a data set. If a model fits the data well, then the following are true.

- The numbers of positive and negative residuals are roughly equal.
- The residuals are randomly distributed about the x-axis on a residual plot.
- The absolute value of the residuals is small relative to the data values.

(A) According to the data, in 2002 there were 147,000,000 Internet hosts. Find the y-value predicted by the model.

$$y = ab^x \quad y = 113(1.27)^1 \quad y = \boxed{?}$$

The actual y-value from the data is $\boxed{?}$.

(B) Find the difference between the data y-value and the model's predicted y-value.

$$\text{data} - \text{model} = 147 - 143 = \boxed{?}$$

(C) On your calculator, enter the regression equation as the rule for equation Y_1. Then view the table to find the y-values predicted by model (y_m). Copy and complete the table.

Number of Internet Hosts			
x	Actual y-value, y_d	Predicted y-value, y_m	Residual $y_d - y_m$
0	110	113	−3
1	147	143	?
2	172	?	?
3	233	?	?
4	318	?	?
5	395	?	?
6	433	?	?

(D) Create a residual scatter plot by plotting the x-values and the residuals in the last column as the second coordinate.

Reflect

3. **Multiple Representations** What does the residual plot reveal about the fit of the model? Does this agree with the correlation coefficient?

4. **Look for Patterns** What can you infer about the accuracy of the model as it moves further away from the initial value? Explain.

⊘ Explain 1   Modeling with Exponential Functions

Exponential regression functions can be used to make predictions.

Example 1   **Find an exponential regression function for the given data, and use the model to make predictions.**

(A)   The table shows the population y of Middleton, where x is the number of years since the end of 2000.

Suppose Middleton's town council decides to build a new high school when its population exceeds 25,000.

When will the population likely exceed 25,000?

Years since 2000, x	Population, y
0	5,005
1	6,010
2	7,203
3	8,700
4	10,521
5	12,420
6	14,982
7	18,010

Enter the x-values into L1 and the y-values into L2 in a graphing calculator and view a scatter plot of the data.

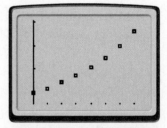

Find the exponential regression model and the regression coefficient for the data. Plot the regression function on the scatter plot.

$y = 5011(1.201)^x \quad r = 0.999$

Use the regression model to construct an equation in one variable to solve in order to determine the time x when the population will reach 25,000.

$25,000 = 5011(1.201)^x$

Enter $y = 25,000$ as Y_2 in the graphing calculator, and find the point of intersection.

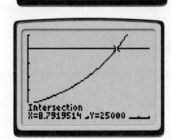

The intersection is at about (8.792, 25,000). The population will reach 25,000 in about 9 years.

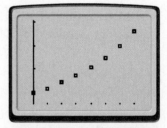

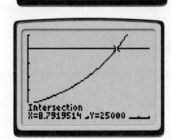

B The table shows the value of a car every year since it was purchased.

The owner plans to sell the car when it reaches 10% of its original value. How long will she have owned the car when she sells it?

Find the exponential regression model and the regression coefficient for the data. Round to four significant digits.

$y =$ $\boxed{25,100(0.8493)^x}$ $\qquad r =$ $\boxed{0.9998}$

Use the regression model to construct an equation in one variable to solve in order to determine the time x when the value will reach 10% of the original value.

$2500 = 25,100(0.8493)^x$

The intersection is at (14.12, 2500). The car will have dropped to a value of $2500 after 15 years.

Age of Car, x	Value, y
0	$25,000.00
1	$21,462.50
2	$17,881.88
3	$15,506.66
4	$12,919.65
5	$11,203.56
6	$9,523.03
7	$7,934.28
8	$6,880.39
9	$5,732.52
10	$4,872.64

Reflect

5. Use the regression model to predict the population at the end of 2015 and at the end of 2030. Round to four significant digits. Which prediction is likely to be more accurate? Explain your reasoning.

6. During what year does the population reach 25,000? Explain your reasoning.

7. Suppose the town will need a new high school already in place when the population reaches 25,000. How will the prediction above help the town make plans?

Your Turn

Create a model from the table of values and answer the questions.

8. The table shows the population of Arizona (in thousands) in each census from 1900–2000.

Use the model to predict the census results from 2010 and compare the estimate to 6,392,017, the actual population according to the 2010 national census.

Years Since 1900 (x)	Population, (y)
0	123
10	204
20	334
30	436
40	499
50	750
60	1302
70	1771
80	2718
90	3665
100	5131

9. The table shows the population of box turtles in a Tennessee wildlife park over a period of 5 years.

Use the model to predict the number of box turtles in the sixth year.

Year, (x)	Population, (y)
1	21
2	27
3	33
4	41
5	48

💬 Elaborate

10. What does a pattern in the plot of the regression data indicate?

11. **Discussion** While it is typically the best model for population growth, what are some factors that cause population growth to deviate from the exponential format?

12. **Essential Question Check-In** What do the variables a and b represent in the regression equation $f(x) = ab^x$?

⭐ Evaluate: Homework and Practice

• Online Homework
• Hints and Help
• Extra Practice

1. The concentration of ibuprofen in a person's blood was plotted each hour. An exponential model fit the data with $a = 400$ and $b = 0.71$. Interpret these parameters.

2. The table shows the temperature of a pizza over three-minute intervals after it is removed from the oven.

a. Find an exponential regression function for the data.

Time	Temperature
0	450
3	350
6	290
9	230
12	190
15	150
18	130
21	110

b. Copy and complete the table to calculate the residuals. Plot the residuals on a scatter plot.

Time	Temperature	Predicted Temperature	Residual
0	450	?	?
3	350	?	?
6	290	?	?
9	230	?	?
12	190	?	?
15	150	?	?
18	130	?	?
21	110	?	?

c. Graph $y = 70$ and the exponential regression function together with the graphing calculator, and find the intersection to predict how long it will take the pizza to cool down to 70 °F.

For Exercises 3 and 4, use a graphing calculator to calculate the exponential regression equation, and use it to solve the problem.

3. The table shows the monthly membership in an online gaming club. When will there be more than 3000 members?

Month	Membership
0	2100
1	2163
2	2199
3	2249
4	2285
5	2329
6	2376
7	2415
8	2464
9	2514
10	2576

4. The table below shows a set of data that can be modeled with an exponential function. When will y be 6000?

x	y
0	15
1	22
2	34
3	50
4	75
5	113
6	170
7	258
8	388
9	575
10	857

5. A researcher is conducting an experiment on the rate that caffeine is eliminated from the body. Three volunteers are given four 8-ounce servings of coffee and asked to consume it as quickly as possible. The researchers then tested the caffeine remaining in each volunteer's blood every 20 minutes for 4 hours to determine the rate of elimination. The table gives the results in milligrams for the three volunteers.

Time (hr)	Student A (mg)	Student B (mg)	Student C (mg)
0	400	400	400
0.33	383	374	387
0.67	365	357	370
1.00	349	341	353
1.33	333	326	337
1.67	318	311	322
2.00	304	297	308
2.33	290	284	294
2.67	277	271	281
3.00	264	259	269
3.33	252	247	257
3.67	241	236	246
4.00	230	225	235

Find the hourly rate at which each student metabolizes caffeine and the time when each student will have 10 mg of caffeine in the blood.

6. The population of Boston, MA in thousands of people is given in the table below.

1990	572	2001	602
1991	561	2002	608
1992	552	2003	608
1993	552	2004	607
1994	551	2005	610
1995	558	2006	612
1996	556	2007	623
1997	556	2008	637
1998	555	2009	645
1999	555	2010	618
2000	590	2011	625

Find a model for the population of Boston as a function of years since 1990 using the even years and a model using the odd years. Compare the models.

Find an exponential model for the radioactive decay of the given isotope.

7. Nobelium-253

Minutes	Mass (grams)
0	10,000.00
1	6651.56
2	4424.33
3	2942.87
4	1957.47
5	1302.02
6	866.05
7	576.06
8	383.17
9	254.87
10	169.53

8. Manganese-52

Weeks	Mass (ounces)
0	200.00
1	83.97
2	35.26
3	14.80
4	6.22
5	2.61
6	1.10
7	0.46
8	0.19
9	0.08
10	0.03

Find an exponential model for the data in the given table.

9.

x	y
0	7
1	10.86
2	16.86
3	26.16
4	40.60
5	63
6	97.77
7	151.72
8	235.44
9	365.37
10	567

10.

x	y
0	2.6
1	3.91
2	5.88
3	8.85
4	13.31
5	20.01
6	30.1
7	45.27
8	68.10
9	102.42
10	154.05

11.

x	y
0	11
1	11.1
2	11.21
3	11.32
4	11.43
5	11.53
6	11.64
7	11.76
8	11.87
9	11.98
10	12.09

12.

x	y
0	4
1	7.36
2	13.54
3	24.92
4	45.85
5	84.36
6	155.23
7	285.62
8	525.54
9	966.99
10	1779.26

13. The yearly profits of Company A are shown in the table. Use the information given to find a function $P(t)$ that models the yearly profits P of the company as a function of t, the number of years since 1995.

Year	Profit (millions)
1995	5.00
1996	5.15
1997	5.30
1998	5.47
1999	5.63
2000	5.79
2001	5.97
2002	6.15
2003	6.33
2004	6.52
2005	6.71

14. Find the Error A student is doing homework and comes to the following question.

The table shows the balance in a student's savings account for 10 years. The student hasn't deposited or withdrawn any money over the time period. Find the exponential model for the student's balance as a function of time.

The student performs exponential regression on the data and compares the result with the answer in the back of the text.

The text gives the solution as $b(t) = 200(1.05)^t$, but the student's model is $b(t) = 190.48(1.05)^t$. Find the error in the student's calculations or explain why the student's model is correct.

Year	Balance
2001	$200.00
2002	$210.00
2003	$220.50
2004	$231.53
2005	$243.10
2006	$255.26
2007	$268.02
2008	$281.42
2009	$295.49
2010	$310.27

15. Determine whether each of the following represents an increasing exponential function, a decreasing exponential function, or a non-exponential function.

a. $f(t) = \frac{1}{2}t^5$

b.

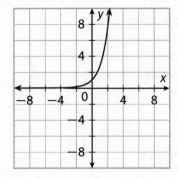

c.

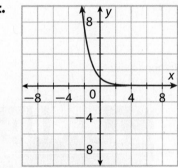

d. $f(x) = 20(0.85)^x$

e. $f(x) = 7(1.16)^x$

f.

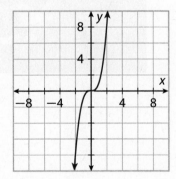

16. Critique Reasoning The absolute values of the residuals in Mark's regression model are less than 20. Working on a different data set, Sandy obtained residuals in the hundreds. This led Mark to conclude his data is a better fit than Sandy's. Explain why Mark is wrong to base his assessment of their regression models on the values of the residuals.

17. Make a Conjecture When Chris used exponential regression on the Arizona population data, he obtained the following results: $a = 186$, $b = 1.026$, $r = 0.813$, which differed from the given exponential regression function of $f(x) = 135.9(1.037)^x$. When he reviewed the data in his lists, he found he had entered a number incorrectly. Is it more likely that his error was in entering the last population value too high or too low? Justify your reasoning.

18. Draw Conclusions Madelyn has recorded the number of bacteria on her growth plate every hour for 3 hours. She finds that a linear model fits her data better than the expected exponential model. What should she do to improve her model?

Lesson Performance Task

A student with an interest-bearing savings account reports the yearly balance in her account in the following table.

Years Since Opening the Account	Balance
1	$6152.42
2	$6305.22
3	$6459.59
4	$6626.83
5	$6793.00
6	$6965.05
7	$7148.27
8	$7322.20
9	$7505.25
10	$7710.33
11	$7906.32
12	$8092.77

Perform an exponential regression on the data. Then estimate the amount of money the student placed in the account initially and the yearly interest rate.

16.4 Comparing Linear and Exponential Models

Essential Question: How can you recognize when to use a linear model or an exponential model?

⊘ Explore 1 Comparing Constant Change and Constant Percent Change

Suppose that you are offered a job that pays you $1000 the first month with a raise every month after that. You can choose a $100 raise or a 10% raise. Which option would you choose? What if the raise were 8%, 6%, or 4%?

Ⓐ Find the monthly salaries for the first three months. Copy the table and record the results, rounded to the nearest dollar.

- For the $100 raise, enter 1000 into your graphing calculator, press ENTER, enter +100, press ENTER, and then press ENTER repeatedly.

- For the 10% raise, enter 1000, press ENTER, enter ·1.10, press ENTER, and then press ENTER repeatedly.

- For the other raises, multiply by 1.08, 1.06, or 1.04.

Monthly Salary after Indicated Monthly Raise					
Month	$100	10%	8%	6%	4%
0	$1000	$1000	$1000	$1000	$1000
1	$1100	$1100	$1080	$1060	$1040
2	?	?	?	?	?
3	?	?	?	?	?

Ⓑ For each option, find how much the salary changes each month, both in dollars and as a percent of the previous month's salary. Round the each percent to the nearest whole number. Copy the table and record the values.

Change in Salary per Month for Indicated Monthly Raise										
Interval	$100		10%		8%		6%		4%	
	$	%	$	%	$	%	$	%	$	%
0 – 1	100	10	100	10	80	8	60	6	40	4
1 – 2	100	?	?	10	?	8	?	6	?	4
2 – 3	100	?	?	10	?	8	?	6	?	4

(C) Continue the calculations you did in Part A until you find the number of months it takes for each salary with a percent raise to exceed the salary with the $100 raise. Copy the table and record the number of months.

Number of Months until Salary with Percent Raise Exceeds Salary with $100 Raise			
10%	8%	6%	4%
2	?	?	?

Reflect

1. **Discussion** Compare and contrast the salary changes per month for the raise options. Explain the source of any differences.

2. **Discussion** Would you choose a constant change per month or a percent increase per month? What would you consider when deciding? Explain your reasoning.

(⊘) **Explore 2** **Exploring How Linear and Exponential Functions Grow**

Linear functions change by equal differences, while exponential functions change by equal factors. Now you will explore the proofs of these statements. $x_2 - x_1$ and $x_4 - x_3$ represent two intervals in the x-values of a function.

(A) Complete the proof that linear functions grow by equal differences over equal intervals.

Given: $x_2 - x_1 = x_4 - x_3$

   f is linear function of the form $f(x) = mx + b$.

Prove: $f(x_2) - f(x_1) = f(x_4) - f(x_3)$

Proof: 1. $x_2 - x_1 = x_4 - x_3$ Given

   2. $m(x_2 - x_1) = \boxed{?} \ (x_4 - x_3)$ Multiplication Property of Equality

   3. $mx_2 - \boxed{?} = mx_4 - \boxed{?}$ Distributive Property

   4. $mx_2 + b - mx_1 - b =$ Addition & Subtraction Properties of Equality
   $mx_4 + \boxed{?} - mx_3 - \boxed{?}$

   5. $mx_2 + b - (mx_1 + b) =$ Distributive property

   $mx_4 + b - \left(\boxed{?}\right)$

   6. $f(x_2) - f(x_1) = \left(\boxed{?}\right)$ Definition of $f(x)$

© Houghton Mifflin Harcourt Publishing Company

(B) Complete the proof that exponential functions grow by equal factors over equal intervals.

Given: $x_2 - x_1 = x_4 - x_3$

g is an exponential function of the form $g(x) = ab^x$.

Prove: $\dfrac{g(x_2)}{g(x_1)} = \dfrac{g(x_4)}{g(x_3)}$

Proof: 1. $x_2 - x_1 = x_4 - x_3$ Given

2. $b^{(x_2 - x_1)} = b^{(x_4 - x_3)}$ If $x = y$, then $b^x = b^y$.

3. $\dfrac{b^{x_2}}{b^{x_1}} = \dfrac{b^{x_4}}{\boxed{?}}$ Quotient of Powers Property

4. $\dfrac{ab^{x_2}}{ab^{x_1}} = \dfrac{ab^{x_4}}{\boxed{?}}$ Multiplication Property of Equality

5. $\dfrac{g(x_2)}{g(x_1)} = \dfrac{g(x_4)}{\boxed{?}}$ Definition of $g(x)$

Reflect

3.   In the previous proofs, what do $x_2 - x_1$ and $x_4 - x_3$ represent?

🖉 Explain 1   Comparing Linear and Exponential Functions

When comparing raises, a fixed dollar increase can be modeled by a linear function and a fixed percent increase can be modeled by an exponential function.

Example 1   **Compare the two salary plans listed by using a graphing calculator. Will Job B ever have a higher monthly salary than Job A? If so, after how many months will this occur?**

(A) • Job A: $1000 for the first month with a $100 raise every month thereafter

• Job B: $1000 for the first month with a 1% raise every month thereafter

Write the functions that represent the monthly salaries. Let t represent the number of elapsed months.

Job A: $S_A(t) = 1000 + 100t$ Job B: $S_B(t) = 1000(1.01)^t$

Graph the functions on a calculator using Y_1 for Job A and Y_2 for Job B. Estimate the number of months it takes for the salaries to become equal using the intersect feature of the calculator. At $x \approx 364$ months, the salaries are equal.

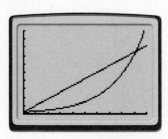
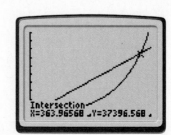

Go to the estimated intersection point in the table feature. Find the first *x*-value at which Y_2 exceeds Y_1. Job B will have a higher monthly salary than Job A after 364 months.

B • Job A: $1000 for the first month with a $200 raise every month thereafter

• Job B: $1000 for the first month with a 4% raise every month thereafter

Write the functions that represent the monthly salaries. Let *t* represent the number of elapsed months.

Job A: $S_A(t) = \boxed{1000} + \boxed{200}\, t$ 　　　　Job B: $S_B(t) = \boxed{1000}\left(\boxed{1.04}\right)^t$

Graph the functions on a calculator and use this graph to estimate the number of months it takes for the salaries to become equal.

At $x \approx \boxed{69}$ months, the salaries are equal.

Job B will have a higher salary than Job A after $\boxed{69}$ months.

Intersection
X=68.547957 .Y=14709.591 .

Reflect

4. In Example 1A, which job offers a monthly salary that reflects a constant change, and which offers a monthly salary that reflects a constant percent change?

5. Describe an exponential increase in terms of multiplication.

Your Turn

Compare the two salary plans listed by using a graphing calculator. Will Job B ever have a higher monthly salary than Job A? If so, after how many months will this occur?

6. • Job A: $2000 for the first month with a $300 raise every month thereafter
    • Job B: $1500 for the first month with a 5% raise every month thereafter

⚙ Explain 2   Choosing between Linear and Exponential Models

Both linear equations and exponential equations and their graphs can model real-world situations. Determine whether the dependent variable appears to change by a common difference or a common ratio to select the correct model. A model may not fit real-world data exactly, so differences or factors between successive intervals may not be constant, but may be nearly so.

Example 2   **Determine whether each situation is better described by an increasing or decreasing function, and whether a linear or exponential regression should be used. Then find a regression equation for each situation by using a graphing calculator. Evaluate the fit.**

Ⓐ   The size of an elk population is studied each year during a period in which there is an increase in its predator population.

	Population over Time	Change per Interval	
Year	Population, P	Difference $P(t_n) - P(t_{n-1})$	Factor $\dfrac{P(t_n)}{P(t_{n-1})}$
0	9739	_____	_____
1	4637	−5102	≈0.48
2	2007	−2630	≈0.43
3	997	−1010	≈0.50
4	458	−539	≈0.46
5	226	−232	≈0.49

The dependent variable is population, and it is decreasing while the number of years is increasing. This means that the function is decreasing.

Note that because the factor changes are relatively close to equal while the difference changes are not, an exponential regression model should be used.

Perform the exponential regression analysis and evaluate the fit.

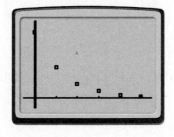

The r-value suggests a good fit.

To draw a residual plot, you can calculate the residuals, enter them in column L3, and make a scatter plot using L1 as the XList and L3 as the YList.

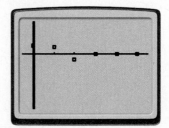

The analysis of residuals suggests a good fit.

The size of a raccoon population is studied each year during a period in which there is a decrease in its predator population.

| | Population over Time | | Change per Interval |
Year	Population, P	Difference $P(t_n) - P(t_{n-1})$	Factor $\dfrac{P(t_n)}{P(t_{n-1})}$
0	190	_____	_____
2	256	66	≈ 1.35
4	338	82	≈ 1.32
6	451	113	≈ 1.33
8	611	160	≈ 1.35
10	801	190	≈ 1.31

Is the function increasing or decreasing? Explain.
Population, which is the dependent variable, is increasing as time increases.
This means that the function is increasing.

Which changes are closer to being equal, the differences or the factors?
the factors

Which type of regression should be used?
exponential regression

Perform the regression analysis and evaluate the fit.

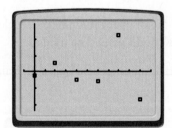

Note that the r-value suggests a good fit. The analysis of residuals suggests a good fit.

Reflect

7. What would the residual plot look like if an exponential regression was not a good fit for a function?

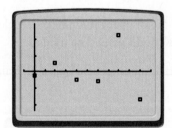

Determine whether this situation is better described by an increasing or decreasing function, and whether a linear or exponential regression should be used. Then find a regression equation. Evaluate the fit.

8. The price of a barrel of oil is recorded each year.

Price over Time		Change per Interval	
Year	Price, P (dollars)	Difference $P(t_n) - P(t_{n-1})$	Factor $\dfrac{P(t_n)}{P(t_{n-1})}$
0	42.00	_____	_____
1	50.40	8.40	$=1.20$
2	60.41	10.01	≈ 1.20
3	72.58	12.17	≈ 1.20
4	87.16	14.58	≈ 1.20
5	105.25	18.09	≈ 1.21

💬 Elaborate

9. In the long term, which type of raise will guarantee a larger paycheck: a fixed raise or a percentage raise?

10. What type of function is typically represented by a linear function?

11. **Essential Question Check-In** An exponential growth model is appropriate when consecutive function values appear to be changing by a constant __?__.

☆ Evaluate: Homework and Practice

- Online Homework
- Hints and Help
- Extra Practice

State whether each situation is best represented by an exponential or linear function. Then write an exponential or linear function for the model and state whether the model is increasing or decreasing.

1. Enrollment at a school is initially 454 students and grows by 3% per year.

2. A salesperson initially earns $50,434 dollars per year and receives a yearly raise of $675.

3. A customer borrows $450 at 5% interest compounded annually.

4. A wildlife park has 35 zebras and sends 1 zebra to another wildlife park each year.

5. The value of a house is $546,768 and decreases by 3% each year.

6. The population of a town is 66,666 people and decreases by 160 people each year.

7. A business has a total income of $236,000 and revenues go up by 6.4% per year.

Use a graphing calculator to answer each question.

8. **Statistics** Companies A and B each have 100 employees. If Company A increases its workforce by 31 employees each month and Company B increases its workforce by an average of 10% each month, when will Company B have more employees than Company A?

9. Finance Employees A and B each initially earn $18.00 per hour. If Employee A receives a $1.50 per hour raise each year and Employee B receives a 4% raise each year, when will Employee B make more per hour than Employee A?

10. Finance Account A and B each start out with $400. If Account A earns $45 each year and Account B earns 5% of its value each year, when will Account B have more money than Account A?

11. Finance Stock A starts out with $900 and gains $50 each month. Stock B starts out with $900 and gains 2% each month. When will Stock B be worth more money than Stock A?

12. Finance Accounts A and B both start out with $800. If Account A earns $110 per year and Account B earns 3% of its value each year, when will Account B have more money than Account A?

13. Finance Two factory workers, A and B, each earn $24.00 per hour. If Employee A receives a $0.75 per hour raise each year and Employee B receives 1.9% raise each year, when will Employee B make more per hour than Employee A?

14. Statistics Two car manufacturers, A and B, each have 500 employees. If Manufacturer A increases its workforce by 15 employees each month and Manufacturer B increases its workforce by 1% each month, when will Manufacturer B have more employees?

15. Finance Stock A is initially worth $1300 and loses $80 each month. Stock B is initially worth $400 and gains 9.5% each month. When will Stock B be worth more than Stock A?

Biology Each table shows an animal population's change over time. Copy and complete the table to determine whether each situation is best described by an increasing or decreasing function and whether a linear or exponential regression should be used. Then find a regression equation for each situation. Evaluate the fit.

16.

x	y	difference $y_n - y_{n-1}$	factor y_n / y_{n-1}
1	49	_____	_____
2	58	?	?
3	70	?	?
4	83	?	?
5	101	?	?

17.

x	y	difference $y_n - y_{n-1}$	factor y_n/y_{n-1}
1	31	_____	_____
2	32	?	?
3	34	?	?
4	35	?	?
5	37	?	?

18.

x	y	difference $y_n - y_{n-1}$	factor y_n/y_{n-1}
1	46	_____	_____
2	61	?	?
3	83	?	?
4	107	?	?
5	143	?	?

19.

x	y	difference $y_n - y_{n-1}$	factor y_n/y_{n-1}
1	22	_____	_____
2	35	?	?
3	60	?	?
4	104	?	?
5	189	?	?

20. Using the given exponential functions, state a and b.

a. $y = 3(4)^x$ 　　　　　**b.** $y = -5(8)^x$ 　　　　　**c.** $y = 4(0.6)^x$

d. $y = -5(0.9)^x$ 　　　　　**e.** $y = 2^x$

21. Suppose that you are offered a job that pays you $2000 the first month with a raise every month after that. You can choose a $400 raise or a 15% raise. Which option would you choose? What if the raise were 10%, 8%, or 5%?

Monthly Salary after Indicated Monthly Raise					
Month	$400	15%	10%	8%	5%
0	$2000	$2000	$2000	$2000	$2000
1	$2400	$2300	$2200	$2160	$2100
2	?	?	?	?	?
3	?	?	?	?	?

Change in Salary per Month for Indicated Monthly Raise										
Interval	$400		15%		10%		8%		5%	
	$	%	$	%	$	%	$	%	$	%
0–1	400	20	300	15	200	10	160	8	100	5
1–2	400	?	?	15	?	10	?	8	?	5
2–3	400	?	?	15	?	10	?	8	?	5

Number of Months until Salary with Percent Raise Exceeds Salary with $400 Raise			
15%	10%	8%	5%
5	?	?	?

22. Draw Conclusions Liam would like to put $6000 in savings for a 5-year period. Should he choose a simple interest account that pays an interest rate of 5% of the principal (initial amount) each year or a compounded interest account that pays an interest rate of 0.4% of the total account value each month?

23. Critical Thinking Why will an exponential growth function always eventually exceed a linear growth function?

24. Explain the Error JoAnn analyzed the following data showing the number of cells in a bacteria culture over time.

Time (min)	0	6.9	10.8	13.5	15.7	17.4
Cells	8	16	24	32	40	48

She concluded that since the number of cells showed a constant change and the time did not, neither a linear function nor an exponential function modeled the number of cells over time well. Was she correct?

Lesson Performance Task

Two major cities each have a population of 25,000 people. The population of City A increases by about 150 people per year. The population of City B increases by about 0.5% per year.

a. Find the population increase for each city for the first 5 years. Round to the nearest whole number, if necessary. Then compare the changes in the populations of each city per year.

b. Will City B ever have a larger population than City A? If so, what year will this occur?

Exponential Equations and Models

Essential Question: How can you use exponential equations to represent real-world situations?

Key Vocabulary

exponential decay
  (decremento exponencial)
exponential growth
  (crecimiento exponencial)
exponential regression
  (regresión exponencial)

KEY EXAMPLE   *(Lesson 16.2)*

A comic book is sold for $3, and its value increases by 6% each year after it is sold. Write an exponential growth function to find the value of the comic book in 25 years. Then graph it and state its domain and range. What does the *y*-intercept represent?

Write the exponential growth function for this situation.

$$y = a(1 + r)^t$$
$$ = 3(1 + 0.06)^t$$
$$ = 3(1.06)^t$$

Find the value in 25 years.

$$y = 3(1.06)^t$$
$$ = 3(1.06)^{25}$$
$$ \approx 12.88$$

After 25 years, the comic book will be worth approximately $12.88.

Create a table of values to graph the function.

t	y	(t, y)
0	3	(0, 3)
5	4.01	(5, 4.01)
10	5.37	(10, 5.37)
15	7.19	(15, 7.19)
20	9.62	(20, 9.62)
25	12.88	(25, 12.88)
30	17.23	(30, 17.23)

The domain is the set of real numbers *t* such that $t \geq 0$.

The range is the set of real numbers *y* such that $y \geq 3$.

The *y*-intercept is the value of *y* when $t = 0$, which is the time when the comic book was sold.

EXERCISES

Solve each equation for *x*. *(Lesson 16.1)*

1. $3(2)^x = 96$

2. $\dfrac{5^x}{25} = 25$

3. The value of a textbook is \$120 and decreases at a rate of 12% per year. Write a function to model the situation, and then find the value of the textbook after 9 years. *(Lesson 16.2)*

Find an exponential model for the data in the given table. *(Lesson 16.3)*

4.

x	0	1	2	3	4	5	6	7	8	9	10
y	9	12.85	16.89	28.15	42.58	65.1	99.34	153	237.6	339.2	478.61

State whether each situation is best represented by an exponential or linear function. Then write an exponential or linear function for the model and state whether the model is increasing or decreasing. *(Lesson 16.4)*

5. A customer borrows \$950 at 6% interest compounded annually.

6. The population of a town is 8548 people and decreases by 90 people each year.

MODULE PERFORMANCE TASK

Half-Life

The half-life of iodine-131 is 8 days, and the half-life of cesium-137 is 30 years. Both of these isotopes can be released into the environment during a nuclear accident.

Suppose that a nuclear reactor accident released 100 grams of cesium-137 and an unknown amount of iodine-131. After 40 days the amount of iodine-131 is equal to the amount of cesium-137. About how much iodine-131 was released by the accident?

Start by listing how you plan to tackle the problem. Then complete the task. Be sure to write down all your data and assumptions. Then use numbers, graphs, tables, or algebra to explain how you reached your conclusion.

(Ready) to Go On?

16.1–16.4 Exponential Equations and Models

• Online Homework
• Hints and Help
• Extra Practice

1. Mike has a savings account with the bank. The bank pays him annual interest of 1.5%. He has $4000 and wonders how much he will have in the account in 5 years. Write an exponential function to model the situation and then find how much he will have. *(Lesson 16.1)*

State each function's domain, range, and end behavior. *(Lesson 16.2)*

2. $f(x) = 900(0.65)^x$

3. $f(x) = 400(1.23)^x$

4. The table shows the temperature of a pizza over four-minute intervals after it is removed from the oven.

Time, (x)	0	4	8	12	16
Temperature, (y)	450	340	240	190	145

Create a model describing the data and use it to predict the temperature after 20 minutes. *(Lesson 16.3)*

5. Account A and B each start out with $600. If Account A earns $50 each year and Account B earns 6% of its value each year, after how many years will Account B have more money than Account A? *(Lesson 16.4)*

ESSENTIAL QUESTION

6. How can you identify an exponential equation?

Assessment Readiness

1. Consider the end behavior of $f(x) = 75(1.25)^x$. Determine if each statement is True or False.

   A. As $x \to -\infty$, $y \to -\infty$.

   B. As $x \to -\infty$, $y \to 0$.

   C. As $x \to \infty$, $y \to \infty$.

2. Tell whether each expression is equivalent to $\sqrt{16^{-\frac{1}{2}}}$.

   A. $\sqrt[4]{\dfrac{1}{16}}$

   B. $16^{\frac{1}{4}}$

   C. $\sqrt{\dfrac{1}{4}}$

3. Solve $36(3)^x = 4$. What is the value of x? Explain how you got your answer.

4. Consider the following situation: enrollment at a school is initially 322 students and grows by 4% per year. Write an equation to represent this situation, and use it to predict the number of students at the school in 5 years.

• Online Homework
• Hints and Help
• Extra Practice

1. Is the given expression equivalent to $\dfrac{x^{\frac{1}{2}}}{16^{-\frac{1}{2}}}$?

   A. $(4x)^{\frac{1}{2}}$

   B. $4x^{\frac{1}{2}}$

   C. $\dfrac{16^{\frac{1}{2}}}{x^{-\frac{1}{2}}}$

2. Consider the graph of $y = \sqrt{4^3 x^2} - 24$. Determine if each statement is True or False.

   A. The x-intercept is -3.

   B. The y-intercept is 4.

   C. The x-intercept is 3.

3. Consider the sequence 8, 4, 0, -4,…. Determine if each statement is True or False.

   A. It is a geometric sequence.

   B. The fifth term is -8.

   C. $f(10) = -28$.

4. Write an explicit and recursive rule for the geometric sequence $-5, 10, -20,$ 40,… and use it to find the 12th term of the sequence. Is each statement correct?

   A. The recursive rule is $f(1) = -2; f(n) = 5 \cdot f(n-1)$.

   B. The explicit rule is $f(n) = -5(-2)^{n-1}$.

   C. The 12th term is $-20{,}480$.

5. Consider the end behavior of $f(x) = -6\left(\dfrac{1}{2}\right)^x$. Determine if each statement is True or False.

   A. As $x \to -\infty$, $y \to -\infty$

   B. As $x \to \infty$, $y \to 0$

   C. As $x \to \infty$, $y \to -\infty$

6. Solve each equation. Tell whether the given is solution correct.

A. $5(2x - 7) = -6x - 27; x = \dfrac{1}{2}$

B. $6 - \dfrac{2}{3}x = -2x - 2; x = -3$

C. $9p = 3(4 - p) + 12; p = 12$

7. Is the set $\{-1, 0, 1\}$ closed under addition? Is it closed under multiplication? Justify your answers.

8. Graph $f(x) = 4\left(\dfrac{1}{2}\right)^x$. What are the domain and range of the function?

9. Solve $3(16)^{\frac{x}{4}} = 192$ for x. Show your work.

Performance Tasks

★**10.** Scientists have found that the life span of a mammal living in captivity is related to the mammal's mass. The life span in years can be approximated by the formula $L = 12m^{\frac{1}{5}}$, where m is the mammal's mass in kilograms. Which animal's life span is about twice the life span of a wolf?

Typical Mass of Mammals	
Mammal	**Mass (kg)**
Koala	8
Wolf	32
Lion	243
Giraffe	1024

★★**11.** Billy earns money by mowing lawns for the summer. He offers two payment plans.

> **Plan 1:** Pay $250 for the entire summer.
> **Plan 2:** Pay $1 the first week, $2 the second week, $4 the third week, and so on.

A. Do the payments for Plan 2 form a geometric sequence? Explain.

B. If you were one of Billy's customers, which plan would you choose? (Assume that the summer is 10 weeks long.) Explain your choice.

★★★**12.** As a promotion, a clothing store draws the name of one of its customers each week. The prize is a coupon for the store. If the winner is not present at the drawing, he or she cannot claim the prize, and the amount of the coupon increases for the following week's drawing. The function $f(x) = 20(1.2)^x$ gives the amount of the coupon in dollars after x weeks of the prize going unclaimed.

A. What is the amount of the coupon after 2 weeks of the prize going unclaimed?

B. After how many weeks of the prize going unclaimed will the amount of the coupon be greater than $100?

C. What is the original amount of the coupon?

D. Find the percent increase each week.

E. Do you think it would be wise for the owner of the store to set a limit on the number of weeks a prize can go unclaimed? Why or why not?

Financial Research Analyst The graph shows the value of two different shares of stock over the period of four years since they were purchased. The values have been changing exponentially.

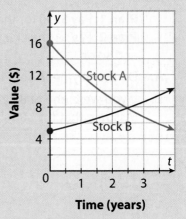

a. For Stock A, which model fits the graph, exponential growth or exponential decay? Find the initial value and the growth or decay factor.

b. For Stock B, which model fits the graph, exponential growth or exponential decay? Find the initial value and the growth or decay factor.

c. According to the graph, after how many years was the value of Stock A about equal to the value of Stock B? What was that value?

d. After how many years was the value of Stock A about twice the value of Stock B? Explain how you found your answer.

UNIT 7

Polynomial Operations

MATH IN CAREERS

Camp Director A camp director is in charge of organizing activities, hiring and supervising staff, and overseeing maintenance of the camp facilities. Camp directors use math for bookkeeping, creating budgets, negotiating vendor contracts, and planning new construction of camp buildings and outdoor spaces.

If you are interested in a career as a camp director, you should study these mathematical subjects:
- Algebra
- Geometry
- Business math

Research other careers that require keeping financial books. Check out the career activity at the end of the unit to find out how **camp directors** use math.

Visualize Vocabulary

Use the ✔ words to complete the chart. Insert one review word for each section.

Vocabulary

Review Words
✔ Associative Property
  (*Propiedad asociativa*)
✔ closure
  (*cerradura*)
✔ Commutative Property
  (*Propiedad conmutativa*)
✔ Distributive Property
  (*Propiedad distributiva*)
✔ like terms
  (*términos semejantes*)
✔ simplify
  (*simplificar*)

Preview Words
binomial (*binomio*)
FOIL (*FOIL*)
monomial (*monomio*)
perfect-square trinomial
  (*trinomio cuadrado perfecto*)
polynomial (*polinomio*)
trinomial (*trinomio*)

The property that states that the sum or product of any two real numbers will equal another real number	The property that states that for all real numbers, the sum is always the same, regardless of their grouping
Properties	
The property that states that for all real numbers, the sum is always the same, regardless of their ordering	The property that states that if you multiply a sum by a number, you will get the same result if you multiply each addend by that number and then add the products

Understand Vocabulary

To become familiar with some of the vocabulary terms in this unit, consider the following. You may refer to the module, the glossary, or a dictionary.

1. The prefix *tri-* is used to identify an item that has three parts, such as a *triangle*. What do you think a **trinomial** might be? __?__

2. The prefix *poly-* is used to identify an item with many elements, such as a *polygon*. What do you think a **polynomial** might be? __?__

Active Reading

Four-Corner Fold Before beginning the unit, create a four-corner fold to help you organize what you learn. Label the flaps "Adding Polynomials," "Subtracting Polynomials," "Multiplying Polynomials," and "Special Products of Binomials." As you study this unit note important ideas and concepts used when performing operations with polynomials under the appropriate flap. You can use your FoldNote later to study for tests and complete assignments.

Adding and Subtracting Polynomials

Essential Question: How can you use adding and subtracting polynomials to solve real-world problems?

REAL WORLD VIDEO
Vehicles, such as planes and cars, are aerodynamically tested in a wind tunnel. The complex factors involved in wind tunnel testing can be modeled with polynomial functions.

MODULE PERFORMANCE TASK PREVIEW
Ozone Levels in the Los Angeles Basin

Ozone in the upper atmosphere helps protect living things from the harmful effects of ultraviolet radiation. However, ozone near the ground is harmful and a major component of air pollution. Suppose you have some data on ozone levels in a community for an entire year. How would you find out the trend in ozone levels for that community? Let's find out!

© Houghton Mifflin Harcourt Publishing Company • Image Credits: ©Joseph McNally/Photonica World/Getty Images

Are (YOU) Ready?

Complete these exercises to review skills you will need for this module.

- Online Homework
- Hints and Help
- Extra Practice

Add and Subtract Integers

Example 1   Add or subtract.

$-9 + (-6)$ Think: Find the sum of 9 and 6.

-15 Same sign, so use the sign of the integers.

$14 + (-17)$ Think: Find the difference of 14 and

-3 17. $17 > 14$, so use the sign of 17.

$3 - (-11)$ Think: Add the opposite of –11.

$3 + 11$ Same sign, so use the sign of the integers.

14

Add or subtract.

1. $-16 + 21$ **2.** $-13 - 12$ **3.** $-23 - (-8)$

Algebraic Expressions

Example 2   Simplify $15 + 9x - 6 - 5x$ by combining like terms.

$15 + 9x - 6 - 5x$

$9x - 5x + 15 - 6$ Reorder, grouping like terms together.

$9x - 5x + 9$ Subtract the integers.

$4x + 9$ Combine the like terms.

Simplify by combining like terms.

4. $8a + 5 - 10a - 11$ **5.** $-7 + d - 6 + 2d$

6. $19z + 14y - y - 3z$ **7.** $21 - 13p + 12q - 5 + 2p - 15q$

Exponents

Example 3   Find the value of $x^3 + x^2$ when $x = 2$.

$x^3 + x^2$

$2^3 + 2^2$ Substitute 2 for x.

$8 + 4$ Evaluate the exponents.

12 Add.

Find the value.

8. $x^3 + x^2$ when $x = -2$ **9.** $x^3 - 4$ when $x = 3$ **10.** $x^3 - 4$ when $x = -3$

17.1 Understanding Polynomial Expressions

Resource Locker

Essential Question: What are polynomial expressions, and how do you simplify them?

⊘ Explore Identifying Monomials

A **monomial** is an expression consisting of a number, variable, or product of numbers and variables that have whole number exponents. *Terms* of an expression are parts of the expression separated by plus signs. (Remember that $x - y$ can be written as $x + (-y)$.) A monomial cannot have more than one term, and it cannot have a variable in its denominator. Here are some examples of monomials and expressions that are not monomials.

Monomials					Not Monomials				
4	x	$-4xy$	$0.25x^3$	$\dfrac{xy}{4}$	$4 + x$	$x - 1$	$0.7x^{-2}$	$0.25x^{-1}$	$\dfrac{y}{x^3}$

Use the following process to determine if $5ab^2$ is a monomial.

Ⓐ $5ab^2$ has ⬚? term(s), so it ⬚? be a monomial.

Ⓑ Does $5ab^2$ have a denominator?

Ⓒ If possible, split it into a product of numbers and variables.

$5ab^2 = 5 \cdot$ ⬚? $\cdot$ ⬚?

Ⓓ List the numbers and variables in the product.

Numbers: ⬚? Variables: ⬚?

Ⓔ Check the exponent of each variable. Complete the following table.

Variable	Exponent
a	?
b	?

Ⓕ The exponents of the variables in $5ab^2$ are all ⬚? .

Therefore, $5ab^2$ ⬚? a monomial.

Ⓖ Is $\dfrac{5}{k^2}$ a monomial?

(H) Complete the table below.

Term	Is this a monomial?	Explain your reasoning.
$5ab^2$	yes	$5ab^2$ is the product of a number, 5, and the variables a and b.
x^2	?	?
$\sqrt{y}$	no	?
2^2	?	?
$\dfrac{5}{k^2}$	no	?
$5x + 7$	?	?
$x^2 + 4ab$	?	?
$\dfrac{k^2}{4}$	?	?

Reflect

1. **Discussion** Explain why $16^{\frac{1}{3}}$ is a monomial but $x^{\frac{1}{3}}$ is not a monomial.

2. **Discussion** Is x^0 a monomial? Justify your answer in two ways.

⚙ Explain 1   Classifying Polynomials

A **polynomial** can be a monomial or the sum of monomials. Polynomials are classified by the number of terms they contain. A monomial has one term, a **binomial** has two terms, and a **trinomial** has three terms. $8xy^2 - 5x^3y^3z$, for example, is a binomial.

Polynomials are also classified by their degree. The **degree of a polynomial** is the greatest value among the sums of the exponents on the variables in each term.

The binomial $8xy^2 - 5x^3y^3z$ has two terms. The variables in the first term are x and y. The exponent on x is 1, and the exponent on y is 2. The number 8 is not a variable, so it has a degree of 0. The first term has a degree of $0 + 1 + 2 = 3$. The degree of the second term is $0 + 3 + 3 + 1 = 7$. Therefore, $8xy^2 - 5x^3y^3z$ is a 7th degree binomial.

Example 1 Classify each polynomial by its degree and the number of terms.

(A) $7x^2 - 5x^3y^3$

Find the degree of each term by adding the exponents of the variables in that term. The greatest degree is the degree of the polynomial. The degree of the term $-5x^3y^3$ is 6, which you obtain by adding the exponents of x and y: $6 = 3 + 3$. Numbers have degree 0.

$7x^2 - 5x^3y^3$

Degree : 6 $7x^2$ has degree 2, and $-5x^3y^3$ has degree $6 = 3 + 3$.

Binomial   There are two terms.

(B) $3^2 + 2n^3 + 8n$

$3^2 + 2n^3 + 8n$

Degree: $\boxed{3}$ 3^2 has degree $\boxed{0}$, $2n^3$ has degree $\boxed{3}$, and $8n$ has degree $\boxed{1}$.

Trinomial   There are $\boxed{3}$ terms.

Reflect

3. What is the degree of $5x^0y^0 + 5$?

4. Is $5x^0y^{0.5} + 5$ a polynomial? Justify your answer.

Your Turn

Classify each polynomial by its degree and the number of terms.

5. $3x^2y^2 + 3xy^2 + 5xy$ 6. $8ab^2 - 3a^2b$

Explain 2 Writing Polynomials in Standard Form

The terms of a polynomial may be written in any order, but when a polynomial contains only one variable there is a standard form in which it can be written.

The **standard form of a polynomial** containing only one variable is written with the terms in order of decreasing degree. The first term will have the greatest degree, the next term will have the next greatest degree, and so on, until the final term, which will have the lowest degree.

When written in this form, the coefficient of the first term is called **the leading coefficient**.

$5x^4 + 4x^2 + x - 2$ is a 4th degree polynomial written in standard form. It consists of one variable, and its first term is $5x^4$. The leading coefficient is 5 because it is in front of the highest-degree term.

Example 2 **Write each polynomial in standard form. Then give the leading coefficient.**

(A) $20x - 4x^3 + 1 - 2x^2$

Find the degree of each term and then arrange them in descending order of their degree.

$$20x \underbrace{}_{1} -4x^3 \underbrace{}_{3} + 1 \underbrace{}_{0} -2x^2 \underbrace{}_{2} \; = \; -4x^3 \underbrace{}_{3} -2x^2 \underbrace{}_{2} + 20x \underbrace{}_{1} + 1 \underbrace{}_{0}$$

Degree:

The standard form is $-4x^3 - 2x^2 + 20x + 1$. The leading coefficient is -4.

(B) $z^3 - z^6 + 4z$

Find the degree of each term and then arrange them in descending order of their degree.

$$z^3 \underbrace{}_{\boxed{3}} -z^6 \underbrace{}_{\boxed{6}} +4z \underbrace{}_{\boxed{1}} = \boxed{-z^6} \underbrace{}_{\boxed{6}} \boxed{+z^3} \underbrace{}_{\boxed{3}} \boxed{+4z} \underbrace{}_{\boxed{1}}$$

Degree:

The standard form is $-z^6 + z^3 + 4z$. The leading coefficient is $\boxed{-1}$.

Your Turn

Write each polynomial in standard form. Then give the leading coefficient.

7. $10 - 3x^2 + x^5 + 4x^3$

8. $18y^5 - 3y^8 + 10y$

9. $10x + 13 - 15x^2$

10. $-3b^2 + 2b - 7 + 6b^3 + 12b^4 + 7$

🔑 Explain 3 Simplifying Polynomials

Polynomials are simplified by combining like terms. Like terms are monomials that have the same variables raised to the same powers. Unlike terms have different powers.

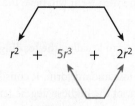

Like Terms:
- Same variable
- Same power

$$r^2 \; + \; 5r^3 \; + \; 2r^2$$

Unlike Terms:
- Different power

Identify like terms and combine them using the Distributive Property. Simplify.

$r^2 + 5r^3 + 2r^2$

$(r^2 + 2r^2) + 5r^3$ Identify like terms by grouping them together in parentheses.

$r^2(1 + 2) + 5r^3$ Combine using the Distributive Property.

$3r^2 + 5r^3$ Simplify.

Example 3   **Combine like terms to simplify each polynomial.**

Ⓐ $-2y^3 - 8y^2 + y^2 + 2y^3$

    $-2y^3 + 2y^3 - 8y^2 + y^2$ Rearrange in descending order of exponents.

    $(-2y^3 + 2y^3) + (-8y^2 + y^2)$ Group like terms.

    $y^3(-2 + 2) + y^2(-8 + 1)$ Combine using the Distributive Property.

    $y^3(0) + y^2(-7)$ Simplify.

    $-7y^2$

Ⓑ $p^2q^3 - 4p^5q^4 - 4p^2q^3 + 3p^5q^4$

    $-4p^5q^4 + 3p^5q^4 + p^2q^3 - 4p^2q^3$ Rearrange in descending order of exponents.

    $(-4p^5q^4 + 3p^5q^4) + (p^2q^3 - 4p^2q^3)$ Group like terms.

    $p^5q^4\left(\boxed{-4 + 3}\right) + p^2q^3\left(\boxed{1 - 4}\right)$ Combine using the Distributive Property.

    $p^5q^4\left(\boxed{-1}\right) + p^2q^3\left(\boxed{-3}\right)$ Simplify.

    $-p^5q^4 - 3p^2q^3$

Reflect

11. Can you combine like terms without formally showing the Distributive Property? Explain.

Your Turn

Simplify.

12. $3p^2q^2 - 3p^2q^3 + 4p^2q^3 - 3p^2q^2 + pq$ **13.** $3(a + b) - 6(b + c) + 8(a - c)$

14. $ab - a^2 + 4^2 - 5ab + 3a^2 + 10$

🎸 Explain 4 Evaluating Polynomials

Given a polynomial expression describing a real-world situation and a specific value for the variable(s), evaluate the polynomial by substituting for the variable(s). Then interpret the result.

Example 4 Evaluate the given polynomial to find the solution in each real-world scenario.

Ⓐ A skyrocket is launched from a 6-foot-high platform with an initial speed of 200 feet per second. The polynomial $-16t^2 + 200t + 6$ gives the height in feet that the skyrocket will rise in t seconds. How high will the rocket rise if it has a 5-second fuse?

$-16t^2 + 200t + 6$	Write the expression.
$-16(5)^2 + 200(5) + 6$	Substitute 5 for t.
$-16(25) + 200(5) + 6$	Simplify using the order of operations.
$-400 + 1000 + 6$	
606	

The rocket will rise 606 feet.

Ⓑ Lisa wants to measure the depth of an empty well. She drops a ball from a height of 3 feet into the well and measures how long it takes the ball to hit the bottom of the well. She uses a stopwatch, starting when she lets go of the ball and ending when she hears the ball hit the bottom of the well. The polynomial $-16t^2 + 0t + 3$ gives the height of the ball after t seconds where 0 is the initial speed of the ball and 3 is the initial height the ball was dropped from. Her stopwatch measured a time of 2.2 seconds. How deep is the well? (Neglect the speed of sound and air resistance).

$-16t^2 + 0t + 3$	Write the expression.
$-16(2.2)^2 + 3$	Substitute 2.2 for t.
$-16(4.84) + 3$	Simplify using order of operations.
-74.44	

The ball goes 74.44 feet below the ground. The well is 74.44 feet deep.

Your Turn

Solve each real-world scenario.

15. Nate's client said she wanted the width w of every room in her house increased by 2 feet and the length $2w$ decreased by 5 feet. The polynomial $(2w - 5)(w + 2)$ or $2w^2 - w - 10$ gives the new area of any room in the house. The current width of the kitchen is 16 feet. What is the area of the new kitchen?

16. A skyrocket is launched from a 20-foot-high platform, with an initial speed of 200 feet per second. If the polynomial $-16t^2 + 200t + 20$ gives the height that the rocket will rise in t seconds, how high will a rocket with a 4-second fuse rise?

💬 Elaborate

17. What is the degree of the expression $-16t^2 + 200t + 20$, where t is a variable? What is the degree of the expression if $t = 1$? Are the expressions monomials, binomials, or trinomials?

18. Two cars drive toward each other along a straight road at a constant speed. The distance between the cars is $\ell - (r_1 + r_2)t$, where r_1 and r_2 are their speeds, t is a variable representing time and ℓ is the length of their original separation. Write the expression in standard form. What is its degree? What is its leading coefficient?

19. The polynomial $-16t^2 + 200t + 20$ gives the height of a projectile launched with an initial speed of 200 feet per second t seconds after launch. A second projectile is launched at the same time but with an initial speed of 300 feet per second, with its height given by the polynomial $-16t^2 + 300t + 20$. How much higher will the second projectile be than the first after 10 seconds?

20. Essential Question Check-In What do you have to do to simplify sums of polynomials? What property do you use to accomplish this?

☆ Evaluate: Homework and Practice

- Online Homework
- Hints and Help
- Extra Practice

1. Is $(5 + 4x^0)2x$ a monomial? What about $(5 + 4x^2)2x$?

2. Is the sum of two monomials always a monomial? Is their product always a monomial?

Classify each polynomial by its degree and the number of terms.

3. $x^2 - 5x^3$

4. $x^2 - x^4 + y^2x^3$

5. $a^4b^3 - a^3b^2 + a^2b$

6. $15 + x\sqrt{2}$

7. $x + y + z$

8. $a^5 + b^2 + a^2b^2$

Write each polynomial in standard form. Then give the leading coefficient.

9. $2x - 40x^3 - 2x^2$

10. $3 + c - c^2$

11. $3b^2 - 2b + b^2$

12. $4a - 3a + 21 + 6$

Simplify each polynomial.

13. $-2y^3 - y^2 + y^2 + y^3$

14. $-y^3x - y^2x + y^2 + y^3x + y^2$

15. $xyz\sqrt[3]{2} + 2^5xyz + 2^{10}xy$

16. $a^3 + a^2 + ab$

Use the information to solve the problem.

17. **Persevere in Problem Solving** Lisa is measuring the depth of a well. She drops a ball from a height of h feet into the well and measures how long it takes the ball to hit the bottom of the well. The polynomial $-16t^2 + 0t + h$ models this situation, where 0 is the initial speed of the ball and h is the height it was dropped from. (This is a different well from the problem you solved before.) She raises her arm very high and drops the ball from a height of 6.0 feet. Her stopwatch measured a time of 3.5 seconds. How deep is the well?

18. **Multi-Step** Claire and Richard are both artists who use square canvases. Claire uses the polynomial $50x^2 + 250$ to decide how much to charge for her paintings, and Richard uses the polynomial $40x^2 + 350$ to decide how much to charge for his paintings. In each polynomial, x is the height of the painting in feet.

   a. How much does Claire charge for a 6-foot painting?

   b. How much does Richard charge for a 5-foot painting?

   c. To the nearest tenth, for what height will both Claire and Richard charge the same amount for a painting? Explain how to find the answer.

   d. When both Claire and Richard charge the same amount for a painting, how much does each charge?

19. **Make a Prediction** The number of cells in a bacteria colony increases according to a polynomial expression that depends on the temperature. The expression for the number of bacteria is $t^2 + 4t + 4$ when the temperature of the colony is 20°C and $t^2 + 3t + 4$ when the colony grows at 30°C. t represents the time in seconds that the colony grows at the given temperature.

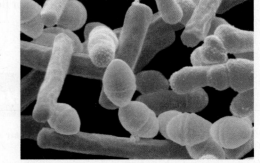

   a. After 1 minute, will the population be greater in a colony at 20°C or 30°C? Explain.

   b. After 10 minutes, how will the colonies compare in size? Explain.

   c. After 1000 minutes, how will the colonies compare in size? Will one colony always have more bacteria? Explain.

20. Two cars are driving toward each other along a straight road. Their separation distance is $\ell - (r_1 + r_2)t$, where ℓ is their original separation distance and r_1 and r_2 are their speeds. Will the cars meet? When? What if they are going in the same direction and not driving toward one another? Will they meet then?

21. Explain the Error Enrique thinks that the polynomial $2^2x^2 + 2^3x + 2^4$ has a degree of 4 since $2 + 2 = 3 + 1 = 4$. Explain his error and determine the correct degree.

22. Analyze Relationships Sewell is doing a problem regarding the area of pairs of squares. Sewell says that the expression $(x + 1)^2$ will be greater than $(x - 1)^2$ for all values of x because $x + 1$ will always be greater than $x - 1$. Why is he correct when the expressions are areas of squares? Is he correct for any real x outside this model?

23. Counterexamples Prove by counterexample that the sum of monomials is not necessarily a monomial.

24. Communicate Mathematical Ideas Polynomials are simplified by combining like terms. When combining like terms, you use the Distributive Property. Prove that the Distributive Property, $a \cdot (b + c) = a \cdot b + a \cdot c$, holds over the positive integers $a, b, c > 0$ from the definition of multiplication: $a \cdot b = \underbrace{a + a + \ldots + a.}_{b \text{ times}}$

25. Analyze Relationships A right triangle has height h and base $h + 8$. Write an expression that represents the area of the triangle. Then calculate the area of a triangle with a height of 16 cm.

Lesson Performance Task

A pyrotechnics specialist is designing a firework spectacular for a company's 75th anniversary celebration. She can vary the launch speed to 200, 250, 300, or 400 feet per second, and can set the fuse on each firework for 3, 4, 5, or 6 seconds. Create a table of the various heights the fireworks can explode at if the height of the firework is modeled by the function $h(t) = -16t^2 + v_0 t$, where t is the time in seconds and v_0 is the initial speed of the firework.

Design a fireworks show using 3 firing heights and at least 30 fireworks. Have some fireworks go off simultaneously at different heights. Describe your display so you will know what needs to be launched and when they will go off.

17.2 Adding Polynomial Expressions

Essential Question: How do you add polynomials?

🧭 Explore Modeling Polynomial Addition Using Algebra Tiles

You have added numbers and variables, which is the same as adding polynomials of degree 0 and degree 1. Adding polynomials of higher degree is similar, but there are more possible like terms to consider.

You can use algebra tiles to model polynomial addition.

Key				
$\boxed{+} = 1$				
$\boxed{-} = -1$	$\boxed{+} = x$ $\boxed{-} = -x$	$\boxed{+} = x^2$	$\boxed{-} = -x^2$	

As the Key shows, a different-sized tile represents each monomial. Like terms have the same shape and size, but if they are positive, they have a $+$ (plus) sign. If they are negative, they have a $-$ (minus) sign. Use these visual aids to add polynomials.

To add polynomials, start by representing each addend with tiles. Add them by placing the tiles for each polynomial next to each other. Cancel out opposite tiles that are of the same size but have a different symbol. Count the remaining tiles of each size and note the symbol. Translate the tiles to a polynomial. This polynomial represents the simplified sum.

Use algebra tiles to find $\left(2x^2 - x\right) + \left(x^2 + 3x - 1\right)$.

(A) Which of the two polynomials in the addition expression do these algebra tiles represent?

Model	Algebra
$\boxed{+}$ $\boxed{+}$ $\boxed{-}$	?

(B) Which polynomial do these algebra tiles represent?

Model	Algebra
$\boxed{+}$ $\boxed{+}$ $\boxed{+}$ $\boxed{-}$	?

Ⓒ Place the algebra tiles representing each expression next to each other. This represents addition/subtraction.

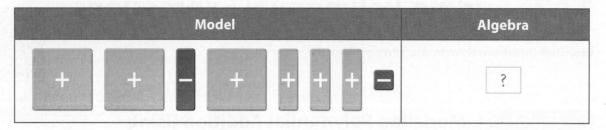

Ⓓ Rearrange tiles so that like tiles are together. *Like tiles* are the same size and shape.

Model	Algebra
(tiles)	?

Ⓔ *Zero pairs* are like tiles with opposite signs. Together they equal zero.

Simplify the sum by ? zero pairs.

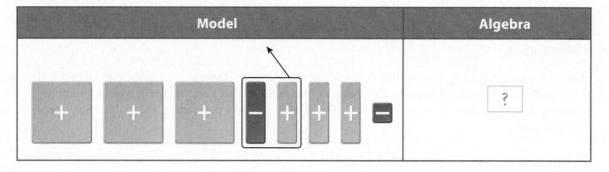

Model	Algebra
(tiles)	?

Reflect

1.   **Discussion** What properties of addition allow you to rearrange the tiles?

⚙ **Explain 1** **Adding Polynomials Using a Vertical Format**

To add polynomials vertically, add like terms in columns. Write the first polynomial in standard form; then write the second polynomial below the first, aligning like terms. Use a monomial with a zero coefficient as a placeholder for missing terms. Add the coefficients of each group and write the sum aligned with the like terms above. Simplify if necessary.

Example 1   Use the vertical format to find the sum.

(A) $5x^2 + 2x - 1$ and $4x^2 - x + 2$

$\left(5x^2 + 2x - 1\right) + \left(4x^2 - x + 2\right)$

Rewrite the problem, vertically aligning the terms.

$$\begin{array}{r} 5x^2 + 2x - 1 \\ +4x^2 - 1x + 2 \\ \hline 9x^2 + 1x + 1 \end{array}$$

Simplify.

$9x^2 + x + 1$

(B) $3y^3 + 2y + 1$ and $y^2 - 1$

$\left(3y^3 + 2y + 1\right) + \left(y^2 - 1\right)$

Rewrite the problem, vertically aligning the terms.

$$\begin{array}{r} 3y^3 + \boxed{0}\ y^2 + \quad 2y + \boxed{1} \\ +0y^3 + \quad 1y^2 + \boxed{0}\ y + \boxed{-1} \\ \hline 3y^3 + \boxed{1y^2} + \quad 2y + \boxed{0} \end{array}$$

Simplify.

$3y^3 + y^2 + 2y$

Reflect

2.   Is the sum of two polynomials always another polynomial? Explain.

Your Turn

Add the given polynomials using the vertical format.

3. $-x^2 - 1$ and $4x^2 - x$

4. $-z^3 - 2z - 1$ and $2z^3 - z^2 + 2z$

5. $x - 1$ and $4x - 6$

⚷ Explain 2   Adding Polynomials Using a Horizontal Format

To add polynomials horizontally, combine like terms. Use the Associative and Commutative Properties to regroup. Place all like terms within the same parentheses. Combine like terms by adding their coefficients, simplifying if necessary.

Example 2 Add the polynomials using the horizontal format.

(A) $5x^2 + 2x + 1$ and $-4x^2 - x - 2$

$\left(5x^2 + 2x + 1\right) + \left(-4x^2 - x - 2\right)$ Add.

$= \left(5x^2 - 4x^2\right) + \left(2x - x\right) + \left(1 - 2\right)$ Group like terms by using the Commutative and Associative Properties.

$= x^2 + x - 1$ Combine like terms.

(B) $-ab + b$ and $ab - a$

$\left(-ab + b\right) + \left(ab - a\right)$ Add.

$= \left(-ab + \boxed{ab}\right) + b + \left(\boxed{-a}\right)$ Group like terms together.

$= \boxed{b - a}$ Combine like terms.

Your Turn

Use the horizontal format to find the sum.

6. $\left(-6x^2 + 2\right)$ and $\left(-4x^2\right)$

7. $\left(-x^3 + 2\right)$ and $\left(-4x^3 + y + x\right)$

8. $\left(y - 7\right)$ and $\left(3y + 18\right)$

⚙ Explain 3   Modeling with Polynomials

You can model many situations using polynomials. Sometimes you can model a new situation by adding two or more polynomials.

For example, a company offers two services. The number of people using each service at a given time can be modeled by polynomials that use the same variable. The total number of people using both services can be modeled by adding the two polynomials.

Example 3 **A box company owns two factories in different parts of the country. The profit for each factory is modeled by a polynomial with x representing the number of boxes each produces. Solve by adding the polynomials. The models needed in each situation are provided.**

Ⓐ The first factory makes a profit of $-0.03x^2 + 20x - 500$, and the second makes $-0.04x^2 + 25x - 1000$. What is the polynomial modeling the box company's total profit if both factories make the same number of boxes?

$(-0.03x^2 + 20x - 500) + (-0.04x^2 + 25x - 1000)$ Add.

$= (-0.03x^2 - 0.04x^2) + (20x + 25x) + (-500 - 1000)$ Group like terms together.

$= -0.07x^2 + 45x - 1,500$ Simplify.

The factories make a total profit of $-0.07x^2 + 45x - 1500$.

Ⓑ The company plans to open a third factory with a projected profit of $-0.03x^2 + 50x - 100$. What will be the total profit of the box company, written as a polynomial, if the projected profit is correct?

The total profit from the first two factories mentioned is $-0.07x^2 + 45x - 1500$. The projected profit from the new factory is $-0.03x^2 + 50x - 100$. Add to solve.

$(-0.07x^2 + 45x - 1,500) + (-0.03x^2 + 50x - 100)$ Add.

$= (-0.07x^2 - 0.03x^2) + (45x + 50x) + (-1,500 - 100)$ Group like terms together.

$= -0.10x^2 + 95x - 1600$ Simplify.

The total projected profit is $-0.10x^2 + 95x - 1600$.

Reflect

9. **Discussion** How could the polynomials be added if the first factory produced x boxes, the second factory produce y boxes, and the third company z boxes? What kind of polynomial would it be?

Your Turn

Model various situations with the sum of polynomials. Simplify their sum.

10. A scientist is growing cell cultures and examining the effects of various substances on them as part of his research. The culture in one petri dish increases according to the expression $t^2 + 4t + 4$ for time t in minutes. Another increases according to $t^2 + 2t + 4$. He needs to feed all the cells equally, so he needs to know the expression for the total number of cells in both dishes because the food is proportional to the total number of cells. Find the expression.

11. A farmer must add the areas of two plots of land to determine the amount of seed to plant. The area of Plot A can be represented by $3x^2 + 7x - 5$, and the area of Plot B can be represented by $5x^2 - 4x + 11$. Write a polynomial that represents the total area of both plots of land.

💬 Elaborate

12. Is adding polynomials horizontally or vertically equivalent? Explain, describing how the steps are similar or different.

13. A car company is analyzing the profits of two car manufacturing plants. The profit of each plant is modeled by a polynomial. What operation would it use to compute the total profit of both plants? The amount of success of one plant versus the other? The total profit of both plants if the polynomials modeling each plant's profits are the same? Will the results be polynomials?

14. Essential Question Check-In What do you have to do to simplify sums of polynomials? What property do you use to accomplish this?

⭐ Evaluate: Homework and Practice

• Online Homework
• Hints and Help
• Extra Practice

1. In adding with tiles, one step corresponds to grouping like terms. Do you think this is more similar to the horizontal or vertical method? Explain your reasoning.

2. Show how to add $(x^2 + x)$ and $(-x^2 - 2x)$ with tiles.

Model	Algebra
	?
	? = ?

Find each sum vertically.

3. $(x^2 - x^4) + (x^4 - x^2)$

4. $(y^2 - x^4) + (x^4 - x^2)$

5. Add $0.5x + 2$ and $x^2 + 1.5x$.

6. $(2x + y + z) + (-x + y - z)$

7. $(x^2 + y + z) + (-x + y - z) + x - y$

8. $-a^5 + (b^2 + a^2b^2) + (a^5 + b^2 - a^2b^2)$

Find each sum horizontally.

9. $(-x^2 + x) + (x^2 - x - 1)$

10. $(a + b - c^2) + (a + b)$

11. $(ab^2 + b^2) + (-2cab^2 + b^2)$

12. $(2x - x^3 - 2x^2) + (-x^3 - 2x)$

13. $(2^{10}a + ab) + (ab\sqrt[3]{2} + ab - 2^{10}a)$

14. $(7q^3r^2 + 6qr^2 + 21q) + (-6qr^2 - qr^2 - 11q - 3q^3r^2)$

© Houghton Mifflin Harcourt Publishing Company

Module 17

646

Lesson 2

Model various situations using the sum of polynomials. Simplify their sum.

15. A pool is being filled with a large water hose. The height of the water in a pool is determined by $8g^2 + 3g - 4$. Previously, the pool had been filled with a different hose. Then, the height was determined by $6g^2 + 2g - 1$. Write an expression that determines the height of the water in the pool if both hoses are on at the same time. Simplify the expression

16. The polynomial $-2x^2 + 500x$ represents the budget surplus of the town of Alphaville. Betaville's surplus is represented by $x^2 - 100x + 10,000$. If x represents the tax revenue in thousands from both towns, which expression represents the total surplus of both towns together?

17. Geometry The length of a rectangle is represented by $4a + 3b$, and its width is represented by $3a - 2b$. Write a polynomial for the perimeter of the rectangle. What is the minimum perimeter of the rectangle if $a = 12$ and b is a non-zero whole number?

18. Multi-Step Tara plans to put wallpaper on the walls of her room. She will not put the wallpaper across the doorway, which is 3 feet wide and 7 feet tall.

  a. Write an expression that represents the number of square feet of wallpaper she will need if the height of her room is x feet, with a length and width that are each 3 times the height of the room. Assume that the walls are four rectangles.

  b. Write the expression for the amount of wallpaper in square feet Tara needs for the living room, which is the same height and width as her bedroom, but has a length that is 5 times the height of the room. The living room has 2 doors that are the same size as the door in her bedroom.

  c. Tara decides to get the same wallpaper for both rooms. Write the expression for the total amount of wallpaper she needs.

  d. If $x = 8$, how much more wallpaper will Tara need for the living room than for the bedroom?

19. Multiple Representations Two polynomials model different financial information for a company. The first polynomial, $40,000 + 3x^2$ represents the gross monthly income from selling x units, while the second one, $0.05x + 100$ represents the monthly production cost of x units.

Which of the following expressions models gross income less production costs?

  a. $40,000 + 3x^2 - 0.05x + 100$

  b. $(40,000 - 100) + 3x^2 - 0.05x$

  c. $3x^2 - 0.05x + 39,900$

  d. $3x^2 - 0.05x + 40,100$

  e. a and b

  f. b and c

20. **Critical Thinking** Subtracting one polynomial from another is the same as adding the opposite of the polynomial by distributing a -1.

Substitute $n = -1$ in $(x^2 + x) + n(x^2 + 2x)$ and simplify.

21. **Explain the Error** Jane and Jill were simplifying the expression $(2x^2 + x) + 2(-x^2 + x)$ and obtained different answers. Who is correct and why?

Jane	Jill
$= (2x^2 + x) + 2(-x^2 + x)$	$= (2x^2 + x) + 2(-x^2 + x)$
$= (2x^2 + x) + (-x^2 + x) + (-x^2 + x)$	$= (2x^2 + x) - 2x^2 + x$
$= (2x^2 - x^2 - x^2) + (x + x + x)$	$= 2x$
$= 3x$	

22. **Critical Thinking** A set is **closed** under an operation if performing that operation on two members of the set results in another member of the set. Is the set of polynomials closed under addition? Is the set of polynomials closed under multiplication by a constant? Explain.

23. **Counterexamples** You can prove that a statement isn't true by finding a single example that contradicts the statement, which is called a *counterexample*. Show that the set of polynomials is not closed under division by finding a counterexample of division of a polynomial by a polynomial that does not result in a polynomial.

24. **Communicate Mathematical Ideas** Simplify $(x^2 + x) + n(x^2 + 2x)$ by distributing the n. Show that it is equivalent for $n = 2$ to $(x^2 + x) + (x^2 + 2x) + (x^2 + 2x)$.

25. **Multiple Representations** Write two polynomials whose sum is $4m^2 + 2m$. Write two polynomials whose difference is $4m^2 + 2m$.

Lesson Performance Task

Swimming pools offer a wide range of activities for both health and leisure. They typically service everyone in the community, from the very young to the elderly. In community pools, the water temperature is often a much debated topic. If the water is too cold, children and older individuals may not be able to use the pool for the length of time they wish. On the other hand, if the pool is too warm, people swimming laps can get overheated.

An architect is working with a health club to design a multi-use aquatics facility that will have two pools. One pool will be primarily used by lap swimmers and local school swim teams. A second pool will be more of a mixed usage pool and have regions of various depths to service the remainder of the community.

Design two swimming pools for the aquatics center and calculate the volume of each pool. The lap pool should be 25 yards long, between 4 and 6 feet deep, and should consist of x lanes, with the width of each lane between 6 and 8 feet. The multi-use pool should have 3 sections. The first section should be a shallow end, where the depth begins between 2.5 and 3.5 feet, and slopes down to a depth equal to one-sixth the width of the pool over about one-third of the pool's length. The last section should slope down to the maximum depth of the pool which should be between 9 and 12 feet. Both pools should have approximately the same width and the multi-use pool should be between 2 and 3 times as long as it is wide.

Produce polynomials representing the volume of each pool and the total volume of water needed by the facility.

© Houghton Mifflin Harcourt Publishing Company

17.3 Subtracting Polynomial Expressions

Essential Question: How do you subtract polynomials?

🧭 Explore Modeling Polynomial Subtraction Using Algebra Tiles

You can also use algebra tiles to model polynomial subtraction.

Key
$+$ = 1
$-$ = -1
$+$ = x $-$ = $-x$ $+$ = x^2 $-$ = $-x^2$

To subtract polynomials, recall that subtraction is equivalent to addition of the opposite.

$5 - 6 = 5 + (-6)$

Polynomial subtraction is the same. To subtract polynomial B from polynomial A, create a new polynomial C that consists of the opposite of each monomial in polynomial B. Add polynomial A and polynomial C.

When using tiles, switch every tile in the polynomial being subtracted for its opposite, the tile of the same size but the opposite sign. Once this is done, place the tiles representing the first polynomial and the new set of tiles next to each other and add like you have done previously. (The opposite of a polynomial is the negative of it. When you add a polynomial to its opposite you get 0.)

(A) Use algebra tiles to find $(2x^2 + 4) - (4x^2)$. Write the polynomial expression for each set of algebra tiles.

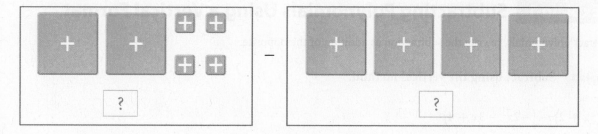

(B) Write the opposite of $4x^2$.

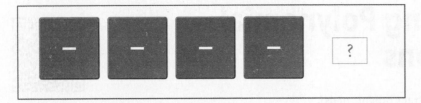

(C) Write the subtraction as addition of the opposite.

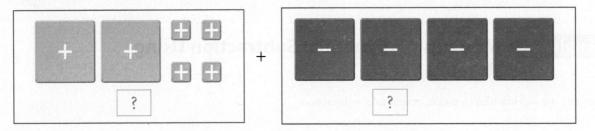

(D) Group like terms and remove zero pairs. Write the resulting expression.

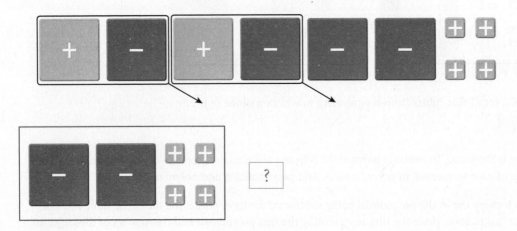

Reflect

1. **Discussion** Explain how removing zero pairs is an application of the additive inverse and the Identity Property of Addition.

🔑 Explain 1 Subtracting Polynomials Using a Vertical Format

To subtract polynomials, rewrite the subtraction as addition of the opposite.

Example 1 Subtract using the vertical method.

(A) $(5x + 2) - (-2x^2 - 3x + 4)$

$(5x + 2) + (2x^2 + 3x - 4)$ Rewrite subtraction as addition of the opposite.

$$\begin{array}{r} 0x^2 + 5x + 2 \\ + \ 2x^2 + 3x - 4 \\ \hline 2x^2 + 8x - 2 \end{array}$$

Use the vertical method. Write $0x^2$ as a placeholder.

Combine like terms.

(B) $\left(y^2 + y - 1\right) - \left(-2y^2 + y + 1\right)$

$\left(y^2 + y - 1\right) + \left(\boxed{+}\, 2y^2 \,\boxed{-}\, y \,\boxed{-}\, 1\right)$ Rewrite subtraction as addition of the opposite.

$$\begin{array}{r} y^2 + y - 1 \\ +\,2y^2 - y - 1 \\ \hline 3y^2 + 0 - 2 \\ 3y^2 - 2 \end{array}$$

Use the vertical method.

Combine like terms and simplify.

Simplify.

Reflect

2. Is the difference of two polynomials always another polynomial? Explain.

Your Turn

Find the difference using a vertical format.

3. $\left(4x^2 - x\right) - \left(-x^2 - 1\right)$ **4.** $\left(-z^3 - 2z - 1\right) - \left(-z^3 + 2z + 1\right)$ **5.** $\left(8y - 7\right) - \left(1 - 3y\right)$

🔑 Explain 2   Subtracting Polynomials Using a Horizontal Format

Once the subtraction problem has been rewritten as a sum, the polynomials can be added using the horizontal method. Recall that this method uses the Associative, Commutative, and Distributive properties to group and combine like terms.

Example 2   **Find the difference of the polynomials horizontally.**

(A) $\left(2q^2 - q - 8\right) - \left(2q^2 + q - 4\right)$

$= \left(2q^2 - q - 8\right) + \left(-2q^2 - q + 4\right)$ Rewrite subtraction as addition of the opposite.

$= \left(2q^2 - 2q^2\right) + \left(-q - q\right) + \left(-8 + 4\right)$ Group like terms together.

$= -2q - 4$ Simplify.

(B) $\left(2ab - b + a\right) - \left(2b^2 + b + a + 4\right)$

$= \left(2ab - b + a\right) + \left(-2b^2 - b - a - 4\right)$ Rewrite subtraction as addition of the opposite.

$= -2b^2 + 2ab + \left(-b - b\right) + \left(a - a\right) + \left(-4\right)$ Group like terms together.

$= -2b^2 + 2ab - 2b - 4$ Simplify.

Find each difference.

6. $\left(-x^3 + y^2 + y - x\right) - \left(-x^3 + y + x\right)$ **7.** $\left(18z + 12\right) - \left(11z - 5\right)$

✏️ Explain 3   Modeling with Polynomials

Some scenarios can be modeled by the difference of two polynomials.

> **Example 3**   **Find the difference between two polynomials to solve a real-world problem.**

(A)   The cost in dollars of producing x toothbrushes is given by the polynomial $400,000 + 3x$, and the revenue generated from sales is given by the polynomial $20x - 0.00004x^2$. Write a polynomial expression for the profit from making and selling x toothbrushes. Then find the profit for selling 200,000 toothbrushes.

Use the formula: Profit $=$ revenue $-$ cost

$\left(20x - 0.00004x^2\right) - \left(400,000 + 3x\right)$

$= \left(20x - 0.00004x^2\right) + \left(-400,000 - 3x\right)$ Add the opposite.

$= -0.00004x^2 + 17x - 400,000$ Combine like terms.

To find the profit for selling 200,000 toothbrushes, evaluate the polynomial when $x = 200,000$.

$-0.00004x^2 + 17x - 400,000$

$= -0.00004(200,000)^2 + 17(200,000) - 400,000 = 1,400,000$

The company will make $1.4 million from the sale of 200,000 toothbrushes.

(B)   The revenue made by a car company from the sale of y cars is given by $0.005y^2 + 10y$. The cost to produce y cars is given by the polynomial $20y + 1,000,000$. Write a polynomial expression for the profit from making and selling y cars. Find the profit the company will make if it sells 30,000 cars.

$\left(0.005y^2 + 10y\right) - \left(20y + 1,000,000\right)$ Profit $=$ revenue $-$ cost

$= \left(0.005y^2 + 10y\right) + \left(-20y - 1,000,000\right)$ Add the opposite.

$= 0.005y^2 \;\boxed{-}\; 10y - 1,000,000$ Combine like terms.

To find the profit for selling 30,000 cars, evaluate the polynomial when $x = 30,000$.

$0.005y^2 - \boxed{10y} - 1,000,000$

$= 0.005(30,000)^2 - \boxed{10(30,000)} - 1,000,000 = \boxed{3,200,000}$

The company will make $3.2 million from the sale of 30,000 cars.

8. What is the addition problem corresponding to profit = revenue − cost? How do you find revenue if you know profit and cost?

Your Turn

Find the difference between two polynomials to solve a real-world problem.

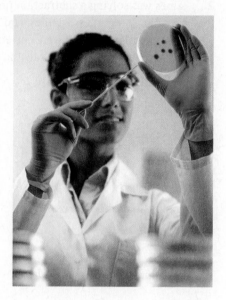

9. Jen, a biologist, is growing bacterial cultures at different temperatures as part of her research. The number of cells in the culture growing at 25 °C is given by the polynomial $t^2 + 4t + 4$, where t is the time elapsed in minutes. The number of cells in the second culture growing at 35 °C is modeled by the polynomial $t^2 + 4$. She needs to measure the success of the 25 °C culture over the 35 °C culture. Find the polynomial representing how many more cells are in the 25 °C culture for time t. How many more cells are there after 15 minutes?

10. The number of gallons of water in a leaking pool is determined by the rate that the water is filling, $8g^2 + 3g − 4$, and the rate that water leaks from the pool, $9g^2 − 2g − 5$, where g represents the number of gallons entering or leaving the pool per minute. Write an expression for the net change in gallons per minute of the water in the pool. Find the change in the amount when the rate, g, is 5 gallons per minute.

⊙ Elaborate

11. You can turn a polynomial subtraction problem into an addition problem. Can you turn a polynomial addition problem into a subtraction problem?

12. **Discussion** Write a pair of polynomials whose sum is $3m^2 + 1$. Write a pair of polynomials whose difference is $3m^2 + 1$. Write a pair of polynomials whose sum and difference are both $3m^2 + 1$.

13. **Essential Question Check-In** What do you have to do to simplify differences of polynomials? What properties do you use to accomplish this?

1. Use algebra tiles to model the difference and organize the steps in a table: $\left(x^2 + x - 3\right) - \left(x^2 + 2x + 1\right)$.

2. James was solving a subtraction problem using algebra tiles, and he ended with 1 x^2-tile, 2 $-x^2$-tiles, 3 1-tiles, and 1 -1-tile. Model these results with algebra tiles. Assuming James' steps were correct up to that point, explain his mistake. Write the algebraic expression and draw the tiles that should be his result.

Find each difference vertically.

3. $\left(2x^2 - 2x^4\right) - \left(x^4 - x^2\right)$

4. $\left(y^2 - x^4\right) - \left(-x^4 - x^2\right)$

5. $\left(0.75x + 2\right) - \left(2.75x + x^2\right)$

6. $\left(x^2 + y^2x + z\right) - \left(-x + xy^2 - z\right)$

7. $\left(m + x + 2z\right) - \left(x - y\right)$

8. $-a^5 - \left(b^2 + a^2b^2\right) - \left(-a^5 - a^2b^2\right)$

Find each difference horizontally.

9. $\left(-2x^2 + x + 1\right) - \left(2x^2 - x - 1\right)$

10. $\left(a + b - 2c\right) - \left(a + b + 2c\right)$

11. $\left(-2cab^2 + ab^2 + b^2\right) - \left(-b^2\right)$

12. $\left(-2cab^2 + ab^2 + b^2\right) - \left[-\left(-b^2\right)\right]$

13. $\left(4^{10}a + ab\sqrt[3]{2}\right) - \left(ab\sqrt[3]{2} + ab + 4^{10}a\right)$

14. $\left(q^3r^2 - 6qr^2 - 21q\right) - \left(-qr^2 - 6qr^2 - 11q - 3q^3r^2\right)$

Model various situations with the difference of polynomials. Simplify.

15. A bicycle company produces y bicycles at a cost represented by the polynomial $y^2 + 10y + 100,000$. The revenue for y bicycles is represented by $2y^2 + 10y + 500$. Find a polynomial that represents the company's profit. If the company only has enough materials to make 300 bicycles, should it make the bicycles?

16. Budget planners in two towns, Alphaville and Betaville, developed models to determine the budget surplus (in dollars) for a year based on the tax revenue (in thousands of dollars) for the year. Using historical data, Alphaville's planner produced the model $-2x^2 + 500x$, while Betaville's planner produced the model $x^2 - 100x + 10,000$. What expression gives how much greater Alphaville's annual budget surplus is than Betaville's for a particular amount of tax revenue? If the tax revenue in each town is $75,000 for a particular year, how much greater is Alphaville's budget surplus than Betaville's that year?

Geometry Mrs. Isabelle is making paper and plastic foam animals for her first-grade class. She is calculating the amount of wasted materials for environmental and financial reasons.

17. Mrs. Isabelle is cutting circles out of square pieces of paper to make paper animals in her class. Write a polynomial that represents the amount of paper wasted if the class cuts out the biggest circles possible in squares of length ℓ.

18. Mrs. Isabelle's class is making plastic foam spheres out of plastic foam cubes. Write a polynomial that represents the amount of plastic foam wasted if the class cuts out the biggest spheres possible from cubes with side lengths of l. The volume of a sphere of radius r is $\frac{4}{3}\pi r^3$.

Persevere in Problem Solving John has yellow, green, and red cubes, each with side length c. Eight yellow cubes are glued together to make a larger cube. An even larger cube is made by gluing on green cubes until no yellow cubes can be seen. After that, John covers the green cubes with red ones so that green also cannot be seen, making an even larger cube. The minimum number of green and red cubes were used to cover previous colors. Use this information for Exercises 19 and 20.

19. What is the volume of the final big red cube?

20. Write an expression for the volume of the final cube after performing this procedure with n colors of cubes.

21. Suppose you have two polynomials regarding the financial situation of a bicycle company. The first polynomial, $20,000 + x^2$, represents revenue from selling x units, and the second, $0.05x + 300$, represents the cost to produce x units.

Which of the following can be the net profit for the company if x units are produced and x units are sold?

a. $20,000 + x^2 - (0.05x + 300)$

b. $\left(20,000 + x^2\right) - (0.05x + 300)$

c. $\left(20,000 + x^2\right) - 0.05x + 300$

d. $\left(20,000 + x^2\right) - 0.05x - 300$

e. $\left(20,000 + x^2\right) + 0.05x + 300$

22. **Explain the Error** Kate performed the following subtraction problem. Explain her error and correct it.

$$(5x^2 + x) - (x^3 + 2x)$$

$$= 5x^2 + x - x^3 + 2x$$

$$= 5x^2 - x^3 + (1 + 2)x$$

$$= -x^3 + 5x^2 + 3x$$

23. **Communicate Mathematical Ideas** Hallie subtracted a quantity from the polynomial $3y^2 + 8y - 16$ and produced the expression $y^2 - 4$. What quantity did Hallie subtract? Explain how you got your answer.

24. **Counterexamples** The Associative Property works for polynomial addition. Does it work for polynomial subtraction? If not, provide a counterexample. Remember, the Associative Property for addition is $(a + b) + c = a + (b + c)$.

25. **Draw Conclusions** Finish a standard proof that the Associative Property does not work for polynomial subtraction.

To show $(a - b) - c \neq a - (b - c)$, take the right side of the Associative Property and simplify it:

$$a - (b - c) = a + \boxed{} + \boxed{} = a - \boxed{} + \boxed{}, \text{ which is not generally the}$$

same as $a - b - c$ unless $c = 0$.

Lesson Performance Task

The profits of two different manufacturing plants can be modeled as shown, where x is the number of units produced at each plant.

Plant 1: $P_1(x) = -0.03x^2 + 25x - 1500$

Plant 2: $P_2(x) = -0.02x^2 + 21x - 1700$

Find polynomials representing the difference in profits between the companies. Find $P_1(x) - P_2(x)$ and $P_2(x) - P_1(x)$. Compare the two differences and draw conclusions.

Adding and Subtracting Polynomials

Essential Question: How can you use adding and subtracting polynomials to solve real-world problems?

KEY EXAMPLE   *(Lesson 17.1)*

Combine like terms to simplify the polynomial.

$5y^2 + 12xy + 10 - y^2 + 6xy - 20$

$5y^2 - y^2 + 12xy + 6xy + 10 - 20$ *Rearrange in descending order of exponents.*

$(5y^2 - y^2) + (12xy + 6xy) + (10 - 20)$ *Group like terms.*

$y^2(5 - 1) + xy(12 + 6) + (10 - 20)$ *Distributive Property*

$y^2(4) + xy(18) + (-10)$ *Simplify.*

$4y^2 + 18xy - 10$

KEY EXAMPLE   *(Lesson 17.2)*

A city planner must add the area of 2 lots to determine the total area of a new park. The area of lot A can be represented by $(2x^2 + 6x + 4)$ ft². The area of lot B can be represented by $(5x^2 - 5x + 10)$ ft². Write an expression that represents the total area of the park.

$(2x^2 + 6x + 4) + (5x^2 - 5x + 10)$ *Add.*

$= (2x^2 + 5x^2) + (6x - 5x) + (4 + 10)$ *Group like terms.*

$= 7x^2 + x + 14$ *Simplify.*

The area of the park is $(7x^2 + x + 14)$ ft².

KEY EXAMPLE   *(Lesson 17.3)*

Find the difference.

$(b^2 + 9ab + 15a) - (3b^2 - 25ab + 1)$

$= (b^2 + 9ab + 15a) + (-3b^2 + 25ab - 1)$ *Rewrite subtraction as addition of the opposite.*

$= (b^2 - 3b^2) + (9ab + 25ab) + 15a - 1$ *Group like terms.*

$= -2b^2 + 34ab + 15a - 1$ *Simplify.*

EXERCISES

Classify each polynomial by degree and number of terms. *(Lesson 17.1)*

1. $z^2 - 12$

2. $r^2 + 8 - 7r^3s$

Combine like terms. *(Lesson 17.1)*

3. $5y - 7y^2 + 10 - 10y^2 + y$

4. $4b(a + b) - 8b^2 + 9ab$

Add or subtract. *(Lessons 17.2, 17.3)*

5. $(7p^2 - 5p + 10) + (p^2 - 8)$

6. $(4r^2 + 9r - 4) - (-2r^2 + 7r + 6)$

7. A student is cutting a square out of a piece of poster board. The area of the poster board can be represented as $(4x^2 + 14x - 8)$ in². The area of the square can be represented as $(x^2 + 8x + 16)$ in². Write an expression to represent the area of the poster board left after the student cuts out the square. *(Lesson 17.3)*

MODULE PERFORMANCE TASK

Ozone Levels in the Los Angeles Basin

You probably know that ozone in the upper atmosphere protects Earth from ultraviolet radiation, but ozone near the ground is harmful and a major component of air pollution. The table below provides maximum and minimum surface-level ozone concentrations in parts per million (ppm) in the Los Angeles Basin area for several months during 2012.

	Jan	Mar	May	June	Aug	Oct	Dec
Max	0.049	0.078	0.097	0.123	0.098	0.076	0.049
Min	0.020	0.040	0.048	0.054	0.053	0.041	0.038

Use the data to find an equation that models the average ozone level by month and use it to predict the average level for the months of February, April, September, and November of 2012.

Complete the task. Be sure to write down all your data and assumptions. Then use numbers, tables, graphs, or algebra to explain how you reached your conclusion.

(Ready) to Go On?

17.1–17.3 Adding and Subtracting Polynomials

- Online Homework
- Hints and Help
- Extra Practice

Simplify each expression by combining like terms. Classify the simplified expression by degree and number of terms. *(Lesson 17.1)*

1. $16 - 5x^2 + 6x - 2x^2 + 10$

2. $p^4 - 5p + 3p(p^3 + 4)$

Add or subtract. Write the expression in standard form. *(Lessons 17.1, 17.2, 17.3)*

3. $(9z^2 + 28) - (z^2 + 8z - 8)$

4. $(12y - 8 + 6y^2) + (9 - 4y)$

5. A community swimming pool has a deep end and a shallow end. The volume of water in the deep end can be represented by $(2x^3 + 12x^2 + 10x)$ ft^3, and the volume of water in the shallow end can be represented by $(4x^3 - 100x)$ ft^3. Write an expression that represents the total volume of water in the pool in ft^3. *(Lesson 17.2)*

ESSENTIAL QUESTION

6. What is one way that adding and subtracting polynomials is similar to adding and subtracting whole numbers and integers?

© Houghton Mifflin Harcourt Publishing Company

Assessment Readiness

1. Is the given polynomial in standard form?

   A. $-10r^3 + 3r - 18$

   B. $-35t^3 - 13t + t^2$

   C. $12x^4 - 12x^2 - 5$

2. Consider the sum of $6m^2n + mn - 15$ and $-10mn^2 + mn + 12$.
Determine if each statement is True or False.

   A. The constant term of the sum is -3.

   B. $6m^2n$ and $-10mn^2$ are like terms.

   C. In simplest form, the sum has 4 terms.

3. A clothing store sells t-shirts and jeans. The store charges customers $15 per t-shirt and $35 per pair of jeans. The store pays $4.50 per t-shirt and $5.00 per pair of jeans, plus a flat fee of $150 per order. Write an expression that represents the store's profit for an order if they sell t t-shirts and j pairs of jeans. Show your work.

4. The value of a company, in millions of dollars, during its first 10 years increased by 2% each year. The original valuation of the company was 2.1 million dollars. Write a function to represent the value of the company x years after being founded. How much more was the company worth, in millions of dollars, after 6 years than after 2 years? Explain how you solved this problem.

Multiplying Polynomials

Essential Question: How can you use multiplying polynomials to solve real-world problems?

REAL WORLD VIDEO
The production of agricultural crops is affected by factors such as weather, pests, and disease. Orange growers can use polynomial expressions to estimate costs, profits, and yield available for consumers.

MODULE PERFORMANCE TASK PREVIEW

Orange Consumption

Do you eat oranges? You probably already know they are high in vitamin C, but they are also good for your skin, eyes, heart, and immune system. Each year the price of oranges increases while the amount consumed varies. In this module, you will explore polynomial operations that will help you model the per capita spending on oranges. So, about how much do Americans spend on oranges each year? Let's find out!

Are (YOU) Ready?

Complete these exercises to review skills you will need for this module.

Multiply and Divide Integers

Example 1

Multiply or divide.

$-7 \cdot (-3)$ Think: Multiply 7 and 3.

21   Same signs, so the product is positive.

$18 \div (-9)$ Think: Divide 18 by 9.

-2 Different signs, so the quotient is negative.

Multiply or divide.

1. $-36 \div 4$ 2. $13 \cdot (-5)$ 3. $-56 \div -8$

Algebraic Expressions

Example 2

Multiply $3(2x - 5)$.

$3(2x - 5)$

$3(2x) - 3(5)$ Distributive Property

$6x - 15$ Multiply.

Multiply.

4. $8(3a + 5)$ 5. $4(6 - 2d)$ 6. $9(2x - 7y)$

Exponents

Example 3

Simplify.

$x^4 \cdot x^2 = x^{4+2} = x^6$ The bases are the same. Add the exponents.

$\dfrac{x^7}{x^3} = x^{7-3} = x^4$ The bases are the same. Subtract the exponents.

Simplify.

7. $y^3 \cdot y^6$ 8. $\dfrac{n^{10}}{n^2}$

9. $\dfrac{a^3 \cdot a^9}{a^4}$ 10. $m^2 \cdot m^5 \cdot m^3$

18.1 Multiplying Polynomial Expressions by Monomials

Resource Locker

Essential Question: How can you multiply polynomials by monomials?

⊘ Explore Modeling Polynomial Multiplication

Algebra tiles can be used to model the multiplication of a polynomial by a monomial.

Rules
1. The first factor goes on the left side of the grid, the second factor on the top.
2. Fill in the grid with tiles that have the same height as tiles on the left and the same length as tiles on the top.
3. Follow the key. The product of two tiles of the same color is positive; the product of two tiles of different colors is negative.

(A) Use algebra tiles to find $2(x + 1)$. Then recount the tiles in the grid and write the expression.

First, fill in the factors.

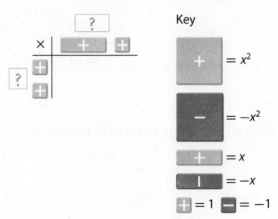

Now fill in the table.

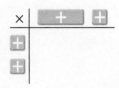

The simplified expression for $2(x + 1) = \boxed{?}\ x + \boxed{?}$.

B Use algebra tiles to model $2x(x - 3)$. Then write the expression.

The simplified expression for

$$2x(x - 3) = \boxed{?} \; x^2 - \boxed{?} \; x.$$

Reflect

1. **Discussion** How do the tiles illustrate the idea of x^2 geometrically?

2. **Discussion** How does the grid illustrate the Distributive Property?

🎸 Explain 1 Multiplying Monomials

When multiplying monomials, variables with exponents may need to be multiplied. Recall the Product of Powers Property, which states that $a^m \cdot a^n = a^{(m+n)}$.

Example 1 Find each product.

A $\left(6x^3\right)\left(-4x^4\right)$

$\left(6x^3\right)\left(-4x^4\right)$

$= (6 \cdot -4)\left(x^3 \cdot x^4\right)$

$= (6 \cdot -4)\left(x^{3+4}\right)$

$= -24x^7$

B $\left(5xy^2\right)\left(7xy\right)$

$\left(5xy^2\right)\left(7xy\right)$

$= \left(5 \cdot \boxed{7}\right)\left(x \cdot \boxed{x}\right)\left(\boxed{y^2} \cdot y\right)$

$= \left(5 \cdot \boxed{7}\right)\left(x^{1+\boxed{1}}\right)\left(y^{\boxed{2}+1}\right)$

$= \boxed{35} \; x^{\boxed{2}} y^{\boxed{3}}$

Reflect

3. In the Product of Powers Property, do the bases need to be the same or can they be different?

Your Turn

4. $\left(18y^2x^3z\right)\left(3x^8y^6z^4\right)$

⚙ Explain 2   Multiplying a Polynomial by a Monomial

Remember that the Distributive Property states that multiplying a term by a sum is the same thing as multiplying the term by each part of the sum then adding the results.

Example 2   Find each product.

Ⓐ $3x(3x^2 + 6x - 5)$

$3x(3x^2 + 6x - 5)$ Distribute and simplify.

$= 3x(3x^2) + 3x(6x) + 3x(-5)$

$= 9x^{1+2} + 18x^{1+1} - 15x^1$

$= 9x^3 + 18x^2 - 15x$

Ⓑ $2xy(5x^2y + 3xy^2 + 7xy)$

$2xy(5x^2y + 3xy^2 + 7xy)$ Distribute and simplify.

$= 2xy(5x^2y) + 2xy\left(\boxed{3xy^2}\right) + 2xy\left(\boxed{7xy}\right)$

$= 10x^{1+2}y^{1+1} + \boxed{6}\,x^{1+\boxed{1}}y^{1+\boxed{2}} + \boxed{14}\,x^{1+\boxed{1}}y^{1+\boxed{1}}$

$= 10x^3y^2 + \boxed{6}\,x^{\boxed{2}}y^{\boxed{3}} + \boxed{14}\,x^{\boxed{2}}y^{\boxed{2}}$

Reflect

5. Is the product of a monomial and a polynomial always a polynomial? Explain. If so, how many terms does it have?

Your Turn

6. $2a^2(5b^2 + 3ab + 6a + 1)$

⚙ Explain 3   Multiplying a Polynomial by a Monomial to Solve a Real-World Problem

Knowing how to multiply polynomials and monomials is useful when solving real-world problems.

Example 3   Write a polynomial equation and solve the problem.

Design Harry is building a fish tank that is a square prism. He wants the height of the tank to be 6 inches longer than the length and width. If he needs the volume to be as close as possible to 3500 in³, what should be the length of the tank? Round to the nearest inch.

Analyze Information

Identify the important information
- Since the bases are squares, the length and width are equal.
- The height of the tank is 6 more inches than the length.
- The total volume of the model should be as close as possible to 3500 in³.

Formulate a Plan

Since the desired volume of the model is given, the volume formula should be used to find the answer. The volume formula for a square prism is

$V =$ | length · width · height | . Use this formula and the given information to write and solve an equation.

Solve

Build the equation.

Since the length and width are equal, let s represent these measurements. The volume will be $V = (s \cdot s)\left(\boxed{s + 6} \right) = s^{\boxed{2}} \left(\boxed{s + 6} \right) = s^{\boxed{3}} + \boxed{6}\, s^{\boxed{2}}$.

s	$s^3 + 6s^2$
11	2057
12	2592
13	3211
14	3920

Justify and Evaluate

3211 is closer to 3500 than any of the other results, so the length of the fish tank to the nearest whole inch should be 13 inches.

Your Turn

7. **Engineering** Diane needs a piece of paper whose length is 4 more inches than the width, and the area is as close as possible to 50 in². To the nearest whole inch, what should the dimensions of the paper be?

Elaborate

8. What is the power if a monomial is multiplied by a constant?

9. **Essential Question Check-In** What properties and rules are used to multiply a multi-term polynomial by a monomial?

☆ Evaluate: Homework and Practice

Find each product.

1. $(3x)(2x^2)$

2. $(19x^5)(8x^3)$

3. $(6x^7)(3x^3)$

4. $(3x^2)(2x^3)$

5. $7xy(3x^2y^3)$

6. $(6xyz^4)(5xy^3)$

7. $(8xy^3)(4y^4z^2)$

8. $(11xy)(x^3y^2)$

9. $(x^2 + x)(x^3)$

10. $(x^3 + 2x^2)(x^4)$

11. $(x^2 + 2x + 5)(x^3)$

12. $(x^4 + 3x^3 + 2x^2 + 11x + 4)(x^2)$

13. $(x^3 + 2y^2 + 3xy)(4x^2y)$

14. $(2x^3 + 5y)(3xy)$

15. $(x^4 + 3x^3y + 3xy^3)(6xy^2)$

16. $(x^4 + 3x^3y^2 + 4x^2y + 8xy + 12x)(11x^2y^3)$

Write a polynomial equation for each situation and then solve the problem.

17. **Design** A bedroom has a length of $x + 3$ feet and a width of x feet. Find the area when $x = 10$.

18. **Engineering** A flat-screen television has a length that is 1 more inch than its width. The area of the television's screen is 1500 in². To the nearest whole inch, what are the dimensions of the television?

19. **Construction** Zach is building a new shed shaped like a square prism. He wants the height of the shed to be 2 feet less than the length and width. If he needs the volume to be as close as possible to 3174 ft³, what should the length be? Round to the nearest foot.

20. State whether each expression is or can be written as a monomial.

    a. x^3

    b. $a^2 + 2a^b + b^c$

    c. $x^3 + 4x^3$

    d. $y^{2^{x'}}$

    e. $xyz + txy + tyz + txz$

21. Draw the algebra tiles that model the factors in the multiplication shown. Then determine the simplified product.

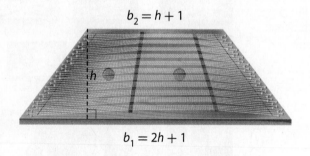

22. Critical Thinking When finding the product of a monomial and a binomial, how is the degree of the product related to the degree of the monomial and the degree of the binomial?

23. Explain the Error Sandy says that the product of x^2 and $x^3 + 5x^2 + 1$ is $x^6 + 5x^4 + x^2$. Explain the error that Sandy made.

24. Communicate Mathematical Ideas What is the lowest degree that a polynomial can have? Explain.

Lesson Performance Task

A craftsman is making a dulcimer with the same dimensions as the one shown. The surface shown requires a special, more durable type of finish. Write a polynomial that represents the area to be finished on the dulcimer shown.

$$b_2 = h + 1$$

h

$$b_1 = 2h + 1$$

18.2 Multiplying Polynomial Expressions

Essential Question: How do you multiply binomials and polynomials?

⊘ Explore   Modeling Binomial Multiplication

Using algebra tiles to model the product of two binomials is very similar to using algebra tiles to model the product of a monomial and a polynomial.

Rules
1. The first factor goes on the left side of the grid, and the second factor goes on the top.
2. Fill in the grid with tiles that have the same height as tiles on the left and the same length as tiles on the top.
3. Follow the key. The product of two tiles of the same color is positive; the product of two tiles of different colors is negative.

Use algebra tiles to model $(x + 1)(x - 2)$. Then write the product. First fill in the factors and mat.

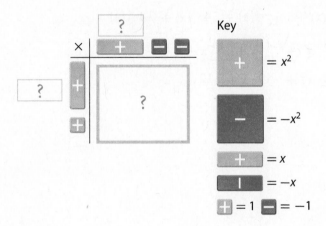

Now remove any zero pairs.

The product $(x + 1)(x - 2)$ in simplest form is $\boxed{?}\ x^2 - \boxed{?}\ x - \boxed{?}$.

1. **Discussion** Why can zero pairs be removed from the product?

2. **Discussion** Is it possible for more than one pair of tiles to form a zero pair?

🔑 Explain 1 Multiplying Binomials Using the Distributive Property

To multiply a binomial by a binomial, the Distributive Property must be applied more than once.

Example 1 Multiply by using the Distributive Property.

Ⓐ $(x + 5)(x + 2)$

$$(x + 5)(x + 2) = x(x + 2) + 5(x + 2) \qquad \text{Distribute.}$$

$$= x(x + 2) + 5(x + 2) \qquad \text{Redistribute and simplify.}$$

$$= x(x) + x(2) + 5(x) + 5(2)$$

$$= x^2 + 2x + 5x + 10$$

$$= x^2 + 7x + 10$$

Ⓑ $(2x + 4)(x + 3)$

$$(2x + 4)(x + 3) = 2x(x + 3) + \boxed{4}\ (x + 3) \qquad \text{Distribute.}$$

$$= 2x(x + 3) + \boxed{4}\ (x + 3) \qquad \text{Redistribute and simplify.}$$

$$= 2x(x) + \boxed{2x}\ (3) + \boxed{4}\ (x) + \boxed{4}\ (3)$$

$$= \boxed{2}\ x^2 + \boxed{6}\ x + \boxed{4}\ x + \boxed{12}$$

$$= \boxed{2}\ x^2 + \boxed{10}\ x + \boxed{12}$$

Your Turn

3. $(x + 1)(x - 2)$

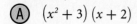

Another way to use the Distributive Property is the *FOIL* method. The **FOIL** method uses the Distributive Property to multiply terms of binomials in this order: First terms, Outer terms, Inner terms, and Last terms.

Example 2 **Multiply by using the FOIL method.**

(A) $(x^2 + 3)(x + 2)$

Use the FOIL method.

$(x^2 + 3)(x + 2) = (x^2 + 3)(x + 2)$ F   Multiply the first terms. Result: x^3

$= (x^2 + 3)(x + 2)$ O   Multiply the outer terms. Result: $2x^2$

$= (x^2 + 3)(x + 2)$ I   Multiply the inner terms. Result: $3x$

$= (x^2 + 3)(x + 2)$ L   Multiply the last terms. Result: 6

Add the result.

$(x^2 + 3)(x + 2) = x^3 + 2x^2 + 3x + 6$

(B) $(3x^2 - 2x)(x + 5)$

Use the FOIL method.

$(3x^2 - 2x)(x + 5) = (3x^2 - 2x)(x + 5)$ F   Multiply the first terms. Result: $\boxed{3x^3}$

$= (3x^2 - 2x)(x + 5)$ O   Multiply the outer terms. Result: $\boxed{15x^2}$

$= (3x^2 - 2x)(x + 5)$ I   Multiply the inner terms. Result: $\boxed{-2x^2}$

$= (3x^2 - 2x)(x + 5)$ L   Multiply the last terms. Result: $\boxed{-10x}$

Add the result.

$(3x^2 - 2x)(x + 5) = \boxed{3}\,x^3 + \boxed{13}\,x^2 - \boxed{10}\,x$

Reflect

4. The FOIL method finds the sum of four partial products. Why does the result from part B only have three terms?

5. Can the FOIL method be used for numeric expressions? Give an example.

Your Turn

6. $(x^2 + 3)(x + 6)$

🔧 Explain 3 Multiplying Polynomials

To multiply polynomials with more than two terms, the Distributive Property must be used several times.

Example 3 **Multiply the polynomials.**

(A) $(x + 2)(x^2 - 5x + 4)$

$(x + 2)(x^2 - 5x + 4) = x(x^2 - 5x + 4) + 2(x^2 - 5x + 4)$ Distribute.

$\qquad\qquad\qquad\qquad = x(x^2 - 5x + 4) + 2(x^2 - 5x + 4)$ Redistribute.

$\qquad\qquad\qquad\qquad = x(x^2) + x(-5x) + x(4) + 2(x^2) + 2(-5x) + 2(4)$ Simplify.

$\qquad\qquad\qquad\qquad = x^3 - 5x^2 + 4x + 2x^2 - 10x + 8$

$\qquad\qquad\qquad\qquad = x^3 - 3x^2 - 6x + 8$

(B) $(3x - 4)(-2x^2 + 5x - 6)$

$(3x - 4)(-2x^2 + 5x - 6) = 3x(-2x^2 + 5x - 6) - \boxed{4}(-2x^2 + 5x - 6)$ Distribute.

$\qquad\qquad\qquad\qquad\qquad = 3x(-2x^2 + 5x - 6) - \boxed{4}(-2x^2 + 5x - 6)$ Redistribute.

$\qquad\qquad\qquad\qquad\qquad = 3x(-2x^2) + 3x\boxed{5x} + 3x\boxed{-6} - 4\boxed{-2x^2} - 4\boxed{5x} - 4\boxed{-6}$

Simplify.

$\qquad\qquad\qquad\qquad\qquad = \boxed{-6}x^{\boxed{3}} + \boxed{15}x^{\boxed{2}} - \boxed{18}x + \boxed{8}x^{\boxed{2}} - \boxed{20}x + \boxed{24}$

$\qquad\qquad\qquad\qquad\qquad = \boxed{-6}x^{\boxed{3}} + \boxed{23}x^{\boxed{2}} - \boxed{38}x + \boxed{24}$

Reflect

7. **Discussion** Is the product of two polynomials always another polynomial?

8. Can the Distributive Property be used to multiply two trinomials?

9. $(3x + 1)(x^3 + 4x^2 - 7)$

⚙ Explain 4 Modeling with Polynomial Multiplication

Polynomial multiplication is sometimes necessary in problem solving.

Ⓐ Gardening Trina is building a garden. She designs a rectangular garden with length $(x + 4)$ feet and width $(x + 1)$ feet. When $x = 4$, what is the area of the garden?

Let y represent the area of Trina's garden. Then the equation for this situation is $y = (x + 4)(x + 1)$.

$y = (x + 4)(x + 1)$

Use FOIL.

$y = x^2 + x + 4x + 4$

$y = x^2 + 5x + 4$

Now substitute 4 for x to finish the problem.

$y = x^2 + 5x + 4$

$y = (4)^2 + 5(4) + 4$

$y = 16 + 20 + 4$

$y = 40$

The area of Trina's garden is 40 ft².

Ⓑ Design Orik has designed a rectangular mural that measures 20 feet in width and 30 feet in length. Laura has also designed a rectangular mural, but it measures x feet shorter on each side. When $x = 6$, what is the area of Laura's mural?

Let y represent the area of Laura's mural. Then the equation for this situation is

$y = (20 - x)(30 - x)$.

$y = (20 - x)(30 - x)$

Use FOIL.

$y = \boxed{600} - \boxed{20}\,x - \boxed{30}\,x + \boxed{1}\,x^2$

$y = \boxed{1}\,x^2 - \boxed{50}\,x + \boxed{600}$

Now substitute $\boxed{6}$ for x to finish the problem.

$y = \boxed{6}^2 - \boxed{50} \cdot \boxed{6} + \boxed{600}$

$y = \boxed{36} - \boxed{300} + \boxed{600}$

$y = \boxed{336}$

The area of Laura's mural is $\boxed{336}$ ft².

10. Landscaping A landscape architect is designing a rectangular garden in a local park. The garden will be 20 feet long and 15 feet wide. The architect wants to place a walkway with a uniform width all the way around the garden. What will be the area of the garden, including the walkway?

💬 Elaborate

11. How is the FOIL method different from the Distributive Property? Explain.

12. Why can FOIL not be used for polynomials with three or more terms?

13. Essential Question Check–In How do you multiply two binomials?

⭐ Evaluate: Homework and Practice

- Online Homework
- Hints and Help
- Extra Practice

Multiply by using the Distributive Property.

1. $(x + 6)(x - 4)$

2. $(2x + 5)(x - 3)$

3. $(x - 6)(x + 1)$

4. $(x^2 + 3)(x - 4)$

5. $(x^2 + 11)(x + 6)$

6. $(x^2 + 8)(x - 5)$

Multiply by using the FOIL method.

7. $(x + 3)(x + 7)$

8. $(4x + 2)(x - 2)$

9. $(3x + 2)(2x + 5)$

10. $(x^2 - 6)(x - 4)$

11. $(x^2 + 9)(x - 3)$

12. $(4x^2 - 4)(2x + 1)$

Multiply the polynomials.

13. $(x - 3)(x^2 + 2x + 1)$

14. $(x + 5)(x3 + 6x2 + 18x)$

15. $(x + 4)(x^4 + x^2 + 1)$

16. $(x - 6)(x^5 + 4x^3 + 6x^2 + 2x)$

17. $(x^2 + x + 3)(x^3 - x^2 + 4)$

18. $(x^3 + x^2 + 2x)(x^4 - x^3 + x^2)$

Write a polynomial equation for each situation.

19. Gardening Cameron is creating a garden. He designs a rectangular garden with a length of $(x + 6)$ feet and a width of $(x + 2)$ feet. When $x = 5$, what is the area of the garden?

20. Design Sabrina has designed a rectangular painting that measures 50 feet in length and 40 feet in width. Alfred has also designed a rectangular painting, but it measures x feet shorter on each side. When $x = 3$, what is the area of Alfred's painting?

21. Photography Karl is putting a frame around a rectangular photograph. The photograph is 12 inches long and 10 inches wide, and the frame is the same width all the way around. What will be the area of the framed photograph?

22. Sports A tennis court is surrounded by a fence so that the distance from each boundary of the tennis court to the fence is the same. If the tennis court is 78 feet long and 36 feet wide, what is the area of the entire surface inside the fence?

23. State the first term of each product.

   a. $(2x + 1)(3x + 4)$

   b. $(x^4 + x^2)(3x^8 + x^{11})$

   c. $x(x + 9)$

   d. $(x^2 + 9)(3x + 4)(2x + 6)$

   e. $(x^3 + 4)(x^2 + 6)(x + 5)$

24. Draw algebra tiles to model the factors in the polynomial multiplication modeled on the mat. Then write the factors and the product in simplest form.

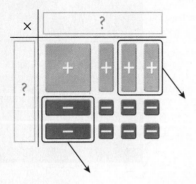

25. Critical Thinking The product of 3 consecutive odd numbers is 2145. Write an expression for finding the numbers.

26. Represent Real-World Problems The town swimming pool is d feet deep. The width of the pool is 10 feet greater than 5 times its depth. The length of the pool is 35 feet greater than 5 times its depth. Write and simplify an expression to represent the volume of the pool.

27. Explain the Error Bill argues that $(x + 1)(x + 19)$ simplifies to $x^2 + 20x + 20$. Explain his error.

Lesson Performance Task

Roan is planning a large vegetable garden in her yard. She plans to have at least six x by x regions for rotating crops and some 2 or 3 feet by x strips for fruit bushes like blueberries and raspberries.

Design a rectangular garden for Roan and write a polynomial that will give its area.

18.3 Special Products of Binomials

Essential Question: How can you find special products of binomials?

⊘ Explore Modeling Special Products

Use algebra tiles to model the special products of binomials.

(A) Use algebra tiles to model $(2x + 3)^2$. Then write the product in simplest form.

$$(2x + 3)^2 = \boxed{?}\; x^2 + \boxed{?}\; x + \boxed{?}\,.$$

(B) Use algebra tiles to model $(2x - 3)^2$. Then write the product in simplest form.

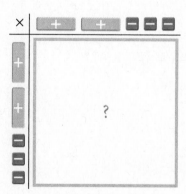

$$(2x - 3)^2 = \boxed{?}\; x^2 - \boxed{?}\; x + \boxed{?}\,.$$

(C) Use algebra tiles to model $(2x + 3)(2x - 3)$. Then recount the tiles in the grid and write the expression.

$$(2x + 3)(2x - 3) = \boxed{?}\; x^2 + \boxed{?}\; x - \boxed{?}\,.$$

1. **Discussion** In Step A, which terms of the trinomial are perfect squares? What is the coefficient of x in the product? How can you use the values of a and b in the expression $(2x + 3)^2$ to produce the coefficient of each term in the trinomial? How can you generalize these results to write a rule for the product $(a + b)^2$?

2. **Discussion** In Step B, which terms of the trinomial are perfect squares? What is the coefficient of x in the trinomial? How can you use the values of a and b in the expression $(2x - 3)^2$ to produce the coefficient of each term in the trinomial? How can you generalize these results to write a rule for the product $(a - b)^2$?

3. **Discussion** In Step C, which terms of the product are perfect squares? What is the coefficient of x in the product? How can you use the values of a and b in the expression $(2x + 3)(2x - 3)$ to produce the coefficient of each term in the product? How can you generalize these results to write a rule for the product $(a + b)(a - b)$?

⚙ Explain 1   Multiplying $(a + b)^2$

In the Explore, you determined a formula for the square of a binomial sum, $(a + b)^2 = a^2 + 2ab + b^2$. A trinomial of the form $a^2 + 2ab + b^2$ is called a *perfect-square trinomial*. A **perfect-square trinomial** is a trinomial that is the result of squaring a binomial.

Example 1   **Multiply.**

(A) $(x + 4)^2$

$$(a + b)^2 = a^2 + 2ab + b^2$$
$$(x + 4)^2 = x^2 + 2(x)(4) + 4^2$$
$$= x^2 + 8x + 16$$

(B) $(3x + 2y)^2$

$$(a + b)^2 = a^2 + 2ab + b^2$$
$$(3x + 2y)^2 = (3x)^2 + 2\boxed{3}\,x\,\boxed{2}\,y + \boxed{2}\,y^2$$
$$= 9x^2 + \boxed{12}\,xy + \boxed{4}\,y^2$$

4. In the perfect square trinomial $x^2 + bx + c$, what is the relationship between b and c? Explain.

Your Turn

Multiply.

5. $(4 + x^2)^2$

6. $(-x + 3)^2$

⚙ Explain 2　Multiplying $(a - b)^2$

In the Explore, you determined the square of a binomial difference, $(a - b)^2 = a^2 - 2ab + b^2$. Because $a^2 - 2ab + b^2$ is the result of squaring the binomial $(a - b)$, $a^2 - 2ab + b^2$ is also a perfect-square trinomial.

Example 2　Multiply.

Ⓐ　$(x - 5)^2$

$$(a - b)^2 = a^2 - 2ab + b^2$$
$$(x - 5)^2 = x^2 - 2(x)(5) + 5^2$$
$$= x^2 - 10x + 25$$

Ⓑ　$(6x - 1)^2$

$$(a - b)^2 = a^2 - 2ab + b^2$$
$$(6x - 1)^2 = \left(\boxed{6}\, x\right) - 2\left(\boxed{6}\, x\right)\left(\boxed{1}\right) + \boxed{1}^2$$
$$= \boxed{36}\, x^2 - \boxed{12}\, x + \boxed{1}$$

Reflect

7.　Why is the last term of a perfect square trinomial always positive?

Your Turn

Multiply.

8.　$(4x - 3y)^2$

9.　$(3 - x^2)^2$

⚙ Explain 3　Multiplying $(a + b)(a - b)$

In the Explore, you determined the formula $(a + b)(a - b) = a^2 - b^2$. A binomial of the form $a^2 - b^2$ is called a **difference of two squares**.

Example 3　Multiply.

Ⓐ　$(x + 6)(x - 6)$

$$(a + b)(a - b) = a^2 - b^2$$
$$(x + 6)(x - 6) = x^2 - 6^2$$
$$= x^2 - 36$$

Ⓑ　$(x^2 + 2y)(x^2 - 2y)$

$$(a + b)(a - b) = a^2 - b^2$$
$$(x^2 + 2y)(x^2 - 2y) = \left(\boxed{x^2}\right)^2 - \left(\boxed{2y}\right)^2$$
$$= \boxed{1}\, x^{\boxed{4}} - \boxed{4}\, y^{\boxed{2}}$$

Reflect

10.　Why does the product of $a + b$ and $a - b$ always include a minus sign?

Your Turn

11.　$(7 + x)(7 - x)$

🔑 Explain 4   Modeling with Special Products

Example 4   **Write and simplify an expression to represent the situation.**

Design A designer adds a border with a uniform width to a square rug. The original side length of the rug is $(x - 5)$ feet. The side length of the entire rug including the original rug and the border is $(x + 5)$ feet. What is the area of the border? Evaluate the area of the border if $x = 10$ feet.

 Analyze Information

Identify the important information.

The answer will be an expression that represents the area of the border.

List the important information:

- The rug is a square with a side length of $\boxed{x - 5}$ feet.
- The side length of the entire square area including the original rug and the border is $\boxed{x + 5}$ feet.

 Formulate a Plan

The area of the rug in square feet is $\boxed{x - 5}^2$. The total area of the rug plus the border in square feet is $\boxed{x + 5}^2$. The area of the rug can be subtracted from the total area to find the area of the border.

🔑 Solve

Find the total area:

$$(x + 5)^2 = \boxed{1}\,x^2 + 2\left(\boxed{x}\right)\left(\boxed{5}\right) + \boxed{5}^{\,2}$$
$$= \boxed{1}\,x^2 + \boxed{10}\,x + \boxed{25}$$

Find the area of the rug:

$$(x - 5)^2 = \boxed{1}\,x^2 - 2\left(\boxed{x}\right)\left(\boxed{5}\right) + \left(\boxed{5}\right)^2$$
$$= \boxed{1}\,x^2 - \boxed{10}\,x + \boxed{25}$$

Find the area of the border:

Area of border = total area − area of rug

$$\text{Area} = \boxed{1}\,x^2 + \boxed{10}\,x + \boxed{25} - \left(\boxed{1}\,x^2 - \boxed{10}\,x + \boxed{25}\right)$$
$$= \boxed{1}\,x^2 + \boxed{10}\,x + \boxed{25} - \boxed{1}\,x^2 + \boxed{10}\,x - \boxed{25}$$
$$= \left(\boxed{1}\,x^2 - \boxed{1}\,x^2\right) + \left(\boxed{10}\,x + \boxed{10}\,x\right) + \left(\boxed{25} - \boxed{25}\right)$$
$$= \boxed{0}\,x^2 + \boxed{20}\,x + \boxed{0}$$
$$= \boxed{20}\,x$$

The area of the border is $\boxed{0}\,x^2 + \boxed{20}\,x + \boxed{0} = \boxed{20x}$ square feet.

Suppose that $x = 10$. The rug is $\boxed{5}$ feet by $\boxed{5}$ feet, so its area is $\boxed{25}$ square feet. The total area is

$\left(\boxed{10} + \boxed{5}\right)^2 = \boxed{225}$ square feet, so the area of the border is $\boxed{225} - \boxed{25} = \boxed{200}$ square feet,

which is $\boxed{20}$ (10) when $x = 10$. So the answer makes sense.

Reflect

12. Critique Reasoning Estelle solved a problem just like the example, except that the value of b in the two expressions was 8. Her expression for the area of the border was $-32x$. How do you know that she made an error? What do you think her error might have been?

Your Turn

Write and simplify an expression.

13. A square patio has a side length of $(x - 3)$ feet. It is surrounded by a flower garden with a uniform width. The side length of the entire square area including the patio and the flower garden is $(x + 3)$ feet. Write an expression for the area of the flower garden.

Elaborate

14. How can you use the formula for the square of a binomial sum to write a formula for the square of a binomial difference?

15. Can you use the formula for the square of a binomial sum to write a formula for a difference of squares?

16. Essential Question Check-In Use one of the special product rules to describe in words how to find the coefficient of xy in the product $\left(5x - 3y\right)^2$.

☆ Evaluate: Homework and Practice

- Online Homework
- Hints and Help
- Extra Practice

Multiply.

1. $(x + 8)^2$

2. $\left(4x + 6y\right)^2$

3. $\left(6 + x^2\right)^2$

4. $(-x + 5)^2$

5. $(x + 11)^2$

6. $\left(8x + 9y\right)^2$

7. $(x - 3)^2$

8. $(5x - 2)^2$

9. $\left(6x - 7y\right)^2$

10. $\left(5 - x^2\right)^2$

11. $\left(5x - 4y\right)^2$

12. $\left(7 - 2x^2\right)^2$

13. $(x + 4)(x - 4)$

14. $(x^2 + 6y)(x^2 - 6y)$

15. $(9 + x)(9 - x)$

16. $(2x + 5)(2x - 5)$

17. $(3x^2 + 8y)(3x^2 - 8y)$

18. $(7 + 3x)(7 - 3x)$

Write and simplify an expression to represent the situation.

19. Design A square swimming pool is surrounded by a cement walkway with a uniform width. The swimming pool has a side length of $(x - 2)$ feet. The side length of the entire square area including the pool and the walkway is $(x + 1)$ feet. Write an expression for the area of the walkway. Then find the area of the cement walkway when $x = 7$ feet.

20. This week Leo worked $(x + 4)$ hours at a pizzeria. He is paid $(x - 4)$ dollars per hour. Leo's friend Frankie worked the same number of hours, but he is paid $(x - 2)$ dollars per hour. Write an expression for the total amount paid to the two workers. Then find the total amount if $x = 12$.

21. Kyra is framing a square painting with side lengths of $(x + 8)$ inches. The total area of the painting and the frame has a side length of $(2x - 6)$ inches. The material for the frame will cost $0.08 per square inch. Write an expression for the area of the frame. Then find the cost of the material for the frame if $x = 16$.

22. Geometry Circle A has a radius of $(x + 4)$ units. A larger circle, B, has a radius of $(x + 5)$ units. Use the formula $A = \pi r^2$ to write an expression for the difference in the areas of the circles. Leave your answer in terms of π. Then use 3.14 for π to approximate to the nearest whole number the difference in the areas when $x = 10$.

23. A square has sides with lengths of $(x - 1)$ units. A rectangle has a length of x units and a width of $(x - 2)$ units. Which statements about the situation are true? Select all that apply.

   a. The area of the square is $(x^2 - 1)$ square units.

   b. The area of the rectangle is $x^2 - 2x$ square units.

   c. The area of the square is greater than the area of the rectangle.

   d. The value of x must be greater than 2.

   e. The difference in the areas is $2x - 1$.

24. Explain the Error Marco wrote the expression $(2x - 7y)^2 = 4x^2 - 49y^2$. Explain and correct his error.

H.O.T. Focus on Higher Order Thinking

25. Critical Thinking Use the FOIL method to justify each special product rule.

   a. $(a + b)^2$

   b. $(a - b)^2$

   c. $(a + b)(a - b)$

26. Communicate Mathematical Ideas Explain how you can use the special product rules and the Distributive Property to write a general rule for $(a - b)^3$. Then write the rule.

Lesson Performance Task

When building a square-shaped outdoor fireplace, the ground needs to be replaced with stone for an additional two feet on each side. Write a polynomial for the area that needs to be excavated to create an x by x fireplace.

Design your ideal space for sitting around a fire pit and relaxing. Add furniture, flowerbeds, rock gardens, and any other desired features.

Evaluate the polynomial for the size fireplace you are including.

Multiplying Polynomials

Essential Question: How can you use multiplying polynomials to solve real-world problems?

KEY EXAMPLE   *(Lesson 18.1)*

Multiply.

$(-3x^2y^4)(-6x^3y)$

$(-3 \cdot -6)(x^2 \cdot x^3)(y^4 \cdot y)$ *Group terms with the same base.*

$(-3 \cdot -6)\ (x^{2+3})(y^{4+1})$ *Apply the Product of Powers Property: $a^m \cdot a^n = a^{m+n}$.*

$18x^5y^5$

KEY EXAMPLE   *(Lesson 18.2)*

Multiply.

$(3x + 7)(x - 1)$ *Multiply using FOIL.*

$= 3x^2 - 3x + 7x - 7$ *First terms $(3x \cdot x)$ Outer terms $(3x \cdot -1)$ Inner terms $(7 \cdot x)$ and Last terms $(7 \cdot -1)$*

$= 3x^2 + 4x - 7$

$(4x - 2)(-2x - 9)$

$= (4x)(-2x) + (4x)(-9) + (-2)(-2x) + (-2)(-9)$

$= -8x^2 - 36x + 4x + 18$

$= -8x^2 - 32x + 18$

KEY EXAMPLE   *(Lesson 18.3)*

Multiply

$(x - 7)(x + 7)$ *The product will be the difference of two squares.*

$= x^2 - 7^2$ $(a + b)(a - b) = a^2 - b^2$

$= x^2 - 49$

$(2x + 5)^2$ *The product will be a perfect-square trinomial.*

$= (2x)^2 + 2(2x)(5) + 5^2$ $(a + b)^2 = a^2 + 2ab + b^2$

$= 4x^2 + 20x + 25$

EXERCISES

Multiply. *(Lessons 18.1, 18.2)*

1. $(7y^5)(-4y^2)$

2. $(3p^4q)(12p^3q^2)$

3. $(x-4)(x+8)$

4. $(4x-1)(2x+6)$

Multiply. Identify each product as a perfect-square trinomial or a difference of squares. *(Lesson 18.3)*

5. $(3x+9)(3x-9)$

6. $(x-8)^2$

MODULE PERFORMANCE TASK

Orange Consumption

About how much do Americans spend per capita on oranges each year? The average price of oranges was $0.57 per pound in 2004 and has been increasing at a rate of $0.02 per year. The table below shows the per capita orange consumption (in pounds) in the United States from 2004–2012.

Year	2004	2005	2006	2007	2008	2009	2010	2011	2012
Pounds Consumed	83.6	80.3	72.8	65.2	62.3	62.7	61.8	62.3	54.9

How can you use this data to find a model and use it to predict how much money the average American spent on oranges in 2014?

Complete the task. Be sure to write down all your data and assumptions. Then use graphs, numbers, words, or algebra to explain how you reached your conclusion.

(Ready) to Go On?

18.1–18.3 Multiplying Polynomials

- Online Homework
- Hints and Help
- Extra Practice

Multiply. Identify each product as a perfect-square trinomial, a difference of squares, or neither. *(Lessons 18.1, 18.2, 18.3)*

1. $(2y - 5)(2y + 5)$

2. $(9r^3s^3)(10r^3s^2)$

3. $(4x + 1)^2$

4. $(3x - 4)(x + 8)$

Use the model of the rectangular prism to answer Exercises 5 and 6. The width of the prism is $(2x - 2)$ ft, and its height is $(x + 6)$ ft. The area of the base of the prism is $(3x^2 + 2x - 4)$ ft².

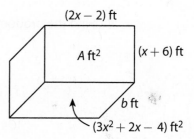

5. Write an expression to represent the area of side A. *(Lesson 18.3)*

6. Could the length of b be $(3x - 1)$ ft? Explain why or why not. *(Lesson 18.3)*

ESSENTIAL QUESTION

7. Is it necessary to use the formulas for special products of binomials to multiply these binomials? Explain.

Assessment Readiness

1. Find the standard form for the product of $(x^2 + 8)$ and $(x^2 - 2)$. Determine if each statement is True or False.
   A. It is a 4th degree polynomial.
   B. The constant term is -16.
   C. It has 3 terms.

2. Multiply $(5x - 9)^2$. Determine if each statement is True or False.
   A. The coefficient of the x-term is -45.
   B. The leading term is $25x^2$.
   C. The constant term is 81.

3. Find the product $(3x + 6)(3x - 6)$. Show your work.

4. Find the product $(x + 10)(4x + 5)$. Show your work.

5. A rectangle has a length $(x + 6)$ m and a width of 7 m. Write expressions to represent the perimeter and area of the rectangle. Explain how you determined your answers.

1. Solve each equation. Tell whether each solution is correct.

   A. $-4(p + 3) = -3p - 7; p = -5$

   B. $8r - 18 = -14; r = \frac{1}{2}$

   C. $\frac{t}{5} - 2 = -5; t = 15$

2. Simplify $5x^2\left(\frac{2}{5} - x\right)$. Determine if each statement is True or False.

   A. The expression is a trinomial.

   B. The expression has a degree of 3.

   C. The expression has a constant term of -2.

3. Is the given polynomial in standard form?

   A. $-5y^2 + 5y + 24$

   B. $7x^5 - 19 + x$

   C. $15z - 3$

4. Simplify $(3x - 8)(x + 2)$. Tell whether each statement is correct.

   A. The coefficient of the x-term is -2.

   B. The leading term is $3x^2$.

   C. The constant term is -16.

5. Is the product of each of the following pairs of factors a difference of squares?

   A. $3(x - 3)$

   B. $4(4x^2 - 1)$

   C. $(5x - 2)(5x + 2)$

6. Write the difference of the following polynomials in standard form: $(11 - 8y + 2y^2) - (y^2 - 15)$. Classify the difference by its degree and number of terms.

7. Sandra has been offered two jobs. Job A pays $25,000 a year with an 8% raise each year. Job B pays $28,000 a year with a $2,500 raise each year. Write a function to represent each salary t years after being hired. Use a graphing calculator to compare the two salary plans. Will Job A ever have a higher salary than Job B? If so, after how many years will this occur? Explain how you solved this problem.

8.

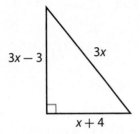

Write an expression that represents the perimeter of the triangle in terms of x and an expression that represents the area of the triangle in terms of x. If the perimeter is 36 cm, what is the area of the triangle? Explain how you solved this problem.

Performance Tasks

★ **9.** The profits of two different manufacturing plants can be modeled as shown.

Eastern: $-0.03x^2 + 25x - 1500$

Southern: $-0.02x^2 + 21x - 1700$

A. Write a polynomial that represents the difference of the profits at the Eastern plant and the profits at the Southern plant.

B. Write a polynomial that represents the total profits from both plants.

© Houghton Mifflin Harcourt Publishing Company

★★**10.** A rectangular swimming pool is 25 feet long and 10 feet wide. It is surrounded by a fence that is *x* feet from each side of the pool.

    A. Draw a diagram of the situation.

    B. Write expressions for the length, width, and area of the fenced region.

★★★**11.** Tammy plans to put a wallpaper border around the perimeter of her room. She will not put the border across the doorway, which is 3 feet wide.

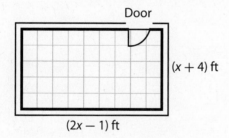

    A. Write a polynomial that represents the number of feet of wallpaper border that Tammy will need.

    B. A local store has 50 feet of the border that Tammy has chosen. What is the greatest whole-number value of *x* for which this amount would be enough for Tammy's room? Justify your answer.

    C. Determine the dimensions of Tammy's room for the value of *x* that you found in part **B**.

Camp Director For the initial year of a summer camp, 44 girls and 56 boys enrolled. Each year thereafter, 5 more girls and 8 more boys enrolled in the camp.

a. Let t be the time (in years) since the camp opened. Write a rule for each of the following functions:

- $g(t)$, the number of girls enrolled as a function of time t

- $b(t)$, the number of boys enrolled as a function of time t

- $T(t)$, the total enrollment as a function of time t

b. The cost per child each year was \$200. Write a rule for each of the following functions:

- $C(t)$, the cost per child as a function of time t

- $R(t)$, the revenue generated by the total enrollment as a function of time t

c. Explain why $C(t)$ is a constant function.

d. What was the initial revenue for the camp? What was the annual rate of change in the revenue?

e. The camp director had initial expenses of \$18,000, which increased each year by \$2,500. Write a rule for the expenses function $E(t)$. Then write a rule for the profit function $P(t)$ based on the fact that profit is the difference between revenue and expenses.

UNIT 8

Quadratic Functions

MATH IN CAREERS

Transportation Engineer

Transportation engineers design and modify plans for transportation systems including airports, trains, highways, and bridges. They use math when preparing budgets and project costs. They also use mathematical models to simulate traffic flow and analyze engineering data.

If you are interested in a career as a transportation engineer, you should study these mathematical subjects:

- Algebra
- Geometry
- Trigonometry
- Calculus
- Differential Equations

Research other careers that require developing and analyzing mathematical models. Check out the career activity at the end of the unit to find out how **transportation engineers** use math.

Visualize Vocabulary

Use the ✔ words to complete the graphic. Write the name of a form of linear equation that best fits each equation.

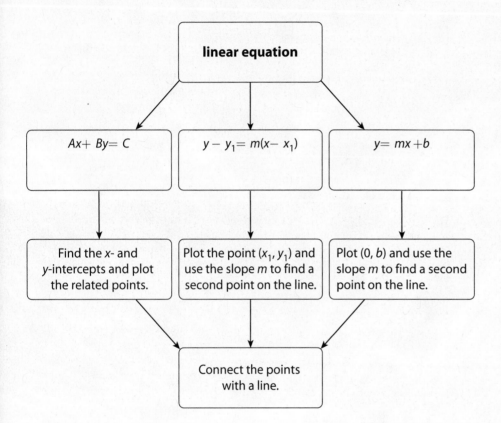

linear equation

$Ax + By = C$ $y - y_1 = m(x - x_1)$ $y = mx + b$

Find the x- and y-intercepts and plot the related points.

Plot the point (x_1, y_1) and use the slope m to find a second point on the line.

Plot $(0, b)$ and use the slope m to find a second point on the line.

Connect the points with a line.

Understand Vocabulary

Match the term on the left to the example on the right.

1. __?__ standard form of a quadratic equation   A. $y = -(x - 2)^2 + 9$

2. __?__ intercept form of a quadratic equation   B. $y = -(x + 1)(x - 5)$

3. __?__ vertex form of a quadratic function   C. $y = -x^2 + 4x + 5$

Active Reading

Tri-Fold Before beginning the unit, create a tri-fold to help you learn the concepts and vocabulary in this unit. Fold the paper into three sections. Label the columns "What I Know," "What I Need to Know," and "What I Learned." Complete the first two columns before you read. After studying the unit, complete the third column.

Graphing Quadratic Functions

Essential Question: How can you use the graph of a quadratic function to solve real-world problems?

REAL WORLD VIDEO
Projectile motion describes the height of an object thrown or fired into the air. The height of a football, volleyball, or any projectile can be modeled by a quadratic equation.

MODULE PERFORMANCE TASK PREVIEW

Throwing for a Completion

Do you wonder how fast a football leaves the hands of a quarterback or how high up it goes? Some professionals can throw approximately 45 miles per hour or faster. The height the ball reaches depends on the initial velocity as well as the angle at which it was thrown. You can use a mathematical model to see how high a football is at different times.

Are (YOU) Ready?

Complete these exercises to review skills you will need for this module.

Linear Functions

Example 1

Tell whether $6x - 2y = 9$ represents a linear function.

When a linear equation is written in standard form, the following are true.

- x and y both have exponents of 1.

- x and y are not multiplied together.

- x and y do not appear in denominators, exponents, or radicands.

$6x - 2y = 9$ represents a linear function.

Tell whether the equation represents a linear function.

1. $y = 3x^2 + 4x + 1$ **2.** $3y = 12 - \frac{1}{2}x$ **3.** $y = 2x + 5$

Algebraic Representations of Transformations

Example 2

The vertices of a triangle are $A(-3, 1)$, $B(0, -2)$, and $C(-4, 2)$. Find the vertices if the figure is translated by the rule $(x, y) \rightarrow (x + 4, y - 3)$.

A $(-3, 1) \rightarrow A'(-3 + 4, 1 - 3)$, so $A'(1, -2)$ Add 4 to each x-coordinate

B $(0, -2) \rightarrow B'(0 + 4, -2 - 3)$, so $B'(4, -5)$ and subtract 3 from each

C $(-4, 2) \rightarrow C'(-4 + 4, 2 - 3)$, so $C'(0, -1)$ y-coordinate.

The vertices of a triangle are $A(0, 3)$, $B(-2, -4)$, and $C(1, 5)$. Find the new vertices.

4. Use the rule $(x, y) \rightarrow (x - 2, y + 4)$ to translate each vertex.

5. Use the rule $(x, y) \rightarrow (x + 1, y - 2)$ to translate each vertex.

Algebraic Expressions

Example 3

Find the value of $x^2 + 5x - 3$ when $x = 2$.

$x^2 + 5x - 3$

$(2)^2 + 5(2) - 3$ Substitute 2 for x.

$4 + 10 - 3$ Follow the order of operations.

11

Find the value.

6. $x^2 - 7x + 9$ when $x = 6$ **7.** $2x^2 + 4x - 7$ when $x = -3$

19.1 Understanding Quadratic Functions

Essential Question: What is the effect of the constant *a* on the graph of $f(x) = ax^2$?

⊘ Explore Understanding the Parent Quadratic Function

A function that can be represented in the form of $f(x) = ax^2 + bx + c$ is called a **quadratic function**. The coefficients *a*, *b*, and *c*, are constants where $a \neq 0$. The greatest exponent of the variable *x* is 2. The most basic quadratic function is $f(x) = x^2$, which is the parent quadratic function.

Ⓐ Here is an incomplete table of values for the parent quadratic function. Complete it.

x	$f(x) = x^2$
−3	$f(x) = x^2 = (-3)^2 = 9$
?	4
−1	?
0	0
1	1
2	?
3	?

Ⓑ Plot the ordered pairs as points on a graph, and connect the points to sketch a curve.

The curve is called a **parabola**. The point through which the parabola turns direction is called its **vertex**. The vertex occurs at $(0, 0)$ for this function. A vertical line that passes through the vertex and divides the parabola into two symmetrical halves is called the **axis of symmetry**. For this function, the axis of symmetry is the *y*-axis.

Reflect

1. **Discussion** What is the domain of $f(x) = x^2$?

2. **Discussion** What is the range of $f(x) = x^2$?

Graphing $g(x) = ax^2$ when $a > 0$

The graph $g(x) = ax^2$, is a vertical stretch or compression of its parent function $f(x) = x^2$. The graph opens upward when $a > 0$.

Vertical Stretch

$g(x) = ax^2$ with $|a| > 1$.

The graph of $g(x)$ is narrower than the parent function $f(x)$.

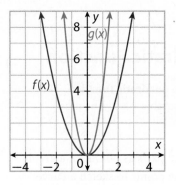

Vertical Compression

$g(x) = ax^2$ with $0 < |a| < 1$.

The graph of $g(x)$ is wider than the parent function $f(x)$.

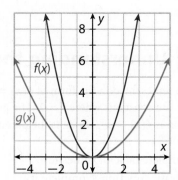

The domain of a quadratic function is all real numbers. When $a > 0$, the graph of $g(x) = ax^2$ opens upward, and the function has a **minimum value** that occurs at the vertex of the parabola. So, the range of $g(x) = ax^2$, where $a > 0$, is the set of real numbers greater than or equal to the minimum value.

Example 1 Graph each quadratic function by plotting points and sketching the curve. State the domain and range.

Ⓐ $g(x) = 2x^2$

x	$g(x) = 2x^2$
−3	18
−2	8
−1	2
0	0
1	2
2	8
3	18

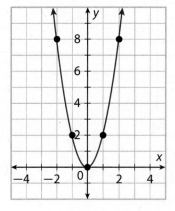

Domain: all real numbers x

Range: $y \geq 0$

(B) $g(x) = \frac{1}{2}x^2$

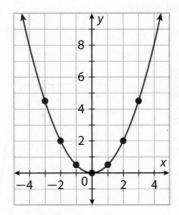

x	$g(x) = \frac{1}{2}x^2$
−3	$4\frac{1}{2}$
−2	2
0	0
2	2
3	$4\frac{1}{2}$

Domain: all real numbers
Range: $y \geq 0$

Reflect

3. For a graph that has a vertical compression or stretch, does the axis of symmetry change?

Your Turn

Graph each quadratic function. State the domain and range.

4. $g(x) = 3x^2$

5. $g(x) = \frac{1}{3}x^2$

🔧 Explain 2 Graphing $g(x) = ax^2$ when $a < 0$

The graph of $y = -x^2$ opens downward. It is a reflection of the graph of $y = x^2$ across the x-axis. So, When $a < 0$, the graph of $g(x) = ax^2$ opens downward, and the function has a **maximum value** that occurs at the vertex of the parabola. In this case, the range is the set of real numbers less than or equal to the maximum value.

Vertical Stretch

$g(x) = ax^2$ with $|a| > 1$.

The graph of $g(x)$ is narrower than the parent function $f(x)$..

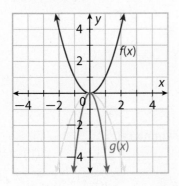

Vertical Compression

$g(x) = ax^2$ with $0 < |a| < 1$.

The graph of $g(x)$ is wider than the parent function $f(x)$.

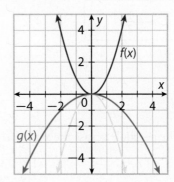

Example 2 Graph each quadratic function by plotting points and sketching the curve. State the domain and range.

(A) $g(x) = -2x^2$

x	$g(x) = 2x^2$
−3	−18
−2	−8
−1	−2
0	0
1	−2
2	−8
3	−18

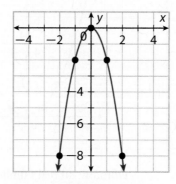

Domain: all real numbers

Range: $y \leq 0$

(B) $g(x) = -\dfrac{1}{2}x^2$

x	$g(x) = -\dfrac{1}{2}x^2$
−3	$-4\dfrac{1}{2}$
−2	−2
−1	$-\dfrac{1}{2}$
0	0
1	$-\dfrac{1}{2}$
2	−2
3	$-4\dfrac{1}{2}$

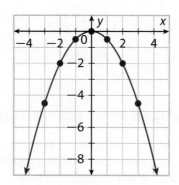

Domain: all real numbers

Range: $y \leq 0$

Reflect

6. Does reflecting the parabola across the x-axis ($a < 0$) change the axis of symmetry?

Your Turn

Graph each function. State the domain and range.

7. $g(x) = -3x^2$

8. $g(x) = -\frac{1}{3}x^2$

You can determine a function rule for a parabola with its vertex at the origin by substituting x and y values for any other point on the parabola into $g(x) = ax^2$ and solving for a.

Example 3 Write the rule for the quadratic functions shown on the graph.

Ⓐ

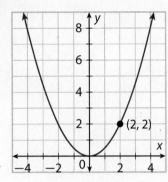

Use the point $(2, 2)$.

Start with the functional form.	$g(x) = ax^2$
Replace x and $g(x)$ with point values.	$2 = a(2)^2$
Evaluate x^2.	$2 = 4a$
Divide both sides by 4 to isolate a.	$\frac{1}{2} = a$
Write the function rule.	$g(x) = \frac{1}{2}x^2$

Ⓑ

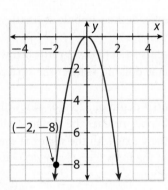

Use the point $\left(-2, \boxed{-8}\right)$.

Start with the functional form.	$g(x) = ax^2$
Replace x and $g(x)$ with point values.	$\boxed{-8} = a\left(\boxed{-2}\right)^2$
Evaluate x^2.	$-8 = \boxed{4}\,a$
Divide both sides by $\boxed{4}$ to isolate a.	$\boxed{-2} = a$
Write the function rule.	$g(x) = \boxed{-2x^2}$

Your Turn

9.

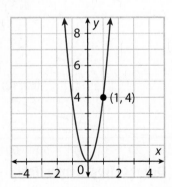

10.

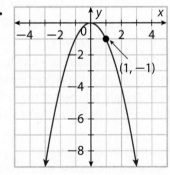

⚙ Explain 4 Modeling with a Quadratic Function

Real-world situations can be modeled by parabolas.

Example 4 For each model, describe what the vertex, *y*-intercept, and endpoint(s) represent in the situation it models, and then determine the equation of the function.

Ⓐ This graph models the depth in yards below the water's surface of a dolphin before and after it rises to take a breath and descends again. The depth *d* is relative to time *t*, in seconds, and $t = 0$ is when dolphin reaches a depth of 0 yards at the surface.

The *y*-intercept occurs at the vertex of the parabola at $(0, 0)$, where the dolphin is at the surface to breathe.

The endpoint $(-4, -32)$ represents a depth of 32 yards below the surface at 4 seconds before the dolphin reaches the surface to breathe.

The endpoint $(4, -32)$ represents a depth of 32 yards below the surface at 4 seconds after the dolphin reaches the surface to breathe.

The graph is symmetric about the *y*-axis with the vertex at the origin, so the function will be of the form $y = ax^2$, or $d(t) = at^2$.

Use a point to determine the equation.

$$d(t) = at^2$$
$$-32 = a(4)^2$$
$$-32 = a \cdot 16$$
$$-2 = a$$

The function is $d(t) = -2t^2$.

Ⓑ Satellite dishes reflect radio waves onto a collector by using a reflector (the dish) shaped like a parabola. The graph shows the height *h* in feet of the reflector relative to the distance *x* in feet from the center of the satellite dish.

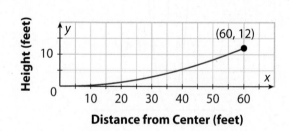

The *y*-intercept occurs at the vertex, which represents the distance $x = 0$ feet from the center of the dish.

The left endpoint represents the height $h = 0$ feet at the center of the dish.

The right endpoint represents the height $h = 12$ feet at the distance $x = 60$ feet from the center of the dish.

The function will be of the form $h(x) = ax^2$. Use $\boxed{60}$, $\boxed{12}$ to determine the equation.

$h(x) = ax^2$

$\boxed{12} = a \left(\boxed{60}\right)^2$

$12 = \boxed{3600}\ a$

$\boxed{a} = \dfrac{1}{300}$

$h(x) = \boxed{\dfrac{1}{300}}\ x^2$

Your Turn

Describe what the vertex, y-intercept, and endpoints represent in the situation, and then determine the equation of the function.

11. The graph shows the height h in feet of a rock dropped down a deep well as a function of time t in seconds.

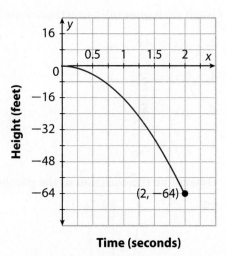

Elaborate

12. Discussion In example 1A the points $(3, 18)$ and $(-3, 18)$ did not fit on the grid. Describe some strategies for selecting points used to guide the shape of the curve.

13. Describe how the axis of symmetry of the parabola sitting on the y-axis can be used to help plot the graph of $f(x) = ax^2$.

14. Essential Question Check-In How can you use the value of a to predict the shape of $f(x) = ax^2$ without plotting points?

⭐ Evaluate: Homework and Practice

• Online Homework
• Hints and Help
• Extra Practice

1. Plot the function $f(x) = x^2$ and $g(x) = -x^2$ on a coordinate grid.

   Which of the following features are the same and which are different for the two functions?

   a. Domain

   b. Range

   c. Vertex

   d. Axis of symmetry

   e. Minimum

   f. Maximum

Graph each quadratic function. State the domain and range.

2. $g(x) = 4x^2$

3. $g(x) = \frac{1}{4}x^2$

4. $g(x) = \frac{3}{2}x^2$

5. $g(x) = 5x^2$

6. $g(x) = -\frac{1}{4}x^2$

7. $g(x) = -4x^2$

8. $g(x) = -\frac{3}{2}x^2$

9. $g(x) = -5x^2$

Determine the equation of the parabola graphed.

10.

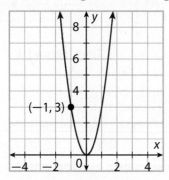

11.

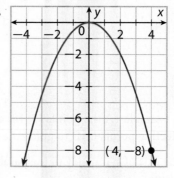

12.

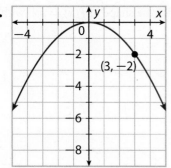

13.

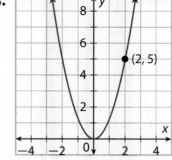

A cannonball fired horizontally appears to travel in a straight line, but drops to earth due to gravity, just like any other object in freefall. The height of the cannonball in freefall is parabolic. The graph shows the change in height of the cannonball (in meters) as a function of distance traveled (in kilometers). Refer to this graph for questions 14 and 15.

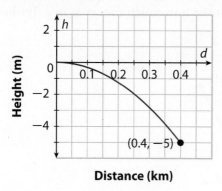

14. Describe what the vertex, y-intercept, and endpoint represent.

15. Find the function $h(d)$ that describes these coordinates.

A slingshot stores energy in the stretched elastic band when it is pulled back. The amount of stored energy versus the pull length is approximately parabolic. Questions 16 and 17 refer to this graph of the stored energy in millijoules versus pull length in centimeters.

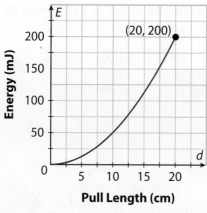

16. Describe what the vertex, y-intercept, and endpoint represent.

17. Determine the function, $E(d)$, that describes this plot.

Newer clean energy sources like solar and wind suffer from unsteady availability of energy. This makes it impractical to eliminate more traditional nuclear and fossil fuel plants without finding a way to store extra energy when it is not available.

One solution being investigated is storing energy in mechanical flywheels. Mechanical flywheels are heavy disks that store energy by spinning rapidly. The graph shows how much energy is in a flywheel, as a function of revolution speed.

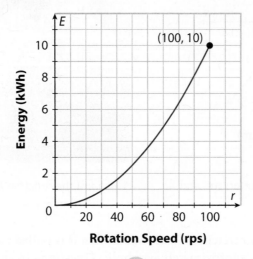

Rotation Speed (rps)

18. Describe what the vertex, y-intercept, and endpoint represent.

19. Determine the function, $E(r)$, that describes this plot.

Phineas is building a homemade skate ramp and wants to model the shape as a parabola. He sketches out a cross section shown in the graph.

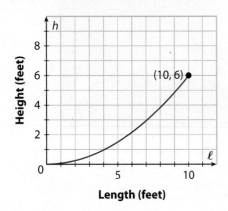

Length (feet)

20. Describe what the vertex y-intercept, and endpoint represent.

21. Determine the function, $h(\ell)$, that describes this plot.

22. Multipart Classification

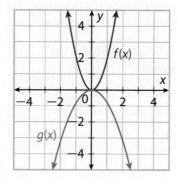

Determine if each statement about $f(x) = x^2$ and $g(x) = ax^2$ is True or False.

a. $a > 1$

b. $a < 0$

c. $a > 0$

d. $|a| < 0$

e. $|a| < 1$

f. The graphs of $f(x)$ and $g(x)$ share a vertex.

g. The graphs share an axis of symmetry.

h. The graphs share a minimum.

i. The graphs share a maximum.

23. Check for Reasonableness The graph of $g(x) = ax^2$ is a parabola that passes through the point $(-2, 2)$. Kyle says the value of a must be $-\frac{1}{2}$. Explain why this value of a is not reasonable.

24. Communicate Mathematical Ideas Explain how you know, without graphing, what the graph of $g(x) = \frac{1}{10}x^2$ looks like.

25. Critical Thinking A quadratic function has a minimum value when the function's graph opens upward, and it has a maximum value when the function's graph opens downward. In each case, the minimum or maximum value is the y-coordinate of the vertex of the function's graph. What can you say about a when the function $f(x) = ax^2$ has a minimum value? A maximum value? What is the minimum or maximum value in each case?

Lesson Performance Task

Kylie made a paper helicopter and is testing its flight time from two different heights. The graph compares the height of the helicopter during the two drops. The graph of the first drop is labeled $g(x)$ and the graph of the second drop is labeled $h(x)$.

a. At what heights did Kylie drop the helicopter? What is the helicopter's flight time during each drop?

b. If each graph is represented by a function of the form $f(x) = ax^2$, are the coefficients positive or negative? Explain.

c. Estimate the functions for each graph.

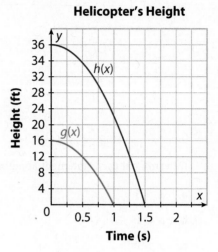

Helicopter's Height

19.2 Transforming Quadratic Functions

Resource Locker

Essential Question: How can you obtain the graph of $g(x) = a(x - h)^2 + k$ from the graph of $f(x) = x^2$?

⊘ Explore   Understanding Quadratic Functions of the Form $g(x) = a(x - h)^2 + k$

Every quadratic function can be represented by an equation of the form $g(x) = a(x - h)^2 + k$. The values of the parameters a, h, and k determine how the graph of the function compares to the graph of the parent function, $y = x^2$. Use the method shown to graph $g(x) = 2(x - 3)^2 + 1$ by transforming the graph of $f(x) = x^2$.

Ⓐ Graph $f(x) = x^2$.

Ⓑ Stretch the graph vertically by a factor of ⬚? to obtain the graph of $y = 2x^2$. Graph $y = 2x^2$.

   Notice that point $(2, 4)$ moves to point ⬚? .

Ⓒ Translate the graph of $y = 2x^2$ right 3 units and up 1 unit to obtain the graph of $g(x) = 2(x - 3)^2 + 1$. Graph $g(x) = 2(x - 3)^2 + 1$.

   Notice that point $(2, 8)$ moves to point ⬚? .

Ⓓ The vertex of the graph of $f(x) = x^2$ is ⬚? while the vertex of the graph of

   $g(x) = 2(x - 3)^2 + 1$ is ⬚? .

Reflect

1. **Discussion** Compare the minimum values of $f(x) = x^2$ and $g(x) = 2(x - 3)^2 + 1$. How is the minimum value related to the vertex?

2. **Discussion** What is the axis of symmetry of the function $g(x) = 2(x - 3)^2 + 1$? How is the axis of symmetry related to the vertex?

⊘ Explain 1   Understanding Vertical Translations

A **vertical translation** of a parabola is a shift of the parabola up or down, with no change in the shape of the parabola.

Vertical Translations of a Parabola
The graph of the function $f(x) = x^2 + k$ is the graph of $f(x) = x^2$ translated vertically.
If $k > 0$, the graph $f(x) = x^2$ is translated k units up.
If $k < 0$, the graph $f(x) = x^2$ is translated $\lvert k \rvert$ units down.

Example 1 Graph each quadratic function. Give the minimum or maximum value and the axis of symmetry.

(A) $g(x) = x^2 + 2$

Make a table of values for the parent function $f(x) = x^2$ and for $g(x) = x^2 + 2$. Graph the functions together.

x	$f(x) = x^2$	$g(x) = x^2 + 2$
−3	9	11
−2	4	6
−1	1	3
0	0	2
1	1	3
2	4	6
3	9	11

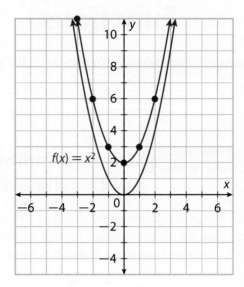

The function $g(x) = x^2 + 2$ has a minimum value of 2.

The axis of symmetry of $g(x) = x^2 + 2$ is $x = 0$.

(B) $g(x) = x^2 - 5$

Make a table of values for the parent function $f(x) = x^2$ and for $g(x) = x^2 - 5$. Graph the functions together.

x	$f(x) = x^2$	$g(x) = x^2 - 5$
−3	9	4
−2	4	−1
−1	1	−4
0	0	−5
1	1	−4
2	4	−1
3	9	4

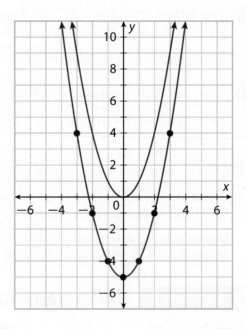

The function $g(x) = x^2 - 5$ has a minimum value of −5.

The axis of symmetry of $g(x) = x^2 - 5$ is $x = 0$.

3. How do the values in the table for $g(x) = x^2 + 2$ compare with the values in the table for the parent function $f(x) = x^2$?

4. How do the values in the table for $g(x) = x^2 - 5$ compare with the values in the table for the parent function $f(x) = x^2$?

Your Turn

Graph each quadratic function. Give the minimum or maximum value and the axis of symmetry.

5. $g(x) = x^2 + 4$

6. $g(x) = x^2 - 7$

🔧 Explain 2 Understanding Horizontal Translations

A **horizontal translation** of a parabola is a shift of the parabola left or right, with no change in the shape of the parabola.

Horizontal Translations of a Parabola

The graph of the function $f(x) = (x - h)^2$ is the graph of $f(x) = x^2$ translated horizontally.

If $h > 0$, the graph $f(x) = x^2$ is translated h units right.

If $h < 0$, the graph $f(x) = x^2$ is translated $|h|$ units left.

Example 2 Graph each quadratic function. Give the minimum or maximum value and the axis of symmetry.

Ⓐ $g(x) = (x - 1)^2$

Make a table of values for the parent function $f(x) = x^2$ and for $g(x) = (x - 1)^2$. Graph the functions together.

x	$f(x) = x^2$	$g(x) = (x-1)^2$
−3	9	16
−2	4	9
−1	1	4
0	0	1
1	1	0
2	4	1
3	9	4

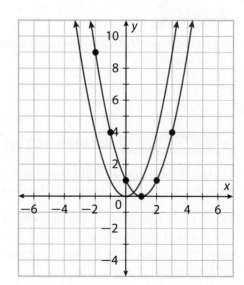

The function $g(x) = (x - 1)^2$ has a minimum value of 0.

The axis of symmetry of $g(x) = (x - 1)^2$ is $x = 1$.

Ⓑ $g(x) = (x + 1)^2$

Make a table of values and graph the functions together.

x	$f(x) = x^2$	$g(x) = (x + 1)^2$
−3	9	4
−2	4	1
−1	1	0
0	0	1
1	1	4
2	4	9
3	9	16

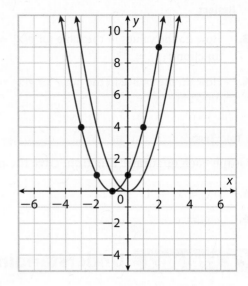

The function $g(x) = (x + 1)^2$ has a minimum value of 0.

The axis of symmetry of $g(x) = (x + 1)^2$ is $x = -1$.

Reflect

7. How do the values in the table for $g(x) = (x - 1)^2$ compare with the values in the table for the parent function $f(x) = x^2$?

8. How do the values in the table for $g(x) = (x + 1)^2$ compare with the values in the table for the parent function $f(x) = x^2$?

Your Turn

Graph each quadratic function. Give the minimum or maximum value and the axis of symmetry.

9. $g(x) = (x - 2)^2$

10. $g(x) = (x + 3)^2$

🎸 **Explain 3** **Graphing $g(x) = a(x - h)^2 + k$**

The **vertex form of a quadratic function** is $g(x) = a(x - h)^2 + k$, where the point (h, k) is the vertex. The *axis of symmetry* of a quadratic function in this form is the vertical line $x = h$.

To graph a quadratic function in the form $g(x) = a(x - h)^2 + k$, first identify the vertex (h, k). Next, consider the sign of a to determine whether the graph opens upward or downward. If a is positive, the graph opens upward. If a is negative, the graph opens downward. Then generate two points on each side of the vertex. Using those points, sketch the graph of the function.

Example 3 **Graph each quadratic function.**

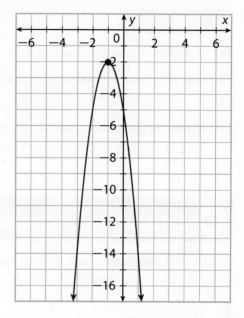

A $g(x) = -3(x+1)^2 - 2$

Identify the vertex.

The vertex is at $(-1, -2)$.

Make a table for the function. Find two points on each side of the vertex.

x	−3	−2	−1	0	1
g(x)	−14	−5	−2	−5	−14

Plot the points and draw a parabola through them.

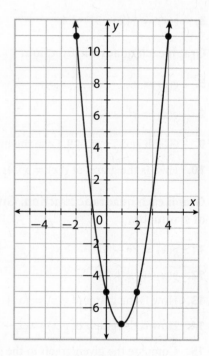

B $g(x) = 2(x-1)^2 - 7$

Identify the vertex.

The vertex is at $(1, -7)$.

Make a table for the function. Find two points on each side of the vertex.

x	−2	0	1	2	4
g(x)	11	−5	−7	−5	11

Plot the points and draw a parabola through them.

Reflect

11. How do you tell from the equation whether the vertex is a maximum value or a minimum value?

Your Turn

Graph each quadratic function.

12. $g(x) = -(x-2)^2 + 4$

13. $g(x) = 2(x+3)^2 - 1$

Elaborate

14. How does the value of k in $g(x) = x^2 + k$ affect the translation of $f(x) = x^2$?

15. How does the value of h in $g(x) = (x - h)^2$ affect the translation of $f(x) = x^2$?

16. In $g(x) = a(x - h)^2 + k$, what are the coordinates of the vertex?

17. **Essential Question Check-In** How can you use the values of a, h, and k, to obtain the graph of $g(x) = a(x - h)^2 + k$ from the graph $f(x) = x^2$?

★ Evaluate: Homework and Practice

• Online Homework
• Hints and Help
• Extra Practice

Graph each quadratic function by transforming the graph of $f(x) = x^2$. Describe the transformations.

1. $g(x) = 2(x - 2)^2 + 5$

2. $g(x) = 2(x + 3)^2 - 6$

3. $g(x) = \frac{1}{2}(x - 3)^2 - 4$

4. $g(x) = 3(x - 4)^2 - 2$

Graph each quadratic function.

5. $g(x) = x^2 - 2$

6. $g(x) = x^2 + 5$

7. $g(x) = x^2 - 6$

8. $g(x) = x^2 + 3$

9. Graph $g(x) = x^2 - 9$. Give the minimum or maximum value and the axis of symmetry.

10. How is the graph of $g(x) = x^2 + 12$ related to the graph of $f(x) = x^2$?

Graph each quadratic function. Give the minimum or maximum value and the axis of symmetry.

11. $g(x) = (x - 3)^2$

12. $g(x) = (x + 2)^2$

13. How is the graph of $g(x) = (x + 12)^2$ related to the graph of $f(x) = x^2$?

14. How is the graph of $g(x) = (x - 10)^2$ related to the graph of $f(x) = x^2$?

15. Compare the given graph to the graph of the parent function $f(x) = x^2$. Describe how the parent function must be translated to get the graph shown here.

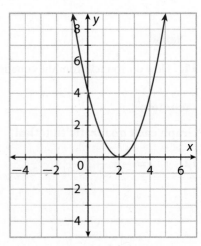

16. For the function $g(x) = (x - 9)^2$ give the minimum or maximum value and the axis of symmetry.

Graph each quadratic function. Give the minimum or maximum value and the axis of symmetry.

17. $g(x) = (x - 1)^2 - 5$

18. $g(x) = -(x + 2)^2 + 5$

19. $g(x) = \frac{1}{4}(x + 1)^2 - 7$

20. $g(x) = -\frac{1}{3}(x + 3)^2 + 8$

21. Compare the given graph to the graph of the parent function $f(x) = x^2$. Describe how the parent function must be translated to get the graph shown here.

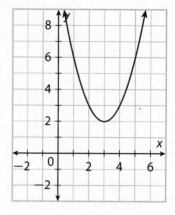

22. Multiple Representations Select the equation for the function represented by the graph of a parabola that is a translation of $f(x) = x^2$. The graph has been translated 11 units to the left and 5 units down.

   a. $g(x) = (x - 11)^2 - 5$

   b. $g(x) = (x + 11)^2 - 5$

   c. $g(x) = (x + 11)^2 + 5$

   d. $g(x) = (x - 11)^2 + 5$

   e. $g(x) = (x - 5)^2 - 11$

   f. $g(x) = (x - 5)^2 + 11$

   g. $g(x) = (x + 5)^2 - 11$

   h. $g(x) = (x + 5)^2 + 11$

H.O.T. Focus on Higher Order Thinking

Critical Thinking Use a graphing calculator to compare the graphs of $y = (2x)^2$, $y = (3x)^2$, and $y = (4x)^2$ with the graph of the parent function $y = x^2$. Then compare the graphs of $y = \left(\frac{1}{2}x\right)^2$, $y = \left(\frac{1}{3}x\right)^2$, and $y = \left(\frac{1}{4}x\right)^2$ with the graph of the parent function $y = x^2$.

23. Explain how the parameter b horizontally stretches or compresses the graph of $y = (bx)^2$ when $b > 1$.

24. Explain how the parameter b horizontally stretches or compresses the graph of $y = (bx)^2$ when $0 < b < 1$.

25. Explain the Error Nina is trying to write an equation for the function represented by the graph of a parabola that is a translation of $f(x) = x^2$. The graph has been translated 4 units to the right and 2 units up. She writes the function as $g(x) = (x + 4)^2 + 2$. Explain the error.

26. Multiple Representations A group of engineers drop an experimental tennis ball from a catwalk and let it fall to the ground. The tennis ball's height above the ground (in feet) is given by a function of the form $f(t) = a(t - h)^2 + k$ where t is the time (in seconds) after the tennis ball was dropped. Use the graph to find the equation for $f(t)$.

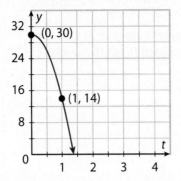

27. Make a Prediction For what values of a and c will the graph of $f(x) = ax^2 + c$ have one x-intercept?

Lesson Performance Task

The path a baseball takes after it has been hit is modeled by the graph. The baseball's height above the ground is given by a function of the form $f(t) = a(t - h)^2 + k$, where t is the time in seconds since the baseball was hit.

Baseball's Height

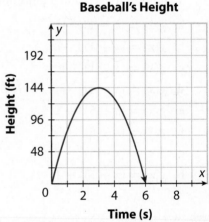

a. What is the baseball's maximum height? At what time was the baseball at its maximum height?

b. When does the baseball hit the ground?

c. Find an equation for $f(t)$.

d. A player hits a second baseball. The second baseball's path is modeled by the function $g(t) = -16(t - 4)^2 + 256$. Which baseball has a greater maximum height? Which baseball is in the air for the longest?

19.3 Interpreting Vertex Form and Standard Form

Essential Question: How can you change the vertex form of a quadratic function to standard form?

Explore   Identifying Quadratic Functions from Their Graphs

Determine whether a function is a quadratic function by looking at its graph. If the graph of a function is a parabola, then the function is a quadratic function. If the graph of a function is not a parabola, then the function is not a quadratic function.

Use a graphing calculator to graph each of the functions. Set the viewing window to show -10 to 10 on both axes. Determine whether each function is a quadratic function.

(A)   Use a graphing calculator to graph $f(x) = x + 1$.

(B)   Determine whether the function $f(x) = x + 1$ is a quadratic function.

The function $f(x) = x + 1$ ⬜?⬜ a quadratic function.

(C)   Use a graphing calculator to graph $f(x) = x^2 + 2x - 6$.

(D)   Determine whether the function $f(x) = x^2 + 2x - 6$ is a quadratic function.

The function $f(x) = x^2 + 2x - 6$ ⬜?⬜ a quadratic function.

(E)   Use a graphing calculator to graph $f(x) = 2^x$.

(F)   Determine whether the function $f(x) = 2^x$ is a quadratic function.

The function $f(x) = 2^x$ ⬜?⬜ a quadratic function.

Ⓖ Use a graphing calculator to graph $f(x) = 2x^2 - 3$.

Ⓗ Determine whether the function $f(x) = 2x^2 - 3$ is a quadratic function.

The function $f(x) = 2x^2 - 3$ ⬚? a quadratic function.

Ⓘ Use a graphing calculator to graph $f(x) = -(x-3)^2 + 7$.

Ⓙ Determine whether the function $f(x) = -(x-3)^2 + 7$ is a quadratic function.

The function $f(x) = -(x-3)^2 + 7$ ⬚? a quadratic function.

Ⓚ Use a graphing calculator to graph $f(x) = \sqrt{x}$.

Ⓛ Determine whether the function $f(x) = \sqrt{x}$ is a quadratic function.

The function $f(x) = \sqrt{x}$ ⬚? a quadratic function.

Reflect

1. How can you determine whether a function is quadratic or not by looking at its graph?

2. **Discussion** How can you tell if a function is a quadratic function by looking at the equation?

⏺ Explain 1 Identifying Quadratic Functions in Standard Form

If a function is quadratic, it can be represented by an equation of the form $y = ax^2 + bx + c$, where a, b, and c are real numbers and $a \neq 0$. This is called the **standard form of a quadratic equation**.

The axis of symmetry for a quadratic equation in standard form is given by the equation $x = -\frac{b}{2a}$. The vertex of a quadratic equation in standard form is given by the coordinates $\left(-\frac{b}{2a}, f\left(-\frac{b}{2a}\right)\right)$.

Example 1   Determine whether the function represented by each equation is quadratic. If so, give the axis of symmetry and the coordinates of the vertex.

(A) $y = -2x + 20$

   $y = -2x + 20$ Compare to $y = ax^2 + bx + c$.

   This is not a quadratic function because $a = 0$.

(B) $y + 3x^2 = -4$

   Rewrite the function in the form $y = ax^2 + bx + c$.

   $y = -3x^2 - 4$

   Compare to $y = ax^2 + bx + c$.

   This is a quadratic function.

   If $y + 3x^2 = -4$ is a quadratic function, give the axis of symmetry. $x = 0$

   If $y + 3x^2 = -4$ is a quadratic function, give the coordinates of the vertex. $\left(0, -4\right)$

Reflect

3.   Explain why the function represented by the equation $y = ax^2 + bx + c$ is quadratic only when $a \neq 0$.

4.   Why might it be easier to determine whether a function is quadratic when it is expressed in function notation?

5.   How is the axis of symmetry related to standard form?

Your Turn

Determine whether the function represented by each equation is quadratic.

6. $y - 4x + x^2 = 0$ 7. $x + 2y = 14x + 6$

⚙ Explain 2   Changing from Vertex Form to Standard Form

It is possible to write quadratic equations in various forms.

Example 2   Rewrite a quadratic function from vertex form, $y = a(x - h)^2 + k$, to standard form, $y = ax^2 + bx + c$.

Ⓐ $y = 4(x - 6)^2 + 3$

$\quad y = 4(x^2 - 12x + 36) + 3 \qquad$ Expand $(x - 6)^2$.

$\quad y = 4x^2 - 48x + 144 + 3 \qquad$ Multiply.

$\quad y = 4x^2 - 48x + 147 \qquad$ Simplify.

The standard form of $y = 4(x - 6)^2 + 3$ is $y = 4x^2 - 48x + 147$.

Ⓑ $y = -3(x + 2)^2 - 1$

$\quad y = -3\left(\boxed{x^2 + 4x + 4} \right) - 1 \qquad$ Expand $(x + 2)^2$.

$\quad y = \boxed{-3x^2 - 12x - 12} - 1 \qquad$ Multiply.

$\quad y = \boxed{-3x^2 - 12x - 13} \qquad$ Simplify.

The standard form of $y = -3(x + 2)^2 - 1$ is $y = \boxed{-3x^2 - 12x - 13}$.

Reflect

8.   If in $y = a(x - h)^2 + k$, $a = 1$, what is the simplified form of the standard form, $y = ax^2 + bx + c$?

Your Turn

Rewrite a quadratic function from vertex form, $y = a(x - h)^2 + k$, to standard form, $y = ax^2 + bx + c$.

9. $y = 2(x + 5)^2 + 3$ **10.** $y = -3(x - 7)^2 + 2$

⚙ Explain 3   Writing a Quadratic Function Given a Table of Values

You can write a quadratic function from a table of values.

Example 3   Use each table to write a quadratic function in vertex form, $y = a(x - h)^2 + k$. Then rewrite the function in standard form, $y = ax^2 + bx + c$.

Ⓐ   The minimum value of the function occurs at $x = -3$.

The vertex of the parabola is $(-3, 0)$.

Substitute the values for h and k into $y = a(x - h)^2 + k$.

$y = a(x - (-3))^2 + 0$, or $y = a(x + 3)^2$

Use any point from the table to find a.

x	y
−6	9
−4	1
−3	0
−2	1
0	9

$y = a(x + 3)^2$

$1 = a(-2 + 3)^2 = a$

The vertex form of the function is $y = 1(x - (-3))^2 + 0$ or $y = (x + 3)^2$.

Rewrite the function $y = (x + 3)^2$ in standard form, $y = ax^2 + bx + c$.

$y = (x + 3)^2 = x^2 + 6x + 9$

The standard form of the function is $y = x^2 + 6x + 9$.

(B) The minimum value of the function occurs at $x = -2$.

The vertex of the parabola is is $(-2, -3)$.

Substitute the values for h and k into $y = a(x - h)^2 + k$.

$y = \boxed{a(x + 2)^2 - 3}$

Use any point from the table to find a. $a = \boxed{4}$

The vertex form of the function is $y = \boxed{4(x + 2)^2 - 3}$.

Rewrite the resulting function in standard form, $y = ax^2 + bx + c$.

$y = \boxed{4x^2 + 16x + 13}$

x	y
0	13
−1	1
−2	−3
−3	1
−4	13

Reflect

11. How many points are needed to find an equation of a quadratic function?

Your Turn

Use each table to write a quadratic function in vertex form, $y = a(x - h)^2 + k$. Then rewrite the function in standard form, $y = ax^2 + bx + c$.

12. The vertex of the parabola is $(2, 5)$.

x	y
−1	59
1	11
2	5
3	11
5	59

13. The vertex of the parabola is $(-2, -7)$.

x	y
0	−27
−1	−12
−2	−7
−3	−12
−4	−27

⚙ Explain 4 Writing a Quadratic Function Given a Graph

The graph of a parabola can be used to determine the corresponding function.

Example 4 Use each graph to find an equation for $f(t)$.

(A) A house painter standing on a ladder drops a paintbrush, which falls to the ground. The paintbrush's height above the ground (in feet) is given by a function of the form $f(t) = a(t - h)^2$ where t is the time (in seconds) after the paintbrush is dropped.

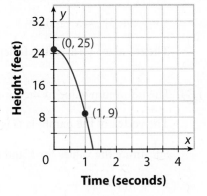

The vertex of the parabola is $(h, k) = (0, 25)$.

$f(t) = a(x - h)^2 + k$

$f(t) = a(t - 0)^2 + 25$

$f(t) = at^2 + 25$

Use the point (1, 9) to find a.

$f(t) = at^2 + 25$

$9 = a(1)^2 + 25$

$-16 = a$

The equation for the function is $f(t) = -16t^2 + 25$.

(B) A rock is knocked off a cliff into the water far below. The falling rock's height above the water (in feet) is given by a function of the form $f(t) = a(t - h)^2 + k$ where t is the time (in seconds) after the rock begins to fall.

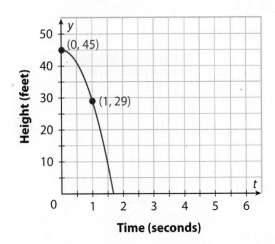

The vertex of the parabola is $(h, k) = \boxed{(0, 40)}$.

$f(t) = a(t - h)^2 + k$

$f(t) = a\left(t - \boxed{0}\right)^2 + \boxed{40}$.

$f(t) = \boxed{at^2 + 40}$

Use the point $(1, 24)$ to find a.

$f(t) = at^2 + \boxed{40}$

$\boxed{24} = a\,\boxed{1}^2 + \boxed{40}$

$a = \boxed{-16}$

The equation for the function is $f(t) = \boxed{-16t^2 + 40}$.

Reflect

14. Identify the domain and explain why it makes sense for this problem.

15. Identify the range and explain why it makes sense for this problem.

Your Turn

16. The graph of a function in the form $f(x) = a(x - h)^2 + k$, is shown. Use the graph to find an equation for $f(x)$.

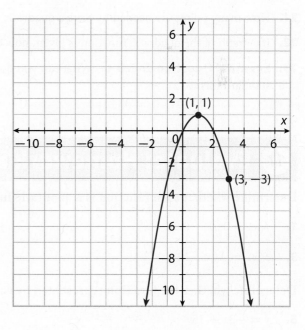

17. A roofer accidentally drops a nail, which falls to the ground. The nail's height above the ground (in feet) is given by a function of the form $f(t) = a(t - h)^2 + k$, where t is the time (in seconds) after the nail drops. Use the graph to find an equation for $f(t)$.

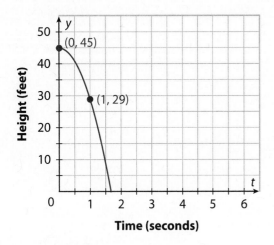

Time (seconds)

💬 Elaborate

18. Describe the graph of a quadratic function.

19. What is the standard form of the quadratic function?

20. Can any quadratic function in vertex form be written in standard form?

21. How many points are needed to write a quadratic function in vertex form, given the table of values?

22. If a graph of the quadratic function is given, how do you find the vertex?

23. **Essential Question Check-In** What can you do to change the vertex form of a quadratic function to standard form?

☆ Evaluate: Homework and Practice

• Online Homework
• Hints and Help
• Extra Practice

Determine whether each function is a quadratic function by graphing.

1. $f(x) = 0.01 - 0.2x + x^2$

2. $f(x) = \frac{1}{2}x - 4$

3. $f(x) = -4x^2 - 2$

4. $f(x) = 2^{x-3}$

Determine whether the function represented by each equation is quadratic.

5. $y = -3x + 15$

6. $y - 6 = 2x^2$

7. $3 + y + 5x^2 = 6x$

8. $y + 6x = 14$

9. Which of the following functions is a quadratic function? Select all that apply.

a. $2x = y + 3$

b. $2x^2 + y = 3x - 1$

c. $5 = -6x + y$

d. $6x^2 + y = 0$

e. $y - x = 4$

10. For $f(x) = x^2 + 8x - 14$, give the axis of symmetry and the coordinates of the vertex.

11. Describe the axis of symmetry of the graph of the quadratic function represented by the equation $y = ax^2 + bx + c$. when $b = 0$.

Rewrite each quadratic function from vertex form, $y = a(x - h)^2 + k$, to standard form, $y = ax^2 + bx + c$.

12. $y = 5(x - 2)^2 + 7$

13. $y = -2(x + 4)^2 - 11$

14. $y = 3(x + 1)^2 + 12$

15. $y = -4(x - 3)^2 - 9$

16. **Explain the Error** Tim wrote $y = -6(x + 2)^2 - 10$ in standard form as $y = 6x^2 + 24x + 14$. Find his error.

17. How do you change from vertex form, $f(x) = a(x - h)^2 + k$, to standard form, $y = ax^2 + bx + c$?

Use each table to write a quadratic function in vertex form, $y = a(x - h)^2 + k$. Then rewrite the function in standard form, $y = ax^2 + bx + c$.

18. The vertex of the function is $(6, -8)$.

x	y
10	24
8	0
6	-8
4	0
2	24

19. The vertex of the function is $(4, 7)$.

x	y
0	-1
2	5
4	7
6	5
8	-1

20. The vertex of the function is $(-2, -12)$.

x	y
2	52
0	4
-2	-12
-4	4
-6	52

21. The vertex of the function is $(-3, 10)$.

x	y
-1	-6
-2	6
-3	10
-4	6
-5	-6

22. **Make a Prediction** A ball was thrown off a bridge. The table relates the height of the ball above the ground in feet to the time in seconds after it was thrown. Use the data to write a quadratic model in vertex form and convert it to standard form. Use the model to find the height of the ball at 1.5 seconds.

Time (seconds)	Height (feet)
0	128
1	144
2	128
3	80
4	0

23. **Multiple Representations** A performer slips and falls into a safety net below. The function $f(t) = a(t - h)^2 + k$, where t represents time (in seconds), gives the performer's height above the ground (in feet) as he falls. Use the graph to find an equation for $f(t)$.

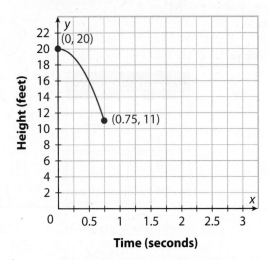

24. Represent Real-World Problems After a heavy snowfall, Ken and Karin made an igloo. The dome of the igloo is in the shape of a parabola, and the height of the igloo in inches is given by the function $f(x) = a(x - h)^2 + k$. Use the graph to find an equation for $f(x)$.

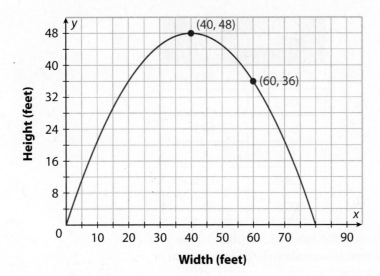

25. Check for Reasonableness Tim hits a softball. The function $f(t) = a(t - h)^2 + k$ describes the height (in feet) of the softball, and t is the time (in seconds). Use the graph to find an equation for $f(t)$. Estimate how much time elapses before the ball hits the ground. Use the equation for the function and your estimate to explain whether the equation is reasonable.

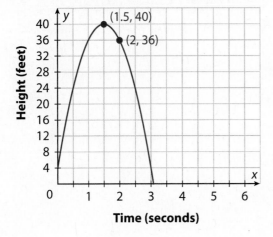

Lesson Performance Task

The table gives the height of a tennis ball t seconds after it has been hit, where the maximum height is 4 feet.

Time (s)	Height (ft)
0.125	3.75
0.25	4
0.375	3.75
0.5	3
0.625	1.75
0.75	0

a. Use the data in the table to write the quadratic function $f(t)$ in vertex form, where t is the time in seconds and $f(t)$ is the height of the tennis ball in feet.

b. Rewrite the function found in part a in standard form.

c. At what height was the ball originally hit? Explain.

Graphing Quadratic Functions

Essential Question: How can you use the graph of a quadratic function to solve real-world problems?

Key Vocabulary

axis of symmetry *(eje de simetría)*

parabola *(parábola)*

quadratic function *(función cuadrática)*

standard form of a quadratic equation *(forma estándar de una ecuación cuadrática)*

vertex *(vértice)*

KEY EXAMPLE   *(Lesson 19.3)*

The graph of a function in the form $f(x) = a(x - h)^2 + k$ is shown. Use the graph to find an equation for $f(x)$.

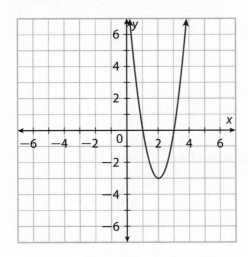

The vertex of the parabola is $(h, k) = (2, -3)$.

$f(x) = a(x - 2)^2 - 3$

From the graph, $f(3) = 0$. Substitute 3 for x and 0 for $f(x)$ and solve for a.

$0 = a(3 - 2)^2 - 3$

$3 = a$

The equation for the function is $f(x) = 3(x - 2)^2 - 3$.

KEY EXAMPLE   *(Lesson 19.2)*

Graph $g(x) = -2(x + 2)^2 + 2$.

The vertex is at $(-2, 2)$.

Make a table for the function. Find two points on each side of the vertex.

x	−4	−3	−2	−1	0
g(x)	−6	0	2	0	−6

Plot the points and draw a parabola through them.

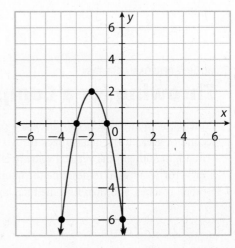

Graph each quadratic function. Give the minimum or maximum value and the axis of symmetry. *(Lessons 19.1, 19.2)*

1. $f(x) = 2x^2$

2. $g(x) = -(x+2)^2 + 4$

Write the equation for the function in each graph, in vertex form. *(Lesson 19.3)*

3.

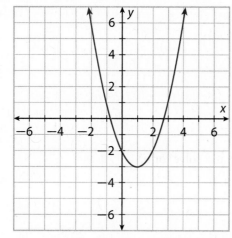

4.

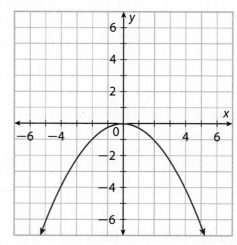

MODULE PERFORMANCE TASK

Throwing for a Completion

Professional quarterbacks can throw a football to a receiver with a velocity of 66 feet per second or greater. If a quarterback throws a pass with that velocity at a 30° angle with the ground, then the initial vertical velocity is 33 feet per second. How can you use the formula $h = -16t^2 + vt + h_0$ to describe the quarterback's pass? Find the maximum height that the football reaches, and then find the total amount of time that the pass is in the air.

(Ready) to Go On?

19.1–19.3 Graphing Quadratic Functions

Personal Math Trainer

• Online Homework
• Hints and Help
• Extra Practice

Graph each quadratic function. *(Lesson 19.1)*

1. $f(x) = -4x^2$

2. $g(x) = \dfrac{1}{2}x^2$

Describe the transformations necessary to get from the graph of the parent function $f(x) = x^2$ to the graph of each of the given functions. *(Lesson 19.2)*

3. $g(x) = (x + 4)^2 - 7$

4. $g(x) = 5(x - 6)^2 + 9$

Rewrite each function in standard form. *(Lesson 19.3)*

5. $f(x) = 2(x + 3)^2 - 6$

6. $f(x) = 3(x - 2)^2 + 3$

ESSENTIAL QUESTION

7. If the only information you have about a parabola is the location of its vertex, what other characteristics of the graph do you know?

Assessment Readiness

1. Consider the graph of $f(x) = \frac{2}{3}(x-3)^2$.
   Determine if each statement is True or False.
   A. The vertex is $(3, 0)$.
   B. The minimum value is 0.
   C. The axis of symmetry is $x = \frac{2}{3}$.

2. Is the given expression equivalent to $16^{\frac{3}{4}} + 32^{\frac{2}{5}}$?
   A. $\left(16^{\frac{1}{4}}\right)^3 + \left(32^{\frac{1}{5}}\right)^2$
   B. $\sqrt[4]{16^3} + \sqrt[5]{32^2}$
   C. $2^3 + 2^2$

3. Write the slope-intercept equation of the line that has the same slope as $y - 3 = \frac{1}{2}(x+3)$ and contains the point $(8, 4)$. Explain how you wrote the equation.

4. Write $f(x) = -2(x-5)^2 + 3$ in standard form. In which form is it easier to determine the maximum value of the graph? Explain.

Connecting Intercepts, Zeros, and Factors

Essential Question: How can you use intercepts of a quadratic function to solve real-world problems?

REAL WORLD VIDEO
Skateboard ramps come in many shapes and sizes. The iconic half-pipe ramp has a flat section in the middle and curved, raised sides. Skateboarders can use a half-pipe ramp to perform tricks, turns, and flips.

MODULE PERFORMANCE TASK PREVIEW

Skateboard Ramp

Skateboard riders often use curved ramps to perform difficult tricks and have fun. In this module, you will imagine that you are a design engineer hired by the local government to help construct a new skateboard ramp for the skateboard riders in the area. How do you model the curve of the ramp? Let's find out!

Are YOU Ready?

Complete these exercises to review skills you will need for this module.

Exponents

Example 1

Simplify.

$$x^5 \cdot x^3 = x^{5+3} = x^8$$

The bases are the same. Add the exponents.

$$\frac{x^9}{x^4} = x^{9-4} = x^5$$

The bases are the same. Subtract the exponents.

Simplify.

1. $b^2 \cdot b^6$

2. $\dfrac{a^{12}}{a^7}$

3. $\dfrac{n^4 \cdot n^7}{n^5}$

Algebraic Expressions

Example 2

Find the value of $3x - 6$ when $x = 2$.

$3x - 6$

$3(2) - 6$ Substitute 2 for *x*.

$6 - 6$ Follow the order of operations.

0

Find the value.

4. $6x + 3$ when $x = -\dfrac{1}{2}$

5. $2x - 5$ when $x = \dfrac{5}{2}$

6. $9x + 6$ when $x = -\dfrac{2}{3}$

Linear Functions

Example 3

Tell whether $y = x^2 - 7$ represents a linear function.

$y = x^2 - 7$ does not represent a linear function because *x* has an exponent of 2.

When a linear equation is written in standard form, the following are true.

- *x* and *y* both have exponents of 1.

- *x* and *y* are not multiplied together.

- *x* and *y* do not appear in denominators, exponents, or radicands.

Tell whether the equation represents a linear function.

7. $y = 3^x + 1$

8. $3x - 2y = 6$

9. $xy + 5 = 8$

20.1 Connecting Intercepts and Zeros

Essential Question: How can you use the graph of a quadratic function to solve its related quadratic equation?

⊘ Explore Graphing Quadratic Functions in Standard Form

A parabola can be graphed using its vertex and axis of symmetry. Use these characteristics, the y-intercept, and symmetry to graph a quadratic function.

Graph $y = x^2 - 4x - 5$ by completing the steps.

(A) Find the axis of symmetry.

$$x = -\frac{b}{2a}$$

$$= -\frac{\boxed{?}}{2 \cdot \boxed{?}}$$

$$= \boxed{?}$$

The axis of symmetry is $x = \boxed{?}$.

(B) Find the vertex.

$$y = x^2 - 4x - 5$$

$$= \boxed{?}^2 - 4 \cdot \boxed{?} - 5$$

$$= \boxed{?} - \boxed{?} - 5$$

$$= \boxed{?}$$

The vertex is $\left(\boxed{?}, \boxed{?} \right)$.

(C) Find the y-intercept.

$$y = x^2 - 4x - 5$$

$$y = \boxed{?}^2 - 4\boxed{?} + \left(\boxed{?} \right)$$

The y-intercept is $\boxed{?}$; the graph passes through $\left(0, \boxed{?} \right)$.

(D) Find two more points on the same side of the axis of symmetry as the y-intercept.

a. Find y when $x = 1$.

$$y = x^2 - 4x - 5$$

$$= \boxed{?}^2 - 4 \cdot \boxed{?} - 5$$

$$= \boxed{?} - \boxed{?} - 5$$

$$= \boxed{?}$$

The first point is $\left(\boxed{?}, \boxed{?} \right)$.

b. Find y when $x = -1$.

$$y = x^2 - 4x - 5$$

$$= \boxed{?}^2 - 4 \cdot \left(\boxed{?} \right) - 5$$

$$= \boxed{?} - \left(\boxed{?} \right) - 5$$

$$= \boxed{?}$$

The second point is $\left(\boxed{?}, \boxed{?} \right)$.

E Graph the axis of symmetry, the vertex, the y-intercept, and the two extra points on the same coordinate plane. Then reflect the graphed points over the axis of symmetry to create three more points, and sketch the graph.

Reflect

1. **Discussion** Why is it important to find additional points before graphing a quadratic function?

 Explain 1 **Using Zeros to Solve Quadratic Equations Graphically**

A **zero of a function** is an x-value that makes the value of the function 0. The zeros of a function are the x-intercepts of the graph of the function. A quadratic function may have one, two, or no zeros.

Quadratic equations can be solved by graphing the related function of the equation. To write the related function, rewrite the quadratic equation so that it equals zero on one side. Replace the zero with y.

Graph the related function. Find the x-intercepts of the graph, which are the zeros of the function. The zeros of the function are the solutions to the original equation.

Example 1 Solve by graphing the related function.

Ⓐ $2x^2 - 5 = -3$

    a. Write the related function. Add 3 to both sides to get $2x^2 - 2 = 0$. The related function is $y = 2x^2 - 2$.

    b. Make a table of values for the related function.

x	-2	-1	0	1	2
y	6	0	-2	0	6

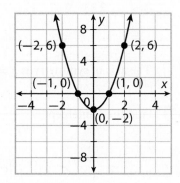

    c. Graph the points represented by the table and connect the points.

    d. The zeros of the function are -1 and 1, so the solutions of the equation $2x^2 - 5 = -3$ are $x = -1$ and $x = 1$.

Ⓑ $6x + 8 = -x^2$

    a. Write the related function. Add x^2 to both sides to get

    $\boxed{x^2} + 6x + 8 = \boxed{0}$. The related function is $\boxed{y} = \boxed{x^2} + 6x + 8$.

    b. Make a table of values for the related function.

x	-5	-4	-3	-2	-1
y	3	0	-1	0	3

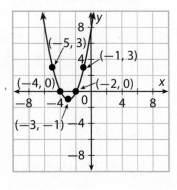

    c. Graph the points represented by the table and connect the points.

d. The zeros of the function are $\boxed{-4}$ and $\boxed{-2}$, so the solutions of the equation

$6x + 8 = -x^2$ are $x = \boxed{-4}$ and $x = \boxed{-2}$.

Reflect

2. How would the graph of a quadratic equation look if the equation has one zero?

Your Turn

Solve by graphing the related function.

3. $x^2 - 4 = -3$

⚙ Explain 2 Using Points of Intersection to Solve Quadratic Equations Graphically

You can solve a quadratic equation by rewriting the equation in the form $ax^2 + bx = c$ or $a(x - h)^2 = k$ and then using the expressions on each side of the equal sign to define a function.

Graph both functions and find the points of intersection. The solutions are the x-coordinates of the points of intersection on the graph. As with using zeros, there may be two, one, or no points of intersection.

Example 2 Solve each equation by finding points of intersection of two related functions.

Ⓐ $2(x - 4)^2 - 2 = 0$

$\qquad 2(x - 4)^2 = 2 \qquad$ Write as $a(x - h)^2 = k$.

a. Let $f(x) = 2(x - 4)^2$. Let $g(x) = 2$.

b. Graph $f(x)$ and $g(x)$ on the same graph.

c. Determine the points at which the graphs of $f(x)$ and $g(x)$ intersect.

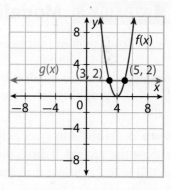

The graphs intersect at two locations: $(3, 2)$ and $(5, 2)$.

This means $f(x) = g(x)$ when $x = 3$ and $x = 5$.

So the solutions of $2(x - 4)^2 - 2 = 0$ are $x = 3$ and $x = 5$.

Ⓑ $3(x-5)^2 - 12 = 0$

$$3(x-5)^2 = \boxed{12}$$

a. Let $f(x) = \boxed{3}(x-5)^2$. Let $g(x) = \boxed{12}$.

b. Graph $f(x)$ and $g(x)$ on the same graph.

c. Determine the points at which the graphs of $f(x)$ and $g(x)$ intersect.

The graphs intersect at two locations:

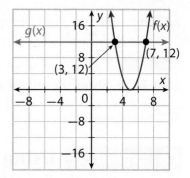

$\left(\boxed{3}, \boxed{12}\right)$ and $\left(\boxed{7}, \boxed{12}\right)$.

This means $f(x) = g(x)$ when $x = \boxed{3}$ and $x = \boxed{7}$.

Therefore, the solutions of the equation $f(x) = g(x)$ are $\boxed{3}$ and $\boxed{7}$.

So the solutions of $3(x-5)^2 - 12 = 0$ are $x = \boxed{3}$ and $x = \boxed{7}$.

Reflect

4. In Part B above, why is the x-coordinates the answer to the equation and not the y-coordinates?

Your Turn

5. Solve $3(x-2)^2 - 3 = 0$ by finding the points of intersection of the two related functions.

⊘ Explain 3 Modeling a Real-World Problem

Many real-world problems can be modeled by quadratic functions.

Example 3 Create a quadratic function for each problem and then solve it by using a graphing calculator.

Nature A squirrel is in a tree holding a chestnut at a height of 46 feet above the ground. It drops the chestnut, which lands on top of a bush that is 36 feet below the squirrel. The function $h(t) = -16t^2 + 46$ gives the height in feet of the chestnut as it falls, where t represents time. When will the chestnut reach the top of the bush?

 Analyze Information

Identify the important information.

- The chestnut is $\boxed{46}$ feet above the ground, and the top of the bush is $\boxed{36}$ feet below the chestnut.

- The chestnut's height as a function of time can be represented by
  $h(t) = \boxed{-16}t^2 + \boxed{46}$, where $(h)t$ is the height of the chestnut in feet as it is falling.

Formulate a Plan

Create a related quadratic equation to find the height of the chestnut in relation to time. Use $h(t) = -16t^2 + 46$ and insert the known value for h.

Solve

Write the equation that needs to be solved. Since the top of the bush is 36 feet below the squirrel, it is 10 feet above the ground.

$-16t^2 + 46 = 10$

Separate the function into $y = f(t)$ and $y = g(t)$. $f(t) = \boxed{-16} \, t^{\boxed{2}} + \boxed{46}$ and $g(t) = \boxed{10}$.

To graph each function on a graphing calculator, rewrite them in terms of x and y.

$y = \boxed{-16} \, x^{\boxed{2}} + \boxed{46}$ and $y = \boxed{10}$

Graph both functions. Use the intersect feature to find the amount of time it takes for the chestnut to hit the top of the bush.

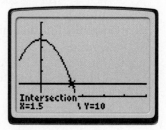

The chestnut will reach the top of the bush in $\boxed{1.5}$ seconds.

Justify and Evaluate

$$-16 \boxed{1.5}^{\,2} + 46 = 10$$

$$\boxed{-36} + 46 = 10$$

$$\boxed{10} = \boxed{10}$$

When t is replaced by 1.5 in the original equation, $-16t^2 + 46 = 10$ is true.

Reflect

6. In Example 3 above, the graphs also intersect to the left of the y-axis. Why is that point irrelevant to the problem?

Your Turn

7. **Nature** An egg falls from a nest in a tree 25 feet off the ground and lands on a potted plant that is 20 feet below the nest. The function $h(t) = -16t^2 + 25$ gives the height in feet of the egg as it drops, where t represents time. When will the egg land on the plant?

🕐 Explain 4   Interpreting a Quadratic Model

The solutions of a quadratic equation can be used to find other information about the situation modeled by the related function.

Example 4   Use the given quadratic function model to answer questions about the situation it models.

Ⓐ **Nature** A dolphin jumps out of the water. The quadratic function $h(t) = -16t^2 + 20t$ models the dolphin's height above the water in feet after t seconds. How long is the dolphin out of the water?

Use the level of the water as a height of 0 feet $h(0) = 0$, so the dolphin leaves the water at $t = 0$. When the dolphin reenters the water again, its height is 0 feet.

Solve $0 = -16t^2 + 20t$ to find the time when the dolphin reenters the water.

Graph the function on a graphing calculator, and find the other zero that occurs at $x > 0$.

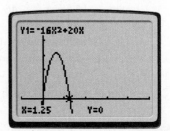

The zeros appear to be 0 and 1.25.

Check $x = 1.25$.

$-16(1.25)^2 + 20(1.25) = 0$ so 1.25 is a solution.

The dolphin is out of the water for 1.25 seconds.

Ⓑ **Sports** A baseball coach uses a pitching machine to simulate pop flies during practice. The quadratic function $h(t) = -16t^2 + 80t + 5$ models the height in feet of the baseball after t seconds. The ball leaves the pitching machine and is caught at a height of 5 feet. How long is the baseball in the air?

To find when the ball is caught at a height of 5 feet, you need to solve $5 = -16t^2 + 80t + 5$.

Graph Y1 = [＿＿＿＿＿] and Y2 = [＿] , and use the intersection feature to find x-values when $y = 5$.

From the graph, it appears that the ball is 5 feet above the ground when

$y = $ [＿] or $y = $ [＿] .

Therefore, the ball is in the air for [＿] − 0 = [＿] seconds.

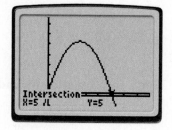

Your Turn

8. **Nature** The quadratic function $y = -16x^2 + 5x$ models the height, in feet, of a flying fish above the water after x seconds. How long is the flying fish out of the water?

💬 Elaborate

9. How is graphing quadratic functions in standard form similar to using zeros to solve quadratic equations graphically?

10. How can graphing calculators be used to solve real-world problems represented by quadratic equations?

11. **Essential Question Check-In** How can you use the graph of a quadratic function to solve a related quadratic equation by way of intersection?

• Online Homework
• Hints and Help
• Extra Practice

Solve each equation by graphing the related function and finding its zeros.

1. $3x^2 - 9 = -6$

2. $2x^2 - 9 = -1$

3. $4x^2 - 7 = -3$

4. $7x + 10 = -x^2$

5. $2x - 3 = -x^2$

6. $-1 = -x^2$

Solve each equation by finding points of intersection of two functions.

7. $2(x - 3)^2 - 4 = 0$

8. $(x + 2)^2 - 4 = 0$

9. $-(x - 3)^2 + 4 = 0$

10. $-(x + 2)^2 - 2 = 0$

11. $(x + 1)^2 - 1 = 0$

12. $(x + 2)^2 - 2 = 0$

Create a quadratic equation for each problem and then solve the equation with a related function using a graphing calculator.

13. Nature A bird is in a tree 30 feet off the ground and drops a twig that lands on a rosebush 25 feet below. The function $h(t) = -16t^2 + 30$, where t represents the time in seconds, gives the height h, in feet, of the twig above the ground as it falls. When will the twig land on the bush?

14. Nature A monkey is in a tree 50 feet off the ground and drops a banana, which lands on a shrub 30 feet below. The function $h(t) = -16t^2 + 50$, where t represents the time in seconds, gives the height h, in feet, of the banana above the ground as it falls. When will the banana land on the shrub?

15. Sports A trampolinist steps off from 15 feet above ground to a trampoline 13 feet below. The function $h(t) = -16t^2 + 15$, where t represents the time in seconds, gives the height h, in feet, of the trampolinist above the ground as he falls. When will the trampolinist land on the trampoline?

16. Physics A ball is dropped from 10 feet above the ground. The function $h(t) = -16t^2 + 10$, where t represents the time in seconds, gives the height h, in feet, of the ball above the ground. When will the ball be 4 feet above the ground?

Use the given quadratic function model to answer questions about the situation it models.

17. **Nature** A shark jumps out of the water. The quadratic function $f(x) = -16x^2 + 18x$ models the shark's height, in feet, above the water after x seconds. How long is the shark out of the water?

18. **Sports** A baseball coach uses a pitching machine to simulate pop flies during practice. The quadratic function $f(x) = -16x^2 + 70x + 10$ models the height in feet of the baseball after x seconds. How long is the baseball in the air if the ball is not caught?

19. The quadratic function $f(x) = -16x^2 + 11x$ models the height, in feet, of a flying fish above the water after x seconds. How long is the flying fish out of the water?

20. A football coach uses a passing machine to simulate 50-yard passes during practice. The quadratic function $f(x) = -16x^2 + 60x + 5$ models the height in feet of the football after x seconds. How long is the football in the air if the ball is not caught?

21. In each polynomial function in standard form, identify a, b, and c.

    a. $y = 3x^2 + 2x + 4$

    b. $y = 2x + 1$

    c. $y = x^2$

    d. $y = 5$

    e. $y = 3x^2 + 8x + 11$

22. Identify the axis of symmetry, y-intercept, and vertex of the quadratic function $y = x^2 + x - 6$ and then graph the function on a graphing calculator to confirm.

H.O.T. Focus on Higher Order Thinking

23. **Counterexamples** Pamela says that if the graph of a function opens upward, then the related quadratic equation has two solutions. Provide a counterexample to refute Pamela's claim.

24. **Explain the Error** Rodney was given the function $h(t) = -16t^2 + 50$ representing the height above the ground (in feet) of a water balloon t seconds after being dropped from a roof 50 feet above the ground. He was asked to find how long it took the balloon to fall 20 feet. Rodney used the equation $-16t^2 + 50 = 20$ to solve the problem. What was his error?

25. **Critical Thinking** If Jamie is given the graph of a quadratic function with only the x-intercepts and a random point labeled, can she determine an equation for the function? Explain.

Lesson Performance Task

Stella is competing in a diving competition. Her height in feet above the water is modeled by the function $f(x) = -16x^2 + 8x + 48$, where x is the time in seconds after she jumps from the diving board. Refer to the graph of the function and solve the related equation $0 = -16x^2 + 8x + 48$. What do the solutions mean in the context of the problem? Are there solutions that do not make sense? Explain.

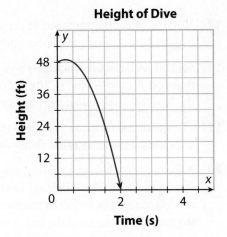

Height of Dive

20.2 Connecting Intercepts and Linear Factors

Essential Question: How are *x*-intercepts of a quadratic function and its linear factors related?

⊘ Explore   Connecting Factors and *x*–Intercepts

Use graphs and linear factors to find the *x*–intercepts of a parabola.

Ⓐ Graph $y = x + 4$ and $y = x - 2$ using a graphing calculator. Then sketch the graphs on a coordinate grid.

Ⓑ Identify the *x*-intercept of each line.

The *x*-intercepts are [?] and [?] .

Ⓒ The quadratic function $y = (x + 4)(x - 2)$ is the product of the two linear factors that have been graphed. Use a graphing calculator to graph the function $y = (x + 4)(x - 2)$. Then sketch a graph of the quadratic function on the same grid with the linear factors that have been graphed.

Ⓓ Identify the *x*-intercepts of the parabola.

The *x*-intercepts are [?] and [?] .

Ⓔ What do you notice about the *x*–intercepts of the parabola?

Reflect

1. Use a graph to determine whether $2x^2 + 5x - 12$ is the product of the linear factors $2x - 3$ and $x + 4$.

2. **Discussion** Make a conjecture about the linear factors and *x*-intercepts of a quadratic function.

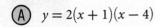 **Explain 1** **Rewriting from Factored Form to Standard Form**

A quadratic function is in **factored form** when it is written as $y = k(x - a)(x - b)$ where $k \neq 0$.

Example 1 Write each function in standard form.

(A) $y = 2(x + 1)(x - 4)$

Multiply the two linear factors.

$y = 2(x^2 - 4x + x - 4)$

$y = 2(x^2 - 3x - 4)$

Multiply the resulting trinomial by 2.

$y = 2x^2 - 6x - 8$

The standard form of $y = 2(x + 1)(x - 4)$ is
$y = 2x^2 - 6x - 8$.

(B) $y = 3(x - 5)(x - 2)$

Multiply the two linear factors.

$y = 3\left(\boxed{x - 5}\right)\left(\boxed{x - 2}\right)$

$y = 3\left(\boxed{x^2 - 7x + 10}\right)$

Multiply the resulting trinomial by 3.

$y = \boxed{3x^2 - 21x + 30}$

The standard form of $y = 3(x - 5)(x - 2)$ is
$y = 3x^2 - 21x + 30$.

Reflect

For the function $y = k(x - a)(x - b)$ when $k > 0$, $a \neq 0$, and $b \neq 0$, consider these questions.

3. For the standard form of the function, will the coefficient of the x-term be positive or negative if a and b are both positive? If a and b are both negative?

4. For the standard form of the function, will the constant term be positive or negative if a and b have the same sign? If a and b have different signs?

Your Turn

Write each function in standard form.

5. $y = (x - 7)(x - 1)$

6. $y = 4(x - 1)(x + 3)$

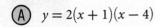 **Explain 2** **Connecting Factors and Zeros**

In the Explore you learned that the factors in factored form indicate the x-intercepts of a function. In a previous lesson you learned that the x-intercepts of a graph are the zeros of the function.

Example 2 Write each function in standard form. Determine x-intercepts and zeros of each function.

(A) $y = 2(x - 1)(x - 3)$

Write the function in standard form.

The factors indicate the x–intercepts.

* Factor $(x - 1)$ indicates an x–intercept of 1.

* Factor $(x - 3)$ indicates an x–intercept of 3.

$y = 2(x^2 - 3x - x + 3)$

$y = 2(x^2 - 4x + 3)$

$y = 2x^2 - 8x + 6$

The x-intercepts of a graph are the zeros of the function.

* An *x*–intercept of 1 indicates that the function has a zero of 1.

* An *x*–intercept of 3 indicates that the function has a zero of 3.

(B) $y = 2(x + 4)(x + 2)$

Write the function in standard form.

The factors indicate the *x*–intercepts.

* Factor $(x + 4)$ indicates an *x*–intercept of −4.

* Factor $(x + 2)$ indicates an *x*–intercept of –2.

The *x*–intercepts of a graph are the zeros of the function.

* An *x*–intercept of –4 indicates that the function has a zero of −4.

* An *x*–intercept of −2 indicates that the function has a zero of −2.

$$y = 2\boxed{x+4}\boxed{x+2}$$

$$y = 2\boxed{x^2 + 6x + 8}$$

$$y = \boxed{2x^2 + 12x + 16}$$

Reflect

7. Discussion What are the zeros of a function?

8. How many *x*-intercepts can quadratic functions have?

Your Turn

Write each function in standard form. Determine *x*–intercepts and zeros of each function.

9. $y = -2(x + 5)(x + 1)$

10. $y = 5(x - 3)(x - 1)$

⚙ Explain 3 Writing Quadratic Functions Given *x*-Intercepts

Given two quadratic functions $f(x) = (x - a)(x - b)$ and $g(x) = k(x - a)(x - b)$, where *k* is any non-zero real constant, examine the *x*-intercepts for each quadratic function.

$f(x) = (x - a)(x - b)$
 $0 = (x - a)(x - b)$
 $x - a = 0$ or $x - b = 0$
     $x = a$ $x = b$
	$g(x) = k(x - a)(x - b)$
	 $0 = k(x - a)(x - b)$
	 $0 = (x - a)(x - b)$
	 $x - a = 0$ or $x - b = 0$
	     $x = a$ $x = b$

Notice that $f(x) = (x - a)(x - b)$ and $g(x) = k(x - a)(x - b)$ have the same *x*-intercepts. You can use the factored form to construct a quadratic function given the *x*–intercepts and the value of *k*.

Example 3   For the two given intercepts, use the factored form to generate a quadratic function for each given constant k. Write the function in standard form.

(A) x-intercepts: 2 and 5; $k = 1$, $k = -2$, $k = 3$

Write the quadratic function with $k = 1$ using $f(x) = k(x - a)(x - b)$.

$f(x) = 1(x - 2)(x - 5)$

$f(x) = (x - 2)(x - 5)$

$f(x) = x^2 - 7x + 10$

Write the quadratic function with $k = -2$.

$f(x) = -2(x - 2)(x - 5)$

$f(x) = -2(x^2 - 7x + 10)$

$f(x) = -2x^2 + 14x - 20$

Write the quadratic function with $k = 3$.

$f(x) = 3(x - 2)(x - 5)$

$f(x) = 3(x^2 - 7x + 10)$

$f(x) = 3x^2 - 21x + 30$

(B) x-intercepts: -3 and 4; $k = 1$, $k = -3$, $k = 2$

Write the quadratic function with $k = 1$.

$f(x) = \boxed{(x + 3)(x - 4)}$

$f(x) = \boxed{x^2 - x - 12}$

Write the quadratic function with $k = -3$.

$f(x) = \boxed{-3(x + 3)(x - 4)}$

$f(x) = \boxed{-3x^2 + 3x + 36}$

Write the quadratic function with $k = 2$.

$f(x) = \boxed{2(x + 3)(x - 4)}$

$f(x) = \boxed{2x^2 - 2x - 24}$

Reflect

11. How are the functions with same intercepts but different constant factors the same? How are they different?

For the given two intercepts and three values of k generate three quadratic functions. Write the functions in factored form and standard form.

12. x-intercepts: 1 and 8; $k = 1, k = -4, k = 5$ **13.** x-intercepts: -7 and 3; $k = 1, k = -5, k = 7$

💬 Elaborate

14. If the x-intercepts of a quadratic function are 3 and 8, what can be said about the x-intercepts of its linear factors?

15. If a quadratic function has only one zero, it has to occur at the vertex of the parabola. Using the graph of a quadratic function, explain why.

16. How are x-intercepts and zeros related?

17. What would the factored form look like if there were only one x-intercept?

18. **Essential Question Check-In** How can you find x-intercepts of a quadratic function if its linear factors are known?

⭐ Evaluate: Homework and Practice

- Online Homework
- Hints and Help
- Extra Practice

Graph each quadratic function and each of its linear factors. Then identify the x-intercepts and the axis of symmetry of each parabola.

1. $y = (x - 2)(x - 6)$ **2.** $y = (x + 3)(x - 1)$

3. $y = (x - 5)(x + 2)$ **4.** $y = (x - 5)(x - 5)$

Write each function in standard form.

5. $y = 5(x - 2)(x + 1)$ **6.** $y = 2(x + 6)(x + 3)$

7. $y = -2(x + 4)(x - 5)$ **8.** $y = -4(x + 2)(x + 3)$

9. Which of the following is the correct standard form of $y = 3(x - 8)(x - 5)$?

   a. $y = 3x^2 + 39x - 120$

   b. $y = x^2 - 13x + 40$

   c. $y = 3x^2 - 39x + 120$

   d. $y = x^2 - 39x + 40$

   e. $y = 3x^2 + 13x + 120$

10. The area of a Japanese rock garden is
    $y = 7(x - 3)(x + 1)$. Write
    $y = 7(x - 3)(x + 1)$ in standard form.

Write each function in standard form. Determine x-intercepts and zeros of each function.

11. $y = -(2x - 4)(x - 2)$

12. $y = 2(x + 4)(x - 2)$

13. $y = -3(x + 1)(x - 3)$

14. $y = 2(x + 2)(x - 1)$

15. A soccer ball is kicked from ground level. The function $y = -16x(x - 2)$ gives the height (in feet) of the ball, where x is time (in seconds). After how many seconds will the ball hit the ground? Use a graphing calculator to verify your answer.

16. A tennis ball is tossed upward from a balcony. The height of the ball in feet can be modeled by the function $y = -4(2x + 1)(2x - 3)$ where x is the time in seconds after the ball is released. Find the maximum height of the ball and the time it takes the ball to reach this height. Determine how long it takes the ball to hit the ground.

For the two given intercepts, use the factored form to generate a quadratic function for each given constant k. Write the function in standard form.

17. x-intercepts: -5 and 3; $k = 1$, $k = -2$, $k = 5$

18. x-intercepts: 4 and 7; $k = 1$, $k = -3$, $k = 5$

H.O.T. Focus on Higher Order Thinking

19. **Explain the Error** For the given two intercepts, 3 and 9, $k = 4$, Kelly wrote a quadratic function in factored form, $f(x) = 4(x + 3)(x + 9)$, and in standard form, $f(x) = 4x^2 + 48x + 108$. What error did she make?

20. **Critical Thinking** How is the graph of $f(x) = 7(x + 3)(x - 2)$ similar to and different from the graph of $f(x) = -7x^2 - 7x + 42$?

21. **Make a Prediction** How could you find an equation of a quadratic function with zeros at -3 and at 1?

Lesson Performance Task

The cross-sectional shape of the archway of a bridge (measured in feet) is modeled by the function $f(x) = -0.5x^2 + 6x$ where $f(x)$ is the height of the arch and x is the horizontal distance from one side of the base. How wide is the arch at its base? Will a box truck that is 8 feet wide and 13.5 feet tall fit under the arch? If not, what is the maximum height a truck that is 8 feet wide and is passing under the bridge can be?

20.3 Applying the Zero Product Property to Solve Equations

Resource Locker

Essential Question: How can you use the Zero Product Property to solve quadratic equations in factored form?

🧭 Explore   Understanding the Zero Product Property

For all real numbers a and b, if the product of the two quantities equals zero, then at least one of the quantities equals zero.

Zero Product Property		
For all real numbers a and b, the following is true.		
Words	**Sample Numbers**	**Algebra**
If the product of two quantities equals zero, at least one of the quantities equals zero.	$9\left(\boxed{?}\right) = 0$ $0(4) = \boxed{?}$	If $ab = 0$, then $\boxed{?} = 0$ or $b = \boxed{?}$.

(A) Consider the equation $(x-3)(x+8) = 0$.   Let $a = x - 3$ and $b = \boxed{?}$.

(B) Since $ab = 0$, you know that $a = 0$ or $b = 0$. $\boxed{?} = 0$ or $x + 8 = 0$

(C) Solve for x.

$x - 3 = 0$ or $x + 8 = 0$

$x = \boxed{?}$ $x = \boxed{?}$

(D) So, the solutions of the equation $(x-3)(x+8) = 0$ are $x = \boxed{?}$ and $x = \boxed{?}$.

(E) Recall that the solutions of an equation are the zeros of the related function. So, the solutions of the equation $(x-3)(x+8) = 0$ are the zeros of the related function $f(x) = \boxed{?}$ because they satisfy the equation $f(x) = 0$. The solutions of the related function $f(x) = \boxed{?}$ are $\boxed{?}$ and $\boxed{?}$.

Reflect

1. Describe how you can find the solutions of the equation $(x-a)(x-b) = 0$ using the Zero Product Property.

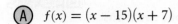

When given a function of the form $f(x) = (x + a)(x + b)$, you can use the Zero Product Property to find the zeros of the function.

Example 1 Find the zeros of each function.

Ⓐ $f(x) = (x - 15)(x + 7)$

Set $f(x)$ equal to zero. $(x - 15)(x + 7) = 0$

Apply the Zero Product Property. $x - 15 = 0$ or $x + 7 = 0$

Solve each equation for x. $x = 15$ $x = -7$

The zeros are 15 and -7.

Ⓑ $f(x) = (x + 1)(x + 23)$

Set $f(x)$ equal to zero. $(x + 1)(x + 23) = \boxed{0}$

Apply the Zero Product Property. $x + \boxed{1} = 0$ or $x + 23 = \boxed{0}$

Solve for x. $x = \boxed{-1}$ $x = \boxed{-23}$

The zeros are $\boxed{-1}$ and $\boxed{-23}$.

Reflect

2. **Discussion** Jordie was asked to identify the zeros of the function $f(x) = (x - 5)(x + 3)$. Her answers were $x = -5$ and $x = 3$. Do you agree or disagree? Explain.

3. How would you find the zeros of the function $f(x) = -4(x - 8)$?

4. What are the zeros of the function $f(x) = x(x - 12)$? Explain.

Your Turn

Find the zeros of each function.

5. $f(x) = (x - 10)(x - 6)$

6. $f(x) = 7(x - 13)(x + 12)$

Solving Quadratic Equations Using the Distributive Property and the Zero Product Property

The Distributive Property states that, for real numbers a, b, and c, $a(b + c) = ab + ac$ and $ab + ac = a(b + c)$. The Distributive Property applies to polynomials, as well. For instance, $3x(x - 4) + 5(x - 4) = (3x + 5)(x - 4)$. You can use the Distributive Property along with the Zero Product Property to solve certain equations.

Example 2 Solve each equation using the Distributive Property and the Zero Product Property.

Ⓐ $3x(x - 4) + 5(x - 4) = 0$

Use the Distributive Property to rewrite the expression $3x(x - 4) + 5(x - 4)$ as a product.

$$3x(x - 4) + 5(x - 4) = (3x + 5)(x - 4)$$

Rewrite the equation.

$$(3x + 5)(x - 4) = 0$$

Apply the Zero Product Property.

$3x + 5 = 0$ or $x - 4 = 0$

Solve each equation for x.

$3x = -5$ $x = 4$

$x = -\dfrac{5}{3}$

The solutions are $x = -\dfrac{5}{3}$ and $x = 4$.

Ⓑ $-9(x + 2) + 3x(x + 2) = 0$

Use the Distributive Property to rewrite the expression $-9(x + 2) + 3x(x + 2)$ as a product.

$$-9(x + 2) + 3x(x + 2) = \left(\boxed{-9} + 3x\right)\left(x + \boxed{2}\right)$$

Rewrite the equation.

$$\left(\boxed{-9} + 3x\right)\left(x + \boxed{2}\right) = 0$$

Apply the Zero Product Property.

$\boxed{-9} + 3x = 0$ or $x + \boxed{2} = 0$

Solve each equation for x.

$3x = \boxed{9}$ $x = \boxed{-2}$

$x = \boxed{3}$

The solutions are $x = \boxed{3}$ and $x = \boxed{-2}$.

Reflect

7. How can you solve the equation $5x(x - 3) + 4x - 12 = 0$ using the Distributive Property?

Your Turn

Solve each equation using the Distributive Property and the Zero Product Property.

8. $7x(x - 11) - 2(x - 11) = 0$

9. $-8x(x + 6) + 3x + 18 = 0$

🎯 Explain 3 Solving Real-World Problems Using the Zero Product Property

Example 3

The height of one diver above the water during a dive can be modeled by the equation $h = -4(4t + 5)(t - 3)$, where h is height in feet and t is time in seconds. Find the time it takes for the diver to reach the water.

Analyze Information

Identify the important information.

- The height of the diver is given by the equation
  $h = -4(4t + 5)(t - 3)$.
- The diver reaches the water when $h = \boxed{0}$.

Formulate a Plan

To find the time it takes for the diver to reach the water, set the equation equal to

$\boxed{0}$ and use the Zero Product Property to solve for t.

Solve

Set the equation equal to zero.	$-4(4t + 5)(t - 3) = 0$
Apply the Zero Product Property.	$4t + 5 = 0 \quad$ or $\quad t - 3 = 0$
Since $-4 \neq 0$, set the other factors equal to 0.	
Solve each equation for x.	$4t + 5 = 0 \quad$ or $\quad t - 3 = 0$
	$4t = \boxed{-5} \qquad\qquad t = \boxed{3}$
	$t = \boxed{-\dfrac{5}{4}}$

The zeros are $t = \boxed{-\dfrac{5}{4}}$ and $t = \boxed{3}$. Since time cannot be negative, the time it takes for the diver to reach the the water is $\boxed{3}$ seconds.

Justify and Evaluate

Check to see that the answer is reasonable by substituting 3 for t in the equation
$-4(4t + 5)(t - 3) = 0$.

$-4(4(3) + 5)((3) - 3) = -4(\boxed{12} + 5)(\boxed{3} - 3)$

$\qquad\qquad\qquad\quad = -4(\boxed{17})(\boxed{0})$

$\qquad\qquad\qquad\quad = \boxed{0}$

Since the equation is equal to $\boxed{0}$ for $t = 3$, the solution is reasonable.

The diver will reach the water after $\boxed{3}$ seconds.

Reflect

10. If you were to graph the function $f(t) = -4(4t + 5)(t - 3)$, what points would be associated with the zeros of the function?

Your Turn

11. The height of a golf ball after it has been hit from the top of a hill can be modeled by the equation $h = -8(2t - 4)(t + 1)$, where h is height in feet and t is time in seconds. How long is the ball in the air?

💬 Elaborate

12. Can you use the Zero Product Property to find the zeros of the function $f(x) = (x - 1) + (2 - 9x)$? Explain.

13. Suppose a and b are the zeros of a function. Name two points on the graph of the function and explain how you know they are on the graph. What are the x-coordinates of the points called?

14. **Essential Question Check-In** Suppose you are given a quadratic function in factored form that is set equal to 0. Why can you solve it by setting each factor equal to 0?

Find the solutions of each equation.

1. $(x - 15)(x - 22) = 0$

2. $(x + 2)(x - 18) = 0$

Find the zeros of each function.

3. $f(x) = (x + 15)(x + 17)$

4. $f(x) = \left(x - \dfrac{2}{9}\right)\left(x + \dfrac{1}{2}\right)$

5. $f(x) = -0.2(x - 1.9)(x - 3.5)$

6. $f(x) = x(x + 20)$

7. $f(x) = \dfrac{3}{4}\left(x - \dfrac{3}{4}\right)$

8. $f(x) = (x + 24)(x + 24)$

Solve each equation using the Distributive Property and the Zero Product Property.

9. $-6x(x + 12) - 15(x + 12) = 0$

10. $10(x - 3) - x(x - 3) = 0$

11. $5x\left(x + \dfrac{2}{3}\right) + \left(x + \dfrac{2}{3}\right) = 0$

12. $-(x + 4) + x(x + 4) = 0$

13. $7x(9 - x) + \dfrac{1}{3}(9 - x) = 0$

14. $-x(x - 3) + 6x - 18 = 0$

Solve using the Zero Product Property.

15. The height of a football after it has been kicked from the top of a hill can be modeled by the equation $h = 2(-2 - 4t)(2t - 5)$, where h is the height of the football in feet and t is the time in seconds. How long is the football in the air?

16. **Football** During football practice, a football player kicks a football. The height h in feet of the ball t seconds after it is kicked can be modeled by the function $h = -4t(4t - 11)$. How long is the football in the air?

17. Physics The height of a flare fired from a platform can be modeled by the equation $h = 8t(-2t + 10) + 4(-2t + 10)$, where h is the height of the flare in feet and t is the time in seconds. Find the time it takes for the flare to reach the ground.

18. Diving The depth of a scuba diver can be modeled by the equation $d = 0.5t(3.5t - 28.25)$, where d is the depth in meters of the diver and t is the time in minutes. Find the time it takes for the diver to reach the surface. Give your answer to the nearest minute.

19. A group of friends tries to keep a small beanbag from touching the ground by kicking it. On one kick, the beanbag's height can be modeled by the equation $h = -2(t - 1) - 16t(t - 1)$, where h is the height of the beanbag in feet and t is the time in seconds. Find the time it takes the beanbag to reach the ground.

20. Elizabeth and Markus are playing catch. Elizabeth throws the ball first. The height of the ball can be modeled by the equation $h = -16t(t - 5)$, where h is the height of the ball in feet and t is the time in seconds. Markus is distracted at the last minute and looks away. The ball lands at his feet. If the ball travels horizontally at an average rate of 3.5 feet per second, how far is Markus standing from Elizabeth when the ball hits the ground?

21. Match the function on the left with its zeros on the right.

A. $f(x) = 11(x - 9) + x(x - 9)$ a. $x = -11$ and $x = -9$

B. $f(x) = (x + 9)(x - 11)$ b. $x = 9$ and $x = -11$

C. $f(x) = 11(x - 9) - x(x - 9)$ c. $x = 9$ and $x = 11$

D. $f(x) = (x - 9)(x + 11)$ d. $x = -9$ and $x = 11$

E. $f(x) = -x(x + 9) - 11(x + 9)$

H.O.T. Focus on Higher Order Thinking

22. Explain the Error A student found the zeros of the function
$f(x) = 2x(x - 5) + 6(x - 5)$. Explain what the student did wrong. Then give the correct answer.
$2x(x - 5) + 6(x - 5) = 0$
$2x(x - 5) = 0$, so $2x = 0$, and $x = 0$, or
$x - 5 = 0$, so $x = 5$, or
$6(x - 5) = 0$, so $x = 5$
Zeros: 0, 5 and 5

23. Draw Conclusions A ball is kicked into the air from ground level. The height h in meters that the ball reaches at a distance d in meters from the point where it was kicked is given by $h = -2d(d - 4)$. The graph of the equation is a parabola.

a. At what distance from the point where it is kicked does the ball reach its maximum height? Explain.

b. Find the maximum height. What is the point $(2, h)$ on the graph of the function called?

24. Justify Reasoning Can you solve $(x - 2)(x + 3) = 5$ by solving $x - 2 = 5$ and $x + 3 = 5$? Explain.

25. Persevere in Problem Solving Write an equation to find three numbers with the following properties. Let x be the first number. The second number is 3 more than the first number. The third number is 4 times the second number. The sum of the third number and the product of the first and second numbers is 0. Solve the equation and give the three numbers.

Lesson Performance Task

The height of a pole vaulter as she jumps over the bar is modeled by the function $f(t) = -1.75(t - 0)(t - 3.5)$, where t is the time in seconds at which the pole vaulter leaves the ground.

a. Find the solutions of the related equation when $f(t) = 0$ using the Zero Product Property. What do these solutions mean in the context of the problem?

b. If the bar is 6 feet high, will the pole vaulter make it over?

Connecting Intercepts, Zeros, and Factors

Essential Question: How can you use intercepts of a quadratic function to solve real-world problems?

KEY EXAMPLE   *(Lesson 20.2)*

Generate the quadratic function with *x*-intercepts 3 and −2 and $k = 3$. Write the function in factored form and standard form.

Write the quadratic function with $k = 3$. Substitute the given values of the *x*-intercepts and *k* into $f(x) = k(x - a)(x - b)$ and simplify.

$f(x) = 3(x + 2)(x - 3)$

Write $f(x) = 3(x + 2)(x - 3)$ in standard form.

$$f(x) = 3(x + 2)(x - 3)$$
$$= 3x^2 - 3x - 18$$

KEY EXAMPLE   *(Lesson 20.3)*

Solve $2x(x - 2) + 4(x - 2) = 0$ by using the Distributive Property and the Zero Product Property.

Use the Distributive Property to rewrite the expression $2x(x - 2) + 4(x - 2)$ as a product of binomials.

$$2x(x - 2) + 4(x - 2) = (2x + 4)(x - 2)$$

Rewrite the equation.

$$(2x + 4)(x - 2) = 0$$

Apply the Zero Product Property.

$2x + 4 = 0$ and $x - 2 = 0$

Solve each equation for *x*.

$2x = -4$ $x = 2$

$x = -2$

The solutions are $x = -2$ and $x = 2$.

EXERCISES

Solve each equation by graphing. *(Lesson 20.1)*

1. $x^2 - 2x - 1 = 2$

2. $(x + 2)^2 - 4 = 0$

Write a function in factored and standard form for each k and set of x-intercepts. *(Lesson 20.2)*

3. x-intercepts: -3 and 4; $k = -2$

4. x-intercepts: 7 and 2; $k = 3$

Find the zeros of each function. *(Lesson 20.3)*

5. $f(x) = x(x + 17)$

6. $f(x) = -4(x - 2.3)(x - 4.6)$

MODULE PERFORMANCE TASK

Designing a Skateboard Ramp

The local government has made partial plans for the construction of a skateboard ramp, which are shown here. Your task is to complete the plans by modeling the parabolic curve of the ramp itself.

First, choose the total width of the parabola from point A to point C, which should be between 3 meters and 6 meters. Then, create an equation that models the parabola that starts at point A, reaches a minimum at point B, and ends at point C. Note that the x- and y-axes are marked in the diagram. Express your equation in standard form.

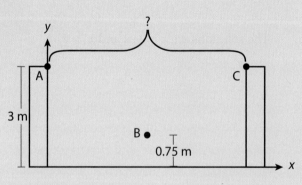

Complete the task, using graphs, numbers, or algebra to explain how you reached your conclusion.

(Ready) to Go On?

20.1–20.3 Connecting Intercepts, Zeros, and Factors

- Online Homework
- Hints and Help
- Extra Practice

Solve each equation by graphing. *(Lesson 20.1)*

1. $-4x + 4 = -x^2$

2. $-x^2 + 1 = 0$

Write a function in factored and standard form for each k and set of x-intercepts. *(Lesson 20.2)*

3. x-intercepts: 5 and -7; $k = -3$

4. x-intercepts: -1 and -8; $k = 4$

Find the zeros of each function. *(Lesson 20.3)*

5. $f(x) = -8(x + 7)(x - 8.6)$

6. $f(x) = x(x - 42)$

7. $f(x) = 9x(x - 4) + 3(x - 4)$

8. $f(x) = -2x(x + 4) + 6x + 24$

ESSENTIAL QUESTION

9. How can you use factoring to solve quadratic equations in standard form?

Assessment Readiness

1. Solve $8x(7 - x) + \frac{1}{5}(7 - x) = 0$. Is each of the following a solution of the equation?

   A. $x = -7$

   B. $x = -\frac{8}{5}$

   C. $x = -\frac{1}{40}$

2. For each statement, determine if it is True or False for the graph of $6x - 3y = 21$.
   A. The x-intercept is $3\frac{1}{2}$.
   B. The y-intercept is -7.
   C. The slope is 3.

3. Is the sequence 6, 3, 0, -3, -6, -9, ... arithmetic, geometric, or neither? Explain your answer. Write a recursive rule for the sequence.

4. Graph $f(x) = (x - 2)^2 - 4$. Describe the relationship between the x-intercepts of the graph and the solutions of $(x - 2)^2 - 4 = 0$.

1. Consider the graph of $f(x) = -2x^2 - \frac{1}{2}$.
   Determine if each statement is True or False.

   A. The vertex is $\left(-2, \frac{1}{2}\right)$.

   B. The maximum value is $-\frac{1}{2}$.

   C. The axis of symmetry is $x = -2$.

2. Does the given statement describe a step in the transformation of the graph of $f(x) = x^2$ that would result in the graph of $g(x) = -5(x + 2)^2$?

   A. The parent function is reflected across the x-axis.

   B. The parent function is stretched by a factor of 5.

   C. The parent function is translated 2 units up.

3. Use the graph of $f(x)$ to determine if each statement is True or False.

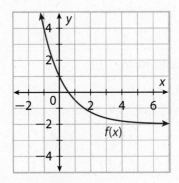

   A. As $x \to \infty, y \to -2$.

   B. The graph represents a quadratic function.

   C. When $f(x) = 1, x = 0$.

4. Solve $\left(2x + \frac{2}{3}\right)(x + 5) = 0$. Is each of the following a solution of the equation?

   A. $x = -\frac{1}{3}$

   B. $x = -5$

   C. $x = \frac{2}{3}$

5. Use the table of values for $h(x)$ to determine if each statement is True or False.

x	−4	−2	0	2	4
$h(x)$	3	0	−3	0	3

    A. A zero of the function is −3.

    B. A zero of the function is −2.

    C. A solution of the equation $h(x) = 0$ is $x = 2$.

6. Graph $y = -2x^2 + 16x - 31$. What is the axis of symmetry of the graph? What is its vertex?

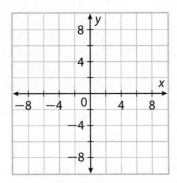

7. Graph $t(x) = \frac{1}{2}(x + 2)(x - 4)$, and write the function in standard form.

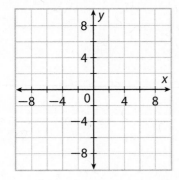

Performance Tasks

★ **8.** A rectangular picture measuring 6 in. by 10 in. is surrounded by a frame with uniform width x.

    A. Write a quadratic function to show the combined area of the picture and frame.

    B. Write a quadratic function for the area of the frame.

© Houghton Mifflin Harcourt Publishing Company

★★ **9. Estimation** The graph shows the approximate height y in meters of a volleyball x seconds after it is served.

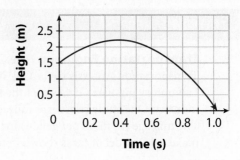

A. Estimate the time it takes for the volleyball to reach its greatest height.

B. Estimate the greatest height that the volleyball reaches.

C. If the domain of a quadratic function is all real numbers, why is the domain of this function limited to nonnegative numbers?

★★★**10.** A rocket team is using simulation software to create and study water bottle rockets. The team begins by simulating the launch of a rocket without a parachute. The table gives data for one rocket design.

A. Show that the data represent a quadratic function.

B. Graph the function.

C. The acceleration due to gravity is 9.8 m/s². How is this number related to the data for this water bottle rocket?

Time (s)	Height (m)
0	0
1	34.3
2	58.8
3	73.5
4	78.4
5	73.5
6	58.8
7	34.3
8	0

Transportation Engineer The Center for Transportation Analysis in the Oak Ridge National Laboratory publishes data about the transportation industry. One study relates gas mileage and a car's speed. The mileage (in miles per gallon) for a particular year, make, and model of car is shown in the table.

Speed (miles per hour)	Gas Mileage (miles per gallon)
40	23.0
50	27.3
55	29.1
60	28.2
70	22.9

a. Identify the independent and dependent variables in this situation. State the units associated with each variable.

b. Make a scatter plot of the data, and sketch a parabola that you think best fits the plotted points. (You will not be able to make the parabola pass through all the points. Instead, you should try to draw the parabola so that some points fall above it and some below it.) Explain why a parabola is a reasonable curve to fit to the data.

c. Write the equation for a function of the form $m(s) = a(s - h)^2 = k$, where s is the speed and m is the gas mileage. Use the coordinates of the vertex of your parabola to determine h and k, and a point on your parabola other than the vertex to solve for the unknown a.

d. Suppose that when the car was driven at a steady speed, its gas mileage was 25 miles per gallon. Describe how you can use your model to find the car's speed. Is only one speed or more than one speed possible? Explain, and then find the speed(s).

Quadratic Equations and Modeling

MATH IN CAREERS

Competitive Diver Diving is the sport of jumping into the water from a springboard or platform. Competitive divers should have a strong understanding of the mathematics of projectile motion, including the time spent in the air, the speed at which they hit the water, and the maximum height of a jump.

If you are interested in a career as a competitive diver, you should study these mathematical subjects:

- Algebra
- Business math

Research other careers that require understanding of the mathematics of projectile motion. Check out the career activity at the end of the unit to find out how **competitive divers** use math.

Visualize Vocabulary

Use the ✔ words to complete the chart.

	a square of a whole number
	one of two equal factors of a number
	the largest common factor of two or more given numbers
	a real number that cannot be expressed as the ratio of two integers
	a number that is multiplied by a variable

Understand Vocabulary

To become familiar with some of the vocabulary terms in this unit, consider the following. You may refer to the module, the glossary, or a dictionary.

1. The ___?___ gives the solutions of a quadratic equation.

2. ___?___ is a process that forms a perfect square trinomial.

3. By the ___?___, $\pm\sqrt{\dfrac{16}{9}} = \pm\dfrac{\sqrt{16}}{\sqrt{9}} = \pm\dfrac{4}{3}$.

Active Reading

Pyramid Before beginning this unit create a pyramid to help you organize what you learn. Label each side with one of the module titles from this unit: "Using Factors to Solve Quadratic Equations," "Using Square Roots to Solve Quadratic Equations," and "Linear, Exponential, and Quadratic Models." As you study each module, write important ideas like vocabulary, properties, and formulas on the appropriate side.

Using Factors to Solve Quadratic Equations

Essential Question: How can you use factoring a quadratic equation to solve real-world problems?

REAL WORLD VIDEO
Ruling out common elements in a scientific experiment is similar to removing common factors in an equation; logically, whatever is common to two samples can't be the cause of differences between them.

MODULE PERFORMANCE TASK PREVIEW

Fitting Through the Arch

An arched doorway is a strong structure that can usually support more weight than a rectangular doorway. An arched opening is also far less likely than a rectangular opening to topple from vibrations of a train passing through it. However, many man-made objects are rectangular, not curved as an arch is curved. So, how big can a rectangular object be and still pass through an arched door? Let's find out!

Are (YOU) Ready?

Complete these exercises to review skills you will need for this module.

• Online Homework
• Hints and Help
• Extra Practice

Exponents

Example 1   Simplify $8^5 \cdot 8^{-2}$.

$$8^5 \cdot 8^{-2} = 8^{5 + (-2)}$$ The bases are the same. Add the exponents.

$$= 8^3$$

$$= 512$$ Multiply.

Simplify.

1. $3^7 \cdot 3^{-3}$

2. $7^7 \cdot 7^{-5}$

3. $6^9 \cdot 6^{-4} \cdot 6^{-5}$

Algebraic Expressions

Example 2   Simplify $13x + 5 - 9x^2 - 8$.

$$13x + 5 - 9x^2 - 8$$

$$-9x^2 + 13x + 5 - 8$$ Reorder in descending order of exponents.

$$-9x^2 + 13x - 3$$ Combine like terms.

Simplify.

4. $12x + 4x^2 - 3 - 7x$

5. $7x^2 - 6 + 8x - 2x^2$

6. $5 + 7x - 2x^2 - 6$

7. $-4x + 6x^2 - 8 + 9x - 3x^2$

Example 3   Multiply $(x + 7)(x - 3)$.

$$(x + 7)(x - 3)$$

$$x(x) - 3(x) + 7(x) + 7(-3)$$ Use FOIL.

$$x^2 - 3x + 7x - 21$$ Simplify.

$$x^2 + 4x - 21$$ Combine like terms.

Multiply.

8. $(x - 4)(x + 5)$

9. $(x - 9)(x - 6)$

10. $(2x - 3)(2x + 3)$

11. $(3x - 2)(2x + 5)$

21.1 Solving Equations by Factoring $x^2 + bx + c$

Essential Question: How can you use factoring to solve quadratic equations in standard form for which $a = 1$?

⊘ Explore 1 Using Algebra Tiles to Factor $x^2 + bx + c$

In this lesson, multiplying binomials using the FOIL process will be reversed and trinomials will be factored into two binomials. To learn how to factor, let's start with the expression $x^2 + 7x + 6$.

(A) Identify and draw the tiles needed to model the expression $x^2 + 7x + 6$.

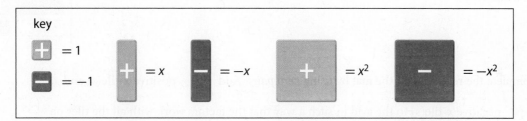

key

$\boxed{+} = 1$

$\boxed{-} = -1$

$\boxed{+} = x$ $\boxed{-} = -x$ $\boxed{+} = x^2$ $\boxed{-} = -x^2$

The tiles needed to model the expression $x^2 + 7x + 6$ are:

$\boxed{?}$ x^2-tiles(s), $\boxed{?}$ x-tile(s), and $\boxed{?}$ unit tile(s).

(B) Arrange and draw the algebra tiles on a grid. Place the $\boxed{?}$ x^2-tile(s) in the upper left corner and arrange the $\boxed{?}$ unit tiles in two rows and three columns in the lower right corner.

(C) Try to complete the rectangle with the x-tiles. Notice that only $\boxed{?}$ x-tiles fit on the grid, which leaves out $\boxed{?}$ tile(s), so this arrangement is not correct.

(D) Rearrange the unit tiles so that all of the $\boxed{?}$ x-tiles fit on the mat.

(E) Complete the multiplication grid by placing the factor tiles on the sides. Then write the factors modeled in this product.

$x^2 + 7x + 6 = \left(x + \boxed{?}\right)\left(x + \boxed{?}\right)$

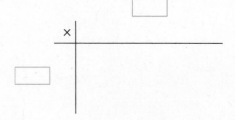

(F) Now let's look at how to factor a quadratic expression with a negative constant term. Use algebra tiles to factor $x^2 + x - 2$. Identify the tiles needed to model the expression.

[?] positive x^2-tile(s), [?] positive x-tile(s), and [?] negative unit tile(s)

(G) Arrange the algebra tiles on the grid. Place the [?] positive x^2-tile(s) in the upper left corner and arrange the [?] negative unit tiles in the lower right corner.

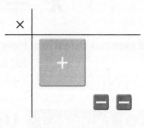

(H) Try to fill in the empty spaces on the grid with x-tiles. There is/are [?] positive x-tile(s) to place on the grid, so there will be [?] empty places for x-tiles.

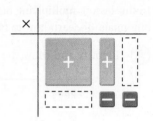

(I) Complete the rectangle on the mat by using *zero pairs*. Add [?] positive x-tile(s) and [?] negative x-tile(s) to the grid in such a way that the factors work with all the tiles on the mat. Which mat shows the correct position of zero pairs?

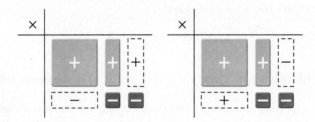

(J) Complete the multiplication grid by placing the factor tiles on the sides. Then write the factors modeled in this product.

$$x^2 + x - 2 = \left(x + \boxed{?}\right)\left(x - \boxed{?}\right)$$

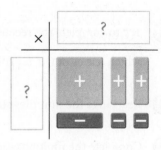

1. Are there any other ways to factor the polynomial $x^2 + 7x + 6$ besides $(x + 6)(x + 1)$? Explain.

2. **Discussion** If c is positive in $x^2 + bx + c$, what sign can the constant terms of the factors have? What about when c is negative?

⊘ Explore 2　Factoring $x^2 + bx + c$

To factor $x^2 + bx + c$, you need to find two factors of c whose sum is b.

Factoring $x^2 + bx + c$	
WORDS	**EXAMPLE**
To factor a quadratic trinomial of the form $x^2 + bx + c$, find two factors of c whose sum is b. If no such Integers exist, the trinomial is not factorable.	To factor $x^2 + 9x + 18$, look for factors of 18 whose sum is 9. Factors of 18　　Sum 　1 and 18　　　19　　x 　2 and 9　　　　11　　x 　3 and 6　　　　9　　✓　$x^2 + 9x + 18 = (x + 3)(x + 6)$

If c is positive, the constant terms of the factors have the same sign.

If c is negative, then one constant term of the factors is positive and one is negative.

(A) First, look at $x^2 + 11x + 30$. Find the values of b and c.　　　$b =$ ⬚?⬚　　$c =$ ⬚?⬚

(B) The sign of c is ⬚?⬚ . The sign of the factors will be the ⬚?⬚ .

(C) List the factor pairs of c, 30, and find the sum of each pair.

Factors of 30	Sum of Factors
1 and ⬚?⬚	$1 +$ ⬚?⬚ $=$ ⬚?⬚
2 and ⬚?⬚	$2 +$ ⬚?⬚ $=$ ⬚?⬚
3 and ⬚?⬚	$3 +$ ⬚?⬚ $=$ ⬚?⬚
5 and ⬚?⬚	$5 +$ ⬚?⬚ $=$ ⬚?⬚

(D) The factor pair whose sum equals b is ⬚?⬚ .

Use this factor pair to factor the polynomial. $x^2 + 11x + 30 = \left(x + \boxed{?}\right)\left(x + \boxed{?}\right)$

(E) Now, look at $x^2 + 13x - 30$. Find the values of b and c.

$b = $ ⬚? $c = $ ⬚?

(F) The sign of c is ⬚? . The sign of the factors will be the ⬚? .

(G) List the factor pairs of c, –30, and find the sum of each pair.

Factors of −30	Sum of Factors
1 and ⬚?	1 + ⬚? = ⬚?
2 and ⬚?	2 + ⬚? = ⬚?
3 and ⬚?	3 + ⬚? = ⬚?
5 and ⬚?	5 + ⬚? = ⬚?
−1 and ⬚?	−1 + ⬚? = ⬚?
−2 and ⬚?	−2 + ⬚? = ⬚?
−3 and ⬚?	−3 + ⬚? = ⬚?
−5 and ⬚?	−5 + ⬚? = ⬚?

(H) The factor pair whose sum equals b is ⬚? .

Use this factor pair to factor the polynomial.

$x^2 + 13x - 30 = \left(x + \boxed{?}\right)\left(x - \boxed{?}\right)$

Reflect

3. **Discussion** When factoring a trinomial of the form $x^2 + bx + c$, where c is negative, one binomial factor contains a positive factor of c and one contains a negative factor of c. How do you know which factor of c should be positive and which should be negative?

Solving Equations of the Form $x^2 + bx + c = 0$ by Factoring

As you have learned, the Zero Product Property can be used to solve quadratic equations in factored form.

Example 1 Solve each equation by factoring. Check your answer by graphing.

Ⓐ $x^2 - 8x = -12$

First, write the equation in the form $x^2 - bx + c = 0$.

$x^2 - 8x = -12$ Original equation

$x^2 - 8x + 12 = 0$ Add 12 to both sides.

The expression $x^2 - 8x + 12$ is in the form $ax^2 + bx + c$, with $b < 0$ and $c > 0$, so the factors will have the same sign and they both will be negative.

Factors of 12	Sum of Factors
-1 and -12	$-1 + (-12) = -13$
-2 and -6	$-2 + (-6) = -8$
-3 and -4	$-3 + (-4) = -7$

The factor pair whose sum equals -8 is -2 and -6. Factor the equation, and use the Zero Product Property.

$$x^2 - 8x + 12 = 0$$

$$(x - 2)(x - 6) = 0$$

$$x - 2 = 0 \quad \text{or} \quad x - 6 = 0$$

$$x = 2 \qquad\qquad\qquad x = 6$$

The zeros of the equation are 2 and 6. Check this by graphing the related function, $f(x) = x^2 - 8x + 12$.

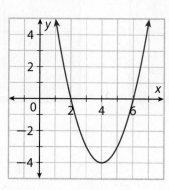

The x-intercepts of the graph are 2 and 6, which are the same as the zeros of the equation. The solutions of the equation are 2 and 6.

Ⓑ $x^2 - 2x = 15$

First, rewrite the expression in the form $x^2 + bx + c = 0$.

$x^2 - 2x = 15$ Original equation

$x^2 - 2x - \boxed{15} = 0$ Subtract 15 from both sides.

To find the zeros of the equation, start by factoring. List the factor pairs of c and find the sum of each pair. Since $c < 0$, the factors will have opposite signs. Since $c < 0$ and $b < 0$, the factor with the greater absolute value will be negative.

Factors of −15	Sum of Factors
1 and $\boxed{-15}$	$1 + \boxed{-15} = \boxed{-14}$
3 and $\boxed{-5}$	$3 + \boxed{-5} = \boxed{-2}$
-1 and $\boxed{15}$	$-1 + \boxed{15} = \boxed{14}$
-3 and $\boxed{5}$	$-3 + \boxed{5} = \boxed{2}$

The factor pair whose sum equals -2 is 3 and -5. Factor the equation, and use the Zero Product Property.

$$x^2 - 2x - 15 = 0$$
$$\left(x + \boxed{3}\right)\left(x - \boxed{5}\right) = 0$$

$x + 3 = 0$ or $x - 5 = 0$

$x = \boxed{-3}$ $x = \boxed{5}$

The zeros of the equation are $\boxed{-3}$ and $\boxed{5}$. Check this by graphing the related function, $f(x) = x^2 - 2x = 15$.

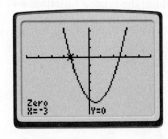
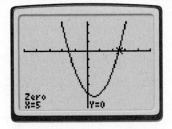

Your Turn

Solve each equation.

4. $x^2 + 15x = -54$ **5.** $x^2 - 13x = -12$ **6.** $x^2 - x = 56$

🔑 Explain 2   Solving Equation Models of the Form $x^2 + bx + c = 0$ by Factoring

Some real-world problems can be solved by factoring a quadratic equation.

Example 2   **Solve each model by factoring.**

Architecture A rectangular porch has dimensions of $(x + 12)$ and $(x + 5)$ feet. If the area of the porch floor is 120 square feet, what are its length and width?

Write an equation for the problem. Substitute 120 for A for the area of the porch.

$$(x + 12)(x + 5) = A$$

$$x^2 + 17x + 60 = A$$

$$x^2 + 17 + 60 = 120$$

$$x^2 + 17x - 60 = 0$$

The factors are of -60 that have a sum of 17 are 20 and -3. Use Zero Product Property to find x.

$$(x + 20)(x - 3) = 0$$

$$x + 20 = 0 \quad \text{or} \quad x - 3 = 0$$

$$x = -20 \qquad\qquad x = 3$$

Since the area cannot be negative, $x = 3$ feet.

Therefore, the dimensions of the porch are $3 + 12 = 15$ feet long and $3 + 5 = 8$ feet wide.

💬 Elaborate

7. How are the solutions of a quadratic equation related to the zeros of the related function?

8. **Essential Question Check-In** How can you solve a quadratic equation by factoring?

Use algebra tiles to model the factors of each expression.

1. $x^2 + 6x + 8$

$$x^2 + 6x + 8 = \left(x\ \boxed{?}\right)\left(x\ \boxed{?}\right)$$

2. $x^2 + 2x - 3$

$$x^2 + 2x - 3 = \left(x\ \boxed{?}\right)\left(x\ \boxed{?}\right)$$

Factor the expressions.

3. $x^2 - 15x + 44$

4. $x^2 + 22x + 120$

5. $x^2 + 14x - 32$

6. $x^2 - 12x - 45$

7. $x^2 + 10x + 24$

8. $x^2 + 7x - 8$

Solve each equation.

9. $x^2 + 19x = -84$

10. $x^2 - 18x = -56$

11. $x^2 - 12x + 27 = 0$

12. $x^2 - 9x - 10 = 0$

13. $x^2 + 6x = 135$

14. $x^2 + 13x = -40$

15. $x^2 + x - 132 = 0$

16. $x^2 - 14x = 32$

17. Construction The area of a rectangular fountain is $\left(x^2 + 12x + 20\right)$ square feet. A 2-foot walkway is built around the fountain. Find the dimensions of the outside border of the walkway.

18. The area of a room is 396 square feet. The length is $(x + 3)$, and the width is $(x + 7)$ feet. Find the dimensions of the room.

19. A rectangular Persian carpet has an area of $(x^2 + x - 20)$ square feet and a length of $(x + 5)$ feet. The Persian carpet is displayed on a wall. The wall has a width of $(x + 2)$ feet and an area of $(x^2 + 17x + 30)$ square feet. Find the dimensions of the rug and the wall if $x = 20$ feet.

20. The area of a poster board is $x^2 + 3x - 10$ square inches. Find the dimensions of the poster board if $x = 14$.

21. Match the equation to its solutions.

A. $x^2 - 3x - 18 = 0$ a. ___?___ 3 and 6

B. $x^2 - 9x + 18 = 0$ b. ___?___ −3 and −6

C. $x^2 + 3x - 18 = 0$ c. ___?___ 3 and −6

D. $x^2 + 9x + 18 = 0$ d. ___?___ −3 and 6

H.O.T. Focus on Higher Order Thinking

22. Explain the Error Amelie found the solutions of the equation $x^2 - x = 42$ to be 6 and −7. Explain why this answer is incorrect. Then, find the correct solutions.

23. Communicate Mathematical Ideas Rico says the expression $x^2 + bx + c$ is factorable when $b = c = 4$. Are there any other values where $b = c$ that make the expression factorable? Explain.

24. Multi-Step A homeowner wants to enlarge a rectangular closet that has an area of $(x^2 + 3x + 2)$ square feet. The length of the closet is greater than the width. After construction, the area will be $(x^2 + 8x + 15)$ square feet.

a. Find the dimensions of the closet before construction.

b. Find the dimensions of the closet after construction.

c. By how many feet will the length and width increase after construction?

25. Critical Thinking Given $x^2 + bx + 64$, find all the values of b for which the quadratic expression has factors $(x + p)$ and $(x + q)$, where p and q are integers.

Lesson Performance Task

Part of the roof of a factory is devoted to mechanical support and part to green space. The area of the roof R of a large building can be modeled by the polynomial $2x^2 - 251x + 80,000$ and the area M that is devoted to mechanical support can be modeled by the polynomial $x^2 + 224x + 31,250$. Given that the area G of the green space is 123,750 square feet, write and solve quadratic equations to find the dimensions of the green space.

21.2 Solving Equations by Factoring $ax^2 + bx + c$

Essential Question: How can you use factoring to solve quadratic equations in standard form for which $a \neq 1$?

⊘ Explore   Factoring $ax^2 + bx + c$ When $c > 0$

When you factor a quadratic expression in standard form $\left(ax^2 + bx + c\right)$, you are looking for two binomials, and possibly a constant numerical factor whose product is the original quadratic expression.

Recall that the product of two binomials is found by applying the Distributive Property, abbreviated sometimes as FOIL:

$$(2x + 5)(3x + 2) = \underbrace{6x^2}_{F} + \underbrace{4x}_{O} + \underbrace{15x}_{I} + \underbrace{10}_{L} = 6x^2 + 19x + 10$$

F   The product of the coefficients of the first terms is a.

O⎫
 ⎬   The sum of the coefficients of the outer and inner products is b.
I⎭

L   The product of the last terms is c.

Because the a and c coefficients result from a single product of terms from the binomials, the coefficients in the binomial factors will be a combination of the factors of a and c. The trick is to find the combination of factors that results in the correct value of b.

Follow the steps to factor the quadratic $4x^2 + 26x + 42$.

(A) First, factor out the largest common factor of 4, 26, and 42 if it is anything other than 1.

$$4x^2 + 26x + 42 = \boxed{?} \left(2x^2 + 13x + 21\right)$$

(B) Next, list the factor pairs of 2.

(C) List the factor pairs of 21.

(D) Make a table listing the combinations of the factors of a and c, and find the value of b that results from summing the outer and inner products of the factors.

Factors of 2	Factors of 21	Outer + inner
1 and 2	1 and 21	$(1)(21) + (2)(1) = 23$
1 and 2	$\boxed{?}$ and 7	$\boxed{?}$
1 and 2	7 and 3	$\boxed{?}$
1 and 2	$\boxed{?}$ and 1	$\boxed{?}$

(E) Copy the pair of factors that resulted in an outer + inner sum of 13 into the binomial factors. Be careful to keep the inner and outer factors from the table as inner and outer coefficients in the binomials.

$$2x^2 + 13x + 21 = \left(\boxed{?}\, x + \boxed{?}\right)\left(\boxed{?}\, x + \boxed{?}\right)$$

(F) Replace the common factor of the original coefficients to complete the factorization of the original quadratic.

$$4x^2 + 26x + 42 = \boxed{?}\,(x + 3)(2x + 7)$$

Reflect

1. **Critical Thinking** Explain why you should use negative factors of c when factoring a quadratic with $c > 0$ and $b < 0$.

2. **What If?** If none of the factor pairs for a and c result in the correct value for b, what do you know about the quadratic?

3. **Discussion** Why did you have to check each factor pair twice for the factors of c (3 and 7 versus 7 and 3) but only once for the factors of a (1 and 2, but not 2 and 1)? Hint: Compare the outer and inner sums of rows two and three in the table, and also check the outer and inner sums by switching the order of both pairs from row 2 (check 2 and 1 for a with 7 and 3 for c).

⊙ Explain 1 Factoring $ax^2 + bx + c$ When $c < 0$

Factoring $x^2 + bx + c$ when $c < 0$ requires one negative and one positive factor of c. The same applies for expressions of the form $ax^2 + bx + c$ as long as $a > 0$. When checking factor pairs, remember to consider factors of c in both orders, **and** consider factor pairs with the negative sign on either member of the pair of c factors.

When you find a combination of factors whose outer and inner product sum is equal to b, you have found the solution. Make sure you fill in the factor table systematically so that you do not skip any combinations.

If $a < 0$, factor out -1 from all three coefficients, or use a negative common factor, so that the factors of a can be left as positive numbers.

Example 1 Factor the quadratic by checking factor pairs.

(A) $6x^2 - 21x - 45$

Find the largest common factor of 6, 21, and 45, and factor it out,
keeping the coefficient of x^2 positive.

$6x^2 - 21x - 45 = 3(2x^2 - 7x - 15)$

Factors of a	Factors of c	Outer Product + Inner Product
1 and 2	1 and -15	$(1)(-15) + (2)(1) = -13$
1 and 2	3 and -5	$(1)(-5) + (2)(3) = 1$
1 and 2	5 and -3	$(1)(-3) + (2)(5) = 7$
1 and 2	15 and -1	$(1)(-1) + (2)(15) = 29$
1 and 2	-1 and 15	$(1)(15) + (2)(-1) = 13$
1 and 2	-3 and 5	$(1)(5) + (2)(-3) = -1$
1 and 2	-5 and 3	$(1)(3) + (2)(-5) = -7$
1 and 2	-15 and 1	$(1)(1) + (2)(-15) = -29$

Use the combination of factor pairs that results in a value of -7 for b.

$2x^2 - 7x - 15 = (x - 5)(2x + 3)$

Replace the common factor of the original coefficients to factor the original quadratic.

$6x^2 - 21x - 45 = 3(x - 5)(2x + 3)$

(B) $20x^2 - 40x - 25$

Factor out common factors of the terms.

$20x^2 - 40x - 25 = \boxed{5}\ (4x^2 - 8x - 5)$

Factors of a	Factors of c	Outer Product + Inner Product
1 and 4	1 and -5	$(1)(-5) + (4)(1) = \boxed{-1}$
1 and 4	5 and -1	$\boxed{(1)(-1)} + \boxed{(4)(5)} = \boxed{19}$
1 and 4	-1 and 5	$\boxed{(1)(5)} + \boxed{(4)(-1)} = \boxed{1}$
1 and 4	-5 and 1	$\boxed{(1)(1)} + \boxed{(4)(-5)} = \boxed{-19}$
2 and 2	1 and -5	$\boxed{(2)(-5)} + \boxed{(2)(1)} = \boxed{-8}$
2 and 2	-1 and 5	$\boxed{(2)(-1)} + \boxed{(2)(5)} = \boxed{8}$

Use the combination of factor pairs that results in a value of $\boxed{-8}$ for b.

$4x^2 - 8x - 5 = \left(\boxed{2}\,x + \boxed{1}\right)\left(\boxed{2}\,x + \boxed{-5}\right)$

Replace the common factor of the original coefficients to factor the original quadratic.

$20x^2 - 40x - 25 = \boxed{5}\ (2x + 1)(2x - 5)$

4. **What If?** Suppose a is a negative number. What would be the first step in factoring $ax^2 + bx + c$?

5. Factor. $-5x^2 + 8x + 4$

🖉 Explain 2 Solving Equations of the Form $ax^2 + bx + c = 0$ by Factoring

For a quadratic equation in standard form, $ax^2 + bx + c = 0$, factoring the quadratic expression into binomials lets you use the Zero Product Property to solve the equation, as you have done previously. If the equation is not in standard form, convert it to standard form by moving all terms to one side of the equation and combining like terms.

Example 2 Change the quadratic equation to standard form if necessary and then solve by factoring.

(A) $2x^2 + 7x - 2 = 4x^2 + 4$

Convert the equation to standard form:

Subtract $4x^2$ and 4 from both sides. $\qquad$ $-2x^2 + 7x - 6 = 0$

Multiply both sides by -1. $\qquad$ $2x^2 - 7x + 6 = 0$

Consider factor pairs for 2 and 6. Use negative factors of 6 to get a negative value for b.

Use the combination pair that results in a sum of -7 and write the equation in factored form. Then solve it using the Zero Product Property.

$$(x - 2)(2x - 3) = 0$$

$$x - 2 = 0 \quad \text{or} \quad 2x - 3 = 0$$

$$x = 2 \qquad\qquad 2x = 3$$

$$x = \frac{3}{2} = 1.5$$

The solutions are 2 and $\frac{3}{2}$, or 1.5.

The solution can be checked by graphing the related function, $f(x) = 2x^2 - 7x + 6$, and finding the x-intercepts.

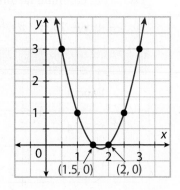

B $3(x^2 - 1) = -3x^2 + 2x + 5$

Write the equation in standard form and factor so you can apply the Zero Product Property.

$$\boxed{3}\ x^2 - \boxed{3} = -3x^2 + 2x + 5$$

$$\boxed{6}\ x^2 - 2x - \boxed{8} = 0$$

$$\boxed{3}\ x^2 - x - 4 = 0$$

Use the combination pair that results in a sum of -1.

$$(x + 1)\left(\boxed{3}\ x + \boxed{-4}\right) = 0$$

$$x + 1 = \boxed{0} \qquad \text{or} \qquad 3x - 4 = 0$$

$$x = \boxed{-1} \qquad\qquad \boxed{3}\ x = 4$$

$$x = \boxed{\dfrac{4}{3}}$$

The solutions are -1 and $\dfrac{4}{3}$.

Use a graphing calculator to check the solutions.

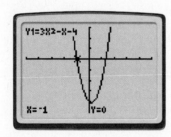
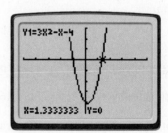

Reflect

6. In the two examples, a common factor was divided out at the beginning of the solution, and it was not used again. Why didn't you include the common term again when solving x for the original quadratic equation?

Your Turn

Solve by factoring.

7. $12x^2 + 48x + 45 = 0$

 **Solving Equation Models of the Form**
$ax^2 + bx + c = 0$ **by Factoring**

A projectile is an object moving through the air without any forces other than gravity acting on it. The height of a projectile at a time in seconds can be found by using the formula $h = -16t^2 + vt + s$, where v is in the initial upwards velocity in feet per second (and can be a negative number if the projectile is launched downwards) and s is starting height in feet. The a term of -16 accounts for the effect of gravity accelerating the projectile downwards and is the only appropriate value when measuring distance with feet and time in seconds.

To use the model to make predictions about the behavior of a projectile, you need to read the description of the situation carefully and identify the initial velocity, the initial height, and the height at time t.

Example 3 **Read the real-world situation and substitute in values for the projectile motion formula. Then solve the resulting quadratic equation by factoring to answer the question.**

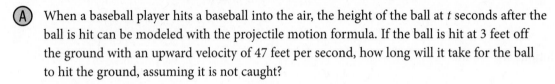 When a baseball player hits a baseball into the air, the height of the ball at t seconds after the ball is hit can be modeled with the projectile motion formula. If the ball is hit at 3 feet off the ground with an upward velocity of 47 feet per second, how long will it take for the ball to hit the ground, assuming it is not caught?

Use the equation $h = -16t^2 + vt + s$. Find the parameters v and s from the description of the problem.

$v = 47$ $\qquad\qquad$ $s = 3$ $\qquad\qquad$ $h = 0$

Substitute parameter values. $\qquad$ $-16t^2 + 47t + 3 = 0$

Divide both sides by -1. $\qquad\qquad$ $16t^2 - 47t - 3 = 0$

Use the combination pair that results in a sum of -47.

$$(t - 3)(16t + 1) = 0$$

$$t - 3 = 0 \qquad \text{or} \qquad 16t + 1 = 0$$

$$t = 3 \qquad\qquad\qquad 16t = -1$$

$$t = -\frac{1}{16}$$

The solutions are 3 and $-\frac{1}{16}$.

The negative time answer can be rejected because it is not a reasonable value for time in this situation. The correct answer is 3 seconds.

B A child standing on a river bank ten feet above the river throws a rock toward the river at a speed of 12 feet per second. How long does it take before the rock splashes into the river?

Find the parameters v and s from the description of the problem.

$$v = -12 \qquad s = \boxed{10} \qquad h = \boxed{0}$$

Substitute parameter values. $\boxed{-16}\, t^2 + \boxed{-12}\, t + \boxed{10} = 0$

Divide both sides by $\boxed{-2}$. $8t^2 + \boxed{6}\, t + \boxed{-5} = 0$

Use the combination pair that results in a sum of 6.

$$\left(\boxed{2}\, t - 1 \right)\left(\boxed{4}\, t + 5 \right) = 0$$

$$2t - 1 = 0 \qquad \text{or} \qquad 4t + 5 = 0$$

$$2t = \boxed{1} \qquad\qquad 4t = \boxed{-5}$$

$$t = \boxed{\tfrac{1}{2}} \qquad\qquad t = \boxed{-\tfrac{5}{4}}$$

The solutions are $\boxed{\tfrac{1}{2}}$ and $\boxed{-\tfrac{5}{4}}$.

The only correct solution to the time it takes the rock to hit the water is $\boxed{\tfrac{1}{2}}$ second.

Your Turn

8. How long does it take a rock to hit the ground if thrown off the edge of a 72-foot tall building roof with an upward velocity of 24 feet per second?

💬 Elaborate

9. **Discussion** What happens if you do not remove the common factor from the coefficients before trying to factor the quadratic equation?

10. Explain how you can know there are never more than two solutions to a quadratic equation, based on what you know about the graph of a quadratic function.

11. **Essential Question Check-In** Describe the steps it takes to solve a quadratic equation by factoring.

Factor the following quadratic expressions.

1. $6x^2 + 5x + 1$

2. $9x^2 + 33x + 30$

3. $4x^2 - 8x + 3$

4. $24x^2 - 44x + 12$

5. $3x^2 - 2x - 5$

6. $-10x^2 + 3x + 4$

7. $12x^2 + 22x - 14$

8. $-15x^2 + 21x + 18$

Solve the following quadratic equations.

9. $5x^2 + 18x + 9 = 0$

10. $12x^2 - 36x + 15 = 0$

11. $6x^2 + 28x - 2 = 2x - 10$

12. $-100x^2 + 55x + 3 = 50x^2 - 55x + 23$

13. $8x^2 - 10x - 3 = 0$

14. $-12x^2 = 34x - 28$

15. $(8x + 7)(x + 1) = 9$

16. $3(4x - 1)(4x + 3) = 48x$

Read the real-world situation and substitute in values for the projectile motion formula. Then solve the resulting quadratic equation by factoring to answer the question.

17. A golfer takes a swing from a hill twenty feet above the cup with an initial upwards velocity of 32 feet per second. How long does it take the ball to land on the ground near the cup?

18. An airplane pilot jumps out of an airplane and has an initial velocity of 60 feet per second downwards. How long does it take to fall from 1000 feet to 900 feet before the parachute opens?

A race car driving under the caution flag at 80 feet per second begins to accelerate at a constant rate after the warning flag. The distance traveled since the warning flag in feet is characterized by $30t^2 + 80t$, where t is the time in seconds after the car starts accelerating again.

19. How long does it take the car to travel 30 feet after it begins accelerating?

20. How long will the car take to travel 160 feet?

Geometry For each rectangle with area given, determine the binomial factors that describe the dimensions.

21.

area = $6x^2 + 17x - 3$

22.

area = $21x^2 + 13x + 2$

23. **Multiple Response** Which of the following expressions in the list describes the complete factorization of the quadratic expression $15x^2 - 25x - 10$?

a. $(3x + 1)(5x - 10)$ **b.** $5(3x + 1)(x - 2)$ **c.** $5(x + 2)(3x - 1)$

d. $5(x - 2)(3x + 1)$ **e.** $5(3x - 1)(x + 2)$ **f.** $(5x - 10)(3x + 1)$

H.O.T. Focus on Higher Order Thinking

24. **Multi-Part Response** A basketball player shoots at the basket from a starting height of 6 feet and an upwards velocity of 20 feet per second. Determine how long it takes for the shot to drop through the basket, which is mounted at a height of 10 feet.

  a. Set up the equation for projectile motion to solve for time and convert it to standard form.

  b. Solve the equation by factoring.

  c. Explain why you got two positive solutions to the equation, and determine how you can rule one of them out to find the answer to the question. Hint: Solving the equation graphically may give you a hint.

25. **Critical Thinking** Find the binomial factors of $4x^2 - 25$.

26. **Communicate Mathematical Ideas** Find all the values of b that make the expression $3x^2 + bx - 4$ factorable.

Lesson Performance Task

The equation for the motion of an object with constant acceleration is $d = d_0 + vt + \frac{1}{2}at^2$, where d is distance from a given point in meters, d_0 is the initial distance from the starting point in meters, v is the starting velocity in meters per second, a is acceleration in meters per second squared, and t is time in seconds.

A car is stopped at a traffic light. When the light turns green, the driver begins to drive, accelerating at a constant rate of 4 meters per second squared. A bus is traveling at a speed of 15 meters per second in another lane. The bus is 7 meters behind the car as it begins to accelerate.

Find when the bus passes the car, when the car passes the bus, and how far each has traveled each time they pass one another.

21.3 Using Special Factors to Solve Equations

Essential Question: How can you use special products to aid in solving quadratic equations by factoring?

Explore **Exploring Factors of Perfect Square Trinomials**

When you use algebra tiles to factor a polynomial, you must arrange the unit tiles on the grid in a rectangle. Sometimes, you can arrange the unit tiles to form a square. Trinomials of this type are called perfect-square trinomials.

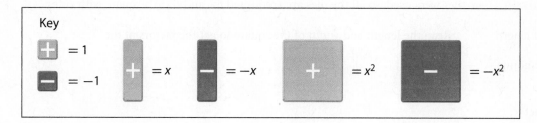

(A) Use algebra tiles to factor $x^2 + 6x + 9$.

Identify the number of tiles you need to model the expression. You need [?] x^2-tiles, [?] x-tiles, and [?] unit tiles.

(B) Arrange the algebra tiles on a grid like the one shown below.. Place the [?] x^2-tile in the upper left corner, and arrange the [?] unit tiles in the lower right corner.

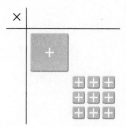

(C) Fill in the empty spaces on a grid with x-tiles.

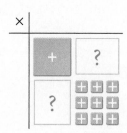

(D) All $\boxed{?}$ x-tiles were used, so all the tiles are accounted for and fit in the square with sides of length $\boxed{?}$. Read the length and width of the square to get the factors of the trinomial $x^2 + 6x + 9 = \left(x + \boxed{?}\right)\left(x + \boxed{?}\right)$.

(E) Now, use algebra tiles to factor $x^2 - 8x + 16$.

You need $\boxed{?}$ x^2-tiles, $\boxed{?}$ $-x$-tiles, and $\boxed{?}$ unit tiles to model the expression.

(F) Arrange the algebra tiles on a multiplication grid. Place the $\boxed{?}$ x^2-tile in the upper left corner, and arrange the $\boxed{?}$ unit tiles in the lower right corner.

(G) Fill in the empty spaces on the grid with $-x$-tiles.

(H) All $\boxed{?}$ $-x$-tiles were used, so all the tiles are accounted for and fit in a square with sides of length $\boxed{?}$. Read the length and width of the square to get the factors of the trinomial $x^2 - 8x + 16 = \left(\boxed{?}\right)\left(\boxed{?}\right)$.

Reflect

1. **What If?** Suppose that the middle term in $x^2 + 6x + 9$ was changed from $6x$ to $10x$. How would this affect the way you factor the polynomial?

2. If the positive unit squares are arranged in a square of unit tiles when factoring with algebra tiles, what will be true about the binomial factors? (The coefficient of the x^2 term is 1 as in the previous problems.)

Recall that a perfect-square trinomial can be represented algebraically in either the form $a^2 + 2ab + b^2$ or the form $a^2 - 2ab + b^2$.

Perfect-Square Trinomials

Perfect-Square Trinomials	
Perfect-Square Trinomial	**Examples**
$a^2 + 2ab + b^2 = (a+b)(a+b)$ $= (a+b)^2$	$x^2 + 6x + 9 = (x+3)(x+3)$ $= (x+3)^2$
	$c^2x^2 + 2cdx + d^2 = (cx)^2 + 2cdx + d^2$ $= (cx+d)(cx+d)$ $= (cx+d)^2$
$a^2 - 2ab + b^2 = (a-b)(a-b)$ $= (a-b)^2$	$x^2 - 10x + 25 = (x-5)(x-5)$ $= (x-5)^2$
	$c^2x^2 - 2cdx + d^2 = (cx)^2 - 2cdx + d^2$ $= (cx-d)(cx-d)$ $= (cx-d)^2$

Example 1 Factor perfect-square trinomials.

Ⓐ $4x^3 - 24x^2 + 36x$

$4x^3 - 24x^2 + 36x = 4x(x^2 - 6x + 9)$ Factor out the common monomial factor $4x$.

$= 4x[x^2 - 2(1 \cdot 3)x + 3^2]$ Rewrite the perfect square trinomial in the form $a^2x^2 - 2abx + b^2$.

$= 4x(x-3)(x-3)$ Rewrite the perfect square trinomial in the form $(ax - b)(ax - b)$ to obtain factors.

The factored form of $4x^3 - 24x^2 + 36x$ is $4x(x-3)(x-3)$, or $4x(x-3)^2$.

Ⓑ $x^2 + 16x + 64$

$x^2 + 16x + 64 = x^2 + 2\left(\boxed{1} \cdot \boxed{8}\right)x + \boxed{8}^2$ Rewrite in the form $a^2x^2 + 2abx + b^2$.

$= \left(x + \boxed{8}\right)\left(x + \boxed{8}\right)$ Rewrite in the form $(ax + b)(ax + b)$.

The factored form of $x^2 + 16x + 64$ is $\left(x + \boxed{8}\right)\left(x + \boxed{8}\right)$, or $\left(x + \boxed{8}\right)^2$.

Factor perfect-square trinomials.

3. $2y^3 + 12y^2 + 18y$

4. $100z^2 - 20z + 1$

⚙ Explain 2 **Factoring $a^2x^2 - b^2 = 0$**

Recall that a difference of squares can be written algebraically as $a^2 - b^2$ and factored as $(a + b)(a - b)$.

Difference of Squares

Difference of Two Squares	
Perfect-Square Trinomial	**Examples**
$a^2 - b^2 = (a + b)(a - b)$	$x^2 - 9 = (x + 3)(x - 3)$ $4x^2 - 9 = (2x + 3)(2x - 3)$ $9x^2 - 1 = (3x + 1)(3x - 1)$ $c^2x^2 - d^2 = (cx)^2 - d^2$ $= (cx + d)(cx - d)$

Example 2 **Factor each difference of squares.**

Ⓐ $x^2 - 49$

$\quad x^2 - 49 = x^2 - 7^2$ Rewrite in the form $a^2x^2 - b^2$.

$\quad\quad\quad = (x + 7)(x - 7)$ Rewrite in the form $(ax + b)(ax - b)$.

The factored form of $x^2 - 49$ is $(x + 7)(x - 7)$.

Ⓑ $49q^2 - 4p^2$

$\quad 49q^2 - 4p^2 = \boxed{7}\,\boxed{q}^{\,2} - \left(\boxed{2p}\right)^2$ Rewrite in the form $a^2x^2 - b^2$.

$\quad\quad\quad = \left(\boxed{7q + 2p}\right)\left(\boxed{7q - 2p}\right)$ Rewrite in the form $(ax + b)(ax - b)$.

The factored form of $49q^2 - 4p^2$ is $\left(\boxed{7q + 2p}\right)\left(\boxed{7q - 2p}\right)$.

Reflect

5. **Discussion** James was factoring a difference of squares but did not finish his work. What steps is he missing?

$\quad 16x^4 - 1 = \left(4x^2\right)^2 - 1$

$\quad\quad\quad = \left(4x^2 + 1\right)\left(4x^2 - 1\right)$

Factor each difference of squares.

6. $x^2 - 144$

7. $81y^4 - 9y^2$

⏺ Explain 3   Solving Equations with Special Factors

Equations with special factors can be solved using the Zero Product Property. Remember, the Zero Product Property states that if the product of two factors is zero, then at least one of the factors must be zero. For example, if $(x + 1)(x + 9) = 0$ then $x + 1 = 0$ or $x + 9 = 0$. Consequently, the solutions for the equation are $x = -1$ or $x = -9$.

Example 3   Solve the following equations with special factors.

Ⓐ $\qquad 4x^2 + 12x + 9 = 0$

$$4x^2 + 12x + 9 = 0$$

$$2^2 x^2 + 2(2 \cdot 3)x + 3^2 = 0 \qquad \text{Rewrite in the form } a^2 x^2 + 2abx + b^2.$$

$$(2x + 3)(2x + 3) = 0 \qquad \text{Rewrite in the form } (ax + b)(ax + b).$$

$$2x + 3 = 0 \qquad \text{Set factors equal to 0 using Zero Product Property.}$$

$$x = -\frac{3}{2} \qquad \text{Solve equation.}$$

Ⓑ $25x^2 - 1 = 0$

$$25x^2 - 1 = 0$$

$$\boxed{5}^2 \ x^2 - \boxed{1}^2 = 0 \qquad \text{Rewrite in the form } a^2 x^2 - b^2.$$

$$\left(\boxed{5x + 1} \right)\left(\boxed{5x - 1} \right) = 0 \qquad \text{Rewrite in the form } (ax + b)(ax - b).$$

$$\boxed{5x - 1} = 0 \text{ or } \boxed{5x + 1} = 0 \qquad \text{Set factors equal to 0 using Zero Product Property.}$$

$$x = \boxed{\tfrac{1}{5}} \text{ or } x = \boxed{-\tfrac{1}{5}} \qquad \text{Solve equation.}$$

Solve the following equations with special factors.

8. $25x^2 - 10x + 1 = 0$

9. $8x^4 - 2x^2 = 0$

Solving Equation Models with Special Factors

For each real-world scenario, solve the model which involves an equation with special factors.

Example 4 **Write the given information and manipulate into a familiar form. Solve the equation to answer a question about the situation.**

As a satellite falls from outer space onto Mars, its distance in miles from the planet is given by the formula $d = -9t^2 + 776$, where t is the number of hours it has fallen. Find when the satellite will be 200 miles away from Mars.

 Analyze Information

Identify the important information
- The satellite's distance in miles is given by the formula $d = -9t^2 + 776$.
- The satellite distance at some time t is $d = \boxed{200}$.

 Formulate a Plan

Substituting the value of the constant $d = \boxed{200}$ into the equation $d = -9t^2 + 776$ you get the equation $200 = -9t^2 + 776$. Simplify the new equation into a familiar form and solve it.

 Solve

Rewrite the equation to be equal to 0.

$\boxed{200} = -9t^2 + 776$ Subtract 200 from both sides.

$0 = -9t^2 + \boxed{576}$ Divide both sides by -1.

$0 = 9t^2 - \boxed{576}$ Factor out 9.

$0 = \boxed{9}\left(t^2 - \boxed{64}\right)$

The equation contains a difference of squares that you can factor.

$0 = 9\left(\boxed{t + 8}\right)\left(\boxed{t - 8}\right)$

Use the Zero Product Property to solve.

$0 = 9\left(t + \boxed{8}\right)\left(t - \boxed{8}\right)$

$\boxed{t + 8} = 0 \text{ or } t - 8 = \boxed{0}$

$t = \boxed{\pm 8}$

The answer is $t = \boxed{8}$ because time must be positive. So, the satellite has fallen for $\boxed{8}$ hours.

$t = \boxed{8}$ makes sense because time must be positive. Check by substituting this value of t into the original equation.

$$-9 \cdot \boxed{8}^2 + 776 = -9 \cdot \boxed{64} + 776$$

$$= 776 - \boxed{576}$$

$$= \boxed{200}$$

This is what is expected from the given information.

Your Turn

Write the given information and manipulate it into a familiar form. Solve the equation to answer a question about the situation.

10. A volleyball player sets the ball in the air, and the height of the ball after t seconds is given in feet by $h = -16t^2 + 12t + 6$. A teammate wants to wait until the ball is 8 feet in the air before she spikes it. When should the teammate spike the ball? How many reasonable solutions are there to this problem? Explain.

11. The height of a model rocket is given (in centimeters) by the formula $h = -490t^2$, where t is measured in seconds and $h = 0$ refers to its original height at the top of a mountain. It begins to fly down from the mountain-top at time $t = 0$. When has the rocket descended 490 centimeters?

💬 **Elaborate**

12. Are the perfect square trinomials $a^2 + 2ab + b^2$ and $a^2 - 2ab + b^2$ very different? How can you get one from the other?

13. How would you go about factoring $a^2 - 2ab + b^2 - 1$?

14. Setting a perfect-square trinomial equal to zero, $a^2x^2 + 2abx + b^2 = 0$, produces how many solutions? How many solutions are produced setting a difference of squares equal to zero, $a^2x^2 - b^2 = 0$?

15. Physical problems involving projectile motion can be modeled using the general equation $h = -16t^2 + v_0t$. Here, h refers to the relative height of the projectile from its initial position, v_0 is its initial vertical velocity, and t is time elapsed from launch. If you are measuring the height of the projectile as it descends from a high place, and it was launched with $v_0 = 0$ (which means it was thrown horizontally or dropped), how would you use special products to find the time at which it reaches a given height? (Assume that the height the projectile has descended is a square number in this question, although this is not a requirement in real life).

16. Essential Question Check-In How can you use special products to solve quadratic equations?

For each trinomial, draw algebra tiles to show the factored form. Then, write the factored form.

1. $x^2 - 10x + 25$

2. $x^2 + 8x + 16$

Factor.

3. $4x^2 + 4x + 1$

4. $9x^2 - 18x + 9$

5. $16x^3 + 8x^2 + x$

6. $32x^3 - 16x^2 + 2x$

7. $x^2 - 169$

8. $4p^2 - 9q^4$

9. $32x^4 - 8x^2$

10. $2y^5 - 32z^4y$

Solve the following equations with special factors.

11. $25x^2 + 20x + 4 = 0$

12. $x^3 - 10x^2 + 25x = 0$

13. $4x^4 + 8x^3 + 4x^2 = 0$

14. $4x^2 - 8x + 4 = 0$

15. $x^2 - 81 = 0$

16. $2x^3 - 2x = 0$

17. $16q^2 - 81 = 0$

18. $4p^4 - 25p^2 = -16p^2$

Jivesh is analyzing the flight of a few of his model rockets with various equations. In each equation, h is the height of the rocket in centimeters, and the rocket was fired from the ground at time $t = 0$, where t is measured in seconds.

19. For Jivesh's Model A rocket, he uses the equation $h = -490t^2 + 1120t$. When is the height of the Model A rocket 640 centimeters?

20. Jivesh also has a more powerful Model B rocket. For this rocket, he uses the equation $h = -490t^2 + 1260t$. When is the height of the Model B rocket 810 centimeters?

21. Jivesh brought his Model B rocket on a camping trip near the top of a mountain. He wants to model how it descends down the mountain. Here, he uses the equation $h = -490t^2$. When has the rocket descended 1000 centimeters?

22. **Geometry** Claire is cutting a square out of a bigger square for an art project. She cuts out a square with an area of 9 cm². The leftover area is 16 cm². What is the length of one of the sides of the bigger square? The area of a square is $A = l^2$ where l is the length of one of its sides.

23. The height of a diver during a dive can be modeled by $h = -16t^2$, where h is height in feet relative to the diving platform and t is time in seconds. Find the time it takes for the diver to reach the water if the platform is 49 feet high.

24. **Physics** Consider a particular baseball player at bat. The height of the ball at time t can be modeled by $h = -16t^2 + v_0t + h_0$. Here, v_0 is the initial upward velocity of the ball, and h_0 is the height at which the ball is hit. If a ball is 4 feet off the ground when it is hit with a negligible upward velocity close to 0 feet per second, when will the ball hit the ground?

25. **Explain the Error** Jeremy factored $144x^2 - 100$ as follows:

$$144x^2 - 100 = (12x + 10)(12x - 10)$$

$$= 2(6x + 5)(6x - 5)$$

What was his error? Correct his work.

26. Which of the following are solutions to the equation $x^5 - 2x^3 + x = 0$? Select all that apply.

a. $x = -1$

b. $x = 2$

c. $x = 1$

d. $x = 0.5$

e. $x = 0$

H.O.T. **Focus on Higher Order Thinking**

27. **Multi-Step** An artist framed a picture. The picture is a square with a side length of $2y$. It is surrounded by a square frame with a side length of $4x$.

a. Find and completely factor the expression for the area of the frame.

b. The frame has an area of 11 square inches and the picture has an area of 25 square inches. Find the width of the frame.

28. **Critical Thinking** Sinea thinks that the fully factored form of the expression $x^4 - 1$ is $(x^2 - 1)(x^2 + 1)$. Is she correct? Explain.

29. **Persevere in Problem Solving** Samantha has the equation $x^3 + 2x^2 + x = x^3 - x$. Explain how she can find the solutions of the equation. Then solve the equation.

30. **Communicate Mathematical Ideas** Explain how to fully factor the expression $x^4 - 2x^2y^2 + y^4$.

Lesson Performance Task

A designer is planning to place a fountain in the lobby
of an art museum. Four artists have each designed
a fountain to fit the space. Some have designed
rectangular fountains and the others designed square
fountains. Given a quadratic equation representing the
area of the fountain and the actual area of the fountain,
find the dimensions of each fountain.

Artist	Artemis	Beatrice	Geoffrey	Daniel
Area equation	$A_A = 9x^2 - 25$	$A_B = 4x^2 - 25$	$A_G = 25x^2 + 80x + 64$	$A_D = 81x^2 + 198x + 121$
Fountain area	39 square feet	$28x - 74$ square feet	$160x$ square feet	$198x + 242$ square feet

Using Factors to Solve Quadratic Equations

Essential Question: How can you use factoring a quadratic equation to solve real-world problems?

Key Vocabulary

difference of two squares
(diferencia de dos cuadrados)
perfect-square trinomial
(trinomio cuadrado perfecto)

KEY EXAMPLE (Lesson 21.1)

Factor $x^2 - 2x - 8$.

Find the factor pair of -8 whose sum is -2.

The factor pair is -4 and 2.

$x^2 - 2x - 8 = (x - 4)(x + 2)$

Factors of -8	Sum of Factors
-1 and 8	7
1 and -8	-7
-2 and 4	2
2 and -4	-2

KEY EXAMPLE (Lesson 21.2)

Solve $4x^2 + 8x + 3 = 0$.

Find the factor pairs of 4 and 3 that result in a sum of 8.

The factor pairs are 2 and 2 and 1 and 3.

$$4x^2 + 8x + 3 = 0$$

$$(2x + 1)(2x + 3) = 0$$

$2x + 1 = 0 \qquad$ or $\qquad 2x + 3 = 0$

$\qquad x = -\dfrac{1}{2} \qquad$ or $\qquad x = -\dfrac{3}{2}$

Factors of 4	Factors of 3	Outer Product + Inner Product
1 and 4	1 and 3	$(1)(3) + (4)(1) = 7$
1 and 4	3 and 1	$(1)(1) + (4)(3) = 13$
2 and 2	1 and 3	$(2)(3) + (2)(1) = 8$

KEY EXAMPLE (Lesson 21.3)

Solve $16x^2 - 25 = 0$.

$$4^2 \cdot x^2 - 5^2 = 0 \qquad\qquad \textit{Rewrite in the form } a^2 x^2 - b^2.$$

$$(4x + 5)(4x - 5) = 0 \qquad \textit{Rewrite in the form } (ax + b)(ax - b).$$

$4x + 5 = 0 \quad$ or $\quad 4x - 5 = 0 \qquad \textit{Set factors equal to 0 using Zero Product Property.}$

$\quad x = -\dfrac{5}{4} \quad$ or $\qquad x = \dfrac{5}{4}$

EXERCISES

Solve each equation. *(Lessons 21.1, 21.2, 21.3)*

1. $x^2 - 81 = 0$

2. $2x^2 - 8x - 10 = 0$

3. $x^2 + 7x + 12 = 0$

4. $x^2 - 14x = -49$

5. $16 - 4x^2 = 0$

6. $6x^2 + 5x + 1 = 0$

7. The area of a rectangular pool is $\left(x^2 + 17x + 72\right)$ square meters. The dimensions of the pool are the factors of this polynomial. There is a 3-meter-wide concrete walkway around the pool. Write expressions to represent the dimensions of the outside border of the walkway. *(Lesson 21.1)*

MODULE PERFORMANCE TASK

Fitting Through the Arch

The Ship-Shape Shipping Company ships items in rectangular crates. At one shipping destination, each crate must be able to fit through an arched doorway. The shape of this arched doorway can be modeled by the quadratic equation $y = -x^2 + 16$, where x is the distance in feet from the center of the arch and y is the height of the arch. Find the width of the archway at its base.

The Ship-Shape Shipping Company just unloaded several crates outside the arch ranging in height from 2 feet to 6 feet. Choose a particular crate height. Then, find the maximum width the crate could have and still fit through the arched doorway.

Start by listing how you will tackle this problem. Then complete the task. Be sure to write down all your data and assumptions. Then use graphs, tables, or algebra to explain how you reached your conclusion.

21.1–21.3 Using Factors to Solve Quadratic Equations

Personal Math Trainer

• Online Homework
• Hints and Help
• Extra Practice

Identify each expression as a perfect-square trinomial, a difference of squares, or neither. Factor each expression. *(Lessons 21.1, 21.2, 21.3)*

1. $4p^2 + 12p + 9$

2. $a^2 - 9a - 36$

Solve each equation. *(Lessons 21.1, 21.2, 21.3)*

3. $x^2 - 4x - 21 = 0$

4. $49x^2 - 100 = 0$

5. $5x^2 - 33x - 14 = 0$

6. $x^2 + 16x + 64 = 0$

7. A golfer hits a ball from a starting elevation of 4 feet with a vertical velocity of 70 feet per second down to a green with an elevation of −5 feet. The number of seconds t it takes the ball to hit the green can be represented by the equation $-16t^2 + 70t + 4 = -5$. How long does it take the ball to land on the green? *(Lesson 21.2)*

ESSENTIAL QUESTION

8. How can you use factoring to solve quadratic equations in standard form?

Assessment Readiness

1. Consider the equation $5x(2x + 1) - 3(2x + 1) = 0$.
   Determine if each statement is True or False.
   A. It is equivalent to $(5x - 3)(2x + 1) = 0$.
   B. A solution of the equation is $x = \dfrac{1}{2}$.
   C. A zero of the equation is $\dfrac{3}{5}$.

2. Factor to solve each equation. Does the equation have a solution of $x = 2$?
   A. $4x^2 - 16 = 0$
   B. $x^2 - 4x + 4 = 0$
   C. $4x^2 + 16x + 16 = 0$

3. Larry thinks the quotient of $\dfrac{4x^2 + 7x - 15}{x + 3}$ is $4x - 5$. Explain how you can check his answer using multiplication. Then, check his answer. Is Larry correct?

4. Marcello is replacing a rectangular sliding glass door with dimensions of $(x + 7)$ and $(x + 3)$ feet. The area of the glass door is 45 square feet. What are the length and width of the door? Explain how you got your answer.

Using Square Roots to Solve Quadratic Equations

Essential Question: How can you use quadratic equations to solve real-world problems?

REAL WORLD VIDEO
The designers of a fireworks display need to make precise timing calculations. An explosion too soon or too late could spell disaster!

MODULE PERFORMANCE TASK PREVIEW
Fireworks Display

As with any other projectile, the relationship between the time since a firework was launched and its height is quadratic. Fireworks must be carefully timed in order to ignite at the most impressive height. In this task, you will figure out how you can use math to launch fireworks that are safe and achieve the maximum possible effect.

Are **YOU** Ready?

Complete these exercises to review skills you will need for this module.

Exponents

Example 1   Simplify $25^{\frac{1}{2}}$.

$25^{\frac{1}{2}} = \sqrt{25} = 5$

A number raised to the $\frac{1}{2}$ power is equal to the square root of the number.

Simplify.

1. $100^{\frac{1}{2}}$

2. $50^{\frac{1}{2}}$

3. $\left(\dfrac{36}{81}\right)^{\frac{1}{2}}$

Algebraic Expressions

Example 2   Evaluate $\left(\dfrac{b}{2}\right)^2$ when $b = 18$.

$\left(\dfrac{b}{2}\right)^2$

$\left(\dfrac{18}{2}\right)^2 = 9^2 = 81$

Substitute 18 for b and evaluate the expression.

Evaluate $\left(\dfrac{b}{2}\right)^2$ for the given value of b.

4. $b = 24$

5. $b = -10$

6. $b = 3$

Example 3   Factor $x^2 + 14x + 49$.

$x^2 + 14x + 49$ $x^2 + 14x + 49$ is a perfect square.

$x^2 + 2(x)(7) + 7^2$ Rewrite in the form $a^2 + 2ab + b^2$.

$(x + 7)(x + 7)$ Rewrite in the form $(a + b)(a + b)$.

$(x + 7)^2$

Factor each perfect square trinomial.

7. $x^2 - 12x + 36$

8. $x^2 + 22x + 121$

9. $4x^2 + 12x + 9$

10. $16x^2 - 40x + 25$

22.1 Solving Equations by Taking Square Roots

Essential Question: How can you solve quadratic equations using square roots?

⊘ Explore Exploring Square Roots

Recall that the **square root** of a nonnegative number a is the real number b such that $b^2 = a$. Since $4^2 = 16$ and $(-4)^2 = 16$, the square roots of 16 are 4 and -4. Thus, every positive real number has two square roots, one positive and one negative. The positive square root is given by $\sqrt{a}$ and the negative square root by $-\sqrt{a}$. These can be combined as $\pm\sqrt{a}$.

Properties of Radicals		
Property	**Symbols**	**Example**
Product Property of Radicals	For $a \geq 0$ and $b \geq 0$, $\sqrt{ab} = \sqrt{a} \cdot \sqrt{b}$.	$\begin{aligned} \sqrt{36} &= \sqrt{9 \cdot 4} \\ &= \sqrt{9} \cdot \sqrt{4} \\ &= 3 \cdot 2 \\ &= 6 \end{aligned}$
Quotient Property of Radicals	For $a \geq 0$ and $b > 0$, $\sqrt{\dfrac{a}{b}} = \dfrac{\sqrt{a}}{\sqrt{b}}$.	$\begin{aligned} -\sqrt{0.16} &= -\sqrt{\dfrac{16}{100}} \\ &= -\dfrac{\sqrt{16}}{\sqrt{100}} \\ &= -\dfrac{4}{10} \\ &= -0.4 \end{aligned}$

Find each square root.

(A) $\pm\sqrt{49} = +\boxed{?}$ and $-\boxed{?}$

(B) $\pm\sqrt{25} = +\boxed{?}$ and $-\boxed{?}$

(C) $\pm\sqrt{12} = \pm\sqrt{\boxed{?} \cdot 3} = \pm\sqrt{\boxed{?}} \cdot \sqrt{\boxed{?}}$
$= \pm\boxed{?} \cdot \sqrt{\boxed{?}}$

(D) $\pm\sqrt{\dfrac{16}{9}} = \pm\dfrac{\sqrt{\boxed{?}}}{\sqrt{\boxed{?}}}$
$= \pm\dfrac{\boxed{?}}{\boxed{?}}$

(E) $\pm\sqrt{0.27} = \pm\sqrt{\dfrac{\boxed{?}}{100}} = \pm\dfrac{\sqrt{\boxed{?}}}{\sqrt{100}} = \pm\dfrac{\sqrt{\boxed{?} \cdot 3}}{\boxed{?}} = \pm\dfrac{\sqrt{\boxed{?}} \cdot \sqrt{3}}{\boxed{?}} = \pm\dfrac{\boxed{?} \cdot \sqrt{\boxed{?}}}{\boxed{?}}$

Reflect

1. **Discussion** Explain why $\sqrt{6^2}$ and $\sqrt{(-6)^2}$ have the same value.

2. **Discussion** Explain why a must be nonnegative when you find $\sqrt{a}$.

3. Does 0 have any square roots? Why or why not?

🎯 Explain 1   Solving $ax^2 - c = 0$ by Using Square Roots

Solving a quadratic equation by using square roots may involve either finding square roots of perfect squares or finding square roots of numbers that are not perfect squares. In the latter case, the solution is irrational and can be approximated.

Example 1   Solve the equation. Give the answer in radical form, and then use a calculator to approximate the solution to two decimal places, if necessary. Use a graphing calculator to graph the related function and compare the roots of the equation to the zeros of the related function.

(A) $4x^2 - 5 = 2$

Solve the equation for x.

$4x^2 - 5 = 2$	Original equation
$4x^2 - 5 + 5 = 2 + 5$	Add 5 to both sides.
$4x^2 = 7$	Simplify.
$\dfrac{4x^2}{4} = \dfrac{7}{4}$	Divide both sides by 4.
$x^2 = 1.75$	Simplify.
$x = \pm\sqrt{1.75}$	Definition of a square root
$x \approx \pm 1.32$	Use a calculator to approximate the square roots.

The approximate solutions of the equation are $x \approx 1.32$ and $x \approx -1.32$.

Use a graphing calculator to graph the related function, $f(x) = 4x^2 - 7$, and find the zeros of the function.

The graph intersects the x-axis at approximately $(1.32, 0)$ and $(-1.32, 0)$. So, the roots of the equation are the zeros of the related function.

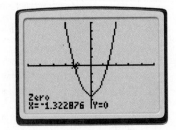

(B) $2x^2 - 8 = 0$

Solve the equation for x.

$2x^2 - 8 = 0$ Original equation

$2x^2 - 8 + \boxed{8} = 0 + \boxed{8}$ Add $\boxed{8}$ to both sides.

$2x^2 = \boxed{8}$ Simplify.

$\dfrac{2x^2}{\boxed{2}} = \dfrac{\boxed{8}}{\boxed{2}}$ Divide both sides by $\boxed{2}$.

$x^2 = \boxed{4}$ Simplify.

$x = \pm\sqrt{\boxed{4}}$ Definition of a square root

$x = \pm\boxed{2}$ Evaluate the square roots.

The solutions of the equation are $x = \boxed{2}$ and $x = \boxed{-2}$.

Use a graphing calculator to graph the related function, $f(x) = 2x^2 - 8$, and find the zeros of the function.

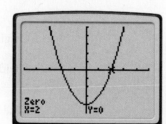 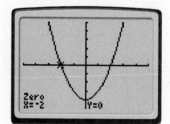

The graph intersects the x-axis at $\left(\boxed{2}, \boxed{0}\right)$ and $\left(\boxed{-2}, \boxed{0}\right)$. So,

the roots of the equation are the zeros of the related function.

Your Turn

Solve the equation. Give the answer in radical form, and then use a calculator to approximate the solution to two decimal places, if necessary. Use a graphing calculator to graph the related function to check your answer.

4. $3x^2 + 6 = 33$

5. $5x^2 - 9 = 2$

⚙ Explain 2 Solving $a(x + b)^2 = c$ by Using Square Roots

Solving a quadratic equation may involve isolating the squared part of a quadratic expression on one side of the equation first.

Example 2 Solve the equation. Give the answer in radical form, and then use a calculator to approximate the solution to two decimal places, if necessary.

Ⓐ $(x + 5)^2 = 36$

$(x + 5)^2 = 36$	Original equation
$x + 5 = \pm\sqrt{36}$	Take the square root of both sides.
$x + 5 = \pm 6$	Simplify the square root.
$x = \pm 6 - 5$	Subtract 5 from both sides.
$x = -6 - 5$ or $x = 6 - 5$	Solve for both cases.
$x = -11$ $x = 1$	

The solutions are $x = -11$ and $x = 1$.

Ⓑ $3(x - 5)^2 = 18$

$3(x - 5)^2 = 18$	Original equation
$(x - 5)^2 = \boxed{6}$	Divide both sides by $\boxed{3}$.
$x - 5 = \pm\sqrt{\boxed{6}}$	Take the square roots of both sides.
$x = \pm\sqrt{\boxed{6}} + \boxed{5}$	Add $\boxed{5}$ to both sides.
$x = \sqrt{\boxed{6}} + 5$ or $x = -\sqrt{6} + \boxed{5}$	Solve for both cases.
$x \approx \boxed{7.45}$ or $x \approx \boxed{2.55}$	

The approximate solutions are $x \approx \boxed{7.45}$ and $x \approx \boxed{2.55}$.

Reflect

6. Find the solution(s), if any, of $2(x - 3)^2 = -32$. Explain your reasoning.

Solve the equation. Give the answer in radical form, and then use a calculator to approximate the solution to two decimal places, if necessary.

7. $4(x + 10)^2 = 24$

8. $(x - 9)^2 = 64$

⚙ Explain 3 Solving Equation Models by Using Square Roots

Real-world situations can sometimes be analyzed by solving a quadratic equation using square roots.

Example 3 Solve the problem.

(A) A contractor is building a fenced-in playground at a daycare. The playground will be rectangular with its width equal to half its length. The total area will be 5000 square feet. Determine how many feet of fencing the contractor will use.

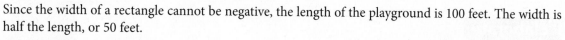

First, find the dimensions.
Let $A = 5000$, $\ell = x$, and $w = \frac{1}{2}x$.

$$A = \ell w$$

$$5000 = x \cdot \frac{1}{2}x$$

$$5000 = \frac{1}{2}x^2$$

$$10{,}000 = x^2$$

$\pm\sqrt{10{,}000} = x$ Take the square root of both sides.

$\pm 100 = x$ Evaluate the square root.

Since the width of a rectangle cannot be negative, the length of the playground is 100 feet. The width is half the length, or 50 feet.

Find the amount of fencing.

$P = 2\ell + 2w$

$\quad = 2(100) + 2(50)$

$\quad = 200 + 100$ Multiply.

$\quad = 300$ Add.

So, the contractor will use 300 feet of fencing.

Ⓑ A person standing on a second-floor balcony drops keys to a friend standing below the balcony. The keys are dropped from a height of 10 feet. The height in feet of the keys as they fall is given by the function $h(t) = -16t^2 + 10$, where t is the time in seconds since the keys were dropped. The friend catches the keys at a height of 4 feet. Find the elapsed time before the keys are caught.

Let $h(t) =$ [4] . Substitute the value into the equation and solve for t.

$h(t) = -16t^2 + 10$	Original equation
$\boxed{4} = -16t^2 + 10$	Substitute.
$4 - \boxed{10} = -16t^2 + 10 - \boxed{10}$	Subtract 10 from both sides.
$-6 = -16t^2$	Simplify.
$\dfrac{-6}{\boxed{-16}} = \dfrac{-16t^2}{\boxed{-16}}$	Divide both sides by -16.
$\boxed{0.375} = t^2$	Simplify.
$\pm\sqrt{\boxed{0.375}} = t$	Take the square root of both sides.
$\pm\boxed{0.61} \approx t$	Use a calculator to approximate the square roots.

Since time cannot be negative, the elapsed time before the keys are caught is approximately [0.61] second(s).

Your Turn

9. A zookeeper is buying fencing to enclose a pen at the zoo. The pen is an isosceles right triangle. There is already a fence along the hypotenuse, which borders a path. The area of the pen will be 4500 square feet. The zookeeper can buy the fencing in whole feet only. How many feet of fencing should he buy?

💬 Elaborate

10. How many real solutions does $x^2 = -25$ have? Explain.

11. Suppose the function $h(t) = -16t^2 + 20$ models the height in feet of an object after t seconds. If the final height is given as 2 feet, explain why there is only one reasonable solution for the time it takes the object to fall.

12. **Essential Question Check-In** What steps would you take to solve $6x^2 - 54 = 42$?

☆ Evaluate: Homework and Practice

- Online Homework
- Hints and Help
- Extra Practice

Use the Product Property of Radicals, the Quotient Property of Radicals, or both to simplify each expression.

1. $\pm\sqrt{0.0081}$

2. $\pm\sqrt{\dfrac{8}{25}}$

3. $\pm\sqrt{96}$

Solve each equation. Give the answer in radical form, and then use a calculator to approximate the solution to two decimal places, if necessary. Use a graphing calculator to graph the related function to check your answer.

4. $5x^2 - 21 = 39$

5. $0.1x^2 - 1.2 = 8.8$

6. $6x^2 - 21 = 33$

7. $6 - \frac{1}{3}x^2 = -20$

8. $5 - 2x^2 = -3$

9. $7x^2 + 10 = 18$

Solve each equation. Give the answer in radical form, and then use a calculator to approximate the solution to two decimal places, if necessary.

10. $5(x - 9)^2 = 15$

11. $(x + 15)2 = 81$

12. $3(x + 1)^2 = 27$

13. $2\_3\ (x - 40)^2 = 24$

14. $(x - 12)2 = 54$

15. $(x + 5.4)2 = 1.75$

16. The area on a wall covered by a rectangular poster is 320 square inches. The length of the poster is 1.25 times longer than the width of the poster. What are the dimensions of the poster?

17. A circle is graphed with its center on the origin. The area of the circle is 144 square units. What are the x-intercepts of the graph? Round to the nearest tenth.

18. The equation $d = 16t\ 2$ gives the distance d in feet that a golf ball falls in t seconds. How many seconds will it take a golf ball to drop to the ground from a height of 4 feet? 64 feet?

19. **Entertainment** For a scene in a movie, a sack of money is dropped from the roof of a 600-foot skyscraper. The height of the sack above the ground in feet is given by $h = -16t^2 + 600$, where t is the time in seconds. How long will it take the sack to reach the ground? Round to the nearest tenth of a second.

20. A lot for sale is shaped like a trapezoid. The bases of the trapezoid represent the widths of the front and back yards. The width of the back yard is twice the width of the front yard. The distance from the front yard to the backyard, or the height of the trapezoid, is equal to the width of the back yard. Find the width of the front and back yards, given that the area is 6000 square feet. Round to the nearest foot.

21. To study how high a ball bounces, students drop the ball from various heights. The function $h(t) = -16t^2 + h$ gives the height (in feet) of the ball at time t measured in seconds since the ball was dropped from a height of h. If the ball is dropped from a height of 8 feet, find the elapsed time until the ball hits the floor. Round to the nearest tenth.

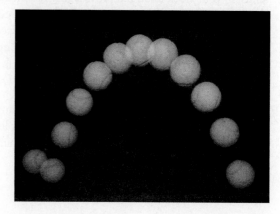

22. Match each equation with its solutions.

A. $2x^2 - 2 = 16$

a. ___?___ $= \pm \dfrac{2\sqrt{33}}{3}$

B. $2(x - 2)^2 = 16$

b. ___?___ $x = \pm 3$

C. $3x^2 + 4 = 48$

c. ___?___ $x = 2 \pm 2\sqrt{2}$

D. $3(x + 4)^2 = 48$

d. ___?___ $x = -8$ and $x = 0$

23. **Explain the Error** Trent and Lisa solve the same equation, but they disagree on the solution of the equation. Their work is shown. Which solution is correct? Explain.

Trent:

$$5x^2 + 1000 = -125$$

$$5x^2 = -1125$$

$$x^2 = -225$$

$$x = \pm\sqrt{-225}$$

$$x = \pm 15$$

Lisa:

$$5x^2 + 1000 = -125$$

$$5x^2 = -1125$$

$$x^2 = -225$$

no real solutions

24. **Multi-Step** Construction workers are installing a rectangular, in-ground pool. To start, they dig a rectangular hole in the ground where the pool will be. The area of the ground that they will be digging up is 252 square feet. The length of the pool is twice the width of the pool.

   a. What are the dimensions of the pool? Round to the nearest tenth.

   b. Once the pool is installed, the workers will build a fence, that encloses a rectangular region, around the perimeter of it. The fence will be 10 feet from the edges of the pool, except at the corners. How many feet of fencing will the workers need?

25. **Communicate Mathematical Ideas** Explain why the quadratic equation $x^2 + b = 0$ where $b > 0$, has no real solutions, but the quadratic equation $x^2 - b = 0$ where $b > 0$, has two real solutions.

26. **Justify Reasoning** For the equation $x^2 = a$, describe the values of a that will result in two real solutions, one real solution, and no real solution. Explain your reasoning.

Lesson Performance Task

You have been asked to create a pendulum clock for your classroom. The clock will be placed on one wall of the classroom and go the entire height of the wall. Choose how large you want the face and hands on your clock to be and provide measurements for the body of the clock. The pendulum will start halfway between the center of the clock face and its bottom edge and will initially end 1 foot above the floor. Calculate the period of the pendulum using the formula $L = 9.78t^2$, where L is the length of the pendulum in inches and t is the length of the period in seconds.

Now, adjust the length of your pendulum so the number of periods in 1 minute or 60 seconds is an integer value. How long is your pendulum and how many periods equal one minute?

22.2 Solving Equations by Completing the Square

Essential Question: How can you use completing the square to solve a quadratic equation?

Explore Modeling Completing the Square

You can use algebra tiles to model a perfect square trinomial.

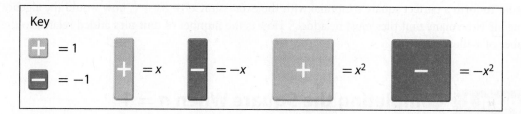

Key

$\boxed{+} = 1$

$\boxed{-} = -1$

$\boxed{+} = x$ $\boxed{-} = -x$ $\boxed{+} = x^2$ $\boxed{-} = -x^2$

(A) The algebra tiles shown represent the expression $x^2 + 6x$. The expression does not have a constant term, which would be represented with unit tiles. Create a square diagram of algebra tiles by adding the correct number of unit tiles to form a square.

(B) How many unit tiles were added to the expression? $\boxed{?}$

(C) Write the trinomial represented by the algebra tiles for the complete square.

$\boxed{?}\ x^2 + \boxed{?}\ x + \boxed{?}$

(D) It should be easily recognized that the trinomial $\boxed{?}\ x^2 + \boxed{?}\ x + \boxed{?}$ is an example of the special case $(a + b)^2 = a^2 + 2ab + b^2$. Recall that trinomials of this form are called perfect-square trinomials. Since the trinomial is a perfect square, it can be factored into two identical binomials.

$\boxed{?}\ x^2 + \boxed{?}\ x + \boxed{?} = \left(\boxed{?}\ x + \boxed{?} \right)^2$

(E) Refer to the algebra tiles in the diagram. What expression is represented by the tiles?

$\boxed{?}\ x^2 + \boxed{?}\ x$

(F) Complete the square in Step E by filling the bottom right corner with unit tiles. How many unit tiles were added to the diagram? $\boxed{?}$

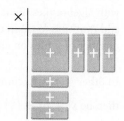

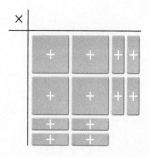

(G) Write the trinomial represented by the algebra tiles for the complete square.

$\boxed{?}\ x^2 + \boxed{?}\ x + \boxed{?}$

(H) The trinomial is a square of a binomial. Use the algebra tiles to write the trinomial in factored form.

$\boxed{?}\ x^2 + \boxed{?}\ x + \boxed{?} = \left(\boxed{?}\ x + \boxed{?}\right)^2$

Reflect

1. **Discussion** When using algebra tiles to model the expression $x^2 + 6x + c$, the x-tiles are divided equally, with 3 tiles on the right and bottom sides of the x^2-tile. How does the number 3 relate to the total number of x-tiles? How does the number 3 relate to the total number of unit tiles that were added?

2. In order to form a perfect square trinomial with the expression $x^2 + 8x + c$, how would the algebra tiles be arranged? How many unit tiles must be added? How is the number of unit tiles added related to the total number of x-tiles?

⊘ Explain 1   Completing the Square When $a = 1$

Completing the square is a process of rewriting a quadratic expression as a perfect square trinomial so that it can be solved by taking square roots. In the Explore, the method for completing the square when $a = 1$ was modeled with algebra tiles. First, place half of the x-tiles along the right side of the x^2-tile and half underneath the tile. Then add unit tiles to fill in the rectangle started with the x^2 - and x-tiles. The number of unit tiles equals the square of the number of x-tiles on either side of the x^2-tile.

In other words, to complete the square for the expression $x^2 + bx + c$, add $\left(\frac{b}{2}\right)^2$. The perfect-square trinomial will then be $x^2 + bx + \left(\frac{b}{2}\right)^2$ and its factored form will be $\left(x + \frac{b}{2}\right)^2$.

Example 1   Complete the square to form a perfect-square trinomial.

(A) $x^2 + 4x$

$x^2 + 4x$

$b = 4$ Identify b.

$\left(\frac{4}{2}\right)^2 = 2^2 = 4$ Find $\left(\frac{b}{2}\right)^2$.

$x^2 + 4x + 4$ Add $\left(\frac{b}{2}\right)^2$ to the expression.

B $x^2 - 8x$

$x^2 - 8x$

$b = \boxed{-8}$ Identify b.

$\left(\dfrac{\boxed{-8}}{2}\right)^2 = \left(\boxed{-4}\right)^2 = \boxed{16}$ Find $\left(\dfrac{b}{2}\right)^2$.

$x^2 - 8x + \boxed{16}$ Add $\left(\dfrac{b}{2}\right)^2$ to the expression.

Reflect

3. When b is negative, why is the result added to the expression still positive?

Your Turn

4. Complete the square: $x^2 + 12x$

⚙ Explain 2   Solving $x^2 + bx + c = 0$ by Completing the Square

Completing the square can also be used to solve equations in the forms $x^2 + bx + c = 0$ or $x^2 + bx = c$.

Example 2   Solve each equation by completing the square. Check the answers.

A $x^2 - 4x = 3$

$x^2 - 4x = 3$

$x^2 - 4x + 4 = 3 + 4$ Add $\left(\dfrac{b}{2}\right)^2 = \left(\dfrac{-4}{2}\right)^2 = 4$ to both sides.

$(x - 2)^2 = 7$ Factor and simplify.

$x - 2 = \pm\sqrt{7}$ Take the square root of both sides.

$x - 2 = \sqrt{7}$ or $x - 2 = -\sqrt{7}$ Write and solve two equations.

$x = 2 + \sqrt{7}$ $x = 2 - \sqrt{7}$ Add 2 to both sides.

Check the answers.

$\left(2 + \sqrt{7}\right)^2 - 4\left(2 + \sqrt{7}\right)$ $\left(2 - \sqrt{7}\right)^2 - 4\left(2 - \sqrt{7}\right)$

$= 4 + 4\sqrt{7} + 7 - 8 - 4\sqrt{7}$ $= 4 - 4\sqrt{7} + 7 - 8 + 4\sqrt{7}$

$= 4 + 7 - 8 + 4\sqrt{7} - 4\sqrt{7}$ $= 4 + 7 - 8 - 4\sqrt{7} + 4\sqrt{7}$

$= 3$ $= 3$

$2 + \sqrt{7}$ and $2 - \sqrt{7}$ are both solutions of the equation $x^2 - 4x = 3$.

B $x^2 + 16x = 36$

$$x^2 + 16x = 36$$

$\boxed{1}\,x^2 + \boxed{16}\,x + \boxed{64} = \boxed{36} + \boxed{64}$ Add $\left(\dfrac{b}{2}\right)^2 = \boxed{64}$ to both sides.

$\left(\boxed{1}\,x + \boxed{8}\right)^2 = \boxed{100}$ Factor and simplify.

$\boxed{1}\,x + \boxed{8} = \pm\,\boxed{10}$ Take the square root of both sides.

$\boxed{1}\,x + \boxed{8} = \boxed{10}$ or $\boxed{1}\,x + \boxed{8} = -\,\boxed{10}$

$x = \boxed{2}$ $x = \boxed{-18}$

Check the answers.

$$x^2 + 16x = 36$$

$(-18)^2 + 16 \cdot \boxed{-18} = 36$

$\boxed{324} - \boxed{288} = 36$

$\boxed{36} = 36$

$x = -18$ is a solution to the equation $x^2 + 16x = 36$.

$$x^2 + 16x = 36$$

$2^2 + 16 \cdot \boxed{2} = 36$

$\boxed{4} + \boxed{32} = 36$

$\boxed{36} = 36$

$x = 2$ is a solution to the equation $x^2 + 16x = 36$

Your Turn

Solve each equation by completing the square. Check the answers.

5. $x^2 - 10x = 11$ **6.** $x^2 + 6x = 2$

Solving $ax^2 + bx + c = 0$ by Completing the Square When a Is a Perfect Square

When a is a perfect square, completing the square is easier than in other cases. Recall that the number of unit tiles needed is equal to the square of b divided by four times a, or $\frac{b^2}{4a}$. This is always the case when a is a perfect square.

Example 3   Solve each equation by completing the square.

(A) $4x^2 - 8x = 21$

$$4x^2 - 8x = 21$$

$$\frac{(-8)^2}{4 \cdot 4} = \frac{64}{16} = 4 \qquad \text{Find } \frac{b^2}{4a}.$$

$$4x^2 - 8x + 4 = 21 + 4 \qquad \text{Add } \frac{b^2}{4a} \text{ to both sides.}$$

$$(2x - 2)^2 = 25 \qquad \text{Factor and simplify.}$$

$$2x - 2 = \pm\sqrt{25} \qquad \text{Take the square root of the both sides.}$$

$$2x - 2 = \pm 5 \qquad \text{Simplify.}$$

$$2x - 2 = 5 \quad \text{or} \quad 2x - 2 = -5 \qquad \text{Write and solve 2 equations.}$$

$$2x = 7 \quad \text{or} \quad 2x = -3 \qquad \text{Add to both sides.}$$

$$x = \frac{7}{2} \quad \text{or} \quad x = -\frac{3}{2} \qquad \text{Divide both sides by 2.}$$

(B) $9x^2 + 6x = 10$

$$9x^2 + 6x = 10$$

$$\frac{\boxed{6}^{\,2}}{4 \cdot \boxed{9}} = \frac{\boxed{36}}{\boxed{36}} = \boxed{1} \qquad \text{Find } \frac{b^2}{4a}.$$

$$\boxed{9}\,x^2 + \boxed{6}\,x + \boxed{1} = 10 + \boxed{1} \qquad \text{Add } \frac{b^2}{4a} \text{ to both sides.}$$

$$\left(\boxed{3}\,x + \boxed{1}\right)^2 = \boxed{11} \qquad \text{Factor and simplify.}$$

$$\boxed{3}\,x + \boxed{1} = \pm\sqrt{\boxed{11}} \qquad \text{Take the square root of the both sides.}$$

$$\boxed{3}\,x + \boxed{1} = \sqrt{\boxed{11}} \quad \text{or} \quad \boxed{3}\,x + \boxed{1} = -\sqrt{\boxed{11}} \qquad \text{Write and solve two equations.}$$

$$\boxed{3}\,x = -\boxed{1} + \sqrt{\boxed{11}} \qquad \boxed{3}\,x = -\boxed{1} - \sqrt{\boxed{11}} \qquad \text{Subtract } \boxed{1} \text{ from both sides.}$$

$$x = \frac{-\boxed{1} + \sqrt{\boxed{11}}}{\boxed{3}} \qquad x = \frac{-\boxed{1} - \sqrt{\boxed{11}}}{\boxed{3}} \qquad \text{Divide both sides by } \boxed{3}.$$

7. In order for the procedure used in this section to work, why does a have to be a perfect square?

Your Turn

Solve each equation by completing the square.

8. $16x^2 - 16x = 5$

9. $4x^2 + 12x = 5$

Explain 4   Solving $ax^2 + bx + c = 0$ by Completing the Square When a Is Not a Perfect Square

When the leading coefficient a is not a perfect square, the equation can be transformed by multiplying both sides by a value such that a becomes a perfect square.

Example 4   Solve each equation by completing the square.

Ⓐ $2x^2 - 6x = 5$

Since the coefficient of x^2 is 2, which is not a perfect square, multiply both sides by a value so the coefficient will have a perfect square. In this case, use 2.

$2x^2 - 6x = 5$	
$2(2x^2 - 6x) = 2(5)$	Multiply both sides by 2.
$4x^2 - 12x = 10$	Simplify.
$\dfrac{(-12)^2}{4 \cdot 4} = \dfrac{144}{16} = 9$	Find $\dfrac{b^2}{4a}$.
$4x^2 - 12x + 9 = 10 + 9$	Add $\dfrac{b^2}{4a}$ to both sides.
$(2x - 3)^2 = 19$	Factor and simplify.
$2x - 3 = \pm\sqrt{19}$	Take the square root of the both sides.
$2x - 3 = \sqrt{19}$ or $2x - 3 = -\sqrt{19}$	Write and solve 2 equations.
$2x = 3 + \sqrt{19}$ $2x = 3 - \sqrt{19}$	Add to both sides.
$x = \dfrac{3 + \sqrt{19}}{2}$ $x = \dfrac{3 - \sqrt{19}}{2}$	Divide both sides by 2.

(B) $3x^2 + 3x = 16$

Since the coefficient of x^2 is 3, which is not a perfect square, multiply both sides by a value so the coefficient will have a perfect square. In this case, use 3.

$$3x^2 + 3x = 16$$

$\boxed{3}\left(3x^2 + 2x\right) = \boxed{3}(16)$ Multiply both sides by $\boxed{3}$.

$\boxed{9}\,x^2 + \boxed{6}\,x = \boxed{48}$ Simplify.

$\dfrac{\boxed{6}^{\,2}}{4\cdot\boxed{9}} = \dfrac{\boxed{36}}{\boxed{36}} = \boxed{1}$ Find $\dfrac{b^2}{4a}$.

$\boxed{9}\,x^2 + \boxed{6}\,x + \boxed{1} = \boxed{48} + \boxed{1}$ Add $\dfrac{b^2}{4a}$ to both sides.

$\left(\boxed{3}\,x + \boxed{1}\right)^2 = \boxed{49}$ Factor and simplify.

$\boxed{3}\,x + \boxed{1} = \pm\sqrt{\boxed{49}} = \pm\boxed{7}$ Take the square root of the both sides.

$\boxed{3}\,x + \boxed{1} = \boxed{7}$ or $\boxed{3}\,x + \boxed{1} = -\boxed{7}$ Write and solve two equations.

$\boxed{3}\,x = \boxed{6}$ $\boxed{3}\,x = -\boxed{8}$ Subtract $\boxed{1}$ from both sides.

$x = \boxed{2}$ $x = -\dfrac{8}{3}$ Divide both sides by $\boxed{3}$.

Reflect

10. Consider the equation $2x^2 + 11x = 12$. Why is 2 the best value by which to multiply both sides of the equation before completing the square?

Your Turn

Solve each equation by completing the square.

11. $\dfrac{1}{2}x^2 + 3x = 14$ **12.** $2x^2 - 4x = 16$

⚙ Explain 5 Modeling Completing the Square for Quadratic Equations

Completing the square can be useful when solving problems involving quadratic functions, especially if the function cannot be factored. In these cases, complete the square to rewrite the function in vertex form: $f(x) = a(x - h)^2 + k$. Completing the square in this situation is similar to solving equations by completing the square, but instead of adding a term to both sides of the equation, you will both add and subtract it from the function's rule.

Recall that the height of an object moving under the force of gravity, with no other forces acting on it, can be modeled by the quadratic function $h = -16t^2 + vt + s$, where t is the time in seconds, v is the initial vertical velocity, and s is the initial height in feet.

Example 5 Write a function in standard form for each model. Then, rewrite the equation in vertex form and solve the problem. Graph the function on a graphing calculator and find the x-intercepts and maximum value of the graph.

(A) **Sports** A baseball is thrown from a height of 5 feet. If the person throws the baseball at a velocity of 30 feet per second, what will be the maximum height of the baseball? How long will it take the baseball to hit the ground?

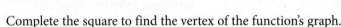

The function for this situation is $h = -16t^2 + 30t + 5$.

Complete the square to find the vertex of the function's graph.

$$h = -16\left(t^2 - \frac{30}{16}t\right) + 5$$ Factor out -16.

$$\frac{\left(-\frac{30}{16}\right)^2}{4} = \frac{\frac{900}{256}}{4} = \frac{900}{256} \cdot \frac{1}{4} = \frac{225}{256}$$ Find $\frac{b^2}{4}$.

$$h = -16\left(t^2 - \frac{30}{16}t + \frac{225}{256} - \frac{225}{256}\right) + 5$$ Complete the square.

$$h = -16\left(\left(t - \frac{15}{16}\right)^2 - \frac{225}{256}\right) + 5$$ Factor the perfect-square trinomial.

$$h = -16\left(t - \frac{15}{16}\right)^2 + \frac{225}{16} + 5$$ Distribute the -16.

$$h = -16\left(t - \frac{15}{16}\right)^2 + \frac{305}{16}$$ Combine the last two terms.

The coordinates of the vertex are $\left(\frac{15}{4}, \frac{305}{16}\right)$, or about $(3.75, 19.06)$. The maximum height will be about 19 feet.

The graph of the function confirms the vertex at about $(3.75, 19.06)$. The t-intercept at about 2.03 indicates that the baseball will hit the ground after about 2 seconds.

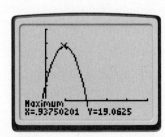

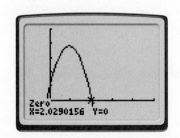

(B) **Sports** A person kicks a soccer ball from the ground with an initial upward velocity of 16 feet per second. What is the maximum height of the soccer ball? When will the soccer ball hit the ground?

An equation for this situation is $h = -16t^2 + \boxed{16}\,t + \boxed{0}$.

Complete the square to find the vertex of the function's graph.

$$h = -16t^2 + \boxed{16}\,t + \boxed{0}$$

$$h = \boxed{-16}\left(\boxed{1}\,t^2 - \boxed{1}\,t\right) + \boxed{0} \qquad \text{Factor out } \boxed{-16}.$$

$$h = \boxed{-16}\left(\boxed{1}\,t^2 - \boxed{1}\,t + \dfrac{\boxed{1}}{4} - \dfrac{\boxed{1}}{4}\right) + 0 \qquad \text{Complete the square.}$$

$$h = \boxed{-16}\left(\left(\boxed{1}\,t - \dfrac{\boxed{1}}{2}\right)^2 - \dfrac{\boxed{1}}{4}\right) + 0 \qquad \text{Factor the perfect-square trinomial.}$$

$$h = \boxed{-16}\left(\boxed{1}\,t - \dfrac{\boxed{1}}{2}\right)^2 + \dfrac{\boxed{16}}{4} + 0 \qquad \text{Distribute the } -16.$$

$$h = \boxed{-16}\left(\boxed{1}\,t - \dfrac{\boxed{1}}{2}\right)^2 + \boxed{4} \qquad \text{Combine the last two terms.}$$

The coordinates of the vertex are $\left(\dfrac{\boxed{1}}{2},\ \boxed{4}\right)$.

The soccer ball will be at its highest when it is at its vertex, or at $\boxed{4}$ feet.

The graph of the function confirms the vertex at (0.5, 4). The *x*-intercept at 1 indicates that the ball will hit the ground after 1 second.

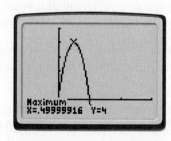
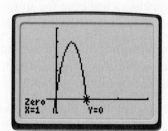

Your Turn

13. **Physics** A person standing at the edge of a cliff 48 feet tall throws a ball up and just off the cliff with an initial upward velocity of 8 feet per second. What is the maximum height of the ball? When will the ball hit the ground?

14. When $b > 0$, the perfect square-trinomial of the expression $x^2 + bx$ is $x^2 + bx + \left(\frac{b}{2}\right)^2$. What is the perfect-square trinomial when $b < 0$? Does the sign of the constant change? Why or why not?

15. Essential Question Check-In What is the first step in completing the square to solve a quadratic equation of the form $ax^2 + bx = c$?

⭐ Evaluate: Homework and Practice

- Online Homework
- Hints and Help
- Extra Practice

Complete the square to form a perfect-square trinomial.

1. $x^2 + 26x$

2. $x^2 - 18x$

3. $x^2 - 2x$

4. $x^2 - 24x$

Solve each equation by completing the square. Check the answers.

5. $x^2 + 8x = 33$

6. $x^2 - 6x = 8$

7. $x^2 + 12x = 5$

8. $x^2 - 14x = 95$

Solve each equation by completing the square.

9. $9x^2 + 12x = 32$

10. $4x^2 + 20x = 2$

11. $16x^2 - 32x = 65$

12. $9x^2 - 24x = 1$

13. $\frac{1}{2}x^2 + 4x = 10$

14. $3x^2 - 4x = 20$

15. $2x^2 + 14x = 4$

16. $\frac{1}{2}x^2 - 5x = 18$

Projectile Motion Write an equation for each model, rewrite the equation into vertex form, and solve the problem. Then graph the function on a graphing calculator and state the x-intercepts of the graph.

17. Sports A person kicks a ball from the ground into the air with an initial upward velocity of 8 feet per second. What is the maximum height of the ball? When will the ball hit the ground?

18. Physics A person reaching out to the edge of a building ledge 85 feet off the ground flicks a twig up and off the ledge with an initial upward velocity of 11 feet per second. What is the maximum height of the twig? When will the twig hit the ground?

19. Volleyball A volleyball player hits a ball from a height of 5 feet with an initial vertical velocity of 16 feet per second. What is the maximum height of the volleyball? Assuming it is not hit by another player, when will the volleyball hit the ground?

20. Lacrosse A lacrosse player throws a ball into the air from a height of 8 feet with an initial vertical velocity of 32 feet per second. What is the maximum height of the ball? When will the ball hit the ground?

21. Identify the value of a in each equation of the form $ax^2 + bx + c = 0$.

   a. $11x^2 + 2x = 4$

   b. $4x^2 + 5 = 0$

   c. $3x^3 = 7$

   d. $5x^2 + 11x = 1$

   e. $3x^2 = 5$

22. The diagram represents the expression $x^2 + 8x$. Use algebra tiles to model completing the square. Then write the perfect square trinomial expression.

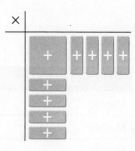

H.O.T. **Focus on Higher Order Thinking**

23. **Explain the Error** A student was instructed to solve the equation $x^2 + 4x = 77$ and produced the following work. Explain the student's error. What is the correct solution?

$$x^2 + 4x = 77$$
$$x^2 + 4x + 4 = 77 + 4$$
$$(x + 2)^2 = 81$$
$$x + 2 = 9$$
$$x = 7$$

24. **Justify Reasoning** Will the equation $x^2 + 6x = -10$ produce an answer that is a real number after the square is completed? Explain.

25. **Draw Conclusions** When solving a quadratic model, why are some solutions considered extraneous? Is this always the case, or can some quadratic models have two solutions?

Lesson Performance Task

An architect is designing the lobby of a new office building. The company that hired her has reclaimed a large quantity of stone floor tiles from the building previously on the site and wishes to use them to tile the lobby. The tiled area needs to be a rectangle 18 feet longer than it is wide to incorporate an information desk. The table below shows the types of tile available, the general color of the tile, and the area that can be covered by the tile.

Stone	Color	Area in Square Feet
Marble	Cream	175
Marble	Cream with gold flecks	115
Marble	Black	648
Marble	White with black flecks	360
Slate	Gray	280
Slate	Gray with blue gray regions	243
Travertine	Caramel	208
Travertine	Latte	760
Adoquin	Dark gray with black regions	319
Adoquin	Light gray with darker gray regions	403
Limestone	Pewter	448
Limestone	Beige	544

Design the lobby using at least all of one type of tile. You can add additional types of tiles to create patterns in the floor. For this exercise, you can decide on the dimensions of the tiles in order to make any pattern you wish. What are the dimensions of the tiled area for your design?

22.3 Using the Quadratic Formula to Solve Equations

Essential Question: What is the quadratic formula, and how can you use it to solve quadratic equations?

⊕ Explore   Deriving the Quadratic Formula

You can complete the square on the general form of a quadratic equation to derive a formula that can be used to solve any quadratic equation.

Ⓐ Write the standard form of a quadratic equation.

$$ax^2 + bx + c = \boxed{?}$$

Ⓑ Subtract c from both sides.

$$ax^2 + bx = \boxed{?}$$

Ⓒ Multiply both sides by $4a$ to make the coefficient of x^2 a perfect square.

$$4a^2x^2 + \boxed{?} = \boxed{?}$$

Ⓓ Add b^2 to both sides of the equation to complete the square.

$$4a^2x^2 + 4abx + b^2 = -4ac + \boxed{?}$$

Ⓔ Factor the left side to write the trinomial as the square of a binomial.

$$\left(\boxed{?} \right)^2 = b^2 - 4ac$$

Ⓕ Take the square roots of both sides.

$$\boxed{?} = \pm \sqrt{\boxed{?}}$$

Ⓖ Subtract b from both sides.

$$2ax = \boxed{?} \pm \sqrt{\boxed{?}}$$

Ⓗ Divide both sides by $2a$ to solve for x.

$$x = \frac{\boxed{?} \pm \sqrt{\boxed{?}}}{\boxed{?}}$$

(I) The formula you just derived, $x = \dfrac{-b \pm \sqrt{b^2 - 4ac}}{2a}$, is called the **quadratic formula**.
It gives you the values of x that solve any quadratic equation where $a \neq 0$.

Reflect

1. **What If?** If the derivation had begun by dividing each term by a, what would the resulting binomial of x have been after completing the square? Does one derivation method appear to be simpler than the other? Explain.

⊘ Explain 1   Using the Discriminant to Determine the Number of Real Solutions

Recall that a quadratic equation, $ax^2 + bx + c = 0$, can have two, one, or no real solutions. By evaluating the part of the quadratic formula under the radical sign, $b^2 - 4ac$, called the **discriminant**, you can determine the number of real solutions.

Example 1   Determine how many real solutions each quadratic equation has.

(A) $x^2 - 4x + 3 = 0$

     $a = 1, b = -4, c = 3$ Identify a, b, and c.

     $b^2 - 4ac$ Use the discriminant.

     $(-4)^2 - 4(1)(3)$ Substitute the identified values into the discriminant.

     $16 - 12 = 4$ Simplify.

     Since $b^2 - 4ac > 0$, the equation has two real solutions.

(B) $x^2 - 2x + 2 = 0$

     $a = \boxed{1}, b = \boxed{-2}, c = \boxed{2}$ Identify a, b, and c.

     $b^2 - 4ac$ Use the discriminant.

     $\left(\boxed{-2}\right)^2 - 4\left(\boxed{1}\right)\left(\boxed{2}\right)$ Substitute the identified values into the discriminant.

     $\boxed{4} - \boxed{8} = \boxed{-4}$ Simplify.

     Since $b^2 - 4ac \boxed{<} 0$, the equation has no real solution(s).

Reflect

2. When the discriminant is positive, the quadratic equation has two real solutions. When the discriminant is negative, there are no real solutions. How many real solutions does a quadratic equation have if its discriminant equals 0? Explain.

Your Turn

Use the discriminant to determine the number of real solutions for each quadratic equation.

3. $x^2 + 4x + 1 = 0$ 4. $2x^2 - 6x + 15 = 0$ 5. $x^2 + 6x + 9 = 0$

🎸 Explain 2 Solving Equations by Using the Quadratic Formula

To use the quadratic formula to solve a quadratic equation, check that the equation is in standard form. If not, rewrite it in standard form. Then substitute the values of a, b, and c into the formula.

Example 2 Solve using the quadratic formula.

Ⓐ $2x^2 + 3x - 5 = 0$

$a = 2, b = 3, c = -5$ Identify a, b, and c.

$x = \dfrac{-b \pm \sqrt{b^2 - 4ac}}{2a}$ Use the quadratic formula.

$x = \dfrac{-3 \pm \sqrt{(3)^2 - 4(2)(-5)}}{2(2)}$ Substitute the identified values into the quadratic formula.

$x = \dfrac{-3 \pm \sqrt{49}}{4}$ Simplify the radicand and the denominator.

$x = \dfrac{-3 \pm 7}{4}$ Evaluate the square root.

$x = \dfrac{-3 + 7}{4}$ or $x = \dfrac{-3 - 7}{4}$ Write as two equations.

$x = 1$ or $x = -\dfrac{5}{2}$ Simplify both equations.

The solutions are 1 and $-\dfrac{5}{2}$.

Graph $y = 2x^2 + 3x - 5$ to verify your answers.

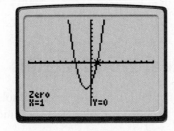
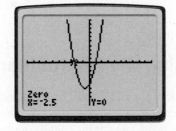

The graph does verify the solutions.

Ⓑ $2x = x^2 - 4$

$x^2 - \boxed{2x} - 4 = 0$ Write in standard form.

$a = \boxed{1}, b = \boxed{-2}, c = \boxed{-4}$ Identify a, b, and c.

$x = \dfrac{-b \pm \sqrt{b^2 - 4ac}}{2a}$ Use the quadratic formula.

$x = \dfrac{-\boxed{-2} \pm \sqrt{\boxed{-2}^2 - 4\boxed{1}\boxed{-4}}}{2\boxed{1}}$ Substitute the identified values into the quadratic formula.

$x = \dfrac{2 \pm \sqrt{\boxed{20}}}{2}$ Simplify the radicand and the denominator.

$$x = \frac{2 \pm \sqrt{\boxed{4} \cdot 5}}{2} = \frac{2 \pm 2\boxed{\sqrt{5}}}{2} = 1 \pm \boxed{\sqrt{5}}$$ Simplify.

$x = \boxed{1 + \sqrt{5}}$ or $x = \boxed{1 - \sqrt{5}}$ Write as two equations.

$x \approx \boxed{3.236}$ or $x \approx \boxed{-1.236}$ Use a calculator to find approximate solutions to three decimal places.

The exact solutions are $\boxed{1 + \sqrt{5}}$ and $\boxed{1 - \sqrt{5}}$. The approximate solutions are

$\boxed{3.236}$ and $\boxed{-1.236}$.

Graph $y = x^2 - \boxed{2x} - 4$ and find the zeros using the graphing calculator. The calculator will give approximate values.

The graph does confirm the solutions.

Reflect

6. **Discussion** How can you use substitution to check your solutions?

Your Turn

Solve using the quadratic formula.

7. $x^2 - 6x - 7 = 0$

8. $2x^2 = 8x - 7$

🔑 Explain 3 Using the Discriminant with Real-World Models

Given a real-world situation that can be modeled by a quadratic equation, you can find the number of real solutions to the problem using the discriminant, and then apply the quadratic formula to obtain the solutions. After finding the solutions, check to see if they make sense in the context of the problem.

In projectile motion problems the projectile height h is modeled by the equation $h = -16t^2 + vt + s$, where t is the time in seconds the object has been in the air, v is the initial vertical velocity in feet per second, and s is the initial height in feet. The -16 coefficient in front of the t^2 term refers to the effect of gravity on the object. This equation can be written using metric units as $h = -4.9t^2 + vt + s$, where the units are converted from feet to meters. Time remains in units of seconds.

Example 3 For each problem, use the discriminant to determine the number of real solutions for the equation. Then, find the solutions and check to see if they make sense in the context of the problem.

Ⓐ A diver jumps from a platform 10 meters above the surface of the water. The diver's height is given by the equation $h = -4.9t^2 + 3.5t + 10$, where t is the time in seconds after the diver jumps. For what time t is the diver's height 1 meter?

Substitute $h = 1$ into the height equation. Then, write the resulting quadratic equation in standard form to solve for t.

$1 = -4.9t^2 + 3.5t + 10$ $\qquad$ $0 = -4.9t^2 + 3.5t + 9$

First, use the discriminant to find the number of real solutions of the equation.

$b^2 - 4ac$ Use the discriminant.

$(3.5)^2 - 4(-4.9)(9) = 188.65$

Since $b^2 - 4ac > 0$, the equation has two real solutions.

Next, use the quadratic formula to find the real number solutions.

$a = -4.9, b = 3.5, c = 9$ Identify a, b, and c.

$t = \dfrac{-b \pm \sqrt{b^2 - 4ac}}{2a}$ Use the quadratic formula.

$t = \dfrac{-3.5 \pm \sqrt{188.65}}{2(-4.9)}$ Substitute the identified values and the value of the discriminant into the quadratic formula.

$t = \dfrac{-3.5 + \sqrt{188.65}}{-9.8}$ or $t = \dfrac{-3.5 - \sqrt{188.65}}{-9.8}$ Write as two equations.

$t \approx -1.04$ or $t \approx 1.76$ Simplify.

Disregard the negative solution because t represents the seconds after the diver jumps and a negative value has no meaning in this context. So, the diver is at height 1 meter after a time of $t \approx 1.76$ seconds.

(B) The height in meters of a model rocket on a particular launch can be modeled by the equation $h = -4.9t^2 + 102t + 100$, where t is the time in seconds after its engine burns out 100 meters above the ground. When will the rocket reach a height of 600 meters?

Substitute $h = \boxed{600}$ into the height equation. Then, write the resulting quadratic equation in standard form to solve for t.

$h = -4.9t^2 + 102t + 100$

$\boxed{600} = -4.9t^2 + 102t + 100$

$0 = -4.9t^2 + 102t - \boxed{500}$

First, use the discriminant to find the number of real solutions of the equation.

$a = -4.9, b = \boxed{102}, c = \boxed{-500}$ Identify a, b, and c.

$b^2 - 4ac$ Use the discriminant.

$\left(\boxed{102}\right)^2 - 4(-4.9)\left(\boxed{-500}\right)$ Substitute the identified values into the discriminant.

$\boxed{10404} - \boxed{9800} = \boxed{604}$ Simplify.

Since $b^2 - 4ac \boxed{>} 0$, the equation has $\boxed{2}$ real solutions.

Next, use the quadratic formula to find the real number solutions.

$$t = \frac{-\boxed{102} \pm \sqrt{\boxed{604}}}{2(-4.9)}$$

Substitute the identified values and the value of the discriminant into the quadratic formula.

$$t = \frac{-102 + \sqrt{\boxed{604}}}{-9.8} \text{ or } t = \frac{-102 - \sqrt{\boxed{604}}}{-9.8}$$

Write as two equations.

$$t \approx \boxed{-7.90} \quad \text{or} \quad t \approx \boxed{12.92}$$

Simplify.

Disregard the negative solution because t represents the seconds after the rocket has launched and a negative value has no meaning in this context. So, the rocket is at height 600 meters after a time of

$t \approx \boxed{12.92}$ seconds.

Your Turn

For each problem, use the discriminant to determine the number of real solutions for the equation. Then, find the solutions and check to see if they make sense in the context of the problem.

9. A soccer player uses her head to hit a ball up in the air from a height of 2 meters with an initial vertical velocity of 5 meters per second. The height h in meters of the ball is given by $h = -4.9t^2 + 5t + 2$, where t is the time elapsed in seconds. How long will it take the ball to hit the ground if no other players touch it?

10. The quarterback of a football team throws a pass to the team's receiver. The height h in meters of the football can be modeled by $h = -4.9t^2 + 3t + 1.75$, where t is the time elapsed in seconds. The receiver catches the football at a height of 0.25 meters. How long does the ball remain in the air until it is caught by the receiver?

💬 Elaborate

11. How can the discriminant of a quadratic equation be used to determine the number of zeros (*x*-intercepts) that the graph of the equation will have?

12. What advantage does using the quadratic formula have over other methods of solving quadratic equations?

13. **Essential Question Check-In** How can you derive the quadratic formula?

⭐ Evaluate: Homework and Practice

Determine how many real solutions each quadratic equation has.

1. $4x^2 + 4x + 1 = 0$

2. $x^2 - x + 3 = 0$

3. $x^2 - 8x^2 - 9 = 0$

4. $2x^2 - x\sqrt{5} + 2 = 0$

5. $\dfrac{x^2}{2} - x + \dfrac{1}{4} = 0$

6. $\dfrac{x^2}{4} - x\sqrt{7} + 7 = 0$

7. $\dfrac{x^2}{2} - x\sqrt{2} + 1 = 0$

8. $x^2\sqrt{2} - x + \dfrac{1}{2} = 0$

Solve using the quadratic formula. Leave irrational answers in radical form.

9. $10x + 4 = 6x^2$

10. $x^2 + x - 20 = 0$

11. $4x^2 = 4 - x$

12. $9x^2 + 3x - 2 = 0$

13. $14x + 3 = -8x^2$

14. $x^2 + 3x^2 + 1 = 0$

For each problem, use the discriminant to determine the number of real solutions for the equation. Then, find the solutions and check to see if they make sense in the context of the problem.

15. **Sports** A soccer player kicks the ball to a height of 1 meter inside the goal. The equation for the height h of the ball at time t is $h = -4.9t^2 - 5t + 2$. Find the time the ball reached the goal.

16. The length and width of a rectangular patio are, $(x + 8)$ feet and $(x + 6)$ feet, respectively. If the area of the patio is 160 square feet, what are the dimensions of the patio?

17. **Chemistry** A scientist is growing bacteria in a lab for study. One particular type of bacteria grows at a rate of $y = 2t^2 + 3t + 500$. A different bacteria grows at a rate of $y = 3t^2 + t + 300$. In both of these equations, y is the number of bacteria after t minutes. When is there an equal number of both types of bacteria?

Use this information for Exercises 18 and 19. A gymnast, who can stretch her arms up to reach 6 feet, jumps straight up on a trampoline. The height of her feet above the trampoline can be modeled by the equation $h = -16x\,2 + 12x$, where x is the time in seconds after her jump.

18. Do the gymnast's hands reach a height of 10 feet above the trampoline? Use the discriminant to explain. (Hint: Since h = height of feet, you must use the difference between the heights of the hands and feet.)

19. Which of the following are possible heights she achieved? Select all that apply.

a. $h = \dfrac{9}{4}$

b. $h = 4$

c. $h = 3$

d. $h = 0.5$

e. $h = \dfrac{1}{4}$

20. Explain the Error Dan said that if a quadratic equation does not have any real solutions, then it does not represent a function. Explain Dan's error.

H.O.T. Focus on Higher Order Thinking

21. Communicate Mathematical Ideas Explain why a positive discriminant results in two real solutions.

22. Multi-Step A model rocket is launched from the top of a hill 10 meters above ground level. The rocket's initial speed is 10 meters per second. Its height h can be modeled by the equation $h = -4.9t^2 + 10t + 10$, where t is the time in seconds.

   a. When does the rocket achieve a height of 100 meters?

   b. How long does it take the rocket to reach ground level?

Lesson Performance Task

A baseball field is next to a building that is 130 feet tall. A series of batters hit pitched balls into the air with the given initial vertical velocities. (Assume each ball is hit from a height of 3 feet.) After the game, a fan reports that several hits resulted in the ball hitting the roof of the building. How can you use the discriminant to determine whether any of the hits described below could be among them? Explain. If any of the balls hit could have hit the roof, identify them. Can you tell if the ball actually did hit the roof?

Player	Initial Vertical Velocity (ft/s)
Janok	99
Jimenez	91
Serrano	88
Sei	89

22.4 Choosing a Method for Solving Quadratic Equations

Essential Question: How can you choose a method for solving a given quadratic equation?

⊘ Explore Comparing Solution Methods for Quadratic Equations

$7x^2 - 3x - 5 = 0$

Try to solve the equation by factoring.

(A) Find the factors of 7 and −5 to complete the table:

Factors of 7	Factors of −5	Outer Product + Inner Product
1, 7	1, −5	2
1, 7	5, −1	?
1, 7	−1, 5	?
1, 7	−5, 1	?

(B) None of the sums of the inner and outer products of the factor pairs of 7 and −5 equal −3.

Does this mean the equation cannot be solved? ? .

Now, try to solve the equation by completing the square.

(C) The leading coefficient is not a perfect square. Multiply both sides by a value that makes the coefficient a perfect square.

$$\boxed{?}\,(7x^2 - 3x - 5) = (0)\,\boxed{?}$$

$$\boxed{?}\,x^2 - \boxed{?}\,x - \boxed{?} = \boxed{?}$$

(D) Add or subtract to move the constant term to the other side of the equation.

$$\boxed{?}\,x^2 - \boxed{?}\,x = \boxed{?}$$

(E) Find $\dfrac{b^2}{4a}$ and reduce to simplest form.

$$\frac{b^2}{4a} = \frac{\boxed{?}^2}{4\left(\boxed{?}\right)} = \frac{\boxed{?}}{\boxed{?}} = \frac{\boxed{?}}{\boxed{?}}$$

(F) Add $\dfrac{b^2}{4a}$ to both sides of the equation,

$$\boxed{?}\,x^2 - \boxed{?}\,x + \dfrac{\boxed{?}}{\boxed{?}} = \boxed{?} + \dfrac{\boxed{?}}{\boxed{?}}$$

$$\boxed{?}\,x^2 - \boxed{?}\,x + \dfrac{\boxed{?}}{\boxed{?}} = \dfrac{\boxed{?}}{\boxed{?}}$$

(G) Factor the perfect-square trinomial on the left side of the equation.

$$\left(\boxed{?}\,x - \dfrac{\boxed{?}}{\boxed{?}}\right)^2 = \dfrac{\boxed{?}}{\boxed{?}}$$

(H) Take the square root of both sides.

$$\boxed{?}\,x - \dfrac{\boxed{?}}{\boxed{?}} = \pm\sqrt{\dfrac{\boxed{?}}{\boxed{?}}}$$

(I) Add the constant to both sides, and then divide by a. Find both solutions for x.

$$\boxed{?}\,x - \dfrac{\boxed{?}}{\boxed{?}} + \dfrac{\boxed{?}}{\boxed{?}} = \pm\sqrt{\dfrac{\boxed{?}}{\boxed{?}}} + \dfrac{\boxed{?}}{\boxed{?}}$$

$$\dfrac{\boxed{?}}{\boxed{?}}\,x = \dfrac{\pm\sqrt{\dfrac{\boxed{?}}{\boxed{?}} + \dfrac{\boxed{?}}{\boxed{?}}}}{\boxed{?}}$$

$$x = \dfrac{\pm\sqrt{\dfrac{\boxed{?}}{\boxed{?}} + \dfrac{\boxed{?}}{\boxed{?}}}}{\boxed{?}}$$

$$x = \dfrac{\sqrt{\dfrac{\boxed{?}}{\boxed{?}} + \dfrac{\boxed{?}}{\boxed{?}}}}{\boxed{?}} \quad \text{or} \quad x = -\dfrac{\sqrt{\dfrac{\boxed{?}}{\boxed{?}} + \dfrac{\boxed{?}}{\boxed{?}}}}{\boxed{?}}$$

(J) Solve both equations to three decimal places using your calculator.

$$x = \boxed{?} \qquad \text{or} \qquad x = \boxed{?}$$

Now use the quadratic formula to solve the same equation.

(K) Identify the values of a, b, and c. $a = \boxed{?}$, $b = \boxed{?}$, $c = \boxed{?}$

(L) Substitute values into the quadratic formula.

$$x = \dfrac{-\boxed{?} \pm \sqrt{\boxed{?}^2 - 4(7)\left(\boxed{?}\right)}}{2\left(\boxed{?}\right)}$$

Ⓜ Simplify the discriminant and the denominator.

$$x = \frac{3 \pm \sqrt{\boxed{?}}}{\boxed{?}}$$

Ⓝ Use your calculator to finish simplifying the expression for x.

$x = \boxed{?}$ or $x = \boxed{?}$

Reflect

1. **Discussion** Another method you learned for solving quadratics is taking square roots. Why would that not work in this case?

🎯 Explain 1 Solving Quadratic Equations Using Different Methods

You have seen several ways to solve a quadratic equation, but there are reasons why you might choose one method over another.

Factoring is usually the fastest and easiest method. Try factoring first if it seems likely that the equation is factorable.

Both completing the square and using the quadratic formula are more general. Quadratic equations that are solvable can be solved using either method.

Example 1 Speculate which method is the most appropriate for each equation and explain your answer. Then solve the equation using factoring (if possible), completing the square, and the quadratic formula.

Ⓐ $x^2 + 7x + 6 = 0$

Factor the quadratic.

Set up a factor table adding factors of c.

Factors of c	Sum of Factors
1, 6	7
2, 3	5

Substitute in factors. $(x + 1)(x + 6) = 0$

Use the Zero Product Property $x + 1 = 0$ or $x + 6 = 0$

Solve both equations for x. $x = -1$ or $x = -6$

Complete the square.

Move the constant term to the right side.	$x^2 + 7x = -6$
Add $\dfrac{b^2}{4a}$ to both sides.	$x^2 + 7x + \dfrac{49}{4} = -6 + \dfrac{49}{4}$
Simplify.	$x^2 + 7x + \dfrac{49}{4} = \dfrac{25}{4}$
Factor the perfect-square trimonial on the left.	$\left(x + \dfrac{7}{2}\right)^2 = \dfrac{25}{4}$
Take the square root of both sides.	$x + \dfrac{7}{2} = \pm\dfrac{5}{2}$
Write two equations.	$x + \dfrac{7}{2} = \dfrac{5}{2}$ or $x + \dfrac{7}{2} = -\dfrac{5}{2}$
Solve both equations.	$x = -1$ or $x = -6$

Apply the quadratic formula.

Identify the values of a, b, and c.	$a = 1, b = 7, c = 6$
Substitute values into the quadratic formula.	$x = \dfrac{-7 \pm \sqrt{7^2 - 4(1)(6)}}{2(1)}$
Simplify the discriminant and denominator.	$x = \dfrac{-7 \pm \sqrt{25}}{2}$
Evaluate the square root and write as two equations.	$x = \dfrac{-7 + 5}{2}$ or $x = \dfrac{-7 - 5}{2}$
Simplify.	$x = -1$ or $x = -6$

Because the list of possible factors that needed to be checked was short, it makes sense to try factoring $x^2 + 7x + 6$ first, even if you don't know if you will be able to factor it. Once factored, the remaining steps are fewer and simpler than either completing the square or using the quadratic formula.

(B) $2x^2 + 8x + 3 = 0$

Factor the quadratic.

Factors of c	Factors of c	Sum of Inner and Outer Products
1, 2	1, 3	5
1, 2	3, 1	7

Can the quadratic be factored? No.

Complete the square.

Move the constant term to the right side.	$2x^2 + 8x = -3$
Multiply both sides by $\boxed{2}$ to make a perfect square.	$\boxed{4}\ x^2 + 16x = \boxed{-6}$
Add $\dfrac{b^2}{4a}$ to both sides.	$4x^2 + 16x + \boxed{16} = 10$
Factor the left side.	$\left(\boxed{2}\ x + \boxed{4}\right)^2 = 10$

Take the square root of both sides.	$2x + 4 = \boxed{\pm\sqrt{10}}$
Write two equations.	$2x + 4 = \boxed{\sqrt{10}}$ or $2x + 4 = -\sqrt{10}$
Solve both equations.	$x = -2 \boxed{+} \dfrac{\sqrt{10}}{2}$ or $x = -2 \boxed{-} \dfrac{\sqrt{10}}{2}$

Apply the quadratic formula.

Identify the values of a, b, and c.	$a = \boxed{2}$, $b = \boxed{8}$, $c = \boxed{3}$
Substitute values into the quadratic formula.	$x = \dfrac{\boxed{-8} \pm \sqrt{\boxed{8}^{2} - 4\boxed{(2)}\boxed{(3)}}}{2\boxed{(2)}}$
Simplify the discriminant and denominator.	$x = \dfrac{-8 \pm \sqrt{\boxed{40}}}{4}$
Evaluate the square root and write as two equations.	$x = \dfrac{-8 \pm \boxed{2}\sqrt{\boxed{10}}}{4}$
Simplify.	$x = \boxed{-2} \pm \dfrac{\sqrt{10}}{\boxed{2}}$

Reflect

2. What are the advantages and disadvantages of solving a quadratic equation by taking square roots?

3. What are the advantages and disadvantages of solving a quadratic equation by factoring?

4. What are the advantages and disadvantages of solving a quadratic equation by completing the square?

5. What are the advantages and disadvantages of solving a quadratic equation by using the quadratic formula?

Your Turn

Solve the quadratic equations by any method you chose. Identify the method and explain why you chose it.

6. $9x^{2} - 100 = 0$

7. $x^{2} + 4x - 7 = 0$

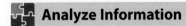

⚙ Explain 2 Choosing Solution Methods for Quadratic Equation Models

Recall that the formula for height, in feet, of a projectile under the influence of gravity is given by $h = -16t^2 + vt + s$, where t is the time in seconds, v is the upward initial velocity (at $t = 0$), and s is the starting height.

Example 2 Marco is throwing a tennis ball at a kite that is stuck 42 feet up in a tree, trying to knock it loose. He can throw the ball at a velocity of 45 feet per second upward at a height of 4 feet. Will his throw reach the kite? How hard does Marco need to throw the ball to reach the kite?

🧩 Analyze Information

The initial velocity is: 45

The starting height is: 4

The height of the kite is: 42

🧩 Formulate a Plan

Use the projectile motion formula to write an equation for the height of the ball t seconds after Marco throws it.

$$h = \boxed{-16}\, t^2 + \boxed{45}\, t + \boxed{4}$$

To determine if the ball can reach the height of the kite, set up the equation to find the time it takes the ball to reach the height of the kite.

$$-16t^2 + 45t + 4 = \boxed{42}$$

Convert the equation to standard form.

$$-16t^2 + 45t + \boxed{-38} = 0$$

This problem will be easiest to solve by using the quadratic formula. To check if the ball reaches the kite, begin by calculating the discriminant. To determine the velocity that Marco must throw the ball to reach the kite, we should find the velocity where the discriminant is equal to 0, which is the exact moment at which the ball changes direction and falls back to earth.

🧩 Solve

Identify values of a, b, and c. $a = \boxed{-16}$, $b = \boxed{45}$, $c = \boxed{-38}$

Evaluate the discriminant first. $b^2 - 4ac = \boxed{45}^2 - 4\left(\boxed{-16}\right)\left(\boxed{-38}\right)$

$$= \boxed{-407}$$

A negative discriminant means that there are 0 solutions to the equation. Marco's throw will not reach as high as the kite.

The velocity with which Marco needs to throw the ball to reach the kite is the coefficient b of the x-term of the quadratic equation.

$b = \boxed{v}$

Substitute v into the discriminant and solve for a discriminant equal to 0 to find the velocity at which Marco needs to throw the ball.

Identify values of a, b, and c. $a = \boxed{-16}$, $b = \boxed{v}$, $c = \boxed{-38}$

Evaluate the discriminant first. $\boxed{v}^2 - 4\left(\boxed{-16}\right)\left(\boxed{-38}\right) = 0$

Simplify. $v^2 - \boxed{2432} = 0$

This quadratic equation should be solved by taking square roots because it has no x-term.

Move the constant term to the right. $v^2 = \boxed{2432}$

Take square roots of both sides. Use your calculator. $v \approx \pm \boxed{49.3}$

The negative velocity represents a downward throw and will not result in the ball hitting the kite. The tennis ball must have a velocity of at about 49.3 feet per second to reach the kite.

Justify and Evaluate

Plot the graph of Marco's throw on your graphing calculator to see that the conclusion you reached (no solution) makes sense because the graphs do not intersect. Sketch the graph.

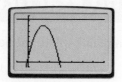

Then plot the height of the ball when the discriminant is equal to zero. The graphs intersect in one point. Sketch the graph.

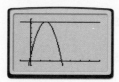

Your Turn

8. The wheel of a remote controlled airplane falls off while the airplane is climbing at 40 feet in the air. The wheel starts with an initial upward velocity of 24 feet per second. How long does it take to fall to the ground? Set up the equation to determine the time and pick one method to solve it. Explain why you chose that method.

9. Marco's brother, Jessie, is helping Marco knock a kite from the tree. He can throw the ball 50 feet per second upwards, from a height of 5 feet. Is he throwing the ball hard enough to reach the kite, and if so, how long does it take the ball to reach the kite?

💬 Elaborate

10. Which method do you think is best if you are going to have to use a calculator?

11. Some factorable quadratic expressions are still quite difficult to solve by factoring rather than using another method. What makes an equation difficult to factor?

12. You are taking a test on quadratic equations and you can't decide which method would be the fastest way to solve a particular problem. How could looking at a graph of the equation on a calculator help you decide which method to use?

13. **Essential Question Check-In** How should you determine a method for solving a quadratic equation?

⭐ Evaluate: Homework and Practice

1. Look at this quadratic equation and explain what you think will be the best approach to solving it. Do not solve the equation.

$$3.38x^2 + 2.72x - 9.31 = 0$$

Solve the quadratic equation by any means. Identify the method and explain why you chose it. Irrational answers may be left in radical form or approximated with a calculator (round to two decimal places).

2. $x^2 - 7x + 12 = 0$

3. $36x^2 - 64 = 0$

4. $4x^2 - 4x - 3 = 2$

5. $8x^2 + 9x + 2 = 1$

6. $5x^2 + 0x - 13 = 0$

7. $7x^2 - 5x - 5 = 0$

8. $3x^2 - 6x = 0$

9. $2x^2 + 4x - 3 = 0$

10. $(x - 5)^2 = 16$

11. $(2x - 1)^2 = x$

12. $2(x + 2)^2 - 5 = 3$

13. $(2x - 3)^2 = 4x$

14. $6x^2 - 5x + 12 = 0$

15. $3x^2 + 6x + 2 = 0$

16. $\frac{1}{2}x^2 + 3x + \frac{5}{2} = 0$

17. $(6x + 7)(x + 1) = 26$

Use the projectile motion formula and solve the quadratic equation by any means. Identify the method and explain why you chose it. Irrational answers and fractions should be converted to decimal form and rounded to two places.

18. Gary drops a pair of gloves off of a balcony that is 64 feet high down to his friend on the ground. How long does it take the pair of gloves to hit the ground?

19. A soccer player jumps up and heads the ball while it is 7 feet above the ground. It bounces up at a velocity of 20 feet per second. How long will it take the ball to hit the ground?

20. A stomp rocket is a toy that is launched into the air from the ground by a sudden burst of pressure exerted by stomping on a pedal. If the rocket is launched at 24 feet per second, how long will it be in the air?

21. A dog leaps off of the patio from 2 feet off of the ground with an upward velocity of 15 feet per second. How long will the dog be in the air?

22. Multipart Classification Determine whether the following statements about finding solutions to quadratic equations with integer coefficients are True or False.

a. Any quadratic equation with a real solution can be solved by using the quadratic formula.

b. Any quadratic equation with a real solution can be solved by completing the square.

c. Any quadratic equation with a real solution can be solved by factoring.

d. Any quadratic equation with a real solution can be solved by taking the square root of both sides of the equation.

e. If the equation can be factored, it has rational solutions.

f. If the equation has only one real solution, it cannot be factored.

23. **Justify Reasoning** Any quadratic equation with a real solution can be solved with the quadratic formula. Describe the kinds of equations where that would not be the best choice, and explain your reasoning.

24. **Critique Reasoning** Marisol decides to solve the quadratic equation by factoring $21x^2 + 47x - 24 = 0$. Do you think she chose the best method? How would you solve this equation?

25. **Communicate Mathematical Ideas** Explain the difference between the statements "The quadratic formula can be used to solve any quadratic equation with a real solution" and "Every quadratic equation has a real solution."

Lesson Performance Task

A landscaper is designing a patio for a customer who has several different ideas about what to make.

Use the given information to set up a quadratic equation modeling the situation and solve it using the quadratic formula. Then determine if another method for solving quadratic equations would have been easier to use and explain why.

a. One of the customer's ideas is to buy bluestone tiles from a home improvement store using several gift cards he has received as presents over the past few years. If the total value of the gift cards is $6500 and the bluestone costs $9 per square foot, what are the dimensions of the largest patio that can be made that is 12 feet longer than it is wide?

b. Another of the customer's ideas is simply a quadratic equation scrawled on a napkin.

$x^2 - 54x + 720 = 0$

c. The third idea is also a somewhat random quadratic polynomial.

$x^2 - 40x + 397 = 0$

22.5 Solving Nonlinear Systems

Resource
Locker

Essential Question: How can you solve a system of equations when one equation is linear and the other is quadratic?

⊘ Explore   Determining the Possible Number of Solutions of a System of Linear and Quadratic Equations

A system of one linear and one quadratic equation may have zero, one, or two solutions.

Ⓐ The graph of the quadratic function $f(x) = x^2 - 2x - 2$ is shown. On the same coordinate plane, graph the following linear functions:

$g(x) = -x - 2, \, h(x) = 2x - 6, \, j(x) = 0.5x - 5$

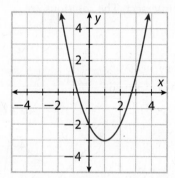

Ⓑ Look at the graph of the system consisting of the quadratic function, $f(x)$, and the linear function, $g(x)$. Based on the intersections of these two graphs, how many solutions exist in a system consisting of these two functions? ☐ ?

Ⓒ Look at the graph of the system consisting of the quadratic function, $f(x)$, and the linear function, $h(x)$. Based on the intersections of these two graphs, how many solutions exist in a system consisting of these two functions? ☐ ?

Ⓓ Look at the graph of the system consisting of the quadratic function, $f(x)$, and the linear function, $j(x)$. Based on the intersections of these two graphs, how many solutions exist in a system consisting of these two functions? ☐ ?

Reflect

1. A system consisting of a quadratic equation and a linear equation can have ☐ ? , ☐ ? , or ☐ ? solutions.

Solving a System of Linear and Quadratic Equations Graphically

A system of equations consisting of a linear and quadratic equation can be solved graphically by finding the points where the graphs intersect.

Example 1 Solve the system of equations graphically.

(A) $\begin{cases} y = (x+1)^2 - 4 \\ y = 2x - 2 \end{cases}$

Graph the quadratic function. The vertex is the point $(-1, -4)$.
The x-intercepts are the points where $y = 0$.

$(x+1)^2 - 4 = 0$

$(x+1)^2 = 4$

$x + 1 = \pm 2$

$x = 1$ or $x = -3$

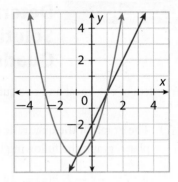

Graph the linear function on the same coordinate plane.

The solutions of the system are the points where the graphs intersect. The solutions are $(-1, -4)$ and $(1, 0)$.

(B) $\begin{cases} y = 2(x-2)^2 - 2 \\ y = -x - 1 \end{cases}$

Graph the quadratic function. The vertex is the point $\left(2, \boxed{-2}\right)$.

The x-intercepts are the points where $y = 0$.

$2(x-2)^2 - 2 = 0$

$2(x-2)^2 = \boxed{2}$

$(x-2)^2 = \boxed{1}$

$\boxed{x-2} = \pm 1$

$x = \boxed{3}$ or $x = \boxed{1}$

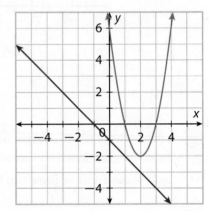

Graph the linear function on the same coordinate plane.

There are 0 intersection points. This system has 0 solution(s).

Your Turn

Solve the system of equations graphically.

2. $\begin{cases} y = -2(x+2)^2 + 8 \\ y = 4x + 16 \end{cases}$

3. $\begin{cases} y = (x+1)^2 - 9 \\ y = 6x - 12 \end{cases}$

Solving a System of Linear and Quadratic Equations Algebraically

Systems of equations can also be solved algebraically by using the substitution method to eliminate a variable. If the system is one linear and one quadratic equation, the equation resulting after substitution will also be quadratic and can be solved by selecting an appropriate method.

Example 2   Solve the system of equations algebraically.

(A) $\begin{cases} y = (x+1)^2 - 4 \\ y = 2x - 2 \end{cases}$

Set the two the expressions for y equal to each other, and solve for x.

$(x+1)^2 - 4 = 2x - 2$

$x^2 + 2x - 3 = 2x - 2$

$x^2 - 1 = 0$

$x^2 = 1$

$x = \pm 1$

Substitute 1 and -1 for x to find the corresponding y-values.

$y = 2x - 2$ $\qquad\qquad\qquad$ $y = 2x - 2$

$y = 2(1) - 2 = 0$ $\qquad\qquad$ $y = 2(-1) - 2 = -4$

The solutions are $(1, 0)$ and $(-1, -4)$.

(B) $\begin{cases} y = (x+4)(x+1) \\ y = -x - 5 \end{cases}$

Set the two the expressions for y equal to each other, and solve for x.

$(x+4)(x+1) = \boxed{-x - 5}$

$x^2 + \boxed{5}\, x + \boxed{4} = -x - 5$

$x^2 + \boxed{6}\, x + \boxed{9} = 0$

$\left(x + \boxed{3}\right)(x + 3) = 0$

$x = \boxed{-3}$

Substitute -3 for x to find the corresponding y-value.

$y = -x - 5$

$y = -\left(\boxed{-3}\right) - 5 = \boxed{-2}$

The solution is $\boxed{(-3, -2)}$.

Reflect

4. **Discussion** After finding the x-values of the intersection points, why use the linear equation to find the y-values rather than the quadratic? What if the quadratic equation is used instead?

Solve the system of equations algebraically.

5. $\begin{cases} y = 2x^2 + 9x + 5 \\ y = 3x - 3 \end{cases}$

🎸 Explain 3 Solving a Real-World Problem with a System of Linear and Quadratic Equations

Systems of equations can be solved by graphing both equations on a graphing calculator and using the Intersect feature.

Example 3 Create and solve a system of equations to solve the problem.

(A) A rock climber is pulling his pack up the side of a cliff that is 175.5 feet tall at a rate of 2 feet per second. The height of the pack in feet after t seconds is given by $h = 2t$. The climber drops a coil of rope from directly above the pack. The height of the coil in feet after t seconds is given by $h = -16t^2 + 175.5$. At what time does the coil of rope hit the pack?

Create the system of equations to solve.

$\begin{cases} h = -16t^2 + 175.5 \\ h = 2t \end{cases}$

Graph the functions together and find any points of intersection.

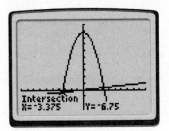

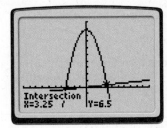

The intersection is at $(-3.375, -6.75)$.

The x-value represents time, so this solution is not reasonable.

The intersection is at $(3.25, 6.5)$.

This solution indicates that the coil hits the pack after 3.25 seconds.

Ⓑ A window washer is ascending the side of a building that is 520 feet tall at a rate of 3 feet per second. The elevation of the window washer after t seconds is given by $h = 3t$. The supplies are lowered to the window washer from the top of the building at the same time that he begins to ascend the building. The height of the supplies in feet after t seconds is given by $h = -2t^2 + 520$. At what time do the supplies reach the window washer?

Create the system of equations to solve.

$$\begin{cases} h = \boxed{-2}\,t^2 + \boxed{520} \\ h = \boxed{3}\,t \end{cases}$$

Graph the functions together and find any points of intersection.

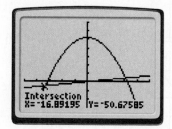

Intersection
X=-16.89195 Y=-50.67585

Intersection
X=15.391948 Y=46.175845

The intersection is at about $\left(\boxed{-16.9}, \boxed{-50.7} \right)$.

The x-value represents time, so this solution is not reasonable.

The intersection is at about $\left(\boxed{15.4}, \boxed{46.2} \right)$.

This solution indicates that the supplies reach the window washer about 15 seconds later.

Reflect

6. How did you know which intersection to use in the example problems?

Your Turn

Create and solve a system of equations to solve the problem.

7. A billboard painter is using a pulley system to hoist a can of paint up to a scaffold at a rate of half a meter per second. The height of the can of paint as a function of time is given by $h(t) = 0.5t$. Five seconds after he starts raising the can of paint, his partner accidentally kicks a paint brush off of the scaffolding, which falls to the ground. The height of the falling paint brush can be represented by $h(t) = -4.9(t - 5)^2 + 30$. When does the brush pass the paint can?

8. **Discussion** When solving a system of equations consisting of a quadratic equation and a linear equation by graphing, why is it difficult to be sure there is one solution as opposed to zero or two?

9. How can you use the discriminant to determine how many solutions a linear-quadratic system has?

Essential Question Check-in How can the graphs of two functions be used to solve How can the graphs of two functions be used to solve a system of a quadratic and a linear equation?

⭐ Evaluate: Homework and Practice

- Online Homework
- Hints and Help
- Extra Practice

1. The graph of the function $f(x) = -\frac{1}{4}(x-3)^2 + 4$ is shown. Graph the functions $g(x) = x + 1$, $h(x) = x + 2$, and $j(x) = x + 3$ with the graph of $f(x)$, and determine how many solutions each system has.

$f(x)$ and $g(x)$

$f(x)$ and $h(x)$

$f(x)$ and $j(x)$

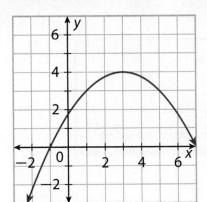

Solve each system of equations graphically.

2. $\begin{cases} y = (x+3)^2 - 4 \\ y = 2x + 2 \end{cases}$

3. $\begin{cases} y = x^2 - 1 \\ y = x - 2 \end{cases}$

4. $\begin{cases} y = (x-4)^2 - 2 \\ y = -2 \end{cases}$

5. $\begin{cases} y = -x^2 + 4 \\ y = -3x + 6 \end{cases}$

6. $\begin{cases} y = -(x-2)^2 + 9 \\ y = 3x + 3 \end{cases}$

7. $\begin{cases} y = 3(x+1)^2 - 1 \\ y = x - 4 \end{cases}$

Solve the system of equations algebraically.

8. $\begin{cases} y = x^2 + 1 \\ y = 5 \end{cases}$

9. $\begin{cases} y = x^2 - 3x + 2 \\ y = 4x - 8 \end{cases}$

10. $\begin{cases} y = (x-3)^2 \\ y = 4 \end{cases}$

11. $\begin{cases} y = -x^2 + 4x \\ y = x + 2 \end{cases}$

12. $\begin{cases} y = 2x^2 - 5x + 6 \\ y = 5x - 6 \end{cases}$

13. $\begin{cases} y = x^2 + 7 \\ y = -9x + 29 \end{cases}$

14. $\begin{cases} y = 4x^2 + 45x + 83 \\ y = 5x - 17 \end{cases}$

15. $\begin{cases} y = (x+2)(x+4) \\ y = 3x + 2 \end{cases}$

Create and solve a linear quadratic system to solve the problem.

16. The height in feet of a skydiver t seconds after deploying her parachute is given by $h(t) = -300t + 1000$. A ball is thrown up toward the skydiver, and after t seconds, the height of the ball in feet is given by $h(t) = -16t^2 + 100t$. When does the ball reach the skydiver?

17. A wildebeest fails to notice a lion that is charging from behind at 65 feet per second until the lion is 40 feet away. The lion's position as a function of time is given by $p(t) = 65t - 40$. The wildebeest has to begin accelerating from a standstill until it is captured or reaches a top speed fast enough to stay ahead of the lion. The wildebeest's position as a function of time is given by $d(t) = 35t^2$. Does the wildebeest escape?

18. An elevator in a hotel moves at 20 feet per second. Leaving from the ground floor, its height in feet after t seconds is given by the formula $h(t) = 20t$. A bolt comes loose in the elevator shaft above, and its height in feet after falling for t seconds is given by $h(t) = -16t^2 + 200$. At what time and at what height does the bolt hit the elevator?

19. A bungee jumper leaps from a bridge 100 meters over a gorge. Before the 40-meter-long bungee begins to slow him down, his height is characterized by $h(t) = -4.9t^2 + 100$. Two seconds after he jumps, a car on the bridge blows out a tire. The sound of the tire blow-out moves down from the top of the bridge at the speed of sound and has a height given by $h(t) = -340(t - 2) + 100$. How high will the bungee jumper be when he hears the sound of the blowout?

20. Explain the Error A student is asked to solve the system of equations $y = x^2 + 2x - 7$ and $y - 2 = x + 1$. For the first step, the student sets the right hand sides equal to each other to get the equation $x^2 + 2x - 7 = x + 1$. Why does this not give the correct solution?

21. Explain the Error After solving the system of equations in Exercise 18 (the elevator and the bolt), a student concludes that there are two different times that the bolt hits the elevator. What is the error in the student's reasoning?

22. Multi-part Classification

The functions listed are graphed here.
$$f_1(x) = 2(x + 3)^2 + 1 \quad \text{and} \quad f_2(x) = -\frac{3}{4}(x - 2)^2 + 3$$
$$g_1(x) = x + 3 \quad \text{and} \quad g_2(x) = 3 \quad \text{and} \quad g_3(x) = -\frac{1}{2}x + 1$$
Use the graph to classify each system as having 0, 1, or 2 solutions.

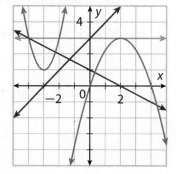

a. $\begin{cases} y = f_1(x) \\ y = g_1(x) \end{cases}$ **b.** $\begin{cases} y = f_1(x) \\ y = g_2(x) \end{cases}$ **c.** $\begin{cases} y = f_1(x) \\ y = g_3(x) \end{cases}$

d. $\begin{cases} y = f_2(x) \\ y = g_1(x) \end{cases}$ **e.** $\begin{cases} y = f_2(x) \\ y = g_2(x) \end{cases}$ **f.** $\begin{cases} y = f_2(x) \\ y = g_3(x) \end{cases}$

23. **Explain the Error** After solving the system of equations in Exercise 16 (the skydiver and the ball), a student concludes there are two valid solutions because they both have positive times. The ball must pass by the skydiver twice. What is the error in the student's reasoning?

24. **Multi-Part Problem** The path of a baseball hit for a home run can be modeled by $y = -\frac{x^2}{484} + x + 3$, where x and y are in feet and home plate is at the origin. The ball lands in the stands, which are modeled by $4y - x = -352$ for $x \geq 400$. Use a graphing calculator to graph the system.

    a. What do the variables x and y represent?

    b. About how far is the baseball from home plate when it lands?

    c. About how high up in the stands does the baseball land?

25. **Draw Conclusions** A certain system of a linear and a quadratic equation has two solutions, $(2, 7)$ and $(5, 10)$. The quadratic equation is $y = x^2 - 6x + 15$. What is the linear equation? Justify your answer.

26. **Justify Reasoning** It is possible for a system of two linear equations to have infinitely many solutions. Explain why this is not possible for a system with one linear and one quadratic equation.

Lesson Performance Task

A race car leaves pit row at a speed of 40 feet per second and accelerates at a constant rate of 44 feet per second squared. Its distance from the pit exit is given by the function $d_r(t) = 22t^2 + 40t$. The race car leaves ahead of an approaching pace car traveling at a constant speed of 120 feet per second. In each case, find out if the pace car will catch up to the race car, and if so, how far down the track it will catch up. If there is more than one solution, explain how you know which one to select.

    a. The pace car passes by the exit to pit row 1 second after the race car exits.

    b. The pace car passes the exit half a second after the race car exits.

Using Square Roots to Solve Quadratic Equations

Essential Question: How can you use quadratic equations to solve real-world problems?

Key Vocabulary

completing the square
(completar el cuadrado)

discriminant *(discriminante)*

quadratic formula
(fórmula cuadrática)

square root *(raíz cuadrada)*

KEY EXAMPLE   *(Lesson 22.1)*

Solve $(x - 8)^2 = 49$ by taking the square root.

$(x - 8)^2 = 49$ *Equations in the form $a(x + b)^2 = c$ can be solved by taking square roots.*

$x - 8 = \pm 7$ *Take the square root of both sides.*

$x = \pm 7 + 8$

$x = 7 + 8$ or $x = -7 + 8$ *Solve both cases.*

$x = 15$ or $x = 1$

KEY EXAMPLE   *(Lesson 22.2)*

Solve $9x^2 - 6x = 20$ by completing the square.

$\dfrac{(-6)^2}{4(9)} = 1$ *Find $\dfrac{b^2}{4a}$.*

$9x^2 - 6x + 1 = 20 + 1$ *Complete the square.*

$(3x - 1)^2 = 21$

$3x - 1 = \pm \sqrt{21}$

$x = \dfrac{\sqrt{21} + 1}{3}$ or $x = \dfrac{-\sqrt{21} + 1}{3}$

KEY EXAMPLE   *(Lesson 22.3)*

Solve $8x^2 - 8x + 2 = 0$ using the quadratic formula.

$a = 8, b = -8, c = 2$ *Identify a, b, and c.*

$x = \dfrac{-b \pm \sqrt{b^2 - 4ac}}{2a}$ *Use the quadratic formula.*

$x = \dfrac{8 \pm \sqrt{(-8)^2 - (4)(8)(2)}}{2(8)}$

$x = \dfrac{8 \pm \sqrt{0}}{16}$ *Since $b^2 - 4ac = 0$, the equation has one real solution.*

$x = \dfrac{1}{2}$

EXERCISES

Solve each equation. *(Lessons 22.1, 22.2, 22.3, 22.4)*

1. $x^2 + 12x = -17$

2. $(4x - 11)^2 = 100$

3. $4x^2 + 8x = 10$

4. $3x^2 + 17x + 10 = 0$

5. A diver jumps off a high diving board that is 33 feet above the surface of the pool with an initial upward velocity of 6 feet per second. The height of the diver above the surface of the pool can be represented by the equation $-16t^2 + 6t + 33 = 0$. How long will the diver be in the air, to the nearest hundredth of a second? Identify the method you used to solve the quadratic equation, and explain why you chose it. *(Lesson 22.4)*

MODULE PERFORMANCE TASK

Fireworks Display

You are planning a fireworks show for a local Fourth of July celebration. Fire officials require that all fireworks explode at a height greater than 70 meters so that debris has a chance to cool off as it falls.

The firing platform for the fireworks is 1.9 meters off the ground. You have the option of firing your fireworks at an initial vertical velocity of anywhere between 35 and 42 meters/second. If every firework is timed to explode when it reaches its maximum height, find two different initial velocities that are acceptable to the local fire officials. Then, figure out how long to delay the firing of the slower firework so that it will explode at the same time as the faster firework.

Complete the task. Be sure to write down all your data and assumptions. Then use graphs, tables, or algebra to explain how you reached your conclusion.

22.1–22.5 Using Square Roots to Solve Quadratic Equations

• Online Homework
• Hints and Help
• Extra Practice

Find the discriminant of each quadratic equation, and determine the number of real solutions of each equation. *(Lesson 22.4)*

1. $3x^2 + 2x + 6 = 0$

2. $4x^2 + 6x = 8$

Solve each equation using the given method. *(Lessons 22.1, 22.2, 22.3, 22.4)*

3. $8x^2 - 72 = 0$; square root

4. $25x^2 + 20x = 6$; completing the square

5. $2x^2 + 14x + 12 = 0$; factoring

6. $3x^2 + 7x + 8 = 0$; quadratic formula

7. Find the solution or solutions of the system of equations $\begin{cases} y = x^2 + 2 \\ y = x + 4 \end{cases}$. *(Lesson 22.5)*

ESSENTIAL QUESTION

8. What are the methods of solving a quadratic equation without factoring? When can you use each method?

Assessment Readiness

1. Is the given expression a perfect-square trinomial?

   A. $x^2 + 24x + 144$

   B. $4x^2 + 36x + 9$

   C. $9x^2 - 6x + 1$

2. Consider the following statements. Determine if each statement is True or False.

   A. $4x^2 - 64 = 0$ has 2 real solutions.

   B. $x^2 - 5x - 9 = 0$ has only 1 real solution.

   C. $3x^2 + 4x + 2 = 0$ has no real solutions.

3. Solve $-2x^2 - 9x = -4$. What are the solutions? Explain how you solved the problem.

4. A landscaper is making a garden bed in the shape of a rectangle. The length of the garden bed is 2.5 feet longer than twice the width of the bed. The area of the garden bed is 62.5 square feet. Find the perimeter of the bed. Show your work.

Linear, Exponential, and Quadratic Models

Essential Question: How can you use linear, exponential, and quadratic models to solve real-world problems?

REAL WORLD VIDEO
The Kemp's Ridley sea turtle is an endangered species of turtle that nests along the Texas coast. Functions can be used to model the survivorship curve of the Kemp's Ridley sea turtle.

MODULE PERFORMANCE TASK PREVIEW
What Model Fits a Survivorship Curve?

Survivorship curves are graphs that show the number or proportion of individuals in a particular population that survive over time. Survivorship curves are used in diverse fields such as actuarial science, demography, biology, and epidemiology. How can you determine what mathematical model best fits a certain type of survivorship curve? Let's find out!

Are (YOU) Ready?

Complete these exercises to review skills you will need for this module.

- Online Homework
- Hints and Help
- Extra Practice

Exponents

Example 1

Find the value of 2^{-5}.

$$2^{-5} = \frac{1}{2^5} = \frac{1}{32}$$

Any nonzero number raised to a negative power is equal to 1 divided by the number raised to the opposite power.

Find the value.

1. 3^{-4}

2. 4^{-3}

3. $\left(\dfrac{2}{3}\right)^{-2}$

Algebraic Expressions

Example 2

Find the value of $y = -2x^2 + 7$ when $x = -3$.

$y = -2x^2 + 7$

$y = -2(-3)^2 + 7$ Substitute -3 for x.

$y = -2(9) + 7$ Evaluate the power.

$y = -18 + 7$ Multiply.

$y = -11$ Add.

Find the value of y for $x = -2$.

4. $y = 5x + 6$

5. $y = 2x^2 - 10$

6. $y = 2^x$

Example 3

Find the product of $(2x^3)(-3x^4)$.

$(2x^3)(-3x^4)$

$\big(2 \cdot (-3)\big)(x^3 \cdot x^4)$ Group factors that use the same variable.

$-6x^7$ The bases are the same, so add the exponents.

Find each product.

7. $\left(-5y^2\right)\left(3y^6\right)$

8. $\left(-6x^6y^2\right)\left(-4x^4y\right)$

9. $\left(7x^4y\right)\left(-5xy\right)$

10. $\left(14ab^3\right)\left(5b^2c^2\right)$

23.1 Modeling with Quadratic Functions

Essential Question: How can you use tables to recognize quadratic functions and use technology to create them?

Explore · Using Second Differences to Identify Quadratic Functions

A linear function is a straight line, a quadratic function is a parabola, and an exponential function is a curve that approaches a horizontal asymptote in one direction and curves upward to infinity in the other direction.

You can determine if a function is linear or exponential when the values of x and y are presented in a table. For a constant change in x-values, if the difference between the associated y-values is constant, then the function is linear. If the ratio of the associated y-values is constant, then the function is exponential.

What if neither the ratio of successive terms nor the first differences are roughly constant? There is a clue in the method for recognizing a linear function. Find the second difference. The second difference is the value obtained by subtracting consecutive first differences. If this number is a non-zero constant, then the function will be quadratic. Examine the graph of the given quadratic function; then construct a table with values for x, y, and the first and second differences.

(A) Graph the function $f(x) = x^2$ on a coordinate plane.

Use the table to complete Steps B, D, and F.

x	$y = f(x)$	First Difference	Second Difference
1	1	————	————
2	$2^2 = $?	$4 - 1 = $?	————
3	$3^2 = $?	$9 - 4 = $?	$5 - 3 = $?
4	$4^2 = $?	? $-$? $= $?	$7 - 5 = $?
5	$5^2 = $?	? $-$? $= $?	? $-$? $= 2$

(B) Complete the $y = f(x)$ column of the table with indicated values of $f(x) = x^2$.

(C) Is there a constant difference between x-values?

(D) Recall that the differences between y-values are called the *first differences*. Complete the First Difference column of the table with the indicated first differences.

(E) Are the first differences constant (the same)?

(F) The differences between the first differences are called the **second differences**. Complete the Second Difference column of the table with the indicated second differences.

(G) Are the second differences constant (the same)?

(H) Complete the table for another quadratic function: $f(x) = -3x^2$.

x	$y = f(x)$	First Difference	Second Difference
1	$-3 \cdot 1 =$?	———	———
2	$-3 \cdot 2^2 =$?	$-12 - (-3) =$?	———
3	$-3 \cdot 3^2 =$?	? $-$? $=$?	$-15 - (-9) =$?
4	$-3 \cdot 4^2 =$?	? $-$? $=$?	? $- (-15) =$?
5	$-3 \cdot 5^2 =$?	? $-$? $=$?	? $-$? $=$?

(I) Is there a constant difference between x-values?

Are the first differences constant (the same)?

Are the second differences constant (the same)?

Reflect

1. **Discussion** When a table of values with constant x-values leads to constant y-values (*first* differences), what kind of function does that indicate? (linear/quadratic)

2. When a table of values with constant x-values leads to constant *second* differences, what kind of function does that indicate? (linear/quadratic)

⚷ Explain 1 Verify Quadratic Relationships Using Quadratic Regression

The second differences for $f(x) = x^2$, the parent quadratic function, are constant for values of y when the corresponding differences between x-values are constant. Now, do the reverse. For a given set of data, verify that the second differences are constant and then use a graphing calculator to find a quadratic model for the data. Enter the independent variable into List 1 and the dependent variable into List 2, and perform a **quadratic regression** on the data. When your calculator performs a quadratic regression, it uses a specific statistical method to fit a quadratic model to the data.

As with linear regression, the data will not be perfect. When finding a model, if the first differences are close but not exactly equal, a linear model will still be a good fit. Likewise, if the second differences aren't exactly the same, a quadratic model will be a good fit if the second differences are close to being the same.

Example 1 **Find a quadratic model for the given situation. Begin by creating a scatter plot of the given data on your graphing calculator, and then find the second differences to verify the data is quadratic. Finally, use a graphing calculator to perform a quadratic regression on the data and graph the regression equation on the scatter plot.**

  A student is measuring the kinetic energy of a pickup truck as it is travels at various speeds. The speed is given in meters per second, and the kinetic energy is given in kilojoules. Use the given data to find a quadratic model for the data.

Speed x	Kinetic Energy y = K(x)	First Difference	Second Difference
20	410	_____	_____
25	640	230	_____
30	922	282	52
35	1256	334	52
40	1640	384	50
45	2076	436	52
50	2563	487	51

Enter the data into a graphing calculator, placing the x-values into List 1 and the y-values into List 2.

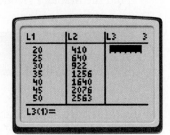

Next view a scatter plot of the data points. The calculator window shown is $15 < x < 55$ with an x-scale of 5 and $0 < y < 3000$ with a y-scale of 500.

Next find the first and second differences and fill in the table.

The first difference of the first and second y-value is found by evaluating the expression below.

$K(25) - K(20)$

$640 - 410$

230

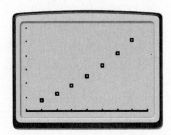

Find the next first difference in the same manner.

$K(30) - K(25)$

$922 - 640$

282

Find the rest of the first differences and fill in the table.

The first of the second differences is the difference between the values in the third and fourth rows of the first difference column.

$282 - 230 = 52$

Find the rest of the second differences and fill in the rest of the table.

Notice that the second differences are very close to being constant.

Use a graphing calculator to find the equation for the quadratic regression. $y \approx 1.026x^2 - 0.0548x + 0.3571$

Note that the correlation coefficient is very close to 1, so the model is a good fit.

Plot the regression equation over the scatter plot.

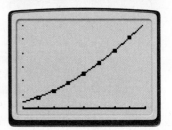

(B) The table shows the speed of a car in meters per second as it accelerates from a stop at a constant rate, measured every 2 seconds.

Time	2	4	6	8	10
Speed	5.1	20.4	45.8	81.2	126.1

Create a scatter plot of the data using a graphing calculator.

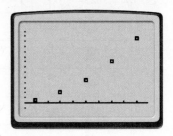

Find the first and second differences and fill out the table.

Time x	Speed y	First Difference	Second Difference
2	5.1	——	——
4	20.4	15.3	——
6	45.8	25.4	10.1
8	81.2	35.4	10
10	126.1	44.9	9.5

Find the regression equation using a graphing calculator. Report the results to 4 significant digits.

$y \approx 1.236x^2 + 0.3114x - 0.52$

Based on the correlation coefficient, the model is a good fit.

Plot the regression equation over the scatter plot.

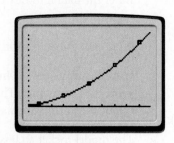

Reflect

3. **Discussion** Give examples of reasons why the second differences in real-world data won't necessarily be equal.

Your Turn

Find a quadratic model for the given situation. Begin by creating a scatter plot of the given data on your graphing calculator, and then find the second differences to verify the data is quadratic. Finally, use a graphing calculator to perform a quadratic regression on the data and graph the regression equation on the scatter plot.

4. The table shows the height of a soccer ball in feet for every half-second after a goalie dropkicks it.

Time	0.5	1.0	1.5	2.0	2.5	3.0	3.5
Height	54	104	142	173	195	208	216

5. A company that makes flying discs to use as promotional materials will produce a flying disc of any size. The table shows the cost of 100 flying discs based on the desired size.

Size	4	4.5	5	5.5	6	6.5	7
Cost	34.99	44.99	54.99	66.99	79.99	92.99	107.99

🔧 Explain 2 Using Quadratic Regression to Solve a Real-World Problem

After performing quadratic regression on a given data set, the regression equation can be used to answer questions about the scenario represented by the data.

Example 2 Use a graphing calculator to perform quadratic regression on the data given. Then solve the problem and identify and interpret the domain and range of the function.

(A) The height of a model rocket in feet t seconds after it is launched vertically is shown in the following table. Determine the maximum height the rocket attains.

Time	1	2	3	4	5	6	7	8
Height	342	667	902	1163	1335	1459	1584	1864

Enter the data into List 1 and List 2 of a graphing calculator and perform the quadratic regression.

Then plot the regression function over a scatter plot of the data.

Increase the values of Xmax and Ymax until you can see the maximum value of the function. Then use the maximum function on your graphing calculator to find the maximum height of the rocket.

The model rocket attains a maximum height of approximately 2150 feet 13.5 seconds after launch.

The domain of the function will be $0 \leq t \leq +\infty$. Because the independent variable is time, it doesn't make sense to consider negative time.

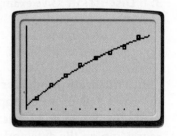

The range of the function is $0 \leq y \leq 2150$ because the height of the rocket should never be negative and it will not go higher than its maximum height.

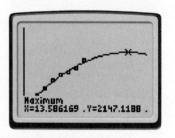

(B) When a rock is thrown into a pond, it makes a series of circular waves. The area enclosed by the first wave is recorded every second and is shown in the table below. If the rock lands 15 meters from shore, when will the first wave reach the shoreline?

Time	1	2	3	4	5	6
Area	9.0	35.8	79.8	145.2	225.1	319.1

Enter the values into List 1 and List 2 of a graphing calculator and use quadratic regression or QuadReg to find the model.

$y \approx$ ⬚ 8.564 ⬚ $x^2 +$ ⬚ 2.444 ⬚ $x +$ ⬚ -2.78 ⬚ $R^2 \approx$ ⬚ 0.9999 ⬚

$y \approx$ ⬚ $8.564x^2 + 2.444x - 2.78$ ⬚

Based on the value of R^2, this function will be a close fit for the data.

The area enclosed by the wave is a circle, so the wave will reach the shore when the radius of the wave is 15 meters.

The area of a circle is given by $A = \pi r^2$.

$A = \pi r^2$

$= \pi$ ⬚ 15 ⬚ $^2 = $ ⬚ 225 ⬚ $\pi \approx$ ⬚ 706.858 ⬚

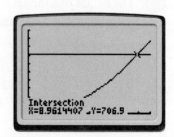

Plot the regression equation as Y_2 and let $Y_2 = $ ⬚ 706.9 ⬚.

Find the intersection of the two lines.

The model intersects the line $y = 706.9$ at $x =$ | 8.9614 |. The first wave will reach the shoreline in 9 seconds.

The function only makes sense while the wave is still circular. Once it reaches the shore, the wave will no longer increase in size in the same way. Therefore, the domain of the function is $0 \leq x < 9.0$ and the range is $0 \leq y \leq 706.9$.

Your Turn

Use a graphing calculator to perform quadratic regression on the data given. Then solve the problem and identify and interpret the domain and range of the function.

6. A company needs boxes to package the goods it produces. One product has a standard shape and thickness but comes in a variety of sizes. The sizes are given as integers. The costs of the various sizes in cents are shown in the table. When the packaging cost reaches $2.00, the company will need to add a surcharge. What is the first size that will have the surcharge added?

Size	1	2	3	4	5	6	7
Cost	7.1	13.8	20.1	29.3	50.1	62.3	86.9

7. A company sells simple circular wall clocks in a variety of sizes. The production cost of each clock is dependent on the diameter of the clock in inches. The costs of making several sizes of clocks in dollars are given in the table. How big would a clock be that costs $4.00 to make? (Round to the nearest eighth.)

Size	8	$8\frac{1}{2}$	9	$9\frac{3}{8}$	$9\frac{1}{2}$	10	12
Cost	1.07	1.16	1.30	1.32	1.36	1.53	2.23

💬 Elaborate

8. Are there any limitations to identifying data that can be modeled by a quadratic function using the method of second differences?

9. A function modeling a situation can be represented as both a function and a graph. Identify some situations where one representation is more helpful than the other.

10. **Essential Question Check-In** When using technology to create a regression model, name two methods for judging the fit of the regression equation.

☆ Evaluate: Homework and Practice

Determine if the function represented in the table is quadratic by finding the second differences.

1.

x	f(x)	First Difference	Second Difference
1	2	————	
2	4	?	————
3	8	?	?
4	16	?	?
5	32	?	?
6	64	?	?

2.

x	f(x)	First Difference	Second Difference
1	3	————	————
2	12	?	————
3	27	?	?
4	48	?	?
5	75	?	?
6	108	?	?

3.

x	f(x)	First Difference	Second Difference
1	9	————	————
2	13	?	————
3	17	?	?
4	21	?	?
5	25	?	?
6	29	?	?

4.

x	f(x)	First Difference	Second Difference
1	2	——	——
2	18	?	——
3	48	?	?
4	92	?	?
5	150	?	?
6	222	?	?

Find the second differences of the given data to verify that the relationship will be quadratic. Then use a graphing calculator to find the quadratic regression equation.

5.

x	1	7	13	19	25	31	37	43	49	55	61	67
y	93	107	125	148	174	203	237	274	316	361	410	462

6.

x	8	11.4	14.8	18.2	21.6	25	28.4	31.8	35.2	38.6	42	45.4
y	24	60	106	161	227	302	387	483	588	703	827	962

7.

x	3.6	17.9	32.2	46.5	60.8	75.1	89.4	103.7	118	132.3	146.6	160.9
y	1946	1684	1442	1219	1012	821	648	494	357	237	133	44

8.

x	9	9.2	9.4	9.6	9.8	10	10.2	10.4	10.6	10.8	11	11.2
y	44	465	844	1180	1475	1728	1941	2117	2255	2355	2409	2416

9.

x	17	20.1	23.2	26.4	29.5	32.7	35.8	38.9	42.1	45.2	48.4	51.5
y	1000	995	974	936	882	814	729	627	510	376	225	58

Find a quadratic model for the given situation. Begin by
creating a scatter plot of the given data on your graphing
calculator, and then find the second differences to verify the
data is quadratic. Finally, use a graphing calculator to perform
a quadratic regression on the data.

10. The table shows the height of an arrow in feet x seconds after
being released toward a target down range by an archery student.

Time	0.25	0.5	0.75	1.0	1.25	1.5	1.75
Height	17	28.7	37.5	44.3	49.6	52.5	52.8

11. The table shows the cost of cleaning a lap pool based on the number of lanes it has.

Number of Lanes	6	8	10	12	14	16
Cleaning Cost	30	95	263	518	875	1299

Use a graphing calculator to find a quadratic model for the given data.

12.

x	2.9	3.9	4.7	5.6	6.9	7.7	8.5
y	8	14	23	29	40	53	70

13.

x	4.7	6.7	8.5	10.1	12.8	14.3	15.9
y	32	17	−27	−94	−193	−321	−499

14.

x	−2.7	−1.9	−0.9	0	0.9	1.9	2.7
y	−13	−8	−6	−4	−5	−8	−13

**Use a graphing calculator to perform quadratic regression on the given data. Then
solve the problem and identify and interpret the domain and range of the function.**

15. The revenue of a company based on the price of its product is in the table below. How much should the
company sell the product for to maximize revenue?

Price ($)	1.00	2.00	2.75	4.00	4.50	6.00	8.00	8.40	9.00
Revenue	90	228	303	384	406	396	282	229	135

16. A scuba diver brought an air-filled balloon 150 feet underwater to the bottom of a lake. The diver conducts an experiment to measure the surface area of the balloon while ascending back to the surface. The results of the measurements are shown in the table. How far will the balloon have risen when it has doubled in surface area?

Distance from Bottom	0	20	40	60	80	100	120
Surface Area	28.6	32.2	35.4	39.5	45.0	52.8	65.4

17. The height of a ski jumper with respect to the low point of the ramp in meters is measured every 0.3 seconds. The results are given in the table. If the skier lands at a point 30 meters below the reference point, how long was the skier in the air?

Time	0.3	0.6	0.9	1.2	1.5	1.8	2.1	2.4
Height	11.2	14.06	16.32	18.47	19.48	20.52	21.01	21.01

H.O.T. Focus on Higher Order Thinking

Use the table for Exercises 18 and 19.

x	1	1.25	1.5	1.75	2	3	4	5	6	7	8	9
y	2	2.378	2.828	3.364	4	8	16	32	64	128	256	512

18. What If? If you perform a quadratic regression on the data, will the value of R^2 be close to 1? Justify your answer.

19. Communicate Mathematical Ideas Perform a quadratic regression on the data; then perform a quadratic regression using only the first four data points. Explain the difference in R^2 values between the two models.

20. Multi-Part A trebuchet is a catapult that was used in the Middle Ages to hurl projectiles during a siege. It is now used in various regions of the United States to throw pumpkins. Teams build trebuchets to compete to see who can throw a pumpkin the farthest. On the practice field, one team has measured the height of its pumpkin after it is launched at 1-second intervals. The results are displayed in the table below.

Time	1	2	3	4	5	6	7	8
Height	152	265	377	441	470	450	396	342

a. Find a quadratic function that models the data.

b. Determine the flight time of the pumpkin.

c. If the pumpkin travels horizontally at a speed of 120 feet per second, how far does it travel before it hits the ground?

d. At the official competition, the trebuchet is situated on a slight rise 10 feet above the targeting area. How far will the pumpkin travel in the competition, assuming the height relative to the base of the trebuchet is modeled by the same function and it moves with the same horizontal speed?

Lesson Performance Task

A student stands at the top of a lighthouse that is 200 feet tall. The base of the lighthouse is an additional 300 feet above the ocean below, and the student has a clear shot to the water below to examine the claims made by Galileo. But, this being the 21st century, the student also has a sophisticated laser tracker that continually tracks the exact height of the dropped object from the ground as well as the length of time elapsed from the drop. At the end of the trial, the student gets sample data in the form of a table.

Time	Height above Ground
0	200
0.5	196
1	184
1.5	164
2	136
2.5	100
3	56
3.5	4
4	−56
4.5	−124
5	−200

Examine the data and determine the relationship between time and height. Then find the function that models the data. (Hint: Negative values represent when the object passes the base of the lighthouse.)

23.2 Comparing Linear, Exponential, and Quadratic Models

Essential Question: How can you determine whether a given data set is best modeled by a linear, quadratic, or exponential function?

⊘ Explore Exploring End Behavior of Linear, Quadratic, and Exponential Functions

Recall that you learned to characterize the end behavior of a function by recognizing what the behavior of the function is as x approaches positive or negative infinity. Look at the three graphs to see what the function does as x approaches infinity or negative infinity.

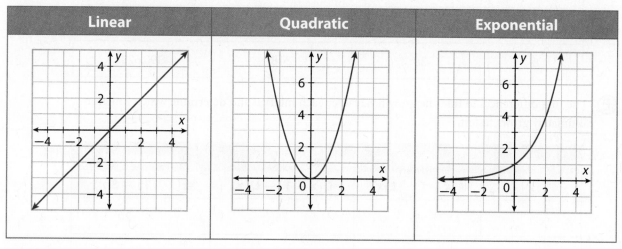

Linear	Quadratic	Exponential

(A) For the linear function, $f(x)$, as x approaches infinity, $f(x)$ [?] , and as x approaches negative infinity, $f(x)$ [?] .

(B) For the quadratic function, $g(x)$, as x approaches infinity, $g(x)$ [?] , and as x approaches negative infinity, $g(x)$ [?] .

(C) For the exponential function, $h(x)$, as x approaches infinity, $h(x)$ [?] , and as x approaches negative infinity, $h(x)$ [?] .

Examine the end behavior and the rate of the change of the three function types by filling in the values of the table.

(D) Fill in the missing values of the table.

x	Linear $L(x) = 5x - 2$	Quadratic $Q(x) = 5x^2 - 2$	Exponential $E(x) = 5^x - 2$
1	3	3	3
2	8	18	?
3	13	43	123
4	?	78	623
5	23	?	3123
6	28	178	15,623
7	33	243	?
8	38	318	390,623

(E) Use first differences to find the growth rate over each interval and determine which function ultimately grows fastest.

x	Linear $L(x+1) - L(x)$	Quadratic $Q(x+1) - Q(x)$	Exponential $E(x+1) - E(x)$
1	5	15	20
2	5	25	?
3	?	35	500
4	5	?	2500
5	5	55	?

(F) The fastest growing function of the three is the [?].

Reflect

1. What is the end behavior of $y = 7x + 12$?

2. What is the end behavior of $y = 5x^2 + x + 2$?

3. What is the end behavior of $y = 3^x - 5$?

4. **Make a Conjecture** Does an increasing exponential function always grow faster than an increasing quadratic function? Will the growth rate of an increasing exponential function eventually exceed that of an increasing quadratic function?

Explain 1 # Justifying a Quadratic Model as More Appropriate Than a Linear Model

The first step in modeling data is selecting an appropriate functional form. If you are trying to decide between a quadratic and a linear model, for example, you may compare interval rates of change or the end behavior. First and second differences are useful for identifying linear and quadratic functions if the data points have equally spaced x-values.

Example 1 Examine the data sets provided and determine whether a quadratic or linear model is more appropriate by examining the graph, the end behavior, and the first and second differences.

x	f(x)
0	3
1	1.5
2	1
3	1.5
4	3
5	5.5
6	9

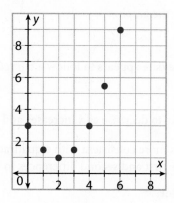

Shape:

The graph of the data appears to follow a curved path that starts downward and turns back upward.

End Behavior:

The path appears to increase without end as x approaches infinity and to increase without end as x approaches negative infinity.

Based on the apparent curvature and end behavior, the function is quadratic.

Interval Behavior:

x	f(x)	First Difference	Second Difference
0	3	——————	——————
1	1.5	−1.5	——————
2	1	−0.5	1
3	1.5	0.5	1
4	3	1.5	1
5	5.5	2.5	1
6	9	3.5	1

The first differences increase as x increases, while the second differences are constant, which is characteristic of a quadratic function.

x	f(x)
0	8
1	6.75
2	5
3	2.75
4	0
5	−3.25
6	−7

Plot the data on the graph.

Shape:

The graph of the data appears to follow a curved, downward path.

End Behavior:

The path appears to decrease as x increases and to increase as x decreases.

The curvature is more consistent with a quadratic than a line, but the apparent end behavior is not. Fill in the first and second differences to discuss interval behavior.

Interval Behavior:

x	f(x)	First Difference	Second Difference
0	8	_____	_____
1	6.75	−1.25	_____
2	5	−1.75	−0.5
3	2.75	−2.25	−0.5
4	0	−2.75	−0.5
5	−3.25	−3.25	−0.5
6	−7	−3.75	−0.5

The absolute values of the first differences increase as x increases, while the second differences are constant, which is characteristic of a quadratic function.

Reflect

5. Was the end behavior helpful in determining that the function in Example 1B was a quadratic? Explain.

6. **Discussion** Can you always tell that a function is quadratic by looking at a graph of it?

Examine the data set and determine whether a quadratic or linear model is more appropriate by examining the graph, the end behavior, and the first and second differences.

7.

x	$f(x)$	First Difference	Second Difference
0	−4	_____	_____
1	−3.8		_____
2	−3.2		
3	−2.2		
4	−0.8		
5	1		
6	3.2		

🎸 Explain 2 Justifying a Quadratic Model as More Appropriate Than an Exponential Model

Previously, you learned to model data with an exponential function. How do you choose between a quadratic and an exponential function to model a given set of data? Graph the given data points and compare the trend of the data with the general shape and end behavior of the parent quadratic and exponential functions. Use the results to decide if the function appears to be quadratic or exponential. Then examine the first and second differences and the ratios of the function using the function values corresponding to x-values separated by a constant amount.

Properties of $f(x) = x^2$ and $g(x) = b^x$		
	$f(x) = x^2$	$g(x) = b^x$ with $b > 1$
End behavior as:		
x approaches infinity	$f(x)$ approaches infinity	$g(x)$ approaches infinity
x approaches negative infinity	$f(x)$ approaches infinity	$g(x)$ approaches zero

Example 2Determine if the function represented in the given table is quadratic or exponential. Plot the given points and analyze the graph. Draw a conclusion if possible. Then find the first and second differences and ratios and either verify your conclusion or determine the family of the function.

(A)

x	f(x)
−3	3
−2	1.5
−1	1
0	1.5
1	3
2	5.5
3	9

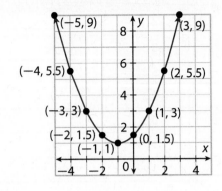

Graph $f(x)$ on the axes provided by plotting the given points and connecting them with a smooth curve.

The data appears to be parabolic.

Also, as x approaches infinity, $f(x)$ appears to increase without end, and as x approaches negative infinity, $f(x)$ appears to increase without end.

It appears that $f(x)$ is a quadratic function.

Now find the first and second differences and the ratio of the values of $f(x)$.

x	f(x)	First Difference	Second Difference	Ratio
−3	3	———	———	———
−2	1.5	−1.5	———	0.5
−1	1	−0.5	1	0.67
0	1.5	0.5	1	1.5
1	3	1.5	1	2
2	5.5	2.5	1	1.83
3	9	3.5	1	1.64

The second differences are constant so the function is quadratic as predicted.

x	f(x)	First Difference	Second Difference	Ratio
−2	4	——	——	——
0	3.5	-0.5	——	0.875
2	2	-1.5	−1	0.571
4	−0.5	-2.5	−1	−0.25
6	−4	-3.5	−1	8
8	−8.5	-4.5	−1	2.125

Graph $f(x)$ on the axes provided by plotting the given points and connecting them with a smooth curve.

The data appears to be either quadratic or exponential.

As x approaches infinity, $f(x)$ appears to decrease without end.

What appears to happen to $f(x)$ as x approaches negative infinity? It cannot be determined.

It appears that $f(x)$ could be either quadratic or exponential.

Now find the first and second differences and the ratio of the values of $f(x)$.

The second differences are constant so the function is quadratic.

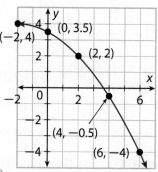

Your Turn

Determine if the function represented in the given table is quadratic or exponential. Plot the given points and analyze the graph. Draw a conclusion if possible. Then find the first and second differences and ratios and either verify your conclusion or determine the family of the function.

8.

x	f(x)	First Difference	Second Difference	Ratio
−3	−5	——	——	——
−2	−3.11	?	——	?
−1	−1.44	?	?	?
0	0	?	?	?
1	1.22	?	?	?
2	2.22	?	?	?
3	3	?	?	?
4	3.56	?	?	?
5	3.89	?	?	?
6	4	?	?	?

9.

x	f(x)	First Difference	Second Difference	Ratio
−2	8.25	——	——	——
0	6	?	——	?
2	4.25	?	?	?
4	3	?	?	?
6	2.25	?	?	?
8	2	?	?	?

🔧 Explain 3 — Selecting an Appropriate Model Given Linear, Exponential, or Quadratic Data

It is important to be able to choose among a variety of models when solving real-world problems.

Example 3 Decide which type of function is best represented by each of the following data sets. Perform the following steps:

1. Graph the data on a scatter plot and draw a fit curve.

2. Identify which function the data appear to represent.

3. Predict the function's end behavior as x approaches infinity.

4. Use a function table to calculate the first differences, second differences, and ratios.

5. Perform the appropriate regression on a graphing calculator. Plot the regression equation and data together to evaluate the fit of regression.

6. Answer any additional questions.

Ⓐ **Demographics** The data table describes the average lifespan in the United States over time.

Year	Average Lifespan (years)
1900	47.3
1910	50.0
1920	54.1
1930	59.7
1940	62.9
1950	68.2
1960	69.7
1970	70.8
1980	73.1
1990	75.4

What was the estimated average lifespan in 2000 according to the model?

Graph the scatter plot and an approximate line of fit to determine the best function to use for this data set.

The data set appears to best fit a linear function.

The end behavior of the data is that as x approaches infinity, $f(x)$ approaches infinity.

Complete the function table for first differences, second differences, and ratios.

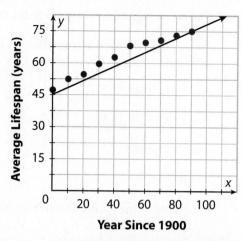

Year Since 1900

Year	Average Lifespan (years)	First Difference	Second Difference	Ratio
1900	47.3	———	———	———
1910	50.0	2.7	———	$\frac{50.0}{47.3} = 1.06$
1920	54.1	4.1	1.4	$\frac{54.1}{50.0} = 1.08$
1930	59.7	5.6	1.5	$\frac{59.7}{54.1} = 1.10$
1940	62.9	3.2	−2.4	$\frac{62.9}{59.7} = 1.05$
1950	68.2	5.3	2.1	$\frac{68.2}{62.9} = 1.08$
1960	69.7	1.5	−3.8	$\frac{69.7}{68.2} = 1.02$
1970	70.8	1.1	−0.4	$\frac{70.8}{69.7} = 1.02$
1980	73.1	2.3	1.2	$\frac{73.1}{70.8} = 1.03$
1990	75.4	2.3	0	$\frac{75.4}{73.1} = 1.03$

Since the ratios are dropping, it is possible that the data set can be modeled by an exponential regression. Since the average of the second differences is around 0, however, it is most likely that the data set should be modeled by a linear regression.

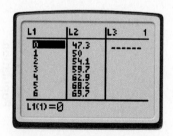

Perform the linear regression by first creating a data table by using the STAT function on a calculator. Use the numbers 0 through 9 to represent the 10-year intervals since 1900, starting with 0 for 1900.

Go to STAT, move over to CALC, type 4, and press ENTER to perform the regression.

Press ZOOM and 9 to fit the data. Plot the line from the regression to test its fit.

The linear regression is a good fit for the data set.

To find the estimated average lifespan in 2000, use the equation $y = 3.23x + 48.57$ and substitute 10 for x.

$y = 3.23x + 48.57$

$y = 3.23(10) + 48.57$

$= 32.3 + 48.57$

$= 80.87$

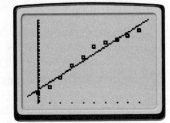

According to the model, the average lifespan in the year 2000 was 80.87 years.

(B) **Biology** The data table lists the whooping crane population in one habitat over time.

Whooping Crane	
Year	**Population**
1940	22
1950	34
1960	33
1970	56
1980	76
1990	146
2000	177
2010	281

What is the expected whooping crane population for 2020?

Graph the scatter plot and an approximate line of fit to determine the best function to use for this data set. Use the numbers 0 through 7 to represent the 10-year intervals since 1940, starting with 0 for 1940.

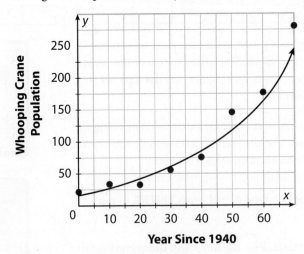

The data set appears to best fit an exponential function.

The end behavior of this data is that as x approaches infinity, $f(x)$, approaches infinity.

Complete the function table for first differences, second differences, and ratios.

Year	Population	First Difference	Second Difference	Ratio
1940	22	————	————	————
1950	34	12	————	$\frac{34}{22} = 1.55$
1960	33	−1	−13	$\frac{33}{34} = 0.97$
1970	56	23	24	$\frac{56}{33} = 1.70$
1980	76	20	−3	$\frac{76}{56} = 1.36$
1990	146	70	50	$\frac{146}{76} = 1.92$
2000	177	31	−39	$\frac{177}{146} = 1.21$
2010	281	104	73	$\frac{281}{177} = 1.59$

Since the ratios are changing and the second difference does not have an average that is close to 0, exponential regression should be used.

Perform the exponential regression by first creating a data table by using the STAT function on a calculator. Use the numbers 0 through 7 to represent the 10-year intervals since 1940, starting with 0 for 1940.

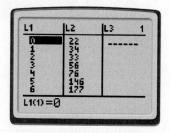

Go to STAT, move over to CALC, type 0, and press ENTER to perform the regression.

Press ZOOM and 9 to fit the data. Plot the line from the regression to test its fit.

The exponential regression is a good fit for the data set.

To find the estimated number of whooping cranes in 2020, use the

equation $y = \boxed{20.05(1.44)^x}$ and substitute 8 for x.

$y = \boxed{20.05(1.44)^x}$

$y = \boxed{20.05(1.44)^8}$

$= \boxed{20.05(18.49)}$

$= \boxed{370.7}$

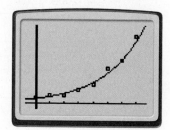

Since it is unrealistic to round up in this situation, the predicted whooping crane population in this habitat in 2020 is 370.

Decide which type of function is best represented by each of the following data sets. Perform the following steps:

1. Graph the data on a scatter plot and draw a fit curve.

2. Identify which function the data appear to represent.

3. Predict the function's end behavior as x approaches infinity.

4. Use a function table to calculate the first differences, second differences, and ratios.

5. Perform the appropriate regression on a graphing calculator. Plot the regression equation and data together to evaluate the fit of regression.

6. Answer any additional questions.

10. **Population** The data table describes the percentage of people living in central cities in the United States over time. According to the model, what percentage of people were living in central cities in the United States in 2000?

Year	% of People
1910	21.2
1920	24.2
1930	30.8
1940	32.5
1950	32.8
1960	32.3
1970	31.4
1980	30.0

11. **Automobiles** The data table describes the car weight versus horsepower for automobiles produced in 2012. If a car weighed 6500 pounds in 2012, how much horsepower should the car have had?

Car Weight (pounds)	Horsepower in 2012
2000	70
2500	105
3000	145
3500	179
4000	259
4500	338
5000	400
5500	557
6000	556

Elaborate

12. In general, what are three possible end behaviors of exponential, linear, and quadratic graphs as x increases without bound? When do these end behaviors occur?

13. What do function tables tell you that graphs don't ? How can this information be used to help you select a model?

14. When does a graph help determine an appropriate model better than examining first and second differences and ratios?

15. Can two different models be created that represent the same set of data?

16. **Essential Question Check-In** How can a graph be used to determine whether a given data set is best modeled by a linear, quadratic, or exponential function?

⭐ Evaluate: Homework and Practice

• Online Homework
• Hints and Help
• Extra Practice

1. For the two functions $f(x) = 2x + 1$ and $g(x) = 2^x + 1$, which function has the greatest average rate of change over the interval from 0 to 1? What about the interval from 2 to 3?

2. Plot the data and describe the observed shape and end behavior. Does it appear linear or quadratic? Calculate first and second differences and identify the type of function.

x	f(x)	First Difference	Second Difference
0	−0.79	_____	_____
1	2.81	?	_____
2	4.41	?	?
3	4.01	?	?
4	1.61	?	?
5	−2.79	?	?

3. Plot the data and describe the observed shape and end behavior. Does it appear to be linear or quadratic? Calculate first and second differences and identify the type of function.

x	f(x)	First Difference	Second Difference
−2	−4	_____	_____
−1	−3.3	?	_____
0	−1.2	?	?
1	2.3	?	?
2	7.2	?	?
3	13.5	?	?

© Houghton Mifflin Harcourt Publishing Company

4. Plot the data and describe the observed shape and end behavior. Does it appear linear or quadratic? Calculate first and second differences and identify the type of function.

x	f(x)	First Difference	Second Difference
0	7.6	————	————
1	6.25	?	————
2	4.6	?	?
3	2.65	?	?
4	0.4	?	?

5. Plot the data and describe the observed shape and end behavior. Does it appear linear or quadratic? Calculate first and second differences and identify the type of function.

x	f(x)	First Difference	Second Difference
1	−7.2	————	————
2	−3.8	?	————
3	0	?	?
4	4.2	?	?
5	8.8	?	?

6. Plot the given points. Describe the general shape and end behavior of the graph. Draw a conclusion about the function, if possible. Then complete the table and use the differences to to verify your conclusions.

x	f(x)	First Difference	Second Difference	Ratio
−2	−5.75	————	————	————
0	1	?	————	?
2	6.25	?	?	?
4	10	?	?	?
6	12.25	?	?	?
8	13	?	?	?
10	12.25	?	?	?
12	10	?	?	?
14	6.25	?	?	?

7. Plot the given points. Describe the general shape and end behavior of the graph. Draw a conclusion about the function, if possible. Then complete the table and use the differences to verify your conclusions.

x	$f(x)$	First Difference	Second Difference	Ratio
−2	9	————	————	————
0	5.5	?	————	?
2	3	?	?	?
4	1.5	?	?	?
6	1	?	?	?

8. Plot the given points. Describe the general shape and end behavior of the graph. Draw a conclusion about the function, if possible. Then complete the table and use the differences to verify your conclusions.

x	$f(x)$	First Difference	Second Difference	Ratio
−5	−3	————	————	————
−2	−2	?	————	?
1	1	?	?	?
4	6	?	?	?
7	13	?	?	?

9. Critical Thinking A set of real-world data was modeled by using the quadratic, linear, and exponential forms of regression. The calculator showed that all three regression equations were close fits for the data provided. Which regression model do you think you should use? Explain.

10. Explain the Error To determine if the data represents a linear model, Louise looked at the difference in y-values: 110, 110, 110, 110.

x	7	9	12	14	18
y	150	260	370	480	590

She decided that since the differences between the y-values are all the same, a linear model would be appropriate. Explain her mistake.

11. Critical Thinking Suppose that the following *r*-values were produced from regressions performed on the same set of data.

r-values	
Linear	**Exponential**
0.15	0.13

What type of regression model should be chosen for this data set? Explain.

Lesson Performance Task

The table shows general guidelines for the weight of a Great Dane at various ages.
Create a function modeling the ideal weight for a Great Dane at any age. Justify your choice of models. How well do you think your model will do when the puppy is one or two years old?

Age (months)	Weight (kg)
2	12
4	23
6	33
8	40
10	45

Linear, Exponential, and Quadratic Models

Essential Question: How can you use linear, exponential, and quadratic models to solve real-world problems?

Key Vocabulary
quadratic regression
(regresión cuadrática)

KEY EXAMPLE   *(Lesson 23.1)*

Find the second differences of the given data to verify that the relationship will be quadratic. Use a graphing calculator to find the quadratic regression equation for the data and R^2 to 4 significant digits.

The table below shows the cost of shipping a box that has a volume of x cubic feet.

Volume	Cost ($)	First Difference	Second Difference
1	$6.15	——————	——————
2	$8.00	$8 - 6.15 = 1.85$	——————
3	$13.90	$13.9 - 8 = 5.9$	$5.9 - 1.85 = 4.05$
4	$23.75	$23.75 - 13.9 = 9.85$	$9.85 - 5.9 = 3.95$
5	$38.25	$38.25 - 23.75 = 14.5$	$14.5 - 9.85 = 4.65$

$a \approx 2.09$

$b \approx -4.54$

$c \approx 8.65$

$R^2 \approx 0.9999$

Enter the volumes, as the x-values, and the costs, as the y-values, into the graphing calculator and perform a quadratic regression.

The quadratic regression equation is $y \approx 2.09x^2 - 4.54x + 8.65$.

KEY EXAMPLE   *(Lesson 23.2)*

Determine which type of function appears to best represents the data shown on the scatter plot: linear, exponential, or quadratic.

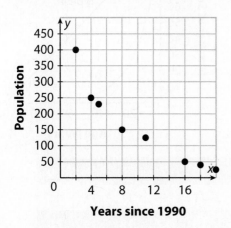

Years since 1990

Based on the curvature of the shape formed by the points, this function appears to be exponential or quadratic.

As x increases, the function that best fits the points appears to decrease to zero. As x decreases, the function appears to increase without end.

Based on the scatter plot, an exponential function appears to are best represent this data.

1. The table below shows the height of a baseball in inches *x* seconds after it was thrown. Complete the table with the first differences and second differences. Then, use a graphing calculator to find the quadratic regression equation for the data. *(Lesson 23.1)*

Time	Height	First Difference	Second Difference
0	60	————	————
0.25	59	?	————
0.5	57	?	?
0.75	52	?	?
1	44	?	?
1.25	35	?	?

2. The scatter plot shown represents a company's profit over 10 years. Which type of function best represents the data? *(Lesson 23.2)*

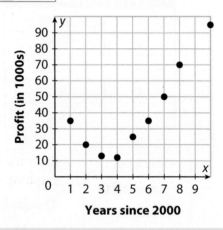

MODULE PERFORMANCE TASK
What Model Fits a Survivorship Curve?

A survivorship curve shows the number of surviving members of a population over time from a given set of births. The graph shows the three types of survivorship curves that commonly occur.

The data table presents the results of a survivorship study for a population of 1000 goats. What type of survivorship curve most closely matches the goat data? Can you find a good mathematical model for these data, using either a linear, quadratic, or exponential function, or a combination of different functions over different parts of the data set?

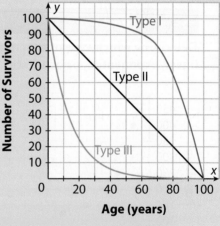

Age (years)	1	2	3	4	5	6	7	8	9	10
Number of Deaths During Year	12	13	9	11	12	11	9	11	11	11
Age (years)	**11**	**12**	**13**	**14**	**15**	**16**	**17**	**18**	**19**	**20**
Number of Deaths During Year	28	14	46	62	52	92	101	133	159	203

(Ready) to Go On?

23.1–23.2 Linear, Exponential, and Quadratic Models

- Online Homework
- Hints and Help
- Extra Practice

1. The height of a plant, in inches, *x* weeks after it was planted is given in the table below. Use a graphing calculator to write a quadratic regression equation for the data set given. About how many weeks did it take the plant to reach a height of 40 inches? *(Lesson 23.1)*

Weeks	5	10	15	20	25
Height	15	31	55	87	127

2. Graph the data represented in the given table. Determine if the function represented in the given table is best represented by a linear, exponential, or quadratic function. Explain your answer. *(Lesson 23.2)*

x	−3	−2	−1	0	1	2	3
f(x)	5.5	3.5	1.5	1	0.6	0.3	0.1

ESSENTIAL QUESTION

3. How can you determine if a function is linear, quadratic, or exponential?

Assessment Readiness

1. Consider each data set and if it is best represented by a linear, exponential, or quadratic model. Determine if each statement is True or False.

   A. $\{(-5, 2), (-3, 6), (-1, 10), (1, 14), (3, 18)\}$ is best represented by a linear model.

   B. $\{(-2, 12), (-1, 6), (0, 3), (1, 1.5), (2, 0.75)\}$ is best represented by a quadratic model.

   C. $\{(-5, 4), (-4, 1), (-3, 0), (-2, 1), (-1, 4)\}$ is best represented by an exponential model.

2. Does the given equation have two real solutions?

   A. $6x^2 + 15 = 0$

   B. $8x^2 - 50 = 0$

   C. $3x^2 + 4x - 10 = 0$

3. Consider data represented by the following points:
   $\{(-2, 0.25), (-1, 1.5), (0, 4), (1, 15), (2, 60)\}$. Determine if the data are best represented by a linear, exponential, or quadratic function. Explain your answer.

4. The equation $2x^2 + 8x + c = 0$ has one real solution. What is the value of c? Explain how you found the value of c.

1. A quadratic equation has the zeros −3 and 6. Can the quadratic equation be the given equation?

   A. $(2x + 6)(x − 6) = 0$

   B. $(6x − 1)(x + 3) = 0$

   C. $− 3x(x − 6) = 0$

2. Factor and solve each equation. Does the equation have a solution of $x = −5$?

   A. $3x^2 + 14x − 5 = 0$

   B. $x^2 + 3x − 40 = 0$

   C. $x^2 − 3x − 40 = 0$

3. Consider the equation $4x^2 − 20 = 0$. Determine if each statement is True or False

   A. The equation has 2 solutions.

   B. A zero of the related function is $− \sqrt{20}$.

   C. A solution of the equation is $\sqrt{5}$.

4. Solve $\left(2x + \frac{2}{3}\right)(x + 5) = 0$. Is the given value a solution of the equation?

   A. $x = −\frac{1}{3}$

   B. $x = − 5$

   C. $x = \frac{2}{3}$

5. The equation $ax^2 + 12x + c = 0$ has one solution. Can a and c equal each of the following values?

   A. $a = 4, c = 9$

   B. $a = 9, c = 16$

   C. $a = 36, c = 1$

6. The table given has been filled out for the function $g(x)$. The values of $g(x)$ are not shown. Is $g(x)$ a linear or quadratic function? Justify your answer.

x	g(x)	First Difference	Second Difference
−2	_____	_____	_____
0	_____	−4	_____
2	_____	−4	0
4	_____	−4	0
6	_____	−4	0

7. The area of a square table top can be represented by $\left(9x^2 - 30x + 25\right)$ square feet. The perimeter of the table top is 34 feet. What is the value of x? Explain how you solved this problem.

8. Solve $4x^2 + 8x = -3$. Which of the following solution methods did you use: factoring, completing the square, or the quadratic formula? Why? Show your work.

Performance Tasks

★ **9.** Abigail has a rectangular quilt with dimensions 36 inches by 48 inches. She decides to sew a border on the quilt, so that the total area of the quilt is 1900 square inches. What will be the width of the border?

★★10. The table shows the average weight of a particular variety of sheep at various ages.

A. None of the three models—linear, quadratic, or exponential—fits the data exactly. Which of these is the best model for the data? Explain your choice.

B. What would you predict for the weight of a sheep that is 1 year old?

C. Do you think you could use your model to find the weight of a sheep any age? Why or why not?

Sheep	
Age (mo)	**Weight (lb)**
2	36
4	69
6	99
8	120
10	135

★★★11. Examine the two models that represent annual tuition for two colleges.

A. Describe each model as linear, quadratic, or exponential.

B. Write a function rule for each model.

C. Both models have the same value for year 0. What does this mean?

D. Why do both models have the same value for year 1?

Years After 2004	Tuition at College 1 ($)	Tuition at College 2 ($)
0	2000.00	2000.00
1	2200.00	2200.00
2	2400.00	2420.00
3	2600.00	2662.00
4	2800.00	2928.20

Competitive Diver Franco and Grace are competitive divers. Grace dives from a 20-meter cliff into the water, with an initial upward speed of 3.2 m/s. Franco dives from a springboard that is 10 meters above the water surface with an initial upward speed of 4.2 m/s.

The height in meters of an object projected into the air with an initial vertical velocity of v meters per second and initial height of h_0 can be modeled by $h(t) = -4.9t^2 + vt + h_0$.

a. Write a function $h_{\text{Grace}}(t)$ that models the height of Grace's dive.

b. Write a function $h_{\text{Franco}}(t)$ that models the height of Franco's dive.

c. Use a graphing calculator to graph both functions on the same screen. Label each function.

d. What are the domain and range of each function in terms of the situation? Explain. Round values to the nearest tenth.

e. Compare the maximum heights and the time that elapses before each diver hits the water.

Inverse Relationships

MATH IN CAREERS

Ichthyologist An ichthyologist is a biologist who specializes in the study of fish. Ichthyologists work in a variety of disciplines relating to fish and their environment, including ecology, taxonomy, behavior, and conservation. Ichthyologists might perform tasks such as monitoring water quality, designing and conducting experiments, evaluating data using statistics, and publishing results in scientific journals. Ichthyologists utilize mathematical models and collect and analyze experimental and observational data to help them understand fish and their environment.

If you are interested in a career as an ichthyologist, you should study these mathematical subjects:
- Geometry
- Algebra
- Statistics
- Calculus

Research other careers that require using mathematical models to understand an organism and its environment. Check out the career activity at the end of the unit to find out how **ichthyologists** use math.

Visualize Vocabulary

Use the ✔ words to complete the graphic. Use one word for each section.

Review Words

✔ cubic function *(función cúbica)*

✔ end behavior *(comportamiento extremo)*

✔ function *(función)*

✔ relation *(relación)*

Preview Words

cube root function *(función raíz cúbica)*

inverse function *(función inversa)*

inverse relation *(relación inversa)*

radical function *(función radical)*

square root function *(function de raíz cuadrada)*

turning point *(punto de inflexión)*

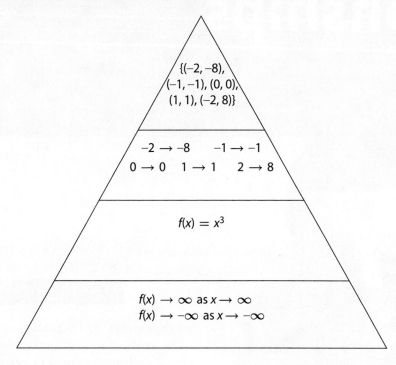

Understand Vocabulary

To become familiar with some of the vocabulary terms in the module, consider the following. You may refer to the module, the glossary, or a dictionary.

1. An ___?___ results from exchanging the input and output values of a one-to-one function.

2. A ___?___ has a rule that contains a variable within a radical.

3. A ___?___ occurs on the graph of a function where the graph changes from increasing to decreasing (or vice versa).

Active Reading

Tri-Fold As you complete each lesson in this unit, create a tri-fold to help you track your progress with the material in the lesson. Organize the lesson topic into what you know, what you want to know, and what you learn. Label the three sections "Know," "Want," and "Learn" and record notes to see how much you have learned after completing the lesson. Be sure to use exact vocabulary and to include specific examples, with corresponding graphs, in your notes.

Functions and Inverses

Essential Question: How can you use functions and inverses to solve real-world problems?

REAL WORLD VIDEO
Balls of different diameters and volumes can present a variety of packaging challenges for sports equipment manufacturers. Check out how inverse functions can help lead to efficient solutions.

MODULE PERFORMANCE TASK PREVIEW

The Smallest Cube

If you know the dimensions of a box that is shaped like a rectangular prism, you can easily find the volume of the box using the formula $v = l \times w \times h$. But what if you know the volume and want to know the dimensions? That's the problem package designers face when they know the size of a new product and must find the dimensions of the package it will be sold in. You'll do just that after you learn to "unpack" functions in this module—that is, find their inverses.

Are (YOU) Ready?

Complete these exercises to review skills you will need for this module.

Squares and Square Roots

Example 1   Evaluate $\sqrt{225}$.

Since $15^2 = 15 \cdot 15 = 225$, the square root of 225 is 15.

Evaluate.

1. $\sqrt{144}$

2. $\sqrt{256}$

3. $\sqrt{\dfrac{4}{9}} \quad \dfrac{2}{3}$

Cubes and Cube Roots

Example 2   Evaluate $\sqrt[3]{-27}$.

Since $(-3)^3 = (-3) \cdot (-3) \cdot (-3) = -27$, the cube root of –27 is –3.

Evaluate.

4. $\sqrt[3]{1000}$

5. $\sqrt[3]{-125}$

6. $\sqrt[3]{-64}$

Linear Functions

Example 3   Write $8x - 2y = 20$ in slope-intercept form.

$$-2y = -8x + 20 \qquad \text{Isolate the } y\text{-term.}$$

$$y = 4x - 10 \qquad \text{Divide both sides by } -2.$$

Write each equation in slope-intercept form.

7. $2x + 3y = 24$

8. $3(2y - x) = -15$

9. $3x + 0.4y = -1$

24.1 Graphing Polynomial Functions

Essential Question: How does the value of *n* affect the behavior of the function $f(x) = x^n$?

⊘ Explore   Exploring Graphs of Cubic and Quartic Functions

The **end behavior** of a function is a description of the values of the function as x approaches positive infinity $(x \to +\infty)$ or negative infinity $(x \to -\infty)$. The degree and leading coefficient of a polynomial function determine its end behavior.

(A) Use your graphing calculator to plot each of the cubic functions in the table, and complete the table to describe each function's general shape and end behavior.

Function	Number of Direction Changes	End Behavior as $x \to +\infty$	End Behavior as $x \to -\infty$
$f(x) = x^3 - 5x$	?	$f(x) \to$?	$f(x) \to$?
$f(x) = -2x^3$	?	$f(x) \to$?	$f(x) \to$?
$f(x) = \frac{3}{2}x^3 + x + 1$	?	$f(x) \to$?	$f(x) \to$?

(B) All three of these functions are cubic, which means that they have degree ⬚? . Their shapes vary, but one feature they all share is the end behavior. Is the end behavior the same or opposite on the two ends? ⬚?

The graphs show quartic functions. Describe each function's general shape and end behavior.

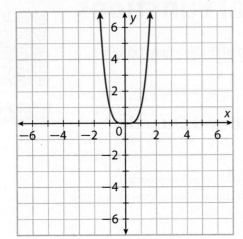

$$f(x) = x^4$$

$\boxed{?}$ direction change(s)

As $x \to +\infty$, $f(x) \to \boxed{?}$.

As $x \to -\infty$, $f(x) \to \boxed{?}$.

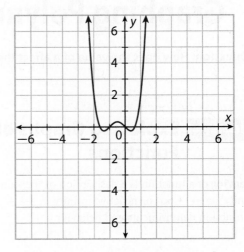

$$f(x) = x^4 + 2x^3 - x$$

$\boxed{?}$ direction change(s)

As $x \to +\infty$, $f(x) \to \boxed{?}$.

As $x \to -\infty$, $f(x) \to \boxed{?}$.

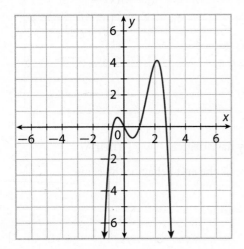

$$f(x) = -x^4 + 3x^3 - 2x$$

$\boxed{?}$ direction change(s)

As $x \to +\infty$, $f(x) \to \boxed{?}$.

As $x \to -\infty$, $f(x) \to \boxed{?}$.

(D) All three of these functions are quartic, which means that they have degree $\boxed{?}$. Their shapes vary, but one feature they all share is the end behavior. Is the

end behavior the same or opposite on the two ends? $\boxed{?}$

Each of the graphs of the functions in Steps A and C change directions at least once. These direction changes are called **turning points**.

Reflect

1. Discussion How many turning points did the cubic functions have? the quartic functions? Do you notice a pattern?

⚙ Explain 1 Even and Odd Degree Polynomial Functions

The degree of a polynomial affects the shape of its graph. The table shows representative graphs for polynomial functions with degrees from 1 through 5. A polynomial of degree n can have up to $n - 1$ turning points.

Notice that for functions with odd degrees (1, 3, 5, …), the end behaviors of graphs are opposite, and for functions with even degrees (2, 4, 6, …), the end behaviors of graphs are the same.

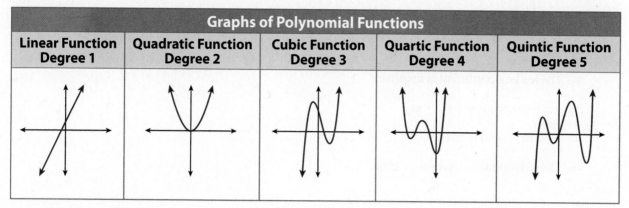

	Graphs of Polynomial Functions			
Linear Function Degree 1	**Quadratic Function Degree 2**	**Cubic Function Degree 3**	**Quartic Function Degree 4**	**Quintic Function Degree 5**

The sign of the leading coefficient determines the end behavior. The table summarizes the end behavior rules for polynomials.

$f(x)$ is a polynomial with…	Odd Degree	Even Degree
Leading coefficient $a > 0$	As $x \to +\infty$, $f(x) \to +\infty$ As $x \to -\infty$, $f(x) \to -\infty$	As $x \to -\infty$, $f(x) \to +\infty$ As $x \to +\infty$, $f(x) \to +\infty$
Leading coefficient $a < 0$	As $x \to -\infty$, $f(x) \to +\infty$ As $x \to +\infty$, $f(x) \to -\infty$	As $x \to -\infty$, $f(x) \to -\infty$ As $x \to +\infty$, $f(x) \to -\infty$

Example 1   For each graph, identify whether the polynomial $f(x)$ is of odd or even degree, and whether the leading coefficient is positive or negative.

(A)

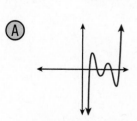

End behavior:

As $x \to +\infty$, $f(x) \to +\infty$.

The leading coefficient is positive.

As $x \to -\infty$, $f(x) \to -\infty$

⇒ Opposite end behaviors

⇒ The polynomial's degree is odd.

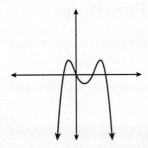

As $x \rightarrow +\infty$, $f(x) \rightarrow \boxed{-\infty}$.

$\Rightarrow$ The leading coefficient is negative.

As of $x \rightarrow -\infty$, $f(x) \rightarrow \boxed{-\infty}$.

$\Rightarrow$ $\boxed{\text{Same}}$ end behaviors

$\Rightarrow$ The polynomial's degree is $\boxed{\text{even}}$.

Reflect

2. **Discussion** Explain why the leading coefficient is the only polynomial coefficient that determines end-behavior.

Your Turn

For each graph, identify whether the polynomial is of odd or even degree, and whether the leading coefficient is positive or negative.

3.

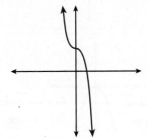

4.

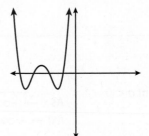

⏺ Explain 2   Classifying Even and Odd Functions

A function is an **even function** if $f(-x) = f(x)$ for all values of x. This means that if the point (x, y) is on the graph, then the point $(-x, y)$ is also on the graph.

A function is an **odd function** if $f(-x) = -f(x)$ for all values of x. This means that if the point (x, y) is on the graph, then the point $(-x, -y)$ is also on the graph.

Even Functions	Odd Functions

Example 2   Classify each graphed polynomial as an odd or even function, and identify whether the leading coefficient is positive or negative.

Ⓐ

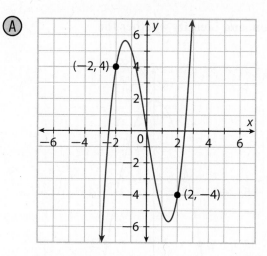

The points $(-2, 4)$ and $(2, -4)$ are on the graph, so the polynomial is an odd function.

End Behavior:

As $x \to +\infty$, $f(x) \to +\infty$, so the leading coefficient is positive.

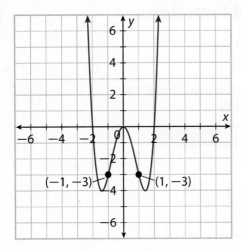

The points $(-1, -3)$ and $(1, -3)$ are on the graph, so the polynomial is an even function.

End Behavior:

As $x \rightarrow +\infty$, $f(x) \rightarrow \boxed{+\infty}$, so the leading coefficient is positive.

Your Turn

Classify each graphed polynomial as an odd or even function, and identify whether the leading coefficient is positive or negative.

5.

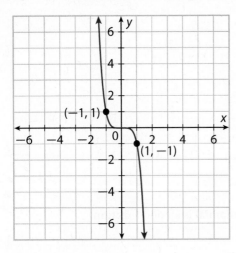

6.

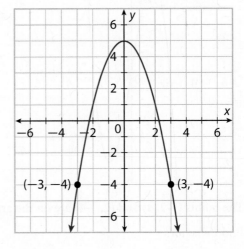

⊙ Elaborate

7. How can you tell based on the end behavior that an odd degree polynomial must have an even number of turning points, and an even degree polynomial must have an odd number?

8. If $f(x)$ is a polynomial and $f(-x) = -f(x)$, how do you know that the polynomial has an odd degree?

9. **Essential Question Check-In** How does the degree of a polynomial affect its end behavior?

⭐ Evaluate: Homework and Practice

1. Use a graphing calculator to plot the function $f(x) = x^3 + 2x^2 - 3x - 4$ and determine how many turning points there are and what the end behavior is.

For each graph, identify whether the polynomial $f(x)$ is of odd or even degree, and whether the leading coefficient is positive or negative.

2.

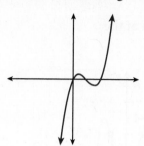

3.

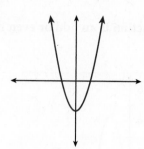

4.

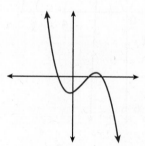

5.

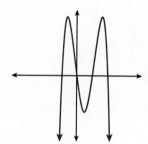

6.

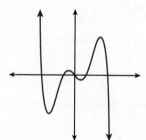

7.

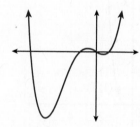

8.

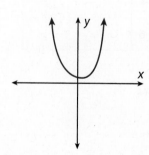

9.

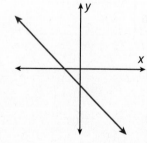

10.

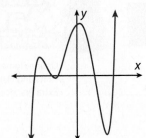

11.

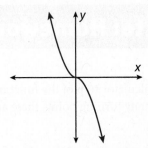

Determine if each function is an odd or even function, and identify the sign of the leading coefficient.

12.

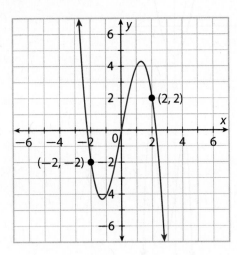

13.

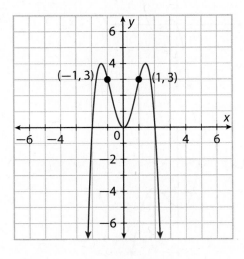

14.

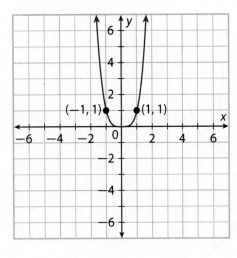

15.

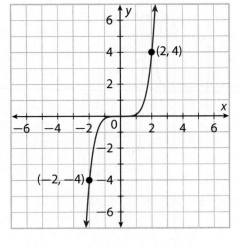

16.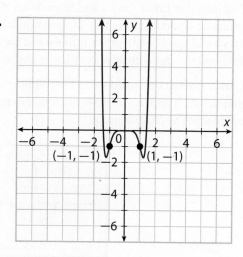

17.

18. Matching Use the end behavior to match each polynomial function to its graph.

A.

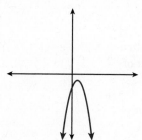

B.

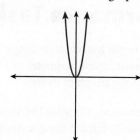

C.

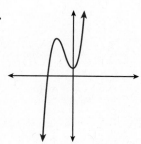

D.

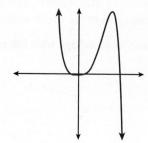

a. ___?___ $f(x) = 5x^3 + 9x^2 + 1$

b. ___?___ $f(x) = 2x^6 + 3x^4 + 5x^2$

c. ___?___ $f(x) = -x^5 + 3x^4 + x$

d. ___?___ $f(x) = -4x^2 + 3x - 1$

H.O.T. Focus on Higher Order Thinking

19. Communicate Mathematical Ideas Predict the end behavior of the polynomial function $f(x) = -x^9$.

20. Communicate Mathematical Ideas Is the function $f(x) = x^3$ an odd or even function? Show your reasoning.

21. **Explain the Error** Carlos and Rhonda are disagreeing over the answer to a math problem. Rhonda claims that the polynomial function $f(x) = \frac{1}{3}x^3 + 6x^2 + 21x + 16$ should approach negative infinity as x approaches negative infinity, because the leading term has a positive coefficient and is of odd degree.

Carlos entered the function on his graphing calculator and produced the following graph, which appears to show the function approaching positive infinity as x approaches negative infinity.

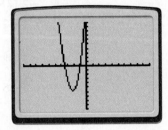

Who is right? Can you figure out what the mistake is?

Lesson Performance Task

A company that specializes in gift baskets is making a pyramid-shaped package with a rectangular base. The base must have a perimeter of 54 centimeters, and the height of the package must be equal to the length of its base.

A. Write a polynomial function, $V(x)$, for the volume of the package, where x is the length of the base. What are the constraints on x for this situation?

B. Use a graphing calculator to find the maximum volume of the package. What value of x corresponds to the maximum volume?

C. What dimensions result in a package with the maximum volume?

24.2 Understanding Inverse Functions

Essential Question: How can you recognize inverses of functions from their graphs and how can you find inverses of functions?

⊘ Explore   Exploring Inverses of Functions

You can use a graphing calculator to explore inverse functions and their relationships to the linear parent function $f(x) = x$.

Ⓐ Using a standard viewing window, graph the function $y = 2^x$ and the linear function $y = x$ on a graphing calculator. Describe the end behavior of $y = 2^x$ as $x \to +\infty$.

Ⓑ Use the DrawInv feature on the calculator to draw the graph of the inverse of $y = 2^x$ along with $y = 2^x$ and $y = x$. How are the graphs of $y = 2^x$ and its inverse related? Is the inverse of $y = 2^x$ a function? Explain your answer.

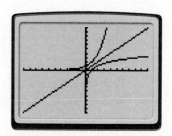

Ⓒ Now graph the function $y = x^2$ and the linear function $y = x$ on a graphing calculator. Use the DrawInv feature to draw the graph of the inverse $y = x^2$ along with $y = x^2$ and $y = x$. How are the graphs of $y = x^2$ and its inverse related? Is the inverse of $y = x^2$ a function? Explain your answer.

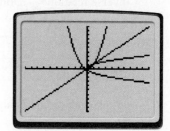

Reflect

1. **Make a Conjecture** Functions and their inverses appear to be reflections across which line?

2. Do you think all inverses of functions are functions? Why or why not?

⏺ Explain 1   Graphing Inverse Relations

You have seen the word *inverse* used in various ways.

The additive inverse of 3 is −3.

The multiplicative inverse of 5 is $\frac{1}{5}$.

You can also find and apply inverses to relations, which are sets of ordered pairs, and functions. To graph the **inverse relation**, you can reflect each point across the line $y = x$. This is equivalent to switching the x- and y-values in each ordered pair of the relation.

Example 1   Graph the relation and connect the points. Then graph the inverse. Identify the domain and range of each relation.

(A)

x	0	1	2	4	8
y	2	4	5	6	7

Graph each ordered pair and connect the points.

Switch the x- and y-values in each ordered pair.

x	2	4	5	6	7
y	0	1	2	4	8

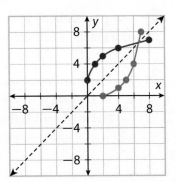

Reflect each point across $y = x$, and connect the new points. Make sure the points match those in the table.

Original relation: Domain: $0 \le x \le 8$ Range: $2 \le y \le 7$

Inverse relation: Domain: $2 \le x \le 7$ Range: $0 \le y \le 8$

(B)

x	1	3	4	5	6
y	0	1	2	3	5

Graph each ordered pair and connect the points.

Switch the x- and y-values in each ordered pair.

x	0	1	2	3	5
y	1	3	4	5	6

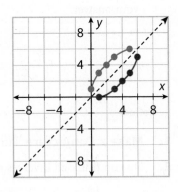

Reflect each point across $y = x$, and connect the new points. Make sure the points match those in the table.

Original relation: Domain: $1 \le x \le 6$ Range: $0 \le y \le 5$

Inverse relation: Domain: $0 \le x \le 5$ Range: $1 \le y \le 6$

3. **Discussion** How are the domain and range of a relation related to the domain and range of its inverse?

Graph the relation and connect the points. Then graph the inverse. Identify the domain and range of each relation.

4.

x	1	2	3	5	7
y	2	4	6	8	9

✪ Explain 2 Writing Inverse Functions by Using Inverse Operations

When a relation is also a function, you can write the inverse of the function $f(x)$ as $f^{-1}(x)$. This notation does *not* indicate a reciprocal.

Functions that undo each other are called **inverse functions**.

You can find the inverse function by writing the original function with x and y switched and solving for y.

Example 2 Use inverse operations to find each inverse. Then check your solution.

Ⓐ $f(x) = 2x$

$$y = 2x \qquad\qquad \text{Write } y \text{ for } f(x).$$

$$x = 2y \qquad\qquad \text{Switch } x \text{ and } y.$$

$$y = \frac{x}{2} \qquad\qquad \text{Solve for } y.$$

The inverse is $f^{-1}(x) = \frac{x}{2}$.

Check:

1. Use the input $x = 7$ in $f(x)$.
$$f(x) = 2x$$
$$f(7) = 2(7) = 14$$
The output is 14.

2. Verify that the output, 14, gives the input, 7.
$$f^{-1}(x) = \frac{x}{2}$$
$$f^{-1}(14) = \frac{14}{2} = 7$$

Since the inverse function *does* undo the original function, $f^{-1}(x) = \frac{x}{2}$ is correct.

B $f(x) = \dfrac{x}{4} - 5$

$y = \dfrac{x}{4} - 5$ \qquad\qquad Write y for $\boxed{f(x)}$.

$\boxed{x} = \dfrac{\boxed{y}}{4} - 5$ \qquad\qquad Switch $\boxed{x}$ and y.

$y = \boxed{4}\left(x + \boxed{5}\right)$ \qquad\qquad Solve for $\boxed{y}$.

Check:

1. Use the input $x = 40$ in $f(x)$.

$f(40) = \dfrac{\boxed{40}}{4} - 5 = \boxed{10} - 5 = \boxed{5}$

The output is $\boxed{5}$.

2. Verify that the output, $\boxed{5}$, gives the input, $\boxed{40}$.

$f^{-1}\!\left(\boxed{5}\right) = 4\left(\boxed{5} + 5\right) = 4\left(\boxed{10}\right) = \boxed{40}$

Since the inverse function does undo the original function, it is correct.

Your Turn

Use inverse operations to find the inverse. Then check your solution.

5. $f(x) = 5x - 7$

⊘ Explain 3 Graphing Inverse Functions

A function and its inverse are reflections across the line $y = x$.

Example 3 Write the inverse of each function. Then graph the function together with its inverse.

A $f(x) = 3x + 6$

$y = 3x + 6$ \qquad\qquad Write y for $f(x)$.

$x = 3y + 6$ \qquad\qquad Switch x and y.

$y = \dfrac{x - 6}{3}$ \qquad\qquad Solve for y.

$y = \dfrac{1}{3}x - 2$ \qquad\qquad Simplify.

The inverse is $f^{-1}(x) = \dfrac{1}{3}x - 2$.

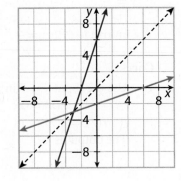

Ⓑ $f(x) = \frac{2}{3}x + 2$

$\boxed{y} = \frac{2}{3}x + 2$ Write y for $f(x)$.

$\boxed{x} = \frac{2}{3}\boxed{y} + 2$ Switch x and y.

$\boxed{y} = \dfrac{3}{\boxed{2}}\left(x - \boxed{2}\right)$ Solve for $\boxed{y}$.

$y = \dfrac{3}{\boxed{2}}x - \boxed{3}$ Simplify.

The inverse is $f^{-1}(x) = \dfrac{3}{\boxed{2}}x - \boxed{3}$.

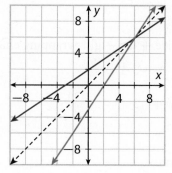

Your Turn

Write the inverse of the function. Then graph the function together with its inverse.

6. $f(x) = 2x - 4$

🔧 **Explain 4**   ## Using Inverse Functions to Solve Real-World Problems

Any time you need to work backward from a result to the original input, you can apply inverse functions.

Example 4   **Solve each problem by finding and evaluating the inverse function.**

Shopping Lloyd is trying to find the original price of a camera he bought as a gift, but he does not have the store receipt. From the bank transaction, he knows that including a $3 gift-wrap charge and 8% tax, the total was $103.14. What was the original price of the camera? Justify your answer.

🧩 **Analyze Information**

Identify the important information.

- Lloyd paid a total of $ $\boxed{103.14}$ for the camera.

- The total includes a gift-wrapping charge of $ $\boxed{3}$ and a sales tax of $\boxed{8}$ % of the original price.

🧩 **Formulate a Plan**

Build a function for the total cost t of the camera. Then determine the inverse of the function, and use it to find the original price p.

total cost = original price + tax + gift-wrapping charge

$$t = p + p \cdot \boxed{8} \% + \boxed{3}$$

$$t = p + \boxed{0.08}\, p + \boxed{3}$$

$$t = \boxed{1.08}\, p + \boxed{3}$$

Find the inverse function.

$$t = \boxed{1.08}\, p + \boxed{3}$$

$$t - \boxed{3} = \boxed{1.08}\, p$$

$$\frac{t - \boxed{3}}{\boxed{1.08}} = p$$

Use the inverse function to find the original price p for a total price of $\$ \boxed{103.14}$.

$$p = \frac{\boxed{103.14} - \boxed{3}}{\boxed{1.08}} \approx \boxed{92.72}$$

The original price of the camera was $\$ \boxed{92.72}$.

Justify and Evaluate

Use the original function to check your answer.

$$t = \boxed{1.08}\, p + \boxed{3}$$

$$t = \boxed{1.08} \cdot \left(\boxed{92.72} \right) + \boxed{3} \approx \boxed{103.14}$$

Since the inverse function does undo the original function, it is correct.

Reflect

7. What are the domain and range of the function for the total cost and its inverse in Example 4?

Your Turn

8. To make tea, use $\frac{1}{6}$ teaspoon of tea per ounce of water plus a teaspoon for the pot. Use the inverse to find the number of ounces of water needed if 7 teaspoons of tea are used. Check your answer.

Elaborate

9. Explain the result of interchanging x and y to find the inverse function of $f(x) = x$. How could you have predicted this from the graph of $f(x)$?

10. Give an example of a function whose inverse is a function. Give an example of a function whose inverse is not a function.

11. Describe what happens when you take the inverse of the inverse of a function. Is the result necessarily a function? Explain.

12. **Essential Question Check-In** Inverses are reflections of functions across which line?

Graph the relation and connect the points. Then graph the inverse. Identify the domain and range of each relation.

1.

x	1	2	3	4
y	1	2	4	8

2.

x	3	4	1	−1
y	−1	−2	−4	−4

3.

x	1	3	5	7
y	0	3	6	9

4.

x	−2	0	3	7
y	0	−1	−4	−9

Use inverse operations to find each inverse. Then check your solution.

5. $f(x) = 5x - 1$

6. $f(x) = \dfrac{x}{2} + 3$

7. $f(x) = 3 - \dfrac{1}{2}x$

8. $f(x) = \dfrac{1}{2}(3 - 3x)$

9. $f(x) = 4(x + 1)$

10. $f(x) = \dfrac{3x - 5}{2}$

Write the inverse of each function. Then graph the function together with its inverse.

11. $f(x) = 5 - 2x$

12. $f(x) = \dfrac{x}{4} + 2$

13. $f(x) = 10 + 0.6x$

14. $f(x) = 2 + 3x$

Solve each problem using an inverse function.

15. Meteorology The formula $C = \dfrac{5}{9}(F - 32)$ gives degrees Celsius as a function of degrees Fahrenheit. Find the inverse of this function to convert degrees Celsius to degrees Fahrenheit, and use it to find 16 °C in degrees Fahrenheit.

16. To make coffee using a home drip coffee maker, use $\dfrac{1}{4}$ tablespoon of coffee grounds per ounce of water plus 2 tablespoons for the coffee pot. Use the inverse to find the number of ounces of water needed if 11 tablespoons of coffee grounds are used.

17. Shopping A shopping attendant needs to price a large jigsaw puzzle returned by a customer. The customer paid a total of $33.14, including a convenience charge of $1.50 and 11% sales tax on the subtotal. Use the inverse to find the original price of the puzzle.

18. Education A student wants to figure out her raw score on a test she recently took. Including a 5-point bonus and a 2% increase after the bonus, the student scored a 94. Use the inverse to find the raw score. $\dfrac{94}{1.02}$

19. Currency At one point, the currency exchange rate between the U.S. dollar and the British pound sterling was 0.600 pound per dollar after a 3-dollar exchange fee. Use the inverse to determine how many U.S. dollars 100 British pounds would be worth.

20. Travel A taxi driver charges \$2 for service plus 65¢ per mile. Use the inverse to determine the number of miles driven if the total charge is \$11.75.

21. Identify whether you need to use an additive inverse, multiplicative inverse, or both to find the inverse of the given function.

　A. $f(x) = 3x$

　B. $f(x) = 3x + 4$

　C. $f(x) = \dfrac{x}{6}$

　D. $f(x) = 5x + 6$

　E. $f(x) = \dfrac{x + 6}{x + 2}$

22. Use a graphing calculator to graph the function $y = 3^x$ on a standard viewing window along with its inverse and the line $y = x$. Is the function's inverse a function? Explain your answer.

> **H.O.T. Focus on Higher Order Thinking**

23. Critical Thinking Find the inverse of $f(x) = \dfrac{x - 3}{x + 4}$. Then use a sample input and output to check your answer.

24. Explain the Error A student produced the following result when attempting to find the inverse of $f(x) = \dfrac{x}{6} + 5$. Explain the student's error and state the correct answer.

$$y = \frac{x}{6} + 5$$

$$x = \frac{y}{6} + 5$$

$$x - 5 = \frac{y}{6}$$

$$6x - 5 = y$$

Lesson Performance Task

The population p in thousands for the state of Oregon can be modeled by the linear function $p = 39.016t + 1039.614$, where t is the time in years since 1940.

　A. Find an equation for the inverse function, rounding the constants and coefficients to three decimal places. What is the meaning of the slope and y-intercept of the inverse function?

　B. Use the inverse function to estimate when the population of Oregon was 3,000,000.

　C. The population of Oregon was estimated as 3,930,065 in 2013. Use the model to predict when the population of Oregon will be 4,800,000. What would have to be assumed for your answer to be valid?

24.3 Graphing Square Root Functions

Essential Question: How can you use transformations of the parent square root function to graph functions of the form $f(x) = a\sqrt{x-h} + k$?

⊘ Explore 1 Exploring the Inverse of $y = x^2$

Use the steps that follow to explore the inverse of $y = x^2$.

(A) Use a graphing calculator to graph $y = x^2$ and $y = x$. Describe the graph.

(B) Use the DrawInv feature to graph the inverse of $y = x^2$ along with $y = x^2$ and $y = x$. Describe the new graph.

(C) State whether the inverse is a function. Explain your reasoning.

(D) Use inverse operations to write the inverse of $y = x^2$.

Switch x and y in the equation. $\qquad x = y^2$

Take the square root of both sides of the equation. $\boxed{\ ?\ } = y$

Reflect

1. **Discussion** Explain why the inverse of $y = x^2$ is not a function.

⊘ Explore 2 Graphing the Parent Square Root Function

The graph shows $y = \pm\sqrt{x}$, $y = x^2$, and $y = x$. You have discovered that $y = \pm\sqrt{x}$ is not a function. You will find out how to alter $y = \pm\sqrt{x}$ so that it becomes a function.

(A) For $y = \pm\sqrt{x}$ can x be negative? Explain your reasoning.

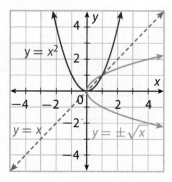

(B) If the domain of $y = x^2$ was restricted to $x \leq 0$, would the inverse be a function? Explain your reasoning.

(C) If the domain of $y = x^2$ was restricted to $x \geq 0$, would the inverse be a function? Explain your reasoning.

(D) Typically the domain of $y = x^2$ is restricted to $x \geq 0$ before findng its inverse to create the parent square root function. What is the equation of the parent square root function?

(E) A **radical function** is a function whose rule is a radical expression. A **square root function** is a radical function involving $\sqrt{x}$.

Graph the parent square root function $y = \sqrt{x}$ by first making a table of values.

x	$y = \sqrt{x}$	(x, y)
0	$\sqrt{0}$	$(0, 0)$
1	?	$(1, ?)$
4	?	$(4, ?)$
9	?	$(9, ?)$

(F) Plot the points and draw a smooth curve through them.

Reflect

2. What are the domain and range of the parent square root function?

✏️ Explain 1 Graphing Translations of the Parent Square Root Function

You discovered in Explore 2 that the parent square root function is $y = \sqrt{x}$. The equation $y = \sqrt{x - h} + k$ is the parent square root function with horizontal and vertical translations, where h and k are constants. The constant h will cause a horizontal shift and k will cause a vertical shift.

Example 1 Graph each function by using a table and plotting the points. State the direction of the shift from the parent square root function, and by how many units. Then state the domain and range. Confirm your graph by graphing with a graphing calculator.

(A) $y = \sqrt{x - 1} + 2$

x	$y = \sqrt{x-1} + 2$	(x, y)
1	$\sqrt{1-1} + 2$	$(1, 2)$
2	$\sqrt{2-1} + 2$	$(2, 3)$
5	$\sqrt{5-1} + 2$	$(5, 4)$
10	$\sqrt{10-1} + 2$	$(10, 5)$

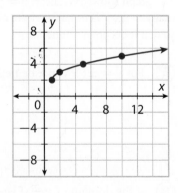

The graph is translated 2 units up and 1 unit right.

Domain: $x \geq 1$ Range: $y \geq 2$

Ⓑ $y = \sqrt{x + 3} - 2$

x	$y = \sqrt{x + 3} - 2$	(x, y)
-3	$\sqrt{-3 + 3} - 2$	$(-3, -2)$
-2	$\sqrt{-2 + 3} - 2$	$(-2, -1)$
1	$\sqrt{1 + 3} - 2$	$(1, 0)$
6	$\sqrt{6 + 3} - 2$	$(6, 1)$
13	$\sqrt{13 + 3} - 2$	$(13, 2)$

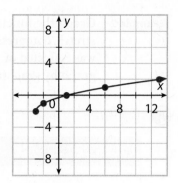

The graph is translated 2 unit(s) down and 3 unit(s) to the left.

Domain: $x \geq -3$ Range: $y \geq -2$

Your Turn

Graph each function by using a table and plotting the points. State the direction of the shift from the parent square root function, and by how many units. Then state the domain and range. Confirm your graph by graphing with a graphing calculator.

3. $y = \sqrt{x + 1}$

x	$y = \sqrt{x + 1}$	(x, y)
-1	?	?
0	?	?
3	?	?
8	?	?

4. $y = \sqrt{x} - 4$

x	$y = \sqrt{x} - 4$	(x, y)
0	?	?
1	?	?
4	?	?
9	?	?

🔑 **Explain 2** **Graphing Stretches/Compressions and Reflections of the Parent Square Root Function**

The equation $y = a\sqrt{x}$, where a is a constant, is the parent square root function with a vertical stretch or compression. If the absolute value of a is less than 1 the graph will be compressed by a factor of $|a|$, and if the absolute value of a is greater than 1 the graph will be stretched by a factor of $|a|$. If a is negative, the graph will be reflected across the x-axis.

Example 2   Graph the functions by using a table and plotting the points. State the stretch/compression factor and whether the graph of the parent function was reflected or not. Then state the domain and range. Confirm your graph by graphing with a graphing calculator.

(A) $y = -2\sqrt{x}$

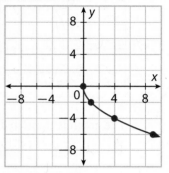

x	$y = -2\sqrt{x}$	(x, y)
0	$-2\sqrt{0}$	(0, 0)
1	$-2\sqrt{1}$	(1, −2)
4	$-2\sqrt{4}$	(4, −4)
9	$-2\sqrt{9}$	(9, −6)

There is a vertical stretch by a factor of 2, and the graph is reflected across the x-axis.

Domain: $x \geq 0$ Range: $y \leq 0$

(B) $y = \frac{1}{2}\sqrt{x}$

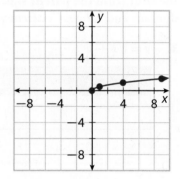

x	$y = \frac{1}{2}\sqrt{x}$	(x, y)
0	$\frac{1}{2}\sqrt{0}$	(0, 0)
1	$-\frac{1}{2}\sqrt{1}$	$\left(1, \frac{1}{2}\right)$
4	$-\frac{1}{2}\sqrt{4}$	(4, 1)
9	$-\frac{1}{2}\sqrt{9}$	$\left(9, \frac{3}{2}\right)$

There is a vertical compression by a factor of $\frac{1}{2}$,

and the graph is not reflected across the x–axis.

Domain: $x \geq 0$ Range: $y \geq 0$

Your Turn

Graph the functions by using a table and plotting the points. State the stretch/compression factor and whether the graph of the parent function was reflected or not. Then state the domain and range. Confirm your graph by graphing with a graphing calculator.

5. $y = 3\sqrt{x}$

6. $y = -\frac{1}{4}\sqrt{x}$

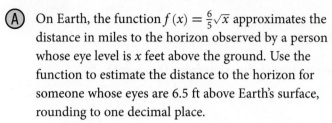

Explain 3 Modeling Real-World Situations with Square Root Functions

You can use transformations of square root functions to model real-world situations.

Example 3 Construct a square root function to solve each problem.

(A) On Earth, the function $f(x) = \frac{6}{5}\sqrt{x}$ approximates the distance in miles to the horizon observed by a person whose eye level is x feet above the ground. Use the function to estimate the distance to the horizon for someone whose eyes are 6.5 ft above Earth's surface, rounding to one decimal place.

$$f(x) = \frac{6}{5}\sqrt{x}$$

$f(6.5) = \frac{6}{5}\sqrt{6.5}$ 　　　Substitute 6.5 for x.

$f(6.5) \approx 3.1$ miles 　　　Simplify.

(B) Using the function from Example 3A, estimate the distance to the horizon for someone whose eyes are 5.8 ft above Earth's surface, rounding to one decimal place.

$$f(x) = \frac{6}{5}\sqrt{x}$$

$f(5.8) = \frac{6}{5}\sqrt{5.8}$ 　　　Substitute 5.8 for x.

$f(5.8) \approx 2.9$ miles 　　　Simplify.

Your Turn

7. On Earth, the function $f(x) = \frac{6}{5}\sqrt{x}$ approximates the distance in miles to the horizon observed by a person whose eye level is x feet above the ground. The graph of the corresponding function for Mars has a vertical stretch relative to $f(x)$ of $\frac{\sqrt{5}}{3}$. Write the corresponding function $g(x)$ for Mars and use it to estimate the distance to the horizon for an astronaut whose eyes are 6.2 ft above Mars's surface, rounding to one decimal place.

8. Using the function from the previous question, estimate the distance to the horizon for an astronaut whose eyes are 5.5 ft above Mars's surface, rounding to one decimal place.

💬 Elaborate

9. What can be said about the inverse of $y = x^2$ when the domain isn't restricted?

10. Are there any square root functions that do not have a restricted domain? Explain.

11. Essential Question Check-In What is the domain and range of the function $f(x) = \sqrt{x - h} + k$?

⭐ Evaluate: Homework and Practice

1. What is the inverse of $y = x^2$? Select the correct answer.

   A. $y = \sqrt{x}$ **B.** $y = \pm\sqrt{x}$ **C.** $y = -\sqrt{x}$ **D.** $y = x$

2. What is the parent square root function? What is its domain and range?

For Exercises 3–14, graph each function, describe any transformation from the parent function, and state the domain and range.

3. $y = \sqrt{x+1} - 4$

x	$y = \sqrt{x+1} - 4$	(x, y)
−1	$\sqrt{-1+1} - 4$	$(-1, -4)$
0	?	?
3	?	?
8	?	?

4. $y = \sqrt{x} + 6$

x	$y = \sqrt{x} + 6$	(x, y)
0	$\sqrt{0} + 6$	$(0, 6)$
1	?	?
4	?	?
9	?	?

5. $y = \sqrt{x+8}$

x	$y = \sqrt{x+8}$	(x, y)
−8	$\sqrt{-8+8}$	$(-8, 0)$
−7	?	?
−4	?	?
1	?	?
8	?	?

6. $y = \sqrt{x-4} + 3$

x	$y = \sqrt{x-4} + 3$	(x, y)
4	$\sqrt{4-4} + 3$	$(4, 3)$
5	?	?
8	?	?

7. $y = \sqrt{x+5} - 7$

x	$y = \sqrt{x+5} - 7$	(x, y)
−5	$\sqrt{-5+5} - 7$	$(-5, -7)$
−4	?	?
−1	?	?
4	?	?

8. $y = \sqrt{x+4} + 7$

x	$y = \sqrt{x+4} + 7$	(x, y)
−4	$\sqrt{-4+4} + 7$	$(-4, 7)$
−3	?	?
0	?	?
5	?	?

9. $y = -\sqrt{x}$

x	$y = -\sqrt{x}$	(x, y)
0	$-\sqrt{0}$	$(0, 0)$
1	?	?
4	?	?
9	?	?

10. $y = \frac{1}{10}\sqrt{x}$

x	$y = \frac{1}{10}\sqrt{x}$	(x, y)
0	$\frac{1}{10}\sqrt{0}$	$(0, 0)$
1	?	?
4	?	?
9	?	?

11. $y = -5\sqrt{x}$

x	$y = -5\sqrt{x}$	(x, y)
0	$-5\sqrt{0}$	$(0, 0)$
1	?	?
4	?	?
9	?	?

12. $y = \frac{1}{3}\sqrt{x}$

x	$y = \frac{1}{3}\sqrt{x}$	(x, y)
0	$\frac{1}{3}\sqrt{0}$	$(0, 0)$
1	?	?
4	?	?
9	?	?

13. $y = 6\sqrt{x}$

x	$y = 6\sqrt{x}$	(x, y)
0	$6\sqrt{0}$	$(0, 0)$
1	?	?
4	?	?
9	?	?
16	?	?

14. $y = -\frac{1}{2}\sqrt{x}$

x	$y = -\frac{1}{2}\sqrt{x}$	(x, y)
0	$-\frac{1}{2}\sqrt{0}$	$(0, 0)$
1	?	?
4	?	?
9	?	?

Construct a square root function to solve the problem.

15. The speed in miles per hour of a tsunami can be modeled by the function $s(d) = 3.86\sqrt{d}$, where d is the average depth in feet of the water over which the tsunami travels. Predict the speed of a tsunami over water with a depth of 1500 feet, rounding to the nearest tenth.

16. Pilots use the function $D(A) = 3.56\sqrt{A}$ to approximate the distance D in kilometers to the horizon from an altitude A in meters. What is the approximate distance to the horizon observed by a pilot flying at an altitude of 11,000 meters? (Round to the nearest tenth of a kilometer.)

17. A pharmaceutical company samples the raw materials it receives before they are used in the manufacture of drugs. For inactive ingredients, the company uses the function $s(x) = \sqrt{x} + 1$ to determine the number of samples s that should be taken from a shipment of x containers. How many samples should be taken from a shipment of 45 containers of an inactive ingredient? (Round to the nearest whole number.)

18. Graph the equation $y = 2\sqrt{x+2} + 2$. Then state the domain and range.

x	$y = 2\sqrt{x+2} + 2$	(x, y)
−2	$2\sqrt{-2+2} + 2$	(−2, 2)
−1	?	?
2	?	?
7	?	?

Write an equation for each graph. Explain your reasoning.

19.

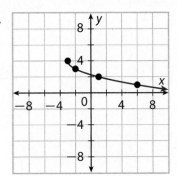

20.

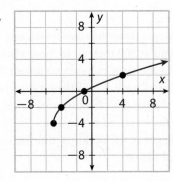

21. Explain the Error A student said the domain and range for the equation $y = \frac{1}{2}\sqrt{x + 10} - 7$ was $x \leq -10$ and $y \geq 7$. Is the student correct? If not, give the mistake and the correct answer.

22. Multi-Step The time t in seconds required for an object to fall from a certain height can be modeled by the function $t(h) = \frac{1}{4}\sqrt{h}$, where h is the initial height of the object in feet. How much longer will it take for a piece of an iceberg to fall into the ocean from a height of 240 ft than from a height of 100 ft? (Round to the nearest hundredth of a second.)

23. Analyze Relationships Describe how a horizontal translation and a vertical translation of the function $f(x) = \sqrt{x}$ each affect the function's domain and range.

24. Represent Real-World Problems Pilots use the function $D(A) = 3.56\sqrt{A}$ to approximate the distance D in kilometers to the horizon from an altitude A in meters on a clear day.

   a. A vertical compression of $D(A)$ by a factor of $\frac{1}{4}$ can be used to model the distance to the horizon on a partly cloudy day. Write the new function and approximate the distance to the horizon observed by a pilot flying at an altitude of 5000 m. (Round to the nearest whole kilometer.)

   b. How will the distance to the horizon on a partly cloudy day change if the pilot descends by 1500 m?

Lesson Performance Task

On a clear day, the ability to see a faraway unobstructed object on flat land is limited by the curvature of Earth. For an object with a height H in meters being observed by a person at height h in meters above the ground, the approximate distance d, in kilometers, at which the object falls below the horizon is given by the function $d(H) = 3.57\sqrt{H} + 3.57\sqrt{h}$.

   A. What is the effect of the observer's height h on the graph of $d(H)$?

   B. An observational tower has two levels, one at 100 meters and the second at 200 meters, so more visitors are able to visit the tower and the visitors have two different perspectives. Several tall buildings are in different directions and are all unobstructed from the observational tower. Plot two functions for the distance required to see a building over the horizon versus the height of the building, one for each level on the observational tower.

   C. Building A is 40 meters tall and 60 kilometers away, building B is 80 meters tall and 62 kilometers away, building C is 110 meters tall and is 68 kilometers away, and building D is 150 meters tall and is 80 kilometers away. Which buildings can be seen from both levels on a clear day? Which buildings can be seen from the top level on a clear day? Explain.

24.4 Graphing Cube Root Functions

Essential Question: How can you use transformations of the parent cube root function to graph functions of the form $f(x) = a\sqrt[3]{x - h} + k$?

Explore 1   Exploring the Inverse of $y = x^3$

The inverse of a function can be found both algebraically and graphically. Explore the graph of the inverse of $y = x^3$ first and then find the functional form.

(A)   Use your graphing calculator to plot the functions $y = x^3$ and $y = x$, with the standard window settings. The graph of ⬚ produces a diagonal line across the screen.

(B)   Use the DrawInv feature to draw the graph of the inverse of $y = x^3$ along with $y = x^3$ and $y = x$. The newly drawn inverse should look like a ⬚ of the graph of $y = x^3$ across the line, $y = x$.

(C)   The inverse graph drawn by the calculator passes the ⬚ line test, indicating that it is a function.

(D)   Cube roots are the inverse operation of cubing. Use inverse operations to write the inverse of $y = x^3$.

Switch x and y in the equation. $x = y^3$

Take the cube root of both sides of the equation.   ⬚ $= y$

Reflect

1.   **Discussion** When you take the cube root of a number or variable, do you have to consider both positive and negative cases? Explain why or why not.

Explore 2   Graphing the Parent Cube Root Function

The graph shows and $y = x^3$ and $y = \sqrt[3]{x}$.

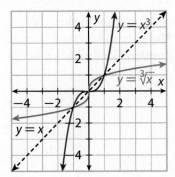

(A) What is the range of $y = x^3$?

$\boxed{?} < y < \boxed{?}$

(B) What values of y cannot result from evaluating the cubic function, $y = x^3$? $\boxed{?}$

(C) If any value of y can result from evaluating the cubic function, $y = x^3$, then $\boxed{?}$ value of x can be used to evaluate the function $y = \sqrt[3]{x}$.

(D) The domain of $y = \sqrt[3]{x}$ is $\boxed{?} < x < \boxed{?}$.

(E) Is there any need to restrict the domain of $y = \sqrt[3]{x}$? $\boxed{?}$

(F) A **cube root function** is a function whose rule is a cube root expression. $y = \sqrt[3]{x}$ is the parent cube root function. Plot the function for yourself by completing the table of values, and plotting the points.

x	$y = \sqrt[3]{x}$
-8	-2
-1	$\boxed{?}$
0	$\boxed{?}$
1	$\boxed{?}$
8	$\boxed{?}$

Reflect

2. Why is it that x can be a negative number in the cube root function, but not the square root function?

⚙ Explain 1 Graphing Translations of the Parent Cube Root Function

Functions of the form $y = \sqrt[3]{x - h} + k$ are translations of the cube root parent function $y = \sqrt[3]{x}$. For example, the graph of $y = \sqrt[3]{x - h} + k$ looks like the graph of $y = \sqrt[3]{x}$ shifted to the right by h units and up by k units. Negative values of h result in a shift to the left, and negative values of k result in a downward shift.

Example 1 Use a table of values to add the graph of the transformed function to the parent function provided. Describe how the graph of the parent function was shifted. State the domain and range. Check your graphs on a graphing calculator.

(A) $y = \sqrt[3]{x - 3} - 4$

x	y
−5	−6
2	−5
3	−4
4	−3
11	−2

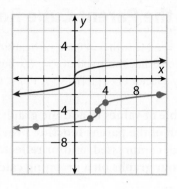

The graph was shifted right by 3 units and down by 4 units.

Domain: $-\infty < x < \infty$

Range: $-\infty < y < \infty$

(B) $y = \sqrt[3]{x + 2} + 8$

x	y
−10	6
−3	7
−2	8
−1	9
6	10

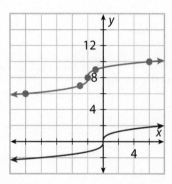

The graph was shifted left by 2 units and up by 8 units.

Domain: $\boxed{-\infty} < x < \boxed{\infty}$

Range: $\boxed{-\infty} < y < \boxed{\infty}$

Your Turn

Graph the function and compare it to the graph of the parent cube root function. State the shift in direction and by how many units. Then state the domain and range.

3. $y = \sqrt[3]{x + 3} - 6$

Graphing Stretches/Compressions and Reflections of the Parent Cube Root Function

Functions of the form $y = a\sqrt[3]{x}$ with $a \neq 0$ are vertical stretches and compressions of the cube root parent function. The graph of $y = a\sqrt[3]{x}$ looks like the graph of $y = \sqrt[3]{x}$ but will be stretched vertically by a factor of $|a|$ if $|a| > 1$ or compressed vertically by a factor of $|a|$ if $|a| < 1$. If $a < 0$, the graph will also be reflected across the x-axis.

Example 2 Use a table of values to add the graph of the transformed function to the graph of the parent function provided. Describe how the graph was stretched, compressed, and/or reflected. State the domain and range. Check your graphs on a graphing calculator.

Ⓐ $y = \frac{1}{2}\sqrt[3]{x}$

x	y
−1	−0.5
0	0
1	0.5

The graph was compressed by a factor of $\frac{1}{2}$ and is not reflected across the x-axis.

Domain: $-\infty < x < \infty$

Range: $-\infty < y < \infty$

Ⓑ $y = -4\sqrt[3]{x}$

x	y
−8	8
−1	4
0	0
1	−4
8	−8

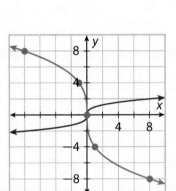

The graph was stretched by a factor of 4 and reflected across the x-axis.

Domain: $\boxed{-\infty} < x < \boxed{\infty}$

Range: $\boxed{-\infty} < y < \boxed{\infty}$

Graph the function and compare it to the parent cube root function. State the stretch/compression factor and whether the graph was reflected or not. Then state the domain and range.

4. $y = 2\sqrt[3]{x}$

💬 Elaborate

5. Does the domain of $y = x^3$ need to be restricted in order for its inverse to be a function? Explain why or why not.

6. How do the transformation parameters a, h, and k affect the domain and range of $y = a\sqrt[3]{x - h} + k$?

7. **Essential Question Check-In** Describe how the parameters a, h, and k affect the graph of $y = a\sqrt[3]{x - h} + k$ as they are changed.

1. Use inverse operations to find the inverse of $y = 8x^3$.

2. Graph $y = \sqrt[3]{x}$ together with $y = \sqrt{x}$ from 0 to 10. For what positive values of x is the cube root of x greater than the square root of x? For what positive values of x is the square root of x greater than the cube root of x?

Graph each function on the same coordinate plane as the parent cube root function.

3. $y = \sqrt[3]{x - 4}$

4. $y = \sqrt[3]{x} - 5$

5. $y = \sqrt[3]{x - 2} - 2$

6. $y = \sqrt[3]{x + 3} + 7$

7. $y = -2\sqrt[3]{x}$

8. $y = \frac{1}{4}\sqrt[3]{x}$

9. $y = 5\sqrt[3]{x}$

10. $y = -\frac{1}{2}\sqrt[3]{x}$

Describe the transformation or transformations of each function from the parent cube root function, $y = \sqrt[3]{x}$.

11. $y = \sqrt[3]{x-1} + 5$

12. $y = \sqrt[3]{x+5} + 7$

13. $y = \sqrt[3]{x-3} - 3$

14. $y = \sqrt[3]{x+7} - 2\frac{1}{2}$

15. $y = 3\sqrt[3]{x}$

16. $y = -\frac{3}{2}\sqrt[3]{x}$

17. $y = -\frac{1}{5}\sqrt[3]{x}$

18. $y = \frac{1}{10}\sqrt[3]{x}$

19. A cylindrical water holding tank with a height equal to its diameter has a height of $h = \sqrt[3]{\frac{4}{\pi}}\sqrt[3]{V}$, where V is the volume of the tank. Graph the height function.

20. **Geometry** The Louvre Palace in Paris has a large glass pyramid in the main court. For a square pyramid with height equal to length, the height is related to the volume by $h = \sqrt[3]{3}\sqrt[3]{V}$. Graph the height of a pyramid as a function of volume.

21. **Geometry** The diameter of a ball as a function of its volume is given by $d = 2\sqrt[3]{\frac{3}{4\pi}}\sqrt[3]{V} \approx 1.24\sqrt[3]{V}$.

Describe the transformations of a graph of the diameter of a sphere compared to the parent cube root function, $d = \sqrt[3]{V}$, and graph the function.

22. The function $y = \frac{1}{3}\sqrt[3]{x+2} - 5$ has been transformed from the parent function, $y = \sqrt[3]{x}$, by which of the following transformations? Select all that apply.

A. vertical stretch by $\frac{1}{3}$

B. vertical compression by $\frac{1}{3}$

C. reflection across the y-axis

D. reflection across the x-axis

E. shifted up by 5

F. shifted down by 5

G. shifted right by 2

H. shifted left by 2

23. **Critical Thinking** If the graph of $y = \frac{1}{2}\sqrt[3]{x}$ is shifted left 2 units, what is the equation of the translated graph?

24. **Communicate Mathematical Ideas** Mitchio says that cube root functions of the form $y = a\sqrt[3]{x}$ should be considered to have a limited domain, because a cannot equal 0. Explain why you do or do not agree with Mitchio.

25. **Multi-step** The length of a cube as a function of total volume is given by $\ell = \sqrt[3]{V_t}$.

   a. Write the function for the length of a cubic box needed to hold a cube-shaped glass vase that has a volume of 125 cubic inches and the packing material that surrounds the vase, which has a volume of V_p.

   b. What are the domain and range of this function?

   c. Graph the function.

Lesson Performance Task

A manufacturer wants to make a ball bearing that is made of a mixture of zinc, iron, and copper and has come down to a choice of two alloys. Alloy A has a density of 7.5 grams per cubic centimeter and alloy B has a density of 8.5 grams per cubic centimeter.

A. Use the formula for the volume of a sphere, $V = \frac{4}{3}\pi r^3$, and the formula for density, $D = \frac{m}{V}$, to write an equation for m as a function of r for each alloy.

B. Find the inverse of each function. Write the function in the form $r = a\sqrt{m}$, where a is rounded to three decimal places.

C. How does the graph of each inverse function compare to the parent cube root function? For a given mass, which alloy would have a greater radius?

D. The manufacturer wants the ball bearings to have a mass of 12 grams and to have a radius as close to 0.7 centimeter as possible. Which alloy would be closer to the manufacturer's desired specifications? Explain.

Functions and Inverses

Essential Question: How can you use functions and inverses to solve real-world problems?

Key Vocabulary

cube root function
(función de raíz cubo)
inverse function
(inverso de una function)
radical function
(radical de una function)
square root function
(función de raíz cuadrada)

KEY EXAMPLE *(Lessons 24.1, 24.2, 24.3)*

Graph $f(x) = x^2 + 1$ **and its inverse.**

$$y = x^2 + 1$$
$$x = y^2 + 1$$

To find the inverse of $f(x)$, or $f^{-1}(x)$, switch x and y, and solve for y.

$$x - 1 = y^2$$
$$\pm\sqrt{x - 1} = y$$

For the inverse to be a function, restrict it to nonnegative numbers, $f^{-1}(x) = \sqrt{x - 1}$.

Fill in a table of values for $f(x)$ and $f^{-1}(x)$.

x	$f(x)$	$f^{-1}(x)$
-2	$(-2)^2 + 1 = 5$	not a real number
-1	$(-1)^2 + 1 = 2$	not a real number
0	$(0)^2 + 1 = 1$	not a real number
1	$(1)^2 + 1 = 2$	$\sqrt{1 - 1} = 0$
2	$(2)^2 + 1 = 5$	$\sqrt{2 - 1} = 1$
3	$(3)^2 + 1 = 10$	$\sqrt{3 - 1} \approx 1.41$
4	$(4)^2 + 1 = 17$	$\sqrt{4 - 1} \approx 1.73$

Graph the ordered pairs.

$f^{-1}(x)$ is a reflection of $f(x)$ over $y = x$ for nonnegative values of x.

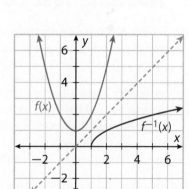

The domain of $f(x)$ is all real numbers, and the range of $f(x)$ is $y \geq 1$.

The domain of $f^{-1}(x)$ is $x \geq 1$, and the range of $f^{-1}(x)$ is $y \geq 0$.

EXERCISES

1. Graph $f(x) = \frac{1}{2}(x + 2)^3$. (*Lesson 24.1*)

Write the inverse of each function. (*Lesson 24.2*)

2. $g(x) = 4x^2 + 7$

3. $t(x) = (x + 15)^3 - 4$

4. Graph $h(x) = \sqrt[3]{x} - 2$. Find the domain and range of $h(x)$. (*Lesson 24.4*)

MODULE PERFORMANCE TASK

The Smallest Cube

Foolish Sports makes sporting equipment for people who play unusual sports like lawnmower racing, pie eating, and cheese rolling. For some reason, companies that make footballs, roller skates, and hockey sticks make a lot more money.

So, Foolish is going into the ordinary-sports business. Its first project is to make and sell baseballs, basketballs, and golf balls. The company's package designer found the typical volumes of the three products and now must determine the dimensions of the boxes they will be sold in. Each box must be cubical and must be the smallest box that can contain the ball.

Basketball	448 in^3
Baseball	14.1 in^3
Golf ball	2.48 in^3

What are the dimensions of the three boxes? Explain how you found the dimensions.

Start by listing the information you will need to solve the problem. Then complete the task. Use numbers, words, or algebra to explain how you reached your conclusion.

© Houghton Mifflin Harcourt Publishing Company

Ready to Go On?

24.1–24.4 Functions and Inverses

- Online Homework
- Hints and Help
- Extra Practice

Graph each function. *(Lesson 24.1)*

1. Graph $g(x) = \frac{1}{4}(x + 1)^3 - 4$.

2. Find and graph the inverse of $f(x) = 2x^2 - 4$.
(Lessons 24.2, 24.3)

3. Graph $h(x) = 2\sqrt[3]{x + 6} + 2$. *(Lesson 24.4)*

ESSENTIAL QUESTION

4. How could you sketch the inverse of an exponential function?

Assessment Readiness

1. Find the solutions of $-2x(x+1)(3x+5) = 0$. Is the given value of x a solution?

   A. $x = -\dfrac{5}{3}$

   B. $x = 0$

   C. $x = 1$

2. Find the inverse of $f(x) = \dfrac{1}{3}x - 2$.

   Use the inverse to determine if each of the following equations is True or False.

   A. $f^{-1}(-2) = 0$

   B. $f^{-1}(0) = 2$

   C. $f^{-1}(3) = 15$

3. Factor $8x^2 - 50$ completely. Is the following expression a factor of this expression?

   A. $(x - 10)$

   B. $(2x + 5)$

   C. 2

4. Graph $f(x) = \dfrac{1}{2}x^3 + 2$. Describe the end behavior of the graph.

1. Consider the system $\begin{cases} y \le \frac{1}{2}x + 3 \\ y \ge 2x \end{cases}$. Is each of the following a solution of the system?

   A. $(-2, -5)$

   B. $(2, 4)$

   C. $(3, -1)$

2. Is −4 a solution of the equation?

   A. $x^2 + 4x + 16 = 0$

   B. $2x^2 - 8x + 32 = 0$

   C. $5x^2 - 80 = 0$

3. Find the inverse of $f(x) = x^2 - 2$. Determine if each statement is True or False.

   A. $f^{-1}(x)$ is a square root function.

   B. The domain of is $f^{-1}(x)$ is $x \ge -2$.

   C. The range of $f^{-1}(x)$ is all real numbers.

4. Does the given statement describe a step in the transformation of the graph of $f(x) = \sqrt[3]{x}$ that would result in the graph of $g(x) = -4\sqrt[3]{x - 1}$?

   A. The graph is reflected across the *x*-axis.

   B. The graph is translated 1 unit down.

   C. The graph is compressed.

5. The graph of $f(x) = \frac{1}{3}x + 1$ is shown. Find and graph the inverse of $f(x)$.

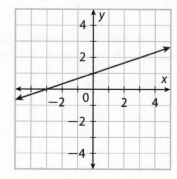

6. The equation that is represented on the graph is a transformation of one of the following parent functions: $y = x^2$, $y = x^3$, $y = \sqrt{x}$, $y = \sqrt[3]{x}$. Write an equation to represent the graph. Explain how you determined which parent function to use.

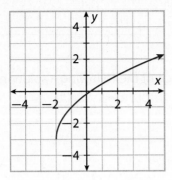

7. Graph $f(x) = (x + 2)^3$. Use the graph to solve $-8 = (x + 2)^3$.

Performance Tasks

★ **8.** The relationship between the radius r, in centimeters, of a solid gold sphere and its mass m, in grams, is given by $r = 0.23 \sqrt[3]{m}$. Graph this relationship for the interval $0 \leq m \leq 10$.

★★ **9.** A grain silo is in the shape of a cylinder with a hemisphere dome on top. The volume of the silo is given by $V = \frac{2}{3}\pi r^3 + \pi r^2 h$. A farmer decides to build a grain silo with a height of 15 feet, and radius between 3 feet and 6 feet.

    A. Write the function $V(r)$ for $h = 15$ ft. Use 3.14 for π. Round all values to two decimal places.

    B. Graph your function from part **A** for the given domain.

    C. What are the minimum and maximum volumes of the silo, to the nearest cubic foot?

★★★**10.** The distance, d, in meters, an object falls after time t, in seconds, is given by $d = 4.9t^2$. Assume that the domain of the function is $t \geq 0$.

    A. Find the inverse of this function.

    B. How much time does it take for a stone dropped from the edge of a cliff to hit the ground 80 meters below? Round your answer to the nearest tenth of a second.

    C. The relationship between the temperature in degrees Fahrenheit and kelvins is given by $F = \frac{9}{5}(K - 273) + 32$. Find the inverse of this function.

    D. If the speed of sound in air is given by $s = 20.1\sqrt{K}$, where s is in meters per second and K is the temperature in kelvins, how long after dropping the stone can the sound of the stone striking the ground be heard at the edge of the cliff, if the temperature is 77°F? Explain how you got your answer.

Ichthyologist A pike is a type of freshwater fish. An ichthyologist uses the function $W(L) = \dfrac{L^3}{3500}$ to find the approximate weight W in pounds of a pike with length L inches.

a. Write the inverse function $L(W)$.

b. Graph the inverse function.

c. What is the significance in the context of the problem of the point at approximately $(6, 28)$ on the graph of $L(W)$?

d. What are the reasonable domain and range of the function $L(W)$?

Focus on Careers

The following Focus on Career pages can be used after you have completed each unit in the book. Each feature shows how mathematics is used in some career.

Quantities and Modeling

Mathematics and Seismology

While earthquakes are neither predictable nor preventable, the area where the earthquake occurred and how strong it was can be determined immediately following the event. This allows emergency management officials to allocate resources and direct emergency aid much more effectively, thereby saving lives and money.

Seismologists in the United States collect data about earthquakes from seismology stations located around the world. The stations are equipped with seismographs, machines that measure the movement of the ground.

Earthquakes originate below the Earth's surface. During an earthquake, the ground moves in circular waves that spread out from its *epicenter*, which is the point on Earth's surface closest to the source of the earthquake. Two types of waves produced by earthquakes are pressure waves (called P waves) and shear waves (called S waves). P waves move the ground back and forth as they travel away from the epicenter, while S waves move the ground sideways as they travel away from the epicenter. The figure below demonstrates the signal that might be recorded by a seismograph. Note that P waves and S waves display different patterns on the seismograph, and that P waves appear first because they travel faster than S waves.

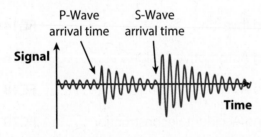

To calculate how far a seismology station is from an earthquake's epicenter, seismologists find the difference between the arrival times of the P waves and S waves. The equation

$$\frac{d}{s} - \frac{d}{p} = t$$

is then used to determine the distance to the epicenter. In the equation, d is the distance in kilometers from the station to the epicenter, p and s are the speeds (in km/s) of the P and S waves, respectively, and t is the time lapse, in seconds, between the S and P waves.

Seismologists need data from at least three seismographs at three different locations in order to locate the epicenter of an earthquake.

• • • • Readings for the Northridge Earthquake • • • • January 17, 1994			
	Average S wave speed (km/s)	Average P wave speed (km/s)	Difference in arrival time (seconds)
Topopah Spring, Nevada	3.3	6.0	49
San Andreas Observatory, California	3.75	7.5	51
Albuquerque, New Mexico	3.5	7.7	169

1. Solve the equation $\dfrac{d}{3.3} - \dfrac{d}{6} = 49$ to estimate the distance d in kilometers from the epicenter of the earthquake to Topopah Spring. Round your answer to the nearest 10 kilometers. (*Hint*: To eliminate the decimal and the fractions, multiply both sides by 66.)

2. Estimate the distance from the epicenter to the San Andreas Observatory. Round your answer to the nearest 10 kilometers. (*Hint*: Use an equation like the equation in Exercise 1. Multiply both sides by 75.)

3. Estimate the distance from the epicenter to Albuquerque. Round your answer to the nearest 100 kilometers. (*Hint*: Use an equation like the equation in Exercise 1. Multiply both sides by 385.)

4. How might a seismologist use the results of Exercises 1–3 and a map of the southwestern United States to locate the epicenter of the earthquake?

5. A seismology station located 500 miles from the epicenter of an earthquake records a difference in arrival times of the S and P waves of 74 seconds. Suppose the average speed of the P waves is exactly twice the average speed of the S waves. What is the average speed of each wave type? Round your answers to the nearest tenth. (*Hint*: Use an equation like the equation in Exercise 1 with $p = 2s$. Multiply both sides by $2s$ to eliminate the denominators.)

Understanding Functions

Mathematics and Bicycle Design

The world of cycling is vast, with over 450 million cyclists in China alone. In the United States, there are 66.5 million cyclists served by a retail market worth an estimated $6.2 billion in 2015.

A bicycle designer's job is to ensure that all of the parts of a bicycle work well together. The main parts of a bicycle are the frame, wheels, seat, handlebars, crankset (where the pedals are mounted), cassettes (the rear gear sprockets), chain, and brake system. A bike designer makes decisions about each part of the bike depending on the desired functionality. For example, when designing a road bike, the designer wants to minimize the weight of the bicycle without affecting its performance.

The largest part of the bike is the frame. The frame consists of several tubes of varying sizes and lengths. The bike designer knows that reducing the weight of the frame will reduce the force needed to accelerate the bike. However, the concern about weight must be balanced against safety, durability of the bike, and the comfort of the rider.

Aerodynamics is another consideration for bike designers. Aerodynamics is concerned with the force of air resistance on a bike rider. This is especially important to cyclists involved in competitive racing. Air resistance can be calculated using the formula

$$\text{air resistance} = 0.00256 \times C_D \times \text{frontal area} \times (\text{relative speed})^2,$$

where C_D is the drag coefficient of the bike, the frontal area is the head-on cross-sectional area of the rider and bike, and the relative speed is the speed of the bike relative to that of still air. To lower a bike's air resistance, a designer can work to reduce both the bike's drag coefficient and the frontal cross-section of the bike.

The gear ratio, or range of gear ratios on a multi-gear bike, is also important in bicycle design. The gear ratio determines how far the bike moves forward for each full turn of the pedals. This forward movement is the product of the gear ratio and the wheel circumference. From this, the speed of the bike can be determined for a given pedaling rate in revolutions per minute (rpm). The following table provides data for a possible "lowest" and "highest" gear ratio on a multi-gear bike.

Number of teeth on front chain wheel	Number of teeth on rear gear	Gear ratio	Forward movement per pedal stroke for 26 in. wheel diameter	Speed at 60 rpm
22	30	22:30 or 0.73	60 in.	3.4 mi/h
44	11	44:11 or 4	326 in.	18.5 mi/h

Exercises

Suppose a bike designer has developed a new road bike frame design. There are 8 tubes of varying sizes and lengths needed to build each frame.

1. **a.** The total number of tubes needed to construct any number of frames is a function of the number of frames needed. Write a function that can be used to calculate the total number of tubes, *y*, needed to construct *x* frames. Determine if the function is continuous or discrete.

b. Use the function from part (a) to determine the total number of tubes required to make 5 frames, 10 frames, and 30 frames.

Use the information about air resistance for various bicycling positions shown in the table below to answer the following questions.

Riding Position	Drag Coefficient C_D	Frontal Area (in ft²)
Upright	1.1	5.5
Racing crouch	0.83	3.9
Closely following another bicycle	0.5	3.9

2. **a.** Write an equation that gives the air resistance *R* on a bicyclist traveling at speed *s* in each situation shown (assuming still air).

b. What is the speed (in miles per hour) of a crouched, racing bicyclist who experiences 4 pounds of air resistance? Round to the nearest tenth.

Use the information regarding gear ratios presented on the previous page to answer the following questions.

3. **a.** A rider has selected a gear that utilizes a 44-tooth front chain wheel and a 15-tooth rear gear. Calculate the gear ratio, rounded to the nearest hundredth.

b. Calculate the forward movement per pedal stroke for a bike with 26-inch wheels for the gear ratio found in part (a). Round to the nearest inch.

c. Calculate the speed of the bike, in miles per hour, at a pedaling rate of 60 rpm for the gear ratio in part (a). Round to the nearest tenth.

4. A certain single-speed, off-road bike with 24-inch diameter wheels has a 25:11 gear ratio. Calculate the forward movement per pedal stroke, rounded to the nearest inch. Then use this value to calculate the speed of the bike, to the nearest tenth of a mile per hour, at a pedaling rate of 40 rpm.

Linear Functions, Equations, and Inequalities

Mathematics and Space Exploration

The International Space Station (ISS) is a large spacecraft that orbits the Earth. Built and used by many countries, it provides living quarters and several science labs for use by a crew of six astronauts at a time. The first piece of the station was launched in 1998, with its construction continuing through 2011. The first crew arrived in November of 2000.

Crewmembers typically spend 6 months at a time on the ISS and include scientists from multiple disciplines who perform research that cannot be done on Earth. For example, one of the lab facilities grows crystals of various proteins. The microgravity environment of the space station results in crystals that are more uniform than those grown on Earth. Once grown, the crystals are sent down to Earth where the arrangement of the protein molecules in the crystal lattice is used to create a better three-dimensional map of the protein. The long-range goal of these experiments is to find a relationship between protein structure and function that can be used to design medications instead of the trial-and-error process used now.

The crew travels to and from the ISS in a spacecraft propelled by a three-stage rocket. The first stage, or section, consists of four identical liquid-booster rockets strapped around the second stage, which is also called the core engine. The third stage is another rocket between the second stage and the spacecraft containing the crew. At liftoff, the rockets in the first and second stages ignite and begin to push the rocket into orbit. About two minutes into the flight, the four booster rockets have exhausted their fuel and are jettisoned to reduce the weight of the spacecraft. The core section continues to fire until it too separates after about 288 seconds. Now, the third stage ignites and propels the spacecraft into orbit before it is jettisoned approximately 9 minutes after liftoff. It generally takes five engine burns over 6 hours for the spacecraft to catch up with the ISS. The following table gives the time and velocity of the rocket until it reaches orbit.

Time after launch (s)	0	118	158	288	528
Velocity (ft/s)	0	5118	6234	12,497	24,580

While some people think there is no gravity outside Earth's atmosphere, the ISS is affected by Earth's gravity. So why do astronauts appear weightless and float around the space station? The answer has to do with the rate at which the ISS travels. To maintain its orbit approximately 250 miles above the Earth's surface, the station travels at about 17,150 miles per hour. Even when traveling at this great speed, the ISS and everything aboard are falling back to Earth. However, the spacecraft is moving fast enough that the path of its fall matches the curvature of the Earth. Because the astronauts are in a constant state of falling, they feel weightless.

© Houghton Mifflin Harcourt Publishing Company • Image Credits: ©NASA

The orbital speed of the International Space Station (ISS) is approximately 17,150 miles per hour.

 a. Approximately how fast is this in feet per second?

b. Which units give you the best idea of the speed of the ISS?

Acceleration is the rate of change in velocity over time. The table on the preceding page shows how the velocity of the rocket that transports astronauts to the ISS changed during its first 9 minutes after takeoff. Velocity is measured in feet per second, so acceleration is measured in feet per second per second. (The units for acceleration are written as ft/s².)

 a. Graph the ordered pairs (time, velocity) from the table, with time shown on the horizontal axis and velocity on the vertical axis. Describe the graph.

b. Find the acceleration between each pair of adjacent points. Round each acceleration to the nearest one.

c. When does the rocket accelerate the most? When does it accelerate the least?

d. The rocket becomes lighter as it rises and the stages separate. Does this seem to affect the rocket's velocity and acceleration over time?

The diameter of Earth is 7918 miles, and the orbital altitude of the ISS is approximately 248 miles above Earth. The ISS is traveling at a rate of roughly 17,150 miles per hour.

 a. Find the distance traveled by the ISS during one orbit around Earth. Round your answer to the nearest mile. Explain how you got your answer.

b. Estimate the number of orbits that the ISS makes in one week.

The force of gravity affects how much you weigh. Astronauts use the letter g to stand for the pull of the Earth's gravity on an object at sea level. Accelerating away from Earth increases the "g-force," making you weigh more than you would ordinarily.

 a. During a launch of the rocket used for transportation to the ISS, the astronauts experience a maximum force of up to 3.5 g's. This makes them weigh 3.5 times their normal weight. Use a graph to show that the maximum weight varies directly with normal weight. What is the slope of the line?

b. The weight of an object on another planet varies directly with its weight on Earth. If the weight of a 100-lb object is 38 lb on Mars, write an equation to calculate the weight on Mars, y, of an object weighing w lb on Earth.

Statistical Models

Mathematics and Urban Planning

Cities have urban planning departments whose purpose is to regulate the types of new development that can occur within the city limits. When developing an urban plan, the considerations are extensive: the environment, housing, public facilities, transportation, public safety, and so on. For a growing city where the city limits are expanding, the planning also includes future land use. Urban planners use statistical models to interpret the current and future status of the city's resources and facilities. With large amounts of data available, mathematics provides a means for making sense of all the data.

Parkland falls under the category of public facilities. In a city, one result of a citywide survey showed the public's desire for more parks. The mayor has asked the city's urban planning department to report on the current parks situation. The city has a development plan that divides the city into nine geographical regions. The tables below show the population of each region, in thousands, and the number of acres of parkland there.

Region	Northwest	North Central	Northeast	West Central	Central
Population (1000's)	28.2	20.8	24.1	27.2	22.7
Acres of parkland	5.8	6.9	5.1	2.4	4.9

Region	East Central	Southwest	South Central	Southeast
Population (1000's)	19.4	25.5	22.2	23.7
Acres of parkland	6.0	2.6	6.8	2.8

The planning department is also currently examining the number of residents in each of the nine regions living in rental properties. The mayor wants to ensure that the city's development plan is providing adequate opportunity for its residents to rent housing in each of the nine regions. The tables below show the number of people in each region, in thousands, who live in a rental property.

Region	Northwest	North Central	Northeast	West Central	Central
Renters (1000's)	3.6	5.4	4.6	6.8	7.9

Region	East Central	Southwest	South Central	Southeast
Renters (1000's)	5.5	4.6	4.9	3.3

Use the data in the tables on the preceding page showing the population and amount of parkland in each of the city's nine regions to answer the following questions.

1. **a.** Calculate the ratio of acres of parkland to population (in 1000's) for each of the nine regions using the data in the table. Round to the nearest hundredth.

  b. Use a graphing calculator to find the mean and standard deviation of the nine ratios that were found in part (a). Round to the nearest hundredth.

  c. Identify the regions with ratios that are at least 0.5 standard deviation below the mean.

  d. Using a graphing calculator, plot the data points (population, acres) and graph the line $y = \mu x$ on the same screen. Observe that three points are significantly below the graphed line. To which regions do these points correspond?

2. **a.** Use a graphing calculator to perform a linear regression for the data points (population, acres). Give the equation of the regression line, rounding values to the hundredths place. In the equation, what do x and y each represent?

  b. Plot the data points and graph the regression line on the same screen. You should observe that three data points fall significantly below the line, suggesting that there are three regions where the amount of parkland is significantly below the linear model for all regions. Are these the same three regions identified in part (d) of Exercise 1?

3. **a.** Suppose you work in the planning department and that the mayor's office has asked you to recommend one region in the city where additional parkland should be acquired. Which region would you recommend? Justify your choice.

Use the data in the tables on the preceding page showing the total population and the number of renters in each of the city's nine regions to answer the following questions.

4. **a.** Calculate the ratio of renting population to total population for each of the nine regions, and then find the mean and standard deviation of the ratios. Round each value to the nearest hundredth. What do these ratios represent?

  b. Use a graphing calculator to perform a linear regression for the data points (total population, renting population) from the tables. Give the equation of the regression line, rounding values to the nearest hundredth.

5. **a.** Suppose the city expands to the east in a similar fashion, with 20,000 people in the new region. Estimate the number of renters in this region, to the nearest hundred, using both the equation $y = \mu x$ and the equation of the regression line found in Exercise 4. Do the estimates agree? If not, which is more credible, and why?

Linear Systems and Piecewise-Defined Functions

Mathematics and Sports Nutrition

Just about everyone knows that being a top athlete takes talent and hard work. But fewer people appreciate the importance of diet in helping athletes perform at their best. For example, high school athletes may not realize how skipping both breakfast and lunch can be detrimental to their performance. When they show up for after-school practice, their body does not have the caloric fuel it needs to operate at its best. A quick energy fix cannot make up for a poor breakfast and lunch, or worse, no breakfast or lunch at all.

As a sports nutritionist will tell you, food is really just fuel, similar to the gasoline you put in your car. Food provides energy from three sources. Proteins build muscles but get used for energy in emergency situations, carbohydrates fuel muscles, and fats contain energy reserves. Of the three, carbohydrates are the most critical for athletes because they provide the body with *glycogen*, a form of sugar that is stored within muscle tissue as a source of energy. Foods such as pasta, rice, potatoes, and bread are high in carbohydrates. Meats and fish, eggs and dairy, and beans, nuts, and seeds are high in protein. Many of these high-protein foods are also high in fat.

A sports nutritionist can help determine the number of calories that a particular athlete should consume. This number depends on many factors including age, height, and activity level. The graph shown below can help an athlete figure out how many calories from carbohydrates to include in a daily diet. Once the athlete's daily calorie needs are known, the number of calories from carbohydrates should be within the shaded region of the graph. The graph itself represents a system of inequalities.

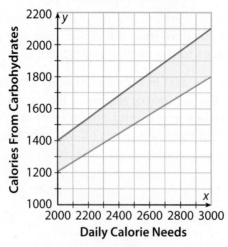

Nutrition for Athletes

One cup of a wheat and barley cereal contains 92 grams (g) of carbohydrates, $\frac{1}{2}$ cup of oatmeal contains 27 g of carbohydrates, $\frac{1}{4}$ cup of raisins contains 25 g of carbohydrates, and one cup of milk contains 10 g of carbohydrates.

1. **a.** How many grams of carbohydrates are in c cups of a wheat and barley cereal?

   b. How many cups of oatmeal x and how many cups of raisins y do you need to eat to get 100 g of carbohydrates? Write an equation and list three possible solutions.

A sports nutrition guidebook advises athletes to choose low-fat sources of calcium. Teenagers need at least 1300 milligrams (mg) of calcium daily to help build strong bones.

2. **a.** One cup of low-fat milk supplies 300 mg of calcium. One cup of vanilla ice cream provides 180 mg of calcium. Write an inequality stating that x cups of milk and y cups of ice cream together supply more than 1300 mg of calcium.

   b. Graph the inequality you wrote in part (a) and list two different solutions.

3. **a.** One cup of low-fat milk contains 5 g of fat. One cup of vanilla ice cream contains 14 g of fat. If you eat 2000 calories per day, you should eat between about 55 g and 65 g of fat. Write an inequality stating that x cups of low-fat milk and y cups of vanilla ice cream contain less than 65 g of fat.

   b. Graph the inequality you wrote in part (a) and list two different solutions.

4. Can you get 1300 milligrams of calcium from low-fat milk and vanilla ice cream without consuming more than 65 g of fat?

Some sports nutritionists stress that a sports diet is healthy for all people, not just athletes. They believe that, regardless of your sport or activity level, 60–70% of the calories you eat should come from carbohydrates.

5. **a.** Let c represent the number of calories from carbohydrates and t represent the total number of calories. Write an inequality that states that at least 60% of the total calories should come from carbohydrates.

   b. Write an inequality that states that at most 70% of calories should come from carbohydrates.

Athletes in training require 70–80% of their calories to be from carbohydrates. Suppose a cyclist in an international cycling stage race uses about 963 calories during one stage of the race.

6. Write an inequality that represents the number of calories c that should come from carbohydrates.

Exponential Relationships

Mathematics and Medicine

Years of education and special training are required to become a medical doctor or surgeon. These medical professionals use math on a daily basis while providing care for their patients. The role of mathematics in the medical field is rich and strongly varied. Math is used for skills such as determining the success of treatments, calculating the dosage amounts of different medicines, and interpreting the results of tests such as CAT scans, X-rays, and ECGs, just to name a few.

Part of a doctor's medical training involves understanding how different medications interact with a patient's body. Doctors need to understand how long a particular medicine will be effective. Once a medicine enters a patient's bloodstream, the amount decreases over time as the body metabolizes the drug and/or eliminates it.

Let's take a look at salicylate, an active ingredient in aspirin. The graph of the amount of salicylate remaining in a patient's bloodstream over time models an exponential function since it decreases by about 80% each hour after the patient takes a small dose of aspirin. Letting A_0 be the original amount of salicylate, an exponential pattern can be seen.

Amount remaining 1 hour after dose $= A_0(0.80)$
Amount remaining 2 hours after dose $= 0.80(A_0(0.80)) = A_0(0.80)^2$
Amount remaining 3 hours after dose $= 0.80[0.80(A_0(0.80))] = A_0(0.80)^3$

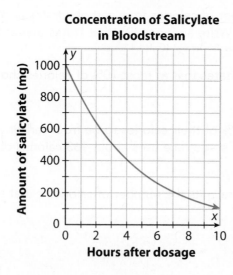

Concentration of Salicylate in Bloodstream

y-axis: Amount of salicylate (mg) — 0, 200, 400, 600, 800, 1000
x-axis: Hours after dosage — 0, 2, 4, 6, 8, 10

The graph shows the exponential relationship between the amount of time after a patient takes the dose of aspirin and the amount of salicylate remaining in the bloodstream. The exponential equation $A(t) = A_0(0.80)^t$ represents the amount of salicylate remaining in the bloodstream t hours after receiving an initial dose of A_0 milligrams (mg).

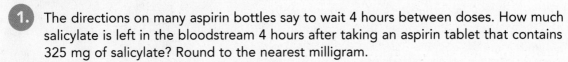
Use the information regarding aspirin and salicylate on the preceding page to answer the following question.

 1. The directions on many aspirin bottles say to wait 4 hours between doses. How much salicylate is left in the bloodstream 4 hours after taking an aspirin tablet that contains 325 mg of salicylate? Round to the nearest milligram.

Doctors use the half-life of medicine to determine dosage times and amounts. The half-life of a drug is the amount of time it takes for half, or 50%, of the medicine to be metabolized or excreted from the body. Assume a doctor administers an initial dose of 800 mg of a medicine with a half-life of 1.5 hours to a patient.

2. **a.** How many milligrams of the drug remain in the patient's bloodstream after 1.5 hours? 3 hours? 4.5 hours?

b. Write an equation that models the amount of medicine remaining in the patient's bloodstream x hours after receiving an 800-mg dose.

c. How would your equation change for a drug with a half-life of 2 hours?

Doctors and surgeons need to protect and treat patients from bacteria that can enter the body and reproduce at an exponential rate. Most single-cell bacteria reproduce by splitting into two new cells. The graphic below shows the increase in a population of bacteria. The amount of time that elapses between each split is called the generation time, or the doubling time for bacteria that divide into two new cells.

3. **a.** By what percent does the population increase during each generation?

b. Suppose one cell of bacteria begins to reproduce by splitting into two. Write an equation that models the bacteria population y after x generations.

c. Look back at your answer to part (b). How does your equation show that the population doubles in one generation?

The most common species of bacteria that infects surgical wounds is the *Staphylococcus aureus* (*S. aureus*). It has a generation time of about 30 minutes. For parts (a) and (b), let x represent the number of generations.

4. **a.** Suppose two *S. aureus* cells have just split into four cells. Write and solve an equation to find the number y of *S. aureus* cells 15.5 hours later.

b. Explain how you chose a value for x in part (a).

Polynomial Operations

Mathematics and Investing

Regardless of your dreams for the future, making them come true will probably take money, and maybe lots of it. How can you save money and make it work for you? You could open a savings account at a bank and make regular deposits. The bank would pay you a small amount of interest on the money in your account. Or, you could ask a financial advisor about investing in the stock market. Some stocks earn 20 percent or more each year, but they can lose that much too, or even more.

You can avoid some of the risk of losing money by investing in a variety of carefully chosen companies through an investment known as a mutual fund. These funds are managed by experts who invest money in a variety of stocks that they think will rise in value. The money comes from thousands of people who share the profits and losses on the stocks owned by the fund. This way, the risk is spread out—if one investment doesn't perform well, hopefully another will. In the end, you shouldn't lose everything because you've invested in a variety of different companies.

Financial advisors encourage people to save and invest on a regular basis. A smart investment today can grow into a future nest egg. For instance, suppose you invest $1000 at the start of each year over a period of three years in a mutual fund that earns 10% annually. You can calculate the total value of your investment after three years by writing an expression like this one:

Total value of investment after three years $= 1000(1 + 0.1)^3 + 1000(1 + 0.1)^2 + 1000(1 + 0.1)$

value of investment made the first year   value of investment made the second year   value of investment made the third year

If the annual growth rate is r, written as a decimal, the expression above becomes:

$$1000(1 + r)^3 + 1000(1 + r)^2 + 1000(1 + r)$$

This is an example of a polynomial. You can verify this by multiplying out the factors of $(1 + r)$ and combining like terms to obtain:

$$1000r^3 + 4000r^2 + 6000r + 3000$$

Use the investment polynomial on the previous page to answer the following questions.

1. Classify the polynomial by its degree. What is its leading coefficient?

2. Calculate the total value of the investment when $r = 0.1$.

3. What will be the value of the investment after four years? Explain.

Sometimes an investor chooses to make a one-time investment. The growth of a one-time investment can be modeled by an exponential function with an annual growth factor $g = (1 + r)$.

4. Does the polynomial on the previous page represent a one-time investment of $1000? Why or why not?

5. **a.** Write a polynomial in terms of g to represent the value of a one-time investment of $2000 at the end of four years.

b. Suppose you invest $2000 at the beginning of each year for four years. Write a polynomial in terms of g to represent the total value of the investment at the end of four years.

c. Find the sum of the polynomials in parts (a) and (b).

A financial investor makes a one-time investment of $5000 for a client at an annual growth rate r, where r is a decimal.

6. **a.** Write an expression to represent the value of the $5000 investment at the end of two years. Then write the polynomial in standard form.

b. Evaluate the polynomial from part (a) when $r = 0.07$.

7. **a.** Suppose a 25-year-old worker invests $5000 at an annual growth rate of 7%. What will her investment be worth when she retires at age 65?

b. Suppose instead that the worker in part (a) invests $5000 at the start of the year at ages 25, 35, 45, and 55. Write an expression that represents the value of her investments when she retires at age 65.

c. If the annual growth rate remains constant at 7% over the entire period, what will her investment from part (b) be worth when she retires at age 65?

UNIT 8

Quadratic Functions

Mathematics and Automotive Design

The global automotive manufacturing industry was valued at nearly 2 trillion dollars in 2015, with nearly 77 million automobiles sold in 2016 and predictions to exceed 100 million units sold worldwide by 2020. Careers in this industry are vast and varied, ranging from automotive design and manufacture to repair. Careers also include sales and marketing and automotive-related services.

Automobile production is a massive industry, with manufacturers employing teams of talented individuals with a diverse set of skills. Bringing a new design through the manufacturing process is an extremely complex task that can only be accomplished by breaking the operation into smaller projects. Multiple teams are called upon to closely collaborate throughout the effort. Mathematics, physics, and engineering skills are required at all stages of the process.

Automotive designers use sophisticated CAD (computer-aided design) software to develop their designs. One of the considerations when designing a vehicle is its aerodynamics. The more aerodynamic a vehicle is, the more efficient it will be, requiring less power from the vehicle's engine to overcome air resistance.

Aerodynamics is concerned with air resistance, or the force that pushes against a car when it moves. The force depends on several variables, all of which are constant for a given car in a given place, except for the speed of the air relative to the car. A drag coefficient, C_D, is a number that describes the aerodynamics of a car—the lower the number, the more aerodynamic the vehicle. The frontal area is determined by the shape of the car. Air resistance is calculated using the formula

$$\text{air resistance} = 0.00256 \times C_D \times \text{frontal area} \times (\text{relative speed})^2,$$

where air resistance is measured in pounds, frontal area is measured in square feet, and the relative speed is measured in miles per hour. Relative speed is a combination of the speed of the car and the speed of the air. In still air, the relative speed is just the car's speed.

Because the air resistance depends on the square of the relative speed, the relationship between air resistance and speed is quadratic. Small changes in the independent variable (speed) can cause large changes in the dependent variable (resistance).

Fuel efficiency is another major consideration for automobile designers. Along with maximizing fuel economy, there has been significant exploration of alternative fuels and/or electric power. In the last several years, vehicles that utilize battery power and alternative fuel sources, such as hydrogen, have become available.

The air resistance that a vehicle encounters depends on the vehicle's drag coefficient, its frontal area, and the square of the relative speed. The table below gives typical values of the drag coefficient and frontal area for several types of vehicles. Use the table and the formula on the preceding page to answer the following questions.

	Sports car	Sedan	Bus
Drag coefficient	0.24	0.32	0.90
Frontal area (ft²)	22	25	85

1. **a.** Write an equation giving the air resistance R on a sedan as a function of the sedan's speed s.

b. Write an equation giving the air resistance on a sports car as a function of its speed.

c. Find the air resistance on both a sedan and a sports car at 30 mph and at 60 mph. What do you notice?

2. **a.** Write an equation giving the air resistance R on a bus as a function of the bus's speed s. Then graph the function.

b. Suppose the air resistance on a bus is 200 lb. About how fast is the bus traveling?

c. By what factor should the bus reduce its speed in order to reduce the air resistance by 50%.

Fuel consumption can be harmful to the environment and expensive as well, so it makes sense to drive at speeds that use fuel most efficiently. The fuel efficiency of an average car is given by

$$y = -0.0177x^2 + 1.48x + 3.39$$

where x is the speed in miles per hour and y is the fuel economy in miles per gallon.

3. **a.** Find the speed(s) at which an average car will get 20 miles per gallon.

b. Determine the range of speeds that yield 32 miles per gallon or better.

c. What speed yields the best fuel economy?

d. What is the best fuel economy for an average car?

UNIT 9
Quadratic Equations and Modeling

Mathematics and Athletic Coaching

You don't have to be a star athlete to pursue a career in sports, but knowing a little math improves your chance of success even more. Athletic coaches and trainers use mathematics to help players optimize their performance on the field. For example, in football the launch angle of a kick and the force with which the football is kicked are factors that impact the flight path of a football when determining the height above the playing surface and the horizontal distance the football travels. A kicking coach might work with a placekicker on kicking the ball with approximately the same force every time. Then the kicker only needs to adjust the launch angle based on the distance to the goalpost.

When a football is kicked, its flight path is governed by the laws of projectile motion. The height of the ball as a function of time is given by the quadratic function

$$h(t) = -16t^2 + v_0 t + h_0,$$

where v_0 is the initial velocity and h_0 is the initial height. However, this function does not provide complete information about the location of the ball. Specifically, it does not tell us the horizontal distance of the ball from the point it was initially kicked. However, if we model the parabolic flight of a football using a pair of *parametric equations*, then we can determine both the height and the horizontal distance with respect to the time, t, since the ball was kicked. The variable t is called the *parameter*.

For simplicity, assume that the wind speed is 0, and therefore the wind resistance is ignored. The football is kicked from the ground, so its initial height, h_0, is 0, and its initial location is modeled by the point (0, 0). Only the vertical component of the football's path is affected by gravity; the horizontal component is not affected by gravity.

The parametric equations modeling the placekicker's kick are

$$x(t) = v_x t \quad \text{and} \quad y(t) = -16t^2 + v_y t$$

where v_x is the horizontal component of the initial velocity (in feet per second), v_y is the vertical component of the initial velocity (in feet per second), and t is the time (in seconds). Greater launch angles yield larger vertical velocity components and smaller horizontal components. Because the path of the football is parabolic, there will be two different times when the ball is at any height below its maximum—one on the ball's way up near the line of scrimmage and another on its way down.

© Houghton Mifflin Harcourt Publishing Company • Image Credits: ©pixelheadphoto digitalskiller/Shutterstock

The top of the crossbar of the goalpost on a football field is 10 feet above the playing surface. Due to the size of the ball, the vertical height of the ball must be at least 10.5 feet when the football reaches the goalpost in order for the ball to clear the crossbar. Suppose that a kicker's typical launch velocity is 80 feet per second. The values of v_x and v_y for this velocity at five different launch angles are given in the table below.

Launch Angle	40°	42°	45°	48°	50°
v_x (in ft/sec)	61.28	59.45	56.57	53.53	51.42
v_y (in ft/sec)	51.42	53.53	56.67	59.45	61.28

  1.
  a. Write the parametric equations using the values in the table for a launch angle of 40°.

  b. Use the parametric equations you wrote in part (a) to determine the times when $y(t) = 10.5$. Round your answers to the nearest hundredth. (*Hint*: Use the quadratic formula and your calculator to solve the equation.)

  c. For each time found in part (b), determine how far the ball is from the point where it was kicked. Convert these distances to yards since a football field is marked in yards. Round your answers to the nearest hundredth of a yard.

The end zone of a football field is 10 yards from the goal line as shown in the diagram. The best launch angle for a kick is 45°.

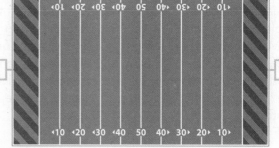

  2.
  a. Write the parametric equations for this angle with an initial velocity of 80 feet per second.

  b. Use the parametric equations you wrote in part (a) to determine the range of times for which the football will be high enough to clear the goalpost.

  c. If the ball is kicked from the 50-yard line (60 yards from the goal post), will it clear the goalpost? Explain your answer.

A young kicker kicks a ball from the 15-yard line (25 yards from the goal post). The parametric equations $x(t) = 40.87t$ and $y(t) = -16t^2 + 36.80t$ describe the horizontal and vertical position of the football t seconds after it was kicked.

  3.
  a. At what time does the ball reach the goalpost? Round your answer to the nearest hundredth.

  b. Does the ball have enough height at the time found in part (a) to clear the goalpost? Explain your answer.

Inverse Relationships

Mathematics and Accident Reconstruction

Many of us think we know from television shows and movies what a police investigation is all about. The detective arrives at the scene of the crime, searching for clues and questioning witnesses until a suspect finally breaks down and confesses. But few people realize the important of mathematics in an investigation, particularly an investigation of a traffic accident.

Tens of thousands of automobile accidents occur each day in the United States. It is the job of an accident reconstructionist to figure out what happened and why. Often the scene of an accident is chaotic, with rescue personnel, police officers, survivors, witnesses, and victims all intermingled. To add to all of that, it is also often dark. The reconstructionist must piece together the parts of the "puzzle" to reconstruct the event. In addition to providing the clues, the information gained from these investigations can highlight safety problems that weren't recognized before, paving the way for safer roads and cars.

Mathematics plays a big role in this process because everything happens according to the laws of physics, and many of these phenomena can be represented by mathematical equations. By examining the position of the vehicles, the nature and extent of the damage they have sustained, and other physical evidence, the reconstructionist works backwards to identify the factors leading up to the crash.

For example, the formula

$$S = \sqrt{30df}$$

is used to calculate the car's minimum speed S in miles per hour at the moment the car begins to skid. In the formula, d is the length in feet of the skid mark left by the car, and f is the coefficient of friction. This coefficient is a measure of the slipperiness or stickiness of the road, and varies with road surface and weather conditions. Values of the friction coefficient may be as high as 0.9 on a dry road and as low as 0.1 on a wet road. The accident reconstructionist measures the distance d manually and determines f with a special device. The following table shows calculated minimum speeds for different combinations of d and f.

Calculated Speed, S			
f \ d	76	98	123
0.1	15.1	17.1	19.2
0.4	30.2	34.3	38.4
0.9	45.3	51.4	57.6

Use the formula on the preceding page to answer the following questions.

1. **a.** If the value of f does not change, what happens to S as d increases?

   b. If the value of S does not change, what happens to f as d increases?

   c. If a car is traveling at 55 miles per hour, will it skid farther on a road with a high coefficient of friction or a low one?

A driver applies the brakes, and the car comes to a stop, leaving a skid mark on the pavement. The greater the initial speed of the car, the longer the skid mark, or stopping distance. Road conditions also affect the stopping distance.

2. Use the formula for minimum speed S to complete the following table. Round values to the nearest tenth.

d	f	S
70	0.4	
70	0.8	
100	0.4	
100	0.8	
	0.4	38.7
150		56.1

3. When the skid distance d remains constant, how does the value of f affect the calculated speed of the car?

One way drivers can avoid getting into accidents is by considering stopping distances. Values of the friction coefficient f are typically 0.7 for dry roads and 0.4 for wet roads.

4. Write the function for the minimum speed S of a vehicle in terms of its stopping distance d in the form $S = a\sqrt{d}$ if the vehicle is driving on a typical dry road. Then graph the function.

5. Write the function for the minimum speed S of a vehicle in terms of its stopping distance d in the form $S = a\sqrt{d}$ if the vehicle is driving on a typical wet road. Then graph the function.

6. Compare the graphs for a vehicle driving on a wet road and on a dry road. For the same speed S, will a car skid farther on a wet road or on a dry road?

UNIT 1 Selected Answers

MODULE 1

Lesson 1.1 Solving Equations

Your Turn

3. $x = 6$
4. $x = 36$
5. The kiwi is 22 inches tall.
6. The kakapo is 26 inches tall.

Evaluate

1. The value 8 is too high. The value 6 is too low. The value 7 is a solution.
3. $a = 2$
5. $-18 = d$
7. $y = 2$
9. $x = 66$
11. $m = \frac{35}{28}$ or $\frac{5}{4}$
13. $m = -12$
15. Addition Property of Equality
    Division Property of Equality
17. Multiplication Property of Equality
    Division Property of Equality
19. Julio's normal hourly rate is $11.80 per hour. Working 35 hours at $12 per hour is 35 · 12 = 420, and $420 is close to $436.60.
21. Paul spent $7 on the discount card.
23. The radius of Mars is 3397 km.
25. The congruent angles each measure 30°.
27. Marietta's hourly wage before the raise was $11.50.

UNIT 1 Selected Answers

MODULE 1

Lesson 1.2 Modeling Quantities

Your Turn

3. The actual heart is about 6 inches long.
4. 2.1
5. 0.9
6. 0.1
8. Alan's go-kart travels approximately 19.5 mi/h. Barry's go-kart travels faster than Alan's go-kart.
10. Alex drove 45 mi/h.

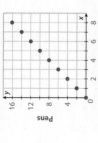

11. Max wrote an average of 2.5 pages per hour.

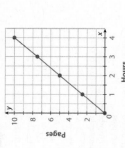

Evaluate

1. The height of the building is 200 ft.
3. The goal post is 45 feet tall.
5. No; $\frac{5}{7}$ is not proportional to $\frac{8}{12}$.

7. The length of the actual car is 185 inches.
9. Reduces; 100 cm > 25 cm
11. Preserves; 12 in. = 1 ft
13. ≈ 0.272 fl oz
15. 589 pounds
17. 10.4 in./min
19. 0.33 kg/L
    ≈ 0.27 kg/L
    Marcia made a more concentrated salt solution.
21. The unit rate is 2 pens per notebook.

23. Graph B because the x-axis goes to 5 and the unit rate is 3.
    Graph D because the x-axis goes to 5 and the unit rate is 3.5.
    Graph A because the x-axis goes to 4 and the unit rate is 4.
    Graph C because the x-axis goes to 4 and the unit rate is 4.5.
25. 0.4 L $= x$

UNIT 1 Selected Answers

MODULE 1

Lesson 1.3 Reporting with Precision and Accuracy

Your Turn

3. Minimum area = 1.35 m · 1.5 m ≈ 2 m²

   Maximum area = 1.45 m · 2.5 m ≈ 4 m²

4. Minimum area = 14.5 ft · 22.65 ft ≈ 328 ft²

   Maximum area = 15.5 ft · 22.75 ft ≈ 353 ft²

6. two

7. one

8. five

11. The perimeter is 31.7 ft. The area is 63 ft².

12. The perimeter is 588 cm. The area is 18,000 cm².

15. about 36

16. about 3600

Evaluate

1. 54.16 cm is more precise because 0.01 is smaller than 0.1 cm.

3. 5 kg; 5212 g

5. 123 cm; 1291 mm

7. a. Scale 3 is the most precise.

   b. Scale 2 is the most accurate.

9. 255 cm² ≤ area < 278 cm²

11. 4 m² ≤ area < 6 m²

13. 123.040 has 6 significant digits.

15. Two significant digits.

17. Eight significant digits.

19. The area is 610 ft².

21. So, on average, about 240 tiles will be needed.

23. The 0 in each dimension, 1.20 cm and 1.40 cm, is significant, so the answer should be given with three significant digits as 1.68 cm² and not as 1.7 cm².

UNIT 1 Selected Answers

MODULE 2

Lesson 2.1 Modeling with Expressions

Your Turn

3. The expression $4.49w + 5p$ represents the total cost of w watermelons and p pineapples.

4. The expression $3p + 2.25(p - 5)$ represents the total cost of pens and pencils.

5. $\dfrac{x+y}{x} > \dfrac{x}{x+y}$

6. $(x + y)^2 > 2(x + y)$

9. $300 + 35m$

10. $p - 0.15p = 0.85p$

Evaluate

1. terms: -20, $5p$, and $-7z$; coefficients: 5 and -7

3. 5; 6 and a; 11 and b

5. The expression represents the total cost of c cucumbers and a apples.

7. The expression represents the total cost of 3 shirts and 2 pairs of pants.

9. The expression represents the price of a sandwich.

11. The factors of the expression are $(y - 2)$ and $(x + 3)$

13. The term $1.4n$ represents the cost of n packages of pencils at \$1.40 per package. The term $1.2m$ represents the cost of m pads of paper at \$1.20 per pad. The expression represents the total cost of n packages of pencils and m pads of paper.

15. $0.5 > \dfrac{b}{a+b}$

17. $\dfrac{a-b}{2} < a - \dfrac{b}{2}$

19. $5(a + b) = (a + b)5$

21. $p - 0.20p = 0.80p$

23. $P + 0.003P = 1.003P$

25. Yes, the student is correct.

   For the rectangle, the perimeter is:
   $(x + 4) + x + (x + 4) + x = 4x + 8$

   For the square, the perimeter is:
   $(x + 2) + (x + 2) + (x + 2) + (x + 2) = 4x + 8$

   Because $(x + 4) + x + (x + 4) + x = 4x + 8 = (x + 2) + (x + 2) + (x + 2) + (x + 2)$, the perimeters are equal.

27. a. There is a total of ten tulips in Border 1. For Border 2, there are eight additional tulips added to the garden plus the ten original tulips from Border 1. $8 + 10$ For Border 3, there are eight additional tulips added to the garden plus the ten original tulips from Border 1. $8(2) + 10$ So, the expression for the number of tulips in the garden with Border b is $8(b - 1) + 10$. So, Jerry's expression is correct.

   b. Elaine's expression is not correct. The correct expression for starting with two rows of four daisies would be $8(b - 1) + 12$.

Selected Answers

UNIT 1 Selected Answers

MODULE 2

Lesson 2.2 Creating and Solving Equations

Your Turn

5. Width = 60 ft, length = 60 + 8 = 68 ft

7. Claire bought 28 feet of fencing.

8. In 7 days, each animal will be consuming 1900 Calories per day.

9. Ian is 180 cm tall now.

Evaluate

Possible answers given.

1. $14 + x = 17$

3. $n - 12 = 20$

5. $\frac{2}{3}x + 4 = 7$

7. $d + 90 = 350$

9. Alice hit 10 home runs and Peter hit $2(10 - 6) = 8$ home runs.

11. Isaac worked 16 hours, Ruby worked 22 hours, and Svetlana worked 88 hours.

13. After 6 months, they will each have 128 stamps.

15. After 15 months, the total amount paid to both gyms is $875.

17. $n = 10$ years

19. In the last year, Sharla earned $2000 more than Paul.

21. Sammie bought 14 meters of fencing.

23. a. Possible answer: You need the length and width of the patio. You can write algebraic expressions for the length and width. Use the expressions in the formula for the perimeter of a rectangle, and then solve to find the length and the width.

b. Find the length and width using the formula for the perimeter of a rectangle. Let ℓ be the length and let $\ell - 5$ be the width. $2\ell + 2(\ell - 5) = 134$; $\ell = 36$. The length of the patio is 36 ft and the width is $36 - 5 = 31$ ft. The area is $36 \times 31 = 1,116$ ft².

25. Initially: A: 260 mi, B: 210 mi; C: 180 mi Zack's answer is the same as Alexa's.

UNIT 1 Selected Answers

MODULE 2

Lesson 2.3 Solving for a Variable

Your Turn

2. The altitude will be 25,000 feet.

3. $\frac{y - b}{x} = m$

Evaluate

1. $\frac{c}{2\pi} = r$

3. $\frac{y - b}{m} = x$

5. $\frac{v}{\pi r^2} = h$

7. $\frac{d}{r} = t$

9. $FV - AT = OV$

11. $p = \frac{q - 5r}{2}$

13. $\frac{a}{c} = b$

15. $x = 5(a + g)$

17. $z = \frac{5}{2}y - 1$

19. $\frac{8 - 3a}{b - a} = n$

21. $E = \frac{9.5}{18} = 2.5$

23. The student only rearranged the formula so the variable was on a side by itself but did not simplify further to remove the coefficient. The formula for ℓ is $\ell = \frac{P - 2w}{2}$

25. The measure of the base is 32 mm.

Selected Answers

MODULE 2

Lesson 2.4 Creating and Solving Inequalities

Your Turn

4. Zachary can spend no more than $45.25 on each video game.

5. $x < -1$

6. $x \le -18$

8. The band members will need to sell at least 34 pizzas.

Evaluate

1. $c > 5$

3. $x < 5$

5. $c \le 3.50$

7. $x > 1$

9. $x > 23$

11. $x > -\dfrac{5}{7}$

13. $x < 4$

15. $x \le -\dfrac{4}{7}$

17. $x \le -4$

19. $x > -10$

21. $8\dfrac{2}{3}$ cubic meters

23. Sven's original inequality is backwards. He should have started with $60 - 5t \ge 35$. Sven should spend 5 minutes or less on each scale.

25. a. $10 > -\dfrac{1}{2} \cdot 4(2x - 3)$

    b. $4 \ge x$

    c. The maximum height is 5 inches.

MODULE 2

Lesson 2.5 Creating and Solving Compound Inequalities

Your Turn

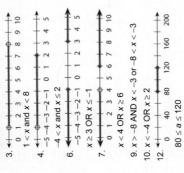

3. $1 < x$ and $x < 8$

4. $-4 < x$ and $x \le 2$

6. $x \ge 3$ OR $x \le -1$

7. $x < 4$ OR $x \ge 6$

9. $x > -8$ AND $x < -3$ or $-8 < x < -3$

10. $x < -4$ OR $x \ge 2$

12. $80 \le a \le 120$

Evaluate

1.

True	True	True
True	False	False
False	True	False
False	False	False

3. $-1 < x \le 3$

5. $x < 8$ OR $x \ge 13$

7. $x < -2$ $x > 5$

9. $-12 < x < 4$

11. $x \le -2$ OR $x \ge 7$

13. $x < 9$ OR $x > 11$

15. $x > 2$ AND $x < 10$, or $2 < x < 10$

17. $70 \le t \le 95$

19. $82.4 \le f \le 659.2$

21. $0 < t$ OR $t > 100$

23. A. C
    B. A
    C. D
    D. B

25. The solutions are $x \ge 5$ AND $x \le 6$.
If the solutions were $x \ge 5$ OR $x \le 6$, then the solutions would be all real numbers. The solution $x \ge 5$ AND $x \le 6$ means the solutions lie between 5 and 6.

UNIT 2 Selected Answers

MODULE 3
Lesson 3.1 Graphing Relationships

Your Turn

3. Graph C

4. Graph A shows the ball thrown from a certain height with the height decreasing until the ball hits the ground and then rolls. Graph B shows the ball thrown from a certain height with the height increasing then decreasing in an arc until the ball is caught at a certain height.

5. The graph is a continuous graph.

The domain is $0 \le t \le 8$.

The range is $0 \le S \le 5$.

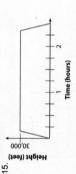

6. The graph is a discrete graph.

The domain is whole numbers from 0 to 10.

The range is whole number multiples of 20 from 0 to 200.

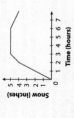

Evaluate

1. Segment 1 is steeper than segment 2. This means more people were entering the arena at a faster rate in segment 1 than in segment 2.

3. Segments 5 and 7 are horizontal, which means no fans are entering or leaving the game.

5. Graph C

7. Graph B

9. Graph A

11. Graph B could represent a rapidly increasing release of water over a dam during a year; graph C could represent a constant release of water over a dam during a year; and graph D could represent a river in a dry climate that almost dries up in the summer and then returns to its original rate due to heavy fall rains.

13. Graph B represents that after a certain number of cups are sold, the profit will reach a limit. Graph C represents when partial cups are being sold, and the profit increases as long as there are cups to sell. Graph D represents that the profit will always stay constant no matter how many cups are sold.

15.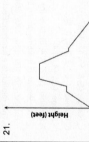

17. The domain is $0 \le t \le 2.5$ and the range is $0 \le H \le 30,000$.

19. Discrete

21.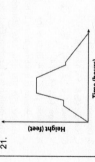

23. Sample answer: The graph is the distance a person driving a car is from a destination. The person is driving on a highway and then exits, where the car slows down and then stops at a red light. The car continues at a slower pace until it stops at another red light. Then the car continues to its destination.

25. The student drew a discrete graph instead of a continuous graph. The height of the skydiver continuously changes so a discrete graph cannot be used. The correct graph is as shown.

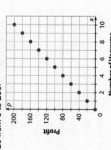

UNIT 2 Selected Answers

MODULE 3

Lesson 3.2 Understanding Relations and Functions

Your Turn

3. Domain: {2, 3, 4, 5}; Books sold.
Range: {4, 6, 7, 9}; Price amounts.
input of 2 books sold, output of $4.00.
input of 3 books sold, output of $6.00.
input of 4 books sold, output of $7.00.
input of 5 books sold, output of $9.00.
This relation is a function. Each domain value is paired with exactly one range value.

4. Domain: {20, 30, 35, 60} times spent exercising.
Range: {50, 85, 100} number of calories;
input of 20 minutes output of 50 calories burned; input of 30 minutes output of 85 calories burned
input of 35 minutes output of 85 calories burned; input of 60 minutes output of 100 calories burned
This relation is a function. Each domain value is paired with exactly one range value.

6. The relation is a function.

7. The relation is not a function.

Evaluate

1.

x	y
5	10
6	20
6	23
7	35

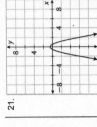

3. Domain: {2, 7, 8, 11, 15}
Range: {5, 8, 15, 12, 19}

5. Domain: {−6, −2, 2, 4, 6, 8}
Range: {−6, −4, 0, 4}

7. Domain: {1, 2, 3, 4, 5}; time (h)
The domain is the time driven in hours.
Range: {50, 100, 150, 200}; distance (mi)
This relation is a function. Each domain value is paired with exactly one range value.

9.

Minutes	Calories
60	360
120	720
180	1080
240	1440

Domain: {60, 120, 180, 240}; minutes bicycling
Range: {360, 720, 1080, 1440}; calories burned
This relation is a function. Each domain value is paired with exactly one range value.

11.

x	y
1	175
2	175
3	225
4	275

Domain: {1, 2, 3, 4}; hours of work
Range: {175, 225, 275}; amount charged
This relation is a function. Each domain value is paired with exactly one range value.

13.

x	y
13	33
17	25
22	22
25	17
33	

The relation is a function. Each domain value is paired with exactly one range value.

15.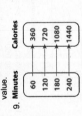

The relation is not a function.

17. The relation is not a function.

19. The relation is a function.

21.

The relation is a function.

23. No; the relation is not a function. The domain value February maps to two range values, 28 and 29. February has 28 days in a regular year and 29 days in a leap year.

25. The student used a horizontal line, rather than a vertical line. A function is allowed to have more than one x-value paired to the same y-value, so there is no horizontal line test. The relation passes the vertical line test and is a function.

UNIT 2 Selected Answers

MODULE 3
Lesson 3.3 Modeling with Functions

Your Turn

4. Dependent: total earnings; Independent: the number of hours h

$f(h) = 7.50h$. $f(8) = 7.50(8) = 60$. Kate earns $60 for working 8 hours.

5. Let h represent the number of hours.
$f(h) = 17 + 2h$

Reasonable domain: {0, 1, 2, 3, 4, 5}
Range: {17 °C, 19 °C, 21 °C, 23 °C, 25 °C, 27 °C}

6. Let h represent the number of hours.
$f(h) = 8.5h$

Reasonable domain: {1, 2, 3, 4, 5}
Range: {$8.50, $17, $25.50, $34, $42.50}

Evaluate

1. A. Independent: expenses;
   Dependent: total cost

   B. Independent: area;
   Dependent: price

   C. Independent: distance;
   Dependent: time

   D. Independent: size of carton;
   Dependent: number of items

3. Almira earns $300 in 6 hours.

5. Bruce charges the cutomer $23.75.

7. Craig owes Allison $88.75 for 5 DVDs.

9. Harold earns $2,250,000 for selling 9 houses.

11. Cindy's total cost for 23 jackets is $1150.

13. $f(t) = $5.00 \cdot t + 40$
A reasonable domain is {0, 1, 2, 3, 4, 5}. The range is {$40, $45, $50, $55, $60, $65}.

15. $f(t) = $100 \cdot h + 300$
A reasonable domain is {1, 2, 3}. The range is {$400, $500, $600}.

17. $f(m) = $50 \cdot m + 200$
A reasonable domain is {1, 2, 3}. The range is {$250, $300, $350}.

19. $f(t) = $9.00 \cdot t + 72$
A reasonable domain is {0, 1, 2, 3, 4, 5, 6}. The range is {$72, $81, $90, $99, $108, $117, $126}.

21. The domain values are 2, 4, 6, and 8.
Sample answer: I substituted each range value for $f(x)$ and solved for x. $f(2) = -1$, $f(4) = -13$, $f(6) = -25$, $f(8) = -37$

23. a. It would take the printer 12.5 minutes.

   b. Since time is continuous, a reasonable domain would be $0 \le t \le 12.5$. The printer starts printing at 0 minutes and finishes printing at 12.5 minutes.

   c. Since there are 100 sheets of paper in the printer and the printer can use them all, a reasonable range would be all whole numbers from 0 to 100.

UNIT 2 Selected Answers

MODULE 3
Lesson 3.4 Graphing Functions

Your Turn

4.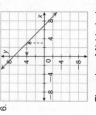

5.

6.

7. The value of $f(x)$ is 4 when x is 3.

7. The cruise ship will be about 42.5 kilometers from port 2.5 hours from now.

Evaluate

1.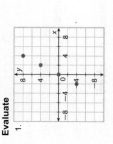

3.

5.

7.

9. $f(3) = -1$

11. $f(-4) = 13$

13. $f(-4) = -77$

15.

$f(0) = 0.5$

Selected Answers

UNIT 2 Selected Answers

MODULE 4

Lesson 4.1 Identifying and Graphing Sequences

Your Turn

6.

n	$f(n) = n^2 - 5$	f(n)
1	$f(1) = 1^2 - 5 = -4$	-4
2	$f(2) = 2^2 - 5 = -1$	-1
3	$f(3) = 3^2 - 5 = 4$	4
4	$f(4) = 4^2 - 5 = 11$	11

The first 4 terms are -4, -1, 4, and 11.

7. The 15th term is 57.

10.

n	$f(n) = f(n - 1) - 2$	f(n)
1	$f(1) = 35$	35
2	$f(2) = 35 - 2 = 33$	33
3	$f(3) = 33 - 2 = 31$	31
4	$f(4) = 31 - 2 = 29$	29
5	$f(5) = 29 - 2 = 27$	27

The first 5 terms are 35, 33, 31, 29, and 27.

11.

n	$f(n) = f(n - 1) - 4$	f(n)
1	$f(1) = 45$	45
2	$f(2) = 45 - 4 = 41$	41
3	$f(3) = 41 - 4 = 37$	37
4	$f(4) = 37 - 4 = 33$	33
5	$f(5) = 33 - 4 = 29$	29

The first 5 terms are 45, 41, 35, 33, and 29.

13.

n	$f(n) = f(n - 1) + 8.5$	f(n)
2	$f(2) = f(1) + 8.5 = 17 + 8.5 = 25.5$	25.5
3	$f(3) = f(2) + 8.5 = 25.5 + 8.5 = 34$	34
4	$f(4) = f(3) + 8.5 = 34 + 8.5 = 42.5$	42.5

The ordered pairs are (1, 17), (2, 25.5), (3, 34), and (4, 42.5).

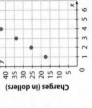

Charges (in dollars) vs Number of pizzas

14.

n	$f(n) = 20n + 100$	f(n)
1	$f(1) = 20(1) + 100 = 120$	120
2	$f(2) = 20(2) + 100 = 140$	140
3	$f(3) = 20(3) + 100 = 160$	160
4	$f(4) = 20(4) + 100 = 180$	180
5	$f(5) = 20(5) + 100 = 200$	200
6	$f(6) = 20(6) + 100 = 220$	220

The ordered pairs are (1, 120), (2, 140), (3, 160), (4, 180), (5, 200), and (6, 220).

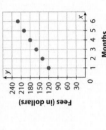

Fees (in dollars) vs Months

17.

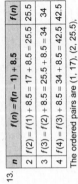

Distance (mi) vs Time (h)

The lava flowed about 27 miles after 4.5 hours.

19.

Distance (mi) vs Time (min)

Joshua drove 2.5 miles in 5 minutes.

21.

Temperature (°F) vs Hour

The temperature after 7 hours is about 92 °F.

23. Student A is incorrect. Student A found the value of x when f(x) is 1. The student moved vertically upward first to get to the graph. The student should have moved horizontally first and then vertically downward to get to the graph.

Evaluate

1.

n	1	2	3	4	5	6
$f(n)$	15	30	45	60	75	90

Domain: {1, 2, 3, 4, 5, 6, . . .}

Range: {15, 30, 45, 60, 75, 90, . . .}

3. 65,536; 256; 16; 4

5. 7; −13; 67; −253

7. 3; 9; 81; 6561

9. The 10th term is 65.

11. The 10th term is −10,190.

13. 25 is the 15th term.

15. 52 is the 26th term.

17. 119 is the 6th term.

19.

21. The reduced fee for each additional round played is $7.

23. No, it is not correct. Shane multiplied each term by 2 to find the next term, and only added 1 at the end instead of adding 1 to each doubled term.

UNIT 2 Selected Answers

MODULE 4

Lesson 4.2 Constructing Arithmetic Sequences

Your Turn

5. The recursive rule is $f(1) = 155$, $f(n) = f(n - 1) - 14$.

The explicit rule is $f(n) = 155 - 14(n - 1)$.

7. Recursive rule: $f(1) = 6$, $f(n) = f(n - 1) + 10$ for $n \geq 2$

Explicit rule: $f(n) = 10(n - 1) + 6$

9. $f(n) = 10 + 8(n - 1)$

Evaluate

1. a. 32; 39; 46; 53

b. Domain: {1, 2, 3, 4} Range: {32, 39, 46, 53}

c. $39 - 32 = 7$

3. The sequence is not arithmetic. There is no common difference.

5. Recursive rule: $f(1) = 58$, $f(n) = f(n - 1) + 7$ for $n \geq 2$

Explicit rule: $f(n) = f(1) + d(n - 1)$, so $f(n) = 58 + 7(n - 1)$

7. Recursive rule: $f(1) = 4567$, $f(n) = f(n - 1) - 1111$ for $n \geq 2$

Explicit rule: $f(n) = f(1) + d(n - 1)$, so $f(n) = 4567 - 1111(n - 1)$

9. Recursive rule: $f(1) = 60$, $f(n) = f(n - 1) + 20$ for $n \geq 2$

Explicit rule: $f(n) = f(1) + d(n - 1)$, so $f(n) = 60 + 20(n - 1)$

11. $f(1) = 63$, $f(n) = f(n - 1) + 7$ for $n \geq 2$

$f(n) = 63 + 7(n - 1)$

13. $f(1) = 112$, $f(n) = f(n - 1) - 2$ for $n \geq 2$

$f(n) = 112 - 2(n - 1)$

15. $f(1) = 67$, $f(n) = f(n - 1) - 30$ for $n \geq 2$

$f(n) = 67 - 30(n - 1)$

17. $f(n) = 38 + 12(n - 1)$

19. $f(n) = 74 + 11(n - 1)$

21. Each term is 3 times the previous term. The sequence is not arithmetic because the difference between consecutive terms is not always the same.

23. The difference between the fourth term and the ninth term in the sequence will be 5 times the common difference. Find the difference between the ninth term and the fourth term and divide the result by 5. The second term in the arithmetic sequence is 41.

Selected Answers

UNIT 2 Selected Answers

MODULE 4

Lesson 4.3 Modeling with Arithmetic Sequences

Your Turn

2. $f(n) = 20 + 12(n - 1)$
   Mila is 128 miles from the store after 10 hours.

3. $f(n) = 4.9 + 4(n - 1)$
   The total cost of 18 battery packs is $72.90.

5. $f(n) = 34 + 17(n - 1)$
   The height of the stack with 7 boxes is 136 inches.

6. $f(n) = 250 + 50(n - 1)$
   Quynh will have saved a total of $800 after 12 months.

7. $f(n) = 3400 + 1200(n - 1)$
   After 5 round-trips, Ruby will have 8200 frequent-flier miles.

8. $f(n) = 100 + 50(n - 1)$
   After 6 months, a person will have spent $350 on their gym membership.

Evaluate

1. a. $7.50; $15.00; $22.50; $30.00
   b. Each shirt costs $7.50, so the common difference is 7.5.
   c. The variable a represents the number of T-shirts. Only nonnegative integers make sense for a in this situation.

3. a. 82; 164; 246; 328
   b. Each day 82 calls are made, so the common difference is 82.
   c. The variable C represents the total number of calls over time, in days. The variable t represents time in days. The reasonable values for both domain and range values is positive integers.

5. a. 487; 476; 465
   b. $f(10) = 421$
   The mile marker at time interval 10 is 421.

7. $f(n) = 20 + 15(n - 1)$
   185; At 12 weeks, Ed will have collected 185 autographs.

9. $f(n) = 100 - 6(n - 1)$
   52; There will be 52 wolves in 9 weeks.

11. $f(n) = 18 - 0.5(n - 1)$
    3.5; At the beginning of Day 30, the weight of the bag is 3.5 pounds.

13. a. The total cost of 15 laps is $35.00.

15. Sam did not write the explicit form of the sequence correctly. The formula should be $f(n) = 75 + 25(n - 1)$. Therefore, 175 people will attend the park on the Day 5 because $f(5) = 75 + 25(4) = 175$.

17. a. The training schedule is an arithmetic sequence because the common difference between each pair of consecutive sessions is 1.5 miles.
    $f(n) = 3.5 + 1.5(n - 1)$
    b. Verona will run 26 miles on the sixteenth session.

19. No, the verbal description does not represent the same sequence.

UNIT 3 Selected Answers

MODULE 5

Lesson 5.1 Understanding Linear Functions

Your Turn

7. The equation is linear.

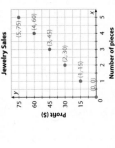

10. The domain is $\{0, 1, 2, 3, 4, \ldots\}$ and the range is $\{0, 6, 12, 18, 24, \ldots\}$.

Umbrella Sales

13. The domain is $\{0, 1, 2, 3, 4, \ldots\}$ and the range is $\{0, 5, 10, 15, 20, \ldots\}$.

Video Game Purchases

15. The domain is $\{0, 1, 2, 3, 4, \ldots\}$ and the range is $\{0, 15, 30, 45, 60, \ldots\}$.

Jewelry Sales

17.

x	1	3	5	7	9
y	85	255	425	595	765

Because y changes by 170 mph between consecutive terms, it has a constant change. x and y are described by a linear function.

19. It will reach 30 km/hr in 18.75 hours.

21. 3; 6; 9; 12; 15
    This pattern follows a linear function and the constant change of 3 for y corresponds to a constant change of 1 for x.

23. The student did not check if x had a constant change with respect to y. Since x from 0 to 2 corresponds to a change in y of 5 and x from 2 to 3 corresponds to a change in y of 5, this cannot be a linear equation.

Evaluate

1. The equation is linear because it is in the standard form of a linear equation:

3. The equation can not be written in standard form, so it is not linear.

5. The equation has a variable with an exponent other than one so it is not linear.

7. Discrete

9. Discrete

11. Continuous

UNIT 3 Selected Answers

MODULE 5
Lesson 5.2 Using Intercepts

Your Turn

3. The x-intercept is $\frac{7}{2}$.
The y-intercept is 4.

4. The x-intercept is -4.
The y-intercept is -3.

6. $28 = x$
So it takes 28 hours to reach 0 °C.
$y = -70$
So the temperature begins at -70 °C.

7. The x-intercept is -6.
The y-intercept is -10.

7. $x = 50$; $y = 60$

9.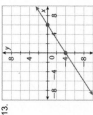

Trout Population

x-intercept: 25; y-intercept: 350
The x-intercept means that it takes 25 years for there to be no trout in the lake. The y-intercept represents the number of trout, 350, that were in the lake at the beginning of the population decrease.

11.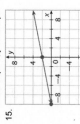

x-intercept: 120; y-intercept: 480
The x-intercept means that it would take 120 cars to run out of brake pads. The y-intercept represents the number of brake pads before any are installed.

Evaluate

1.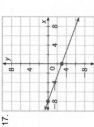

The y-intercept 140 means that the manufacturer started with 140 capacitors. The x-intercept 35 means that when 35 circuit boards have been made, there are no capacitors remaining.

3. $x = -3$; $y = 2$
5. $x = -7$; $y = -14$

13.

15. x-intercept: 6; y-intercept: -4

17. x-intercept: -10; y-intercept: 2

19. The equation of the function is $f(x) = 35x - 245$.
x-intercept: 7; y-intercept: -245
The x-intercept means that it takes Kim 7 weeks to repay the amount completely. The y-intercept represents the amount Kim owes her friend, $245, before she starts making payments.

21. A. y-intercept
B. both
C. x-intercept
D. neither
E. x-intercept

23. a. $f(x) = 2 - \frac{1}{5}x$
b. x-intercept: 30; y-intercept: 2
The x-intercept means that it takes Kathryn 30 minutes to complete her walk. The y-intercept represents the distance remaining when Kathryn begins, 2 mi.

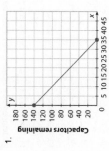

25. If A is not zero, the x-intercept is $\frac{C}{A}$, and if B is not zero, the y-intercept is $\frac{C}{B}$.

UNIT 3 Selected Answers

MODULE 5

Lesson 5.3 Interpreting Rate of Change and Slope

Your Turn

7. $\frac{6}{5}$

8. −5

9. The slope is negative. The line falls from left to right.

10. The slope is zero and the line is horizontal.

11. The slope is $\frac{5}{9}$ which means that if the temperature increases by 1 degree Fahrenheit, the temperature increases $\frac{5}{9}$ degree Celsius.

12. The slope is 50, which means that the amount of water in the reservoir is increasing at a rate of 50 cubic feet each hour.

Evaluate

1. 3

3. The slope is undefined.

5. $-\frac{5}{2}$

7. 1; The slope is positive.

9. 0; The slope is zero.

11. $\frac{-1}{2}$; The slope is negative.

13. The slope is 15. The money earned increases by $15 for each hour worked.

15. The slope is $\frac{3}{50}$ or 0.06. The cost to print each page is $0.06 after an initial charge of $250.

17. a.

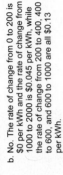

b. 4; 2; 6

c. The line segment from 2 hours to 3 hours has the greatest slope and it appears to be the steepest line segment.

19. 0.775 or $\frac{31}{40}$; discrete; because you make one movement forward and one up (or down) for each step, the function is discrete.

21. a. 40 to 50: 4
   50 to 60: 4
   60 to 70: 4
   70 to 80: 4
   80 to 90: 4

b. Yes, the graph is a line because the slope is constant. The slope is 4.

23. No; when lines have the same slope, the ratio of the rise to the run of those lines is the same but the lines do not necessarily pass through the same points.

25. a.

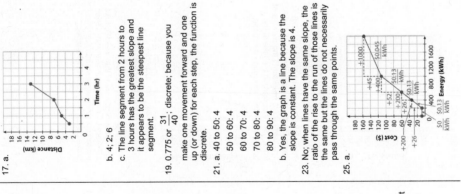

b. No. The rate of change from 0 to 200 is $0 per kWh and the rate of change from 1000 to 2000 is $0.045 per kWh, while the rate of change from 200 to 400, 400 to 600, and 600 to 1000 are all $0.13 per kWh.

c. The cost for 1 kilowatt-hour.

d. Sample answer: There is a flat fee of $8 for up to the first 200 kilowatt-hours. From 200 to 1000 kilowatt-hours, the cost is $0.13 for each additional kilowatt-hour. For over 1000 kilowatt-hours, the cost is $0.045 for each additional kilowatt-hour.

UNIT 3 Selected Answers

MODULE 6

Lesson 6.1 Slope-Intercept Form

Your Turn

3. $y = -x + 5$

4. $y = 7x - 3$

5. $y = -2x + 4$

6. $y = -\dfrac{2}{3}x + 2$

8. $m = 59$; so the rate of change in the cost is \$59 per month. The initial cost is \$100, so the y-intercept, b, is 100. The equation is $y = 59x + 100$. (4, 336) is a solution.

Evaluate

1. The slope is 200.
   The y-intercept is 500.

3.

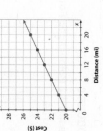

Cost of a Rental Truck

5. $y = 3x + 2$

7. $y = \dfrac{1}{4}x + 1$

9. $y = -\dfrac{2}{3}x - 9$

11. $y = 3x - 8$

13. $y = \dfrac{1}{2}x + 3$

15. $y = 2x + 3$; 2; 3

17. $y = \dfrac{2}{3}x - 4$; $\dfrac{2}{3}$; -4

19. $y = 2x + 5$; 2; 5

21. $y = -\dfrac{5}{2}x - 4$; $-\dfrac{5}{2}$; -4

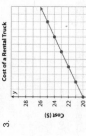

23. The cost per lesson is \$25, so the slope of the equation that represents the situation is 25. The initial cost of the lessons (that is, before any lessons are paid for), is \$30. So the y-intercept is 30. An equation is $y = 25x + 30$. The cost for 6 lessons is $25(6) + 30 = 180$. A \$200 gift certificate would pay for the lessons, and \$20 would be left.

25. Jake will have 48 more pages left to read. For Jake, the number of pages to read after 0 days is 168, and the rate of change is -24, so the equation is $y = -24x + 168$. Because $-24(5) + 168 = 48$, Jake will have 48 pages left to read after 5 days.

   Julio's pace is $\dfrac{5}{4}$ (24), so the equation for Julio is $y = -30x + 180$. Then after 5 days, Julio will have $-30(5) + 180 = 30$ pages left to read, and $48 - 30 = 18$. So, Jake has $48 - 30 = 18$ more pages to read.

27. No; it is not possible to write the equation of a vertical line in slope-intercept form. The equation of a vertical line has form $x = a$, where a is a real number. The slope of a vertical line is undefined.

UNIT 3 Selected Answers

MODULE 6
Lesson 6.2 Point-Slope Form

Your Turn

3. $y - 2 = 6(x - 1)$

4. $y - 1 = \frac{1}{3}(x + 3)$

6. The signup fee is $15.

8. $(y - 1) = -3(x - 3)$ or $(y - 4) = -3(x - 2)$

9. $(y - 1) = 0(x - 0)$ or $(y - 1) = 0(x - 1)$

10. A member would pay $61 for 22 gallons of gas.

11. A party for 12 skaters would cost $119.

Evaluate

1. Yes; the equation is equivalent to $y - (-1) = 7(x - (-2))$.

3. $y - 1 = (-2)(x - 1)$

5. $y - 2 = \left(\frac{1}{4}\right)(x - 1)$

7. $y - 1 = (-1)(x + 1)$ or $y + 1 = (-1)(x - 1)$

9. $y - 3 = \left(\frac{1}{2}\right)(x - 0)$ or $y - 4 = \left(\frac{1}{2}\right)(x - 2)$

11. If he finishes the race, James will raise $300.

13. Lizzy took 10.5 days to place all the tiles.

15. The boiling point at 6000 feet is 200 °F.

17. The balloon will not reach an altitude of 2500 feet in 4 minutes.

19. It will take about 100 minutes to fill the pool completely.

21. a. c
b. b
c. a
d. d

23. If the slope is undefined, there is no equation of the line in point-slope form. Otherwise, there are at least two equations in point-slope form for every pair of points on the line.

UNIT 3 Selected Answers

MODULE 6
Lesson 6.3 Standard Form

Your Turn

4. $2x + y = -24$

5. $-4x + y = 12$

7. $2x + y = 1$

8. $x - y = -4$

10. $4.5x - y = -1.5$

11. $2750x + y = 18,000$

Evaluate

1. a. standard form
b. point-slope form
c. slope-intercept form
d. standard form

3. $x + y = -5$

5. $7x - 3y = 9$

7. $2x + y = 11$

9. $y = 5$

11. $3x + 2y = 12$

13. $2x - y = 1$

15. $-8x + 5y = -30$

17. $4x - y = -12$

19. An equation is $10x + 6y = 150$. Other possible combinations are (15, 0), (9, 10), (6, 15), (3, 20), and (0, 25).

21. Cody made an error while finding the slope: $-\frac{3}{\frac{1}{6}} = -3(6) = -18$. Cody also should have multiplied both sides of the equation by 6, not 3, and should have multiplied all the terms. The equation should be $18x + y = 13$.

UNIT 3 Selected Answers

MODULE 6

Lesson 6.4 Transforming Linear Functions

Your Turn

6. The graph will have the same slope, but it has a y-intercept of 0.

7. No; the domain still starts at 0 and continues for any number of months. Yes; the range has a new minimum value equal to the new joining fee.

Evaluate

1.
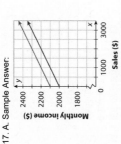

3.

5. g(x); m(x); h(x); n(x)

7. The graph of the parent function is reflected across the y-axis and is translated 9 units up.

9. The parent function is shrunk vertically and becomes less steep.

11. The graph of the parent function is reflected across the y-axis and is less steep. The graph is then translated 5 units up.

13. The function after reflecting the graph of $f(x) = x - 1$ will be $h(x) = -x - 1$. Then translating the graph 4 units down will result in the graph of the function $g(x) = -x - 5$.

15. The graph will be translated 2 units down if the number of parents is reduced to 0. The graph becomes steeper than the parent function if the number of teachers is raised to 1 for every 3 students. The new function is $g(x) = \dfrac{1}{3}x$.

17. A. Sample Answer:

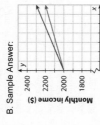

The salesperson's base monthly salary is increased.

B. Sample Answer:

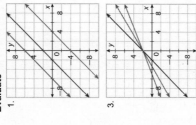

The salesperson's commission percentage rate is decreased.

19. a. $y = 12x + 20$

b. $y = 12x + 30$

c. Both functions have the same slope but have a different value for b.

21. The student has confused the values of b and m. In this situation, the cost to play each week, m, has increased. This will cause the graph to become steeper. The cost to join the league, b, decreases. This will cause the graph to shift down.

23. The graph of $y = x + 3$ is a horizontal translation of the graph of $y = x + 1$, 2 units to the left.

25. The graph will be translated three units to the left.

Selected Answers

UNIT 3 Selected Answers

MODULE 6

Lesson 6.5 Comparing Properties of Linear Functions

Your Turn

3. The rate of change is 7.

4. The slope of $f(x)$ is greater than the slope of $g(x)$. The y-intercepts are different because the y-intercept of $f(x)$ is 0 and the y-intercept of $g(x)$ is 11.

6. The rate of change for $g(t)$ is 0.25 centimeters per day, which is less than the rate of change for $f(t)$, which is 0.3 centimeters each day.

Evaluate

1. The initial value of $f(x)$ is 5.
The initial value of $g(x)$ is 8.
The range of $f(x)$ is all real numbers such that $5 \le f(x) \le 11$.
The range of $g(x)$ is all real numbers such that $8 \le g(x) \le 11$.

3. The initial value of $f(x)$ is 1.
The initial value of $g(x)$ is 10.
The range of $f(x)$ is all real numbers such that $1 \le f(x) \le 7$.
The range of $g(x)$ is all real numbers such that $7 \le g(x) \le 10$.

5. The initial value of $f(x)$ is 22.
The initial value of $g(x)$ is 17.
The range of $f(x)$ is all real numbers such that $22 \le f(x) \le \dfrac{53}{2}$.
The range of $g(x)$ is of all real numbers such that $17 \le g(x) \le \dfrac{37}{2}$.

7. $f(x) = 6x + 20$
$g(x) = 5x - 8$
The domain and range of the functions are the same.
The slope of $f(x)$ is greater than $g(x)$.
The y-intercept of $f(x)$ is greater than the y-intercept of $g(x)$.

9. $J(t) = 32t + 25$, $0 \le t \le 5.5$
$B(t) = 30t + 40$, $0 \le t \le 4$
The domain for both functions is real numbers that start at 0, but $B(t)$ ends at 4 and $J(t)$ ends at 5.5.
The range for $B(t)$ is the set of all real numbers $B(t)$, where $40 \le B(t) \le 160$. The range for $J(t)$ is the set of all real numbers $J(t)$, where $25 \le J(t) \le 201$.
The slope of $J(t)$ is greater than the slope of $B(t)$.
The y-intercept of $B(t)$ is greater than the y-intercept of $J(t)$.

11. $g(t) = 19t$, $0 \le t \le 6$
$m(t) = 37.5t$, $0 \le t \le 8$
The domain for both functions is real numbers that begin at 0, but $g(t)$ ends at 6 and $m(t)$ ends at 8.
The range for $g(t)$ is real numbers $g(t)$, where $0 \le g(t) \le 114$. The range for $m(t)$ is real numbers $m(t)$, where $0 \le m(t) \le 300$.
The slope of $m(t)$ is greater than the slope of $g(t)$
The y-intercept of both functions is 0.

13. a. 0(0, 0); 4(20, 4); 8(40, 8);
0.10d + 10
10(0, 10); 12(20, 12) 14(40, 14)

b.

c. Sample answer: the graphs have different slopes and different y-intercepts.

15. a. The domain of $g(t)$ is the set of real numbers t, where $20 \le t \le 30$.
The domain of $e(t)$ is the set of real numbers t, where $15 \le t \le 25$.
The range of $g(t)$ is the set of real numbers $g(t)$, where $250 \le g(t) \le 375$.
The range of $e(t)$ is the set of real numbers $e(t)$, where $195 \le e(t) \le 325$.

b. Gillian earns less per hour than Emily. Gillian earns from $250 to $375 per week and Emily earns from $195 to $325 per week.

17. The domains, ranges, slopes and y-intercepts are the same for $f(x)$ and $g(x)$. They represent the same function.

-1, 3, 7, 11

19. The functions do not have the same domain. The domain of $f(x)$ includes all real numbers between 6 and 8, while the domain of $g(x)$ is {6, 7, 8}.

21. a. The domain and range of both $f(x)$ and $g(x)$ is the set of all real numbers.

b. The slope is $-\dfrac{1}{4}$ and the y-intercept is 6 for $f(x)$, and the slope is $-\dfrac{1}{4}$ and the y-intercept is -6 for $g(x)$.

23. The functions do not have to be identical. Each could have a different domain.

25. The domains are not the same because the domain of $f(x)$ is all real numbers between 0 and 5, while the domain of $g(x)$ is only the integers between 0 and 5. The range of $f(x)$ is $-17 \le f(x) \le 18$ while the range of $g(x)$, {-17, -10, -3, 4, 11, 18}. Both have a y-intercept of -17. The function $f(x)$ is linear, but the function $g(x)$ is not linear because it is not a line or a line segment.

UNIT 3 Selected Answers

MODULE 7

Lesson 7.1 Modeling Linear Relationships

Your Turn

5. An equation for the sales goal is $5s + w = 100$, where s is the number of sandwiches sold, and w is the number of waters sold. If no waters are sold, the shop must sell 20 sandwiches.

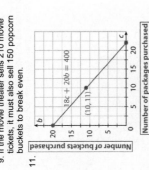

Evaluate

1. A linear equation that describes this problem is $3b + r = 24$, where b is the number of loaves of bread sold, and r is the number of rolls sold.

3. If 12 rolls are sold, the baker must sell 4 loaves of bread.

5.

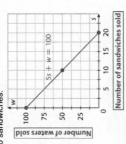

7. A linear equation that describes this problem is $10t + 6p = 3000$, where t is the number of tickets sold, and p is the number of containers of popcorn sold.

9. If the movie theater sells 210 movie tickets, it must also sell 150 popcorn buckets to break even.

11.

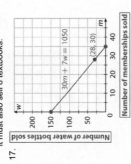

13. A linear equation that describes the problem is $80t + 4n = 800$, where t is the number of textbooks sold, and n is the number of notebooks sold.

15. If the bookstore sells 40 notebooks, it must also sell 8 textbooks.

17.

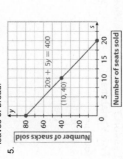

19. The units for a card are points.

21. 20; 8; 20

23. Sample answer: The point represents a slight profit after a two-month period of time.

25. Juan assigned the wrong coefficient to x. He should have written the equation $y = 6x + 35$.

UNIT 3 Selected Answers

MODULE 7

Lesson 7.2 Using Functions to Solve One-Variable Equations

Your Turn

5. The solution must be between 16 and 17 hours. From the graph, the solution to the nearest tenth is 16.7 hours.

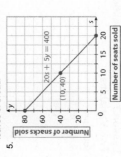

8. From the table, the value of the account would be 0 between 2 and 3 months. From the graph, the x-intercept is about 2.2.

Evaluate

1. The two actors will charge the same amount of money after 5 days.

3. The two designers will charge the same amount of money after 2 hours.

5. The two mimes will charge the same amount of money after 3 hours.

7. The two coaches will charge the same amount of money after 4 hours.

9. in 4 months

11. in 6 months

13. in 5 months

15. At 5 hours, both waiters will charge the same amount, $51.25.

17. At approximately 7.7 hours, both singers will charge the about the same amount.

19.*about 8.3

21. about 2.9

23. $45x + 12 = 244x + 234$
$13x + 48 = 24x + 47$
$71x + 145 = 43x + 17$
$8x + 11 = 55x + 123$

25. Quadrants II and III are never used for a real-world problem in one variable.

Selected Answers

Selected Answers

25. a. $2.5x + 0.75y \leq 22$

b. $2.5\,(3) + 0.75y \leq 22$

$7.5 + 0.75y \leq 22$

$0.75y \leq 14.5$

$y \leq 19\frac{1}{3}$

They can travel $19\frac{1}{3}$ miles.

c. $x \leq 5.8$

Since the number of passengers has to be a whole number, at most 5 friends can ride in the taxi.

UNIT 3 Selected Answers

MODULE 7

Lesson 7.3 Linear Inequalities in Two Variables

Your Turn

3.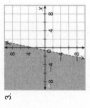

4.

5. $\leq$

6. $5.5x + 2y \leq 18$

$y \leq 9 - \frac{11}{4}x$

Evaluate

1. Boundary line: $y = \frac{4}{5}x - 6$ above; boundary included

3. Boundary line: $y = \frac{3}{2}x - \frac{5}{2}$ above; boundary included

5.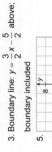

7.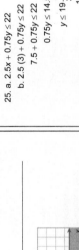

9. Boundary line: $y = -\frac{1}{5}x + 5$ below; boundary not included

11. Boundary line: $y = \frac{1}{2}x + \frac{1}{3}$ above; boundary included

13.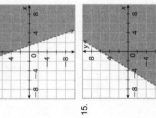

15.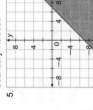

17. $5x + 4y \leq 120$
(10, 8)

19. $y \leq -\frac{2}{3}x - 6$

21. $\geq$

23. No; When you solve this equation for y, you must divide both sides of the equation by a negative number, which reverses the inequality symbol. $y \leq -\frac{5}{2} + \frac{3}{2}x$, so you must shade below the line.

UNIT 4 Selected Answers

MODULE 8

Lesson 8.1 Two-Way Frequency Tables

Your Turn

5. 45, 15, 15, 18, 21, 6, 60

6. 74, 26, 77, 23, 100

8. 21, 25, 51, 46, 27, 27, 100

9. 43, 57, 101

Evaluate

1. categorical, quantitative

3. 69, 61, 62, 24, 44, 130

5. 38, 36, 13, 32, 29, 74

7. 50, 49, 48, 34, 17, 99

9. 95, 90, 81, 67, 37, 185

11. 44, 42, 21, 32, 33, 86

13. 96 boys: 104 of the 200 students were girls, so 200 − 104 = 96 of them were boys.

15. 10, 14, 62, 29, 89, 18, 14, 150; Students own more laptops.

17. 12, 13, 55, 29, 40, 31 Students preferred mint the most and vanilla the least.

19. 7, 22, 5, 12, 14, 14, 40

21.

Gender	Likes Tennis		
	Yes	No	Total
Girl	15	35	50
Boy	30	20	50
Total	45	55	100

23. B, C, D, F

25. a. Charles only surveyed boys, so there is only one categorical variable: color. You need two categorical variables to make a two-way frequency table.

b. He can make a table, but he cannot complete it. There are now two categorical variables, color and gender, but there is not enough information about the girls' preferences. In addition to the information provided, you need to know how many girls were surveyed or how many prefer red to complete the table.

UNIT 4 Selected Answers

MODULE 8

Lesson 8.2 Relative Frequency

Your Turn

4. $\frac{12}{40} = 0.3$ or 30%

5. $\frac{21}{40} = 0.525$ or 52.5%

6. $\frac{14}{21} = 0.667$ or 66.7%

7. $\frac{7}{19} = 0.368$ or 36.8%

9. Possible answer: 36.8% of respondents who like aerobics like weight lifting, while 52.5% of all respondents like weight lifting. Those who like aerobics are less likely than those who do not like aerobics to like weight lifting.

Evaluate

1. 0.083, 0.208, 0.042, 0.25, 0.333, 0.083, 1

3. 0.333

5. 23.5%, 23.5%, 47.1%, 29.4%, 23.5%, 52.9%, 52.9%, 47.1%, 100%

7. 52.9%; a marginal relative frequency

9. $\frac{4}{15} \approx 0.267$

11. 64%, 18%, 82%, 10%, 8%, 18%, 74%, 26%, 100%

13. 74%

15. $\frac{12}{27} \approx 44.4\%$

17. $\frac{12}{27} = 0.444$

19. $\frac{160}{185} = 86.5\%$

21. No, both genders are equally likely to be taking Spanish.

23. The conditional relative frequency of obeying the law, given knowledge of the law, is 86.5% (from Exercise 19), and the percent of all drivers who obey the law is 82%. There is a slight difference, though both frequencies are greater than 50%, so there is a possible association between knowledge of the law and obeying it.

25. Millie missed the fact that there are more boys than girls in the survey, so a 50% conditional relative frequency of a student who likes an orange being a girl is higher than the 43.5% marginal relative frequency of girls in the whole survey. This means girls in the survey actually had a higher preference for oranges than boys.

27. Cole should have divided 45 by the total number of drivers that obey the law, 205.

Selected Answers

UNIT 4 Selected Answers

MODULE 9

Lesson 9.1 Measures of Center and Spread

Your Turn

4. The mean is 76, and the median is 72.5.

5. The mean is 89.3, and the median is 90.

7. The median is 26. Range = 31 − 21 = 10
IQR = 28 − 24 = 4

8. The median is 73. Range = 79 − 68 = 11
IQR = 75 − 71 = 4

10. The standard deviation is approximately 3.1.

11. The standard deviation is approximately 2.8.

Evaluate

1. No. The day the trip took 24 minutes will skew the value of the average to be too high.

3. mean ≈ 137.2
The median is 139.5.

5. mean = 522.008 or $522.01
The median is $427.23.

7. mean = 14.25
The median is 13.5.

9. Range = 4
The interquartile range is 3.

11. Range = 27
The interquartile range is 17.5.

13. Range = 5
The interquartile range is 2.

15. Range = 8
The interquartile range is 5.5

17. The standard deviation is $\sqrt{140.5} \approx 11.9$.

19. The standard deviation is $\sqrt{57,258} \approx 239.3$.

21. The standard deviation is approximately 2.1.

23. The standard deviation is $\sqrt{41.33} \approx 6.4$.

25. No, the highest and lowest values both increase by 10, so their difference, the range, will stay the same.

27. The data set must have an even number of values. When a data set has an odd number of values, the median is always found in the data set.

UNIT 4 Selected Answers

MODULE 9

Lesson 9.2 Data Distributions and Outliers

Your Turn

3. 72 is not an outlier.

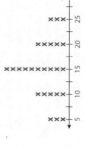

Pitching Speeds (mph)

4. 43.81, 39.5, 30, 16.42, 40.67, 42, 21.5, 10.84

The mean is lower for Arizona, which means that, on average, members of Congress tend to be younger in Arizona than in Illinois. However, the median is lower in Illinois, which means that there are more young members of Congress in Illinois despite the differences in average age. Finally, the IQR and standard deviation are lower for Arizona, which means that the ages of members of Congress are closer together than they are in Illinois.

9.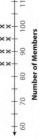

Team A

Number of Free Throws

Team B

Number of Free Throws

The data for team A show a symmetric distribution. This means that the number of free throws shot is evenly distributed about the mean.

The data for team B show a distribution skewed to the right. This means that fewer than half of the team members shot a number of free throws that were greater than the mean.

Evaluate

1. Possible plot shown.

Number of Members

3. Possible plot shown.

Number of Feet

5. Possible plot shown.

Number of Students

7. Possible plot shown.

Bowling Scores

9. 38.1, 37, 18.5, 9.27, 43.1, 45, 20.5, 11.33

11. 2.6, 2.9, 1.2, 0.59, 2.6, 2.6, 1.1, 0.57

13. Possible plot shown.

Team A

Miles

The data for team A show a symmetric distribution. The distances run are evenly distributed about the mean.

Team B

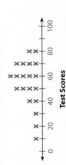

Miles

The data for team B show a right-skewed distribution. This means that fewer than half of the team members ran a distance greater than the mean.

15. symmetric
right-skewed
symmetric
symmetric
symmetric

17. An extreme value such as the max or min value can be an outlier, but by definition, no value between Q_1 and Q_3 can be an outlier.

19.

Test Scores

The data for school A show a symmetric distribution. This means that the test scores were evenly distributed about the mean test score.

Test Scores

The data for school B show a left-skewed distribution. This means that more than half of the classes received a test score that was above the mean.

UNIT 4 Selected Answers

MODULE 9

Lesson 9.3 Histograms and Box Plots

Your Turn

4. Possible table and histogram shown.

Height Interval	Frequency
63–66	2
67–70	4
71–74	6
75–78	2
79–82	1

Heights of Basketball Players

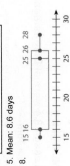

Height

5. Mean: 8.6 days

8.

9.

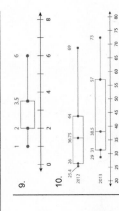

10.

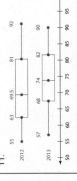

The medians are close, but the median for 2013 is slightly greater than that of 2012. The ranges are close, but the interquartile range for 2013 is much greater than that of 2012.

11.

The median for 2013 is much greater than the median for 2012. Both the range and interquartile range for 2013 are less than those of 2012, so the ages were more varied in 2012.

Evaluate

1. The vertical axis shows the frequency for each interval, and the horizontal axis shows the bowlers' scores.

3. 30 bowlers competed.

UNIT 4 Selected Answers

MODULE 9

Lesson 9.4 Normal Distributions

Your Turn

6. 99.7% of these pennies have a mass between 2.44 g and 2.56 g.

7. 47.5% of these pennies have a mass between 2.46 g and 2.50 g.

8. 97.5%

9. 99.85%

Evaluate

1. 97.5%

3. 50%

5. 16%

7. 50%

9. 95% of the data fall between 7 and 13.

11. 2.5%

13. 2.5%

15. 95%

17. a. 7

b. 6 data points are below, and 3 are above.

c. No; the data set has 3 values greater than the mean but 6 values less than the mean, so the distribution is not symmetric.

19. 97.5%

21. 71 inches is 8 inches below the mean of 79 inches.
The standard deviation is 4 inches, so 8 inches below the mean is 2 standard deviations below the mean.

23. $39.4 - 34.8 = 4.6$; so 34.8 is 2 standard deviations below the mean.
$41.7 - 39.4 = 2.3$; so 41.7 is 1 standard deviation above the mean.
The percent of adult males with an upper-arm length between 34.8 cm and 41.7 cm is $13.5\% + 34\% + 34\% = 81.5\%$.

25. Use a normal distribution to approximate characteristics for the "Heads Up" experiment because the distribution is symmetric and bell-shaped.

---

5. Possible tables and histograms shown.

7.

9. Mean: = 3.19

11. Mean: ≈ 48.8

13.

15.

17.

19.

Carlos scored a maximum number of 19 points in a game versus Mario's maximum of 15. Between these two games, Carlos scored 4 more points than Mario.

21. Because the minimum and the first quartile are the same, the box plot would have no "whisker" on the left side.

UNIT 4 Selected Answers

MODULE 10

Lesson 10.1 Scatter Plots and Trend Lines

Your Turn

2. r is close to 0.5.

3. r is close to −1.

5. The equation of this line of fit is $y = \frac{8}{5}x + 2$.

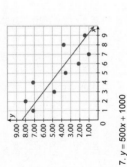

Tree height (ft.) — Year after planting

7. 18ft

9. The variables are the number of minutes of exercise per week and the HDL cholesterol count. The greater number of minutes of exercise per week corresponds to a greater HDL cholesterol count, so there is a positive correlation. Causation is possible but it is unknown which variable causes the other. Having a greater HDL cholesterol count may cause a person to exercise more per week. It is also possible that another factor causes a greater number of minutes of exercise per week and a higher HDL cholesterol count.

Evaluate

1. The value of r for this data is closest to −0.5.

3. The value of r for this data is closest to 1.

5. Possible answer: $y = -\frac{4}{5}x + \frac{42}{5}$ or $y = -0.8x + 8.4$

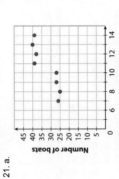

7. $y = 500x + 1000$

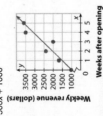

Weekly revenue (dollars) — Weeks after opening

9. 4.8 Interpolation

11. $5000 Extrapolation

13. The variables are the population of wolves and the population of deer. The greater population of wolves corresponds to a lower population of deer, so there is a negative correlation. Causation is possible but it is unknown which variable causes the other.

15. The variables are the number of musical instruments played and the grade in math. The greater number of musical instruments played corresponds to a higher grade in math, so there is a positive correlation. Causation is possible, but it is unknown which variable causes the other.

17. The variables are the number of centimeters of snowfall and the number of visitors. The greater number of centimeters of snowfall corresponds to a higher number of visitors, so there is a positive correlation. Causation is possible but it is unlikely that the number of visitors affects the amount of snowfall during a season. However, it is also possible that other factors affect both variables.

19. The slope is a measure of fuel efficiency in miles per gallon, and a value of 35 is a reasonable value for a car. The intercept is how many miles she can drive with 0 gallons of gas and should be 0. However, fits are not perfect and an intercept of 0.83 is close enough to 0 to be considered reasonable.

21. a.

Number of boats — Years since 2000

b. There is no correlation between the variables. The number of boats in the marina is neither increasing nor decreasing over time. The trend since 2011 is for the number of boats to be around 40.

23. No, even if one variable affects the second variable, as the first variable increases, the second variable could increase and then decrease.

25. No, if the two data sets have very different lines of fit, the combined r value could be closer to zero than either of the original sets.

UNIT 4 Selected Answers

MODULE 10

Lesson 10.2 Fitting a Linear Model to Data

Your Turn

7.

x	y (Actual)	y Predicted by y = x + 4	Residual for y = x + 4	y Predicted by y = x + 4.2	Residual for y = x + 4.2
1	4	5	−1	5.2	−1.2
2	7	6	1	6.2	0.8
3	8	7	1	7.2	0.8
4	6	8	−2	8.2	−2.2

$y = x + 4$: $(-1)^2 + (1)^2 + (1)^2 + (-2)^2 = 7$

$y = x + 4.2$: $(-1.2)^2 + (0.8)^2 + (0.8)^2 + (-2.2)^2 = 7.56$

The sum of the squared residuals for $y = x + 4$ is smaller, so it provides a better fit.

10. The temperature in Trenton, New Jersey, should be around 40 degrees Fahrenheit. The correlation coefficient is about −0.99, which indicates a very strong correlation. Therefore, the line of best fit is reliable for estimating temperatures within the same range of latitudes.

Evaluate

1. $y = x + 5$: $(-6)^2 + (-6)^2 + (-6)^2 + (-6)^2 = 36 + 36 + 36 + 36 = 144$

$y = x + 4.9$: $(-5.9)^2 + (-5.9)^2 + (-5.9)^2 + (-5.9)^2 = 139.24$

The sum of the squared residuals for $y = x + 4.9$ is smaller, so it provides a better fit for the data.

3. $y = 3x + 4$: $(-8)^2 + (-8)^2 + (-18)^2 + (-22)^2 = 936$

$y = 3x + 4.1$: $(-8.1)^2 + (-8.1)^2 + (-18.1)^2 + (-22.1)^2 = 947.24$

The sum of the squared residuals for $y = 3x + 4$ is smaller, so it provides a better fit.

5. $y = 3x + 1.2$: $(-6.2)^2 + (-8.2)^2 + (-15.2)^2 + (-22.2)^2 = 829.56$

$y = 3x + 1$: $(-6)^2 + (-8)^2 + (-15)^2 + (-22)^2 = 809$

The sum of the squared residuals for $y = 3x + 1$ is smaller, so it provides a better fit.

7. $y = 2x + 1$: $(-2)^2 + (-3)^2 + (-9)^2 + (-12)^2 = 238$

$y = 2x + 1.4$: $(-2.4)^2 + (-3.4)^2 + (-9.4)^2 + (-12.4)^2 = 259.44$

The sum of the squared residuals for $y = 2x + 1$ is smaller, so it provides a better fit.

9. $y = x + 3$: $(-4)^2 + (-2)^2 + (-2)^2 + (-8)^2 = 88$

$y = x + 2.6$: $(-3.6)^2 + (-1.6)^2 + (-1.6)^2 + (-7.6)^2 = 75.84$

The sum of the squared residuals for $y = x + 2.6$ is smaller, so it provides a better fit.

11. $y = 2x + 3.1$: $(-3.1)^2 + (1.9)^2 + (-2.1)^2 + (0.9)^2 = 18.44$

$y = 2x + 3.5$: $(-3.5)^2 + (1.5)^2 + (-2.5)^2 + (0.5)^2 = 21$

The sum of the squared residuals for $y = 2x + 3.1$ is smaller, so it provides a better fit.

13. $y = x + 5$: $(1)^2 + (-2)^2 + (3)^2 + (-1)^2 = 15$

$y = 1.3x + 5$: $(0.7)^2 + (-2.6)^2 + (2.1)^2 + (-2.2)^2 = 16.5$

The sum of the squared residuals for $y = x + 5$ is smaller, so it provides a better fit.

15. $y \approx -0.95x + 71.14$

The correlation coefficient is about −0.997 ≈ −1, which indicates a very strong correlation. Therefore, the line of best fit is reliable for estimating temperatures within the same range of latitudes.

The temperature in Panama City should be around 63 degrees Fahrenheit.

17. $y \approx -0.86x + 85.19$

The correlation coefficient is about −0.999 ≈ −1, which indicates a very strong correlation. Therefore, the line of best fit is reliable for estimating temperatures within the same range of latitudes.

The temperature in Jerusalem should be around 58 degrees Fahrenheit.

19. Since the residuals are large, the line $y = 0.5x + 20$ is not a good fit.

21. 2, 2.3, −2.6, 3.6

23. This means that either all of the residuals are either the same as each other or the opposite of each other.

UNIT 5 Selected Answers

MODULE 11

Lesson 11.1 Solving Linear Systems by Graphing

Your Turn

3.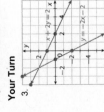

4. The solution is (−2, 2).

5. The solution is (−2, 4).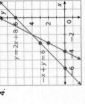

6. The two lines coincide, so there are infinitely many solutions.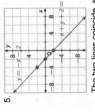

The two lines don't intersect, so there is no solution.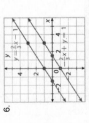

7. about (2.5, −1.5).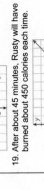

8. about (−1.5, −1.5).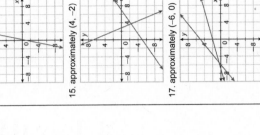

10. $\begin{cases} y = 4x + 10 \\ y = 3x + 15 \end{cases}$

The lines appear to intersect at (5, 30). The cost will be the same for renting 5 movies, and that cost will be $30.

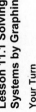

Evaluate

1. No, if the graphs of the two equations are coincident lines, the system has infinitely many solutions.

---

3. (−6, 4)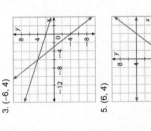

5. (6, 4)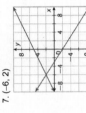

7. (−6, 2)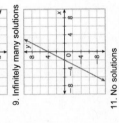

9. Infinitely many solutions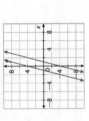

11. No solutions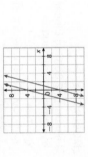

13. Infinitely many solutions

15. approximately (4, −2)

17. approximately (−6, 0)

19. After about 45 minutes, Rusty will have burned about 450 calories each time.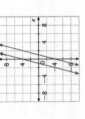

UNIT 5 Selected Answers

MODULE 11

Lesson 11.2 Solving Linear Systems by Substitution

Your Turn

5. The solution of the system is (3, 5).

7. infinitely many solutions

8. no solutions

10. The second boat will catch up in 8.5 hours, and they will be 187 km from their port.

Evaluate

1. a. The solution is (8, 12).

   b.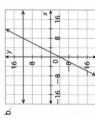

   The solutions are the same.

3. The solution is (−2, −4).

5. The solution is (3, −2).

7. The solution is (2, 5).

9. There are infinitely many solutions.

11. There is no solution.

13. There is no solution.

15. Both plans would cost $78 if 6 gigabytes of data are used.

17. Michelle will catch up in 80 minutes, and they will be 35.2 km from the start.

19. a. Both providers will cost $629 in 7 months.

    b. Satellite would be less expensive because it costs less per month than cable and 12 months is after 7 months.

21. Adrienne invested $600 in account A and $1300 in account B.

23. $3x + 5y = 90$; The solution is (20, 6).

25. No, the equation of a horizontal line is in the form $y = a$ and the equation of a vertical line is in the form $x = b$. The horizontal line equation has no x-term and the vertical line equation has no y-term.

21. Account A have a balance at least as great as Account B in about 37 months. The balance will be about $750.

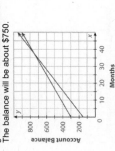

23. Inconsistent systems have the same slope, but different y-intercepts. This system is consistent and independent.

25. The variable x represents the number of weeks from now, and y represents the total number of miles run by each person. after 2 weeks; 17 miles

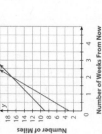

UNIT 5 Selected Answers

MODULE 11

Lesson 11.3 Solving Linear Systems by Adding or Subtracting

Your Turn

5. Solution: $(-2, -4)$

6. Solution: $(3, -2)$

7. $0 = 5$

The resulting equation is false, so the system has no solutions.

8. $0 = 0$

The resulting equation is true, so the system has infinitely many solutions.

9. The length is 21 inches and the width is 10 inches.

Evaluate

1. The addition method would be best because the y-values are opposites, or additive inverses.

3. Solution: $(1, 5)$

5. Solution: $\left(-\dfrac{1}{3}, \dfrac{5}{3}\right)$

7. Solution: $(-2, -2)$

9. Solution: $(6, 2)$

11. $0 = -5$

No solution

13. $0 = 0$

Infinitely many solutions

15. $0 = 0$

Infinitely many solutions

17. The length of the garden is 48 feet and the width is 12 feet.

19. Max exercises 13 hours a week and Sasha exercises 7 hours a week.

21. The pool is 32 feet long and 15 feet wide.

23. You can add $-2x + 2y = 10$ since subtracting is the same as adding the opposite.

25. Julia will pay $48.

UNIT 5 Selected Answers

MODULE 11

Lesson 11.4 Solving Linear Systems by Multiplying First

Your Turn

4.

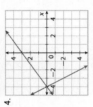

5.

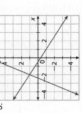

The solution is $(-4, 0)$.

The solution is $(-2, 1)$.

6. Adult tickets cost $12 each and student tickets cost $8 each.

Evaluate

1. a. 24

   b. $y = 2x + 4$

3. a. 24

   b. $y = -\dfrac{4}{7}x + \dfrac{8}{7}$

5. $-8x + 16y = 32$

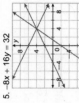

7. The solution is $(3, 2)$.

9. The solution is $(-1, 4)$.

11. The solution is $(14, 23)$.

13. The measures of the angles are 138° and 42°.

15. Jamian bought 15 bagels and 25 donuts.

17. Bath towels cost $32 each and hand towels cost $18 each.

19. a. Yes
    b. Yes
    c. No
    d. No
    e. No
    f. No

21. You could multiply the first equation by 4 and the second equation by -11, and then add the resulting equations to eliminate y. You might choose to eliminate x instead because the numbers you would multiply by are easier to work with.

23. a. $4 on shelf A and $2 on shelf B
    b. You save $8 when buying the first package.

    You save $7 for buying the second package.

Selected Answers

UNIT 5 Selected Answers

MODULE 12
Lesson 12.1 Creating Systems of Linear Equations

Your Turn

3. Both will charge $860 for 10 months.

4. Both will charge $136 for 3 months.

5. Both companies charge $285 for 7 cubic yards of pea stone.

6. Both companies charge $148 for 7 hours of surfboard rental.

7. initial cost $57; $y = x + 57$
   initial cost $15; $y = 7x + 15$
   Solution: $(7, 64)$
   The solution represents $64 that both cabins cost to rent for 7 days.

8. The slope represents the rate of change of the dependent variable with respect to the independent variable.

9. All three methods will give approximately the same solution, but not always. A table of prices may have a small degree of rounding to make prices more appealing, either rounding to the nearest ten or hundred or making the prices end in 9.99 or 9.95. A system created from a graph may not be as exact if specific points are not identified.

10. Translate verbal statements or tables of prices into linear equations that can then be used as a system of equations to solve a problem.

Evaluate

1. The slope of $f(t)$ represents the speed of the first vehicle and the y-intercept represents the starting distance. The slope of $g(t)$ represents the speed of the second vehicle and the y-intercept represents the starting distance.

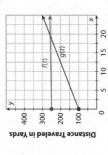

5. The boys club sold 48 bags of hardwood mulch and 128 bags of pine bark mulch.

7. Both iSpice and Spice Magic charge $98 for 8 pounds of paprika.

9. Both Company 1 and Company 2 charge $136.25 for cleaning 25 garments. For cleaning fewer than 25 garments, Company 2 is less expensive.

11. Both Restaurant Warehouse and Supply Side charge $1020 for 25 cases of paper towels.

13. The system is $\begin{cases} f(t) = 7t + 22 \\ g(t) = 10t + 4 \end{cases}$.
    The solution $(6, 64)$ represents a total of 64 gallons of water by both functions after 6 minutes.

15. The system is $\begin{cases} f(t) = 17.5t + 125 \\ g(t) = 35t + 20 \end{cases}$.
    The solution $(6, 230)$ represents a total cost of $230 from either company for making a film with a running time of 6 minutes.

17. The student used an incorrect ordered pair to calculate the model for Company B. One possible correct ordered pair is $(4, 834)$, not $(2, 834)$. So, $m = 206$ and $b = 10$.

19. Sample answer: Plot the data. Then use linear regression to find a function modeling each set of data. Finally, set up and solve a linear system with the two models.

UNIT 5 Selected Answers

MODULE 12
Lesson 12.2 Graphing Systems of Linear Inequalities

Your Turn

3.
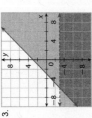

$(2, -4)$ and $(-2, -8)$ are solutions.
$(0, 0)$ and $(-8, -4)$ are not solutions.

4.
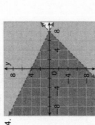

$(0, 0)$ and $(-8, -4)$ are solutions.
$(-2, 8)$ and $(8, -6)$ are not solutions.

5.
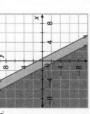

The solutions are the same as the solutions of $y \le -2x - 3$.

6.
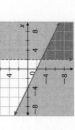

This system has no solution.

Evaluate

1. a. b
   b. d
   c. b
   d. e
   e. d
   f. a

3. The point is a solution of the system.

5. The point $(6, -2)$ is a solution.

7.
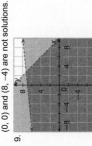

$(4, -4)$ and $(8, -8)$ are solutions.
$(0, 0)$ and $(8, -4)$ are not solutions.

9.

$(0, 0)$ and $(4, 4)$ are solutions.
$(0, 8)$ and $(8, 6)$ are not solutions.

UNIT 5 Selected Answers

MODULE 12

Lesson 12.3 Modeling with Linear Systems

Your Turn

4. $550x + 390y = 8160$

$x + y = 16$

So, the company bought 12 computers and 4 printers.

5. $x + y \geq 6$

$2x + 3y \leq 27$

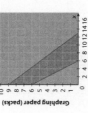

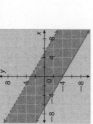

6. $x + y \geq 7$

$2x + 3y \leq 30$

The point (8, 4) is not a solution because it does not lie in the region shared by the two inequalities and it does not satisfy both inequalities.

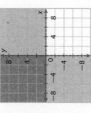

The point (8, 4) is a solution because it lies in the region shared by the two inequalities, and it does satisfy both inequalities.

Evaluate

1. $x + y = 12$

$75x + 50y = 775$

3. $a + c = 30$

$200a + 300c = 7000$

5. $n + d = 12$

$0.05n + 0.10d = 1$

7. $d + b = 8$

$2.29d + 5.69b = 28.52$

9. $80x + 45y = 645$

$x + y = 12$

Jan spent 3 months at the first gym and 9 months at the second gym.

11. $150a + 225c = 5100$

$a + c = 31$

The adult tickets cost $25 and the child tickets cost $6.

13. $0.05n + 0.10d = 1.20$

$n + d = 15$

Nicole has 6 nickels and 9 dimes.

15. $2.65d + 6.29b = 30.46$

$d + b = 6$

Meaghan bought 2 packages of hot dogs and 4 packages of hamburgers.

17. $8x + 10y \leq 70$

$x + y \geq 4$

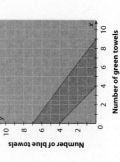

11.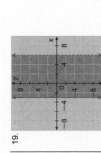

(0, 0) and (10, −6) are solutions.

(8, −2) and (8, 6) are not solutions.

13.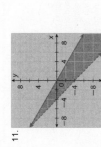

(4, −6) and (6, −1) are solutions.

(0, 0) and (8, 6) are not solutions.

15.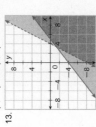

The solutions are the same as the solutions of $y < 3x - 8$.

17.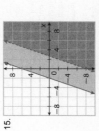

The solutions are the same as the solutions of $y \geq \frac{5}{4}x$.

19.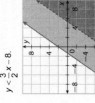

The solutions are all points between the parallel lines, including points on the line $x \geq -3$.

21. The solutions are all points between the parallel lines and on the solid line.

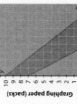

23. $\begin{cases} y > 0 \\ x < 0 \end{cases}$

25. The student switched the inequality signs when graphing them. The correct solution set is the same as the solutions of $y < \frac{3}{2}x - 8$.

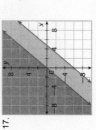

The possible solutions are points with integer coordinates that lie in the shaded region shared by the inequalities and on the solid boundary lines. One possible solution is Angelique can buy 4 green towels and 2 blue towels.

19. $3x + 8y \geq 48$
$x + y \leq 12$

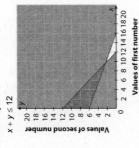

Values of first number

The possible solutions lie in the shaded region shared by the inequalities and on the solid boundary lines. One possible solution is the first number is 4 and the second number is 6.

21. $14x + 12y \leq 720$
$x + y \geq 40$

Selling Tickets

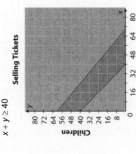

The possible solutions are points with integer coordinates that lie in the shaded region shared by the inequalities and on the solid boundary lines. One possible solution is 24 adults and 32 children.

23. The student graphed the system of equations as a system of inequalities. When graphing a system of equations, the solution is the point of intersection. So the solution should be (4, 2).

25. One possible solution is Chris buys 3 daisy arrangements and 3 rose arrangements. Substitute these values into the inequalities to check for reasonableness.
Since the number of arrangement is greater than 4 and the cost is less than $39, the answer is reasonable.

UNIT 5 Selected Answers

MODULE 13

Lesson 13.1 Understanding Piecewise-Defined Functions

Your Turn

3. $f(-2) = 2$; $f(-0.4) = 0.4$; $f(3.7) = 10.4$; $f(5) = 25$

6.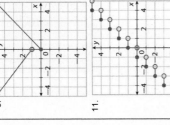

7. $p(d) = \begin{cases} 0.014d & \text{if } 0 \leq d \leq 100 \\ 0.024d - 1 & \text{if } 100 < d \leq 500 \\ 0.034d - 6 & \text{if } 500 < d \end{cases}$

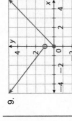

Annual Interest ($) / **Balance ($100s)**

8. $y = \begin{cases} \frac{1}{2}x - 4 & \text{if } x \leq 4 \\ 4 & \text{if } x > 4 \end{cases}$

Evaluate

1. $f(-4) = -4$ and $f(-3.1) = -4$; $f(1.2) = 1$; $f(2.8) = 2$

3. $f(-4) = -5$; $f(-2.9) = -0.9$; $f(1.9) = 10.61$

5. $f(-3) = -\frac{2}{3}$; $f(-1) = -1$; $f(1) = 1$

7. $f(-2.8) = 9$; $f(-1.2) = 4$; $f(0.4) = 0$; $f(1.6) = 1$

9.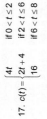

11.

13. $y = \begin{cases} x + 1 & \text{if } x < 0 \\ 2 & \text{if } x \geq 0 \end{cases}$

15. $y = \begin{cases} 1 & \text{if } x < 0 \\ 2 & \text{if } x \geq 0 \end{cases}$

17. $c(t) = \begin{cases} 4t & \text{if } 0 < t \leq 2 \\ 2t + 4 & \text{if } 2 < t \leq 6 \\ 16 & \text{if } 6 < t \leq 8 \end{cases}$

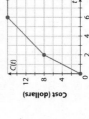

Cost (dollars) / **Time (hours)**

0; 4; 8; 10; 12
14; 16; 16; 16

19. $c(t) = \begin{cases} 30t & \text{if } 0 < t \le 3 \\ 35t - 15 & \text{if } 3 < t \le 8 \\ 265 & \text{if } 8 < t \le 10 \end{cases}$

Cost (dollars) vs *Time (hours)*

60; 125; 195; 265; 265

21. A. D: all real numbers $x > 0$,
   R: $y = 0$ and $y = 5$
   B. D: all real numbers x,
   R: all real numbers $y \ge 0$
   C. D: all real numbers x,
   R: all real numbers $y \ge 0$
   D. D: all real numbers x,
   R: all real numbers $y \ge -8$
   E. D: all real numbers x,
   R: $y = 1$

23. Clara needed to include the weight already lost when writing an equation for the second and third rays of the piecewise function. The correct answer is

$W(t) = \begin{cases} 0.5t & \text{if } 0 \le t \le 1 \\ 0.7t - 0.2 & \text{if } 1 \le t < 4 \\ 0.1t + 2.2 & \text{if } t \ge 4 \end{cases}$

25. A piecewise function is not a function if it contains a vertical line because a vertical line contains more than one y-value for a single x-value, which goes against the definition of a function.

UNIT 5 Selected Answers

MODULE 13

Lesson 13.2 Absolute Value Functions and Transformations

Your Turn

5.
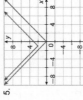

7. $h = -2$
   $k = 1$
   $g(x) = |x + 2| + 1$

10.
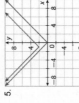

11.
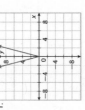

Evaluate

1.
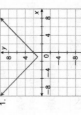

3.
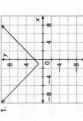

5.

7. $g(x) = |x - 5| + 1$

9. $g(x) = |x + 2| + 3$

11. $g(x) = |x - 2| + 1$

13. Domain = {real numbers}
    Range = $\{y | y \ge -1\}$

15. Domain = {real numbers}
    Range = $\{y | y \ge 1\}$

17.

UNIT 5 Selected Answers

MODULE 13

Lesson 13.3 Solving Absolute Value Equations

Your Turn

3. $x = 18$ or $x = -22$

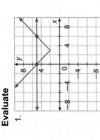

4. $x = \frac{8}{3}$ or $x = \frac{4}{3}$

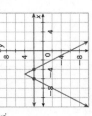

5. No solution

6. $x = \frac{3}{2}$

Evaluate

1.

$x = 0$ or $x = 6$

3.

$x = -4$ or $x = -6$

5.

$x = \frac{3}{2}$ or $x = -\frac{3}{2}$

7.

$x = \frac{5}{3}$ or $x = \frac{4}{3}$

9. No solution

11.

$x = -4$

13. No solution

15.

$x = -\frac{3}{2}$ or $x = -\frac{11}{2}$

17. The buoys should be placed at 150 ft and 330 ft from the left-hand shore.

19. The points are $(-2, 0)$ and $(8, 0)$.

21. No Solution. Terry does not have a spot on his roof that is 30 feet high.

23. $3|x - 2| - 5|x - 2| = -7$ Subtraction Property of Equality

$(3 - 5)|x - 2| = -7$ Distributive Property

$|x - 2| = \frac{7}{2}$ Division Property of Equality

$x - 2 = \frac{7}{2}$ or $x - 2 = -\frac{7}{2}$ Definition of absolute value

$x = \frac{11}{2}$ or $x = -\frac{3}{2}$ Addition Property of Equality

25. Answers will vary. Sample answer: time, distance, height, length, speed

19.

21. A. $h = 2$, $k = 2$, and $a = 3$

B. $h = 3$, $k = 4$, and $a = -0.2$

C. $h = -6$, $k = -1$, and $a = -5$

D. $h = -2$, $k = -7$, and $a = 0.5$

E. $h = 0$, $k = 3$, and $a = 0.8$

23. $d(x) = |x - 69.3|$; the graph of $d(x)$ is a horizontal translation of the graph of $f(x) = |x|$ to the right 69.3 units.

25. $g(x) = \frac{2}{5}|x|$

27.

$f(x) = \frac{3}{4}|x - 4| + 6$ or $f(x) = 0.75|x - 4| + 6$

UNIT 5 Selected Answers

MODULE 13
Lesson 13.4 Solving Absolute Value Inequalities

Your Turn

6. $x \geq -3$ and $x \leq 1$.

9. The solution is $x \leq 4$ or $x \geq 10$.

$$-4 \;-2 \;\;0 \;\;2 \;\;4 \;\;6 \;\;8 \;10 \;12 \;14 \;16 \;18$$

10. The solution is $-4 < x < 1$.

$$-5 \;-4 \;-3 \;-2 \;-1 \;\;0 \;\;1 \;\;2 \;\;3 \;\;4 \;\;5$$

11. The inequality that models the situation is $|w - 13.8| \leq 0.1$.
The range of acceptable weights of the cereal (in ounces) is $13.7 \leq w \leq 13.9$.

Evaluate

1. The integers from −5 to 5 that satisfy the inequality are −5, −4, −3, −2, −1, 3, 4, and 5.

$$-5 \;-4 \;-3 \;-2 \;-1 \;\;0 \;\;1 \;\;2 \;\;3 \;\;4 \;\;5$$

3.

The solution is $-3 \leq x \leq 3$.

5.

The solution is $-2 < x < 2$.

7. C. The solution is $x < -2$ or $x > 2$.

9. B. The solution is $-\dfrac{5}{2} < x < \dfrac{1}{2}$.

11.

$$-2 \;-1 \;\;0 \;\;1 \;\;2 \;\;3 \;\;4 \;\;5 \;\;6 \;\;7 \;\;8 \;\;9$$

The solution is $x < 3$ or $x > 4$.

13. The solution is $x \leq -5$ or $x \geq -3$.

$$-9 \;-8 \;-7 \;-6 \;-5 \;-4 \;-3 \;-2 \;-1 \;\;0 \;\;1$$

15. all real numbers

$$-10 \;-8 \;-6 \;-4 \;-2 \;\;0 \;\;2 \;\;4 \;\;6 \;\;8 \;10$$

17. The range of house temperatures (in degrees Fahrenheit) is $66 \leq T \leq 70$.

19. The range of ages (in years) that a squirrel lives is $5 \leq a \leq 8$.

21. The range of typical speeds (in miles per hour) is $25 \leq s \leq 35$.

23. The student identified where the graph of $g(x)$ lies above the graph of $f(x)$, but the student should have identified where the graph of $f(x)$ lies above the graph of $g(x)$ because the inequality has the form $f(x) > g(x)$. So, the solution of the inequality is $x < -3$ or $x > 5$.

UNIT 6 Selected Answers

MODULE 14
Lesson 14.1 Understanding Rational Exponents and Radicals

Your Turn

3. 2

4. 7

5. 8

6. 24

Evaluate

1. $\dfrac{1}{100}$

3. $\dfrac{1}{16}$

5. 1

7. 9

9. 5

11. 343

13. 89

15. $\dfrac{1}{5}$

17. 1

19. $1\dfrac{2}{3}$

21. 8

23. 1000 cm³

25. It needs to be moving at about 1400 miles per hour.

27. No, he is not correct. It is only even numbers in the denominator of an exponent that cannot be evaluated with a negative base. With an odd denominator and an even numerator in the exponent, there is no problem. The correct answer is:

$$(-8)^{\frac{2}{3}} = \left(\sqrt[3]{-8}\right)^2$$
$$= \left(\sqrt[3]{(-2)^3}\right)^2$$
$$= (-2)^2$$
$$= 4$$

29. No one: Xia mistook the "2" for the root instead of the "3," and negative numbers have cube roots. Yen's last parenthesis should be after the "3." The calculator found the −2 power, then divided by 3. Zane's first step is wrong. When he rewrote the power as positive, he mistakenly also wrote the reciprocal of the exponent when he wrote the reciprocal of the quantity. Also, the negative sign should be inside the parentheses. He could have more simply solved the problem like this:

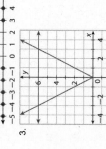

$$\left(-\dfrac{1}{64}\right)^{-\frac{2}{3}} = \left(\dfrac{1}{-\frac{1}{64}}\right)^{\frac{2}{3}} = (-64)^{\frac{2}{3}} = \left(\sqrt[3]{-64}\right)^2 = (-4)^2 = 16.$$

UNIT 6 Selected Answers

MODULE 14

Lesson 14.2 Simplifying Expressions with Rational Exponents and Radicals

Your Turn

5. $x^4 y^3$

6. $\sqrt{x}$

8. $\dfrac{2}{x^4}$

9. $\dfrac{1}{3x^4}$

10. a. $3 \times 10^8 = fw \Rightarrow f = \dfrac{3 \times 10^8}{w}$

b. $f = \dfrac{3 \times 10^8}{w} = (3 \times 10^8)w^{-1}$

c. The frequency of violet light with a wavelength of 400 nanometers is 7.5×10^{14} cycles per second.

11. 36π
The sphere has surface area of 36π cm squared. While the units are different, the number is the same.

Evaluate

1. Addition and multiplication are commutative. A subtraction table would not be symmetric because subtraction is not commutative.

3. $81x^4$

5. $64y^8$

7. $2x\sqrt[4]{2y}$

9. 0

11. $\dfrac{5}{x^4}$

13. $8x^3$

15. $x^8 y^5$

17. $xy^2 z^4$

19. $\dfrac{1}{x^2}$

21. $x^8 \sqrt[4]{y^{17}} = x^8 y^4 \sqrt[4]{y}$

23. The brain of the mouse has an approximate mass of 2 grams.

25. They should plan on buying approximately 1.59a liters of paint.

27. a. Rational
b. Irrational
c. Rational
d. Irrational
e. Irrational
f. Rational
g. Rational

29. Because both $\dfrac{1}{a}$ and c are rational numbers and the set of rational numbers is closed under multiplication, $b = \left(\dfrac{1}{a}\right) \cdot c$ must be rational. This contradicts the given statement that b is irrational, so the product of a nonzero rational number and an irrational number must be irrational.

31. $\left(\sqrt[3]{x}\right)^3 = x$ Definition of cube root

$\left(x^k\right)^3 = x$ Substitute x^k for $\sqrt[3]{x}$.

$x^{3k} = x^1$ Power of a Power Property
Equate the exponents.

$3k = 1$

$k = \dfrac{1}{3}$ Solve for k.

Because x^k was substituted for $\sqrt[3]{x}$,

$x^{\frac{1}{3}} = \sqrt[3]{x}$.

UNIT 6 Selected Answers

MODULE 15

Lesson 15.1 Understanding Geometric Sequences

Your Turn

5. $4 = r$
The next three terms are 1280, 5120, and 20,480.

6. $-\dfrac{1}{3} = r$
The next three terms are $\dfrac{1}{9}, -\dfrac{1}{27},$
and $\dfrac{1}{81}$.

8. The ball bounces about 2.5 meters on the 4th bounce.

Evaluate

1. $3 = r$
The next three terms of the sequence are 405, 1215, and 3645.

3. $5 = r$
The next three terms of the sequence are 2500, 12,500, and 62,500.

5. $-\dfrac{1}{2} = r$
The next three terms of the sequence are 4.5, −2.25, and 1.125.

7. $3 = r$
The next three terms of the sequence are 810, 2430, and 7290.

9. $2 = r$
The next three terms of the sequence are 288, 576, and 1152.

11. 4096

13. −0.405

15. 192.08 centimeters

17. 24,000 ants

19. $4230.14

21. e. B, C, D, and E all apply.

23. The value that Alicia gave is correct, but it is not the only correct value. x could also be −8, 8, −8, 8, −8, … is also a geometric sequence, so Miguel is correct.

UNIT 6 Selected Answers

MODULE 15

Lesson 15.2 Constructing Geometric Sequences

Your Turn

5. Recursive rule: $f(1) = 7$ and
$f(n) = f(n - 1) \cdot 2$ for $n \geq 2$
Explicit rule: $f(n) = 7 \cdot 2^{n-1}$

6. Recursive rule: $f(1) = 128$ and
$f(n) = f(n - 1) \cdot 0.25$ for $n \geq 2$
Explicit rule: $f(n) = 128 \cdot (0.25)^{(n-1)}$

9. Find the common ratio.

Numbers	Algebra
6, 12, 24, 48, 96, …	$f(1), f(2), f(3), f(4), f(5), …$
Common ratio = 2	Common ratio = r

Write a recursive rule.

Numbers	Algebra
$f(1) = 6$ and	Given $f(1)$,
$f(n) = f(n - 1) \cdot 2$	$f(n) = f(n - 1) \cdot r$
for $n \geq 2$	for $n \geq 2$

Write an explicit rule.

Numbers	Algebra
$f(n) = 6 \cdot 2^{n-1}$	$f(n) = f(1) \cdot r^{n-1}$

11. $a^n = \frac{1}{3}\left(\frac{1}{3}\right)^{n-1}$

13. Yes; you can divide the second term by the common ratio to get the first term. Then, you can substitute the first term and the common ratio into the general explicit rule to get the explicit rule for the sequence.

14. Use the first term of the sequence and the common ratio as given in the recursive rule. Use these values in the form $f(n) = f(1) \cdot r^{n-1}$.

Evaluate

1. Recursive rule: $a_1 = 2$ and $a_n = 3a_{n-1}$ for $n \geq 2$; Explicit rule: $a_n = 2(3)^{n-1}$

3. Recursive rule: $a_1 = 5$ and $a_n = 4a_{n-1}$ for $n \geq 2$; Explicit rule: $a_n = 5 (4)^{n-1}$

5. Recursive rule: $a_1 = 9$ and $a_n = \frac{2}{3} a_{n-1}$ for $n \geq 2$; Explicit rule: $a_n = 9\left(\frac{2}{3}\right)^{n-1}$

7. Recursive rule: $a_1 = 4$ and $a_n = 6a_{n-1}$ for $n \geq 2$; Explicit rule: $a_n = 4(6)^{n-1}$

9. Recursive rule: $a_1 = 3$ and $a_n = 7a_{n-1}$ for $n \geq 2$; Explicit rule: $a_n = 3(7)^{n-1}$

11. Recursive rule: $a_1 = 6$ and $a_n = 5a_{n-1}$ for $n \geq 2$; Explicit rule: $a_n = 6(5)^{n-1}$

13.

	Numbers	Algebra
Common ratio:	10, 40, 160, 640, 2560, …	$f(1), f(2), f(3), f(4), f(5), …$
	Common ratio = 4	Common ratio = r
Recursive rule:	$f(1) = 10$ and	Given $f(1)$,
	$f(n) = f(n - 1) \cdot 4$ for $n \geq 2$	$f(n) = f(n - 1) \cdot r$ for $n \geq 2$
Write an explicit rule:	$f(n) = 10 \cdot 4^{n-1}$	$f(n) = f(1) \cdot r^{n-1}$

15.

	Numbers	Algebra
Common ratio:	18, 90, 450, 2250, 11,250, …	$f(1), f(2), f(3), f(4), f(5), …$
	Common ratio = 5	Common ratio = r
Recursive rule:	$f(1) = 18$ and	Given $f(1)$,
	$f(n) = f(n - 1) \cdot 5$ for $n \geq 2$	$f(n) = f(n - 1) \cdot r$ for $n \geq 2$
Explicit rule:	$f(n) = 18 \cdot 5^{n-1}$	$f(n) = f(1) \cdot r^{n-1}$

17. $a_n = 187.5(0.8)^{n-1}$

19. $a_n = 256\left(\frac{1}{2}\right)^{n-1}$

21. $a_n = 1000\left(\frac{6}{5}\right)^{n-1}$

23. $a_n = 57(1.07)^{n-1}$

25. a. $f(n) = 3.2 \cdot 1.04^{n-1}$; the cost in year 1, $f(1)$, is \$3.20. An increase of 4% means the cost is multiplied by 1.04, that is, $f(n) = f(n - 1) \cdot 1.04$

b. \$3.60; it represents the cost of the box of cereal in year 4. $f(4) = 3.2 \cdot 1.04^3 \approx 3.60$

27. Francis used the square of the common ratio. For the given sequence, $a_2 = 64$, and $a_4 = 16$, so $16 = 64 \cdot r^2$. Then $r^2 = \frac{1}{4}$ and $r = \frac{1}{2}$.

UNIT 6 Selected Answers

MODULE 15

Lesson 15.3 Constructing Exponential Functions

Your Turn

4.

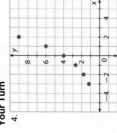

x	f(x)	(x, f(x))
-3	$\left(\frac{32}{27}\right) = 1\frac{5}{27}$	$\left(-3, 1\frac{5}{27}\right)$
-2	$\left(\frac{16}{9}\right) = 1\frac{7}{9}$	$\left(-2, 1\frac{7}{9}\right)$
-1	$\left(\frac{8}{3}\right) = 2\frac{2}{3}$	$\left(-1, 2\frac{2}{3}\right)$
0	4	(0, 4)
1	6	(1, 6)
2	9	(2, 9)

6. $t(n) = 0.2 \cdot 2^n$

7. $f(x) = 10 \cdot 5^x$

Evaluate

1.

3.

x	f(x)	(x, f(x))
-2	$\frac{1}{32}$	$\left(-2, \frac{1}{32}\right)$
-1	$\frac{1}{8}$	$\left(-1, \frac{1}{8}\right)$
0	$\frac{1}{2}$	$\left(0, \frac{1}{2}\right)$
1	2	(1, 2)
2	8	(2, 8)

x	f(x)	(x, f(x))
-1	9	(-1, 9)
0	6	(0, 6)
1	4	(1, 4)
2	$2\frac{2}{3}$	$\left(2, 2\frac{2}{3}\right)$
3	$1\frac{7}{9}$	$\left(3, 1\frac{7}{9}\right)$
4	$1\frac{5}{27}$	$\left(4, 1\frac{5}{27}\right)$

5. $v(n) = 100 \cdot 5^n$

7. $p(n) = 5(0.99)^n$

9. $f(x) = 10^x$

11. $f(x) = \frac{24}{25} \cdot \left(\frac{5}{6}\right)^x$

13. $f(x) = 14 \cdot \left(\frac{1}{7}\right)^x$

15. $f(x) = 3 \cdot 2^x$

17. $h(n) = 9 \cdot \left(\frac{2}{3}\right)^n$

19. The ratio between successive function values is $\frac{4}{5}$, so this is consistent with an exponential function.

$3200 \cdot \frac{4}{5} = 2560$

21. $p(n) = \left(\frac{1}{2}\right)^n$

23. No; Biff's test scores do not increase by a constant ratio. Instead they go up by 2 points each test. His scores are not consistent with an exponential function.

© Houghton Mifflin Harcourt Publishing Company

UNIT 6 Selected Answers

MODULE 15

Lesson 15.4 Graphing Exponential Functions

Your Turn

5. $a = 2$
$b = 2$
y-intercept: (0, 2)
End Behavior: As $x \to \infty$, $y \to \infty$ and as $x \to -\infty$, $y \to 0$.

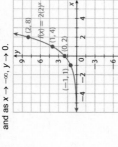

7. $a = -3$
$b = 3$
y-intercept: (0, -3)
End Behavior: As $x \to \infty$, $y \to -\infty$ and as $x \to -\infty$, $y \to 0$.

9. $a = 3$
$b = 0.5$
y-intercept: (0, 3)
End Behavior: As $x \to \infty$, $y \to 0$ and as $x \to -\infty$, $y \to \infty$.

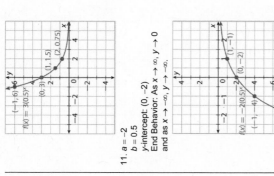

11. $a = -2$
$b = 0.5$
y-intercept: (0, -2)
End Behavior: As $x \to \infty$, $y \to 0$ and as $x \to -\infty$, $y \to -\infty$.

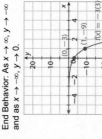

Evaluate

1. $a = 2$
$b = 3$
y-intercept: (0, 2)

3. $a = -5$
$b = 0.5$
y-intercept: (0, -5)

---

5. $a = 6$
$b = 3$
y-intercept: (0, 6)

7. $a = 7$
$b = 0.9$
y-intercept: (0, 7)

9. $a = 3$
$b = 3$
y-intercept: (0, 3)
End Behavior: As $x \to \infty$, $y \to \infty$ and as $x \to -\infty$, $y \to 0$.

11. $a = -6$; $b = 0.7$
y-intercept: (0, -6)
End Behavior: As $x \to \infty$, $y \to 0$ and as $x \to -\infty$, $y \to -\infty$.

13. $a = 5$; $b = 2$
y-intercept: (0, 5)
End Behavior: As $x \to \infty$, $y \to \infty$ and as $x \to -\infty$, $y \to 0$.

15. $a = 9$; $b = 3$
y-intercept: (0, 9)
End Behavior: As $x \to \infty$, $y \to \infty$ and as $x \to -\infty$, $y \to 0$.

17. $a = 7$; $b = 0.4$
y-intercept: (0, 7)
End Behavior: As $x \to \infty$, $y \to 0$ and as $x \to -\infty$, $y \to \infty$.

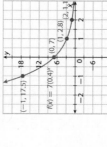

19. Domain: $\{x|-\infty < x < \infty\}$, Range: $\{y|y > 0\}$

Domain: $\{x|-\infty < x < \infty\}$, Range: $\{y|y > 0\}$

Domain: $\{x|-\infty < x < \infty\}$, Range: $\{y|y < 0\}$

Domain: $\{x|-\infty < x < \infty\}$, Range: $\{y|y < 0\}$

Domain: $\{x|-\infty < x < \infty\}$, Range: $\{y|y > 0\}$

21. The ball will be rolling at a rate of about 10 inches per minute after 20 minutes.

23. The graph of the exponential function will be a horizontal line at $y = a$.

25. $f(x) = 4(5)^x$

UNIT 6 Selected Answers

MODULE 15

Lesson 15.5 Transforming Exponential Functions

Your Turn

3.

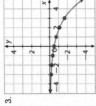
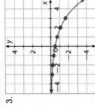

End behavior:
$f(x) \to -\infty$ as $x \to \infty$
$f(x) \to 0$ as $x \to -\infty$
y-intercept: −0.5

4.

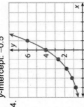

End behavior:
$f(x) \to \infty$ as $x \to \infty$
$f(x) \to 0$ as $x \to -\infty$
y-intercept: 4

6.

End behavior:
$f(x) \to 0$ as $x \to \infty$
$f(x) \to \infty$ as $x \to -\infty$
y-intercept: 2

7.

End behavior:
$f(x) \to 0$ as $x \to \infty$
$f(x) \to -\infty$ as $x \to -\infty$
y-intercept: −0.25

9.

The y-intercept of $f(x)$ is 1.
The y-intercept of $g(x)$ is 5.
The y-intercept of $g(x)$ is 4 more than that of $f(x)$ because $g(x)$ is a vertical translation of $f(x)$ up by 4 units.

10.

The y-intercept of $f(x)$ is 2.
The y-intercept of $g(x)$ is −1.
The y-intercept of $g(x)$ is 3 less than that of $f(x)$ because $g(x)$ is a vertical translation of $f(x)$ down by 3 units.

Evaluate

1. $f_2(x)$

3. $f_1(x)$

5. vertical compression, no reflection

7. vertical compression and reflection

9. 0.7

11. −0.5

13. $g(x)$ is translated up by 5 units from $f(x)$.

15. $g(x)$ is translated down by 3 units from $f(x)$.

17. $h(n) = 5(0.8)^n$

19. The function is translated up by 3 feet.
$k = 3$ $h(n) = 10(0.8)^n + 3$

21. a

23. b

25. a vertical compression

27. The y-intercept equals a for all values of $b > 1$ because $ab^0 = a$. As the value of b increases, the graph rises more quickly as x increases to the right of 0, and it falls more quickly as x decreases to the left of 0.

29. $f_1(x)$ decreases more quickly. $f_1(x)$ has the greater decay rate (6% rather than 2%), so you would expect $f_1(x)$ to decrease more quickly as x increases to the right of 0.

UNIT 6 Selected Answers

MODULE 16

Lesson 16.1 Using Graphs and Properties to Solve Equations with Exponents

Your Turn

6. $x = 3$

7. $x = 2$

8. The wolf population will reach 500 in approximately 5.7 years.

9. The deer population will reach 300 in approximately 4.8 years.

Evaluate

1. Yes, $3(2)^x = 96$ becomes $(2)^x = 32$ after dividing both sides of the equation by 3 and 32 is an integer power of 2.

In general, the input-output tables for $f(x)$ and $g(x)$ have integers in the domain and the values in the range are easy to calculate.

3. Yes, you can solve algebraically if you can rewrite the equation to have the same base on both sides and then equate the exponents. If not, then you can always solve graphically by treating each side of the equation as a function and graphing the two functions to see where the graphs intersect.

5. $x = 2$

7. $x = 2$

9. $x = 3$

11. $x = 2$

13. $x = 3$

15. $x = 2$

17. The population will reach half of its original value in approximately 9.6 years.

19. The population of the fish will double in 18 years.

The population will be 80 in 54 years $(3 \cdot 18)$.

21. Both accounts will reach $5200 in about 4 years. Switching won't make much difference.

23. a. The population will reach 300,000 in approximately 5.7 years.

b. The second city's population will reach 300,000 sooner.

25. The equation $\frac{1}{3}(3)^x = 243$ has a greater solution. Since the values of the powers of 3 increase less quickly than the values of the powers of 9, the value of x in $\frac{1}{3}(3)^x = 243$ will be greater than the value of x in $\frac{1}{3}(9)^x = 243$.

Selected Answers

UNIT 6 Selected Answers

MODULE 16

Lesson 16.2 Modeling Exponential Growth and Decay

Your Turn

10. After 8 years, the coin will be worth approximately $3.51.

The domain is the set of real numbers t such that $t \geq 0$.

The range is the set of real numbers y such that $y \geq 3$.

The y-intercept is the value of the coin when $t = 0$, which is the value of the coin when it was sold.

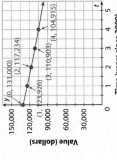

Value (dollars) — Time (years)
(2, 3.12), (4, 3.25), (6, 3.38), (8, 3.51), (0, 3)

13. After 7 years, the boat will be worth approximately $9,198.35. The domain is the set of real numbers t such that $t \geq 0$. The range is the set of real numbers y such that $0 < y \leq 17,800$. The y-intercept is 17,800, the value of y when $t = 0$, which is the original value of the boat.

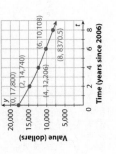

Value (dollars) — Time (years since 2006)
(0, 17,800), (2, 14,740), (4, 12,206), (6, 10,108), (8, 8370.5)

15. $A(t) = 150(0.3)^t$

$B(t) = 5(3)^t$

The value of Stock A is going down over time. The value of Stock B is going up over time. The initial value of Stock A is greater than the initial value of Stock B. However, after about 1.5 years, the value of Stock B becomes greater than the value of Stock A.

Evaluate

1. Domain: $\{x \mid -\infty < x < \infty\}$ Range: $\{y \mid y > 0\}$
End behavior: As $x \to -\infty$, $y \to 0$ and as $x \to \infty$, $y \to \infty$ Asymptote: $y = 0$

3. Domain: $\{x \mid -\infty < x < \infty\}$ Range: $\{y \mid y > 0\}$
End behavior: As $x \to -\infty$, $y \to 0$ and as $x \to \infty$, $y \to \infty$ Asymptote: $y = 0$

5. $309,845.72

7. $349.47

9. $59,068.21

11. 28,584

13. $y = a(1 - r)^t = 192,000 (0.93)^t$
$y = 192,000(0.93)^9 \approx 99,918.93$
After 9 years, the boat will be worth approximately $99,918.93.
Domain: $\{t \mid t \geq 0\}$
Range: $\{y \mid 0 < y \leq 192,000\}$
The y-intercept is 192,000, the original value of the boat in 2004.

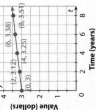

Value (dollars) — Time (years since 2004)
(0, 192,000), (4, 143,626), (8, 107,440), (12, 80,370)

15. $y = a(1 - r)^t = 51.5(0.93)^t$
$y = 51.5(0.93)^9 \approx 26.8$
After 9 years, the airplane will be worth approximately $26.8 million.
Domain: $\{t \mid t \geq 0\}$ Range: $\{y \mid 0 < y \leq 51.5\}$
The y-intercept is 51.5, the original value in millions of dollars of the airplane in 2004.

Value (millions of dollars) — Time (years since 2004)
(0, 51.5), (2, 44.5), (4, 38.5), (6, 33.3), (8, 28.8), (10, 24.9)

17. $y = a(1 - r)^t = 1232(0.938)^t$
$y = 1232(0.938)^7 \approx 787.10$
After 7 years, the couch will be worth approximately $787.10.
Domain: $\{t \mid t \geq 0\}$ Range: $\{y \mid 0 < y \leq 1232\}$
The y-intercept is 1232, the original value of the couch in 2007.

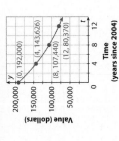

Value (dollars) — Time (years since 2007)
(0, 1232.00), (2, 1083.97), (4, 953.72), (6, 839.19), (8, 738.30)

19. $y = a(1 - r)^t = 131,000(0.946)^t$
$y = 131,000(0.946)^{10} \approx 75,194$
After 10 years, the house will be worth about $75,194.
Domain: $\{t \mid t \geq 0\}$
Range: $\{y \mid 0 < y \leq 131,000\}$

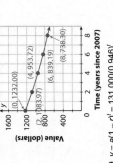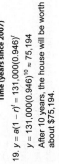

The y-intercept is 131,000, the original value of the house in 2009.

Value (dollars) — Time (years since 2009)
(0, 131,000), (1, 123,926), (2, 117,234), (3, 110,903), (4, 104,915)

21. The value of $A(t)$ is decreasing. The value of $B(t)$ is increasing. The initial value of $A(t)$ is greater than the initial value of $B(t)$. However, after about .7 units, the value of $B(t)$ becomes greater than the value of $A(t)$.

23. The value of $A(t)$ is decreasing. The value of $B(t)$ is increasing. The initial value of $A(t)$ is greater than the initial value of $B(t)$. However, for t greater than about 2.7 units, the value of $B(t)$ becomes greater than the value of $A(t)$.

25. a. 3123
b. 76
c. 45

27. The value of the function will never be 0 because the right side of the function is a product of positive numbers. Although the value can become extremely close to 0, it can never equal 0.

UNIT 6 Selected Answers

MODULE 16

Lesson 16.3 Using Exponential Regression Models

Your Turn

8. 7,394

The model is significantly off from the actual value.

9. 61

Evaluate

1. The initial amount of ibuprofen was approximately 400 units. 71% of the previous hour's amount of ibuprofen remains after each hour.

3. The club will have 3000 members in about 18 months.

5. Student A metabolizes caffeine at a rate of 12.95% per hour and will have 10 mg of caffeine in the blood after approximately 26.6 hours.

Student B metabolizes caffeine at a rate of 13.09% per hour and will have 10 mg of caffeine in the blood after approximately 26.2 hours.

Student C metabolizes caffeine at a rate of 12.62% per hour and will have 10 mg of caffeine in the blood after approximately 27.4 hours.

7. $y = 10,000(0.665)^x$

9. $y = 7(1.552)^x$

11. $y = 11(1.010)^x$

13. $P(t) = 5.00(1.03)^t$

15. a. Non-exponential
    b. Increasing exponential
    c. Decreasing exponential
    d. Decreasing exponential
    e. Increasing exponential
    f. Non-exponential

17. too low; The growth rate is too small and the initial value is too large. Entering a lower value for the last population value would have caused the modeled curve to shift "down" at the end and thus "up" at the beginning.

UNIT 6 Selected Answers

MODULE 16

Lesson 16.4 Comparing Linear and Exponential Models

Your Turn

6. Job B will have a higher salary than Job A after 50 months.

8. Increasing function; exponential regression; $y = 41.93(1.20)^x$; $r \approx 1$, and analysis of the residual plot would also suggest a good fit.

Evaluate

1. exponential; $E(t) = 454(1.03)^t$; increasing

3. exponential; $C(t) = 450(1.05)^t$; increasing

5. exponential; $H(t) = 546, 768(.97)^t$; decreasing

7. exponential; $I(t) = 236, 000(1.064)^t$; increasing

9. Employee B will make more than Employee A after 35 years.

11. Stock B will be worth more than Stock A after 91 months.

13. Employee B will make more than Employee A after 50 years.

15. Stock B will be worth more than Stock A after 7 months.

17. Since the values of y are increasing over time, the function is increasing. Since both the factor changes and the difference changes are close together, neither choice is clearly better than the other. Linear regression equation is $y = 1.5x + 29.3$, with $r \approx 0.993$; exponential regression equation is $y \approx 29.53 (1.05)^x$, with $r \approx 0.994$. Both residual plots would show a good fit.

19. Since the values of y are increasing over time, the function is increasing. Since the factor changes are relatively close together and the difference changes are not, an exponential regression should be used; regression equation:
    $y \approx 12.3 (1.71)^x$; $r \approx 1$, and analysis of the residual plot would also suggest a good fit.

21. The salary chosen would depend on the length of the job and the percentage change in salary offered.

23. Since the exponential growth function eventually curves upward while a linear growth function continues in a straight line with a positive slope, the exponential growth function will eventually exceed the linear growth function.

Selected Answers

Selected Answers

Selected Answers

UNIT 7 Selected Answers

MODULE 17

Lesson 17.1 Understanding Polynomial Expressions

Your Turn

5. 4th degree trinomial

6. 3rd degree binomial

7. $x^5 + 4x^3 - 3x^2 + 10$, 1

8. $-3y^8 + 18y^5 + 10y$, -3

9. $-15x^2 + 10x + 13$, -15

10. $12b^4 + 6b^3 - 3b^2 + 2b$, 12

12. $-q^3p^2 + pq$

13. $11a - 3b - 14c$

14. $2a^2 - 4ab + 26$

15. The area of the new kitchen is 486 square feet.

16. The rocket will rise 564 feet.

Evaluate

1. $(5 + 4x^6)$ 2x is a monomial, but $(5 + 4x^2)$ 2x is a binomial.

3. 3rd degree trinomial

5. 7th degree trinomial

7. 1st degree binomial

9. $-40x^3 - 2x^2 + 2x$; -40

11. $4b^2 - 2b$; 4

13. $-y^3$

15. $xyz\left(\sqrt[3]{2} + 2^5\right) + 2^{10}xy$

or

$\left(32 + \sqrt[3]{2}\right)xyz + 1024xy$

17. The well is 190 feet deep.

19. a. When t is 60 seconds, the colony at 20°C will have 60 more bacteria.

b. The colony at 20°C will have 600 more bacteria after 10 minutes.

c. The colony at 20°C will have 60,000 more bacteria after 1000 minutes. After $t = 0$, the 20°C colony will always have t more bacteria.

21. Enrique treated the numbers like variables, but their degree is 0. The degree of the polynomial is 2 from the exponent of 2 over the x in the term $2^2 x^2$.

23. By counterexample, $x + y$ is not a monomial, although it is a sum of monomials.

25. $\frac{1}{2}h(h + 8)$; area = 192 cm²

UNIT 7 Selected Answers

MODULE 17

Lesson 17.2 Adding Polynomial Expressions

Your Turn

3. $3x^2 - x - 1$

4. $z^3 - z^2 - 1$

5. $5x - 7$

6. $-10x^2 + 2$

7. $-5x^3 + x + y + 2$

8. $4y + 11$

10. $(t^2 + 4t + 4) + (t^2 + 2t + 4)$

The total number of cells is $2t^2 + 6t + 8$ for time t.

11. $(3x^2 + 7x - 5) + (5x^2 - 4x + 11)$

$8x^2 + 3x + 6$

Evaluate

1. This is a lot like the horizontal method, but you can make an argument for either. The algebra in the Explore is written using the horizontal method.

3. 0

5. $x^2 + 2x + 2$

7. $x^2 + y$

9. -1

11. $-2cab^2 + ab^2 + 2b^2$

13. $\left(2 + \sqrt[3]{2}\right)ab$

15. $(8g^2 + 3g - 4) + (6g^2 + 2g - 1)$

$14g^2 + 5g - 5$

17. $14a + 2b$

170

19. $-x$

21. Jane is correct. Jill distributed the 2 incorrectly. She should have written

$= (2x^2 + x) + 2(-x^2 + x)$

$= 2x^2 + x - 2x^2 + 2x$

$= 3x$

23. Sample answer: $\frac{1}{x}$ is the quotient of two monomials but is not a monomial.

25. Sample answers:

$(3m^2 + m) + (m^2 + m) = 4m^2 + 2m$

$= 5(m^2 + m) - (m^2 + 3m)$

$= (5m^2 - m^2) + (5m - 3m) = 4m^2 + 2m$

UNIT 7 Selected Answers

MODULE 17

Lesson 17.3 Subtracting Polynomial Expressions

Your Turn

3. $5x^2 - x + 1$

4. $-4z - 2$

5. $11y - 8$

6. $y^2 - 2x$

7. $7z + 17$

9. The 25 °C culture has $4t$ more cells at time t. There are 60 more cells in the 25 °C culture after 15 minutes.

10. $-g^2 + 5g + 1$

At a rate of 5 gallons per minute, the change of the volume will be 1 gallon per minute.

Evaluate

1. $(x^2 + x - 3) + (-x^2 - 2x - 1)$

$x^2 + (-x^2) + x + (-2x) - 3 + (-1)$

$-x - 4$

3. $-3x^4 + 3x^2$

5. $-x^2 - 2x + 2$

7. $m + 2z + y$

9. $-4x^2 + 2x + 2$

11. $-2cab^2 + ab^2 + 2b^2$

13. $-ab$

15. $y^2 - 99,500$

If the company can only make 300 bicycles, they will lose money.

17. $\ell^2 \left(1 - \dfrac{\pi}{4}\right)$

19. The volume of the cube is $(6c)^3 = 216c^3$.

21. c is incorrect because the −1 was distributed incorrectly. e is incorrect because $0.05x + 300$ was added instead of subtracted. a, b, and d are correct because they are algebraically equivalent.

23. You can write $(3y^2 + 8y - 16) - P_1 = y^2 - 4$ for some polynomial P_1. Just rewrite the equation and solve for P_1. By the Subtraction Property of Equality, $(3y^2 + 8y - 16) - P_1 = y^2 - 4$ is equivalent to $(3y^2 + 8y - 16) - (y^2 - 4) = P_1$.

Simplify the left side.

$(3y^2 + 8y - 16) - (y^2 - 4) = P_1$

$(3y^2 + 8y - 16) + (-y^2 + 4) = P_1$

$(3y^2 - y^2) + 8y + (-16 + 4) = P_1$

$2y^2 + 8y - 12 = P_1$

Hallie subtracted the quantity $2y^2 + 8y - 12$.

25. −b; c; b; c

UNIT 7 Selected Answers

MODULE 18

Lesson 18.1 Multiplying Polynomial Expressions by Monomials

Your Turn

4. $54x^{11}y^8z^5$

6. $10a^2b^2 + 6a^3b + 12a^3 + 2a^2$

7. $x = 5$ inches is the closest possible answer.

$x + 4 = 5 + 4 = 9$

The width should be 5 inches and the length should be 9 inches.

Evaluate

1. $6x^3$

3. $18x^{10}$

5. $21x^3y^4$

7. $32xy^7z^2$

9. $x^5 + x^4$

11. $x^5 + 2x^4 + 5x^3$

13. $4x^5y + 8x^2y^3 + 12x^3y^2$

15. $6x^5y^2 + 18x^4y^3 + 18x^2y^5$

17. When $x = 10$, the area is 130 square feet.

19. $x = 15$ feet is the closest possible answer.

21. $-x^2 + 3x - 2$

23. Sandy multiplied the exponents for x^2 and x^3 instead of adding them.

UNIT 7 Selected Answers

MODULE 18

Lesson 18.2 Multiplying Polynomial Expressions

Your Turn

3. $x^2 - x - 2$

6. $x^3 + 6x^2 + 3x + 18$

10. The area, including the walkway, is $(4x^2 + 70x + 300)$ft².

Evaluate

1. $x^2 + 2x - 24$

3. $x^2 - 5x - 6$

5. $x^3 + 6x^2 + 11x + 66$

7. $x^2 + 10x + 21$

9. $6x^2 + 19x + 10$

11. $x^3 - 3x^2 + 9x - 27$

13. $x^3 - 3x^2 - 5x - 3$

15. $x^5 + 4x^4 + x^3 + 4x^2 + x + 4$

17. $x^5 + 2x^3 + x^2 + 4x + 12$

19. Let y represent the area of Cameron's garden. Then the equation for this situation is $y = (x + 6)(x + 2)$.
    The area of Cameron's garden is 77 ft².

21. Let x be the width of the frame.
    $(12 + 2x)(10 + 2x)$
    The area of the framed photograph is $(4x^2 + 44x + 120)$ in².

23. a. $6x^2$
    b. $3x^{12}$
    c. x^2
    d. $6x^4$
    e. x^6

25. $n^3 + 6n^2 + 8n$

27. Bill added the constants in the binomials. He should have multiplied the constant of each binomial together instead.

UNIT 7 Selected Answers

MODULE 18

21. $3x^2 - 40x - 28$

23. \$8.

25. a. $(a + b)^2 = a^2 + ab + ab + b^2$
    $= a^2 + 2ab + b^2$

    b. $(a - b)^2 = a^2 - ab - ab - b^2$
    $= a^2 - 2ab + b^2$

    c. $(a + b)(a - b) = a^2 + ab - ab - b^2$
    $\qquad\qquad\qquad = a^2 - b^2$

Lesson 18.3 Special Products of Binomials

Your Turn

5. $16 + 8x^2 + x^4$

6. $x^2 - 6x + 9$

8. $16x^2 - 24xy + 9y^2$

9. $9 - 6x^2 + x^4$

11. $49 - x^2$

13. Total area
    $(x + 3)^2 = x^2 + 2(x)(3) + 3^2 = x^2 + 6(x) + 9$
    Area of patio
    $(x - 3)2 = x^2 - 2(x)(3) + 3^2 = x^2 - 6(x) + 9$
    Area of flower garden = total area − area of patio
    $= x^2 + 6x + 9 - (x^2 - 6x + 9)$
    $12x$

Evaluate

1. $x^2 + 16x + 64$

3. $36 + 12x^2 + x^4$

5. $x^2 + 22x + 121$

7. $x^2 - 6x + 9$

9. $(36x^2) - 84xy + 49y^2$

11. $25x^2 - 40xy + 16y^2$

13. $x^2 - 16$

15. $81 - x^2$

17. $9x^4 - 64y^2$

19. Area of walkway = Total area − area of pool
    $\qquad\qquad\qquad = (x + 1)^2 - (x - 2)^2$
    $\qquad\qquad\qquad\quad 6x - 3$
    When $x = 7$ feet, the area of the walkway is $6(7) - 3 = 39$ square feet.

UNIT 8 Selected Answers

MODULE 19
Lesson 19.1 Understanding Quadratic Functions

Your Turn

4. 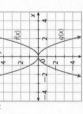 D: all real; R: $y \geq 0$

5. D: all real; R: $y \geq 0$

7. D: all real; R: $y \leq 0$

8. D: all real; R: $y \geq 0$

9. $g(x) = 4x^2$

10. $g(x) = -x^2$

11. The y-intercept occurs at the left end-point, which is also the vertex, and

represents the height $h = 0$ at which the rock was released at ground level.

The right endpoint represents the height $h = -64$ feet at which the rock hits the bottom of the well $t = 2$ seconds after it was released.

$h(t) = -16t^2$

Evaluate

1.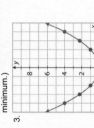

Domain, vertex, and axis of symmetry are the same. Range, maximum, and minimum are different. ($f(x)$ doesn't have a maximum, and $g(x)$ doesn't have a minimum.)

3. 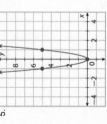 D: all real; R: $y \geq 0$

5. D: all real; R: $y \geq 0$

7. D: all real; R: $y \leq 0$

9. D: all real; R: $y \leq 0$

11. $g(x) = -\frac{1}{2}x^2$

13. $g(x) = \frac{5}{4}x^2$

15. $h(d) = -31.25d^2$

17. $E(d) = \frac{1}{2}d^2$

19. $E(r) = 0.001r^2$

21. $E(\ell) = 0.06\ell^2$

23. When a is negative, the y values cannot be positive. Since the y-value is positive, a must be positive.

25. When $f(x)$ has a minimum value, it means $a > 0$. When it has a maximum value, $a < 0$. In either case, the minimum or the maximum value will be 0.

Selected Answers

UNIT 8 Selected Answers

MODULE 19
Lesson 19.2 Transforming Quadratic Functions

Your Turn

5. The function $g(x) = x^2 + 4$ has a minimum value of 4.

The axis of symmetry for $g(x) = x^2 + 4$ is $x = 0$.

6. The function $g(x) = x^2 - 7$ has a minimum value of -7.

The axis of symmetry for $g(x) = x^2 - 7$ is $x = 0$.

10.

12.

13.

9.

Evaluate

1.

3. The parent function has been translated 2 units right and 5 units up. It has been stretched vertically by a factor of 2.

5. The parent function has been translated 3 units right and 4 units down. It has been vertically compressed by a factor of $\frac{1}{2}$.

7.

9. The function has a minimum value of -9.

The axis of symmetry is $x = 0$.

11.

The function has a minimum value of 0.

The axis of symmetry is $x = 3$.

13. The graph of $g(x) = (x + 12)^2$ is the graph of $f(x) = x^2$ translated 12 units left.

15. Translate the graph of the parent function 2 units *to the right*.

Selected Answers

UNIT 8 Selected Answers

MODULE 19

Lesson 19.3 Interpreting Vertex Form and Standard Form

Your Turn

6. $y - 4x + x^2 = 0$ is a quadratic function.

7. This is not a quadratic function because $a = 0$.

9. The standard form of
$y = 2(x + 5)^2 + 3$ is $y = 2x^2 + 20x + 53$.

10. The standard form of
$y = -3(x - 7)^2 + 2$ is $y = -3x^2 + 42x - 145$.

12. Vertex form $y = 6(x - 2)^2 + 5$.
Standard form $y = 6x^2 - 24x + 29$.

13. Vertex form $y = -5(x + 2)^2 - 7$.
Standard form $y = -5x^2 - 20x - 27$.

16. The equation for the function is
$f(x) = -(x - 1)^2 + 1$.

17. The equation for the function is
$f(t) = -16t^2 + 45$.

Evaluate

1. The graph is a parabola. It is quadratic.

3. The graph is a parabola. It is quadratic.

5. No, $a = 0$

7. Yes, $a \neq 0$, b, and c are real numbers.

9. b, d

11. The axis of symmetry is the y-axis,
or $x = 0$.

13. The standard form of
$y = -2(x + 4)^2 - 11$ is $y = -2x^2 - 16x - 43$.

15. The standard form of
$y = -4(x - 3)^2 - 9$ is $y = -4x^2 + 24x - 45$.

17. Sample answer: Expand the squared
term. Then distribute the a-value. Finally,
combine like terms.

19. Vertex form $y = -\dfrac{1}{2}(x - 4)^2 + 7$.

Standard form $y = -\dfrac{1}{2}x^2 + 4x - 1$.

21. Vertex form $y = -4(x + 3)^2 + 10$.
Standard form $y = -4x^2 - 24x - 26$.

23. The equation for the function is
$f(t) = -16t^2 + 20$.

25. The equation for the function is
$f(t) = -16(t - 1.5)^2 + 40$.
The curve appears to intersect the x-axis
at 3.1.
So, evaluate the function $f(t)$ at 3.1;
$f(3.1) = -16(3.1 - 1.5)^2 + 40 = -0.96$
-0.96 is close to the expected value of 0,
so the equation is reasonable.

17.

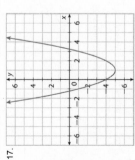

The function has a minimum value of -5.
The axis of symmetry is $x = 1$.

19.

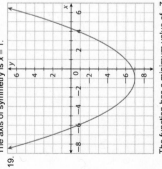

The function has a minimum value of -7.
The axis of symmetry is $x = -1$.

21. Translate the graph of the parent function
3 units to the right and 2 units up.

23. When $b > 1$, the graph of $y = (bx)^2$ is
compressed horizontally by a factor of $\dfrac{1}{b}$.

25. Nina should have subtracted 4 from x in
the equation instead of adding it.

27. For any real value of a with $a \neq 0$, the
function will have one x-intercept when
$c = 0$.

UNIT 8 Selected Answers

MODULE 20

Lesson 20.1 Connecting Intercepts and Zeroes

Your Turn

3. The related function is $y = x^2 - 1$.

The zeros of the function are 1 and -1, so the solutions of the equation are $x = -1$ and $x = 1$.

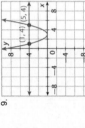

5. The graphs intersect at two locations: (1, 3) and (3, 3).

This means $f(x) = g(x)$ when $x = 1$ and $x = 3$.

So the solutions of $3(x - 2)^2 - 3 = 0$ are 1 and 3.

7. The egg will hit the plant after about 1.12 seconds.

8. The fish is out of the water for 0.3125 second.

Evaluate

1.

The zeros of $y = 3x^2 - 3$ are 1 and -1, so $x = -1$ or $x = 1$.

3.

The zeros of $y = 4x^2 - 4$ are 1 and -1, so $x = -1$ or $x = 1$.

5.
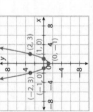

The zeros of $y = x^2 + 2x - 3$ are -3 and -1, so $x = -3$ or $x = 1$.

7.

9.
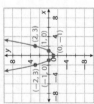

The graphs of $f(x) = 2(x - 3)^2$ and $g(x) = 4$ intersect at (1.59, 4) and (4.41, 4). So $x = 1.59$ or $x = 4.41$.

11.

The graphs of $f(x) = (x - 3)^2$ and $g(x) = 4$ intersect at (5, 4) and (1, 4). So $x = 5$ or $x = 1$.

13. The graphs of $y = -16x^2 + 30$ and $y = 5$ intersect at about (1.25, 5). The twig will hit the rosebush after about 1.25 seconds.

15. The graphs of $y = -16x^2 + 15$ and $y = 2$ intersect at about (0.9, 2). The trampolinist will land on the trampoline after about 0.9 second.

17. The graph of $f(x) = -16x^2 + 18x$ shows a zero of 1.125. The shark is out of the water for 1.125 seconds.

19. The graph of $f(x) = -16x^2 + 11x$ shows a zero of about 0.7. The flying fish is in the air for about 0.7 seconds.

21. a. $a = 3, b = 2, c = 4$

b. $a = 0, b = 2, c = 1$

c. $a = 1, b = 2, c = 0$

d. $a = 0, b = 0, c = 5$

e. $a = 3, b = 8, c = 11$

23. Sample answer: The graph of $f(x) = x^2$ opens upward, but the related equation, $x^2 = 0$, has only one solution.

25. Yes; Jamie can find the zeros of the function using the x-intercepts, and write the equation in the factored form $f(x) = k(x - a)(x - b)$, where a and b are the zeros. She can then substitute the coordinates of the given point to find the value of k.

UNIT 8 Selected Answers

MODULE 20

Lesson 20.2 Connecting Intercepts and Linear Factors

Your Turn

5. $y = x^2 - 8x + 7$

6. $y = 4x^2 + 8x - 12$

9. $y = -2x^2 - 12x - 10$

The factored form shows that x-intercepts are −5 and −1.; the zeros are −5 and −1.

10. $y = 5x^2 - 20x + 15$

The factored form shows that x-intercepts are 1 and 3; the zeros are 1 and 3.

12. $k = 1$:
$f(x) = x^2 - 9x + 8$

$k = -4$:
$f(x) = -4x^2 + 36x - 32$

$k = 5$:
$f(x) = 5x^2 - 45x + 40$

13. $k = 1$:
$f(x) = x^2 + 4x - 21$

$k = -5$:
$f(x) = -5x^2 - 20x + 105$

$k = 7$:
$f(x) = 7x^2 + 28x - 147$

Evaluate

1.

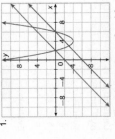

The x-intercepts are 2 and 6.
The axis of symmetry is x = 4.

3.

The x-intercepts are −2 and 5.
The axis of symmetry is x = 1.5.

5. $y = 5x^2 - 5x - 10$

7. $y = -2x^2 + 2x + 40$

9. c

11. $y = -2x^2 + 12x - 16$
x-intercepts are 2 and 4. The zeros are 2 and 4.

13. $y = -3x^2 + 6x + 9$
x-intercepts are −1 and 3. The zeros are −1 and 3.

15. The x-intercepts are 0 and 2. The ball will hit the ground in 2 seconds

17. $k = 1$: $f(x) = 1(x + 5)(x - 3)$
$f(x) = x^2 + 2x - 15$

$k = -2$: $f(x) = -2(x + 5)(x - 3)$
$f(x) = -2x^2 - 4x + 30$

$k = 5$: $f(x) = 5(x + 5)(x - 3)$
$f(x) = 5x^2 + 10x - 75$

19. The factored form is $f(x) = 4(x - 3)(x - 9)$ and the standard form is $f(x) = 4x^2 - 48x + 108$. Kelly substituted negative values for the x-intercepts.

21. Find the product $(x - (-3))(x - 1)$, or $(x + 3)(x - 1)$. Then write a quadratic function using this product. So a possible quadratic function is $y = x^2 + 2x - 3$.

UNIT 8 Selected Answers

MODULE 20

Lesson 20.3 Applying the Zero Product Property to Solve Equations

Your Turn

5. The zeros are 10 and 6.

6. The zeros are 13 and −12.

8. $x = \frac{2}{7}$ $x = 11$

9. $x = \frac{3}{8}$ $x = -6$

11. The ball is in the air for 2 seconds.

Evaluate

1. $x = 15$ $x = 22$

3. $x = -15$ $x = -17$

5. $x = 1.9$ $x = 3.5$

7. $x = \frac{3}{4}$

9. $x = -12$ $x = -\frac{15}{6}$

11. $x = -\frac{2}{3}$ $x = -\frac{1}{5}$

13. $9 = x$ $x = -\frac{1}{21}$

15. The solutions are $t = -\frac{1}{2}$ and $t = \frac{5}{2}$. Since time cannot be negative, the football is in the air for 2.5 seconds.

17. The solutions are $t = -0.5$ and $t = 5$. Since time cannot be negative, the flare is in the air for 5 seconds.

19. The solutions are $t = -0.125$ and $t = 1$. Since time cannot be negative, the time it takes for the beanbag to reach the ground is 1 second.

21. A. E
    B. A, D
    C. C
    D. B

23. a. Since the ball starts at $d = 0$, it will hit the ground at $d = 4$. Since the curve is symmetric, the ball will be at its maximum height at half this distance, or 2 meters.

    b. The maximum height is 8 meters. The point (2, h), or (2, 8), is the vertex of the graph of the function.

25. First number: x
    Second number: x + 3
    Third number: 4(x + 3)
    $4(x + 3) + x(x + 3) = 0$
    $x = -4$, or $x = -3$
    The three numbers are either −4, −1, and −4, or −3, 0, and 0.

UNIT 9 Selected Answers

MODULE 21

Lesson 21.1 Solving Equations by Factoring $x^2 + bx + c$

Your Turn

4. $x = -6$ or $x = -9$
5. $x = 12$ or $x = 1$
6. $x = -7$ or $x = 8$

Evaluate

1.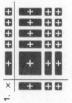

$+4$ $+2$

3. $(x - 4)(x - 11)$
5. $(x - 2)(x + 16)$
7. $(x + 4)(x + 6)$
9. $x = -7$ or $x = -12$
11. $x = 3$ or $x = 9$
13. $x = 9$ or $x = -15$
15. $x = 11$ or $x = -12$
17. The dimensions of the outside border of the walkway are $(x + 6)$ feet and $(x + 14)$ feet.
19. Rug:
Length: 25 feet
Width: 16 feet
Wall:
Width: 22 ft
Length: 35 ft
21. b
d
c
a

23. There are no other values where $b = c$ that make the expression factorable. The expression $x^2 + 4x + 4$ is factorable because $2 + 2 = 4$ and $2 \cdot 2 = 4$. The only number that has equal factors which sum to the number itself is 4, so no other factorable expressions exist where $b = c$.
25. The possible values of b are the sums of the factors of 64: ±65, ±34, ±20, and ±16.

UNIT 9 Selected Answers

MODULE 21

Lesson 21.2 Solving Equations by Factoring $ax^2 + bx + c$

Your Turn

5. $-1(x - 2)(5x + 2)$
7. $x = -\dfrac{3}{2}$ and $x = -\dfrac{5}{2}$
8. The rock lands 3 seconds after it is thrown.

Evaluate

1. $(3x + 1)(2x + 1)$
3. $(2x - 1)(2x - 3)$
5. $(x + 1)(3x - 5)$
7. $2(2x - 1)(3x + 7)$
9. $x = -3$ or $x = -\dfrac{3}{5}$
11. $x = -4$ or $x = -\dfrac{1}{3}$
13. $x = \dfrac{3}{2}$ or $x = -\dfrac{1}{4}$
15. $x = -2$ or $x = \dfrac{1}{8}$
17. It takes the ball $2\dfrac{1}{2}$ seconds to land.
19. It takes $\dfrac{1}{3}$ second to travel 30 more feet.
21. length = $(6x - 1)$, width = $(x + 3)$
23. b. $5(3x + 1)(x - 2)$
d. $5(x - 2)(3x + 1)$
25. $(2x + 5)(2x - 5)$

UNIT 9 Selected Answers

MODULE 21

Lesson 21.3 Using Special Factors to Solve Equations

Your Turn

3. $2y(y + 3)^2$

4. $(10z - 1)^2$

6. $(x + 12)(x - 12)$

7. $9y^2(3y + 1)(3y - 1)$

8. $x = \dfrac{1}{5}$

9. $x = 0$ or $x = -\dfrac{1}{2}$ or $x = \dfrac{1}{2}$

10. $t = \dfrac{1}{4}$ $t = \dfrac{1}{2}$

At 0.25 second or 0.5 second the ball will be 8 ft high. There are two solutions because both occur after $t = 0$, when the ball is set.

11. $t = \pm 1$

After one second, the rocket will have descended a distance of 490 centimeters. The negative time cannot be used in this context.

Evaluate

1.

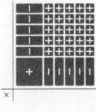

$(x - 5)(x - 5)$

3. $(2x + 1)^2$

5. $x(4x + 1)^2$

7. $(x + 13)(x - 13)$

9. $8x^2(2x + 1)(2x - 1)$

11. $x = -\dfrac{2}{5}$

13. $x = 0$ $x = -1$

15. $x = -9$ $x = 9$

17. $q = -\dfrac{9}{4}$ $x = \dfrac{9}{4}$

19. After $t = \dfrac{8}{7} \approx 1.14$ seconds, the rocket will have reached a height of 640 centimeters.

21. After $t = \dfrac{10}{7} \approx 1.43$ seconds, the rocket will have descended a distance of 1000 centimeters. The negative value of t cannot be used in this context.

23. After $t = \dfrac{7}{4} = 1.75$ seconds, the diver will have reached the water.

25. He factored out a 2 from both $(12x + 10)$ and $(12x + 10)$, which is the same as factoring out a 4 from the whole expression. It should be $4(6x + 5)(6x - 5)$.

$144x^2 - 100 = (12x + 10)(12x - 10)$
$= 2(6x + 5) \cdot 2(6x - 5)$
$= 4(6x + 5)(6x - 5)$

27. The area of the frame is $4(2x + y)(2x - y)$.

29. She can factor each side of the equation, and then subtract the right side from both sides so one side of the equation is 0. She can then simplify the equation and set the factors equal to 0 to solve for x.

The solutions are 0 and –1.

UNIT 9 Selected Answers

MODULE 22

Lesson 22.1 Solving Equations by Taking Square Roots

Your Turn

4. $x = \pm\sqrt{9}$

The solutions are 3 and –3.

The graph intersects the x-axis at (3, 0) and (–3, 0).

5. $x = \pm\sqrt{2.2}$

The approximate solutions are 1.48 and –1.48.

The graph intersects the x-axis at approximately (1.48, 0) and (–1.48, 0).

7. $x = -\sqrt{6} - 10$ or $x = \sqrt{6} - 10$

$x \approx -12.45$ $x \approx -7.55$

8. $x = 1$ $x = 17$

9. The zookeeper should buy 95 + 95, or 190, feet of fencing.

Evaluate

1. ± 0.09

3. $\pm 4\sqrt{6}$

5. $x = \pm\sqrt{100}$

$x = \pm 10$

The graph intersects the x-axis at (10, 0) and (–10, 0).

7. $x = \pm\sqrt{78}$

$x = \pm 8.83$

The graph intersects the x-axis at approximately (8.83, 0) and (–8.83, 0).

9. $x = \pm\sqrt{\dfrac{8}{7}}$

$x = \pm 1.07$

The graph intersects the x-axis at approximately (1.07, 0) and (–1.07, 0).

11. $x = -24$ $x = -6$

13. $x = 34$ $x = 46$

15. $x = \dfrac{\sqrt{7}}{2} - 5.4$ or $x = \dfrac{\sqrt{7}}{2} - 5.4$

$x \approx -6.72$ $x \approx -4.08$

17. The x-intercepts occur 6.8 units from the origin. So, they are located at (–6.8, 0) and (6.8, 0).

19. It will take the sack approximately 6.1 seconds to reach the ground.

21. The ball will hit the ground after approximately 0.7 second.

23. Lisa's solution is correct. By the definition of a square root of $ax^2 = a$, so the square of a real number is always nonnegative. So, a must be nonnegative. In the equation $x^2 = -225$, a is negative. So, there are no real solutions of the equation.

25. When $b > 0$, the solution of $x^2 + b = 0$ is the square root of a negative number, which is not real; but the solution of $x^2 - b = 0$ is the square root of a positive number, which has 2 possible values.

Selected Answers

UNIT 9 Selected Answers

MODULE 22

Lesson 22.2 Solving Equations by Completing the Square

Your Turn

4. $x^2 + 12x + 36$

5. $x = 11$ $x = -1$

6. $x = -3 + \sqrt{11}$ $x = -3 - \sqrt{11}$

8. $x = \dfrac{5}{4}$ $x = -\dfrac{1}{4}$

9. $x = \dfrac{-3+\sqrt{14}}{2}$ $x = \dfrac{-3-\sqrt{14}}{2}$

11. $x = -3 + \sqrt{37}$ $x = -3 - \sqrt{37}$

12. $x = 4$ $x = -2$

13. 49 feet; after 2 seconds

Evaluate

1. $x^2 + 26x + 169$

3. $x^2 - 2x + 1$

5. $x = 3$ $x = -11$

7. $x = -6 + \sqrt{41}$ $x = -6 - \sqrt{41}$

9. $x = \dfrac{4}{3}$ $x = -\dfrac{8}{3}$

11. $x = \dfrac{13}{4}$ $x = \dfrac{5}{4}$

13. $x = 2$ $x = -10$

15. $x = \dfrac{-7+\sqrt{57}}{2}$ $x = \dfrac{-7-\sqrt{57}}{2}$

17. $h = -16\left(t - \dfrac{1}{4}\right)^2 + 1$

The ball will be at its highest when it is at its vertex, or at 1 foot.

The graph of the function confirms the vertex at (0.25, 1). The x-intercept at 0.5 indicates that the ball will hit the ground after 0.5 second.

19. The maximum height is 9 feet. The volleyball will hit the ground after 1.25 seconds.

21. $a = 11$

    $a = 4$

    $a = 0$

    $a = 5$

    $a = 3$

23. The student forgot that the square root of 81 has two solutions:
    -9 and 9. The correct solution is
    $x + 2 = \pm9$, or $x = 7$ and $x = -11$.

25. When solving a quadratic model, some solutions are considered extraneous because they have a negative value, which is not useful in a real-world context. However, this is not always the case, as some quadratic models will have two valid solutions.

17. There is an equal number of both types of bacteria at $t \approx 15.18$ minutes.

19. a. d. e.

    The letters A, D, and E are possible heights of the gymnast

21. Because every positive number has two square roots, a positive discriminant results in two solutions to a quadratic equation.

UNIT 9 Selected Answers

MODULE 22

Lesson 22.3 Using the quadratic formula to Solve Equations

Your Turn

3. two real solutions

4. no real solutions

5. one real solution

7. The solutions are 7 and -1.

8. The solutions are $2 + \dfrac{\sqrt{2}}{2}$ and $2 - \dfrac{\sqrt{2}}{2}$

9. The soccer ball reached the ground after about $t \approx 1.33$ seconds.

10. The ball was in the air for $t \approx 0.94$ second.

Evaluate

1. Since $b^2 - 4ac = 0$, the equation has one real solution.

3. Since $b^2 - 4ac > 0$, the equation has two real solutions.

5. Since $b^2 - 4ac > 0$, the equation has two real solutions.

7. Since $b^2 - 4ac = 0$, the equation has one real solution.

9. The solutions are 2 and $-\dfrac{1}{3}$.

11. The solutions are $\dfrac{-1+\sqrt{65}}{8}$ and $\dfrac{-1-\sqrt{65}}{8}$.

13. The solutions are $-\dfrac{1}{4}$ and $-\dfrac{3}{2}$.

15. Since $b^2 - 4ac > 0$, the equation has two real solutions.

    $t \approx -1.19$ or $t \approx 0.17$

    Disregard the negative solution because there is no negative time in this context. The soccer ball reached the goal after about $t \approx 0.17$ seconds.

© Houghton Mifflin Harcourt Publishing Company

UNIT 9 Selected Answers

MODULE 22

Lesson 22.4 Choosing a Method for Solving Quadratic Equations

Your Turn

Sample explanations given.

6. Take the square roots because $b = 0$.

$$x = \pm \frac{10}{3}$$

7. Complete the square, because it is not factorable, but the coefficients are small and will not lead to a lot of fractional terms

$$x = -2 \pm \sqrt{11}$$

8. $0 = -16t^2 + 24t + 40$

The wheel will not hit the ground before it falls off, so the answer must be the positive, and the time is 2.5 seconds. I chose to solve by factoring because after 8 was factored out, the quadratic was easy to factor.

9. The ball reaches the same height as the kite at about 1.20 seconds, and then again on the way back down at 1.92 seconds.

Evaluate

1. This formula is expressed with two digit decimal coefficients. Factoring and completing the squares could be attempted by multiplying the equation by 100 to get to integer coefficients, but the amount of work in either method would be unreasonable. The quadratic formula, on the other hand, can be used easily with a calculator to evaluate the coefficients without any further manipulation.

3. Taking square roots, because $b = 0$.

$$x = \pm \frac{4}{3}$$

5. Factoring, because there are not many factors to check, and in this case, it works.

$$x = -\frac{1}{8} \quad \text{or} \quad x = -1$$

7. The quadratic formula, because the equation cannot be factored and completing the square will be complicated.

$$x = 1.27 \quad \text{or} \quad x = -0.56$$

9. Completing the square, because it is not factorable, but the coefficients are small and will not lead to a lot of fractional terms.

$$x = -1 \pm \frac{\sqrt{10}}{2}$$

11. Factoring, because there are not too many factors to check, and in this case, it works.

$$x = 1 \quad \text{or} \quad x = \frac{1}{4}$$

13. Completing the square, because it is not factorable, but the coefficients are small and will not lead to a lot of fractional terms.

$$x = 2 \pm \frac{\sqrt{7}}{2}$$

15. The quadratic formula, because the equation cannot be factored and completing the square will be complicated.

$$x = -1 \pm \frac{\sqrt{3}}{3}$$

17. The quadratic formula, because factoring and completing the square may be time-consuming.

$$x = 1 \quad \text{or} \quad x = -\frac{19}{6}$$

19. The quadratic formula, because the equation cannot be factored and completing the square will be complicated.

1.54 seconds after it is headed.

21. The quadratic formula, because the equation cannot be factored and completing the square will be complicated.

1.06 seconds.

23. Equations that can be solved by taking square roots or by factoring are usually solved that way because there is less computation involved in both of those methods. The answer will usually be found in less time and with fewer errors. If an equation cannot be factored, but can be solved by completing the square without large or fractional terms, it will probably be easier to solve by completing the square rather than using the quadratic formula.

25. The second statement is false. Some quadratic equations cannot be solved for a real value of x. If there are real solutions, then the quadratic formula can be used to find them. Either way, the first statement is true.

UNIT 9 Selected Answers

MODULE 22

Lesson 22.5 Solving Nonlinear Systems

Your Turn

2. Solution: (−4, 0) or (−2, 8)

3. Solution: (2, 0)

5. The discriminant is negative, so there are no real solutions.

7. The paint brush passes by the can about 7.3 seconds after the painter starts hoisting it up or about 2.3 seconds after the paintbrush starts to fall.

Evaluate

1. 2; 1; 0

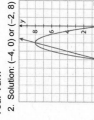

3. No Solutions

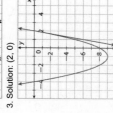

5. (2, 0) (1, 3)

7. No Solutions

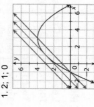

9. (2, 0) (5, 12)

11. (2, 4) (1, 3)

13. (2, 11) (−11, 128)

15. There are no real solutions.

17. The wildebeest escapes.

19. The jumper hears the tire blow-out at a height of about 79.2 meters.

21. One solution has a negative value of t, which would mean the bolt hit the elevator before it began to fall.

23. The second intersection point at 22.18 seconds corresponds to a height −5654.74 feet, or under the ground. The second intersection point is outside the range of the model even though it has a positive time, and it cannot be a valid solution.

25. The two solutions are points on the line and can be used to solve for the line.

$$m = \frac{10 - 7}{5 - 2} = 1$$

$$y = mx = b$$
$$10 = 1(5) + b$$
$$b = 5$$

The line is $y = x + 5$. Two points define a line, so there is no need to use the quadratic equation.

UNIT 9 Selected Answers

MODULE 23

Lesson 23.1 Modeling with Quadratic Functions

Your Turn

4. $y = -16.8x^2 + 120.6x - 1.143$

5. $y = -2x^2 + 2.286x - 6.081$

6. The first size with the surcharge will be size 11.
The function represents the cost of specific sizes so the domain will be integer values of x with $x > 0$ and the range will be $y > 0$.

7. A clock with diameter of $15\frac{1}{4}$ inches can be made for $4.00.
The function represents the cost of different sizes of clocks, so the domain will be $x > 0$ and the range will be $y > 0$.

Evaluate

1. is not

3. is not

5. Second Difference: 4, 5, 3, 3, 5, 3, 5, 3, 6, 3
$y = 0.0531x^2 + 1.990x + 90.67$

7. Second Difference: 20, 19, 16, 16, 18, 19, 17, 17, 16, 15
$y = 0.0423x^2 - 19.03x + 2012$

9. Second Difference: -16, -17, -16, -14, -17, -17, -15, -17, -17, -16
$y = -0.8172x^2 - 28.73x - 747.5$

11. Second Difference: 103, 87, 102, 67
$y = 11.39x^2 - 122.8x + 353.6$

13. $y = -4.645x^2 + 50.89x - 113.4$

15. If the company sells its product for $5.19, it will maximize its revenue.
The model is for selling price and revenue, so the domain will be $x > 0$ and the range will be $0 < y \le 413.57$.

17. The skier was in the air for 6.6 seconds.
The function models height based on a reference point after an event begins, the jump height has a maximum and a minimum (the landing point) so the domain will be $0 < x \le 6.6$ and the range is $-30 \le y \le 21.06$

19. Full Set: $y = 13.84x^2 - 86.13x + 104.6$
$R^2 = 0.9493$
Four points: $y = 0.632x^2 + 0.0788x + 1.290$
$R^2 = 1$
The value of R^2 reflects how well the equation models the data. When only a few data points are used, the equation may model those few data points well, but may not do so for the entire data set.

UNIT 9 Selected Answers

MODULE 23

Lesson 23.2 Comparing Linear, Exponential, and Quadratic Models

Your Turn

7.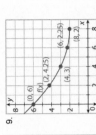

The function appears to be quadratic based on the curvature, although the apparent end behavior is not consistent with either a linear or a quadratic function. The function has increasing first differences and constant second differences so it is a quadratic function.

8.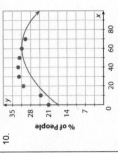

The end behavior of the function as x approaches negative infinity cannot be determined. As x approaches negative infinity, $f(x)$ appears to decrease without end. Based on the graph, the data could be either quadratic or exponential. The second differences are nearly constant. Therefore, the function is quadratic.

9.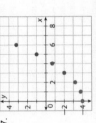

Based on the graph, the data could be either quadratic or exponential. The second differences are constant. Therefore, the function is quadratic.

10.

The function appears to best fit a quadratic function.
The end behavior of the data is as x approaches infinity, $f(x)$ approaches negative infinity.
Since the ratios increase quickly and then decrease quickly, a quadratic function should probably be used for this data set. The quadratic regression is a good fit for the data set.
By the year 2000, 20.62% of people were living in central cities in the United States.

11.

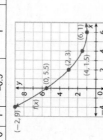

2012 Horsepower vs. Car Weight (pounds)

The data set appears to best fit a linear function.

The end behavior of the data is that as x approaches infinity, f(x) approaches infinity.

The changing ratios suggest that the data set is best described by a quadratic or linear function. However, the average of the second differences is close to 0, so a linear regression should be used.

The linear regression is a good fit for the data set.

A car weighing 6500 pounds in 2012 should have had 606 horsepower.

Evaluate

1. f(x) increases faster from 0 to 1. g(x) increases faster from 2 to 3.

3.

x	f(x)	First Differences	Second Differences
-2	-4		
-1	-3.3	0.7	
0	-1.2	2.1	1.4
1	2.3	3.5	1.4
2	7.2	4.9	1.4
3	13.5	6.3	1.4

The shape appears slightly curved upward.

f(x) appears to increase without end as x approaches infinity and to decrease without end as x approaches negative infinity.

The function appears to be quadratic because of the curvature, but the apparent end behavior is not consistent with a quadratic function.

The function has constant second differences and decreasing first differences, so it is quadratic.

5.

x	f(x)	First Differences	Second Differences
1	-7.2		
2	-3.8	3.4	
3	0	3.8	0.4
4	4.2	4.2	0.4
5	8.8	4.6	0.4

The shape appears straight.

f(x) appears to increase without end as x increases and todecrease as x decreases.

The function appears to be linear.

The function has constant second differences so it is quadratic.

7.

x	f(x)	First Difference	Second Difference	Ratio
-2	9			
0	5.5	-3.5		0.61
2	3	-2.5	1	0.55
4	1.5	-1.5	1	0.5
6	1	-0.5	1	0.67

Based on the graph, the data could be either quadratic or exponential.

Since f(x) has not been defined for x > 6, the end behavior of the function as x approaches infinity cannot be determined. As x approaches negative infinity, f(x) appears to increase without end. No conclusions can be drawn about f(x) from the graph.

The second differences are constant. Therefore, the function is quadratic.

9. Possible answer: Consider the data. For example, quadratic models are not the best choice for cost data, because costs don't usually increase as the number of items increases, then reach a maximum and decrease as the number of items continues to increase.

11. Since both regression models extremely low r^2-values, neither should be chosen for this data set.

Selected Answers

UNIT 10 Selected Answers

MODULE 24

Lesson 24.1 Graphing Polynomial Functions

Your Turn

3. Odd degree, negative leading coefficient

4. Even degree, positive leading coefficient

5. odd function; the leading coefficient is negative

6. even function; the leading coefficient is negative

Evaluate

1. There are two turning points.
   As $x \to -\infty$, $f(x) \to -\infty$.
   As $x \to +\infty$, $f(x) \to +\infty$.

3. even degree, positive leading coefficient

5. even degree, negative leading coefficient

7. even degree, positive leading coefficient

9. odd degree, negative leading coefficient

11. odd degree, negative leading coefficient

13. even function; negative leading coefficient

15. odd function, positive leading coefficient

17. even function, positive leading coefficient

19. As $x \to -\infty$, $f(x) \to +\infty$.
    As $x \to +\infty$, $f(x) \to -\infty$.

21. Rhonda is correct. The end behavior of a polynomial is entirely determined by the term with the highest degree. Carlos missed a turning point because he did not adjust the graph window from the default settings. (To see all of the important features of the graph, adjust Ymax to 80 and Xmin to –20).

Selected Answers

UNIT 10 Selected Answers

MODULE 24

Lesson 24.2 Understanding Inverse Functions

Your Turn

4.

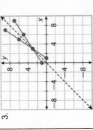

Original: Domain: $1 \le x \le 7$ Range: $2 \le y \le 9$
Inverse: Domain: $2 \le x \le 9$ Range: $1 \le y \le 7$

5. $f^{-1}(x) = \dfrac{x + 7}{5}$

Sample check: $f(5) = 5(5) - 7 = 25 - 7 = 18$

$f^{-1}(18) = \dfrac{18 + 7}{5} = \dfrac{25}{5} = 5$

6.

$f^{-1}(x) = \dfrac{1}{2}x + 2$

8. For 7 teaspoons, 36 ounces of water are needed.

Check: $t = \dfrac{1}{6}(36) + 1 = 7$

Evaluate

1.

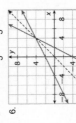

Original: Domain: $1 \le x \le 4$ Range: $1 \le y \le 8$
Inverse: Domain: $1 \le x \le 8$ Range: $1 \le y \le 4$

3. Original: Domain: $1 \le x \le 7$ Range: $0 \le y \le 9$
   Inverse: Domain: $0 \le x \le 9$ Range: $1 \le y \le 7$

5. $f^{-1}(x) = \dfrac{x + 1}{5}$

Sample check: $f(4) = 5(4) - 1 = 19$ and

$f^{-1}(19) = \dfrac{19 + 1}{5} = 4$

7. $f^{-1}(x) = -2\,(x - 3)$

Sample check:

$f(8) = 3 - \dfrac{1}{8}(8) = -1$ and

$f^{-1}(-1) = -2(-1 - 3) = 8$

9. $f^{-1}(x) = \dfrac{x - 4}{4}$

Sample check: $f(3) = 4(3 + 1) = 4 \cdot 4 = 16$

and $f^{-1}(16) = \dfrac{16 - 4}{4} = \dfrac{12}{4} = 3$

UNIT 10 Selected Answers

MODULE 24

Lesson 24.3 Graphing Square Root Functions

Your Turn

3.

x	$y = \sqrt{x+1}$	(x, y)
-1	$\sqrt{-1+1}$	(-1, 0)
0	$\sqrt{0+1}$	(0, 1)
3	$\sqrt{3+1}$	(3, 2)
8	$\sqrt{8+1}$	(8, 3)

There is a horizontal translation 1 unit to the left. Domain: $x \geq -1$ Range: $y \geq 0$

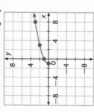

4.

x	$y = \sqrt{x} - 4$	(x, y)
0	$\sqrt{0} - 4$	(0, -4)
1	$\sqrt{1} - 4$	(1, -3)
4	$\sqrt{4} - 4$	(4, -2)
9	$\sqrt{9} - 4$	(9, -1)

There is a vertical translation 4 units down. Domain: $x \geq 0$ Range: $y \geq -4$

5.

x	$y = 3\sqrt{x}$	(x, y)
0	$3\sqrt{0}$	(0, 0)
1	$3\sqrt{1}$	(1, 3)
4	$3\sqrt{4}$	(4, 6)
9	$3\sqrt{9}$	(9, 9)

There is a vertical stretch by a factor of 3, and there is no reflection across the x-axis. Domain: $x \geq 0$ Range: $y \geq 0$

6.

x	$y = -\dfrac{1}{4}\sqrt{x}$	(x, y)
0	$-\dfrac{1}{4}\sqrt{0}$	(0, 0)
1	$-\dfrac{1}{4}\sqrt{1}$	$\left(1, -\dfrac{1}{4}\right)$
4	$-\dfrac{1}{4}\sqrt{4}$	$\left(4, -\dfrac{1}{2}\right)$
9	$-\dfrac{1}{4}\sqrt{9}$	$\left(9, -\dfrac{3}{4}\right)$

Vertical compression by a factor of $\dfrac{1}{4}$, and its graph is reflected across the x-axis. Domain: $x \geq 0$ Range: $y \leq 0$

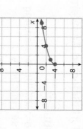

11.

13.

$f^{-1}(x) = -\dfrac{1}{2}x + \dfrac{5}{2}$

$f^{-1}(x) = \dfrac{x-10}{0.6}$ or $\dfrac{5}{3}x - \dfrac{50}{3}$

15. $F = 60.8$; $\dfrac{9}{5}c + 32 = F$

17. $p = 28.36$; $\dfrac{t}{1.11} - 1.5 = p$

19. $d \approx 169.67$; $\dfrac{p}{0.600} + 3 = d$

21. a. Multiplicative Inverse
b. Both
c. Multiplicative Inverse
d. Both
e. Both

23. $f(6) = \dfrac{6-4}{6+4} = \dfrac{3}{10}$

$f^{-1}\left(\dfrac{3}{10}\right) = 6$

$y = \dfrac{-4x-3}{x-1}$

7. $g(x) = \frac{2\sqrt{5}}{5}\sqrt{x}$

$g(6.2) \approx 2.2$ miles

$g(5.5) \approx 2.1$ miles

Evaluate

1. B

3.

5. The graph is translated 4 units down and 1 unit to the right.
Domain: $x \geq -1$ Range: $y \geq -4$

7. The graph is translated to the left 8 units.
Domain: $x \geq -8$ Range: $y \geq 0$

9. The graph is translated down 7 units and 5 units to the left.
Domain: $x \geq -5$ Range: $y \geq -7$.

11. The graph is reflected across the x-axis.
Domain: $x \geq 0$ Range: $y \leq 0$

13. The graph is stretched by a factor of 5 and is reflected across the x-axis.
Domain: $x \geq 0$ Range: $y \leq 0$

13. The graph is stretched by a factor of 6.
Domain: $x \geq 0$ Range: $y \geq 0$

15. The speed of the tsunami is about 149.5 mph.

17. ≈ 8 samples

19. $y = -\sqrt{x+3} + 4$

Since the graph is translated 3 units to the left, reflected across the x-axis, and translated 4 units up.

21. Both the domain and range are incorrect. The correct domain is $x \geq -10$ and the correct range is $y \geq -7$.

23. Possible Answer: A horizontal translation affects the domain, but not the range. The domain of the translated function is $x \geq h$, where h is the number of units the function is translated horizontally. A vertical translation affects the range, but not the domain. The range of the translated function is $f(x) \geq k$, where k is the number of units the function is translated vertically.

117

UNIT 10 Selected Answers

MODULE 24

Lesson 24.4 Graphing Cube Root Functions

Your Turn

3.

The transformed function was shifted left by 3 units and down by 6 units.
Domain: $-\infty < x < \infty$
Range: $-\infty < y < \infty$

4.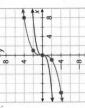

The transformed plot was stretched by a factor of 2 and is not reflected across the x-axis.
Domain: $-\infty < x < \infty$
Range: $-\infty < y < \infty$

Evaluate

1. The inverse of $y = 8x^3$ is $y = \frac{\sqrt[3]{x}}{2}$ or

$y = \frac{1}{2}\sqrt[3]{x}$.

3.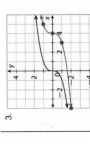

5.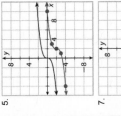

7.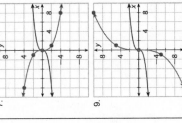

9.

11. translated right by 1 unit and up by 5 units

13. translated right by 3 units and down by 3 units

15. stretched vertically by a factor of 3

17. compressed vertically by a factor of $\frac{1}{5}$, and reflected across the x-axis

118

Selected Answers

Selected Answers

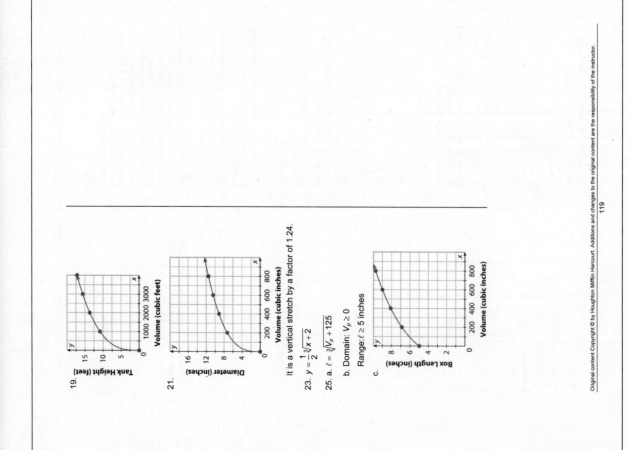

19.

Tank Height (feet)

Volume (cubic feet)

21.

Diameter (inches)

Volume (cubic inches)

It is a vertical stretch by a factor of 1.24.

23. $y = \frac{1}{2}\sqrt[3]{x+2}$

25. a. $\ell = \sqrt[3]{V_p + 125}$

b. Domain: $V_p \geq 0$

Range: $\ell \geq 5$ inches

c.

Box Length (inches)

Volume (cubic inches)

Glossary/Glosario

A

ENGLISH	SPANISH	EXAMPLES
absolute value The absolute value of x is the distance from zero to x on a number line, denoted $|x|$. $$|x| = \begin{cases} x & \text{if } x \geq 0 \\ -x & \text{if } x < 0 \end{cases}$$	**valor absoluto** El valor absoluto de x es la distancia de cero a x en una recta numérica, y se expresa $|x|$. $$|x| = \begin{cases} x & \text{si } x \geq 0 \\ -x & \text{si } x < 0 \end{cases}$$	$|3| = 3$ $|-3| = 3$
absolute-value equation An equation that contains absolute-value expressions.	**ecuación de valor absoluto** Ecuación que contiene expresiones de valor absoluto.	$|x + 4| = 7$
absolute-value function A function whose rule contains absolute-value expressions.	**función de valor absoluto** Función cuya regla contiene expresiones de valor absoluto.	$y = |x + 4|$
absolute-value inequality An inequality that contains absolute-value expressions.	**desigualdad de valor absoluto** Desigualdad que contiene expresiones de valor absoluto.	$|x + 4| > 7$
accuracy The closeness of a given measurement or value to the actual measurement or value.	**exactitud** Cercanía de una medida o un valor a la medida o el valor real.	
Addition Property of Equality For real numbers a, b, and c, if $a = b$, then $a + c = b + c$.	**Propiedad de igualdad de la suma** Dados los números reales a, b y c, si $a = b$, entonces $a + c = b + c$.	$\begin{array}{r} x - 6 = 8 \\ \underline{+6 +6} \\ x = 14 \end{array}$
Addition Property of Inequality For real numbers a, b, and c, if $a < b$, then $a + c < b + c$. Also holds true for $>$, $\leq$, $\geq$, and $\neq$.	**Propiedad de desigualdad de la suma** Dados los números reales a, b y c, si $a < b$, entonces $a + c < b + c$. Es válido también para $>$, $\leq$, $\geq$ y $\neq$.	$\begin{array}{r} x - 6 < 8 \\ \underline{+6 \phantom{<} +6} \\ x < 14 \end{array}$
additive inverse The opposite of a number. Two numbers are additive inverses if their sum is zero.	**inverso aditivo** El opuesto de un número. Dos números son inversos aditivos si su suma es cero.	The additive inverse of 5 is -5. The additive inverse of -5 is 5.
algebraic expression An expression that contains at least one variable.	**expresión algebraica** Expresión que contiene por lo menos una variable.	
AND A logical operator representing the intersection of two sets.	**Y** Operador lógico que representa la intersección de dos conjuntos.	$A = \{2, 3, 4, 5\}$ $B = \{1, 3, 5, 7\}$ The set of values that are in A AND B is $A \cap B = \{3, 5\}$.

Glossary/Glosario

ENGLISH	SPANISH	EXAMPLES
arithmetic sequence A sequence whose successive terms differ by the same nonzero number d, called the common difference.	**sucesión aritmética** Sucesión cuyos términos sucesivos difieren en el mismo número distinto de cero d, denominado *diferencia común*.	4, 7, 10, 13, 16, … $+3\ +3\ +3\ +3$ $d = 3$
Associative Property of Addition For all numbers a, b, and c, $(a + b) + c = a + (b + c)$.	**Propiedad asociativa de la suma** Dados tres números cualesquiera a, b y c, $(a + b) + c = a + (b + c)$.	$(5 + 3) + 7 = 5 + (3 + 7)$
Associative Property of Multiplication For all numbers a, b, and c, $(a \cdot b) \cdot c = a \cdot (b \cdot c)$.	**Propiedad asociativa de la multiplicación** Dados tres números cualesquiera a, b y c, $(a \cdot b) \cdot c = a \cdot (b \cdot c)$.	$(5 \cdot 3) \cdot 7 = 5 \cdot (3 \cdot 7)$
asymptote A line that a graph gets closer to as the value of a variable becomes extremely large or small.	**asíntota** Línea recta a la cual se aproxima una gráfica a medida que el valor de una variable se hace sumamente grande o pequeño.	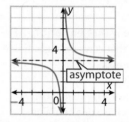
axis of symmetry A line that divides a plane figure or a graph into two congruent reflected halves.	**eje de simetría** Línea que divide una figura plana o una gráfica en dos mitades reflejadas congruentes.	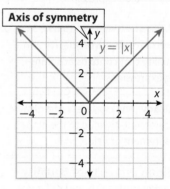

B

base of a power The number in a power that is used as a factor.	**base de una potencia** Número de una potencia que se utiliza como factor.	$3^4 = 3 \cdot 3 \cdot 3 \cdot 3 = 81$ 3 is the base.
base of an exponential function The value of b in a function of the form $f(x) = ab^x$, where a and b are real numbers with $a \neq 0$, $b > 0$, and $b \neq 1$.	**base de una función exponencial** Valor de b en una función del tipo $f(x) = ab^x$, donde a y b son números reales con $a \neq 0$, $b > 0$ y $b \neq 1$.	In the function $f(x) = 5(2)^x$, the base is 2.
binomial A polynomial with two terms.	**binomio** Polinomio con dos términos.	$x + y$ $2a^2 + 3$ $4m^3n^2 + 6mn^4$

Glossary/Glosario

ENGLISH	SPANISH	EXAMPLES
boundary line A line that divides a coordinate plane into two half-planes.	**línea de límite** Línea que divide un plano cartesiano en dos semiplanos.	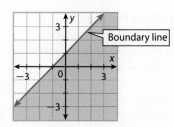

C

ENGLISH	SPANISH	EXAMPLES
categorical data Data that are qualitative in nature, such as "liberal," "moderate," and "conservative."	**datos categóricos** Datos de índole cualitativa, como "liberal", "moderado" y "conservador".	
closure A set of numbers is said to be closed, or to have closure, under a given operation if the result of the operation on any two numbers in the set is also in the set.	**cerradura** Se dice que un conjunto de números es cerrado, o tiene cerradura, respecto de una operación determinada, si el resultado de la operación entre dos números cualesquiera del conjunto también está en el conjunto.	The natural numbers are closed under addition because the sum of two natural numbers is always a natural number.
coefficient A number that is multiplied by a variable.	**coeficiente** Número que se multiplica por una variable.	In the expression $2x + 3y$, 2 is the coefficient of x and 3 is the coefficient of y.
common difference In an arithmetic sequence, the nonzero constant difference of any term and the previous term.	**diferencia común** En una sucesión aritmética, diferencia constante distinta de cero entre cualquier término y el término anterior.	In the arithmetic sequence 3, 5, 7, 9, 11, …, the common difference is 2.
common factor A factor that is common to all terms of an expression or to two or more expressions.	**factor común** Factor que es común a todos los términos de una expresión o a dos o más expresiones.	Expression: $4x^2 + 16x^3 - 8x$ Common factor: $4x$ Expressions: 12 and 18 Common factors: 2, 3, and 6
common ratio In a geometric sequence, the constant ratio of any term and the previous term.	**razón común** En una sucesión geométrica, la razón constante entre cualquier término y el término anterior.	In the geometric sequence 32, 16, 8, 4, 2, . . ., the common ratio is $\frac{1}{2}$.
Commutative Property of Addition For any two numbers a and b, $a + b = b + a$.	**Propiedad conmutativa de la suma** Dados dos números cualesquiera a y b, $a \cdot b = b \cdot a$.	$3 + 4 = 4 + 3 = 7$
Commutative Property of Multiplication For any two numbers a and b, $a \cdot b = b \cdot a$.	**Propiedad conmutativa de la multiplicación** Dados dos números cualesquiera a y b, $a \cdot b = b \cdot a$	$3 \cdot 4 = 4 \cdot 3 = 12$

Glossary/Glosario

ENGLISH	SPANISH	EXAMPLES

ENGLISH	SPANISH	EXAMPLES
completing the square A process used to form a perfect-square trinomial. To complete the square of $x^2 + bx$, add $\left(\frac{b}{2}\right)^2$.	**completar el cuadrado** Proceso utilizado para formar un trinomio cuadrado perfecto. Para completar el cuadrado de $x^2 + bx$, hay que sumar $\left(\frac{b}{2}\right)^2$.	$x^2 + 6x +$ 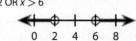 Add $\left(\frac{6}{2}\right)^2 = 9$. $x^2 + 6x + 9$
compound inequality Two inequalities that are combined into one statement by the word *and* or *or*.	**desigualdad compuesta** Dos desigualdades unidas en un enunciado por la palabra *y* u *o*.	$x \geq 2$ AND $x < 7$ (also written $2 \leq x < 7$) 0 2 4 6 8 $x < 2$ OR $x > 6$ 0 2 4 6 8
compound interest Interest earned or paid on both the principal and previously earned interest. The formula for compound interest is $A = P\left(1 + \frac{r}{n}\right)^{nt}$, where A is the final amount, P is the principal, r is the interest rate expressed as a decimal, n is the number of times interest is compounded, and t is the time.	**interés compuesto** Intereses ganados o pagados sobre el capital y los intereses ya devengados. La fórmula de interés compuesto es $A = P\left(1 + \frac{r}{n}\right)^{nt}$, donde A es la cantidad final, P es el capital, r es la tasa de interés expresada como un decimal, n es la cantidad de veces que se capitaliza el interés y t es el tiempo.	If \$100 is put into an account with an interest rate of 5% compounded monthly, then after 2 years, the account will have $100\left(1 + \frac{0.05}{12}\right)^{12\cdot2} = \$110.49$.
compound statement Two statements that are connected by the word *and* or *or*.	**enunciado compuesto** Dos enunciados unidos por la palabra *y* u *o*.	The sky is blue and the grass is green. I will drive to school or I will take the bus.
conditional relative frequency The ratio of a joint relative frequency to a related marginal relative frequency in a two-way table.	**frecuencia relativa condicional** Razón de una frecuencia relativa conjunta a una frecuencia relativa marginal en una tabla de doble entrada.	
consistent system A system of equations or inequalities that has at least one solution.	**sistema consistente** Sistema de ecuaciones o desigualdades que tiene por lo menos una solución.	$\begin{cases} x + y = 6 \\ x - y = 4 \end{cases}$ solution: $(5, 1)$
constant A value that does not change.	**constante** Valor que no cambia.	$3, 0, \pi$
constant of variation The constant k in direct and inverse variation equations.	**constante de variación** La constante k en ecuaciones de variación directa e inversa.	$y = 5x$ constant of variation
continuous function A function whose graph is an unbroken line or curve with no gaps or breaks.	**función continua** Función cuya gráfica es una línea recta o curva continua, sin espacios ni interrupciones.	$f(x) = 2^x$ 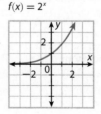

© Houghton Mifflin Harcourt Publishing Company

ENGLISH	SPANISH	EXAMPLES
continuous graph A graph made up of connected lines or curves.	**gráfica continua** Gráfica compuesta por líneas rectas o curvas conectadas.	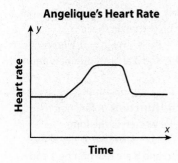
conversion factor The ratio of two equal quantities, each measured in different units.	**factor de conversión** Razón entre dos cantidades iguales, cada una medida en unidades diferentes.	$\frac{12 \text{ inches}}{1 \text{ foot}}$
correlation A measure of the strength and direction of the relationship between two variables or data sets.	**correlación** Medida de la fuerza y dirección de la relación entre dos variables o conjuntos de datos.	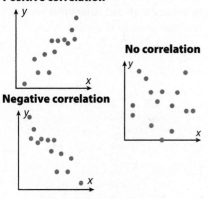
correlation coefficient A number r, where $-1 \leq r \leq 1$, that describes how closely the points in a scatter plot cluster around the least-squares line.	**coeficiente de correlación** Número r, donde $-1 \leq r \leq 1$, que describe a qué distancia de la recta de mínimos cuadrados se agrupan los puntos de un diagrama de dispersión.	An r-value close to 1 describes a strong positive correlation. An r-value close to 0 describes a weak correlation or no correlation. An r-value close to -1 describes a strong negative correlation.
cross products In the statement $\frac{a}{b} = \frac{c}{d}$, bc and ad are the cross products.	**productos cruzados** En el enunciado $\frac{a}{b} = \frac{c}{d}$, bc y ad son productos cruzados.	$\frac{1}{2} = \frac{3}{6}$ Cross products: $2 \cdot 3 = 6$ and $1 \cdot 6 = 6$
Cross Product Property For any real numbers a, b, c, and d, where $b \neq 0$ and $d \neq 0$, if $\frac{a}{b} = \frac{c}{d}$, then $ad = bc$.	**Propiedad de productos cruzados** Dados los números reales a, b, c y d, donde $b \neq 0$ y $d \neq 0$, si $\frac{a}{b} = \frac{c}{d}$, entonces $ad = bc$.	If $\frac{4}{6} = \frac{10}{x}$, then $4x = 60$, so $x = 15$.
cube root A number, written as $\sqrt[3]{x}$, whose cube is x.	**raíz cúbica** Número, expresado como $\sqrt[3]{x}$, cuyo cubo es x.	$\sqrt[3]{64} = 4$, because $4^3 = 64$; 4 is the cube root of 64.
cube-root function The function $f(x) = \sqrt[3]{x}$.	**función de raíz cúbica** La función $f(x) = \sqrt[3]{x}$.	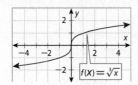

ENGLISH	SPANISH	EXAMPLES
cubic equation An equation that can be written in the form $ax^3 + bx^2 + cx + d = 0$, where $a, b, c,$ and d are real numbers and $a \neq 0$.	**ecuación cúbica** Ecuación que se puede expresar como $ax^3 + bx^2 + cx + d = 0$, donde $a, b, c,$ y d son números reales y $a \neq 0$.	$4x^3 + x^2 - 3x - 1 = 0$
cubic function A function that can be written in the form $f(x) = ax^3 + bx^2 + cx + d$, where $a, b, c,$ and d are real numbers and $a \neq 0$.	**función cúbica** Función que se puede expresar como $f(x) = ax^3 + bx^2 + cx + d$, donde $a, b, c,$ y d son números reales y $a \neq 0$.	$f(x) = x^3 + 2x^2 - 6x + 8$
cubic polynomial A polynomial of degree 3.	**polinomio cúbico** Polinomio de grado 3.	$x^3 + 4x^2 - 6x + 2$
cumulative frequency The frequency of all data values that are less than or equal to a given value.	**frecuencia acumulativa** Frecuencia de todos los valores de los datos que son menores que o iguales a un valor dado.	For the data set 2, 2, 3, 5, 5, 6, 7, 7, 8, 8, 8, 9, the cumulative frequency table is shown below.

For the cumulative frequency table:

Data	Frequency	Cumulative Frequency
2	2	2
3	1	3
5	2	5
6	1	6
7	2	8
8	3	11
9	1	12

D

ENGLISH	SPANISH	EXAMPLES
data Information gathered from a survey or experiment.	**datos** Información reunida en una encuesta o experimento.	
degree of a monomial The sum of the exponents of the variables in the monomial.	**grado de un monomio** Suma de los exponentes de las variables del monomio.	$4x^2y^5z^3$ Degree: $2 + 5 + 3 = 10$ $5 = 5x^0$ Degree: 0
degree of a polynomial The degree of the term of the polynomial with the greatest degree.	**grado de un polinomio** Grado del término del polinomio con el grado máximo.	$3x^2y^2 \quad + \quad 4xy^5 \quad - \quad 12x^3y^2 \qquad$ Degree 6 Degree 4 Degree 6 Degree 5
dependent system A system of equations that has infinitely many solutions.	**sistema dependiente** Sistema de ecuaciones que tiene infinitamente muchas soluciones.	$\begin{cases} x + y = 2 \\ 2x + 2y = 4 \end{cases}$
dependent variable The output of a function; a variable whose value depends on the value of the input, or independent variable.	**variable dependiente** Salida de una función; variable cuyo valor depende del valor de la entrada, o variable independiente.	For $y = 2x + 1$, y is the dependent variable. input: x output: y
difference of two cubes A polynomial of the form $a^3 - b^3$, which may be written as the product $(a - b)(a^2 + ab + b^2)$.	**diferencia de dos cubos** Polinomio del tipo $a^3 - b^3$, que se puede expresar como el producto $(a - b)(a^2 + ab + b^2)$.	$x^3 - 8 = (x - 2)(x^2 + 2x + 4)$

ENGLISH	SPANISH	EXAMPLES

difference of two squares A polynomial of the form $a^2 - b^2$, which may be written as the product $(a + b)(a - b)$.

diferencia de dos cuadrados Polinomio del tipo $a^2 - b^2$, que se puede expresar como el producto $(a + b)(a - b)$.

$x^2 - 4 = (x + 2)(x - 2)$

---

dimensional analysis A process that uses rates to convert measurements from one unit to another.

análisis dimensional Un proceso que utiliza tasas para convertir medidas de unidad a otra.

$12 \text{ pt} \cdot \frac{1 \text{ qt}}{2 \text{ pt}} = 6 \text{ qt}$

---

direct variation A linear relationship between two variables, x and y, that can be written in the form $y = kx$, where k is a nonzero constant.

variación directa Relación lineal entre dos variables, x e y, que puede expresarse en la forma $y = kx$, donde k es una constante distinta de cero.

---

discrete function A function whose graph is made up of unconnected points.

función discreta Función cuya gráfica compuesta de puntos no conectados.

---

discrete graph A graph made up of unconnected points.

gráfica discreta Gráfica compuesta de puntos no conectados.

Theme Park Attendance

---

discriminant The discriminant of the quadratic equation $ax^2 + bx + c = 0$ is $b^2 - 4ac$.

discriminante El discriminante de la ecuación cuadrática $ax^2 + bx + c = 0$ es $b^2 - 4ac$.

The discriminant of $2x^2 - 5x - 3 = 0$ is $(-5)^2 - 4(2)(-3)$ or 49.

Distance Formula In a coordinate plane, the distance from (x_1, y_1) to (x_2, y_2) is
$$d = \sqrt{(x_2 - x_1)^2 + (y_2 - y_1)^2}.$$

Fórmula de distancia En un plano cartesiano, la distancia desde (x_1, y_1) hasta (x_2, y_2) es
$$d = \sqrt{(x_2 - x_1)^2 + (y_2 - y_1)^2}.$$

The distance from $(2, 5)$ to $(-1, 1)$ is
$$d = \sqrt{(-1 - 2)^2 + (1 - 5)^2}$$
$$= \sqrt{(-3)^2 + (-4)^2}$$
$$= \sqrt{9 + 16} = \sqrt{25} = 5.$$

Distributive Property For all real numbers a, b, and c, $a(b + c) = ab + ac$, and $(b + c)a = ba + ca$.

Propiedad distributiva Dados los números reales a, b y c, $a(b + c) = ab + ac$, y $(b + c)a = ba + ca$.

$3(4 + 5) = 3 \cdot 4 + 3 \cdot 5$
$(4 + 5)3 = 4 \cdot 3 + 5 \cdot 3$

Division Property of Equality For real numbers a, b, and c, where $c \neq 0$, if $a = b$, then $\frac{a}{c} = \frac{b}{c}$.

Propiedad de igualdad de la división Dados los números reales a, b y c, donde $c \neq 0$, si $a = b$, entonces $\frac{a}{c} = \frac{b}{c}$.

$4x = 12$
$\frac{4x}{4} = \frac{12}{4}$
$x = 3$

Division Property of Inequality
If both sides of an inequality are divided by the same positive quantity, the new inequality will have the same solution set. If both sides of an inequality are divided by the same negative quantity, the new inequality will have the same solution set if the inequality symbol is reversed.

Propiedad de desigualdad de la división Cuando ambos lados de una desigualdad se dividen entre el mismo número positivo, la nueva desigualdad tiene el mismo conjunto solución.Cuando ambos lados de una desigualdad se dividen entra el mismo número negativo, la nueva desigualdad tiene el mismo conjunto solución si se invierte el símbolo de desigualdad.

$$4x \geq 12$$
$$\frac{4x}{4} \geq \frac{12}{4}$$
$$x \geq 3$$

$$-4x \geq 12$$
$$\frac{-4x}{-4} \leq \frac{12}{-4}$$
$$x \leq -3$$

---

domain The set of all first coordinates (or x-values) of a relation or function.

dominio Conjunto de todos los valores de la primera coordenada (o valores de x) de una función o relación.

The domain of the function $\{(-5, 3), (-3, -2), (-1, -1), (1, 0)\}$ is $\{-5, -3, -1, 1\}$.

---

dot plot A number line with marks or dots that show frequency.

diagrama de puntos Recta numérica con marcas o puntos que indican la frecuencia.

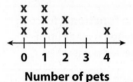

Number of pets

E

elimination method A method used to solve systems of equations in which one variable is eliminated by adding or subtracting two equations of the system.

eliminación Método utilizado para resolver sistemas de ecuaciones por el cual se elimina una variable sumando o restando dos ecuaciones del sistema.

---

empty set A set with no elements.

conjunto vacío Conjunto sin elementos.

The solution set of $|x| < 0$ is the empty set, $\{\ \}$, or $\emptyset$.

---

end behavior The trends in the y-values of a function as the x-values approach positive and negative infinity.

comportamiento extremo Tendencia de los valores de y de una función a medida que los valores de x se aproximan al infinito positivo y negativo.

Equality of Bases Property Two powers with the same positive base other than 1 are equal if and only if the exponents are equal.

Propiedad de igualdad de las bases Dos potencias con la misma base positiva distinta de 1 son iguales si y solo si los exponentes son iguales.

If $b > 0$ and, $b \neq 1$, then $b^x = b^y$ if and only if $x = y$.

---

equation A mathematical statement that two expressions are equivalent.

ecuación Enunciado matemático que indica que dos expresiones son equivalentes.

$$x + 4 = 7$$
$$2 + 3 = 6 - 1$$
$$(x - 1)^2 + (y + 2)^2 = 4$$

---

equivalent ratios Ratios that name the same comparison.

razones equivalentes Razones que expresan la misma comparación.

$\frac{1}{2}$ and $\frac{2}{4}$ are equivalent ratios.

Glossary/Glosario

ENGLISH	SPANISH	EXAMPLES
evaluate To find the value of an algebraic expression by substituting a number for each variable and simplifying by using the order of operations.	**evaluar** Calcular el valor de una expresión algebraica sustituyendo cada variable por un número y simplificando mediante el orden de las operaciones.	Evaluate $2x + 7$ for $x = 3$. $2x + 7$ $2(3) + 7$ $6 + 7$ 13
even function A function in which $f(-x) = f(x)$ for all x in the domain of the function.	**función par** Función en la que para todos los valores de x dentro del dominio de la función.	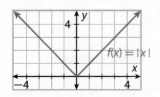 $f(x) = \|x\|$ is an even function.
explicit rule for *n*th term of a sequence A rule that defines the nth term a_n, or a general term, of a sequence as a function of n.	**fórmula explícita** Fórmula que define el enésimo término a_n, o término general, de una sucesión como una función de n.	
exponent The number that indicates how many times the base in a power is used as a factor.	**exponente** Número que indica la cantidad de veces que la base de una potencia se utiliza como factor.	$3^4 = 3 \cdot 3 \cdot 3 \cdot 3 = 81$ 4 is the exponent.
exponential decay An exponential function of the form $f(x) = ab^x$ in which $0 < b < 1$. If r is the rate of decay, then the function can be written $y = a(1 - r)^t$, where a is the initial amount and t is the time.	**decremento exponencial** Función exponencial del tipo $f(x) = ab^x$ en la cual $0 < b < 1$. Si r es la tasa decremental, entonces la función se puede expresar como $y = a(1 - r)^t$, donde a es la cantidad inicial y t es el tiempo.	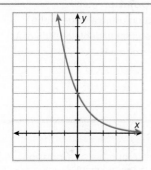
exponential expression An algebraic expression in which the variable is in an exponent with a fixed number as the base.	**expresión exponencial** Expresión algebraica en la que la variable está en un exponente y que tiene un número fijo como base.	2^{x+1}
exponential function A function of the form $f(x) = ab^x$, where a and b are real numbers with $a \neq 0$, $b > 0$, and $b \neq 1$.	**función exponencial** Función del tipo $f(x) = ab^x$, donde a y b son números reales con $a \neq 0$, $b > 0$ y $b \neq 1$.	$f(x) = 3 \cdot 4^x$ 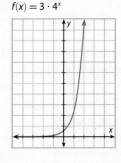

Glossary/Glosario

ENGLISH	SPANISH	EXAMPLES

exponential growth An exponential function of the form $f(x) = ab^x$ in which $b > 1$. If r is the rate of growth, then the function can be written $y = a(1 + r)^t$, where a is the initial amount and t is the time.

crecimiento exponencial Función exponencial del tipo $f(x) = ab^x$ en la que $b > 1$. Si r es la tasa de crecimiento, entonces la función se puede expresar como $y = a(1 + r)^t$, donde a es la cantidad inicial y t es el tiempo.

$f(x) = 2^x$

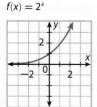

---

exponential regression A statistical method used to fit an exponential model to a given data set.

regresión exponencial Método estadístico utilizado para ajustar un modelo exponencial a un conjunto de datos determinado.

---

expression A mathematical phrase that contains operations, numbers, and/or variables.

expresión Frase matemática que contiene operaciones, números y/o variables.

$6x + 1$

---

extraneous solution A solution of a derived equation that is not a solution of the original equation.

solución extraña Solución de una ecuación derivada que no es una solución de la ecuación original.

To solve $\sqrt{x} = -2$, square both sides; $x = 4$.
Check $\sqrt{4} = -2$ is false; so 4 is an extraneous solution.

---

extrapolation Making a prediction using a value of the independent variable outside of a model's domain.

extrapolación Hacer una predicción con un valor de la variable independiente que esté fuera del dominio de un modelo.

F

factor A number or expression that is multiplied by another number or expression to get a product. *See also factoring.*

factor Número o expresión que se multiplica por otro número o expresión para obtener un producto. *Ver también* factoreo.

$12 = 3 \cdot 4$
3 and 4 are factors of 12.
$x^2 - 1 = (x - 1)(x + 1)$
$(x - 1)$ and $(x + 1)$ are factors of $x^2 - 1$.

---

factored form A quadratic function written as $y = k(x - a)(x - b)$ where $k \neq 0$.

forma factorizada Función cuadrática expresada en la forma $y = k(x - a)(x - b)$ donde $k \neq 0$.

$f(x) = x^2 + 2x - 8$
$\quad = (x + 4)(x - 2)$

---

factoring The process of writing a number or algebraic expression as a product.

factorización Proceso por el que se expresa un número o expresión algebraica como un producto.

$x^2 - 4x - 21 = (x - 7)(x + 3)$

---

family of functions A set of functions whose graphs have basic characteristics in common. Functions in the same family are transformations of their parent function.

familia de funciones Conjunto de funciones cuyas gráficas tienen características básicas en común. Las funciones de la misma familia son transformaciones de su función madre.

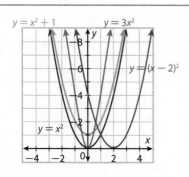

Glossary/Glosario

ENGLISH	SPANISH	EXAMPLES
first differences The differences between *y*-values of a function for evenly spaced *x*-values.	**primeras diferencias** Diferencias entre los valores de *y* de una función para valores de *x* espaciados uniformemente.	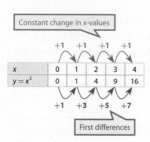
first quartile The median of the lower half of a data set, denoted Q_1. Also called *lower quartile*.	**primer cuartil** Mediana de la mitad inferior de un conjunto de datos, expresada como Q_1. También se llama *cuartil inferior*.	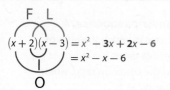
FOIL A mnemonic (memory) device for a method of multiplying two binomials: Multiply the **First** terms. Multiply the **Outer** terms. Multiply the **Inner** terms. Multiply the **Last** terms.	**FOIL** Regla mnemotécnica para recordar el método de multiplicación de dos binomios: Multiplicar los términos **Primeros** (*First*). Multiplicar los términos **Externos** (*Outer*). Multiplicar los términos **Internos** (*Inner*). Multiplicar los términos **Últimos** (*Last*).	$$(x+2)(x-3) = x^2 - 3x + 2x - 6$$ $$= x^2 - x - 6$$
formula A literal equation that states a rule for a relationship among quantities.	**fórmula** Ecuación literal que establece una regla para una relación entre cantidades.	$A = \pi r^2$
fractional exponent *See* rational exponent.	**exponente fraccionario** *Ver* exponente racional.	
frequency The number of times the value appears in the data set.	**frecuencia** Cantidad de veces que aparece el valor en un conjunto de datos.	In the data set 5, 6, 6, 7, 8, 9, the data value 6 has a frequency of 2.
frequency table A table that lists the number of times, or frequency, that each data value occurs.	**tabla de frecuencia** Tabla que enumera la cantidad de veces que ocurre cada valor de datos, o la frecuencia.	Data set: 1, 1, 2, 2, 3, 4, 5, 5, 5, 6, 6, 6, 6 Frequency table: Data: 1 2 3 4 5 6 / Frequency: 2 2 1 1 3 4
function A relation in which every domain value is paired with exactly one range value.	**función** Relación en la que a cada valor de dominio corresponde exactamente un valor de rango.	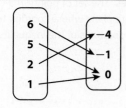

For the frequency table example:

Data	Frequency
1	2
2	2
3	1
4	1
5	3
6	4

Glossary/Glosario

ENGLISH	SPANISH	EXAMPLES
function notation If x is the independent variable and y is the dependent variable, then the function notation for y is $f(x)$, read "f of x," where f names the function.	**notación de función** Si x es la variable independiente e y es la variable dependiente, entonces la notación de función para y es $f(x)$, que se lee "f de x," donde f nombra la función.	equation: $y = 2x$ function notation: $f(x) = 2x$
function rule An algebraic expression that defines a function.	**regla de función** Expresión algebraica que define una función.	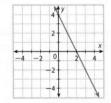

Glossary/Glosario

G

geometric sequence A sequence in which the ratio of successive terms is a constant r, called the common ratio, where $r \neq 0$ and $r \neq 1$.	**sucesión geométrica** Sucesión en la que la razón de los términos sucesivos es una constante r, denominada razón común, donde $r \neq 0$ y $r \neq 1$.	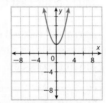
graph of a function The set of points in a coordinate plane with coordinates (x, y), where x is in the domain of the function f and $y = f(x)$.	**gráfica de una función** Conjunto de los puntos de un plano cartesiano con coordenadas (x, y), donde x está en el dominio de la función f e $y = f(x)$.	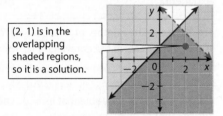
graph of a system of linear inequalities The region in a coordinate plane consisting of points whose coordinates are solutions to all of the inequalities in the system.	**gráfica de un sistema de desigualdades lineales** Región de un plano cartesiano que consta de puntos cuyas coordenadas son soluciones de todas las desigualdades del sistema.	$(2, 1)$ is in the overlapping shaded regions, so it is a solution.
graph of an inequality in one variable The set of points on a number line that are solutions of the inequality.	**gráfica de una desigualdad en una variable** Conjunto de los puntos de una recta numérica que representan soluciones de la desigualdad.	
graph of an inequality in two variables The set of points in a coordinate plane whose coordinates (x, y) are solutions of the inequality.	**gráfica de una desigualdad en dos variables** Conjunto de los puntos de un plano cartesiano cuyas coordenadas (x, y) son soluciones de la desigualdad.	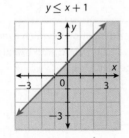

ENGLISH	SPANISH	EXAMPLES
greatest common factor (monomials) (GCF) The product of the greatest integer and the greatest power of each variable that divide evenly into each monomial.	**máximo común divisor (monomios) (MCD)** Producto del entero mayor y la potencia mayor de cada variable que divide exactamente cada monomio.	The GCF of $4x^3y$ and $6x^2y$ is $2x^2y$.
greatest common factor (numbers) (GCF) The largest common factor of two or more given numbers.	**máximo común divisor (números) (MCD)** El mayor de los factores comunes compartidos por dos o más números dados.	The GCF of 27 and 45 is 9.
greatest integer function A function denoted by $f(x) = [x]$ in which the number x is rounded down to the greatest integer that is less than or equal to x.	**función de entero mayor** Función expresada como $f(x) = [x]$ en la cual el número x se redondea hacia abajo hasta el entero mayor que sea menor o igual a x.	
grouping symbols Symbols such as parentheses ( ), brackets [ ], and braces { } that separate part of an expression. A fraction bar, absolute-value symbols, and radical symbols may also be used as grouping symbols.	**símbolos de agrupación** Símbolos tales como paréntesis ( ), corchetes [ ] y llaves { } que separan parte de una expresión. La barra de fracciones, los símbolos de valor absoluto y los símbolos de radical también se pueden utilizar como símbolos de agrupación.	$6 + \{3 - [(4 - 3) + 2] + 1\} - 5$ $6 + \{3 - [1 + 2] + 1\} - 5$ $6 + \{3 - 3 + 1\} - 5$ $6 + 1 - 5$ 2

H

half-plane The part of the coordinate plane on one side of a line, which may include the line.	**semiplano** La parte del plano cartesiano de un lado de una línea, que puede incluir la línea.	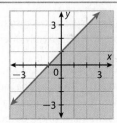
Heron's Formula A triangle with side lengths a, b, and c has area $A = \sqrt{s(s - a)(s - b)(s - c)}$, where s is one-half the perimeter, or $s = \frac{1}{2}(a + b + c)$.	**fórmula de Herón** Un triángulo con longitudes de lado a, b y c tiene un área $A = \sqrt{s(s - a)(s - b)(s - c)}$, donde s es la mitad del perímetro ó $s = \frac{1}{2}(a + b + c)$.	
histogram A bar graph used to display data grouped in intervals.	**histograma** Gráfica de barras utilizada para mostrar datos agrupados en intervalos de clases.	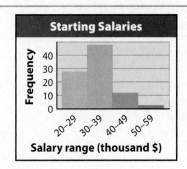

ENGLISH	SPANISH	EXAMPLES

horizontal line A line described by the equation $y = b$, where b is the y-intercept.

línea horizontal Línea descrita por la ecuación $y = b$, donde b es la intersección con el eje y.

$y = 4$

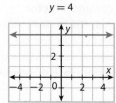

---

horizontal translation (of a parabola) is a shift of the parabola left or right, with no change in the shape of the parabola.

traslación horizontal (de una parábola) Desplazamiento de la parábola hacia la izquierda o hacia la derecha, sin producir cambios en la forma de la parábola.

---

hypotenuse The side opposite the right angle in a right triangle.

hipotenusa Lado opuesto al ángulo recto de un triángulo rectángulo.

hypotenuse

---

identity An equation that is true for all values of the variables.

identidad Ecuación verdadera para todos los valores de las variables.

$3 = 3$
$2(x - 1) = 2x - 2$

---

inconsistent system A system of equations or inequalities that has no solution.

sistema inconsistente Sistema de ecuaciones o desigualdades que no tiene solución.

$\begin{cases} x + y = 0 \\ x + y = 1 \end{cases}$

---

independent system A system of equations that has exactly one solution.

sistema independiente Sistema de ecuaciones que tiene sólo una solución.

$\begin{cases} x + y = 7 \\ x - y = 1 \end{cases}$
Solution: $(4, 3)$

---

independent variable The input of a function; a variable whose value determines the value of the output, or dependent variable.

variable independiente Entrada de una función; variable cuyo valor determina el valor de la salida, o variable dependiente.

For $y = 2x + 1$, x is the independent variable.

---

index In the radical $\sqrt[n]{x}$, which represents the nth root of x, n is the index. In the radical $\sqrt{x}$, the index is understood to be 2.

índice En el radical $\sqrt[n]{x}$, que representa la enésima raíz de x, n es el índice. En el radical $\sqrt{x}$, se da por sentado que el índice es 2.

The radical $\sqrt[3]{8}$ has an index of 3.

---

indirect measurement A method of measurement that uses formulas, similar figures, and/or proportions.

medición indirecta Método de medición en el que se usan fórmulas, figuras semejantes y/o proporciones.

---

inequality A statement that compares two expressions by using one of the following signs: $<, >, \leq, \geq$, or $\neq$.

desigualdad Enunciado que compara dos expresiones utilizando uno de los siguientes signos: $<, >, \leq, \geq,$ o $\neq$.

$x \geq 2$

---

input A value that is substituted for the independent variable in a relation or function.

entrada Valor que sustituye a la variable independiente en una relación o función.

For the function $f(x) = x + 5$, the input 3 produces an output of 8.

---

input-output table A table that displays input values of a function or expression together with the corresponding outputs.

tabla de entrada y salida Tabla que muestra los valores de entrada de una función o expresión junto con las correspondientes salidas.

Input	x	1	2	3	4
Output	y	4	7	10	13

---

intercept *See x*-intercept and *y*-intercept.

intersección *Ver* intersección con el eje *x* e intersección con el eje *y*.

---

interest The amount of money charged for borrowing money or the amount of money earned when saving or investing money. *See also* compound interest, simple interest.

interés Cantidad de dinero que se cobra por prestar dinero o cantidad de dinero que se gana cuando se ahorra o invierte dinero. *Ver también* interés compuesto, interés simple.

---

interpolation Making a prediction using a value of the independent variable from within a model's domain.

interpolación Hacer una predicción con un valor de la variable independiente a partir del dominio de un modelo.

---

interquartile range (IQR) The difference of the third (upper) and first (lower) quartiles in a data set, representing the middle half of the data.

rango entre cuartiles Diferencia entre el tercer cuartil (superior) y el primer cuartil (inferior) de un conjunto de datos, que representa la mitad central de los datos.

Lower half   Upper half
18, (23,) 28, 29, (36,) 42
First quartile   Third quartile
Interquartile range: $36 - 23 = 13$

---

intersection The intersection of two sets is the set of all elements that are common to both sets, denoted by ∩.

intersección de conjuntos La intersección de dos conjuntos es el conjunto de todos los elementos que son comunes a ambos conjuntos, expresado por ∩.

$A = \{1, 2, 3, 4\}$
$B = \{1, 3, 5, 7, 9\}$
$A \cap B = \{1, 3\}$

---

inverse of a function The relation that results from exchanging the input and output values of a function.

inverso de una función La relación que se genera al intercambiar los valores de entrada y de salida de una función.

---

inverse operations Operations that undo each other.

operaciones inversas Operaciones que se anulan entre sí.

Addition and subtraction of the same quantity are inverse operations:
$5 + 3 = 8, 8 - 3 = 5$
Multiplication and division by the same quantity are inverse operations: $2 \cdot 3 = 6$, $6 \div 3 = 2$

---

inverse relation The relation that results from exchanging the input and output values of a relation.

relación inversa La relación que se genera al intercambiar los valores de entrada y de salida de una relación.

Glossary/Glosario

Glossary/Glosario

inverse variation A relationship between two variables, x and y, that can be written in the form $y = \frac{k}{x}$, where k is a nonzero constant and $x \neq 0$.

variación inversa Relación entre dos variables, x e y, que puede expresarse en la forma $y = \frac{k}{x}$, donde k es una constante distinta de cero y $x \neq 0$.

$y = \frac{8}{x}$

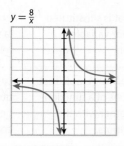

irrational number A real number that cannot be expressed as the ratio of two integers.

número irracional Número real que no se puede expresar como una razón de enteros.

$\sqrt{2}, \pi, e$

isosceles triangle A triangle with at least two congruent sides.

triángulo isósceles Triángulo que tiene al menos dos lados congruentes.

J

joint relative frequency The ratio of the frequency in a particular category divided by the total number of data values.

frecuencia relativa conjunta La línea de ajuste en que la suma de cuadrados de los residuos es la menor.

L

leading coefficient The coefficient of the first term of a polynomial in standard form.

coeficiente principal Coeficiente del primer término de un polinomio en forma estándar.

$3x^2 + 7x - 2$
Leading coefficient: 3

least common denominator (LCD) The least common multiple of the denominators of two or more given fractions or rational expressions.

mínimo común denominador (MCD) Mínimo común múltiplo de los denominadores de dos o más fracciones dadas o expresionnes racionales.

The LCD of $\frac{3}{4}$ and $\frac{5}{6}$ is 12.

least common multiple (monomials) (LCM) The product of the smallest positive number and the lowest power of each variable that divide evenly into each monomial.

mínimo común múltiplo (monomios) (MCM) El producto del número positivo más pequeño y la menor potencia de cada variable que divide exactamente cada monomio.

The LCM of $6x^2$ and $4x$ is $12x^2$.

least common multiple (numbers) (LCM) The smallest whole number, other than zero, that is a multiple of two or more given numbers.

mínimo común múltiplo (números) (MCM) El menor de los números cabales, distinto de cero, que es múltiplo de dos o más números dados.

The LCM of 10 and 18 is 90.

least-squares line The line of fit for which the sum of the squares of the residuals is as small as possible

línea de mínimos cuadrados La línea de ajuste en que la suma de cuadrados de los residuos es la menor.

ENGLISH	SPANISH	EXAMPLES
like terms Terms with the same variables raised to the same exponents.	**términos semejantes** Términos con las mismas variables elevadas a los mismos exponentes.	
line graph A graph that uses line segments to show how data changes.	**gráfica lineal** Gráfica que se vale de segmentos de recta para mostrar cambios en los datos.	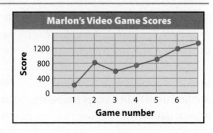
line plot A number line with marks or dots that show frequency.	**diagrama de acumulación** Recta numérica con marcas o puntos que indican la frecuencia.	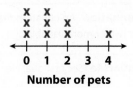
line of best fit The line that comes closest to all of the points in a data set.	**línea de mejor ajuste** Línea que más se acerca a todos los puntos de un conjunto de datos.	
line of fit *See trend line.*	**línea de ajuste** *Ver línea de tendencia.*	
linear equation in one variable An equation that can be written in the form $ax = b$ where a and b are constants and $a \neq 0$.	**ecuación lineal en una variable** Ecuación que puede expresarse en la forma $ax = b$ donde a y b son constantes y $a \neq 0$.	$x + 1 = 7$
linear equation in two variables An equation that can be written in the form $Ax + By = C$ where A, B, and C are constants and A and B are not both 0.	**ecuación lineal en dos variables** Ecuación que puede expresarse en la forma $Ax + By = C$ donde A, B y C son constantes y A y B no son ambas 0.	$2x + 3y = 6$
linear function A function that can be written in the form $y = mx + b$, where x is the independent variable and m and b are real numbers. Its graph is a line.	**función lineal** Función que puede expresarse en la forma $y = mx + b$, donde x es la variable independiente y m y b son números reales. Su gráfica es una línea.	$y = x - 1$ 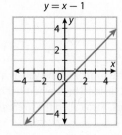
linear inequality in one variable An inequality that can be written in one of the following forms: $ax < b, ax > b, ax \leq b, ax \geq b$, or $ax \neq b$, where a and b are constants and $a \neq 0$.	**desigualdad lineal en una variable** Desigualdad que puede expresarse de una de las siguientes formas: $ax < b, ax > b, ax \leq b,$ $ax \geq b$ o $ax \neq b$, donde a y b son constantes y $a \neq 0$.	$3x - 5 \leq 2(x + 4)$

Glossary/Glosario

ENGLISH	SPANISH	EXAMPLES
linear inequality in two variables An inequality that can be written in one of the following forms: $Ax + By < C$, $Ax + By > C$, $Ax + By \leq C$, $Ax + By \geq C$, or $Ax + By \neq C$, where A, B, and C are constants and A and B are not both 0.	**desigualdad lineal en dos variables** Desigualdad que puede expresarse de una de las siguientes formas: $Ax + By < C$, $Ax + By > C$, $Ax + By \leq C$, $Ax + By \geq C$ o $Ax + By \neq C$, donde A, B y C son constantes y A y B no son ambas 0.	$2x + 3y > 6$
linear regression A statistical method used to fit a linear model to a given data set.	**regresión lineal** Método estadístico utilizado para ajustar un modelo lineal a un conjunto de datos determinado.	
literal equation An equation that contains two or more variables.	**ecuación literal** Ecuación que contiene dos o más variables.	$d = rt$ $A = \frac{1}{2}h(b_1 + b_2)$
lower quartile *See* first quartile.	**cuartil inferior** *Ver* primer cuartil.	

M

ENGLISH	SPANISH	EXAMPLES
mapping diagram A diagram that shows the relationship of elements in the domain to elements in the range of a relation or function.	**diagrama de correspondencia** Diagrama que muestra la relación entre los elementos del dominio y los elementos del rango de una función.	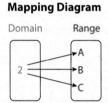 **Mapping Diagram**
marginal relative frequency The sum of the joint relative frequencies in a row or column of a two-way table.	**frecuencia relativa marginal** La suma de las frecuencias relativas conjuntas en una fila o columna de una tabla de doble entrada.	
maximum value of a function The y-value of the highest point on the graph of the function.	**máximo de una función** Valor de y del punto más alto en la gráfica de la función.	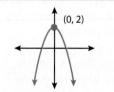 $(0, 2)$ The maximum of the function is 2.
mean The sum of all the values in a data set divided by the number of data values. Also called the *average*.	**media** Suma de todos los valores de un conjunto de datos dividida entre el número de valores de datos. También llamada *promedio*.	Data set: 4, 6, 7, 8, 10 Mean: $\frac{4 + 6 + 7 + 8 + 10}{5} = \frac{35}{5} = 7$
measure of central tendency A measure that describes the center of a data set.	**medida de tendencia dominante** Medida que describe el centro de un conjunto de datos.	mean, median, or mode

ENGLISH	SPANISH	EXAMPLES
median For an ordered data set with an odd number of values, the median is the middle value. For an ordered data set with an even number of values, the median is the average of the two middle values.	**mediana** Dado un conjunto de datos ordenado con un número impar de valores, la mediana es el valor medio. Dado un conjunto de datos con un número par de valores, la mediana es el promedio de los dos valores medios.	8, 9, (9), 12, 15 Median: 9 4, 6, (7, 10), 10, 12 Median: $\frac{7+10}{2} = 8.5$
midpoint The point that divides a segment into two congruent segments.	**punto medio** Punto que divide un segmento en dos segmentos congruentes.	A $\quad$ B $\quad$ C Point B is the midpoint of $\overline{AC}$.
minimum value of a function The y-value of the lowest point on the graph of the function.	**mínimo de una función** Valor de y del punto más bajo en la gráfica de la función.	 (0, -2) The minimum of the function is -2.
mode The value or values that occur most frequently in a data set; if all values occur with the same frequency, the data set is said to have no mode.	**moda** El valor o los valores que se presentan con mayor frecuencia en un conjunto de datos. Si todos los valores se presentan con la misma frecuencia, se dice que el conjunto de datos no tiene moda.	Data set: 3, 6, 8, 8, 10 Mode: 8 Data set: 2, 5, 5, 7, 7 Modes: 5 and 7 Data set: 2, 3, 6, 9, 11 No mode
monomial A number or a product of numbers and variables with whole-number exponents, or a polynomial with one term.	**monomio** Número o producto de números y variables con exponentes de números cabales, o polinomio con un término.	$3x^2y^4$
Multiplication Property of Equality If a, b, and c are real numbers and $a = b$, then $ac = bc$.	**Propiedad de igualdad de la multiplicación** Si a, b y c son números reales y $a = b$, entonces $ac = bc$.	$\frac{1}{3}x = 7$ $(3)\left(\frac{1}{3}x\right) = (3)(7)$ $x = 21$
Multiplication Property of Inequality If both sides of an inequality are multiplied by the same positive quantity, the new inequality will have the same solution set. If both sides of an inequality are multiplied by the same negative quantity, the new inequality will have the same solution set if the inequality symbol is reversed.	**Propiedad de desigualdad de la multiplicación** Si ambos lados de una desigualdad se multiplican por el mismo número positivo, la nueva desigualdad tendrá el mismo conjunto solución. Si ambos lados de una desigualdad se multiplican por el mismo número negativo, la nueva desigualdad tendrá el mismo conjunto solución si se invierte el símbolo de desigualdad.	$\frac{1}{3}x > 7$ $(3)\left(\frac{1}{3}x\right) > (3)(7)$ $x > 21$ $-x \leq 2$ $(-1)(-x) \geq (-1)(2)$ $x \geq -2$
multiplicative inverse The reciprocal of the number.	**inverso multiplicativo** Recíproco de un número.	The multiplicative inverse of 5 is $\frac{1}{5}$.

N

Glossary/Glosario

---

negative correlation Two data sets have a negative correlation if one set of data values increases as the other set decreases.

correlación negativa Dos conjuntos de datos tienen una correlación negativa si un conjunto de valores de datos aumenta a medida que el otro conjunto disminuye.

---

negative exponent For any nonzero real number x and any integer n, $x^{-n} = \frac{1}{x^n}$.

exponente negativo Para cualquier número real distinto de cero x y cualquier entero n, $x^{-n} = \frac{1}{x^n}$.

$x^{-2} = \frac{1}{x^2}; 3^{-2} = \frac{1}{3^2}$

---

negative number A number that is less than zero. Negative numbers lie to the left of zero on a number line.

número negativo Número menor que cero. Los números negativos se ubican a la izquierda del cero en una recta numérica.

−2 is a negative number.

−4 −3 −2 −1 0 1 2 3 4

---

net A diagram of the faces of a three-dimensional figure arranged in such a way that the diagram can be folded to form the three-dimensional figure.

plantilla Diagrama de las caras de una figura tridimensional que se puede plegar para formar la figura tridimensional.

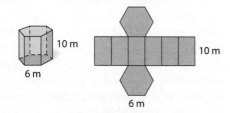

---

no correlation Two data sets have no correlation if there is no relationship between the sets of values.

sin correlación Dos conjuntos de datos no tienen correlación si no existe una relación entre los conjuntos de valores.

---

nonlinear system of equations A system in which at least one of the equations is not linear.

sistema no lineal de ecuaciones Sistema en el cual por lo menos una de las ecuaciones no es lineal.

A system that contains one quadratic equation and one linear equation is a nonlinear system.

---

normal curve The graph of a probability density function that corresponds to a normal distribution; bell-shaped and symmetric about the mean, with the x-axis as a horizontal asymptote.

curva normal La gráfica de una función de densidad de probabilidad que corresponde a la distribución normal; con forma de campana y simétrica con relación a la media, el eje x es una asíntota horizontal.

---

normal distribution A distribution of data that varies about the mean in such a way that the graph of its probability density function is a normal curve.

distribución normal Distribución de datos que varía respecto de la media de tal manera que la gráfica de su función de densidad de probabilidad es una curva normal.

ENGLISH	SPANISH	EXAMPLES
nth root The *n*th root of a number *a*, written as $\sqrt[n]{a}$ or $a^{\frac{1}{n}}$, is a number that is equal to *a* when it is raised to the *n*th power.	**enésima raíz** La enésima raíz de un número *a*, que se escribe $\sqrt[n]{a}$ o $a^{\frac{1}{n}}$, es un número igual a *a* cuando se eleva a la enésima potencia.	$\sqrt[5]{32} = 2$, because $2^5 = 32$.
numerical expression An expression that contains only numbers and operations.	**expresión numérica** Expresión que contiene únicamente números y operaciones.	

O

ENGLISH	SPANISH	EXAMPLES
obtuse triangle A triangle with one obtuse angle.	**triángulo obtusángulo** Triángulo con un ángulo obtuso.	
odd function A function in which $f(-x) = -f(x)$ for all *x* in the domain of the function.	**función impar** Función en la que $f(-x) = -f(x)$ para todos los valores de *x* dentro del dominio de la función	$f(x) = x^3$ $f(x) = x^3$ is an odd function.
opposite The opposite of a number *a*, denoted $-a$, is the number that is the same distance from zero as *a*, on the opposite side of the number line. The sum of opposites is 0.	**opuesto** El opuesto de un número *a*, expresado $-a$, es el número que se encuentra a la misma distancia de cero que *a*, del lado opuesto de la recta numérica. La suma de los opuestos es 0.	5 units 5 units $-6\ -5\ -4\ -3\ -2\ -1\ 0\ 1\ 2\ 3\ 4\ 5\ 6$ 5 and -5 are opposites.
opposite reciprocal The opposite of the reciprocal of a number. The opposite reciprocal of any nonzero number *a* is $-\frac{1}{a}$.	**recíproco opuesto** Opuesto del recíproco de un número. El recíproco opuesto de *a* es $-\frac{1}{a}$.	The opposite reciprocal of $\frac{2}{3}$ is $-\frac{3}{2}$.
OR A logical operator representing the union of two sets.	**O** Operador lógico que representa la unión de dos conjuntos.	$A = \{2, 3, 4, 5\}$ $B = \{1, 3, 5, 7\}$ The set of values that are in *A* OR *B* is $A \cup B = \{1, 2, 3, 4, 5, 7\}$.
outlier A data value that is far removed from the rest of the data.	**valor extremo** Valor de datos que está muy alejado del resto de los datos.	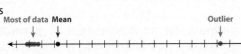
output The result of substituting a value for a variable in a function.	**salida** Resultado de la sustitución de una variable por un valor en una función.	For the function $f(x) = x^2 + 1$, the input 3 produces an output of 10.

Glossary/Glosario

Glossary/Glosario

P

parabola The shape of the graph of a quadratic function.

parábola Forma de la gráfica de una función cuadrática.

parallel lines Lines in the same plane that do not intersect.

líneas paralelas Líneas en el mismo plano que no se cruzan.

parameter One of the constants in a function or equation that may be changed. Also the third variable in a set of parametric equations.

parámetro Una de las constantes en una función o ecuación que se puede cambiar. También es la tercera variable en un conjunto de ecuaciones paramétricas.

parent function The simplest function with the defining characteristics of the family. Functions in the same family are transformations of their parent function.

función madre La función más básica que tiene las características distintivas de una familia. Las funciones de la misma familia son transformaciones de su función madre.

$f(x) = x^2$ is the parent function for $g(x) = x^2 + 4$ and $h(x) = (5x + 2)^2 - 3$.

perfect square A number whose positive square root is a whole number.

cuadrado perfecto Número cuya raíz cuadrada positiva es un número cabal.

36 is a perfect square because $\sqrt{36} = 6$.

perfect-square trinomial A trinomial whose factored form is the square of a binomial. A perfect-square trinomial has the form $a^2 - 2ab + b^2 = (a - b)^2$ or $a^2 + 2ab + b^2 = (a + b)^2$.

trinomio cuadrado perfecto Trinomio cuya forma factorizada es el cuadrado de un binomio. Un trinomio cuadrado perfecto tiene la forma $a^2 - 2ab + b^2 = (a - b)^2$ o $a^2 + 2ab + b^2 = (a + b)^2$.

$x^2 + 6x + 9$ is a perfect-square trinomial, because $x^2 + 6x + 9 = (x + 3)^2$.

permutation An arrangement of a group of objects in which order is important.

permutación Arreglo de un grupo de objetos en el cual el orden es importante.

For objects A, B, C, and D, there are 12 different permutations of 2 objects.
AB, AC, AD, BC, BD, CD
BA, CA, DA, CB, DB, DC

perpendicular Intersecting to form 90° angles.

perpendicular Que se cruza para formar ángulos de 90°.

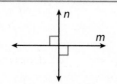

perpendicular lines Lines that intersect at 90° angles.

líneas perpendiculares Líneas que se cruzan en ángulos de 90°.

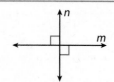

piecewise function A function that is a combination of one or more functions.

función a trozos Función que es una combinación de una o más funciones.

---

plane A flat surface that has no thickness and extends forever.

plano Una superficie plana que no tiene grosor y se extiende infinitamente.

---

point A location that has no size.

punto Ubicación exacta que no tiene ningún tamaño.

$P \bullet$
point P

---

point-slope form The point-slope form of a linear equation is $y - y_1 = m(x - x_1)$, where m is the slope and (x_1, y_1) is a point on the line.

forma de punto y pendiente La forma de punto y pendiente de una ecuación lineal es $y - y_1 = m(x - x_1)$, donde m es la pendiente y (x_1, y_1) es un punto en la línea.

$y - 3 = 2(x - 3)$

---

polynomial A monomial or a sum or difference of monomials.

polinomio Monomio o suma o diferencia de monomios.

$2x^2 + 3xy - 7y^2$

---

polynomial long division A method of dividing one polynomial by another.

división larga polinomial Método por el que se divide un polinomio entre otro.

$$\begin{array}{r} x+1 \\ x+2 \overline{)\ x^2 + 3x + 5} \\ -(x^2 + 2x) \\ \hline x + 5 \\ -(x+2) \\ \hline 3 \end{array}$$

$\frac{x^2 + 3x + 5}{x+2} = x + 1 + \frac{3}{x+2}$

---

population The entire group of objects or individuals considered for a survey.

población Grupo completo de objetos o individuos que se desea estudiar.

In a survey about the study habits of high school students, the population is all high school students.

---

positive correlation Two data sets have a positive correlation if both sets of data values increase.

correlación positiva Dos conjuntos de datos tienen correlación positiva si los valores de ambos conjuntos de datos aumentan.

Power of a Power Property If a is any nonzero real number and m and n are integers, then $(a^m)^n = a^{mn}$.

Propiedad de la potencia de una potencia Dado un número real a distinto de cero y los números enteros m y n, entonces $(a^m)^n = a^{mn}$.

$(6^7)^4 = 6^{7 \cdot 4}$
$= 6^{28}$

Power of a Product Property If a and b are any nonzero real numbers and n is any integer, then $(ab)^n = a^n b^n$.

Propiedad de la potencia de un producto Dados los números reales a y b distintos de cero y un número entero n, entonces $(ab)^n = a^n b^n$.

$(2 \cdot 4)^3 = 2^3 \cdot 4^3$
$= 8 \cdot 64$
$= 512$

Glossary/Glosario

Power of a Quotient Property
If a and b are any nonzero real numbers and n is an integer, then $\left(\frac{a}{b}\right)^n = \frac{a^n}{b^n}$.

Propiedad de la potencia de un cociente Dados los números reales a y b distintos de cero y un número entero n, entonces $\left(\frac{a}{b}\right)^n = \frac{a^n}{b^n}$.

$$\left(\frac{3}{5}\right)^4 = \frac{3}{5} \cdot \frac{3}{5} \cdot \frac{3}{5} \cdot \frac{3}{5}$$
$$= \frac{3 \cdot 3 \cdot 3 \cdot 3}{5 \cdot 5 \cdot 5 \cdot 5}$$
$$= \frac{3^4}{5^4}$$

---

precision The level of detail of a measurement, determined by the unit of measure.

precisión Detalle de una medición, determinado por la unidad de medida.

A ruler marked in millimeters has a greater level of precision than a ruler marked in centimeters.

---

prediction An estimate or guess about something that has not yet happened.

predicción Estimación o suposición sobre algo que todavía no ha sucedido.

---

prime factorization A representation of a number or a polynomial as a product of primes.

factorización prima Representación de un número o de un polinomio como producto de números primos.

The prime factorization of 60 is $2 \cdot 2 \cdot 3 \cdot 5$.

---

prime number A whole number greater than 1 that has exactly two positive factors, itself and 1.

número primo Número cabal mayor que 1 que es divisible únicamente entre sí mismo y entre 1.

5 is prime because its only positive factors are 5 and 1.

---

principal An amount of money borrowed or invested.

capital Cantidad de dinero que se pide prestado o se invierte.

Product of Powers Property
If a is any nonzero real number and m and n are integers, then $a^m \cdot a^n = a^{m+n}$.

Propiedad del producto de potencias Dado un número real a distinto de cero y los números enteros m y n, entonces $a^m \cdot a^n = a^{m+n}$.

$$6^7 \cdot 6^4 = 6^{7+4}$$
$$= 6^{11}$$

Product Property of Radicals For $a \geq 0$ and $b \geq 0$, $\sqrt{ab} = \sqrt{a} \cdot \sqrt{b}$.

Propiedad del producto de radicales Dados $a \geq 0$ y $b \geq 0$, $\sqrt{ab} = \sqrt{a} \cdot \sqrt{b}$.

$$\sqrt{9 \cdot 25} = \sqrt{9} \cdot \sqrt{25}$$
$$= 3 \cdot 5 = 15$$

---

proportion A statement that two ratios are equal; $\frac{a}{b} = \frac{c}{d}$.

proporción Ecuación que establece que dos razones son iguales; $\frac{a}{b} = \frac{c}{d}$.

$$\frac{2}{3} = \frac{4}{6}$$

Pythagorean Theorem If a right triangle has legs of lengths a and b and a hypotenuse of length c, then $a^2 + b^2 = c^2$.

Teorema de Pitágoras Dado un triángulo rectángulo con catetos de longitudes a y b y una hipotenusa de longitud c, entonces $a^2 + b^2 = c^2$.

13 cm   5 cm   12 cm

$$5^2 + 12^2 = 13^2$$
$$25 + 144 = 169$$

Pythagorean triple A set of three positive integers a, b, and c such that $a^2 + b^2 = c^2$.

Tripleta de Pitágoras Conjunto de tres enteros positivos a, b y c tal que $a^2 + b^2 = c^2$.

The numbers 3, 4, and 5 form a Pythagorean triple because $3^2 + 4^2 = 5^2$.

Q

quadrant One of the four regions into which the *x*- and *y*-axes divide the coordinate plane.

cuadrante Una de las cuatro regiones en las que los ejes *x* e *y* dividen el plano cartesiano.

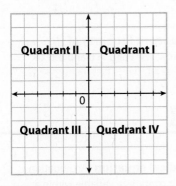

quadratic equation An equation that can be written in the form $ax^2 + bx + c = 0$, where *a*, *b*, and *c* are real numbers and $a \neq 0$.

ecuación cuadrática Ecuación que se puede expresar como $ax^2 + bx + c = 0$, donde *a*, *b* y *c* son números reales y $a \neq 0$.

$x^2 + 3x - 4 = 0$
$x^2 - 9 = 0$

Quadratic Formula The formula $x = \frac{-b \pm \sqrt{b^2 - 4ac}}{2a}$, which gives solutions, or roots, of equations in the form $ax^2 + bx + c = 0$, where $a \neq 0$.

fórmula cuadrática La fórmula $x = \frac{-b \pm \sqrt{b^2 - 4ac}}{2a}$, que da soluciones, o raíces, para las ecuaciones del tipo $ax^2 + bx + c = 0$, donde $a \neq 0$.

The solutions of $2x^2 - 5x - 3 = 0$ are given by
$$x = \frac{-(-5) \pm \sqrt{(-5)^2 - 4(2)(-3)}}{2(2)}$$
$$= \frac{5 \pm \sqrt{25 + 24}}{4} = \frac{5 \pm 7}{4}$$
$x = 3$ or $x = -\frac{1}{2}$

quadratic function A function that can be written in the form $f(x) = ax^2 + bx + c$, where *a*, *b*, and *c* are real numbers and $a \neq 0$.

función cuadrática Función que se puede expresar como $f(x) = ax^2 + bx + c$, donde *a*, *b* y *c* son números reales y $a \neq 0$.

$f(x) = x^2 - 6x + 8$

quadratic polynomial A polynomial of degree 2.

polinomio cuadrático Polinomio de grado 2.

$x^2 - 6x + 8$

quadratic regression A statistical method used to fit a quadratic model to a given data set.

regresión cuadrática Método estadístico utilizado para ajustar un modelo cuadrático a un conjunto de datos determinado.

quantitative data Numerical data.

datos cuantitativos Datos numéricos.

quartile The median of the upper or lower half of a data set. *See also* first quartile, third quartile.

cuartil La mediana de la mitad superior o inferior de un conjunto de datos. *Ver también* primer cuartil, tercer cuartil.

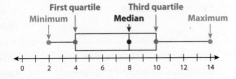

Glossary/Glosario

ENGLISH	SPANISH	EXAMPLES
Quotient of Powers Property If a is a nonzero real number and m and n are integers, then $\frac{a^m}{a^n} = a^{m-n}$.	**Propiedad del cociente de potencias** Dado un número real a distinto de cero y los números enteros m y n, entonces $\frac{a^m}{a^n} = a^{m-n}$.	$\frac{6^7}{6^4} = 6^{7-4} = 6^3$
Quotient Property of Radicals For $a \geq 0$ and $b > 0$, $\sqrt{\frac{a}{b}} = \frac{\sqrt{a}}{\sqrt{b}}$.	**Propiedad del cociente de radicales** Dados $a \geq 0$ y $b > 0$, $\sqrt{\frac{a}{b}} = \frac{\sqrt{a}}{\sqrt{b}}$.	$\sqrt{\frac{9}{25}} = \frac{\sqrt{9}}{\sqrt{25}} = \frac{3}{5}$

R

ENGLISH	SPANISH	EXAMPLES
radical equation An equation that contains a variable within a radical.	**ecuación radical** Ecuación que contiene una variable dentro de un radical.	$\sqrt{x+3} + 4 = 7$
radical expression An expression that contains a radical sign.	**expresión radical** Expresión que contiene un signo de radical.	$\sqrt{x+3} + 4$
radical function A function whose rule contains a variable within a radical.	**función radical** Función cuya regla contiene una variable dentro de un radical.	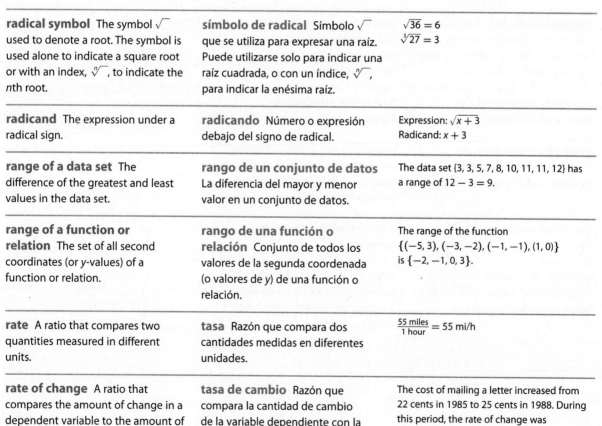 $f(x) = \sqrt{x}$
radical symbol The symbol $\sqrt{}$ used to denote a root. The symbol is used alone to indicate a square root or with an index, $\sqrt[n]{}$, to indicate the nth root.	**símbolo de radical** Símbolo $\sqrt{}$ que se utiliza para expresar una raíz. Puede utilizarse solo para indicar una raíz cuadrada, o con un índice, $\sqrt[n]{}$, para indicar la enésima raíz.	$\sqrt{36} = 6$ $\sqrt[3]{27} = 3$
radicand The expression under a radical sign.	**radicando** Número o expresión debajo del signo de radical.	Expression: $\sqrt{x+3}$ Radicand: $x+3$
range of a data set The difference of the greatest and least values in the data set.	**rango de un conjunto de datos** La diferencia del mayor y menor valor en un conjunto de datos.	The data set {3, 3, 5, 7, 8, 10, 11, 11, 12} has a range of $12 - 3 = 9$.
range of a function or relation The set of all second coordinates (or y-values) of a function or relation.	**rango de una función o relación** Conjunto de todos los valores de la segunda coordenada (o valores de y) de una función o relación.	The range of the function $\{(-5, 3), (-3, -2), (-1, -1), (1, 0)\}$ is $\{-2, -1, 0, 3\}$.
rate A ratio that compares two quantities measured in different units.	**tasa** Razón que compara dos cantidades medidas en diferentes unidades.	$\frac{55 \text{ miles}}{1 \text{ hour}} = 55$ mi/h
rate of change A ratio that compares the amount of change in a dependent variable to the amount of change in an independent variable.	**tasa de cambio** Razón que compara la cantidad de cambio de la variable dependiente con la cantidad de cambio de la variable independiente.	The cost of mailing a letter increased from 22 cents in 1985 to 25 cents in 1988. During this period, the rate of change was $\frac{\text{change in cost}}{\text{change in year}} = \frac{25-22}{1988-1985} = \frac{3}{3}$ = 1 cent per year.

ENGLISH	SPANISH	EXAMPLES
ratio A comparison of two quantities by division.	**razón** Comparación de dos cantidades mediante una división.	$\frac{1}{2}$ or 1:2
rational exponent An exponent that can be expressed as $\frac{m}{n}$ such that if m and n are integers, then $b^{\frac{m}{n}} = \sqrt[n]{b^m} = \left(\sqrt[n]{b}\right)^m$.	**exponente racional** Exponente que se puede expresar como $\frac{m}{n}$ tal que si m y n son números enteros, entonces $b^{\frac{m}{n}} = \sqrt[n]{b^m} = \left(\sqrt[n]{b}\right)^m$.	$64^{\frac{1}{6}} = \sqrt[6]{64}$
rational expression An algebraic expression whose numerator and denominator are polynomials and whose denominator has a degree ≥ 1.	**expresión racional** Expresión algebraica cuyo numerador y denominador son polinomios y cuyo denominador tiene un grado ≥ 1.	$\frac{x+2}{x^2+3x-1}$
rational number A number that can be written in the form $\frac{a}{b}$, where a and b are integers and $b \neq 0$.	**número racional** Número que se puede expresar como $\frac{a}{b}$, donde a y b son números enteros y $b \neq 0$.	$3, 1.75, 0.\overline{3}, -\frac{2}{3}, 0$
rationalizing the denominator A method of rewriting a fraction by multiplying by another fraction that is equivalent to 1 in order to remove radical terms from the denominator.	**racionalizar el denominador** Método que consiste en escribir nuevamente una fracción multiplicándola por otra fracción equivalente a 1 a fin de eliminar los términos radicales del denominador.	$\frac{1}{\sqrt{2}} \cdot \frac{\sqrt{2}}{\sqrt{2}} = \frac{\sqrt{2}}{2}$
real number A rational or irrational number. Every point on the number line represents a real number.	**número real** Número racional o irracional. Cada punto de la recta numérica representa un número real.	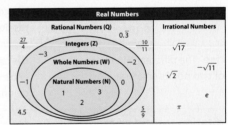
reciprocal For a real number $a \neq 0$, the reciprocal of a is $\frac{1}{a}$. The product of reciprocals is 1.	**recíproco** Dado el número real $a \neq 0$, el recíproco de a es $\frac{1}{a}$. El producto de los recíprocos es 1.	Number | Reciprocal (see table below)
recursive rule for nth term of a sequence A rule for a sequence in which one or more previous terms are used to generate the next term.	**fórmula recurrente para hallar el enésimo término de una sucesión** Fórmula para una sucesión en la cual uno o más términos anteriores se usan para generar el término siguiente.	
reflection A transformation that reflects, or "flips," a graph or figure across a line, called the line of reflection.	**reflexión** Transformación en la que una gráfica o figura se refleja o se invierte sobre una línea, denominada la línea de reflexión.	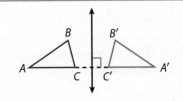

Number	Reciprocal
2	$\frac{1}{2}$
1	1
-1	-1
0	No reciprocal

Glossary/Glosario

ENGLISH	SPANISH	EXAMPLES
relation A set of ordered pairs.	**relación** Conjunto de pares ordenados.	$\{(0, 5), (0, 4), (2, 3), (4, 0)\}$
relative frequency The relative frequency of a category is the frequency of the category divided by the total of all frequencies.	**frecuencia relativa** La frecuencia relativa de una categoría es la frecuencia de la categoría dividido por el total de todas las frecuencias.	
repeating decimal A rational number in decimal form that has a nonzero block of one or more digits that repeat continuously.	**decimal periódico** Número racional en forma decimal que tiene un bloque de uno o más dígitos que se repite continuamente.	$1.\overline{3}, 0.\overline{6}, 2.1\overline{4}, 6.77\overline{3}$
replacement set A set of numbers that can be substituted for a variable.	**conjunto de reemplazo** Conjunto de números que pueden sustituir una variable.	
residual The signed vertical distance between a data point and a line of fit.	**residuo** La diferencia vertical entre un dato y una línea de ajuste.	
residual plot A scatter plot of points whose x-coordinates are the values of the independent variable and whose y-coordinates are the corresponding residuals.	**diagrama de residuos** Diagrama de dispersión de puntos en el que la coordenada x representa los valores de la variable independiente y la coordenada y representa los residuos correspondientes.	
rise The difference in the y-values of two points on a line.	**distancia vertical** Diferencia entre los valores de y de dos puntos de una línea.	For the points $(3, -1)$ and $(6, 5)$, the rise is $5 - (-1) = 6$.
rotation A transformation that rotates or turns a figure about a point called the center of rotation.	**rotación** Transformación que rota o gira una figura sobre un punto llamado centro de rotación.	
run The difference in the x-values of two points on a line.	**distancia horizontal** Diferencia entre los valores de x de dos puntos de una línea.	For the points $(3, -1)$ and $(6, 5)$, the run is $6 - 3 = 3$.

S

ENGLISH	SPANISH	EXAMPLES
sample A part of the population.	**muestra** Una parte de la población.	In a survey about the study habits of high school students, a sample is a survey of 100 students.
scale The ratio between two corresponding measurements.	**escala** Razón entre dos medidas correspondientes.	1 cm : 5 mi

Glossary/Glosario

ENGLISH	SPANISH	EXAMPLES

scale drawing A drawing that uses a scale to represent an object as smaller or larger than the actual object.

dibujo a escala Dibujo que utiliza una escala para representar un objeto como más pequeño o más grande que el objeto original.

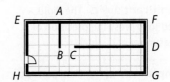

A blueprint is an example of a scale drawing.

---

scale factor The multiplier used on each dimension to change one figure into a similar figure.

factor de escala El multiplicador utilizado en cada dimensión para transformar una figura en una figura semejante.

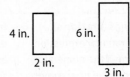

Scale factor: $\frac{3}{2} = 1.5$

---

scale model A three-dimensional model that uses a scale to represent an object as smaller or larger than the actual object.

modelo a escala Modelo tridimensional que utiliza una escala para representar un objeto como más pequeño o más grande que el objeto real.

---

scatter plot A graph with points plotted to show a possible relationship between two sets of data.

diagrama de dispersión Gráfica con puntos que se usa para demostrar una relación posible entre dos conjuntos de datos.

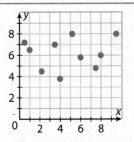

---

second differences Differences between first differences of a function.

segundas diferencias Diferencias entre las primeras diferencias de una función.

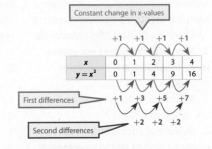

---

second quartile The median of an entire data set, denoted Q_2.

segundo cuartil Mediana de un conjunto de datos completo, expresada como Q_2.

8, 9, ⑨, 12, 15 Q_2: 9

4, 6, ⑦, ⑩, 10, 12

Q_2: $\frac{7 + 10}{2} = 8.5$

---

sequence A list of numbers that often form a pattern.

sucesión Lista de números que generalmente forman un patrón.

1, 2, 4, 8, 16, …

---

set A collection of items called elements.

conjunto Grupo de componentes denominados elementos.

$\{1, 2, 3\}$

---

set-builder notation A notation for a set that uses a rule to describe the properties of the elements of the set.

notación de conjuntos Notación para un conjunto que se vale de una regla para describir las propiedades de los elementos del conjunto.

$\{x \mid x > 3\}$ is read "The set of all x such that x is greater than 3."

significant digits The digits used to express the precision of a measurement.

dígitos significativos Dígitos usados para expresar la precisión de una medida.

---

simple interest A fixed percent of the principal. For principal P, interest rate r, and time t in years, the simple interest is $I = Prt$.

interés simple Porcentaje fijo del capital. Dado el capital P, la tasa de interés r y el tiempo t expresado en años, el interés simple es $I = Prt$.

---

simplest form of a rational expression A rational expression is in simplest form if the numerator and denominator have no common factors.

forma simplificada de una expresión racional Una expresión racional está en forma simplificada cuando el numerador y el denominador no tienen factores comunes.

$$\frac{x^2 - 1}{x^2 + x - 2} = \frac{(x-1)(x+1)}{(x-1)(x+2)}$$
$$= \frac{x+1}{x+2}$$

Simplest form

---

simplest form of a square root expression A square root expression is in simplest form if it meets the following criteria:
1. No perfect squares are in the radicand.
2. No fractions are in the radicand.
3. No square roots appear in the denominator of a fraction. *See also* rationalizing the denominator.

forma simplificada de una expresión de raíz cuadrada Una expresión de raíz cuadrada está en forma simplificada si reúne los siguientes requisitos:
1. No hay cuadrados perfectos en el radicando.
2. No hay fracciones en el radicando.
3. No aparecen raíces cuadradas en el denominador de una fracción. *Ver también* racionalizar el denominador.

Not Simplest Form	Simplest Form
$\sqrt{180}$	$6\sqrt{5}$
$\sqrt{216a^2b^2}$	$6ab\sqrt{6}$
$\frac{\sqrt{7}}{\sqrt{2}}$	$\frac{\sqrt{14}}{2}$

---

simplest form of an exponential expression An exponential expression is in simplest form if it meets the following criteria:
1. There are no negative exponents.
2. The same base does not appear more than once in a product or quotient.
3. No powers, products, or quotients are raised to powers.
4. Numerical coefficients in a quotient do not have any common factor other than 1.

forma simplificada de una expresión exponencial Una expresión exponencial está en forma simplificada si reúne los siguientes requisitos:
1. No hay exponentes negativos.
2. La misma base no aparece más de una vez en un producto o cociente.
3. No se elevan a potencias productos, cocientes ni potencias.
4. Los coeficientes numéricos en un cociente no tienen ningún factor común que no sea 1.

Not Simplest Form	Simplest Form
$7^8 \cdot 7^4$	7^{12}
$\left(x^2\right)^{-4} \cdot x^5$	$\frac{1}{x^3}$
$\frac{a^5b^9}{(ab)^4}$	ab^5

---

skewed distribution A type of distribution in which the right or left side of its display indicates frequencies that are much greater than those of the other side. In a distribution skewed to the left, more than half the data are greater than the mean. In a distribution skewed to the right, more than half the data are less than the mean.

distribución sesgada Tipo de distribución en la que el lado derecho o izquierdo muestra frecuencias mucho mayores que las del otro lado. En una distribución sesgada a la izquierda, más de la mitad de los datos son menores que la media. En una distribución sesgada a la derecha, más de la mitad de los datos son menores que la media.

Glossary/Glosario

slope A measure of the steepness of a line. If (x_1, y_1) and (x_2, y_2) are any two points on the line, the slope of the line, known as m, is represented by the equation $m = \frac{y_2 - y_1}{x_2 - x_1}$.

pendiente Medida de la inclinación de una línea. Dados dos puntos (x_1, y_1) y (x_2, y_2) en una línea, la pendiente de la línea, denominada m, se representa con la ecuación $m = \frac{y_2 - y_1}{x_2 - x_1}$.

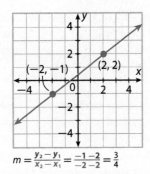

$m = \frac{y_2 - y_1}{x_2 - x_1} = \frac{-1 - 2}{-2 - 2} = \frac{3}{4}$

---

slope formula If (x_1, y_1) and (x_2, y_2) are any two points on a line, the slope of the line is $m = \frac{y_2 - y_1}{x_2 - x_1}$.

fórmula de la pendiente Dados dos puntos (x_1, y_1) y (x_2, y_2) en una línea, la pendiente de la línea es $m = \frac{y_2 - y_1}{x_2 - x_1}$.

---

slope-intercept form The slope-intercept form of a linear equation is $y = mx + b$, where m is the slope and b is the y-intercept.

forma de pendiente-intersección La forma de pendiente-intersección de una ecuación lineal es $y = mx + b$, donde m es la pendiente y b es la intersección con el eje y.

$y = -2x + 4$
The slope is -2.
The y-intercept is 4.

---

solution of a linear inequality in one variable A value or values that make the inequality true.

solución de una desigualdad lineal en una variable Valor o valores que hacen que la desigualdad sea verdadera.

Inequality: $x + 2 < 6$
Solution: $x < 4$

---

solution of a linear equation in two variables An ordered pair or ordered pairs that make the equation true.

solución de una ecuación lineal en dos variables Un par ordenado o pares ordenados que hacen que la ecuación sea verdadera.

$(4, 2)$ is a solution of $x + y = 6$.

---

solution of a system of linear equations Any ordered pair that satisfies all the equations in a linear system.

solución de un sistema de ecuaciones lineales Cualquier par ordenado que resuelva todas las ecuaciones de un sistema lineal.

$\begin{cases} x + y = -1 \\ -x + y = -3 \end{cases}$

The solution of the system is the ordered pair $(1, -2)$.

---

solution of a system of linear inequalities Any ordered pair that satisfies all the inequalities in a linear system.

solución de un sistema de desigualdades lineales Cualquier par ordenado que resuelva todas las desigualdades de un sistema lineal.

$\begin{cases} y \leq x + 1 \\ y < -x + 4 \end{cases}$

$(2, 1)$ is in the overlapping shaded regions, so it is a solution.

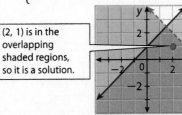

---

solution of an inequality in two variables An ordered pair or ordered pairs that make the inequality true.

solución de una desigualdad en dos variables Un par ordenado o pares ordenados que hacen que la desigualdad sea verdadera.

$(3, 1)$ is a solution of $x + y < 6$.

Glossary/Glosario

ENGLISH	SPANISH	EXAMPLES
solution set The set of values that make a statement true.	**conjunto solución** Conjunto de valores que hacen verdadero un enunciado.	Inequality: $x + 3 \geq 5$ Solution set: $\{x \mid x \geq 2\}$
square root A number that is multiplied by itself to form a product is called a square root of that product.	**raíz cuadrada** El número que se multiplica por sí mismo para formar un producto se denomina la raíz cuadrada de ese producto.	A square root of 16 is 4, because $4^2 = 4 \cdot 4 = 16$. Another square root of 16 is -4 because $(-4)^2 = (-4)(-4) = 16$.
standard form of a linear equation $Ax + By = C$, where A, B, and C are real numbers and A and B are not both 0.	**forma estándar de una ecuación lineal** $Ax + By = C$, donde A, B y C son números reales y A y B no son ambos cero.	$2x + 3y = 6$
standard form of a polynomial A polynomial in one variable is written in standard form when the terms are in order from greatest degree to least degree.	**forma estándar de un polinomio** Un polinomio de una variable se expresa en forma estándar cuando los términos se ordenan de mayor a menor grado.	$4x^5 - 2x^4 + x^2 - x + 1$
standard form of a quadratic equation $ax^2 + bx + c = 0$, where a, b, and c are real numbers and $a \neq 0$.	**forma estándar de una ecuación cuadrática** $ax^2 + bx + c = 0$, donde a, b y c son números reales y $a \neq 0$.	$2x^2 + 3x - 1 = 0$
standard deviation A measure of dispersion of a data set. The standard deviation σ is the square root of the variance	**desviación estándar** Medida de dispersión de un conjunto de datos. La desviación estándar σ es la raíz cuadrada de la varianza	Data set: $\{6, 7, 7, 9, 11\}$ Mean: $\frac{6+7+7+9+11}{5} = 8$ Variance: $\frac{1}{5}(4 + 1 + 1 + 1 + 9) = 3.2$ Standard deviation: $\sigma = \sqrt{3.2} \approx 1.8$
statistics Numbers that describe a sample or samples.	**estadísticas** Números que describen una o varias muestras.	
step function A piecewise function that is constant over each interval in its domain.	**función escalón** Función a trozos que es constante en cada intervalo en su dominio.	
subset A set that is contained entirely within another set. Set B is a subset of set A if every element of B is contained in A, denoted $B \subset A$.	**subconjunto** Conjunto que se encuentra dentro de otro conjunto. El conjunto B es un subconjunto del conjunto A si todos los elementos de B son elementos de A; se expresa $B \subset A$.	
substitution method A method used to solve systems of equations by solving an equation for one variable and substituting the resulting expression into the other equation(s).	**sustitución** Método utilizado para resolver sistemas de ecuaciones resolviendo una ecuación para una variable y sustituyendo la expresión resultante en las demás ecuaciones.	

ENGLISH	SPANISH	EXAMPLES
Subtraction Property of Equality If a, b, and c are real numbers and $a = b$, then $a - c = b - c$.	**Propiedad de igualdad de la resta** Si a, b y c son números reales y $a = b$, entonces $a - c = b - c$.	$$\begin{array}{r} x + 6 = 8 \\ \underline{-6 \quad -6} \\ x \quad\; = 2 \end{array}$$
Subtraction Property of Inequality For real numbers a, b, and c, if $a < b$, then $a - c < b - c$. Also holds true for $>$, $\leq$, $\geq$, and $\neq$.	**Propiedad de desigualdad de la resta** Dados los números reales a, b y c, si $a < b$, entonces $a - c < b - c$. Es válido también para $>$, $\leq$, $\geq$ y $\neq$.	$$\begin{array}{r} x + 6 < 8 \\ \underline{-6 \quad -6} \\ x \quad\; < 2 \end{array}$$
symmetric distribution A type of distribution in which the right and left sides of its display indicate frequencies that are mirror images of each other.	**distribución simétrica** Tipo de distribución en la que los lados derecho e izquierdo muestran frecuencias que son idénticas.	
system of linear equations A system of equations in which all of the equations are linear.	**sistema de ecuaciones lineales** Sistema de ecuaciones en el que todas las ecuaciones son lineales.	$$\begin{cases} 2x + 3y = -1 \\ x - 3y = 4 \end{cases}$$
system of linear inequalities A system of inequalities in which all of the inequalities are linear.	**sistema de desigualdades lineales** Sistema de desigualdades en el que todas las desigualdades son lineales.	$$\begin{cases} 2x + 3y > -1 \\ x - 3y \leq 4 \end{cases}$$

T

term of a sequence An element or number in the sequence.	**término de una sucesión** Elemento o número de una sucesión.	5 is the third term in the sequence 1, 3, 5, 7, …
term of an expression The parts of the expression that are added or subtracted.	**término de una expresión** Parte de una expresión que debe sumarse o restarse.	$3x^2 + 6x - 8$ Term Term Term
third quartile The median of the upper half of a data set. Also called *upper quartile*.	**tercer cuartil** La mediana de la mitad superior de un conjunto de datos. También se llama *cuartil superior*.	**Lower half** **Upper half** 18, 23, 28, 29, (36,) 42 **Third quartile**
tolerance The amount by which a measurement is permitted to vary from a specified value.	**tolerancia** La cantidad por que una medida se permite variar de un valor especificado.	
transformation A change in the position, size, or shape of a figure or graph.	**transformación** Cambio en la posición, tamaño o forma de una figura o gráfica.	Preimage / Image $\triangle ABC \rightarrow \triangle A'B'C'$

ENGLISH	SPANISH	EXAMPLES

translation A transformation that shifts or slides every point of a figure or graph the same distance in the same direction.

traslación Transformación en la que todos los puntos de una figura o gráfica se mueven la misma distancia en la misma dirección.

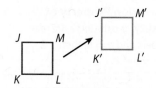

---

trend line A line on a scatter plot that helps show the correlation between data sets more clearly.

línea de tendencia Línea en un diagrama de dispersión que sirve para mostrar la correlación entre conjuntos de datos más claramente.

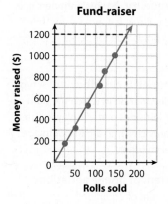

---

trinomial A polynomial with three terms.

trinomio Polinomio con tres términos.

$4x^2 + 3xy - 5y^2$

---

turning point A point on the graph of a function that corresponds to a local maximum (or minimum) where the graph changes from increasing to decreasing (or vice versa).

punto de inflexión Punto de la gráfica de una función que corresponde a un máximo (o mínimo) local donde la gráfica pasa de ser creciente a decreciente (o viceversa).

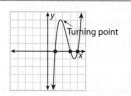

---

two-variable data A collection of paired variable values, such as a series of measurements of air temperature at different times of day.

datos de dos variables Conjunto de valores variables agrupados en pares, como una serie de mediciones de la temperatura del aire en diferentes momentos del día.

Time	Temperature (°F)
8 A.M.	65
9 A.M.	69
10 A.M.	72

---

two-way frequency table A frequency table that displays two-variable data in rows and columns.

table de frecuencia de doble entrada Una tabla de frecuencia que muestra los datos de dos variables organizados en filas y columnas.

		Preference		
		inside	Outside	Total
Pet	Cats	35	15	50
	Dogs	20	30	50
	Total	55	45	100

U

---

union The union of two sets is the set of all elements that are in either set, denoted by ∪.

unión La unión de dos conjuntos es el conjunto de todos los elementos que se encuentran en ambos conjuntos, expresado por ∪.

$A = \{1, 2, 3, 4\}$
$B = \{1, 3, 5, 7, 9\}$
$A \cup B = \{1, 2, 3, 4, 5, 7, 9\}$

---

unit rate A rate in which the second quantity in the comparison is one unit.

tasa unitaria Tasa en la que la segunda cantidad de la comparación es una unidad.

$\frac{30 \text{ mi}}{1 \text{ h}} = 30 \text{ mi/h}$

Glossary/Glosario

ENGLISH	SPANISH	EXAMPLES
unlike radicals Radicals with a different quantity under the radical sign.	**radicales distintos** Radicales con cantidades diferentes debajo del signo de radical.	$2\sqrt{2}$ and $2\sqrt{3}$
unlike terms Terms with different variables or the same variables raised to different powers.	**términos distintos** Términos con variables diferentes o las mismas variables elevadas a potencias diferentes.	$4xy^2$ and $6x^2y$
upper quartile *See* third quartile.	**cuartil superior** *Ver* tercer cuartil.	

V

ENGLISH	SPANISH	EXAMPLES
value of a function The result of replacing the independent variable with a number and simplifying.	**valor de una función** Resultado de reemplazar la variable independiente por un número y luego simplificar.	The value of the function $f(x) = x + 1$ for $x = 3$ is 4.
value of a variable A number used to replace a variable to make an equation true.	**valor de una variable** Número utilizado para reemplazar una variable y hacer que una ecuación sea verdadera.	In the equation $x + 1 = 4$, the value of x is 3.
value of an expression The result of replacing the variables in an expression with numbers and simplifying.	**valor de una expresión** Resultado de reemplazar las variables de una expresión por un número y luego simplificar.	The value of the expression $x + 1$ for $x = 3$ is 4.
variable A symbol used to represent a quantity that can change.	**variable** Símbolo utilizado para representar una cantidad que puede cambiar.	In the expression $2x + 3$, x is the variable.
vertex form of a quadratic function A quadratic function written in the form $f(x) = a(x - h)^2 + k$, where a, h, and k are constants and (h, k) is the vertex.	**forma en vértice de una función cuadrática** Una function cuadrática expresada en la forma $f(x) = a(x - h)^2 + k$, donde a, h y k son constantes y (h, k) es el vértice.	
vertex of a parabola The highest or lowest point on the parabola.	**vértice de una parábola** Punto más alto o más bajo de una parábola.	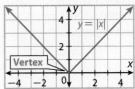 The vertex is $(0, -2)$.
vertex of an absolute-value graph The point on the axis of symmetry of the graph.	**vértice de una gráfica de valor absoluto** Punto en el eje de simetría de la gráfica.	

ENGLISH	SPANISH	EXAMPLES
vertical compression A transformation that pushes the points of a graph toward the *x*-axis.	**vertical compresión** Transformación que desplaza los puntos de una gráfica hacia el eje *x*.	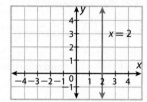
vertical line A line whose equation is $x = a$, where *a* is the *x*-intercept.	**línea vertical** Línea cuya ecuación es $x = a$, donde *a* es la intersección con el eje *x*.	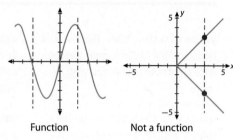
vertical-line test A test used to determine whether a relation is a function. If any vertical line crosses the graph of a relation more than once, the relation is not a function.	**prueba de la línea vertical** Prueba utilizada para determinar si una relación es una función. Si una línea vertical corta la gráfica de una relación más de una vez, la relación no es una función.	Function Not a function
vertical stretch A transformation that pulls the points of a graph away from the *x*–axis.	**vertical estiramiento** Transformación que desplaza los puntos de una gráfica en forma vertical alejándolos del eje *x*.	
vertical translation (of a parabola) is a shift of the parabola up or down, with no change in the shape of the parabola.	**traslación vertical (de una parábola)** Desplazamiento de la parábola hacia arriba o hacia abajo, sin producir cambios en la forma de la parábola.	

X

***x*-intercept** The *x*-coordinate(s) of the point(s) where a graph intersects the *x*-axis.	**intersección con el eje *x*** Coordenada(s) *x* de uno o más puntos donde una gráfica corta el eje *x*.	The *x*-intercept is 2.

Y

***y*-intercept** The *y*-coordinate(s) of the point(s) where a graph intersects the *y*-axis.	**intersección con el eje *y*** Coordenada(s) *y* de uno o más puntos donde una gráfica corta el eje *y*.	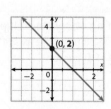 The *y*-intercept is 2.

Z

zero exponent For any nonzero real number x, $x^0 = 1$.

exponente cero Dado un número real distinto de cero x, $x^0 = 1$.

$5^0 = 1$

---

zero of a function For the function f, any number x such that $f(x) = 0$.

cero de una función Dada la función f, todo número x tal que $f(x) = 0$.

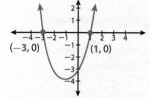

The zeros are -3 and 1.

Zero Product Property For real numbers p and q, if $pq = 0$, then $p = 0$ or $q = 0$.

Propiedad del producto cero Dados los números reales p y q, si $pq = 0$, entonces $p = 0$ o $q = 0$.

If $(x - 1)(x + 2) = 0$, then $x - 1 = 0$ or $x + 2 = 0$, so $x = 1$ or $x = -2$.

Glossary/Glosario

Index

Index locator numbers are in Module. Lesson form. For example, 2.1 indicates Module 2, Lesson 1 as listed in the Table of Contents.

Index

Index

completing the square, 22.2
exponential decay, 16.2
   with exponential functions, 16.3
exponential growth, 16.2
exponential regression, 16.3
using a function graph, 3.4
with functions, 3.3, 24.3
linear, 10.2
linear relationships, 7.1
with linear systems, 12.1, 12.2, 12.3
use of piecewise-defined functions in, 13.1
with polynomials, 17.2, 17.3
with quadratic functions, 19.1, 23.1
quantities, 1.2

models, 1.2. *See also* **modeling**
   algebraic, 2.1, 2.2
   comparing, 23.2
   exponential, 16.1, 16.4
   and functions, 3.1, 3.3, 3.4
   linear, 6.2, 6.3, 16.4
   with linear inequalities, 7.3
   linear system, 11.2, 11.3, 12.1
   quadratic, 20.1
monomials, 17.1, 18.1
movies, 7.1
multiplication
   and linear systems, 11.4
Multiplication Property of Equality, 1.1
multiplying first, 11.4
music, 2.5

N

nature, 20.1
negative discriminant, 22.5
nonlinear systems, solving, 22.5
normal curve, 9.4
normal distributions, 9.4
numbers
   irrational, 14.2
   rational, 14.2
   term, 15.2
numerator, 8.2
numerical expressions, 2.1
   simplifying, 14.1
numerical measurements, 8.1

O

odd functions, 24.1
one-variable data distributions, 9.1
optics, 15.3
ordered pairs, 3.4
outliers of data, 9.2

P

paired values, frequency of, 8.1
parabolas, 19.1
   translations of, 19.2

parallel lines
   boundary lines, 12.2
parameters, 6.4, 15.5
   changing, 12.1
parent functions, 6.4, 24.3
   absolute value, 13.2
   cube root, 24.4
   exponential, 15.5
patterns, 4.1, 4.2, 4.3
   of graphs, 24.1
perfect-square trinomials, 18.3, 21.3, 22.2
perimeters
   and significant digits, 1.3
photography, 15.2, 18.2
physical science, 15.1
physics, 2.4, 5.1, 15.4, 16.4, 20.1, 20.3,
   21.2, 22.2
piecewise-defined functions, 13.1, 13.2
   differentiation, 13.1
   intervals in, 13.1
   use in defining situations, 13.1
   use of in modeling, 13.1
point-slope form, 6.2
points of intersection, 20.1
   finding by graphing, 22.5
   finding with quadratic equations, 22.5
polynomial expressions, 17.1, 17.2, 17.3,
   18.1, 18.2
polynomial functions
   graphing, 24.1
   levels of degree, 24.1
polynomials
   adding, 17.2
   multiplying, 18.1, 18.2
   simplifying, 17.1
   subtracting, 17.3
population, 23.2
population statistics, 13.2
precision of measurements, 1.3
probability, 15.3
Product Property of Radicals, 22.1
projectile motion, 22.2
Properties
   Addition Property of Equality, 1.1
   Associative Property, 17.3
   Distributive Property, 18.2, 20.3
   Division Property of Equality, 1.1
   Equality of Bases Property, 16.1
   Multiplication Property of Equality, 1.1
   Product Property of Radicals, 22.1
   Quotient Property of Radicals, 22.1
   Subtraction Property of Equality, 1.1
   Zero Product Property, 20.3
Properties of Equality, 1.1
proportion, 1.2

Q

quadratic equations
   choosing a method for solving, 22.4

solving, 20.1, 21.2, 22.4, 22.5
   algebraically, 22.5
   by graphing, 22.5
   with square roots, 22.1, 22.5
   with the Zero Product Property, 20.3
quadratic formula, 22.3
   solving equations with, 22.3
quadratic functions, 19.1, 23.2
   creating, 23.1
   factored form of, 20.2
   graphing, 19.3, 20.1
   identifying, 19.3
   modeling with, 23.1
   path of, 19.3
   transforming, 19.2
   understanding, 19.1
   writing, 19.3
   and x-intercept, 20.2
quadratic models
   comparing, 23.2
quadratic regression, 23.1
quadratic systems, 22.5
quadratics, possible number of
   solutions in, 22.5
qualitative data. *See* **categorical data**
quantitative data. *See* **numerical**
   measurements
quantitative reasoning, 1.1, 1.2, 1.3, 2.3
quartile, 9.1
   finding, 9.2
Quotient Property of Radicals, 22.1

R

radical expression, 14.1
radical functions, 24.3
radicals, 14.1
   simplifying expressions with, 14.2
radicand, 14.1
range, 3.2, 9.1
   of absolute value functions, 13.2
   comparing, 6.5
   of functions, 24.4
   interquartile (IQR), 9.1
rate, 1.2
rate of change, interpreting, 5.3
ratio, 1.2
   numerical expression of, 8.2
rational exponents, 14.1
   properties of, 14.2
   simplifying expressions with, 14.2
rational numbers, 14.2
rays
   in absolute value functions, 13.2
   compared to lines, 13.1
   use of, 13.1
reading, 7.1, 9.2
rectangles, area of, 1.3

Index

Table of Measures

LENGTH

1 inch = 2.54 centimeters

1 meter = 39.37 inches

1 mile = 5,280 feet

1 mile = 1760 yards

1 mile = 1.609 kilometers

1 kilometer = 0.62 mile

MASS/WEIGHT

1 pound = 16 ounces

1 pound = 0.454 kilograms

1 kilogram = 2.2 pounds

1 ton = 2000 pounds

CAPACITY

1 cup = 8 fluid ounces

1 pint = 2 cups

1 quart = 2 pints

1 gallon = 4 quarts

1 gallon = 3.785 liters

1 liter = 0.264 gallons

1 liter = 1000 cubic centimeters

Symbols

$\neq$	is not equal to	π	pi: (about 3.14)
$\approx$	is approximately equal to	$\perp$	is perpendicular to
10^2	ten squared; ten to the second power	$\parallel$	is parallel to
		$\overleftrightarrow{AB}$	line AB
$2.\overline{6}$	repeating decimal 2.66666...	$\overrightarrow{AB}$	ray AB
$\lvert-4\rvert$	the absolute value of negative 4	$\overline{AB}$	line segment AB
$\sqrt{}$	square root	m$\angle A$	measure of $\angle A$

Formulas

Triangle	$A = \frac{1}{2}bh$	Pythagorean Theorem	$a^2 + b^2 = c^2$
Parallelogram	$A = bh$	Quadratic Formula	$x = \dfrac{-b \pm \sqrt{b^2 - 4ac}}{2a}$
Circle	$A = \pi r^2$	Arithmetic Sequence	$a_n = a_1 + (n-1)d$
Circle	$C = \pi d$ or $C = 2\pi r$	Geometric Sequence	$a_n = a_1 r^{n-1}$
General Prisms	$V = Bh$	Geometric Series	$S_n = \dfrac{a_1 - a_1 r^n}{1 - r}$ where $r \neq 1$
Cylinder	$V = \pi r^2 h$	Radians	$1\ radian = \frac{180}{\pi}\ degrees$
Sphere	$V = \frac{4}{3}\pi r^3$	Degrees	$1\ degree = \frac{\pi}{180}\ radians$
Cone	$V = \frac{1}{3}\pi r^2 h$	Exponential Growth/Decay	$A = A_0\, e^{k(t - t_0)} + B_0$
Pyramid	$V = \frac{1}{3}Bh$		